GREATER MANCHESTER STREET ATLAS

CONTENTS

Key to Map Pages	2-3
Enlarged City Centre at 6" to 1 mile	4-5
Map Pages at 4.25" to 1 mile	6-121
Postcode Map	122-123
Index to Places & Areas	124
Index to Streets	125 onwards

REFERENCE

Motorway M63

A Road A57

Under Construction

Proposed

B Road B5228

Dual Carriageway

One Way Street
Traffic flow on 'A' Roads is indicated by a heavy line on the drivers left.

Restricted Access

Map Continuation 24 Large Scale City Centre 4

B.R. Railway (Level Crossing, ECCLES)

Private Railway (RAMSBOTTOM)

Metrolink (LRT) (G. Mex)
The boarding of Metrolink trains at stations may be limited to a single direction, indicated by the arrow.

Built Up Area

County Boundary

District Boundary

Posttown Boundary
By arrangement with the Post Office

Postcode Boundary
Within Posttowns

Ambulance Station

Car Park Selected

Church or Chapel

Fire Station

Hospital

House Numbers
'A' and 'B' Roads only (48, 5)

Information Centre

National Grid Reference ³80

Police Station

Post Office

Toilet

SCALE

Map Pages 6-121 1:15,000 (4.25 inches to 1 mile)

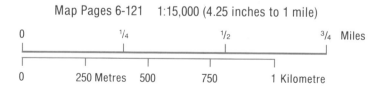

Enlarged City Centre 4-5 1:10,560 (6 inches to 1 mile)

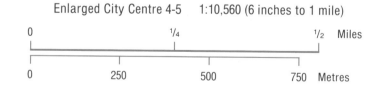

Geographers' A-Z Map Company Ltd.

Head Office :
Fairfield Road, Borough Green, Sevenoaks, Kent. TN15 8PP
Telephone 0732-781000

Showrooms :
44 Gray's Inn Road, London. WC1X 8LR
Telephone 071-242 9246

Edition 1 1993
An A to Z Publication

The representation on the Maps of a road, track or footpath is no evidence of the existence of a Right of Way.

Every possible care has been taken to ensure that the information given in this Atlas is accurate and whilst the publishers would be grateful to learn of any errors, they regret they cannot accept any responsibility for loss thereby caused.

The Maps in this Atlas are based upon the Ordnance Survey 1:10,560 Maps with the permission of the Controller of Her Majesty's Stationery Office.

The grid on these maps is the National Grid taken from the Ordnance Survey Maps with the permission of the Controller of Her Majesty's Stationery Office.

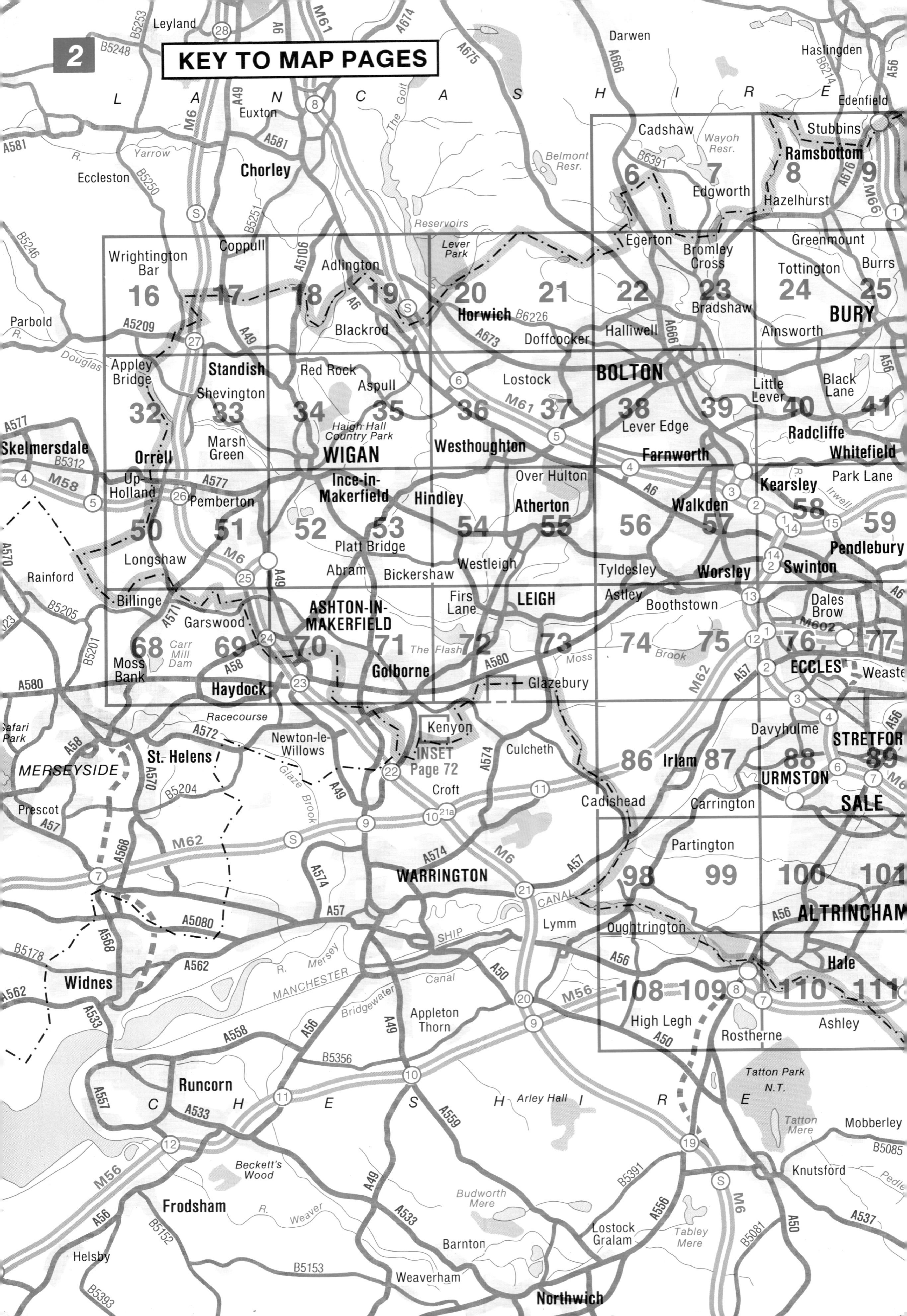

KEY TO MAP PAGES

2

LANCASHIRE

MERSEYSIDE

CHESHIRE

Leyland · Euxton · Chorley · Eccleston · Parbold · Darwen · Haslingden · Edenfield · Stubbins · Ramsbottom · Hazelhurst · Cadshaw · Edgworth · Egerton · Bromley Cross · Greenmount · Tottington · Burrs

Wrightington Bar · Coppull · Adlington · Blackrod · Horwich · Doffcocker · Halliwell · Bradshaw · **BURY** · Ainsworth

| 16 | 17 | 18 | 19 | 20 | 21 | 22 | 23 | 24 | 25 |

Appley Bridge · Standish · Shevington · Red Rock · Aspull · Lostock · **BOLTON** · Little Lever · Black Lane · Radcliffe · Whitefield · Lever Edge · Farnworth

| 32 | 33 | 34 | 35 | 36 | 37 | 38 | 39 | 40 | 41 |

Skelmersdale · Orrell · Marsh Green · **WIGAN** · Westhoughton · Over Hulton · Walkden · Kearsley · Park Lane · Up-Holland · Pemberton · Ince-in-Makerfield · Hindley · Atherton

| 50 | 51 | 52 | 53 | 54 | 55 | 56 | 57 | 58 | 59 |

Rainford · Longshaw · Billinge · Platt Bridge · Abram · Bickershaw · Westleigh · Tyldesley · Worsley · Swinton · Pendlebury · Astley · Boothstown · Dales Brow

| 68 | 69 | 70 | 71 | 72 | 73 | 74 | 75 | 76 | 77 |

Moss Bank · Garswood · **ASHTON-IN-MAKERFIELD** · Golborne · Firs Lane · **LEIGH** · Haydock · Glazebury · **ECCLES** · Weaste

Racecourse · Newton-le-Willows · Kenyon · Culcheth · Davyhulme · **STRETFORD**

ST. Helens · Croft · **INSET Page 72** · **IRLAM** · **URMSTON** · **SALE**

| 86 | 87 | 88 | 89 |

Prescot · **WARRINGTON** · Cadishead · Carrington · Partington

| 98 | 99 | 100 | 101 |

Lymm · Oughtrington · **ALTRINCHAM**

Widnes · Appleton Thorn · High Legh · Hale · Ashley · Rostherne

| 108 | 109 | 110 | 111 |

Runcorn · Frodsham · Helsby · Barnton · Weaverham · Arley Hall · Tatton Park N.T. · Tatton Mere · Mobberley · Knutsford · Lostock Gralam · Tabley Mere · **Northwich**

Beckett's Wood · Budworth Mere

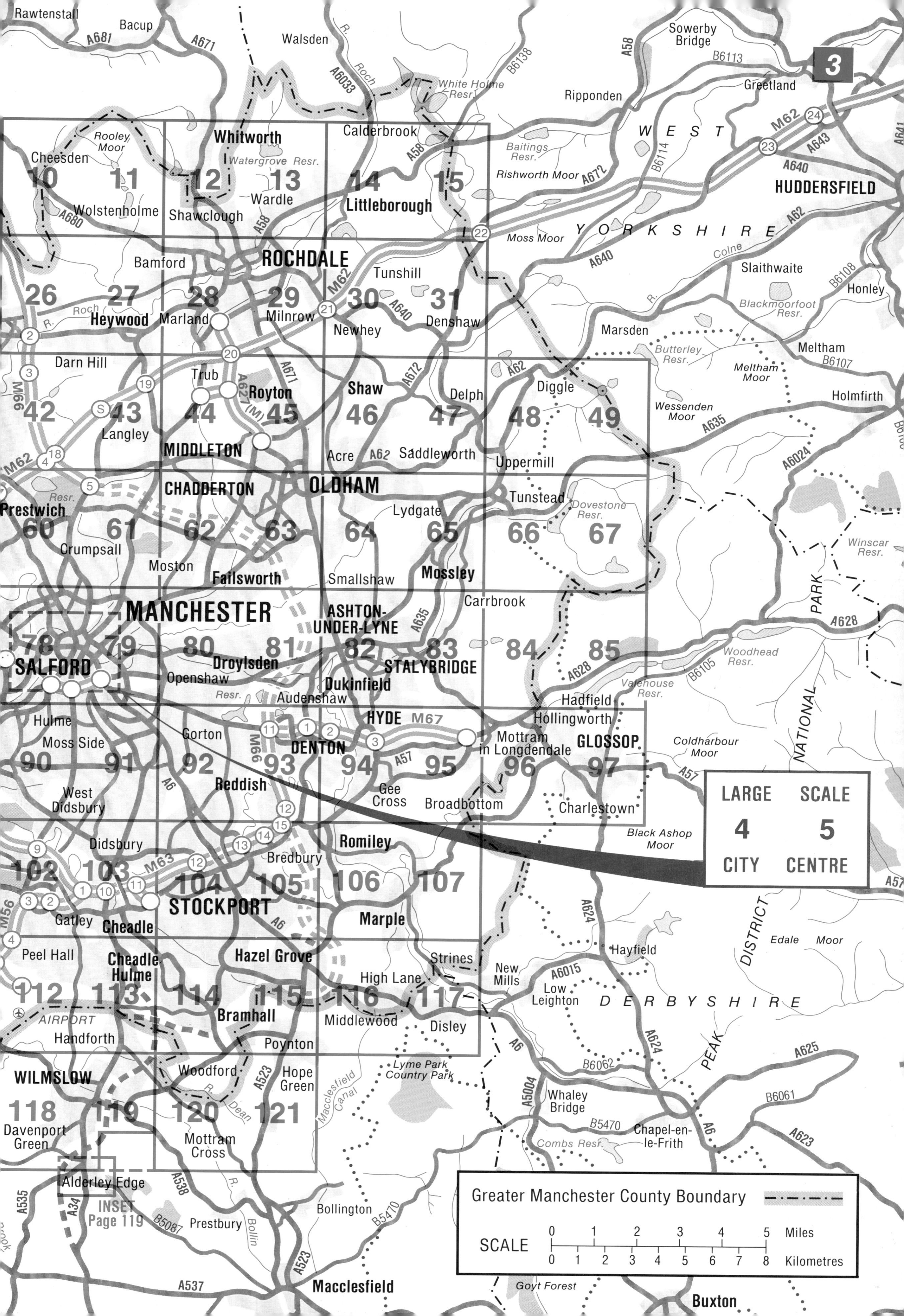
3
LARGE SCALE
4 CITY
5 CENTRE
Greater Manchester County Boundary
SCALE
0 1 2 3 4 5 Miles
0 1 2 3 4 5 6 7 8 Kilometres
MANCHESTER
SALFORD
ROCHDALE
OLDHAM
STOCKPORT
HUDDERSFIELD
MIDDLETON
CHADDERTON
ASHTON-UNDER-LYNE
STALYBRIDGE
HYDE
DENTON
GLOSSOP
WILMSLOW
WEST YORKSHIRE
DERBYSHIRE
PEAK DISTRICT NATIONAL PARK
INSET Page 119

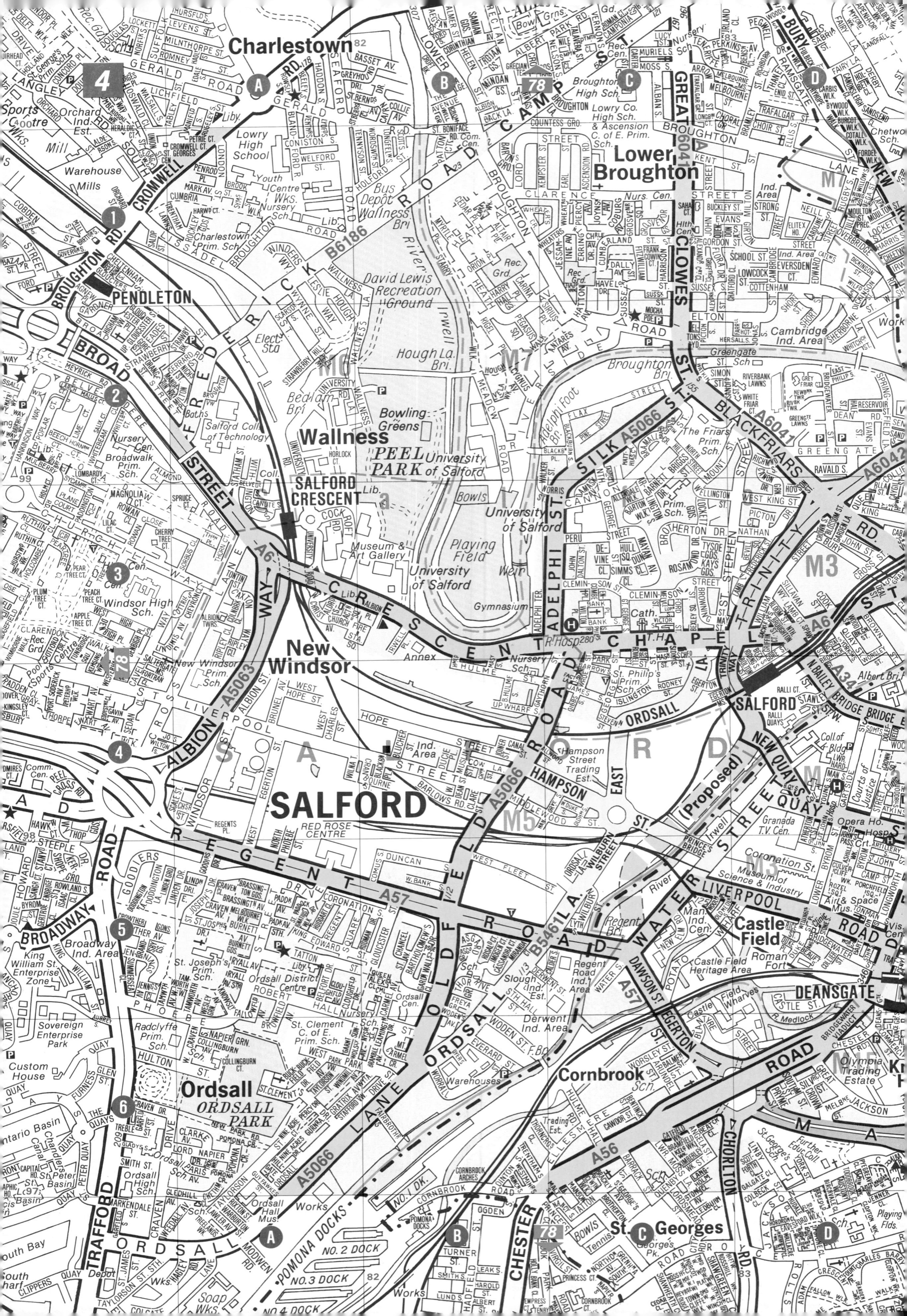
4
Charlestown
A
B
C
D
78
Lower Broughton
PENDLETON
Lowry High School
Warehouse Mills
Orchard Ind. Est.
Sports Centre
CROMWELL RD.
BROUGHTON RD.
BROAD ST.
FREDERICK ROAD
B6186
Bus Depôt
Wallness Bri.
Charlestown Prim. Sch.
Broughton High Sch.
Lowry Co. High Sch.
GREAT CLOWES ST.
A6041
David Lewis Recreation Ground
River Irwell
Hough La. Bri.
Elect. Sta.
Bedlam Bri.
Bowling Greens
Wallness
PEEL PARK
University of Salford
SALFORD CRESCENT
Salford Coll. of Technology
Museum & Art Gallery
Playing Field
Weir
Gymnasium
Broughton Bri.
Adelphi Foot Br.
SILK ST.
A5066
BLACKFRIARS
A6042
The Friars Prim. Sch.
Cambridge Ind. Area
TRINITY WAY
M3
M6
M7
M5
CRESCENT
CHAPEL ST.
A6
New Windsor
New Windsor Prim. Sch.
Windsor High Sch.
Broadwalk Prim. Sch.
ALBION WAY
A5063
SALFORD
RED ROSE CENTRE
REGENT ROAD
A57
HAMPSON ST.
Hampson Street Trading Est.
ORDSALL LA.
NEW QUAY ST.
(Proposed)
QUAY ST.
Granada T.V. Cen.
Museum of Science & Industry
Air & Space Mus.
LIVERPOOL ROAD
Castle Field
Roman Fort
Castle Field Heritage Area
DEANSGATE
WATER ST.
DAWSON ST.
B5461
Cornbrook
Ordsall
ORDSALL PARK
Ordsall District Centre
St. Joseph's Prim. Sch.
St. Clement C. of E. Prim. Sch.
Radclyffe Prim. Sch.
Ordsall High Sch.
Ordsall Hall Mus.
BROADWAY
Broadway Ind. Area
King William St. Enterprise Zone
Sovereign Enterprise Park
Custom House
TRAFFORD ROAD
ORDSALL LANE
POMONA DOCKS
NO. 1 DK.
NO. 2 DOCK
NO. 3 DOCK
NO. 4 DOCK
CORNBROOK ROAD
CHESTER ROAD
A56
CHORLTON RD.
St. Georges
Olympia Trading Estate
MANCUNIAN WAY
Further Educ. Coll.
St. George's Sch.
Ontario Basin
St. Peter Basin
South Bay
South Wharf
Soap Wks.
Wks.
82
83
97
98
99
Salford Central
Warehouses
Trading Est.
Playing Flds.
Albert Bri.
Courts of Justice
Opera Ho.
Castle Field Wharves

5
MANCHESTER
Strangeways
H.M. PRISON
H.M. Prison
Magistrates Crt.
Great Horrocks
Newtown
Ancoats
Gaythorn
University
University of Manchester
VICTORIA
PICCADILLY
Piccadilly Gs.
Mosley St.
High St.
Mkt. St.
ARNDALE SHOPPING CENTRE
Central Retail Park
Piccadilly Trading Estate
University of Manchester Inst. of Science & Technology
UMIST
G.MEX Cen.
Palace Theatre
Apollo Theatre
Business Sch.
Victoria Ind. Est.
Crown Ind. Est.
Poland St. Ind. Est.
Aged Persons Day Centre
Ancoats Hosp.
St. Thomas More High Sch. (Lower)
St.Thomas More High Sch.
Abbott Prim. Sch.
St.Patrick's R.C. Prim. Schs
St. Malachy's R.C. Prim. Sch.
St.Gregory's Sec.Sch.
Goods Sta.
Playing Field
John Dalton Coll.
Coll. of Music
78
79
E
F
G
H
1
2
3
4
5
6
M1
M4
M8
M12
M13
A56
A62
A664
A665
A662
A6
A34
A57(M)
B6469
GRT. DUCIE ST.
CHEETHAM HILL RD.
ROCHDALE RD.
OLDHAM RD.
GREAT ANCOATS STREET
POLLARD STREET
CORPORATION ST.
DEANSGATE
PORTLAND ST.
OXFORD RD.
OXFORD ST.
WHITWORTH ST.
PRINCESS ST.
PICCADILLY
LONDON RD.
FAIRFIELD ST.
DOWNING ST.
ARDWICK GREEN STH.
HYDE RD.
UPPER BROOK ST.
GROSVENOR ST.
MANCUNIAN WAY
MILLER ST.
SHUDEHILL
ST. PETER ST.
CHANCELLOR LA.
DEVONSHIRE ST. N.
STOCKPORT RD.
NEW BRI. ST.

6
Wives' Hill
Sugar Leach
Dickinsons
Bull Hill Maternity Home
High Tom Barn
Tom Barn
Smith's Height
Darwen
BB3
Bolton Barn Farm
Green Lowe
Cadshaw Clough Brook
Top o'th' Brow
Cranshaws
Cadshaw Farm
Lowe Hill
Black Hill
Cadshaw Cottages
Cadshaw Bridge
Cadshaw
Whewell's
Fairy Battery
TURTON MOOR
Grindle End
Andrew's Buttery
Yarnsdale Delph (disused)
Simms Clough
Greens Arms
Brownfield Quarry (disused)
Yarnsdale
Fox Hill
Simms Meadow Plantation
Cooper's
Rabbit Warren
Brownfield
Fox Hill Plantation
Turton
BLACKBURN ROAD
BOLTON ROAD
A666
Track of Old Tramway
Rushton's Brook
Shaft (dis)
Green Walls
GREENS ARMS
B6391
Holden's
Tarkingtons
Little Moor Clough
Top o'th' Brow
Owshaw Clough Brook
Stepping Stones
Old Man's
STONES BANK ROAD
Charter's Moss Plantation
Moss Side Plantation
BL7
Three Lowes
Whittles
Turton Heights
Stones Bank Brook
LANCASHIRE
GREATER MANCHESTER
Stones Bank Plantation
Top o'th' Meadow Plantation
STONES BANK BROW
Stones Bank Bridge
Rostrones
Broad Hill
Delph Brook
Valentines
Hole Bottoms (disused Quarry)
Moss Cottages
Horridge's Farm
EGERTON RD
Slate Brook
Slate Brook Bridge
Buffs
LONGWORTH
Hall Shore
The Hall Wood
Longworth Hall Plantation
Dimple
Dimple Hall
Dimple House
Chee
COX GREEN
Victoria Farm
Delph Reservoir
Longworth Clough
Lower Folds
Howarth's Fold Farm
Lynwood
Oak Field
School
New Butterworth's Farm
BOLTON
Siss Hey
Higher Fold Farm
Three Nooked Shaw Wood
Cricket Ground
Whittle Hill Farm
Works
Hey
Belmont or Eagley Brook
Higher Critchley Fold
Longworth Clough
Little Stanrose Farm
Spring Side Cottages
Lower Critchley Fold
Dewhurst Clough
Springs Reservoir
Hampsons Gate House
Pingle House
Egerton Ho.
Dingle Reservoir
Egerton
BELMONT
A675
BL1
Longworth Cottages
Egerton Lodge
Cox Green Quarries
Works
Dunscar Golf Course
Water Works Cottage
Hampson's Pasture
Shootersiee Wood
Prospect Place
22
School
BELMONT ROAD
69
370
71
19
18
17
16
415
1
2
3
4
5
6
7
8
9
A
B
C
D
E
F

7
72
73
74
375
19
18
17
16
15
G
H
J
K
L
M
1
2
3
4
5
6
7
8
9
Pike House
Round Barn Quarry (disused)
Round Barn
The Naze
Naze Clough
Orrell's Farm
Higher Barn Clough
Springside Farm
BLACKBURN
Wittlestone
Round Barn Farm
Poultry Farm
Orrell Cote Farm
Little Edge Farm
Cote Farm
Stanley Hill
Stanley Farm
Head
Bank Wood
Entwistle Rifle Range (disused)
Nevill's Fold
Wayoh Farm
Wayoh Fold Farm
Broadhead
Bisley Moor Side Farm
Edgeworth Moor
Slacks Farm
Crowthorn Farm
Edge Fold Delf
Edge Fold
Edgefold Farm
Delf Farm
Edge Foot Farm
Fold
Burton Hill
Fairfield
Moor Side Farm
MOORSIDE
ROAD
Wayoh Brow
Wayoh Bridge
Longworth Bank
School View
Green Alders
Crooked Walls
Ainsworth Recreation Ground
Gardeners Cottage
Agricultural Cottages
Willows Farm
Greystokes
Crowthorn School
Crowthorn Reservoir
Crowthorn End
CROWTHORN
School Cottages
Recreation Ground
Edge Moor Farm
Broad Meadow Farm
Brook
Hill Top Bungalow
Hill Top
Pleasant View
LANE
Entwistle
New House Farm
New Hall
ENTWISTLE
Dingle Farm
Dingle Cottage
Croft Gate
Wheatsheaf
Hob Lane Bridge
Paragon Nursing Home
Wheatsheaf Farm
Wheatsheaf Hill Farm
PLANTATION
Hall Shores Plantation
Entwistle
Railway Terrace
OVERSHORES
ENTWISTLE HALL LANE
Entwistle Hall Farm
Hob Lane Farm
SCHOOL
Hazel Clough Farm
Barons Farm
Holly Bank
CROW TREES
HOB
Nursery Farm
BATRIDGE RD
Higher Crow Trees
ISHERWOOD FOLD
Horrocks Fold Farm
Greenthorne
Batridge Clough
Armsgrove Clough
Bradshaw Brook Viaduct
Armsgrove Bridge
HORROCKS
MIDDLE FOLD
BROADHEAD
GREENTHORNE CL.
Wickenlow Hill Farm
8
B6391
Nabbs Farm
Horrocks Fold
AINSDALE AV.
FOXDALE CL.
Armsgrove Farm
Wayoh Reservoir
Edgworth Quarry (disused)
BURY
BROOKY MOOR
Hey Head Cottage
Hey Head
News Heys Farm
Sandy Bank
Edgworth
Recreation Ground
Quarlton
Lowes Moor
GREENS
Turton
Windy Harbour
Spring Bank Farm
Brandwood Fold
Temple Farm
Higher Barn Farm
ARMS
The Old Vicarage
Works
Turton Edgeworth C. of E. Methodist School
Hillock Farm
Lower Pelton Fold
Billy
EMBANKMENT RD
Fir Trees
Meadowcroft's Farm
Saltpie
Mill
Sports Ground
Works
Turton Bottoms Bridge
Clough House Farm
Close
Chapeltown
ROAD
HIGH ST
Pallet
Top of Quarlton
School
Mill
STATION
KAY ST
The Bungalow
WELLINGTON
Turton Bottoms
BIRCHES
KNOTTS BROW
Works
Stone Mill Cottages
Knotts Cottage
Low Hou
Birches
Bradshaw
Bottom o'th' Knotts Brow
Quarlton Fold Farm
Swine
Yard
Brook
Turton Tower
Tower Farm
Litherman's Bridge
LANCASHIRE
GREATER MANCHESTER
Jumbles
Walves Reservoir
TOWER DRIVE
Tower Rakes
Tunnel Mouth
RAMSBOTTOM
BOLTON
Horrobin Lodge
Jumbles Country Park
New House
B6213
TOTTINGTON RD.
Torra Barn
THE COPSE
THE SPINNEY
HORROBIN LA
Lees Cottages
Reservoir
WATLING
TURTON RD.
A676
BL8
Hazelhurst
Hazelhurst Wood
Walsh Fold Farm
Farnworth Hall Farm
Turton Golf Course
Club House
Horrobin Fold
BL2
Wood End
Walsh Fold
Fletchers
Jumbles Reservoir
23
Bradshaw Head
Moor Gate
Toy Farm
BRADSHAW
STREET
CHAPELTOWN
Holts Fold
Reservoir
Wittsende Farm
Top of Turton
Last Drop Village

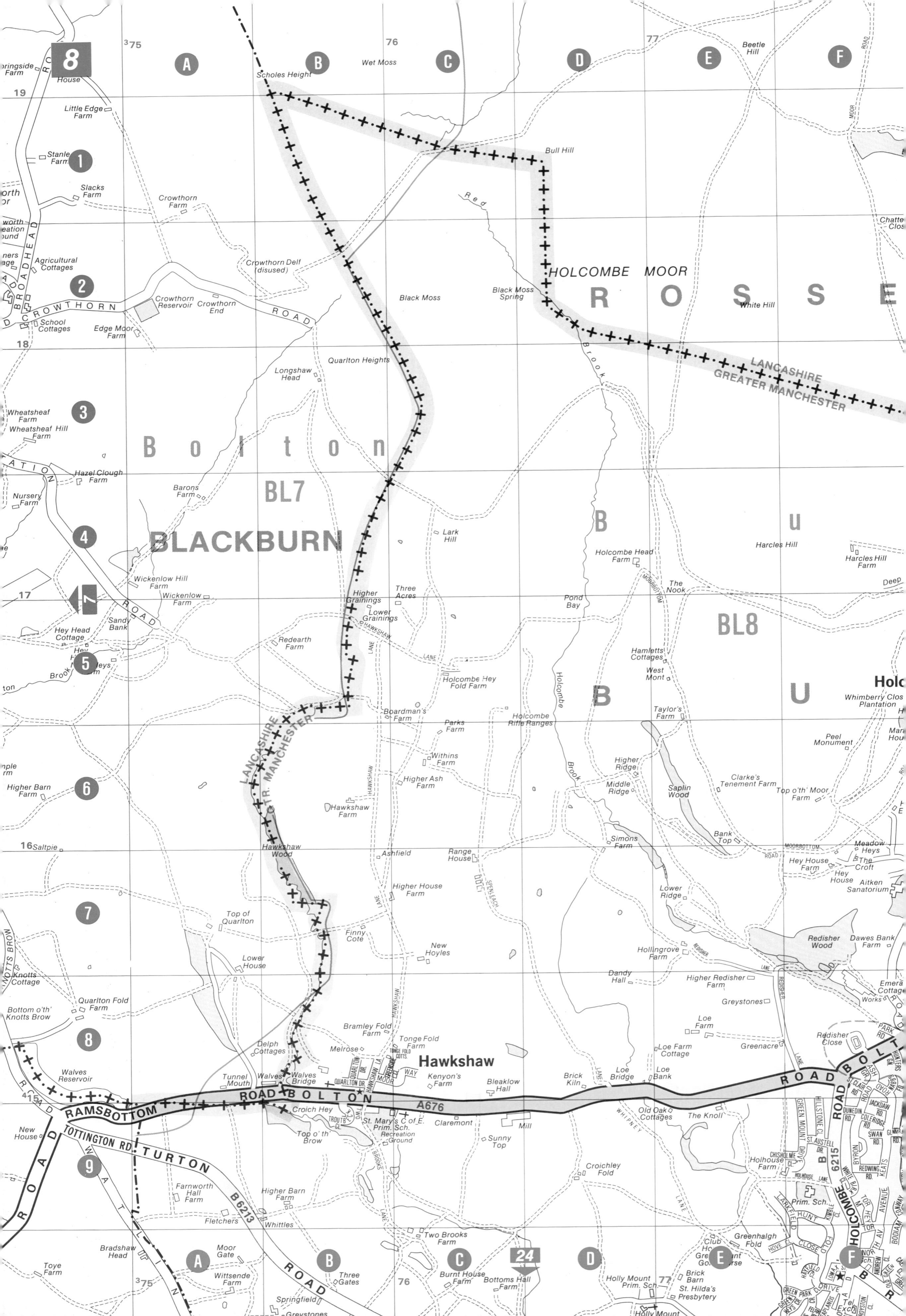

8
A
B
C
D
E
F
Scholes Height
Wet Moss
Beetle Hill
House
Little Edge Farm
Bull Hill
Slacks Farm
Crowthorn Farm
Red
HOLCOMBE MOOR
Agricultural Cottages
Crowthorn Delf (disused)
Black Moss
Black Moss Spring
ROSSE
White Hill
CROWTHORN ROAD
Crowthorn Reservoir
Crowthorn End
School Cottages
Edge Moor Farm
Brook
LANCASHIRE
GREATER MANCHESTER
Quarlton Heights
Longshaw Head
Wheatsheaf Farm
Wheatsheaf Hill Farm
Bolton
Hazel Clough Farm
Barons Farm
BL7
Nursery Farm
BLACKBURN
Lark Hill
Bu
Holcombe Head Farm
Harcles Hill
Harcles Hill Farm
Wickenlow Hill Farm
Wickenlow Farm
The Nook
Deep
Higher Grainings
Three Acres
Lower Grainings
Pond Bay
Sandy Bank
ROAD
Hey Head Cottage
Redearth Farm
HAWKSHAW LANE
Hamletts Cottages
BL8
West Mont
Holcombe Hey Fold Farm
Holcombe
BU
Taylor's Farm
Whimberry Clos Plantation
Boardman's Farm
Parks Farm
Holcombe Rifle Ranges
LANCASHIRE GTR. MANCHESTER
Withins Farm
Peel Monument
Higher Ridge
Higher Barn Farm
Higher Ash Farm
Middle Ridge
Saplin Wood
Clarke's Tenement Farm
Top o'th' Moor Farm
Hawkshaw Farm
Bank Top
16 Saltpie
Hawkshaw Wood
Ashfield
Range House
Simons Farm
MOORBOTTOM ROAD
Meadow Heys
Hey House Farm
The Croft
Hey House
Aitken Sanatorium
Higher House Farm
SPENLEACH
Lower Ridge
Top of Quarlton
Finny Cote
New Hoyles
Redisher Wood
Dawes Bank Farm
Hollingrove Farm
REDISHER LANE
Lower House
Dandy Hall
Higher Redisher Farm
Knotts Cottage
Quarlton Fold Farm
Greystones
Bottom o'th' Knotts Brow
Loe Farm
Redisher Close
Bramley Fold Farm
Tonge Fold Farm
Greenacre
Delph Cottages
Melrose
Loe Farm Cottage
Walves Reservoir
Hawkshaw
Brick Kiln
Loe Bridge
Loe Bank
Tunnel Mouth
Walves
Walves Bridge
Kenyon's Farm
Bleaklow Hall
ROAD BOLTON
ROAD BOLTON
Croich Hey
A676
Old Oak Cottages
The Knoll
RAMSBOTTOM
St. Mary's C of E. Prim. Sch.
Recreation Ground
Claremont
Mill
Top o' th' Brow
New House
TOTTINGTON RD.
TURTON
Sunny Top
Croichley Fold
Holhouse Farm
9
ROAD
Farnworth Hall Farm
B6213
Higher Barn Farm
Prim. Sch.
Fletchers
Whittles
Bradshaw Head
Moor Gate
Two Brooks Farm
Greenhalgh Fold
24
Toye Farm
Wittsende Farm
Three Gates
Burnt House Farm
Bottoms Hall Farm
Holly Mount Prim. Sch.
Brick Barn
St. Hilda's Presbytery
Springfield
ROAD
Greystones
Holly Mount
HOLCOMBE ROAD B6215
375
76
77
19
18
17
16
15
1
2
3
4
5
6
7

9
Edenfield
Strongstry
Chatterton
Stubbins
Ramsbottom
RAMSBOTTOM
Shuttleworth
Turn
Carr
Peel Brow
Fletcher Bank
Nuttall Lane
Nuttall
Tanners
Hazelhurst
Woodhey
Brooksbottom's
Summerseat
Lower Summerseat
Higher Summerseat
Holcombe Brook
Rowlands
Junction 1
Baldingstone
Wood
BL0
BL9
M66
M66 MOTORWAY
A56
A676
A680
B6214
HELMSHORE ROAD
BOLTON ROAD NORTH
ROCHDALE ROAD
MANCHESTER ROAD
WALMERSLEY ROAD
BURY OLD ROAD
BOLTON ROAD WEST
CARR ROAD
ROSSENDALE
LANCASHIRE
GREATER MANCHESTER
Chatterton Hey Wood
Buckden Cottage
Lower Buckden
Higher Buckden
Broadwood Edge Farm
Gibbon Green
Eaves Farm
Middle Red Lees
Lower Red Lees
Higher Red Lees
The Bungalow
Higher Stubbins
Ox Hey Wood
Carr Barn Wood
Higher Dick Field
Lower Dick Field
Hillcrest
Top Farm
Higher Tops
Old Bar House
Kibboth Crew
Top Wood
Woodhill House
Sheep Hey
Windy Bank Farm
Grave Yard
Anthony Fold
Green Hill Farm
Cross Bank Reservoir
Leach Barn
Moor Side Farm
Kay Barn Farm
Smithy Carr Farm
Bleakholt Farm
Recreation Ground
Top o'th' Lea
Dry Gap
Scout Fold
Lowes Farm Cottages
Cote Farm House
Scout Barns
New Gate
Acre Nook Farm
Hollin's Quarry (disused)
Hillcrest Hollins Villas
Moorgarth
Bouville
The Mount
Plunge Farm
Grime Cote
Dearden Clough Bridge
Fletcher Bank Quarry
Grime Height
Shipper Bottom Farm
Whitelow Hillock
Park House
Pike Farm
Pike Wood
Park Wood Farm
Pinfold
Grant's Tower
Grant's Wood
Bent House Farm
Top o'th' Hoof Farm
Hoof Farm
Butcher Acre Farm
Mam Hill
Ridshaw
Higher Sedger Hey
Snape Hill
High Hope
Nangreaves
Whitewall Farm
Lower Longcroft Cottages
Longcroft House
Throstle Hill
Gollinrod
Red Hall
Tower View
Higher Gollinrod
Gollinrod Wood
Bast House
Bassfield Farm
Crag Farm
Robinson Kay Home
Cricket Ground
Sewage Works
Twist Bridge
Chest Well Bridge
Higher Wood Road Farm
Nabbs Farm
Summerseat Residential School
Lammy Bank
Play Area
Rylston Wood Hey
Woodhey Comp. Sch.
Broad Hey Wood
Cemetery
Ramsbottom Cottage Hosp.
Tag Wood
Tower View
Half Acres
Higher House
Higher Barn
Quarry (dis)
Carr Brae
The Old Rectory
Square River Bridge
Bowling Green
Nuttall Park
Playground
Crow Lumb Wood
Acre Bottom Cricket Ground
Swimming Pool
Rosebank House
Stubbins Cnty. Prim. Sch.
Chatterton Farm
Highbury
The Cliffe
Springfield
Lower Park
Park Wood
Brook
Well Bank
Higher Fold
Bank Lane
Cross Bank Brook
Brook Bottom Brook
Lane End
Croft Hey
Sunny Clough
River Irwell
East Lancashire Railway
Brooksbottom Tunnel
10
25
78
79
380
81
19
18
17
16
415
G
H
J
K
L
M
1
2
3
4
5
6
7
8
9

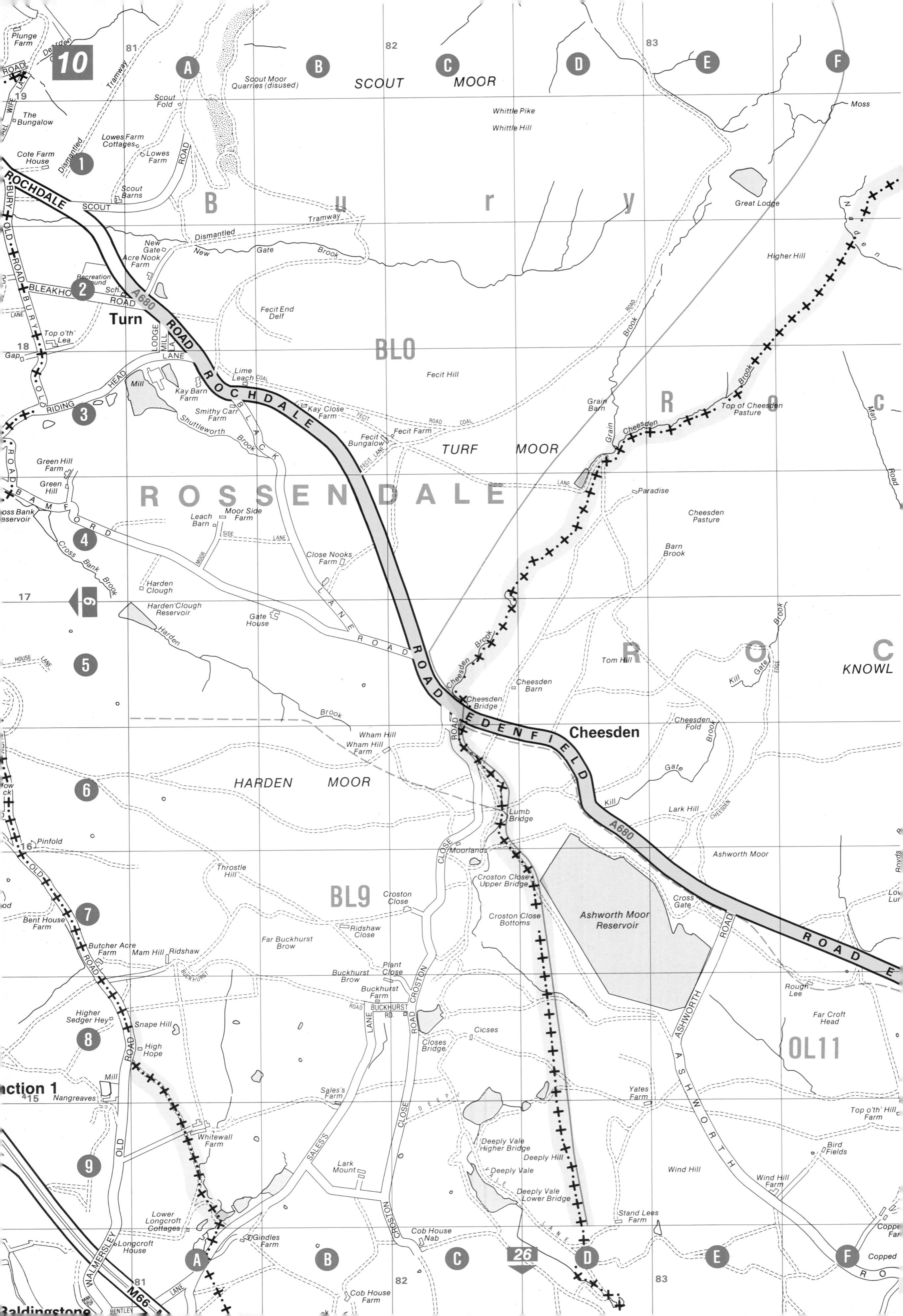
10
Plunge Farm
Dearden
ROAD
WIFE LA
19
The Bungalow
Tramway
81
82
83
A
B
C
D
E
F
Scout Moor Quarries (disused)
SCOUT
MOOR
Scout Fold
Whittle Pike
Whittle Hill
Moss
Lowes Farm Cottages
Lowes Farm
Cote Farm House
Dismantled
1
ROAD
Scout Barns
ROCHDALE
SCOUT
B
u
r
y
Great Lodge
Tramway
Dismantled
New Gate
New
Gate
Brook
Acre Nook Farm
Higher Hill
Naden
Recreation Ground
Sch.
BLEAKHO
2
ROAD
A680
Turn
Fecit End Delf
ROAD
Brook
LANE
Top o'th' Lea
18
Gap
LODGE
MILL LA
ROAD
LANE
BLO
Fecit Hill
Lime Leach
COAL
HEAD
Mill
Kay Barn Farm
ROCHDALE
Kay Close Farm
Grain Barn
R
g
C
RIDING
3
Smithy Carr Farm
BLACK
FECIT
ROAD
COAL
Cheesden
Top of Cheesden Pasture
Man
Shuttleworth
Brook
Fecit Bungalow
Fecit Farm
Grain
TURF
MOOR
Green Hill Farm
Green Hill
FECIT LANE
LANE
Road
ROAD
BAMFORD
ROSSENDALE
Paradise
Cross Bank Reservoir
Leach Barn
Moor Side Farm
SIDE
LANE
Cheesden Pasture
4
MOOR
Close Nooks Farm
Barn Brook
Cross Bank Brook
Harden Clough
17
9
Harden Clough Reservoir
Gate House
LANE
ROAD
Brook
Brook
HOUSE LANE
5
Harden
ROAD
Cheesden
R
O
C
Tom Hill
KNOWL
Cheesden Barn
Kill
Gate
EDGE
Cheesden Bridge
Brook
Wham Hill
Wham Hill Farm
ROAD
EDENFIELD
Cheesden
Cheesden Fold
Brook
Gate
6
HARDEN
MOOR
Kill
Lumb Bridge
Lark Hill
CHEESDEN
A680
Pinfold
16
CLOSE
Moorlands
Ashworth Moor
Roads
Throstle Hill
OLD
Croston Close Upper Bridge
BL9
Croston Close
Cross Gate
7
Bent House Farm
Ashworth Moor Reservoir
Croston Close Bottoms
Ridshaw Close
ROAD
Butcher Acre Farm
Mam Hill
Ridshaw
Far Buckhurst Brow
ROAD
BUCKHURST
Plant Close
Buckhurst Brow
ROAD
Higher Sedger Hey
Buckhurst Farm
ROAD
BUCKHURST RD.
LANE
ROAD
CROSTON
Rough Lee
Snape Hill
Cicses
Far Croft Head
8
High Hope
Closes Bridge
ASHWORTH
OL11
ROAD
Mill
nction 1
415
Nangreaves
Sales's Farm
DEEPLY
Yates Farm
CLOSE
ASHWORTH
Top o'th' Hill Farm
Whitewall Farm
Deeply Vale Higher Bridge
Deeply Hill
Bird Fields
9
OLD
SALES'S
Deeply Vale
Wind Hill
Lark Mount
Wind Hill Farm
Deeply Vale Lower Bridge
Lower Longcroft Cottages
CROSTON
Stand Lees Farm
Coppe Fa
Gindles Farm
Cob House Nab
LANE
Longcroft House
A
B
C
26
D
E
F
Copped
WALMERSLEY
81
82
83
RO
M66
LANE
Cob House Farm
BANK TOP
BENTLEY
aldingstone

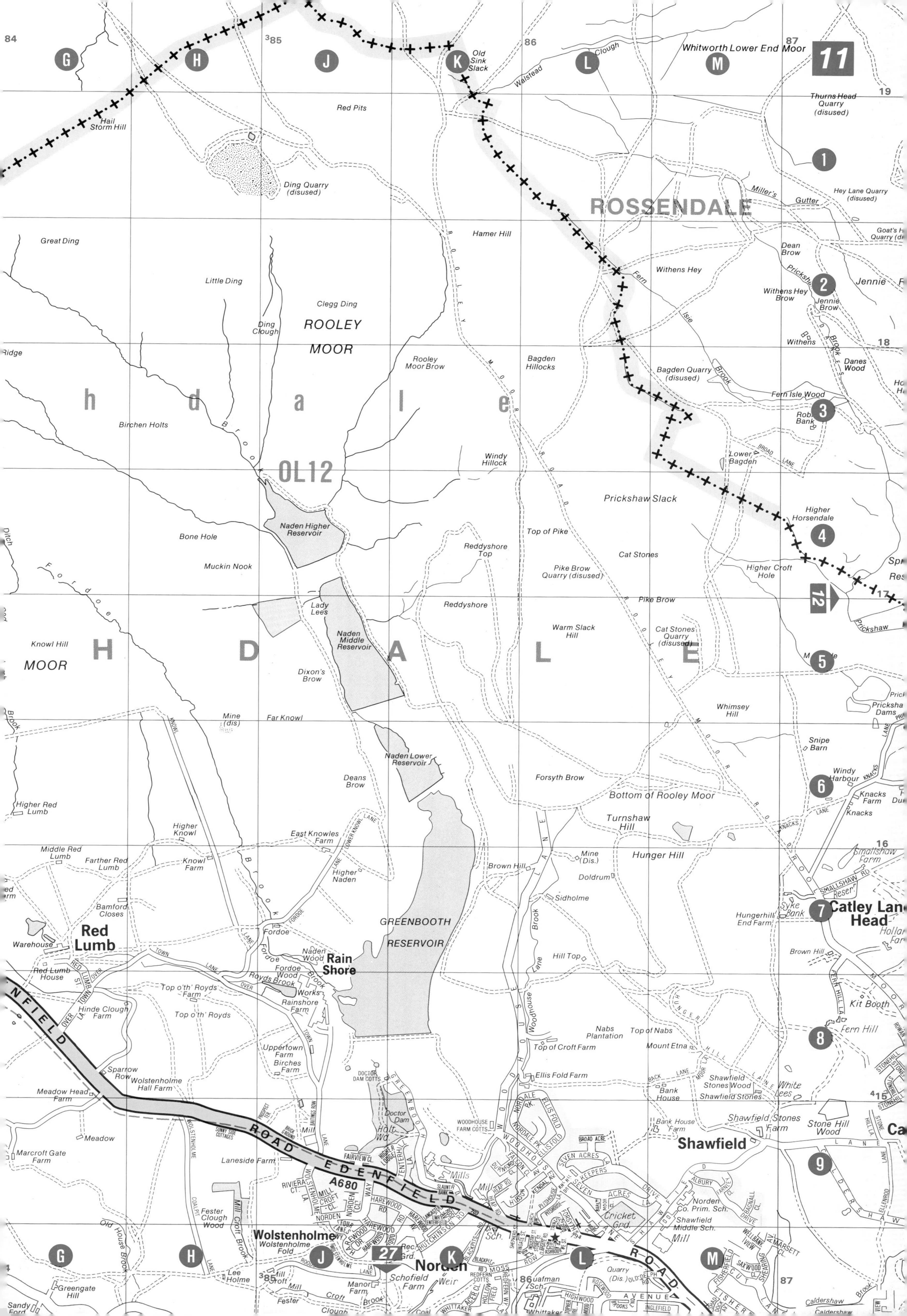

84
385
86
87
11
19
18
17
16
15
G
H
J
K
L
M
Old Sink Slack
Walstead
Clough
Whitworth Lower End Moor
Thurns Head Quarry (disused)
Hail Storm Hill
Red Pits
Ding Quarry (disused)
ROSSENDALE
Miller's
Gutter
Hey Lane Quarry (disused)
Great Ding
Hamer Hill
Dean Brow
Prickshaw
Little Ding
Withens Hey
Jennie
Clegg Ding
Withens Hey Brow
Jennie Brow
Fern
Isle
Ding Clough
ROOLEY MOOR
Withens
Ridge
Rooley Moor Brow
Bagden Hillocks
Bagden Quarry (disused)
Brook
Danes Wood
Fern Isle Wood
h d a l e
Birchen Holts
Robin Bank
Broad Lane
Lower Bagden
Windy Hillock
OL12
Prickshaw Slack
Higher Horsendale
Naden Higher Reservoir
Bone Hole
Top of Pike
Reddyshore Top
Cat Stones
Muckin Nook
Pike Brow Quarry (disused)
Higher Croft Hole
12
Fordoe
Lady Lees
Reddyshore
Pike Brow
Naden Middle Reservoir
Warm Slack Hill
Cat Stones Quarry (disused)
Prickshaw
Knowl Hill
MOOR
H D A L E
Dixon's Brow
Rooley Moor Road
Whimsey Hill
Prickshaw Dams
Mine (dis)
Far Knowl
Snipe Barn
Naden Lower Reservoir
Windy Harbour
Knacks
Deans Brow
Forsyth Brow
Bottom of Rooley Moor
Knacks Farm
Knacks
Higher Red Lumb
Turnshaw Hill
Higher Knowl
East Knowles Farm
Lower Knowl Lane
Middle Red Lumb
Farther Red Lumb
Knowl Farm
Brown Hill
Mine (Dis.)
Hunger Hill
Smallshaw Farm
Smallshaw Rd
Higher Naden
Doldrum
Bamford Closes
Sidholme
Syke Bank
Catley Lane Head
Hungerhill End Farm
Red Lumb
GREENBOOTH RESERVOIR
Warehouse
Fordoe
Naden Wood
Rain Shore
Hill Top
Brown Hill
Red Lumb House
Town Lane
Fordoe Wood
Royds Brook
Top o'th' Royds Farm
Works
Rainshore Farm
Hinde Clough Farm
Top o'th' Royds
Woodhouse Lane
Hunger Hill
Kit Booth
Nabs Plantation
Top of Nabs
Fern Hill
Mount Etna
Top of Croft Farm
Uppertown Farm
Birches Farm
Sparrow Row
Wolstenholme Hall Farm
Doctor Dam Cotts
Ellis Fold Farm
Back Lane
Shawfield Stones Wood
Shawfield Stones
White Lees
Meadow Head Farm
Bank House
Doctor Dam
Holt Wd
Woodhouse Farm Cotts
Bank House Farm
Shawfield Stones Farm
Stone Hill Wood
Meadow
ROAD
EDENFIELD
Marcroft Gate Farm
Laneside Farm
Fairview Cl
A680
Shawfield
Mills
Cricket Grd
Norden Co. Prim. Sch.
Shawfield Middle Sch.
Fester Clough Wood
Mill Croft Brook
Old House Brook
Wolstenholme
Wolstenholme Fold
27
Norden
Rec Grd
Quarry (Dis.)
G
H
J
K
L
M
Lee Holme
Hill Croft
Mill
Manor Farm
Schofield Farm
Weir
Greengate Hill
Sandy Ford
Fester
Croft
Clough
Brook
Caldershaw
INFIELD

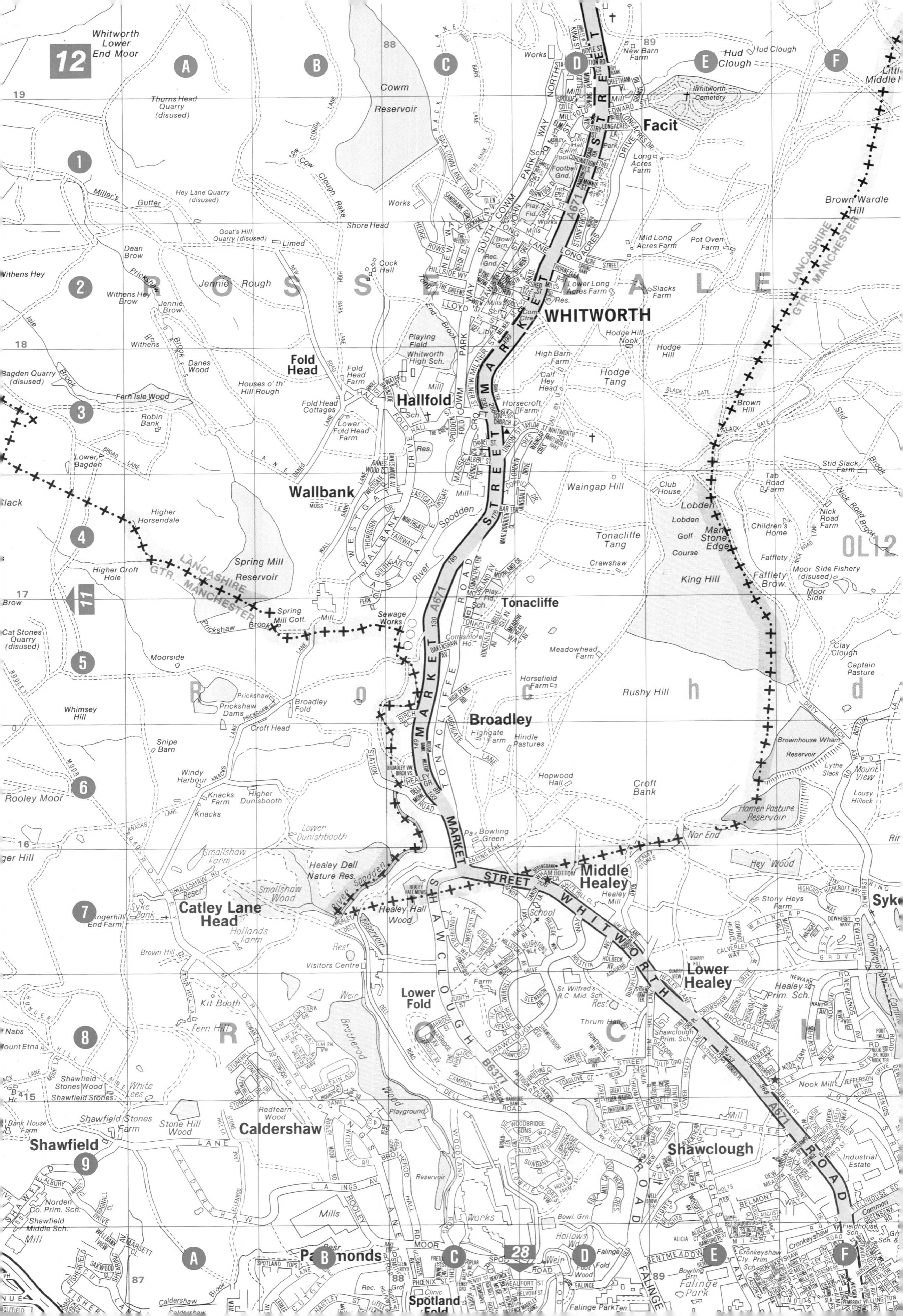
12
Whitworth Lower End Moor
Thurns Head Quarry (disused)
Cowm Reservoir
Hud Clough
Whitworth Cemetery
Facit
Long Acres Farm
New Barn Farm
Miller's Gutter
Hey Lane Quarry (disused)
Goat's Hill Quarry (disused)
Shore Head
Dean Brow
Withens Hey
Withens Hey Brow
Jennie Rough
Jennie Brow
Cock Hall
Mid Long Acres Farm
Pot Oven Farm
Lower Long Acres Farm
Slacks Farm
Brown Wardle Hill
ROSSENDALE
WHITWORTH
Hodge Hill Nook
Hodge Hill
Hodge Tang
Withens
Bagden Quarry (disused)
Danes Wood
Fold Head
Houses o' th' Hill Rough
Fern Isle Wood
Robin Bank
Lower Bagden
Playing Field
Whitworth High Sch.
Hallfold
Fold Head Farm
Fold Head Cottages
Lower Fold Head Farm
High Barn Farm
Calf Hey Head
Horsecroft Farm
Brown Hill
Wallbank
Waingap Hill
Club House
Lobden
Lobden Golf Course
Man Stone Edge
Stid Slack Farm
Tab Road Farm
Nick Road Farm
Children's Home
Higher Horsendale
Higher Croft Hole
Spring Mill Reservoir
LANCASHIRE GTR. MANCHESTER
Tonacliffe Tang
Crawshaw
King Hill
Faffley
Faffley Brow
Moor Side Fishery (disused)
Moor Side
OL12
11
Spring Mill Cott.
Sewage Works
Tonacliffe
Cat Stones Quarry (disused)
Moorside
Meadowhead Farm
Horsefield Farm
Rushy Hill
Clay Clough
Captain Pasture
Prickshaw
Prickshaw Dams
Broadley Fold
Croft Head
Whimsey Hill
Rochdale
Broadley
Highgate Farm
Hindle Pastures
Brownhouse Wham Reservoir
Snipe Barn
Windy Harbour
Knacks Farm
Knacks
Higher Dunisbooth
Lower Dunishbooth
Hopwood Hall
Croft Bank
Lythe Slack
Mount View
Lousy Hillock
Hamer Pasture Reservoir
Rooley Moor
Nor End
Bowling Green
Smallshaw Farm
Healey Dell Nature Res.
Smallshaw Wood
Middle Healey
Healey Mill
Hey Wood
Stony Heys Farm
Catley Lane Head
Syke Bank
Ingerhill End Farm
Hollands Farm
Healey Hall Wood
School
Lower Healey
Healey Prim. Sch.
Brown Hill
Visitors Centre
Lower Fold
St. Wilfred's R.C. Mid. Sch.
Thrum Hall
Shawclough Prim. Sch.
Kit Booth
Fern Hill
Brotherod
Nabs
Mount Etna
Shawfield Stones Wood
White Lees
Shawfield Stones
Redfearn Wood
Playground
Nook Mill
Industrial Estate
Bank House Farm
Shawfield Stones Farm
Stone Hill Wood
Caldershaw
Shawfield
Shawclough
Norden Co. Prim. Sch.
Shawfield Middle Sch.
Mills
Works
Reservoir
Palmonds
Spotland Fold
Falinge Fold
Falinge Park
Cronkeyshaw Cty. Prim. Sch.
Fieldhouse Sch.
Caldershaw Brook
A671
B6377
MARKET STREET
WHITWORTH ROAD
SHAWCLOUGH ROAD
A B C D E F
1 2 3 4 5 6 7 8 9
88 89 87
19 18 17 16 415
28

13
14
29
Crook Moor
Allenden Hill
Turn Slack Hill
Fox Stones Hill
Turn Slack Dam
Old Charles Hill
Blue Pot Brook
Long Shoot Clough
Higher Slack Brook
Clay Pots Hill
Flight Hill
Lower Turn Slack Hill
Dearden's Pasture
Turn Slack Clough
Ringing Pots Hill
Wardle Brook
Hills Clough
Grimes
Higher Stone Pits
Stansfield Hill
Dobbin Hill
Watergrove Reservoir
Lower Stone Pits
Long Clough
Littleborough
Stony Brook
High Lee Slack
Ratcliffe Hill
Long Clough Brook
Quarry (disused)
Trap Farm
Higher Pemmin
Clough
OL15
Heights Farm
Clough Ter.
Lower Newgate
Works
Stid Fold
Lower House
Lower Pemmin
East Hill
Higher Shore Wood
Middle Wood Brook
Green Hill
High Lea
Benthead Farm
Benthead Bungalow
Wardle Farm
Wardle Fold
Higher Shore
Higher Shore House
Nick Road Brook
Hurstead Nook
Clough House Farm
Wardle Mill
East Top Farm
Wardle
Shore Fold
Shore
Stid Hey Bottom
Clough Ho. Farm Cotts.
Hunger Hill
Woodend La.
Pedler Brow
Caldermoor
Clough House Brook
Pedler Brow
Starring Wood
Higher Starring Farm
Birch Hill
Featherstall Brook
Rydings Mount
Rydings Farm
Bench Carr
Starring Hill
Middle Starring
Sports Gnd.
Stubley
St. Mary's Prim. Sch.
Rydings Dam
Fanny Brook
Wardle High School
Birch Hill Hospital
Cemetery
Birchen Head Farm
Great Howarth
Ashbrook Hey
C. of E. Prim. Sch.
Featherstall Road
Stubley New Hall
Dearnley
St. John's Prim. Sch.
Rydings Sch.
Comm. Cen.
Ashbrook Hey Farm
Works
Council Offices
Hurstead
Lows Lane
Reservoir
Buckley Brook
Buckley Wood
Weirs
Ash Brook
Play Field
Roch
Calliards Ho. Fm.
Lodge Bri
Brown Brow Hill
Lower Cleggswood Farm
Rochdale Canal (Dis.)
Reservoir
Buckley Hall (H.M. Detention Cen.)
Resr.
Play Fld.
Smallbridge
Greengate
Wuerdle
Yea Bri.
Smithy Bridge Prim. Sch.
Holl
Cross Lees Farm
Greenfield
Higher Eafield Farm
Smithy Bridge
Buckley
Moss Cottages
OL16
Lower Eafield
Ball Barn Farm
School
Alice Ingham R.C. Prim. Sch.
Hamar Prim. Sch.
Howarth Cross
Youth Club
Little Clegg
All Saints C. of E. Prim. Sch.
Halifax Road
Albert Royds St.
Clegg Hall Bridge
Clegg Hall
Branch Road
Peanock Farm
Hey Brook
Clover
Beal
Weir
Shaw Moss
Shaw La.
Works
G
H
J
K
L
M
1
2
3
4
5
6
7
8
9
90
91
92
93
19
18
17
16
15
A58
A664
B6225
D
L

14
13
30
Summit
Timbercliffe
Calderbrook
Clough
Gale
Shore
Caldermoor
Stubley
Durn
Ealees
Lydgate
LITTLEBOROUGH
Dearnley
Hollingworth
Smithy Bridge
Whittaker
Rakewood
Little Clegg
HOLLINGWORTH LAKE
WHITTAKER GOLF COURSE
CHELBURN MOOR
CLEGG MOOR
Calderbrook Moor
OL15
TODMORDEN ROAD
HALIFAX ROAD
CHURCH ST.
FEATHERSTALL ROAD
HOLLINGWORTH ROAD
LAKE BANK
RAKEWOOD ROAD
MILNROW ROAD
WILD HOUSE LANE
BLACKSTONE EDGE
M62 MOTORWAY
A58
A6033
B6225
Littleborough

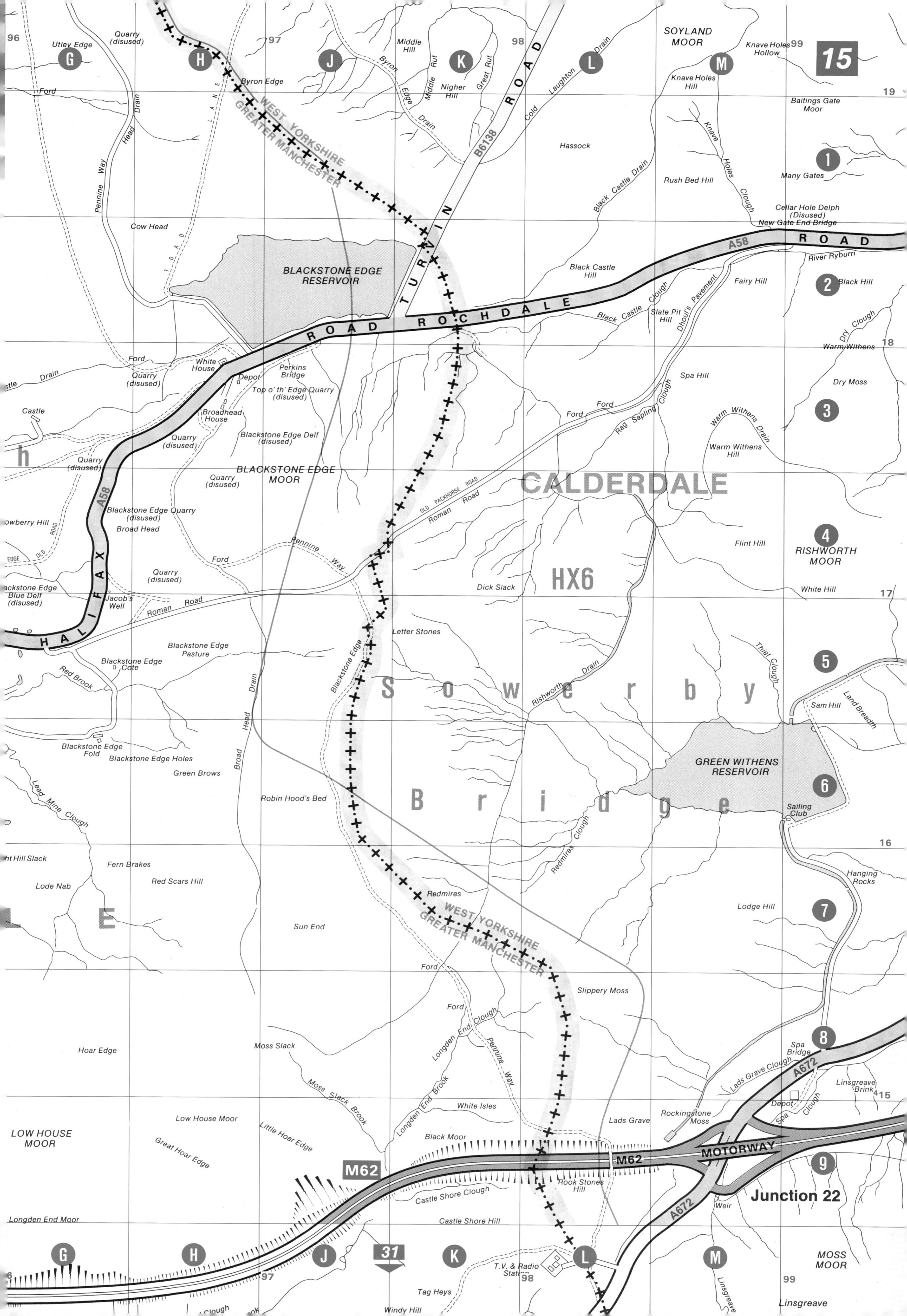
15
96
97
98
99
19
18
17
16
15
G
H
J
K
L
M
1
2
3
4
5
6
7
8
9
Utley Edge
Quarry (disused)
Ford
Byron Edge
WEST YORKSHIRE
GREATER MANCHESTER
Middle Hill
Byron Edge Drain
Middle Rut
Great Rut
Nigher Hill
ROAD
B6138
Cold Laughton Drain
SOYLAND MOOR
Knave Holes Hollow
Knave Holes Hill
Baitings Gate Moor
Hassock
Knave Holes Clough
Many Gates
Rush Bed Hill
Black Castle Drain
Cellar Hole Delph (Disused)
New Gate End Bridge
Head Drain
Pennine Way
LANE
TOAD
Cow Head
BLACKSTONE EDGE RESERVOIR
TURVIN
A58
ROAD
River Ryburn
Black Castle Hill
Fairy Hill
Black Hill
ROAD ROCHDALE
Black Castle Clough
Slate Pit Hill
Dhoul's Pavement
Dry Clough
Warm Withens
Ford
White House
Quarry (disused)
Depot
Perkins Bridge
Top o' th' Edge Quarry (disused)
Spa Hill
Dry Moss
Drain
Castle
Broadhead House
Quarry (disused)
Blackstone Edge Delf (disused)
Ford
Ford
Rag Sapling Clough
Warm Withens Drain
Warm Withens Hill
Quarry (disused)
BLACKSTONE EDGE MOOR
Quarry (disused)
CALDERDALE
OLD PACKHORSE ROAD
Roman Road
Blackstone Edge Quarry (disused)
Broad Head
Flint Hill
RISHWORTH MOOR
Pennine Way
Ford
Quarry (disused)
Dick Slack
HX6
Blackstone Edge Blue Delf (disused)
Jacob's Well
Roman Road
HALIFAX
White Hill
Letter Stones
Blackstone Edge Pasture
Blackstone Edge Cote
Red Brook
Blackstone Edge
Thief Clough
Sowerby
Rishworth Drain
Sam Hill
Land Breadth
Broad Head Drain
Blackstone Edge Fold
Blackstone Edge Holes
Green Brows
GREEN WITHENS RESERVOIR
Lead Mine Clough
Robin Hood's Bed
Bridge
Sailing Club
Redmires Clough
Fern Brakes
Red Scars Hill
Lode Nab
Redmires
Hanging Rocks
Lodge Hill
E
Sun End
Ford
Slippery Moss
Ford
Longden End Clough
Pennine Way
Hoar Edge
Moss Slack
Moss Slack Brook
Longden End Brook
White Isles
Spa Bridge
Lads Grave Clough
A672
Linsgreave Brink
Depot
Spa Clough
Low House Moor
LOW HOUSE MOOR
Little Hoar Edge
Great Hoar Edge
Black Moor
Lads Grave
Rockingstone Moss
MOTORWAY
M62
M62
Rook Stones Hill
Junction 22
Castle Shore Clough
Weir
A672
Longden End Moor
Castle Shore Hill
31
MOSS MOOR
T.V. & Radio Station
Tag Heys
Linsgreave
Windy Hill
Linsgreave

16
RIDLEY
SALT PIT LA
Mawdesley R.C. School
School Farm
EAST
BACK LANE
Tootles Farm
Andertons' Mill
BENTLEY LANE
Three Posts Green
Myrtle House
Ormskirk
L40
Windy Ridge
Gauger's Farm
Gauger's House
Harrock Windmill (dis.)
Harrock Hill
Mine (dis.)
Quarry (dis.)
Halliwell's o'th' Hill
Dwerry House
Cross (rems. of)
SANDERSON LANE
Sanderson House
Threaper's Green
Swift's House
Rivington View
Fisher's Cottages
Anglefield Cottages
Barmskin Hall Farm
The Oaks
Cragg's Farm
Spencer House
BARMSKIN LANE
TOWN LANE
Howe Brook
Wrennall's Lower House
Higher Wrennall
Charity Farm
Grundy's Farm
COOPERS HILL
Vicarage
SMITHY LANE
BROW
CHURCH LANE
Heskin Gorse
Kingsley House
WOOD LANE
B5250
Martin House
School Farm
Chisnall's o'th' Brow
Wakefield House
Tan Pitt Farm
HOUSE
Hargreaves Farm
Copyhold Farm
Manor House
CARR
Cowling's Farm
Sandhole Farm
Wrightington Bar
North Tunley
Stringer's Farm
Cowling's Spout
BROADHURST LA.
Higher Broadhurst Farm
Lower Broadhurst Farm
Raby Fold
MOSSY LEA
BROADHURST
Toogood Farm
TOOGOOD LANE
Wrights Coverts
Howe Brook
13
OLD MILL LANE
Bow Wood
Harrock Hill Reservoir
WEST LANCASHIRE
Mossy Lea
ROAD MOSSY
School
Moat
CHISNALL AV.
MANSE AV.
Well Wood
Harrock Hall
Butteries Wood
HARROCK LANE
Higher Barn
Hesketh House
Stone Leach
TUNLEY LANE
Hill House Fold
Pine Covert
South Tunley Hall
South Tunley Farm
Diglake Farm
Pumping Stat
Rigby's Bridge
Lathom's Charity Farm
Brook
Tunley
HILL HOUSE FOLD LANE
LOW LANE
12
WHITTLE LA.
High Moor
High Moor Club
HARROCK
STONY LA.
HIGH
Stony Lane Farm
BROAD HEY LANE
Bowling Green House Farm
MOOR LANE
High Moor Farm
Cardwell's House
Baron's Farm
Tunley Moss Farm
Nursery
TUNLEY MOSS
Moss View Farm
Lassell Far
Brown's Farm
COURAGE LOW
Poultry Houses
Boggart House
Olive House
Robin Hood Farm
Bury Hey Wood
Robin Hood
MOSS LANE
Moss House
Tunley Lane Farm
LEA
Courage Low Wood
Primrose Woods
Wigan
ROBIN HOOD LANE
Boar's Den Farm
Boar's Den
Coal Gate Cottages
Black Field Plantation
WN6
11
Sprodley Wood
Runshaw Pit
Dangerous Corner
Old Pond
Wrightington Bridge
HALL LANE
HILL
A5209
SPARROW
Parbold Hall
GLENSIDE
GLENS DE
APPLEY CL.
APPLEY LANE
Fairy Glen
Sprodley Brook
SPRODLEY DR.
GRESHAM DR.
NORTH DR.
SOUTH DR.
GROVE AV.
Waterfall
STONEYGATE LA.
West Lodge
Grove Houses
Wrightington Hospital
East Lodges
Wrightington Pond
The Rookery
CROW ORCHARD R
Boat House
New Pond
Foumart's Hill
The Dingle
Parbold Hill
Parbold Beacon
Parbold Quarries (Sandstone)
Delf House
Delf House Quarry (dis.)
Delf House Wood
Park House
Finch Farm
Big Wood
The Woods Nursery
FINCH LANE
LANE B5375
The Mount
Close Wood
Poultry Houses
Appley Bridge
Gillibrand House
WN8
NORTH
Richardson's Farm
Draper's Farm
School
Liby.
SKULL HOUSE
Engineering Works
Coal Pit Hey Plantation
Pumping Station
Worthington's Farm
BEACON VW
BACK SKULL HO. LA.
Works
32
Wood's Farm
410
Hand L Bridge
Pichill Wood
Sprodley
Dawber Delf
Depot
The Glen
Dawber Delf Farm
ASHFIELD TER.
RIVER
LEEDS
51
52
53
14
A
B
C
D
E
F
1
2
3
4
5
6
7
8
9

Whittle Mill Farm
Willow Cottage
Chisnall House
CROSTON LA.
Guest's Farm
Knob Farm
M6
CHORLEY LA.
Heaton's Farm
Depot
Barker Bridge
Whittle Bridge Farm
Whalleys Farm
A49 WHITTLE BROW
PRESTON
Haydock Farm
Four Acre Wood
Syd Brook
DOWN LANE
Coppull Ring Mill
Reservoir
Orchard Heyes
Vicarage
TANSLEY AV.
SPENDMORE
B5251
School
Health Cen.
Liby
Coppull
B5251 LANE
Coppull Parish Sch.
LANCASTER ST.
Yew Tree House
HALL
Works
Coppull Old Hall
Depot
Blainscough Wood
Green Lane Farm
C H O R L E Y
Moat
Blainscough Hall
Bernhey House
Works
Wet Oaks Wood
Vause Farm
Elmhurst Farm
Coppull Moor Farm
Coppull Cross Roads
JOLLY TAR
Fiddler's Nook
Jolly Tar Farm
The Nook
Bridge Farm
C h o r l e y
Sand Pit
Troy Fold Farm
Moss House
Patrick Farm
St. John's C. of E. School
Chisnall Wood
COPPULL MOOR
Coppull Moor
A49 ROAD
White Hill Farm
BOGBURN
HIC-BIBI
Moor House Farm
Coppull Hill
PR7
Chisnall Hall
18
The Grange
BOGBURN LANE
Bogburn Hall
(SPRINGS BROW)
Dark Lane Bridge
Stars Brook
Talbot House
Langtree Hall West
Langtree Old Hall
Sand Pit
LANCASHIRE
GREATER MANCHESTER
Workings
Bibby's Farm
Sand Pit
(STARS BROW)
Cross Farm
Workings
Cross Hey Wood
WN1
Sand Pit
Gorse Hall
Chadwick Farm
M6 MOTORWAY
Lane Farm
W I G A N
Sand Pit
Thompson House
Hunger Hill
School
Potters Farm
Depot
B5250
Pepper Lane Farm
Langtree
w a n
PEPPER LANE
BOUNDARY
Almond
Langtree Hall
Moat
Saddle Hill Farm
Dam House
BRADLEY HALL TRADING ESTATE
Robin Hill Farm East
Robin Hill Farm West
Shevington Moor
Standish High School
Factory
Factory
Barrowcroft Wood
BRADLEY
St. Marie's R.C. Junior & Infant School
GREENWOOD STREET
SHEVINGTON MOOR
CROW ORCHARD RD.
A5209
Chamberlain's Farm
ALMOND BROOK
Cat i'th' Window Farm
Rectory Farm
Black Horse Farm
STANDISH
RECTORY LANE
B5239
Reservoir
St. Wilfrid's Jun. and Inf. Sch.
Lark Hill
Kitchen Carr Wood
The Beeches
SCHOOL LA.
A5209
MARKET ST.
HIGH STREET
Playing Field
SHEVINGTON LANE
B5206
Aspinalls Farm
Gunnell's Fold Farm
Bowling Green House
Prim. Sch.
White Hill Farm
Pumping Station
33
Merrybone Farm
Cricket Ground
WIGAN

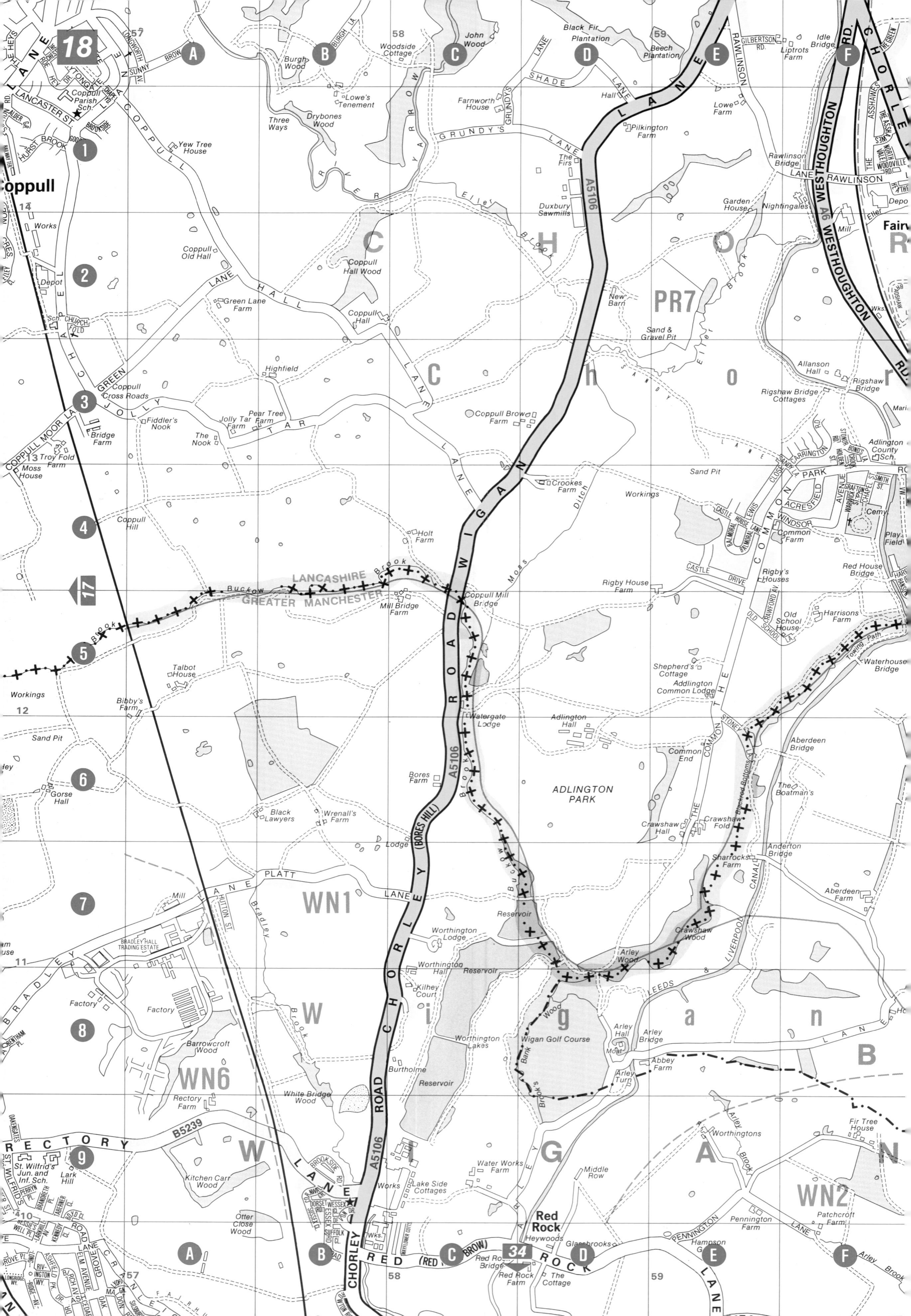
A
B
C
D
E
F
1
2
3
4
5
6
7
8
9
57
58
59
14
13
12
11
10
Coppull
Longworth
Tongate
Coppull Parish Sch.
Lancaster St.
Hurst Brook
Brookside
Sunny Av.
Brow
Burgh La.
Burgh Wood
Woodside Cottage
John Wood
Black Fir Plantation
Beech Plantation
Rawlinson Rd.
Gilbertson Rd.
Liptrots Farm
Idle Bridge
Lowe's Tenement
Drybones Wood
Three Ways
River Yarrow
Farnworth House
Grundy's Lane
Shade Lane
Hall
Pilkington Farm
Lowe Farm
Yew Tree House
Coppull Lane
The Firs
Duxbury Sawmills
A5106
Rawlinson Bridge
Rawlinson Lane
Garden House
Nightingales
Westhoughton Rd.
A6 Westhoughton Rd.
Mill
Depo
Works
Coppull Old Hall
Ellers Brook
C
H
O
R
Coppull Hall Wood
Depot
Hall Lane
Green Lane Farm
Coppull Hall
New Barn
PR7
Sand & Gravel Pit
Sandy
Church Fold
Chapel Lane
Green Lane
Coppull Cross Roads
Jolly Tar Lane
Highfield
Pear Tree Farm
Jolly Tar Farm
Fiddler's Nook
The Nook
Bridge Farm
Coppull Moor La.
Troy Fold Farm
Moss House
Coppull Brow Farm
Allanson Hall
Rigshaw Bridge
Rigshaw Bridge Cottages
Adlington County Sch.
Sand Pit
Workings
Park Rd.
Crookes Farm
Moss Ditch
Common Lane
Acresfield
Avenue
Windsor
Common Farm
Cemy.
Play Field
Coppull Hill
Holt Farm
Castle Drive
Lancashire
Greater Manchester
Buckow Brook
Coppull Mill Bridge
Mill Bridge Farm
Rigby House Farm
Rigby's Houses
Red House Bridge
Harrisons Farm
Old School House
Old School La.
Wigan Road
Talbot House
Bibby's Farm
Workings
Shepherd's Cottage
Addlington Common Lodge
Towing Path
Waterhouse Bridge
Sand Pit
Watergate Lodge
Adlington Hall
Common End
Aberdeen Bridge
The Common
Gorse Hall
Bores Farm
Chorley Road (Bores Hill)
Adlington Park
The Boatman's
Black Lawyers
Wrenall's Farm
Crawshaw Hall
Crawshaw Fold
Lodge
Anderton Bridge
Sharrocks Farm
Platt Lane
WN1
Mill
Hutton St.
Bradley Brook
Reservoir
Aberdeen Farm
Canal
Bradley Hall Trading Estate
Worthington Lodge
Crawshaw Wood
Arley Wood
Liverpool
Leeds
Bradley Lane
Worthington Hall
Reservoir
Kilhey Court
Factory
W
i
g
a
n
Barrowcroft Wood
Worthington Lakes
Wigan Golf Course
Arley Hall
Arley Bridge
Moat
B
WN6
Burtholme
Abbey Farm
Arley Turn
Bank Wood
Brook's
Reservoir
Rectory Farm
White Bridge Wood
Rectory Lane
B5239
St. Wilfrid's Jun. and Inf. Sch.
Lark Hill
Kitchen Carr Wood
W
I
G
A
N
Worthingtons
Arley Brook
Fir Tree House
Water Works Farm
Middle Row
Brookside Rd.
Works
Lake Side Cottages
WN2
Otter Close Wood
Red Rock
Heywoods
Glasbrooks
Pennington Lane
Pennington Farm
Patchcroft Farm
Hampson
Chorley Road
Red Rock Lane
Red Rock Bridge
Red Rock Farm
The Cottage
Arley Brook
Elm Avenue
Grove
Lane
Oak
Cedar
34
17

Rivington
Upper Rivington Reservoir
Pilkington Wd.
Pilkington Embankment
Dean Brook
Chapel House
Fisher House
Rivington Sch.
Croff Bri.
Waterhey Cott.
Rivington Hall Barn
Spring Cott.
Rivington Embankment
Horrobin Quarry (Dis.)
Dawber Quarry (Dis.)
Cunliffe Farm
Shaw Place
Bent House
Bay Horse Hotel
Slack's Farm
Lonsdale Farm
New House
Hole House Farm
Springfield Farm
Newlands
Major Bottoms
Windy Rannets
Home Farm
Anderton Park
Lower Rivington Reservoir
Great House Barn
Lever Park
Top o'th' Hill Farm
Ward's Cott.
Crosses
Brown Cot
The Castle
The Nursery
King George's Field
Tennis Crt.
Greenhalgh Farm
Rothwells Farm
PR6
Anderton
St. Joseph's R.C. Sch.
St. Paul's Sch.
Liby.
Adlington
ADLINGTON
Roscoe Lowe Hill
Roscoe Lowe
Tan Pits Farm
The Shawes
Throstle's Nest Farm
Woodward House
Headless Cross
Millstone Hotel
Mill Farm
Grimeford Village
Brown House Fm.
Crosse's Wood
Crosse's Creek
Quarry (Dis.)
Rivington Lodge
Hamer's Cott.
Lower Rivington Embankment
Anderton Manor Farm
Berne House
Lakeland Farm
Dryfield
Squirrel Hotel
Anderton Ford Bri.
Woodward Wood
Warehouses
Reservoirs
Huyton Fold
Edgewood
Goodman's Fold Farm
Crow's Nest
Grimeford Bri.
Grimeford Farm
White Hill
White Hill Farm
Markland Farm
Denton's Farm
Greenland's Farm
Great Ryeley
Anderton Service Area
Anderton Old Hall Farm
Mill Bri.
Crown Clough
Depot
Pumping Station
LANCASHIRE
GREATER MANCHESTER
BL6
Anderton House
Bolton
Crowshaw House
Crowshaw Farm
Pennington Hill
Pennington Fold
Holmes
Little Scotland
Rollinson House Farm
Rigby Hill
School
Cricket Grd.
Blackrod
Makinson's Fm.
Sibbering's Farm
Wood's Barn Farm
Blackrod Junction
BLACKROD
Cemy.
Hotel
Highfield Farm
Brown Fold
Copperas House
Borsdane Brook
Tucker's Hill Farm
Nightingale's Farm
Willoughby Farm
Freezeland Farm
Edge's Farm
Playing Field
Blackrod Prim. Sch.
Leigh Tenement Farm
Ridgway Bri.
Red Moss Bri.
Park Hall Farm
Barker's Fm.
Warehouses
Gibb Farm
Subway
Vale Farm
Vale Ho
Resr.
Reservoir
Works
Playing Fields
A673
A6
M61
M61 MOTORWAY
B5408
B5238 ROAD
BOLTON ROAD
CHORLEY ROAD
BLACKROD BY-PASS
MANCHESTER ROAD
STATION ROAD
CROWN LANE
HORROBIN LANE
ROSCOE LOWE BROW
SCOTLAND LANE
DARKING LANE
LITTLE SCOTLAND
TUCKERS HILL BROW
RIVER DOUGLAS
20
35

20
Rivington
63
64
365
A
B
C
D
E
F
Old Kate's Dingle
Noon Hill
Douglas Springs
CATTER NAB
Chapel House
Fisher House
Rivington Hall Barn
Hall Wood
Spring Cott.
Old Kate's Close
Rivington Sch.
Croft Bri.
RIVINGTON
MOOR
River Douglas
CHORLEY
Clump
Breres Meadow Pit
Hall Closes
The Nursery
14
LEVER PARK
Great House
Tower
RIVINGTON PIKE
Top o'th' Hill Farm
Ward's Cott.
Gilsbrook
BROWN HILL
Crooked Edge Clough
CROOKED EDGE HILL
LANCASHIRE
GREATER MANCHESTER
Crosses
Brown Cot
Higher Derbyshires
BOLTON
Two Lads
Pall Mall
Higher Knoll
Pike Cott.
The Castle
RESERVOIR
13
Middle Derbyshires
Knowle House
Shaw's Clough
Shaw's Wood
WILDER'S MOOR
Weirs
Quarries (Dis.)
Crosse's Wood
Crosse's Creek
Quarry (Dis.)
Playing Field
School
Waterfall
Knoll Wood
Rivington Lodge
Douglas Diversion
Old Lord's Farm
Old Lord's Height
Ormstons Farm
Wilder's Wood
Makinson Moor
Hamer's Creek
Hamer's Cott.
Red Cot
Reservoir
Wilderswood
19
Lower Rivington Embankment
Jepson's Bri.
Wilderswood Farm
Well Cott.
Montcliffe
Montcliffe Stone Quarries
Anderton Manor Farm
Berne House
Dryfield
Hodgkinson's Fold
Stony Croft
Hart's Houses
Bowling Grn.
Lakeland Farm
Pendennis
Firs Cottage
Markland's Ho.
BL6
Squirrel Bri.
Reservoir
12
Squirrel Hotel
Anderton Ford Bri.
Ridgeway Delf (Dis.)
Grundy Cotts.
Mill Bri.
Hopwood Hill
Edge Hill
Foxholes Wood
Works
Depot
Wallsuches
Anderton Old Hall Farm
Top of Wallsuches
Park Reservoir
CHURCH STREET
CHORLEY OLD ROAD
B6226
Old Station Pk.
Ridgmont Cemetery
Ridgmont
Ridgmont Park
Playing Fields
Leisure Centre
Football Grd.
HORWICH
Cricket Grd.
White Croft
Ridgmont Nurseries
Boardman's Farm
Knowles Farm
Vale Ho.
Vale Farm
Reservoir
11
HORWICH GOLF COURSE
Club
Reservoir
Nellie's Clough
Bolton Fold
The Ferns
New Chapel Cott.
Claypool Farm
Claypool Cotts.
Subway
Travelling Crane
A673
College
Barker's Fm.
M61 MOTORWAY
Warehouses
Gibb Farm
Leigh Tenement Farm
M61
Ridgway Bri.
Lower House Farm
The Homestead
Higher Austin's
Austin's Farm
Lower Austin's
RED MOSS
10
Red Moss Bri.
New Close Fa
36
Playing Field
Works
Park Hall Farm
Warehouse
Sefton Fold Farm
CHORLEY NEW ROAD

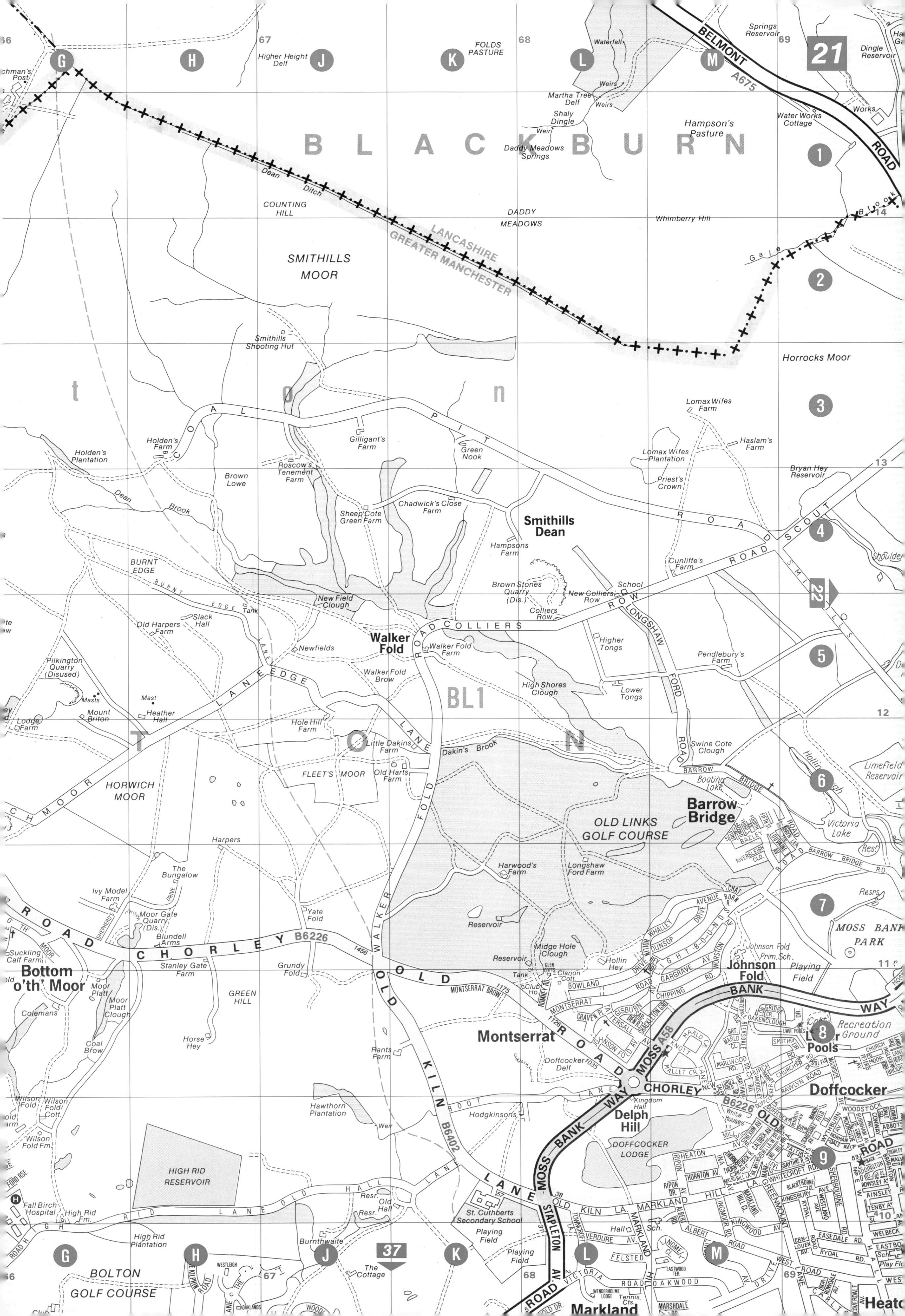
21
BLACKBURN
Springs Reservoir
Dingle Reservoir
BELMONT ROAD
A675
Waterfall
Weirs
Martha Tree Delf
Shaly Dingle
Weir
Daddy Meadows Springs
Hampson's Pasture
Water Works Cottage
Works
Higher Height Delf
FOLDS PASTURE
Dean Ditch
COUNTING HILL
DADDY MEADOWS
Whimberry Hill
LANCASHIRE
GREATER MANCHESTER
Gale Brook
SMITHILLS MOOR
Smithills Shooting Hut
Horrocks Moor
Lomax Wifes Farm
Lomax Wifes Plantation
Haslam's Farm
Bryan Hey Reservoir
Priest's Crown
COAL PIT ROAD
Holden's Farm
Holden's Plantation
Gilligant's Farm
Green Nook
Roscow's Tenement Farm
Brown Lowe
Dean Brook
Chadwick's Close Farm
Sheep Cote Green Farm
Smithills Dean
Hampsons Farm
SCOUT ROAD
Cunliffe's Farm
BURNT EDGE
Brown Stones Quarry (Dis.)
School
New Colliers' Row
Colliers Row
New Field Clough
COLLIERS ROW ROAD
LONGSHAW FORD ROAD
22
Slack Hall
Old Harpers Farm
Tank
Newfields
Walker Fold
Walker Fold Farm
Higher Tongs
Pilkington Quarry (Disused)
Masts
Mast
Walker Fold Brow
High Shores Clough
Lower Tongs
Pendlebury's Farm
Mount Briton
Heather Hall
Lodge Farm
EDGE LANE
BL1
Hole Hill Farm
Little Dakins Farm
Dakin's Brook
Swine Cote Clough
Limefield Reservoir
HORWICH MOOR
FLEET'S MOOR
Old Harts Farm
BARROW BRIDGE
Boating Lake
Barrow Bridge
Victoria Lake
OLD LINKS GOLF COURSE
Harpers
Harwood's Farm
Longshaw Ford Farm
The Bungalow
Ivy Model Farm
Moor Gate Quarry (Dis.)
Yate Fold
Reservoir
MOSS BANK PARK
Blundell Arms
CHORLEY ROAD
B6226
Midge Hole Clough
Johnson Fold
Playing Field
Suckling Calf Farm
Stanley Gate Farm
Grundy Fold
Hollin Hey
Bottom o'th' Moor
Moor Platt
Moor Platt Clough
GREEN HILL
MONTSERRAT BROW
OLD ROAD
MOSS BANK WAY
Recreation Ground
Colemans
Lower Pools
Montserrat
Coal Brow
Horse Hey
Rants Farm
Doffcocker Delf
A58
Doffcocker
Kingdom Hall
Delph Hill
Wilson Fold
Wilson Fold Cott.
Wilson Fold Fm.
Hawthorn Plantation
Weir
BOOT LANE
Hodgkinsons
DOFFCOCKER LODGE
OLD KILN LANE
B6402
HIGH RID RESERVOIR
Fall Birch Hospital
High Rid Fm.
HIGH RID LANE
OLD HALL LANE
Resr.
Old Hall
St. Cuthberts Secondary School
Playing Field
MARKLAND HILL
STAPLETON AV.
High Rid Plantation
Burnthwaite
37
The Cottage
BOLTON GOLF COURSE
Markland
Heaton
66
67
68
69
14
13
12
11
10
G
H
J
K
L
M
1
2
3
4
5
6
7
8
9

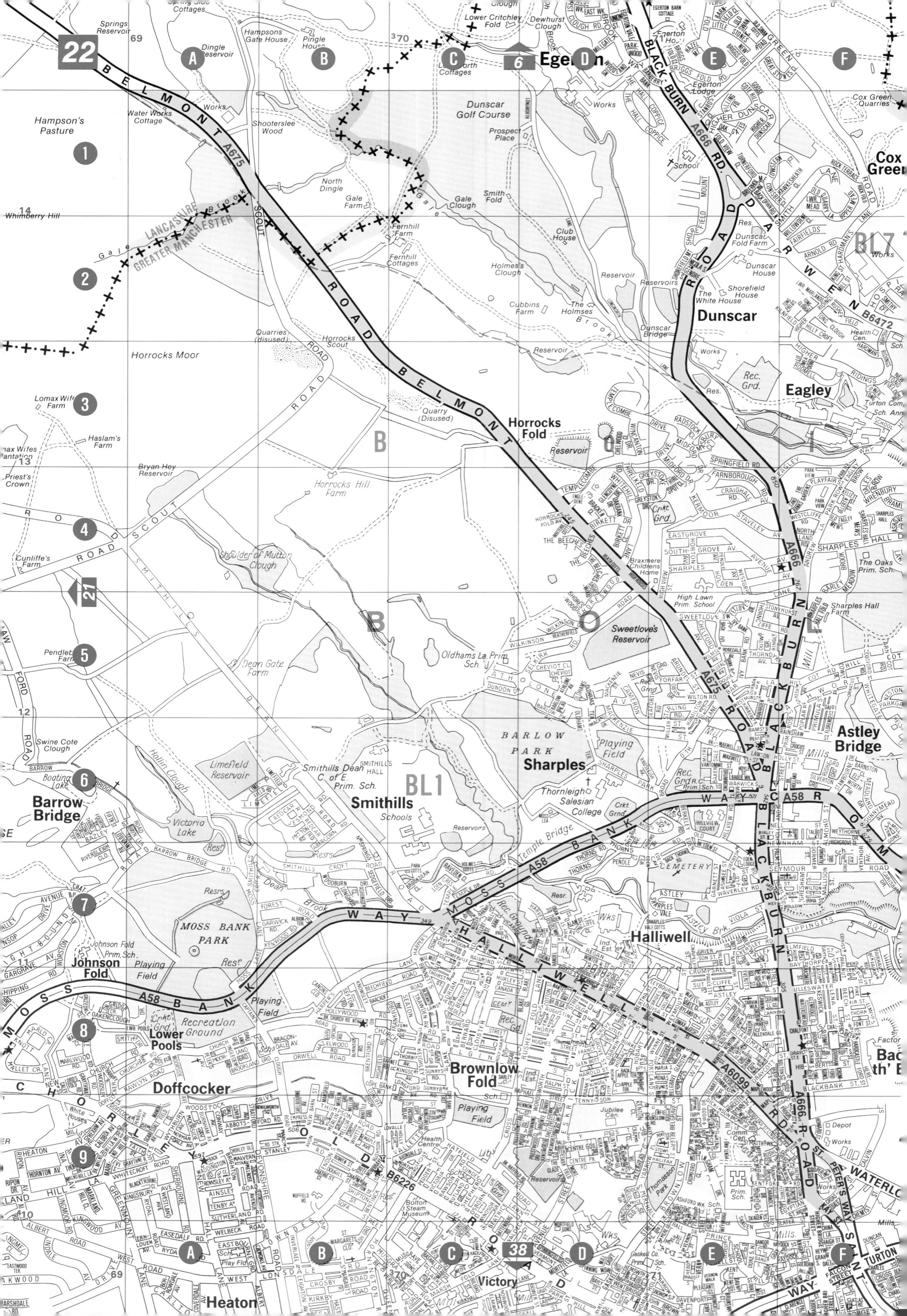

22
Springs Reservoir
Hampsons Gate House
Pingle House
Lower Critchley Fold
Dewhurst Clough
Egerton
6
Dingle Reservoir
Water Works Cottage
Works
Hampson's Pasture
Shooterslee Wood
Dunscar Golf Course
Prospect Place
North Dingle
Gale Farm
Gale Clough
Smith Fold
Whimberry Hill
LANCASHIRE
GREATER MANCHESTER
Fernhill Farm
Fernhill Cottages
Club House
Holmes's Clough
Reservoir
Reservoirs
Cubbins Farm
The Holmses
Dunscar Bridge
Dunscar
Dunscar Fold Farm
Dunscar House
Shorefield House
The White House
Egerton Lodge
Cox Green
Cox Green Quarries
BL7
Quarries (disused)
Horrocks Scout
Horrocks Moor
BELMONT ROAD
A675
A666
BLACKBURN ROAD
Lomax Wife Farm
Haslam's Farm
Quarry (Disused)
Horrocks Fold
Rec. Grd.
Eagley
Bryan Hey Reservoir
Horrocks Hill Farm
SCOUT ROAD
Cunliffe's Farm
21
Shoulder of Mutton Clough
Braxmere Childrens Home
High Lawn Prim. School
The Oaks Prim. Sch.
Sharples Hall Farm
Sweetlove's Reservoir
Oldhams La Prim Sch.
Dean Gate Farm
Pendlebury Farm
Swine Cote Clough
BARLOW PARK
Playing Field
Sharples
Astley Bridge
Limefield Reservoir
Smithills Dean C. of E. Prim. Sch.
Smithills Hall
BL1
Smithills Schools
Thornleigh Salesian College
Boating Lake
Barrow Bridge
Hollin Clough
Victoria Lake
Reservoirs
Temple Bridge
A58
MOSS BANK WAY
CEMETERY
Halliwell
MOSS BANK PARK
Johnson Fold Prim. Sch.
Johnson Fold
Recreation Ground
Lower Pools
HALLIWELL ROAD
A6099
Brownlow Fold
Doffcocker
CHORLEY OLD ROAD
B6226
Jubilee Cen.
Health Centre
Bolton Steam Museum
Playing Field
Thomasson Park
Gaskell Co. Prim. Sch.
Victory
38
Heaton
ST. PETER'S WAY
WATERLOO
Depot
Works
Mills
A B C D E F
1 2 3 4 5 6 7 8 9

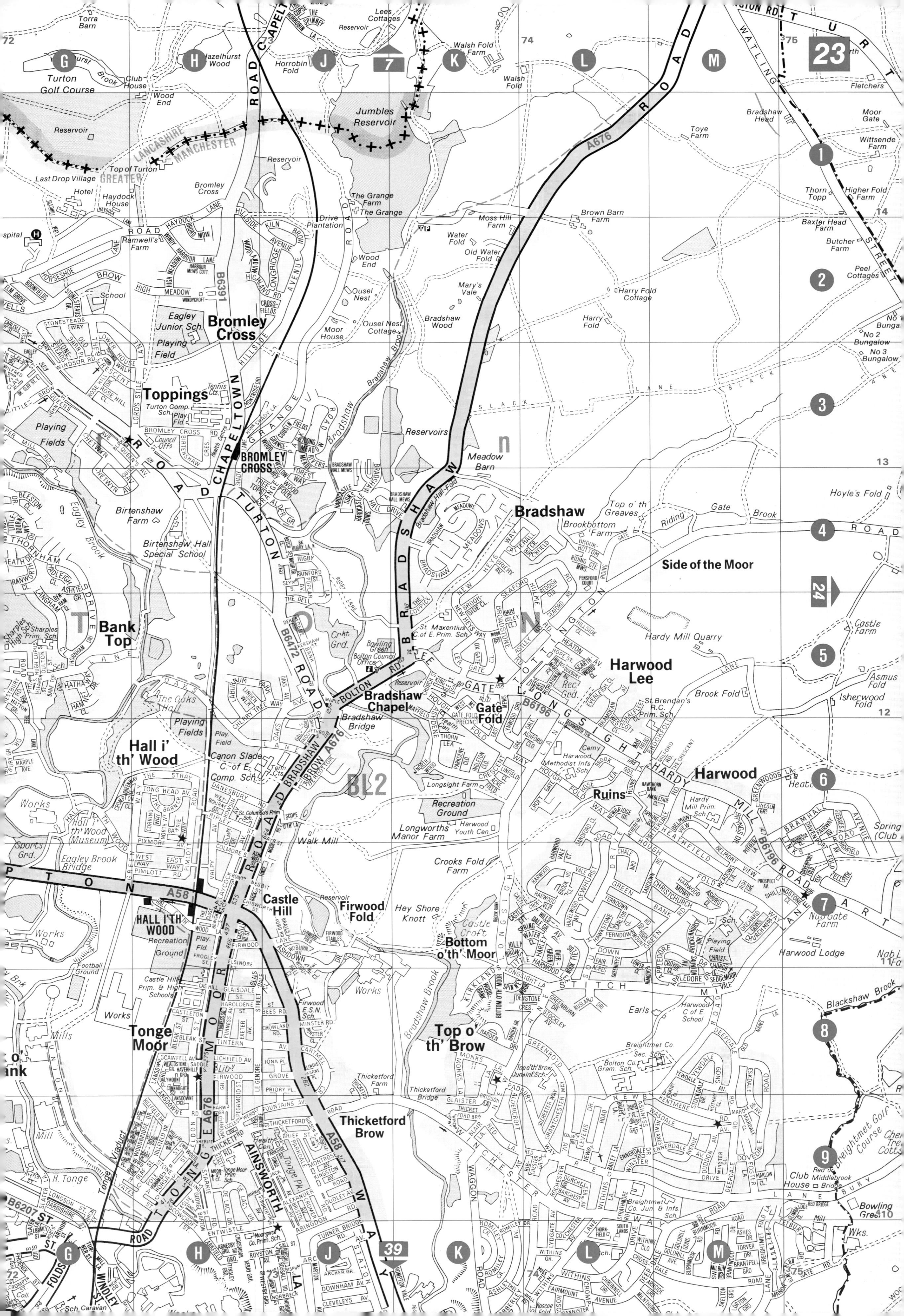

23
7
24
39
Torra Barn
Turton Golf Course
Club House
Hazelhurst Wood
Wood End
Horrobin Fold
Lees Cottages
Reservoir
Walsh Fold Farm
Walsh Fold
Jumbles Reservoir
LANCASHIRE
GREATER MANCHESTER
Top of Turton
Last Drop Village
Hotel
Haydock House
Bromley Cross
The Grange Farm
The Grange
Drive Plantation
Moss Hill Farm
Brown Barn Farm
Toye Farm
Bradshaw Head
Fletchers
Moor Gate
Wittsende Farm
Thorn Topp
Higher Fold Farm
Baxter Head Farm
Butcher Farm
Peel Cottages
Water Fold
Old Water Fold
Wood End
Ousel Nest
Ousel Nest Cottages
Moor House
Mary's Vale
Bradshaw Wood
Harry Fold Cottage
Harry Fold
No 2 Bungalow
No 3 Bungalow
Ramwell's Farm
Eagley Junior Sch.
Playing Field
Bromley Cross
Toppings
Turton Comp. Sch.
Council Offs
Playing Fields
BROMLEY CROSS
Reservoirs
Meadow Barn
Bradshaw
Top o' th' Greaves
Brookbottom Farm
Hoyle's Fold
Side of the Moor
Birtenshaw Farm
Birtenshaw Hall Special School
Bank Top
Sharples High Sch.
Sharples Prim. Sch.
Crkt. Grd.
Bowling Green
Bolton Council Office
St. Maxentius C. of E. Prim. Sch.
Hardy Mill Quarry
Castle Farm
Harwood Lee
Brook Fold
Asmus Fold
Isherwood Fold
St. Brendan's R.C. Prim. Sch.
The Oaks Hall
Playing Fields
Bradshaw Chapel
Bradshaw Bridge
Gate Fold
Hall i' th' Wood
Canon Slade C. of E. Comp. Sch.
BL2
Harwood Methodist Infs Sch.
Harwood
Ruins
Hardy Mill Prim. Sch.
Longsight Farm
Recreation Ground
Longworths Manor Farm
Harwood Youth Cen.
Works
Hall i' th' Wood (Museum)
Sports Grd.
Eagley Brook Bridge
Walk Mill
Crooks Fold Farm
Castle Hill
Firwood Fold
Hey Shore Knott
Castle Croft
Bottom o'th' Moor
Nab Gate Farm
Harwood Lodge
HALL I'TH WOOD
Recreation Ground
Football Ground
Castle Hill Prim. & High Schools
Works
Firwood E.S.N. Sch.
Tonge Moor
Top o' th' Brow
Earls
Harwood C. of E. School
Blackshaw Brook
Breightmet Co. Sec. Sch.
Bolton Co. Gram. Sch.
Top o'th' Brow Jun.& Inf. Sch.
Thicketford Farm
Thicketford Bridge
Thicketford Brow
Tonge Moor Prim. Sch.
Tonge Viaduct
R. Tonge
Breightmet Co. Jun & Infs. Sch.
Club House
Middlebrook Bridge
Breightmet Golf Course
Bowling Green
Wks.
Moorgate Co. Prim. Sch.
Sch. Caravan
A676
A58
B6391
B6472
B6196
B6207

24
8
23
40
Affetside
Tottington
Four Lane Ends
Side of the Moor
BOLTON
BL2
Walshaw
Starling
Ainsworth
Greenmount
Harwood
TURTON ROAD
B6213
WATLING STREET
TOTTINGTON ROAD
BRADSHAW ROAD
HARWOOD ROAD
BENTLEY HALL ROAD
ARTHUR LANE
B6196
BURY OLD RD.
CHURCH ST.
COCKEY MOOR ROAD
STARLING ROAD
B6292
HOLCOMBE RD.
B6215
MARKET ST.
HIGH STREET
Farnworth
Higher Barn Farm
Fletchers
Whittles
Bradshaw Head
Moor Gate
Toye Farm
Wittsende Farm
Three Gates
Springfield
Greystones Farm
Thorn Topp
Higher Fold Farm
Tom Nook Farm
Holcombe Villa Farm
Baxter Head Farm
Butcher Farm
Spring Bank Farm
Buckley Close Farm
Peel Cottages
Two Brooks Farm
Burnt House Farm
Bottoms Hall Farm
Bottom Hall Cottages
Old Bates
Reynards Bank
Meadow Nook
Windmill Farm
Hillcrest
Leeside
Ralph Moor
Claybank
Ferns
Croichley Fold
Holly Mount R.C. Prim. Sch.
Holly Mount Convent
Claremont
Holly Mount Farm
Brick Barn
St. Hilda's Presbytery
Club House Greenmount Golf Course
Greenhalgh Fold
Brook House Bridge
Old Kays
Brookfield
The Whitehead Garden
Affetside Prim. Sch.
Mum's Harris Farm
No 1 Bungalow
No 2 Bungalow
No 3 Bungalow
Yeoman's
Howarth's Farm
Hoyle's Fold
Old Ned's
Top of Raikes
Hill End
Bowstone Hill
High Barn
Castle Farm
Asmus Fold
Isherwood Fold
The Height
Height Barn
Rodger Lake
Gorsey Clough
Hey Head
Meadow Head Cottage
Bannisters Farm
Walshaw Hall Farm
Reservoir
Walshaw Hall
Sheep Gate Farm
Brook Fold
Heatons
Springfield (Club Ho.)
Harwood Golf Course
Higher Bury Meadows
Old Holts
Bentley Hall
High Crompton
Meadow Croft
Nab Gate Farm
Harwood Lodge
Nab Lane Farm
Blackshaw Brook
Arthur Lane Fm
Barrack Fold
Ainsworth Isolation Hospital
Old Barn
Knowsley
Brown Hill
Reservoirs
Breightmet Golf Course
Cherry Tree Cotts
Club House
Red or Middlebrook Bridge
Bowling Green
Dearden Fold
Cockey Moor
Pilkington Fold
Kiln Clough
Newington
Tottington Sec. School
Christ Church C of E Prim. Sch.
Cricket Grd
School Playing Fields
Hardy Mill Prim. Sch.
Harwood C of E School

25
Holcombe Brook
Summerseat
Lower Summerseat
Higher Summerseat
Twist Bridge
Sewage Works
Cricket Ground
9
ROWLANDS ROAD
Robinson Kay Home
Nabbs Farm
M66
M66 MOTORWAY
Lower Longcroft Cottages
Longcroft House
WALMERSLEY OLD ROAD
Baldingstone
Reservoir
Carr Bank
Bevis Green
Walmersley
Springside Prim. Sch.
WALMERSLEY ROAD
A56
Chest Well Bridge
Higher Wood Road Farm
Wood Road
Mill
BL0
LONGSIGHT
B6214
B6215
BRANDLESHOLME ROAD
HAZEL HALL LANE
WOOD ROAD LANE
River Irwell
Bank Top Farm
Springside Farm
Springside View
Banks Farm
Old Hall Prim. Sch.
Brandlesholme Hall Farm
Brandlesholme Old Hall
Brandlesholme
Brandlesholme Ho.
Our Lady of Lourdes Prim. Sch.
Lower Brandlesholme
Castle Steads (Site of Camp)
East Lancashire Railway
Canal Feeder
Works
Burrs
BL9
BL8
Recreation Ground
Playing Field
Resr
Res
Garside Hey
Kirklees Brook
Pigs Lee Bridge
Touch Road
Pigsden Fm.
Hillside Prim. Sch.
Top o'th' Hill
Gorses Quarry
Lowes Park Golf Course
Club Ho.
Limefield
Clay Pit
Summerseat (Limefield) Prim. Sch.
Bury General Hosp.
26
Lido
Littlewood
Seedfield Comm. Cen.
Playing Fields
Seedfield
Clarence Recreation Ground
Chesham
TOTTINGTON ROAD
Woolfold
Viaduct
Higher Woodhill
Cricket Ground
St. John's Prim. Sch.
Bolholt
Walshaw Brk
Elton High School
Owler Barrow
B6213
Elton Nursery Sch.
Woodhill
ROAD
Woodhill Fold
Fernhill
Wood Fields
Subway
Freetown
MOORGATE
R.C. Prim. Sch.
Scholes Nursery
Sports Field
Elton Brook
Elton Ho.
Chantlers Co. Primary Sch.
B6212
Elton
King George V Playing Fields
Recrn Grd.
Bury Ground
PEEL (INNER RELIEF RD.) WAY
East Lancs Railway Museum
BOLTON ST.
Bury Bolton St.
B6216
ROCHDALE ROAD
BURY
JUBILEE WAY
ANGOULEME WAY
A58
A56
Tentersfield
Bury Grammar Schools
Town Hall
Bury Technical College
Townside Fields
Recreation Ground
Reservoir
Reg. Mus.
Daisyfield
Florence Nightingale Hospital
Buckley Wells
St. Gabriels R.C. Secondary Sch.
Playing Fields
Peel Sixth Form College
Play. Flds.
Tennis Ct.
Bury Tech Play. Fld.
Playing Flds.
Bowling Greens
Bury C. of E. High Sch.
Tennis & Basketball Cts.
Grundy Centre
Fishpool
B6218
B6219
WELLINGTON
MANCHESTER
B6196
BOLTON ROAD
41
School Playing Fields
Derby High School
Bury Sports Ct.
Lower
Recreation Grd.
G
H
J
K
L
M
1
2
3
4
5
6
7
8
9

26
ROSSENDALE
M66 MOTORWAY
M66
Lower Longcroft Cottages
Longcroft House
Gindles Farm
Lark Mount
Cob House Nab
Cob House Farm
Deeply Vale
Higher Bridge
Wind Hill
Wind Hill Farm
Bird Fields
Stand Lees Farm
Copped Hill Farm
Shepherd Hey
Leaches
Cockshouse
Deep Moss
Dunham Farm
Club House (Garrett's Close)
Walmersley Golf Course
Broomses Farm
Cheesden
Cleggs Wood
Wood Barn
Old Birtle
New Birtle Farm
Penn Green Farm
Birtle Green
Mt. Pleasant Farm
Marcroft Farm
Birtle
Delph House Farm
Castle Hill Farm
Castle Hill Quarry (Dis.)
Harwood Fields
BL9
Hercules Farm
Gorsey Brow Farm
Top o'th' Hill
Lowes Park Golf Course
Gorses Quarry
Club Ho.
Limefield
Clay Pit
Chesham Co. Prim. Sch.
Bury General Hosp.
Lido
Clarence Recreation Ground
Chesham
Green Bank
Riddings Farm
Woodgate Hill
Freetown
St. Joseph's Jun & Inf. Schs
Playing Fields
Bowling Greens
Fern Grove
Jericho
Isolation Hosp.
Fairfield General Hosp.
Broad Oak Farm
Broad Oak Wood
Smethurst Wd.
Lomax Wood
Lower Lomax
Fairfield
Fairfield Prim. Sch.
Football Grd
Works
Hillside Prim. Sch.
Bowling Green
Carr Bank
Reservoir
BURY EASTERLY BY-PASS
B6222
B6221
B6219
A58
The Geoffrey Kershaw Cen.
East Ward Prim. Sch.
Broad Oak High Sch.
Bridge Hall Indus. Est.
Mill
Prettywood
Summit
Heady Hill
Top of Heap
Sand Pit
Boohole Sand Pit
Goods Sta.
Heap Bridge
Heap Bri Prim. Sch.
Heap Fold Fm.
Our Lady & St. Paul's R.C. Prim. Sch.
Heywood High Sch.
Play Flds.
Tennis Courts
Darn Hill
Playing Fields
Darnhill Co. Inf. & Jun. Sch.
BURY
ROCHDALE ROAD
BURY NEW ROAD
Junction 2
Rochdale Rd. Rec. Grd.
River Roch
Water Fold Fm.
Heap Bridge Junc.
Spout Bank Farm
Pimhole
Viaduct
Sewage Works
Water Farm
Reservoir
Moor Hole Farm
Fishpool
The Grundy Centre
Bury Tech. Play. Fld.
Tennis Ct.
Lake Mosses Ho
10
42
25
A B C D E F
1 2 3 4 5 6 7 8 9
81 82 83
13 12 11 10

27
Shawfield
Wolstenholme
Wolstenholme Fold
Norden
Schofield Farm
OL11
OL12
A680
Caldershaw
Caldershaw Cty. Prim. Sch.
St. Vincent's R.C. Prim. Sch.
Cutgate
ROCHDALE GOLF COURSE
Bagslate Moor
Clay Lane Storage Reservoir
Electricity Sub. Station
Childrens Hospital
Whittaker Moss Sch.
Alf Kuafman Sch.
Fester Clough Wood
Lee Holme
Greengate Hill
Sandy Ford
Marcroft Gate Farm
Laneside Farm
Manor Farm
Paper House Farm
Seddons Farm
Ashworth Wood
Duckworth Farm
Dairy House
Black Dad
Black Dad Wood
Kershaw Bridge
Nab Wife
Mine
Higher Clough
Lower Clough
Waterloo Farm
Lower Jowkin Farm
Higher Jowkin Farm
Naden Brk
Jowkin Wood
Carr Wood
Dobb Wood
Windy Cliff Bridge
Windy Cliff Wood
Heywood's Farm
Fernises
Gelder Wood
Bamford Wood
Cheesden Brook
Gelder Clough Caravan Park
Bamford Hall
Knowl View Sch.
Bamford
Broadhalgh
Rugby Grd
Play.
Kenyon Fold
Wrigley Carr Farm
Gristlehurst Farm
Top o' th' Wood
Simpson Clough
Bird i'th' Hand
B6222
ROCHDALE OLD ROAD
BURY ROAD
Simpson Clough Bri.
Reservoirs
Hooley Bridge
St. Michael's C. of E. Prim. Sch.
Plumpton Hall
Hazelhurst
Plumpton Wood
Crimble Hall Farm
Crimble
Springfield Public Golf
Running Track
Springfield Cotts.
HEYWOOD CEMETERY
Primrose Hill Farm
Tack Lee Wood
Tack Lee Brook
Gristlehurst Wood
Elbut Wood
Hooley Bridge Ind. Est.
QUEEN'S PARK
Boating Lake
Cricket Ground
Captain Fold
Ryecroft Ho.
Ryecroft Farm
All Souls C. of E. Prim. Sch.
OL10
Bottom o' th' Brow
Back o' th' Moss
Playing Fields
Hooley Brow
St. Luke's Prim. Sch.
Sports Cen.
Swim. Pool
A58
ROCHDALE ROAD
BURY NEW RD.
BURY ST.
BRIDGE ST.
MARKET ST.
YORK ST.
CHURCH ST.
MANCHESTER ST.
Harefield Hall
Harefield Farm
HEYWOOD
Roeacre Brook
Wilderness
Castle Hawk Golf Course
Club Ho.
Works
Mills
Public Baths
Mkt.
Rec. Grnd
St. Margarets Prim. Sch.
Broadfield
Recreation Ground
St. Joseph's R.C. Prim. Sch.
St. Joseph's R.C. Sec. Sch.
Higher Broadfield Farm
PHOENIX PARK IND. EST.
Hopwood
HEYWOOD BUSINESS PARK
43
28
11
G
H
J
K
L
M
1
2
3
4
5
6
7
8
9
385
86
87

28
12
27
44
OL12
OL11
OL10
Shawfield
Shawclough
Passmonds
Spotland Fold
Spotland Bri.
Cutgate
Town Head
Bagslate Moor
Greave
Mitchell Hey
Broadhalgh
Rochdale Golf Course
Rochdale Cemetery
Crematorium
Denehurst Park
Falinge Park
Springfield Park Public Golf Course
Running Track
Heywood Cemetery
Marland
Sudden
Stoneyfield
Castleton
Heywood
Junction 20
Kirk
Mandale Park
Broadfield Park
Town Hall
Castle Hawk Golf Course
Rail Welding Depot
Royal Pennine Trading Estate
Lyntown Trans-Pennine Trading Estate
Edenfield Road
Spotland Road
Bury Road
Bolton Road
Rochdale Road
Manchester Road
Queens Way
Edinburgh Way
Sandy Lane
Roch Valley Way
Mellor Street
St. Mary's Gate
Drake Street
A680
A6060
A58
A664
A627(M)
A627(M) Motorway
B6222
B6452
B6377
M62 Motorway
River Roch
Rochdale Canal
Rochdale
Castleton
Industrial Estate
Phoenix Park Ind. Est.
Castleton Wood Junction
Top O' Th' Hill
Sand Hole
87
88
89

G
H
J
K
L
M
13
Howarth Cross
Little Clegg
Clegg Hall
Littleborough
OL15
Mayfield
Clover Hall
Belfield
Newbold Brow
ROCHDALE
Newbold
Firgrove
Milnrow
MILNROW
Butterworth Hall
Lady House
OL16
Lower Place
Turf Hill
Balderstone
Buersil
Pleasant View
Green Gate
Junction 21
M62
M62 MOTORWAY
Buersil Head
Burnedge
OLDHAM
Oldham OL2
Green Hill
Moss Gate
Higher Rushcroft
Gravel Hole
45
30
1
2
3
4
5
6
7
8
9
A664
A640
A671
A58
B6266
B6225
B6194
ROYDS STREET
KINGSWAY
ROCHDALE ROAD
ELIZABETHAN WAY
WILD HOUSE LANE
ROCHDALE LANE
STANNEY BROOK PARK
Football Ground
Community Centre
Mayfields Farm
Fenns Farm Equestrian Centre
Rochdale Canal (Disused)
Waith Field
Lower Moss Side
Moss Side Farm
Rochdale Hornets R.L.F.C. Ground
Sacred Heart R.C. Prim. Sch.
Kingsway Middle Sch.
St. Joseph's R.C. Middle Sch.
Balderstone Community High Sch.
Holy Family R.C. Prim. Sch.
St. Cuthbert's R.C. High Sch.
Hill Top Prim. Sch.
Milnrow C of E Inf & Jun Sch.
Hollingworth High Sch.
Crossgates Prim. Sch.
Belfield Comm. Prim. Sch.
Heybrook Cty Prim. Sch.
Eagle Technology Park
Tithe Barn
Silver Hill
Castle
White Horse
Ginnell
Calf Hey
Beet
Burnedge Farm
Bryney Heys
Knott Booth
Hey Farm
Green Hill Farm
Snipe Leach
Plumpton
Thornham
Peanock Farm
Shaw Moss
Bib Knowl Plantation
Birchinley Hall
Cronshaw
Plumb Ho.
Wild Ho.
Dobfield
Recreation Ground
Belfield Trading Est.
Belfield Bridge
Clegg Hall Bridge
Branch Road Farm
Shaw La. Cotts.
Buckley Hill Farm
Dig Gate
Garside
Ellenroad
Broad Shaw
Chadwick Fold
Dear Farm
Newhey

30
14
46
29
Little Clegg
Higher Fold
Benny Hill
Hollingworth Lake Country Park
Peanock Farm
Branch Road Farm
Turnough Hill
Rakewood
Turnough
Higher Abbots
Antioch
Lower Abbots
Schofield Hall
Schofield Hall Farm
Higher Booth Hollings Hill
Higher Booth Hollings
Lower Booth Hollings
M62 MOTORWAY
New Nook
Works
Shaw Moss
Shaw La. Cotts
Bib Knowl Plantation
Nigher Bib Knowl
Bib Knowl
Dickey Steps
Round House
Sports Ground
Roadfield Wood
Birchinley Hall
Annis Hill
Annis Hill Farm
Rakewood Viaduct
Castle Hill
Schofield Hall Hill
Booth Hollings Mill Bridge
Mill Race
Weir
Nicholas Pike
Heights Barn Farm
Reservoir
Wild Ho.
WILD HOUSE LANE
Broad Carr
Higher Crow Nest
Tunshill Hill
Lower Crow Nest
Crossgates Prim. Sch.
Dick Hill
Tunshill Farm
Hen Carr Farm
Higher Tunshill
Higher Tunshill Farm
Rag Hole Clough
TUNSHILL GOLF COURSE
Carr Farm
Spring Holes
Milnrow C of E Inf & Jun Sch.
Hollingworth High Sch.
Kitcliffe
Kitcliffe Farm
Horse Barn
Ogden Reservoir
Butterworth Hall
Playing Fields
Lark Hill
Piethorne
OGDEN LANE
Higher Ogden
The Bungalow
Charity Farm
Manor House Farm
Tame Barn
Rough Farm
Rough Bank Farm
Moy Hill
Spring Mill
Cricket Ground
Walk Bank
Lane Bottom
Lower Ogden
Cliffe Plantation
Quarry (dis.)
A640
HUDDERSFIELD ROAD
Wicken Hall Farm
Memorial Park
Newhey
Rec. Gnd.
NEWHEY
Bethany Farm
OL16
Junction 21
Haugh
Bye Carr Farm
Wicken Hall Clough
Far Wicken Hall Farm
Helpet Edge
Bentgate
Whitfield Bottoms
Further Whitfield Bottoms Farm
Top O'Th' Hill
Haugh Hey
Jep Wood
Jubilee
Ley Wood
OL2
Heys
Whitfield Park Farm
Slences Hey
A663
Whitfield Hall
Dun Wood Park
Whitesides
Hey Farm
Whitfield Dairy Farm
Crow Knowl
Park Farm
Jordan Brow
Top o'th' Green Quarry (dis.)
Brushes Clough Quarry (dis.)
Moss Gate
Lower Rushcroft
Crompton Rushcroft Cnty. Prim. Sch.
BUCKSTONES ROAD
Brushes
Higher Rushcroft
Crompton Fold
Brushes Clough Res.
Shore Edge
Way Moss
MILNROW ROAD
R O C H D A L E
O L D H A M

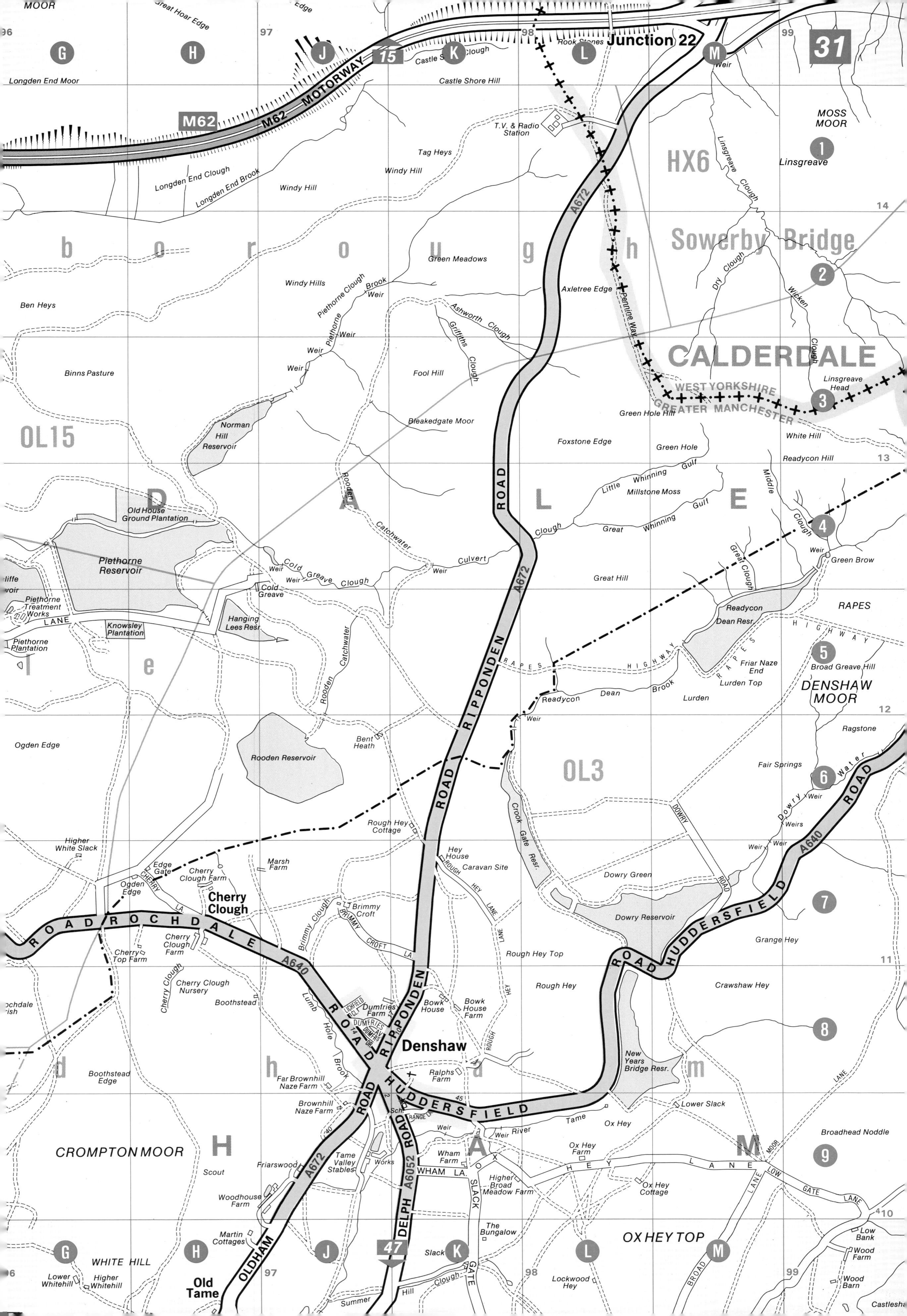

Junction 22
M62
15
MOTORWAY
Castle Shore Hill
Longden End Moor
T.V. & Radio Station
Tag Heys
Windy Hill
Longden End Clough
Longden End Brook
HX6
MOSS MOOR
Linsgreave
Sowerby Bridge
Green Meadows
Windy Hills
Ben Heys
Axletree Edge
A672
CALDERDALE
WEST YORKSHIRE
GREATER MANCHESTER
Pennine Way
Binns Pasture
Fool Hill
Norman Hill Reservoir
Bleakedgate Moor
OL15
Green Hole Hill
Foxstone Edge
Green Hole
White Hill
Readycon Hill
Millstone Moss
Old House Ground Plantation
Piethorne Reservoir
Piethorne Treatment Works
Knowsley Plantation
Hanging Lees Resr.
Piethorne Plantation
Great Hill
Green Brow
Readycon Dean Resr.
RAPES
RAPES HIGHWAY
Friar Naze End
Lurden Top
Broad Greave Hill
DENSHAW MOOR
Readycon Dean Brook
Lurden
Ragstone
Ogden Edge
Rooden Reservoir
Bent Heath
OL3
Fair Springs
RIPPONDEN ROAD
Rough Hey Cottage
Higher White Slack
Hey House
Caravan Site
Dowry Green
Marsh Farm
Cherry Clough Farm
Edge Gate
Ogden Edge
Cherry Clough
Dowry Reservoir
Brimmy Croft
ROCHDALE ROAD
HUDDERSFIELD ROAD
Cherry Top Farm
Cherry Clough Farm
Grange Hey
Rough Hey Top
Cherry Clough Nursery
Rough Hey
Crawshaw Hey
Boothstead
Dumfries Farm
Bowk House
Bowk House Farm
Denshaw
New Years Bridge Resr.
Boothstead Edge
Far Brownhill Naze Farm
Ralphs Farm
Brownhill Naze Farm
Lower Slack
Ox Hey
Broadhead Noddle
CROMPTON MOOR
Scout
Friarswood
Tame Valley Stables
Wham Farm
Ox Hey Farm
Higher Broad Meadow Farm
Ox Hey Cottage
OX HEY LANE
Woodhouse Farm
Martin Cottages
The Bungalow
Low Bank
Wood Farm
OX HEY TOP
47
Slack
WHITE HILL
Lower Whitehill
Higher Whitehill
Old Tame
OLDHAM ROAD
DELPH ROAD
A6052
A640
Lockwood Hey
Wood Barn
Castleshaw

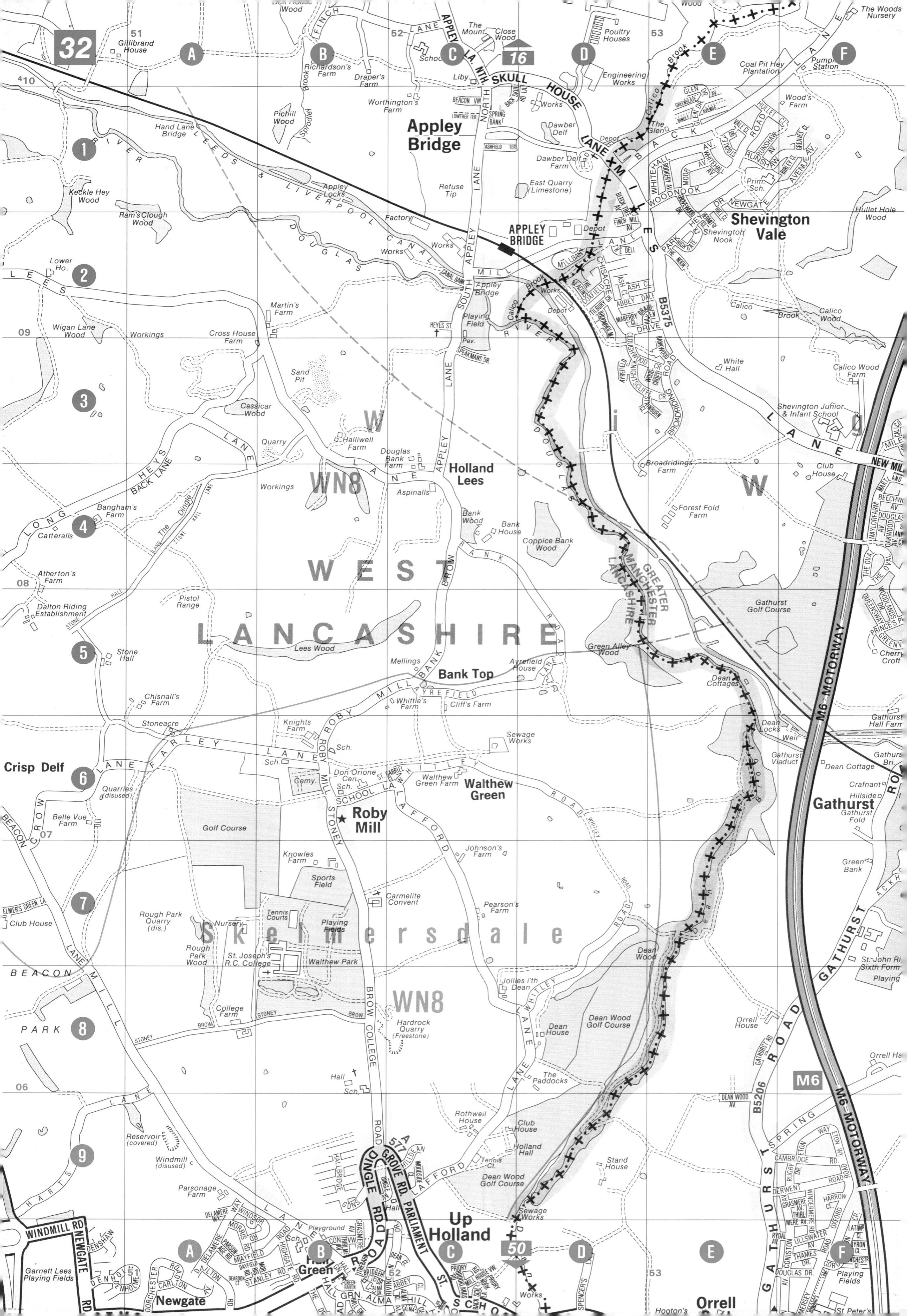

32
16
50
A
B
C
D
E
F
1
2
3
4
5
6
7
8
9
51
52
53
410
09
08
07
06
Gillibrand House
Richardson's Farm
Draper's Farm
Worthington's Farm
Pichill Wood
The Mount
Close Wood
Poultry Houses
Engineering Works
Coal Pit Hey Plantation
Pumping Station
The Woods Nursery
Wood's Farm
Appley Bridge
APPLEY BRIDGE
Hand Lane Bridge
RIVER
LEEDS & LIVERPOOL CANAL
DOUGLAS
Keckle Hey Wood
Ram's Clough Wood
Appley Locks
Factory
Works
Refuse Tip
Dawber Delf
Dawber Delf Farm
East Quarry (Limestone)
Shevington Vale
Shevington Nook
Hullet Hole Wood
Lower Ho.
Martin's Farm
Wigan Lane Wood
Workings
Cross House Farm
Sand Pit
Playing Field
Calico Brook
Calico Wood
White Hall
Calico Wood Farm
Shevington Junior & Infant School
Cassicar Wood
Quarry
Halliwell Farm
Douglas Bank Farm
Holland Lees
Aspinalls
WN8
Broadridings Farm
Club House
Forest Fold Farm
Bangham's Farm
Catteralls
Bank Wood
Bank House
Coppice Bank Wood
WEST
LANCASHIRE
GREATER MANCHESTER
LANCASHIRE
Atherton's Farm
Dalton Riding Establishment
Pistol Range
Lees Wood
Gathurst Golf Course
Stone Hall
Mellings
Bank Top
Ayrefield House
Green Alley Wood
Dean Cottages
Chisnall's Farm
Whittle's Farm
Cliff's Farm
Stoneacre
Knights Farm
Sewage Works
Dean Locks
Weir
Gathurst Viaduct
Dean Cottage
Crisp Delf
Cemy.
Don Orione Cen.
Walthew Green Farm
Walthew Green
Quarries (disused)
Belle Vue Farm
Golf Course
Roby Mill
Gathurst
Gathurst Fold
Knowles Farm
Sports Field
Johnson's Farm
Carmelite Convent
Pearson's Farm
Green Bank
Club House
Rough Park Quarry (dis.)
Nursery
Tennis Courts
Playing Fields
Skelmersdale
Rough Park Wood
St. Joseph's R.C. College
Walthew Park
Dean Wood
St. John Rigby Sixth Form
BEACON
PARK
College Farm
WN8
Hardrock Quarry (Freestone)
Jollies i'th Dean
Dean House
Dean Wood Golf Course
Orrell House
Hall
Sch.
The Paddocks
M6
M6 MOTORWAY
Reservoir (covered)
Windmill (disused)
Rothwell House
Club House
Holland Hall
Tennis Ct.
Stand House
Dean Wood Golf Course
Parsonage Farm
Sewage Works
Up Holland
Garnett Lees Playing Fields
Newgate
Hall Green
Orrell
Hooton's
Works
Playing Fields
St Peter's
B5375
B5206
A577

33
STANDISH
RECTORY
MARKET ST.
HIGH ST.
SCHOOL LA.
BROOK RD.
ALMOND
ARBOUR
Black Horse Farm
Aspinalls Farm
Gunnell's Fold Farm
Bowling Green House
Reservoir
The Beeches
Beech Lodge
Playing Field
Prim. Sch.
St. Wilfrid's Jun. and Inf. Sch.
GROVE
Pumping Station
White Hill Farm
Merrybone Farm
Almond Brook
Mill Brook
M6 MOTORWAY
M6
B5206
WIGAN
A49
Cricket Ground
Nursery
Offices
Ashfield House
Tennis Cts.
Playing Fields
Shevington High Sch.
Stockley Hill Wood
Paradise Farm
Beech Walk Plantation
Strickland House Farm
Lime Vale
Reservoir (cov.)
Convent
Playing Field
STANDISH WOOD
WN6
Calico Wood
Mill Dam Wood Cotts.
Hot House Wood
Standish Hall Farm
Wakefields
Roundmoor Farm
Boar's Head
SHEVINGTON
CHURCH
LONGBROOK
Elnup Wood
Prim. Sch.
St. Bernadette's R.C. Junior & Infant School
Rec. Grd.
B5375
WIGAN
STANDISH PARK
Cross (rems. of)
W I G A N
Upper Wood Farm
Wood Folds
Lower Wood Farm
Birley Wood
New Plantation
Monument
Ridges Wood
Frodsham's Wood
Brockhurst Farm
Frodsham's House
Giant's Hall Farm
Brimelow
Greaves Wood
Works
Otters Croft Wood
Crooke Wood
Lawns Wood
Follent Wood
Christopher Park Play. Field
Ten. Courts
Standish Lower Ground
LEEDS & LIVERPOOL CANAL
Crooke
River Douglas
Crooke Bridge
Crooke Hall Farm
LOWER
Jun. & Inf. Sch.
Coronation Park
Depot
Towing Path
Beech Hill
Beech Hill Sch.
GATHURST
Ackhurst Hall
Martland Mill
Martland Mill Bridge
Martland Mill Farm
Ricstan Villa
WOODHOUSE
WOODHOUSE DRIVE
St. John Fisher R.C. High Sch.
Cuthbert Scotts Farm
Warehouse
Works
Lock
Wigan Athletic F.C.
Springfield
Porters Wood
Play. Fld.
Playing Fields
WN5
Walthew House Wood
WALTHEW HOUSE LANE
Factory
Marsh Green
Sports Ground
Pagefield Indus. Est.
PARK RD.
Bowling Green
Playing Fields
Depot
Marsh Green Sch.
Laithwaite
Latham House Farm
Depot
Stadium
Sports Ground
ROBIN PARK
Playing Fields
The Bell
Kitt Green
Pemberton Community High
Montrose School
Recreation Ground
St. Edwards R.C. Sch.
St. Thomas More Sch.
Bell House Farm
Worsley Hall
Lamberhead Green
17
34
51

34
18
33
52
Kitchen Carr Wood
Otter Close Wood
Water Works Farm
Middle Row
Red Rock
Heywoods
Glassbrooks
RED ROCK (RED ROCK BROW)
B5239
Red Rock Bridge
Red Rock Farm
The Cottage
Pennington Farm
Hampson Green
Patchcroft Farm
Arley Brook
MEADOW PIT
Red Rock Lodge
Barkers
Fairclough Wood
LEEDS & LIVERPOOL CANAL
Winstanleys
School Coverts
Old Haigh School
Sandstone Wood
Pendlebury House
Astleys
WN2
Sennicar Covert
Grimshaws
Pendlebury Bridge
Samuel's Fold Cottage
Callands Fold
Home Farm
Zoological Gardens
Sennicar Bridge
Crow Orchard
Haigh Hall
Haigh Hall Golf Course
HAIGH HALL COUNTRY PARK
Rothwells Farm
Bank House
Brock Wood
Brock Mill Farm
Rugby Ground
Wingate Wood
Basin Quay
Longhurst
Hanfield
Hall Lane Lodge
HAIGH UP PLANTATI
Haigh Cottage
Leyland Mill Farm
Leyland Mill Brow
The Receptacle
Leyland Mill Bridge
HAIGH LOWER PLANTATIONS
Shedfield Bridge
Marylebone
Bottling Wood
Park House
St. John the C of E Jun.
New Springs
Swinley
WN1
Whelley
Longshoot
Water Heyes
Central Park
Scholes
Rose Bridge
Rose Bridge High Sch.
Playing Field
Peel Hall Bridge
MANCHESTER
DARLINGTON
Whalley's Basin
Gas Works
NORTH WESTERN
WALLGATE
Wallgate
WIGAN
Depot
Stadium
Sports Ground
ROBIN PARK
St. Edwards R.C. Sch.
St. Thomas More Sch.
POTTERY
WN3
Bull Hey
Cricket Ground
Deanery C of E High Sch.
The Galleries Shop. Cen.
NORTHWAY
CENTRAL PARK WAY
Mesnes Park
Bowling Grns.
Bandstand
MESNES
Royal Albert Edward Infirmary
Gidlow
Springfield
St. John Fisher R.C. High Sch.
Beech Hill
Beech Hill Sch.
Whitley
Playing Field
Reservoir
Factory
Greenfields
WN6
Brimelow Farm
Brockhurst Farm
Cemetery
Barley Brook
Thorn Hill
Res. (covered)
Mere Oaks Sch.
Bowl. Green
Cemy.
Boar's Head
WN1
CHORLEY ROAD
A5106
A49
WIGAN LANE
WIGAN ROAD
Victoria Industrial Estate
Pipe Lines
Works
Roundmoor Farm
Wakefields
Convent
Playing Field
Ashfield Playing Fields
Tennis Cts.
Ashfield House
Playing Fields
Reservoir (cov.)
Nursery
Offices
St. Wilfrid's Jun. and Inf. Sch.
Otter Close Wood
Lake Side Cottage
Pageffield Indus. Est.
Offices
Playgrd.
Sports Ground
Woodhouse
LEEDS & LIVERPOOL CANAL
PARSON'S WALK
B5357
B5356
B5238
Longshoot
Whelley Hosp.
St. Stephen's Sch.
Emp. Indus. Estate
Towing Path
Rec. Grd.

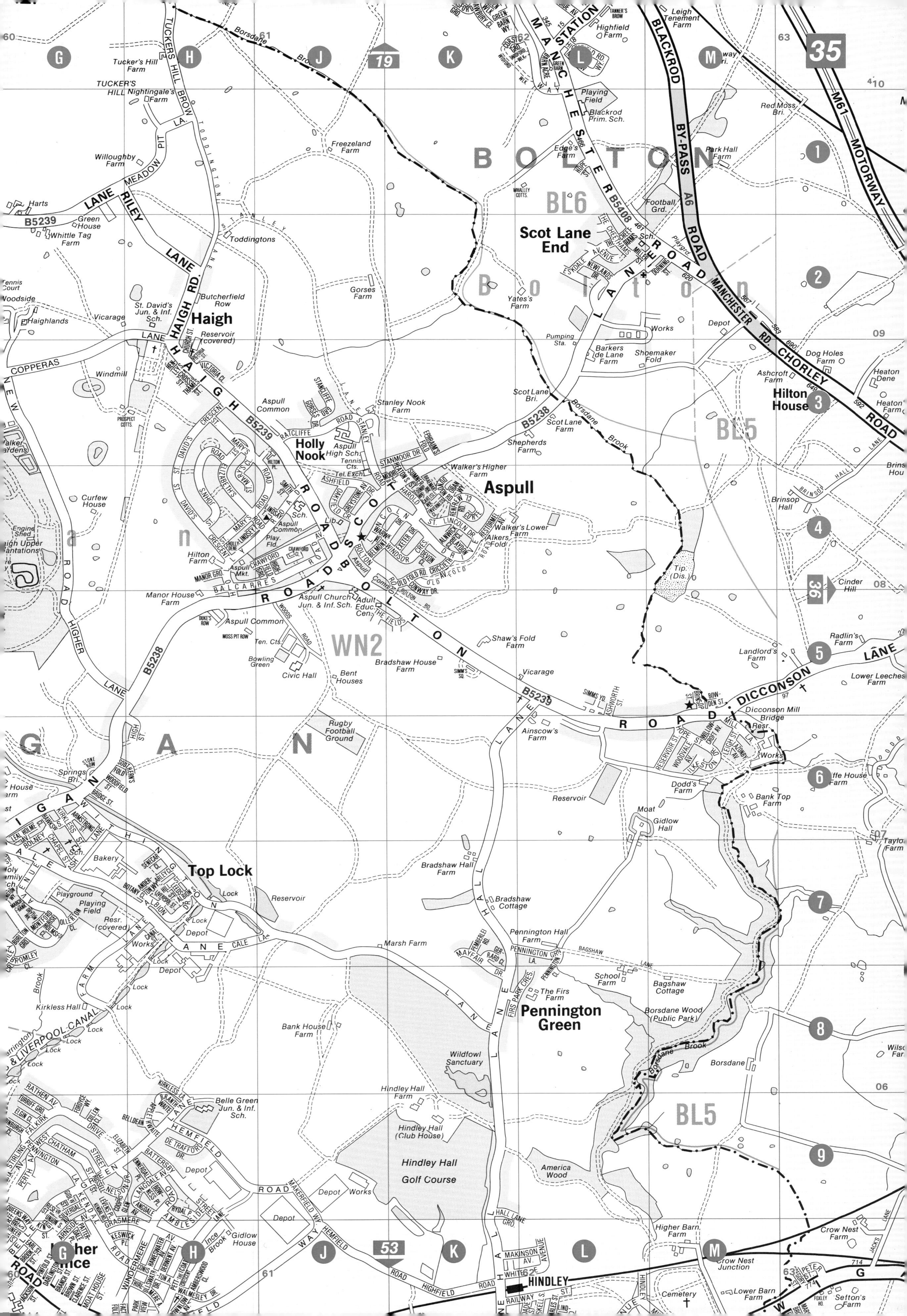

35
19
36
53
G
H
J
K
L
M
1
2
3
4
5
6
7
8
9
60
61
62
63
10
09
08
07
06
BOLTON
Bolton
WIGAN
Wigan
BL6
BL5
WN2
Tucker's Hill Farm
TUCKER'S HILL
Nightingale's Farm
TUCKERS HILL BROW
Borsdane Brook
Freezeland Farm
Willoughby Farm
MEADOW PIT LA.
RILEY LANE
B5239
Harts
Green House
Whittle Tag Farm
Toddingtons
STANLEY
Tennis Court
Woodside
Haighlands
Vicarage
Butcherfield Row
St. David's Jun. & Inf. Sch.
Haigh
HAIGH RD.
Reservoir (covered)
COPPERAS LANE
Windmill
Prospect Cotts.
Aspull Common
Holly Nook
Aspull High Sch.
Stanley Nook Farm
Gorses Farm
Yates's Farm
Pumping Sta.
Barkers de Lane Farm
Shoemaker Fold
Works
Depot
Scot Lane Bri.
Scot Lane Farm
Shepherds Farm
Walker's Higher Farm
Aspull
Walker's Lower Farm
Alkers Fold
Curfew House
Engine Shed
Hilton Farm
Manor House Farm
Aspull Mkt.
BALCARRES ROAD
Aspull Church Jun. & Inf. Sch.
Adult Educ. Cen.
Aspull Common
Ten. Cts.
Bowling Green
Civic Hall
Bent Houses
Bradshaw House Farm
Shaw's Fold Farm
Vicarage
BOLTON ROAD
B5238
HIGHER LANE
Rugby Football Ground
Ainscow's Farm
Reservoir
DICCONSON LANE
Dicconson Mill Bridge
Resr.
Dodd's Farm
Bank Top Farm
Moat
Gidlow Hall
Springs Bri.
Bakery
Top Lock
Lock
Reservoir
Playground
Playing Field
Resr. (covered)
Depot
Works
CALE LANE
Marsh Farm
Bradshaw Hall Farm
Bradshaw Cottage
Pennington Hall Farm
PENNINGTON GRN
BAGSHAW LANE
School Farm
Bagshaw Cottage
The Firs Farm
Pennington Green
Borsdane Wood (Public Park)
Borsdane
Kirkless Hall
LEEDS & LIVERPOOL CANAL
Bank House Farm
Wildfowl Sanctuary
Hindley Hall Farm
Hindley Hall (Club House)
Hindley Hall Golf Course
America Wood
Belle Green Jun. & Inf. Sch.
HEMFIELD ROAD
Depot
Works
Higher Barn Farm
Crow Nest Farm
Crow Nest Junction
Lower Barn Farm
Cemetery
Sefton's Farm
HINDLEY
HIGHFIELD ROAD
Gidlow House
Higher Ince
Leigh Tenement Farm
Highfield Farm
STATION ROAD
MANCHESTER ROAD
B5408
BLACKROD BY-PASS
A6
Playing Field
Blackrod Prim. Sch.
Edge's Farm
Scot Lane End
Football Grd.
Park Hall Farm
Red Moss Bri.
M61 MOTORWAY
CHORLEY ROAD
Dog Holes Farm
Ashcroft Farm
Heaton Dene
Hilton House
Heaton Farm
Brinsop Hall
Tip (Dis.)
Cinder Hill
Radlin's Farm
Landlord's Farm
Lower Leeches Farm

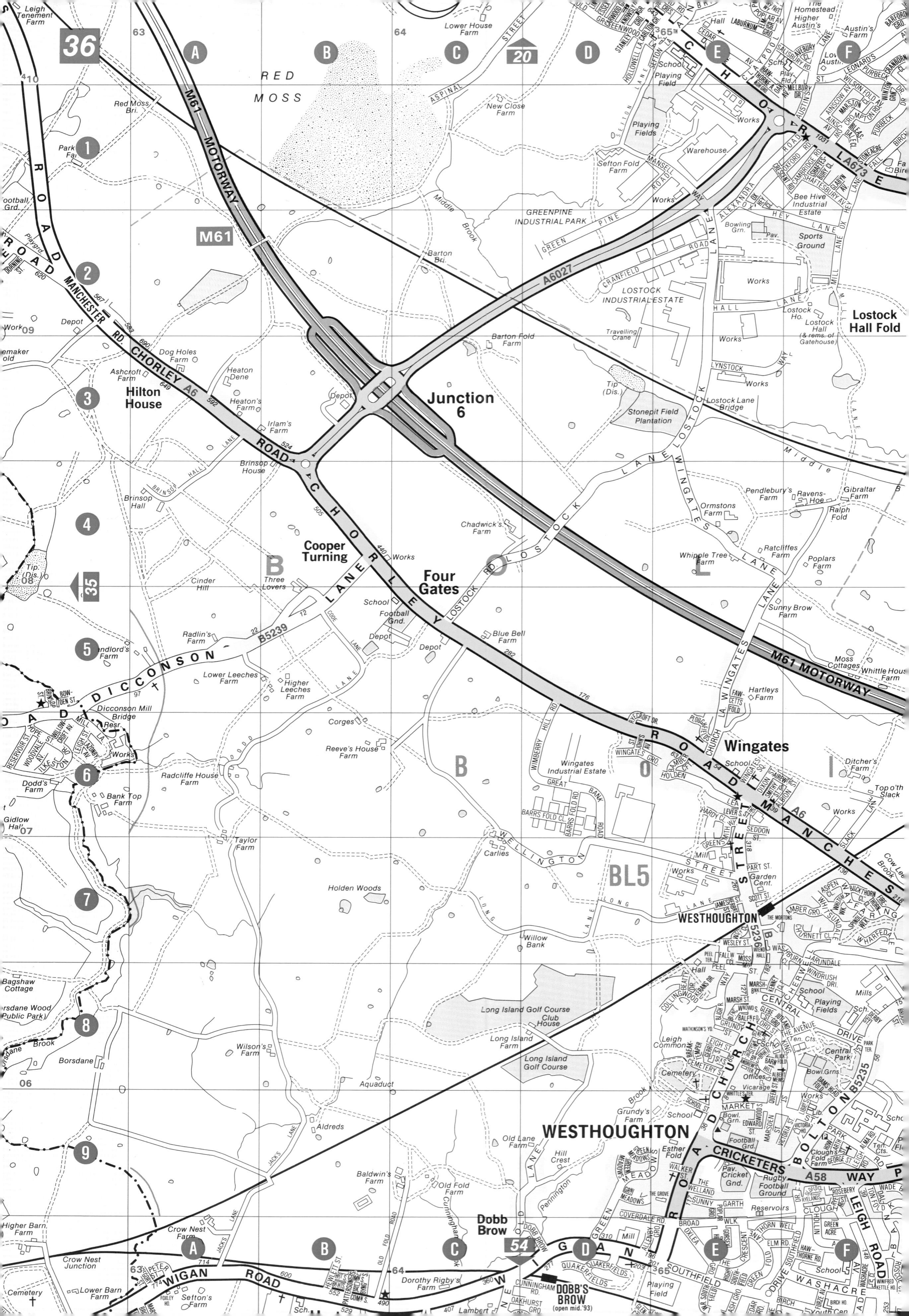

36
20
35
54
RED MOSS
M61 MOTORWAY
M61
Junction 6
CHORLEY ROAD
MANCHESTER RD.
A6
A6027
B5239
DICCONSON
LOSTOCK LANE
WINGATES LANE
Lostock Hall Fold
GREENPINE INDUSTRIAL PARK
LOSTOCK INDUSTRIAL ESTATE
Hilton House
Cooper Turning
Four Gates
Wingates
Wingates Industrial Estate
WELLINGTON
BL5
WESTHOUGHTON
Long Island Golf Course
Dobb Brow
DOBB'S BROW
WIGAN ROAD
CRICKETERS WAY
A58
LEIGH ROAD
CHURCH STREET
B5235
BOLTON
A673
Crow Nest Junction
Red Moss Bri.
Lower House Farm
New Close Farm
Sefton Fold Farm
Barton Bri.
Barton Fold Farm
Dog Holes Farm
Heaton Dene
Heaton's Farm
Irlam's Farm
Brinsop House
Brinsop Hall
Three Lovers
Cinder Hill
Radlin's Farm
Lower Leeches Farm
Higher Leeches Farm
Dicconson Mill Bridge
Radcliffe House Farm
Bank Top Farm
Taylor Farm
Corges
Reeve's House Farm
Holden Woods
Willow Bank
Carlies
Blue Bell Farm
Chadwick's Farm
Stonepit Field Plantation
Pendlebury's Farm
Ormstons Farm
Ratcliffes Farm
Whipple Tree Farm
Sunny Brow Farm
Hartleys Farm
Poplars Farm
Ravens-Hoe
Gibraltar Farm
Ralph Fold
Moss Cottages
Whittle House Farm
Ditcher's Farm
Top o'th Slack
Wilson's Farm
Borsdane
Aquaduct
Aldreds
Baldwin's Farm
Old Fold Farm
Old Lane Farm
Hill Crest
Dorothy Rigby's Farm
Crow Nest Farm
Higher Barn Farm
Lower Barn Farm
Sefton's Farm
Cemetery
Leigh Common
Esther Fold
Pav. Cricket Gnd.
Rugby Football Ground
Reservoirs
Playing Field
Central Park
Vicarage
Market St.
Bee Hive Industrial Estate
Sports Ground
Lostock Hall
Lostock Lane Bridge
Leigh Tenement Farm
Park Fa
Ashcroft Farm
Depot
School
Football Gnd.
Works
Tip (Dis.)
Gidlow Hall
Dodd's Farm
Bagshaw Cottage
Borsdane Wood (Public Park)
Playing Fields
Warehouse
Travelling Crane

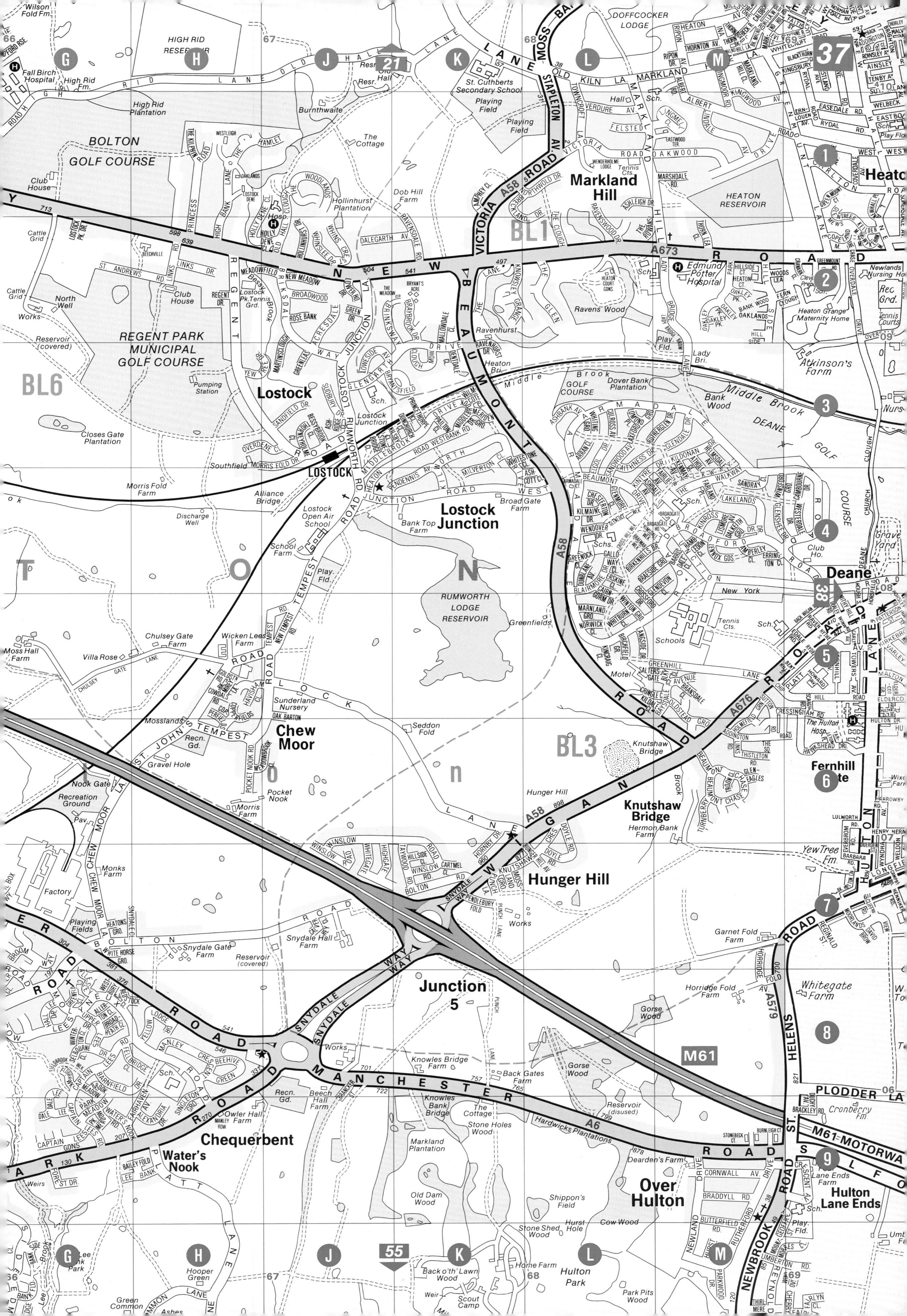

38
Heaton
Heaton Reservoir
Chorley New Road
A673
Edmund Potter Hospital
Bolton School
Gilnow Park
Playing Fields
Heaton Cemetery
Atkinson's Farm
Middle Brook
Deane Golf Course
Haslam Park
Pocket
Gilnow
Victory
Chorley Old Road
Bolton Steam Museum
B6226
Bolton Royal Infirmary
Queen's Park
BOLTON
BL1
St. George's Road
Marsden Road
Mayor St.
College Way
Institute of Technology
Trinity Street
Lecturers Closes
Industrial Estate
Deane
Deane Road
A676
Willows
Derby Street
A579
Recreation Ground
Pike Mill Estate
BL3
Fernhill Gate
Hulton Lane
A6145
The Hulton Hosp.
Hulton Lane Estate
Daubhill
St. Helens Road
Lever Edge
Great Lever
Morris Green
Hayward Grammar Sch.
Club House
Will Hill Brook
Grt. Lever & Farnworth Golf Course
Top o' th' Height
Whitegate Farm
Water Towers
Top o' Cow
Garnet Fold Farm
Horridge Fold Farm
Bolton District General Hospital
Reservoir
Scot Meadow
Townleys Farm
Plodder Lane
B6199
Cranberry Fm.
Heathfield Farm
Stone House
Water Gate La.
BL5
M61
M61 Motorway
Manchester Road
Hulton Lane Ends
Four Lane Ends Farm
Salford Road
A6
Junction 4
Sewage Works
Moss Hall Farm
Umberton's Farm
Adises Farm
Highfield Road
Highfield Youth Centre
High
Newbrook Road
37
22
56

Breightmet
Roscow Fold
Mill Hill
Tonge Fold
Oaken Bottom
BL2
Springfield
Rose Hill
Darcy Lever
Burnden
Moses Gate
Harper Green
BL4
FARNWORTH
Nob End
Prestolee
KEARSLEY
New Bury
M26
A58
A666
A6053
B6209
23
40
57

40
24
39
58
A
B
C
D
E
F
1
2
3
4
5
6
7
8
9
Ainsworth
Cockey Moor
CHURCH ST.
Bowling Green
Breightmet
Industrial Estate
Reservoir
Kiln Clough
Ainsworth Hall Farm
Top o'th' Carrs
Pilkington Fold
Rothwells
Plane Trees
Taylors Farm
Halfway Houses
Openshaw Fold
Ainsworth Lo.
BURY ROAD
BURY AND BOLTON ROAD
A58
NEW ROAD
BURY NEW ROAD
RADCLIFFE A665
MOOR ROAD
STARLING ROAD
B6292
HIGHER AINSWORTH ROAD
BL2
Reservoirs
Coggra Fold
Football Ground
Blackshaw Prim.Sch.
BLENHEIM ROAD ESTATE
Bradley Fold Works
Moss Shaw Farm
Bradley Fold Junction
Davenport Farm
RADCLIFFE ROAD
Five Acre Farm
RADCLIFFE MOOR RD.
COUNTESS LANE
A665
Bradley Fold Pottery
Grundy Fold
Masefield Jun.& Inf. Sch.
Stopes Farm
Little Lever
STOPES ROAD
BOLTON ROAD
A6053
Radcliffe Jun.& Inf. Schs.
Playing Fields
Youth Centre
Football Ground
Bolton Rd. Park
M26
Cricket Grd.
Health Cen.
RADCLIFFE
Radcliffe High Sch
Cams Lane Prim. School
Bowness School
CHURCH ST.
HALL LA.
A6053
BL3
St.Matthews Prim.Sch.
Bolton Council Area Office
HIGH ST.
Comm. Cen. Health Cen.
Playing Fields
Play ground
Football Ground
Works
BOLTON
Harper Fold
Rush Acre
Manchester, Bolton & Bury Canal
Mount Sion
Nickernoie Bridge
River Irwell
Mine
Weir
Mill
Nob End
Wellfield
FARNWORTH CEMETERY
Lower Farley
Wilsons Bridge
Nearer Shore Top
Oak Hill
Seddon's Fold
PRESTOLEE ROAD
Langley Brow
Shore Top Farm
Outwood Sidings
Sewage Works
Outwood
Resrs.
Clammerclough Tunnel
Prestolee Prim. Sch.
Manchester, Bolton & Bury Canal (Dis)
Ringley Lock
Ringley Bridge
Ringley Canal Bridge
Bottom of Croft
KEARSLEY ROAD
RINGLEY ROAD
A667
Prestolee
Horridge Brook
MARKET ST.
S. RINGLEY RD.
KEARSLEY
Stoneclough
Europa Trading Estate
STONECLOUGH ROAD
Ringley
Ringley Old Br.
Ringley Prim. Sch.
Higher Heaps
Playing

41
42
25
59
Daisyfield
Buckley Wells
Florence Nightingale Hospital
Recreation Grd
BOLTON A58
BL8
BL9
School Playing Fields
Lower Hinds
Derby High School
Warth Fold
Bury Sports Ground
Bury Football Ground
WELLINGTON
Fishpool
Peel Sixth Form College
Bury C. of E. High Sch.
MANCHESTER BOLTON & BURY RESERVOIR
Old Hall Farm
Doffer Fold
Withins Reservoir
Recreation Grd
CEMETERY
Crow Trees Farm
Coney Green
Manchester, Bolton & Bury Canal
River Irwell
Irwell Bank Farm
Redvales
Fletcher Fold
CEMETERY
Roach Farm
Weir
Gigg
Paper Mill
Sports Ground
Hardy's Gate Bri.
Works
Barlow Fold
White Brow
Hollins Vale
Hollins
Bury Golf Course
Blackford Bridge
Blackford Old Bri.
Unsworth Hall (Club House)
Mountains Farm
Sunny Bank
CLOSE PARK
River Irwell
Radcliffe
A6053
SPRING LA.
CROSS LANE
BURY ST.
DUMERS LANE
A6053
PILKINGTON WAY
A665
CORONATION PARK
RADCLIFFE NEW ROAD
A665
Lily Hill
MANCHESTER ROAD
A56
BURY NEW ROAD
BURY NEW ROAD
A56
Elms Fm
Moss Lane Industrial Estate
Whitefield
Higher Barn
King George's Field
Reservoir
Chapel Field
Old Manchester Golf Club
Stand Golf Course
M25
Stand Golf Course
Outwood Gate Farm
Clarke's Hill Reservoir
Hillsden Farm
A667
ROAD
WEST A667
HIGHER LANE A665
DALES LANE
CHURCH LA.
WHITEFIELD
Stand
Philip's High School
Oak Bank
Besses o' th' Barn
G
H
J
K
L
M
1
2
3
4
5
6
7
8
9
78
79
80
81
10
09
08
07
06

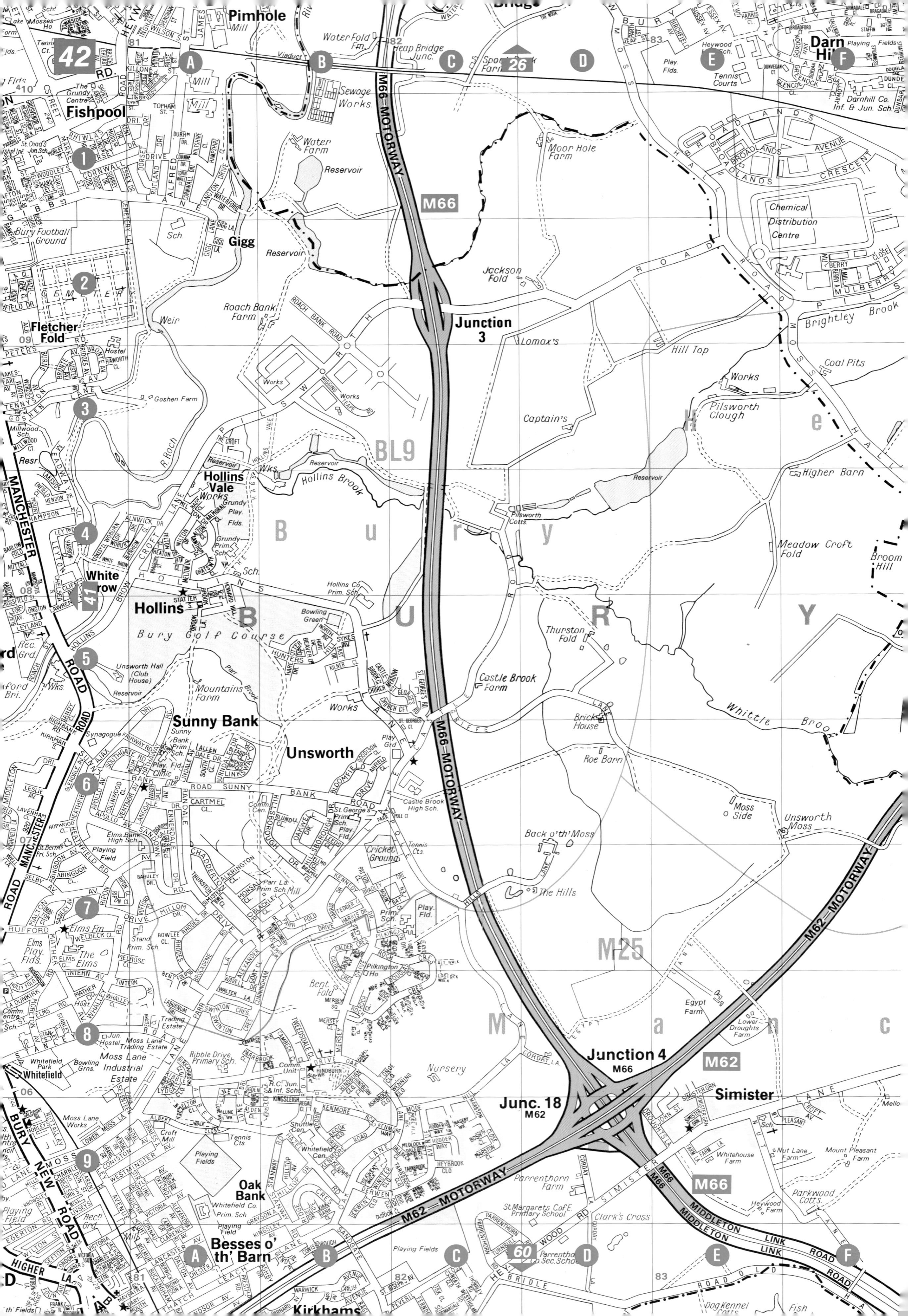

42
Pimhole
Mill
Water Fold Fm.
Heap Bridge Junc.
82
26
Sports Ground Farm
83
Heywood Sch.
Play. Flds.
Tennis Courts
Darn Hill
Playing Fields
Darnhill Co. Inf. & Jun. Sch.
Viaduct
A
B
C
D
E
F
The Grundy Centre
Fishpool
Sewage Works
Water Farm
Reservoir
Moor Hole Farm
Broadlands Avenue
Broadlands Crescent
Chemical Distribution Centre
M66
M66 MOTORWAY
Bury Football Ground
Sch.
Gigg
Gigg Lane
Cemetery La.
Reservoir
Jackson Fold
Pilsworth Road
Mulberry
Brightley Brook
Roach Bank Farm
Roach Bank Road
Weir
Junction 3
Lomax's
Hill Top
Coal Pits
Fletcher Fold
Hostel
Goshen Farm
Works
Wiggins Teape Rd.
Captain's
Pilsworth Clough
Tennyson Av.
Millwood Sch.
R. Roch
BL9
Reservoir
Hollins Brook
Higher Barn
Resr.
Hollins Vale Works
Grundy Play. Flds.
Grundy Prim. Sch.
Pilsworth Cotts.
Bury
MANCHESTER ROAD
White Brow
41
Meadow Croft Fold
Broom Hill
Hollins
Hollins Lane
Hollins Brow
Bury Golf Course
Hollins Co. Prim. Sch.
Bowling Green
BURY
Thurston Fold
Rec. Grd.
Unsworth Hall (Club House)
Reservoir
Mountains Farm
Parr Brook
Castle Brook Farm
Church Cft.
Whittle Brook
Wks.
Synagogue
Sunny Bank
Sunny Bank Prim. Sch.
Unsworth
Works
Brick House
Roe Barn
Play. Fld.
Clinic
Sunny Bank Road
Castle Brook High Sch.
St. George's Prim. Sch.
Moss Side
Unsworth Moss
Elms Bank High Sch.
Playing Field
Cricket Ground
Tennis Cts.
Back o'th' Moss
M62 MOTORWAY
St. Bernard's Pri. Sch.
Parr La. Prim. Sch.
Mill
The Hills
Play. Fld.
Prim. Sch.
Elms Fm.
The Elms
Elms Play. Flds.
Stand Prim. Sch.
Pilkington Ho.
M25
Bent Fold
Egypt Farm
Manchester
Trading Estate
Moss Lane Trading Estate
Jun. Hostel
Moss Lane Industrial Estate
Whitefield
Bowling Grns.
Ribble Drive Primary Sch.
Comm. Unit
R.C. Jun. & Inf. Schs.
Nursery
Junction 4
M66
Junc. 18
M62
Lower Droughts Farm
M62
Simister
Simister Lane
Mount Pleasant Farm
Nut Lane Farm
Whitehouse Farm
Moss Lane Works
Croft Mill Av.
Tennis Cts.
Playing Fields
Shuttle Cen.
Whitefield Cen.
Parrenthorn Farm
M66
Parkwood Cotts.
Heywood Farm
BURY NEW ROAD
Playing Field
Rec. Grd.
Oak Bank
Whitefield Co. Prim. Sch.
Playing Field
St. Margarets C of E Primary School
Clark's Cross
Middleton Link Road
Besses o' th' Barn
Playing Fields
60
Parrenthorn Sec. School
Higher La.
Kirkhams
Bridle Road
Dog Kennel Cotts.
Old Road

43
27
44
61
Broadfield
Hopwood
Heywood Business Park
Higher Broadfield Farm
Siddal Moor
Siddal Moor Depot
Siddal Moor High Sch.
Lane End
M62
M62 MOTORWAY
Junction 19
OL10
Hares Hill Farm
Collop Gate Farm
Siddal Moor Farm
Brightley Brook
Higher Fields
Stock Nook
New Gap Farm
Saxons Fm.
Yew Tree Farm East
Yew Tree Farm South
Glade Wood
Oaken Bank Wood
Birch Industrial Estate
Doctor Fold
Lower Whittle
Siddal Fold
Hatters Fm.
Birch Service Area
Mills
Top o'th' Hill
Woodside Farm
Hopwood College
Queen Elizabeth's High Sch.
Leighs
Whittle Fold
Birch
Langley Lane Farm
Playing Fields
ROCHDALE
The Grange
Greenhill Fm.
Top of Hebers
Hollins
M24
Langley Brook Adult Training Centre
Langley High School
Langley Co. Inf. Jun. & Nursy. Schools
Langley
Green Lane End
Sand Field
Mere Brook
Simon Lane Farm
Mill
Golf Driving Range
Council Depot
Saxon Nook Sch.
St. Mary's R.C. Inf. & Jun. Schs.
Parish C.E. Sch.
Cricket Grnd.
Parkside Fm.
Demesne Jun. & Inf. Sch.
Parkside Cen.
Truffet Park Rec. Grnd.
Bowlee
Cambashaw
Burial Ground
North Manchester Golf Course
Asker Dam
Cobler's Dam
Franks Dam
Rhodes Green Fm.
Rhodes Green
Reservoir
Bradley Hall Farm
Sunny Brow Nursery Sch.
Parkfield Prim. Sch.
Lime Field
Recreation Ground
Council Offs.
Rhodes Ho. (Club Ho.)
Resrs
Arndale Centre
Middleton
Little Park
McBride Riverside Park
Little Nook
Little Heaton Prim. Sch.
Reservoirs
Lever Bri.
Bird Sanctuary
Alkrington Hall
Rhodes
HEYWOOD OLD ROAD
MANCHESTER OLD ROAD
MIDDLETON ROAD
HOLLIN ROAD
HOLLIN LANE
A6045
A6046
A576
NEW ROAD
MANCHESTER NEW RD.
MIDDLETON WAY
OLDHAM RD.
LANGLEY LANE
WHITTLE LANE
WORTH ROAD
DOCTOR FOLD LANE
OAKEN BANK ROAD
STOTT LA.
BOARDMAN LANE
ELLIS LANE
LONG ST.

44
Works
PHOENIX PARK IND. EST.
A
B
C
D
E
F
87
88
89
Rail Welding
Spin Threads
Castleton Worth Junction
Lock
28
Prim. Sch.
Trows House
Trows Fm.
Mill Pond
Works
Res.
Junction 20
Weir
M62 MOTORWAY
M62
St. Gabriel's R.C. Sch.
1
Hope Cott.
Lane End Fm.
Ley Farm
Lane End
M62 MOTORWAY
Works
Fox Hill
Trub
Rochdale
OL11
Rec. Grd.
Avondale Ct.
M62
Depot
2
Heywood
Brook
OL10
MANCHESTER RD.
Towing Path
Garden Centre
A627(M)
Thornfields
Thornham Fold
Thornham Fold Farm
A627(M) MOTORWAY
MANCHESTER
GOLF CLUB
Trub
A664
Crkt. Grd.
Slattocks
Middleton Thornham C. of E. School
3
Glade Wood
Round Hill
Reservoir
Gerrard Wood
Brook
Whit
Hopwood Cottage Club Ho.
Hopwood Hall Farm
SLATTOCKS LINK ROAD
Yew Tree Farm South
Oaken Bank Wood
OAKEN BANK ROAD
Lord's Wood
ROCHDALE
Locks
Stake Hill
Reservoirs
Whit Brook
4
Hopwood Hall
Hopwood Hall College
The Butts
Works
Slattocks
Manchester
08
43
Playing Field
Woodside Farm
Works
STAKEHILL INDUSTRIAL ESTATE
Park View
Three Gates Farm
Higher Stake Hill
Queen Elizabeth's High Sch.
5
ROCHDALE
Hopwood Clough
Playing Fields
Playing Fields
Alderman Kay School
Cardinal Langley R.C. High Sch.
Whit Brook
Works
Chadderton Heights
Stanycliffe
Hollins
6
HOLLIN
St. John Fisher R.C. Prim. Sch.
Acresfield Nursy. Sch.
Stanycliffe Bri.
Hollin Jun. & Inf. Schs.
M24
Mount Pleasant Farm
Nod
Healds Green
Healds Green Farm
07
A6046
LANE
Cricket Grnd.
BOARSHAW CEMETERY
Kenyon's Fm.
Higher Boarshaw
Acres Fm.
Acres
7
Recreation Ground
Resr.
Chadderton Fold
Playing Field
Parish C.E. Sch.
Playing Fld.
Lime Field
Scowcroft Fm.
Whit Brook
Lock
Lock
Little Green
8
Clinic
A664
LONG
Cromer Indust. Estate
Mill
River Irk
Chadderton Hall Park
Weir
CHADDERTON
B6195
Burial Ground
John Lee Fold
A669
MIDDLETON
ROAD
Chadderton Park
06
Elm St. Jun. & Inf. Schs.
MILLS HILL
Factory
Mills Hill
Mills Hill Junior & Infant Schools
Training Centre
9
Lark Hill
MIDDLETON
Bus Sta.
Little Park
Playing Field
Middleton High Sch.
GRIMSHAW
B6189
McBride Riverside Park
Ind. Est.
Res.
Ramsden Farm
Bowling Green
Moss Close
62
Ferney Field House Fm.
Kitchen Wood
St. Peter's R.C. Prim. Sch.
Radcliffe Comprehensive Upper School
Ferney Field Farm
Playing Field
87
88
89

Burnedge
29
Buersil Head
Green Hill
Green Hill Farm
Moss Gate
Lower Rushcroft
OL16
Buersil Reservoir
Gravel Hole
Higher Rushcroft
Plumpton
Thornham
Thornham St. James Jun. & Inf. Sch.
Summit
Narrow Gate Brow
High Crompton
High Gate
Hanging Chadder
Narrow Gate
Firbank Co. Prim. Sch
OL2
Low Crompton
Sewage Works
Newbarn Jun. & Inf. Sch.
Cowlishaw
Source of River Irk
River Irk
Tandle Hill Countryside Park
Oozewood
Lower Oozewood Farm
Paddling Pool
Crompton & Royton Golf Course
Cowlishaw Fm.
OLDHAM
Thorp
Royton Cemetery
Dogford Park
Greenbank Special Sch.
Diamond Rope Works
A.T.C. Headquarters
Reservoir
Luzley Brook
46
Royton Park
Highbarn Junior School
Royton Crompton Comp Sch
Playing Field
Head o' th' Heys
Crofters
ROYTON
Cricket Grd.
Blackshaw Jun. & Inf. Sch.
Playing Fields
Heyside
Millfields Farm
Haggate
B6195
Lower Gillotts
Gillotts
Race Field
Street Bridge
MIDDLETON RD.
Royley
Sewage Wks
St. Paul's C. of E. Jun. Sch.
Nether Hey Fm
Ten. Cts.
Playing Field
Broadway Playground
Dr Kershaw's Cott. Hospice
Industrial Estate
Warehouse
Buckley Wood
River Irk
A627(M) MOTORWAY
A627(M)
Holden Fold
Elk Mill
Monarch Mill
Sun Fields
Rhos Mill
Salmon Fields
OL1
A663
BROADWAY
Long Clough
Higginshaw
Chadderton Hall Junior School
Football Grd.
Clayton Playing Fields
The Clayton Arms Sports Hall
Boundary Park
Oldham Athletic FC
Long Sight
Gas Wks.
CHADDERTON WAY
A627
The Royal Oldham Hospital
WESTWOOD PARK
Westwood Running Track
West Hulme
Shaw Road Estate
OL9
West Pennine College of Health Studies
Burnley Brow
Coldhurst Hollow Estate
Sarah Moor
DERKER
North Chadderton Comp. Lwr. Sch.
Bare Trees County Primary School
CHADDERTON CEMETERY
Busk
Open Space
Oldham Edge
Higginshaw Youth Cen.
Oldham Central Trading Park
Cold Hurst
A669
A663D
A671
ROCHDALE ROAD
OLDHAM ROAD
SHAW ROAD
A66
B6194
Blue Coat Comp. Sch.
Lower Moor
North Moor
63
Fra Hill
Mumps
Bus Depot
MIDDLETON
FEATHERSTALL
St. Herbert's Inf. & Jun.
College of Technology
Civic Centre
Market
Baths
G
H
J
K
L
M
1
2
3
4
5
6
7
8
9
90
91
92
93
10
09
08
07
06

46
Moss Gate
Lower Rushcroft
Higher Rushcroft
Crompton Rushcroft Cnty. Prim. Sch.
Wood End
Goats
Crompton Fold
Shore Edge
Brushes Clough Res.
Brushes Clough Quarry (dis.)
Top o'th' Green Quarry (dis.)
Way Moss
Jordan Brow
30
Nook
Lane Side
Dog Hill
Top O'th' Dog Hill
Burn Farm
Chapel Farm
SHAW & CROMPTON
New Town
Moss Hey
SHAW
OL2
Clough
Fullwood
Cowlishaw
Crompton
Newbarn Jun. & Infs. Sch.
Playing Field
Shaw Side
Moss Farm
Birshaw House
Shaw Edge
Luzley Brook
45
Sholver
Besom Hill
Besom Hill Reservoir
Slack Farm
Carrchief Nook Farm
Alderney Farm
Sholver Moor Farm
Heyside
Brownlow
Bullcote Farm
Intake Farm
Harleyroad
Woodstock Factory
Moorside
Count Hill
Hodge Clough
Higher Barrowshaw
Higher Count Hill
Lower Count Hill
Reservoir
Roebuck
Green Lane Farm
OL1
Barrowshaw Fm.
Higginshaw
Salmon Fields
Sun Fields
Broadbent
Watersheddings
Near Barrowshaw
Stoneleigh Park
Spring Hill
Waterhead
Sarah Moor
Oldham Edge
Derker
Acre
Greenacres Hill
Top Of Moor
Birks
Lower Moor
Greenacres Moor
Mumps
Cross Bank
Sun Hill
Greenacres
Greenacres Cemetery
64
A672
A663
A62
B6194
B6197

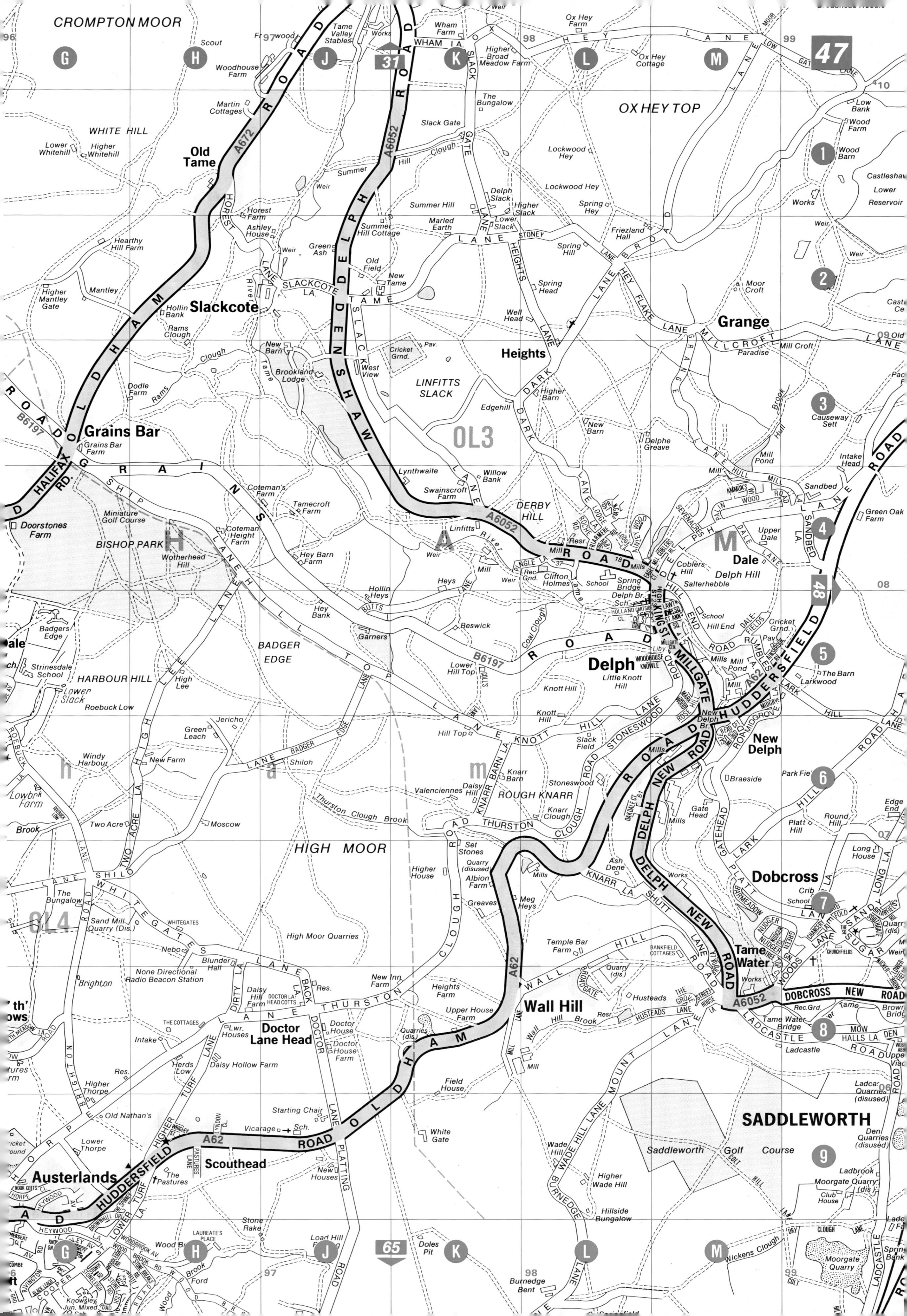

47
CROMPTON MOOR
Scout
Woodhouse Farm
Tame Valley Stables
Works
31
Wham Farm
WHAM LA.
Ox Hey Farm
HEY LANE
Higher Broad Meadow Farm
Ox Hey Cottage
LOW GATE LANE
Low Bank
Wood Farm
Wood Barn
Castleshaw Lower Reservoir
Martin Cottages
The Bungalow
OX HEY TOP
WHITE HILL
Lower Whitehill
Higher Whitehill
Old Tame
A672
A6052
Slack Gate
SLACK GATE
Lockwood Hey
Summer
Weir
Hill Clough
Summer Hill
Marled Earth
Delph Slack
Higher Slack
Lower Slack
Spring Hey
Works
Friezland Hall
Horest Farm
Ashley House
Summer Hill Cottage
Green Ash
Old Field
New Tame
HORSE LANE
Hearthy Hill Farm
STONEY LANE
HEIGHTS LANE
Spring Hill
Spring Head
Moor Croft
Mantley
Higher Mantley Gate
Hollin Bank
Slackcote
SLACKCOTE LA.
TAME
Rams Clough
Well Head
Grange
MILLCROFT LANE
Mill Croft
Paradise
Old Lane
Clough
New Barn
Tame
Cricket Grnd.
Pav.
West View
Heights
Brookland Lodge
LINFITTS SLACK
DARK LANE
Higher Barn
Dodle Farm
Rams
Edgehill
Causeway Sett
New Barn
Delphe Greave
OL3
Grains Bar
Grains Bar Farm
B6197
HALIFAX RD.
GRAINS ROAD
DENSHAW
OLDHAM ROAD
Mill Pond
Intake Head
Lynthwaite
Willow Bank
Coteman's Farm
Swainscroft Farm
Sandbed
Tamecroft Farm
Miniature Golf Course
SHIP LANE
Doorstones Farm
DERBY HILL
Green Oak Farm
Coteman Height Farm
Linfitts
River
Upper Dale
Dale
Delph Hill
BISHOP PARK
Wotherhead Hill
Hey Barn Farm
Weir
Mill
Rec. Gnd.
Clifton Holmes
School
Spring Bridge
Cobblers Hill
Salterhebble
Heys
Hollin Heys
Hey Bank
BUTTS
Beswick
Delph Br.
Sch.
HOLLAND CL.
School
Hill End
Cricket Grnd.
Badgers Edge
Garners
Coal Clough
Liby
WOODHOUSE KNOWLE
Delph
Little Knott Hill
Mills
Mill Pond
BADGER EDGE
Strinesdale School
HARBOUR HILL
Lower Hill Top
The Barn
Larkwood
High Lee
Lower Slack
Roebuck Low
Knott Hill
MILLGATE
New Delph Br.
HUDDERSFIELD
A62
New Delph
Jericho
Knott Hill
Green Leach
Hill Top
KNOTT HILL
Slack Field
STONESWOOD ROAD
Windy Harbour
New Farm
BADGER LANE
Shiloh
Mills
Knarr Barn
Braeside
Park Field
Lowbrook Farm
Daisy Hill
ROUGH KNARR
Stoneswood
Valenciennes
Thurston Clough Brook
Knarr Clough
Gate Head
Edge End
Brook
Two Acre
Moscow
THURSTON CLOUGH
DELPH NEW ROAD
Mills
Round Hill
Platt Hill
HIGH MOOR
Set Stones
Quarry (disused)
Albion Farm
Higher House
Long House
Ash Dene
KNARR LA.
Works
Dobcross
The Bungalow
Mills
Greaves
Meg Heys
Crib
School
OL4
Sand Mill Quarry (Dis.)
WHITEGATES
High Moor Quarries
Temple Bar Farm
Nebo
Blunder Hall
None Directional Radio Beacon Station
WALL HILL
BANKFIELD COTTAGES
Quarry (dis)
Tame Water
Brighton
Daisy Hill Farm
DOCTOR LA. HEAD COTTS.
Res.
New Inn Farm
Heights Farm
Wall Hill
Husteads
Works
CHURCHFIELDS
A6052
DOBCROSS NEW ROAD
THE COTTAGES
Doctor Lane Head
Doctor House
Doctor House Farm
Lwr. Houses
Upper House Farm
Quarries (dis)
Resr.
Hill Brook
HUSTEADS LANE
Rec.Grd.
Tame
Tame Water Bridge
MOW HALLS LA.
LADCASTLE ROAD
Intake
Herds Low
Daisy Hollow Farm
Res.
Mill
Ladcastle
Higher Thorpe
Field House
Starting Chair
Sch.
Vicarage
OLDHAM ROAD
MOUNT LANE
SADDLEWORTH
Ladcastle Quarries (disused)
Old Nathan's
Lower Thorpe
Scouthead
White Gate
Saddleworth Golf Course
Den Quarries (disused)
Austerlands
The Pastures
New Houses
Wade Hill
WADE HILL LANE
Higher Wade Hill
Ladbrook
Moorgate Quarry (dis)
Club House
Stone Rake
BURNEDGE LANE
Hillside Bungalow
LAUREATE'S PLACE
Wood Brow
Load Hill
65
Doles Pit
Wickens Clough
Moorgate Quarry
Spring Bank
Brook
Ford
97
98
Burnedge Bent
99
Knowsley Jun. Mixed
G
H
J
K
L
M
1
2
3
4
5
6
7
8
9
48

48
47
66
WEST YORKSHIRE
GREATER MANCHESTER
Castleshaw Upper Resr.
Castleshaw Lower Reservoir
Castle Shaw
Bleak Hey Nook
Grange
Harrop Ridge
Harrop Dale
Diggle Edge
HARROP EDGE
Harrop Green
Carr
Kiln Green
Diggle
Dale
New Delph
Holly Grove
Marslands
Dobcross
Tame Water
Running Hill Head
Pobgreen
Saddleworth Fold
Heathfields
Uppermill
SADDLEWORTH
Saddleworth Golf Course
HUDDERSFIELD ROAD
STANDEDGE ROAD
A62
A670
A6052
DOBCROSS NEW ROAD
HIGH STREET
Huddersfield Narrow Canal
LOWER KNOLL
BILLY GRO
Ravenstone Rocks
OL3
Big Rough
Broadstone Hill
Broad Stones
Slades
Primrose Hill
Shaw Rochar
Shaw Rocks
Pilling Slack
Sugar Loaf
Dick Hill
Kinder Stones
Rocher Brow
Slades Rocks
Moorgate Quarry
Ladcastle
Ballgrove
Churchill Fields

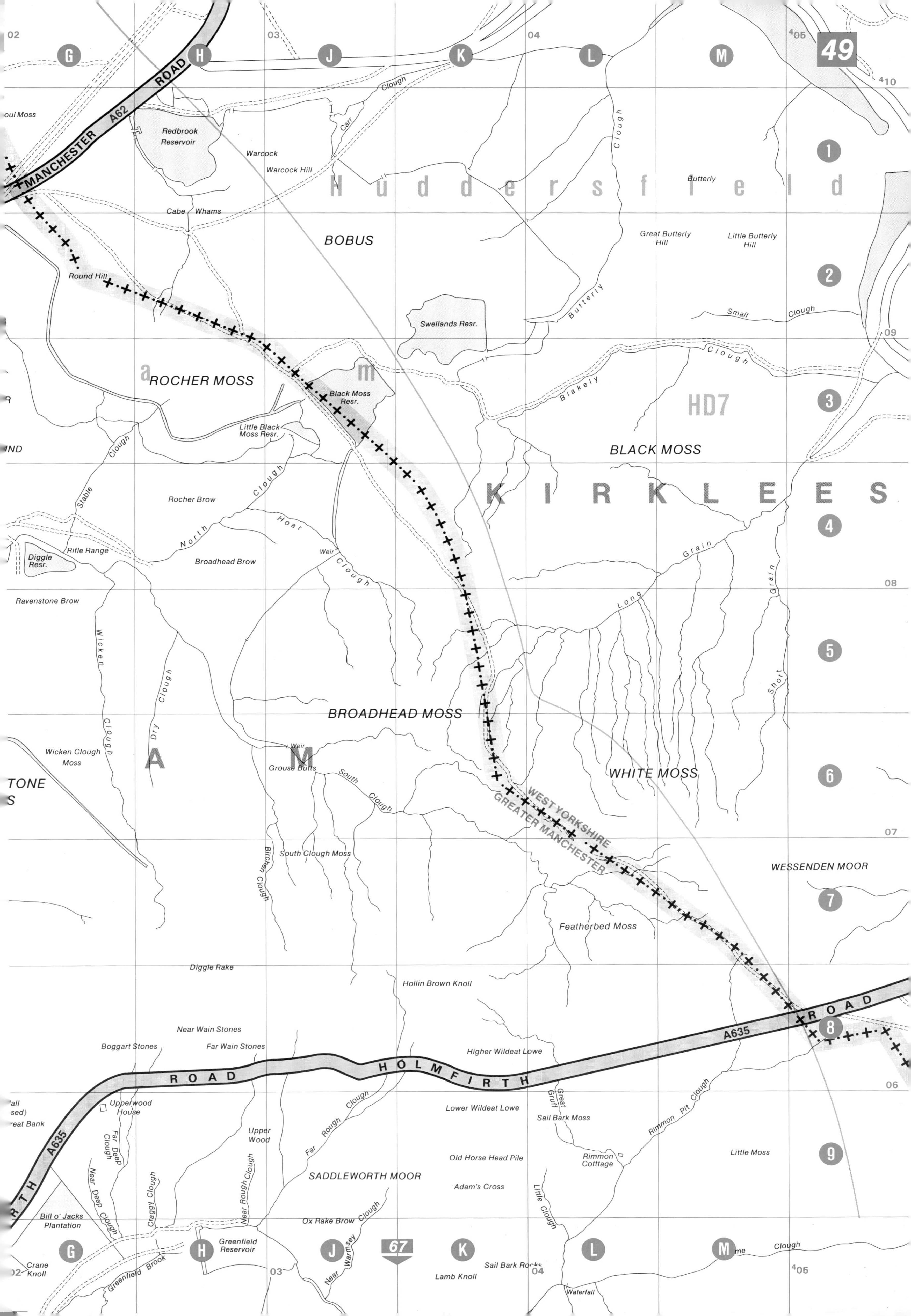

02   03   04   405   410

1

2

09

3

08

4

5

07

6

7

06

8

9

oul Moss

MANCHESTER ROAD A62

Redbrook Reservoir

Warcock

Warcock Hill

Cabe Whams

Round Hill

a ROCHER MOSS

m

Black Moss Resr.

Little Black Moss Resr.

Rocher Brow

Stable Clough

North Clough

Hoar Clough

Weir

Broadhead Brow

Rifle Range

Diggle Resr.

Ravenstone Brow

Wicken Clough

Dry Clough

A

Wicken Clough Moss

Weir

Grouse Butts

BROADHEAD MOSS

M

South Clough

Birchen Clough

South Clough Moss

Diggle Rake

Near Wain Stones

Boggart Stones

Far Wain Stones

Near Deep Clough

Far Deep Clough

Upperwood House

Craggy Clough

Upper Wood

Near Rough Clough

Far Rough Clough

SADDLEWORTH MOOR

Ox Rake Brow

Bill o' Jacks Plantation

Crane Knoll

Greenfield Brook

Greenfield Reservoir

Near Warmsey Clough

ROAD HOLMFIRTH ROAD A635

H u d d e r s f i e l d

BOBUS

Swellands Resr.

Butterly

Great Butterly Hill

Little Butterly Hill

Small Clough

Butterly Clough

Blakely Clough

HD7

BLACK MOSS

K I R K L E E S

Long Grain

Short Grain

WHITE MOSS

WEST YORKSHIRE
GREATER MANCHESTER

Featherbed Moss

WESSENDEN MOOR

Hollin Brown Knoll

Higher Wildeat Lowe

Lower Wildeat Lowe

Sail Bark Moss

Great Gruff

Rimmon Pit Clough

Little Clough

Old Horse Head Pile

Adam's Cross

Rimmon Cotttage

Little Moss

A635 ROAD

me Clough

Sail Bark Rocks

Lamb Knoll

Waterfall

03   04   405

50
Windmill (disused)
51
52
53
A
B
C
D
E
F
32
68
Up Holland
Holland Hall
Stand House
Dean Wood Golf Course
Sewage Works
Hall Green
Newgate
Garnett Lees Playing Fields
WINDMILL RD.
NEWGATE RD.
ORMSKIRK RD.
ORMSKIRK
A577
DINGLE RD.
PARLIAMENT ST.
SCHOOL LA.
ORRELL
Orrell Post
Hooton's Farm
GATHURST ROAD
M6 MOTORWAY
M6
St Peter's R.C. High School
Playing Fields
Blackledge Ho.
Works
Lower Tower Hill Farm
Higher Tower Hill Farm
TOWER HILL
Quarry
Skelmersdale
Dean Brook Bridge
CINNAMON BROW
TONTINE
ST. HIGHER LANE
Health Cen.
M58 MOTORWAY
M58
Well Cross Farm
Chequer Lane Playing Fields
Junc. 5
Playing Field
Fairhurst House
Giant House Farm
TOWER LANE
Sefton House Farm
Tontine
Sefton Farm
SEFTON RD.
SANDBROOK ROAD
The Lawns Farm
The Lawns
ORRELL
Holgate Jun. & Inf. Sch.
Farmoor
Junction 26
Rugby Football Ground
Edge Wood Hall
Smithy Brook
Sewage Works
WN8
Upholland
Tunnel
UPHOLLAND
WEST LANCASHIRE
Reservoir (covered)
School
Far Moor
St. James' R.C. Jun. & Inf. Sch.
St. James' Rd. Jun. & Inf. Sch.
JAMES ST.
ST. LUKE'S DR.
LODGE ROAD
Cricket Ground
Athertons Farm
WINSTANLEY ROAD
Lower Balcony Farm
Lower Pimbo
Higher Pimbo
LONG LA.
PIMBO
Millets
Captain Leigh's Farm
Pimbo Bushes
LANCASHIRE
GREATER MANCHESTER
Higher End
UPHOLLAND ROAD
B5206
Farrar's Farm
Gorsey Hill Wood
Winstanley College
Playing Field
Upholland Lodges
Swift Gate Farm
Bowling Green
Greenslate Farm
GREENSLATE RD.
Gautley Ho.
Works
SMETHURST ROAD
Billinge Hospital
Playing Field
Oak Wood
Moss Wood
Moss House
Hesketh House
Birch Wood
Black Brook
Sankey Brook
Hollin Wood
Maddocks Wood
Higher Heaton Farm
Heaton House
Bispham Hall
Daisy Wood
Hangman's Wood
Maddocks
Brownlow Farm
Coppice Wood
The Hoofons
Brownlow
CRANK ROAD
Longshaw Farm
Longshaw Bottom
LONGSHAW PARK ROAD
WN5
Paddock Wood
Promised Land Farm
St. Helens
Plane Tree Farm
Billinge Plants
Longshaw Common
Chair Wood
Moss Vale Cottages
Beacon Farm
WA11
Shaley Brow Farm
Billinge Hall
Victoria Quarry (dis.)
Billinge Hill
Billinge Beacon
Wiswall's Farm
Moss Vale Farm
Derbyshire House
Crow's Nest
Fir Tree Farm
Billinge Brook Farm
King's Moss Farm
GREATER MANCHESTER
MERSEYSIDE
Mine (dis.)
ST. HELENS
Billinge Hill Quarry
BEACON RD.
Vicarage
Longshaw House
Mount Pleasant Farm
Upper Castle
WIGAN ROAD
A571
Maddox House
Rainford Brook Farm
King's Bridge
King's Bridge Farm
Old Bull Cottages
Red Barn Farm
Great Houghwood
Houghwood Farm
OAKLEY AV.
Recreation Ground
Ash Grove Farm
NEW STREET
PIMBO ROAD
CRANK LANE

51
33
69
52
The Bell
Kitt Green
Norley
Worsley Hall
Rose Hill
Spring Bank
Redwood
Lamberhead Green
Pemberton
Newtown
Worsley Mesnes
Highfield
Goose Green
Winstanley
WINSTANLEY PARK
Marus Bri.
New Houses
Windy Arbour
Land Gate
Junction 25
North Ashton
Rose Hill
ROBIN PARK
WN5
WN3
WN4
ORMSKIRK ROAD
WARRINGTON ROAD
PEMBERTON ROAD
BILLINGE ROAD
VICTORIA STREET
WIGAN ROAD
POOLSTOCK
M6 MOTORWAY
A577
A571
A49
B5238
PEMBERTON
Playing Fields
Pemberton Community High Sch.
Montrose School
Recreation Ground
Opencast Coal Disposal Centre
Winstanley Hall
Duke's Wood
Little Wood
Lea Wood
Glead Wood
Tan Pit Slip
Appleton Farm
Elm Farm
Wheatlea Farm
Derbyshire House Farm
Cranberry Lea Farm
Ryecroft Farm
Brocstedes Farm
Booth's Brow Farm
Barton Clough
Haslemere Ind. Est.
Summersales Indus. Est.
Lamberhead Indus. Est.
Warrington Road Indus. Est.
Camp Hill
Mossey Croft Wood
Spring Pool Wood
Captain's Clough

52
WIGAN
Wallgate
WALLGATE
NORTH WESTERN
WN5
Newtown
Poolstock
Worsley Mesnes
Hawkley
Marus Bri.
Land Gate
Rose Hill
INCE-IN-MAKERFIELD
INCE
Lower Ince
Spring View
Bryn Gates
Bamfurlo
Scholes
Bridge
WN3
WN4
Scotman's Flash
Pearson's Flash
LEEDS & LIVERPOOL CANAL (LEIGH BRANCH)
Wigan Borough Cemetery
Westwood Park
Westwood Hall
Home Farm
Westwood Park Gardens
Westwood Cemy.
Sewage Works
Ince Moss
Manchester Junction
Liverpool Junction
Springs Branch Junction
Coal Depot
Ince Cemetery
Three Sisters Recreation Area
Boating Lake
Bryn Hall
Bryn Hall Farm
Park Brook Bri.
Wood Cottage
Park House
Gravel Pit
Rough Wood
Derbyshire House Farm
Wheatlea Farm
Link Farm
Haslemere Ind. Est.
Park Lane Farm
Perry Brook Bridge
Land Gate Farm
Perry Brook Sch.
Rose Hill Sch.
Edmund Collins Park
Baldwins
Lily Lane Farm
Tip (disused)
Whalley's Basin
William Foster Playing Fields
Empress Industrial Estate
Acton's Wlk. Trad. Cen.
Recreation Ground
Skew Bridge
Timber Yard
Research Cen.
St. Mary's C of E Jun. & Inf. Sch.
Rose Bridge High Sch.
WARRINGTON ROAD
POOLSTOCK LANE
WIGAN ROAD
BOLTON RD.
BRYN LANE
GATES LANE
LILY LANE
A49
A577
A573
A58
B5238
34
51
70
57
58
59
01
02
03
04
05

Higher Ince
Hindley Hall Golf Course
America Wood
Higher Barn Farm
Crow Nest Farm
Crow Nest Junction
HINDLEY
Cemetery
Lower Barn Farm
Sefton's Farm
Greyhound Stadium
Rayner Park
Reservoir
Marsh Brook
Brownlow
Walmesley Park
Burrow's Farm
Ince Farm
Playing Field
Cardinal Newman R.C. High Sch.
Rec. Grd.
St. Benedict's R.C. Sch.
HINDLEY
Hypermarket
Moss Hall Farm
Dodhurst Farm
Chapel Fields
The Hollins
AMBERSWOOD COMMON
St. Peter's C of E Jun. & Inf Sch.
Tanfield Sch.
Mornington High Sch.
Thorley House
Stoney Lane Bri.
Borsdane Brook Sch.
Ince Moss
Dog Pool Weir
Park High Sch.
Intack Farm
Low Hall Park
Bus Depot
Low Hall Sch.
WN2
Alder Farm
Mine (disused)
Close Lane Farm
Close House Farm
Scowcroft Farm
Leyland Ten. Ct.
Playing Fields
Hall Lane Farm
Platt Bridge
H.M. Prison
Barlow's Farm
Sewage Works
Holy Family R.C. Sch.
Brookside Farm
Pear Tree Farm
Goods Cheap Farm
Factories
Football Field
Bickershaw
Naylor's Farm
Lee Lane Park
Lee Lane Farm
Morris's Farm
Bickersall C. of E. Jun. & Inf. School
Recn. Grnd.
Abram
Abram Brow
Fields Farm Cottages
Maypole Industrial Estate
Park Lane Farm
Maypole Farm
Lygoe's Farm
Dover
Dover Bridge
Lee Lane Farm
LEEDS & LIVERPOOL CANAL (LEIGH BRANCH)
A58
A577
A573
B5237
35
71
54

54
36
53
72
A
B
C
D
E
F
1
2
3
4
5
6
7
8
9
Crow Nest Junction
Higher Barn Farm
Crow Nest Farm
Lower Barn Farm
Cemetery
Sefton's Farm
Greyhound Stadium
Reservoir
Baldwin's Farm
Dorothy Rigby's Farm
Hart Common
Hart Common Farm
Playing Field
Dobb Brow
DOBB'S BROW
(open mid.'93)
Old Lane Farm
Hill Crest
Esther Fold
Pennington
Cunningham Brook
WIGAN ROAD
A58
CRICKETERS WAY
Rugby Football Ground
Pav. Cricket Gnd.
Reservoirs
SOUTHFIELD
Daisy Hill
Lambert's Sales Farm
Banks Farm
Marshes Farm
Harts i'th' Hole
Hosker's Nook
BL5
The Pungle
Bugle Horn
Edges Farm
Schools
Cricket Ground
Old Sirs
Gillibrands
Works
Land Farm
Sewage Works
Astleys
Speakman's Farm
Carr Common Cottages
Belvedere Farm
Subway
Marsh Brook
Small Brook
Hall Lee Brook
Dodhurst Brow Farm
Maxwell Farm
Alder Farm
Nursery
The Hollins
Hollins Jun. & Inf. Sch.
St. Margaret Jun. & Inf. Sch.
Mornington High Sch.
Swim. Baths
Pond
Training Centre
Sacred Heart Jun. & Inf. Sch.
ATHERTON ROAD
A577
Dog Pool Brook
Alder Farm
Close Lane Farm
Close House Farm
Scowcroft Farm
Barlow's Farm
Goods Cheap Farm
Playing Field
Hindley Green Sch.
Hindley Green
WN2
ROAD CORNER LA. SMALLBROOK LANE WIGAN
Dangerous Corner
Bowker's Bridge
Lower Snipes
Smith's Farm
Sports Ground
Factories
Football Field
Recreation Ground
Park Farm
Owen's Farm
Wigan
LEIGH ROAD
Westleigh
Playing Fields
Parsonage Bridge
Pickley Green
War Mem.
Westleigh High Lower Sch.
Westleigh Methodist School
Hampson's Fold Farm
Jun. & Inf. Sch.
Nel Pan Bri.
WN7
Bickershaw
BICKERSHAW LANE
SMITH'S LANE
B5237
Nursery
Bickershaw C. of E. Jun. & Inf. School
Recn. Grnd.
BOLTON HOUSE RD.
Tamer Lane End
A578
WIGAN ROAD
Hurst House Farm
Fir Tree Flash
Dunster's Farm
Depot
Super-store
Football Grd.
Health Centre
Parsonage Colliery
Res.
ATHERLEIGH WAY
A579
B5215
B5235
LOWER LEIGH ROAD
SCHOFIELD LANE
Factory

55
Chequerbent
Water's Nook
Markland Plantation
37
Old Dam Wood
Over Hulton
Dearden's Farm
Shippon Field
Hurst Hole
Cow Wood
Stone Shed Wood
Hall Lee Bank Park
Hooper Green
Green Common
Ashes Farm
Yew Tree Farm
Back o'th' Lawn Wood
Scout Camp
Home Farm
Hulton Park
Park Pits Wood
BL5
Belgrave Spinney
Mill Dam Stream
Dog Kennel Wood
Mill Dam Stream
The Firs
DAISY HILL
Rawsthorne Wood
Lower Whittles
Langley Hall Farm
Resr. (covered)
Mountain Farm
Assessment Centre
Wood End Farm
Mill Dam Wood
Mill Dam
New Park Wood
Kearsley Plantation
Park End Farm
Spout Fold Farm
Ashes Farm
Mill's Brow
Hag Fold
HAG FOLD
ATHERTON
Green Hall Sch.
Football Gnd.
Play. Fld.
Shams Farm
56
ATHERTON
Coal Yard
MEALHOUSE
MARKET
Hyper-market
Central Park
Cemetery
Hatton Fold
Gadbury Fold
Parklee Jun. & Inf. Sch.
Chanters Industrial Estate
Works Depot
Shakerley
Shakerley C. of E. Jun. & Inf. Sch.
Hindsford
Howe Bridge
M29
Recreation Ground
Lodge Farm
Sacred Heart R.C. Inf. Sch.
Hindsford C. of E. Jun. & Inf. Sch.
Fred Longworth High School
Hindsford Bridge
Opencast Workings
Omnibus Depot
Crab Fold Farm
Atherton Brook
Langley Platt Bridge
Hindsford Brook
Nuttall's Farm
Astley Street Park
Old Hall Mill Farm
Leigh C. of E. High School
Atherton Wood
Atherton Hall
Atherton Old Hall Farm
Atherton Lake Brook
Bedford or Hough Wood
Lilford Park
Higher Folds Jun. & Inf. School
Walmsley Farm
Cemetery House
Football Ground
Cricket Ground
Gin Pit
LEIGH INFIRMARY
Miniature Golf Course
Playing Fields
73
Bates Farm
Higher Folds
Lilford
Livesley's Cott.
A579
A577
B5212
B5235
ATHERLEIGH WAY
NEWBROOK ROAD
BOLTON OLD ROAD
TYLDESLEY ROAD
SHUTTLE ST.
ELLIOT ST.
CASTLE ST.
HALL LANE
RICHMOND DRIVE
CORONATION

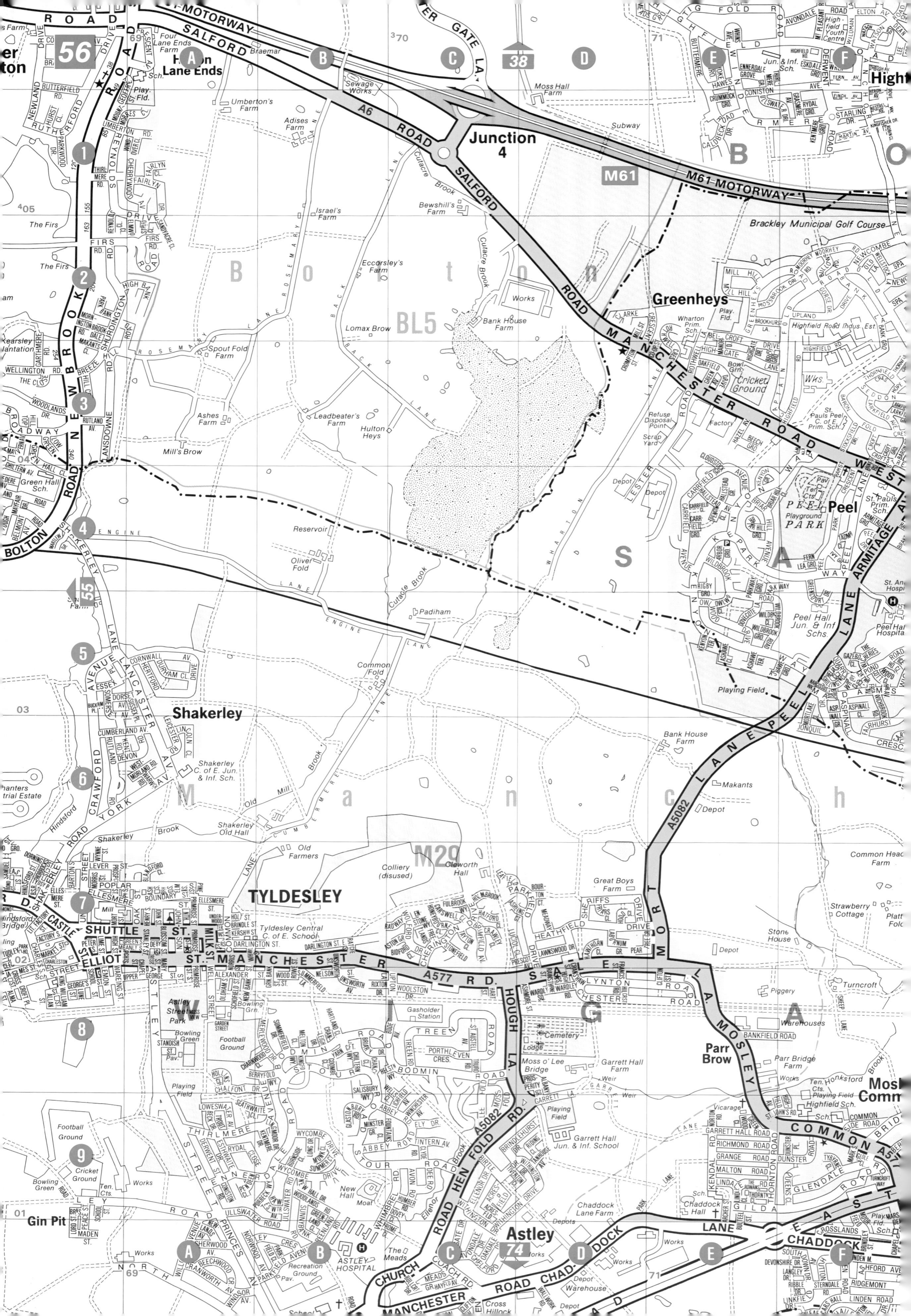

56
38
55
74
Hulton Lane Ends
Junction 4
M61 MOTORWAY
A6 SALFORD ROAD
MANCHESTER ROAD WEST
Greenheys
Peel
PEEL PARK
Brackley Municipal Golf Course
BL5
Shakerley
TYLDESLEY
M29
Astley
Parr Brow
Gin Pit
A577 MANCHESTER RD.
A5082 PEEL LANE
HOUGH LA.
HEN FOLD RD.
MOSLEY COMMON ROAD
CHADDOCK LANE
ENGINE LANE
LANCASTER AV.
NEWBROOK ROAD
Bolton
Manchester
Tyldesley Central C. of E. School
Shakerley C. of E. Jun. & Inf. Sch.
Peel Hall Jun. & Inf. Schs.
Garrett Hall Jun. & Inf. School
ASTLEY HOSPITAL
Cemetery
Gasholder Station
Colliery (disused)
Reservoir
Oliver Fold
Common Fold
Bank House Farm
Lomax Brow
Eccorsley's Farm
Israel's Farm
Leadbeater's Farm
Hulton Heys
Ashes Farm
Mill's Brow
Spout Fold Farm
Adises Farm
Umberton's Farm
Bewshill's Farm
Moss Hall Farm
Padiham
Cleworth Hall
Great Boys Farm
Makants
Stone House
Strawberry Cottage
Common Head Farm
Piggery
Turncroft
Warehouses
Parr Bridge Farm
Highfield Sch.
Chaddock Lane Farm
Chaddock Hall
Moss o' Lee Bridge
Garrett Hall Farm
Shakerley Old Hall
Old Farmers
Playing Field
Football Ground
Cricket Ground
Bowling Green
Recreation Ground
Astley Street Park
The Firs
Green Hall Sch.
Works
Depot
Sewage Works

57
39
58
75
M61
M28
BL4
FARNWORTH
New Bury
Highfield Primary School
Green Fold School
Playing Fields
Green Fold
Our Lady of Lourdes R.C. Primary Sch.
St. James C. of E. Comp. Sch.
Reservoir
Playing Field
Mill
Kearsley Park
Kearsley
Horridge Brook
Prestolee
Prestolee Rd.
STONECLOUGH
A667
A666
A5082
A575
A6
A580
B5232
LONG CAUSEWAY
BOLTON ROAD
Singing Clough
George Tomlinson Sec. Sch.
Sports Hall & Pool
Town Hall
Alderbank (Home for Aged)
St. John Fisher Sch.
Kearsley Moor C. of E. Prim. Sch.
Kearsley Moss
Bent Spur Farm
Junction 3
Junction 2
Junction 14 (M62)
M61 MOTORWAY
Express Trading Estate
Oakhill Trading Estate
Works
Coal Yard
Depot
Springfield
St. Josephs R.C. Prim. Sch.
Brynheys (Old Peoples Home)
Dukesgate Prim. Sch.
Little Hulton
Hulton High Sch.
Playing Fields
MANCHESTER ROAD
EAST HIGH ST.
Rec. Grd.
Sports Ground
Hill Top
Blackleach Reservoir
St Mary's Park
Linnyshaw Moss
Moss Bank Trading Estate
Nursery
Linnyshaw Industrial Estate
Linnyshaw
Re-establishment Centre
Reservoir
Football Grnd.
Cricket Grd.
WALKDEN
St. Paul's C. of E. Prim. Sch.
Youth Cen.
Grave Yard
Christ the King R.C. Prim. Sch.
Whittle Brook
Linnyshaw Farm
Joseph-Eastham County High School
Playing Fields
St. George's R.C. High Sch.
Swim Pool
Depot
Jubilee Houses
Sludge Bed
Playing Field
Burgess Farm
HILTON LANE
Walkden High Sch.
Town Hall
Bowling Green
Putting Grn.
PARR FOLD PARK
Tennis Courts
Parr Fold
Worsley Coll. of Further Edn.
Mesne Lea Prim. Sch.
Worsley Haysbrook Sch.
Playing Fields
Ellesmere Golf Course
Club Ho.
Running Track
Recreation Ground
Leyland Farm
New Manchester
Mosley Common
Ellenbrook
EAST LANCASHIRE ROAD
NEWEARTH ROAD
Ellesmere Sports Club
Hotel
Cricket Ground
Beesley Green
Beesley Community Centre
Crick. Grd
Roe Green
Kempnough Brook
Ponds
New Plantation
Lady Hill
Old Hall Farm
Worsley Old Hall
WORSLEY
Ryecroft Children's Home
St. Mark's C. of E. Prim. Sch.
Rands Clough Wood
Memorial
Mill Brow
Comm. Cen. & Liby.
Shaw Brook
LEIGH ROAD
SIMPSON RD.
Booth's Bank Farm
Old Warke Dam
The Aviary
The Lodge

58
Prestolee
Kearsley
Stoneclough
Europa Trading Estate
Ringley
Ringley Lock
Ringley Canal Bridge
Bottom of Croft
Manchester Bolton & Bury Canal (Dis)
KEARSLEY
M26
Ringley Wood
Higher Heaps
Lower Heaps
Heaps Cottage
Giants Seat House
Giant's Seat Wood
Little Hurst Wood
Sewage Works
Cooling Towers
Playing Field
River Irwell
Clifton Marina
Clifton House Farm
Weir
Rhodes Lock
Electricity Sub Station
Depot
Unity Brook Farm
Golf Driving Range
Kearsley Moss
Bent Spur Farm
Spindle Point Prim. Sch.
Unity Brook
Ryder's Farm
Kearsley Golf Centre
Manor Farm
BL4
Junction 3
Junction 2
Junction 1 (M61)
Junction 14 (M62)
Junction 15
Junction 2 (M61)
M61
M61 MOTORWAY
M62 MOTORWAY
M62
M28
A666
A667
A6
A580
A572
B5231
Nursery
57
Linnyshaw Industrial Estate
Linnyshaw
Reservoir
New Hill Farm
Linnyshaw Farm
MANCHESTER ROAD
Whittle Brook
Clifton
Clifton Moss Farm
Sports Ground
Wardley
Wardley Grange
Salford College of Further Education Wardley Campus
Wardley Industrial Estate
Wardley Hall
Wardley Wood
Cemetery
Moorside
MOORSIDE
Newtown
SWINTON
Deans
Hazelhurst
Egerton Park
Broad Oak
Roe Green
Ellesmere Golf Course
Club Ho.
Beesley Green
Beesley Community Centre
Kempnough Brook
Ponds
WORSLEY
Ryecroft Children's Home
St. Marks C. of E. Prim. Sch.
New Plantation
Old Warke Dam
The Lodge
Granada Superbowl
Superstore
Industrial Estate
Moorside Park
Civic Cen.
Elmstead School
Clinic
Playing Fields
Shopping Precinct
76
77

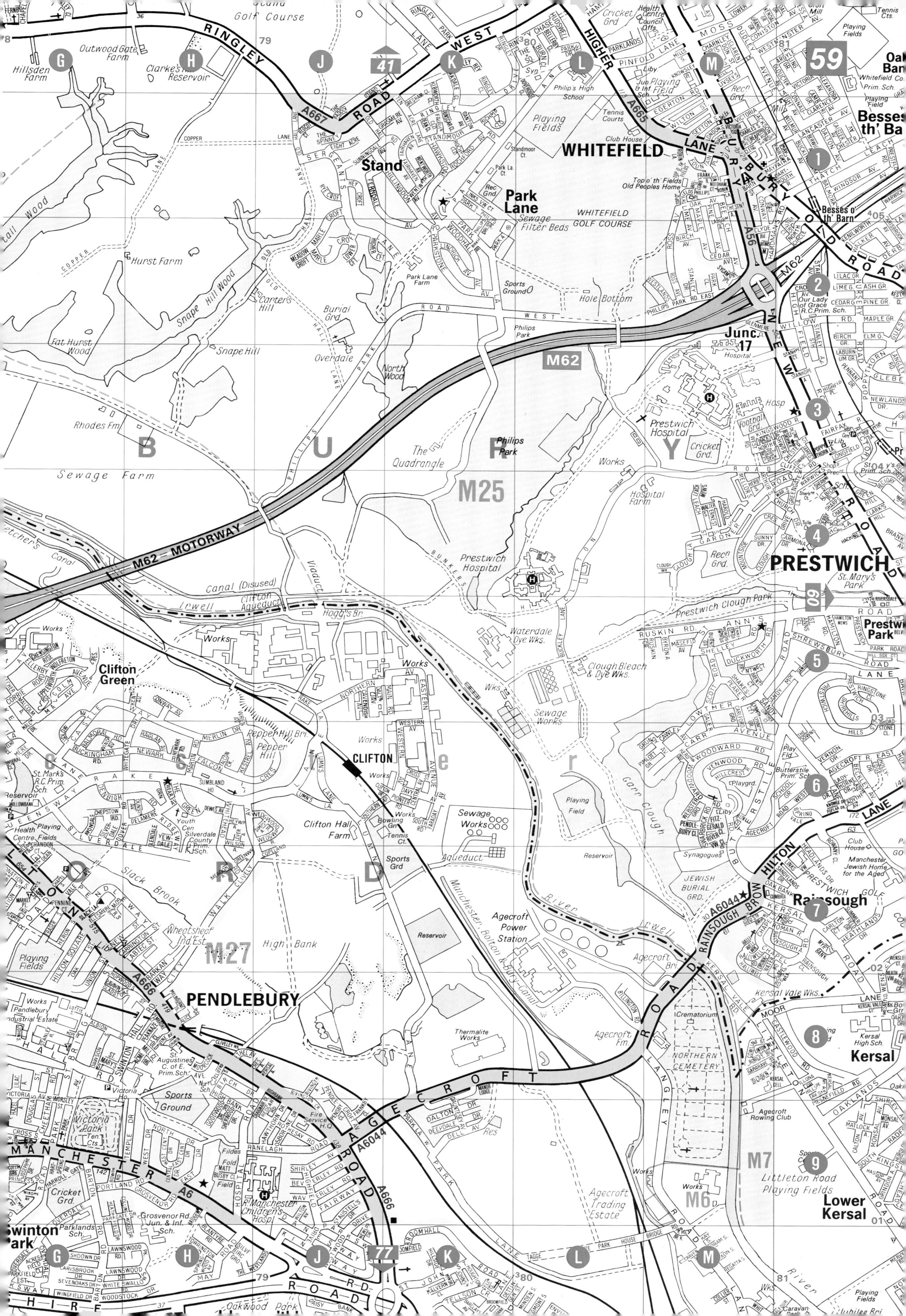

59
60
41
77
G
H
J
K
L
M
1
2
3
4
5
6
7
8
9
WHITEFIELD
PRESTWICH
PENDLEBURY
CLIFTON
Stand
Park Lane
Besses o' th' Barn
Clifton Green
Prestwich Park
Rainsough
Kersal
Lower Kersal
Swinton Park
B U R Y
S a l f o r d
M62 MOTORWAY
M62
M25
M27
M7
M6
RINGLEY ROAD WEST
A667
A665
A56
A6044
A666
A6
AGECROFT ROAD
MANCHESTER ROAD
BURY OLD ROAD
BURY NEW ROAD
HIGHER LANE
RAINSOUGH BROW
KERSAL VALE
HILTON LANE
Outwood Gate Farm
Hillsden Farm
Clarke's Hill Reservoir
Golf Course
Hurst Farm
Snape Hill Wood
Fat Hurst Wood
Snape Hill
Carters Hill
Rhodes Fm.
Sewage Farm
Burial Grd.
Overdale
North Wood
Park Lane Farm
Sewage Filter Beds
WHITEFIELD GOLF COURSE
Playing Fields
Philip's High School
Tennis Courts
Club House
Topo' th' Fields Old Peoples Home
Hole Bottom
Sports Ground
Philips Park
The Quadrangle
Junc. 17
Hospital
Prestwich Hospital
Cricket Grd.
Hospital Farm
Works
Bunkers
Canal (Disused)
Clifton Aqueduct
Irwell
Viaduct
Hogg's Br.
Waterdale Dye Wks.
Clough Bleach & Dye Wks.
Sewage Works
Prestwich Clough Park
St. Mary's Park
Pepper Hill
Pepper Hill Bri.
Clifton Hall Farm
Bowling Gn.
Tennis Ct.
Sports Grd
Aqueduct
Playing Field
Reservoir
Carr Clough
Synagogues
JEWISH BURIAL GRD.
Agecroft Power Station
River Irwell
Manchester, Bolton & Bury Canal
High Bank
Wheatsheaf Ind. Est.
Slack Brook
Agecroft Bri.
Agecroft Fm.
Crematorium
NORTHERN CEMETERY
Thermalite Works
Fire Service H.Q.
Sports Ground
Victoria Park
R. Manchester Children's Hospl.
Grosvenor Rd. Jun. & Inf. Sch.
Parklands Sch.
Cricket Grd.
Agecroft Trading Estate
PARK HOUSE BRIDGE ROAD
Agecroft Rowing Club
Littleton Road Playing Fields
Kersal High Sch.
Kersal Vale Wks.
Manchester Jewish Home for the Aged
Butterstile Prim. Sch.
Pendlebury Industrial Estate
St. Augustines C. of E. Prim. Sch.
St. Mark's R.C. Prim. Sch.
Silverdale County Prim. Sch.
Oakwood Park
Our Lady of Grace R.C. Prim. Sch.

60
42
59
78
M66
M62
M62 MOTORWAY
MIDDLETON LINK ROAD
Oak Bank
Besses o' th' Barn
Kirkhams
Half Acre
Junc. 17
Prestwich Hospital
PRESTWICH
St. Mary's Park
Prestwich Park
Hilton Park
Rainsough
Kersal
Lower Kersal
Sedgley Park
Heaton Park
HEATON PARK RESERVOIR
Heaton Park Golf Course
HEATON PARK
Heaton Hall (Museum)
Boating Lake
Heaton Park Tramway
Tramway Depot (Museum)
Miniature Golf Course
Crumpsall
Bowker Vale
Broughton Park
Higher Broughton
Kersal Dale
The Cliff
Hightown
Kersal Moor (Recreation Grd)
PRESTWICH GOLF COURSE
Crematorium
NORTHERN CEMETERY
Littleton Road Playing Fields
Agecroft Rowing Club
Sports Centre
University Halls of Residence
Carmelite Monastery
Rugby Football Grd
Manchester Jewish Home for the Aged
Parrenthorn Farm
Parrenthorn Co Sec. School
St. Margarets C of E Primary School
Whitefield Co. Prim. Sch.
Clark's Cross
Nut Lane Farm
Whitehouse Farm
Mount Pleasant Farm
Heywood Farm
Parkwood Cotts.
Dog Kennel Cotts.
Fish Pond
Oak Croft Hill
Blackfish Pond
Temple
Heaton Ho.
Heaton Farm
Parkside School
A665
A56
A6044
A576
SHEEPFOOT LANE
SCHOLES LANE
HILTON LANE
BURY NEW ROAD
BURY OLD ROAD
MIDDLETON ROAD
LEICESTER ROAD
CHEETHAM HILL ROAD
OLD ROAD
BURY ROAD
Manchester
Salford
SALFORD
M25
M7
M6
M8
M9
A B C D E F
1 2 3 4 5 6 7 8 9

61
43
79
G
H
J
K
L
M
1
2
3
4
5
6
7
8
9
84
85
86
87
Rhodes Green
Reservoir
Little Nook
Junc. 5
Rhodes
ROCHDALE
M24
Lime Field
Middleton
Little Park
Kitchen Wood
Alkrington Wood
Bird Sanctuary
Pike Fold Golf Course
M66 MOTORWAY
(Proposed)
Heaton Mills
Alkrington Garden Village
St. Clares Sec. Sch.
St. Clare's Inf. Sch.
Convent
Nut Bank Farm
Higher Blackley
BLACKLEY CEMETERY
Crematorium
Plant Hill High Sch.
Plant Hill Park
Telford Sch. (Orthopaedic)
JEWS CEMY
Crosslee Prim. Sch.
Knottley Hill
M A N C H E S T E R
M9
Pike Fold Prim. Sch.
St. Peter's C of E. Sch.
Booth Hall Childrens Hospital
Baileys Wood
Crumpsall Green
Delaunay's Day Hospital
Limbert Ho. (Nurses Home)
Crumpsall Hosp
North Manchester General Hospital
Springfield Hospital
Higher Crumpsall
Crumpsall Park
Crumpsall
War Memorial
BOGGART HOLE CLOUGH
Fish Pond
Boating Lake
David Lewis Rec Grd
Blackley
Barnes Green
Mount Carmel Prim.Sch.
Lower Crumpsall
M8
Jews Cemy.
Abraham Moss Centre
Woodlands Playing Field
Harpurhey District Centre
Ashley Lane Playing Fields
Margaret Ashton Coll.
M40
Northern Hospital
Cheetham Hill
Woodlands Road
Smedley Fields Recreation Grd.
Manchester General Cemetery
McCartney House
Concastrian Ind. Est.
Harpurhey
Burgess Becker Prim. Sch.
Harpurhey High School (Lower)
St. Edmund's R.C. Prim. Sch.
Monsall Hospital
Museum Art Gall'y
QUEENS PARK
Smedley
VICTORIA AVENUE EAST
VICTORIA AVENUE
A6104
A664
A576
A665
ROCHDALE ROAD
CHARLESTOWN ROAD
MANCHESTER OLD ROAD
MANCHESTER NEW ROAD
HEYWOOD OLD ROAD

62
44
67
80
A
B
C
D
E
F
1
2
3
4
5
6
7
8
9
MIDDLETON
Lark Hill
Little Park
Mills Hill
CHADDERT
Moorclose
Green Hill
Middleton Junction
Alkrington Garden Village
ROCHDALE
M24
M66 MOTORWAY
(Proposed)
VICTORIA AVENUE EAST
A6104
Charlestown
M9
Chain Bar
CHADDERTON INDUSTRIAL ESTATE
Blackley Golf Course
Thatch Leach
White Gate End
MOSTON
New Moston
MANCHESTER
Manchester
M10
Moston
BROADHURST PARK
ST. JOSEPH'S CEMETERY
FAILSWORTH
M35
DEAN LANE
Booth Hall Childrens Hospital
Knottley Hill
Sewage Works
Oldham Broadway Business Park
H.M. Stationery Office
Lower Memorial Park
Golf Driving Range
Lancaster Sports & Social Club
Radclyffe Comprehensive Upper School
Radclyffe Comprehensive Lower School
Foxdenton Hall Pk.
B6189
B6393
A663
A62

63
64
45
81
Chadderton Cemetery
Busk
Cold Hurst
Oldham Edge
Lower Moor
North Moor
Frank Hill
Mumps
OL1
Westwood
Westwood Ind. Estate
West Point Industrial Est.
Stock Brook
Alder Root
Cowhill
Crossley Estate
Oldham Werneth
Bank Top
Rhodes Bank
OLDHAM
OL4
Alexandra Park
Boating Lake
Nimble Nook
Primrose Bank
OL9
Butler Green
Werneth Park
Werneth
Coppice
Glodwick Brook
Hathershaw
Copster Hill
OL8
Hollins Green
Hollins
The Edge
Moss Grove
HOLLINWOOD
Hollinwood
Lime Gate
Lime Side
Hollinwood Cemetery
Werneth Golf Course
Coal Pit Lane
Wood Park
Knott Lanes
Street End
Cutler Hill
Woodhouse Green
Crime Lake
Holt Lane End
Woodhouses
Daisy Nook
Daisy Nook Country Park
Medlock Vale Country Park
OL7
Ashton-under-Lyne
Limehurst
Barsley
Marland Fold
Bardsley Vale Mills
Springwood Hall
M66 MOTORWAY (Proposed)
MIDDLETON ROAD
MANCHESTER STREET
ASHTON ROAD
OLDHAM ROAD
HOLLINS ROAD
A62
A627
A6104
A669
A671
A663
B6190
B6189
A6048

64
46
63
82
Oldham Edge
Acre
Greenacres Hill
Top Of Moor
Birks
Lower Moor
Greenacres Moor
Cross Bank
Mumps
Greenacres
Sun Hill
Cooke
OLDHAM
OLDHAM MUMPS
Moorhey
Bank Top
Leesbrook
Salem
Leesfield
County End
New Earth
Nether Lees
Lees
Roxbury
Glodwick
Roundthorn
ALEXANDRA PARK
Low Side
Glodwick Brook
Fenny Hill
Pitses
Holts
OL1
OL4
OL8
OL6
OL7
Alt
Hathershaw
Fitton Hill
Park Bridge
Higher Hartshead
Bardsley
Alt Hill
Hartshead Green
Limehurst
Hurst Nook
Oldham Golf Course
Wildmoor Leach Wood
Ashton-under-Lyne Golf Course
T A M E
Ashton-under-Lyne
HUDDERSFIELD ROAD
OLDHAM WAY
LEES ROAD
HIGH ST
OLDHAM ROAD
LEES NEW ROAD
ABBEY HILLS ROAD
A62
A669
A627
B6194
River Medlock
Holden Clough
Knott Hill Res.
Rowton Clough
Thornley Brook

65
47
83
99
Austerlands
Scouthead
Shelderslow
Stone Breaks
Springhead
Grotton
Lydgate
Grasscroft
Grasscroft Clough
Greenfield
Shaw Hall
Shaw Hall Bank
Sharon
Friezland
Dacres
Quick
Quick Edge
Roaches
Roughtown
Quickwood
Sandbed
Brook Bottom
Broad Carr
Woodend
MOSSLEY
Mossley Brow
Mossley Cross
Fox Platt
Bottoms
Micklehurst
Heyheads
Luzley
Stalybridge
Moorgate
Carrbrook
OL3
OL5
SK15
A669
A670
A6050
A635
B6175
OLDHAM ROAD
STOCKPORT ROAD
MANCHESTER ROAD
MOSSLEY ROAD
HUDDERSFIELD ROAD
Saddleworth Golf Course
Stamford Golf Course

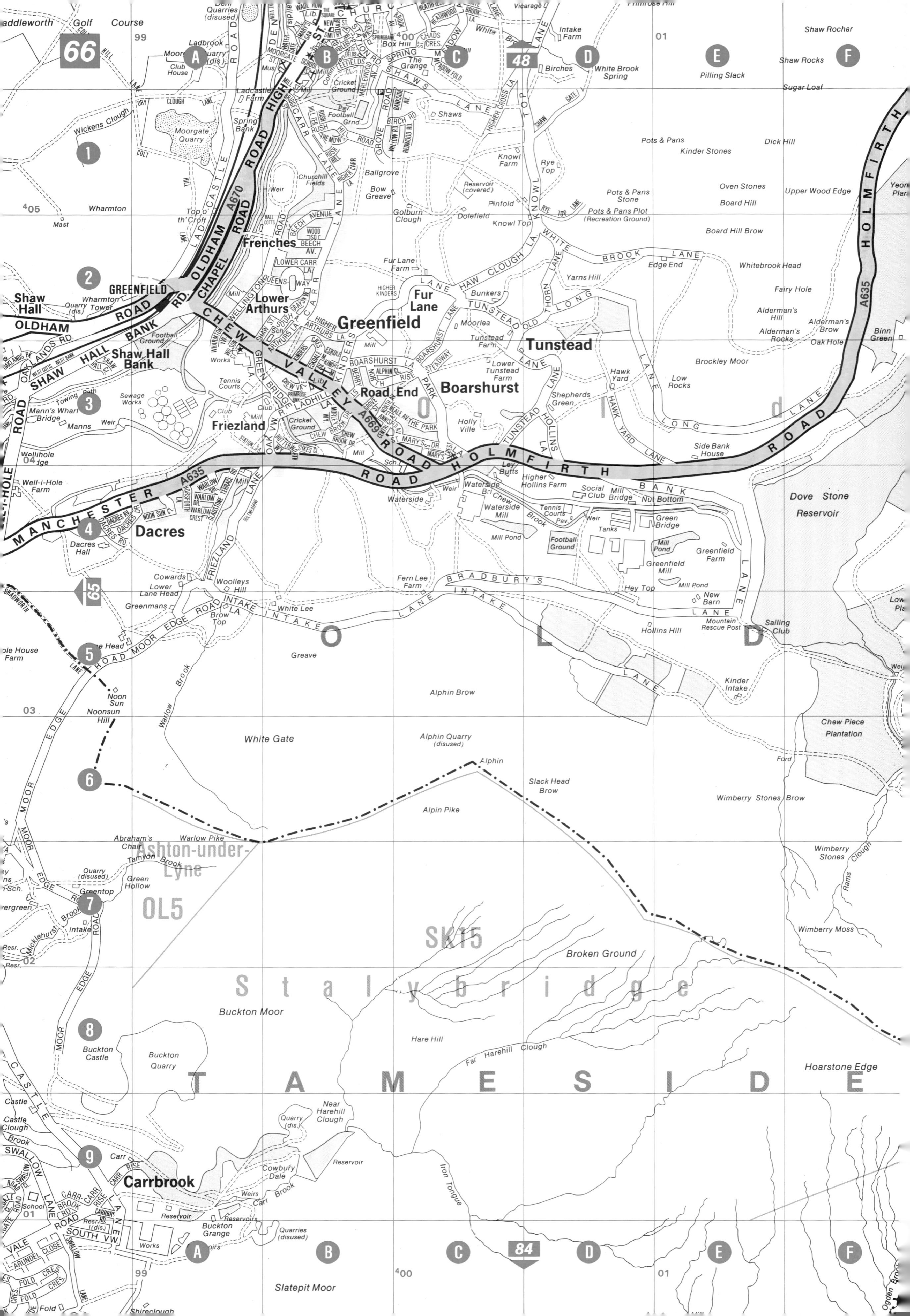
66
48
65
84
A
B
C
D
E
F
99
400
01
05
04
03
02
01
Golf Course
Ladbrook Quarry (dis)
Moorgate Quarry
Wickens Clough
Shaw Rochar
Shaw Rocks
Pilling Slack
Sugar Loaf
White Brook Spring
Birches
Intake Farm
Box Hill
The Grange
Shaws
Pots & Pans
Kinder Stones
Dick Hill
Oven Stones
Board Hill
Upper Wood Edge
Pots & Pans Stone
Pots & Pans Plot (Recreation Ground)
Board Hill Brow
Whitebrook Head
Fairy Hole
Alderman's Hill
Alderman's Rocks
Alderman's Brow
Oak Hole
Binn Green
Brockley Moor
Low Rocks
Knowl Farm
Rye Top
Knowl Top
Dolefield
Pinfold
Reservoir (covered)
Golburn Clough
Ballgrove
Bow Greave
Churchill Fields
Wharmton
Mast
Top o' th' Croft
Frenches
GREENFIELD
Lower Arthurs
Greenfield
Fur Lane
Fur Lane Farm
Tunstead
Boarshurst
Road End
Friezland
Shaw Hall
Shaw Hall Bank
Wharmton Tower
Quarry (dis)
Sewage Works
Mann's Wharf Bridge
Manns
Wellihole Bridge
Well-i-Hole Farm
Dacres
Dacres Hall
Moorlea
Tunstead Farm
Lower Tunstead Farm
Hawk Yard
Shepherds Green
Holly Ville
Yarns Hill
Edge End
Bunkers
Side Bank House
Ley Butts
Higher Hollins Farm
Social Club
Mill Bridge
Nut Bottom
Waterside
Waterside Mill
Chew Brook
Mill Pond
Football Ground
Green Bridge
Greenfield Farm
Greenfield Mill
Hey Top
New Barn
Mountain Rescue Post
Hollins Hill
Sailing Club
Dove Stone Reservoir
Kinder Intake
Chew Piece Plantation
Fern Lee Farm
Cowards
Lower Lane Head
Woolleys Hill
White Lee
Greenmans
Brow Top
Greave
Noon Sun
Noonsun Hill
Alphin Brow
White Gate
Alphin Quarry (disused)
Alphin
Slack Head Brow
Alpin Pike
Wimberry Stones Brow
Wimberry Stones
Wimberry Moss
Warlow Brook
Abraham's Chair
Warlow Pike
Ashton-under-Lyne
OL5
SK15
Tamyon Brook
Quarry (disused)
Green Hollow
Greentop
Micklehurst Brook
Intake
Broken Ground
Stalybridge
Buckton Moor
Hare Hill
Harehill Clough
Hoarstone Edge
Buckton Castle
Buckton Quarry
TAMESIDE
Near Harehill Clough
Quarry (dis)
Reservoir
Cowbury Dale
Carr Brook
Weirs
Iron Tongue
Carr
Carrbrook
Reservoirs
Buckton Grange
Quarries (disused)
Works
Slatepit Moor
Shireclough
Castle
Castle Clough
CHAPEL ROAD
OLDHAM ROAD
A670
HIGH STREET
CHEW VALLEY ROAD
A669
HOLMFIRTH ROAD
A635
MANCHESTER ROAD
OLDHAM ROAD
SHAW HALL BANK ROAD
MOOR EDGE ROAD
INTAKE LANE
BRADBURY'S LANE
LONG LANE
BROOK LANE
HAW CLOUGH LANE
TUNSTEAD LANE
HOLLINS LANE
HAWK YARD LANE
SHAWS LANE
KNOWL TOP LANE
SWALLOW LANE
SOUTH VW.
CARR BROOK ROAD

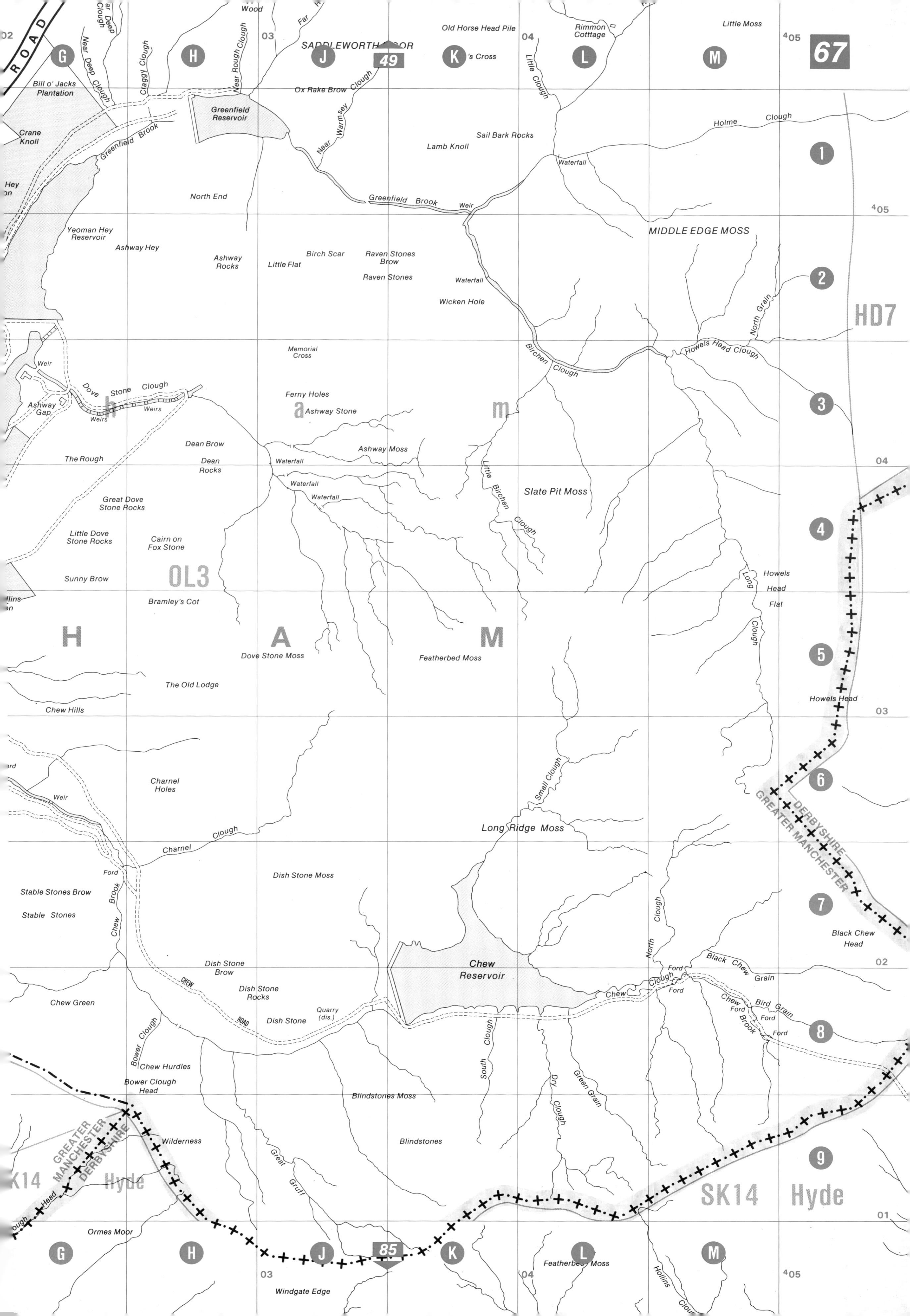
67
ROAD
Wood
Far
03
SADDLEWORTH MOOR
49
Old Horse Head Pile
's Cross
04
Rimmon Cottage
Little Moss
405
Near Deep Clough
Craggy Clough
Near Rough Clough
Little Clough
Bill o' Jacks Plantation
Greenfield Reservoir
Ox Rake Brow
Near Warmsey Clough
Crane Knoll
Greenfield Brook
Sail Bark Rocks
Lamb Knoll
Holme Clough
Waterfall
North End
Greenfield Brook
Weir
Yeoman Hey Reservoir
Ashway Hey
Ashway Rocks
Birch Scar
Little Flat
Raven Stones Brow
Raven Stones
MIDDLE EDGE MOSS
Waterfall
Wicken Hole
North Grain
HD7
Memorial Cross
Birchen Clough
Howels Head Clough
Weir
Dove Stone Clough
Ashway Gap
Weirs
Ferny Holes
Ashway Stone
Dean Brow
Dean Rocks
Ashway Moss
Waterfall
The Rough
Little Birchen Clough
Slate Pit Moss
Great Dove Stone Rocks
Little Dove Stone Rocks
Cairn on Fox Stone
Sunny Brow
OL3
Bramley's Cot
Long Clough
Howels Head Flat
H A M
Dove Stone Moss
Featherbed Moss
The Old Lodge
Chew Hills
Howels Head
03
Charnel Holes
Small Clough
Long Ridge Moss
DERBYSHIRE
GREATER MANCHESTER
Charnel Clough
Ford
Stable Stones Brow
Chew Brook
Stable Stones
Dish Stone Moss
North Clough
Black Chew Head
Chew Reservoir
Black Chew Grain
Dish Stone Brow
Dish Stone Rocks
CHEW ROAD
Quarry (dis.)
Dish Stone
Chew Clough
Chew Ford
Bird Grain
Chew Brook
Chew Green
Bower Clough
Chew Hurdles
South Clough
Dry Clough
Green Grain
Bower Clough Head
Blindstones Moss
Blindstones
Wilderness
Great Gruff
SK14 Hyde
Ormes Moor
85
Featherbed Moss
Windgate Edge
Hollins Clough
01

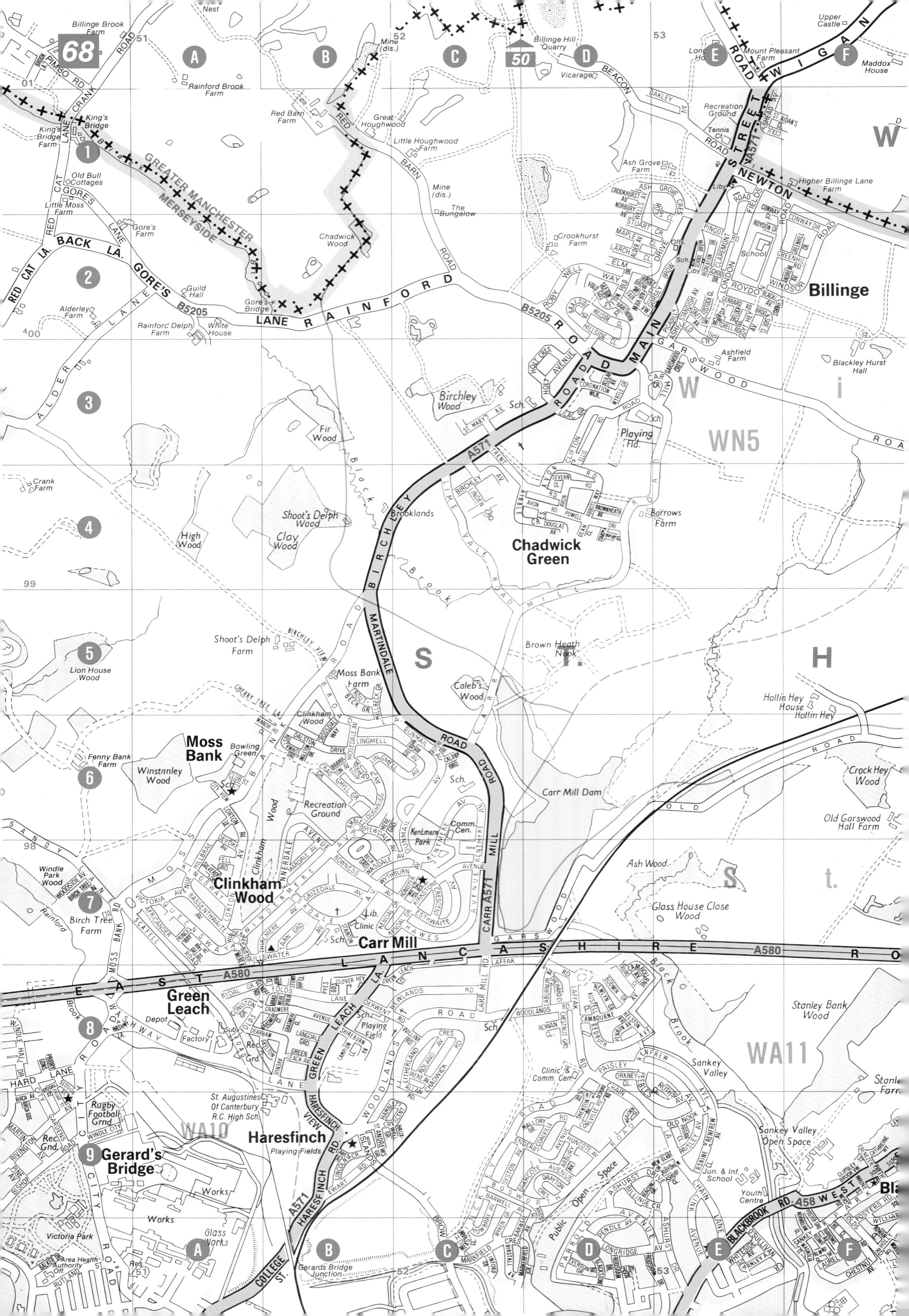
68
50
Billinge
Chadwick Green
Moss Bank
Clinkham Wood
Carr Mill
Green Leach
Haresfinch
Gerard's Bridge
WN5
WA11
WA10
GREATER MANCHESTER
MERSEYSIDE
EAST LANCASHIRE ROAD
A580
A571
B5205
RAINFORD LANE
Carr Mill Dam
Shoot's Delph Wood
Clay Wood
High Wood
Birchley Wood
Fir Wood
Winstanley Wood
Lion House Wood
Windle Park Wood
Crock Hey Wood
Ash Wood
Glass House Close Wood
Stanley Bank Wood
Sankey Valley
Sankey Valley Open Space
Public Open Space
Rugby Football Grnd
Victoria Park
Gerards Bridge Junction
St. Augustines Of Canterbury R.C. High Sch.
Haresfinch Playing Fields
Chadwick Wood
Rainford Brook Farm
Red Barn Farm
Great Houghwood
Little Houghwood Farm
Billinge Hill Quarry
Mount Pleasant Farm
Upper Castle
Maddox House
Recreation Ground
Ash Grove Farm
Higher Billinge Lane Farm
Crookhurst Farm
Ashfield Farm
Blackley Hurst Hall
Barrows Farm
Brown Heath Nook
Caleb's Wood
Hollin Hey House
Old Garswood Hall Farm
Moss Bank Farm
Shoot's Delph Farm
Fenny Bank Farm
Birch Tree Farm
Crank Farm
Alderley Farm
Guild Hall
Gore's Farm
Old Bull Cottages
Little Moss Farm
King's Bridge
King's Bridge Farm
Rainford Delph Farm
White House
Gore's Bridge
Billinge Brook Farm
Playing Fld.
Kentmere Park
Comm. Cen.
Recreation Ground
Clinic & Comm. Cen.
Jun. & Inf. School
Youth Centre
Area Health Authority Off.
Glass Works
Works
Depot
Factory

69
51
70
Junction 25
North Ashton
Junction 24
M6
M6 MOTORWAY
Rose Hill
Bryn
BRYN
Leyland Green
Downall Green
Simm's Lane End
Garswood
GARSWOOD
WN4
Ashton Cross
Garswood Park
Ashton-in-Makerfield Golf Course
Pewfall
North Florida
HAYDOCK
New Boston
Old Boston
Cemetery
Deer House Farm
Old Garswood Park
Carter's Fold Farm
Torpen Wood
Montrey Reservoir
Charity Farm
Arch Lane Farm
Manor House Farm
Tithe Barn Hillock
Tithe Barn Farm
Seneley Green Farm
Barton Clough
Tatlock's Hillock
Lower Billinge Lane Farm
Billinge Lane Farm
Leyland Green Farm
Gladden Hey Brow
Coal Mine
Booth's Brow Farm
Brocstedes Farm
Highfield House
Mill Farm
The Clough
Skitters
Long Covert
Coal Yard
Saw Mill
Depots
Warehouse
Rookery Plantation
Vista Plantation
Club House
Haydock Boundary Plantation
New Hall Wood
Millfield Farm
Reservoir (covered)
Yew Tree Trading Estate
Waggon Road Plantation
Garswood Gates Farm
Wood Pit Covert
Tip (disused)
Heyes Park House
Lyme House
Heyescroft
GREATER MANCHESTER
MERSEYSIDE
WIGAN
ST. HELENS
B5207
A58
A580
A599
EAST LANCASHIRE ROAD
LIVERPOOL ROAD
BILLINGE ROAD
DOWNALL GREEN ROAD
WIGAN ROAD
CLIPSLEY LANE
CHURCH ROAD
PENNY LANE
VISTA ROAD
GARSWOOD ROAD
GARSWOOD OLD ROAD
WINSTANLEY ROAD
SPINDLE HILLOCK
CAMP ROAD
GIBBONS ROAD
MILLFIELD LANE
KENYONS LANE
VICARAGE RD.
LOW BANK RD.
OLD ROAD
TITHEBARN LANE
ARCH LANE
STATION ROAD
SCHOOL LANE
STRANGE ROAD

70
52
ASHTON-IN-MAKERFIELD
Bryn
Rose Hill
Bryn Gates
Bamfurlong
Stubshaw Cross
Town Green
Edge Green
Bank Heath
Old Boston
New Boston
Junction 23
Three Sisters Recreation Area
South Lancashire Industrial Estate
Haydock Park Race Course
Haydock Park
Haydock Park Golf Course
Lady Hill Plantation
Park Plantation
Yew Tree Trading Estate
St. Helens
Newton - le - Willows
ST. HELENS
WN4
WA12
WA11
GTR. MANCHESTER
MERSEYSIDE
M6 MOTORWAY
A49
A58
A580
A599
B5207
B5209
69
M6
Ashton Heath
Junction 24

71
53
72
Dover
Dover Bridge
Maypole Industrial Estate
Park Lane Farm
Maypole House Farm
Lygoe's Farm
Lee Lane Farm
WN2
Chadwick's Farm
Aye Bridge Farm
Aye Bridge
Scotson's Farm
Leigh
Bickershaw Sidings
WN7
Crankwood House
Crank Wood
Crankwood
New Bear Hey
Old Bear Hey
Gerrard's Bridge
Smith's Bridge
Works
Bickershaw Colliery
Conveyors
Ackers Whitley's Basin
Plank Lane Bri.
Leeds & Liverpool
Balmer's Farm
Hillcroft
Windy Bank Farm
Lightshaw Hall
Houghton Coat Bridge (north)
Houghton Coat Br. (south)
Critchley House
Dam Lane Farm
Wigan Road Farm
Haydock Branch Junction
Mossley Hall
Byrom Hall
Little Byrom Hall
Saddletree Fold Farm
Belle-vue
Lowton Sailing Club
Leigh Sailing Club
Elm House Farm
Wilton Cottages
New Barn Farm
Factory
Depot
B5207
WA3
Stack House Farm
Rothwell's Farm
Playing Field
Golborne High Sch.
Laburnum Cottage
Red House Farm
Goldborne Colliery
St. Thomas Jun. & Inf. Sch.
All Saints Jun. & Inf. Sch.
Golborne Jun. & Inf. Sch.
Millingford Brook
Barn Lane Bridge
GOLBORNE
Millfield Farm
Lawson's Farm
Town Farm
Recreation Ground
Lowton W. Jun. & Inf. Sch.
Lowton
Lowton Common
Cheetham Fold
The Meadows
Civic Hall
St. Catherines R.C. Jun. & Inf. Sch.
St. Luke's C of E Jun. & Inf. School
Little Lowes Fold
Stirrups Farm
Lowton Heath House
Thompson's Farm
Lowton St. Mary's
A572
A580
A573
A579
Lowton Heath
Grange Farm
Lane Head
Offices
Hayes Farm
Dickinson's Farm
Johnson's Farm
Five Acres
Locking Stoop Farm
Depot
Golborne Junction
Lancashire Road
Newton Road
Warrington Road
Winwick La.
Kenyon Road
Church La.
Heath Lane
Stone Cross Lane
Byrom Lane
Lightshaw Lane
Crankwood Road
Park Lane
Wigan Road
Aye Bridge Road
Church Street
High St.
Golborne Rd.
Church Lane
Newton Road
Sandy Lane
Pocket Nook Lane
Liverpool Canal (Leigh Branch)

72
A
B
C
D
E
F
54
71
1
2
3
4
5
6
7
8
9
Fir Tree Flash
Dunster's Farm
Firsdale Industrial Estate
Westleigh Heath Farm
Recn. Grnd.
Jun. & Inf. School
Firs Park
Firs Lane
Playing Fields
Parsonage Colliery
Bickershaw Sidings
Bickershaw Colliery
Conveyors
Plank Lane
CRANKWOOD
Gerrard's Bridge
Ackers Whitley's Basin
Plank Lane Bri.
LEEDS & LIVERPOOL CANAL (LEIGH BRANCH)
Strange Common Farm
Workings
The Flash
Pennington Flash Country Park
W
I
G
A578
A579
A572
A580
B5215
B5207
WIGAN ROAD
ATHERLEIGH WAY
TWIST LA.
BRADSHAWGATE
KING STREET
ST. HELENS ROAD
BYROM LANE
Lowton Sailing Club
Leigh Sailing Club
Elm House Farm
Saddletree Fold Farm
Belle-vue
Wilton Cottages
Sorrowcow Farm
New Barn Farm
Rowe Farm
Laburnum Cottage
Red House Farm
SANDY LANE
GREEN LANE
Depot
Taylor's Hole
Pennington Park
Pennington
Playing Field
Bowling Green
Cricket Grd.
Aspull Common
Liptrot Farm
Moss Industrial Estate
Warehouses
Works
Lowton Common
Cheetham Fold
Gilded Hollins Jun. & Inf. Sch.
Albion Nurseries
Lowton Jun. & Inf. School
Lowton High School
Wash End
Fair House
Pocket Nook
POCKET NOOK LANE
Carr Farm
Pocket Nook Farm
Yates Farm
LOWTON ST. MARY'S BY-PASS
Land Side
Landside Farm
Collier's Farm
Dean's Farm
Yew Tree Farm
Collier's Tenement
Old Carr House
Wood's Farm
Football Ground
The Meade
Civic Hall
School
Playing Fields
Lowton St. Mary's
NEWTON ROAD
EAST LANCASHIRE ROAD
Warrington
WA3
WN7
GREATER MANCHESTER
CHESHIRE
Diggle Green Farm
Layland's Farm
Hall Farm
Pumping Sta.
Broseley Bridge
Broseley Hall
BROSELEY LANE
Birchall's Farm
WILTON LANE
Dickinson's Farm
Johnson's Farm
Five Acres
KENYON LANE
INSET
Wilton Grange
Mole End
Kenyon
Peak's Farm
Barrow's Farm
Lowe's Farm
Heath Lane Farm
STONE PIT LANE
WIGAN
63
64
65
97
98
99
400
01

LEIGH
Lilford
Siddow Common
Bedford
Hooten Gardens
Higher Folds
Gin Pit
Blackmoor
Marsland Green
Town Lane
Lately Common
Glazebury
WARRINGTON
WA3
Manchester
M29
Leigh Infirmary
Bedford Moss
Windy Bank Wood
Knowle's Wood
Hitchfield Wood
Old Woods
Bridgewater Canal
Greater Manchester
Cheshire
A572
A574
A580
East Lancashire Road
Manchester Road
Warrington Road
Chapel St.
Light Oaks Road
Old Moss Lane
Moss Lane
Jennet's Lane
Hurst Lane
Coronation Drive
Queensway
Bedford Hall Farm
Sandy Pool Farm
Grange Farm
Crompton House
Crompton Fold
Magpie's Nest
Netherbarrow Farm
Hawk Hurst Farm
Speakman House
Manor House Farm
Choughey Hill Farm
Boarded Barn
Windy Bank Farm
Light Oaks Moss Farm
Red House
Morley Hall
Sales House
Turf Nest Farm
Kay House
Hurst Hall
Duckinfield House
Bowland Field
Three Acres
Ward's End
Ward's Place
Old Field Farm
Bonny Well
Hope Carr Terrace
The Oaks Farm
Walmsley 55
74
66
67
68
69
96
97
98
99
400
G
H
J
K
L
M
1
2
3
4
5
6
7
8
9

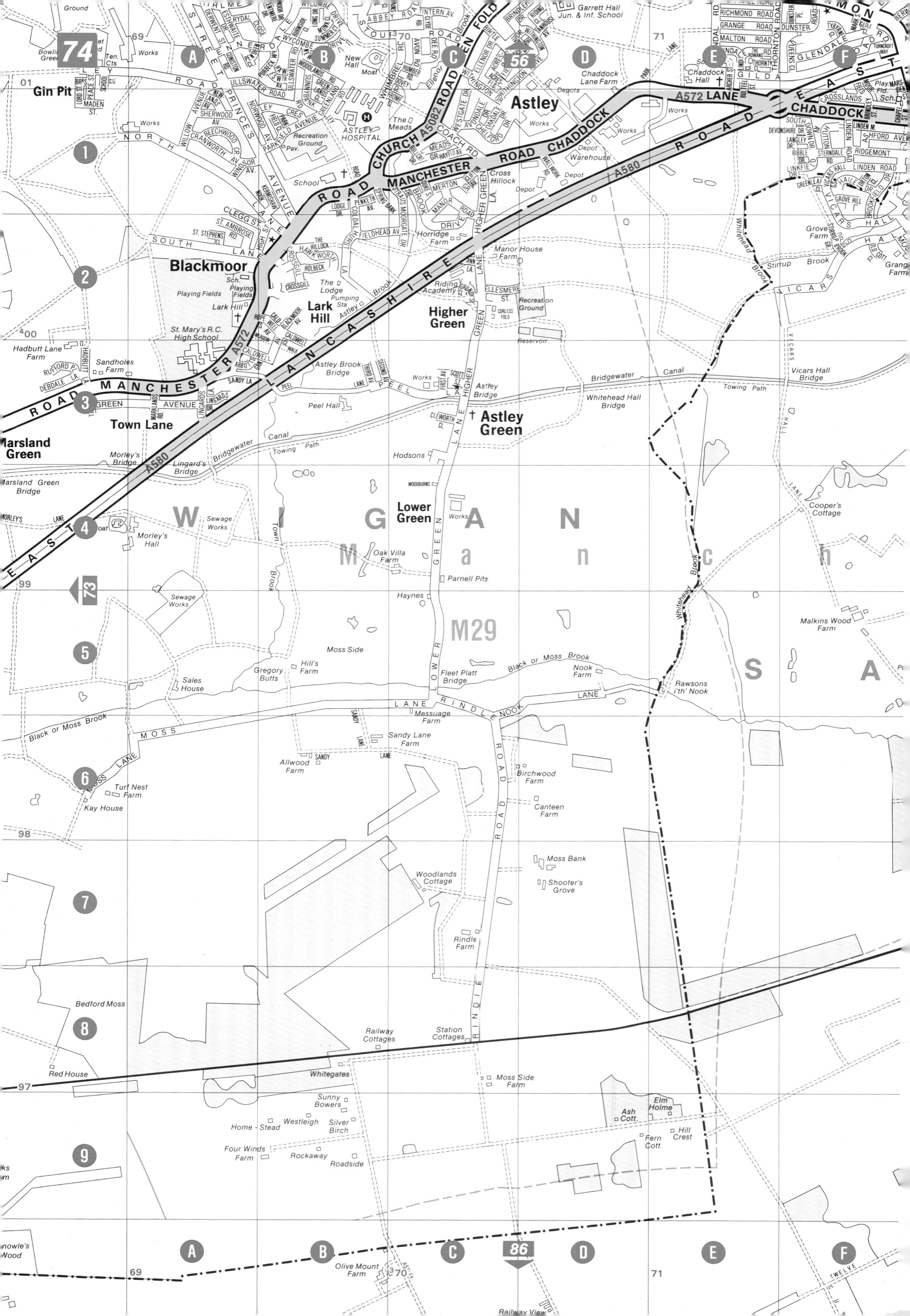

74
Gin Pit
Ten. Cts.
Works
A
B
C
D
E
F
56
71
70
69
01
Garrett Hall Jun. & Inf. School
RICHMOND ROAD
GRANGE ROAD
MALTON ROAD
DUNSTER
GLENDALE
Chaddock Hall
Chaddock Lane Farm
Depots
Astley
A572 LANE
CHADDOCK
EAST
ROAD
New Hall
Moat
The Meads
ASTLEY HOSPITAL
Recreation Ground
Pav.
School
ULLSWATER ROAD
PRINCE'S
SHERWOOD AV.
BEECHWOOD
CRANWORTH AV.
WINDSOR AV.
NORTH
1
2
3
4
5
6
7
8
9
CHURCH A5082 ROAD
COACH RD
MANCHESTER ROAD CHADDOCK
Warehouse
Depot
Cross Hillock
A580
Whitehead Brook
Stirrup Brook
VICARS
Grove Farm
CROSSLANDS
RIDGEMONT
LINDEN ROAD
SOUTH
Blackmoor
Sch.
Playing Fields
Lark Hill
St. Mary's R.C. High School
Lark Hill
The Lodge
Pumping Sta
Horridge Farm
Manor House Farm
Riding Academy
ELLESMERE ST.
Recreation Ground
Higher Green
Reservoir
Hadbutt Lane Farm
Sandholes Farm
MANCHESTER
ROAD
GREEN AVENUE
Town Lane
Marsland Green
LANCASHIRE
Astley Brook Bridge
PEEL LANE
Works
Astley Bridge
Astley Green
Bridgewater Canal
Whitehead Hall Bridge
Vicars Hall Bridge
Towing Path
Peel Hall
Morley's Bridge
Lingard's Bridge
Marsland Green Bridge
Hodsons
Lower Green
WIGAN
Manch
Sewage Works
Morley's Hall
Oak Villa Farm
Parnell Pits
Cooper's Cottage
99
73
Haynes
Sewage Works
M29
Malkins Wood Farm
Moss Side
Gregory Butts
Hill's Farm
Fleet Platt Bridge
Black or Moss Brook
Nook Farm
Rawsons i'th' Nook
SA
Sales House
LANE RINDLE NOOK
Messuage Farm
Sandy Lane Farm
MOSS LANE
Allwood Farm
Turf Nest Farm
Kay House
Birchwood Farm
Canteen Farm
98
Moss Bank
Shooter's Grove
Woodlands Cottage
Rindle Farm
RINDLE ROAD
Bedford Moss
Railway Cottages
Station Cottages
Red House
97
Whitegates
Moss Side Farm
Sunny Bowers
Home - Stead
Westleigh
Silver Birch
Elm Holme
Ash Cott.
Hill Crest
Fern Cott.
Four Winds Farm
Rockaway
Roadside
86
Olive Mount Farm
TWELVE
Railway View

75
57
87
76
WORSLEY
Mill Brow
Boothstown
Booth's Bank
Alder Forest
Junction 13
Junction 12
Junction 1
LEIGH ROAD
A572
WALKDEN RD.
A575
M62 MOTORWAY
STRETFORD
M62
M63
BY PASS
WORSLEY ROAD
B 5211
BARTON
LIVERPOOL ROAD
A57
M28
M30
SALFORD
Rands Clough Wood
Booth's Bank Farm
Alder Wood
Middle Wood
Boating Lake
Worsley Hall Nurseries
Worsley Old Hall
Ryecroft Children's Home
Novotel
Bridgewater Canal
Towing Path
Hollin Wood
Bittern Pits Wood
Moss House Farm
Boothstown Bridge
Booth's Hall Bridge
Moss Cottage
The Grange
BOTANY BAY WOOD
WORSLEY MOSS
Eccles Corporation Tip
Brookhouse Sports Centre
Eccles C. of E. High Sch.
Eccles Cemetery
Crematorium
Woodside Farm
Moss Side Farm
Brighton Grange
Nursery Farm
Manor Farm
Tunnel Farm
Barton Moss
Barton Aerodrome
Lancashire Aero Club
Control Tower
Research Lab.
Park House
Marriots Farm
Storage Depot
Parkhall
Black Wood
Bartonmoss Farm
Barton Locks
Sewage Works
Salteye Sewage Works
Moat Hall Sports Cen.
Playing Fields

76
WORSLEY
Ryecroft Children's Home
St. Marks C. of E. Prim. Sch.
Plantation
Egerton Park
Hazelhurst
Deans
58
Moorside Sec. Sch.
EAST LANCASHIRE ROAD
A580
A572
WORSLEY ROAD
Junction 13
M28
Broad Oak
Old Warke Dam
The Aviary
The Lodge
Bridgewater Sch.
Worsley Green
Worsley High School
Broadoak Park
Broadoak Jun. & Inf. Sch.
Dales Brow
M27
Swinton Golf
Sewage Works
Bacteria Beds
Pumping Sta.
Chorlton Fold
Eccles Sixth Form College
M62 MOTORWAY
STRETFORD ROAD
Bridgewater Canal
Broadoak Park
WORSLEY GOLF COURSE
Dukes Drive Recreation Ground
Alder Forest
Cricket Ground
Alder Park Prim. & Nursy. Schs.
Westwood Park
Monton
Club Ho.
Pav. Cricket Grd.
Ellesmere Park
Tennis Courts
Playing Fields
John Bradley School
MONTON LANE
B5229
M602 MOTORWAY
Playing Fields
Grange
Junction 12
Moss Cottage
Winton
WINTON PARK
Winton Nursy. Cen.
Lyn Town Trading Estate
M602
ECCLES BY PASS
M30
PATRICROFT
M62 MOTORWAY
Junction 1
Playing Field
St. Gilberts R.C. Prim. Sch.
St. Patricks R.C. High Sch.
Rugby Football Ground
Bridgewater Hosp.
GREEN LANE B5231
CHURCH ROAD A57
Baths
M63 BY PASS
Playing Fields
Tennis Courts
Eccles C. of E. High Sch.
Barton Moss Prim. Sch.
Schofield
Peel Green
Patricroft
Recreation Ground
Bowls
Moat Hall Sports Cen.
LIVERPOOL ROAD
Junc. 2
Eccles Cemetery
Godfrey Ermen Mem. Schs.
B5230
B5211
Barton upon Irwell
Barton Aqueduct
Barton Bri. (Swing)
Land. Stage
Works
Depot
A57
Salteye Brook
Sewage Works
Eccles Sewage Works
MANCHESTER SHIP CANAL
Cemetery
Dumplington
Kedclyffe Manor
REDCLYFFE ROAD
ASHBURTON ROAD
Broad Oak Ind. Est. & Bus. Pk.
Royce Ind. Estate
Bridgewater Canal
Sports Ground
Bowl. Grn.
M31
M63
West Point Enterprise Park
River Irwell (Old Course)
B5214
BARTON DOCK ROAD B5211
Junction 3
M63 MOTORWAY
Wilderspool Ho.
Barton Locks
Wharf
Sewage Works
88
Barton Kennels
Croft Fm.
Depot
1 2 3 4 5 6 7 8 9
A B C D E F

77
78
59
89
Swinton Park
Lower Kersal
Irlams o'th' Height
Brindle Heath
Pendleton
Seedley
Weaste
ECCLES
Little Bolton
Salford Quays
Trafford Park
Agecroft Trading Estate
Oakwood Park
Buile Hill Park
Museum
Band Stand
Tennis Crts.
Bolton Road Playing Fields
Open Air Sch
Duncan Mathieson Playing Fields
Running Track
Cricket Ground
Recreat'n Grd.
Lightoaks Park
Hope Hospital
Ladywell Hospital
Ladywell Trading Est.
Weaste Cemetery
Engineering Works
Sewage Works
Filter Beds
Pumping Sta.
Trafford Ecological Park
Mode Wheel Locks
Dry Docks
MANCHESTER SHIP CANAL
North Bay
Central Wharf
Trafford Wharf
Erie Basin
Huron Basin
Ontario Basin
Custom House
Sovereign Enterprise Park
Metroplex Bus. Park
Timber Yard
Westbrook Industrial Estate
Springfield Trading Estate
Central Park Estate
Monde Trading Estate
Guinness Road Trading Estate
Enterprise Trading Estate
Orion Trading Estate
Manchester United Football Ground
White City Retail Park
Trafford Enterprise Cen.
Broadway Ind. Area
King William St. Enterprise Zone
Salford Technical High Sch.
Salford Grammar Sch.
Salford Football Grd.
Weaste Trading Estate
CITY OF SALFORD OFFICES
R. Manchester Children's Hosp
Pope John Paul II R.C. High School
Refuse Treatment Plant
Orchard Trading Estate
Duchy Caravan Park
Jubilee Bri.
River Irwell
M602 MOTORWAY
M602
M6
M5
M17
A580
A6
A576
A57
A5185
A5186
A5081
A5181
B5228
B5214
A666
ASHBURTON ROAD EAST
TRAFFORD PARK ROAD
ECCLES NEW ROAD
LIVERPOOL STREET
BOLTON RD.
BROAD STREET
LANCASTER ROAD
STOTT LANE
ECCLES OLD ROAD
WEASTE LANE
LANGWORTHY ROAD
MOSLEY ROAD
TRAFFORD ROAD
WESTINGHOUSE ROAD
BROADWAY
(Under Construction)
Const. Est. Comp. June 1994

78
60
77
90
4
A
B
C
D
E
F
1
2
3
4
5
6
7
8
9
81
82
83
97
Broughton
The Cliff
Lower Kersal
Littleton Road Playing Field
M7
River Irwell
Jubilee Bri.
Playing Fields
Caravan Park
Pope John Paul II R.C. High School
Lower Kersal Prim. Sch.
Littleton Bri.
Castle Irwell Student Village
Refuse Treatment Plant
Orchard Trading Estate
Charlestown
Duchy Caravan Park
Brindle Heath
Sports Centre
Orchard Ind. Est.
Mills
Warehouse
Lowry High School
Halton Bank Prim. Sch.
PENDLETON
M6
Pendleton
Langworthy Park
West Liverpool St. Prim. Sch.
Windsor High Sch.
M602 MOTORWAY
ECCLES NEW RD.
A57
A6
A576
A5063
A5066
A56
A6041
A6010
A6144
B6186
B6187
B6180
B6469
B5461
Holland St.
Broadway Ind. Area
Sovereign Enterprise Park
Custom House
Erie Basin
Swing Bridge
Huron Basin
Salford Quays
Ontario Basin
Central Bay
East Wharf North
East Wharf South
South Bay
South Wharf
SHIP CANAL
Waterway Enterprise Park
Monarch Trading Estate
TRAFFORD PARK ROAD
Manchester United Football Ground
White City Retail Park
Trafford Bar
Old Trafford
STRETFORD
M16
Ordsall
ORDSALL PARK
Ordsall Hall Mus.
POMONA DOCKS
NO.2 DOCK
NO.3 DOCK
NO.4 DOCK
Cornbrook
St. Georges
Hulme
Knott Hill
Gaythorn
Olympia Trading Estate
DEANSGATE
WHITWORTH ST.
OXFORD
G.MEX
M2
M3
M1
M4
M5
M15
Castle Field
Castle Field Heritage Area
Roman Fort
Museum of Science & Industry
Granada T.V. Cen.
Coronation St.
LIVERPOOL ROAD
QUAY ST.
PETER ST.
REGENT ROAD
SALFORD
RED ROSE CENTRE
New Windsor
SALFORD CRESCENT
CRESCENT
CHAPEL
Wallness
PEEL PARK
University of Salford
Museum & Art Gallery
Salford Coll. of Technology
David Lewis Recreation Ground
Hough La. Bri.
Bowling Greens
Playing Field
Gymnasium
Broughton Bri.
Lower Broughton
Albert Park
GREAT CHEETHAM ST.
BURY NEW ROAD
GREAT CLOWES ST.
LOWER BROUGHTON ROAD
Cheetham
Hightown
Strangeways
H.M. PRISON
H.M. Prison
Magistrates Crt.
Cambridge Ind. Area
Emperor House
NEW BRI. ST.
GREENGATE
TRINITY WAY
BLACKFRIARS
VICTORIA ST.
Albert Bri. Ho.
SALFORD CENTRAL
Colloff Bldg
Opera Ho.
Hampson Street Trading Est.
HAMPSON
ORDSALL
(Proposed)
Manchester Ind. Cen.
Regent Road Ind. Area
Derwent Ind. Area
Warehouses
Tennis Courts
Sports Ground
St. Joseph's R.C. Prim. Sch.
Birley High Sch.
Industrial Estate
ELIZABETH ST.
CHORLTON ROAD
PRINCESS
MANCUNIAN

79
Cheetham Hill
Northern Hospital
Harpurhey
Smedley
QUEEN'S PARK
Museum Art Gall'y
Collyhurst
Moston Brook High School
Monsall Hospital
Recreation Ground
Concrete Works
M8
M9
M10
M11
M12
M13
M4
M1
Great Horrocks
MANCHESTER
Newtown
MILES PLATTING
Miles Platting
Recreation Ground
Gas Plant Wks.
Park Engineering Works
PARK
Philips Park
PHILIPS PARK CEMETERY
Gas Works
Holt Town
Electricity Generating Stn.
Bradford
Ancoats
Central Retail Park
Piccadilly Gs.
PICCADILLY
Piccadilly Trading Estate
Beswick
University of Manchester Inst. of Science & Technology
A57(M)
Ardwick
ARDWICK
ASHBURYS
West Gorton
University
University of Manchester
Greenheys
Exhibition Hall
ROCHDALE ROAD
QUEENS ROAD
OLDHAM ROAD
GREAT ANCOATS STREET
POLLARD ST
ASHTON NEW ROAD
ASHTON OLD ROAD
HYDE ROAD
STOCKPORT ROAD
UPPER BROOK ST
OXFORD ROAD
PLYMOUTH GROVE
PLYMOUTH STREET
DEVONSHIRE ST.
CHANCELLOR LA
FORGE LANE
GREY MARE LANE
HULME HALL LANE
POTTERY LANE
A6010
A664
A665
A662
A62
A635
A57
A34
A6
B6469
B5117
5
61
80
91

62
79
92
A
B
C
D
E
F
1
2
3
4
5
6
7
8
9
Newton Heath
M10
Culcheth
Clayton Bridge
Philips Park
PHILIPS PARK CEMETERY
PHILIPS PARK
River Medlock
Clayton Vale
Greenside
Bradford
Clayton
M11
Openshaw
MANCHESTER
Beswick
Higher Openshaw
West Gorton
M12
M18
GORTON
ASHBURYS
BELLE VUE
DEAN LANE
PARK
BROOKDALE PARK
Brookdale Park High School
St. Wilfred's Prim. Sch.
St. Willibrord's R.C. Prim Sch.
Moston Brook High School
Concrete Works
Diesel Depot
Broadhurst Co. Prim. Sch.
Lancaster Sports & Social Club
Hardman Fold Sch.
Propps Hall Infant & Junior Schools
St Mary's Infant & Junior Schools
South Failsworth Jun. & Inf. Schs.
Failsworth Cemetery
Park Engineering Works
Recreat'n Ground
Sports Ground
Sewage Wks
Gartside Fm.
Clayton Vale Bri.
Electricity Generating Stn.
Gas Works
Abattoir
Hewlett Playing Fields
Sunny Bank Park
Droylesden High Sch. For Girls
Corporation Yard
Chemical Works
Clayton Industrial Est
Manchester and Ashton-u-Lyne Canal
St. Brigid's R.C. Prim.Sch.
Parkhouse Street Industrial Estate
Openshaw Prim. Sch.
City Course Trading Estate
Crossley Wks.
Openshaw Tech. Coll.
New Smithfield Market
Openshaw Complex
Highbank Trading Estate
Lees St. Enterprise Trading Estate
King George V Play. Fld
Bishop Greer High Sch.
Recreation Ground
All Saints Prim Sch.
Motor Wks
Delamere Park
St.Gregory's R.C. Prim.Sch.
Abbey Hey Prim.Sch.
Exhibition Hall
Bowling Alley
Snooker Club
Cinema
Depot
Sports Ground
A62
A662
A635
A6010
B6393
ASHTON OLD ROAD
OLDHAM ROAD
ASHTON NEW ROAD
HYDE ROAD
POTTERY LANE

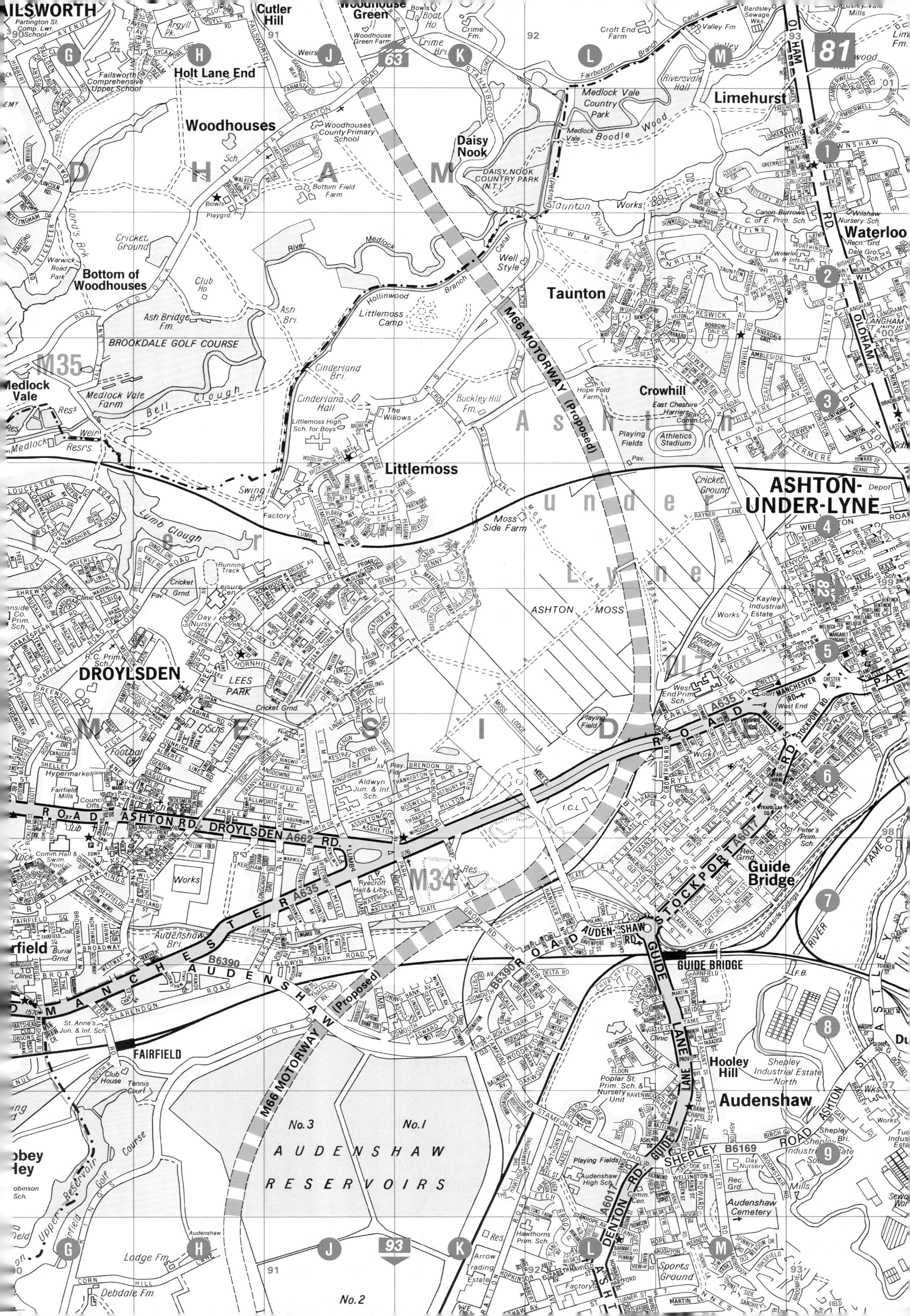

82
64
94
81
A
B
C
D
E
F
1
2
3
4
5
6
7
8
9
Limehurst
Waterloo
Smallshaw
Hurst Knoll
Hurst
Hurst Nook
Higher Hurst
Hurst Brook
ASHTON-UNDER-LYNE
Cockbrook
STAMFORD PARK
STALYBRIDGE
Hydes
DUKINFIELD
Tame Valley
Guide Bridge
GUIDE BRIDGE
Hooley Hill
Audenshaw
SHEPLEY
Dukinfield Hall
Newton Wood
HYDE NORTH
Yew Tree
Ashton-under-Lyne Golf Course
Limehurst Fm.
Knott Hill Res.
Gorsey Fm.
King George V Playing Fields
Tameside Gen. Hosp.
Boating Lake
DUKINFIELD PARK
Dewsnap Sidings
Shepley Industrial Estate North
Shepley Industrial Estate South
Globe Lane Industrial Estate
Tudor Industrial Estate
Kayley Industrial Estate
Audenshaw Cemetery
Playing Fields
OLDHAM RD. A627
OLDHAM ROAD
MOSSLEY RD.
STAMFORD ST.
PARK PARADE
KING ST.
STOCKPORT RD.
CAVENDISH ST.
RIVER TAME
A635
A670
B6194
B6445
B6169
B6170
B6175
OL6
OL7
SK16

83
65
84
95
Luzley
Smithy Farm
Springfield Farm
Dirk Farm
Miller Hey
Lock
Tunnel
Fershaw Hey
Moorfield Ter.
Brook
Swallow Lane
School La.
Carr
Carrbrook
Castle Lane
Carr Rise
Moorgate
Oakfield House (Club Ho.)
Reservoir
Resr. (dis)
Buckton Grange
Reservoirs
Works
South Vw.
Luzley End Farm
Crows i'th' Wood
Stamford Golf Course
OL5
Manchester Road
A670
Mossley Road
Luzley Road
Whitehall House
Hazelhurst
Buckton Vale
Buckton Vale Road
Huddersfield Road
B6175
Little Bank
Higher Little Bank
Shireclough
Shire Clough
Winterhill
Hopkins Fm.
Spout
Riding School
Standrick Hill
Brook Rd.
John St.
Weir
Works
Spring Bank
A635
Harridge Hall
Golf Course
School
Reservoir
Higher Hydegreen
Hydegreen
Harridge Pike
Arlies Prim. & Nursery Sch.
Heyrod
Staley House
Broadhill Rd.
Lower Hyde Green Farm
Sun Green
Cooper Farm
Sun Green Farm
Crickt. Grd.
Millbrook
Mill
Staley Hall
Huddersfield Canal
Oakwood
Staveleigh
Cote Farm
Woodfield Primrose Wood
Printworks
Sour Acre Fold
Besom La.
Reservoir
Higher Glent Quarry
R. Tame
Mills
North End Rd.
Swineshaw Brk.
Brushes
Brushes Road
Brushes Reservoir
Walkerwood Reservoir
Filter Hous
Cocker Hill
SK15
Factory
Huddersfield Road
St. Pauls Prim. Sch.
Clock Houses
Comm. Cen.
Recreation Centre
Copley High Sch.
Quarry (Disused)
Cock Wood
Football Ground
Cricket Grnd.
Range House
STALYBRIDGE
Copley
Wakefield Road
Market Street
Town Hall
Lib.
Swimming Baths
Sports Club
Mottram Road
Brushes Rifle Ranges (Disused)
Resr.
Flaxfield
Wild Bank
Wild Bank Primary School
Stocks La.
Playing Fields
High Street
Gorse Hall Prim. Sch.
Hollingworth Moor
Fern Bank
Castle Hall
Cheetham Park
Old Gorse Hall
Bower Fold
Football Grd.
Lower Hough Hill Farm
Hough Hill Rd.
Hough Hill
Shutts Lane
Ashtonhill Cross
Shawmoor
Wind Pump (Disused)
Shaw Moor
Woodlands
A6018
Stalyhill Jun. Sch.
Mottram Rise
Early Bank Wood
Broadbent Fold Farm
Hobson Moor
Quarry (Disused)
Acres Brook
Nailons
Gallows Clough
Gallowsclough
Lyne Edge (Club Ho.)
Golf Course
SK14
Hyde
Roe Cross Road
Bardsley Gate
Matley
Wrigleyfold
Matley Lane
Works
Oak
Hobson Moor Road
Lumb Farm
Dewsnap
Dewsnap Farm
Rabbit Lane
Roe Cross
Lower Roe Cross
Old Road
Shawhall
Edge Lane
Lwr. Roe Cross Farm
Quarries (Disused)
Res. (Covered)
Mottram Old Hall
Cheetham
Harrop Edge Road
Hall Drive

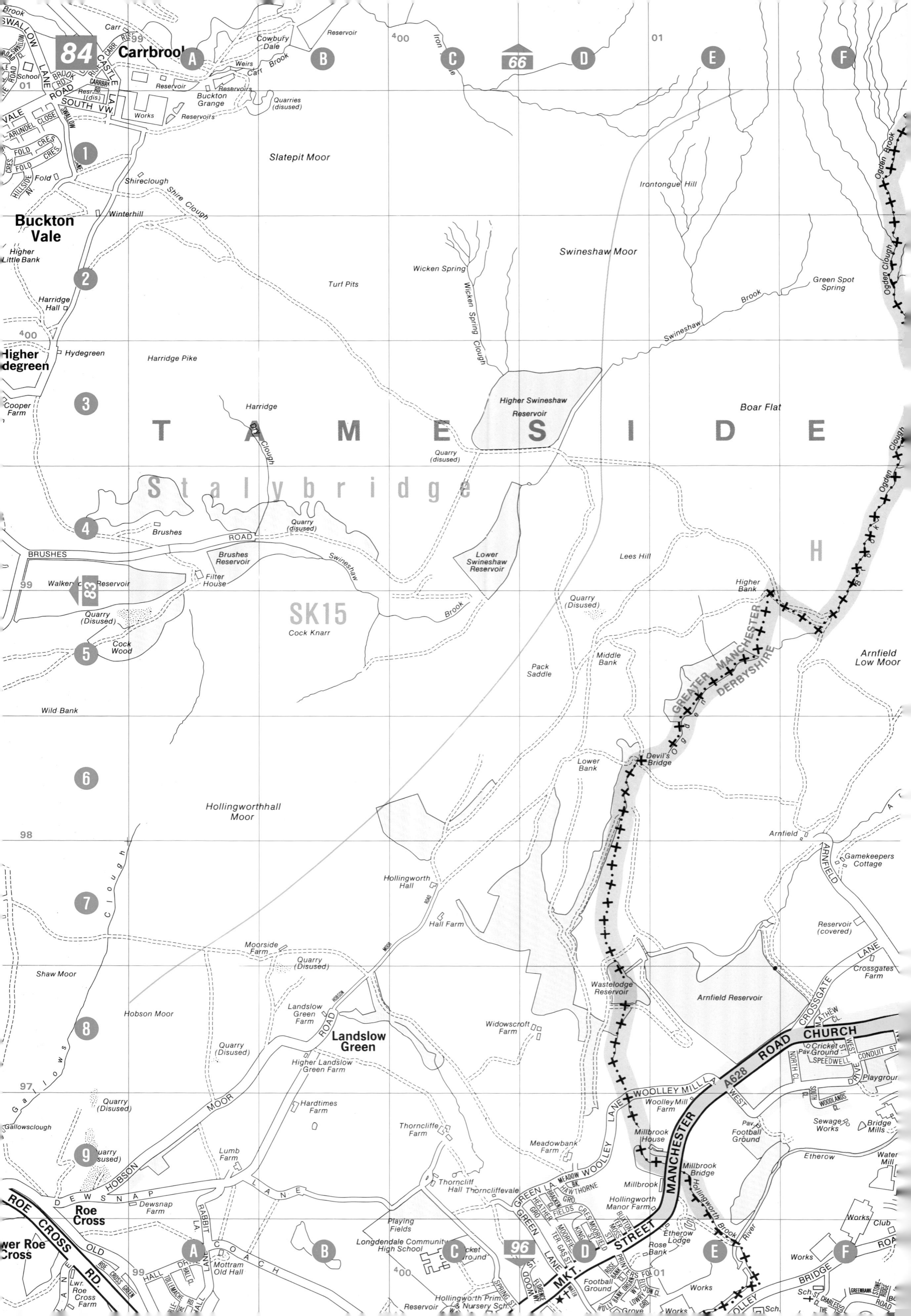

84
Carrbrook
A
B
C
D
E
F
66
Cowbury Dale
Reservoir
Weirs
Carr Brook
Reservoirs
Buckton Grange
Quarries (disused)
Works
School
SOUTH VW.
ARUNDEL CLOSE
Slatepit Moor
Shireclough
Shire Clough
Winterhill
Buckton Vale
Higher Little Bank
Harridge Hall
Hydegreen
Higher degreen
Harridge Pike
Turf Pits
Wicken Spring
Wicken Spring Clough
Irontongue Hill
Swineshaw Moor
Green Spot Spring
Swineshaw Brook
Higher Swineshaw Reservoir
Boar Flat
Cooper Farm
Harridge
Dry Clough
T A M E S I D E
Stalybridge
Quarry (disused)
Brushes
BRUSHES ROAD
Brushes Reservoir
Lower Swineshaw Reservoir
Lees Hill
Walkerwood Reservoir
83
Filter House
SK15
Cock Knarr
Quarry (Disused)
Cock Wood
Higher Bank
GREATER MANCHESTER
DERBYSHIRE
Ogden Brook
Ogden Clough
Middle Bank
Pack Saddle
Arnfield Low Moor
Wild Bank
Devil's Bridge
Lower Bank
Hollingworthhall Moor
Arnfield
Gamekeepers Cottage
ARNFIELD
Hollingworth Hall
Hall Farm
Reservoir (covered)
Moorside Farm
Quarry (Disused)
Shaw Moor
Wastelodge Reservoir
Arnfield Reservoir
Crossgates Farm
CROSSGATE LANE
Hobson Moor
Landslow Green Farm
Landslow Green
Widowscroft Farm
A628 ROAD
CHURCH
Higher Landslow Green Farm
Hardtimes Farm
Woolley Mill Farm
WOOLLEY MILL LA
Cricket Ground
Playground
Gallows Clough
Gallowsclough
Thorncliffe Farm
Millbrook House
Sewage Works
Bridge Mills
Football Ground
Lumb Farm
HOBSON MOOR ROAD
Meadowbank Farm
MANCHESTER
Millbrook Bridge
Etherow
Water Mill
DEWSNAP
Dewsnap Farm
Roe Cross
Thorncliff Hall
Thorncliffevale
Millbrook
Hollingworth Manor Farm
Hollingworth Brook
River
Works
Club
ROE CROSS RD.
Lower Roe Cross
RABBIT LA.
COACH
LANE
Playing Fields
Longdendale Community High School
Cricket Ground
96
MKT. STREET
Etherow Lodge
Rose Bank
Football Ground
Works
BRIDGE
Mottram Old Hall
Lwr. Roe Cross Farm
Hollingworth Prim. & Nursery Sch.
Reservoir
Sch.

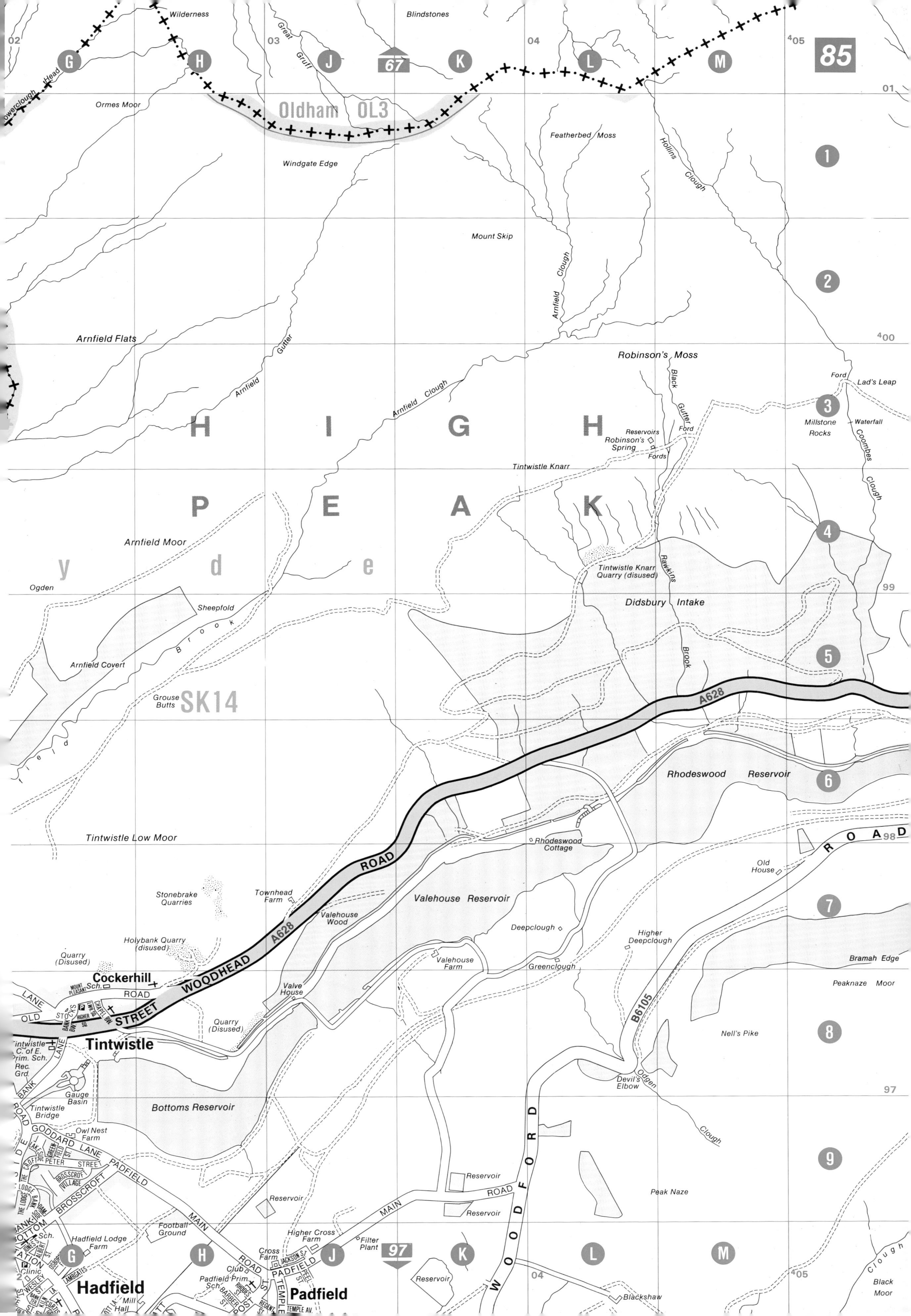
Wilderness
Blindstones
Great Gruff
67
Ormes Moor
Oldham OL3
Windgate Edge
Featherbed Moss
Hollins Clough
Mount Skip
Arnfield Clough
Arnfield Flats
Arnfield Gutter
Robinson's Moss
Black Gutter
Ford
Lad's Leap
Millstone Rocks
Waterfall
Coombes Clough
Reservoirs
Robinson's Spring
Fords
Tintwistle Knarr
HIGH PEAK
Arnfield Moor
Ogden
Tintwistle Knarr Quarry (disused)
Rawkins Brook
Didsbury Intake
Sheepfold
Arnfield Covert
Grouse Butts
SK14
A628
Rhodeswood Reservoir
Tintwistle Low Moor
Rhodeswood Cottage
Old House
ROAD
Stonebrake Quarries
Townhead Farm
Valehouse Reservoir
Valehouse Wood
Holybank Quarry (disused)
Deepclough
Higher Deepclough
Quarry (Disused)
Valehouse Farm
Greenclough
Bramah Edge
Peaknaze Moor
Cockerhill
WOODHEAD ROAD
Valve House
B6105
Nell's Pike
Tintwistle
Tintwistle C. of E. Prim. Sch.
Rec. Grd.
Gauge Basin
Devil's Elbow
Odden Clough
Bottoms Reservoir
Tintwistle Bridge
Owl Nest Farm
GODDARD LANE
PADFIELD
WOODFORD ROAD
Reservoir
Peak Naze
MAIN ROAD
Football Ground
Higher Cross Farm
Filter Plant
97
Hadfield Lodge Farm
Cross Farm
Club
Padfield Prim. Sch.
Hadfield
Padfield
Mill Hall
Blackshaw
Black Moor
Clough

86
74
98
M29
M62
M30
M62 MOTORWAY
Warrington
WARRINGTON
WA3
S A L F O R D
C H A T M O S S
Manchester
Knowle's Wood
Four Winds Farm
Rockaway
Roadside
Fern Cott.
Crest
Olive Mount Farm
Railway View Farm
Red House Farm
Moss Lodge Farm
Mosslands Farm
New Farm
Woodbarn Farm
Birch View Farm
Oakfield
Moss Farm
Four Lane Ends Farm
Ebenezer Farm
Larkhill Farm
Retreat Cottage
Westholme
Hope Cottage
Hephzibah
Little Woolden Moss
IRLAM MOSS
Woodstock Farm
Jenny Green
Springfield Farm
Ringing Pits Farm
Plant Cottage Farm
Birch Covert
Mosshall Farm
Worsley View
Brackley Farm
Woodland Farm
Prospect Grange
Great Woolden Wood
Keepers Cottage
Woolden View Farm
Nook Farm
CHAT MOSS
Mill Drain Farm
Rose Bank Farm
Great Woolden Hall
Cadishead Moss
Ryefield Farm
Lower Stanley Bank Farm
New Farm
Ash Farm
Higher Stanley Bank Farm
Railway View Farm
Ellesmere Farm
Bridge House Farm
Glazebrook Exchange Sidings
Glazebrook East Junction
Glazebrook
GLAZEBROOK
Rose Cottage
Glazebrook Country Club
Brush Farm
Sewage Works
Sports Ground
Lower Irlam
Council Off.
Astley Road Farm
Irlam High Sch.
Thames Trading Centre
IRLAM STATION
BRINELL
NORTHBANK INDUSTRIAL ESTATE
Northbank Industrial Estate
Cadishead Jun. Sch.
Playing Field
Recn. Grnd.
Sports Centre
Recreation Ground
Cadishead
Bandstand
Rec. Grnd.
Works
Viaduct
Partington Coal Basin
Mersey Farm
Inglewood Caravan Park
Townley Brow Farm
Hollingreave Farm
Lea Brook Farm
Great Woolden
GREATER MANCHESTER
CHESHIRE
Boundary
Drain
GLAZEBROOK
LIVERPOOL ROAD
A57
ASTLEY ROAD
MOSS ROAD
WOOLDEN ROAD
ROSCOE
TWELVE
BRINELL
HUNTSMAN
(Proposed)
B5212
DAM LANE
HEAD
STREET
LANE
A B C D E F
1 2 3 4 5 6 7 8 9
69 370 71 96 95 94 93 92

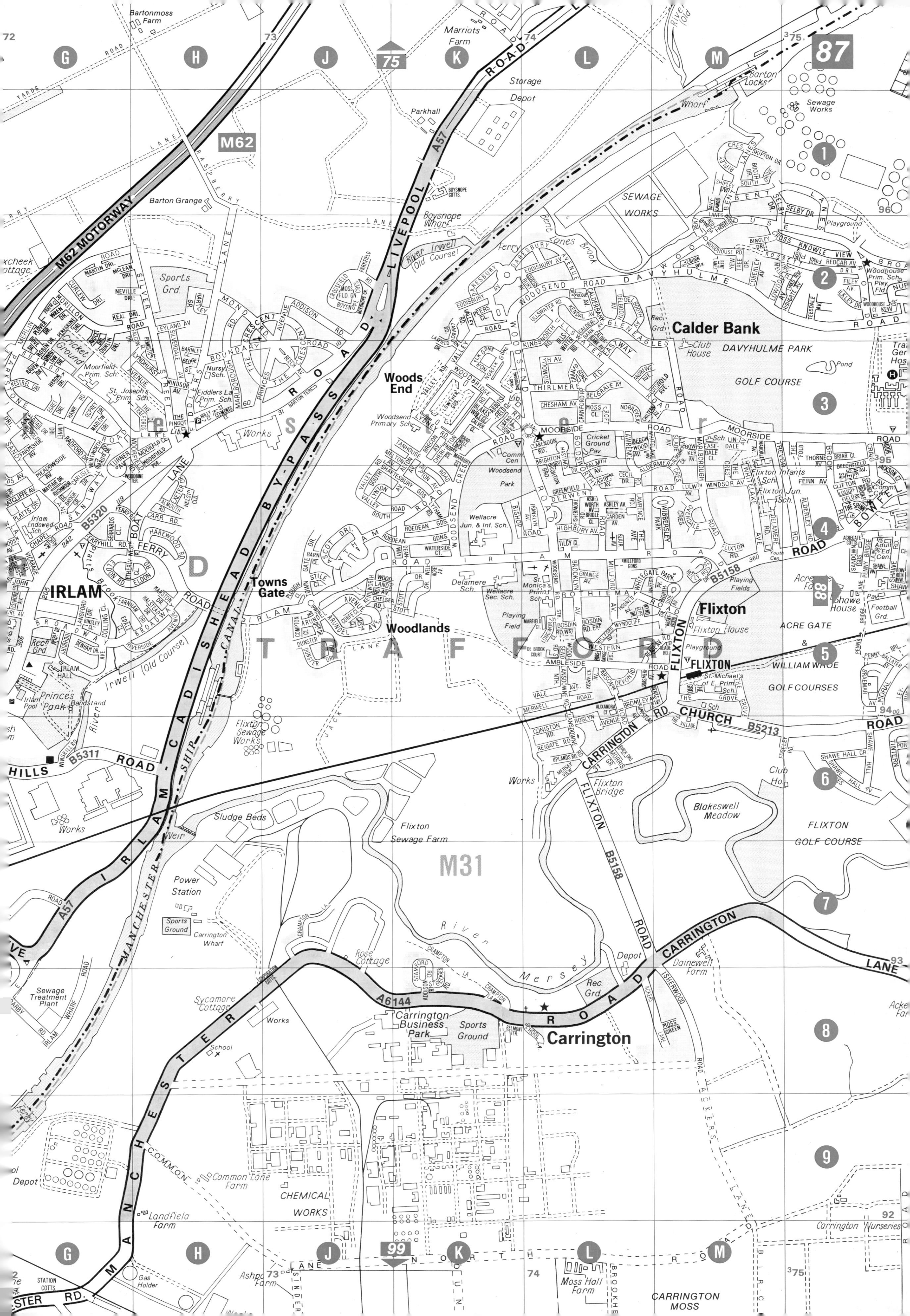
75
M62
M62 MOTORWAY
LIVERPOOL ROAD
A57
Bartonmoss Farm
Marriots Farm
Storage Depot
Parkhall
Barton Locks
Wharf
Sewage Works
Barton Grange
Boysnope Wharf
Boysnope Cotts.
River Irwell (Old Course)
SEWAGE WORKS
DAVYHULME ROAD
WOODSEND ROAD
Calder Bank
DAVYHULME PARK
GOLF COURSE
Club House
Pond
Woodhouse Prim. Sch.
Woods End
Woodsend Primary Sch.
Sports Grd.
Cricket Ground
Moorfield Prim. Sch.
St. Joseph's Prim. Sch.
Fiddlers La Prim. Sch.
Nursy Sch.
BOUNDARY ROAD
THE CRESCENT
MOORSIDE ROAD
Cricket Ground Pav.
Comm. Cen
Woodsend Park
Flixton Infants Sch.
Flixton Jun. Sch.
Wellacre Jun. & Inf. Sch.
CADISHEAD BY-PASS
SHIP CANAL
IRLAM ROAD
B5320
B5158
IRLAM
Towns Gate
Delamere Sch.
Wellacre Sec. Sch.
St. Monica's Prim. Sch.
Playing Field
Woodlands
Flixton
Flixton House
Playing Fields
ACRE GATE & WILLIAM WROE GOLF COURSES
Shawe House
Football Grd.
T R A F F O R D
FLIXTON
St. Michael's C of E. Prim. Sch.
CHURCH RD.
B5213
Irlam Hall
Princes Park
Bandstand
Irlam Endowed Sch.
Irwell (Old Course)
River
Flixton Sewage Works
B5311
HILLS ROAD
Works
Sludge Beds
Weir
Flixton Sewage Farm
M31
CARRINGTON RD.
FLIXTON ROAD
Flixton Bridge
Blakeswell Meadow
FLIXTON GOLF COURSE
Club Ho.
Power Station
Sports Ground
Carrington Wharf
River Mersey
Rose Cottage
CRAMPTON LA
Depot
Dainewell Farm
CARRINGTON LANE
A6144
Rec. Grd
Carrington
Carrington Business Park
Sports Ground
Sycamore Cottage
Sewage Treatment Plant
MANCHESTER ROAD
MANCHESTER SHIP CANAL
School
CHEMICAL WORKS
Common Lane Farm
Landfield Farm
Gas Holder
Ashpo Farm
Moss Hall Farm
CARRINGTON MOSS
Carrington Nurseries
NORTH ROAD
99
G H J K L M
1 2 3 4 5 6 7 8 9
88

M63 MOTORWAY
Junction 3
M63
Barton Locks
Wharf
Sewage Works
Barton Kennels
Croft Fm.
Depot
BARTON B5211
A5081
Clarke Ind. Est
Works
Crofts Bank
Parklands Sch.
G.Carnall Sports Centre
Kingsway Prim.Sch.
Barton Clough Prim. S
Junction 4
LOSTOCK B5158 ROAD
DAVYHULME
Calder Bank
Club House
DAVYHULME PARK
GOLF COURSE
Pond
Trafford General Hospital
Woodhouse Prim. Sch.
Broadway Park
Our Lady of the Rosary Prim. Sch.
St Mary's Prim. Sch.
Davyhulme
DAVYHULME PARK
Community Centre
Davyhulme Jun. & Inf. Sch.
MOORSIDE ROAD
Flixton Infants Sch.
Flixton Jun. Sch.
Sports Cen.
Flixton Sec. Sch. for Girls
Baths
Sports Ground
Playing Field
Grammar School
Urmston Jun. Sch.
Urmston Inf. Sch.
Golden Hill Park
Court Offs.
B5214 ROAD STATION RD
Nursing Home
Club
Football Grd.
Warehouse
St. Paul's Sec. Sch.
Highfield Prim. Sch.
Acregate Farm
Shawe House
Club
CHASSEN ROAD
Mini Rly.
URMSTON
Flixton
Flixton House
ACRE GATE & WILLIAM WROE GOLF COURSES
FLIXTON
St. Michael's C of E. Prim. Sch.
Football Grd.
Bradshaw Bridge
St. Clement's Sch.
B5213
STRETFORD ROAD
Training Centre
URMSTON
M63
ECCLES
M63 MOTORWAY
Ousel Brook
Sports Ground
CEMETERY
M31
TRAFFORD
Hilliam Farm
Junction 6
SPUR
Club Ho.
Blakeswell Meadow
FLIXTON GOLF COURSE
Old Eea Brook
River Mersey
Newcroft Farm
A6144(M)
A6144(M) MOTORWAY
Cricket Grd.
Tanks
Tennis Cts.
ASHTON-ON-MERSEY GOLF COURSE
Club Ho.
Stromford
Sewage Works
Sports Ground
Sports Grd.
CARRINGTON A6144
ACKERS COTTAGES
Ackers Farm
Ashton Hall Farm
Barracks Farm
Mersey Farm
All Saints Pri. Sch
CARRINGTON LANE
A6144
Wellfield Jun. Sch.
Wellfield Inf. Sch.
ASHTON PARK
Hlth Cen.
Carrington Nurseries
Sale West Sec. Sch.
Ashton upon Mersey
Brook Wood
B5166
CARRINGTON MOSS
76
100
87

89
77
90
101
Trafford Park
TRAFFORD PARK
HUMPHREY PARK
Gorse Hill
Old Trafford
Firswo
STRETFORD
STRETFORD CEMETERY
LONGFORD PARK
Chorlton-cum-Hardy
MANCHESTER
Chorlton Ees
SALE WATER PARK
SALE
WORTHINGTON PARK
SALE GOLF COURSE
Junction 7
Junction 8
M63
M63 MOTORWAY
SALE EASTERN & NORTHENDEN BY-PASS
M16
M17
M21
M32
M33
A5181
A56
A5067
A5145
B5211
B5213
B5215
B5397
B5166
A6144
MOSLEY ROAD
PARK ROAD
TRAFFORD PARK ROAD
WESTINGHOUSE ROAD
ASHBURTON ROAD EAST
TALBOT ROAD
CHESTER ROAD
KINGSWAY
EDGE LANE
WILBRAHAM ROAD
BARTON ROAD
SANDY LANE
URMSTON LANE
DOCK ROAD
CROSS STREET
WASHWAY RD.
NORTHENDEN ROAD
DANE ROAD
OLD HALL ROAD
WYTHENSHAW
Manchester United Football Ground
Old Trafford Cricket Ground
White City Retail Park
Lostock Park
Bridgewater Canal
Freightliner Terminal
Turn Moss
Playing Fields
Recreation Ground
Ivy Green
Longford Hall
Barrow Brook
Jackson's Bri.
River Mersey
Sewage Farm
Sale Lodge (Club Ho)
CHORLTON
F
O
R
D
G
H
J
K
L
M
1
2
3
4
5
6
7
8
9

90
78
89
102
A
B
C
D
E
F
1
2
3
4
5
6
7
8
9
Old Trafford
Hulme
Moss Side
Whalley Range
Firswood
Darley Park
Manley Park
Alexandra Park
Chorlton-cum-Hardy
Chorltonville
Barlow Moor
West Didsbury
Junction 8
TRAFFORD PARK RD.
STRETFORD ROAD
CHESTER ROAD
TALBOT ROAD
SEYMOUR GROVE
UPPER CHORLTON ROAD
CHORLTON ROAD
MOSS LA. WEST
MOSS LANE EAST
PRINCESS ROAD
WILBRAHAM ROAD
HIGH LANE
BARLOW MOOR ROAD
MANCHESTER ROAD
EDGE LANE
MAULDETH ROAD WEST
KINGS ROAD
Manchester United Football Ground
White City Retail Park
Old Trafford Cricket Ground
Trafford Bar
Town Hall
Seymour Park
Alexandra Park
Chorlton Park
Longford Park
Manchester Crematorium
Manchester Southern Cemetery
Chorlton-cum-Hardy Golf Course
Sale Golf Course
Chorlton Water Park
Houghend Playing Fields
Withington Hospital
River Mersey
Chorlton Brook
M17
M16
M21
M32
M33
A56
A5067
A6010
A5103
A5145
B5217
B5218
B5219
B5224
TRAFFORD
MANCHESTER

91
92
79
103
G
H
J
K
L
M
1
2
3
4
5
6
7
8
9
University
University of Manchester
Greenheys
Holy Name R.C. Prim. Sch.
Infirmary
Royal Infirmary
St. Mary's Hosp.
Whitworth Art Gallery
WHITWORTH PARK
Chorlton upon Medlock
Victoria Park
Coll. of Higher Education
Hulme Hall
Xaverian Coll.
Rusholme
BIRCHFIELDS PARK
Manchester City Football Ground
Platt Hall (Art Gall. & Mus.)
PLATT FIELDS PARK
Recreation Ground
Boating Lake
Fallowfield
Owens Park
Hall of Residence
Athletic Ground
Playing Fields
Tennis Courts
Football Lacrosse Grd.
Grammar School
Longsight
Longsight Dist. Cen. Shopping Centre
Exhibition Hall
Depot
Rushford Park
Levenshulme
Alma Park
Thirlmere Aqueduct
Levenshulme High School
CRINGLE FIELDS
Heaton Moor Golf Course
Mauldeth Home
Ladybarn
MAULDETH RD.
Ladybarn Park Recreation Ground
Burnage High School
Burnage
Burnage High Sch. (Upper)
Green End
Withington
Christie Hospital
Whalley Range High School
Albert Park
FOG LANE PARK
BURNAGE
M13
M12
M14
M15
M19
M20
SK4
UPPER BROOK STREET
PLYMOUTH GROVE
OXFORD ROAD
STOCKPORT ROAD
HYDE ROAD
WILMSLOW ROAD
DICKENSON ROAD
BIRCHFIELDS ROAD
KINGSWAY
MOSELEY ROAD
SLADE LANE
ANSON ROAD
PALATINE ROAD
A6
A34
A5184
A6010
A5079
B5093
B5117
B5219
B5167

92
80
104
91
A
B
C
D
E
F
1
2
3
4
5
6
7
8
9
HYDE RD.
A57
BELLE VUE
Belle Vue
Belle Vue Greyhound Race Course
Exhibition Hall
Bowling Alley
Snooker Club
Cinema
Gorton Park
Baths
Motor Wks.
Recreation Ground
Gorton
Gorton Lower Resr.
Debdale Park
Debdale
Miniature Golf Course
Band Stand
Gorton Ho.
Sports Ground
Abbey Hey Prim. Sch.
Longsight
Kirkmanshulme La.
Stockport Rd.
St. John's Rd.
Dickenson Rd.
Nutsford Vale
Ryder Brow
RYDER BROW
Brook Green
CEMETERY
MANCHESTER
M12
M18
M19
Corporation Yard
Sunny Brow Park
Crowcroft Park
Melland Playing Field
Playing Field
Spurley Hey Upr. High Sch.
Melland Sch.
Saints Peter & Paul R.C. Sec. Sch.
Sports Grd. Club
Bowling Grn.
Nico Ditch
B6178
A6
Rushford Park
Coston Park
Levenshulme
LEVENSHULME
B5093
Levenshulme High School
Alma Park
Thirlmere Aqueduct
Recreation Ground
Baths
Reservoir
Fir Tree Nursery Sch.
Fir Tree Jun. & Infs. Sch.
Wingate House (Club Ho.)
Houldsworth Golf Course
Highfield Farm
Nelstrop Road North
REDDISH NORTH
North Reddish Park
North Reddish
North Reddish Clinic
B6167
REDDISH
Reddish Green
Reddish Mills
REDDISH STH.
B5169
Hurstfield Indus. Est.
Warehouse
Whitehill Indus. Est.
Haigh Park
Heaton Chapel
HEATON CHAPEL
A626
Broadstone Rd.
Wellington Rd. North
Manchester Rd.
Biscuit Wks.
Errwood Park Works
Cringle Fields
Peel Moat
Heaton Moor Golf Course
Mauldeth Home
Heaton Moor
Heaton Mr. Pk.
Playing Fields North Area Coll. & Adult Educ. Cen.
Leisure Cen.
Heaton Day Sch.
Burnage
Green End
Kingsway
Acacias Prim. Sch.
Children's Hosp.
Depot
SK4
SK5

AUDENSHAW RESERVOIRS
81
93
Abbey Hey
Audenshaw Lodge
Lodge Fm.
Debdale Fm.
No.2
Valve House
M66 MOTORWAY (Proposed)
Dodgeleach Brook
DENTON GOLF COURSE
Thirlmere
Club House
Aqueduct
Junction 11
MANCHESTER ROAD
A57
Denton Reservoirs No.1 No.2
DENTON
Arrow Trading Estate
Hawthorns Prim. Sch.
Playing Fields
Audenshaw Cemetery
Sports Ground
SHEPLEY RD.
Egerton Pk. Sec. Sch.
Russell Scott Prim. Sch.
Cricket Gnd.
M67 MOTORWAY
Junc. 1
DENTON RELIEF ROAD
HYDE RD.
M67
Works
Skill Centre
WINDMILL LANE INDUSTRIAL ESTATE
Play. Field
Victoria Park
DENTON
Football Grnd.
Playing Fields
Linden Prim. Sch.
West End Jun. & Inf. Sch.
Dane Bank
Cricket Ground
Dane Bank Prim. Sch.
The City
Res.
TAMESIDE
Denton Hall Farm
St. Thomas More R.C. High Sch.
Cricket Grd.
94
Playing Fields
Two Trees High Sch.
Hyde Hall
Denton Wood
M66
Horse Close Wood
Hardy Wood
Recreation Ground
Haughton Green
Holt Wood
Hulme's Wood
DENTON CEMETERY
Sewage Works
Reddish
Weir
River Tame
STOCKPORT ROAD
Beight Bri.
Reddish Vale
Vale Farm
Arden Hall
Horse Shoe Farm
Millhill Farm
Castle Hill Farm
Castle Hill
Bakery
Tame Valley Prim. Sch.
BRINNINGTON
Reddish Vale Golf Course
Arden Bri.
SK6
Playing Fields
Brinnington Secondary Sch.
Engineering Works
Maycroft Prim. Schs.
South Reddish
Bredbury Industrial Estate
Brick Works
Sports Ground
Brinnington Park
Brinnington
Junc. 12 (M66)
A6(M) MOTORWAY (Proposed)
Woodley
Junc. 15 (M63)
105
Crookilley Wood
BREDBURY
STOCKPORT RD. WEST
Junc. 14 (M63)

94
82
106
A
B
C
D
E
F
1
2
3
4
5
6
7
8
9
SHEPLEY
Shepley Industrial Estate South
Audenshaw Cemetery
Sports Ground
Playing Field
Sewage Works
Globe Lane Industrial Estate
Prim. & Nursery Sch.
Peak Forest Canal
SK96
Newton Wood
Works
Ind. Est.
Depot
HYDE NORTH
DUKINFIELD
A627
B6170
FLOWERY FIELD
Flowery Field
Oakfield Hall
Playing Field
Courts
Newton
Sports Gound
St. Paul's R.C. Prim. Sch.
NEWTON FOR HYDE
Bayley Hall
HYDE PARK
Hyde Sixth Form Coll.
River Tame
Dunkirk Farm
DENTON
RELIEF ROAD
Junction 2
M67 MOTORWAY
M67
HYDE BY-PASS
A57
MANCHESTER RD.
Linden Rd. Prim. Sch.
Kingston
Playing Fields
HYDE
Junc. 3
Godley
HYDE CENTRAL
Rec. Grd.
Works
Cricket Grd.
Playing Field
Two Trees High Sch.
M34
Manchester
St. John Fisher R.C. Prim. Sch.
Dan Wood
Gower Hey Wood
Tameside Coll. of Tech.
Sports Grd.
MARKET ST.
STOCKPORT RD.
Hyde Hospital
Cemetery
Hardy Wood
Haughton Green
Recreation Ground
DENTON CEMETERY
Gibraltar Row
Dowson Jun. Sch.
Dowson Inf. Sch.
Gee Cross
A560
Aethorn Fold
Pear Tree Farm
Pole Bank Hall
Longacre Farm
Haughton Dale
Nursery
Arden Bri.
River Tame
Tame Valley
Bowlacre Home
Tennis Courts
Reservoir (Covered)
Bowlacre Farm
Wood Cottages
Sports Ground
Swing Br. (Foot)
Mill
Ash Tree
Birches
Werneth Low
WOODLEY
SK6
Stockport
Back o' th' Hill
Werneth-Hall
Woodley
Rec. Grd.
Civic Hall
BREDBURY
Sports Ground
Highlane Farm
Heald Wd.
Greavefold Res.
Greavefold
Lowtop
Lowbank Cott.
Anglestone Ho.
Rose Cott.
Beech Cott.
The Cottage
Spring Wood
Springwood Farm
STOCKPORT

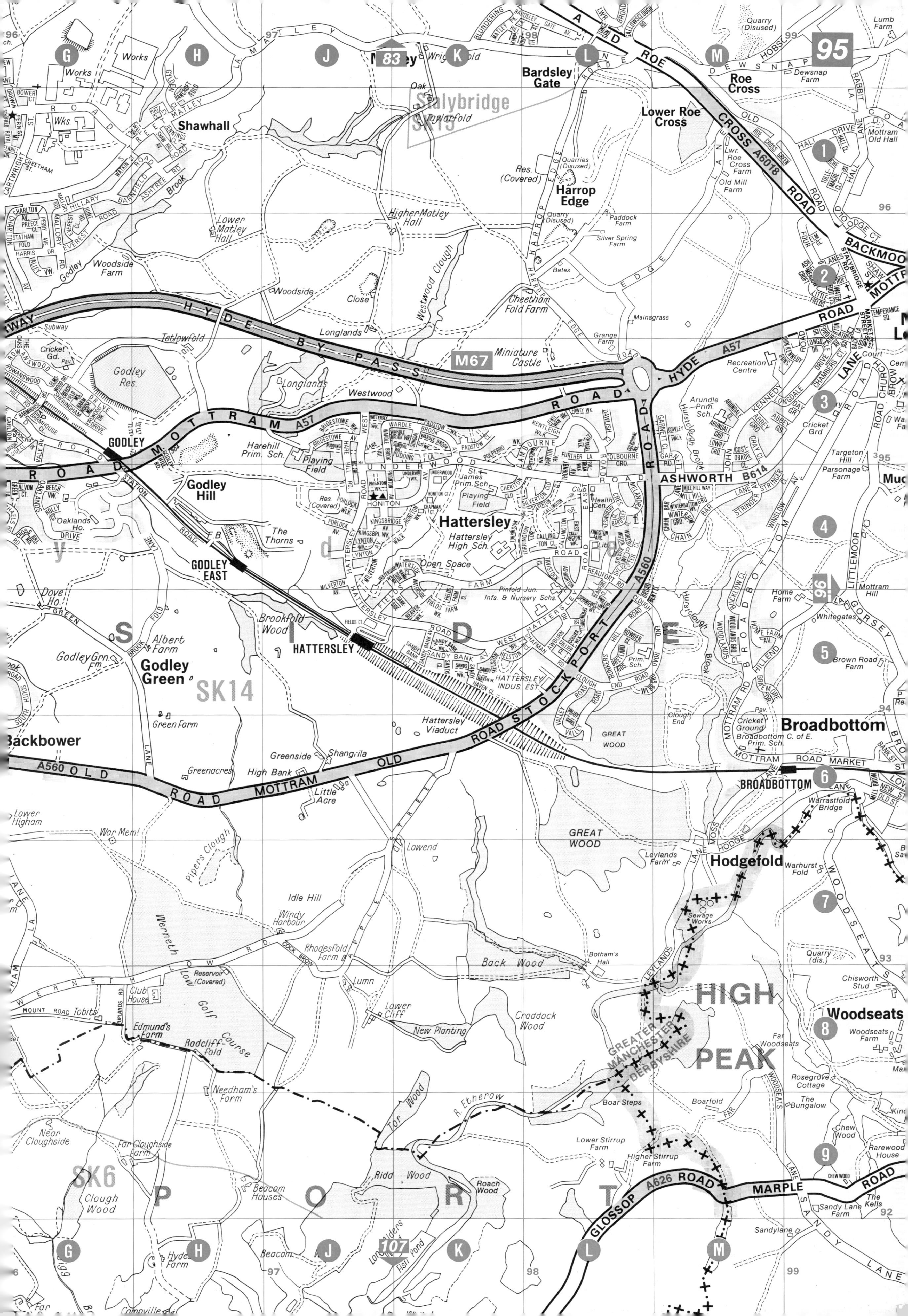

95
83
96
107
SK15
SK14
SK6
Stalybridge
Shawhall
Works
Wks.
Bardsley Gate
Roe Cross
Lower Roe Cross
Dewsnap Farm
Lumb Farm
Mottram Old Hall
Quarry (Disused)
ROE CROSS ROAD
A6018
HOBSON
DEWSNAP
OLD ROE CROSS RD
Lwr. Roe Cross Farm
Old Mill Farm
Res. (Covered)
Harrop Edge
Quarries (Disused)
Paddock Farm
Silver Spring Farm
Bates
HARROP EDGE
Mainsgrass
Grange Farm
Cheetham Fold Farm
Higher Matley Hall
Lower Matley Hall
Oak
Taylorfold
Wrigley Fold
MATLEY LANE
Woodside Farm
Woodside
Close
Longlands
Westwood Clough
Tetlowfold
Cricket Gd.
Godley Res.
HYDE BY-PASS
M67
Miniature Castle
HYDE ROAD
A57
Westwood
MOTTRAM ROAD
GODLEY
GODLEY EAST
Godley Hill
Harehill Prim. Sch.
Playing Field
UNDERWOOD
St. James Prim. Sch.
Hattersley
Hattersley High Sch.
Open Space
Pinfold Jun. Infs. & Nursery Schs.
Res. (Covered)
The Thorns
Oaklands Ho.
Dove Ho.
Brookfold Wood
HATTERSLEY
Albert Farm
Godley Grn. Fm
Godley Green
Green Farm
HATTERSLEY INDUS. EST.
Hattersley Viaduct
STOCKPORT ROAD
A560
ASHWORTH
B614
Recreation Centre
Arundle Prim. Sch.
Cricket Grd
Targeton Hill
Parsonage Farm
Health Cen.
Lib.
Club
Hurstclough Brook
Home Farm
Whitegates
Mottram Hill
Brown Road Farm
LITTLEMOOR
GORSEY
Clough End
GREAT WOOD
Cricket Ground
Broadbottom
Broadbottom C. of E. Prim. Sch.
MOTTRAM ROAD
MARKET ST
BROADBOTTOM
Warrastfold Bridge
Hodgefold
Warhurst Fold
Leylands Farm
Sewage Works
Backbower
OLD ROAD
Greenside
Shangrila
Greenacres
High Bank
OLD MOTTRAM ROAD
Little Acre
Lower Higham
War Mem!
Pipers Clough
Lowend
Idle Hill
Windy Harbour
Rhodesfold Farm
Werneth Low
Reservoir (Covered)
Club House
Golf Course
Tobits
Edmund's Farm
Radcliff Fold
Needham's Farm
Lumn
Lower Cliff
New Planting
Back Wood
Botham's Hall
Craddock Wood
HIGH PEAK
GREATER MANCHESTER
DERBYSHIRE
Quarry (dis.)
Chisworth Stud
Woodseats
Woodseats Farm
Far Woodseats
Rosegrove Cottage
The Bungalow
Boar Steps
Boarfold
R. Etherow
Tor Wood
Near Cloughside
Far Cloughside Farm
Lower Stirrup Farm
Higher Stirrup Farm
Chew Wood
Rarewood House
Ridd Wood
Roach Wood
Beacom Houses
Clough Wood
GLOSSOP ROAD
A626
MARPLE ROAD
Sandy Lane Farm
The Kells
Sandylane
SANDY LANE
Hyde Farm
Beacom
Fish Pond
Campville

Roe Cross
Lower Roe Cross
Mottram in Longdendale
Broadbottom
Hodgefold
Woodseats
Chisworth
Higher Chisworth
Holehouse
Lee Head
Charlesworth
Bankwood Gate
Higher Gamesley
Gamesley
The Hague
Mudd
Warhill
Hollingworth
Woolley Bridge
Brookfield
Dinting Vale
Simmondley
TAMESIDE
HIGH PEAK
GREATER MANCHESTER
DERBYSHIRE
SK14
SK12
A57
A626
A628
A6018
B6174
MARPLE ROAD
GLOSSOP ROAD
MOTTRAM MOOR
WOOLLEY LANE
MARKET STREET
MANCHESTER ROAD
DINTING ROAD
BROOKFIELD
BACKMOOR
HYDE ROAD
Longdendale Community High School
Broadbottom C. of E. Prim. Sch.
Charlesworth C. of E. Prim Sch.
Mottram C. of E. Prim. Sch.
St. Mary's R.C. Primary School
Melandra Castle Roman Fort
Robin Wood
Tom Wood
Chew Wood
Close Wood
Coombes Edge
Coombes Rocks
Coombes
Mares Back
Cloud Farm
Moorside
Monks Road
Slack Edge
84
95

85
Hadfield
Padfield
HADFIELD
Glossop
GLOSSOP
Old Glossop
Higher Dinting
Lower Dinting
Whitfield
Simmondley Village
Charlestown
Chunal
Moorfield
SHEFFIELD ROAD
WOODCOCK RD.
HIGH STREET WEST
HIGH STREET EAST
WOODHEAD ROAD
B6105
A57
A6016
A624
Reservoir
Peak Naze
Black Moor
Blackshaw
Swineshaw Reservoir
Upper Swineshaw Reservoir
Cemetery
Cat Wood
Broom Hill
Shire Hill Hospital
Wood's Hospital
Edge Plantation
Blakemoor Plantation
Shire Hill
Stone Quarry
Glossop & District Golf Course
Glossopdale Community College
Mouselow Quarry
Castlehill Wood
Dinting Railway Museum
Herod Farm
Herod Clough
Oak Wood
Shaw Moor Plantation
The Twitchlings
Grouse Butts
Bray Clough
Kidd Road
Kydd Road Farm
Whiteley Nab
Hobroyd Farm
Lean Town
Lees Hall Farm
Gnathole Wood
Horseshoe Farm
Sheepfold
Shepley Farm
P
E
A
K

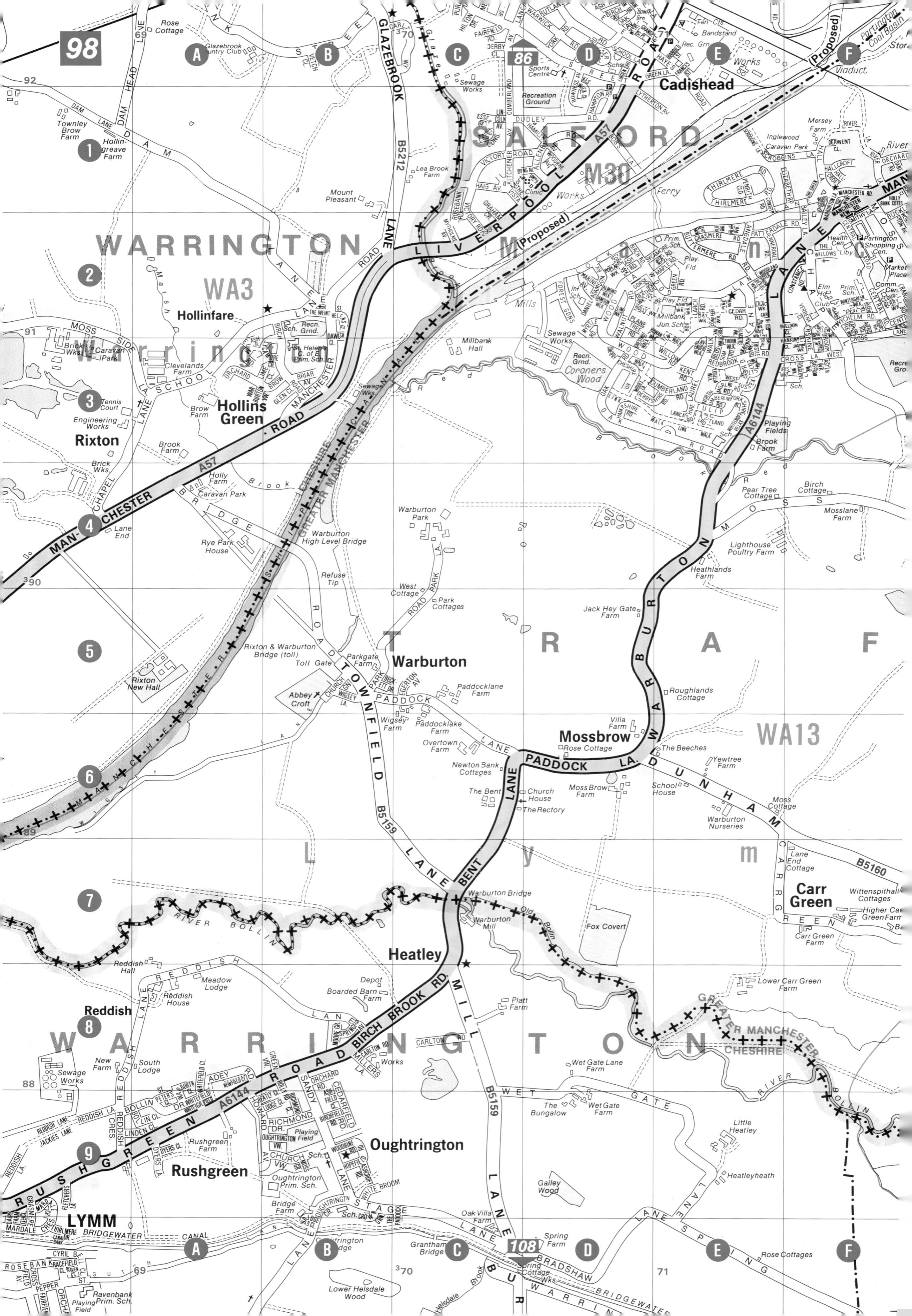
WARRINGTON
WA3
Hollinfare
Hollins Green
Rixton
Cadishead
SALFORD
M30
A57
B5212
Warburton
Mossbrow
WA13
Heatley
Carr Green
Reddish
Oughtrington
Rushgreen
LYMM
A6144
B5159
B5160
Warburton High Level Bridge
Rixton & Warburton Bridge (toll)
Rixton New Hall
Warburton Park
River Bollin
Greater Manchester
Cheshire
Fox Covert
Gailey Wood
Coroners Wood
Glazebrook Country Club
Rose Cottage
Townley Brow Farm
Hollingreave Farm
Clevelands Farm
Brow Farm
Brook Farm
Holly Farm
Caravan Park
Rye Park House
Lea Brook Farm
Mount Pleasant
Millbank Hall
Sewage Works
Recreation Ground
Sports Centre
Abbey Croft
Parkgate Farm
Wigsey Farm
Paddocklake Farm
Overtown Farm
Newton Bank Cottages
The Bent
Church House
The Rectory
Moss Brow Farm
School House
Warburton Nurseries
Moss Cottage
Roughlands Cottage
Villa Farm
Jack Hey Gate Farm
Heathlands Farm
Lighthouse Poultry Farm
Mosslane Farm
Pear Tree Cottage
Birch Cottage
Warburton Bridge
Warburton Mill
Reddish Hall
Meadow Lodge
Reddish House
Boarded Barn Farm
Platt Farm
Wet Gate Lane Farm
The Bungalow
Wet Gate Farm
Little Heatley
Heatleyheath
Lower Carr Green Farm
Carr Green Farm
Wittenspithall Cottages
South Lodge
New Farm
Rushgreen Farm
Oughtrington Prim. Sch.
Bridge Farm
Oak Villa Farm
Spring Farm
Grantham Bridge
Rose Cottages
Lower Helsdale Wood
Ravenbank Prim. Sch.
Bridgewater Canal
Manchester Road
Liverpool Road
Warburton Lane
Paddock La.
Dunham
Birch Brook Rd.
Rushgreen Road
Mill Lane
Townfield Lane
Bent Lane
Wet Gate Lane
Spring Lane
Partington Coal Basin
Viaduct
Ferry
Mills
Works

86
108

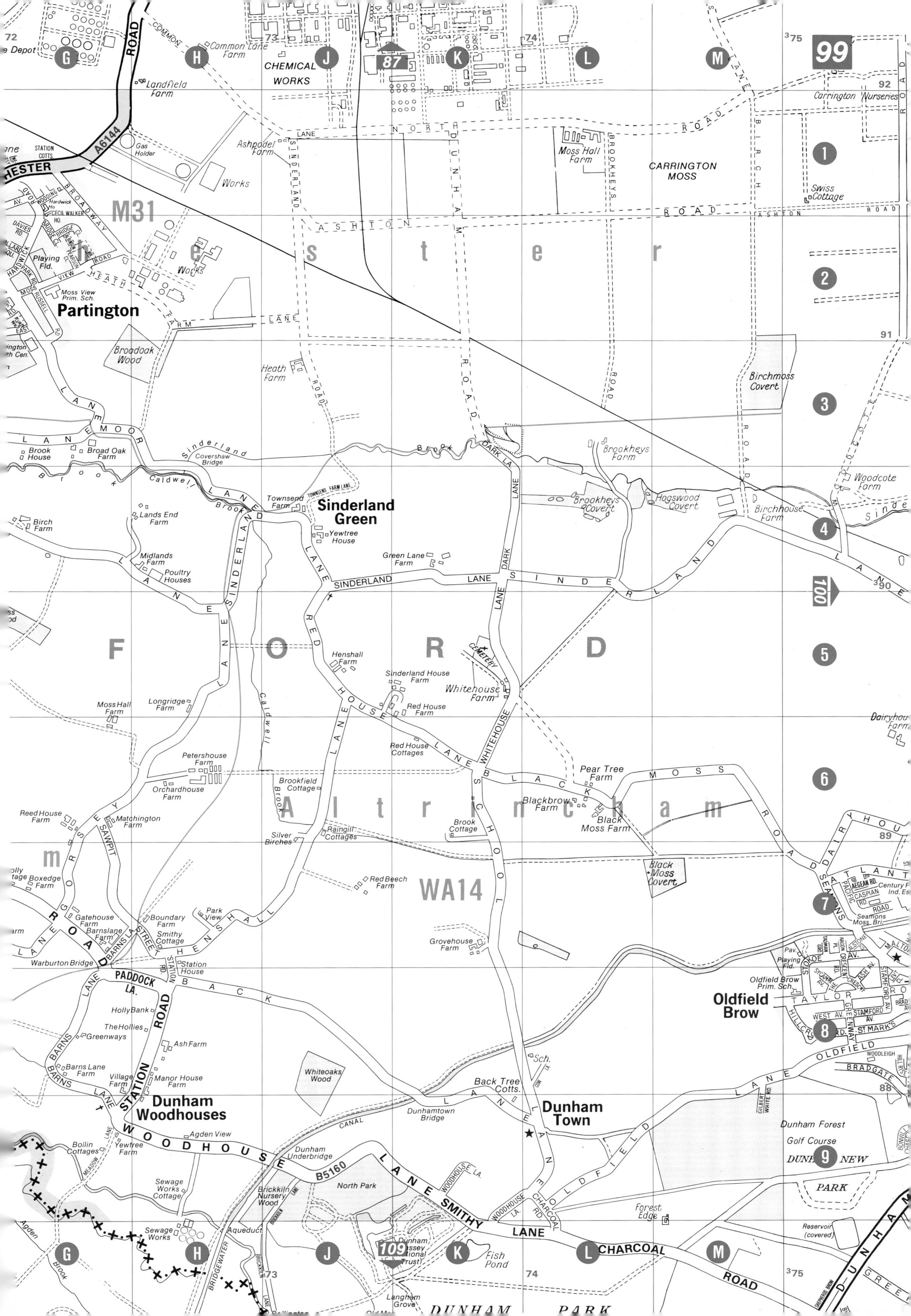

99
87
109
100
Partington
Sinderland Green
Oldfield Brow
Dunham Woodhouses
Dunham Town
CHEMICAL WORKS
CARRINGTON MOSS
Carrington Nurseries
Swiss Cottage
Moss Hall Farm
Common Lane Farm
Landfield Farm
Ashpodel Farm
Gas Holder
Works
STATION COTTS.
A6144
M31
Moss View Prim. Sch.
Playing Fld.
Broadoak Wood
Heath Farm
Birchmoss Covert
Brookheys Farm
Brookheys Covert
Hogswood Covert
Birchhouse Farm
Woodcote Farm
Brook House
Broad Oak Farm
Covershaw Bridge
Townsend Farm
Yewtree House
Lands End Farm
Birch Farm
Midlands Farm
Poultry Houses
Green Lane Farm
Henshall Farm
Sinderland House Farm
Whitehouse Farm
Red House Farm
Red House Cottages
Longridge Farm
Moss Hall Farm
Petershouse Farm
Orchardhouse Farm
Brookfield Cottage
Pear Tree Farm
Blackbrow Farm
Black Moss Farm
Reed House Farm
Matchington Farm
Silver Birches
Raingill Cottages
Brook Cottage
Black Moss Covert
Red Beech Farm
Boxedge Farm
Gatehouse Farm
Barnslane Farm
Boundary Farm
Smithy Cottage
Park View
Grovehouse Farm
Warburton Bridge
Station House
Holly Bank
The Hollies
Greenways
Ash Farm
Barns Lane Farm
Village Farm
Manor House Farm
Whiteoaks Wood
Back Tree Cotts.
Dunhamtown Bridge
Agden View
Bollin Cottages
Yewtree Farm
Sewage Works Cottage
Sewage Works
Aqueduct
Dunham Underbridge
Brickkiln Nursery Wood
North Park
Dunham Massey (National Trust)
Fish Pond
Langham Grove
Forest Edge
Reservoir (covered)
Dunham Forest Golf Course
DUNHAM NEW PARK
DUNHAM PARK
Oldfield Brow Prim. Sch.
Seamons Moss Bri.
Century Ind. Es.
Dairyhouse Farm
F O R D
Altrincham
WA14
CHARCOAL ROAD
WOODHOUSE LANE
SMITHY LANE
B5160
BACK LANE
SINDERLAND LANE
SINDERLAND ROAD
RED HOUSE LANE
WHITEHOUSE LANE
SCHOOL LANE
BLACK MOSS ROAD
DARK LANE
DUNHAM ROAD
ASHTON ROAD
NORTH ROAD
BIRCH ROAD
MOSS LANE
STATION ROAD
PADDOCK LA.
BARNS LANE
SAWPIT STREET
GORSEY LANE
HENSHALL LANE
OLDFIELD LANE
OLDFIELD ROAD
TAYLOR RD.
DAIRYHOUSE LANE
ATLANTIC ST.
CANAL
Caldwell Brook
Sinderland Brook
Agden Brook
BRIDGEWATER
72 73 74 75 92 91 90 89 88
G H J K L M
1 2 3 4 5 6 7 8 9

100
Ashton upon Mersey
Woodhouses
Manchester
M31
Carrington Nurseries
Carrington Moss
Swiss Cottage
Birchmoss Covert
Woodcote Farm
Hogswood Covert
Birchhouse Farm
Brookside Farm
Sinderland Brook
Broadheath
WA14
Trading Est.
Stag Industrial Estate
Bridgewater Canal
Century Park Ind. Est.
Seamons Moss Bri.
Dairyhouse Farm
Oldfield Brow
Oldfield Brow Prim. Sch.
Dunham Forest Golf Course
DUNHAM NEW PARK
Reservoir (covered)
CHARCOAL RD.
JOHN LEIGH PARK
ALTRINCHAM
NAVIGATION ROAD
Timperley
STAMFORD PARK
Hale
Altrincham Grammar Sch
Ashton-on-Mersey Sec. Sch.
Sale West Sec. Sch.
Firs Plantation
Sale Boys' Gram. Sch.
Woodheys Prim. Sch.
Woodheys Park
Tyntesfield Prim. Sch.
S. Trafford Coll. of Further Educ.
Broadheath Prim. Sch.
Gibson Ho Hosp
Shopping Precinct
K. George V Pool
Playing Fields
Football Ground
Sports Ground
A56
A6144
A560
A538
B5164
B5165
88
99
110

Junction 8
SALE GOLF COURSE
M63
M63 MOTORWAY
WORTHINGTON PARK
Sale
Brooklands
MARSLAND RD.
A6144
NORTHENDEN ROAD
B5166
WYTHENSHAWE ROAD
SALE ROAD
Northern Moor
Sale Grammar School (Girls)
Sale Moor Sec. Sch.
Sale Cem.
Bridgewater Canal
M33
MANCHESTER
Manchester
Timperley
Baguley
ALTRINCHAM ROAD
A560
SHAFTESBURY AVENUE
B5165
B5167
Roundthorn
ROUNDTHORN INDUSTRIAL ESTATE
Mill Brook Indus. Est.
M23
WA15
Wythenshawe Hospital
Baguley Hospital
WYTHENSHAWE PARK
Wythenshawe College
Brookway High School
Royal Oak Recreation Ground
Nan Nook Wood
Fir Coppice
Newall Green
Newall Green High Sch.
Green Lane High Sch.
GROVE PARK
Timperley Brook
Baguley Brook
Fairywell Brook
Delahays Farm
Holly Tree Farm
Holly Tree Cottage
Manor Farm
Clay Ho.
Municipal Course
Rodger Park
Baguley Park
Recreation Ground
89
102
111

Junction 8
102
90
Barlow Moor
West Didsbury
Sale Golf Course
Sale
TRAFFORD
Chorlton Water Park
M21
Christie Playing Fields
Lancasterian School
Fielden Park
Fielden Park Coll. of Further Education
Mersey Bank Open Space
Parkway Playing Fields
Mersey Bank Playing Fields
M33
Sports Ground
River Mersey
Northenden Golf Course
Junction 9
SALE EASTERN & NORTHENDEN BY-PASS
Kenworthy
M63 MOTORWAY
M63
Withington Golf Course
Northern Moor
Button Lane Prim. Sch.
Northenden
PRINCESS PARKWAY
A5103
A5145
B5167
B5166
WYTHENSHAWE ROAD
101
WYTHENSHAWE PARK
Wythenshawe Hall (Art Gal. & Mus.)
Fir Coppice
The Big Round
M23
Wythenshawe Horticultural Centre
Baguley Brook
Royal Oak Recreation Ground
Wythenshawe College
MANCHESTER
Baguley
ALTRINCHAM ROAD
A560
Rose Hill (Assessment Centre)
M22
Sharston Industrial Area
Junction 3
Junc. 2
Blackcarr Wood
Princes Spinney
M56 MOTORWAY
Refuse Treatment Plant
Sharston
Baguley Hall Prim. School
Newall Green High School (Lower)
Benchill
Hollyhedge Park
Rodger's Park
Wythenshawe Hospital
M56
Newall Green
Newall Green High Sch.
St. Peter's Prim. Sch.
Junction 4
Wythenshawe
112
Poundswick High Sch.
South Wythenshawe High Sch.
Park Wood
Crossacres Prim. Sch.
Woodside Special Sch.

103
Heaton Moor Golf Course
Mauldeth Home
Green End
Albert Park
Ewing School
Synagogue
PALATINE B5167
Tennis Ground
WILMSLOW RD.
B5093
FOG LANE PARK
Tennis Courts
Bowling Green
Recreation Ground
91
BURNAGE
Burnage High Sch (Upper)
M19
M20
Didsbury
Didsbury Park
Lawnhurst
Simon Playing Field
Fletcher Moss Museum
Didsbury College (Manchester Poly)
Children's Home
Cricket Grd.
A5145
Fletcher Moss Playing Fields
Stenner Farm
Bowls
Tennis Cts.
The Towers Business Park
EAST DIDSBURY
East Didsbury
Parr's Wood High Sch.
Superstore
PARRS WOOD LANE
DIDSBURY ROAD
Recreation Ground
Heaton Mersey
St. John's Prim. Sch.
Golf Range
Cricket Ground
Priestnall Hey
Priestnall Sec. School
Sports Centre
Heaton Mersey Park
Sports Grd.
SK4
Heaton Mersey Bleach Works
Reservoirs
Vale Rd. Farm
104
River Mersey
Cheadle Bri
Filter Beds
Viaduct
Sewage Works
Cheadlewood
Millgate Farm
Underbank House
Play. Fields
Broad Oak Prim. Sch.
M63 MOTORWAY
Junction 11
Junction 10
MANCHESTER ROAD
B5095
Bridge Fm.
Fish Pond
Abney Hall
Abney Hall Park
Barnes Hospital
Cheadle Bleach Wks.
Offices
Recreation Ground
STOCKPORT ROAD
A560
Cheadle Heath
Cheadle Heath Prim. Sch.
M56
Recreation Ground
Sports Centre
SK8
GATLEY
Gatley
Gatley Hill Bri. Liby.
Gatley Prim. Sch.
Athletic Grnd.
Scholes Park
KINGSWAY
A34
Sports Ground
Play. Fields
The Kingsway Lower Sec. Sch.
The Kingsway Upper Sec. Sch.
Playing Flds.
CHEADLE
Demmings Infants Sch.
Stadium
Recreation Ground
Demmings Indus. Est.
Public Open Space
Playing Flds.
Brookfields Park
Club Ho.
Sports Cen.
Cheadle Golf Course
Adult Ed. Cent.
WILMSLOW ROAD
A5149
CHEADLE ROAD
Sports Field
Tennis Cts.
Sports Ground
113
Gatley Golf Course
Highfield House
South View
BRUNTWOOD PARK
Grammar School for Girls
Tennis Courts
Lacrosse Ground
G
H
J
K
L
M
1
2
3
4
5
6
7
8
9

104
92
114
103
Green End
Heaton Moor Golf Course
Heaton Chapel
Heaton Moor
Priestnall Sports Centre
Thornfield Park
Norris Bank
Norris Hill
Heaton Norris
SK4
Heaton Mersey Park
Heaton Mersey Bleach Works
Craig Road Playing Fields
Stockport Trading Estate
Junc.12
M63 MOTORWAY
M63
A5145
A6
A626
A560
B5465
B5169
B6167
DIDSBURY ROAD
BRINKSWAY
WELLINGTON ROAD
Lancashire Hill
Cheadle Heath
Edgeley
Alexandra Park
Stockport Co. F.C.
STOCKPORT
Shaw Heath
Hollywood Park
Sewage Works
Filter Beds
SK3
SK8
Sports Field
Pumping Sta.
Lawnhurst Indus. Est.
Adswood
Adswood Park
Davenport
Cale Green
Recreation Ground
Lady Bri. Ladybridge
Adswood Brick & Tile Works
Demmings Indus. Est.
Public Open Space
Cheadle
Playing Fields
Viaduct
Mersey Bank

105
106
93
115
Brinnington
Brinnington Park
Woodley
Junc. 15 (M63)
Junc. 14 (M63)
Junc. 13
M63
(M66)
River Tame
Weir
St. Bernadette's Prim. Sch.
Brindale Prim. Sch.
SK5
SK6
SK7
SK1
SK2
Crookilley Wood
Crookilley Way
Motorway
Arden Park
Welkin Mill
Lower Bredbury
Arden Prim. Sch.
Bredbury
Bredbury Hall
Bredbury Green
Stockport Rd. West
Stockport Rd.
Whitefield Road
Ashton Rd.
A560
A6017
A6(M) Motorway (Proposed)
Portwood
Portwood Indus. Est.
Worth Meadow Mills
Carrington Rd.
New Zealand Road
Vernon Park
Museum
Woodbank Memorial Park
River Goyt
Swan Pool Res.
Sports Ground
Stringer's Weir
Pear Mill Indus. Est.
C.E.G.B. Bow. Sub Station
Middle Farm
Goyt Hall Farm
Goyt Hall
King George's Field
Stockport Little Moor
Cricket Ground
Swim'g Pool
Woodlands Park
Offerton High Sch.
Fairway Prim. Sch.
CKPORT
St. Marys Way
A626
Turncroft La.
Hall Street
Offerton Lane
Marple Rd.
St. Thomas Park
Football Grd.
Banks La. Prim. Sch.
Bus Depot
Crematorium
Borough Cemetery
Hillcrest Road
B6171
Nangreave
Aquinas R.C. Coll.
Sports Grd.
Mile End
Heaviley
Stockport Great Moor
Cherry Tree Hosp.
The Dialstone Centre
Playing Field
Offerton
Offerton Hall
Offerton Hall Prim. Sch.
Offerton Ho. Hospital
Offerton Prim. Sch.
Holliday Farm
Foggbrook
Foggbrook Bri.
Offerton Green
Wood Cottage
Warren Wood
Shadyoak Fm.
Brooklands Farm
Poise Brook
Bunkers Hill Recreation Ground
Lower Waterside
Waterside Farm
Sewage Works
Sewage Works (Disused)
Ford
Overdale Sch.
Werneth Sec. Sch.
Highfield Cemetery
Playing Fields
Davenport Park
Davenport
Stockport Gramm. Sch.
Stockport High Sch.
Stockport Sec. Sch.
London Road
A6
Woodsmoor
Gt. Moor Park
Club Ho.
Mirrlees Golf Course
Woods Moor
Recreation Ground
Stepping Hill
Stepping Hill Hospital
Stepping Hill Link (Proposed)
Dial Park Prim. Sch.
Open Space
Reservoir
National Trad. Est.
Advice Bureau
St. Simons Prim. Sch.
Offerton Road
Dial Park Road
Bosden Fold
G
H
J
K
L
M
1
2
3
4
5
6
7
8
9

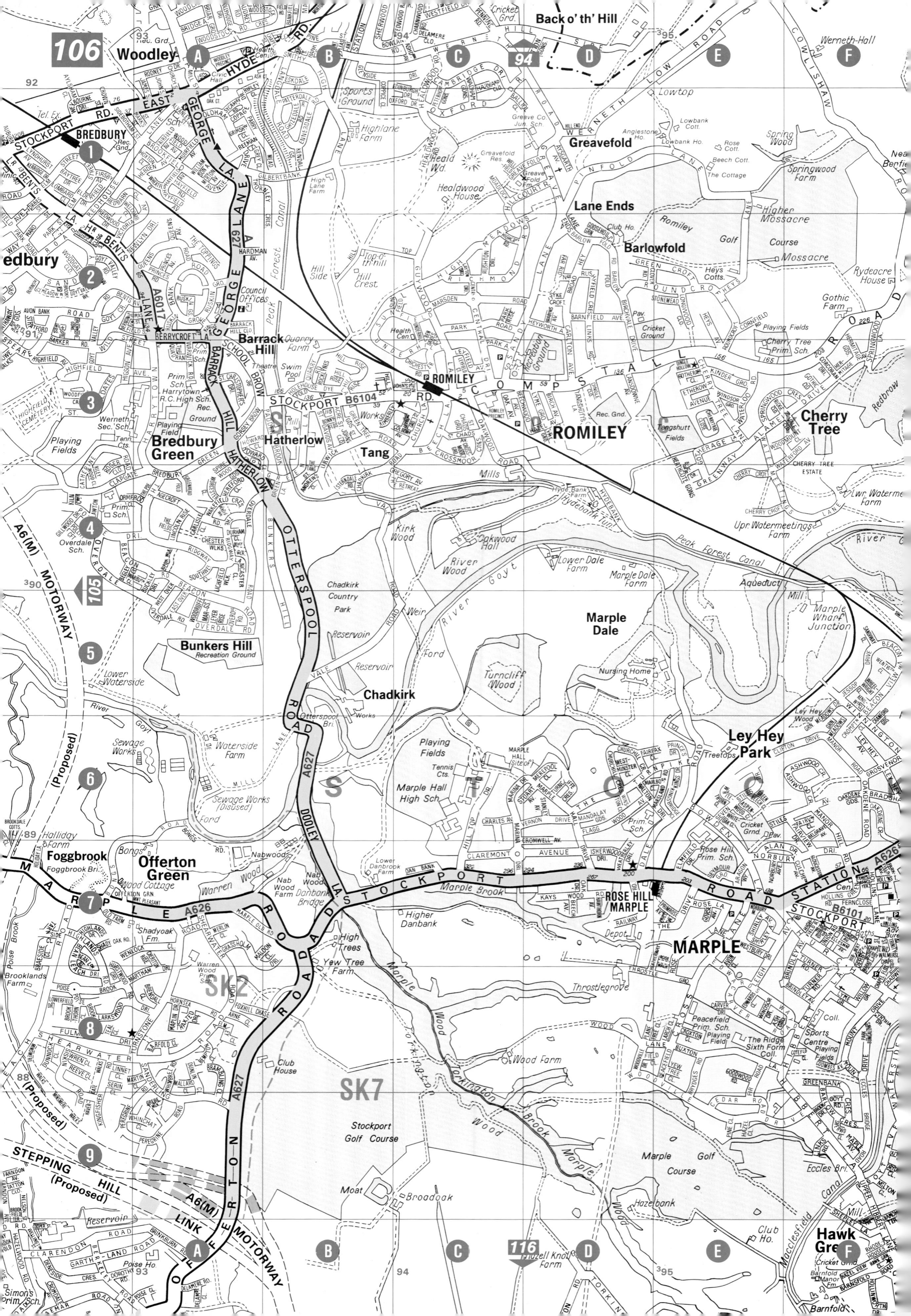
Woodley
Back o' th' Hill
Bredbury
Greavefold
Lane Ends
Barlowfold
Bredbury Green
Hatherlow
Tang
Romiley
Cherry Tree
Barrack Hill
Bunkers Hill
Chadkirk
Marple Dale
Ley Hey Park
Foggbrook
Offerton Green
Rose Hill Marple
Marple
Hawk Green
Stockport Golf Course
Marple Golf Course
Peak Forest Canal
River Goyt
SK2
SK6
SK7

Cloughside
Far Cloughside Farm
Clough Wood
Gigg Brook
Beacom Houses
Beacom Wood
Hyde's Farm
Long Alders Wood
Fish Pond
Roach Wood
95
107
Lower Stirrup Farm
Higher Stirrup Farm
MARPLE ROAD
Sandy Lane Farm
The Kells
Sandylane
SANDY LANE
Hyde
SK14
HIGH PEAK
DERBYSHIRE
GTR. MANCHESTER
Far Benfield
Benfield Clough
Compville Farm
Whitebottom
Woodheys
A626
Martin Clough
Mortin Farm
School Lane Farm
Yew Tree Cotts.
The Mount
Weir Cottages
Rabbit Warren
Etherow Country Park
Ernocroft Wood
Ernocroft
ERNOCROFT
Intakes Farm
Brown Low
Resr.
Dirtylane
Compstall
COMPSTALL B6104 ROAD
Compstall Hall
Library
Reservoir
Mills
Compstall Bridge
Cricket Ground
Bowling Green
Lwr. Ernocroft Farm
Works
Cowhey Farm
GLOSSOP ROAD
SANDHILL LANE
Rest
Brownlow
Larkhill
SMITHY LANE
Smithylane
Cote Green
COTE GREEN
Lane Ends
SK6
Iron Bridge
Weir
Bowling Green
Sun Hill
Broadstone
Hollywood End
Brook Bottom
Norton Lea Farm
Recreation Ground
Mill Brow
HOLLYWOOD ROAD
Sportsmans Farm
CHATTERTON LANE
Chatterton Lane Farm
Horsepool
Recreation Grd.
Ludworth Prim. Sch.
LOWER FOLD
MILL LANE
Marple Bridge
MARPLE
St. Martins Cott.
BRABYNS BROW
Tennis Cts.
Cattle Mkt.
St. Mary's Prim. Sch.
HOLLINS LANE
FERN WOOD
Greenhill
Weir
Primrose Mill
Blackberry Hall
Mill Pond
Mellor Hall
Hambleton Fold
Heathy Bank
LONGHURST LANE
TOWNSCLIFFE LANE
Lea Farm
Townscliffe
Vicarage
CHURCH ROAD
Mellor Prim. Sch.
Meadows
Cataract Bridge
Mills
Podnor
Hilltop Farm
Knowle Wood
KNOWLE ROAD
Sports Ground
Pav.
Ten. Cts.
Reservoir
Mellor
Rec. Grd.
Lower Hall
Brook Bottom
Moorend
Cheetham Hill
MOOR END ROAD
Recreation Ground
STRINES ROAD B6102
ARKWRIGHT ROAD
Lime Kiln
Chapel Ho.
BRICKBRIDGE
All Saints Prim. Sch. Playing Fields
Brick Bridge
Bottoms Bridge
Reservoir
Bottom's Hall
Damsteads Farm
Tarden
Longshaw Clough
Linnet Clough
Club Ho.
GIBB
WHETMORHURST
Birchenough
Roman Bri. Lake
Mellor & Townscliffe Golf Course
Whetmorhurst
EDGE ROAD
Whitehouse Farm
River Goyt
B6101
Mill Lade
Cobden Farm
Cobden Edge
Cobdenedge Farm
Mellor Moor
Weir
Barlow Wood
Windybottom Wood
Snape Hey
RIDGE AVE.
Hill Top Farm
Strawberry Hill
Forest Canal
Paradise
BLACK LANE
COBDEN EDGE
117
Windybottom Farm
The Banks
Bull Hill
Cross Gates
Quarry (Disused)
Spring Mount
Peak
G H J K L M
1 2 3 4 5 6 7 8 9
97 98 99
92 91 90 89 88

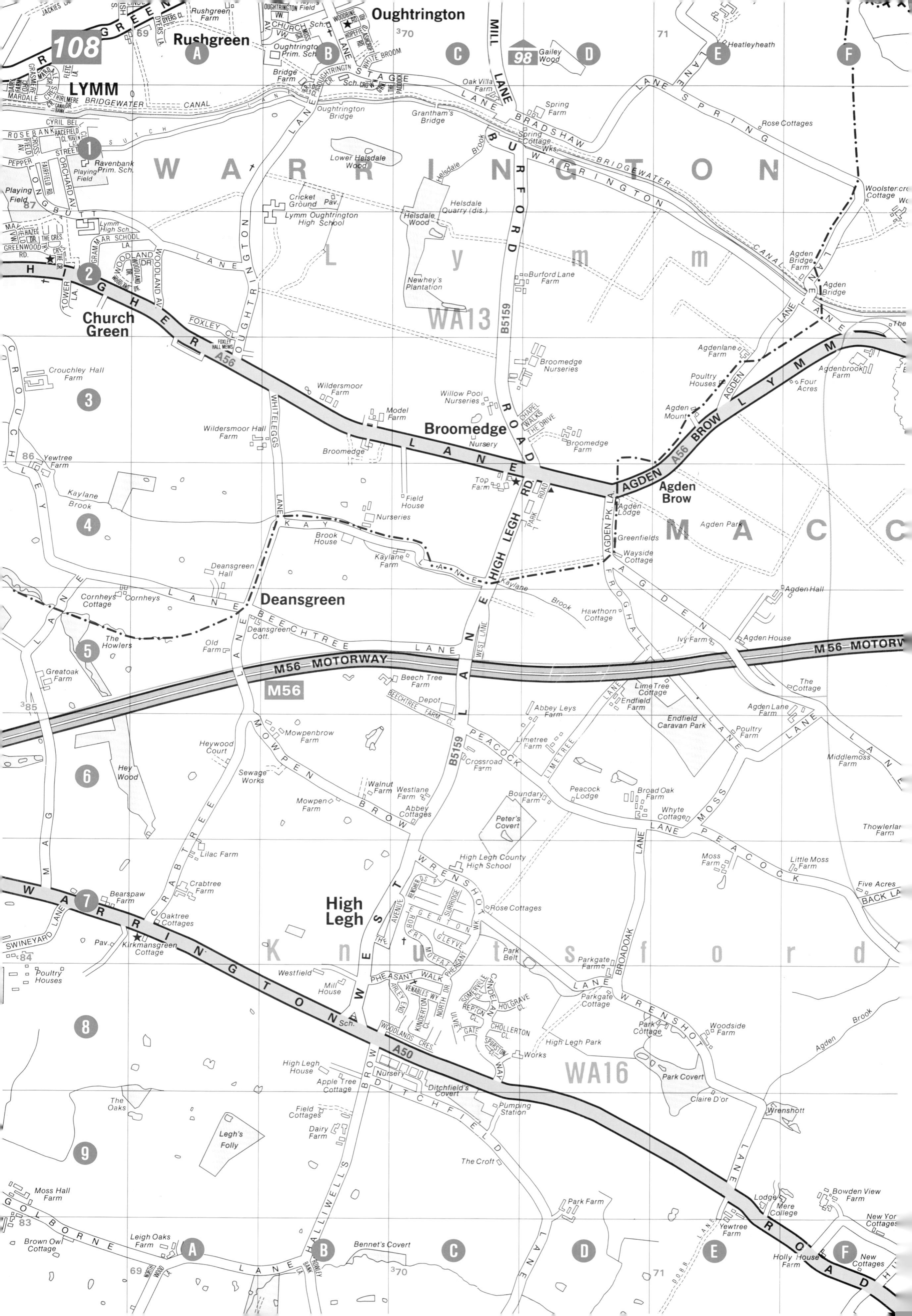
108
98
Oughtrington
Rushgreen
Rushgreen Farm
LYMM
BRIDGEWATER CANAL
Oughtrington Bridge
Grantham's Bridge
Bridge Farm
Oughtrington Prim. Sch.
Oak Villa Farm
MILL LANE
Gailey Wood
Heatleyheath
Spring Farm
BRADSHAW LANE
SPRING LANE
Rose Cottages
Spring Cottage
Lower Helsdale Wood
Ravenbank Prim. Sch.
Playing Field
WARRINGTON
Woolster Cottage
Cricket Ground
Pav.
Lymm Oughtrington High School
Lymm High Sch.
GRAMMAR SCHOOL LA.
Helsdale Quarry (dis.)
Helsdale Wood
BURFORD ROAD
Lymm
Burford Lane Farm
Agden Bridge Farm
Agden Bridge
Newhey's Plantation
Church Green
HIGHER LANE
FOXLEY CL.
A56
WA13
B5159
Agdenlane Farm
Agdenbrook Farm
Crouchley Hall Farm
Broomedge Nurseries
Poultry Houses
Four Acres
Wildersmoor Farm
Willow Pool Nurseries
Model Farm
Broomedge
Agden Mount
Wildersmoor Hall Farm
Nursery
Broomedge Farm
Broomedge
Yewtree Farm
LANE
Agden Brow
AGDEN BROW
Top Farm
HIGH LEGH RD.
Kaylane Brook
Field House
Agden Lodge
Nurseries
Agden Park
MACC
Brook House
KAY LANE
Greenfields
Kaylane Farm
Wayside Cottage
Deansgreen Hall
Kaylane Brook
Agden Hall
Cornheys Cottage
Cornheys
Deansgreen
Hawthorn Cottage
The Howlers
Deansgreen Cott.
BEECHTREE LANE
Old Farm
Ivy Farm
Agden House
M56 MOTORWAY
M56
Greatoak Farm
Beech Tree Farm
Depot
Lime Tree Cottage
Endfield Farm
The Cottage
Endfield Caravan Park
Abbey Leys Farm
Agden Lane Farm
Mowpenbrow Farm
Heywood Court
Poultry Farm
Limetree Farm
Hey Wood
Sewage Works
PEACOCK LANE
Middlemoss Farm
Crossroad Farm
Peacock Lodge
Broad Oak Farm
Walnut Farm
Westlane Farm
Boundary Farm
Mowpen Farm
Abbey Cottages
Whyte Cottage
MOWPEN BROW
Peter's Covert
MOSS LANE
Thowlerlane Farm
Lilac Farm
High Legh County High School
Moss Farm
Little Moss Farm
Crabtree Farm
Bearspaw Farm
Five Acres
BACK LANE
High Legh
Rose Cottages
Oaktree Cottages
SWINEYARD LANE
Pav.
Kirkmansgreen Cottage
Knutsford
Park Belt
Parkgate Farm
Poultry Houses
Westfield
PHEASANT WALK
Mill House
Parkgate Cottage
BROADOAK
WRENSHOT LANE
Woodside Farm
Park Cottage
High Legh Park
Works
Agden Brook
High Legh House
Nursery
A50
WA16
Apple Tree Cottage
Ditchfield's Covert
Park Covert
The Oaks
Field Cottages
Pumping Station
Claire D'or
Wrenshott
Dairy Farm
Legh's Folly
DITCHFIELD LANE
HALLIWELLS BROW
The Croft
Moss Hall Farm
Lodge
Mere College
Bowden View Farm
Park Farm
New York Cottages
GOLBORNE LANE
Leigh Oaks Farm
Yewtree Farm
Brown Owl Cottage
Bennet's Covert
Holly House Farm
New Cottages
ROAD
WARRINGTON ROAD
A
B
C
D
E
F
1
2
3
4
5
6
7
8
9
69
370
71
87
86
385
84
83

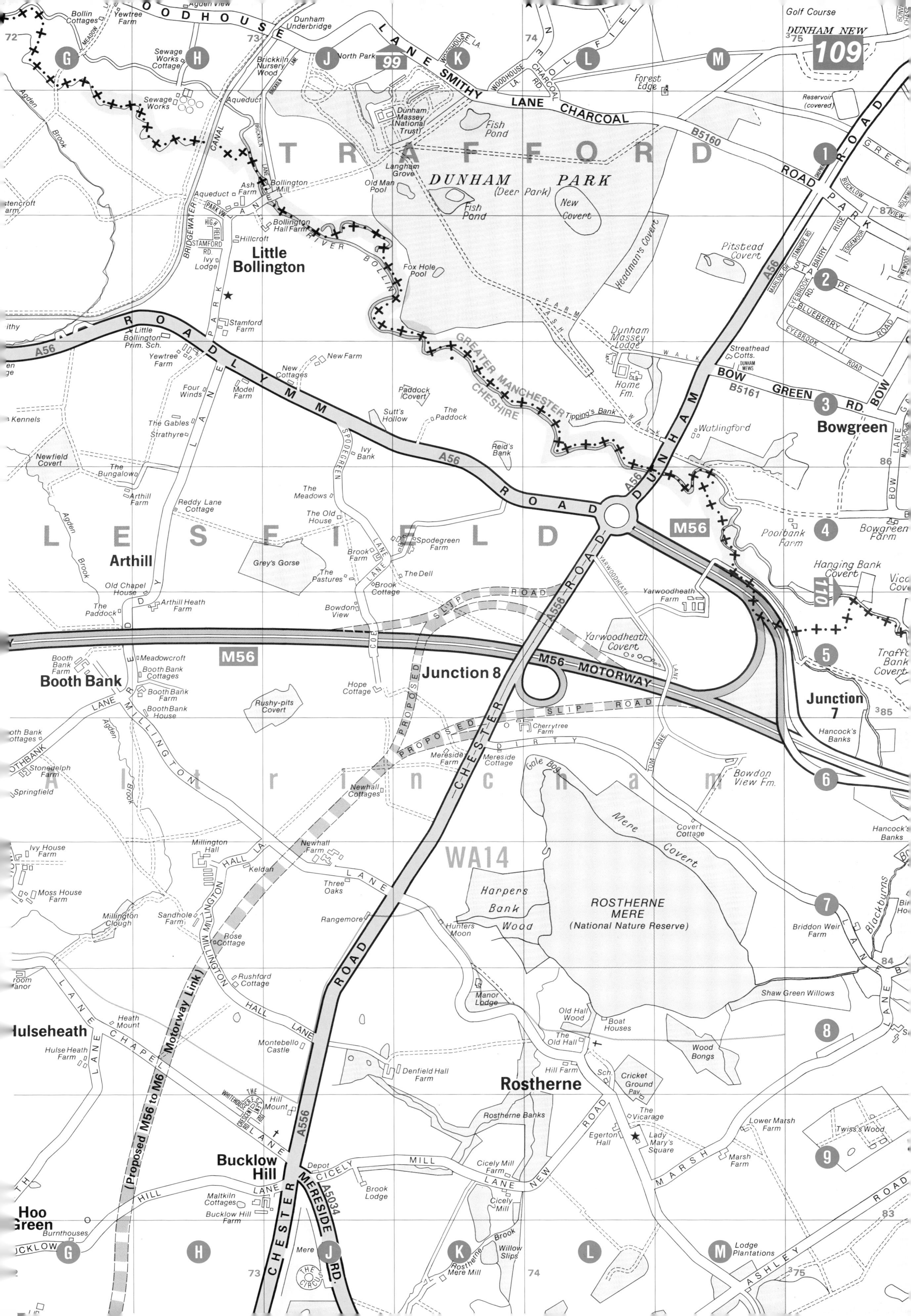
109
99
110
TRAFFORD
LESEFIELD
Altrincham
WA14
DUNHAM PARK
(Deer Park)
Little Bollington
Arthill
Booth Bank
Junction 8
Junction 7
Bowgreen
Rostherne
Bucklow Hill
Hulseheath
Hoo Green
ROSTHERNE MERE
(National Nature Reserve)
Dunham Massey (National Trust)
Dunham Underbridge
WOODHOUSE LANE
SMITHY LANE
CHARCOAL ROAD
B5160
DUNHAM ROAD
A56
A556
M56
M56 MOTORWAY
CHESTER ROAD
LYMM ROAD
BOW GREEN RD.
B5161
MERESIDE RD.
A5034
CICELY MILL LANE
NEW ROAD
MARSH LANE
ASHLEY ROAD
CHAPEL LANE
BUCKLOW HILL LANE
MILLINGTON LANE
MILLINGTON HALL LANE
DIRTY LANE
PROPOSED SLIP ROAD
(Proposed M56 to M6 Motorway Link)
GREATER MANCHESTER
CHESHIRE
RIVER BOLLIN
BRIDGEWATER CANAL
Fish Pond
New Covert
Pitstead Covert
Headman's Covert
Fox Hole Pool
Old Man Pool
Langham Grove
Dunham Massey Lodge
Home Fm.
Streathead Cotts.
Watlingford
Tipping's Bank
Reid's Bank
Poolbank Farm
Bowgreen Farm
Hanging Bank Covert
Yarwoodheath Farm
Yarwoodheath Covert
Hancock's Banks
Bowdon View Fm.
Gale Bog
Mere Covert
Covert Cottage
Harpers Bank Wood
Hunters Moon
Manor Lodge
Old Hall Wood
Boat Houses
The Old Hall
Hill Farm
Cricket Ground
Wood Bongs
The Vicarage
Lady Mary's Square
Egerton Hall
Lower Marsh Farm
Marsh Farm
Twiss's Wood
Lodge Plantations
Shaw Green Willows
Briddon Weir Farm
Blackburns
Rostherne Banks
Cicely Mill Farm
Cicely Mill
Rostherne Brook
Willow Slips
Rostherne Mere Mill
Denfield Hall Farm
Montebello Castle
Rangemore
Three Oaks
Newhall Farm
Keldan
Millington Hall
Sandhole Farm
Rose Cottage
Rushford Cottage
Millington Clough
Moss House Farm
Ivy House Farm
Springfield
Stonedelph Farm
Booth Bank Farm
Meadowcroft
Booth Bank Cottages
Rushy-pits Covert
Hope Cottage
Newhall Cottages
Mereside Farm
Mereside Cottage
Cherrytree Farm
Bowdon View
Brook Cottage
The Dell
The Pastures
Brook Farm
Spodegreen Farm
Grey's Gorse
The Old House
The Meadows
Ivy Bank
Sutt's Hollow
The Paddock
Paddock Covert
New Cottages
New Farm
Model Farm
Four Winds
Yewtree Farm
Little Bollington Prim. Sch.
Stamford Farm
The Gables
Strathyre
The Bungalow
Arthill Farm
Reddy Lane Cottage
Old Chapel House
Arthill Heath Farm
Newfield Covert
Kennels
Agden Brook
Hillcroft
Ivy Lodge
Bollington Hall Farm
Bollington Mill
Ash Farm
Aqueduct
Sewage Works
Sewage Works Cottage
Bollin Cottages
Yewtree Farm
Brickkiln Nursery Wood
North Park
Forest Edge
Reservoir (covered)
Golf Course
Heath Mount
Hulse Heath Farm
Hill Mount
Maltkiln Cottages
Bucklow Hill Farm
Burnthouses
Depot
Brook Lodge
Mere
THE CIRCUS
72
73
74
75
83
84
85
86
87
G H J K L M
1 2 3 4 5 6 7 8 9

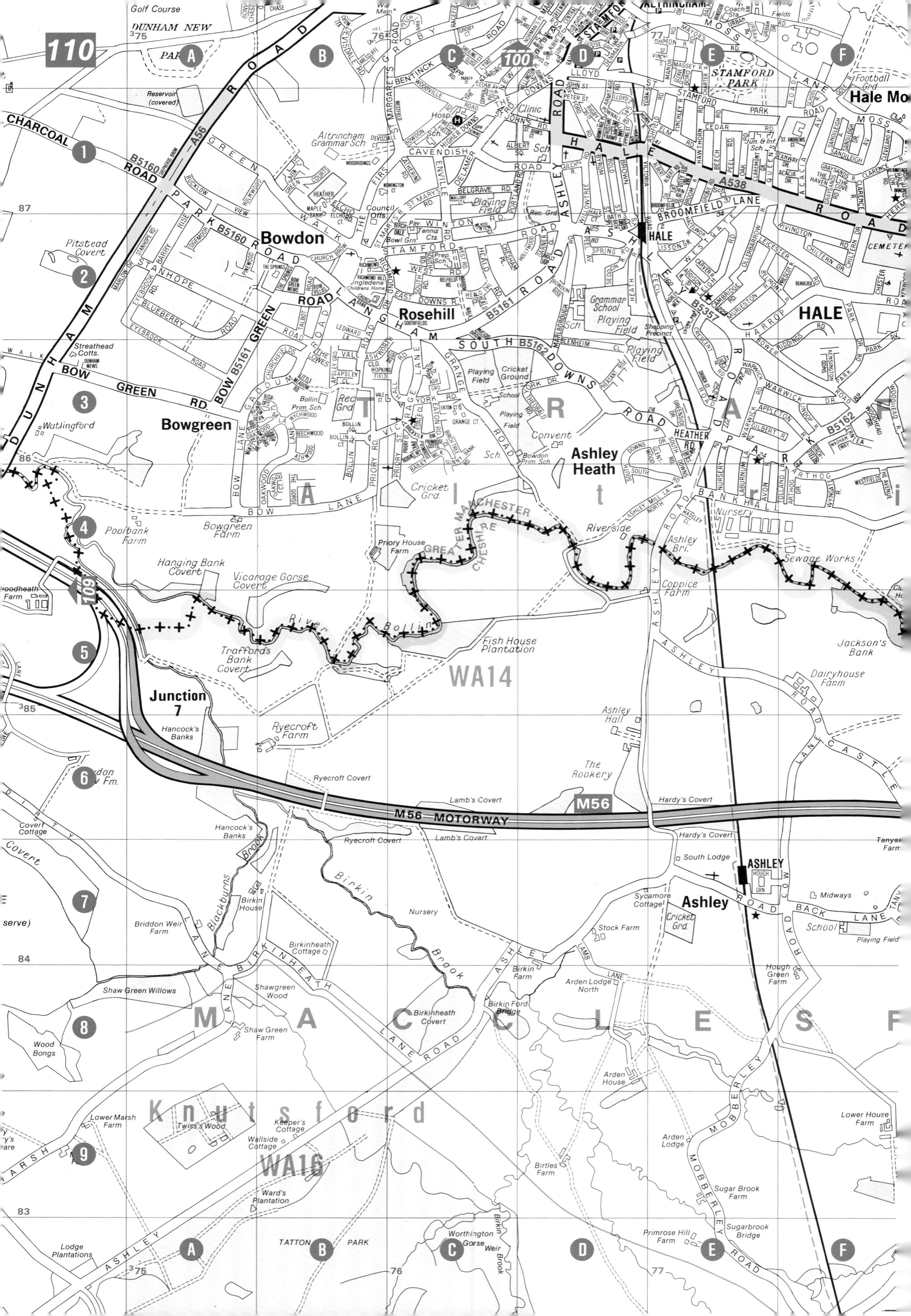
110
100
109
A
B
C
D
E
F
1
2
3
4
5
6
7
8
9
87
86
385
84
83
375
76
77
Golf Course
DUNHAM NEW PARK
DUNHAM ROAD
A56
Reservoir (covered)
CHARCOAL ROAD
B5160
Pitstead Covert
Streathead Cotts.
BOW GREEN RD.
Watlingford
Bowdon
Rosehill
Bowgreen
Altrincham Grammar Sch
Council Offs.
Clinic
Hosp.
STAMFORD PARK
Hale Moss
HALE
Ashley Heath
Grammar School
Playing Field
Cricket Ground
Convent
Bowdon Prim. Sch.
A538
B5161
B5162
B5357
CEMETERY
Poolbank Farm
Bowgreen Farm
Hanging Bank Covert
Vicarage Gorse Covert
Priory House Farm
GREATER MANCHESTER
CHESHIRE
River Bollin
Riverside
Ashley Bri.
Coppice Farm
Sewage Works
Jackson's Bank
Dairyhouse Farm
Trafford's Bank Covert
Fish House Plantation
WA14
Junction 7
Hancock's Banks
Ryecroft Farm
Ryecroft Covert
Lamb's Covert
Hardy's Covert
M56 MOTORWAY
M56
Ashley Hall
The Rookery
South Lodge
ASHLEY
Ashley
Sycamore Cottage
Midways
School
Playing Field
Stock Farm
Covert Cottage
Birkin House
Briddon Weir Farm
Blackburns Brook
Birkin Brook
Birkinheath Cottage
Nursery
Birkin Farm
Arden Lodge North
Birkin Ford Bridge
Shawgreen Wood
Shaw Green Willows
Shaw Green Farm
Birkinheath Covert
Wood Bongs
MACCLESFIELD
Knutsford
WA16
Lower Marsh Farm
Twiss's Wood
Keeper's Cottage
Wallside Cottage
Ward's Plantation
Arden House
Arden Lodge
Birtles Farm
Lower House Farm
Sugar Brook Farm
Sugarbrook Bridge
Primrose Hill Farm
Hough Green Farm
MOBBERLEY ROAD
ASHLEY ROAD
Lodge Plantations
TATTON PARK
Worthington Gorse
Weir
Birkin Brook

111
101
112
Timperley Brook
Delahays Farm
Holly Tree Farm
Green Lane High Sch
GROVE PARK
Manchester Playing Field
M23
Baguley Hospital
Newall Green High Sch.
Well Green
Ash Farm
Clay Ho.
Roaring Gate Farm
Butteryhouse Farm
Davenport Green
Davenport Hall
Junction 5
Isolation Hospital
Playing Field
Oakland Ct.
Clinic
Halemount (Club Ho.)
Halebarns
Ringway Golf Course
Davenportgreen Wood
Playing Fields
F O R D
n c h a m
Flaxhigh Covert
Cricket Grd.
Pav.
Elmridge Prim. Sch.
WA15
Golf Hale Course
Tomfield Bank
Bently Bank
Junction 6
M56
Remote Pier
Passenger Subway (Under Construction) Open Spring
Transit Sheds
Cargo Cen.
Ringway
Hale Golf Course
Jackson's Bank
River Bollin
M56 MOTORWAY
Oak Fm.
Recn. Grnd.
Hanger
Lane End Cottage
Halebank
Yewtree Ho.
Broadoak Cottages
MANCHESTER
Little Thorns Green Farm
Back Lane Farm
Thorns Green
Higher Thornsgreen Farm
Sunbank Wood
GREATER MANCHESTER
CHESHIRE
Ashlar
Chapel House Farm
Hunters Close
Mill Wood
Castle Mill Bridge
Cotteril Clough
I E L D
Ecclesfield Wood
Brickhill Wood
Hillside
Top Field
Castlehill Farm
Castle Hill
Well Wood
Middle House
Higherhouse Farm
Meadow Cott
Meadowlands
Castlehill Farm
Double Wood
Round Covert
Oversley Ford Bridge Works
WILMSLOW RD.
ALTRINCHAM RD.
WA16
Blackshaw Heys Farm
Woodend
A538
A5144
HALE ROAD
WILMSLOW ROAD

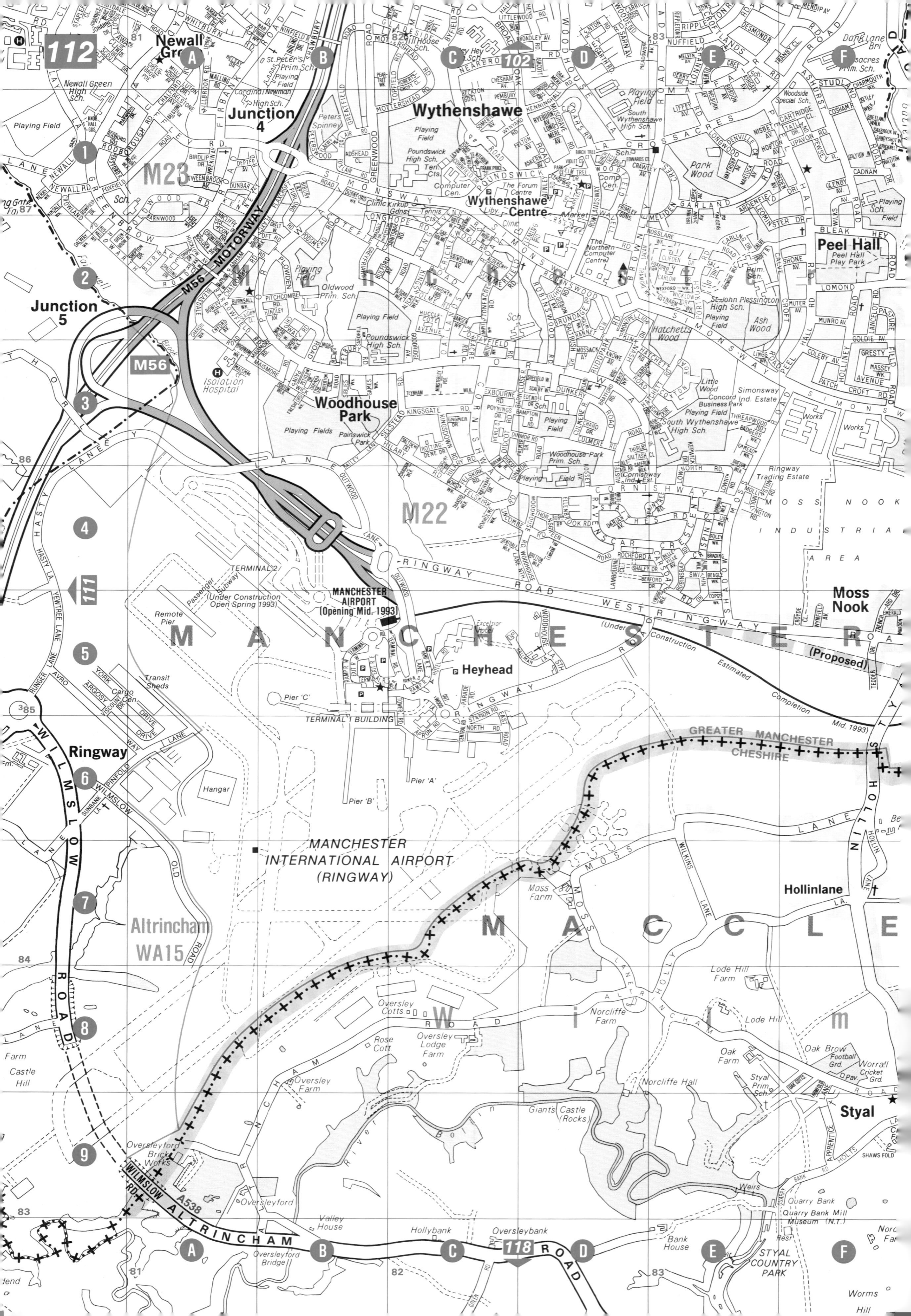

112
102
111
118
A
B
C
D
E
F
1
2
3
4
5
6
7
8
9
Newall Green
Wythenshawe
Junction 4
Junction 5
M23
M22
M56
M56 MOTORWAY
Wythenshawe Centre
Woodhouse Park
Peel Hall
Moss Nook
Heyhead
Ringway
Hollinlane
Styal
MANCHESTER
MACCLESFIELD
Wilmslow
Altrincham WA15
MANCHESTER AIRPORT (Opening Mid. 1993)
MANCHESTER INTERNATIONAL AIRPORT (RINGWAY)
TERMINAL 2
TERMINAL 1 BUILDING
Passenger Subway (Under Construction Open Spring 1993)
Remote Pier
Pier 'A'
Pier 'B'
Pier 'C'
Transit Sheds
Cargo Cen.
Hangar
Isolation Hospital
Newall Green High Sch.
Playing Field
Playing Fields
Peters Spinney
Poundswick High Sch.
Oldwood Prim. Sch.
Painswick Park
Park Wood
Ash Wood
Hatchetts Wood
Little Wood
Simonsway Ind. Estate
Concord Business Park
South Wythenshawe High Sch.
St. John Plessington High Sch.
The Northern Computer Centre
Computer Cen.
The Forum Centre
Woodhouse Park Prim. Sch.
Cornishway Ind. Est.
Ringway Trading Estate
MOSS NOOK INDUSTRIAL AREA
Peel Hall Play Park
Woodside Special Sch.
Excelsior Hotel
WEST RINGWAY ROAD (Under Construction Estimated Completion Mid. 1993)
(Proposed)
RINGWAY ROAD
SIMONSWAY
GREATER MANCHESTER
CHESHIRE
WILMSLOW ROAD
ALTRINCHAM ROAD
A538
MOSS LANE
HOLLIN LANE
HASTY LA.
YEWTREE LANE
RUNGER LANE
OUTWOOD LANE
Moss Farm
Lode Hill Farm
Lode Hill
Norcliffe Farm
Norcliffe Hall
Oversley Cotts
Oversley Lodge Farm
Rose Cott
Oversley Farm
Oversleyford Brick Works
Oversleyford
Oversleyford Bridge
Valley House
Hollybank
Oversleybank
Bank House
Giants Castle (Rocks)
River Bollin
Weirs
Oak Farm
Oak Brow
Football Grd.
Worrall Cricket Grd.
Pav.
Styal Prim. Sch.
Quarry Bank
Quarry Bank Mill Museum (N.T.)
STYAL COUNTRY PARK
Worms Hill
Farm
Castle Hill
81
82
83
84
85
86
87

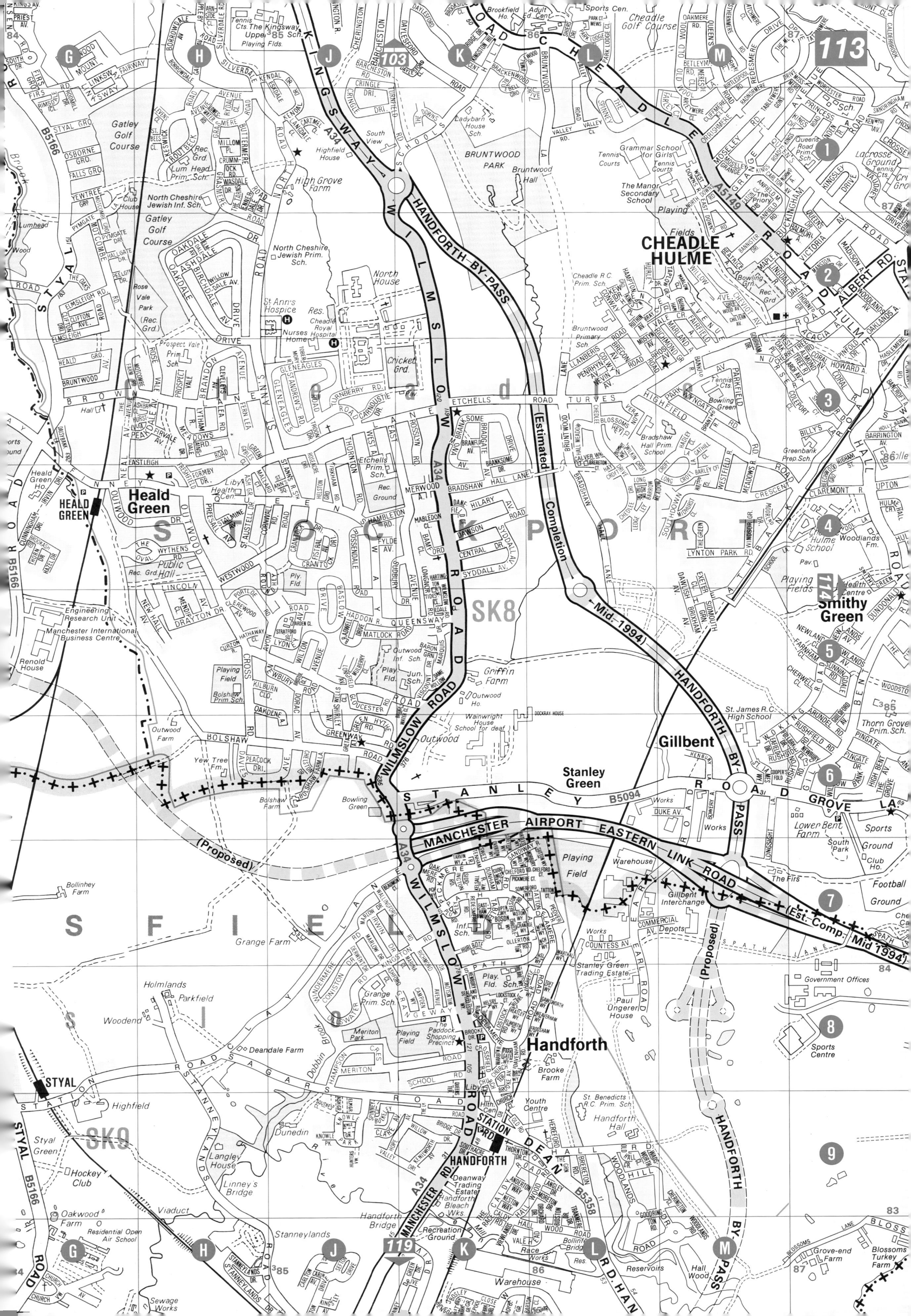
103
119
114
G
H
J
K
L
M
1
2
3
4
5
6
7
8
9
84
85
86
87
83
SK8
SK9
CHEADLE HULME
Heald Green
HEALD GREEN
Gillbent
Stanley Green
Smithy Green
Handforth
HANDFORTH
STYAL
S T O C K P O R T
Cheadle
S F I E L D
KINGSWAY
A34
WILMSLOW ROAD
HANDFORTH BY-PASS
(Estimated Completion Mid-1994)
MANCHESTER AIRPORT EASTERN LINK ROAD
(Est. Comp. Mid 1994)
(Proposed)
STANLEY ROAD
B5094
B5166
B5358
A5149
ETCHELLS ROAD
TURVES ROAD
BRADSHAW HALL LANE
STYAL ROAD
STATION ROAD
SAGARS ROAD
DEAN ROAD
MANCHESTER RD.
FINNEY LANE
BOLSHAW ROAD
GROVE LA.
SPATH LANE
EARL ROAD
HALL ROAD
BRUNTWOOD LA.
HULME HALL ROAD
ALBERT RD.
ACACIA AV.
Gatley Golf Course
Cheadle Golf Course
BRUNTWOOD PARK
Bruntwood Hall
North Cheshire Jewish Inf. Sch.
North Cheshire Jewish Prim. Sch.
St Ann's Hospice
Cheadle Royal Hospital
North House
High Grove Farm
Highfield House
South View
Ladybarn House Sch.
Grammar School for Girls
The Manor Secondary School
Cheadle R.C. Prim. Sch.
Bruntwood Primary Sch.
Bradshaw Hall Prim. School
Greenbank Prep. Sch.
Cheadle Hulme School
Woodlands Fm.
St. James R.C. High School
Thorn Grove Prim. Sch.
Engineering Research Unit
Manchester International Business Centre
Renold House
Outwood Farm
Yew Tree Fm.
Bolshaw Farm
Bowling Green
Griffin Farm
Outwood Ho.
Wainwright House School for deaf
Outwood
Gillbent Interchange
Stanley Green Trading Estate
Government Offices
Sports Centre
Paul Ungerer House
Grange Farm
Bollinhey Farm
Holmlands
Parkfield
Woodend
Deandale Farm
Highfield
Styal Green
Hockey Club
Oakwood Farm
Residential Open Air School
Langley House
Linney's Bridge
Viaduct
Stanneylands
Dunedin
Sewage Works
Meriton Park
Grange Prim. Sch.
The Paddock Shopping Precinct
Brooke Farm
Youth Centre
St. Benedicts R.C. Prim. Sch.
Handforth Hall
Deanway Trading Estate
Handforth Bleach Wks.
Handforth Bridge
Recreation Ground
Race Works
Bollin Bridge
Reservoirs
Hall Wood
Warehouse
Grove-end Farm
Blossoms Turkey Farm
Lower Bent Farm
Sports Ground
Football Ground
South Park
Club Ho.
The Firs
Works
Depots
Playing Field
Playing Fields
Lacrosse Ground
Etchells Prim. Sch.
Public Hall
Rose Vale Park
Prospect Vale Prim. Sch.
Lum Head Prim. Sch.
Tennis Cts.
Bolshaw Prim. Sch.
Outwood Inf. Sch.
Jun. Sch.

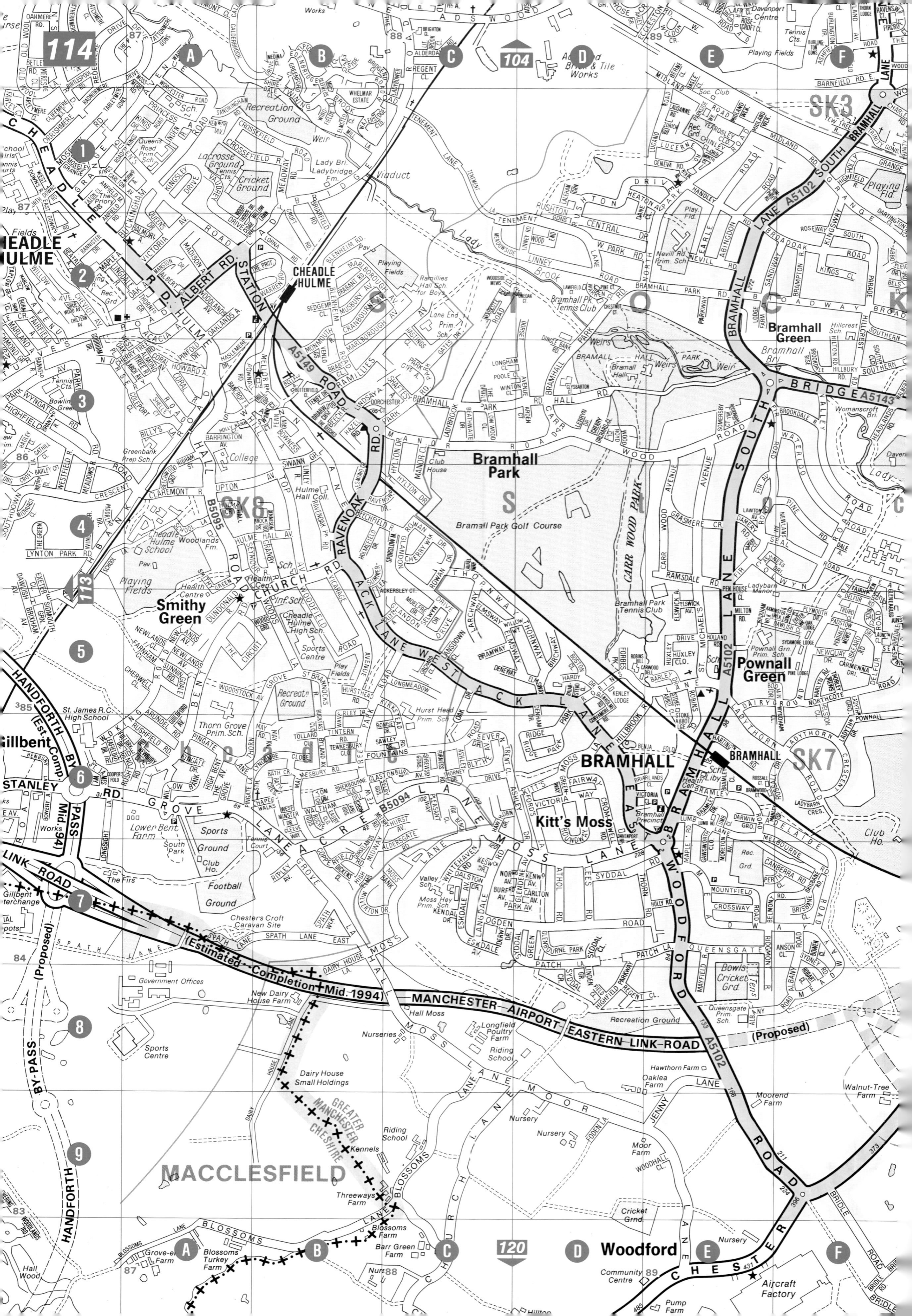

114
104
113
120
A
B
C
D
E
F
1
2
3
4
5
6
7
8
9
SK3
SK8
SK7
CHEADLE HULME
CHEADLE HULME
BRAMHALL
Bramhall Park
Bramhall Green
Pownall Green
Smithy Green
Kitt's Moss
Gilbent
Woodford
MACCLESFIELD
Recreation Ground
Lacrosse Ground
Cricket Ground
Playing Fields
Viaduct
Lady Bri. Ladybridge Fm.
Ramillies Hall Sch for Boys
Lane End Prim. Sch.
Bramhall Pk Tennis Club
Bramhall Hall
Weirs
Bramall Park Golf Course
CARR WOOD PARK
Bramhall Park Tennis Club
Cheadle Hulme School
Cheadle Hulme High Sch.
Hulme Hall Coll.
Sports Centre
Thorn Grove Prim. Sch.
St. James R.C. High School
Lower Bent Farm
Sports Ground
Football Ground
Chesters Croft Caravan Site
Government Offices
New Dairy House Farm
Hall Moss
Longfield Poultry Farm
Riding School
Dairy House Small Holdings
Sports Centre
Recreation Ground
Queensgate Prim. Sch.
Bowls Cricket Grd
Hawthorn Farm
Oaklea Farm
Moorend Farm
Walnut-Tree Farm
Moor Farm
Nursery
Kennels
Threeways Farm
Blossoms Farm
Barr Green Farm
Grove-end Farm
Blossoms Turkey Farm
Hall Wood
Cricket Grnd
Community Centre
Aircraft Factory
Pump Farm
GREATER MANCHESTER
CHESHIRE
MANCHESTER AIRPORT EASTERN LINK ROAD
(Estimated Completion Mid. 1994)
(Proposed)
HANDFORTH BY-PASS
LINK ROAD
STATION ROAD
A5149
A5102
A5143
B5094
B5095
BRAMHALL LANE SOUTH
BRIDGE LANE
WOODFORD ROAD
CHESTER ROAD
MOSS LANE
ACRE LANE
ACK LANE EAST
ACK LANE WEST
RAVENOAK RD.
HULME HALL RD.
ALBERT RD.
CHURCH RD.
CARR WOOD
MOOR LANE
CHURCH LANE
BLOSSOMS LANE
SPATH LANE
GROVE LANE
STANLEY RD.

115
Woodsmoor
Woods Moor
Mirrlees Golf Course
Stepping Hill
Stepping Hill Hospital
105
Hazel Grove
HAZEL GROVE
Torkington
Torkington Park
Stepping Hill Link (Proposed)
Offerton
A627
Torkington Rd.
Buxton Road
A6
London Road
Macclesfield Road
A523
Jacksons Lane
Dean Lane
A5143
Norbury Moor
Norbury Brook
A6(M) Motorway
116
Hazel Grove Golf Course
Hazel Grove High Sch. Sports Centre
Great Reddish Wood
Bramhall High Sch. & Sports Centre
Further Dairyground
Millhill Farm
Sewage Works
Millbank
Towers Farm
Long Plantation
Black Hole
Serpentine Wood
Park Pit Plantation
Barlowfold
North Road
Poynton Lake
Boat House
Park House Fm.
Bramhall Golf Course
GREATER MANCHESTER
CHESHIRE
MACCLESFIELD
Poynton Park
Fish Pond
Towers Yard Farm
Rabbit Bank Farm
Round Nursery
Lady's Wood
Petre Bank
Poynton
POYNTON
Chester Road
A5149
Hazelbadge Bridge
SK12
Cricket Ground
South Park Drive
Wigwam Wood
Long Furrow
Lostockhall Farm
Upper Swineseye
(Proposed)
Hockley
Midway
121
Poynton County High School
Lynden
G
H
J
K
L
M
1
2
3
4
5
6
7
8
9
90
91
92
93
83
84
385
86
87

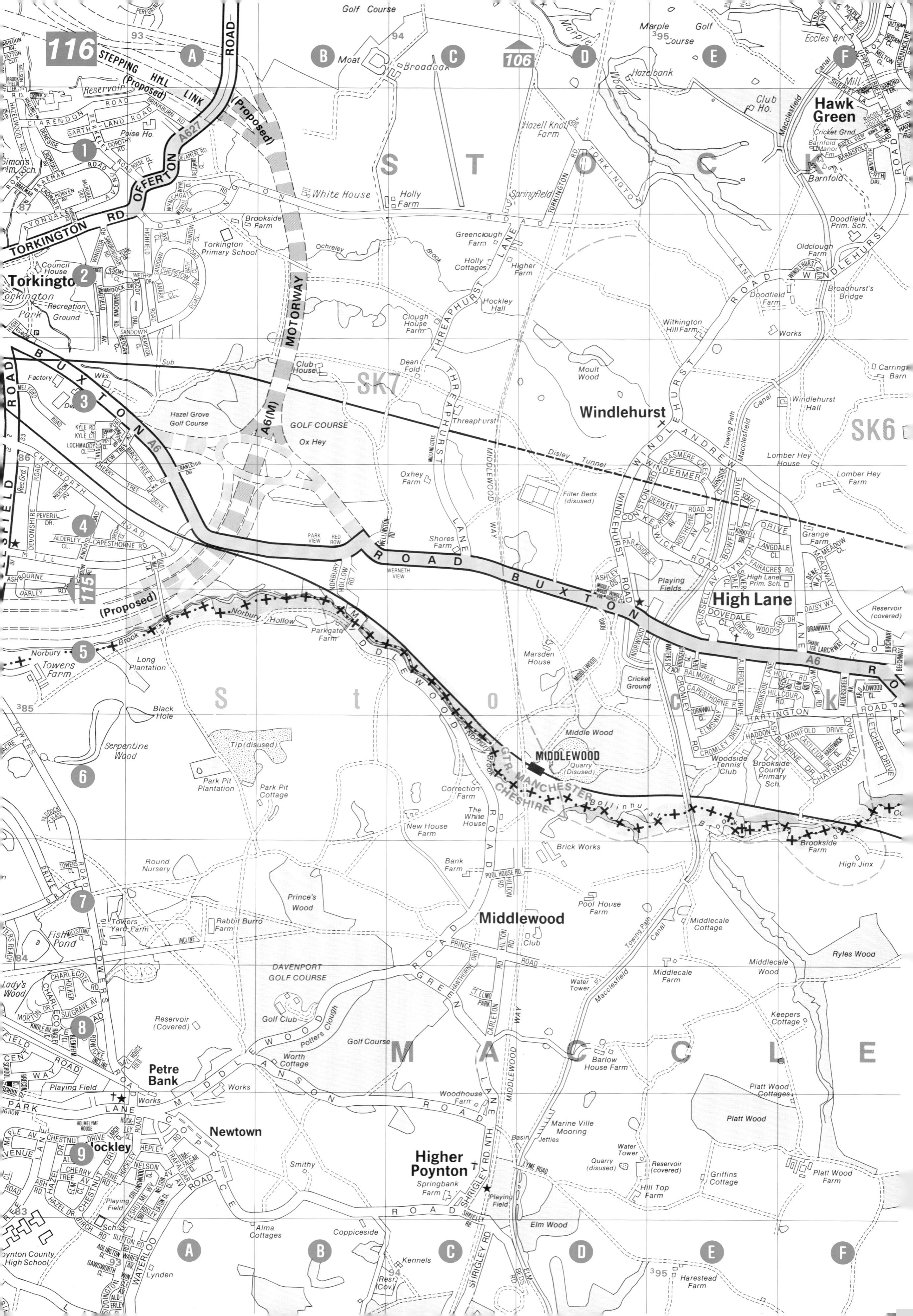

116
A
B
C
D
E
F
106
115
1
2
3
4
5
6
7
8
9
STEPPING HILL LINK (Proposed)
(Proposed)
OFFERTON ROAD
A627
TORKINGTON RD
Reservoir
Poise Ho.
Torkington
Torkington Park
Recreation Ground
Council House
Torkington Primary School
Brookside Farm
White House
Holly Farm
Moat
Broadoak
Golf Course
Marple Golf Course
Hazelbank
Club Ho.
Hazell Knoll Farm
Springfield
TORKINGTON LANE
Hawk Green
Cricket Grnd
Barnfold Manor Fm
Barnfold
Doodfield Prim. Sch.
Oldclough Farm
WINDLEHURST ROAD
Broadhurst's Bridge
Doodfield Farm
Withington Hill Farm
Works
Carrington Barn
Windlehurst Hall
Lomber Hey House
Lomber Hey Farm
Grange Farm
STOCK
SK7
SK6
MOTORWAY
A6(M)
Greenclough Farm
Holly Cottages
Higher Farm
Hockley Hall
Clough House Farm
Dean Fold
Threaphurst
THREAPHURST LANE
Ochreley
Club House
Moult Wood
Windlehurst
Disley Tunnel
Filter Beds (disused)
Oxhey Farm
Shores Farm
GOLF COURSE
Ox Hey
Hazel Grove Golf Course
BUXTON ROAD
A6
Factory
Wks.
Sub.
High Lane
High Lane Prim. Sch.
Playing Fields
Reservoir (covered)
Cricket Ground
Marsden House
Norbury Hollow
Parkgate Farm
Norbury
Towers Farm
Long Plantation
Black Hole
Serpentine Wood
Tip (disused)
Park Pit Plantation
Park Pit Cottage
Stockport
MIDDLEWOOD
Middle Wood
Quarry (Disused)
GTR. MANCHESTER
CHESHIRE
Bollinhurst Brook
Correction Farm
The White House
New House Farm
Brick Works
Brookside Farm
High Jinx
Woodside Tennis Club
Brookside County Primary Sch.
Round Nursery
Bank Farm
Prince's Wood
Pool House Farm
Middlewood
Middlecale Cottage
Rabbit Burrow Farm
Towers Yard Farm
Fish Pond
INCLINE
DAVENPORT GOLF COURSE
Golf Club
Golf Course
Potters Clough
Worth Cottage
Middlecale Wood
Middlecale Farm
Ryles Wood
Water Tower
Keepers Cottage
Macclesfield Canal
Towing Path
Lady's Wood
Reservoir (Covered)
MACCLESFIELD
Barlow House Farm
Platt Wood Cottages
Platt Wood
Petre Bank
Playing Field
Works
MIDDLEWOOD WAY
Woodhouse Farm
Newtown
Hockley
Marine Ville Mooring
Basin
Jetties
Quarry (disused)
Reservoir (covered)
Higher Poynton
Springbank Farm
Smithy
Playing Field
Hill Top Farm
Griffins Cottage
Platt Wood Farm
Elm Wood
Alma Cottages
Coppiceside
Kennels
Rest (Cov.)
Harestead Farm
Poynton County High School
Lynden
SHRIGLEY RD
PARK LANE
MIDDLEWOOD ROAD
POYNTON ROAD

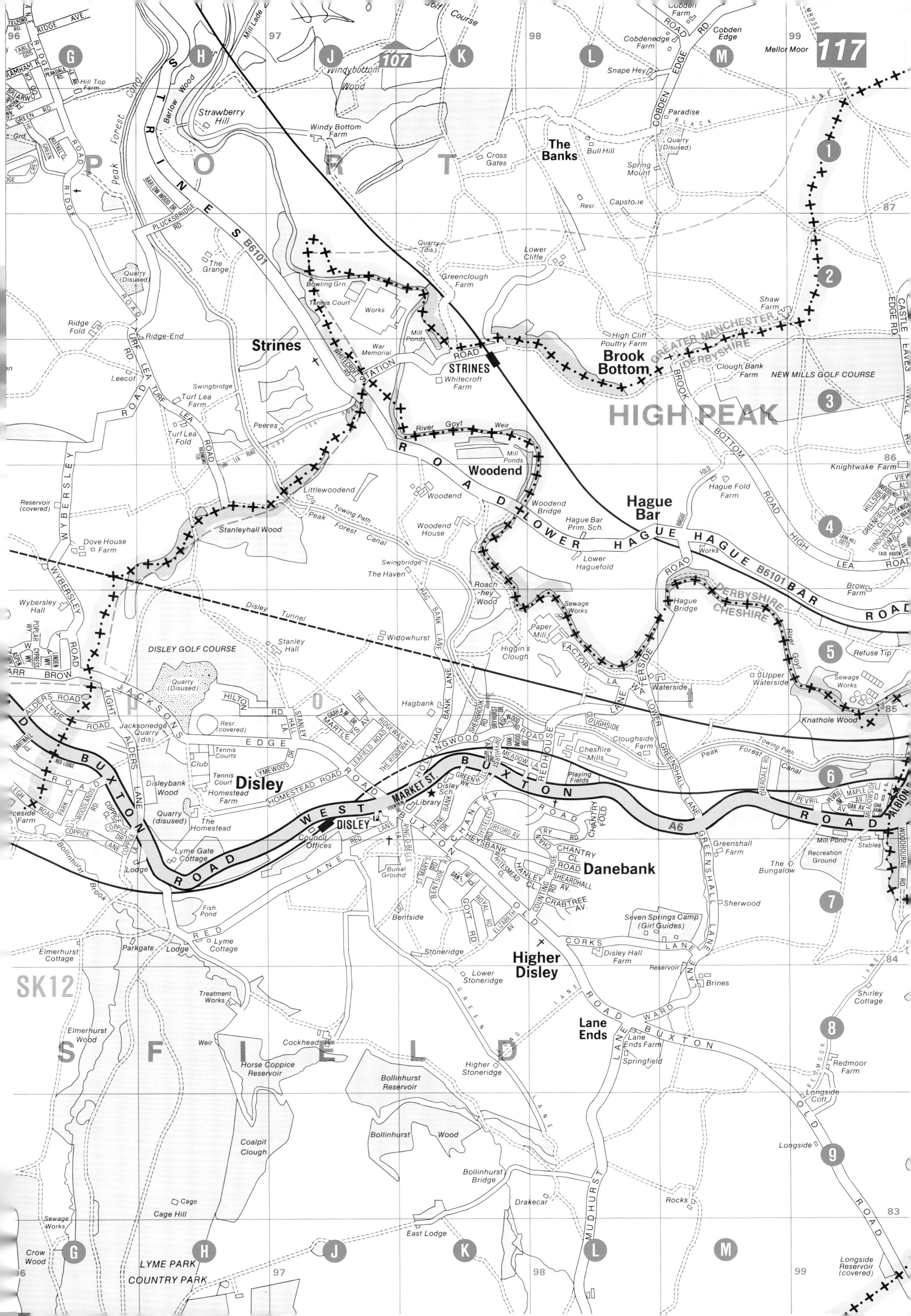

117
107
Strines
Disley
Woodend
Brook Bottom
Hague Bar
The Banks
Danebank
Higher Disley
Lane Ends
HIGH PEAK
DISLEY GOLF COURSE
NEW MILLS GOLF COURSE
LYME PARK COUNTRY PARK
SK12
GREATER MANCHESTER
DERBYSHIRE
CHESHIRE
Strawberry Hill
Windy Bottom Farm
Windybottom Wood
Stanleyhall Wood
Littlewoodend
Peak Forest Canal
Disley Tunnel
Bollinhurst Reservoir
Horse Coppice Reservoir
Bollinhurst Wood
Elmerhurst Wood
Cage Hill
Longside Reservoir (covered)
A6
B6101

112
A
B
C
D
E
F
1
2
3
4
5
6
7
8
9
81
82
83
Oversleyford Brick Works
WILMSLOW RD.
ALTRINCHAM RD
A538
Oversleyford
Valley House
Hollybank
Oversleybank
Oversleyford Bridge
Bank House
Weirs
Weir
Quarry Bank
Quarry Bank Mill Museum (N.T.)
Resr
STYAL COUNTRY PARK
Norcliff Farm
Worms Hill
Sand Pit
Willow Ground Wood
Burned Hey Wood
Shaws Fold
Holts
Beehive Farm
Hooksbank Wood
Bollinhouse Farm
oodend
Shadygrove
DOOLEYS LA
Morley
MORLEY GREEN RD
Nansmoss
NANSMOSS LA
Cash's Farm
Stamford Lodge
Wood Farm
Burleyhurst Wood
Mossbrow
School
Nursery
Jim Evison Memorial Rec. Grd.
Rugby Football Grd.
Morley Green
Club
CHAPEL COTTAGES
MOBBERLEY RD
SANDY LA
Oak Farm
Ash Tree Farm
Pownall Hall Prep. Sch.
Pownall Hall
Pownall Park
Carr Wood
WA16
SK9
W i l m
M A C C L E S F I E L D
Platt Cottage
Burleyhurst Bridge
Burleyhurst Farm
Mossway Cott
ECCUPS LANE
MOBBERLEY LANE
GREAVES LA
LINDOW MOSS
Bowers Folly
LINDOW COMMON
Gorsey Bank Prim. Sch.
The Carnival Field Football Grd
Blakeley Farm
BLAKELEY LA
Boundary Lodge
Lindow Moss
NEWGATE
Black Lake
RACECOURSE RD
Sunnyside Farm
BURLEYHURST LA
Saltersley Farm
Newgate Ho
ROTHERWOOD RD
Lindow Ho.
LINDOW LANE
WESTWARD RD
CAMBRIDGE AV
WINDSOR AV
Benkeyhurst Farm
Moat
Hollingee
Maple Farm
STRAWBERRY LANE
WINGFIELD AVENUE
WING-FIELD DR.
THE ELMS
WOODACRES CT.
NORTHWARD RD
BUCKINGHAM RD
CLIFFORD RD
BOURNE
CHAPEL LA
Fulshaw C. of E. Sch.
SOUTH OAK LA
NURSERY LA
CHURCH WLK
Caravan Park
Sugar Brook
Coppock House Farm
Lindow Farm Caravan Site
BURFORD CRES
ARLINGTON CR.
ARLINGTON WAY
Yew Tree Farm
Rec. Grd.
GRAVEYARD LA
Graveyard Farm
Oakbank Farm
Barlow House Farm
Lindow Farm
MOOR LANE
Lea Farm
Kennels
SPRINGFIELD DR.
Hetlee Farm
ASHDENE RD
Ashdene Cty. Jun. Sch.
Play Fld.
K n u t s f o r d
Moss Farm
Mount Pleasant Farm
Ivy House Farm
LEIGH RD
LINDOW FOLD DR
CUMBER LANE
THE CIRCUIT
MOORWAY
B5086
Sunnybank Farm
MEADOW CL.
MEADOW WAY
Yewtree Farm
Moss Mount Farm
Five Acres
Nursery
The Yew
CLAY LANE
High Lea
Paddock Cottage
PADDOCKHILL LANE
MOSS LA
DAVENPORT AV
VILLA
STOCKTON RD
FULSHAW
COBBETT'S WAY
Stockton Farm
CHESHAM RD
WELTON
Margis
Paddockhill Farm
Paddockhill
Lindow C.P. Sch.
Chorley Cricket Grd.
Pav.
Hall
Football Grd.
Smithy
Club Ho.
Davenport Green
Alderley Edge Golf Course
Clayhouse Farm
CLAY LANE
Poultry House
Clay Lane Farm
Blue Ball
Gore Lane Farm
Heathside
Shenston Cottage
Nursery
Cottage Farm
School
Kennels
KNUTSFORD ROAD
BROOK LA
BROOKSIDE TER
DINGLE AV
Brookfield Bridge
Cobbles
Moss Meadow Farm
Yewtree Farm
Hillfield Farm
Brownhouse
Edgeview Farm
GORE LANE
BESWICKS LA
Row-of-Trees
A d l e r l e y
CARR LA
Brook House
Sunninghey
Chesham Knoll
B5085
BY-PASS
Kelsall House
Gorse House
Davenport House
Whitehall Brook
EDGE VIEW
Smithy
PADDOCK HILL
Brookside
KNUTSFORD RD
B5085
Pear Tree Farm
Lindow End
STANLEY TER
SK9
Sewage Works
Carr Bank Farm
Whim
Lindow End Farm
FODEN LANE
Foden House
Common Carr Farm
ALDERLEY EDGE
ALDFORD PL
WILTON CRES
EATON
Beech Mount
Mobberley Brook
NOAHS ARK LANE
Tall Trees
Pownall House Farm
WARFORD LA
Pownallbrow (Club Ho.)
WILMSLOW GOLF COURSE
The Ryleys Prep.
RYLEYS LA
CHELFORD RD
CHORLEY
WINDERMERE

119
113
120
HANDFORTH
Styal Green
Langley House
Linney's Bridge
Hockey Club
Oakwood Farm
Residential Open Air School
Viaduct
Stanneylands
River Dean
Handforth Bridge
Handforth Bleach Wks.
Recreation Ground
Race Works
Bollinfee Bridge
Res.
Reservoirs
Hall Wood
Grove-end Farm
Blossoms Turkey Farm
SK7
(Proposed)
Warehouse
H.M. PRISON
Sewage Works
Lacey Green
Finney Green
Deadman's Clough
Lacey Green Prim. Sch.
Sewage Works
Recreation Gnd.
Twinnies Bridge
Colshaw Co. Prim. Sch.
Playing Fields
Grammar Sch.
Cemetery
Dean Row Jun. Sch.
Oaklands Inf. Sch.
Playing Fields
HANDFORTH BY-PASS
B5358 RD.
HANDFORTH ROAD
DEAN ROW
B5166
River Bollin
THE CARRS
Hill Top
Dean Row
Wilmslow Park
Dean Bank
Upton House
WOODFORD RD.
A5102
WILMSLOW
Hawthorn Hall
Wilmslow Bridge
Mill Lade
River Bollin
Weir
Bollin Hall
Leisure Centre
Little Lindow
WATER LA.
STATION RD.
MACCLESFIELD A538 ROAD
ADLINGTON
Vardon Bridge
Varden House Farm
The Hollies Farm
River Bollin
Playing Fields
Harefield High Sch.
Council Offs
Styal Line Junc.
High Sch.
PRESTBURY ROAD LINK (Proposed)
PRESTBURY A538 ROAD
Hough Hall Farm
Bowling Green
Chorlton Ho.
Harefield Farm
Fulshaw Hall
Fulshaw Park
Harefield
Lloyd House
Whitehall Bridge
White Hall
WILMSLOW BY-PASS
College Flats
HARDEN PARK
Brynwood
Harden Park
Harden Park Playing Fields
Tennis Cts.
Jenny Hayes
Whitehall Brook
Rufford
Bel Air
Elmgrove
INSET
Belmont
Moss Farm
ALDERLEY EDGE
Endsleigh
Mnt. Carmel School
A34 ROAD
Chesham Knoll
Sunninghey
Oakhurst
ALDERLEY EDGE BY-PASS (Proposed)
Alderley Edge Prim. Sch.
War Mem.
Beech Mount
The Ryley's Prep. Sch.
Burnside
Chorley Hall
Moat
Rustic Cott.
RYLEYS LA. A535
CHELFORD RD.
WILMSLOW
Hosp.
Liby.
Bowling Grn.
Hall
MACCLESFIELD
Cricket & Sports Ground
MOTTRAM
Swiss Villa
The Hollies
The Cedars
The Gables
Rockwood
Woodbrook
Firwood
Fernhill
Springfield
St. Hilary's Sch.
SK9
MACCLESFIELD B5087 ROAD
Greylands
The Hurst
The Skerries
Armstrong Farm
Oatlands
The Whins
Broomfield House
The Quinta
Elmbank
CONGLETON RD.
LONDON RD.
WHITEBARN ROAD
White Barn Farm
Fields Farm
Alderley Edge
INSET

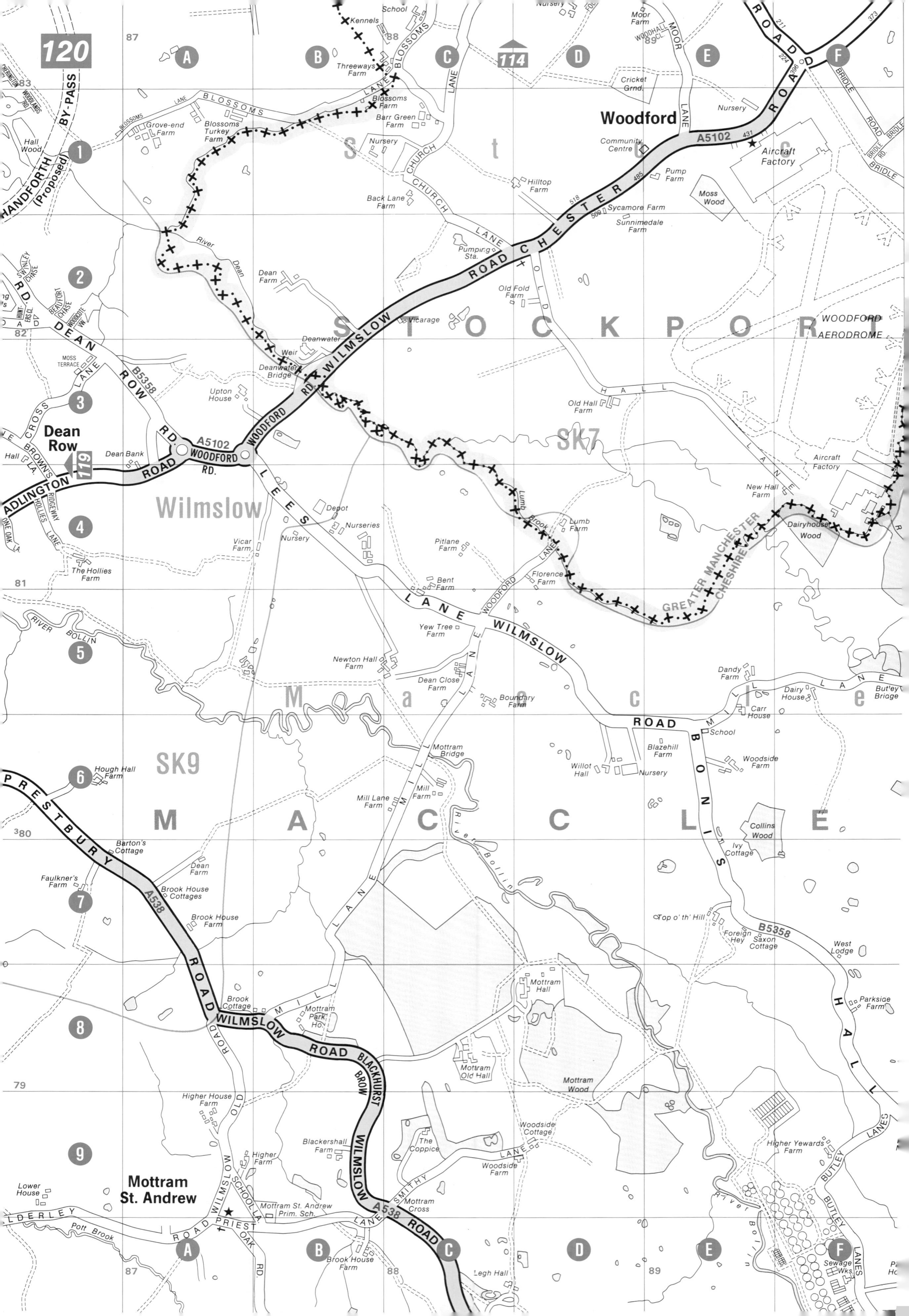
Woodford
Dean Row
Wilmslow
Mottram St. Andrew
WOODFORD AERODROME
Aircraft Factory
STOCKPORT
MACCLESFIELD
SK7
SK9
114
119
HANDFORTH BY-PASS (Proposed)
A5102
A538
B5358
CHESTER ROAD
WILMSLOW ROAD
WOODFORD ROAD
ADLINGTON ROAD
DEAN ROW RD.
PRESTBURY ROAD
LEES LANE
WILMSLOW ROAD
BONIS HALL
MILL LANE
BLOSSOMS LANE
CHURCH LANE
OLD HALL LANE
BLACKHURST BROW
SMITHY LANE
PRIEST LANE
ALDERLEY ROAD
BUTLEY LANES
MOOR LANE
BRIDLE ROAD
GREATER MANCHESTER
CHESHIRE
River Dean
Lumb Brook
River Bollin
Pott Brook
Kennels
School
Threeways Farm
Blossoms Farm
Barr Green Farm
Nursery
Grove-end Farm
Blossoms Turkey Farm
Hall Wood
Moor Farm
Cricket Grnd.
Community Centre
Pump Farm
Moss Wood
Hilltop Farm
Back Lane Farm
Sycamore Farm
Sunnimedale Farm
Pumping Sta.
Old Fold Farm
Dean Farm
Vicarage
Deanwater
Weir
Deanwater Bridge
Upton House
Dean Bank
Old Hall Farm
New Hall Farm
Dairyhouse Wood
Depot
Nurseries
Vicar Farm
The Hollies Farm
Pitlane Farm
Lumb Farm
Florence Farm
Bent Farm
Yew Tree Farm
Newton Hall Farm
Dean Close Farm
Boundary Farm
Dandy Farm
Dairy House
Butley Bridge
Carr House
Blazehill Farm
Willot Hall
Woodside Farm
Mottram Bridge
Hough Hall Farm
Mill Farm
Mill Lane Farm
Collins Wood
Ivy Cottage
Barton's Cottage
Dean Farm
Faulkner's Farm
Brook House Cottages
Brook House Farm
Top o' th' Hill
Foreign Hey
Saxon Cottage
West Lodge
Parkside Farm
Mottram Hall
Brook Cottage
Mottram Park Ho.
Mottram Old Hall
Mottram Wood
Higher House Farm
Woodside Cottage
The Coppice
Blackershall Farm
Higher Farm
Higher Yewards Farm
Lower House
Mottram St. Andrew Prim. Sch.
Mottram Cross
Brook House Farm
Legh Hall
Sewage Wks.

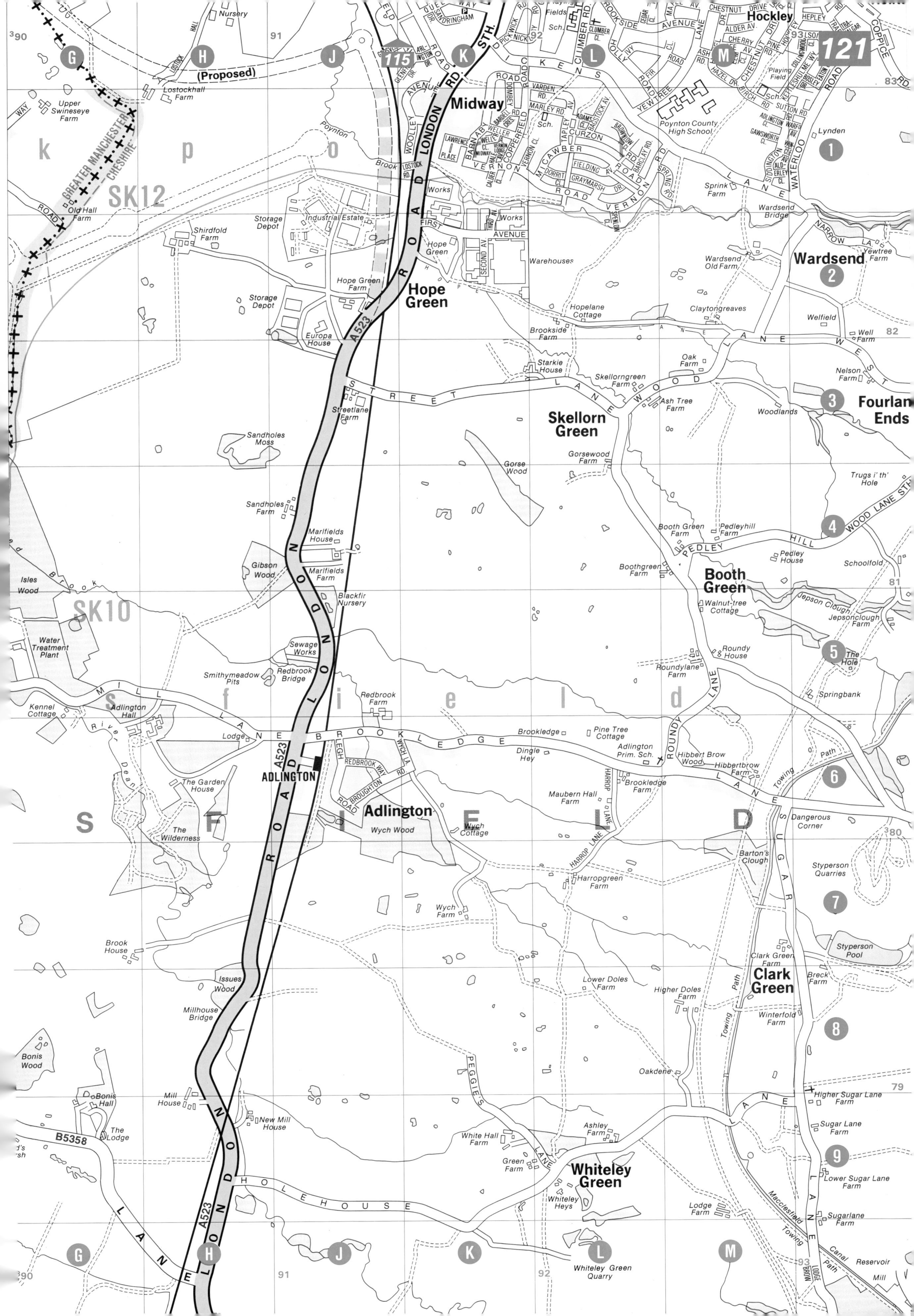
121
Hockley
Midway
Hope Green
Wardsend
Fourlane Ends
Skellorn Green
Booth Green
Adlington
Clark Green
Whiteley Green
ADLINGTON
SK12
SK10
A523
B5358
LONDON ROAD
Poynton County High School
Lostockhall Farm
Upper Swineseye Farm
Old Hall Farm
Shirdfold Farm
Sandholes Moss
Gibson Wood
Isles Wood
Water Treatment Plant
Adlington Hall
Kennel Cottage
The Garden House
The Wilderness
Brook House
Issues Wood
Millhouse Bridge
Bonis Wood
Bonis Hall
The Lodge
Mill House
New Mill House
White Hall Farm
Ashley Farm
Green Farm
Whiteley Heys
Whiteley Green Quarry
Lodge Farm
Lower Sugar Lane Farm
Sugarlane Farm
Higher Sugar Lane Farm
Sugar Lane Farm
Winterfold Farm
Breck Farm
Styperson Pool
Styperson Quarries
Dangerous Corner
Barton's Clough
Oakdene
Higher Doles Farm
Lower Doles Farm
Harropgreen Farm
Wych Farm
Wych Cottage
Maubern Hall Farm
Brookledge Farm
Hibbertbrow Farm
Hibbert Brow Wood
Adlington Prim. Sch.
Pine Tree Cottage
Dingle Hey
Redbrook Farm
Roundylane Farm
Roundy House
Springbank
The Hole
Jepsonclough Farm
Jepson Clough
Walnut-tree Cottage
Boothgreen Farm
Booth Green Farm
Pedleyhill Farm
Pedley House
Schoolfold
Trugs i' th' Hole
Gorsewood Farm
Gorse Wood
Ash Tree Farm
Skellorngreen Farm
Starkie House
Oak Farm
Woodlands
Nelson Farm
Well Farm
Welfield
Claytongreaves
Wardsend Old Farm
Yewtree Farm
Wardsend Bridge
Sprink Farm
Lynden
Hopelane Cottage
Brookside Farm
Warehouses
Works
Industrial Estate
Storage Depot
Hope Green Farm
Europa House
Streetlane Farm
Sandholes Farm
Marlfields House
Marlfields Farm
Blackfir Nursery
Sewage Works
Smithymeadow Pits
Redbrook Bridge
Wych Wood
Reservoir
Mill
Nursery
(Proposed)
Playing Field
Macclesfield Canal
Towing Path
GREATER MANCHESTER
CHESHIRE
S F I E L D
115

122
POSTCODE MAP
PR4
Leyland
Wheelton
Darwen
BB3
BB4
Haslingden
PR5
L A N C A S H I R E
Euxton
PR6
Edenfield
Cadshaw
Stubbins
Ramsbottom
Eccleston
Chorley
PR7
BL7
Edgworth
Hazelhurst
BL8
L40
Coppull
Lever Park
Egerton
Bromley Cross
Greenmount
Wrightington Bar
Adlington
Tottington
Burrs
16
17
18
19
20
21
22
23
24
25
WN6
Blackrod
Horwich
BL6
Doffcocker
BL1
Halliwell
Bradshaw
BL2
Ainsworth
BURY
Parbold
WN8
Appley Bridge
Standish
Shevington
Red Rock
Aspull
Lostock
BOLTON
Little Lever
Black Lane
32
33
34
35
36
37
38
39
40
41
BL3
M26
Marsh Green
WN1
Haigh Hall Country Park
WIGAN
Westhoughton
Lever Edge
Radcliffe
Skelmersdale
WN8
Orrell
Farnworth
BL4
Whitefield
Up-Holland
WN5
Pemberton
Ince-in-Makerfield
Hindley
BL5
Over Hulton
Park Lane
Kearsley
Atherton
Walkden
WN2
50
51
WN3
52
53
54
55
56
57
58
59
Platt Bridge
M29
M28
Pendlebury
Longshaw
Westleigh
Tyldesley
Rainford
Abram
Bickershaw
Worsley
Swinton
M27
Billinge
Astley
Boothstown
Dales Brow
M6
WN4
ASHTON-IN-MAKERFIELD
Firs Lane
LEIGH
Garswood
WN7
SALFORD
M602
WA11
68
69
70
71
72
73
74
75
76
77
Moss Bank
Golborne
ECCLES
Weaste
Haydock
Glazebury
M17
Racecourse
WA12
M30
Safari Park
WA10
Kenyon
Davyhulme
Newton-le-Willows
STRETFORD
St. Helens
INSET Page 72
Culcheth
86
Irlam
87
M31
88
89
M32
MERSEYSIDE
WA3
L34
URMSTON
WA9
Croft
Prescot
Cadishead
Carrington
SALE
Burtonwood
L35
WA2
Partington
M33
WA5
98
99
100
101
WARRINGTON
WA1
ALTRINCHAM
WA14
WA8
Lymm
Oughtrington
WA15
WA13
Bowden
Hale
Widnes
108
109
110
111
WA6
High Legh
Appleton Thorn
Rostherne
Ashley
WA4
Tatton Park N.T.
Runcorn
C H E S H I R E
Arley Hall
WA7
WA16
Mobberley
Beckett's Wood
CW9
Knutsford
Frodsham
M56
Lostock Gralam
Helsby
WA8
Barnton
CW8
Weaverham
Northwich

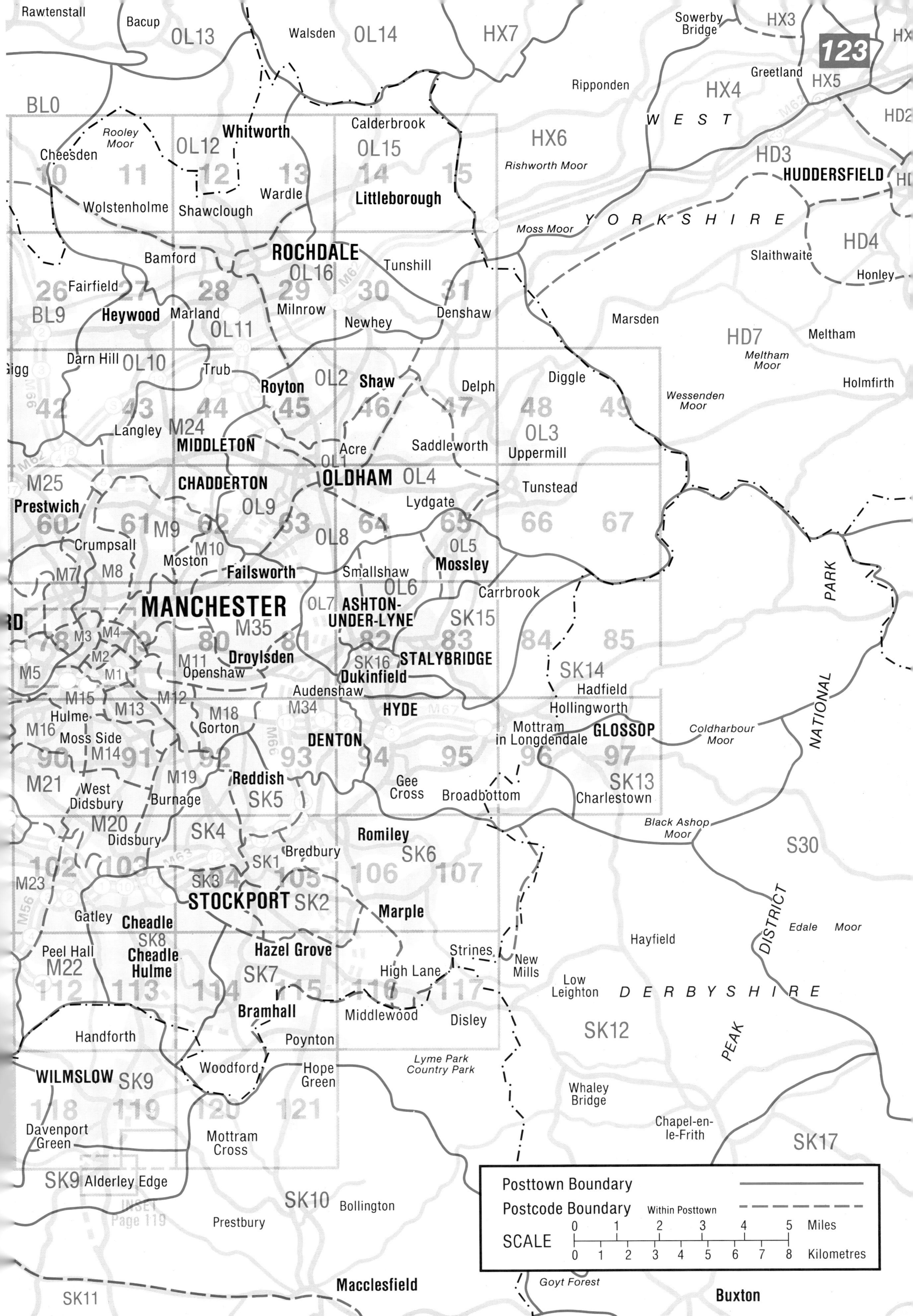
123
Rawtenstall
Bacup
OL13
Walsden
OL14
HX7
Sowerby Bridge
HX3
Ripponden
Greetland
HX4
HX5
HD2
BL0
Rooley Moor
Whitworth
Calderbrook
OL12
OL15
HX6
W E S T
HD3
Cheesden
Rishworth Moor
HUDDERSFIELD
10
11
12
13
14
15
Wolstenholme
Shawclough
Wardle
Littleborough
Moss Moor
Y O R K S H I R E
HD4
ROCHDALE
Bamford
OL16
Tunshill
Slaithwaite
Honley
26
Fairfield
27
28
29
30
31
BL9
Heywood
Marland
Milnrow
Denshaw
Marsden
OL11
Newhey
HD7
Meltham
Meltham Moor
Darn Hill
OL10
Trub
Royton
OL2
Shaw
Delph
Diggle
Holmfirth
42
43
44
45
46
47
48
49
Wessenden Moor
Langley
M24
MIDDLETON
Acre
Saddleworth
OL3
Uppermill
OL1
M25
CHADDERTON
OLDHAM
OL4
Tunstead
Prestwich
OL9
Lydgate
60
61
M9
62
63
64
65
66
67
OL8
OL5
Crumpsall
M10
Moston
Mossley
M7
M8
Failsworth
Smallshaw
PARK
OL6
Carrbrook
MANCHESTER
OL7
ASHTON-UNDER-LYNE
SK15
M35
M3
M4
80
81
82
83
84
85
M2
Droylsden
STALYBRIDGE
M5
M1
M11
Openshaw
SK16
SK14
Dukinfield
Hadfield
NATIONAL
M15
M12
Audenshaw
Hollingworth
Hulme
M13
M18
M34
HYDE
Gorton
Mottram in Longdendale
GLOSSOP
Coldharbour Moor
M16
Moss Side
DENTON
M14
90
91
92
93
94
95
96
97
M21
West Didsbury
M19
Reddish
Gee Cross
Broadbottom
SK13
Charlestown
Burnage
SK5
M20
Didsbury
SK4
Black Ashop Moor
Romiley
S30
Bredbury
SK6
102
103
SK1
105
106
107
M23
SK3
STOCKPORT
SK2
Marple
Gatley
Cheadle
DISTRICT
Edale
Moor
SK8
Hayfield
Peel Hall
Cheadle Hulme
Hazel Grove
Strines
New Mills
M22
SK7
High Lane
Low Leighton
D E R B Y S H I R E
112
113
114
115
116
117
Bramhall
Middlewood
Disley
SK12
PEAK
Handforth
Poynton
Lyme Park Country Park
Woodford
Hope Green
WILMSLOW
SK9
Whaley Bridge
118
119
120
121
Chapel-en-le-Frith
Davenport Green
Mottram Cross
SK17
SK9
Alderley Edge
INSET Page 119
SK10
Bollington
Prestbury
Posttown Boundary
Postcode Boundary
Within Posttown
SCALE
0
1
2
3
4
5
Miles
0
1
2
3
4
5
6
7
8
Kilometres
Goyt Forest
Macclesfield
Buxton
SK11

Names in this index shown in CAPITAL LETTERS, followed by their Postcode District(s), are Posttowns.

INDEX TO STREETS

HOW TO USE THIS INDEX

1. Each name is followed by its Postcode District and then by its map reference; e.g. Abberley Dri. M10—6D 62 is in the M10 Postcode District and appears in map square 6D on Page 62. The Postcode Districts are illustrated on the map on Pages 122 & 123. It is not recommended that this index be used as a means of addressing mail.

2. A strict alphabetical order is followed in which Avenue, Road, Street, etc., (even though abbreviated) are read as part of the name preceding them; e.g. Aber Rd. appears after Abernethy St. but before Abersoch Av.

3. Street and subsidiary names not shown on the Maps, appear in the index in *Italics* with the thoroughfare to which it is connected shown in brackets.

POSTCODE ABBREVIATIONS

BB : Blackburn
BL : Bolton
HD : Huddersfield
HX : Halifax
M : Manchester
OL : Oldham
PR : Preston
SK : Stockport
WA : Warrington
WN : Wigan

GENERAL ABBREVIATIONS

All : Alley
App : Approach
Arc : Arcade
Av : Avenue
Bk : Back
Boulevd : Boulevard
Bri : Bridge
B'way : Broadway
Bldgs : Buildings
Bus : Business
Cen : Centre
Chu : Church
Chyd : Churchyard
Circ : Circle
Cir : Circus
Clo : Close
Comn : Common
Cotts : Cottages
Ct : Court
Cres : Crescent
Dri : Drive
E : East
Embkmt : Embankment
Est : Estate
Gdns : Gardens
Ga : Gate
Gt : Great
Grn : Green
Gro : Grove
Ho : House
Ind : Industrial
La : Lane
Lit : Little
Lwr : Lower
Mnr : Manor
Mans : Mansions
Mkt : Market
M : Mews
Mt : Mount
N : North
Pal : Palace
Pde : Parade
Pk : Park
Pas : Passage
Pl : Place
Rd : Road
S : South
Sq : Square
Sta : Station
St : Street
Ter : Terrace
Up : Upper
Vs : Villas
Wlk : Walk
W : West
Yd : Yard

INDEX TO STREETS

bberley Dri. M10—6D 62
bberley Way. WN3—4H 51
bberton Rd. M20—8G 91
bbey Clo. M26—4E 40
bbey Clo. M32—3F 88
bbey Clo. WA14—3A 110
bbey Clo. WN8—1C 50
bbey Ct. M18—9E 80
bbey Ct. M26—5E 40
bbey Ct. SK1—5H 105
bbey Cres. OL10—6H 27
bbeydale. OL12—2E 28 (off Spotland Rd.)
bbey Dale. WN6—2D 32
beydale Clo. OL6—1E 82
beydale Gdns. M28—5J 57
bey Dri. BL8—9G 25
bey Dri. M27—7E 58
bey Dri. OL15—8M 13
bey Dri. WN5—2E 50
beyfield Sq. M11—7B 80 (off Herne St.)
bey Gdns. SK14—3M 95
bey Gro. M30—5E 76
bey Gro. OL9—3G 63
bey Gro. PR6—3G 19
bey Gro. SK1—5H 105
bey Gro. SK14—3M 95
bey Hey La. M11—8E 80
bey Hey La. M18—1E 92
bey Hills Rd. OL8 & OL4 —3B 64
bey La. WN7—7D 54
bey Rd. M24—5M 43
bey Rd. M29—9B 56
bey Rd. M33—8G 89
bey Rd. M35—4F 80 (Droylsden)
bey Rd. M35—8H 63 (Failsworth)
bey Rd. OL3—4L 47
bey Rd. SK8—8A 104
bey Rd. WA3—7C 72
bey Rd. WA11—8L 69
ey Sq. WN7—7D 54
ey St. WN7—1F 72
eyville Wlk. M15—1E 90
eyway N. WA11—8A 70
eyway S. WA11—8A 70
eywood Av. M18—2E 92 (in two parts)
ingdon Way. WN7—7D 54
ot Croft. BL5—2F 54
otsbury Clo. M12—9A 80
otsbury Clo. SK12—7K 115
ots Clo. M33—9K 89
ots Ct. M33—9K 89
otsfield Clo. M31—3K 87
ot's Fold Rd. M28—9H 57
otsford. OL12—1D 12 (off Millfold)
otsford Clo. WA3—6K 71
otsford Dri. M24—5K 43
otsford Gro. WA14—5E 100
otsford Rd. BL1—9A 22
otsford Rd. M21—4B 90
otsford Rd. OL1—8B 46
otsford Rd. OL9—9E 44
otside Clo. M16—3D 90
otsleigh Dri. SK7—2F 114
ot St. BL3—4E 38
ot St. BL6—6B 20
ots Way. WN5—4D 68
otts Grn. M29—3A 74
ott St. OL9—2L 63
tt St. OL11—7B 28
tt St. WN2—2J 53
n St. M26—6G 41
s La. OL3—9C 48
Av. SK2—9J 105
carn Clo. M8—9G 61
corn Rd. BL1—6B 22
corn St. OL4—2D 64
dare Wlk. M9—3L 61 (off Brockford Dri.)
daron Wlk. M13—6G 5 & 8H 79
deen. M30—5E 76 (off St Andrews Ct.)
deen Cres. SK3—5D 104
deen Gro. SK3—5D 104
deen Ho. M15—1H 91
deen St. M15—1H 91
ord Rd. M23—8A 102
ale St. SK2—8G 105
ele Rd. M14—6L 91
ele St. SK2—8G 105
ant Clo. M11—6M 79
ethy St. BL6—8D 20
Rd. SK8—7A 104
och Av. M14—6L 91
don Av. M25—7M 41
don Clo. M25—7M 41
don Clo. OL9—4H 63
don Clo. OL11—5E 28
don Dri. WN2—7G 53
don Rd. BL2—1J 39
don Rd. M31—3E 88
don Rd. SK5—7F 92
don Rd. SK7—2E 114
don St. M1—5F 5 & 7G 79
don St. OL6—5D 82
er Rd. WN4—3K 69
er Wlk. M10—3D 80
on Rd. M33—2H 101
Rd. OL5—8J 65
Rd. SK4—9C 92
r St. OL16—2H 29
am St. BL6—6B 20
am St. OL4—8C 46
Clo. M14—5G 91
St. M6—1M 77
m Dri. M8—8F 60
St. OL1—8J 45
Av. M27—1E 76
Av. M34—3A 94
Av. SK8—2A 114
Av. SK9—6F 118
Acacia Av. WA15—1F 110
Acacia Cres. WN6—6M 33
Acacia Dri. M6—4H 77
Acacia Dri. WA15—1F 110
Acacia Gro. SK5—1F 104
Acacia Rd. OL8—7K 63
Academy Wlk. M15—1E 90
Acer Clo. OL11—1K 27
Acer Gro. M7—9D 60
Aches St. M18—1D 92
Ackers La. M31—8L 87 (in two parts)
Ackersley Ct. SK8—4B 114
Ackers St. M13—1H 91
Acker St. OL16—2F 28
Ackhurst La. WN5—7F 32
Ack La. E. SK7—5C 114
Ack La. W. SK8—4B 114
Ackroyd Av. M18—9F 80
Ackroyd St. M11—8E 80 (in two parts)
Ackworth Dri. M23—7A 102
Ackworth Rd. M27—7E 58
Acme Dri. M27—8H 59
Acomb St. M14—3H 91
Acomb St. M15—1H 91
Acorn Av. SK8—8L 103
Acorn Av. SK14—6E 94
Acorn Bus. Cen. SK4—4D 104
Acorn Clo. M19—6M 91
Acorn Clo. WN7—4F 72
Acorn St. OL4—2E 64
Acorn Way. OL1—1L 63
A Court. WN4—5B 70
Acre Barn. OL2—1L 45
Acre Clo. BL0—1K 9
Acre Ct. SK13—7J 97
Acre Field. BL2—6K 23
Acre Field. M33—2G 101
Acrefield Av. M31—5F 88
Acrefield Av. SK4—1A 104
Acregate. M31—4A 88
Acre La. OL1—8A 46
Acre La. SK8—7B 114
Acresbrook Av. BL8—5F 24
Acresbrook Wlk. BL8—5F 24
Acresdale. BL6—2J 37
Acres Dri. S. OL12—2D 12
Acresfield. M29—9C 56
Acresfield. PR7—4F 18
Acresfield Av. M34—6J 81
Acresfield Clo. BL6—7J 19
Acresfield Clo. M27—1G 77
Acresfield Mall. BL1—2F 38 (off Arndale Cen.)
Acresfield Rd. M6—2K 77
Acresfield Rd. M24—6B 44
Acresfield Rd. M28—4H 57
Acresfield Rd. SK14—1F 94
Acresfield Rd. WA15—5G 101
Acres La. SK15—6H 83
Acres Pass. M21—6A 90
Acres Rd. M21—6A 90
Acres Rd. SK8—8G 103
Acres St. BL8—5F 24
Acre St. M26—6E 40
Acre St. M34—3L 93
Acre St. OL12—2D 12
Acre St. SK6—3B 106
Acre St. SK13—7J 97
Acreswood Clo. PR7—2L 17
Acre Top Rd. M9—3H 61
Acre View. BL0—1K 9
Acreville Gro. WA3—8J 73
Acton Av. M10—3B 80
Acton Ho. WN1—9D 34
Acton Sq. M5—3A 4 & 5B 78
Acton St. OL12—1G 29
Acton St. WN1—8C 34
Acton's Wlk. WN3—1C 52
Actons Wlk. Trading Cen. WN3 —1C 52
Acton Ter. WN1—8C 34
Adair St. M1—5H 5 & 7J 79
Adair St. OL11—8B 28
Adam Clo. SK8—9B 104
Adams Av. M21—8B 90
Adams Clo. SK12—1L 121
Adamson Gdns. M20—2F 102
Adamson Rd. M30—7C 76
Adamson St. SK16—9C 82
Adamson St. WN4—4A 70
Adamson Wlk. M14—3H 91
Adam St. BL3—4F 38
Adam St. OL6—4C 82
Adam St. OL8—6M 63
Ada St. BL0—6H 9
Ada St. M9—7K 61
Ada St. OL4—2A 64
Ada St. OL12—9G 13
Adcroft St. SK1—6F 104
Adderley Pl. SK13—5F 96
Adderley Rd. SK13—5F 96
Addingham Clo. M9—3H 61
Addington Rd. BL3—6M 37
Addington St. M4—3G 5 & 5H 79
Addison Av. OL6—4D 82
Addison Clo. M13—9J 79
Addison Cres. M16—2B 90
Addison Dri. M24—7C 44
Addison Grange. M33—2J 101
Addison Rd. M30—2J 87
Addison Rd. M31—8K 87 (Carrington)
Addison Rd. M31—5D 88 (Urmston)
Addison Rd. M32—3H 89
Addison Rd. WA15—2E 110
Addison St. WN3—1B 52
Addison Ter. M13—2K 91
Adelaide Ct. OL11—5D 28 (off Manchester Rd.)
Adelaide Rd. SK3—5C 104
Adelaide Rd. SK7—6F 114
Adelaide St. BL0—7G 9
Adelaide St. BL3—5D 38
Adelaide St. M8—1F 78
Adelaide St. M24—9A 44
Adelaide St. M27—9D 58
Adelaide St. M30—6D 76
Adelaide St. OL10—8K 27
Adelaide St. PR6—2G 19
Adelaide St. E. OL10—8L 27
Adeline St. M4—2F 5 & 4G 79
Adelphi Ct. M3—2C 4 & 4D 78
Adelphi Dri. M28—3H 57
Adelphi Gro. M28—3H 57
Adelphi St. M3—3C 4 & 5D 78
Adelphi St. M26—4F 40
Adelphi St. WN6—8L 17
Adelphi Ter. M3—3B 4 & 5C 78
Aden Clo. M12—7K 79
Aden St. OL4—3D 64
Aden St. OL12—1G 29
Adey Rd. WA13—8A 98
Adisham Dri. BL1—9F 22
Adlington Clo. BL8—9G 25
Adlington Clo. SK12—1M 121
Adlington Clo. WA15—7K 101
Adlington Dri. M32—2M 89
Adlington St. BL3—5D 38
Adlington St. M12—7K 79
Adlington St. OL4—8D 46
Adlington Wlk. SK1—3E 104
Adlington Way. M34—5A 94
Admel Sq. M15—9G 79
Adrian Gro. SK1—5F 104
Adrian Rd. BL1—8C 22
Adrian St. M10—9A 62
Adrian Ter. OL16—4J 29
Adria Rd. M20—1J 103
Adscombe Wlk. M16—2E 90
Adshall Rd. SK8—8A 104
Adshead Clo. M22—1B 112
Adstock Wlk. M10—2H 5 & 4J 79
Adstone Clo. M4—6K 79
Adswood Gro. SK3—7D 104
Adswood La. E. SK2—7F 104
Adswood La. W. SK3—7F 104
Adswood Old Hall Rd. SK8 —9D 104
Adswood Old Rd. SK3—7E 104
Adswood Rd. SK3—7E 104 (in two parts)
Adswood St. M10—5L 79
Adswood Ter. SK3—7E 104
Aegean Gdns. M7—2C 78
Aegean Rd. WA14—7A 100
Affetside Dri. BL8—8E 24
Affleck Av. M26—9A 40
Afghan St. OL1—9B 46
Africander Rd. WA11—7A 68
Agden La. WA13, WA16 & WA14 (in two parts) —4D 108
Age Croft. OL8—5C 64
Agecroft Rd. M27—9J 59
Agecroft Rd. SK6—4A 106
Agecroft Rd. E. M25—6A 60
Agecroft Rd. W. M25—6M 59
Agecroft Trading Est. M27 —9L 59
Agincourt St. OL10—8H 27
Agnes Clo. OL9—4J 63
Agnes Ct. M14—7J 91
Agnes St. BL3—4K 39
Agnes St. M8—9F 60
Agnes St. M19—4A 92
Agnes St. OL9—2H 63
Agnes St. OL16—4G 29
Agnew Pl. M6—3A 78
Agnew Rd. M18—1C 92
Aigburth Gro. SK5—4E 92
Ailsa Clo. M10—2K 79
Aimson Pl. WA15—6J 101
Aimson Rd. WA15—6J 101 (in two parts)
Aines St. M12—8A 80
Ainley Rd. M22—1D 112
Ainley Wood. OL3—4L 47
Ainsbrook Av. OL3—5M 47
Ainsbrook Ter. OL3—4D 48 (off Harrop Ct. Rd.)
Ainscoughs Ct. WN7—3E 72
Ainscow Av. BL6—1F 36
Ainscow St. WN2—7L 53
Ainscow St. WN3—3E 52
Ainsdale Av. BL7—5L 7
Ainsdale Av. BL8—8H 25
Ainsdale Av. M7—7D 60
Ainsdale Av. M29—4J 55
Ainsdale Clo. OL8—4K 63
Ainsdale Clo. SK7—5F 114
Ainsdale Cres. OL2—7L 45
Ainsdale Dri. M33—3E 100
Ainsdale Dri. OL12—4D 12
Ainsdale Dri. SK8—3H 113
Ainsdale Gro. SK5—6F 92
Ainsdale Rd. BL3—7E 38 (in two parts)
Ainsdale Rd. SK5—5G 93
Ainsdale St. M12—9M 79
Ainse Rd. BL6—7H 19
Ainsford Rd. M20—9K 91
Ainsley Gro. M28—6K 57
Ainsley Rd. BL1—9A 22
Ainsley St. M10—2C 80
Ainsty Rd. M14—2G 91
Ainsworth Av. BL6—9E 20
Ainsworth Clo. M34—3H 93
Ainsworth Clo. OL2—5M 45
Ainsworth Ct. BL2—2J 39
Ainsworth Hall Rd. BL2—2B 40
Ainsworth La. BL2—9H 23
Ainsworth Rd. BL3—6A 40
Ainsworth Rd. BL8—9F 24
Ainsworth Rd. M26—3F 40
Ainsworth St. BL1—8C 22
Ainsworth St. M26—5K 41
Ainsworth St. OL16—4G 29
Ainthorpe Wlk. M10—2D 80
Aintree Av. M33—2C 100
Aintree Clo. SK7—2M 115
Aintree Dri. OL11—2L 27
Aintree Gro. SK3—7E 104
Aintree Rd. BL3—7A 40
Aintree St. M11—6B 80
Aintree Wlk. OL9—1J 63
Airedale Clo. SK8—7J 103
Airedale Ct. WA14—8E 100
Aireworth St. BL5—6E 36
Air Hill Ter. OL12—1C 28
Airley St. WN3—4E 52
Airton Clo. M10—2H 5 & 4J 79
Airton Pl. WN3—5B 52
Aitken Clo. BL0—6H 9
Aitken St. M19—5C 92
Ajax Dri. BL9—6M 41
Ajax St. BL0—6H 9
Ajax St. OL11—7B 28
Aked Clo. M12—9K 79
Akesmoor Dri. SK2—7J 105
Alamein Dri. SK6—3E 106
Alan Av. M35—2F 80
Alandale Av. M34—8L 81
Alandale Dri. OL2—4J 45
Alandale Rd. SK3—6C 104
Alan Dri. SK6—7E 106
Alan Dri. WA15—4G 111
Alan Rd. M20—8J 91
Alan Rd. SK4—2A 104
Alan St. BL1—7D 22
Alban St. M7—2D 78
Albany Av. M11—8F 80
Albany Clo. M28—2H 57
Albany Ct. M20—8G 91
Albany Ct. M31—3B 88
Albany Dri. BL9—2M 41
Albany Gro. M29—8D 56
Albany Rd. M21—5B 90
Albany Rd. M30—4B 76
Albany Rd. SK7—8E 114
Albany Rd. SK9—6F 118
Albany St. M24—1B 62
Albany St. OL4—8D 46
Albany St. OL11—5G 29
Albany Trading Est. M21 —5B 90
Albany Way. M6—4A 78
Alba Pl. M15—6D 4 & 8E 78
Alba Way. M32—1G 89
Albemarle Av. M20—8G 91
Albemarle Rd. M21—6A 90
Albemarle Rd. M27—9E 58
Albemarle St. M14—2G 91
Albemarle Ter. OL6—4C 82
Albermarle St. OL6—4C 82
Alberta St. BL3—4C 38
Alberta St. SK1—5F 104
Albert Av. M18—2F 92
Albert Av. M25—7C 60
Albert Av. M28—3J 57
Albert Av. M31—4E 88
Albert Av. OL2—4A 46
Albert Clo. M25—9A 42
Albert Clo. SK8—2A 114
Albert Ct. WA14—9D 100
Albert Fildes Wlk. M8—9F 60
Albert Gdns. M10—2D 80
Albert Gro. BL4—9K 39
Albert Gro. M12—2A 92 (in two parts)
Albert Hill St. M20—2H 103
Albert M. BL5—8E 36
Albert Pk. Rd. M7—2C 78
Albert Pl. M13—3M 91
Albert Pl. M25—8B 42
Albert Pl. OL4—2E 64
Albert Pl. WA14—8D 100
Albert Rd. BL1—1B 38 (Bolton)
Albert Rd. BL1—9M 21 (Markland Hill)
Albert Rd. BL4—9J 39
Albert Rd. M19—5M 91
Albert Rd. M25—8A 42
Albert Rd. M30—4F 76
Albert Rd. M33—1J 101
Albert Rd. SK4—2A 104
Albert Rd. SK8—2A 114
Albert Rd. SK9—5G 119
Albert Rd. SK14—4D 94
Albert Rd. WA15—1E 110
Albert Rd. E. WA15—1E 110
Albert Rd. W. BL1—1M 37
Albert Royds St. OL16—9H 13
Albert Sq. M2—4E 5 & 6F 78 (in two parts)
Albert Sq. SK15—6F 82
Albert Sq. WA14—1C 110
Albert St. BL0—5H 9
Albert St. BL3—6B 40
Albert St. BL4—1K 57 (Farnworth)
Albert St. BL4—9L 39 (Kearsley)
Albert St. BL6—6B 20
Albert St. BL7—8D 6
Albert St. BL9—8A 26
Albert St. M11—6L 79 (in three parts)
Albert St. M16—9C 78
Albert St. M24—9A 44
Albert St. M25—3C 60
Albert St. M26—6H 41
Albert St. M30—8E 86 (Cadishead)
Albert St. M30—5F 76 (Eccles)
Albert St. M34—3M 93
Albert St. M35—6H 81
Albert St. OL2—5K 45 (Royton)
Albert St. OL2—2A 46 (Shaw)
Albert St. OL4—3E 64
Albert St. OL8—7H 63
Albert St. OL9—5H 63
Albert St. OL10—8H 27
Albert St. OL12—3C 12
Albert St. OL15—6B 14
Albert St. OL16—5A 30
Albert St. SK3—4D 104
Albert St. SK7—1K 115
Albert St. SK14—1G 97 (Hadfield)
Albert St. SK14—3F 94 (Hyde)
Albert St. WA14—9D 100
Albert St. WN1—1F 52
Albert St. WN2—3K 53
Albert St. WN4—4B 70
Albert St. WN5—2M 51
Albert St. W. M35—1D 80
Albert Ter. SK1—4F 104
Albine St. M10—8M 61
Albinson Wlk. M31—2G 99
Albion Clo. SK4—2E 104
Albion Ct. BL8—8K 25
Albion Dri. M35—5G 81
Albion Dri. WN2—7H 35
Albion Gdns. SK15—5H 83
Albion Gro. M30—7B 76
Albion Gro. M33—1G 101
Albion Pl. M5—3B 4 & 5C 78
Albion Pl. M7—2C 78
Albion Pl. M25—4A 60
Albion Pl. SK7—1K 115
Albion Rd. M14—5J 91
Albion Rd. OL11—4D 28
Albion Rd. SK12—6M 117
Albion St. BL3—4F 38
Albion St. BL4—1A 58
Albion St. BL5—6F 36
Albion St. BL8—8K 25
Albion St. M1—6E 5 & 8F 78
Albion St. M5—4A 4 & 6B 78
Albion St. M16—2D 90
Albion St. M26—8H 41
Albion St. M27—8G 59
Albion St. M33—1H 101
Albion St. M35—9E 62
Albion St. OL1—1L 63 (in two parts)
Albion St. OL5—7J 65
Albion St. OL6—4C 82 (in two parts)
Albion St. OL9—1G 63
Albion St. OL11—9C 28
Albion St. OL15—6A 14
Albion St. SK14—4D 94
Albion St. SK15—5H 83
Albion St. WN2—6G 53
Albion St. WN7—3F 72
Albion Ter. BL1—7B 22
Albion Towers. M5—3A 4 & 5B 78
Albion Trading Est. OL6—4D 82
Albion Way. M5—4A 4 & 6A 78
Albury Dri. M19—3K 103
Albury Dri. OL12—9M 11
Albury Way. WN2—7F 34
Albyns Av. M8—9G 61
Alcester Av. SK3—6M 103
Alcester Clo. BL8—7H 25
Alcester Clo. M24—2B 62
Alcester Rd. M33—3H 101
Alcester Rd. SK8—9H 103
Alcester St. OL9—5G 63
Alcester Wlk. M9—3J 61
Alconbury Wlk. M9—2H 61
Aldborough Clo. M20—8H 91
Aldbourne Clo. M10—2K 79
Aldbury Ter. BL1—9D 22
Aldcliffe. WA3—7M 71
Aldcroft St. M18—9F 80
Alden Clo. M25—9A 42
Alden Wlk. SK4—7D 92
Alder Av. BL9—7C 26
Alder Av. SK12—9M 115
Alder Av. WN4—2M 69
Alder Av. WN5—2D 68 (Billinge)
Alder Av. WN5—2K 51 (Wigan)
Alderbank. BL6—7M 19
Alderbank. OL12—4J 13
Alderbank Clo. BL4—2M 57
Alder Clo. OL6—9B 64
Alder Clo. SK16—8G 83
Alder Clo. WN7—5F 72
Aldercroft Av. BL2—9K 23
Aldercroft Av. M22—2C 112
Alderdale Clo. SK4—9A 92
Alderdale Dri. M35—5D 80
Alderdale Dri. SK4—9A 92
Alderdale Dri. SK6—5E 116
Alderdale Gro. SK9—6E 118
Alderdale Rd. SK8—9C 104
Alder Dri. M27—7C 58
Alder Dri. WA15—8L 101
Alder Edge. M21—5M 89
Alderfield Ho. M21—5M 89
Alderfield Rd. M21—5M 89
Alderfold St. M29—5K 55
Alderford Pde. M8—1F 78
Alder Forest Av. M30—3A 76
Aldergate Ct. M27—9C 58
Aldergate Gro. OL6—2F 82
Alderglen Rd. M8—1F 78
Alder Gro. BL7—4J 23
Alder Gro. M32—4L 89
Alder Gro. M34—3A 94
Alder Gro. PR7—1M 17
Alder Gro. SK3—5C 104
Alder Ho. M29—5K 55
Alder La. OL8—6K 63
Alder La. WA11—2A 68
Alder La. WN2—3A 54
Alderley Av. BL1—5E 22
Alderley Av. WA3—8K 71
Alderley Clo. SK7—4M 115
Alderley Clo. SK12—1M 121
Alderley Dri. SK6—2L 105
Alderley La. WN7—4H 73
Alderley Lodge. SK9—6G 119
Alderley Rd. M31—4A 88
Alderley Rd. M33—3L 101
Alderley Rd. SK5—9F 92
Alderley Rd. SK9—6G 119
Alderley Rd. WN2—3A 54
Alderley St. OL6—2D 82
Alderley Ter. SK16—6B 82
Alderman Sq. M12—7L 79
Aldermary Rd. M21—9D 90
Aldermaston Gro. M9—2H 61
Aldermere Cres. M31—4L 87
Alderminster Av. M28—3G 57
Alderney Dri. WN3—5A 52
Alderney Wlk. M10—4K 79
Alder Rd. M24—7C 44
Alder Rd. M35—2F 80
Alder Rd. OL11—8D 28
Alder Rd. SK8—8K 103
Alder Rd. WA3—7M 71
Alders Av. M22—8C 102
Alders Ct. OL8—8A 64
Aldersgate Rd. SK2—7H 105
Aldersgate Rd. SK8—7C 114
Aldersgreen Av. SK6—5F 116
Alders Grn. Rd. WN2—3A 54
Aldershot Wlk. M11—6M 79
Alderside Rd. M9—8K 61
Aldersley Av. M9—3H 61
Alderson St. M6—3A 78
Alderson St. OL9—1L 63
Alders Rd. M22—8C 102
Alders Rd. SK12—5G 117
Alders Rd. SK15—4K 83
Alder St. BL3—6F 38
Alder St. M6—5M 77
Alder St. M29—5K 55
Alder St. M30—3A 76
Aldersyde St. BL3—6D 38
Alderton Dri. WN4—4M 69
Alderue Av. M22—7D 102
Alderway. BL0—2J 9
Alderwood Av. SK4—4A 104
Alderwood Wlk. M8—1F 78
Aldfield Rd. M23—4L 101
Aldford Clo. M20—2J 103
Aldford Dri. M29—3L 55
Aldford Gro. BL2—4B 40
Aldford Pl. SK9—7K 119
Aldford Way. WN6—1L 33
Aldham Av. M10—3C 80
Aldington Rd. SK9—5K 119
Aldred Clo. M8—1H 79
Aldred St. BL3—6B 38
Aldred St. M5—3A 4 & 5B 78
Aldred St. M30—6C 76
Aldred St. M35—9E 62
Aldred St. WN2—4K 53
Aldred St. WN7—8E 54
Aldridge Clo. WN3—5B 52
Aldridge Wlk. M11—7M 79
Aldsworth Dri. BL3—5E 38
Aldsworth Dri. M10—1L 79
Aldwick Av. M20—2J 103
Aldwinians Clo. M34—1L 93
Aldwych. OL11—7F 28
Aldwych Av. M14—3H 91
Aldwyn Clo. M34—1L 93
Aldwyn Cres. SK7—2J 115
Aldwyn Pk. Rd. M34—7J 81
Alexander Av. M35—8G 63
Alexander Dri. BL9—7A 42
Alexander Dri. OL16—4L 29
Alexander Dri. WA15—7G 101
Alexander Gdns. M7—1C 4 & 3D 78
Alexander Rd. BL2—9J 23
Alexander St. M6—5L 77
Alexander St. M29—8A 56
Alexander St. OL11—8B 28
Alexandra Av. M14—4F 90
Alexandra Av. M25—9A 42
Alexandra Av. SK14—4C 94
Alexandra Cen. Retail Pk. OL4 —2M 63
Alexandra Clo. SK3—7C 104
Alexandra Cres. OL1—8B 46
Alexandra Cres. WN5—2L 51
Alexandra Dri. M19—7M 91
Alexandra Gro. M30—6F 86
Alexandra Ho. OL1—9B 46
Alexandra M. OL8—3A 64
Alexandra Rd. BL4—1A 58
Alexandra Rd. BL6—1E 36
Alexandra Rd. M16—3E 90
Alexandra Rd. M26—9A 40
Alexandra Rd. M28—3J 57
Alexandra Rd. M30—6B 76
Alexandra Rd. M33—1J 101
Alexandra Rd. M34—2A 94
Alexandra Rd. OL6—4B 82
Alexandra Rd. OL8—4A 64
Alexandra Rd. SK4—2C 104
Alexandra Rd. WN4—3B 70
Alexandra Rd. S. M16—3E 90
Alexandra St. BL4—1K 57
Alexandra St. M7—2C 4 & 4D 78
Alexandra St. OL6—3D 82
Alexandra St. OL8—3A 64
Alexandra St. OL10—1L 43
Alexandra St. SK14—5C 94
Alexandra St. WN2—8H 53
Alexandra St. WN5—1M 51
Alexandra Ter. M19—5A 92
Alexandra Ter. M33—8G 89
Alexandra Ter. OL4—6D 46
Alexandria Dri. BL5—9H 37
Alford Av. M20—6G 91
Alford Gro. BL2—3M 39
Alford Rd. SK4—8B 92
Alford St. OL9—6H 63
Alfred Av. M28—9A 58
Alfred James Clo. M10—4J 79
Alfred Rd. WA3—7A 72
Alfred Rd. WA11—8M 69
Alfred St. BL0—6H 9
Alfred St. BL3—5H 39
Alfred St. BL4—7K 39 (Farnworth)
Alfred St. BL4—9M 39 (Kearsley)
Alfred St. BL7—8D 6
Alfred St. BL9—1A 42
Alfred St. M9—8K 61
Alfred St. M28—5K 57
Alfred St. M30—8E 86 (Cadishead)
Alfred St. M30—4D 76 (Eccles)
Alfred St. M35—8F 62
Alfred St. OL2—2A 46
Alfred St. OL6—3D 82
Alfred St. OL9—2J 63 (Oldham, in two parts)
Alfred St. OL9—5G 63 (White Gate)
Alfred St. OL12—1D 12
Alfred St. OL15—5A 14
Alfred St. SK14—3C 94
Alfred St. WN1—7B 34
Alfred St. WN2—5G 53
Alfred St. WN3—2D 52
Alfreton Av. M34—6A 94
Alfreton Rd. SK2—7K 105
Alfreton Wlk. M10—1A 80 (off Thorpebrook Rd.)
Alfriston Dri. M23—3A 102
Algernon Rd. M28—4J 57
Algernon St. BL4—7K 39
Algernon St. M27—8D 58
Algernon St. M30—4D 76
Algernon St. OL6—5D 82
Algernon St. WN2—3K 53
Algernon St. WN3—4A 52
Alger St. OL6—3D 82
Algreave Rd. SK3—5A 104
Alice Ingram Ct. OL12—1B 28
Alice St. BL3—4C 38
Alice St. M27—8H 59
Alice St. M33—1K 101
Alice St. M35—7G 81
Alice St. OL12—1H 29
Alice St. SK14—7E 94
Alicia Ct. OL12—1E 28
Alicia Dri. OL12—1E 28
Alicia St. BL3—4K 39
Alick's Fold. BL5—8E 36
Alison St. M14—3F 90
Alison St. OL2—1A 46
Alixandra Ct. M31—5L 87
Alker Rd. M10—4K 79
Alker St. WN5—2M 51
Alkrington Clo. BL9—7A 42
Alkrington Ct. M24—3B 62
Alkrington Grn. M24—2M 61
Alkrington Hall Rd. N. M24 —1M 61
Alkrington Hall Rd. S. M24 —2L 61
Alkrington Pk. Rd. M24—1L 61
Allams St. M11—5L 79
Allanbrooke Wlk. M15—1E 90
Allan Ct. M21—7A 90
Allandale Ct. M7—7E 60
Allandale Rd. M19—5M 91
Allan Roberts Clo. M9—7K 61
Allanson Rd. M22—4E 102
Allan St. M29—8M 55
Alldis St. SK2—8H 105
Allebry Way. WA3—7L 71
Allen Av. SK14—6F 94
Allenby Gro. BL5—1D 54
Allenby Rd. M27—1C 76
Allenby Rd. M30—1D 98
Allenby St. M29—6H 55
Allenby St. OL2—2A 46
Allenby Wlk. M10—2J 79
Allen Clo. OL2—3A 46
Allendale Dri. BL9—6A 42
Allendale Gdns. BL1—8E 22
Allendale Wlk. M3—3C 4 & 5D 78
Allen Rd. M31—4F 88
Allen St. BL3—6A 40
Allen St. BL8—7J 25
Allen St. M26—6E 40 (in two parts)
Allen St. OL8—2K 63
Allen St. OL16—4G 29
Allerdean Wlk. SK4—2L 103
Allerford Clo. M16—2E 90
Allerton Clo. BL5—8G 37
Allerton Ho. BL1—1E 38 (off Duke St. N.)
Allerton Wlk. M13—9H 79
Allesley Clo. BL5—8G 37
Alley St. OL4—3C 64
Allgreave Clo. M33—3L 101
Alliance St. WN1—9D 34
Allingham St. M13—2L 91
Allington. OL11—4E 28
Allington Dri. M30—3E 76
Alliott Wlk. M15—1E 90
Allison Gro. M30—6B 76
Allison St. M8—2F 78
Allonby Wlk. M24—7J 43
Allotment Rd. M30—8D 86
Alloway Wlk. M10—1A 80
All Saint's Clo. OL2—4K 45
All Saints Ct. M32—4H 89
All Saints Gro. WN2—3L 53
All Saints' Rd. SK4—1E 104
All Saints St. BL1—1F 38
All Saints St. M10—2C 80
All Saints Ter. OL16—9H 13
Allscott Way. WN4—4C 70
Allwood St. M5—4C 4 & 6D 78
Alma Clo. WN8—1C 50
Alma Ct. WN8—1C 50
Alma Grn. WN8—1B 50
Alma Gro. WN3—6L 51
Alma Hill. WN8—1B 50
Alma Ind. Est. OL12—1F 28
Alma La. SK9—5G 119
Alma Pde. WN8—1C 50
Alma Rd. BL5—9F 36
Alma Rd. M19—6A 92
Alma Rd. M33—3E 100
Alma Rd. SK4—9B 92
Alma Rd. SK7—4A 116
Alma Rd. WN8—1C 50
Alma St. BL3—5C 38 (Bolton)
Alma St. BL3—6B 40 (Little Lever)
Alma St. BL4—3B 58
Alma St. M26—4F 40
Alma St. M29—5J 55 (Atherton)
Alma St. M29—8M 55 (Tyldesley)
Alma St. M30—6F 76
Alma St. OL12—1F 28
Alma St. SK14—3C 94
Alma St. SK15—5H 83
Alma St. WN7—8E 54
Alma Wlk. WN8—1C 50
Alminstone Clo. M10—3D 80
Almond Av. BL9—7C 26
Almond Brook Rd. WN6—9H 17
Almond Clo. M6—2A 4 & 4A 78
Almond Clo. M35—1F 80
Almond Clo. OL15—5M 13
Almond Clo. SK3—5C 104
Almond Clo. WA11—9F 68
Almond Ct. SK16—6C 82
Almond Cres. WN6—2M 33
Almond Dri. M33—8F 88
Almond Gro. BL1—7F 22
Almond Gro. M16—1B 90
Almond Gro. WN5—2L 51
Almond Rd. OL4—8D 46
Almond St. BL1—6F 22
Almond St. BL4—9J 39
Almond St. M10—1G 5 & 3H 79
Almond Tree Rd. SK8—3A 114
Almond Wlk. M31—2D 98
Alms Hill Rd. M8—1G 79
Almshouses. M33—1L 101
Alness Rd. M16—3E 90
Alnwick Clo. WN2—4K 35
Alnwick Dri. BL9—4A 42
Alnwick Rd. M9—3K 61
Alperton Wlk. M10—3D 80
Alpha Ct. M34—3J 93
Alpha Pl. M15—8E 78
Alpha Rd. M32—4J 89
Alpha St. M6—4M 77
Alpha St. M11—8E 80
Alpha St. M26—5F 40
Alpha St. W. M6—4L 77
Alphin Clo. OL3—3B 66
Alphin Clo. OL5—5L 65
Alphin Sq. OL5—7K 65
Alphonsus St. M16—2C 90
Alpine Dri. OL2—6J 45
Alpine Dri. OL12—5J 13
Alpine Dri. OL16—3A 30
Alpine Dri. WN7—8C 54
Alpine Rd. SK1—3G 105
Alpine St. M11—4B 80
Alpine Ter. BL4—9L 39
Alpington Wlk. M10—6C 62
Alport Av. M16—4C 90
Alport Gro. SK13—4E 96 (off Melandra Castle Rd.)
Alport Lea. SK13—4E 96 (off Hathersage Cres.)
Alport Way. SK13—4E 96 (off Melandra Castle Rd.)
Alresford Rd. M6—2K 77
Alresford Rd. M24—3M 61
Alric Wlk. M22—4E 112
Alsfield Way. SK12—4M 117
Alsham Wlk. M8—1G 79
Alsop Av. M7—9B 60
Alstead Av. WA15—1G 111
Alston Av. M32—3H 89
Alston Av. M33—2F 100
Alston Av. OL2—1B 46
Alston Clo. SK7—3G 115
Alstone Dri. WA14—7A 100
Alstone Rd. SK4—8C 92
Alston Gdns. M19—9M 91
Alston Lea. M29—4L 55
Alston Rd. M18—1E 92
Alston Rd. WN2—7F 34
Alston St. BL3—6E 38
Alston St. BL8—6J 25
Alston Wlk. M24—7J 43
Altair Av. M22—3D 112
Altair Pl. M7—1B 4 & 3C 78
Altcar Gro. SK5—4E 92
Altcar Wlk. M22—2C 112 (in two parts)
Alt Fold Dri. OL8—5D 64
Alt Gro. OL6—1B 82
Altham Clo. BL9—2K 41
Altham Wlk. M10—1A 80 (off Craiglands Av.)
Alt Hill La. OL6—8C 64
Alt Hill Rd. OL6—7C 64
Althorn Wlk. M23—8A 102
Althorpe Wlk. M10—3D 80
Alt La. OL8—6C 64
Alton Av. M31—3K 87
Alton Clo. BL9—4A 42
Alton Clo. OL6—9C 64
Alton Clo. WN4—3A 70
Alton Rd. SK9—3F 118
Alton Sq. M11—8E 80
Alton St. M9—1K 79
Alton St. OL8—5M 63
Altrincham Rd. M23, M22 & SK8 (in four parts) —6K 101
Altrincham Rd. SK9—9A 112
Altrincham St. M1— (in two parts) 5G 5 & 7H 79
Altrincham St. OL9—9K 45
Alt Rd. OL6—1B 82
Alt Wlk. M25—7C 42
Alum Cres. BL9—6A 42
Alvanley Clo. M33—4H 101
Alvanley Clo. WN5—8J 33
Alvanley Cres. SK3—7C 104
Alvanley St. SK6—1A 106
Alvan Sq. M11—8E 80
Alva Rd. OL4—7D 46
Alvaston Av. SK4—2B 104
Alvaston Rd. M18—2E 92
Alveley Av. M20—9J 91
Alverstone Rd. M20—8J 91
Alvington Gro. SK7—3G 115
Alvon Ct. SK14—4G 95
Alwin Rd. OL2—1A 46
Alwinton Av. SK4—2L 103
Alworth Rd. M9—4J 61
Alwyn Clo. WN7—6F 72
Alwyn Dri. M13—2L 91
Alwyn St. WN1—8D 34
Alwyn Ter. WN1—8D 34
Amar St. WN2—1F 52
Ambassador Pl. WA15—8E 100
Amber Gdns. SK16—7B 82
Ambergate St. M11—5M 79
Amber Gro. BL5—7F 36
Amberidge Wlk. M15—1G 91 (off Duxbury Sq.)
Amberley Clo. BL3—4M 37
Amberley Clo. WN2—7F 34
Amberley Dri. M23—9A 102
Amberley Dri. M30—5G 87
Amberley Dri. WA15—4H 111
Amberley Rd. M33—9E 88
Amberley Wlk. OL9—1J 63
Amber St. M4—3F 5 & 5G 79
Amberswood. WN2—2K 53
Amberswood Clo. WN2—1H 53
Amberwood. OL9—9E 44
Amberwood Dri. M23—7K 101
Amblecote Dri. E. M28—2G 57
Amblecote Dri. W. M28—2G 57
Ambleside. SK15—4G 83
Ambleside. WN2—9H 35
Ambleside. WN5—1J 51
Ambleside Av. OL7—3M 81
Ambleside Av. WA15—8J 101
Ambleside Clo. BL2—6M 23
Ambleside Clo. M24—8L 43
Ambleside Pl. WA11—6B 68
Ambleside Rd. M31—5L 87
Ambleside Rd. SK5—7F 92
Ambleside Way. M9—6A 62
Ambrose Av. WN7—7E 54
Ambrose Cres. OL3—6B 48
Ambrose Dri. M20—1D 102
Ambrose Gdns. M20—1D 102
Ambrose St. M12—8A 80
Ambrose St. OL11—5F 28
Ambrose St. SK14—7E 94
Ambush St. M11—8F 80
Amelia St. SK14—4E 94
Amelia St. W. M34—2M 93
Amersham Clo. M31—1B 88
Amersham Pl. M19—8A 92
Amersham St. M5—6M 77
Amesbury Dri. WN3—6J 51
Amesbury Gro. SK5—9F 92
Amesbury Rd. M9—4L 61
Amherst Rd. M20 & M14—7J 91
Amlwch Av. SK2—7K 105
Ammon's Way. OL3—4M 47
Ammon Wrigley Clo. OL1 —1M 63
Amory St. M12—5H 5 & 7J 79
Amos Av. M10—3C 80
Amos St. M6—5L 77
Amos St. M9—9L 61
Ampleforth Gdns. M26 —4E 40
Ampney Clo. M30—6B 76
Amport Wlk. M10—6C 62
Amwell St. M8—9H 61
Amy St. M24—8B 44
Amy St. OL12—1B 28
Ancaster Wlk. M10—6C 62
Anchorage Quay. M5—7A 78
Anchorage Rd. M31—5G 89
Anchorage Wlk. M18—9C 80
Anchor Clo. M19—5C 92
Anchor Ct. M8—7F 60
Anchor Ct. SK9—3H 119
Anchor La. BL4 & M28—9F 38
Anchor St. OL1—9M 45
Ancoats Gro. M4—6K 79
Ancoats Gro. N. M4—6K 79
Ancoats St. OL4—2E 64
Ancroft Gdns. BL3—6C 38
Anderton Clo. BL8—9F 24
Anderton Gro. OL6—2E 82
Anderton La. BL6—7L 19 (in two parts)
Anderton Pl. M7—2D 78
Anderton St. WN2—1F 52
Anderton Way. SK9—9K 113
Anderton Way. WN2—7H 35
Andoc Av. M30—5G 77
Andover Av. M24—3B 62
Andover Cres. WN3—6J 51
Andover St. M30—6C 76
Andover Wlk. M8—7G 61
Andre St. M11—5C 80
Andrew Av. WN5—2F 68
Andrew Clo. BL8—1F 24
Andrew Clo. M26—8J 41
Andrew Ct. M20—8H 91
Andrew Gro. SK16—7D 82
Andrew La. BL1—4F 22
Andrew La. SK6—3E 116
Andrew Rd. M9—6K 61
Andrews Av. M31—3L 87
Andrew's Brow. M10—3D 80
Andrews Clo. M34—6B 94
Andrews La. M4—4F 5 & 6G 79
Andrew's Ter. BL5—8E 36
Andrew St. BL9—8A 26
Andrew St. M9—1K 79
Andrew St. M24—1C 62
Andrew St. M35—3J 81 (Droylsden)
Andrew St. M35—8E 62 (Failsworth)
Andrew St. OL5—8J 65
Andrew St. OL6—2D 82
Andrew St. OL9—9H 45
Andrew St. SK4—3D 104
Andrew St. SK6—3G 107
Andrew St. SK14—3F 94
Andrew St. WN6—9B 34

Andy Nicholson Wlk. M9 —8M 61
Anerley Rd. M20—1H 103
Anfield Clo. BL9—6B 42
Anfield M. SK8—1M 113
Anfield Rd. BL3—6E 38
Anfield Rd. M10—7D 62
Anfield Rd. M33—9J 89
Angela Av. OL2—7L 45
Angela St. M15—6C 4 & 8D 78
Angel Clo. SK16—2B 82
Angelico Rise. OL1—6D 46
Angelo St. BL1—7D 22
(in two parts)
Angel St. M4—2F 5 & 4G 79
Angel St. M34—2A 94
Angel St. SK7—1K 115
Angier Gro. M34—3M 93
Anglesea Av. M9—8K 61
Anglesea Av. SK2—7F 104
Anglesey Clo. OL7—1A 82
Anglesey Dri. SK12—6L 117
Anglesey Gro. SK8—7M 103
Anglesey Rd. OL7—1M 81
Angleside Av. M19—1L 103
Anglia Gro. BL3—5C 38
Angouleme Way. BL9—8L 25
Angus Av. OL10—9G 27
Angus Av. WN7—1C 72
Angus St. M34—5D 4 & 7E 78
Aniline St. M11—1L 57
Anita St. M4—3G 5 & 5H 79
Annable Rd. M18—9D 80
Annable Rd. M30—6F 86
Annable Rd. M35—6H 81
Annable St. BL6—2K 105
Annald Sq. M35—5G 81
Annan Gro. M34—2E 70
Annan St. M34—2M 93
Annecy Clo. BL8—6K 25
Annersley Av. OL2—3A 46
Annesley Cres. WN3—5M 51
Annesley Gdns. M18—9D 80
Annesley Rd. M10—7E 62
Anne St. SK16—7D 82
Annie Darby Ct. M9—9N 61
Annie St. BL0—7G 9
Annie St. M5—5L 77
Annis Clo. SK9—2L 119
Annisdale Clo. M30—5B 76
Annisfield Av. WA15—3H 66
Annis Rd. BL3—5B 38
Annis Rd. SK9—1M 119
Ann La. M29—2C 74
Ann Sq. OL4—9D 64
Ann's Rd. M25—5M 59
Ann St. BL4—1L 57
Ann St. M34—3L 93
Ann St. OL7—7M 81
Ann St. OL10—7K 27
Ann St. OL16 & OL12—4F 28
Ann St. SK14—3C 94
Ann St. SK14—1E 104
Ann St. WN7—8E 54
Anscombe Clo. M10—4K 79
Anscombe Wlk. M10—4K 79
Ansdell Av. M21—6C 90
Ansdell Dri. M35—5E 80
Ansdell Rd. BL6—6C 20
Ansdell Rd. OL16—6H 29
Ansdell Rd. WN5—3K 51
Ansdell St. M8—6G 61
Ansford Wlk. M9—9J 61
(off Westmere Dri.)
Ansleigh Av. M8—7G 61
Ansley Gro. SK4—2B 104
Anslow Clo. M10—2K 79
Anson Av. M27—1E 76
Anson Clo. SK7—7F 114
Anson Pl. WN5—9J 33
Anson Rd. M14—2K 91
Anson Rd. M27—1E 76
Anson Rd. M34—4G 93
Anson Rd. SK9—2L 119
Anson Rd. SK12—8B 116
Anson St. BL1—7F 22
Anson St. M30—4B 76
Anson WN5—1M 51
Anson View. M14—3K 91
Ansty Clo. WA11—9D 68
Answell Av. M8—6G 61
Antares Av. M7—2C 4 & 4D 78
Anthistle Ct. M5—5K 77
Anthony St. BL3—7F 38
Anthony Rd. WN5—5L 51
Anton Wlk. M9—9K 61
Antrim Clo. M19—4K 103
Antrim Clo. WA11—9J 69
Antrim Clo. WN5—6J 51
Anvil St. BL4—1K 57
Anvil St. M1—6E 5 & 8F 78
Anvil Way. OL1—1L 63
Apethorn La. SK14—7C 94
Apfel La. OL9—1H 63
Apollo Av. BL9—8M 41
Apollo Wlk. M12—9A 80
Appelthwaite. WN2—9H 35
Apperley Grange. M30—3E 76
Appian Way. M7 & M8—1E 78
Appleby Av. M12—3A 92
Appleby Av. SK14—1C 94
Appleby Av. WA15—8J 101
Appleby Gdns. BL2—9G 23
Appleby Lodge. M14—4N 91
Appleby Rd. SK8—9H 103
Appleby Wlk. OL2—5L 45
Apple Clo. OL8—5K 63
Applecross Wlk. M11—7C 80
Appledore Dri. M7M 23
Appledore Dri. M23—6K 101
Appledore Wlk. OL9—1H 63
Appleford Dri. M8—1H 79
Apple St. SK14—7J 95
Apple Ter. BL1—8D 22
Appleton Ct. M33—1H 101
Appleton Dri. SK13—6M 97
Appleton Gro. M33—3E 100
Appleton Rd. SK4—8D 92
Appleton St. WN3—9B 34
Appleton Wlk. SK9—2L 119
Apple Tree Ct. M5—5E 104
Apple Tree La. SK16—9C 82
Apple Tree Wlk. M33—9C 88
Applewood. OL9—1E 62
Appley Clo. WN6—8C 16
Appley La. N. WN6—8C 16 —3C 32
Appley La. S. WN8 & WN6 —3C 32
Apprentice La. SK9—9F 112
Approach Rd. M31—1F 88
Apron Rd. M22—6C 112
Apsley Clo. M14—3B 110
Apsley Gro. M12—9J 79
Apsley Gro. M34—3B 110
Apsley Pl. OL6—5A 82
Apsley Rd. M34—2N 93
Apsley Side. OL5—8J 65
Aqueduct Rd. BL3—5J 39
Aragon Dri. OL10—8J 27
Aragon Way. SK6—7E 106
Arbor Av. M19—7M 103
Arbor Clo. M6—4M 77
Arbor Gro. M28—7M 61
Arbor Gro. OL10—7M 27
Arbor Lo. WN2—7J 73
Arbor Rd. OL4—4E 64
Arbour La. OL9—1L 25
Arbroath St. M11—6D 80
Arbury Av. OL11—5C 28
Arbury Av. SK3—6M 103

Arcade, The. SK15—7F 82
Arcadia Av. M33—4G 101
Archer Av. BL2—1J 39
Archer Gro. BL2—1J 39
Archer St. M11—5A 80
Archer St. M28—9E 56
Archer St. OL5—6J 65
Archer St. SK2—8J 105
Arch La. WN4—4G 69
Archie St. BL1—9G 23
Arclid Clo. SK9—2L 119
Arcon Clo. M16—1E 29
Arcon Pl. SK14—2H 105
Arcon Rd. PR7—1L 17
Ardale Av. M10—6C 62
Ardcombe Av. M9—3J 61
Ardeen Wlk. M13—9J 79
Arden Av. M34—3B 62
Arden Clo. BL9—1L 41
Arden Clo. BL6—1F 82
Arden Clo. SK13—6G 97
Arden Ct. SK7—3D 114
Ardenfield. M34—7A 94
Ardenfield Dri. M22—1E 112
Arden Gro. M10—7C 62
Arden Lodge Rd. M23—6K 101
Arden Rd. SK6—7L 93
Arden St. OL9—9C 63
Arderne Rd. WA15—5G 101
Ardern Field St. SK1—6F 104
Ardern Rd. M8—4E 60
Ardingly Wlk. M23—5K 101
Ardley Rd. BL6—6C 20
Ardsley Clo. BL2—3A 40
Ardwick Grn. N. M12—6H 5 & —8J 79
Ardwick Grn. S. M13—6H 5 & —8J 79
Ardwick Ter. M12—9K 79
Argo St. OL8—7J 63
Argosy Dri. M30—8M 75
Argosy Dri. WA15—5M 111
Argus St. OL8—7J 63
Argyle Av. M14—2L 91
Argyle Av. M25—9A 42
Argyle Av. M33—2J 57
Argyle Cres. OL10—9H 27
Argyle St. BL9—5M 25
Argyle St. M18—9D 80
Argyle St. M29—9E 58
Argyle St. M35—6G 81
Argyle St. M35—9D 46
Argyle St. OL6—2H 81
Argyle St. OL5—7J 65
Argyle St. SK7—2L 115
Argyle St. WN5—2M 51
Ariel Wlk. WA3—7M 71
Arkholme. M28—8G 57
Arkholme Wlk. M9—9H 79
Arkle Wlk. M13—9H 79
Ark St. M19—4J 103
Arkwright Dri. SK6—7G 107
Arkwright Rd. SK6—6G 107
Arkwright St. OL9—9C 63
Arkwright Ter. SK14—5C 94
Arkwright Way. M4—5G 79
(off Arndale Cen.)
Arkwright Way. OL11—8G 29
Arkwright St. BL4—4F 38
Arlen Rd. BL2—4H 39
Arlen Way. OL10—8H 27
Arley Av. BL9—4L 25
Arley Av. M20—9F 90
Arley Clo. WN2—7H 35
Arley Dri. OL2—1C 46
Arley End. WA16—6C 108
Arley Gro. SK3—9D 104
Arleymere Clo. SK8—1M 113
Arley Moss Wlk. M13—6G 5 & —8H 79
Arley St. M26—8H 41
Arley St. SK14—3C 94
Arley Way. M34—5A 94
Arlies La. SK15—3G 83
Arlies St. OL6—3D 82
Arlington Av. M25—6C 60
Arlington Av. M27—1D 76
Arlington Av. M34—4A 94
Arlington Clo. OL11—6E 28
Arlington Cres. SK9—6E 118
Arlington Dri. SK2—1G 115
Arlington Dri. SK12—9K 115
Arlington Dri. WN7—7C 72
Arlington Rd. SK8—6F 38
Arlington St. BL3—6F 38
Arlington St. M3—3D 4 & 4D 78
Arlington St. M8—8F 60
Arlington St. OL6—4C 82
Arliss Av. M19—4A 92
Arlow Rd. M22—1B 112
Armadale Av. M9—8G 61
Armadale Clo. SK3—8F 104
Armadale Ct. BL3—4L 37
Armadale Rd. BL3—3L 37
Armadale Rd. SK16—7C 82
Armadale Rise. OL4—8E 46
Armentieres Sq. SK15—6G 83
Armhope Ter. SK9—5E 104
Armit Rd. OL3—4L 65
Armitage Av. M24—1K 61
Armitage Gro. M28—6E 94
Armitage Ho. M6—5L 77
Armitage Owen Wlk. M10 —9A 62
Armitage Pl. WA14—1D 110
Armitage Rd. WA14—1D 110
Armitage St. M30—6C 76
Armour Pl. M9—6J 61
Armoury Bank. WN4—4B 70
Armour St. OL15—7L 13
Armstrong Hurst Clo. OL12 —8H 13
Armstrong St. BL6—8C 20
Armstrong St. WN2—6G 35
Arncliffe Ct. BL4—8K 79
Arncliffe Dri. M23—1A 112
Arncliffe Rise. OL4—8E 46
Arncot Rd. BL1—5F 22
Arncot Clo. OL2—5A 46
Arndale Cen. M24—9M 43
Arndale Shopping Cen. M4 & —2F 5 & 5G 79
Arndale Shopping Cen. M32 —5J 89
Arne Clo. SK2—8A 106
Arneside Rd. M9—8J 79

Arnold Av. OL10—2L 43
Arnold Av. SK14—7F 94
Arnold Clo. SK16—8G 83
Arnold Dri. M24—6C 44
Arnold Dri. M35—6G 81
Arnold Rd. M16—5E 90
Arnold St. BL1—8C 22
Arnold St. OL1—9A 46
Arnold St. SK3—6E 104
Arnold Wlk. M34—7A 94
Arnott Cres. M15—7F 90
Arnside Av. OL9—2G 63
Arnside Av. SK4—8D 92
Arnside Av. SK7—2J 115
Arnside Clo. OL2—2D 46
Arnside Clo. SK6—9H 103
Arnside Clo. SK8—9H 103
Arnside Dri. M6—4L 77
Arnside Dri. OL11—5L 27
Arnside Gro. BL2—4M 39
Arnside Gro. M33—8H 89
Arnside Rd. WN6—9H 33
Arnside St. M14—3H 91
Arran Av. M32—4G 89
Arran Av. M33—2J 101
Arran Av. OL8—5M 63
Arran Clo. BL3—3L 37
Arran Clo. WN6—2D 32
Arrandale Ct. M31—3D 88
Arran Gdns. M31—1D 88
(in three parts)
Arrandale Av. M32—2A 40
Arran Rd. SK16—8C 82
Arran St. M7—1D 78
Arran St. M10—8M 61
Arran Wlk. OL10—9M 27
Arras Gro. M34—3F 92
Arreton Sq. M14—3K 91
Arrowfield Rd. M21—8D 90
Arrowhill Rd. M26—1F 40
Arrowscroft Way. SK14—1D 96
Arrowsmith St. BL6—9E 20
Arrowsmith Wlk. M11—6M 79
(off Redfield Clo.)
Arrow St. BL1—1E 38
Arrow St. M7—2D 78
Arrow St. WN7—4H 73
Arrow Trading Est. M34—1K 93
Art Clo. WN7—1D 72
Arthington St. OL16—2H 29
Arthog Dri. WA15—4F 110
Arthog Rd. M20—9K 91
Arthog Rd. WA15—4F 110
Arthur Av. M28—2J 57
Arthur La. BL2—7A 24
Arthur Pits. OL11—3M 27
Arthur Rd. M16—3C 90
Arthurs & Alice Kenyon Ind. Est. OL4—2D 64
Arthurs La. BL1—1G 39
Arthur St. BL1—5M 25
Arthur St. M18—9D 80
Arthur St. M30—6C 76
Arthur St. M35—6L 81
Arthur St. OL10—8K 27
Arthur St. SK5—7E 92
Arthur St. SK14—5C 94
Arthur St. WN2—3L 53
Arthur St. WN7—3E 72
Arthur Ter. SK5—7E 92
Arthur St. M28—7L 57
(Walkden)
Arthur St. M30—6C 76
(Worsley)
Artillery Pl. M22—9F 102
Artillery St. BL3—4F 38
Artillery St. M3—5D 4 & 7E 78
Arundale. BL5—7F 36
Arundale Av. M16—5E 90
Arundale Clo. SK14—3M 95
Arundale Gro. SK14—3M 95
Arundel Av. M25—1B 60
Arundel Av. M41—3J 35
Arundel Av. WA15—9E 101
Arundel Clo. BL8—4J 25
Arundel Clo. SK15—1M 83
Arundel Clo. WA13—3J 111
Arundel Ct. M9—3G 61
Arundel Dri. WN7—1F 72
Arundel Grange. SK13—6G 97
Arundel Gro. SK2—9H 105
Arundel Rd. SK8—5A 114
Arundel St. BL1—5E 22
Arundel St. M15—6E 4 & 8D 78
Arundel St. M27—7C 58
Arundel St. OL4—1C 64
Arundel St. OL11—6E 28
Arundel St. SK13—5J 97
Arundel St. WN2—3L 53
Arundel Wlk. OL9—2G 63
Asby Clo. M24—2A 44
Ascension Rd. M7—1C 4 & —3D 78
Ascot Av. M32—3M 89
Ascot Av. M33—2C 100
Ascot Clo. BL2—6L 23
Ascot Clo. OL9—1J 63
Ascot Clo. OL11—2C 28
Ascot Dri. M33—2D 100
Ascot Dri. SK7—2A 116
Ascot M. M7—1D 78
Ascot Pde. M19—8M 91
Ascot Rd. BL3—6B 38
Ascot Rd. M10—3B 62
Ascot Wlk. OL9—2H 63
Ascroft Av. WN6—6L 33
Ascroft Ct. OL1—2M 63
Ascroft St. WN1—1E 52
Asgard Dri. M5—5B 4 & 7C 78
Asgard Gro. M5—5B 4 & 7C 78
Ash Av. M30—9D 86
Ash Av. WA14—8A 100
Ashawe Clo. M28—5E 56
Ashawe Ter. M28—5E 56
Ashbank Av. BL3—3L 37
Ashbee St. BL1—7E 22
Ashberry Clo. SK9—3K 119
Ashborne Dri. BL9—9N 9
Ashbourne Av. BL2—3H 39
Ashbourne Av. M24—6C 44
Ashbourne Av. M31—4L 87
Ashbourne Av. M34—7M 103
Ashbourne Av. WN2—3N 53
(Hindley)
Ashbourne Av. WN2—7F 34
(Wigan)
Ashbourne Clo. OL12—5K 13
Ashbourne Ct. SK13—6M 97
Ashbourne Dri. BL6—1F 82
Ashbourne Gdns. WN2—3M 53
Ashbourne Gro. M6—2G 77
Ashbourne Gro. M25—8K 41
Ashbourne Gro. M45—5F 80
Ashbourne Rd. M31—4D 88
Ashbourne Rd. M34—8M 81
Ashbourne Rd. SK3—3G 103
Ashbourne Rd. SK7—4M 115

Ashbourne Sq. OL8—3L 63
Ashbourne St. OL11—1L 27
Ashbridge. M35—1H 81
Ashbridge Rd. M34—3H 93
Ashbrook Clo. M45—9B 42
Ashbrook Clo. M34—3H 93
Ashbrook Clo. SK8—3H 113
Ashbrook Cres. OL16—8J 13
Ashbrook Farm Clo. SK5 —4F 92
Ashbrook Hey La. OL12—7J 13
Ashbrook La. SK5—4F 92
Ashbrook St. M11—8G 81
Ashburn Av. M19—9M 91
Ashburn Clo. BL6—4L 37
Ashburner St. BL1—3E 38
Ashburn Gro. SK4—2D 104
Ashburton Clo. SK14—4L 95
Ashburton Rd. SK3—9E 104
Ashburton Rd. E. M17—9H 77
Ashburton Rd. W. M31 & M17 —8D 76
Ashbury Clo. BL3—4E 38
Ashbury Pl. M10—3L 79
Ashby Av. M19—1L 103
Ashby Clo. BL3—6J 39
Ashby Gro. M25—1B 60
Ashby Rd. WN3—5B 52
Ash Clo. OL6—2D 82
Ash Clo. OL12—7J 13
Ashcombe Dri. BL2—3A 40
Ashcombe Dri. M26—4D 40
Ashcombe Wlk. M11—6M 79
(off Aldershot Wlk.)
Ashcott Av. M22—9D 102
Ashcott Clo. BL6—4L 37
Ash Ct. SK6—9A 94
Ashcroft. OL12—7K 13
Ashcroft Av. M6—3L 77
Ashcroft Clo. SK9—6F 118
Ashcroft St. WN2—4L 53
Ashdale Av. BL3—4L 37
Ashdale Clo. SK5—9F 82
Ashdale Dri. M20—9K 91
Ashdale Dri. SK8—2H 113
Ashdene. OL12—7D 12
Ashdene Cres. BL2—5K 23
Ashdene Rise. OL1—5D 46
Ashdene Rd. M20—8K 91
Ashdown Av. M9—4K 61
Ashdown Av. SK6—9C 94
Ashdown Dri. M27—1G 77
Ashdown Dri. M28—9G 57
Ashdown Dri. WA3—4N 61
Ashdown Rd. SK4—2C 104
Ashdown Ter. M9—4K 61
Ashdown Way. OL2—1L 45
Ash Dri. M27—7C 58
Ashenhurst Ct. M9—5G 61
Asher St. BL3—7C 38
Ashes Clo. SK15—7J 83
Ashes Dri. BL2—1M 39
Ashes La. OL4—2F 64
Ashes La. SK13—4H 97
Ashes La. SK15—7J 83
Ashfell Ct. M21—5M 89
Ashfield. M29—4J 55
Ashfield Av. OL11—5F 28
Ashfield Clo. M34—4M 53
Ashfield Clo. M6—4L 77
Ashfield Cres. OL11—5F 28
Ashfield Cres. SK8—7K 103
Ashfield Dri. M10—3D 80
Ashfield Dri. M41—4J 35
Ashfield Gro. M18—2F 92
Ashfield Gro. M30—8E 86
Ashfield Gro. SK6—4H 107
Ashfield Ho. OL11—5F 28
Ashfield La. OL16—6M 29
Ashfield Lodge. M20—3F 102
Ashfield Pk. Dri. WN6—1M 33
Ashfield Rd. M13—3L 91
Ashfield Rd. M31—4D 88
Ashfield Rd. M33—9H 89
Ashfield Rd. OL6—2H 19
Ashfield Rd. SK8—7K 103
Ashfield Rd. SK14—7G 83
Ashfield Ter. OL16—1C 32
Ashfield Ter. PR6—2H 19
Ashford. M33—1C 100
Ashford Av. M27—1C 76
Ashford Av. M30—7C 76
Ashford Av. SK5—4F 92
Ashford Clo. BL2—6L 23
Ashford Clo. BL8—9H 25
Ashford Clo. SK7—2A 116
Ashford Ct. M33—2D 100
Ashford Grn. SK13—5E 96
(off Ashford M.)
Ashford M. SK13—5E 96
Ashford Rise. WN1—5B 34
Ashford Rd. M20—7G 91
Ashford Rd. SK4—8D 92
Ashford Rd. E. M35—8F 62
Ashford Wlk. OL9—2H 63
Ashgate. M22—9E 102
Ashgill Wlk. M9—4J 61
(off Fernclough Rd.)
Ash Gro. BL0—8F 8
Ash Gro. BL1—1B 38
Ash Gro. OL10—3J 27
Ash Gro. OL11—5E 28
Ash Gro. SK6—8C 94
Ash Gro. SK7—1J 97
Ash Gro. SK14—9A 82
Ash Gro. WN1—9C 34
Ash Gro. OL4—2F 64
(Springhead)
Ash Gro. OL5—5D 104
Ash Gro. SK14—1H 95
(Milnrow)
Ash Gro. WN2—7F 34

Ashkirk St. M18—1D 92
Ashland Av. WN1—7C 34
Ashlands. M33—9G 89
Ashlands Av. M10—7C 62
Ashlands Av. M33—2E 100
Ashlands Av. WN1—7C 34
Ashlands Clo. BL0—1K 9
Ashlands Dri. M34—8H 53
Ashlands Rd. WA15—4G 101
Ash La. WA15—3J 111
Ashlar Dri. M12—7K 79
Ashleigh Clo. OL2—7L 45
Ashleigh Dri. BL1—3E 38
Ashleigh Rd. WA15—5H 101
Ashley Av. BL3—1K 39
Ashley Av. M16—2D 90
Ashley Clo. OL11—6C 28
Ashley Ct. M10—7F 62
Ashley Ct. OL12—1D 12
Ashley Ct. WA15—3E 110
Ashley Ct. Dri. M10—7F 62
Ashley Cres. M27—9D 58
Ashley Dri. M27—9D 58
Ashley Dri. M33—3E 100
Ashley Dri. SK7—6C 14
Ashley Gro. BL4—9J 39
Ashley La. M9—4M 61
Ashley Mill La. N. WA15 —4D 110
Ashley Rd. M35—5E 80
Ashley Rd. SK2—5J 105
Ashley Rd. WA14 & WA15 —1D 110
Ashley St. M4—2G 5 & 4H 79
Ashley St. OL11—6C 28
Ashley Wlk. M35—5E 80
Ashling Ct. M29—7C 56
Ashlor St. BL9—9L 25
Ashlyn Gro. M14—6K 91
Ashmead. M33—1M 101
Ashmill Wlk. M9—1J 79
Ashmond Rd. OL4—2F 64
Ashmoor St. M3—1E 5 & 3F 78
Ashmoor Rd. M22—3E 112
Ashmore Wlk. M22—3E 112
Ashmore St. M29—8D 56
Ashness Dri. BL2—9L 23
Ashness Dri. M24—6L 43
Ashness Pl. BL2—9L 23
Ashop Wlk. M15—6D 4 & 8E 78
Ashover Av. M12—3M 91
Ashover Clo. BL1—4F 22
Ashover St. M32—3L 89
Ashridge Dri. M30—7D 76
Ashridge Dri. SK7—4E 114
Ash Rd. BL4—3D 57
Ash Rd. M31—2F 92
Ash Rd. M34—3F 92
Ash Rd. OL2—2G 45
Ash Rd. PR7—2L 17
Ash Rd. SK12—9M 115
Ash Rd. WA3—3A 98
Ash Sq. OL4—9D 46
Ashstead Rd. M33—4J 101
Ash St. BL2—3G 39
Ash St. BL9—8A 26
Ash St. M6—5M 77
Ash St. M24—9C 44
Ash St. M34—8K 81
Ash St. M35—8E 62
Ash St. OL10—7H 27
Ash St. OL11—8C 23
Ash St. SK3—5B 104
Ash St. SK7—1K 115
Ash St. WA3—5H 71
Ashton Av. WA14—7E 100
Ashton Clo. M33—1E 100
Ashton Clo. M34—9M 81
Ashton Cres. OL9—5G 63
Ashton Field Dri. M28—6D 56
Ashton Gallery. WN1—9C 34
(off Galleries, The)
Ashton Gdns. SK13—5E 28
Ashton Gdns. WN3—7J 91
Ashton Heath. WN4—5C 70
Ashton Hill La. M35—7B 81
Ashton Ho. OL6—4B 82
Ashton La. M33—4K 89
Ashton New Rd. M11—6L 79
—7L 79
Ashton Old Rd. M12 & M11
Ashton Rd. M9—3K 61
Ashton Rd. M31 & M33—2J 99
Ashton Rd. M34—7M 93
Ashton Rd. M35—6E 81
(Droylsden)
Ashton Rd. M35—1J 81
(Failsworth)
Ashton Rd. OL8—3L 63
Ashton Rd. OL11—3A 28
Ashton Rd. SK4—9D 82
Ashton Rd. E. M35—8F 62
Ashton Rd. W. M35—9E 62
Ashton's La. SK15—9E 62
Ashton's Pl. SK15—9F 62
Ashton St. BL3—63 40
(Bolton)
Ashton St. BL3—5G 63
(Little Lever)
Ashton St. OL10—3J 27
Ashton St. OL11—5E 28
Ashton St. SK6—8C 94
Ashton St. SK7—1J 97
Ashton St. WN1—9C 34
Ashton Sq. WN1—9C 34
(off Galleries, The)
Ashurst Av. M11—5B 80
Ashurst Clo. BL2—7J 23
Ashurst Clo. M22—9E 68
Ashurst Dri. SK3—8B 104
Ashurst Gdns. OL6—2J 82
Ashurst Rd. M22—9E 102
Ashville Ter. M10—7M 61
Ashwater Wlk. M9—3L 61
(off Brockford Dri.)
Ashway Clough N. SK2—8K 105
Ashway Clough S. SK2—8L 105
Ashwell Rd. M23—4M 101
Ashwell St. BL2—2H 39
Ashwin Wlk. M8—1F 78
Ashwood. WA14—3C 100

Ashwood Av. M20—1E 102
Ashwood Av. M28—2E 100
Ashwood Av. M33—2E 100
Ashwood Av. WN2—3J 73
Ashwood Clo. OL7—2A 82
Ashwood Cres. SK6—6F 106
Ashwood Dri. BL8—4H 25
Ashwood Dri. OL2—4J 45
Ashwood Dri. OL15—6K 13
Ashwood Rd. SK12—6M 117
Ashworth Av. BL3—6L 40
Ashworth Av. M31—4L 87
Ashworth Av. M34—8L 81
Ashworth Clo. OL3—2B 46
Ashworth Clo. OL15—4A 14
Ashworth Clo. WA14—3B 110
Ashworth Clo. OL11—8E 10
Ashworth Ct. M26—1C 40
Ashworth La. BL1—5F 22
Ashworth La. SK14—4M 95
Ashworth Rd. OL11—8E 10
Ashworth St. M34—2J 93
Ashworth St. M35—1D 80
Ashworth St. OL1—2M 63
(in two parts)
Ashworth St. OL11—2D 28
Ashworth St. SK14—1E 104
Ashworth St. BL8—7J 25
Ashworth Ter. BL2—6L 23
Ashworth View. M5—8B 78
(off Ordsall Dri.)
Ashway Clough S. SK2—8L 105
Asia St. BL3—6G 39
Askern Av. M22—1D 112
Askill Dri. M24—8K 43
Askrigg Wlk. M13—2M 91
Aspen Av. WA15—8L 101
Aspen Clo. WA15—8L 101
Aspen Grn. M34—4A 94
Aspen Way. SK6—5G 117
Aspenwood. WA14—5A 70
Aspenwood Clo. SK6—6E 106
Aspenwood Dri. M33—1C 100
Aspenwood Dri. OL9—1G 62
Aspinal Clo. OL12—9E 12
Aspinall Ct. BL6—8C 20
Aspinall Cres. M28—5F 56
Aspinall Rd. WN6—9H 17
Aspinall St. BL6—1C 36
Aspinall St. M24—1C 62
Aspinall St. M28—5F 56
Aspland Rd. SK4—4G 103
Aspley Pl. M34—2D 100
Aspull Arc. WN1—9C 34
(off Galleries, The)
Aspull Comn. WN7—6C 72
Aspull St. OL4—3C 64
Asquith Av. SK16—6F 83
Asquith Rd. M19—8M 91
Asquith St. SK5—5P 92
Asquith St. BL8—5L 25
Assheton Av. M34—4M 93
Assheton Clo. OL6—4B 82
Assheton Cres. M10—3B 80
Assheton Rd. OL2—2M 45
Assheton Rd. M10—2D 80
Assheton Way. M24—9A 44
Astan Av. M35—4E 80
Astbury Av. M34—6K 81
Astbury Av. WA14—4B 70
Astbury Clo. WA15—7E 100
Astbury Cres. SK3—7D 104
Astbury Wlk. SK8—8A 104
Aster Av. BL4—8G 39
Aster St. OL1—4L 45
Astley Clo. OL2—9M 45
Astley Gdns. SK16—4F 82
Astley Gro. OL6—5E 86
Astley La. BL1—7E 22
Astley M. SK16—6B 82
Astley Rd. BL2—5L 23
Astley Rd. SK16—9A 82
Astley St. BL1—8E 22
Astley St. M11—6D 80
Astley St. M34—9B 80
Astley St. SK4—4G 103
Astley St. SK16—9A 82
Astley Ter. SK16—6C 82
Aston Av. M14—4F 90
Aston Clo. SK3—8D 104
Aston Gdns. BL4—8K 39
Aston Gro. M29—7C 56
Aston Way. SK9—7K 113
Astor Rd. M19—7L 91
Astra Business Pk. M17—2G 77
Astral M. M14—3K 91
Atcham Gro. M9—6J 61
Athens Dri. M28—6E 56
Athens St. SK1—4G 105
Atherfield. BL2—5L 23
Atherfield Clo. M18—9F 80
Atherleigh Gro. M28—6G 56
Atherleigh Way. WN7 & M29 —5D 72
Atherley Gro. M10 & OL9—6G 63
Atherstone. OL12—2E 28
(off Spotland Rd.)
Atherstone Av. M8—6F 60
Atherstone Clo. BL8—6J 25
Atherton Av. M31—3F 88
Atherton Gro. SK14—2A 96
Atherton Ho. M29—4K 55
Atherton Lodge. M33—2H 101
Atherton Rd. BL4—9F 38
Atherton Rd. WN2—2L 41
Atherton Sq. WN1—9C 34
(off Galleries, The)
Atherton St. M3—2D 4 & 4D 78
Atherton St. M30—6H 75
Atherton St. SK1—1H 105
Atherton St. WN1—7C 34
(Lees)
Atherton St. OL4—2F 64
(Springhead)
Atherton St. PR7—3G 16
Atherton St. SK14—5D 104
Atherton St. WN2—4L 53
Athlone Av. BL1—5C 22
Athlone Av. BL9—6A 26
Athlone Av. M33—4D 100
Athlone Av. OL9—6G 63
Athol Cres. WN2—4B 54
Athole St. M5—6M 77
Athol Rd. M16—9M 89
Athol Rd. SK7—2J 115
Athol St. M18—3A 92
Athol St. M30—6C 76
Athol St. OL6—8H 81
Athol St. SK4—3H 103
Athol St. WN3—9B 34
Athos Wlk. M10—2C 62
Atkin St. M28—6C 56
Atkinson Av. BL3—4D 39
Atlanta Av. M22—7M 111

Atkinson St. M3—4D 4 & 6E 78
Atkinson St. OL9—9K 45
Atkinson St. M28—3J 57
Atkinson St. SK1—8C 28
Atkinson St. SK16—6G 105
Atkin St. M28—6M 57
Atlantic St. WA14—7A 100
Atlantic Wlk. M11—6M 79
(off Yeoman Wlk.)
Atlas St. BL1—1F 38
Atlas St. OL7—2A 82
Atlas St. OL8—2L 63
Atlas St. SK16—7D 82
Atlee Way. M12—6J 79
Attenburys La. M34—5E 100
Attenbury's Pk. Est. WA14 —5E 100
Attercliffe Rd. M21—7A 90
Attingham Rd. M34—3H 93
Attingham Wlk. M10—9A 62
Attleboro Rd. M10—9A 62
Attwood St. M12—3A 92
Atwood Rd. M20—2H 103
Atwood St. M1—7G 5 & 1G 79
Aubrey Rd. M20—2J 91
Aubrey St. M5—7A 78
Aubrey St. M6—2J 77
Auburn Av. SK6—1M 105
Auburn Dri. WN7—8C 54
Auburn Rd. M16—2D 90
Auburn Rd. M34—4K 93
Auburn St. BL1—9F 22
Auburn St. M1—4K 5 & 5G 79
Auckland Dri. M6—2A 78
Auckland Rd. M19—6M 91
Audax Wlk. M10—3B 80
Auden Clo. M11—6A 80
Audenshaw Hall Gro. M34 —8H 81
Audenshaw Rd. M34—8H 81
Audlem Clo. M10—5K 79
Audlem Wlk. SK8—8A 104
Audley Av. M32—3M 89
Audley Rd. M19—4B 92
Audley St. OL11—5K 65
(in two parts)
Audley St. OL6—5E 82
Audlum Ct. BL9—4A 26
Audrey Av. M18—1E 92
Audrey St. M9—8M 61
Augusta Clo. OL12—9E 12
Augusta St. OL12—9E 12
Augustus Clo. WN5—3K 51
Augustus St. BL3—5G 39
Augustus St. M3—1E 5 & 3F 78
Augustus Way. M15—2D 90
Austell Rd. M22—4D 112
Austell Ct. WA11—8D 68
Austen Av. BL9—3M 41
Austen Rd. M30—6D 76
Austen Wlk. OL1—5E 46
Auster Clo. M14—4L 91
Austin Av. WA11—9J 69
Austin Dri. M20—1J 103
Austin Gro. M19—6M 91
Austin's La. BL6—1F 36
Austin St. BL8—5L 25
Austonley Wlk. M15—6D 4 & —8E 78
Avalon Dri. M20—5J 103
Avebury Clo. BL6—9F 20
Avebury Clo. M7—3B 78
Avebury Rd. M23—8A 102
Aveham Clo. M15—1F 90
Avenham Clo. M15—1F 90
Avens Rd. M31—2F 98
Avenue St. BL1—1D 38
Avenue St. SK1—3F 104
Avenue, The. BL5—2H 39
Avenue, The. BL9—5M 25
Avenue, The. M7—2C 78
Avenue, The. M28—4J 75
Avenue, The. M31—2D 100
Avenue, The. M41—1L 87
Avenue, The. OL2—3A 46
Avenue, The. SK6—1K 105
Avenue, The. SK9—8J 113
Avenue, The. WA14—4F 110
Avenue, The. WA15—7K 108
Avenue, The. WN1—7D 34
Avenue, The. WN5—5D 50
Avenue, The. WN2—5L 33
Averham Clo. M28—6B 70
Averhill. M28—8F 57
Averill St. M10—2J 79
Avery Clo. BL6—3M 37
Avery Cres. WA11—8J 69
Avian Av. WA11—8J 69
Avian Dri. M14—6H 91
Aviary Rd. M28—1H 75
Avis St. OL2—2B 46
Avocet Dri. M20—5B 80
Avocet Dri. WA14—5B 100
Avon Business Pk. M10—6F 62
Avonbrook Dri. M10—6F 62
Avoncliffe Clo. BL1—9A 22
Avon Clo. M26—6G 57
Avon Clo. OL16—4A 30
Avon Clo. SK6—7E 106
Avon Clo. WN5—4C 68
Avoncourt Dri. M20—1G 103
Avondale. WN2—1G 35
Avondale Av. BL9—6L 25
Avondale Av. SK7—2M 115
Avondale Clo. SK6—2B 106
Avondale Cres. M31—3C 88
Avondale Dri. BL0—1H 9
Avondale Dri. M6—2H 77
Avondale Lodge. M33—2H 101
Avondale Rd. BL4—9F 38
Avondale Rd. M32—2L 89
Avondale Rd. SK3—4D 104
Avondale Rd. SK7—2M 115
Avondale Rd. WN1—7C 34
Avondale St. BL1—1C 38
Avondale St. M8—2G 61
Avon Flats. OL10—8J 27
(off Kay St.)
Avon Gdns. M19—8A 92
Avonhead Clo. BL6—4K 37
Avonlea Dri. M19—1K 103
Avonlea Rd. M33—4D 100
Avonleigh Gdns. OL1—4M 63
Avon Rd. BL4—9M 39
Avon Rd. M19—8M 91
Avon Rd. M29—3C 56
Avon Rd. OL2—1L 45
Avon Rd. SK8—5J 113
Avon Rd. WA15—4C 110
Avon Rd. WN5—4C 68
(Billinge)
Avon Rd. WN5—5M 51
(Wigan)
Avon St. BL1—9B 22
Avon St. OL8—4M 63
Avon St. SK3—7F 104
Avril Clo. SK5—6F 92
Avril Ct. WN3—4E 52

Avro Clo. M14—5H 91
Avroe Rd. M30—8M 75
Avro Way. WA15—5M 111
Awburn St. SK14—5L 95
Axbridge Wlk. M10—5K 79
Axford Clo. M7—1E 78
Axminster Wlk. SK7—3E 114
Axon Sq. M16—2F 90
Aycliffe Av. M21—9D 90
Aycliffe Gro. M13—9L 79
Aye Bri. Rd. WN2—2H 71
Aylesbury Av. M34—5M 93
Aylesbury Av. M41—3A 88
Aylesbury Clo. M5—7A 78
Aylesbury Cres. WN2—6C 54
Aylesbury Gro. M24—7C 44
Aylesby Av. M18—2B 92
Aylesford Rd. M14—3H 91
Aylestone Wlk. M10—9A 62
Aylsham M. M27—2D 76
Aylsham Clo. SK6—9P 93
Aylwin Dri. M33—2J 101
Ayr Av. OL8—5M 63
Ayr Clo. SK7—2A 116
Ayrefield. M16—3D 32
Ayrefield La. WN8—5C 32
Ayres Rd. M16—2C 90
Ayrshire Rd. M7—1B 78
Ayr St. BL2—6J 23
Ayrton Gro. M28—2G 57
Aysgarth Av. M18—1E 92
Aysgarth Av. SK6—1D 106
Aysgarth Clo. M33—4D 100
Aysgarth Av. SK8—7J 103
Ayshford Clo. WA14—7B 100
Ayton Gro. M14—3G 91
Ayton St. M1—4F 5 & 6G 79
Azalea Av. M18—9D 80

Babbacombe Gro. M9—3H 61
Babbacombe Rd. SK2—7J 105
Baber Wlk. BL1—6E 22
Babylon La. PR6—2H 19
Bk. Acton St. M1—5G 5 & 7H 79
Bk. Albany St. OL11—5C 65
Bk. Adley Rd. M19—4B 92
Bk. Adrian St. OL5—7K 65
(two parts)
Bk. Audley St. OL6—5E 82
Bk. All Saints St. BL1—1F 38
(off Bark St.)
Bk. Apple Ter. BL1—8D 22
Bk. Argyle St. BL9—5M 25
Bk. Ashley St. M4—2G 5 & 4H 79
Bk. Ashworth St. BL8—7J 25
Bk. Astley St. BL1—9C 22
Bk. Avondale St. BL1—1C 38
Bk. Baldwin St. N. BL3—4E 38
Bk. Balloon St. M4—2F 5 &
Bk. Bank St. M8—1F 5 & 3G 79
Bk. Belfast St. BL1—8E 22
Bk. Bennett's La. BL1—8C 22
Bk. Birch St. BL9—7M 25
(in two parts)
Bk. Bolton Rd. S. BL9—6M 25
Bk. Bower La. SK14—6F 94
Bk. Bowness Rd. BL3—5D 38
Bk. Bradshaw St. SK16—2G 29
Bk. Bridge St. M3—3E 4 & 5E 78
Bk. Brierley Rd. BL9—L 41
Bk. Brook St. N. BL9—6A 26
(in two parts)
Bk. Broom St. BL2—2G 39
Back Brow. BL8—1C 50
Bk. Burgess Ter. M12—8K 79
Bk. Burnley Rd. BL9—9N 9
Bk. Burton St. M12—6H 5 & —8J 79
Bk. Bury Rd. S. BL2—2J 39
(in two parts)
Bk. Byrom St. S. BL8—6H 25
Bk. Cambridge St. BL1—9E 22
Bk. Cambridge St. OL7—6M 81
Bk. Camp St. M7—2D 78
Bk. Canada St. BL2—7B 20
Bk. Canning St. BL9—6M 25
Bk. Cateaton St. BL9—6M 25
Bk. Chapel St. BL6—7C 20
Bk. Chapel St. M19—4J 103
Bk. Chapel St. M30—5F 76
Bk. Chapel St. M19—5A 92
Bk. Chapel St. WN5—5D 50
Bk. Chapel St. WA15—4F 110
Bk. Cheapside. BL1—2F 38
Bk. Chesham Rd. N. BL9—5A 26
(off Chesham Rd.)
Bk. Chesham Rd. BL9—5A 26
Bk. China La. M1—4G 5 & 6H 79
Bk. Chorley Old Rd. S. BL1 —9A 22
Bk. Church Rd. N. BL1—8B 22
Bk. Church St. N. BL1—2G 97
Bk. Clay St. E. BL7—3G 23
Bk. Clifton St. BL9—6M 25
Bk. Common St. BL5—1B 54
Bk. Cowm La. OL12—1C 12
Bk. Crostons Rd. BL8—7C 25
Bk. Crown St. BL6—6A 20
Bk. Dale St. OL16—5M 29
Bk. Darwen Rd. N. BL7—1G 22
Bk. Deacon's Dri. M6—1K 77
Bk. Deane Chu. La. BL3—5B 38
Bk. Delamere St. S. BL9—5A 26
(off Delamere St.)
Bk. Demesne St. SK15—5J 83
Bk. Denton St. BL9—6A 26
Bk. Devonshire Rd. BL1—9A 22
Bk. Devon St. N. BL3—6J 39
Bk. Deyne Av. M25—4B 60
Bk. Dumers La. BL9—6K 41
Bk. Duncan St. M7—9C 60
Bk. Duncan St. WN7—2G 73
Bk. East St. BL9—9M 25
Bk. Edenfield Rd. OL12—9J 11
Bk. Eden St. BL1—6C 22
Bk. Eldon St. BL9—6M 25
Bk. Elsworth St. M3—2F 5 & —4G 79
Bk. Emmett St. BL6—7B 20
Bk. Everton St. N. BL1—8D 22
Bk. Fairhaven Rd. BL1—7F 22
Bk. Fern St. BL3—3D 38
Bk. Fletcher St. M26—9D 40
Bk. Foundry St. M4—3G 5 & —4G 79
Bk. Garden St. M3—3D 4 & 5E 78
Bk. George St. M1—5F 5 & 7G 79
Bk. Georgiana St. BL9—8M 25
Bk. Gigg La. BL9—8N 25
Bk. Grafton St. WA14—9D 100
Bk. Grantham Clo. BL1—9E 22
Bk. Grosvenor St. BL3—1M 41
Bk. Hamel St. SK14—1F 94
Bk. Hamilton St. M7—9D 60
Bk. Hanover St. M4—3F 5 & —5G 79
Bk. Hanson St. BL9—6M 25
Bk. Hart St. BL5—1B 54
Bk. Harvey St. BL1—7D 22
Bk. Haslam St. BL9—6A 26
Bk. Hatfield Rd. BL1—9D 22
Bk. Heywood St. BL9—9A 26
Bk. Higher Swan La. BL3—6E 38
Bk. High St. BL7—2J 7
Bk. Hilton St. BL2—6M 25
Bk. Hilton St. M7—9D 60
Bk. Holland St. BL1—6F 22
Bk. Hope St. M7—9D 60
Bk. Hope St. OL1—1B 64
Bk. Hornby St. BL9—6M 25
Bk. Horne St. BL9—6M 25
Bk. Horne St. BL9—1L 41
Bk. Hotel St. BL1—2F 38
Bk. Howe St. M7—9C 60

Bk. Hulme St. M5—4B 4 & 6C
Bk. Hulton La. S. BL3—7A 38
Bk. Huntley Mt. Rd. BL9—6B
Bk. Ingham St. BL9—9A 26
Bk. Ivy Bank Rd. BL1—5E 22
Bk. Ivy Rd. BL1—9G 22
Bk. James St. BL3—4B 40
Bk. James St. OL15—6M 13
Bk. Johnson St. M4—2F 5 & —4G
Bk. John St. BL3—3E 38
Bk. Kingholm Gdns. BL1—9D
Bk. King St. OL1—2L 63
Bk. Knowl St. SK15—5H 83
Back La. BL1—7C 20
Back La. BL5—2B 56
Back La. M7—2C 78
Back La. OL4 & OL6—5G 65
(Oldham)
Back La. OL4—8J 47
(Scouthead)
Back La. OL12—3K 81
(in two parts)
Back La. OL12—1C 12
(Rochdale)
Back La. OL12—1C 12
(Whitworth)
Back La. SK14—8D 96
(Charlesworth)
Back La. SK14—3A 96
(Mottram)
Back La. WA11—2A 68
Back La. WA14—8H 99
(Dunham Town)
Back La. WA14—7F 108
(Hulseheath)
Back La. WA15—7F 110
Bk. Lark Hill. BL1—1E 32
Back La. WN8—4A 32
Bk. Lee St. OL3—9B 48
Bk. Lever St. BL3—5M 25
Bk. Lightburne Av. BL1—9A 22
Bk. Linton Av. BL9—5M 25
Bk. Louise St. OL12—8H 13
Bk. Lucas St. BL3—7A 26
Bk. Lydia St. BL2—2G 39
Bk. Manchester Old Rd. BL9
Bk. Manchester Rd. E. BL9
(off Parkhills Rd.) —1L
Bk. Manchester Rd. W. BL9
(Blackford Bridge) —4M
Bk. Manchester Rd. W. BL9
(Bury)
Bk. Manor St. BL9—8A 26
Bk. Market St. M26—9B 40
Bk. Market St. SK16—3K 53
Bk. Market St. WN7—2E 72
Bk. Markland Hill La. BL1 —9M
Bk. Markland Hill La. W. BL1 —9M
Bk. Maskill St. N. BL9—6M
Bk. Massie St. SK8—7K 103
Bk. Mawdsley St. BL1—2F 2
Bk. Maxwell St. BL1—6E 22
Bk. Melbourne St. SK15—5G
Bk. Mere Gdns. BL1—1E 38
Bk. Merton St. BL8—7K 25
Bk. Milner Av. BL9—6A 26
Bk. Mirey La. BL6—5H 37
Bk. Monmouth St. BL9—6A 26
Bk. Nelson St. BL6—7C 20
Bk. Nelson St. N. BL9—1M
Bk. Nelson St. S. BL9—1M
Bk. Newton St. BL1—8E 22
Bk. Nook Ter. OL12—8F 12
Bk. Oldham Rd. OL16—4G 2
Bk. Olga St. BL1—8D 22
Bk. Olive Bank. BL8—6K 25
Back o' th' Low Rd. OL4—4
Back o' th' Moss La. OL10
(in two parts) —8
Bk. Parkfield View. OL16 —8
Bk. Parkhills Rd. BL9—9A 2
Bk. Parkhills Rd. N. BL9—1
Bk. Parkhills Rd. S. BL9—1
Bk. Patience St. OL12—1C 2
Bk. Piccadilly. M4 & M1—4F 6
Bk. Pine St. BL9—7B 30
(off Pine St.)
Bk. Platting La. OL11—6G 2
Bk. Pool Fold. M2—4E 5 & 6
Bk. Porter St. BL9—6M 25
Bk. Portland St. BL6—6A 20
Bk. Prestbury Clo. BL8—9A 2
Bk. Quay St. M3—4D 4 & 6
Bk. Queen St. BL8—8B 22
Bk. Queen St. WN7—2G 73
(off Brown St.)
Bk. Quickwood. OL8—5K 6
Bk. Rake St. BL9—6K 60
Bk. Ramsden Rd. OL12—4J
Bk. Rawlinson St. BL6—6A 2
Bk. Red Bank. M4—2F 5 & 4
Bk. Rigby La. N. BL2—1J 39
Bk. Roman Rd. M7—1E 78
Bk. Rooley Moor Rd. OL12
Bk. Rossini St. BL1—7D 22
Bk. Rowena St. BL3—6J 39
Bk. Royds St. OL16—5G 29
Bk. St Anne's St. BL9—6A 2
Bk. St George's Rd. BL1—1
Bk. St George's Rd. M4—2C
Bk. Salford St. BL9—6A 26
Bk. Salford St. WN7—2F 71
Bk. Sandy Bank Rd. BL7—
Bk. Sapling Rd. S. BL3—8C
Bk. School St. WN8—1C 5
Bk. School La. M20—6G 91
Bk. Scott St. OL8—3M 63
Bk. Settle St. N. BL3—6D 3
Bk. Shakerley Rd. M29—7
Bk. Shepard St. BL9—8A 2
Bk. Shipton St. BL1—7F 22
Bk. Short St. M29—7M 55
Bk. Skull Ho. La. WN6—1C
Bk. Somerset Rd. W. BL1 4G
Bk. South Pde. M3—4E 5 &
Bk. Spear St. M1—3G 5 & 5
Bk. Spring Gdns. BL1—2F 3
Bk. Spring St. W. BL9—6A 2
Bk. Spring Mill. OL16—5G 2
Bk. Stanley St. BL9—6L 25
Bk. St. M20—3F 5
Bk. Thomasson Clo. BL1—8
Bk. Thomas St. M4—3F 5 &
Bk. Thorns Rd. BL1—7E 22
Bk. Tonge Moor Rd. BL2— 5G
Bk. Tootal Rd. M5—5K 77
Bk. Tottington Rd. BL8—6
(off Sawyer St.)
Bk. Tottington Rd. N. BL8
Bk. Tottington Rd. S. BL8
Bk. Turner St. M4—3F 5 &
Bk. Union Rd. OL12—1L 1
Bk. Vernon St. BL9—6M 2
Bk. Vernon St. M7—
Bk. Walmersley Rd. E. BL9
(in three parts)
Bk. Walmersley Rd. W. BL
(in five parts)
Bk. Walshaw Rd. N. EL8—
Bk. Walshaw Rd. S. EL8—
Bk. Walshaw Rd. S. BL8
(off Wellington Rd.)

ckwell Wlk. M4—5J 79 *(off Marsworth Dri.)*
. Whitegate. OL15—7L 13
. Wigan Rd. N. BL3—5A 38
(in two parts)
. Willows La. BL3—5C 38
. Woking Gdns. BL1—9E 22
. Wood St. BL6—7C 20
. Wright St. BL6—6B 20
. Young St. BL4—1L 57
claw Clo. WN1—8F 34
con Av. M34—7A 94
con St. M10—8A 62
dby Clo. M4—6K 79
ddeley Clo. SK3—8D 104
dder St. BL1—1F 38
den St. M11—7L 79
der Dri. OL10—2K 43
dger Edge La. OL4—6J 47
dger La. OL16—8H 29
in three parts)
dger St. BL9—7M 25
dgers Wlk. M22—3E 112
dminton Rd. M21—5C 90
g La. M29—4H 55
gnall Clo. OL3—8C 48
gnall Clo. OL12—9M 11
gnall Ct. M22—4E 102
gnall Wlk. M22—5E 102
got St. BL4—2A 58
got St. M11—5C 80
got St. M27—7C 58
gshaw La. WN2—7L 35
gshaw St. SK14—1E 94
gslate Moor La. OL11
—2M 27
gslate Moor Rd. OL11
—3M 27
gstock Av. SK12—1L 121
uley Cres. M24—1G 61
uley Cres. SK2—7D 104
uley Dri. BL9—7A 42
uley La. M33—3L 101
n three parts)
uley Rd. M33—1L 101
uley St. M35—6H 81
ama Clo. WA11—7K 69
ama Rd. WA11—7K 69
don Rd. OL12—1B 28
don St. M10—7A 62
ey Field. BL5—9G 37
ey La. BL2—9L 23
n two parts)
ey La. M22—3B 112
ey La. M31—2F 98
ey Rd. M17—8G 77
ey's Ct. WN1—9C 34
ey St. M11—6D 80
ey St. M25—3C 60
ey St. OL1—1A 64
ey Wlk. WA14—3C 110
ie St. OL16—3F 28
n four parts)
ie St. E. OL16—2G 29
abridge Clo. M12—9K 79
aes Av. M30—6F 86
aes St. BL1—1B 38
St. M27—9F 58
ton Wlk. M9—3J 61
d St. M1—5G 5 & 7H 79
ngs Row. OL12—9J 11
er Ho. OL2—5L 45
ff Royton Hall Wlk.)
ers La. OL3—7E 48
er St. BL0—6H 9
er St. BL4—2B 58
er St. M24—9B 44
er St. OL7—1A 82
er St. OL10—1L 43
er St. SK4—2E 104
er St. SK15—6H 83
er St. WA15—6J 101
er St. WN3—2B 52
er St. WN7—9E 54
er Ter. M34—2H 93
ewell Av. M34—6A 94
ewell Av. OL6—1F 82
ewell Bank. SK13—5D 96
ff Bakewell Gdns.)
ewell Clo. SK13—5D 96
ff Bakewell M.)
ewell Fold. SK13—5D 96
f Bakewell M.)
ewell Gdns. SK13—5D 96
ewell Grn. SK13—5D 96
f Bakewell Gdns.)
well Gro. SK13—5D 96
well Lea. SK13—5D 96
f Bakewell M.)
well M. SK13—5D 96
well Rd. M30—7C 76
well Rd. M32—3G 89
well Rd. M35—5E 80
well Rd. SK7—4L 115
well St. M18—2C 92
well St. SK3—5D 104
well Wlk. SK13—5D 96
f Bakewell Gdns.)
arres Av. WN1—7E 34
arres Rd. WN2—4H 35
ary Gro. BL1—1B 38
mbe Clo. BL8—3J 25
rstone Rd. OL11—8F 28
ck Rd. M20—2K 103
ine Dri. WN2—3B 54
vin Rd. M19—8M 91
vin St. BL3—4D 38
vin St. WN1—9D 34
vin St. WN2—5B 54
vin St. WN3—1D 52
vin St. WN5—2H 51
St. M2—5E 5 & 7F 78
n Clo. BL5—8E 36
n Fold. BL5—8E 36
ur Gro. SK5—5F 92
ur Rd. M31—3B 88
ur Rd. OL12—1C 28
ur Rd. WA14—6D 100
ur St. BL3—3D 38
ur St. M6—1A 78
ur St. M8—8G 61
ur St. OL2—2B 46
ur St. OL4—1C 64
m Wlk. M12—9M 79
r Dri. WA10—9A 68
ntine St. M10—3C 80
d Clo. OL15—4B 14
er Av. M31—5A 88
er Clo. OL10—9H 27
er Wlk. M8—9F 60
ook Av. M20—9G 91
ook Clo. M20—1H 103
att St. M19—5A 92
Clo. SK6—1C 106
St. M8—8G 61
St. M27—8E 58
Way. WN4—3M 69
n St. M4—3F 5 & 5G 79
Cotts. WN3—5F 52
. OL16—2G 29
. WN6—7L 23
reen. OL11—7C 28
in Av. M18—3C 92
in Rd. M31—3B 88
Dri. M23—9B 102
eld St. M8—1G 79
orth St. M15—6C 4 &
8D 78
ral. PR7—4E 18
ral Av. BL3—6A 40
ral Av. M25—1A 60
ral Av. M31—5B 88
ral Av. M32—3K 89
ral Av. M34—8K 81
ral Av. OL2—5M 45
ral Av. OL11—2B 28
ral Av. SK8—2A 114
ral Av. SK14—6E 94
ral Av. WA3—6K 71
ral Clo. BL6—8E 20
ral Clo. BL8—1G 25
ral Clo. BL9—4A 42
ral Clo. OL16—4A 30
Balmoral Ct. M9—3F 60
Balmoral Dri. M34—2G 93
Balmoral Dri. OL10—9G 27
Balmoral Dri. SK6—5E 116
Balmoral Dri. SK12—9K 115
Balmoral Dri. SK15—4G 83
Balmoral Dri. WA14—5F 100
Balmoral Dri. WN2—4J 53
Balmoral Dri. WN7—1K 73
(in two parts)
Balmoral Grange. M25—5E 60
Balmoral Gro. SK7—1M 115
Balmoral Ho. M30—5C 76
(off Police St.)
Balmoral Rd. BL4—1J 57
Balmoral Rd. M14—6K 91
Balmoral Rd. M27—6G 59
Balmoral Rd. M31—5A 88
Balmoral Rd. SK4—2A 104
Balmoral Rd. WA15—9E 100
Balmoral Rd. WN4—3A 70
Balmoral Rd. WN5—2L 51
Balmoral St. M18—2C 92
Balmoral Way. SK9—5G 119
Balmore Clo. OL10—9E 26
Balm St. BL0—7G 9
(in two parts)
Balniel Wlk. WN1—6E 34
Balsam Clo. M13—6H 5 & 8J 79
Balshaw Av. M30—4F 86
Balshaw Clo. BL3—4C 38
Balshaw Ct. M30—4G 87
Baltic St. M5—5L 77
Baltimore St. M10—2M 79
Bamber Av. M33—2L 101
Bamber Croft. BL5—6E 36
Bamburgh Clo. M26—4C 40
Bamburgh Dri. OL7—2L 81
Bamburgh Pl. WN4—2A 70
Bamburg St. BL9—7M 25
Bamford Av. M24—7A 44
Bamford Av. M34—6M 93
Bamford Clo. BL9—6E 26
Bamford Clo. SK8—4K 113
Bamford Ct. OL11—4B 28
(off Half Acre M.)
Bamford Dri. WN2—7F 34
Bamford Fold. SK13—5E 96
(off Castleton Cres.)
Bamford Gdns. WA15—7K 101
Bamford Grn. SK13—5E 96
(off Castleton Cres.)
Bamford Gro. M20—2G 103
Bamford Gro. OL6—1F 82
Bamford La. SK13—5E 96
Bamford M. SK13—5E 96
Bamford Pl. OL12—1E 28
Bamford Rd. BL0—3L 9
Bamford Rd. M9—3K 61
Bamford Rd. M20—2G 103
Bamford Rd. OL10—6J 27
Bamfords Pas. OL15—5A 14
Bamford St. M11—5B 80
Bamford St. OL2—5L 45
Bamford St. OL9—9J 45
Bamford St. OL15—5M 13
(Caldermoor)
Bamford St. OL15—6M 13
(Stubley)
Bamford St. SK1—5F 104
Bamford Way. OL11—4M 27
Bampton Clo. SK2—6H 105
Bampton Rd. M22—3D 112
Bampton Wlk. M24—7L 43
Banbury Dri. WA14—5E 100
Banbury M. M27—7D 58
Banbury Rd. M23—8M 101
Banbury Rd. M24—3M 61
Banbury St. BL2—9J 23
Banbury St. SK1—4F 104
Bancroft Av. SK8—3A 114
Bancroft Clo. SK6—2C 105
Bancroft Ct. WA15—1F 110
Bancroft Fold. SK14—1H 95
Bancroft Rd. M27—7E 58
Bancroft Rd. WA15—1G 111
Banff Gro. OL10—9G 27
Banff Rd. M14—2J 91
Bangor Fold. WN7—3J 73
Bangor Rd. SK8—7M 103
Bangor St. BL1—1E 38
Bangor St. OL6—5E 82
Bangor St. OL16—4H 29
Bangor St. SK5—1F 104
Banham Av. WN3—5J 51
Banham St. M9—7K 61
Bank. OL12—4J 13
Bank Av. WN5—3D 50
Bank Barn La. OL12—4K 13
Bankbottom. SK14—1G 97
Bank Bri. Rd. M11—4B 80
Bank Brow. SK14—8G 85
Bank Brow. WN8—5C 32
Bank Clo. OL15—8A 14
Banker St. BL3—4J 39
Bankes Av. WN5—2G 51
Bankfield. BL5—1G 55
Bankfield Av. M13—3L 91
Bankfield Av. M30—9D 86
Bankfield Av. M35—5G 81
Bankfield Av. SK4—3C 104
Bankfield Clo. BL2—9C 24
Bankfield Cotts. OL3—7M 47
Bankfield Cotts. SK6—9A 94
Bankfield Dri. M28—9H 57
Bankfield Dri. OL8—6B 64
Bankfield Ho. SK6—9B 94
Bankfield La. OL11—2L 27
Bankfield M. BL9—2M 41
Bankfield Rd. M29—8E 56
Bankfield Rd. M33—8E 88
Bankfield Rd. SK6—9B 94
Bankfield Rd. SK8—3M 113
Bankfield St. BL3—4C 38
(in two parts)
Bankfield St. M9—7K 61
Bank Field St. M26—1D 58
Bankfield St. SK5—1E 104
Bankfield Trading Est. SK5
—1E 104
Bank Gro. M28—2F 56
Bankhall La. WA15—4E 110
Bankhall Rd. SK4—2A 104
Bankhall Wlk. M9—9L 61
(off Broadwell Dri.)
Bank Hill St. OL4—1C 64
Bankhouse Rd. BL8—5J 25
Bank Ho. Rd. M9—4H 61
Banklands Clo. M30—9D 86
Bank La. M6 & M27—2K 77
Bank La. M28—2F 56
Bank La. OL3—4D 66
Bank La. OL12—4K 13
Bank La. SK14—8G 85
Bankley St. M19—5A 92
Bank Meadow. BL6—6C 20
Bankmill Clo. M13—6G 5 &
8H 79
Bank Pl. BL8—7J 25
Bank Pl. M3—3C 4 & 5D 78
Bank Pl. WA3—6G 71
Bank Rd. M8—6G 61
Bank Rd. SK6—2A 106
Bank Rd. SK15—2L 83
Bank Rd. WN8—4C 32
Banks Ct. WA15—8K 101
Bank Side. BL5—1F 54
Bank Side. OL5—8J 65
Bankside. SK14—5K 95
Bankside. WA15—6K 111
Bankside Av. M26—5K 41
Bankside Av. OL3—1C 66
Bankside Av. WN4—8A 52
Bankside Clo. OL9—2K 63
Bankside Clo. SK6—4H 107
Bankside Clo. SK9—2K 119
Bankside Ct. SK4—3A 104
Bankside Rd. M20—6H 103
Bankside Wlk. SK14—4K 95
Banks La. SK1—5H 105
Bank Sq. SK9—4H 119
Banks St. WN7—2D 72
Bank St. BL1—2F 38
Bank St. BL4—9K 39
Bank St. BL7—7J 7
Bank St. BL8—6F 24
Bank St. BL9—8L 25
Bank St. M3—3C 4 & 5D 78
Bank St. M8—8F 60
Bank St. M11—4B 80
(in two parts)
Bank St. M25—8L 41
Bank St. M26—7H 41
Bank St. M33—9J 89
Bank St. M34—9M 81
(Audenshaw)
Bank St. M34—6A 94
(Denton)
Bank St. M35—7F 80
Bank St. OL2—2A 46
Bank St. OL4—2D 64
Bank St. OL5—8J 65
Bank St. OL7—5B 82
Bank St. OL10—8H 27
(in two parts)
Bank St. SK6—9B 94
Bank St. SK8—7L 103
Bank St. SK13—6K 97
Bank St. SK14—6A 96
(Broadbottom)
Bank St. SK14—1G 97
(Hadfield)
Bank St. SK14—3D 94
(Hyde)
Bank St. WA3—9A 86
Bank St. WN2—5G 53
Bank St. WN5—2L 51
Bankswood Clo. SK14—2G 97
Bank Ter. OL12—3C 12
Bank Ter. SK14—1G 97
Bank, The. OL16—3F 28
Bank Top. BL9—1M 25
Bank Top. OL6—5C 82
Bank Top Gro. BL1—5G 23
Bank Top Pk. OL4—2D 64
Bank Top St. OL10—7H 27
Bank View. BL4—1L 57
Bankwell Clo. M15—1E 90
Bank Wood. BL1—2M 37
Bankwood. WN6—3E 32
Banky La. M33—8C 88
Bannatyne Clo. M40—7E 62
Bannerdale Clo. M13—2M 91
Bannerman Av. M25—5B 60
Bannerman Rd. M35—6H 81
Bannerman Sq. M16—2F 90
Bannerman St. M7—9E 60
Banner St. WN2—3L 53
Banner St. WN3—3E 52
Banner Wlk. M11—6M 79
Bannister Dri. SK8—2M 113
Bannister St. BL2—1L 39
Bannister St. SK1—6F 104
Bann St. SK3—5E 104
Banstead Av. M22—6D 102
Bantock St. M14—3J 91
Bantry Dri. M9—5H 61
Bantry St. BL3—4E 38
Bantry St. OL12—9G 13
Baptist St. M4—2G 5 & 4H 79
Barathea Clo. OL11—7A 28
Barbara Rd. BL3—7A 38
Barbara St. BL3—5D 38
Barbeck Clo. M10—4L 79
Barberry Bank. BL7—9D 6
Barberry Clo. WA14—6B 100
Barberry Wlk. M31—2F 98
Barber St. SK14—1H 97
Barbican St. M20—7H 91
Barbirolli Mall. M4—5G 79
(off Arndale Cen.)
Barbirolli Sq. M4—5G 79
(off Arndale Cen.)
Barbon Wlk. M4—3H 5 & 5J 79
Barchester Av. BL2—9L 23
Barcheston Rd. SK8—9J 103
Barcicroft Rd. M19 & SK4
—1L 103
Barcicroft Wlk. M19—1L 103
Barclay Dri. M30—4E 76
Barclay Rd. SK12—1L 121
Barclays Av. M6—1K 77
Barcliffe Av. M10—6C 62
Barclyde St. OL11—5E 28
Barcombe Clo. OL4—7D 46
Barcombe Wlk. M9—9K 61
(in two parts)
Barcroft Rd. BL1—8B 22
Barcroft St. BL9—7M 25
Bardale Gro. WN4—4A 70
Bardell Cres. SK12—1K 121
Bardon Clo. BL1—9D 22
Bardon Rd. M23—7M 101
Bardsea Av. M22—3D 112
Bardsley Av. M35—9F 62
Bardsley Clo. BL2—5K 23
Bardsley Clo. SK14—4L 95
Bardsley Clo. WN8—1A 50
Bardsley Ga. Av. SK15—9L 83
Bardsley St. M10—2D 80
Bardsley St. M24—8A 44
Bardsley St. OL4—3E 64
(Lees)
Bardsley St. OL4—8E 46
(Oldham)
Bardsley St. OL9—5F 62
Bardsley St. SK4—2D 104
Bardsley Vale Av. OL8
—8A 64
Barehill St. OL15—5B 14
Bare St. BL1—1G 39
Barff Rd. M5—5J 77
Barfold Clo. SK2—8A 106
Barfold Wlk. M15—9E 78
Barford Dri. WA3—7A 72
Barford Gro. BL6—9F 20
Barford Wlk. M23—9B 102
Bar Gap Rd. OL1—9J 45
Baric Clo. M30—6F 76
Baring St. M1—5G 5 & 7H 79
Barker Rd. SK6—2M 105
Barkers La. M33—9F 88
Barker St. BL9—9L 25
Barker St. M3—1E 5 & 3F 78
Barker St. OL10—9H 27
Barker St. WN7—2C 72
Barke St. OL15—8L 13
Barking St. M10—4L 79
Bark St. BL1—2E 38
(in two parts)
Bark Wlk. M15—9F 78
Barkway Rd. M32—4G 89
Barkwell La. OL5—7H 65
Barkworth Wlk. M10—1B 80
Bar La. BL1—5E 22
Barlborough Rd. WN5—3K 51
Barlby Wlk. M10—1B 80
Barlea Av. M10—7D 62
Barley Brook Meadow. BL1
—4F 22
Barley Brook St. WN6—8A 34
Barleycorn Clo. M33—2M 101
Barley Ct. SK14—2F 96
Barley Croft. SK8—4M 113
Barleycroft Clo. M16—2F 90
Barley Croft Rd. SK14—9E 82
Barley Dri. SK7—5E 114
Barleyfield Wlk. M24—8M 43
Barley Hall St. OL10—7L 27
Barleywood Wlk. SK15—8K 83
Barlow Ct. BL7—6L 7
Barlow Cres. SK6—8F 106
Barlow Fold. BL9—4M 41
Barlow Fold. SK5—6F 92
Barlow Fold. SK6—2D 106
Barlow Fold Clo. BL9—4M 41
Barlow Fold Rd. SK5—6F 92
Barlow Fold Rd. SK6—2D 106
Barlow Hall Rd. M21—9C 90
Barlow Ho. OL8—3M 63
Barlow La. M30—5C 76
Barlow La. N. SK5—6F 92
Barlow Moor Clo. OL12—9L 11
Barlow Moor Ct. M20—1F 102
Barlow Moor Rd. M21—4B 90
Barlow Moor Rd. M21 & M20
—6B 90
Barlow Pk. Av. BL1—5D 22
Barlow Rd. M19—5A 92
Barlow Rd. M32—2M 89
Barlow Rd. SK9—2H 119
Barlow Rd. SK16—7D 82
Barlow Rd. WA14—5B 100
Barlow's Croft. M3—3E 5 &
5E 78
Barlow's La. S. SK7—1J 115
Barlows Rd. M5—4B 4 & 6C 78
Barlow St. BL1—2G 39
Barlow St. BL6—8C 20
Barlow St. BL9—7M 25
Barlow St. M26—6H 41
Barlow St. M28—4K 57
Barlow St. M30—6D 76
Barlow St. OL4—2A 64
Barlow St. OL10—1L 43
Barlow St. OL16—3G 29
Barlow Ter. M21—9D 90
Barlow Wlk. SK5—6F 92
Barlow Wood Dri. SK6—1H 117
Barmeadow. OL3—7M 47
Barmhouse Clo. SK14—3G 95
Barmouth St. M11—7M 79
Barmouth Wlk. OL8—6H 63
Barnaskin La. PR7—1B 16
Barnaby Rd. SK12—1K 121
Barn Acre. BL6—9L 19
Barnacre Av. BL2—2M 39
Barnacre Av. M23—1M 111
Barnard Av. M25—1B 60
Barnard Av. SK4—3B 104
Barnard Clo. OL7—2M 81
Barnard Rd. M18—3B 92
Barnard St. BL2—1J 39
Barnbrook St. BL9—7A 26
Barnby St. M12—3A 92
Barn Clo. M31—4J 87
Barn Clo. SK13—7K 97
Barnclose Rd. M22—3D 112
Barncroft Clo. SK6—2L 105
Barncroft Dri. BL6—7F 20
Barncroft Gdns. M22—8C 102
Barncroft Rd. BL4—9K 39
Barndale Clo. BL2—1C 40
Barnes Av. SK4—3A 104
Barnes Clo. BL0—8G 9
Barnes Clo. BL4—9L 39
Barnes Meadows. OL15—2C 14
Barnes Pas. M29—5L 55
Barnes St. BL4—8H 39
Barnes St. OL4—9E 46
Barnes Ter. BL4—1A 58
Barnet Rd. BL1—8C 22
Barnett Av. M20—8H 91
Barnett Ct. OL10—8J 27
Barnett Dri. M3—3C 4 & 5D 78
Barnfield. M31—5B 88
Barnfield. OL15—5D 14
Barnfield Av. SK6—2D 106
Barnfield Clo. BL7—9E 6
Barnfield Clo. M5—6M 77
Barnfield Clo. M26—6E 40
Barnfield Cres. M33—8F 88
Barnfield Dri. BL5—8G 37
Barnfield Dri. M28—1H 75
Barnfield Rise. OL2—9A 30
Barnfield Rd. M19—1L 103
Barnfield Rd. M27—6D 58
Barnfield Rd. SK14—1G 95
Barnfield Rd. E. SK3—9F 104
Barnfield Rd. W. SK3—9D 104
Barnfield St. M34—2K 93
Barnfield St. OL10—8L 27
Barnfield St. OL12—9F 12
Barnfield Wlk. WA15—8J 101
(in two parts)
Barn Fold. OL4—3E 64
Barngate Dri. OL5—8J 65
Barngate Rd. SK8—7G 103
Barngill Gro. WN3—5L 51
Barn Gro. M34—8L 81
Barnham Wlk. M23—5L 101
Barn Hill. BL5—8E 36
Barnhill Av. M25—6B 60
Barnhill Dri. M25—6B 60
Barnhill Rd. M25—5A 60
Barnhill St. M14—2F 90
Barn Hill Ter. BL5—8E 36
Barn La. WA3—8F 70
Barnley Clo. M30—3H 87
Barn Meadow. BL7—5K 7
Barnsdale Dri. M8—1G 79
Barnsfold Av. M14—6J 91
Barnsfold Rd. SK6—1F 116
Barnside. OL12—3C 12
Barnside Av. M28—6L 57
Barnside Clo. BL9—2L 25
Barnside Way. M35—9J 63
Barns La. WA14 & WA13—8G 99
Barnsley St. SK1—5G 105
Barnsley St. WN6—6A 34
Barns Pl. WA15—4J 111
Barnstaple Dri. M10—1J 79
Barnstead Av. M20—9K 91
Barnston Av. M14—4H 91
Barnston Clo. BL1—6F 22
Barn St. BL1—2E 38
Barn St. M25—1M 59
Barn St. OL1—2L 63
Barn St. SK1—2F 104
Barnswell St. M10—2C 80
Barn Wlk. M11—8E 80
Barnway Wlk. M10—6C 62
Barnwell Clo. M34—1L 93
Barnwood Clo. BL1—9E 22
(off Barnwood Dri.)
Barnwood Dri. BL1—9E 22
Barnwood Rd. M23—1A 112
Barnwood Ter. BL1—9E 22
(off Barnwood Dri.)
Baroness Gro. M7—1B 4 & 3C 78
Baron Fold. M28—3G 57
Baron Fold Cres. M28—3F 56
Baron Fold Gro. M28—3F 56
Baron Fold Rd. M28—3F 56
Baron Grn. SK8—5K 113
Barons Ct. M35—1D 80
Baron St. BL9—9K 25
(in three parts)
Baron St. OL4—3B 64
Baron St. OL16—3F 28
Baron St. SK14—7F 94
Baron Wlk. BL3—6C 40
Barrack Hill. SK6—3A 106
Barrack Hill Clo. SK6—2A 106
Barracks La. M33—8D 88
Barrack Sq. WN1—9C 34
(off Library St.)
Barracks Rd. WN2—7K 53
Barrack St. BL3—3E 38
Barrack St. M15—6C 4 & 8D 78
Barracks Yd. WN1—9C 34
Barra Dri. M31—1D 88
Barrass St. M11—8D 80
Barratt Gdns. M24—5K 43
Barrett Av. BL4—1M 57
Barrett St. BL9—8A 26
Barrett St. OL4—3B 64
Barrfield Rd. M6—3L 77
Barr Hill Av. M6—2L 77
Barrie St. WN7—8D 54
Barrie Way. BL1—6H 23
Barrington Av. M35—6F 80
Barrington Av. SK8—3A 114
Barrington Clo. WA14—7D 100
Barrington Rd. WA14—7D 100
Barrington St. M11—5C 80
Barrisdale Clo. BL3—4M 37
Barrow Bri. Rd. BL1—6M 21
Barrow Brook. M33—8M 89
Barrowdale Rd. WA3—7H 71
Barrowfield Rd. M22—2A 112
Barrowfields. M24—7A 44
Barrow Hill Rd. M8—2F 78
Barrow La. WA15—5H 111
Barrow Meadow. SK8—4L 113
Barrow Meadow. WN7—9D 54
Barrows Ct. BL1—3F 38
Barrow St. M3—4C 4 & 6D 78
Barrow St. WN4—2D 70
Barrs Fold Clo. BL5—6D 36
Barrs Fold Rd. BL5—6D 36
Barr St. BL4—3B 58
Barrule Av. SK7—3L 115
Barry Ct. M20—8H 91
Barry Cres. M28—5G 57
Barry Dri. M29—8B 56
Barrygate Clo. M15—1G 91
Barry Lawson Clo. M8—9F 60
Barry Rise. WA14—2A 110
Barry Rd. M23—3B 102
Barry Rd. SK5—9F 92
Barry St. OL1—9B 46
Barsham Dri. BL3—4D 38
Bar St. WN2—7G 53
Bar Ter. OL12—4C 12
Bartlam Pl. OL1—1M 63
Bartlemore St. OL1—8A 46
Bartlett Rd. OL2—3A 46
Bartlett St. M11—8B 80
Bartley Rd. M22—5C 102
Barton Arc. M3—5F 78
(off Deansgate)
Barton Av. M31—4B 88
Barton Av. WN1—7B 34
Barton Clo. SK9—1K 119
Barton Clo. WA3—4L 71
Barton Clough. WN5—2E 68
Barton Dock Rd. M31 & M32
—9E 76
Barton Fold. SK14—5D 94
Barton Hall Av. M30—6A 76
Barton Ho. M6—3J 77
Barton La. M30—7D 76
Barton Moss Rd. M30—7J 75
Barton Rd. BL4—1H 57
Barton Rd. M24—9M 43
Barton Rd. M27—1G 77
Barton Rd. M28—2M 75
Barton Rd. M30—6C 76
Barton Rd. M31—2C 88
Barton Rd. M32—2F 88
Barton Rd. SK4—4L 103
Barton Sq. M2—4E 5 & 6F 78
Barton St. BL4—1L 57
Barton St. M3—5D 4 & 7E 78
(in two parts)
Barton St. M27—6F 58
Barton St. M29—7M 55
Barton St. OL1—9K 45
Barton St. WA3—6G 71
Barton St. WN2—5H 53
Barton Ter. M30—3J 87
Barton Wlk. BL4—1H 57
Barway Rd. M21—5M 89
Barwell Av. WA11—9C 68
Barwell Clo. SK5—6F 92
Barwell Rd. M33—9E 88
Barwell Sq. BL4—7H 39
Barwick Pl. M33—1G 101
Basford Rd. M16—3B 90
Bashall St. BL1—1C 38
Basil Ct. OL16—4H 29
Basildon Clo. M13—1K 91
Basil St. BL3—4E 38
Basil St. M14—3J 91
Basil St. OL16—4H 29
Basil St. SK4—2D 104
Basle Clo. SK7—9E 104
Baslow Av. M19—4B 92
Baslow Clo. SK13—5E 96
(off Baslow M.)
Baslow Dri. SK7—4M 115
Baslow Dri. SK8—5J 113
Baslow Fold. SK13—5E 96
(off Castleton Cres.)
Baslow Grn. SK13—5E 96
(off Castleton Cres.)
Baslow Gro. SK5—9F 92
Baslow M. SK13—5E 96
Baslow Rd. M32—3G 89
Baslow Rd. M34—6M 93
Baslow Rd. M35—4E 80
Baslow St. M11—6L 79
Baslow Way. SK13—5E 96
(off Castleton Cres.)
Bassenthwaite Av. WA11
—7A 68
Basset Av. M6—2C 78
Bassett Clo. OL12—8E 12
Bassett Gdns. OL12—8E 12
Bassett Gro. WN3—6J 51
Bassett Way. OL12—9E 12
Bassey Wlk. M16—2E 90
Bass La. BL9—8K 9
Bass St. BL2—2J 39
Bass St. SK16—7B 82
Basswood Grn. WN2—5A 54
Basten Dri. M7—1E 78
Batchelor Clo. M21—7E 90
Bateman St. BL6—8D 20
Bates Clo. OL11—9D 28
Bateson Dri. OL4—2F 64
Bateson St. SK1—3G 105
Bateson Way. OL8—3M 63
Bates St. M13—2M 91
Bates St. SK16—7C 82
Bath Clo. SK7—2A 116
Bath Cres. M16—1C 90
Bath Cres. SK8—6B 114
Batheaston Gro. WN7—8D 54
Bath Pl. WA14—2D 110
Bath St. BL1—1F 38
Bath St. M29—5G 55
Bath St. OL9—1H 63
(Chadderton)
Bath St. OL9—3J 63
(Oldham)
Bath St. OL12—1G 29
Bath St. WA14—1D 110
Bath St. WN2—7F 34
Batley St. M9—8L 61
Batley St. OL5—7H 65
Batridge Rd. BL7—4G 7
Battenberg Rd. BL1—1C 38
Battersbay Gro. SK7—2L 115
Battersby Ct. SK2—7L 105
Battersby St. BL9—7D 26
Battersby St. M11—8E 80
Battersby St. OL11—4B 28
Battersby St. WN2—9H 35
Battersby St. WN7—3H 73
Battersea Rd. SK4—4L 103
Battle La. SK5—7K 93
Batty St. M8—2J 79
Baucher Rd. WN3—3M 51
Baum, The. OL16—2F 28
Baxendale St. BL1—6E 22
Baxter Gdns. M23—6A 102
Baxter Rd. M33—1H 101
Baxter St. WN6—9M 17
Baybutt St. M26—6J 41
Baycliffe Wlk. M8—1F 78
Baycroft Gro. M23—4A 102
Baydon Av. M8—1F 78
Bayfield Gro. M10—7A 62
Bayford St. M10—9B 62
Bayley Ind. Est. SK15—6F 82
Bayley St. BL1—1D 38
Bayley St. SK15—5E 82
Baynard Wlk. M9—4H 61
Baynham Av. M20—2H 103
Baysdale Av. BL3—5M 37
Baysdale Dri. OL2—4J 45
Baysdale Wlk. M11—6M 79
Bayston Wlk. M12—9M 79
(off Gortonvilla Wlk.)
Bay St. OL9—1K 63
Bay St. OL10—7H 27
Bay St. OL12—1G 29
Bay St. SK1—5F 104
Bayswater Av. M10—3B 80
Bayswater St. BL3—7C 38
Bayswell Ho. WN1—9D 34
Baythorpe St. BL1—7F 22
Bay Tree Av. M28—2A 76
Baytree Av. OL9—9E 44
Baytree Dri. SK6—1M 105
Baytree Gro. BL0—9H 9
Baytree La. M24—8D 44
Baytree Rd. WN6—7M 33
Baywood St. M9—8K 61
Bazaar St. M6—3A 78
Bazley Rd. M22—4D 102
Bazley St. BL1—6M 21
B Court. WN4—5B 70
Beacon Clo. M29—6G 55
Beacon Dri. M23—2A 112
Beaconfield. SK6—2G 107
Beaconfield Av. SK14—4E 94
Beacon Gro. WA11—9D 68
Beacon La. WN8—6A 32
Beacon Rd. SK6—4M 105
Beacon Rd. WN2—8A 54
Beacon Rd. WN5—9D 50
Beacon Rd. WN6—8H 17
Beaconsfield. M14—7J 91
Beaconsfield Rd. WA14
—6D 100
Beaconsfield St. BL3—3D 38
Beaconsfield St. WN1—7E 34
Beaconsfield Ter. OL5—7H 65
Beacons, The. WN6—2D 32
Beacon View. SK6—5F 106
Beacon View. WN6—1C 32
Beacon View Dri. WN8—1B 50
Beadham Dri. M9—3G 61
Beaford Clo. WN5—3H 51
Beaford Dri. M22—4E 112
Beagle Wlk. M22—4E 112
Beal Clo. SK4—2K 103
Beal Cres. OL16—1J 29
Bealcroft Clo. OL16—3L 29
Bealcroft Wlk. OL16—3L 29
Beal Dri. WN2—6G 53
Beale Gro. M21—6B 90
Bealey Av. M26—4L 41
Bealey Clo. M18—9B 80
Bealey Clo. M26—5K 41
Bealey Dri. BL9—2K 41
Beal La. OL2—3C 46
Beal Ter. OL16—4M 29
Beal View. OL2—2D 46
Beal Wlk. M25—9C 42
Beaminster Av. SK4—2A 104
Beaminster Clo. SK4—2A 104
Beaminster Ct. SK4—2A 104
(off Beaminster Clo.)
Beaminster Rd. SK4—2M 103
Beaminster Wlk. M13—1J 91
Beamish Clo. M13—9J 79
Beamsley Dri. M22—2B 112
Beanfields. M28—2M 75
Beanfield Ter. M28—2M 75
Bean Leach Av. SK2—7M 105
Bean Leach Dri. SK2—7M 105
Bean Leach Rd. SK7 & SK2
—9L 105
Beard Rd. M18—2C 92
Beard St. M35—6F 80
Beard St. OL2—6L 45
Beardwood Rd. M9—4K 61
Bearwood Clo. SK14—5F 94
Beathwaite Dri. SK7—3C 114
Beatrice Av. M18—2F 92
Beatrice Av. SK8—2M 113
Beatrice M. BL6—6B 20
Beatrice Rd. BL1—1C 38
Beatrice Rd. M28—9B 58
Beatrice St. BL4—9H 39
Beatrice St. M27—7D 58
Beatrice St. M34—3L 93
Beatrice St. OL11—3D 28
Beatrice Wignall St. M35
—7G 81
Beatson Wlk. M4—5J 79
(off Caroline Dri.)
Beattock Clo. M15—6C 4 &
8D 78
Beatty Dri. BL5—8E 36
Beauchamp St. OL6—3C 82
Beaufont Dri. OL4—3C 64
Beaufort Av. M20—9G 91
Beaufort Av. M27—9D 58
Beaufort Av. M33—2J 101
Beaufort Chase. SK9—2M 119
Beaufort Clo. SK9—7M 119
Beaufort Clo. SK14—5L 95
Beaufort Rd. M33—2J 101
Beaufort Rd. OL6—4D 82
Beaufort Rd. SK2—9K 105
Beaufort Rd. SK14—4L 95
Beaufort St. M3—5D 4 & 7E 78
Beaufort St. M25—4C 60
Beaufort St. M30—4B 76
Beaufort St. OL12—1C 28
Beaufort St. WN2—3K 53
Beaufort St. WN5—2L 51
Beaulieu. WA15—2F 110
Beaumaris Clo. M12—9M 79
Beaumaris Clo. WN7—2C 72
Beaumaris Cres. SK7—4J 115
Beaumaris Rd. WN2—5A 54
Beaumonds Way. OL11—4A 28
Beaumont Av. BL6—6C 20
Beaumont Chase. BL3—6M 37
Beaumont Clo. OL15—6M 13
Beaumont Ct. SK9—7J 113
Beaumont Dri. BL3—4L 37
Beaumont Gro. WN5—9H 33
Beaumont Rd. BL1, BL6 & BL3
—2K 37
Beaumont Rd. BL6—6C 20
Beaumont Rd. M21—7B 90
Beaumont St. OL6—4C 82
Beauvale Av. SK2—6J 105
Beaver Ct. WN4—1C 70
Beaver Dri. BL9—5B 42
Beaver Ho. SK1—5H 105
Beaver Rd. M20—2H 103
Beaver St. M1—5F 5 & 7G 79
Beaver Wlk. SK14—5K 95
Bebbington Clo. M33—2M 101
Bebbington St. M11—6C 80
Beccles Rd. M33—4H 101
Beckenham Clo. BL8—9H 25
Beckenham Rd. M8—9G 61
Becket Av. M7—1E 78
Becket Meadows. OL4—2B 64
Becket Meadow St. OL4—2B 64
Beckett Dri. WA13—5B 98
Beckett St. M18—1C 92
Beckett St. OL4—1E 64
Beckfield Rd. M23—8A 102
Beckfoot Dri. M13—3L 91
Beckford St. M10—2L 79
Beck Gro. M28—7L 57
Beck Gro. OL2—1D 46
Beck Gro. WA11—7B 68
Beckhampton Clo. M13—1J 91
Beckley Av. M25—6A 60
Beckley Clo. OL2—4A 46
Beckside. M29—8L 55
Beckside. SK5—5G 93
Beck St. M3—3D 4 & 5E 78
Beck St. M11—8E 80
Beckton Gdns. M22—1C 112
Beckwith. WN2—5H 53
Becontree. M23—6L 101
Becontree Av. M34—2A 94
Beddell's La. SK9—5G 119
Bede St. BL1—8C 22
Bedfont Wlk. M9—7L 61
(off Polworth Rd.)
Bedford Av. M16—4D 90
Bedford Av. M27—9E 58
Bedford Av. M28—7J 57
Bedford Av. M33—3K 101
Bedford Av. OL2—2M 45
Bedford Av. SK14—3E 94
Bedford Ct. M7—7D 60
Bedford Ct. WA15—7J 101
Bedford Dri. M29—7G 55
Bedford Dri. WA15—6J 101
Bedford Gdns. WN2—2M 53
Bedford Gro. M30—8B 86
Bedford Pl. WN4—2A 70
Bedford Rd. M16—3A 90
Bedford Rd. M30—4E 76
Bedford Rd. M31—2C 88
Bedford Sq. WN7—3G 73
Bedford St. BL1—1D 38
Bedford St. BL7—9D 6
Bedford St. BL9—6A 26
Bedford St. M25—3C 60
Bedford St. OL6—5C 82
Bedford St. OL10—8L 27
Bedford St. SK5—6E 92
Bedford St. SK15—6F 82
Bedford St. WN1—8E 34
Bedford St. WN5—3J 51
Bedford St. WN7—2G 73
Bedford Wlk. M34—5M 93
Bedlam Grn. BL9—8M 25
Bedlington Clo. M23—7K 101
Bednal Av. M10—3L 79
Bedwell Clo. M16—3F 90
Bedworth Clo. BL2—4H 39
Beechacre. BL0—6K 9
Beech Av. BL3—7B 40
Beech Av. BL4—9G 39
(Farnworth)
Beech Av. BL4—3B 58
(Kearsley)
Beech Av. BL6—9E 20
Beech Av. M6—3L 77
Beech Av. M22—5D 102
Beech Av. M25—1M 59
Beech Av. M26—9F 40
Beech Av. M28—1G 75
Beech Av. M29—5L 55
Beech Av. M30—3J 87
Beech Av. M31—4C 88
Beech Av. M32—5L 89
Beech Av. M34—2K 93
Beech Av. M35—6F 80
Beech Av. OL1—7G 45
Beech Av. OL3—2B 66
Beech Av. OL4—9D 46
Beech Av. PR6—2H 19
Beech Av. SK3—7F 104
Beech Av. SK6—7D 106
Beech Av. SK7—2L 115
Beech Av. SK8—8H 103
Beech Av. SK13—6G 97
Beech Av. WA3—8M 71
Beech Av. WA11—8M 69
Beech Av. WA15—5H 101
Beech Clo. BL2—4J 23
Beech Clo. M25—5C 60
Beech Clo. M31—2F 98
Beech Clo. OL12—2C 12
Beech Clo. SK9—8H 119
Beech Cotts. SK9—9L 119
Beech Ct. M6—4A 78
Beech Ct. M8—7F 60
Beech Ct. M14—6J 91
Beech Ct. M21—5M 89
Beech Ct. M33—1F 100
Beech Ct. SK9—5K 119
Beech Cres. SK12—8L 115
Beech Cres. WN6—1L 33
Beech Cres. WN7—4E 72
Beechcroft. M25—5C 60
Beechcroft Av. BL2—3L 39
Beechcroft Clo. M10—4K 79
Beechcroft Gro. BL2—3L 39
Beech Dri. WN7—5F 72
Beecher Wlk. M9—1K 79
(off Kelvington Dri.)
Beeches, The. BL1—4D 22
Beeches, The. M20—1F 102
Beeches, The. M29—5K 55
(off George St.)
Beeches, The. M30—4F 76
Beeches, The. OL5—7L 65
Beeches, The. OL10—8J 27
Beeches, The. OL12—2C 12
Beeches, The. SK8—3B 114
Beechey Sq. OL1—9A 46
Beechfield. M33—3F 100
Beechfield. OL4—2K 65
Beechfield. OL11—4L 27
Beechfield. WA14—1C 110
Beechfield Av. M26—8J 41
Beechfield Av. M28—3G 57
Beechfield Av. M31—3A 88
Beechfield Av. SK9—6E 118
Beechfield Av. WN2—4A 54
Beechfield Clo. OL11—4L 27
Beechfield Ct. BL9—2L 41
Beechfield Dri. BL9—2L 41
Beechfield Dri. WN7—4F 72
Beechfield Rd. BL1—8B 22
Beechfield Rd. M27—2D 76
Beechfield Rd. OL16—5L 29
Beechfield Rd. SK3—9F 104
Beechfield Rd. SK8—4B 114
Beechfield Rd. SK9—9L 119
Beechfield Rd. SK14—3E 96
Beechfield St. M8—1G 79
Beech Gro. BL8—1G 25
Beech Gro. M6—3L 77
Beech Gro. M14—7K 91
Beech Gro. M28—3E 56
Beech Gro. M33—1F 100
Beech Gro. OL7—6M 81
Beech Gro. SK9—5G 119
Beech Gro. SK15—7F 82
Beech Gro. WN2—9J 53
Beech Gro. WN6—6L 33
Beech Gro. WN7—5E 72
Beech Gro. Clo. BL9—6B 26
Beech Hall St. WN6—7A 34
Beech Hill Av. WN6—6M 33
Beech Hill La. WN6—7L 33
Beech Hill Rd. OL4—2K 65
Beech Holme Gro. SK2—5J 105
Beech Ho. M30—6B 76
Beech Ho. OL2—4B 46
Beech Hurst Clo. M16—4D 90
Beech La. OL4—3K 65
Beech La. SK6—3C 106
Beech La. SK9—5G 119
Beech Lawn. WA14—9C 100
Beech M. M21—6A 90
Beech M. SK2—8G 105
Beech M., The. M20—2F 102
Beech Mt. M9—8K 61
Beech Mt. OL7—1A 82
Beechpark Av. M22—6C 102
Beech Range. M19—5A 92
Beech Rd. M21—6A 90
Beech Rd. M33—1K 101
Beech Rd. SK3 & SK1—7F 104
Beech Rd. SK6—5F 116
Beech Rd. SK8—3B 114
Beech Rd. SK9—8H 119
Beech Rd. WA3—6G 71
Beech Rd. WA15—1E 110
Beech St. BL1—8F 22
Beech St. BL7—6K 7
Beech St. BL9—8B 26
(Bury)
Beech St. BL9—8J 9
(Summerseat)
Beech St. M24—9M 43
Beech St. M26—8J 41
Beech St. M27—9F 58
Beech St. M29—5L 55
Beech St. M30—6B 76
Beech St. M35—8E 62
Beech St. OL1—1A 64
Beech St. OL2—2B 46
Beech St. OL9—5H 63
Beech St. OL11—4D 28
Beech St. OL16—6A 30
Beech St. SK14—3D 94
Beech St. WN2—9F 52
Beech St. WN4—1A 70
Beech Tree Av. WN6—1D 32
Beech Tree Bank. M25—4A 60
Beechtree La. WA13—5B 108
Beechurst Rd. SK8—8B 104
Beech View. SK14—4G 95
Beech Vs. M33—1K 101
Beechville. BL6—2H 37
Beech Wlk. M24—2M 61
Beech Wlk. M32—5J 89
Beech Wlk. WN6—1K 33
Beech Wlk. WN7—5E 72
Beechway. SK6—5F 116
Beechway. SK9—6G 119
Beech Wlks. WN3—6J 51
Beechwood. OL2—1D 46
Beechwood. SK13—7F 96
Beechwood. WA14—3B 110
Beechwood Av. BL0—5K 9
Beechwood Av. M21—6C 90
Beechwood Av. M31—3L 87
Beechwood Av. OL15—8A 14
Beechwood Av. SK5—1F 104
Beechwood Av. SK6—3C 106
Beechwood Av. SK15—3J 83
Beechwood Av. WN4—5A 70
Beechwood Av. WN6—4F 32
Beechwood Cres. M29—1A 74
Beechwood Cres. WN5—2E 50
Beechwood Dri. M28—1B 76
Beechwood Dri. M33—1C 100
Beechwood Dri. OL2—3J 45
Beechwood Dri. OL5—6J 65
Beechwood Dri. SK6—7G 107
Beechwood Dri. SK9—3L 119
Beechwood Gro. M9—9L 61
Beechwood Gro. SK8—4A 114
Beechwood La. SK15—3J 83
Beechwood Rd. M25—5D 60
Beechwood Rd. OL8—6M 63
Beechwood St. BL3—6F 38
Beede St. M11—7B 80
Beedon Av. BL3—5A 40
Bee Fold La. M29—6H 55
(in three parts)
Beehive Grn. BL5—8H 37
Bee Hive Ind. Est. BL6—1F 36
Beehive St. OL8—5M 63
Beeley St. M6—2B 78
Beeley St. SK14—4E 94
Beeston Av. M7—1B 78
Beeston Av. WA15—7F 100
Beeston Clo. BL1—4G 23
Beeston Gro. M25—1B 60
Beeston Gro. SK3—8E 104
Beeston Gro. WN7—9K 55
Beeston Rd. M33—1E 100
Beeston Rd. SK9—7K 113
Beeston St. M9—8L 61
Beeth St. M11—8D 80
Beeton Gro. M13—2L 91
Beever St. M16—1C 90
Beever St. OL1—1A 64
Beggar's Wlk. WN6 & WN1
—6B 34
Begley Clo. SK6—4M 105
Begonia Av. BL4—8H 39
Begonia Wlk. M12—9M 79
Beightons Wlk. OL12—7D 12
Belbeck St. BL8—8J 25
Belcroft Dri. M28—2E 56
Belcroft Gro. M28—3E 56
Belding Av. M10—7F 62
Beldon Rd. M9—4H 61
Belfield Clo. OL16—2J 29
Belfield Ho. WA14—2C 110
Belfield La. OL15—3K 29
Belfield La. OL16—3J 29
(in two parts)
Belfield Lawn. OL16—2K 29
Belfield Mill La. OL16—2J 29
Belfield Old Rd. OL16—2J 29
Belfield Rd. M20—1H 103
Belfield Rd. M25—5E 60
Belfield Rd. OL16—2H 29
Belfield Rd. SK5—3F 92
Belfield Trading Est. OL16
—2K 29
Belford Av. M34—3G 93
Belford Dri. BL3—5E 38
Belford Rd. M32—3K 89
Belford Wlk. M23—7A 102
Belfort Dri. M5—5A 4 & 7B 78
Belfry Clo. SK9—3K 119
Belgate Clo. M12—2A 92
Belgian Ter. OL2—5M 45
Belgium St. OL11—3L 27
Belgrave Av. M14—3L 91
Belgrave Av. M31—3L 87
Belgrave Av. M35—8H 63
Belgrave Av. OL8—4A 64
Belgrave Av. SK6—6F 106
Belgrave Clo. M26—5G 41
Belgrave Clo. WN3—5K 51
Belgrave Clo. WN7—7C 72
Belgrave Ct. M34—2K 93
Belgrave Ct. OL8—3M 63
Belgrave Cres. BL6—7D 20
Belgrave Cres. M30—4F 76
Belgrave Cres. SK2—9H 105
Belgrave Dri. M26—5G 41
Belgrave Gdns. BL1—8E 22
Belgrave Rd. M10—7E 62
Belgrave Rd. M30—9D 86
Belgrave Rd. M33—1G 101
Belgrave Rd. OL8—4M 63
Belgrave Rd. WA14—1C 110
Belgrave St. BL1—9E 22
(in two parts)
Belgrave St. M26—5F 40
Belgrave St. M29—6G 55
Belgrave St. M34—2K 93
Belgrave St. OL10—9J 27
(in two parts)
Belgrave St. OL12—1D 28
Belgrave St. S. BL1—9E 22
Belgrave Ter. M10—1L 79
Belgravia Gdns. M21—6A 90
Belgravia M. OL2—2C 46
Belhaven Rd. M8—6F 60
Bellairs St. BL3—6C 38
Bellamy Ct. M18—1E 92
Bella St. BL3—5C 38
Bell Clough Rd. M35—4H 81
Bell Cres. M11—7L 79
Belldale Clo. SK4—3A 104
Belldean. WN2—9H 35
Belle Grn. La. WN2—1G 53
Belle Isle Av. OL12—5C 12
Bellerby Clo. M25—9L 41
Belleville Av. M22—4E 112
Belle Vue Av. M12—1M 91
Belle Vue St. M12—9A 80
Belle Vue St. WN5—3K 51
Belle Vue Ter. BL9—9L 25
Bellew St. M11—7L 79
Bellfield Av. OL8—6M 63
Bellfield Av. SK8—3B 114
Bellingham Av. WN1—7D 34
Bellingham Clo. BL8—8F 24
Bellingham Dri. WN1—7D 34
Bellingham Mt. WN1—6D 34
Bellingham St. M8—2G 79
Bellis Clo. M12—6L 79
Bell La. BL9—7A 26
Bell La. WN5—1H 51
Bell Meadow Dri. OL11—5M 27
Bellott St. M8—1G 79
Bellot Wlk. OL1—9L 45
Bellpit Clo. M28—9J 57
Bellscroft Av. M10—9B 62
Bellshill Cres. OL16—2J 29
Bell St. M35—5H 81
Bell St. OL1—1A 64
Bell St. OL16—2F 28
Bell St. WN2—2L 53
Bell St. WN7—7D 54
Bell Ter. M30—7C 76
Belmont Av. M6—4G 77
Belmont Av. M27—3D 58
Belmont Av. M29—4M 55
Belmont Av. M34—2K 93
Belmont Av. OL4—1F 64
Belmont Av. WA3—6J 71
Belmont Av. WN2—7M 53
Belmont Av. WN5—5D 50
Belmont Clo. SK4—2E 104
Belmont Dri. BL8—9G 25
Belmont Dri. SK6—3H 107
Belmont Dri. WN2—4J 35
Belmont Rd. BL6—1C 20
Belmont Rd. BL7 & BL1—9A 6
Belmont Rd. M26—8G 41
Belmont Rd. M33—8G 89
Belmont Rd. PR6—3G 19
Belmont Rd. SK7—7E 114
Belmont Rd. SK8—7H 103
Belmont Rd. WA15—2E 110
Belmont Rd. WN2—2M 53
Belmont Shopping Cen. SK4
—3E 104
Belmont St. M5—6K 77
Belmont St. M16—1D 90
Belmont St. M30—4D 76
Belmont St. OL1—9L 45
Belmont St. OL4—3E 64
Belmont St. SK4—2D 104
Belmont St. WN5—2H 51
Belmont Ter. M31—8K 87
Belmont View. BL2—6M 23
Belmont Wlk. M13—9J 79
Belmont Way. OL9—9J 45
Belmont Way. OL12—9E 12
Belmont Way. SK4—3D 104
Belmore Av. M8—7F 60
Belper Rd. M30—7B 76
Belper Rd. SK4—4M 103
Belper St. BL3—4J 39
Belper St. OL6—3B 82
Belper Wlk. M18—9C 80
Belper Way. M34—6A 94
(in two parts)
Belsay Dri. M23—9A 102
Belstone Av. M23—1A 112
Belstone Clo. SK7—2F 114
Belsyde Wlk. M9—9L 61
(off Norbet Wlk.)
Belthorne Av. M9—6A 62
Belton Av. OL16—1J 29
Beltone Clo. M32—5H 89
Belton Wlk. M8—1G 79
Belton Wlk. OL9—2K 63
Belvedere Av. BL8—1G 25
Belvedere Av. M29—4M 55
Belvedere Av. SK5—4F 92
Belvedere Clo. WN7—9K 55
Belvedere Ct. M25—5A 60
Belvedere Dri. SK6—2J 105
Belvedere Dri. SK16—6E 82
Belvedere Pl. WN3—3M 51
Belvedere Rise. OL1—6D 46
Belvedere Rd. M6—2A 4 & 4A 78
Belvedere Rd. M14—6L 91
Belvedere Rd. WA12—9B 70
Belvedere St. M6—2A 4 & 4B 78
Belverdere Rd. WN4—3C 70
Belvoir Av. M19—4A 92
Belvoir Av. SK7—4L 115
Belvoir Ct. WN1—9E 34
Belvoir St. BL2—2J 39
Belvoir St. OL12—1C 28
Belvoir St. WN1—9E 34
Belvor Av. M34—8L 81
Belwood. BL5—2C 54
Belwood Rd. M21—7A 90
Bembridge Clo. M14—3J 91
Bembridge Dri. BL3—4K 39
Bembridge Rd. M34—6B 94
Bempton Clo. SK2—8A 106
Bemrose Av. WA14—7C 100
Benbecula Way. M31—1C 88
Benbow Av. M12—1M 91
Benbow St. M33—9H 89
Ben Brierley Way. OL1—1M 63
Benbrook Gro. SK9—1L 119
Bench Carr. OL12—1E 28
Benchill Av. M22—8D 102
Benchill Ct. Rd. M22—9E 102
Benchill Cres. M22—8C 102
Benchill Dri. M22—8C 102
Benchill Rd. M22—7C 102
Bendall St. M11—7E 80
Ben Davies Ct. SK6—2C 106
Bendemeer. M31—3C 88
Bendix St. M4—3G 5 & 4H 79
Benfield Av. M10—6C 62
Benfield St. OL10—8K 27
Benfield Wlk. M24—6K 43
Benfleet Clo. M12—9A 80
Bengal La. OL6—3C 82
Bengal Sq. OL6—3C 82
Bengal St. M4—3G 5 & 5H 79
Bengal St. SK3—5E 104
Bengal St. WN7—2F 72
Bengarin Clo. WN1—8F 34
Benhale Wlk. M8—1G 79
(off Tamerton Dri.)
Benham Clo. BL4—8K 39
Benham Clo. M20—2J 103
Benin Wlk. M10—2C 80
Benja Fold. SK7—6D 114
Benjamin Wilson Ct. M7—3D 78
(off Fitzwilliam St.)
Benmore Clo. OL10—8G 27
Benmore Rd. M9—4M 61
Bennet St. M26—5D 40
Bennett Clo. SK3—5C 104
Bennett Dri. M7—1E 78
Bennett Rd. M8—7F 60
Bennett's La. BL1—7C 22
Bennett St. M12—9L 79
Bennett St. M32—5J 89
Bennett St. OL7—6M 81
Bennett St. OL11—5G 29
Bennett St. SK3—5C 104
Bennett St. SK14—1C 94
Bennett St. SK15—6G 83
Benny La. M35—4J 81
Benson Clo. M7—2E 78
Benson St. BL7—6K 7
Benson St. BL9—9A 26
Benson Wlk. SK9—1K 119
Ben St. M11—5B 80
Bentcliffe Way. M30—6F 76
Bentfield Cres. OL16—6A 30
Bentfold Dri. BL9—7A 42
Bentgate Clo. OL16—6A 30
Bentgate St. OL16—7A 30
Benthall Wlk. M34—6L 93
Bentham Clo. BL8—7E 24
Bentham Pl. WN6—8M 17
Bentham Rd. WN6—9L 17
Bentham St. PR7—1L 17
Bent Hill S. BL3—5A 38
Bentinck Ho. OL6—5A 82
Bentinck Rd. WA14—9C 100
Bentinck St. BL1—9B 22
Bentinck St. BL4—8J 39
Bentinck St. M15—6C 4 & 8D 78
Bentinck St. OL6 & OL7—4A 82
(in two parts)
Bentinck St. OL8—4M 63
Bentinck St. OL12—1C 28
Bentinck St. WN3—4L 51
Bentinck Ter. OL6—5A 82
Bent La. M8—9F 60
Bent La. M25—4C 60
Bent La. WA13—7C 98
Bent Lanes. M31—1M 87
(in four parts)
Bentley Av. M24—4D 44
Bentley Clo. M26—5K 41
Bentley Ct. M7—8E 60
Bentley Hall Rd. BL8—6C 24
Bentley La. BL9—1M 25
Bentley La. L40 & PR7—1A 16
Bentley Rd. M7—8E 60
Bentley Rd. M21—5A 90
Bentley Rd. M34—3M 93
Bentleys, The. SK5—2F 104
Bentley St. BL2—4J 39
Bentley St. BL4—8K 39
Bentley St. OL1—9B 46
Bentley St. OL9—1H 63
Bentley St. OL12—9D 12
Bentmeadows. OL12—1E 28
Benton Dri. SK6—5H 107
Benton St. M9—9M 61
Bents Av. M31—5M 87
Bents Av. SK6—2M 105
Bentside Rd. SK12—7K 117
Bents La. SK6—2M 105
Bent Spur Rd. BL4—3A 58
Bent St. BL4—1L 57
Bent St. M8—1F 5 & 3G 79
Bent Ter. M31—2C 88
Bentworth Wlk. M9—9L 61
Benville Wlk. M10—1B 80
(off Troydale Dri.)
Benwick Ter. BL1—8E 22
Benyon St. OL4—2E 64
Berberis Wlk. M33—8C 88
Beresford Av. BL3—4C 38
Beresford Cres. OL4—9D 46
Beresford Cres. SK5—3E 92

Beresford Rd. M13—3M 91
Beresford Rd. M32—2L 89
Beresford St. M14—3F 90
Beresford St. M35—9E 62
Beresford St. OL4—9D 46
Beresford St. OL16—6B 30
Beresford St. WN6—8A 34
Berger St. M10—2D 80
Bergman Wlk. M10—1B 80
(off Harmer Clo.)
Berigan Clo. M12—1L 91
Berisford Clo. WA15—6E 100
Berkeley Av. M14—2L 91
Berkeley Av. M32—2G 89
Berkeley Av. OL9—5F 62
Berkeley Av. WN3—6K 51
Berkeley Clo. SK2—5J 105
Berkeley Clo. SK14—5D 94
Berkeley Clo. WN7—7C 72
Berkeley Ct. M8—7E 60
Berkeley Ct. M20—2F 102
Berkeley Cres. M26—4C 40
Berkeley Cres. SK14—5D 94
Berkeley Dri. OL2—7K 45
Berkeley Rd. BL1—6E 22
Berkeley Rd. SK7—1M 115
Berkeley St. OL2—4K 45
Berkley Av. M19—5A 92
Berkley Dri. OL16—6H 29
Berkley St. OL6—4A 82
Berkley Wlk. OL15—6M 13
Berkshire Clo. OL9—3H 63
Berkshire Ct. BL9—1M 41
Berkshire Dri. M30—9C 86
Berkshire Pl. OL9—3J 63
Berkshire Rd. M10—4K 79
Berlin Rd. SK3—7D 104
Berlin St. BL3—3C 38
Bernard Gro. BL1—8C 22
Bernard St. M9—8K 61
Bernard St. OL12—8E 12
Bernard St. SK13—5J 97
Bernard Walker Ct. SK6
—3H 107
Berne Av. BL6—7A 20
Berne Clo. OL9—2J 63
Berne Clo. SK7—9E 104
Bernice Av. OL9—2H 63
Bernice St. BL1—8C 22
Bernington Wlk. BL2—9G 23
Berrie Gro. M19—6B 92
Berrington Gro. WN4—4A 70
Berry Brow. M10—3D 80
Berryfold Way. M29—8B 56
Berry St. M1—5G 5 & 7H 79
Berry St. M27—6F 58
Berry St. M30—7B 76
Berry St. OL3—3B 66
Berry St. SK15—7J 83
Bertha Rd. OL16—3J 29
Bertha St. BL1—8D 22
Bertha St. M11—7B 80
Bertha St. OL2—4B 46
Bertie St. OL11—6D 28
Bertram St. M12—9A 80
Bertram St. M33—1L 101
Bertrand Rd. BL1—2C 38
Bert St. BL3—6B 38
Berwick Av. M25—1A 60
Berwick Av. M31—4G 89
Berwick Av. SK4—2K 103
Berwick Clo. M28—9F 56
Berwick Clo. OL10—9G 27
Berwick Pl. WN1—8E 34
Berwick St. OL16—4H 29
Berwyn Av. M9—3H 61
Berwyn Av. M24—9C 44
Berwyn Av. SK8—8B 104
Beryl Av. BL8—3F 24
Beryl St. BL1—7F 22
Besom La. SK15—4K 83
Bessemer Rd. M30—7F 86
Bessemer St. M11—8C 80
Bessemer Way. OL1—1L 63
Bessie's Well Pl. WN6—1M 33
Bessybrook Clo. BL6—3J 37
Beswick Dri. M35—1G 81
Beswicke Royds St. OL16
—1H 29
Beswicke St. OL12—2E 28
Beswicke St. OL15—6C 14
Beswick Row. M4—2F 5 & 4G 79
Beswicks La. SK9—8C 118
Beswick St. M4—5K 79
Beswick St. M35—8M 81
Beswick St. OL2—7L 45
Beta Av. M32—5J 89
Beta St. BL1—1E 38
Bethany La. OL16—6C 30
Bethel Av. M35—9E 62
Bethel Grn. OL15—2C 14
(off Calderbrook Rd.)
Bethel St. M11—6B 80
Bethel St. OL10—8J 27
Bethersden Rd. WA11—4B 34
Bethesda Ho. M8—8E 60
Bethesda St. OL8—4M 63
Bethnall Dri. M14—5G 91
Betjeman Pl. OL2—1D 46
Betleymere Rd. SK8—9M 103
Betley Rd. SK5—5F 92
Betley St. M1—5H 5 & 7J 79
Betley St. M26—5J 41
Betley St. OL10—9J 27
Betnor Av. SK1—4H 105
Betony Clo. OL12—8D 12
Betison Av. WN7—4J 73
Bettwood Dri. M8—6E 60
Betty Nuppy's La. OL16—5J 29
Betula Gro. M7—1D 78
Betula M. OL11—1K 27
Beulah Av. WN5—3D 68
Beulah St. M11—8C 80
Bevan Clo. M12—6L 79
Bevendon Sq. M7—1E 78
Beverdale Clo. M11—7A 80
Beverleley Clo. OL6—1B 82
Beveridge St. M14—3G 91
Beverley Av. M31—2E 88
Beverley Av. M34—4A 94
Beverley Av. WN5—7E 50
Beverley Av. WN7—1G 73
Beverley Flats. OL10—8J 27
(off Wilton St.)
Beverley Pl. OL16—2G 29
Beverley Rd. BL1—1B 38
Beverley Rd. BL3—6M 39
Beverley Rd. M27—9J 59
Beverley Rd. SK2—5G 105
Beverley Rd. WN5—9H 33
Beverley St. M9—7L 61
Beverley Wlk. OL8—3L 63
Beverley Wlk. SK6—4A 106
Beverly Rd. M14—7K 91
Beverston. OL11—4E 28
Beverston Dri. M7—1E 78
Bevill Sq. M3—3D 4 & 5E 78
Bevington St. WN4—2M 69
Bevis Grn. BL9—2M 25
Bewick St. BL2—7H 23
Bewley Gro. WN7—1G 73
Bewley St. OL8—6K 63
Bewley Wlk. M10—1A 80
Bexhill Av. WA15—7F 100
Bexhill Clo. BL3—6C 40
Bexhill Dri. M13—3L 91
Bexhill Rd. SK3—9E 104
Bexhill Wlk. OL9—2H 63
Bexington Wlk. M16—3E 90
Bexley Clo. M31—2B 88
Bexley Clo. SK13—3J 97
Bexley Dri. BL8—9H 25
Bexley Dri. M28—4J 57
Bexley Sq. M3—3C 4 & 5D 78
Bexley St. OL9—3J 63
Bexley St. WN2—5B 54
Bexley Wlk. M10—1B 80
(off John Foran Clo.)
Beyer Clo. M18—1C 92
Bibby La. M19—8M 91
Bibby St. BL9—4M 41
Bibby St. SK14—1D 94
Bickerdike Av. M12—3A 92
Bickershaw La. WN2—7H 53
Bickershaw St. WN7—3A 72
Bickerstaffe Clo. OL2—3A 46
Bickerton Ct. OL9—5J 63
Bickerton Dri. SK7—3G 115
Bickerton Rd. WA14—8B 100
Bickley Wlk. M16—2F 90
Bickley Av. M22—1B 112
Biddall Dri. M23—7B 102
Biddisham Wlk. M10—2K 79
Biddulph Av. SK2—8J 105
Bideford Dri. BL2—3A 40
Bideford Dri. M23—5M 101
Bideford Dri. OL11—7B 28
Bideford Rd. SK2—4J 105
Bidford Clo. M29—7C 56
Bidston Av. M14—4H 91
Bidston Clo. OL2—3D 46
Bidston Dri. SK9—9L 113
Bidworth La. SK13—5D 96
Bigginwood Wlk. M10—9A 62
(off Halliford Rd.)
Bignor St. M8—1G 79
Bilbao St. BL1—1C 38
Bilberry St. OL16—4G 29
Bilbrook St. M4—2G 5 & 4H 79
Billing Av. M12—6H 5 & 8J 79
Billinge Arc. WN1—9C 34
(off Galleries, The)
Billinge Clo. BL1—1F 38
Billinge Cres. WA11—9D 68
Billinge Rd. WN3 & WN5—4J 51
Billinge Rd. WN4—2H 69
Billington Av. WA12—9B 70
Billington Rd. M27—8L 59
Bill La. M25—9M 41
Bill Williams Clo. M11—7C 80
Billy La. M27—6F 58
Billy Meredith Clo. M14—3G 91
Billy's La. SK8—3A 114
Billy Whelan Wlk. M10—2B 80
Bilsland Wlk. M10—2C 80
Bilson Dri. SK3—6B 104
Bilson Sq. OL16—5A 30
Bilton Wlk. M8—8K 61
Binbrook Wlk. BL3—5F 38
Bincombe Wlk. M13—1J 91
Bindloss Av. M30—4G 77
Bindon Wlk. M9—9K 61
(off Carisbrook St.)
Bingham Dri. M23—7M 101
Bingham St. M27—8F 58
Bingley Clo. M11—7M 79
Bingley Dri. M31—2M 87
Bingley Rd. OL16—3J 29
Bingley Sq. OL16—3J 29
Bingley Ter. OL16—3J 29
Bingley Wlk. M27—8M 59
Binns Nook Rd. OL12—9G 13
Binns Pl. M4—4G 5 & 6H 79
Binns St. SK15—6E 82
Binn's Ter. OL15—5B 14
(off Barehill St.)
Binsley Clo. M30—5G 87
Binstead Clo. M14—3L 91
Birchacre Gro. M14—7K 91
Birchall Grn. SK6—9M 93
Birchall Way. M15—9F 78
Birch Av. BL5—1F 54
Birch Av. BL8—5G 25
Birch Av. M6—2L 77
Birch Av. M16—2A 90
Birch Av. M24—1A 62
Birch Av. M25—3H 59
Birch Av. M30—9D 86
Birch Av. M33—2H 101
Birch Av. M35—1F 80
Birch Av. OL1—7G 45
Birch Av. OL8—6K 63
Birch Av. OL12—7K 13
Birch Av. SK4—1B 104
Birch Av. SK6—3D 106
Birch Av. SK9—5G 119
Birch Av. WA10—9A 68
Birch Av. WN6—1M 33
Birchbrook Rd. WA13—8B 98
Birch Clo. OL12—5C 12
Birch Ct. M13—3L 91
Birch Ct. SK16—7D 82
Birch Cres. OL16—7A 30
Birchdale. WA14—2C 110
Birchdale Av. SK8—2H 113
Birch Dri. M27—8H 59
Birch Dri. OL4—3F 64
Birch Dri. SK7—2J 115
Birchenall St. M10—3M 61
Birchen Bower Dri. BL8—5F 24
Birchen Bower Wlk. BL8—5F 24
Birchenlea St. OL9—5G 63
Birches Rd. BL7—7K 7
Birches, The. M33—9E 88
Birches, The. OL5—7H 65
Birchfield. BL2—4L 23
Birchfield Av. BL9—9E 26
Birchfield Av. M29—4H 55
Birchfield Dri. M28—9G 57
Birchfield Dri. OL11—5C 28
Birchfield Gro. BL3—5L 37
Birchfield Rd. SK3—6A 104
Birchfield Rd. WA13—9B 98
Birchfields. WA15—3F 110
Birchfields Av. M13—3L 91
Birchfields Rd. M13 & M14
—3L 91
Birchfold. M28—4H 57
Birchfold Clo. M28—4H 57
Birchfold Gdns. WA10—9A 68
Birchgate Wlk. BL3—5E 38
Birch Grn. SK13—5L 97
Birch Gro. BL0—8G 9
Birch Gro. M14—3K 91
Birch Gro. M25—2A 60
Birch Gro. M31—6L 87
Birch Gro. M34—9M 81
(Audenshaw)
Birch Gro. M34—3L 93
(Denton)
Birch Gro. WA15—8L 101
Birch Gro. WN2—2J 69
Birch Hall La. M13—4L 91
Birch Hey Clo. OL12—7J 13
Birch Hill Cres. OL12—7K 13
Birch Hill La. OL12—5K 13
Birch Hill Wlk. OL15—6M 13
Birch Ho. BL5—1F 54
Birch Ho. M16—2A 90
Birch Ind. Est. OL10—4G 43
Birchington Rd. M14—6G 91
Birchin La. M4—4F 5 & 6G 79
Birchinlee Av. OL2—6H 45
Birch La. M13—3L 91
Birch La. SK16—7D 82
(in two parts)
Birch Lea Clo. BL9—2M 41
Birchleaf Gro. M5—5J 77
Birchley Av. WN5—4C 68
Birchley Rd. WN5—4B 68
Birchley View. WA11—5B 68
Birch Mt. OL12—7K 13
Birch Polygon. M14—3K 91
Birch Rd. BL4—2M 57
Birch Rd. M8—7H 61
Birch Rd. M24—7C 44
Birch Rd. M27—2D 76
Birch Rd. M28—7K 57
Birch Rd. M29—5L 55
Birch Rd. M31—1M 99
(Carrington)
Birch Rd. M31—2D 98
(Partington)
Birch Rd. OL3—1C 66
Birch Rd. OL12—5J 13
Birch Rd. PR7—1L 17
Birch Rd. SK8—8G 103
Birch Rd. SK12—1M 121
Birch Rd. WA3—2B 98
Birch Rd. WA11—8L 69
Birch Rd. WN2—9H 53
Birch Rd. WN7—9E 54
Birchside Av. SK13—4H 97
Birch St. BL2—3G 39
Birch St. BL9—6M 25
Birch St. M12—9A 80
Birch St. M26—4L 41
Birch St. M29—7A 56
Birch St. M35—6H 81
Birch St. OL7—6L 81
Birch St. OL10—9K 27
Birch St. OL12—5J 13
Birch St. SK15—3J 83
Birch St. WN2—3K 53
Birch St. WN6—8A 34
Birch Tree Av. SK7—3A 116
Birch Tree Av. WA11—7A 68
Birch Tree Clo. WA14—3C 110
Birch Tree Ct. M22—1D 112
Birch Tree Dri. M22—1D 112
Birch Tree Rd. WA3—7M 71
Birch Tree Way. BL6—9E 20
Birchvale Clo. M15—6D 4 &
8E 78
Birchvale Dri. SK6—2D 106
Birch Vs. OL12—6C 12
Birchway. SK6—5F 116
Birchway. SK7—5D 114
Birchwood. OL9—1E 62
Birchwood Clo. SK4—4A 104
Birchwood Clo. WN7—4F 72
Birchwood Dri. SK9—3K 119
Birchwood Rd. M24—9C 44
Birchwood Way. SK16—9D 82
Birdcage Cotts. WA11—8L 69
(off Church Rd.)
Bird Hall Av. SK8—9C 104
Birdhall Gro. M19—6A 92
Bird Hall La. SK3—6B 104
Bird Hall Rd. SK8—8B 104
Birdlip Dri. M23—1A 112
Bird St. WN2—1F 52
Birkbeck St. SK15—6F 82
Birkby Dri. M24—7L 43
Birkdale Av. M25—2K 59
Birkdale Av. M29—3J 55
Birkdale Av. OL2—7L 45
Birkdale Clo. BL8—7E 24
Birkdale Clo. OL10—1K 43
Birkdale Clo. SK7—5F 114
Birkdale Clo. SK14—1E 94
Birkdale Dri. BL8—8H 25
Birkdale Dri. M33—3E 100
Birkdale Gdns. BL3—4D 38
Birkdale Gro. M30—5F 76
Birkdale Gro. SK5—9F 92
Birkdale Pl. M28—5G 57
Birkdale Rd. OL16—6J 29
Birkdale Rd. SK5—9E 92
Birkdale St. M8—3G 61
Birkenhills Dri. BL3—4L 37
Birkett Bank. WN1—9E 34
Birkett Bank Ter. WN1—9E 34
Birkett Clo. BL1—4D 22
Birkett Dri. BL1—4D 22
Birkett St. WN1—9E 34
Birkinbrook Clo. M25—8A 42
Birkinheath La. WA14—7A 110
Birkleigh Wlk. BL2—3L 39
Birks Av. OL4—9F 46
Birks Dri. BL8—4H 25
Birkside Clo. WN3—7A 52
Birkworth Ct. SK2—7K 105
Birley Clo. WA15—6F 100
Birley Clo. WN6—1F 32
Birley Ct. M5—5A 78
Birley Pk. M20—2F 102
Birley St. BL1—6E 22
Birley St. BL9—5M 25
Birley St. OL12—1G 29
Birley St. WN7—1G 73
Birling Dri. M23—9B 102
Birnham Gro. OL10—9G 27
Birstall Av. WA11—9C 68
Birstall Wlk. M23—6K 113
Birtenshaw Cres. BL7—3H 23
Birtle Dri. M29—9C 56
Birtle Rd. BL9—3E 26
Birtles Av. SK5—3F 92
Birtles Clo. SK8—8A 104
Birtlespool Rd. SK8—9M 103
Birtles, The. M22—1D 112
Birtles Way. SK9—6K 113
Birtley Wlk. M10—2H 5 & 4J 79
Birt St. M10—3K 79
Birwood Rd. M8—6H 61
Biscay Clo. M11—6M 79
Bishop Clo. M16—2E 90
Bishop Clo. OL7—2A 82
Bishopgate. WN1—9C 34
Bishop Marshall Clo. M10
—2K 79
Bishop Marshall Way. M24
—5K 43
Bishop Reeves Rd. WA11
—8L 69
Bishop Rd. M6—3H 77
Bishop Rd. M31—4K 87
Bishop Rd. WA10—9A 68
Bishopsbridge Clo. BL3—5F 38
Bishop's Clo. BL3—7G 39
Bishops Clo. SK8—8A 104
Bishops Clo. WA14—3B 110
Bishopscourt. M7—7E 60
Bishopsgate. M2—5E 5 & 7F 78
Bishops Ga. St. OL9—2G 63
Bishops M. M33—8E 88
Bishop's Rd. BL3—7G 39
Bishops Rd. M25—5C 60
Bishops St. SK1—4G 105
Bishop St. M24—1D 62
Bishop St. OL16—1H 29
Bishopton Clo. M19—5C 92
Bishop Wlk. OL7—6A 82
Bisley Av. M23—7M 101
Bisley St. BL6—2K 63
Bismark St. OL4—3A 64
Bispham Av. BL2—2M 39
Bispham Av. SK5—4F 92
Bispham Clo. BL8—9F 24
Bispham Dri. WN4—2M 69
Bispham Dri. M7—9E 60
Bispham St. BL2—1J 39
Bittern Clo. OL11—3M 27
Bittern Clo. SK12—8G 115
Bittern Dri. M35—4J 81
Blackbank St. BL1—8F 22
Blackberry Clo. WA14—5B 100
Blackberry La. SK5—7H 93
Black Brook Rd. SK4—7D 92
Blackbrook Rd. WA11—9E 68
Blackburn Clo. WA3—7L 71
Blackburn Gdns. M20—1G 103
Blackburn Old Rd. BL7—7C 6
Blackburn Pl. M3—2C 4 & 4D 78
Blackburn Pl. M5—4B 4 & 6C 78
Blackburn Rd. BL1 & BL7
—6E 22
Blackburn Rd. BL7—4B 6
(Edgeworth)
Blackburn Rd. BL7—1G 7
(Turton)
Blackburn St. M3—2C 4 & 4D 78
Blackburn St. M16—1C 90
Blackburn St. M25—4C 60
Blackburn St. M26—6G 41
Blackcap Clo. M28—9H 57
Blackcarr Rd. M23—8B 102
Black Dad La. OL11—2G 27
Blackden Wlk. SK9—2K 119
Blackett St. M12—7K 79
Blackfield La. M7—8C 60
Blackfields. M7—8C 60
Blackford Av. BL9—5M 41
Blackford Rd. SK4—7B 92
Blackford Wlk. M10—4K 79
Blackfriars Rd. M3—2D 4 &
4E 78
Blackfriars St. M3—3E 5 &
5F 78
Blackhill Clo. M13—6G 5 &
8H 79
Blackhorse Av. BL6—8J 19
Blackhorse Clo. BL6—7J 19
Black Horse St. BL1—2E 38
Black Horse St. BL4—1L 57
Black Horse St. BL6—7J 19
Blackhurst Brow. SK10
—8B 120
Black La. BL0—3A 10
Black La. SK6 & SK12—1M 117
Black La. WN7—2K 73
Black Leach. OL4—1G 65
Blackleach Dri. M28—3K 57
Blackledge St. BL3—5C 38
Blackley Clo. BL9—7A 42
Blackley Ct. M9—5G 61
Blackleyhurst Av. WN5—2E 68
Blackley New Rd. M9—5F 60
Blackley Pk. Rd. M9—7K 61
Blackley St. M16—1C 90
Blackley St. M24—1H 61
Blacklock St. M8—1E 5 & 3F 78
Blackmoor. SK14—2A 96
Blackmoor Av. M29—2B 74
Black Moss Clo. M26—6D 40
Black Moss Rd. WA14—6K 99
Blackpits Rd. OL11—1K 27
Blackpool St. M11—5C 80
(in two parts)
Blackrock Cotts. OL5—1J 83
Blackrock St. M11—6M 79
Blackrod Brow. BL6—6H 19
Blackrod By-Pass Rd. BL6
—6J 19
Blackrod Dri. BL8—9F 24
Black Sail Wlk. OL1—8A 46
Blackshaw Ho. BL3—3C 38
Blackshaw La. BL3—3C 38
Blackshaw La. OL2—5M 45
Blackshaw La. SK9—8K 119
Blackshaw Rd. SK13—4L 97
Blackshaw Row. BL3—4C 38
Blackshaw St. SK3—5E 104
Blacksmith La. OL11—6B 28
Blackstock St. M13—2J 91
Blackstone Av. OL16—2J 29
Blackstone Av. WA11—9D 68
Blackstone Edge Ct. OL15
—5C 14
Blackstone Edge Old Rd. OL15
—5C 14
Blackstone Rd. SK2—8K 105
Blackstone Wlk. M9—1K 79
Blackthorn Av. M19—7A 92
Blackthorn Av. WN6—6M 33
Blackthorn Clo. OL12—9E 12
Blackthorne Clo. BL1—9A 22
Blackthorne Dri. M33—3D 100
Blackthorn Rd. SK14—8E 94
Blackthorn Wlk. M31—3E 98
Blackwin St. M12—9A 80
Blackwood Dri. M23—5K 101
Blackwood St. BL3—5G 39
Bladen Clo. SK8—9A 104
Blainscough Rd. PR7—2L 17
Blair Av. M28—4H 57
Blair Av. M31—4L 87
Blair Av. WN2—5B 54
Blair Clo. M33—4C 100
Blair Clo. OL2—2B 46
Blair Clo. SK7—4J 115
Blairhall Av. M40—9A 62
Blair La. BL2—9K 23
Blairmore Dri. BL3—4L 37
Blair Rd. M16—5E 90
Blair St. BL4—2B 58
Blair St. BL7—2F 22
Blair St. M16—1D 90
Blair St. OL12—1D 28
Blake Av. M29—3K 55
Blakeborough Ho. M29—5K 55
(off Elizabeth St.)
Blake Clo. WN3—5A 52
Blakedown Wlk. M12—1L 91
(off Cochrane Av.)
Blake Dri. SK2—6L 105
Blakefield Dri. M28—7L 57
Blake Gdns. BL1—8D 22
Blakeley La. WA16—3A 118
Blakelock St. OL2—2A 46
Blakemere Av. M33—2L 101
Blakemore Wlk. M12—6L 79
Blake St. BL1—8D 22
Blake St. BL7—3G 23
Blake St. OL16—2G 29
Blakeswell Clo. M31—3K 87
Blakey Clo. BL3—5M 37
Blakey St. M12—2A 92
Blanche St. OL12—9G 13
Blanche Wlk. OL1—9A 46
Bland Clo. M35—9E 62
Blandford Av. M28—8M 57
Blandford Clo. BL8—5K 25
Blandford Clo. M29—7A 56
Blandford Ct. SK15—5G 83
Blandford Dri. M10—6D 62
Blandford Rise. BL6—9F 20
Blandford Rd. M6—1A 4 & 2B 78
Blandford Rd. M30—5B 76
Blandford Rd. SK4—3B 104
Blandford St. OL6—4A 82
Blandford St. SK15—5G 83
Bland Rd. M25—6B 60
Bland St. BL9—7M 25
Bland St. M16—2E 90
Bland Wlk. M16—2E 90
Blanshard Wlk. M15—9F 78
Blantyre Av. M28—6L 57
Blantyre Rd. M27—1H 77
Blantyre St. M15—6C 4 & 8D 78
Blantyre St. M27—8D 58
Blantyre St. M30—4K 75
Blantyre St. WN2—2L 53
Blanwood Dri. M8—9H 61
Blaven Clo. SK3—8F 104
Blaydon Clo. WN2—4K 35
Blaydon Ho. WN1—8K 35
Blazemoss Bank. SK2—8K 105
Bleach St. M8—9K 61
Bleackley St. BL8—6J 25
Bleak Hey Rd. M22—2F 112
Bleakholt Rd. BL0—2M 9
Bleakledge Gro. WN2—2L 53
Bleakledge St. WN2—1M 53
Bleaklow Clo. WN3—6B 52
Bleaklow Fold. SK13—5E 96
(off Castleton Cres.)
Bleaklow Gdns. SK13—5E 96
(off Castleton Cres.)
Bleaklow La. SK13—5E 96
Bleaklow Wlk. SK13—5E 96
(off Castleton Cres.)
Bleak St. BL2—8H 23
Bleasby St. OL4—1C 64
Bleasdale Clo. BL6—1F 36
Bleasdale Clo. BL9—6A 42
Bleasdale Rd. M22—2A 112
Bleasdale Rd. WN2—3A 54
Bleasdale St. OL2—4K 45
Bleasedale Rd. BL1—8M 21
Bleatarn Rd. SK1—6H 105
Bledlow Clo. M30—4E 76
Blencarn Wlk. M9—9K 61
Blendworth Clo. M8—9F 60
Blenheim Av. M16—4D 90
Blenheim Av. OL1—6D 46
Blenheim Clo. BL9—4M 41
Blenheim Clo. OL10—8L 27
Blenheim Clo. SK12—8M 115
Blenheim Clo. SK9—4K 119
Blenheim Clo. WA14—2D 110
Blenheim Ct. M9—3G 61
(off Deanswood Dri.)
Blenheim Dri. WN7—9L 55
Blenheim Rd. BL2—2K 39
Blenheim Rd. M16—3A 90
Blenheim Rd. SK8—2B 114
Blenheim Rd. WN4—5D 70
Blenheim Rd. WN5—9J 33
Blenheim Rd. Est. BL2—3M 39
Blenheim St. M29—7M 55
Blenheim St. OL12—1C 28
Blenmar Clo. M26—4J 41
Bleriot St. BL3—6D 38
Bletchley Clo. M13—1K 91
Bletchley Clo. SK4—4L 103
Blethyn Clo. BL3—7B 38
Bligh Rd. BL5—8E 36
Blinco Rd. M31—5F 88
Blind La. M12—8K 79
Blindsill Rd. BL4—1H 57
Blissford Clo. WN2—4K 53
Blisworth Av. M30—7E 76
Blisworth Clo. M4—6K 79
Blithfield Wlk. M34—4L 93
Block La. OL9—4H 63
Blocksage St. SK16—8D 82
Blodwell St. M6—5M 77
Blofield Ct. BL4—1K 57
Blomley St. OL11—8C 28
Bloomfield Dri. BL9—6B 42
Bloomfield Dri. M28—9G 57
Bloomfield Rd. BL4—2K 57
Bloomfield St. BL1—7E 22
Bloomsbury Gro. WA15
—7G 101
Bloomsbury La. WA15—7G 101
Bloom St. BL0—7G 9
Bloom St. M1—5F 5 & 7G 79
(in two parts)
Bloom St. M3—3D 4 & 5E 78
Bloom St. SK3—5C 104
Blossom Pl. OL16—2F 28
Blossom Rd. M31—3E 98
Blossoms Hey. SK8—3L 113
Blossoms Hey Wlk. SK8
—3L 113
Blossoms La. SK7—1A 120
Blossom St. M3—3D 4 & 5E 78
Blossom St. M4—3G 5 & 5H 79
Blossom St. M29—7A 56
Blow St. BL4—4M 61
Blucher St. M5—4B 4 & 6C 78
Blucher St. M12—9L 79
Blucher St. OL7—1A 32
Blue Bell Av. M10—7A 62
Bluebell Av. WA11—8L 69
Bluebell Av. WN6—5M 33
Blue Bell Clo. SK14—1F 94
Bluebell Dri. OL11—7B 28
Bluebell Dri. SK6—7K 107
Bluebell Gro. SK8—9K 103
Blueberry Dri. OL2—2D 46
Blueberry Rd. WA14—2A 110
Bluefields. OL2—1D 46
Bluestone Dri. SK4—2L 103
Bluestone Rd. M10—8A 62
Bluestone Rd. M34—4G 93
Bluestone Ter. M34—4G 93
Blundell Clo. BL9—6B 42
Blundell La. BL6—8G 19
Blundell St. BL1—2E 38
Blundering La. SK15—9K 83
Blunn St. OL8—4M 63
Blyth Av. M23—3C 102
Blyth Av. OL15—8M 13
Blyth Clo. WA15—7L 101
Blythe Av. SK7—6C 114
Blyth Rd. M31—4H 87
Blyth St. M15—1H 91
Blyton Way. M34—6M 93
Boad St. M1—5G 5 & 7H 79
Boardale Dri. M24—8L 43
Boardman Clo. BL1—8E 22
Boardman Clo. SK5—1F 104
Boardman Fold Clo. M24
—3A 62
Boardman Fold Rd. M24
—3M 61
Boardman La. M24—3H 43
Boardman Rd. M8—6F 60
Boardman St. BL1—8E 22
Boardman St. BL6—6K 19
Boardman St. M30—6E 76
Boardman St. SK14—4D 94
Board St. BL3—3C 38
Board St. OL6—8L 63
Boar Grn. Clo. M10—8C 62
Boarshaw Clough. M24—7B 44
Boarshaw Cres. M24—7C 44
Boarshaw La. M24—6D 44
Boarshaw Rd. M24—8A 44
Boars Head Av. WN6—2A 34
Boarshurst La. OL3—3B 66
Boat La. M22—4E 102
Boat La. M30—4H 87
Boat La. OL3—4D 48
Bobbin Wlk. M4—6J 79
(off Cardroom Rd.)
Bobbin Wlk. OL4—2A 64
Bob Massey Clo. M11—6C 80
Bob's La. M30—1D 98
Boddens Hill Rd. SK4—4A 104
Bodden St. WA3—6A 72
Boddington Rd. M30—6A 76
Bodiam Rd. BL8—1F 24
Bodley St. M11—5C 80
Bodmin Clo. OL2—3A 46
Bodmin Cres. SK5—5H 93
Bodmin Dri. SK7—5E 114
Bodmin Dri. WN2—7G 53
Bodmin Gro. WA11—8D 68
Bodmin Rd. M29—8B 56
Bodmin Rd. M33—9D 88
Bodmin Wlk. M23—8A 102
Bodney Way. M9—5H 61
Bogburn La. PR7—4K 17
Boggard La. SK14—8D 96
Bognor Rd. SK3—6E 104
Bolam Clo. M23—4L 101
Boland Dri. M14—6L 91
Bolderrod Pl. OL1—9A 46
Bolderstone Pl. SK2—9L 105
Bolderwood Dri. WN2—4K 53
Bold Row. M27—9F 58
Bold St. BL1—2F 38
Bold St. BL9—7A 26
Bold St. M15—1E 90
Bold St. M16—2E 90
Bold St. M27—8F 58
Bold St. WA14—1D 110
Bold St. WN5—3K 51
Bold St. WN7—1F 72
(in two parts)
Bolesworth Clo. M21—6M 89
Boleyn Ct. OL10—3J 27
Boleywood Ct. SK3—2H 119
Bolholt Ter. BL8—6H 25
Bolivia St. M5—5J 77
Bollin Av. WA14—4B 110
Bollin Clo. BL4—2A 58
Bollin Clo. M15—9C 78
Bollin Clo. SK9—3J 119
Bollin Clo. WA13—9A 98
Bollin Ct. M15—9D 78
Bollin Ct. SK9—4L 119
Bollin Ct. WA14—3B 110
Bollin Dri. M33—3H 101
Bollin Dri. WA13—9A 98
Bollin Dri. WA14—5E 100
Bollings Yd. BL1—3F 38
Bollington Rd. M10—5K 79
Bollington Rd. SK4—9D 92
Bollington St. OL7—6A 82
Bollingwood Chase. SK9
—4K 119
Bollin Hill. SK9—3G 119
Bollin Sq. WA14—3B 110
Bollin Wlk. SK5—9F 92
Bollin Wlk. SK9—4H 119
Bollin Way. M25—7C 42
Bollinway. WA15—1G 111
Bolney St. WN2—6G 35
Bolney Wlk. M10—3K 79
Bolshaw Farm La. SK8—6J 113
Bolshaw Rd. SK8—6H 113
Boltmeadow. OL3—4A 66
Bolton Av. M19—3K 103
Bolton Clo. M25—6M 59
Bolton Clo. M26—8K 115
Bolton Clo. WA3—7B 72
Bolton Ho. Rd. WN2—9M 53
Bolton Old Rd. M29—5K 55
Bolton Rd. BL2—5J 23
Bolton Rd. BL4—7K 39
(Farnworth)
Bolton Rd. BL4—1L 57
(Kearsley)
Bolton Rd. BL5 & BL3—9F 36
Bolton Rd. BL7—9K 7
Bolton Rd. BL8—1G 41
(Bury)
Bolton Rd. BL8—8B 8
(Hawkshaw)
Bolton Rd. M6—1K 77
Bolton Rd. M26—5D 40
Bolton Rd. M27—6F 58
Bolton Rd. M28—4K 57
Bolton Rd. M29—5K 55
Bolton Rd. OL11—6A 28
Bolton Rd. PR6 & BL6—2H 19
Bolton Rd. WN2—4J 35
(in two parts)
Bolton Rd. WN4 & WN2—4B 70
Bolton Rd. N. BL0—3J 9
(Ramsbottom)
Bolton Rd. W. BL0—8F 8
Bolton Sq. WN1—8E 34
Bolton St. BL0—6H 9
Bolton St. BL1—8E 22
Bolton St. BL9—8K 25
Bolton St. M3—4D 4 & 5E 78
Bolton St. M26—6F 40
Bolton St. OL4—2B 64
(in two parts)
Bolton St. SK5—7E 92
Bolton St. WN1—1F 52
Bolton St. WN4—2K 69
Bolton Yd. OL3—9B 48
Bombay Rd. SK3—6C 104
Bombay Rd. WN5—9J 33
Bombay Sq. M1—7G 79
(off Whitworth St.)
Bombay St. M1—5F 5 & 7G 79
Bombay St. OL6—3D 82
Bonar Clo. SK3—6C 104
Bonar Rd. SK3—5C 104
Boncarn Dri. M23—9A 102
Bonchurch Wlk. M18—9B 80
Bond Clo. BL6—7C 20
Bondmark Rd. M18—9C 80
Bond's La. PR7—3F 18
Bond Sq. M7—1E 78
Bond St. BL0—1L 9
Bond St. BL9—8A 26
Bond St. M12—5H 5 & 8J 79
Bond St. M34—3M 93
Bond St. OL12—9G 13
Bond St. SK15—4G 83
Bond St. WN7—2F 72
Bongs Rd. SK2—7M 105
(in two parts)
Bonhill Wlk. M11—5B 80
Bonington Rise. SK6—5H 107
Bonis Cres. SK2—9J 105
Bonis Hall La. SK10—6E 120
Bonny Brow St. M24—1H 61
Bonnyfields. SK6—3B 106
Bonnywell Rd. WN7—4E 72
Bonsall Bank. SK13—4E 96
(off Melandra Castle Rd.)
Bonsall Clo. SK13—4E 96
(off Melandra Castle Rd.)
Bonsall Fold. SK13—4E 96
(off Melandra Castle Rd.)
Bonsall St. M15—9F 78
Bonscale Cres. M24—6L 43
Bonthe St. M30—6F 76
Bonville Chase. WA14—9A 100
Bonville Rd. WA14—8A 100
Boodle St. OL6—4B 82
Bookham Wlk. M9—8L 61
Boond St. M3—3D 4 & 5E 78
Boond St. M4—6K 79
Boonfields. BL7—3G 23
Booth Av. M14—7K 91
Boothbank La. WA14—6G 109
Boothby Ct. M27—7D 58
Boothby Rd. M27—7E 58
Boothby St. SK2—9J 105
Booth Clo. SK15—6F 82
Boothcote. M34—9K 81
Booth Ct. BL4—9K 39
Booth Dri. M31—1M 87
Boothfield. BL4—7J 25
Boothfield. M30—4K 76
Boothfield Av. M22—7D 102
Boothfield Dri. M22—7D 102
Boothfield Rd. M22—7C 102
Booth Hall Rd. M9—5A 62
Booth Hill. OL1—8L 45
Booth La. M9—4G 61
Booth Rd. BL3—7B 40
Booth Rd. M16—3C 90
Booth Rd. M33—8H 89
Booth Rd. M34—8B 81
Booth Rd. SK9—2G 119
Booth Rd. WA14—9C 100
Boothroyden Clo. M24—1H 61
(in two parts)
Boothroyden Rd. M24 & M9
(in two parts)—1J 61
Boothroyden Ter. M9—2J 61
Boothsbank Av. M28—1H 75
Booth's Brow Rd. WN4—1K 69
Booth's Hall Gro. M28—1H 75
Booth's Hall Rd. M28—1H 75
Booth's Hall Way. M28—1H 75
Booth St. BL1—7C 22
Booth St. BL8—4F 24
Booth St. M2—4E 5 & 6F 78
Booth St. M24—2D 62
Booth St. M33—3E 5 & 5F 78
Booth St. M34—1M 93
Booth St. M35—9E 62
Booth St. OL4—2E 64
Booth St. OL6—5B 82
Booth St. OL9—2L 63
Booth St. SK3—6E 104
Booth St. SK14—1C 96
(Hollingworth)
Booth St. SK14—5E 94
(Hyde)
Booth St. SK15—7E 82
Booth St. E. M13—9H 79
Booth St. W. M15—9G 79
Booth Way. BL8—5E 24
Boothway. M30—6E 76
Boot La. BL1—9K 21
Bootle St. M2—4E 5 & 6F 78
Bor Av. WN3—4B 52
Bordale Av. M9—9M 61
Bordan St. M11—7M 79
Borden Clo. WN2—7F 34
Bordesley Av. M28—2G 57
Bordley Wlk. M23—4L 101
Bordon Rd. SK3—6B 104
Bores Hill. WN1—7C 18
Boringdon Clo. M10—1B 80
Borland Av. M10—7C 62
Borough Arc. SK14—3D 94
Borough Av. M26—4K 41
Borough Av. M27—7G 59
Borough Rd. M5—6K 77
Borough Rd. WA15—9E 100
Borough St. SK15—6G 83
Borron Rd. WA12—9B 70
Borron St. SK1—3G 105
Borrowdale Av. BL1—1A 38
Borrowdale Av. SK8—3C 114
Borrowdale Clo. OL2—3K 45
Borrowdale Cres. M20—1E 102
Borrowdale Cres. OL7—2M 81
Borrowdale Dri. BL9—6A 42
Borrowdale Dri. OL11—6B 28
Borrowdale Rd. M24—7K 43
Borrowdale Rd. SK2—6H 105
Borrowdale Ter. SK15—3G 83
Borsdane Av. WN2—4L 53
Borsden St. M27—6D 58
Borth Av. SK2—6H 105
Borth Wlk. M23—7M 101
Borwell St. M18—9D 80
Boscobel Rd. BL3—7H 39
Boscombe Av. M30—7C 76
Boscombe Dri. SK7—2J 115
Boscombe St. M14—4H 91
Boscombe St. SK5—4F 92
Boscow Rd. BL3—7A 40
Bosden Av. SK7—1L 115
Bosden Clo. SK1—5F 104
(off Bosden Fold)
Bosden Clo. SK9—7K 113
Bosden Fold. SK1—5F 104
Bosdenfold Rd. SK7—1L 115
Bosden Hall Rd. SK7—1L 115
Bosdin Rd. E. M31—5L 87
Bosdin Rd. W. M31—5L 87
Bosley Av. M20—6G 91
Bosley Clo. SK9—1K 119
Bosley Dri. SK12—9A 116
Bosley Rd. SK3—5A 104
Bossall Av. M9—4L 61
Bossington Clo. SK2—5J 105
Bostock Wlk. M13—6G 5 &
8H 79
Boston Clo. M35—7F 62
Boston Clo. SK7—5D 114
Boston Ct. M5—7L 77
Boston Gro. WN7—8E 54
Boston St. BL1—8E 22
Boston St. BL8—4M 63
Boston St. SK14—3E 94
Boston Wlk. M34—5A 94
Boswell Av. M34—6K 81
Boswell Pl. WN3—4M 51
Boswell Way. M24—5E 44
Bosworth Clo. M25—9C 42
Bosworth Rd. WA11—9C 68
Bosworth Sq. OL11—6D 28
Bosworth St. BL6—6B 20
Bosworth St. M11—7A 80
Bosworth St. OL11—6D 28
Botanical Av. M16—1A 90
Botanical Ho. M16—1A 90
Botany Clo. OL10—7H 27
Botany Clo. WN2—7H 35
Botany La. OL6—3C 82
Botany Rd. M30—3A 76
Botany Rd. SK6—8A 94
Botha Clo. M11—8D 80
Botham Clo. M15—1G 91
Botham Ct. M30—4B 76
Bothwell Rd. M10—2H 5 & 4J 79
Bottesford Av. M20—9F 90
Bottomley Side. M9—6J 61
Bottom o' th' Moor. BL2—8K 23
Bottom o' th' Moor. BL6—7F 20
Bottom o' th' Moor. OL1—1B 64
Bottom St. SK14—3E 94
Boughey St. WN7—2E 72
Boulder Dri. M23—2A 112
Boulderstone Rd. SK15—3G 83
Bouldon Dri. BL8—5J 25
Boulevard, The. SK7—2L 115
Boulevard, The. SK14—2D 96
Bouley Wlk. M12—9A 80
Boulton St. M3—5E 78
Boundary Clo. OL5—1J 83
(in two parts)
Boundary Clo. SK6—9C 94
Boundary Dri. BL2—4A 40
Boundary Gdns. BL1—8D 22
Boundary Gdns. OL1—8L 45
Boundary Grn. M34—1L 93
Boundary Gro. M33—2M 101
Boundary La. M15—9G 79
Boundary La. WN6—7G 17
Boundary Pk. Rd. OL1—8J 45
Boundary Rd. M27—7F 58
Boundary Rd. M30—3H 87
Boundary Rd. SK8—7M 103
Boundary St. BL1—8D 22
Boundary St. BL9—7M 25
Boundary St. M12—1A 92
Boundary St. M29—7A 56
Boundary St. OL11—5B 28
Boundary St. OL15—5A 14
Boundary St. WN1—1D 52
Boundary St. WN7—3H 73
Boundary St. E. M13—6F 5 &
8G 79
Boundary St. W. M15—9G 79
Boundary, The. M27—4E 58
Boundary Wlk. OL11—5E 28
Bourdon St. M10—4K 79
Bourget St. M8—8F 60
Bournbrook Av. M28—2G 57
Bourne Av. M27—9F 58
Bourne Av. WA3—7K 71
Bourne Dri. M10—7B 62
Bourne Ho. M5—5M 77
Bournelea Av. M19—8M 91
Bourne Rd. OL2—1A 46
Bourne St. OL9—6H 63
Bourne St. SK4—1E 104
Bourne St. SK9—5F 118
Bourne Wlk. BL1—9F 22
Bournville Av. SK4—1M 103
Bournville Gro. M19—5B 92
Bourton Clo. BL8—7H 25
Bourton Ct. M29—7D 56
Bourton Dri. M18—2B 92
Bowden Clo. OL11—1D 44
Bowden Clo. WN7—5H 73
Bowden La. SK6—6E 106
Bowden Rd. M27—9J 59
Bowden Rd. SK13—3J 97
Bowden St. BL1—9B 22
Bowden St. M27—5B 58
Bowden St. M34—3L 93
Bowden St. SK7—1L 115
Bowden St. SK14—1D 94
Bowden St. WN2—5M 35
Bowden View. M31—4B 88
Bowder Clo. SK14—5L 95
Bowdon Av. M14—5F 90
Bowdon Rise. WA14—2D 110
Bowdon Rd. WA14—1C 110
Bowdon St. SK3—5D 104
(in two parts)
Bowen Clo. SK7—7F 114
Bowen St. BL1—9B 22
Bower Av. OL12—7K 13
Bower Av. SK4—2C 104
Bower Av. SK7—3K 115
Bower Ct. WA14—1G 95
Bowerfield Av. SK7—4K 115
Bowerfield Cres. SK7—4K 115
Bowerfold La. SK4—3C 104
Bower Gro. SK15—5J 83
Bower La. OL9—6G 63
Bower Rd. WA15—3E 110
Bowers Av. M31—2B 88
Bowers St. M14—7L 91
Bower St. BL9—7C 26
Bower St. M8—9E 60
Bower St. M10—2M 79
Bower St. OL1—1A 64
Bower St. SK5—4F 92
Bower Ter. M35—4J 81
Bowery Av. SK8—1E 114
Bowes Clo. BL8—5H 25
Bowes St. M14—3F 90
Bowfell Circ. M31—3B 88
Bowfell Dri. SK6—4E 116
Bowfell Gro. M9—4H 61
Bowfell Rd. M31—4A 88
Bowfell Wlk. M10—2C 80
Bowgreave Av. BL2—2M 39
Bow Grn. M. WA14—2B 110
Bow Grn. Rd. WA14—3M 109
Bowgreen Wlk. M15—9D 78
Bowker Av. M31—3M 87
Bowker Bank Av. M8—6F 60
Bowker Clo. OL11—1L 27
Bowker Ct. M7—1D 78
Bowkers Row. BL1—2F 38
Bowker St. M7—1D 78
Bowker St. M26—6G 41
Bowker St. M28—5H 57
Bowker St. SK14—3E 94
Bowker Vale Gdns. M9—5F 60
Bowlacre Rd. SK14—8D 94
Bowland Av. WN4—3B 70
Bowland Clo. BL8—7E 24
Bowland Clo. OL6—9C 64
Bowland Clo. SK2—8L 105
Bowland Ct. M33—1H 101
Bowland Dri. BL1—8L 21
Bowland Gro. OL16—6M 29
Bowland Rd. M23—7M 101
Bowland Rd. M34—3H 93
Bowland Rd. SK6—9B 94
Bowland Rd. SK13—6G 97
Bow La. M2—4E 5 & 6F 78
Bow La. OL10—8K 27
Bow La. WA14—4A 110
Bowlee Clo. BL9—7A 42
Bowler St. M19—6B 92
Bowler St. OL2—2B 46
Bowlers Wlk. OL12—9F 12
Bowley Av. M22—2A 112
Bowling Grn. St. BL0—4K 9
(in two parts)
Bowling Grn. St. OL10—8K 27
Bowling Grn. St. SK14—4D 94
Bowling Grn. Way. OL11
—3M 27
Bowling Rd. M18—3E 92
Bowlings, The. WN6—7A 34
Bowling St. OL9—6H 63
Bowman Cres. OL6—4D 82
Bowmeadow Grange. M12
—2M 91
Bowmead Wlk. M8—1F 78
Bowmont Clo. SK8—9A 104
Bowness Av. M30—1D 98
Bowness Av. OL12—1C 28
Bowness Av. SK4—8E 92
Bowness Av. SK8—3B 114
Bowness Av. WA11—7B 68
Bowness Ct. M24—7K 43
Bowness Dri. M33—9F 88
Bowness Pl. WN2—9H 35
Bowness Rd. BL3—5D 38
(Bolton)
Bowness Rd. BL3—5M 39
(Little Lever)
Bowness Rd. M24—7J 43
Bowness Rd. OL7—3M 81
Bowness Rd. WA15—8K 101
Bowness St. M11—8F 80
Bowness St. M32—3K 89
Bow Rd. WN7—4H 73
Bowscale Clo. M13—2M 91
Bowstone Hill Rd. BL2—5B 24
Bow St. BL1—2F 38
Bow St. M2—4E 5 & 6F 78
Bow St. OL1—1M 63
Bow St. OL6—5C 82
(off Nelson St.)
Bow St. OL6—4B 82
(off Warrington St.)
Bow St. OL11—7D 28
Bow St. SK3—5C 104
Bow Vs. WA14—2B 110
Boxgrove Rd. M33—9E 88
Boxgrove Wlk. M8—1F 78
Boxhill Dri. M23—4A 102
Box St. BL0—5K 9
Box St. OL15—6A 14
Boxtree Av. M18—2D 92
Box Wlk. M31—2E 98
Boyd Clo. WN6—9M 17
Boydell St. WN7—1F 72
Boyd St. M12—8A 80
Boyd's Wlk. SK16—8C 82
Boyer St. M16—1B 90
Boyle St. BL1—9A 22
Boyle St. M8—1H 79
Boysnope Cotts. M30—1K 87
Boysnope Cres. M30—2J 87
Brabant Clo. SK8—3B 114
Brabant Rd. SK8—2B 114
Brabazon Pl. WN5—9J 33
Brabham Clo. M21—6B 90
Brabyns Av. SK6—2D 106
Brabyns Brow. SK6—6G 107
Brabyns Rd. SK14—7E 94
Bracadale Dri. SK3—9E 104
Bracadale Dri. SK3—8E 104
Bracewell Clo. M12—1A 92
Bracken Av. M28—5L 57
Brackenbury Wlk. M15—1G 91
Bracken Clo. BL1—4D 22
Bracken Clo. M24—6K 55
Bracken Clo. M33—3C 88
Bracken Clo. M35—5J 81
Bracken Clo. OL4—2F 64
Bracken Clo. OL10—1K 43
Bracken Clo. SK6—6H 107
Bracken Clo. SK14—9D 84
Bracken Dri. M23—8B 102
Brackenfield Wlk. WA15
—7K 101
Brackenhall Ct. OL10—8G 27
Brackenhurst Av. WN5—6F 50
Bracken Lea. BL5—3F 54
Bracken Rd. WN7—2B 72
Brackenside. SK5—6G 93
Bracken Way. SK13—7M 97
Brackenwood Dri. SK8—9K 103
Brackenwood M. SK9—3L 119
Brackley Av. M15—6C 4 & 8D 78
Brackley Av. M30—8D 86
Brackley Ct. M22—5D 102
Brackley Lodge. M30—4F 76
Brackley Rd. BL2—9A 38
Brackley Rd. M30—3D 76
Brackley Rd. SK4—1C 104
Brackley Sq. OL1—9A 46
Brackley St. BL4—9K 39
(in two parts)
Brackley St. M28—4J 57
Brackley St. OL1—9A 46
Bracknell Dri. M9—5G 61
Bracondale Av. BL1—8B 22
Bradbourne Clo. BL3—4E 38
Bradburn Av. M30—6D 76
Bradburn Clo. M30—5D 76
Bradburn Gro. M30—6D 76
Bradburn Rd. M30—7E 76
Bradburn St. M30—6D 76
Bradburn Wlk. M8—1H 79
(off Moordown Clo.)
Bradbury Av. WA14—8A 100
Bradbury's La. OL3—4C 66
Bradbury St. BL4—4A 40
Bradbury St. OL7—3A 82
Bradbury St. SK14—5E 94
Bradbury Wlk. OL2—5L 45
(off Shaw St.)
Bradda Mt. SK7—2G 115
Braddan Av. M33—2J 101
Braddocks Clo. OL12—7K 13
Braddon Av. M31—4D 88
Braddon Rd. SK6—9A 94
Braddon St. M11—6C 80
Braddyll Rd. BL5—9M 37
Bradfield Av. M6—5J 77
Bradfield Clo. SK5—4E 92
Bradfield Rd. M31 & M32—4F 88
Bradford Av. BL3—6H 39
Bradford Ct. M10—7C 62
Bradford Cres. BL3—6H 39
Bradford Pk. Dri. BL2—3H 39
Bradford Rd. BL4 & BL3—9G 39
Bradford Rd. M10—5K 79
Bradford Rd. M30—2E 76
Bradford Sq. BL3—6H 39
Bradford St. BL2—3G 39
Bradford St. OL1—9L 45
Bradford St. WN3—2E 52
Bradford Ter. BL9—9K 25
Bradgate Av. SK8—3L 113
Bradgate Clo. M22—5E 102
Bradgate Rd. M33—3H 101
Bradgate Rd. WA14—8A 100
Bradgate St. OL7—6A 82
Brading Wlk. M22—4E 112
Bradley Av. M7—9B 60
Bradley Clo. M34—8L 81
Bradley Clo. WA15—6E 100
Bradley Dri. BL9—7B 42
Bradley Fold. SK15—5H 83
Bradley Fold Rd. BL2—3B 40
Bradley Grn. Rd. SK14—9F 84
Bradley Hall Trading Est. WN6
—7A 18
Bradley Ho. OL8—3M 63
Bradley La. BL2—4B 40
Bradley La. M32—7H 89
Bradley La. OL16—6B 30
Bradley La. WN6 & WN1
—8M 17
Bradley's Ct. M1—4G 5 & 5H
Bradley St. M1—5H 79
Bradley St. OL16—6B 30
Bradley St. SK16—8A 82
Bradnor Rd. M22—6D 102
Bradshaw Av. M20—7H 91
Bradshaw Av. M25—1E 41
Bradshaw Av. M35—2E 80
Bradshaw Brow. BL2—6L 23
Bradshaw Cres. SK6—6G 107
Bradshaw Fold Av. M10—5D
Bradshawgate. BL1 & BL2
—2F
Bradshaw Ga. WN1—9D 34
Bradshawgate. WN7—2F 72
Bradshawgate Diversion. WN
—3F
Bradshaw Hall Dri. BL2—4J
Bradshaw Hall La. SK8—4K 1
(in two parts)
Bradshaw Hall M. BL2—3J 2
Bradshaw La. M32—5K 89
Bradshaw La. PR6—2F 18
Bradshaw La. WA13—1C 108
Bradshaw Meadows. BL2
—4K
Bradshaw Rd. BL2—5K 23
Bradshaw Rd. BL8—4C 24
Bradshaw Rd. SK6—6F 106
Bradshaw St. BL2—3F 33
Bradshaw St. M4—3F 5 & 5G
Bradshaw St. M7—1E 7E
Bradshaw St. M24—1C 62
Bradshaw St. M26—6F 40
Bradshaw St. M29—5K 55
Bradshaw St. OL1—1M 63
Bradshaw St. OL10—8L 27
(in two parts)
Bradshaw St. OL16—2G 29
Bradshaw St. WN1—7D 34
Bradshaw St. WN5—2G 51
Bradshaw St. N. M7—9D 60
Bradshaw Trading Est. M24
—2C
Bradstock Clo. M16—3E 90
Bradstone Rd. M8—2F 78
Bradwell Av. M20—8F 90
Bradwell Av. M32—3G 89
Bradwell Dri. SK8—5J 113
Bradwell Fold. SK13—5E 96
(off Buxton M.)
Bradwell Lea. SK13—4E 96
(off Buxton M.)
Bradwell Pl. BL2—9H 23
Bradwell Rd. SK7—4L 115
Bradwell Rd. WA3—8L 71
Bradwell Ter. SK13—5E 96
(off Buxton M.)
Bradwell Wlk. M31—3K 87
Bradwen Av. M8—7G 61
Bradwen Clo. M34—5A 94
Bradwin Rd. SK6—6A 94
Brady St. SK1—3G 105
Bradbury Ct. WN7—2D 72
Braemar Av. M31—5A 88
Braemar Av. M32—4G 89
Braemar Ct. M9—3G 61
Braemar Dri. BL9—8D 26
Braemar Dri. M33—3C 100
Braemar Gro. OL10—9G 27
Braemar La. M28—1H 75
Braemar Rd. M14—6L 91
Braemar Rd. SK7—1M 115
Braemar Wlk. BL3—4J 39
Braemar Wlk. WN2—4K 35
Braemore Clo. OL2—1C 46
Braemore Clo. WN3—6J 51
Braemore Dri. SK14—5M 95
Braeside. M32—5G 89
Brae Side. OL8—6L 63
Braeside Clo. SK2—7M 105
Braeside Cres. WN5—2H 69
Braeside Gro. BL3—4L 37
Braewood Clo. BL9—7G 26
Brafferton Clo. OL7—9F 26
Brageham St. M18—1C 92
Braidhaven. WN6—2D 32
Brailsford Av. SK13—4E 96
Brailsford Clo. SK13—4E 9
(off Hathersage Cres.)
Brailsford Gdns. SK13—4E
(off Hathersage Cres.)
Brailsford Grn. SK13—4E 9
(off Melandra Castle Rd.
Brailsford M. SK13—4E 96
Brailsford Rd. BL2—7J 23
Brailsford Rd. M14—6L 91
Braintree Rd. M22—4E 112
Braithwaite. WN6—3G 33
Braithwaite Rd. M24—5K 4
Braithwaite Rd. WA3—6K
Brakehouse Clo. OL16—4L
Brakesmere Gro. M28—4F
Braley St. M12—6G 5 & 8H
Bramall Clo. BL9—7B 42
Bramall Ct. M3—2C 4 & 4D
Bramall St. M3—2C 4 & 4
Bramall Mt. SK2—8F 104
Bramber Way. OL9—2H 63
Bramble Av. M5—6B 4 & 8
Bramble Av. OL4—8D 46
Bramble Clo. OL15—6M 13
Bramble Gro. WN5—1L 51
Bramble Meadow. M5—8B
(off W. Park St.)
Bramble Wlk. M22—2C 11
Bramble Wlk. M33—9C 88
Bramblewood. OL9—4A 62
Brambling Clo. M34—5J 8
Brambling Clo. SK2—8A 1
Brambling Dri. BL5—2D 5
Bramcote Av. BL2—4H 39
Bramcote Av. M23—7B 10
Bramcote Av. WA11—9D 6
Bramdean Av. BL2—5L 23
Bramfield Wlk. M15—6C 4
Bramhall Av. BL2—6A 24
Bramhall Clo. M33—2L 10
Bramhall Clo. OL16—4L 2
Bramhall Clo. WA15—7K
Bramhall La. SK2 & SK3
—7
Bramhall La. SK7—2E 114
Bramhall La. S. SK7—6E
Bramhall Moor La. SK7
—3
Bramhall Pk. Rd. SK7—3D
Bramhall Rd. SK7—3C 11
Bramhall St. BL3—3H 39
Bramhall St. M18—1E 92
Bramhall St. SK14—2D 9
Bramhall Wlk. M34—4L 9
Bramhope Wlk. M9—9K 6
Bramley Av. M19—6A 92
Bramley Av. M32—4H 89
Bramley Clo. M27—1C 76
Bramley Clo. SK7—6E 114
Bramley Cres. SK4—4B 10
Bramley Dri. BL8—4J 25
Bramley Dri. SK7—6E 114
Bramley Meade. M7—9D
Bramley Rd. BL1—4F 22
Bramley Rd. OL11—2L 27
Bramley Rd. SK7—6E 114
Bramley St. M7—1D 4 & 3
Brammall La. SK3—1F 1
Brammay Dri. BL8—4E 2
Brampton Av. WA11—6B
Brampton Clo. WN2—7F
Brampton Rd. BL3—6A 3
Brampton Rd. SK7—2F 1
Brampton St. M29—5K
Brampton Wlk. M10—1B
Bramway. SK6—5F 116
Bramway. SK7—5C 114
Bramwell Dri. M13—9J 7
Bramwell St. SK1—5H 10
Bramwood Ct. SK7—6E 1
Bramworth Av. BL0—5H
Brancaster Rd. M1—6F 5

Burnell Clo. M10—4K 79
Burnell Ct. OL10—2K 43
Burnett Av. M5—5A 4 & 7B 78
Burnett Clo. M10—2K 79
Burnett Gdns. M5—5A 6 & 7B 78
Burnfell. WA3—8L 71
Burnfield Rd. M18—3D 92
Burnfield Rd. SK5—3E 92
Burnham Av. BL1—9A 22
Burnham Av. SK5—5F 92
Burnham Clo. SK8—2M 113
Burnham Dri. M19—6M 91
Burnham Dri. M31—3C 88
Burnham Gro. WN2—7F 34
Burnham Wlk. BL4—8K 39
Burnleigh Ct. BL5—9M 37
Burnley La. OL9 & OL1—7G 45
Burnley Rd. BL9—2L 25
(in two parts)
Burnley St. M35—8G 63
Burnley St. OL9—1H 63
Burnmoor Rd. BL2—1M 39
Burnsall Av. M25—9L 41
Burnsall Av. WA3—7M 71
Burnsall Gro. OL2—5K 45
Burnsall Wlk. M22—2A 112
Burns Av. BL9—3M 41
Burns Av. M27—7D 58
Burns Av. M29—3K 55
Burns Av. SK8—7M 103
Burns Av. WN7—8C 54
Burns Clo. M11—6L 79
Burns Clo. OL1—4E 46
Burns Clo. WN3—4A 52
Burns Clo. WN4—9M 51
Burns Clo. WN5—7D 50
Burns Cres. SK2—6L 105
Burns Fold. SK16—8G 83
Burns Gdns. M25—5M 59
Burns Gro. M35—5G 81
Burnside. BL0—1K 9
Burnside. OL2—1D 46
Burnside. SK14—2F 96
Burnside. SK15—8K 83
Burnside Av. M6—2H 77
Burnside Av. SK4—8E 92
Burnside Clo. M26—2F 40
Burnside Clo. M29—9B 56
Burnside Clo. OL10—9K 27
Burnside Clo. SK6—2M 105
Burnside Clo. SK15—8K 83
Burnside Cres. M24—6L 43
Burnside Dri. M19—7L 91
Burnside Rd. BL1—8B 22
Burnside Rd. OL16—4J 29
Burnside Rd. SK8—8G 103
Burns Rd. M28—3H 57
Burns Rd. M34—7A 94
Burns Rd. WN2—7H 53
Burns St. BL3—3F 38
Burns St. OL10—9K 27
Burnt Edge La. BL6—4H 21
Burnthorpe Av. M9—5H 61
Burnthorpe Clo. OL11—4L 27
Burntwood Wlk. M9—8L 61
(off Naunton Wlk.)
Burnvale. WN3—6K 51
Burran Rd. M22—4D 112
Burrell St. M13—8H 79
(off Hanworth Clo.)
Burrington Dri. WN7—9D 54
Burrows Av. M21—8B 90
Burrows Av. WA11—9F 68
Burrows St. WA11—9G 69
Burrswood Av. BL9—4M 25
Burrwood Dri. SK3—8D 104
Burslem Av. M20—6G 91
Burstead St. M18—8E 80
Burstock St. M4—2G 5 & 4H 79
Burston St. M18—9C 80
Burtinshaw St. M18—1D 92
Burton Av. BL8—6F 24
Burton Av. M20—8G 91
Burton Av. M32—5H 89
Burton Av. WA15—4G 101
Burton Dri. SK12—8K 115
Burton Gro. M28—8C 58
Burton Ho. SK9—4H 119
Burton Rd. M20—1F 102
Burton St. M10—1H 5 & 3H 79
Burton St. M24—9M 43
Burton St. OL4—2E 64
Burton St. SK4—2E 104
Burton Wlk. M3—3C 4 & 5D 78
Burton Wlk. SK4—2E 104
(off Heskith St.)
Burtonwood Ct. M24—8M 43
Burtree St. M12—9A 80
Burwell Av. PR7—2K 17
Burwell Clo. OL12—8D 12
Burwell Clo. SK13—6G 97
Burwell Gro. M23—6M 101
Bury Av. M16—4C 90
Bury & Bolton Rd. M26—2C 40
Bury Easterly By-Pass. BL9
—5B 26
Bury New Rd. BL2—2G 39
(Bolton)
Bury New Rd. BL2—2A 40
(Breightmet)
Bury New Rd. BL9 & OL10
—8C 26
Bury New Rd. M25 M7 & M8
—9M 41
Bury Old Rd. BL0—1M 9
Bury Old Rd. BL2—9A 24
(Ainsworth)
Bury Old Rd. BL2—2G 39
(Bolton, in two parts)
Bury Old Rd. BL9 & OL10—9E 26
(Heap)
Bury Old Rd. BL9—6M 9
(Walmersley)
Bury Old Rd. M25 & M8—5C 60
Bury Pl. M11—5C 80
Bury Rd. BL0—1K 9
Bury Rd. BL2—2H 39
Bury Rd. BL7—9L 7
Bury Rd. BL8—4F 24
Bury Rd. M26—5H 41
Bury Rd. OL11—5L 27
Bury & Rochdale Old Rd. BL9 &
OL10—6F 26
Bury St. BL1—2G 39
Bury St. M3—3D 4 & 5E 78
Bury St. M26—5J 41
Bury St. OL5—8J 65
Bury St. OL10—8H 27
Bury St. SK5—2F 104
Bushell St. BL3—5B 38
Bushey Dri. M23—8A 102
Busheyfield Clo. SK14—1D 94
Bushfield Wlk. M23—6L 101
Bushgrove Wlk. M9—3K 61
(off Claygate Dri.)
Bushmoor Wlk. M13—1K 91
Bushnell Wlk. M9—3K 61
(off Eastlands Rd.)
Bush St. M10—2L 79
Bushton Wlk. M10—2J 79
Bushway Wlk. M8—1H 79
(off Geneva Wlk.)
Bushycroft. SK14—2A 96
Busk Rd. OL9—9J 45
Busk Wlk. OL9—9J 45
Butcher La. BL9—8M 25
Butcher La. M23—6K 101
(in two parts)
Butcher La. OL2—4J 45
Butchers La. WN4—5B 70
Bute Av. OL8—5M 63
Bute St. BL1—9B 22
Bute St. M5—6K 77
Bute St. M10—8M 61
Bute St. M30—7B 76
Bute St. SK13—4L 97
Butler Ct. M10—2H 5 & 4J 79
Butler Ct. M32—5K 89
Butler Grn. OL9—4G 63
Butler La. M4—2H 5 & 4J 79
Butler St. BL0—7G 9
Butler St. M4—2H 5 & 4J 79
Butler St. WN1—9D 34

Butley Lanes. SK10—9F 120
Butley St. SK7—9L 105
Butman St. M18—9F 80
Buttercup Av. M28—5F 56
Buttercup Dri. OL11—7B 28
Buttercup Dri. SK3—9D 104
Butterfield Clo. SK8—3B 114
Butterfield Rd. BL5—9M 37
Butterhouse La. OL3—7C 48
Butter La. M3—4E 5 & 6F 78
Butterley Clo. SK16—8F 82
Buttermere. OL11—6F 28
Buttermere Av. M27—1F 76
Buttermere Av. OL10—1K 43
Buttermere Av. WA11—7A 68
Buttermere Av. WN4—2B 70
Buttermere Clo. BL3—5M 39
Buttermere Dri. BL0—4H 9
Buttermere Dri. M24—7L 43
Buttermere Dri. WA15—6K 111
Buttermere Gro. OL2—2K 45
Buttermere Rd. BL4—9E 38
Buttermere Rd. M31—2E 98
Buttermere Rd. OL4—9D 46
Buttermere Rd. OL7—3A 82
Buttermere Rd. SK8—1H 113
Buttermere Rd. WN5—1J 51
Buttermere Ter. SK15—4G 83
Butterstile La. M25—7M 59
Butterwick Clo. M12—3B 92
Butterworth Hall. OL16—5A 30
Butterworth La. OL9—5E 62
Butterworth Pl. OL15—5A 14
Butterworth St. M11—7A 80
Butterworth St. M24—1C 62
Butterworth St. M26—5H 41
Butterworth St. OL2—6A 46
Butterworth St. OL9—9H 45
Butterworth St. OL15—6A 14
Butterworth Way. OL3—3B 66
Buttery Ho. La. WA15—2L 111
Butt Hill Av. M25—5B 60
Butt Hill Ct. M25—5B 60
Butt Hill Dri. M25—5B 60
Butt Hill Rd. M25—5B 60
Butt La. OL5—4H 65
Button Hole. OL2—2D 46
Button La. M23—3A 102
Buttress St. M18—9C 80
Butts Av. WN7—4J 73
Butts La. OL3—5J 47
Butts St. WN7—4H 73
Butts, The. OL16—3F 28
Buxted Rd. OL1—8B 46
Buxton Av. M20—8F 90
Buxton Av. OL6—1F 82
Buxton Clo. M29—4L 55
Buxton Clo. SK13—4E 96
(off Buxton M.)
Buxton Cres. M33—4K 101
Buxton Cres. OL16—6H 29
Buxton La. M35—6E 80
Buxton La. SK6—8E 106
Buxton M. SK13—4E 96
Buxton Old Rd. SK12—6K 117
Buxton Pl. OL8—3L 63
Buxton Rd. M32—3G 89
Buxton Rd. SK2—7G 105
Buxton Rd. SK7, SK6 & SK12
—3M 115
Buxton Rd. SK12—6K 117
Buxton Rd. W. SK12—6G 117
Buxton St. BL8—8J 25
Buxton St. M1—5G 5 & 7H 79
Buxton St. OL10—9K 27
Buxton St. SK7—1K 115
Buxton St. SK8—8G 103
Buxton Ter. SK14—9D 84
Buxton Wlk. SK13—5E 96
(off Buxton M.)
Buxton Way. M34—6M 93
Bycroft Wlk. M10—3D 80
Byer Clo. M33—2A 102
Bye Rd. BL0—4L 9
Bye St. M34—8M 81
Byfield Rd. M22—9C 102
Byland Av. OL4—4D 64
Byland Av. SK8—6B 114
Byland Clo. BL1—8E 22
Byland Gdns. M26—5E 40
Bylands Clo. SK12—8K 115
Bylands Fold. SK16—9D 82
Byland Wlk. M22—3D 112
Byley Rise. WN6—1L 33
Byng Av. M30—1D 98
Byng St. BL4—9K 39
Byng St. BL5—1B 54
Byng St. OL10—1L 43
Byng St. E. BL2—3F 38
Byng St. W. BL3—3F 38
Byre Clo. M33—2A 102
Byrness Clo. M29—4L 55
Byrom Av. M19—5C 92
Byrom Ct. M35—6F 80
Byrom La. WA3—5M 71
Byrom Pde. M19—5C 92
Byrom St. BL8—6H 25
Byrom St. M3—5D 4 & 7E 78
Byrom St. M5—7A 78
Byrom St. M16—2D 90
Byrom St. SK15—6F 82
Byrom St. WA14—1D 110
Byron Av. M25—5M 59
Byron Av. M26—5D 40
Byron Av. M27—8E 58
Byron Av. M35—5G 81
Byron Clo. WN2—7H 53
Byron Clo. WN5—1F 50
Byron Clo. WN6—6L 33
Byron Cres. PR7—1M 17
Byron Dri. SK8—7M 103
Byron Gro. M29—3K 55
Byron Gro. SK5—5E 92
Byron Gro. WN7—9F 54
Byron Rd. M24—7B 44
Byron Rd. M32—3L 89
Byron Rd. M34—6M 93
Byron St. M30—5D 76
Byron St. OL2—5L 45
Byron St. OL8—6H 63
Byron St. WN2—3K 53
Byron St. WN7—1F 72
Byron Wlk. BL4—1H 57
Byrth Rd. OL8—8M 63
Bywell Wlk. M8—9F 60
(off Levenhurst Rd.)
Bywood Wlk. M7—2E 78

Cabin La. OL4—6F 46
Cablestead Wlk. M11—7M 79
(off Cotteridge Wlk.)
Cable St. BL1—1F 38
Cable St. M3—3D 4 & 5E 78
Cable St. M4—3G 5 & 5H 79
Cabot Pl. SK5—1F 104
Caddington Rd. M21—6C 90
Cadleigh Wlk. M10—9A 62
Cadman Gro. WN2—4K 53
Cadman St. M12—8K 79
Cadmium Wlk. M18—2C 92
Cadnam Dri. M22—1F 112
Cadogan Dri. WN3—6K 51
Cadogan Pl. M7—7E 60
Cadogan St. M14—2G 91
Cadum Wlk. M13—9J 79
Caen Av. M10—5C 62
Caernarvon Clo. BL8—1F 24
Caernarvon Dri. SK7—3J 115
Caernarvon Rd. WN2—5A 54
Caernarvon Way. M34—5M 93
Caesar St. OL11—8G 29
Cairn Dri. M6—2C 78
Cairn Dri. OL11—4L 27
Cairngorm Dri. BL3—4L 37
Cairns Pl. OL6—2D 82
Cairn Wlk. M11—6M 79
Caister Av. M25—1A 60
Caister Clo. M31—5J 87
Caistor St. SK1—2H 105
Caistor Wlk. OL1—1M 63
Caithness Dri. BL3—3L 37
Caithness Rd. OL11—5L 27

Cajetan ho. M24—3M 61
Cakebread St. M12—6H 5 &
8J 79
Calbourne Cres. M12—3B 92
Calcot Wlk. M23—7M 101
Calcutta Rd. SK3—6C 104
Caldbeck Av. BL1—9M 21
Caldbeck Av. M33—9L 89
Caldbeck Clo. WN2—6H 53
Caldbeck Clo. WN4—3B 70
Caldbeck Dri. BL4—1E 56
Caldbeck Dri. M24—8L 43
Caldbeck Gro. WA11—6C 68
Caldecott Rd. M9—3G 61
Calder Av. M22—5D 102
Calder Av. M30—5F 86
Calder Av. OL15—4A 14
Calder Av. WN2—5C 54
Calderbank. WN5—2G 51
Calderbank Av. M31—2L 87
Calderbank St. WN5—3L 51
Calderbrook Dri. SK8—9A 104
Calderbrook Rd. OL15—5A 14
(Littleborough)
Calderbrook Ter. OL15—3C 14
Calderbrook Wlk. M9—9K 61
Calder Clo. SK5—9F 92
Calder Clo. SK12—1K 121
Caldercourt. M31—2L 87
Calder Cres. M25—7B 42
Calder Dri. BL4—3B 58
Calder Dri. BL9—2A 26
Calder Dri. M27—7E 58
Calder Dri. M28—6G 57
Calder Dri. WN2—6G 53
Calder Flats. OL10—8J 27
(off Wilton St.)
Calder Gro. OL2—1A 46
Calder Pl. WN5—1J 51
Calder Rd. BL3—6E 38
Caldershaw La. OL12—9A 12
Caldershaw Rd. OL12—1A 28
Calder St. M5—5C 4 & 7D 78
Calder St. OL16—9H 13
Caldervale Av. M21—1C 102
Calder Wlk. M24—7J 43
Calder Wlk. M25—7B 42
Calder Way. M25—7B 42
Caldey Rd. M23—8L 101
Caldwell Av. M29—3A 74
Caldwell Clo. M29—2B 74
Caldwell St. BL5—3F 54
Caldwell St. SK5—5F 92
Caldy Dri. BL0—8G 9
Caldy Gro. WA11—7G 69
(Haydock)
Caldy Gro. WA11—9D 68
(St Helens)
Caldy Rd. M6—2K 77
Caldy Rd. SK9—9K 113
Caledon Av. M10—8A 62
Caledonian Dri. M30—7E 76
Caledonia St. BL3—4C 38
Caledonia St. M26—5J 41
(in two parts)
Caledonia Way. M32—1G 89
Cale Grn. SK2—7F 104
Cale La. WN2—7G 35
Cale St. SK2—6F 104
Calf Hey. OL12—4J 13
Calf Hey. OL15—5M 13
Calf Hey Clo. M26—6D 40
Calf Hey La. OL12—3D 12
Calf Hey N. OL11—6G 29
Calf Hey Rd. OL2—1D 46
Calf Hey S. OL11—6G 29
Calgarth Dri. M24—6K 43
Calico Wood Av. WN6—3F 32
Calland Av. SK14—3F 94
Callender Sq. OL10—9F 26
Callender St. BL0—5H 9
Calliards La. OL15—7L 13
Calliard's Rd. OL16—7L 13
Callingdon Rd. M21—9D 90
Callington Clo. SK14—4L 95
Callington Dri. SK14—4L 95
(in two parts)
Callington Wlk. SK14—4L 95
Callis Rd. BL3—3C 38
Callum Wlk. M13—9J 79
Calne Wlk. M23—8A 102
Calow Clo. SK13—4E 96
Calow Dri. WN7—4J 73
Calow Grn. SK13—5E 96
Calshot Wlk. M7—1F 78
Caltha St. BL0—5H 9
Calthorpe Av. M9—9J 61
Calton Av. M7—9A 60
Calton Wlk. M15—9E 78
Calve Croft Rd. M22—2E 112
Calveley Way. WN6—1L 33
Calver Av. M30—7C 76
Calver Bank. SK13—4E 96
(off Eyam La.)
Calver Clo. M31—3K 87
Calver Clo. SK13—4E 96
Calver Fold. SK13—4D 96
(off Eyam La.)
Calverhall Wlk. M12—9M 79
Calverhall Way. WN4—4A 70
Calver Hey Clo. BL3—7J 37
Calverley Av. M19—7M 91
Calverley Rd. SK8—8A 104
Calverley Way. OL12—7E 12
Calver M. SK13—4D 96
Calver Pl. SK13—4D 96
Calverton Dri. M10—9C 62
Calvert Rd. BL3—6E 38
Calvert St. M5—5K 77
Calver Wlk. M10—2H 5 & 4J 79
Calver Wlk. M34—6A 94
Calver Wlk. SK8—3L 113
Calvine Wlk. M10—2H 5 & 4J 79
Calvin St. BL1—9F 22
Cambeck Clo. M25—8B 42
Cambeck Wlk. M25—8A 42
Cambell Rd. M30—5B 76
Camberley Clo. SK7—5G 115
Camberley Dri. OL11—4M 27
Cambert La. M18—1D 92
(Gorton)
Cambert La. M18—1C 92
(Manchester)
Camberwell Cres. WN2—7F 34
Camberwell Dri. OL7—1A 82
Camberwell St. M8—1F 5 &
3G 79
Camberwell St. OL8—4L 63
Camberwell Way. OL2—5J 45
Camborne Rd. SK14—3L 95
Camborne St. M14—3H 91
Cambourne Av. WA11—8D 68
Cambourne Dri. BL3—4A 38
Cambourne Dri. WN2—6C 54
Cambo Wlk. SK4—2L 103
Cambrai Cres. M30—3A 76
Cambrian Cres. WN3—6J 51
Cambrian Dri. OL2—6J 45
Cambrian Dri. OL16—4A 30
Cambrian Rd. SK3—5C 104
Cambrian St. M10—5L 79
Cambria St. BL3—4C 38
Cambria St. OL4—1D 64
Cambridge Av. M16—4C 90
Cambridge Av. OL11—4A 28
Cambridge Av. SK9—4F 118
Cambridge Clo. BL4—8F 38
Cambridge Dri. BL3—5B 40
Cambridge Dri. M34—3G 93
Cambridge Dri. SK6—9C 94
Cambridge Gro. M25—9A 42
Cambridge Gro. M30—5F 76
Cambridge Ind. Area. M7
(in two parts) —2D 4 & 4E 78
Cambridge Rd. BL6—1F 36
Cambridge Rd. M9—7K 61
Cambridge Rd. M31—5B 88
Cambridge Rd. M35—4F 80
(Droylsden)
Cambridge Rd. M35—2F 80
(Failsworth)
Cambridge Rd. SK4—9C 92
Cambridge Rd. SK8—7H 103

Cambridge Rd. WA15—2E 110
Cambridge Rd. WN5—9F 32
Cambridge St. M1 & M15
(in two parts) —6E 5 & 8F 78
Cambridge St. M7—1D 4 & 3E 78
Cambridge St. M29—6J 55
Cambridge St. OL7—6M 81
Cambridge St. OL9—3J 63
Cambridge St. SK2—7G 105
Cambridge St. SK15—5G 83
Cambridge St. SK16—6C 82
Cambridge St. WN1—1E 52
Cambridge Ter. SK2—7G 105
(off Russell St.)
Cambridge Ter. SK15—3K 83
Cambridge Way. WN1—9D 34
Camdale Wlk. M8—1F 78
(off Ermington Dri.)
Camden Av. M10—3C 80
Camden Clo. BL2—9C 24
Camelford Clo. M15—9G 79
Camelia Rd. M9—9J 61
Camellia Clo. BL1—2B 38
Cameron Ct. OL2—3K 45
Cameron Pl. WN5—9L 33
Cameron St. BL1—5D 22
Cameron St. BL8—8J 25
Cameron St. M1—7F 78
Cameron St. WN7—9D 54
Camley Wlk. M8—1H 79
(off Appleford Dri.)
Camm St. WN2—8H 53
Camomile Wlk. M31—2F 98
Campania St. OL2—7L 45
Campanula Wlk. M8—1G 79
(off Magnolia Dri.)
Campbell Ct. BL4—7J 39
Campbell Ho. BL4—8H 39
Campbell Rd. BL3—7A 38
Campbell Rd. M13—4M 91
Campbell Rd. M27—1E 76
Campbell Rd. M33—2F 100
Campbell St. BL4—7H 39
Campbell St. M35—6G 81
Campbell St. OL12—9E 12
Campbell St. SK5—5F 92
Campbell St. WN5—3K 51
Campbell Wlk. BL4—7J 39
Campbell Way. M28—5J 57
Campden St. OL5—5K 65
Campden Way. SK9—8K 113
Campfield Av. Arc. M3—7E 78
(off Camp St.)
Camphill Wlk. M15—9F 78
Campion Clo. WA11—8B 68
Campion Gro. WN4—3M 69
Campion Wlk. M11—6M 79
Campion Way. M34—6A 94
Campion Way. OL12—8C 12
Camponia Gdns. M7—2D 78
Camp Rd. WN4—4L 69
Camp St. BL8—7J 25
Camp St. M3—5D 4 & 7E 78
Camp St. M7—2C 78
Camp St. OL6—4B 82
Camrose Wlk. M13—1K 91
Cams Acre Clo. M26—6E 40
Cams La. M26—7E 40
Canaan. WA3—7C 72
Canada St. BL1—8C 22
Canada St. BL6—7B 20
Canada St. M10—3L 79
Canada St. SK2—7G 105
Canal Bank. M30—4C 76
Canal Bank. WA13—1A 108
Canal Bank. WN6—2C 32
Canal Bank. WN7—3E 72
Canal Cotts. WN3—1B 52
Canal Rd. WA14—6E 100
Canalside Ind. Est. OL16—5H 29
Canal St. M1—5F 5 & 7G 79
Canal St. M5—4B 4 & 6C 78
Canal St. M30—4C 76
Canal St. M35—6G 81
Canal St. OL9—5H 63
Canal St. OL10—1L 43
Canal St. OL11—5G 29
Canal St. OL15—6B 14
Canal St. SK1—4F 104
Canal St. SK14—3C 94
Canal St. SK15—6G 83
Canal St. WN2—7H 35
(Aspull)
Canal St. WN2—2F 52
(Ince)
Canal St. WN6—8M 33
Canal St. WN7—3E 72
Canal Wharf. SK4—2E 104
Canberra Rd. SK7—7E 114
Canberra Rd. WN5—9J 33
Canberra St. M11—5C 80
Candahar St. BL3—6G 39
Candelan Way. WA16—8C 108
Candleford Pl. SK2—9L 105
Candleford Rd. M20—8H 91
Canfield Wlk. M8—1F 78
(off Ermington Dri.)
Canley Clo. SK1—5F 104
Cannel Fold. M28—9H 57
Canning Clo. M4—5K 79
Canning Dri. BL1—8E 22
Canning St. BL1—8E 22
Canning St. BL9—6M 25
Canning St. SK4—3E 104
Canniswood Rd. WA11—9G 69
Cannock Dri. SK4—3M 103
Cannon Ct. M3—5F 78
(off Cateaton St.)
Cannon Gro. BL3—3D 38
Cannon St. BL0—7G 9
Cannon St. BL3—4D 38
Cannon St. M3—3C 4 & 5D 78
Cannon St. M4—3E 5 & 5F 78
Cannon St. M29—5K 55
Cannon St. M30—5E 76
Cannon St. OL9—1L 63
Cannon St. SK14—1C 96
Cannon St. N. BL3—3D 38
Cannon Wlk. M34—4L 93
Cann St. BL8—2D 24
Canon Flynn Ct. OL16—3J 29
Canon Grn. Dri. M3—2D 4 &
4E 78
Canons Clo. BL1—8B 22
Canons Gro. M10—2L 79
Canonsleigh Clo. M8—2E 78
Canon St. BL9—6A 26
Canon St. OL16—9H 13
Canonsway. M27—8E 58
Canon Tighe Ct. OL9—1G 63
Canon Wilson Clo. WA11
—9K 69
Cansfield Gro. WN4—3A 70
Canterbury Clo. M29—4L 55
Canterbury Clo. OL11—3A 28
Canterbury Clo. SK16—9D 82
Canterbury Dri. BL8—6K 25
Canterbury Dri. M25—6C 60
Canterbury Gdns. M5—5G 77
Canterbury Gro. BL3—6D 38
Canterbury Pk. M20—2F 102
Canterbury Rd. M31—3C 88
Canterbury Rd. SK1—4G 105
Canterbury Rd. WA3—6K 71
Canterbury Rd. WA15—1J 111
Canterbury St. OL6—3C 82
Canterfield Clo. M35—5K 81
Canton Wlk. M16—2E 90
Cantrell St. M11—6B 80
Canute Ct. M32—3L 89
Canute Rd. M32—3L 89
Canute St. BL2—9J 23
Canute St. M6—3A 4 & 5B 78
Canute St. M26—6E 40
Capella Wlk. M7—1B 4 & 3C 78
Capenhurst Clo. M23—9M 101
Capesthorne Clo. SK7—4M 115
Capesthorne Dri. OL2—2M 45
Capesthorne Rd. SK6—5E 116
Capesthorne Rd. SK7—4M 115
Capesthorne Rd. SK9—6E 118
Capesthorne Rd. WA15—7K 101
Capesthorne Wlk. M34—4L 93

Cape St. M20—7J 91
Capethorne Rd. SK16—9D 82
Capital Ho. M5—8A 78
Capital Rd. M11—8E 80
Capstan St. M9—8L 61
Captain Clarke Rd. SK14—1B 94
Captain Fold. OL10—8L 27
Captain Fold Rd. M28—3E 56
Captain Lees Gdns. BL5—9G 37
Captain Lees Rd. BL5—8G 37
Captain's Clough Rd. BL1
—8A 22
Captain's La. WN4—4C 70
Captain St. BL6—6B 20
Capton Clo. SK7—2G 115
Caradoc Av. M8—1H 79
Car Bank Av. M29—4K 55
Car Bank Cres. M29—4K 55
Car Bank Sq. M29—4K 55
Car Bank St. M29—4H 55
(in four parts)
Carberry Rd. M18—1D 92
Carbis Wlk. M7—2E 78
Cardale Wlk. M9—9K 61
(off Middlewood Wlk.)
Carden Av. M27—9D 58
Carden Av. M31—4L 87
Cardenbrook Gro. SK9—1K 119
Carder Clo. M27—9E 58
Cardew Av. M22—9E 102
Cardiff Clo. OL8—6H 63
Cardiff St. M7—9E 60
Cardiff Wlk. M34—5M 93
Cardigan Dri. BL9—2L 41
Cardigan Rd. OL8—6H 63
Cardigan St. M6—5L 77
Cardigan St. M26—3F 40
Cardigan St. OL2—5L 45
Cardigan St. OL12—8E 12
Cardigan Ter. M14—2F 90
Cardinal St. M8—1H 79
Cardinal St. OL1—1A 64
Cardroom Rd. M4—4H 5 & 6J 79
Cardus St. M19—5A 92
Cardwell Gdns. BL1—8E 22
Cardwell Rd. M30—6A 76
Cardwell St. OL8—5M 63
Careless La. WN2—1F 52
Carey Clo. M7—1C 4 & 3D 78
Carey Clo. WN3—6K 51
Carey Wlk. M15—1F 90
(off Arnott Cres.)
Carfax St. M18—1D 92
Carforth Av. OL9—2G 63
Cargate Wlk. M8—1F 78
Carill Dri. M14—6K 91
Carina Pl. M7—1B 4 & 3C 78
Carisbrook Av. M25—1A 60
Carisbrook Av. M31—4C 88
Carisbrook Dri. M27—1G 77
Carisbrooke Av. SK7—3K 115
Carisbrooke Dri. BL1—7F 22
Carisbrooke Rd. WN7—1K 73
Carisbrook St. M9—1K 79
Carlburn St. M11—5D 80
Carleton Clo. M28—7J 57
Carleton Rd. SK12—8C 116
Carley Gro. M9—4H 61
Carlford Gro. M25—5M 59
Carlin Ga. WA15—7G 101
Carling Dri. M22—2E 112
Carlingford Clo. SK3—8E 104
Carlisle Clo. BL3—7A 40
Carlisle Clo. M25—1B 60
Carlisle Clo. SK6—4A 106
Carlisle Cres. OL6—9C 64
Carlisle Dri. M30—4G 87
Carlisle Dri. WA14—5E 100
Carlisle St. BL7—2G 23
Carlisle St. M27—6F 58
Carlisle St. OL9—4J 63
(in two parts)
Carlisle St. OL12—8E 12
Carlisle St. SK3—5E 104
Carlisle St. SK9—8L 119
Carlisle St. WN2—2L 53
Carlisle St. WN5—2K 51
Carlisle Wlk. WN2—4K 35
Carlisle Way. M34—5M 93
Carloon Rd. M23—4B 102
Carlow Dri. M22—2E 112
Carl St. BL1—8D 22
Carlton Av. BL3—5A 38
Carlton Av. M14—3H 91
Carlton Av. M16—2B 90
Carlton Av. M25—6E 60
(Prestwich)
Carlton Av. M25—8K 41
(Whitefield)
Carlton Av. OL4—8D 46
Carlton Av. SK6—2D 106
Carlton Av. SK7—7D 114
Carlton Av. SK8—1M 113
Carlton Av. SK9—1J 119
Carlton Av. WN3—3A 52
Carlton Av. WN8—1A 50
Carlton Clo. BL2—7L 23
Carlton Clo. BL6—3K 19
Carlton Clo. WN4—2A 70
Carlton Ct. M25—7A 60
Carlton Ct. WA15—3H 111
Carlton Cres. M31—5D 88
Carlton Cres. SK1—3G 105
Carlton Dri. M25—6E 60
Carlton Dri. SK8—7G 103
Carlton Flats. OL10—8J 27
(off Brunswick St.)
Carlton Gdns. BL4—8K 39
Carlton Gro. BL6—9D 20
Carlton Gro. WN2—5M 53
Carlton Range. M18—2F 92
Carlton Rd. BL1—1A 38
Carlton Rd. M6—3L 77
Carlton Rd. M16—3D 90
Carlton Rd. M28—7J 57
Carlton Rd. M31—5D 88
Carlton Rd. M33—8G 89
Carlton Rd. OL6—2C 82
Carlton Rd. SK4—3A 104
Carlton Rd. SK14—3G 95
Carlton Rd. WA3—6K 71
Carlton Rd. WA13—8B 98
(in two parts)
Carlton Rd. WA15—3H 111
Carlton St. BL2—3F 38
Carlton St. BL4—8K 39
Carlton St. BL9—1M 41
Carlton St. M16—2C 90
Carlton St. M30—4D 76
Carlton St. WN3—2B 52
Carlton Way. OL2—7K 45
Carlton Way. WA3—9C 86
Carlyle Clo. M8—1G 79
Carlyle Gro. WN7—8C 54
Carlyle St. BL9—7L 25
Carlyn Av. M33—1K 101
Carmel Av. M5—5B 4 & 7C 78
Carmel Clo. M5—5B 4 & 7C 78
Carmel Ct. M8—6F 60
Carmenna Dri. SK7—5F 114
Carmichael Clo. M31—2E 98
Carmichael St. SK3—5C 104
Car Mill Cres. WN5—3E 68
Carmona Dri. M25—4A 60
Carmona Gdns. M7—7C 60
Carnaby St. M9—7M 61
Carna Rd. SK5—4E 92
Carnarvon St. M3—1E 5 & 3F 78
Carnarvon St. M7—9E 60
Carnarvon St. OL8—6H 63
Carnarvon St. SK1—4G 105
Carnation Rd. BL4—8G 39
Carnation Rd. OL4—4E 64
Carnation St. M3—2E 5 & 4F 78
Carnegie Av. M19—5B 92
Carnforth Av. OL11—2D 44
Carnforth Av. WN2—3A 54
Carnforth Dri. BL8—9G 9
Carnforth Dri. M33—2G 101
Carnforth Rd. SK4—8C 92
Carnforth Rd. SK8—9B 104
Carnforth Sq. OL11—2D 44
Carnforth St. M14—3H 91

Carnoustie Clo. M10—9C 62
Carnoustie Clo. SK9—3K 119
Carnoustie Dri. BL0—6H 9
Carnoustie Dri. SK8—3J 113
Carnoustie Gro. WA11—9H 69
Carnwood Clo. M10—3D 80
Carnwood Gro. BL6—9D 20
Caroline Dri. M4—4H 5 & 6J 79
Caroline St. BL3—5D 38
Caroline St. M7—1D 4 & 3E 78
Caroline St. M30—6F 86
Caroline St. OL6—4C 82
Caroline St. SK3—6D 104
Caroline St. SK15—6G 83
Caroline St. WN1—9E 34
Caroline St. WN3—1C 52
Carpenters La. M4—3F 5 &
5G 79
Carradale Dri. M33—9C 88
Carradale Wlk. M10—1A 80
Carr Av. M25—6M 59
Carr Bank Av. BL0—4H 9
Carr Bank Av. M9—5F 60
Carr Bank Dri. BL0—4H 9
Carr Bank Rd. BL0—4H 9
Carrbrook Clo. SK15—1L 83
Carrbrook Cres. SK15—1L 83
Carr Brook Dri. M29—4L 55
Carrbrook Rd. SK15—9M 65
(in two parts)
Carrbrook Ter. M26—5H 41
Carr Brow. SK6—5G 117
Carr Clo. SK1—5H 105
Carr Comn. Rd. WN2—5C 54
Carrfield Av. M28—4E 56
Carrfield Av. SK3—9G 105
Carrfield Av. WA15—7K 101
Carrfield Clo. M28—4E 56
Carrfield Gro. M28—4E 56
Carrgate Rd. M34—5B 94
Carrgreen Clo. M19—9M 91
Carrgreen La. WA13—7E 98
Carr Gro. OL16—4A 30
Carr Head. OL3—3C 48
Carrhill Quarry Clo. OL5—6J 65
Carrhill Rd. OL5—6J 65
Carr Ho. La. WN6—2F 16
Carr Ho. Rd. OL4—1F 64
Carriage Dri., The. SK14—1F 96
Carriage St. M16—1D 90
Carrick Gdns. M22—9D 102
Carrie St. BL1—1B 38
Carrill Gro. M19—5A 92
Carrill Gro. E. M19—5A 92
Carrington Bus. Pk. M31—8K 87
Carrington Dri. BL3—4F 38
Carrington Field St. SK1
—6F 104
Carrington Gro. WN7—9F 54
Carrington La. M31 & M33
—7M 87
Carrington Rd. M14—6J 91
Carrington Rd. M31—6L 87
Carrington Rd. PR7—3E 18
Carrington Rd. SK1—2G 105
Carrington Spur. M33 & M31
—8C 88
Carrington St. M27—7H 59
Carrington St. OL9—5H 63
Carrington St. WN7—9F 54
Carr La. OL3—4C 48
(Diggle)
Carr La. OL3—2B 66
(Greenfield)
Carr La. OL16—4C 30
Carr La. SK9—8D 118
Carr La. WA3—8A 72
Carr La. WN3—5A 52
Carr La. WN7—7E 72
Carr Mill Rd. WA11—8C 68
Carr Mill Rd. WA11 & WN5
—7C 68
Carrmoor Rd. M13—1J 91
Carrock Wlk. M24—8H 43
Carron Av. M9—7M 61
Carron Gro. BL2—2M 39
Carroway St. M10—2L 79
Carr Rise. SK15—9M 65
Carr Rd. BL6—5B 20
Carr Rd. M30—4H 87
Carr Rd. WA15—2H 111
Carrs Av. SK8—7A 104
Carrsfield Rd. M22—7E 102
Carrslea Clo. M26—4E 40
Carrs Rd. SK8—7M 103
Carr St. BL0—4H 9
Carr St. M27—9D 58
Carr St. OL6—2D 82
Carr St. WN2—2K 53
Carr St. WN7—2C 72
Carrsvale Av. M31—3B 88
Carrswood Rd. M23—5J 101
Carruthers Clo. OL10—7M 27
Carruthers St. M4—5K 79
Carrwood. WA15—5H 111
Carr Wood Av. SK7—4E 114
Carrwood Hey. BL0—7G 9
Carr Wood Rd. SK7—3D 114
Carrwood Rd. SK9—2F 118
Carsdale Rd. M22—4E 112
Carslake Av. BL1—1C 38
Carslake Rd. M10—2K 79
Carson Rd. M19—6A 92
Carstairs Av. SK2—9G 105
Carstairs Clo. M8—9F 60
Car St. OL1—1A 64
Car St. WN2—7G 53
Carswell Clo. M29—7C 56
Carter Clo. M34—4M 93
Carter Pl. SK14—1D 94
Carter St. BL3—5G 39
Carter St. BL4—1L 57
Carter St. M7—2D 78
Carter St. OL5—8J 65
Carter St. SK14—1D 94
Carter St. SK15—5G 83
Carter St. WN3—2E 52
Carthage St. OL8—4M 63
Carthorpe Arch. M5—6M 77
Cart House La. BL0—5M 9
Cartleach Gro. M28—6G 57
Cartleach La. M28—6F 56
Cartledge St. M1—5G 5 & 7H 79
Cartmel. OL12—2E 28
(off Spotland Rd.)
Cartmel Av. OL16—6M 29
Cartmel Av. SK4—8E 92
Cartmel Av. WN1—6B 34
Cartmel Clo. BL3—7K 37
Cartmel Clo. BL9—6A 42
Cartmel Clo. OL8—5K 63
Cartmel Clo. SK7—1J 115
Cartmel Clo. SK8—1J 113
Cartmel Cres. BL2—8J 23
Cartmel Cres. OL9—6F 62
Cartmel Dri. WA15—7K 101
Cartmel Gro. M28—9B 58
Cartmell Ct. M9—4A 62
Cartmel Wlk. M9—9K 61
Cartmel Wlk. M24—7L 43
Cartridge Clo. M22—9F 102
Cartridge St. OL10—8J 27
Cartwright Gro. WN7—7D 54
Cartwright Rd. M21—6M 89
Cartwright St. M34—9M 81
Cartwright St. OL4—2B 64
Cartwright St. SK14—1G 95
Carver Av. M25—3C 60
Carver Clo. M16—1B 90
Carver Dri. SK6—8E 106
Carver Rd. SK6—8E 106
Carver Rd. WA15—2E 110
Carver St. M16—1B 90
Carver Wlk. M15—1F 90
(off Arnott Cres.)
Carwood Dell. SK7—5E 114
Cashmere Rd. SK3—6C 104
Cashmore Dri. WN2—4K 53
Cashmore Wlk. M12—9L 79
Caspian Rd. WA14—7A 100
Cassandra Ct. M5—5B 4 & 7C 78
Cassidy Clo. M4—3G 5 & 5H 79
Cassidy Ct. M5—7L 77

Cassidy Gdns. M24—5K 43
Casson Ga. OL12—1E 28
Casson St. M35—9F 62
Castle Av. M34—4L 93
Castle Av. OL11—4E 28
Castlebrook Clo. BL9—5B 42
Castle Ct. OL6—9B 64
Castle Croft. BL2—7K 23
Castlecroft Av. BL6—8K 19
Castlecroft Rd. BL9—8L 25
Castledene Av. M6—4L 77
Castle Dri. PR7—4E 18
Castle Edge Rd. SK12—2M 117
Castle Farm Dri. SK2—8H 105
Castle Farm La. SK2—7H 105
Castlefield Av. M7—8E 60
Castleford Clo. BL1—1D 38
Castleford St. OL1—8J 45
Castleford Wlk. M21—7D 90
Castle Gro. BL0—9G 9
Castle Gro. BL6—5C 20
Castle Gro. WN7—1K 73
Castle Hall Clo. SK15—6G 83
Castle Hill. OL11—4E 28
Castle Hill. SK6—7L 93
Castle Hill. SK13—3L 97
Castle Hill Cres. OL11—4E 28
Castle Hill Pk. WN2—1M 53
Castle Hill Rd. BL9—4B 26
Castle Hill Rd. M25—6D 60
Castle Hill Rd. WN2—2L 53
Castle Hill St. BL2—7H 23
(in two parts)
Castle Ho. La. PR7—4E 18
Castle La. SK15—8L 65
Castlemere Dri. OL2—1D 46
Castlemere Rd. M9—5J 61
Castlemere St. OL11—4E 28
Castlemere Ter. OL11—4F 28
Castle M. BL4—1K 57
Castle Mill La. WA15—6F 110
Castle Mill St. OL1—1B 64
Castlemoor Av. M7—8B 60
Castlerigg Dri. M24—6J 43
Castlerigg Dri. OL2—3J 45
Castle Rise. WN2—3L 53
(in three parts)
Castle Rd. BL9—6C 42
Castleshaw Rd. SK2—8K 105
Castle St. BL2—2G 39
Castle St. BL4—1K 57
Castle St. BL9—8L 25
(Bury)
Castle St. BL9—9K 9
(Summerseat)
Castle St. M3—5D 4 & 7E 78
Castle St. M24—1D 62
Castle St. M29—7M 55
Castle St. M30—5F 76
Castle St. M35—5H 81
Castle St. SK3—6D 104
Castle St. SK14—2G 97
(Hadfield)
Castle St. SK14—3F 94
(Hyde)
Castle St. SK15—6G 83
Castle St. WN2—2L 53
Castleton Av. M32—2H 89
Castleton Bank. SK13—5E 96
(off Castleton Cres.)
Castleton Ct. M29—7M 55
(off Castle St.)
Castleton Ct. M34—6A 94
Castleton Cres. SK13—5E 96
Castleton Dri. SK6—6F 116
Castleton Grn. SK13—5E 96
(off Castleton Cres.)
Castleton Gro. OL6—1F 82
Castleton Gro. SK13—5E 96
(off Castleton Cres.)
Castleton Rd. M7—7E 60
Castleton Rd. OL2—1J 45
Castleton Rd. SK7—3L 115
Castleton Rd. S. OL11—7D 28
Castleton St. BL2—8H 23
Castleton St. OL9—2J 63
Castleton St. WA14—6C 100
Castleton Ter. SK13—5E 96
Castleton Wlk. M11—6M 79
Castleton Way. M34—6A 94
Castleton Way. WN3—6J 51
Castle Wlk. OL6—9B 64
Castle Wlk. SK15—6G 83
Castleway. M6—3L 77
Castle Way. M27—6G 59
Castleway. OL11—9B 28
Castleway. WA15—5J 111
Castle Way. WN2—3M 53
Castlewood Gdns. SK2—8J 105
Castlewood Rd. M7—8A 60
Castlewood Sq. BL2—9J 23
Castle Yd. SK1—3F 104
Caston Clo. M16—2E 90
Catchdale Clo. M9—3J 61
Catches Clo. OL11—2B 28
Catches La. OL11—2B 28
Cateaton St. BL9—7M 25
Cateaton St. M3—3E 5 & 5F 78
Caterham St. M4—6K 79
Catesby Rd. M16—3D 90
Catfield Wlk. M15—6C 4 & 8D 78
Catford Rd. M23—8L 101
Cathedral App. M3—3E 5 &
5F 78
Cathedral Clo. SK16—9D 82
Cathedral Gates. M3—5F 78
Cathedral Rd. OL9—8F 44
Cathedral St. M4—3E 5 & 5F 78
Cathedral Yd. M3—3E 5 & 5F 78
Catherine Rd. M8—7E 60
Catherine Rd. M27—9C 58
Catherine Rd. SK6—4M 105
Catherine Rd. WA14—1C 110
Catherine St. BL3—7B 38
Catherine St. BL9—3L 41
Catherine St. M11—8E 80
Catherine St. M30—4A 76
Catherine St. M34—3K 93
Catherine St. OL4—2E 64
Catherine St. SK7—1L 115
Catherine St. SK14—3D 94
Catherine St. WN1—9E 34
Catherine St. WN7—1F 72
Catherine St. E. BL6—6B 20
Catherine St. E. M34—3K 93
Catherine St. W. BL6—5B 20
Catherine Ter. WN1—9E 34
Catherston Clo. M16—3E 90
Cathreine Way. WA11—9F 68
Catlow La. M4—3F 5 & 5G 79
Catlow St. M7—1D 4 & 3E 78
Caton Clo. BL9—1L 41
Caton St. OL16—4F 28
Cato St. BL0—7G 9
Catterall Cres. BL2—4K 23
Catterick Av. M20—2J 103
Catterick Av. M33—3C 100
Catterick Dri. BL3—6A 40
Catterick Rd. M20—2J 103
Catterwood Dri. SK6—2H 107
Catterwood Rd. SK6—3H 107
Cattlin Way. OL8—6J 63
Caunce Av. WA3—8G 71
Caunce Av. WA11—9H 69
Caunce Rd. WN1—9E 34
Caunce St. WN1—9E 34
Causeway, The. WA14—9D 100
Causewood Clo. OL4—5E 46
Causey Dri. M24—6K 43
Cavalier St. M10—5K 79
Cavalry St. M4—2F 5 & 4G 79
Cavanagh Clo. M13—9K 79
Cavan Clo. SK3—6M 103
Cavell Way. M5—6A 78
Cavendish Av. M20—8F 90
Cavendish Av. M27—5J 59
Cavendish Ct. M7—7D 60
Cavendish Ct. M9—3G 61
(off Deanswood Dri.)
Cavendish Ct. M31—4E 88
(off Cavendish Rd.)
Cavendish Ct. M32—2L 89
Cavendish Ct. SK4—3M 103

Cavendish Dri. WN3—6K 51
Cavendish Gdns. M20—8F 90
Cavendish Gro. M30—4E 76
Cavendish Ho. M30—3E 76
Cavendish M. SK9—5G 119
Cavendish Pl. M11—5A 80
Cavendish Pl. M27—8G 59
Cavendish Rd. M7—7C 60
Cavendish Rd. M20—8F 90
Cavendish Rd. M28—1B 76
Cavendish Rd. M30—4E 76
Cavendish Rd. M31—4E 88
(in two parts)
Cavendish Rd. M32—2L 89
Cavendish Rd. OL11—7E 28
Cavendish Rd. SK4—3M 103
Cavendish Rd. SK7—3K 115
Cavendish Rd. WA14—1C 110
Cavendish St. M15
(in two parts) —6F 5 & 9G 79
Cavendish St. OL6—4A 82
Cavendish St. OL8—2L 63
Cavendish St. WN7—9F 54
Cavendish Ter. M21—6B 90
Cavenham Gro. BL1—1C 38
Cavenham Wlk. M9—9J 61
(off Hendham Vale)
Caversham Dri. M9—8L 61
Cawdor Av. BL4—7H 39
Cawdor Ct. BL4—7J 39
Cawdor Ho. M30—7D 76
(off Enfield Clo.)
Cawdor Pl. WA15—7J 101
Cawdor Rd. M14—5J 91
Cawdor St. M15—6C 4 & 8D 78
Cawdor St. M27—8D 58
Cawdor St. M28—6L 57
Cawdor St. M30—6C 76
Cawdor St. WN2—3L 53
Cawdor St. WN5—2M 51
Cawdor St. WN7—3F 72
Cawdor Wlk. BL4—7J 39
Cawley Av. M25—6M 59
Cawood Sq. SK5—7J 93
Cawston Wlk. M8—1G 79
Cawthorne Ct. M27—7D 58
Caxton Rd. M14—5H 91
Caxton St. OL10—8K 27
Caxton St. OL11—8C 28
Caxton Way. M5—3A 4 & 5B 78
Caygill St. M3—3D 4 & 5E 78
Cayley St. OL16—3H 29
C Court. WN4—5B 70
Caythorpe St. M14—3G 91
Cayton St. M12—3A 92
Ceal, The. SK6—3H 107
Cecil Av. M33—2E 100
Cecil Av. WN6—7A 34
Cecil Ct. SK3—5B 104
Cecil Dri. M31—4L 87
Cecil Gro. M18—1D 92
Cecilia Ct. N. BL3—5G 39
Cecilia Ct. S. BL3—5G 39
Cecilia St. BL3—5G 39
Cecil Rd. M9—3K 61
Cecil Rd. M30—6E 76
Cecil Rd. M32—5J 89
Cecil Rd. WA15—2E 110
Cecil St. BL2—2G 39
Cecil St. BL9—9M 25
Cecil St. M15—1H 91
Cecil St. M28—5K 57
(Walkden)
Cecil St. M28—7K 57
(Worsley)
Cecil St. OL2—6J 45
Cecil St. OL5—8J 65
Cecil St. OL7—6A 82
Cecil St. OL8—3L 63
Cecil St. OL11—5F 28
Cecil St. OL15—6M 13
Cecil St. SK3—6E 104
Cecil St. SK15—6H 83
Cecil St. SK16—7B 82
Cecil St. WN1—9E 34
Cecil St. WN3—4E 52
Cecil St. WN7—3G 73
Cecil Wlk. OL7—6M 81
Cecil Walker Ho. M31—1G 99
Cedar Av. BL3—7B 40
Cedar Av. BL6—9E 20
Cedar Av. M25—2M 59
Cedar Av. M29—4H 55
Cedar Av. OL6—2D 82
Cedar Av. OL10—7J 27
Cedar Av. SK7—2L 115
Cedar Av. WA14—9C 100
Cedar Av. WN2—5M 53
Cedar Av. WN6—1M 33
Cedar Clo. M15—9D 78
Cedar Clo. SK12—9L 115
Cedar Clo. SK13—4H 97
Cedar Ct. M14—6J 91
Cedar Cres. BL0—4J 9
Cedar Cres. OL9—9H 45
Cedar Dri. M27—4D 58
Cedar Dri. M31—5C 88
Cedar Dri. M35—5J 81
Cedar Dri. WN1—7D 34
Cedarfield. WA13—9B 98
Cedar Gro. BL4—9H 39
Cedar Gro. BL5—1E 54
Cedar Gro. M14—6K 91
Cedar Gro. M25—2A 60
Cedar Gro. M34—3L 93
Cedar Gro. OL2—3K 45
(Royton)
Cedar Gro. OL2—3B 46
(Shaw)
Cedar Gro. SK4—9C 92
Cedar Gro. SK16—7F 82
Cedar Gro. WA11—8L 69
Cedar Gro. WN4—2K 69
Cedar Gro. WN5—2F 50
Cedar La. OL4—2K 65
Cedar La. OL16—7A 30
Cedar Lawn. SK8—2A 114
Cedar Pl. M7—1B 4 & 3C 78
Cedar Rd. M24—9C 44
Cedar Rd. M31—2E 98
Cedar Rd. M33—8D 88
Cedar Rd. M35—1F 80
Cedar Rd. SK2—9H 105
Cedar Rd. SK6—9E 106
Cedar Rd. SK8—8G 103
Cedar Rd. WA3—8M 71
Cedar Rd. WA15—1E 110
Cedar Rd. WN7—8E 54
Cedars Rd. M22—1D 112
Cedar St. BL9—7B 26
Cedar St. OL4—1C 64
(in two parts)
Cedar St. OL6—3D 82
Cedar St. OL12—1F 28
Cedar St. SK14—1E 94
Cedarway. SK9—7F 118
Cedarwood Av. SK4—4A 104
Cedric Rd. M8—6E 60
Cedric Rd. OL4—1C 64
Cedric St. M5—5K 77
Celandine Clo. OL15—5M 13
Celandine Clo. WN3—4H 51
Celia St. M8—8J 61
Cellini Sq. BL1—9D 22
Celtic St. SK1—5G 105
Cemetery La. BL9—1M 41
Cemetery Rd. BL0—7G 9
Cemetery Rd. BL2—2H 39
Cemetery Rd. BL4—8M 39
Cemetery Rd. M5—6L 77
Cemetery Rd. M26—5F 40
Cemetery Rd. M27—7E 58
Cemetery Rd. M34—9M 81
(Audenshaw)
Cemetery Rd. M34—5M 93
(Denton)
Cemetery Rd. M35—6F 80
(Droylsden)
Cemetery Rd. M35—1F 80
(Failsworth)
Cemetery Rd. OL2—4J 45
Cemetery Rd. OL5—9K 65
Cemetery Rd. SK13—2J 97

Cemetery Rd. WN3—4E 52
Cemetery St. BL5—8E 36
Cemetery St. M24—8A 44
Cennick Clo. OL4—2D 64
Ceno St. OL1—8A 46
Centaur Clo. M27—6F 58
Centaur Way. M8—9F 60
Central Av. BL0—1K 9
Central Av. BL4—9G 39
Central Av. BL9—2K 41
Central Av. M6—1L 77
Central Av. M19—4A 92
Central Av. M27—6K 59
Central Av. M28—3J 57
Central Av. M29—4L 55
Central Av. M31—9E 76
(in two parts)
Central Av. M33—4D 100
Central Av. OL3—3B 66
Central Av. OL15—5B 14
Central Av. WN7—4J 73
Central Dri. BL5—8E 36
Central Dri. BL9—2M 25
Central Dri. M27—9H 59
Central Dri. M31—4D 88
Central Dri. SK5—9F 92
Central Dri. SK6—2C 106
Central Dri. SK7—2D 114
Central Dri. SK8—4K 113
Central Dri. WA11—9H 69
Central Dri. WN6—3H 33
Central Ho. M9—3L 61
Central Ind. Est. M24—9M
Central Pk. Est. M17—9K 7
Central Pk. Way. WN1—8D
Central Retail Pk. M4—4H
6
Central Rd. M20—9G 91
Central Rd. M22—6C 112
Central Rd. M31—2F 98
Central St. BL1—2E 38
Central St. M2—4E 5 & 6F
Central Way. WA14—9D 1
Centre Gdns. BL1—9D 22
Centre Pk. Rd. BL1—9D 22
Centre Vale. OL15—4C 14
Centre Vale Clo. OL15—4C
Centurion Gro. M7—1E 78
Century Gdns. OL12—2F 2
Century Pk. Ind. Est. WA14
—7
Century St. M3—5D 4 & 7E
Cestrian St. BL3—6F 38
Ceylon St. M10—1A 80
Ceylon St. OL4—3D 64
Chadderton Clo. M20—8J
Chadderton Dri. BL9—7A
Chadderton Hall Rd. OL9
Chadderton Heights. OL1
Chadderton Ind. Est. M24
Chadderton Pk. Rd. OL9—
Chadderton St. M4—3G 5
Chadderton Way. OL1 & O
Chaddesley Wlk. M11—7
Chaddock La. M28—1D 74
Chadkirk Rd. SK6—4B 10
Chadvil Rd. SK8—8J 103
Chadwell Rd. SK2—6L 10
Chadwick Clo. M14—3H 9
Chadwick Clo. OL16—5A
Chadwick Fold. BL9—3M
Chadwick Hall Rd. OL11—
Chadwick La. OL10 & OL1
Chadwick La. OL16—8J 2
Chadwick Rd. M30—5E 7
Chadwick Rd. WA11—8C
Chadwick St. BL2—3G 39
Chadwick St. BL3—6B 40
Chadwick St. BL9—6E 26
Chadwick St. M27—8F 58
Chadwick St. OL6—5E 82
Chadwick St. OL9—1K 63
Chadwick St. OL10—8M
Chadwick St. OL11—3D 2
Chadwick St. OL16—3L 2
Chadwick St. SK1—5F 10
Chadwick St. SK6—8F 10
Chadwick St. SK13—6H
Chadwick St. SK14—3F 9
Chadwick St. WN2—2K 5
Chadwick St. WN3—2B 5
Chadwick St. WN7—1F 7
Chadwick Ter. OL12—7D
Chadwick Wlk. M27—8F
Chadworth Clo. OL5—4L
Chaffinch Clo. M22—8F
Chaffinch Clo. M35—4J
Chaffinch Dri. BL9—3C 2
Chain Bar La. SK14—4M
Chainhurst Wlk. M13—9
(off Ardeen Wlk.)
Chain La. WA11—8D 68
Chain Rd. M9—3K 6
Chain St. M1—4F 5 & 6G
Chain Wlk. M9—3L 61
Chalbury Clo. WN2—4K
Chalcombe Grange. M12
Chale Clo. M10—4K 79
Chale Dri. M24—2C 62
Chale Grn. BL2—7L 23
Chalfont Av. M31—4E 8
Chalfont Clo. OL8—4B 6
Chalfont Dri. M8—9G 61
Chalfont Dri. M28—8L 5
Chalfont Dri. M29—3A 5
Chalfont Ho. M5—5M 77
Chalfont St. BL1—8F 22
(in two parts)
Chalford Rd. M23—1A 1
Challenor Sq. M12—9A
Challinor St. BL1—B 38
Chalter Wlk. M7—1F 78
Chamber Hall Clo. OL8—
Chamberhall St. BL9—7
Chamber Ho. Dri. OL11—
Chamberlain Rd. SK15—
Chamberlain St. BL3—3
Chamber Rd. OL2—2A 4
Chamber Rd. OL8—5J 6
Chambers Ct. SK14—3A
Chambersfield Ct. M5—
Champagnole Ct. SK16—
(off Astley St.)
Champneys Wlk. M9—
Chancel Av. M5—5B 4 &
Chancel Clo. SK16—9C
Chancel La. SK9—3H 11
Chancellor La. M12—7K
Chancel Pl. M1—4F 5 &
Chancel Pl. OL16—3F 2
Chancery Clo. M29—8B
Chancery La. BL1—2F 3
Chancery La. M2—4E 5
Chancery La. OL2—2C
Chancery La. OL3—7A
Chancery Pl. M2—4E 5
Chancery St. OL4—2C 6
Chancery St. OL9—9J 4
Chancery Wlk. OL9—9J
Chandley Ct. SK1—6G
(off Ward St.)
Chandley St. SK8—7K
Chandos Gro. M5—5K 7
Chandos Rd. M21—5C
Chandos Rd. M25—6B
Chandos Rd. SK4—8B
Chandos Rd. S. M21—6
Chandos St. OL2—2C 4
Channing Ct. OL16—4H
Channing Sq. OL16—4H
Channing St. OL16—4H
Chanters Av. M29—6L
Chanters Ind. Est. M29
Chantler's Av. BL8—9G
Chantler's St. BL8—8G
Chantry Brow. BL6—7J

try Clo. BL5—3F 54
try Clo. SK5—7E 92
try Clo. SK12—7L 117
try Fold. SK12—6L 117
try Rd. SK12—6K 117
try Wlk. WN4—2M 69
el All. BL1—2F 38
(Deansgate)
el Brow. SK14—8D 96
arlesworth)
el Brow. SK14—8G 85
ntwistle)
el Clo. SK16—7C 82
el Clo. WN3—2D 53
el Cotts. SK9—2D 118
l Ct. M33—8E 88
l Ct. SK6—8F 106
l Ct. SK9—5G 119
l Ct. SK14—5C 94
l Ct. WA14—9D 100
l Croft. OL2—5K 45
l Dri. WA15—5J 111
elfield. M26—8J 41
elfield Clo. M35—3K 83
elfield Dri. M28—5H 57
elfield Rd. M12—5H 5 & 7J 79
elfield Rd. M34—3M 93
l Fields. BL7—7J 7
l Fields. SK6—8F 106
l Fields La. WN2—3L 53
l Field St. BL1—7E 22
l Ga. OL16—4M 29
l Grn. M34—3M 93
l Grn. Rd. WN2—2L 53
l Gro. M31—4E 88
l Hill. OL15—5B 14
hill Dri. M9—5J 61
l Ho. SK6—8G 107
l Ho. SK7—9J 105
l La. BL8—5G 9
l La. M9—4H 61
l La. M31 & WA13—2F 98
l La. M32—5J 89
l La. M33—8E 88
l La. OL2—5K 45
l La. OL11—2H 27
l La. PR7—3M 17
l La. SK9—5F 118
l La. SK14—1F 96
l La. WA3—4A 98
l La. WA15—4H 111
l La. WA16—8G 109
l La. WN3 & WN1—2C 52
Meadow. M28—9H 57
l Pl. BL2—4J 39
l Pl. M31—7D 76
l Pl. WN4—4B 70
Rd. M22—5D 102
Rd. M24—7M 59
Rd. M27—9C 58
Rd. M30—4G 87
Rd. M33—9H 89
Rd. OL3—2A 66
Rd. OL8—5J 63
Rd. SK9—8L 119
stead. BL5—3F 54
St. BL1—1G 39
St. BL3—6B 40
St. BL4—9L 39
St. BL6—8K 19
ckrod)
St. BL6—7C 20
wich)
St. BL7—8D 6
St. BL8—3E 24
St. BL9—8M 25
St. M3—3C 4 & 5D 78
St. M19—5K 92
St. M24—8M 43
dleton, in two parts)
St. M24—1J 61
des)
St. M25—4A 60
St. M26—9B 40
St. M27—7G 59
St. M28—1F 74
St. M29—5K 55
erton)
St. M29—7A 56
esley)
St. M30—6C 76
St. M34—9M 81
St. M35—6H 81
St. OL2—5K 45
ton)
St. OL2—2B 46
w)
St. OL3—9B 48
wo parts)
St. OL4—2E 64
St. OL5—7J 65
St. OL6—4C 82
St. OL10—8K 27
wo parts)
St. OL11—6G 29
St. OL12—4J 13
dle)
St. OL12—3C 12
worth)
St. OL15—1D 14
St. PR7—4F 18
ngton)
St. PR7—1L 17
ull)
St. SK4—3K 103
St. SK6—9B 94
dley)
St. SK7—1L 115
St. SK8—8K 103
St. SK9—8L 119
St. SK13—5J 97
St. SK14—9B 84
St. SK15—5G 83
St. SK16—7B 82
St. WN2—7L 53
ershaw)
St. WN2—3K 53
ey)
St. WN2—6G 53
Bridge)
St. WN2—6G 35
ock)
St. WN3—2D 52
r Ince)
St. WN3—1C 52
gate)
St. WN4—4B 70
St. WN5—2H 51
St. WN5—3H 51
erton)
St. WN7—3G 73
er. M20—7H 91
er. WA3—6B 72
wn Rd. BL7—3H 23
wn Rd. M26—9G 41
wn St. M1—5G 5 & 7H 79
Wlk. M24—1J 61
Wlk. M25—8A 60
Wlk. M25—8B 42
field)
Wlk. M30—5F 76
Wlk. SK6—7F 106
Wlk. SK14—1F 96
Wlk. SK15—6H 83
Wlk. WA3—6B 72
Wlk. WA13—3D 108
alks. M2—4E 5 & 6F 78
Valks. M33—9H 89
Valks. SK8—6B 114
ay Gdns. OL2—4K 45
d. PR7—1M 17
n Ct. SK14—4K 95
n M. M18—1D 92
n Rd. SK14—5L 95
n St. BL1—9B 22
n St. M18—9D 80
Rd. M35—5G 81
St. M10—3M 79
Rd. WA14—9L 99

Charcon Wlk. OL2—5L 45
Chard Dri. M22—3D 112
Chardin Av. SK6—5J 107
Chard St. M26—6G 41
Charfield St. M10—2D 80
Charges St. OL7—6M 81
Chariot St. M11—7D 80
Charlbury Av. M25—5E 60
Charlbury Av. SK5—7F 92
Charlbury Way. OL2—4A 46
Charlecote Rd. SK12—8H 115
Charles Av. M34—8G 81
Charles Av. SK6—6C 106
Charles Barry Cres. M15—9E 78
Charles Ct. WA15—7H 101
(in two parts)
Charles Craddock Dri. M7 —1F 78
Charles Halle Rd. M15—1G 91
Charles Holden St. BL1—3D 38
Charles Ho. BL1—1F 38
Charles La. OL16—5A 30
Charles La. SK13—4L 97
Charles M. OL16—5A 30
Charles Morris Clo. M35—8H 63
Charles Rupert St. BL1—8F 22
Charles St. BL1—1F 38
Charles St. BL4—1L 57
(Farnworth)
Charles St. BL4—8L 39
(Kearsley)
Charles St. BL7—8D 6
Charles St. BL9—7M 25
Charles St. M1—6F 5 & 8G 79
Charles St. M6—3M 77
(in two parts)
Charles St. M25—1M 59
Charles St. M27—7D 58
Charles St. M29—7M 55
Charles St. M30—8E 86
Charles St. M34—1M 93
Charles St. M35—6E 80
Charles St. OL2—5K 45
Charles St. OL7—5B 82
Charles St. OL9—2J 63
Charles St. OL10—1L 43
Charles St. OL12—1D 12
Charles St. OL15—6A 14
Charles St. SK1—6F 104
Charles St. SK7—1K 115
Charles St. SK13—5J 97
Charles St. SK16—7B 82
Charles St. WA3—6G 71
Charles St. WN1—8C 34
Charles St. WN2—1L 53
(Hindley)
Charles St. WN2—1F 52
(Ince)
Charles St. WN7—2F 72
(in two parts)
Charleston Clo. OL8—5M 63
Charleston Ct. M29—7M 55
Charleston St. OL8—4M 63
Charlestown Clo. OL6—4B 82
Charlestown Ind. Est. OL6 —3B 82
Charlestown Rd. M9—6K 61
Charlestown Rd. SK13—6J 97
Charlestown Rd. E. SK2 —1G 115
Charlestown Rd. W. SK3 —1F 114
Charles Whittaker St. OL12 —1M 27
Charlesworth Av. M34—6M 93
Charlesworth St. M11—7M 79
Charlesworth St. SK1—6F 104
Charley Av. M7—1C 4 & 3D 78
Charlock Av. BL5—2E 54
Charlock Sq. WA14—5B 100
Charlock Wlk. M31—2F 98
Charlotte St. BL0—6H 9
Charlotte St. BL1—8E 22
Charlotte St. BL7—7J 7
Charlotte St. M1—4F 5 & 6G 79
Charlotte St. OL16—6H 29
Charlotte St. SK1—2H 105
Charlotte St. SK8—8K 103
Charlsworth Av. BL3—6H 39
Charlton Av. M25—5B 60
Charlton Av. M30—6D 76
Charlton Av. SK14—1G 95
Charlton Ct. M25—5B 60
Charlton Dri. M27—6D 58
Charlton Dri. M33—1J 101
Charlton Pl. M12—6G 5 & 8H 79
Charlton Rd. M19—4B 92
Charmouth Wlk. M22—9F 102
Charnley Clo. M10—4L 79
Charnley St. M25—9M 41
Charnock Dri. BL1—9E 22
Charnock St. WN2—7H 53
Charnville Rd. SK8—8F 102
Charnwood Av. M34—3H 93
Charnwood Clo. M28—6J 57
Charnwood Clo. M29—8A 56
Charnwood Clo. OL2—1L 45
Charnwood Clo. OL6—9C 64
Charnwood Cres. SK7—4K 115
Charnwood Rd. M9—3K 61
Charnwood Rd. SK6—9C 94
Charter. M30—6F 76
Charter Av. M26—7J 41
Charterhouse Rd. WN3—2D 52
Charter Rd. WA15—9E 100
Charter St. M3—2E 5 & 4F 78
Charter St. OL1—9A 46
Charter St. OL16—6G 29
Chartwell Clo. M5—5M 77
Chartwell Dri. M23—6K 101
Chaseley Rd. M6—3L 77
Chaseley Rd. OL12—2E 28
Chase St. M4—2F 5 & 4G 79
Chase, The. BL1—2A 38
Chase, The. M28—2A 76
Chasetown Clo. M23—7K 101
Chassen Av. M31—4A 88
Chassen Ct. M31—5B 88
Chassen Rd. BL1—2B 38
Chassen Rd. M31—4B 88
Chataway Rd. M8—8J 61
Chatburn Av. OL11—2D 44
Chatburn Av. WA3—6J 71
Chatburn Ct. OL2—1B 46
Chatburn Gdns. OL10—8F 26
Chatburn Rd. BL1—7M 21
Chatburn Rd. M21—6C 90
Chatburn Sq. OL11—1D 44
Chatcombe Rd. M22—2A 112
Chatfield Rd. M21—6B 90
Chatford Clo. M7—1D 4 & 3E 78
Chatham Ct. M20—8G 91
Chatham Gdns. BL3—4D 38
Chatham Gro. M20—8G 91
Chatham Pl. BL3—4D 38
Chatham Rd. M16—3B 90
Chatham Rd. M18—3E 92
Chatham St. M1—4G 5 & 6H 79
Chatham St. SK3—5C 104
Chatham St. SK14—7E 94
Chatham St. WN1—1E 52
Chatham St. WN2—9G 35
Chatham St. WN7—9F 54
Chatley Rd. M30—6M 75
Chatley St. M3—1E 5 & 3F 78
Chatswood Av. SK2—7F 104
Chatsworth Av. M25—3B 60
Chatsworth Av. WN3—4F 52
Chatsworth Clo. BL9—4A 42
Chatsworth Clo. M31—4E 88
Chatsworth Clo. OL2—1D 46
Chatsworth Clo. WA15—8J 101
Chatsworth Clo. WN4—3M 69
Chatsworth Ct. M9—3G 61
(off Deanswood Dri.)
Chatsworth Ct. SK2—8G 105
Chatsworth Cres. M32—3F 88
Chatsworth Dri. WN7—9K 55
(in two parts)
Chatsworth Gro. BL3—5A 40
Chatsworth Gro. M16—4D 90
Chatsworth Rd. M18—1C 92
Chatsworth Rd. M26—4D 40

Chatsworth Rd. M28 & M27 —1B 76
Chatsworth Rd. M30—3F 76
Chatsworth Rd. M32—3G 89
Chatsworth Rd. M35—4E 80
Chatsworth Rd. SK6—6F 116
Chatsworth Rd. SK7—3M 115
Chatsworth Rd. SK8—9B 104
Chatsworth Rd. SK9—7E 118
Chatsworth St. OL4—3C 64
Chatsworth St. OL12—8E 12
Chatsworth St. WN5—3J 51
Chatteris Clo. WN2—4L 53
Chatterton La. SK6—5M 107
Chatterton Old La. BL0—1J 9
Chatterton Rd. BL0—1J 9
Chattock Clo. M16—3E 90
Chatton Clo. BL8—8F 24
Chatwell Ct. OL16—6C 30
Chatwood Rd. M10—6D 62
Chaucer Av. M26—5E 40
Chaucer Av. M34—7A 94
Chaucer Av. M35—6G 81
Chaucer Av. SK5—5D 92
Chaucer Gro. M29—3K 55
Chaucer Gro. WN7—8C 54
Chaucer Ho. SK5—6D 92
Chaucer M. SK1—4H 105
Chaucer Pl. WN1—6C 34
Chaucer Pl. WN2—7H 53
Chaucer Rise. SK16—8G 83
Chaucer Rd. M24—7B 44
Chaucer St. BL1—8D 22
Chaucer St. OL1—2L 63
Chaucer St. OL2—4L 45
Chaucer St. OL11—8C 28
Chaucer Wlk. M13—9J 79
Chaumont Way. OL6—4B 82
Chaunce Rd. WN1—9E 34
Chauncy Rd. M10—8E 62
Chaytor Av. M10—9A 62
Cheadle Av. M7—9A 60
Cheadle Grn. SK8—7K 103
Cheadle Old Rd. SK3—6B 104
Cheadle Rd. SK8—9L 103
Cheadle St. BL1—2E 38
Cheadle St. M11—7D 80
Cheam Clo. M11—8B 80
Cheam Rd. WA15—5F 100
Cheapside. M2—4E 5 & 6F 78
Cheap Side. M24—7A 44
Cheapside. OL1—1L 63
Cheddar St. M18—1D 92
Chedlee Dri. SK8—3L 113
Chedlin Dri. M23—9A 102
Chedworth Cres. M28—2G 57
Chedworth Gro. BL3—4E 38
(off Parrot St.)
Cheeryble St. M11 & M35 —8F 80
Cheesden Edge. OL12—6E 10
Cheesden Wlk. M25—8C 42
Cheetham Av. M24—8B 44
Cheetham Fold Rd. SK14 —6D 94
Cheetham Gdns. SK15—6H 83
Cheetham Gro. WN3—2M 51
Cheetham Hill. OL2—3B 46
Cheetham Hill. OL12—1D 12
Cheetham Hill Rd. M4 & M8 —2F 5 & 4G 79
Cheetham Hill Rd. M8—8F 60
Cheetham Hill Rd. SK16 & SK15 —9D 82
Cheetham Pde. M8—8F 60
Cheetham Rd. M27—9G 59
Cheethams Cres. OL2—5A 46
Cheethams, The. BL6—2L 35
Cheetham St. M10—2L 79
Cheetham St. M24—9M 43
Cheetham St. M26—6J 41
Cheetham St. M35—8G 63
(in two parts)
Cheetham St. OL1—1B 64
Cheetham St. OL2—3C 46
Cheetham St. OL16—2F 28
Cheetham St. SK14—1G 95
Cheetham Wlk. SK14—3E 94
Cheetwood Rd. M8—1E 5 & 3F 78
Cheetwood St. M8—1D 4 & 3E 78
Chelburn Clo. SK2—8K 105
Chelburn Way. OL15—2C 14
Chelden Wlk. M10—1C 80
Chelford Av. BL1—5E 22
Chelford Av. WA3—8K 71
Chelford Clo. M13—1K 91
Chelford Clo. M24—7C 44
Chelford Clo. WA15—7E 100
Chelford Clo. WN4—6H 51
Chelford Ct. SK9—7L 113
Chelford Dri. M27—6E 58
Chelford Dri. M29—1C 74
Chelford Gro. SK3—8C 104
Chelford Rd. M16—3C 90
Chelford Rd. M33—3L 101
Chelford Rd. SK9—8K 119
(Alderley Edge)
Chelford Rd. SK9—7K 113
(Handforth)
Chelford Rd. WA16—9F 118
Chellow Dene. OL5—7H 65
Chelmarsh Av. WN4—4C 70
Chelmer Clo. BL5—8F 36
Chelmer Gro. OL10—7G 27
Chelmorton Gro. WN3—6J 51
Chelmsford Av. M10—3B 80
Chelmsford Av. WN3—4A 52
Chelmsford M. WN1—7B 34
Chelmsford Rd. SK3—5C 104
Chelmsford St. OL8—2K 63
Chelmsford Wlk. M34—5A 94
Chelsea Av. M26—5D 40
Chelsea Clo. OL2—2B 46
Chelsea Rd. BL3—6D 38
Chelsea Rd. M10—2B 80
Chelsea Rd. M31—5J 87
Chelsea St. BL9—4M 41
Chelsea St. OL11—5D 28
Chelsfield Gro. M21—6D 90
Chelston Av. M10—6D 62
Chelston Dri. SK8—6J 113
Cheltenham Av. WN3—2D 52
Cheltenham Cres. M7—8E 60
Cheltenham Dri. M33—1J 101
Cheltenham Dri. WN5—6D 50
Cheltenham Grn. M24—2A 62
Cheltenham Rd. M21—4B 90
Cheltenham Rd. M24—2A 62
Cheltenham Rd. SK3—6A 104
Cheltenham St. M6—3A 78
Cheltenham St. OL1—8B 46
Cheltenham St. OL11—6D 28
Cheltenham St. WN2—7F 34
Chelt Wlk. M22—2B 112
Chelwood Clo. BL1—3D 22
Chemist St. BL1—9F 22
Cheney Clo. M11—8D 80
Chepstow Av. M33—2C 100
Chepstow Clo. OL11—2M 27
Chepstow Dri. OL1—8B 46
Chepstow Dri. SK7—2A 116
Chepstow Gro. WN7—9L 55
Chepstow Rd. M21—5A 90
Chepstow Rd. M27—6G 59
Chepstow St. M1—7F 78
Chepstow St. N. M1—5E 5 & 7F 78
Chepstow St. S. M1—5E 5 & 7F 78
Chequer La. WN8—1A 50
Chequer Rd. M21—6B 90
Chequers Rd. WN1—9B 34
Cherington Dri. M29—7C 56
Cherington Rd. SK8—9J 103
Cheriton Av. M33—9J 89
Cheriton Clo. SK14—4K 95
Cheriton Dri. BL2—3L 39
Cheriton Gdns. BL6—4B 20
Cheriton Rise. SK2—7A 106
Cheriton Rd. M31—3K 87
Cherrington Clo. M23—3B 102

Cherrington Dri. OL11—1D 44
Cherry Av. BL9—7C 26
Cherry Av. OL6—1B 82
Cherry Av. OL8—5C 64
Cherry Ct. M33—1G 101
Cherry Croft. SK6—4E 106
(in two parts)
Cherry Dri. M27—8G 59
Cherry Gro. OL2—3J 45
Cherry Gro. OL11—2A 28
Cherry Gro. SK15—7G 83
Cherry Gro. WN6—6M 33
Cherry Gro. WN7—8F 54
Cherry Hall Dri. OL2—2L 45
Cherry Holt Av. SK4—1M 103
Cherry La. M33—3C 100
Cherry La. OL3—7H 31
Cherry Orchard Clo. SK7 —3D 114
Cherry St. M25—3C 60
Cherryton Wlk. M13—9J 79
Cherry Tree Av. BL4—9F 38
Cherry Tree Av. SK12—9M 115
Cherrytree Clo. SK6—3E 106
Cherry Tree Clo. SK9—2L 119
Cherry Tree Clo. WA11—9G 69
Cherry Tree Ct. M6—5A 78
Cherry Tree Ct. SK2—9J 105
Cherry Tree Ct. WN6—8K 17
Cherry Tree Dri. SK7—4M 115
Cherry Tree Est. SK6—3F 106
Cherry Tree Gro. M29—4J 55
Cherry Tree Gro. WN7—1D 72
Cherry Tree La. SK2—8J 105
Cherry Tree La. SK6—3E 106
Cherry Tree La. WA11—5A 68
Cherrytree Rd. M23—4M 101
Cherry Tree Rd. SK8—3M 113
Cherry Tree Rd. WA3—7M 71
Cherry Tree Wlk. M32—5J 89
Cherry Tree Wlk. OL5—7H 65
Cherry Tree Way. BL2—6H 23
Cherry Tree Way. BL6—9E 20
Cherry Wlk. M31—3D 98
Cherry Wlk. SK8—4C 114
Cherrywood. OL9—1D 62
Cherrywood Av. BL5—1A 56
Cherrywood Clo. M28—7H 57
Chertsey Clo. M18—1E 92
Chertsey Clo. OL2—1B 46
Cherwell Av. OL10—7G 27
Cherwell Clo. OL8—7J 63
Cherwell Clo. SK8—5A 114
Cherwell Rd. BL5—8F 36
Cheryls Bank. SK13—6H 97
Chesham Av. BL1—8E 22
Chesham Av. M22—9C 102
Chesham Av. OL11—2D 44
Chesham Clo. SK9—7F 118
Chesham Cres. BL9—7A 26
Chesham Fold Rd. BL9—7B 26
Chesham Ho. M5—5M 77
Chesham Pl. WA14—2C 110
Chesham Rd. BL9—6M 25
Chesham Rd. M30—7C 76
Chesham Rd. OL4—2C 64
Chesham Rd. SK9—7F 118
Chesham St. BL3—7B 38
Cheshire Clo. M32—5H 89
Cheshire Ct. BL0—5K 9
Cheshire Rd. M31—3D 98
Cheshire Rd. SK15—2L 83
Cheshire Sq. SK15—2L 83
Cheshires, The. OL5—7K 65
Cheshire St. OL5—8K 65
Chesney Av. OL9—6E 62
Chesshyre Av. M4—6K 79
Chessington Rise. M27 —5G 59
Chester Av. BL3—5B 40
Chester Av. M25—1A 60
Chester Av. M31—3E 88
Chester Av. M33—4B 100
Chester Av. OL11—4A 28
Chester Av. SK15—4K 83
Chester Av. SK16—8E 82
Chester Av. WA3—7K 71
Chester Av. WA15—2F 110
Chester Clo. BL3—5B 40
Chester Clo. M30—9D 86
Chester Clo. SK9—2L 119
Chester Dri. BL0—7G 9
Chester Dri. WN4—5D 70
Chesterfield Gro. OL6—4D 82
Chesterfield St. OL4—2B 64
Chesterfield Way. M34—6M 93
Chestergate. SK3 & SK1 —4D 104
Chester Pl. OL2—5K 45
Chester Pl. PR6—2G 19
Chester Rd. M29—8D 56
Chester Rd. M32, M16 & M15 —7J 89
Chester Rd. SK7—5K 115
(Hazel Grove)
Chester Rd. SK7 & SK12
(Woodford & Poynton)—2D 120
Chester Rd. WA16 & WA14 —9J 109
Chester Sq. OL6—5A 82
Chester St. BL1—9F 22
Chester St. BL9—6A 26
Chester St. M15 & M1—6E 5 & 8F 78
Chester St. M25—3A 60
Chester St. M27—9E 58
Chester St. M29—6L 55
Chester St. M34—4M 93
Chester St. OL9—3J 63
Chester St. OL11—4G 29
Chester St. SK3—4D 104
Chester St. WN2—6B 54
Chesterton Clo. WN3—3A 52
Chesterton Dri. BL3—4L 37
Chesterton Gro. M35—5G 81
Chesterton Rd. M23—5K 101
Chesterton Rd. OL1—7B 46
Chesterton Wlk. M23—6L 101
Chester Wlk. BL1—8E 22
(off Boardman St.)
Chester Walks. SK6—4A 106
Chestnut Av. BL8—5G 25
Chestnut Av. BL9—8B 26
Chestnut Av. M21—6B 90
Chestnut Av. M25—1M 59
Chestnut Av. M28—6K 57
Chestnut Av. M29—4J 55
Chestnut Av. M30—9D 86
Chestnut Av. M35—4E 80
Chestnut Av. SK8—8L 103
Chestnut Av. WA11—9F 68
Chestnut Av. WN7—4E 72
Chestnut Clo. BL3—5B 38
Chestnut Clo. OL4—9D 46
Chestnut Clo. SK15—7G 83
Chestnut Ct. SK7—2D 114
Chestnut Cres. OL8—6A 64
Chestnut Dri. BL5—1F 54
Chestnut Dri. M33—4D 100
Chestnut Dri. SK12—9M 115
Chestnut Dri. WN7—4F 72
Chestnut Dri. S. WN7—5F 72
Chestnut Gdns. M34—4L 93
Chestnut Gro. M26—9F 40
Chestnut Gro. M35—5G 81
Chestnut Gro. WA3—7M 71
Chestnut Gro. WA11—8D 68
Chestnut Gro. WN2—4A 54
Chestnut Gro. WN4—3D 70
Chestnut La. WN7—5F 72
Chestnut Pl. OL16—2H 29
Chestnut Rd. M30—3A 76
Chestnut Rd. WN1—7D 34
Chestnuts, The. PR7—1M 17
Chestnut St. OL9—5F 62
Chestnut Vs. SK4—3C 104
Chestnut Wlk. M31—3D 98
Chestnut Way. OL15—5M 13
Chesworth Clo. SK1—5F 104
Chesworth Ct. M35—6F 80
Chesworth Fold. SK1—5F 104

Chesworth Wlk. M15—8E 78
(off Jackson Cres.)
Chetham Clo. M5—6A 4 & 8B 78
Chetwode Av. WN4—6B 70
Chetwyn Av. BL7—3G 23
Chetwyn Av. OL2—5J 45
Chetwynd Av. M31—4C 88
Chetwynd Clo. M33—8E 88
Chevin Gdns. SK7—5G 115
Chevington Dri. M9—1K 79
Chevington Dri. SK4—2K 103
Chevington Gdns. BL1—7E 22
Cheviot Av. OL2—6J 45
Cheviot Av. OL8—5L 63
Cheviot Av. SK8—2M 113
Cheviot Clo. BL0—7J 9
Cheviot Clo. BL1—5D 22
Cheviot Clo. BL6—5C 20
Cheviot Clo. BL8—7G 25
Cheviot Clo. M6—4L 77
Cheviot Clo. M24—9D 44
Cheviot Clo. OL9—3G 63
Cheviot Clo. OL16—4A 30
Cheviot Clo. SK4—2D 104
Cheviot Clo. WN3—6J 51
Cheviot Ct. OL8—4L 63
Cheviot Rd. SK7—3H 115
Cheviots Rd. OL2—1A 46
Cheviot St. M3—2E 5 & 4F 78
Cheviot Wlk. WN2—6H 53
Chevithorne Clo. WA14—7B 100
Chevril Clo. M15—9G 79
Chevril Wlk. WN3—4L 51
Chevron Clo. M6—3A 4 & 5B 78
Chevron Clo. OL11—7B 28
Chew Brook Dri. OL3—3B 66
Chew Moor La. BL5—7G 37
Chew Vale. OL3—3B 66
Chew Vale. SK16—8F 82
Chew Valley Rd. OL3—2A 66
Chew Wood. SK14—9A 96
Chichester Av. M29—6G 55
Chichester Clo. OL15—8M 13
Chichester Cres. OL9—8G 45
Chichester Rd. M15—1E 90
Chichester Rd. SK6—3C 106
Chichester St. OL16—3G 29
Chichester Way. M34—5A 94
Chidlow Av. M20—7G 91
Chidwall Rd. M22—2B 112
Chief St. OL4—2A 64
Chigwell Clo. M22—8D 102
Chilcombe Wlk. M9—3L 61
(off Brockford Dri.)
Chilcote Av. M33—1D 100
Chilgrove Av. BL6—9K 19
Chilham Rd. M28—6L 57
Chilham Rd. M30—3F 76
Chilham St. BL3—6B 38
Chilham St. M27—1E 76
Chillingham Dri. WN7—3J 73
Chillington Wlk. M34—5L 93
Chillingworth St. M8—1G 79
Chilmark Dri. M23—7A 102
Chiltern Av. M29—3M 55
Chiltern Av. M31—3L 87
Chiltern Av. SK8—2M 113
Chiltern Clo. BL0—7J 9
Chiltern Clo. BL6—5C 20
Chiltern Clo. M28—8L 57
Chiltern Clo. OL2—1M 45
Chiltern Clo. SK7—3H 115
Chiltern Clo. WN5—5C 70
Chiltern Dri. BL2—2H 39
Chiltern Dri. BL8—6H 25
Chiltern Dri. M27—1F 76
Chiltern Dri. OL2—5J 45
Chiltern Dri. SK2—9G 105
Chiltern Dri. WA15—2F 110
Chiltern Dri. WN3—6K 51
Chiltern Gdns. M33—5J 101
Chiltern Rd. BL0—7J 9
Chiltern Way. M29—8B 56
Chilton Av. OL9—2G 63
Chilton Dri. M24—1C 62
Chilworth St. M14—4H 91
Chime Bank. M8—9H 61
Chimes Rd. WN4—1M 69
Chimney Hall St. SK4—1E 104
China La. BL1—1F 38
China La. M1—4G 5 & 6H 79
Chingford Wlk. M13—2M 91
(off St John's Rd.)
Chinley Av. M10—8A 62
Chinley Av. M32—2G 89
Chinley Clo. M33—2K 101
Chinley Clo. SK4—2B 104
Chinley Clo. SK7—1E 114
Chinley St. M6—2B 78
Chinwell View. M19—5A 92
Chip Hill Rd. BL3—5M 37
Chippendale Pl. OL6—2E 82
Chippenham Av. SK2—6K 105
Chippenham Ct. M4—5K 79
Chippenham Rd. M4—3H 5 & 5J 79
Chipping Fold. OL16—5M 29
Chipping Rd. BL1—8M 21
Chipstead Wlk. M12—1L 91
Chirmside St. BL8—9H 25
Chirton Wlk. M10—9A 62
Chisacre Dri. WN6—2D 32
Chiseldon Clo. BL3—4E 38
(off Bantry St.)
Chiselhurst St. M8—8G 61
Chisholm Clo. WN6—7H 17
Chisholme Clo. BL8—9F 8
Chisholm St. M11—8D 80
Chisledon Av. M8—1F 78
Chislehurst Av. M33—3C 88
Chislehurst Clo. BL8—9H 25
Chisnall Av. WN6—5F 16
Chisnall La. PR7—1G 17
(Coppull)
Chisnall La. PR7—5G 17
(Mossy Lea)
Chisolm Ct. M24—8M 43
Chiswell St. WN5—3J 51
Chiswick Dri. M26—4B 40
Chiswick Rd. M20—2J 103
Chisworth Clo. SK7—1E 114
Chisworth St. BL2—7H 23
Chisworth Wlk. M34—6A 94
Choir St. M7—1D 4 & 3E 78
Chokeberry Clo. WA14—5B 100
Chollerton Clo. WA16—8C 108
Cholmondeley Av. WA14 —4E 100
Cholmondeley Rd. M6—3H 77
Cholsey Av. M7—9B 60
Chomlea. WA14—9B 100
Chomlea Manor. M6—3J 77
Choral Gro. M7—2D 78
Chorley Clo. BL8—9F 24
Chorley Hall Clo. SK9—8K 119
Chorley Hall La. SK9—8K 119
Chorley La. PR7—1J 17
Chorley New Rd. BL6 & BL1 —6A 20
Chorley Old Rd. BL1—8M 21
Chorley Old Rd. BL6 & BL1 —6C 20
Chorley Rd. BL5—3A 36
Chorley Rd. BL6—4G 19
Chorley Rd. M27—7E 58
Chorley Rd. M33—3L 101
Chorley Rd. PR6—1F 18
Chorley Rd. WN6 & WN1—3B 34
Chorley St. BL1—1E 38
Chorley St. M32—2M 89
Chorley St. WN3—2E 52
Chorley Wood Av. M19—8M 91
Chorlton Brook. SK8—7L 103
Chorlton Dri. SK8—7L 103
Chorlton Fold. M30—2D 76
(in two parts)
Chorlton Fold. SK6—9C 94
Chorlton Grn. M21—6A 90
Chorlton Gro. SK1—6H 105
Chorlton Pl. M21—5B 90
Chorlton Rd. M16 & M15—6C 4 & 2D 90
Chorlton St. M1—5F 4 & 7G 79
Chorlton St. M16—1C 90

Chowbent Clo. M29—5L 55
Chretien Rd. M22—3D 102
Chrisleton Av. SK4—9D 92
Christ Chu. Av. M5—3A 4 & 5B 78
Christchurch Clo. BL2—7M 23
Christchurch La. BL2—7M 23
Christchurch Rd. M33—9C 88
Christie Rd. M32—3L 89
Christie St. SK1—5G 105
Christine St. OL2—3H 46
(in two parts)
Christleton. WN6—3H 33
Christleton Way. SK9—7K 113
Christopher Acre. OL11—1L 27
Christopher St. M5—4A 4 & 6A 78
Christopher St. M10—3D 80
Christopher St. WN3—2E 52
Chronnell Dri. BL2—1L 39
Chudleigh Clo. SK7—1G 115
Chudleigh Clo. WA14—7B 100
Chudleigh Rd. M8—6G 61
Chulsey Ga. La. BL6—5G 37
Chulsey St. BL3—5B 38
Chunal La. SK13—8J 97
Church Av. BL3—5C 38
Church Av. M6—5K 77
Church Av. M10—2C 80
Church Av. M24—3D 44
Church Av. SK9—1G 119
Church Av. SK14—6F 94
Church Av. WN2—8M 53
Church Bank. BL1—2G 39
Churchbank. SK15—4K 83
Church Bank. WA14—2B 110
Church Brow. M24—8A 44
Church Brow. SK14—5D 94
(Hyde)
Church Brow. SK14—3A 96
(Mottram)
Church Brow. WA14—2B 110
Church Clo. M34—8M 81
Church Clo. SK9—9K 113
Church Clo. SK13—4L 97
Church Ct. OL9—3J 63
Church Ct. SK16—6B 82
Church Ct. WA15—3E 110
Church Ct. WN1—9E 34
Church Croft. BL9—5B 42
Churchdale Rd. M9—4H 61
Church Dri. M25—4A 60
Church Dri. WN5—3D 50
Churchfield. WN6—3G 33
Churchfield Clo. M26—8F 40
Churchfield Rd. M6—2K 77
Churchfields. M34—8L 81
Churchfields. OL3—7A 48
Churchfields. WA14—3B 110
Churchfield Wlk. M11—7A 80
(off Outrington Dri.)
Church Fold. PR7—2M 17
Church Fold. SK14—7C 96
Churchgate. BL1—2F 38
Churchgate. M41—5E 88
Churchgate. SK1—4F 104
Churchgate Bldgs. M1—5H 5 & 7J 79
Church Grn. M6—4M 77
Church Grn. M26—5K 41
Church Grn. WA13—5B 98
Church Gro. M30—6E 76
Church Gro. SK7—2L 115
Church Gro. WN1—9E 34
Churchill Av. BL2—9D 24
Churchill Av. M16—4D 90
Churchill Clo. OL10—1L 43
Churchill Ct. M6—5M 77
Churchill Cres. SK5—5E 92
Churchill Cres. SK6—6D 106
Churchill Dri. BL3—6C 40
Churchill Ho. M16—2A 90
Churchill Rd. WA14—6D 100
Churchill St. BL2—2J 39
Churchill St. OL4—2A 64
Churchill St. OL12 & OL11 (in two parts) —1C 28
Churchill St. SK4—2D 104
Churchill St. E. OL4—2A 64
Churchill Way. M6—3A 4 & 5A 78
Churchill Way. M17—8J 77
Church La. BL5—6E 36
Church La. M7—7C 60
Church La. M9—8K 61
(in two parts)
Church La. M19—8M 91
Church La. M25—4A 60
(Prestwich)
Church La. M25—9L 41
(Whitefield)
Church La. M33—7E 88
Church La. OL1—1M 63
Church La. OL3—8D 48
Church La. OL16—3F 28
Church La. SK6—7F 106
(Marple)
Church La. SK6—3C 106
(Romiley)
Church La. SK7—1C 120
Church La. SK9—7L 119
Church La. WA3—7K 71
Church La. WN6—3G 33
(Shevington)
Church La. WN6—2D 16
(Wrightington)
Churchley Clo. SK3—7A 104
Churchley Rd. SK3—6A 104
Church Manor. SK4—1B 104
Church Meadow. BL9—5B 42
Church Meadow. OL3—3L 65
Church Meadows. BL2—7M 23
Church M. M34—3L 93
Church M. SK7—2L 115
Church Pl. OL1—1M 63
Church Pl. OL10—8K 27
Church Rd. BL0—3L 9
Church Rd. BL1—8A 22
Church Rd. BL4—9L 39
Church Rd. M22—4D 102
Church Rd. M24—1D 62
Church Rd. M26—9A 40
Church Rd. M28—5K 57
Church Rd. M30—1E 74
Church Rd. M30—5F 76
Church Rd. M31—5M 87
Church Rd. M33—1K 101
Church Rd. OL2—3B 46
Church Rd. OL3—3L 65
(Greenfield)
Church Rd. OL3—9B 48
(Uppermill)
Church Rd. OL16—4H 29
Church Rd. SK4—3D 104
Church Rd. SK6—7L 107
Church Rd. SK8—4B 114
(Cheadle Hulme)
Church Rd. SK8—8G 103
(Gatley)
Church Rd. SK9—8K 113
(Handforth)
Church Rd. SK9—7E 118
(Wilmslow)
Church Rd. SK14—2D 96
Church Rd. WA11—9L 69
Church Rd. WN2—5H 53
Church Rd. E. M33—1K 101
Church Rd. W. M33—1J 101
Churchside Clo. M9—6K 61
Church Stile. OL16—3F 28
(in two parts)
Churchstoke Wlk. M23—6L 101
Church St. BL2—9C 24
(Ainsworth)
Church St. BL2—5K 23
(Bradshaw)
Church St. BL3—6M 39
Church St. BL4—9L 39
(Farnworth)
Church St. BL4—1L 57
(Kearsley, in two parts)
Church St. BL6—7J 19
(Blackrod)

Church St. BL6—6C 20
(Horwich)
Church St. BL8—6F 24
Church St. BL9—7A 26
Church St. M4—5F 4 & 5G 79
Church St. M26—6H 41
Church St. M27—8H 59
(Pendlebury)
Church St. M27—8E 58
(Swinton)
Church St. M29—5K 55
Church St. M30—5E 76
(in three parts)
Church St. M32—5J 89
Church St. M34—8L 81
Church St. M35—6H 81
(Droylsden)
Church St. M35—8F 62
(Failsworth)
Church St. OL1—1M 63
Church St. OL2—5K 45
Church St. OL3—5L 47
Church St. OL4—3E 64
Church St. OL5—7K 65
Church St. OL6—5B 82
Church St. OL10—8K 27
Church St. OL11—3E 28
Church St. OL12—3C 12
Church St. OL15—6A 14
Church St. OL16—6B 30
(Newhey)
Church St. OL16—8K 13
(Smallbridge)
Church St. PR7—3G 19
Church St. SK4—2D 104
(in two parts)
Church St. SK6—9A 94
(Bredbury)
Church St. SK6—7F 106
(Marple)
Church St. SK8—7K 103
Church St. SK9—4H 119
Church St. SK13—4K 97
Church St. SK14—2G 97
(Hadfield)
Church St. SK14—5D 94
(Hyde)
Church St. SK14—8F 84
(Tintwistle)
Church St. SK16—6B 82
Church St. WA3—6H 71
Church St. WA14—8D 100
Church St. WN1—9C 34
Church St. WN2—3H 35
(Aspull)
Church St. WN2—3K 53
(Hindley)
Church St. WN3—2F 52
Church St. WN5—3D 50
(Orrell)
Church St. WN5—2H 51
(Wigan)
Church St. WN6—9L 17
Church St. WN7—2F 72
Church St. WN8—1C 50
Church St. E. M26—6J 41
(in two parts)
Church St. E. OL4—9E 46
Church St. S. SK13—4L 97
Church St. W. M26—6H 41
Church Ter. M33—8G 89
Church Ter. OL1—1M 63
Church Ter. OL16—5A 30
Church Ter. SK4—3D 104
Church Ter. SK9—8K 113
Church Ter. SK13—4K 97
Church Ter. WN4—5B 70
(off Heath Rd.)
Churchtown Av. BL2—2M 39
Church View. M30—4G 87
Church View. M35—6H 81
(Droylsden)
Church View. M35—8F 62
(Failsworth)
Church View. OL12—9L 11
Church View. SK9—1G 119
Church View. SK14—5D 94
Church View. WA13—9B 98
Church Wlk. BL4—9J 39
Church Wlk. M27—4F 58
Church Wlk. OL2—5K 45
Church Wlk. SK9—5F 118
Church Wlk. SK13—4L 97
Church Wlk. SK15—5G 83
(in two parts)
Church Wlk. WA14—8D 100
Churchward Sq. BL6—8C 20
Churchwood Rd. M20—2H 103
Churning St. M10—2K 79
Churnet Clo. BL5—7F 36
Churston Av. M9—4L 61
Churston Av. SK7—2F 114
Churton Av. M14—4H 91
Churton Av. M33—2F 100
Churton Gro. WN6—8H 17
Churton Rd. M18—3C 92
Churwell Av. SK4—1M 103
Cicely Mill La. WA16—9J 109
Cicero St. M9—8M 61
Cicero St. OL1—8A 46
Cilder's Villas. OL4—4H 65
Cinder Hill La. OL1—5G 45
Cinnamon Av. WN2—4M 53
Cinnamon Clo. OL12—2D 28
Cinnamon Pl. M29—6J 55
Cinnamon St. OL12—2D 28
Cipher St. M4—2H 5 & 4J 79
Circle Ct. M32—2F 88
Circle, The. M32—2F 88
Circuit, The. M20—9H 91
Circuit, The. SK3—7B 104
Circuit, The. SK8—5A 114
Circuit, The. SK9—9H 119
(Alderley Edge)
Circuit, The. SK9—6D 118
(Wilmslow)
Circular Rd. M20—9H 91
Circular Rd. M25—6B 60
Circular Rd. M34—4L 93
Circus, The. WA16—9J 109
Cirencester Clo. M28—2G 57
Ciss La. M31—4E 88
City Av. M34—4L 93
City Course Trading Est. M11 —7A 80
City Gdns. M34—4K 93
City Gdns. WA10—9A 68
City Rd. M15—9C 78
City Rd. M28—8G 57
City Rd. WA10—9A 68
City Rd. WN5—1H 51
City Rd. E. M15—6E 5 & 8F 78
City View. WA11—6A 68
City Wlk. M27—8H 59
Civic Wlk. OL10—8K 27
Clacton Wlk. M13—9J 79
(off Ardeen Wlk.)
Clague St. M11—5A 80
Claife Av. M10—6B 62
Clammerclough Rd. BL4 —9M 39
Clandon Av. M30—5B 76
Clandon Clo. M12—9K 79
Clanwood Clo. WN3—6L 51
Clapgate. SK6—4M 105
Clap Ga. La. WN3—5L 51
Clapgate Rd. OL11—1L 27
Clapham St. M10—8C 62
Clara Gorton Ct. OL16—4H 29
Clara St. OL9—4J 63
Clara St. OL11—5F 28
Clara St. OL12—2D 12
Clare Av. SK9—9J 113
Clare Clo. BL8—5K 25
Clare Ct. SK1—4G 105
Claremont Av. M20—9G 91
Claremont Av. SK4—9C 92
Claremont Av. SK6—7C 106
Claremont Av. WA14—5D 100
Claremont Av. WN2—3M 53
Claremont Dri. M28—3H 57
Claremont Dri. WA14—5D 100
Claremont Gro. M20—2G 103
Claremont Gro. WA15—1E 110

Claremont Range. M18—2F 92
Claremont Rd. M6—1J 77
Claremont Rd. M16 & M14 —3E 90
Claremont Rd. M33—9H 89
Claremont Rd. OL11—3C 28
Claremont Rd. OL16—5L 29
Claremont Rd. SK2—8H 105
Claremont Rd. WN5—2E 68
Claremont St. M35—8F 62
Claremont St. OL6—3E 82
(in two parts)
Claremont St. OL8—6M 63
Claremont St. OL9—8J 45
Clarence Arc. OL6—5B 82
Clarence Av. M17—8F 76
Clarence Av. M25—1A 60
Clarence Av. M33—2E 100
Clarence Av. OL8—4K 63
Clarence Ct. BL1—1E 38
Clarence Ct. SK9—5G 119
Clarence Gro. M15—2E 90
Clarence Ho. WN1—9D 34
Clarence Rd. M13—3L 91
Clarence Rd. M27—9C 58
Clarence Rd. OL6—3C 82
Clarence Rd. SK4—9B 92
Clarence Rd. WA15—1F 110
Clarence St. BL1—1F 38
(in two parts)
Clarence St. BL4—8L 39
Clarence St. M2—4D 5 & 6F 78
Clarence St. M7—1B 4 & 3C 78
Clarence St. M29—6L 55
Clarence St. OL2—6A 46
Clarence St. OL12—9D 12
Clarence St. SK14—2E 94
Clarence St. SK15—6E 82
Clarence St. WA3—6G 71
Clarence St. WN1—9D 34
Clarence St. WN2—1G 53
Clarence St. WN4—2M 69
Clarence St. WN7—3H 73
Clarence Yd. WN1—9C 34
Clarendon Av. SK4—2B 104
Clarendon Av. WA15—8E 100
Clarendon Cres. M30—4F 76
Clarendon Cres. M33—9K 89
Clarendon Gdns. M30—4F 76
Clarendon Gro. BL2—3H 39
Clarendon Pl. SK14—4E 94
Clarendon Rd. BL2—2J 39
Clarendon Rd. M16—4C 90
Clarendon Rd. M27—8F 58
Clarendon Rd. M30—4F 76
(Eccles)
Clarendon Rd. M30—7F 86
(Irlam)
Clarendon Rd. M31—3L 87
Clarendon Rd. M33—1K 101
Clarendon Rd. M34—8G 81
(Audenshaw)
Clarendon Rd. M34—4B 94
(Denton)
Clarendon Rd. SK7—1M 115
Clarendon Rd. SK14—3D 94
Clarendon Rd. W. M21—4B 90
Clarendon St. BL3—5E 38
Clarendon St. BL9—6A 26
Clarendon St. M15—6E 5 & 9F 78
(in two parts)
Clarendon St. M25—9M 41
Clarendon St. OL5—8K 65
Clarendon St. OL16—6H 29
Clarendon St. SK5—2F 104
Clarendon St. SK14—3D 94
(in two parts)
Clarendon St. SK16—7A 82
(in two parts)
Clarendon St. WN3—3E 52
Clarendon Wlk. M5—5A 78
Clare Rd. M19—6A 92
Clare Rd. SK5—1F 104
Clare St. M5—4B 4 & 6C 78
Clare St. M34—2L 93
Clare St. WN3—1B 52
Claribel St. M11—7L 79
Claridge Rd. M21—4A 90
Clarington Gro. WN1—1E 52
Clarion St. M4—2H 5 & 4J 79
Clark Av. M18—1E 92
Clarke Av. M5—6A 4 & 8B 78
Clarke Brow. M24—8A 44
Clarke Cres. M28—2D 56
Clarke Cres. WA15—1H 111
Clarke Ind. Est. M32—1F 88
Clarkenwell Clo. OL1—9L 45
Clarkes Croft. BL9—7C 26
Clarke's La. OL12—2D 28
Clarke St. BL1—1C 38
Clarke St. BL4—1L 57
Clarke St. M4—3H 5 & 5J 79
Clarke St. OL7—7M 81
Clarke St. OL10—8K 27
Clarke St. OL16—9H 13
Clarke St. WA14—6D 100
Clarke St. WN7—3E 72
Clarkethorn Ter. SK5—2E 104
Clarksfield Rd. OL4—2C 64
Clarksfield St. OL4—2C 64
Clark's Hill. M25—4A 60
Clarkson Clo. M24—1J 61
Clarkson Clo. M34—4K 93
Clark Way. SK14—3C 94
Clatford Wlk. M9—9K 61
(off Fernclough Rd.)
Claude Av. M27—8D 58
Claude Rd. M21—7A 90
Claude St. M8—7G 61
Claude St. M27—8D 58
Claude St. WN5—2K 51
Claudia Sq. SK15—2L 83
Claughton Av. BL2—2M 39
Claughton Av. M28—8J 57
Claughton Rd. BL8—5F 24
Clavendon Rd. M26—2E 40
Claverham Wlk. M23—6L 101
Claverton Rd. M23—2M 111
Claxton Av. M9—5K 61
Claybank Dri. BL8—3D 24
Clay Bank St. OL10—7J 27
Claybrook Wlk. M11—6A 80
Clay Croft Ter. OL15—4A 14
Claydon Dri. M28—4B 40
Claydon Dri. WN3—3F 52
Clayfield Dri. OL11—2M 27
Claygate Dri. M9—3K 61
Clayhill Wlk. M9—7K 61
Claylands Clo. SK14—2D 96
Clay La. M23—9M 101
Clay La. OL11—2K 27
Clay La. SK9—8H 113
(Handforth)
Clay La. SK9—7C 118
(Wilmslow)
Clay La. WA15—8H 101
Claymore St. M18—9E 80
Claypool Rd. BL6—9E 20
Clay St. BL7—3G 23
Clay St. OL8—4L 63
Clay St. OL15—6M 13
Claythorpe Wlk. M8—6E 60
Clayton Av. BL2—4J 39
Clayton Av. M20—1H 103
Clayton Av. WA3—7L 71
Claytonbrook Rd. M11—7C 80
Clayton Clo. BL8—9F 24
Clayton Clo. M15—1E 90
Claytongate. PR7—1M 17
Clayton Hall Rd. M11—5C 80
Clayton Ind. Est. M11—6C 80
Clayton La. M11—7B 80
Clayton La. S. M12—8A 80
Clayton's Clo. OL4—1F 64
Clayton St. BL2—4J 39
Clayton St. M11—4B 80
(in two parts)
Clayton St. M34—4M 93
Clayton St. M35—9F 62
Clayton St. OL9—5G 63

Clayton St. OL12—9H 13
Clayton St. SK16—7D 82
Clayton St. WN3—9B 34
Cleadon Av. M18—2C 92
Cleadon Dri. BL8—5J 25
Cleadon Dri. S. BL8—5J 25
Cleavley St. M30—5B 76
Clee Av. M13—4M 91
Cleethorpes Av. M9—5H 61
Cleeve Av. WN7—9D 54
Cleeve Rd. M23—3A 102
Cleeve Rd. OL4—2C 64
Cleeve Way. SK8—6B 114
Clegg Hall Rd. OL15—9K 13
Clegg Pl. OL6—3D 82
Clegg's Arc. OL12—1C 12
(off Clegg St.)
Clegg's Bldgs. BL1—2E 38
Clegg's Ct. M3—3E 5 & 5F 78
Clegg's Ct. OL12—1C 12
(off Clegg St.)
Clegg's La. M28—4G 57
Clegg St. BL2—2J 39
Clegg St. M25—1M 59
Clegg St. M29—1A 74
(Astley)
Clegg St. M29—7M 55
(Tyldesley)
Clegg St. M35—6F 80
(Droylsden)
Clegg St. OL1—2M 63
Clegg St. OL4—2M 63
(Oldham)
Clegg St. OL4—2G 65
(Springhead)
Clegg St. OL12—1C 12
Clegg St. OL15—4M 13
Clegg St. OL16—5A 30
Clegg St. SK6—2M 105
Cleggswood Av. OL15—8A 14
Clelland St. BL4—1L 57
Clematis Wlk. M27—6E 58
Clement Ct. OL16—4H 29
Clementina St. OL12—1F 28
Clement Pl. OL12—2E 28
Clement Pl. OL15—6C 14
Clement Rd. SK6—6H 107
Clement Royds St. OL12—2E 28
Clements Av. M29—6G 55
Clements St. M11—8E 80
Clement Stott Clo. M9—4M 61
Clement St. SK4—2E 104
Cleminson St. M3—3C 4 & 5D 78
Clemshaw Clo. OL10—9J 27
Clerewood Av. SK8—5H 113
Clerke St. BL9—8M 25
Clerk's Ct. M5—5H 77
Clevedon Av. M31—4G 89
Clevedon Dri. WN3—4J 51
Clevedon Rd. OL9—8G 45
Clevedon St. M9—9L 61
Cleveland Av. M6—4J 77
Cleveland Av. M19—4B 92
Cleveland Av. SK14—4C 94
Cleveland Av. WN3—6J 51
Cleveland Clo. BL0—8J 9
Cleveland Clo. M27—6G 59
Cleveland Dri. OL16—4A 30
Cleveland Dri. WA3—7K 71
Cleveland Gdns. BL3—5B 38
Cleveland Gro. OL2—6J 45
Cleveland Rd. M8—7H 61
Cleveland Rd. SK4—1A 104
Cleveland Rd. WA15—1F 110
Clevelands Clo. OL2—1A 46
Cleveland St. BL3—5B 38
Cleveland St. PR7—1L 17
Cleveleys Av. BL2—1J 39
Cleveleys Av. BL9—1L 41
Cleveleys Av. M21—6J 91
Cleveleys Av. OL16—7H 29
Cleveleys Av. SK8—3H 113
Cleveleys Gro. M7—9E 60
Cleves Ct. OL10—9J 27
Cleworth Clo. M29—3C 74
Cleworth Rd. M24—7M 43
Cleworth Wlk. M15—6C 4 & 8D 78
Clibran St. M8—1H 79
Clifden Dri. M22—2E 112
Cliff Av. BL9—9J 9
Cliff Av. M7—1C 78
Cliffbrook Gro. SK9—1K 119
Cliff Cres. M7—9D 60
Cliffdale Dri. M8—7G 61
Cliffe Dale. SK15—7F 82
Cliffe Rd. SK13—7K 97
Cliffe St. OL15—1D 14
Cliff Grange. M7—9D 60
Cliff Gro. SK4—1B 104
Cliff Hill. OL2—9D 30
Cliff Hill Rd. OL2—9D 30
Cliffmere Clo. SK8—1M 113
Cliff Mt. BL0—4H 9
Clifford Av. M34—1L 93
Clifford Av. WA15—7G 101
Clifford Ct. M15—1E 90
Clifford Ct. SK2—8H 105
Clifford Rd. BL3—7A 38
Clifford Rd. SK9—5F 118
Clifford Rd. SK12—8J 115
Clifford St. M27—8H 59
Clifford St. M30—6B 76
Clifford St. OL11—5F 28
Clifford St. WN7—3H 73
Cliff Rd. BL9—4M 41
Cliff Rd. SK9—3H 119
Cliff Side. SK9—3H 119
Cliff St. OL16—1H 29
Clifton Av. M14—6K 91
Clifton Av. M29—1C 74
Clifton Av. M30—4D 76
Clifton Av. OL4—3B 64
Clifton Av. SK8—2G 113
Clifton Av. WA15—8E 100
Clifton Clo. M16—1D 90
Clifton Clo. OL4—3B 64
Clifton Clo. OL10—9J 27
Clifton Ct. BL4—7H 39
Clifton Ct. M27—4E 58
Clifton Ct. SK4—2B 104
Clifton Cres. OL2—6A 46
Clifton Cres. WN1—7C 34
Clifton Dri. BL6—7H 19
Clifton Dri. M27—6J 59
(Clifton)
Clifton Dri. M27—7D 58
(Swinton)
Clifton Dri. SK6—6F 106
Clifton Dri. SK8—8F 102
(Gatley)
Clifton Dri. SK8—2G 113
(Heald Green)
Clifton Dri. SK9—7E 118
Clifton Gro. M27—6C 58
Clifton Ho. WN3—3B 52
Clifton Ho. Rd. M27—4E 58
Clifton Lodge. SK2—8G 105
Clifton Pk. Rd. SK2—8G 105
Clifton Rd. M16—1D 90
Clifton Rd. M21—6C 90
Clifton Rd. M24—3D 44
Clifton Rd. M25—4L 59
Clifton Rd. M30—4D 76
Clifton Rd. M31—4A 88
Clifton Rd. M33—2H 101
Clifton Rd. SK4—2A 104
Clifton Rd. WN4—1M 69
Clifton Rd. WN5—3D 68
Clifton Rd. WN7—5E 72
Clifton St. BL1—8E 22
Clifton St. BL4—7H 39
(Farnworth)
Clifton St. BL4—1M 57
(Kearsley)
Clifton St. BL9—6M 25
Clifton St. M10—4M 79
Clifton St. M16—1D 90
Clifton St. M29—8E 56
Clifton St. M35—7G 63
Clifton St. OL6—8L 63
Clifton St. OL16—4M 29
Clifton St. SK9—8L 119

Clifton St. WN1—8C 34
Clifton St. WN3—4A 52
Clifton St. WN7—2D 72
Clifton View. M27—4E 58
Clifton Vs. M35—7G 63
Cliftonville Dri. M27 & M6 —1G 77
Cliftonville Rd. OL16—1J 45
Clifton Wlk. M24—6K 43
Clinton Av. M14—4F 90
Clinton Gdns. M14—4G 91
Clinton Ho. M5—6M 77
Clinton St. OL6—3D 82
Clinton Wlk. OL4—2A 64
Clippers Quay. M5—9A 78
Clipsley Brook View. WA11 —9F 68
Clipsley Cres. OL4—5F 46
Clipsley Cres. WA11—8G 69
Clipsley La. WA11—9H 69
Cliston Wlk. SK7—2G 115
Clitheroe Clo. OL10—7K 27
Clitheroe Dri. BL8—8F 24
Clitheroe Rd. M13—3M 91
Clito St. M9—8M 61
Clive Av. M25—8L 41
Cliveley Wlk. M27—8H 59
Clive Rd. BL5—2E 54
Clive Rd. M35—9E 62
Clive St. BL1—2F 38
Clive St. M4—2G 5 & 4H 79
Clive St. OL7—2A 82
Clive St. OL8—6K 63
(in two parts)
Clivia Gro. M7—1D 78
Cloak St. M1—6F 5 & 8G 79
Clock Ho. Av. M35—4E 80
Clockhouse M. M35—4E 80
Clock Houses. SK15—5J 83
Clock Tower Clo. M28—5F 56
Cloister Av. WN7—7D 54
Cloister Clo. SK16—9C 82
Cloister Rd. SK4—3K 103
Cloisters, The. BL5—3E 54
Cloisters, The. OL16—1H 29
Cloisters, The. SK8—8A 104
Cloister St. BL1—8C 22
Clopton Wlk. M15—9E 78
(in four parts)
Closebrook Rd. WN5—2K 51
Closeburn Wlk. M11—7M 79
Close La. WN2—5M 53
(in two parts)
Close St. WN2—2M 53
Close, The. BL2—7H 23
Close, The. BL8—4J 25
Close, The. M24—6B 44
Close, The. M34—2K 93
Close, The. OL3—3M 55
Close, The. SK6—4H 107
Close, The. SK15—3F 82
(in two parts)
Close, The. WA11—9F 68
Close, The. WA14—8C 100
(Altrincham)
Close, The. WA14—9C 100
(Bowdon)
Clothorn Rd. M20—1H 103
Cloudberry Wlk. M31—2F 98
Cloudstock Gro. M28—3E 56
Clough. OL2—3D 46
Clough Av. BL5—9F 36
Clough Av. M33—4D 100
Clough Av. SK6—6J 107
Clough Av. SK9—1H 119
Clough Bank. M9—6K 61
Clough Bank. OL15—3A 14
Clough Ct. M24—7B 44
Clough Croft. OL4—2L 65
Clough Dri. M25—4M 59
Clough End Rd. SK14—5L 95
Clough Field. OL15—7A 14
Cloughfield Av. M5—5A 4 & 7B 78
Cloughfield Dri. M5—5A 4 & 7B 78
Clough Flats. OL10—8J 27
(off Brunswick St.)
Clough Fold Av. SK14—5D 94
Clough Fold Rd. SK14—5C 94
Clough Ga. OL8—6K 63
Clough Ga. SK14—6E 94
Clough Gro. WN4—2M 69
Clough Head. OL15—1C 14
(off Calderbrook Rd.)
Clough La. M25—4M 59
Clough La. OL4—2K 65
Clough Meadow. BL1—3K 37
Clough Meadow. SK6—9G 94
Clough Meadow Rd. M26 —6E 40
Clough Pk. Av. OL4—2L 65
Clough Rd. M9—8M 61
Clough Rd. M24—7A 44
Clough Rd. M35—5G 81
(Droylsden)
Clough Rd. M35—9G 63
(Failsworth)
Clough Rd. OL1—6D 46
Clough Rd. OL2—3D 46
Clough Rd. OL15—3A 14
Cloughs Av. OL9—9D 44
Clough Side. M9—7M 61
Clough Side. SK6—6H 107
Cloughside. SK12—6L 117
Clough St. BL4—1M 57
Clough St. M11—2C 80
Clough St. M24—7B 44
Clough St. M26—8J 41
Clough St. OL12—5J 13
Clough, The. BL1—2L 37
Clough, The. SK5—8H 93
Clough Wlk. M10—2D 80
Clough Top Rd. M9—6A 62
Clough Wlk. M25—4M 59
Clough Wlk. SK5—8H 93
Cloughwood Cres. WN6—3D 32
Clovelly Av. OL8—6J 63
Clovelly Av. WN7—8F 54
Clovelly Rd. M21—6C 90
Clovelly Rd. M27—9C 58
Clovelly Rd. SK2—5J 105
Clovelly St. M10—2D 80
Clovelly St. OL11—7B 28
Clover Av. SK3—8D 104
Cloverbank Av. M19—1K 103
Clover Cres. OL8—5D 64
Clover Croft. M33—4K 101
Cloverdale Sq. BL1—9A 22
Cloverfield Wlk. M28—5K 57
(off Bolton Rd.)
Clover Hall Cres. OL16—1J 29
Clover Hey. WA11—8B 68
Cloverley. M33—3H 101
Cloverley Dri. WA15—9G 101
Clover Rd. SK6—2E 106
Clover Rd. WA15—8G 101
Clover St. OL12—2E 28
Clover St. WN6—7A 34
Clover View. OL16—2J 29
Clowes St. M3—3D 4 & 5E 78
Clowes St. M7—2D 78
Clowes St. M12—9M 79
(in two parts)
Clowes St. OL9—6H 63
Club St. M11—8F 80
Club St. WA11—6A 68
Clumber Clo. SK12—9L 115
Clumber Rd. M18—2F 92
Clumber Rd. SK12—9L 115
Clunton Av. BL3—4B 38
Clutha Rd. SK3—9F 104
Clwyd Av. SK3—6D 104
Clyde Av. M25—2M 59
Clyde Ct. OL16—4H 29
Clyde Rd. M20—1F 102
Clyde Rd. M26—4F 40
Clyde Rd. M29—9C 56
Clyde Rd. SK3—6C 104
Clydesdale Rise. OL3—4D 48
Clydesdale St. OL8—4L 63
Clyde St. BL1—8E 22
Clyde St. OL1—8C 46
Clyde St. OL7—6M 81
Clyde St. WN7—3H 73
Clyde Ter. M26—4F 40
Clyne Ho. M32—2M 89
Clyne St. M32—1M 89
Clysbarton Ct. SK7—3D 114
Coach Ho. Dri. WN6—3H 33
Coach Ho., The. SK9—7M 119
Coach Rd. M22—5C 112
Coach Rd. M29—1C 74
Coach St. BL2—4G 39
Coach St. M29—5K 55
Coalbrook Wlk. M12—6L 79
(off Aden Clo.)
Coalburn St. M12—9A 80
Coal Pit La. M29—4H 55
(in two parts)
Coal Pit La. OL8—9J 63
Coal Pit La. WN2—7B 54
Coal Pit La. WN7—8E 54
Coal Pit Rd. BL1—3H 21
Coal Rd. BL0—3A 10
Coalshaw Grn. Rd. OL9—5G 63
Coalville Rd. WA11—9D 68
Coatbridge St. M11—5C 80
Cobalt Av. M31—9F 76
Cobb Clo. M8—5E 60
Cobbett's Way. SK9—7F 118
Cobble Bank. M9—5J 61
Cobblers Yd. SK9—8L 119
Cobden Edge Rd. SK6—9M 107
Cobden St. BL1—7D 22
Cobden St. BL7—9D 6
Cobden St. BL9—7A 26
Cobden St. M6—3A 78
Cobden St. M9—8L 61
Cobden St. M26—3F 40
Cobden St. M29—7A 56
Cobden St. OL4—9D 46
Cobden St. OL6—5D 82
Cobden St. OL9—1H 63
Cobden St. OL10—9K 27
Coberley Av. M31—2M 87
Cob Hall Rd. M32—5J 89
Cobham Av. BL3—6D 38
Cobham Av. M10—5C 62
Coblers Hill. OL3—4M 47
Cob Moor Av. WN5—7D 50
Cob Moor Rd. WN5—7D 50
Cobourg St. M1—5G 5 & 7H 79
Coburg Av. M7—1C 4 & 3D 78
Cochrane Av. M12—1L 91
Cochrane St. BL3—4F 38
Cochrane St. OL1—9A 46
Cock Brow. SK14—7J 95
Cock Clod St. M26—6J 41
Cockcroft St. M9—7K 61
Cocker Hill. SK15—5G 83
Cocker Mill La. OL2—4M 45
Cockers La. SK15—7K 83
Cocker St. M28—4G 57
Cockey Moor Rd. BL2 & BL8 —9D 24
Cockhall La. OL12—2C 12
Cock Hollow. BL9—6A 26
Cockinstones. BL8—7H 25
Cockroft Rd. M5—3A 4 & 5B 78
Codale Dri. BL2—9M 23
Coddington Av. M11—7E 80
Code La. BL5—5B 36
Cody Ct. M5—7L 77
Coe La. WA14—5J 109
Coe St. BL3—4F 38
Coffin La. WN2—1D 70
Coghlan Clo. M11—5B 80
Cohen St. M8—8F 60
Coke St. M7—1E 78
Colbeck Clo. M15—6D 4 & 9E 78
Colborne Av. M30—5B 76
Colborne Av. SK5—3F 92
Colborne Av. SK6—3B 106
Colbourne Av. M8—6F 60
Colbourne Gro. SK14—3L 95
Colbourne Wlk. SK14—3L 95
Colburn Clo. WN3—6A 52
Colby Rd. WN3—5B 52
Colby Wlk. M10—9A 62
Colchester Av. BL2—1L 39
Colchester Av. M25—6C 60
Colchester Clo. M23—4L 101
Colchester Dri. BL4—8F 38
Colchester Pl. SK4—2B 104
Colchester St. M10—3K 79
Colchester Wlk. OL1—1M 63
Colclough Clo. M10—1B 80
Coldalhurst La. M29—1B 74
Coldfield Dri. M23—7M 101
Cold Greave Clo. OL16—6C 30
Coldhurst Hollow Est. OL1 —8L 45
Coldhurst St. OL1—9L 45
Coldstone Dri. WN4—4K 69
Coldstream Av. M9—4K 61
Coldstream Ho. M16—1C 90
Coldwall St. OL12—2D 28
Colebrook Dri. M10—1A 80
Colebrook Rd. WA15—7G 101
Coleby Av. M16—2C 90
Coleby Av. M22—3F 112
Coledale Dri. M24—7J 43
Coleford Clo. BL1—3E 38
Coleford Wlk. M16—3E 90
(off Maclure Clo.)
Colegate Cres. M14—6H 91
Colenso Gro. SK4—2B 104
Colenso Rd. BL2—2K 39
Colenso St. OL8—5K 63
Coleport Clo. SK8—3A 114
Coleridge Av. M24—6C 44
Coleridge Av. M26—6E 40
Coleridge Av. WN5—2G 51
Coleridge Clo. SK5—5E 92
Coleridge Dri. OL15—9M 13
Coleridge Pl. WN3—5M 51
Coleridge Rd. BL8—9F 8
Coleridge Rd. M16—3C 90
Coleridge Rd. OL1—5D 46
Coleridge Rd. SK5—5E 92
Coleridge Rd. WN5—7D 50
Coleridge St. M10—3C 80
Coleridge Way. SK5—5E 92
Colerne Way. WN3—6K 51
Colesbourne Clo. M28—2G 57
Coleshill Rise. WN3—6J 51
Coleshill St. M10—4L 79
Colesmere Wlk. M10—7D 62
Cole St. M10—8M 61
Colgate La. M5—9A 78
Colgrove Av. M10—6C 62
Colindale Av. M9—4L 61
Colindale Clo. BL3—4C 38
Colin Rd. SK4—1D 104
Colin St. WN1—8D 34
Colinton Clo. BL1—9D 22
Colinwood Clo. BL9—6M 41
Collard St. M29—4H 55
Coll Dri. M31—1D 88
College Av. M35—7F 80
College Av. OL8—5K 63
College Av. WN1—9C 34
College Clo. BL3—3E 38
College Clo. SK2—7G 105
College Clo. SK9—3F 118
College Croft. M30—5F 76
College Dri. M16—4C 90
College Land. M3—4E 5 & 6F 78
College Rd. M16—3C 90
College Rd. M30—5G 77
College Rd. OL8—4K 63
College Rd. OL12—3D 28
College Rd. WN8—8B 32
College St. WA10—9B 68
College St. WN7—2G 73
College Way. BL3—3D 38
Collen Cres. BL8—4H 25
Collett St. OL1—9C 46
Colley St. M32—1M 89
Colley St. OL16—1G 29
Collie Av. M6—2C 78
Collier Av. OL16—3M 29
Collier Clo. SK14—5L 95
Collier Hill. OL8—5K 63
Collier Hill Av. OL8—5J 63
Collier's Ct. OL11—9H 29
Colliers Row Rd. BL1—5K 21
Collier St. M3—5D 4 & 7E 78
(Manchester)
Collier St. M3—2D 4 & 4E 78
(Salford)
Collier St. M6—1M 77
Collier St. M26—6H 41
Collier St. M27—9E 58
Collier St. SK13—6J 97
Collier St. WN2—2K 53
Collier Wlk. SK14—5L 95
Colliery St. M11—6A 80
(in two parts)
Collin Av. M18—2C 92
Collingburn Av. M5—6A 4 & 8B 78
Collingburn Ct. M5—6A 4 & 8B 78
Colling Clo. M30—5G 87
Collinge Av. M24—9C 44
Collinge St. BL8—6H 25
Collinge St. M24—1D 62
Collinge St. OL2—2B 46
Collinge St. OL10—8J 27
Collinge St. WN2—6G 53
Collingham St. M8—1G 5 & 3G 79
Collings St. BL1—8E 22
Colling St. BL0—6H 9
Collington Clo. M12—1A 92
Collingwood Av. M35—4E 80
Collingwood Clo. SK12—9A 116
Collingwood Dri. M27—9H 59
Collingwood Rd. M19—5M 91
Collingwood St. OL11—1C 44
Collingwood St. WN6—9L 17
Collingwood Way. BL5—8E 36
Collingwood Way. OL1—9M 45
Collins La. BL5—2F 54
Collins St. BL8—6F 24
Collisdene Rd. WN5—2D 50
Collop Dri. OL10—2L 43
Coll's La. OL3—5K 47
Collyhurst Av. M28—6L 57
Collyhurst Rd. M10—1G 5 & 3H 79
Collyhurst St. M10—1H 5 & 3J 79
Colmar Way. SK14—4D 94
Colmore Av. M20—2K 103
Colmore Dri. M9—4A 62
Colmore Gro. BL2—6H 23
Colmore St. BL2—7H 23
Colnbrook Clo. M5—3A 4 & 5B 78
Colne St. OL11—9D 28
Colonel's La. WA12—9F 70
Colonial Rd. SK2—7G 105
Colshaw Clo. E. M26—5F 40
Colshaw Clo. S. M26—5F 40
Colshaw Dri. SK9—2K 119
Colshaw Rd. M23—9A 102
Colshaw Wlk. SK9—2K 119
Colson Dri. M24—1M 61
Colt Hill La. OL3—9M 47
Coltness Wlk. M10—2C 80
Colts Acre. M5—8C 78
(off Bramble Av.)
Coltsfoot Dri. WA14—5B 100
Columbia Av. M18—2F 92
Columbia Rd. BL1—1C 38
Columbia St. OL8—4M 63
Columbine Clo. OL12—8C 12
Columbine St. M11—8D 80
Columbine Wlk. M31—2F 98
Columbus St. WN4—2M 69
(off Priory Rd.)
Colville Dri. BL8—9H 25
Colville Gro. M33—4E 100
Colville Gro. WA15—7G 101
Colville Rd. OL1—8K 45
Colwell Av. M32—4H 89
Colwell Wlk. M9—3H 61
Colwick Av. WA14—7E 100
Colwith Av. BL2—9L 23
Colwood Wlk. M8—1F 78
(off Elizabeth St.)
Colwyn Av. M14—6L 91
Colwyn Av. M24—2A 62
Colwyn Cres. SK5—9F 92
Colwyn Dri. WN2—6C 54
Colwyn Gro. BL1—9D 22
Colwyn Gro. M29—3J 55
Colwyn Rd. M27—9C 58
Colwyn Rd. SK7—4E 114
Colwyn Rd. SK8—3L 113
Colwyn St. M6—4M 77
Colwyn St. OL7—1A 82
Colwyn St. OL9—1K 63
Colwyn St. OL11—8B 28
Colwyn Ter. OL7—1A 82
Colyton Wlk. M22—1F 112
Combe Clo. M11—4B 80
Combe Clo. SK12—4M 117
Combermere Av. M20—7G 91
Combermere Clo. SK8—9M 103
Combermere St. SK16—6C 82
Combs Bank. SK13—5D 96
(off Melandra Castle Rd.)
Combs Fold. SK13—4D 96
(off Brassington Cres.)
Combs Gdns. SK13—5D 96
(off Brassington Cres.)
Combs Gro. SK13—4D 96
(off Brassington Cres.)
Combs Lea. SK13—5D 96
Combs M. SK13—4D 96
(off Brassington Cres.)
Combs Ter. SK13—5D 96
(off Melandra Castle Rd.)
Combs Way. SK13—4D 96
Comer Ter. M33—1G 101
Comet Rd. WN5—9J 33
Comet St. M1—4G 5 & 6H 79
Commercial Av. SK8—7L 113
Commercial Brow. SK14—2E 94
Commercial Rd. OL1—2M 63
Commercial Rd. SK7—1K 115
Commercial St. M15—6D 4 & 8E 78
Commercial St. OL9—2J 63
Commercial St. SK14—3E 94
Commodore Pl. WN5—8L 33
Common La. M29—7A 56
Common La. WN7—3B 72
Common La. N. M31—9H 87
Common Nook. WN2—2G 53
Common Side Rd. M28—9F 56
Common St. BL5—1B 54
Common, The. PR7—6E 18
Como Wlk. M18—9B 80
Compass St. M11—8C 80
Compstall Av. M14—4H 91
Compstall Gro. M18—9E 80
Compstall Rd. SK6—3C 106
(in two parts)
Compton Clo. M31—5J 87
Compton Dri. M23—2A 112
Compton St. SK15—6H 83
Compton Way. M24—1C 62
Comrie Wlk. M23—8A 102
Comus St. M5—5B 4 & 7C 78
Concastrian Ind. Est. M9—9J 61
Concert La. M2—4F 5 & 6G 79
Concord Bus. Pk. M22—3E 112
Concorde Av. WN3—5B 52
Concord Pl. M6—2A 78
Concord Way. SK16—7C 82
(in two parts)
Condor Clo. M35—4J 81
Condor Pl. M6—2A 78
Conduit St. OL1—6D 46
Conduit St. OL6—5C 82
Conduit St. SK14—8F 84
Conewood Wlk. M13—9J 79
Coney Gro. M23—6A 102
Coneymead. SK15—3G 83
Congham Rd. SK3—5C 104
Congleton Av. M14—4G 91
Congleton Clo. SK9—9L 119
Congleton Rd. SK9—8L 119
Congou St. M1—6J 79
Congreave St. OL1—9L 45
Congresbury Rd. WN7—9D 54
Conifer Wlk. M31—2E 98
Conifer Wlk. WN7—2B 72
Coningsby Dri. M9—8K 61
Conisborough. OL11—4E 28
Conisborough Pl. M25—1B 60
Coniston Av. BL4—9E 38
Coniston Av. M9—8K 61
Coniston Av. M25—9M 41
Coniston Av. M28—3G 57
Coniston Av. M29—3K 55
Coniston Av. M33—3J 101
Coniston Av. OL8—5K 63
Coniston Av. PR6—1H 19
Coniston Av. SK14—2C 94
Coniston Av. WN1—6B 34
Coniston Av. WN2—1H 53
Coniston Av. WN4—3B 70
Coniston Av. WN5—1F 50
Coniston Clo. BL0—3J 9
Coniston Clo. BL3—5A 40
Coniston Clo. M34—4H 93
Coniston Clo. OL9—1G 63
Coniston Dri. BL9—2L 41
Coniston Dri. M24—7L 43
Coniston Dri. SK9—8J 113
Coniston Dri. SK15—3G 83
Coniston Dri. WN2—8H 53
Coniston Gro. M28—4G 57
Coniston Gro. OL2—3K 45
Coniston Gro. OL7—3A 82
Coniston Gro. OL10—1K 43
Coniston Gro. WA11—8A 68
Coniston Pk. Dri. WN6—3A 34
Coniston Rd. BL6—7K 19
Coniston Rd. M27—1F 76
Coniston Rd. M29—9A 56
Coniston Rd. M31—1E 98
(Partington)
Coniston Rd. M31—6L 87
(Urmston)
Coniston Rd. M32—3J 89
Coniston Rd. SK5—8F 92
Coniston Rd. SK6—4D 116
Coniston Rd. SK8—7H 103
Coniston Rd. WN2—4L 53
Coniston St. BL1—7F 22
Coniston St. M6—1A 4 & 3B 78
Coniston St. M10—2C 80
Coniston St. WN7—2E 72
Coniston Wlk. WA15—8K 101
Conmere Sq. M15—6E 5 & 8F 78
Connaught Av. M19—7M 91
Connaught Av. M25—9A 42
Connaught Av. OL16—7H 29
Connaught Clo. SK9—3J 119
Connaught Pl. M6—5M 77
Connaught Sq. BL2—8H 23
Connaught St. BL8—9H 25
Connaught St. OL8—2L 63
Connel Clo. BL2—3M 39
Connell Rd. M23—7A 102
Connell Way. OL10—7M 27
Connery Cres. OL6—1D 82
Connie St. M11—7C 80
Connington Av. M9—7K 61
Connington Clo. OL2—5J 45
Connor Way. SK8—9F 102
Conquest Clo. M12—9M 79
Conrad Clo. OL1—5E 46
Conrad Clo. WN3—3A 52
Conrad St. BL1—1E 38
Conran St. M9—9K 61
Consett Av. M23—7A 102
Consiber Clo. BL7—1E 22
Consort Av. OL2—3J 45
Constable Clo. BL1—9D 22
Constable Dri. SK6—5H 107
Constable Dri. SK9—3L 119
Constable St. M18—9E 80
Constable Wlk. M34—7A 94
Constable Wlk. OL1—5D 46
Constance Gdns. M5—6M 77
Constance Rd. BL3—5C 38
Constance Rd. M31—2F 98
Constance St. M15—6D 4 & 8E 78
Constantia St. WN3—4F 52
Constantine Rd. OL16—3F 28
Constantine St. OL4—2D 64
Consul St. M22—4E 102
Convamore Rd. SK7—5D 114
Convent St. OL4—4C 64
Conway Av. BL1—9A 22
Conway Av. M25—1M 59
Conway Av. M27—5H 59
Conway Av. M30—6F 86
Conway Clo. BL0—5H 9
Conway Clo. M16—3B 90
Conway Clo. M24—1A 62
Conway Clo. M25—1M 59
Conway Clo. OL10—7G 27
Conway Clo. WN5—1E 68
Conway Clo. WN7—1L 73
Conway Cres. BL8—9F 8
Conway Dri. BL9—8D 26
Conway Dri. SK7—3J 115
Conway Dri. SK15—4G 83
Conway Dri. WA15—7J 101
Conway Dri. WN2—4K 35
Conway Dri. WN5—2F 68
Conway Gro. OL9—8F 44
Conway Gro. WN7—9L 55
Conway Rd. M31—2D 88
Conway Rd. M33—2K 101
Conway Rd. SK8—2L 113
Conway Rd. WN2—4M 53
Conway Rd. WN4—2E 70
Conway St. BL4—1K 57
Conway St. SK5—1E 104
Conway St. WN5—3J 51
Conway Towers. SK5—7J 93
Conyngham Rd. M14—2K 91
Cook Av. WA11—8L 69
Cooke St. BL4—1L 57
Cooke St. BL6—6D 20
Cooke St. M34—3L 93
Cooke St. M35—8F 62
Cooke St. SK7—1K 115
Cooke St. SK14—1F 94
Cooks Croft. OL4—1G 65
Cook St. BL9—8M 25
Cook St. M3—3D 4 & 5E 78
Cook St. M30—5C 76
Cook St. M34—9M 81
Cook St. OL4—1C 64
Cook St. OL16—1H 29
Cook St. SK3—4E 104
Cook St. WN2—7G 53
Cook St. WN7—2F 72
Cook Ter. OL16—1H 29
Cook Ter. SK16—6B 82
(off Astley St.)
Cooling La. M29—8L 55
Coomassie St. M26—6G 41
Coomassie St. OL10—8J 27
Coombe Clo. M29—8B 56
Coombes Av. SK6—8F 106
Coombes Av. SK14—5F 94
Coombes La. SK14—9C 96
Coombes St. SK2—8H 105
Co-operation St. M35—7F 62
Co-operative St. M6—5M 77
Co-operative St. M26—5G 41
Co-operative St. M28—3E 56
Co-operative St. OL2—2B 46
Co-operative St. OL3—9B 48
Co-operative St. OL4—2F 64
Co-operative St. SK7—1L 115
Co-operative St. WN7—2D 72
Cooper Fold. M24—5A 44
Cooper Ho. M15—9G 79
Cooper La. M9—3K 61
Cooper La. M24—6M 43
Cooper La. WA11—9H 69
Cooper La. WN4 & WA11—9J 69
Cooper Rd. M30—7E 86
Coopers Fold. SK8—6M 113
Coopers Glen. WN2—9G 35
Cooper's La. PR7—2B 16
Coopers Row. BL1—2F 38
Coopers Row. WN1—9C 34
Cooper St. BL1—9F 22
Cooper St. BL6—6B 20
Cooper St. BL9—8L 25
Cooper St. M2—4E 5 & 6G 79
Cooper St. M32—5K 89
Cooper St. OL4—1G 65
Cooper St. OL12—7K 13
Cooper St. SK1—6F 104
Cooper St. SK7—1M 115
Cooper St. SK13—5H 97
Cooper St. SK16—6B 82
Cooper Ter. OL16—2H 29
Coop St. BL1—6E 22
Coop St. M4—3G 5 & 5H 79
Coop St. WN1—8D 34
Coop Ter. OL16—3K 29
Copage Dri. SK6—1A 106
Cope Bank. BL1—9C 22
Cope Bank E. BL1—9C 22
Cope Bank W. BL1—8B 22
Cope Clo. M11—8E 80
Copeland Av. M27—7J 59
Copeland Clo. M24—8J 43
Copeland M. BL1—2A 38
Copeland St. SK14—1D 94
Copeman Clo. M13—9J 79
Copenhagen Sq. OL16—2G 29
Copenhagen St. OL16—2G 29
Cope St. BL1—9C 22
Copgrove Rd. M21—7B 90
Copgrove Wlk. M22—5E 112
Copley Av. SK15—5J 83
Copley Pk. M. SK15—5J 83
Copley Rd. M21—4A 90
Copley St. OL2—1C 46
Copley St. SK15—5J 83
Copperas Clo. WN6—2G 33
Copperas La. M35—7E 80
Copperas La. WN2—3G 35
(Haigh)
Copperas La. WN2—9H 19
(Little Scotland)
Copperas St. M4—3F 5 & 5G 79
Copperbeech Clo. M22—4E 102
Copperbeech Dri. WN6—3B 34
Copperfield. WN1—7C 34
Copperfield Ct. WA14—1C 110
Copperfield Rd. SK8—7B 114
Copperfield Rd. SK12—1K 121
Copperfields. BL6—5H 37
Copperfields. SK9—3J 119
Copper La. M25—2G 59
Copperways. M20—9H 91
Coppice Av. M33—3D 100
Coppice Clo. SK6—9B 94
Coppice Clo. SK12—6G 117
Coppice Dri. M22—4D 102
Coppice Dri. OL12—4C 12
Coppice Dri. SK12—6G 117
Coppice Dri. WN3—5M 51
Coppice Dri. WN5—6D 50
Coppice La. SK12—6G 117
Coppice Rd. SK12—9A 116
Coppice St. BL9—7C 26
Coppice St. OL8—3K 63
(in two parts)
Coppice, The. BL0—7G 9
Coppice, The. BL2—5K 23
Coppice, The. M24—2B 62
Coppice, The. M27—2C 76
Coppice, The. M28—3M 57
Coppice, The. WA15—4H 111
Coppice Wlk. M34—4K 93
Copping St. M12—9M 79
Coppins, The. SK9—7E 118
Coppleridge Dri. M8—7G 61
Copplestone Dri. M33—9C 88
Coppull Hall La. PR7—1A 18
Coppull La. WN1—7D 34
Coppull Moor La. PR7—4K 17
Cop Rd. OL1—5C 46
Copse Av. M22—1E 112
Copse Dri. BL9—4M 25
Copse, The. BL7—9L 7
Copse, The. SK6—2J 117
Copse, The. WA15—5K 111
Copse Wlk. OL15—6M 13
Copson St. M20—7H 91
Copster Av. OL8—5L 63
Copster Hill Rd. OL8—5L 63
Copster Pl. OL8—5L 63
Copthall La. M8—8F 60
Copthorne Clo. OL10—1K 43
Copthorne Cres. M13—4L 91
Copthorne Dri. BL2—3L 39
Copthorne Wlk. BL8—5F 24
Coptrod Head Clo. OL12—7E 12
Coral Av. SK8—3A 114
Coral Gro. WN7—3E 72
Coral Rd. SK8—3A 114
Coral St. M13—6H 5 & 8J 79
Coral St. WN6—6A 34
Coram St. M18—9F 80
Corbar Rd. SK2—8G 105
Corbett Ct. WN2—3L 53
Corbett St. M11—5A 80
(in two parts)
Corbett St. OL16—2G 29
Corbridge Wlk. M8—1H 79
Corbrook Rd. OL9—8E 44
Corby St. M12—9A 80
Corcoran Clo. OL10—7J 27
Corcoran Dri. SK6—3F 106
Corda Av. M22—5D 102
Corday La. M25—8D 42
Cordingley Av. M35—7F 80
Cordova Av. M34—3F 92
Corelli St. M10—3M 79
Corfe Clo. M31—5J 87
Corfe Clo. WN2—4K 35
Corfe Cres. SK7—3J 115
Corhampton Cres. M29—3L 55
Corinthian Av. M7—2C 78
Corinth Wlk. M28—6K 57
Corkland Clo. OL6—5D 82
Corkland Rd. M21—6B 90
Corkland St. OL6—5E 82
Corks La. SK12—7L 117
Cork St. BL9—8A 26
Cork St. M12—7K 79
Cork St. OL6—4C 82
Corless Fold. M29—2C 74
Corley Av. SK3—6M 103
Corley Wlk. M11—6M 79
Cormallon Gro. M35—9G 63
Cormorant Clo. M28—5J 57
Cormorant Wlk. M12—9A 80
Cornall St. BL8—7J 25
Cornbrook Arches. M15—6B 4 & 8C 78
Cornbrook Clo. OL12—5J 13
Cornbrook Ct. M15—9D 78
Cornbrook Gro. M16—1D 90
Cornbrook Pk. Rd. M15—9C 78
Cornbrook Rd. M15—6B 4 & 9C 78
Cornbrook St. M16 & M15 —1D 90
Cornbrook Way. M16—1D 90
Corn Clo. M13—1J 91
Cornell St. M4—3G 5 & 5H 79
Corner Croft. SK9—7G 119
Corner Ga. BL5—3E 54
Corner La. WN7—5D 54
Corner St. OL6—5C 82
Cornerways. SK14—1G 97
(off Albert St.)
Cornet St. M7—1D 78
Corn Exchange. M4—3E 5 & 5F 78
Cornfield. SK15—8L 83
Cornfield Clo. BL9—3M 25
Cornfield Clo. M33—2M 101
Cornfield Dri. M22—1C 112
Cornfield Rd. SK6—2E 106
Cornfield St. OL16—5M 29
Cornford Av. M18—3B 92
Cornhey Rd. M33—3C 100
Cornhill Av. M31—3B 88
Corn Hill La. M34—1G 93
Cornhill Rd. M31—2B 88
Cornhill St. OL1—7D 46
Cornishway. M22—3C 112
Cornish Way. OL2—6M 45
Cornishway Ind. Est. M22 —4D 112
Corn Mill Clo. OL12—7J 13
Corn St. M35—1C 80
Corn St. OL4—1A 64
Corn St. SK13—5L 97
Corn St. WN7—2D 72
Cornwall Av. BL5—9M 37
Cornwall Av. M19—6B 92
Cornwall Av. M29—5A 56
Cornwall Clo. BL9—1A 42
Cornwall Clo. SK6—5E 116
Cornwall Cres. OL3—5B 48
Cornwall Cres. SK5—8J 93
Cornwall Cres. WN1—9B 18
Cornwall Dri. BL9—1M 41
Cornwall Dri. WN2—2M 53
Cornwallis Rd. WN3—3M 51
Cornwall Pl. WN5—2J 51
Cornwall Rd. M30—9D 86
Cornwall Rd. M35—4G 81
Cornwall Rd. SK8—4H 113
Cornwall St. M11—8D 80
Cornwall St. M30—6C 76
Cornwall St. OL9—3H 63
Cornwell Clo. SK9—3K 119
Cornwood Clo. M8—9F 60
Corona Av. OL8—5K 63
Corona Av. SK14—3E 94
Coronation Av. M29—3J 55
Coronation Av. OL10—1L 43
Coronation Av. SK14—5E 94
Coronation Av. SK16—9F 82
Coronation Av. WA3—8J 73
Coronation Bldgs. M4—1G 5 & 3H 79
Coronation Dri. WA11—8A 70
Coronation Dri. WN7—1K 73
Coronation Gdns. M26—4E 40
Coronation Rd. M26—4E 40
Coronation Rd. M35—4F 80
(Droylsden)
Coronation Rd. M35—1E 80
(Failsworth)
Coronation Rd. OL6—1C 82
Coronation Rd. WN6—6K 33
Coronation Sq. BL3—6B 40
Coronation Sq. M12—5H 5 & 7J 79
Coronation Sq. M34—8K 81
Coronation St. BL1—3F 38
(off Gt. Moor St.)
Coronation St. M5—5A 4 & 7B 78
Coronation St. M11—7C 80
Coronation St. M27—7G 59
Coronation St. M34—3J 93
Coronation St. SK5—1E 104
Coronation St. WN3—5F 52
(Ince)
Coronation St. WN3—2B 52
(Poolstock)
Coronation St. WN4—1K 69
Coronation Vs. OL12—1D 12
Coronation Wlk. M26—4E 40
Coronation Wlk. WN5—3D 68
Corporation Cotts. M31—8J 87
Corporation Rd. M30—5E 76
Corporation Rd. M34—1K 93
Corporation Rd. OL11—4D 28
Corporation St. BL1—2F 38
Corporation St. M4—3E 5 & 5F 78
Corporation St. M24—9A 44
Corporation St. SK1—3F 104
Corporation St. SK14—4D 94
Corporation St. SK15—6G 83
Corporation St. WN3—2B 52
Corporation Yd. SK4—2A 104
Corporation Yd. SK5—6F 92
Corran Clo. M30—5B 76
Corrie Clo. M34—5M 93
Corrie Cres. BL4—3D 58
Corrie Dri. BL4—4D 58
Corrie Rd. M27—5G 59
Corrie St. M28—4G 57
Corrie Way. SK6—9L 93
Corrigan St. M18—9E 80
Corringham Rd. M19—7C 92
Corring Way. BL1—6H 23
Corrin Rd. BL2—4H 39
Corris Av. M9—3G 61
Corry St. OL10—8L 27
Corsey Rd. WN2—4L 53
Corsock Dri. WN1—8E 34
Corson St. BL3—7K 39
(in two parts)
Corston Gro. BL6—9K 19
Corston Wlk. M10—1B 80
Corwen Clo. OL8—6H 63
Corwen St. M9—8L 61
Cosgrove Cres. M35—2E 80
Cosgrove Rd. M35—2E 80
Cosham Rd. M22—1F 112
Costabeck Wlk. M10—3D 80
Costessey Way. WN3—5J 51
Costobadie Clo. SK14—3M 95
Cosworth Clo. WN7—3H 73
Cotaline Clo. OL11—7B 28
Cotall Wlk. M7—1D 4 & 3E 78
Cotefield Av. BL3—6F 38
Cotefield Clo. SK6—8F 106
Cotefield Rd. M22—2B 112
Cote Grn. Rd. SK6—4H 107
Cote Grn La. SK6—4H 107
Cote La. OL3—1B 48
Cote La. OL5—5L 65
Cote La. OL15—5M 13
Cotford Rd. BL1—5F 22
Cotham St. M3—1E 5 & 3F 78
Cotman Dri. SK6—5J 107
Cotswold Av. M31—3M 87
Cotswold Av. OL2—1M 45
Cotswold Av. OL9—3G 63
Cotswold Av. SK7—3H 115
Cotswold Av. WA3—9K 71
Cotswold Av. WN5—3H 51
Cotswold Clo. BL0—7J 9
Cotswold Clo. M25—3C 60
Cotswold Clo. SK13—6G 97
Cotswold Cres. BL8—7G 25
Cotswold Cres. OL16—3A 30
Cotswold Dri. BL6—5C 20
Cotswold Dri. M6—4M 77
Cotswold Dri. OL2—6H 45
Cotswold Rd. SK4—2D 104
Cottage Gdns. SK6—2K 105
Cottage La. SK13—5E 96
Cottage, The. OL10—5J 43
Cottage Wlk. OL12—7C 12
Cottam Cres. SK6—5H 107
Cottam Gro. M27—9G 59
Cottam St. BL8—7J 25
Cottam St. OL1—9K 45
Cottenham La. M7 & M3—1D 4 & 3E 78
Cottenham St. M13—9H 79
Cotteridge Wlk. M11—7M 79
Cotterill Clo. M23—4J 101
Cotter St. M12—6H 5 & 8J 79
Cottesmore Dri. M8—8J 61
Cottesmore Gdns. WA15 —4J 111
Cottesmore Way. WA3—6H 71
Cottingham Dri. OL6—3C 82
Cottonfield Rd. M20—8J 91
Cotton Hill. M20—9J 91
Cotton La. M20—8H 91
Cotton La. OL11—6C 28
Cotton St. BL1—8D 22
Cotton St. M4—3G 5 & 5H 79
Cotton St. SK14—3E 94
Cotton St. WN7—2D 72
Cotton St. E. OL6—5A 82
Cotton St. W. OL6—5A 82
Cotton Tree Clo. OL4—9D 46
Cotton Tree St. SK4—4E 104
Cottonwood Dri. M33—9C 88
Cottrell Rd. WA15—5K 111
Cottrill St. M6—3A 4 & 5B 78
Coucill Sq. BL4—9L 39
Coulsden Dri. M9—5K 61
Coulthart St. OL6—4B 82
Coulthurst St. BL0—5H 9
Coulton Clo. OL1—9A 46
Coulton Wlk. M6—5M 77
Coultshead Av. WN5—1E 68
Council Av. WN4—4B 70
Councillor La. SK8—7M 103
Councillor St. M12—6L 79
Countess Av. SK8—7L 113
Countess Gro. M7—1C 4
Countess La. M26—4D 40
Countess Pl. M25—4C 60
Countess Rd. M20—2H 103
Countess St. OL6—5D 82
Countess St. SK2—8F 104
Counthill Dri. M8—6E 60
Counthill Rd. OL4—8D 46
Counting Ho. Rd. SK12—7L 117
Count St. OL16—5G 29
County Av. OL6—3E 82
County Police St. WN2—1F 52
County Rd. M28—4G 57
County St. M2—4E 5 & 6F 78
County St. OL8—6J 63
Coupland Dri. OL4—5F 46
Coupland Rd. WN2—4C 54
Couplands, The. PR7—2L 17
Coupland St. M15—1G 91
Coupland St. OL12—3C 12
Coupland St. E. M15—9G 79
Courage Low La. WN6—6D 16
Courier Pl. WN5—8L 33
Courier St. M18—8E 80
Course View. OL4—5E 64
Court Dri. M10—3E 80
Courtfield Av. M9—4K 61
Courthill St. SK1—5G 105
Court Ho. Way. OL10—8K 27
(off Longford St.)
Court St. BL2—2G 39
Court St. OL3—9B 48
Court, The. M25—4B 60
Cousin Fields. BL7—3J 23
Covall Wlk. M8—1H 79
Covell Rd. SK12—7L 115
Covent Garden. SK1—4F 104
Coventry Av. SK3—6M 103
Coventry Gro. OL9—8G 45
Coventry Rd. M26—4F 40
Coventry St. OL11—4F 28
Coverdale Av. BL1—1A 38
Coverdale Av. OL2—4J 45
Coverdale Clo. OL10—9J 27
Coverdale Cres. M12—9K 79
Coverdale Rd. BL5—9D 36
Coverham Av. OL4—4D 64
Coverhill Rd. OL4—3H 65
Covert Rd. M22—8E 102
Covert Rd. OL4—5D 64
Cove, The. WA15—1F 110
Cowan St. M10—5K 79
Cowbrook Av. SK13—5M 97
Cowbrook Ct. SK13—5M 97
Cowbrook Pk. SK13—5M 97
Cowburn St. M3—2E 5 & 4F 78
Cowburn St. OL10—9L 27
Cowburn St. WN2—1M 53
Cowburn St. WN7—1D 72
Cowdals Rd. BL6—5H 37
Cowesby St. M14—3G 91
Cowhill La. OL6—4C 82
Cowie St. OL2—1B 46
Cow La. BL3—7B 38
Cow La. M5—4B 4 & 6C 78
Cow La. M33—8L 89
Cow La. M35—9E 62
Cow La. OL4—1C 64
Cow La. SK7—9K 105
Cow La. SK9—4J 119
Cow La. WA14—8L 99
Cow La. WA15—7F 110
Cow Lees. BL5—8G 37
Cowley Gro. SK14—3M 95
Cowley Rd. BL1—5F 22
Cowling St. M27—8M 59
Cowling St. OL8—4M 63
Cowling St. WN3—2B 52
Cowlishaw. OL2—4A 46
Cowlishaw La. OL2—4A 46
Cowlishaw Rd. SK14 & SK6 —9F 94
Cowm Pk. Way N. OL12—1C 12
Cowm Pk. Way S. OL12—3C 12
Cowm Top La. OL11—9D 28
(in two parts)
Cowper Av. M29—3K 55
Cowper St. M24—9D 44
Cowper St. OL6—4C 82
Cowper St. WN7—2D 72
Cowper Wlk. M11—6M 79
Coxfield. WN6—2D 32
Cox Grn. Clo. BL7—8D 6
Cox Grn. Rd. BL7—8D 6
Coxton Rd. M22—3E 112
Coxwold Gro. BL3—6C 38
Crabbe St. M4—1F 5 & 4G 79
Crab La. M9—4H 61
Crabtree Av. SK12—7L 117
Crabtree Av. WA15—5K 111
Crabtree La. M11—7D 80
(in two parts)
Crab Tree La. M29—5K 55
Crabtree La. WA16 & WA13 —7A 108
Crabtree Rd. OL1—9B 46
Crabtree Rd. WN5—1K 51
Crabtree St. BL9—7B 26
Craddock Rd. M33—3J 101
Craddock St. OL5—7H 65
Cradley Av. M11—7D 80
Crag Av. BL9—9K 9
Cragg Pl. OL15—6B 14
Cragg Rd. OL1—7F 44
(in two parts)
Crag Gro. WA11—6B 68
Crag La. BL9—9K 9
Craig Av. BL8—9H 25
Craig Av. M31—3A 88
Craig Clo. SK4—4B 104
Craigend Dri. M9—9L 61
Craig Hall. M30—7F 86
Craighall Av. M19—6M 91
Craighall Rd. BL1—4E 22
Craigie St. M8—2F 78
Craiglands. OL16—8H 29
Craiglands Av. M10—1A 80
Craigmore Av. M20—1D 102
Craigner Ct. M27—9J 59
Craig Rd. M18—2C 92
Craig Rd. SK4—4M 103
Craig Wlk. OL8—3L 63
Craigweil Av. M20—2J 103
Craigwell Rd. M25—6E 60
Craigwell Wlk. M13—6G 5 & 8H 79
Crail Pl. OL10—9F 26
Cramer St. M10—2M 79
Crammond Clo. M10—1D 80
Cramond Clo. BL1—9D 22
Cramond Wlk. BL1—9D 22
Crampton Dri. WA15—4J 111
Crampton La. M31—7J 87
(in three parts)
Cranage Rd. M19—6B 92
Cranage Way. SK9—7K 113
Cranark Clo. BL1—2A 38
Cranberry Av. WN6—6M 33
Cranberry Clo. WA14—5B 100
Cranberry Rd. M31—2F 98
Cranberry St. OL4—2B 64
Cranborne Clo. BL6—9F 20
Cranbourne Av. SK8—2B 114
Cranbourne Clo. OL7—3A 82
Cranbourne Ct. SK4—1B 104
Cranbourne Rd. M16—2C 90
Cranbourne Rd. M21—6B 90
Cranbourne Rd. OL7—3A 82
Cranbourne Rd. OL11—4L 27
Cranbourne Rd. SK4—1B 104
Cranbourne St. M5—4B 4 & 6C 78
Cranbourne Ter. OL6—2B 82
Cranbrook Av. WN4—3A 70
Cranbrook Clo. BL1—9F 22
(off Lindfield Dri.)
Cranbrook Dri. M25—6C 60
Cranbrook Pl. OL4—2C 64
Cranbrook Rd. M18—3E 92
Cranbrook Rd. M30—3A 76
Cranbrook St. M26—4J 41
Cranbrook St. OL4—2B 64
Cranbrook St. OL7—3B 82
Cranbrook Wlk. OL9—2G 63
Cranbrook Way. WN1—5B 34
Cranby St. WN2—3K 53
Crandon Ct. M27—6G 59
Crandon Dri. M20—5J 103
Crane St. BL3—6B 38
Crane St. M12—5H 5 & 7J 79
Crane St. PR7—4K 17
Cranfield Rd. BL6—2D 36
Cranfield Rd. WN3—5A 52
Cranfield Wlk. M10—5L 79
Cranford Av. M20—1K 103
Cranford Av. M25—7L 41
Cranford Av. M32—3M 89
Cranford Av. M33—8J 89
Cranford Clo. M25—7L 41
Cranford Clo. M27—1H 77
Cranford Dri. M30—3F 86
Cranford Gdns. M31—3L 87
Cranford Gdns. SK6—6F 106
Cranford Rd. M31—3L 87
Cranford Rd. SK9—2G 119
Cranford St. BL3—7C 38
Cranham Av. WA3—8L 71
Cranham Clo. BL8—7H 25
Cranham Clo. M28—2G 57
Cranham Rd. M23—2A 112
Crank Rd. WA11 & WN1—9A 50
Crank Rd. WN5—7D 50
Crankwood Rd. WN2 & WN7 —1H 71
Cranleigh. WN6—1M 33
Cranleigh Av. SK4—1M 103
Cranleigh Clo. BL6—9K 19
Cranleigh Dri. M28—8L 57
Cranleigh Dri. M29—8B 56
Cranleigh Dri. M33—4J 101
(Brooklands)
Cranleigh Dri. M33—9G 89
(Sale)
Cranleigh Dri. SK7—4A 116
Cranleigh Dri. SK8—7M 103
Cranlington Dri. M8—1F 78
Cranmer Ct. OL10—9J 27
Cranmere Av. M19—4C 92
Cranmere Dri. M33—3D 100
Cranmer Rd. M20—1H 103
Cranshaw St. M29—8D 56
Cranstal Dri. WN2—3A 54
Cranston Dri. M20—5H 103
Cranston Dri. M33—2L 101
Cranston Gro. SK8—8F 102
Cranswick St. M14—3G 91
Crantock Dri. SK8—4J 113
Crantock Dri. SK15—4K 83
Crantock St. M12—3B 92
Cranwell Dri. M19—1L 103
Cranworth Av. M29—1A 74
Cranworth St. SK15—6H 83
Craston Rd. M13—4L 91
Crathie Ct. BL1—9B 22
Craven Av. M5—5A 4 & 7B 78
Craven Av. WA3—8L 71
Craven Clo. M5—5A 4 & 7B 78
Craven Ct. BL6—8D 20
Craven Dri. M5—9A 78
Craven Dri. WA14—5C 100
Craven Gdns. OL11—5E 28
Cravenhurst Av. M10—3B 80
Craven Pl. BL1—8L 21
Craven Pl. M11—5C 80
Craven Rd. SK5—8F 92
Craven Rd. WA14—6C 100
(in two parts)
Craven St. BL6—8D 20
Craven St. BL9—7B 26
Craven St. M5—4B 4 & 6C 78
Craven St. M6—1M 77
Craven St. M35—6G 81
Craven St. OL1—8L 45
Craven St. OL6—1D 82
Craven Ter. M33—1J 101
Cravenwood Rd. M8—8G 61
Crawford Av. BL2—3H 39
Crawford Av. M28—8M 57
Crawford Av. M29—6M 55
Crawford Av. PR7—5E 18
Crawford Av. WN2—4J 35
Crawford Clo. WN2—4J 35
Crawford Sq. OL10—9G 27
Crawford St. BL2—3H 39
Crawford St. M10—2C 80
Crawford St. M30—4D 76
Crawford St. OL6—5D 82
Crawford St. OL16—5G 29
Crawford St. WN1—9C 34
Crawley Av. M22—1D 112
Crawley Av. M30—4G 77
Crawley Clo. M29—7C 56
Crawley Gro. SK2—6H 105
Crawley Way. OL9—2G 63
Craybridge Rd. M12—9K 79
Craydon St. M11—7B 80
Crayfield Rd. M19—6B 92
Crayford Rd. M10—3B 80
Cray, The. OL16—4L 29
Cray Wlk. M13—6G 5 & 8H 79
Creation Way. M24—5J 43
Creden Av. M22—1F 112
Crediton Clo. M15—1F 90
Crediton Clo. WA14—7B 100
Crediton Dri. BL2—2A 40
Crediton Dri. WN2—7G 53
Creel Clo. M9—4H 61
Cresbury St. M12—7K 79
Crescent. M5—3A 4 & 5B 78
Crescent Av. BL1—1D 38
Crescent Av. BL4—2J 57
Crescent Av. BL5—9A 38
Crescent Av. M8—8G 61
Crescent Av. M25—6B 60
Crescent Av. M27—8J 59
Crescent Av. WN4—3A 70
Crescent Clo. SK3—8F 104
Crescent Clo. SK16—6C 82
Crescent Ct. M21—5M 89
Crescent Ct. M33—2H 101
Crescent Dri. M28—3H 57
Crescent Gro. M19—5A 92
Crescent Gro. M25—6B 60
Crescent Gro. SK8—7J 103
Crescent Pk. SK4—3B 104
Crescent Range. M14—3J 91
Crescent Rd. BL3—5G 39
Crescent Rd. BL4—2M 57
Crescent Rd. BL6—1E 36
Crescent Rd. M8—8F 60
Crescent Rd. OL9—6E 62
Crescent Rd. OL11—6B 28
Crescent Rd. SK1—2H 105
Crescent Rd. SK8—7J 103
Crescent Rd. SK9—7M 119
Crescent Rd. SK16—6C 82
Crescent Rd. WA14—7A 100
Crescent Rd. WA15—2E 110
Crescent Rd. WA16—9H 109
Crescent St. M8—8J 61
Crescent, The. BL2—6M 23
Crescent, The. BL3—7B 40
Crescent, The. BL5—1E 54
Crescent, The. BL6—9E 20
Crescent, The. BL7—3G 23
Crescent, The. M19—5A 92
Crescent, The. M24—9L 43
Crescent, The. M25—4B 60
Crescent, The. M26—4D 40
Crescent, The. M30—2H 87
Crescent, The. M31—4M 87
Crescent, The. M35—6F 80
Crescent, The. OL5—7H 65
Crescent, The. OL12—3C 12
Crescent, The. SK3—9G 105
Crescent, The. SK6—1K 105
Crescent, The. SK8—7J 103
Crescent, The. SK16—7C 82
Crescent, The. WA13—2A 10
Crescent, The. WA14—8A 10
Crescent, The. WA15—6F 10
Crescent, The. WA16—9H 10
Crescent, The. WN2—1H 53
Crescent, The. WN5—2K 51
Crescent View. SK16—6C 82
(off Astley St.)
Crescent Way. SK3—8G 105
Cresgarth Ho. SK3—9G 105
Cressell Pk. WN6—9H 17
Cressfield Way. M21—7D 90
Cressingham Rd. BL3—5A 3
Cressingham Rd. M32—4H 8
Cressington Clo. M5—5L 77
Cresswell Gro. M20—9G 91
Crestfield. M28—4G 57
Crestfold. M28—4G 57
Crest St. M3—2F 5 & 4G 79
Crest, The. M35—8G 81
Crest, The. OL2—3A 46
Crestwood Av. WN3—5L 51
Crestwood Wlk. M10—1J 79
Crete St. OL8—4M 63
Crewe Rd. M23—5L 101
Crib Fold. OL3—7A 48
Crib La. OL3—7A 48
Criccieth Av. WN2—4K 35
Criccieth Rd. SK3—6A 104
Criccieth Way. M16—2F 90
Crickets La. OL6—4C 82
Cricket St. BL3—4D 38
Cricket St. M34—2A 94
Cricket View. OL16—5M 29
Cricklewood Rd. M22—2C 1
Crimble La. OL11 & OL10—5
Crimbles St. OL4—9E 46
(in two parts)
Crimble St. OL12—3D 28
Crime La. M35 & OL8—9K 6
Crimsworth Av. M16—4B 9
Crinan Sq. OL10—9F 26
Crinan Wlk. M10—4K 79
Crinan Way. BL2—3M 39
Cringle Clo. BL3—5L 37
Cringle Dri. SK8—1J 113
Cringleford Wlk. M12—1L 9
Cringle Hall Rd. M19—6M 9
Cringle Rd. M19—7B 92
Cringle St. M10—1A 80
Crippen St. M29—7G 55
Cripplegate. WN6—8F 16
Cripple Ga. La. OL11—9E 2
Crispin Rd. M22—4E 112
Critchley Clo. SK14—5F 94
Criterion St. SK5—4F 92
Croal Av. WN2—6G 53
Croal St. BL1—3D 38
Croal Wlk. M25—8B 42
Croasdale St. BL1—9F 22
(in two parts)
Crocker Wlk. M9—9L 61
Crocus St. BL1—6F 22
Crocus Wlk. M7—1D 78
(off Hilton St. N.)
Croftacres. BL0—1K 9
Croft Av. M25—9F 42
Croft Av. M29—6K 55
Croft Av. WA3—5F 70
Croft Bank. M7—2C 78
Croft Bank. M18—1E 92
Croft Bank. OL12—1D 12
Croft Bank. SK15—3K 83
Croft Brow. OL8—6L 63
Croft Clo. WA15—6J 111
Croft Dri. BL8—4E 24
Crofters Brook. M26—5J 4
Crofters Grn. SK9—5F 118
Crofters Hall Wlk. M10—9
Crofters, The. M33—2M 10
Croft Ga. BL2—6L 23
Croft Gates Rd. M24—1K 6
Croft Gro. M28—3F 56
Crofthead. OL15—4B 14
Croft Head Dri. OL16—3M
Crofthill Ct. OL12—7K 13
Croft Hill Rd. M10—7A 62
Croftlands. BL0—8G 9
Croftlands Rd. M22—9E 1
Croft La. BL3—4H 39
Croft La. BL9—4A 42
Croft La. M26—5J 41
Croft Mnr. SK13—5L 97
Crofton Av. WA15—4G 10
Crofton St. M14—3H 91
Crofton St. M16—2D 90
Crofton St. OL8—5L 63
(in two parts)
Croft Pl. M29—8M 55
Croft Rd. M33—3K 101
Croft Rd. SK8—1B 114
Croft Rd. SK9—7E 118
Crofts Bank Rd. M31—2C
Croftside Av. M28—5L 57
Croftside Clo. M28—5L 57
Croftside Gro. M28—5L 57
Croft Sq. OL12—8J 13
Croft St. BL3—5H 39
Croft St. BL9—8A 26
Croft St. M7—2C 78
Croft St. M11—5B 80
Croft St. M28—3F 56
Croft St. M35—7G 63
Croft St. OL5—8J 65
Croft St. OL12—8J 13
Croft St. SK14—4C 94
Croft St. SK15—5H 83
Croft St. WA3—7G 7
Croft, The. BL9—3A 42
Croft, The. OL8—6L 63
Croft, The. SK2—7H 105
Croft, The. SK14—9G 85
Croft, The. WN5—5D 50
Cromar Rd. SK7—1M 115
Cromarty Av. OL9—5F 62
Cromarty Sq. OL10—9G 2
Cromarty Wlk. M11—6M
Crombie Av. M22—6D 10
Crombouke Dri. WN7—7
Crombouke Fold. M28—
Cromdale Av. BL1—1B 3
Cromdale Av. SK7—1M 1
Cromedale Cres. WN6—
Cromer Av. BL2—9J 23
Cromer Av. M20—8H 91
Cromer Av. M34—3G 93
Cromer Dri. M29—6F 54
Cromer Ind. Est. M24—8
Cromer Rd. BL8—5J 25
(in two parts)
Cromer Rd. M33—2J 101
Cromer Rd. SK8—7L 103
Cromer Rd. WN3—4L 51
Cromer St. M11—6D 80
Cromer St. M24—8E 44
Cromer St. OL12—2E 28
Cromer St. SK1—3H 105
Cromford Av. M32—3H 8
Cromford Bank. SK13—4
(off Grassmoor Cres.)
Cromford Clo. BL1—9E 2
Cromford Clo. SK13—4D
(off Grassmoor Cres.)
Cromford Ct. M4—5G 79
(off Arndale Cen.)
Cromford Courts. M4—3
Cromford Dri. WN5—3H
Cromford Fold. SK13—4
(off Grassmoor Cres.)
Cromford Gdns. BL1—8
Cromford Grn. SK13—4D
(off Grassmoor Cres.)
Cromford Gro. SK13—4D
(off Grassmoor Cres.)
Cromford Lea. SK13—4
Cromford Pl. SK13—4D
(off Grassmoor Cres.)
Cromford St. OL1—9A 4
Cromford Way. SK13—4
Cromhall Wlk. M8—1G 7

132 Greater Manchester

nhurst St. M8—7G 61
nley Dri. SK6—6E 116
nley Rd. SK2—1G 115
nley Rd. SK6—5E 116
npton Av. BL2—1L 39
npton Av. OL16—7H 29
npton Clo. BL1—6G 23
npton Clo. M26—9H 41
npton Clo. SK6—6F 106
npton Ho. M27—8E 58
npton Ho. WN1—9D 34
npton Rd. BL6—1F 36
npton Rd. M19—6A 92
npton Rd. M26—9A 40
nptons St. OL2—6L 45
npton St. BL1—1G 39
npton St. BL4—1L 57
npton St. BL9—8L 25
npton St. M27—8E 58
npton St. M28—3D 56
eenheys)
npton St. M28—6M 57
alkden)
npton St. OL1—9L 45
npton St. OL2—6K 45
oyton, in three parts)
npton St. OL2—2B 46
naw)
npton St. OL6—3E 82
pton St. OL9—1J 63
pton St. WN1—9C 34
pton St. WN2—4H 53
pton St. WN3—5F 52
pton Vale. BL2—1K 39
pton Way. BL1 & BL2
—6F 22
pton Way. OL2—3B 46
well Av. M16—4C 90
well Av. SK6—6D 106
well Av. SK8—7G 103
well Ct. M6—1A 4 & 3B 78
well Ct. M30—7E 86
well Gro. M7—2C 78
well Gro. M19—5A 92
well Range. M14—4K 91
well Rd. M6—1A 4 & 3A 78
well Rd. M25—4C 60
estwich)
well Rd. M25—7K 41
hitefield)
well Rd. M27—7E 58
well Rd. M30—5C 76
cles)
well Rd. M30—7E 86
am)
well Rd. M32—5L 89
well Rd. OL2—3J 45
well Rd. SK6—8K 93
well Rd. SK7—6D 114
well St. BL1—2E 38
well St. OL1—2M 63
well St. OL10—9K 27
well St. SK4—2D 104
ale Wlk. M13—9J 79
Watkin Clo.)
all St. M14—3G 91
field Wlk. M16—3F 90
eyshaw Rd. OL12—1E 28
haw St. M19—6B 92
e Rd. WN6—6J 33
hall St. WN4—3C 70
hill Dri. M8—9F 60
hilley Way. SK1
—2G 105
hurst Av. WN5—1D 68
St. BL3—3F 38
St. M26—6H 41
St. OL16—2G 29
St. PR7—3F 18
St. SK14—4D 94
St. WN1—9B 34
St. WN2—4K 53
Wlk. M10—4K 79
Av. M28—6M 57
Gro. M29—4L 55
Ho. BL1—1F 38
Haydock St.)
Rd. BL1—1B 38
Rd. M6—2K 77
Rd. M10—2C 80
Rd. M26—2E 40
St. M29—4L 55
St. OL12—9F 12
St. SK2—6F 104
eld Gro. M18—1D 92
acres Rd. M22—1D 112
Av. M25—2A 60
ank Av. OL4—1F 64
ank Clo. M13—1K 91
ank St. OL8—2L 63
wo parts)
ank Way. M24—8M 43
Bri. Rd. SK14—4G 95
y Clo. M24—3M 61
Cliffe. SK13—6K 97
Cliffe. SK14—6C 94
liffe Clo. M16—2F 90
ale Rd. BL2—1L 39
ale Rd. M9—4M 61
ale Rd. WN2—3M 53
wo parts)
ale Way. WA11—6B 68
field Rd. SK8—1A 114
n St. BL3—4J 39
ll Av. M9—3H 61
eld Av. BL9—9J 9
eld Av. WA13—1A 108
eld Clo. M34—4A 94
eld Clo. OL12—4J 13
eld Clo. SK15—6G 83
field Dri. M26—6E 40
eld Dri. M27—7E 58
eld Dri. M28—9M 57
eld Gro. SK2—9H 105
eld Gro. SK6—4H 107
eld Pl. OL11—5G 29
eld Rd. M30—2J 87
eld Rd. OL12—5J 13
eld Rd. SK9—8K 113
eld Rd. WA15—2H 111
elds. BL7—2J 23
eld St. BL9—5M 41
rd Ct. M33—8J 89
rd Dri. BL3—4L 37
rd St. M32—5K 89
ate Av. M22—7D 102
ate La. SK14—8F 84
ate M. SK4—2L 103
ates Rd. OL16—3M 29
ll. M29—2B 74
lebe St. OL6—4C 82
ro. WA15—5F 100
ll. OL11—5F 28
ll Clo. M16—2F 90
ill Wlk. BL3—4L 37
ope St. OL8—3D 82
eys St. M4—3G 5 &
5H 79
nowle View. M31
—2M 87
nd Rd. M21—6A 90
nd Rd. M35—5H 81
nds Clo. SK13—6K 97
nds Rd. M28—1F 74
a. BL8—6G 9
a. M5—4A 4 & 6A 78
a. M18—1D 92
a. M26—5J 41
a. M35—3K 81
a. SK6—8E 106
a. SK9—3M 119
a. WN5—5D 50
a. E. M31—3F 98
a. W. M31—3F 98
ees. OL12—8G 13
Cres. OL6—1D 82
Est. OL9—2H 63
Rd. M19 & SK4—7M 91
Rd. M33—8G 89
St. BL3—6A 40
St. M18—9B 80
St. OL2—7L 45
on)

Crossley St. OL2—2C 46
(Shaw)
Crossley St. OL16—4L 29
Crossley St. SK15—5F 82
Crossley St. SK16—6D 82
Crossmead Dri. M9—3L 61
Crossmoor Cres. SK6—3C 106
Crossmoor Dri. BL2—1H 39
Crossmoor Gro. SK6—3C 106
Cross Ormrod St. BL3—3D 38
Cross Rd. M21—6B 90
Cross Rd. SK8—5H 113
Cross St. BL1—1F 38
Cross St. BL3—6B 40
Cross St. BL4—8K 39
(Farnworth)
Cross St. BL4—3B 58
(Kearsley)
Cross St. BL7—3F 22
Cross St. BL9—8M 25
Cross St. M2—4E 5 & 6F 78
Cross St. M3—3D 4 & 5E 78
Cross St. M16—1D 90
Cross St. M24—9M 43
(in two parts)
Cross St. M25—7L 41
Cross St. M26—6H 41
Cross St. M27—6K 59
Cross St. M28—9C 58
Cross St. M29—4H 55
(Atherton)
Cross St. M29—8M 55
(Tyldesley)
Cross St. M31—5C 88
Cross St. M32—4K 89
Cross St. M33—9H 89
Cross St. M34—1L 93
Cross St. OL4—2E 64
(Lees)
Cross St. OL4—1B 64
(Oldham)
Cross St. OL4—2G 65
(Springhead)
Cross St. OL5—6J 65
Cross St. OL6—5A 82
Cross St. OL10—9L 27
Cross St. OL11—8D 28
Cross St. OL16—3K 29
Cross St. SK13—5J 97
Cross St. SK14—1G 97
(Hadfield)
Cross St. SK14—2D 96
(Hollingworth)
Cross St. SK14—4D 94
(Hyde)
Cross St. SK15—3K 83
Cross St. WA3—8G 71
Cross St. WA14—9D 100
Cross St. WN2—3H 35
(Aspull)
Cross St. WN2—3K 53
(Hindley)
Cross St. WN3—4E 52
(Ince)
Cross St. WN3—1C 52
(Poolstock)
Cross St. WN5—2H 51
(Orrell)
Cross St. WN5—2H 51
(Pemberton)
Cross St. WN6—9L 17
Cross St. WN7—3G 73
Cross, The. SK14—1G 97
Crosswaite Rd. SK2—7K 105
Crossway. M20—2H 103
Crossway. M35—8G 81
Crossway. SK2—9G 105
Crossway. SK7—7E 114
Crossway Clo. WN4—2E 70
Crossway Rd. M33—4F 100
Cross Ways. OL8—7A 64
Croston Av. PR6—2G 19
Croston Clo. M16—1D 90
Croston Clo. SK9—8M 119
Croston Clo. Rd. BL9—1C 26
Croston La. PR7—1H 17
Crostons Rd. BL8—7K 25
Croston St. BL3—5C 38
Croston St. WN2—2J 53
Croston St. S. M16—2D 90
Croston Wlk. M11—6L 79
Croton St. SK4—3L 103
Crouchley La. WA13—3A 108
Croughton Clo. M11—8D 80
Crowbank Wlk. M10—2A 80
Crowborough Wlk. M15—1G 91
Crowbrook Gro. SK9—2K 119
Crowcombe Wlk. M16—2E 90
Crowcroft Rd. M13 & M12
—3A 92
Crowden Rd. M10—6B 62
Crow Hill. SK15—2L 83
Crow Hill N. M24—2M 61
Crowhill Rd. OL7—3M 81
Crow Hill S. M24—2M 61
Crow Hill View. OL4—4E 64
Crowhurst Dri. WN1—6B 34
Crowhurst Wlk. M23—6L 101
(off Sandy La.)
Crowland Gdns. SK8—6B 114
Crowland Rd. BL2—8J 23
Crowland Rd. M23—1M 111
Crowland St. OL8—4C 64
Crow La. BL0—5J 9
Crow La. WN8—6A 32
Crowley La. OL4—8D 46
Crowley Rd. M9—8M 61
Crowley Rd. WA15—7H 101
Crowndale. BL7—4K 7
Crowneast St. OL11—3C 28
Crown Gdns. BL7—5K 7
Crown Gdns. OL16—5G 29
Crown Grn. WA13—9B 98
Crown Gro. WN7—1K 73
Crown Hill. OL5—8K 65
Crown Ind. Est. M4—3H 5 &
5J 79
Crown Ind. Est. WA14—6E 100
Crown La. BL6—8M 19
Crown La. M4—2F 5 & 4G 79
Crown M. SK2—9J 105
Crown Pas. WA15—2E 110
Crown Point. BL7—5K 7
Crown Point Av. M10—2C 80
Crown Rd. OL10—8H 27
Crown Royal Ind. Est. SK1
—5F 104
Crown Sq. M3—4D 4 & 6E 78
Crown St. BL1—2F 38
Crown St. M3—3D 4 & 5E 78
Crown St. M15—6D 4 & 8E 78
Crown St. M29—5J 55
Crown St. M34—2L 93
Crown St. M35—8F 62
Crown St. OL2—2B 46
Crown St. OL6—5B 82
Crown St. OL16—5G 29
Crown St. SK6—9M 93
(Bredbury)
Crown St. SK6—1F 116
(Marple)
Crown St. WN2—2J 53
Crown St. WN3—2B 52
Crownswood Dri. SK15—1K 83
Crow Orchard Rd. WN6—8F 16
(in two parts)
Croworchard Ter. WN3—3E 52
Crowsdale Pl. SK2—9L 105
Crowshaw Dri. OL12—8E 12
Crowther Av. M5—7A 78
Crowther Clo. OL15—7L 13
Crowther Gdns. M5—7A 78
Crowther St. M18—1D 92
Crowther St. OL15—6L 13
Crowther St. OL16—6H 29
Crowther St. SK1—4F 104
Crowthorn Dri. M23—2A 112
Crowthorn Rd. BL7—2M 7
Crowthorn Rd. OL7—6M 81
Crowthorn Rd. SK4—7D 92
Crowton Av. M33—3D 100
Crow Trees La. BL7—4J 7
Crow Wood Rd. WA3—6K 71

Croxdale Clo. OL7—2L 81
Croxdale Wlk. M9—3K 61
(off Claygate Dri.)
Croxton Av. OL16—2H 29
Croxton Clo. M33—2D 100
Croxton Clo. SK6—8E 106
Croxton Wlk. M13—9J 79
Croyde Clo. BL2—7M 23
Croyde Clo. M22—5F 112
Croydon Av. OL2—3J 45
Croydon Av. OL11—2D 44
Croydon Av. WN7—8F 54
Croydon Dri. M10—3B 80
Croydon Sq. OL11—1D 44
Crummock Clo. BL3—6M 39
Crummock Dri. M24—6L 43
Crummock Dri. WN3—5L 51
Crummock Gro. BL4—1E 56
Crummock Rd. SK8—1H 113
Crumpsall Cres. M8—8G 61
Crumpsall La. M8—7F 60
Crumpsall St. BL1—7E 22
Crumpsall Vale. M9—6J 61
Crundale Rd. BL4—6G 23
Cruttenden Rd. SK2—9K 105
Cryer St. M35—3J 81
Cuba St. M24—9C 44
Cubley Rd. M7—8E 60
Cuckoo Gro. M25—2B 60
Cuckoo La. BL9—8C 26
Cuckoo La. M25—2B 60
Cuddington Av. M20—6G 91
Cuddington Cres. SK3—7D 104
Cuddington Way. SK9—7K 113
Cudworth Rd. M9—3G 61
Cuerdon Wlk. M22—5E 102
Culand St. M12—9L 79
Culbert Av. M20—2J 103
Culcheth Av. SK6—7F 106
Culcheth Av. WN2—7H 53
Culcheth La. M10—2C 80
Culcheth Rd. WA14—1D 110
Culcombe Wlk. M13—1J 91
Culcross Av. WN3—4J 51
Culford Clo. M12—1L 91
Culgaith Wlk. M9—9K 61
Culham Clo. BL1—8D 22
Cullen Clo. WN2—9G 35
Cullen Gro. M9—5M 61
Cullercoats Wlk. M12—3B 92
Culmere Rd. M22—3D 112
Culmington Clo. M15—1E 90
Culross Av. BL3—3L 37
Culross Av. M10—7E 62
Culvercliff Wlk. M3—5D 4 &
7E 78
Culverden Av. M6—1M 77
Culverden Wlk. M6—1M 77
Culver Rd. SK3—8D 104
Culvert St. OL4—9E 46
Culvert St. OL16—8H 29
Culvert St. WN6—6A 34
Culzean Clo. WN7—3H 73
Cumber Clo. SK9—7D 118
Cumber Dri. SK9—7D 118
Cumberland Av. M27—6F 58
Cumberland Av. M29—6M 55
Cumberland Av. M30—1C 98
Cumberland Av. OL10—8G 27
Cumberland Av. SK5—1J 105
Cumberland Av. SK16—7E 82
Cumberland Clo. BL9—3L 41
Cumberland Cres. WA11
—9G 69
Cumberland Dri. OL1 & OL2
—8K 45
Cumberland Gro. OL7—3B 82
Cumberland Rd. M9—7K 61
Cumberland Rd. M29—4L 55
Cumberland Rd. M31—3E 98
(Partington)
Cumberland Rd. M31—5C 88
(Urmston)
Cumberland Rd. M33—3J 101
Cumberland Rd. OL11—8F 28
Cumberland St. M7—1C 4 &
3D 78
Cumberland St. SK15—5F 82
Cumberland St. WN1—8E 34
Cumber La. SK9—6D 118
Cumbermere La. M29—6B 56
Cumbrae Gdns. M5—6K 77
Cumbrae Rd. M19—5C 92
Cumbria Ct. M25—7M 59
Cumbrian Clo. M13—9J 79
Cumbrian Clo. OL2—1M 45
Cumbria Clo. WN2—6H 53
Cumbria Wlk. M6—1A 4 & 3B 78
Cummings St. OL8—6J 63
Cunard Clo. M13—9J 79
Cundall Wlk. M23—4M 101
Cundey St. BL1—9C 22
Cundiff Ct. M19—5C 92
Cundiff Rd. M21—8B 90
Cundy St. SK14—2E 94
Cunliffe Av. BL0—7G 9
Cunliffe Brow. BL1—8B 22
Cunliffe Dri. M33—2J 101
Cunliffe Dri. OL2—2C 46
Cunliffe St. BL2—3F 38
Cunliffe St. M26—6J 41
Cunliffe St. SK3—5C 104
Cunliffe St. SK14—2C 94
Cunliffe St. WN7—2C 72
Cunnah's Gro. M16—1B 90
Cunningham Dri. BL9—8B 42
Cunningham Dri. M22—4G 113
Cunningham Rd. BL5—1D 54
Cunningham Way. OL1—9M 45
Curate St. SK1—4G 105
Curlew Clo. OL11—3M 27
Curlew Dri. M30—2G 87
Curlew Rd. OL4—4E 64
Curlew Wlk. M12—1L 91
Currier La. OL6—5C 82
Curtels Clo. M28—9C 58
Curtis Gro. SK14—1G 97
Curtis Rd. SK4—3A 104
Curtis St. BL3—7C 38
Curtis St. M19—5C 92
Curzon Av. M14—2L 91
Curzon Clo. OL11—8F 28
Curzon Dri. WA15—7H 101
Curzon Grn. SK2—5K 105
Curzon M. SK9—5G 119
Curzon Rd. BL1—2C 38
Curzon Rd. M7—9D 60
Curzon Rd. M32—3G 89
Curzon Rd. M33—9H 89
Curzon Rd. OL6—3D 82
Curzon Rd. SK2—6K 105
Curzon Rd. SK8—5H 113
Curzon Rd. SK12—1L 121
Curzon St. OL1—1M 63
Curzon St. OL5—7J 65
Cutgate Clo. M23—4L 101
Cutgate Rd. OL12—1B 28
Cuthbert Av. M19—4B 92
Cuthbert Mayne Ct. OL16
—4E 28
Cuthbert Rd. SK8—7L 103
Cuthbert St. BL3—7B 38
Cuthbert St. WN5—2K 51
Cuthill Wlk. M10—3D 80
Cutland St. M10—1A 80
Cut La. OL12—1M 27
Cutler Hill Rd. M35—9H 63
Cutler St. OL9—1J 63
Cutnook La. M30—1F 86
Cycle St. M11—7B 80
Cyclone St. M11—7M 79
Cygnet St. WN3—2B 52
Cygnus Av. M7—2B 4 & 4C 78
Cymbal Ct. SK5—2F 104
Cynthia Dri. SK6—8F 106
Cypress Av. OL9—9H 45
Cypress Clo. SK3—5C 104
Cypress Gro. BL4—1M 57
Cypress Gro. M34—3A 94
Cypress Rd. M30—3A 76
Cypress Rd. M35—4G 81
Cypress Rd. OL4—9D 46

Cypress Rd. WN5—2L 51
Cypress St. M9—9K 61
Cypress St. M24—1C 62
Cypress Wlk. M33—8C 88
Cypress Way. SK6—5G 117
Cyprus Clo. M5—6M 77
Cyprus Clo. OL4—2D 64
Cyprus St. M32—5K 89
Cyril Bell Clo. WA13—1A 108
Cyril St. BL3—4G 39
Cyril St. M14—3H 91
Cyril St. OL2—2C 46
Cyrus St. M10—5K 79

Daccamill Dri. M27—9F 58
Dacre Av. M16—4B 90
Dacre Clo. M24—8H 43
Dacre Rd. OL11—6F 28
Dacres Av. OL3—4M 65
Dacres Dri. OL3—4M 65
Dacres Rd. OL3—4M 65
Daffodil Clo. OL12—8E 12
Daffodil Rd. BL4—8G 39
Daffodil St. BL1—5F 22
Dagenham Rd. M14—2J 91
Dagmar St. M28—4J 57
Dagnall Av. M21—7B 90
Dahlia Clo. OL12—8D 12
Dailton Rd. WN8—1A 50
Daimler St. M8—1G 79
Dain Clo. SK16—7E 82
Daine Av. M23—4B 102
Dainton St. M12—7K 79
Daintry Clo. M15—9F 78
Daintry Rd. OL9—1J 63
Dairybrook Gro. SK9—2L 119
Dairy Farm Clo. WA13—1A 108
Dairyground Rd. SK7—5E 114
Dairy Ho. La. SK7—9A 114
Dairyhouse La. WA14—7A 100
Dairy St. OL9—1H 63
Daisey Bank Av. M27—1J 77
Daisey Hill Ct. OL4—9E 46
(off Howard St.)
Daisey St. SK1—6F 104
Daisy Av. BL4—8G 39
Daisy Av. M13—2L 91
Daisy Bank. M10—2C 80
Daisy Bank. SK14—6C 94
Daisybank La. SK8—3G 113
Daisy Bank Rd. M14—2K 91
Daisyfield Ct. BL8—9J 25
Daisyfield Wlk. M28—5K 57
Daisy Hall Dri. BL5—2E 54
Daisy Hill Clo. M33—1L 101
Daisy Hill Dri. PR6—1G 19
Daisy Hill Rd. OL5—7K 65
Daisy M. SK3—9D 104
Daisy Rd. WN5—2L 51
Daisy Row. OL15—8M 13
Daisy St. BL3—5C 38
Daisy St. BL8—8J 25
Daisy St. OL9—9G 45
(Chadderton)
Daisy St. OL9—1K 63
(Oldham)
Daisy St. OL12—2E 28
Daisy Way. SK6—5F 116
Dakerwood Clo. M10—2C 80
Dakins Rd. WN7—5H 73
Dakota Av. M5—7L 77
Dalbeattie Rise. WN1—8F 34
Dalbeattie St. M9—7L 61
Dalberg St. M12—8K 79
Dalbury Dri. M10—2J 79
Dalby Av. M27—9E 58
Dalby Gro. SK1—4G 105
Dalby Rd. WN2—3B 54
Dale Av. M30—4C 76
Dale Av. OL5—5L 65
Dale Av. SK7—4F 114
Dalebank. M29—3J 55
Dale Bank M. M27—3D 58
Dalebeck Clo. M25—9C 42
Dalebeck Wlk. M25—9C 42
Dalebrook Av. SK16—9D 82
Dalebrook Clo. BL3—5A 40
Dalebrook Rd. M33—3J 101
Dale Ct. M34—4M 93
Dalecrest. WN5—7D 50
Dale End. OL8—6A 64
Dalefields. OL3—5M 47
Daleford Sq. M13—6G 87 &
8H 79
Dalegarth Av. BL1—2J 37
Dale Gro. M30—8E 86
Dale Gro. OL7—2A 82
Dale Gro. WA15—6F 100
Dale Gro. WN7—3C 72
Dalehead Clo. M18—9F 80
Dalehead Dri. OL2—2D 46
Dalehead Pl. WA11—6B 68
Dale Ho. M24—8B 44
Dale Ho. OL2—3B 46
Dale Ho. Fold. SK12—8A 116
Dale La. OL3—4M 47
Dale Lee. BL5—9G 37
Dale Rd. M24—7B 44
Dale Rd. SK6—7D 106
Dale Rd. WA3—8G 71
Dales Av. M8—6F 60
Dales Av. M25—8K 41
Dales Brow. BL1—4F 22
Dales Brow. M27—1D 76
Daleside Cres. OL5—7L 65
Dalesford Clo. WN7—7C 72
Dales Gro. M28—7M 57
Daleside Av. WN4—8A 52
Dales La. M25—8K 41
Dalesman Wlk. M15—9G 79
(off Wilmott St.)
Dales Pk. Dri. M27—1D 76
Dale Sq. OL2—5M 45
Dale Sq. WA14—6D 100
Dale St. BL0—3J 9
Dale St. BL1—1F 38
(in two parts)
Dale St. BL4—8L 39
Dale St. BL8—6J 25
Dale St. M1—4G 5 & 6H 79
(in two parts)
Dale St. M24—1B 62
Dale St. M25—8L 41
Dale St. M26—7G 41
(in two parts)
Dale St. M27—1E 76
Dale St. OL2—3B 46
Dale St. OL6—1G 83
Dale St. OL16—4M 29
(Milnrow)
Dale St. OL16—3J 29
(Rochdale)
Dale St. SK3—7D 104
Dale St. SK15—6F 82
Dale St. WA14—6D 100
Dale St. WN2—5F 52
Dale St. WN7—2C 72
Dale St. E. BL6—8D 20
Dale St. E. OL6—5A 82
Dale St. Ind. Est. M26—7G 41
Dale St. W. BL6—8D 20
Dale St. W. OL6—5A 82
Daleswood Av. M25—8K 41
Dale View. M34—7A 94
Dale View. OL16—9M 13
Dale View. SK14—6D 94
Dalham Av. M9—6A 62
Dalkeith Av. SK5—7F 92
Dalkeith Gro. BL3—4M 37
Dalkeith Rd. SK5—7F 92
Dalkeith Rd. WN2—3A 54
Dalkeith Sq. OL10—9G 27
Dallas Ct. M5—7L 77
Dalley Av. M7—1C 4 & 3D 78
Dallimore Rd. M23—7L 101
Dalmahoy Clo. M10—8C 62
Dalmain Wlk. M8—1F 78
Dalmeny Ter. OL11—6F 28
Dalmorton Rd. M21—6D 90
Dalny St. M19—5B 92
Dalry Wlk. M23—7A 102
Dalston Av. M35—8H 63

Dalston Dri. M20—3H 103
Dalston Dri. SK7—7C 114
Dalston Dri. WA11—6B 68
Dalston Gdns. BL1—9E 22
(off Gladstone St.)
Dalston Gro. WN3—5K 51
Dalton Av. M14—4G 91
Dalton Av. M25—1A 60
Dalton Av. M27—5J 59
Dalton Av. M32—2F 88
Dalton Av. OL16—3K 29
Dalton Clo. BL0—7G 9
Dalton Clo. OL16—3K 29
Dalton Clo. WN5—1H 51
Dalton Dri. M27—9K 59
Dalton Dri. WN3—5L 51
Dalton Fold. BL5—9F 36
Dalton Gdns. M31—3B 88
Dalton Gro. SK4—1C 104
Dalton Gro. WN4—2A 70
Dalton Rd. M9—3K 61
Dalton Rd. M24—1H 61
Dalton St. BL8—8J 25
(in two parts)
Dalton St. M4 & M10—1G 5 &
3H 79
Dalton St. M30—4D 76
Dalton St. M33—8J 89
Dalton St. M35—8E 62
Dalton St. OL1—1B 64
Dalton St. OL9—1H 63
Daltrey St. OL1—9A 46
Dalveen Av. M31—2C 88
Dalveen Dri. WA15—6F 100
Dalymount Clo. BL2—8H 23
Damask Av. M3—5D 78
Dame Hollow. SK8—5K 113
Damery Ct. SK7—4E 114
Damery Rd. SK7—4E 114
Dame St. OL9—9K 45
Dam Head Dri. M9—5L 61
Dam Head La. WA3—1A 98
Damien St. M12—4A 92
Dam La. WA3—1A 98
Dam La. WN4 & WA3—4F 70
Dams Head Fold. BL5—8F 36
Damside. SK14—9G 85
Damson Wlk. M31—2D 98
Dan Bank. SK6—7C 106
Danbers. WN8—2A 50
Danbury Wlk. M23—5K 101
Danby Clo. SK14—2F 94
Danby Ct. OL1—9L 45
Danby Pl. SK14—2F 94
Danby Rd. BL3—4E 38
Danby Rd. SK14—2F 94
Danby Wlk. M9—7L 61
(off Polworth Rd.)
Dane Av. M31—1F 98
Dane Av. SK3—5A 104
Dane Bank Dri. SK12—6K 117
Danebank Wlk. M13—6G 5 &
8H 79
Danebury Clo. WN2—4K 53
Dane Clo. SK7—1D 114
Danecroft Clo. M13—9K 79
Dane Dri. SK9—5K 119
Danefield Ct. SK8—4K 113
Danefield Rd. M33—8J 89
Dane Hill Clo. SK12—7K 117
Daneholme Rd. M19—9L 91
Dane M. M33—8H 89
Dane Rd. M33—8H 89
Dane Rd. M34—4G 93
Dane Rd. Ind. Est. M33—8J 89
Danes Av. WN2—2L 53
Danesbury Rise. SK8—8K 103
Danesbury Rd. BL2—6H 23
Daneshill. M25—2B 60
Daneshot St. M34—4H 93
Danes La. OL12—2A 12
Danesmoor Dri. BL9—6B 26
Danesmoor Rd. M20—9G 91
Danes Rd. M14—4K 91
Danes, The. M8—7F 60
Dane St. M11—8E 80
Dane St. OL4—1C 64
Dane St. OL5—5K 65
Dane St. OL11—3E 28
Danesway. M25—6D 60
Danesway. M27—9J 59
Danesway. WN1—6B 34
Daneswood Av. M9—4M 61
Daneswood Av. OL12—3C 12
Daneswood Clo. OL12—3B 12
Danett Clo. M12—9B 80
Dane Wlk. SK5—9F 92
Danforth Gro. M19—6B 92
Daniel Adamson Av. M31
—2D 98
Daniel Adamson Rd. M5—6K 77
Daniel Fold. OL12—9B 12
Daniel's La. SK1—3E 104
Daniel St. OL1—9B 46
Daniel St. OL2—6A 46
Daniel St. OL10—8H 27
Daniel St. OL12—1D 12
Daniel St. SK7—2L 115
Danisher La. OL8—8M 63
Dannywood Clo. SK14—6C 94
Danson St. M10—4L 79
Dantall Av. M9—5A 62
Dante Clo. M30—3G 77
Danty St. SK16—6B 82
Dantzic St. M4—3F 5 & 5G 79
Danwood Clo. M34—4B 94
Darbishire St. BL1—9G 23
Darby La. WN2—2J 53
Darby Rd. M30—8G 87
Darbyshire Clo. BL1—1C 38
Darbyshire Ho. WA15—6J 101
Darbyshire Wlk. M26—6H 41
Darcy Wlk. M14—2G 91
Darden Clo. SK4—2L 103
Darell Wlk. M8—1H 79
Darenth Clo. M15—9F 78
Daresbury. M31—2K 87
Daresbury Av. M31—2K 87
Daresbury Av. WA15—8E 100
Daresbury Clo. M33—2M 101
Daresbury Clo. SK3—8D 104
Daresbury Rd. M21—5M 89
Daresbury St. M8—8G 61
Darfield. WN8—1A 50
Darfield Wlk. M10—4K 79
Dargai St. M11—6D 80
Dargle Rd. M33—8H 89
Darian Av. M22—4D 112
Daric Clo. WN7—6C 72
Dark La. BL6—6H 19
Dark La. M12—7K 79
Dark La. OL3—3L 47
Dark La. OL5—6K 65
(in two parts)
Dark La. SK6—2K 105
Dark La. WA14—4K 99
Darlbeck Wlk. M21—9C 90
Darley Av. BL4—8L 39
Darley Av. M21 & M20—8B 90
(in two parts)
Darley Av. M30—7C 76
Darley Av. SK8—8H 103
Darley Ct. BL1—8C 22
Darley Gro. BL4—8L 39
Darley Rd. M16—3B 90
Darley Rd. OL11—6F 28
Darley Rd. SK7—5M 115
Darley Rd. WN3—5B 52
Darley St. BL1—9D 22
Darley St. BL4—9L 39
Darley St. BL6—5B 20
Darley St. M11—6M 79
Darley St. M32—2K 89
Darley St. M33—1H 101
Darley St. SK4—2C 104
Darley Ter. BL1—9E 22
Darlington Clo. BL8—5H 25
Darlington Rd. M20—8G 91
Darlington Rd. OL11—6F 28
Darlington St. M4—3H 5 & 5J 79
Darlington St. M29—7A 56
Darlington St. PR7—1K 17

Darlington St. WN1—1C 52
Darlington St. WN2—1G 53
Darlington St. E. M29—7B 56
Darlington St. E. WN1—1D 52
Darliston Av. M9—3G 61
Darlton Wlk. M9—8L 61
Darnall Av. M20—6G 91
Darnbrook Dri. M22—3B 112
Darncombe Clo. M16—2F 90
Darnhall St. WN3—4F 52
Darnley Av. M28—7J 57
Darnley St. M16—2D 90
Darnton Rd. OL6 & SK15—3E 82
Darran Av. WN3—5M 51
Darras Rd. M18—3C 92
Darsham Wlk. M16—2E 90
Dart Clo. OL9—9F 44
Dartford Av. M30—5B 76
Dartford Av. SK5—8H 93
Dartford Clo. M12—9K 79
Dartford Rd. M31—5C 88
Dartington Clo. M23—7K 101
Dartington Clo. SK7—1F 114
Dartington Cres. SK5—9J 93
Dartmouth Rd. M21—6C 90
Dartmouth Rd. M25—1A 60
Dartnall Clo. SK12—6G 117
Darton Av. M10—4L 79
Darvel Av. WN4—3J 69
Darvel Clo. BL2—3M 39
Darwell Av. M30—7C 76
Darwen Rd. BL7—1E 22
Darwen Rd. BL8—1G 25
Darwen St. M16—9C 78
Darwin Gro. SK7—6F 114
Darwin St. BL1—8D 22
Darwin St. OL4—3C 64
Darwin St. SK14—1G 95
Dashwood Rd. M25—3A 60
Dashwood Wlk. M12—9A 80
Datchet Ter. OL11—6F 28
Dauntesey Av. M27—8K 59
Davehall Av. SK9—4G 119
Davenfield Gro. M20—2H 103
Davenfield Rd. M20—2H 103
Davenham Rd. M33—8E 88
Davenham Rd. SK5—4F 92
Davenham Rd. SK9—8K 113
Davenhill Rd. M19—6A 92
Davenport Av. M20—7H 91
Davenport Av. M26—3F 40
Davenport Av. SK9—7E 118
Davenport Dri. SK6—8B 94
Davenport Fold. BL2—7A 24
Davenport Fold Rd. BL2—6A 24
Davenport Gdns. BL1—1E 38
Davenport Ho. SK7—6D 114
Davenport La. WA14—6C 100
Davenport Lodge. SK2—8F 104
Davenport Pk. Rd. SK2—8G 105
Davenport Rd. SK7—1K 115
Davenport Rd. WA14—6C 100
Davenport St. BL1—1E 38
Davenport St. M34—7L 81
Davenport St. M35—6E 80
Davenport Ter. M9—5L 61
Daventry Rd. M21—6D 90
Daventry Rd. OL11—6F 28
Daventry Way. OL11—7F 28
Daveylands. SK9—4K 119
Davey La. SK9—7L 119
David Brow. BL3—7A 38
David M. M14—7J 91
David Pegg Wlk. M10—1B 80
David's Farm Clo. M24—1C 62
David's La. OL4—1F 64
Davidson Dri. M24—2B 62
Davidson Wlk. WN5—1L 51
David's Rd. M35—5E 80
David St. BL8—7J 25
(in two parts)
David St. M34—4A 94
David St. OL1—2L 63
David St. OL12—1F 28
David St. N. OL12—1F 28
Davies Av. SK8—6H 113
Davies Rd. M31—2G 99
Davies Rd. SK6—2K 105
Davies Sq. M14—2G 91
Davies St. BL4—1A 58
Davies St. OL1—9K 45
Davies St. OL7—6M 81
Davies St. WN2—6G 53
Davis St. M30—6E 76
Davy Av. M27—6K 59
Davyhulme Circ. M31—2C 88
Davyhulme Rd. M31—2L 87
Davyhulme Rd. M32—3J 89
Davyhulme Rd. E. M32—3K 89
Davyhulme St. OL12—1H 29
Davylands. M31—1M 87
Davy St. M10—1G 5 & 3H 79
Daw Bank. SK3—4E 104
Dawbers Ter. WN3—9B 34
(off York St.)
Dawber St. WN4—3D 70
Dawes St. BL3—3F 38
Dawley Clo. BL3—3C 38
Dawley Clo. WN4—4A 70
Dawley Flats. OL10—8J 27
(off Brunswick St.)
Dawlish Av. M35—5E 80
Dawlish Av. OL9—8F 44
Dawlish Av. SK5—9J 93
Dawlish Av. SK8—4M 113
Dawlish Clo. SK7—5F 114
Dawlish Clo. SK14—3L 95
Dawlish Clo. WA3—2B 98
Dawlish Rd. M21—6C 90
Dawlish Rd. M33—9E 88
Dawnay St. M11—7B 80
Dawn St. OL2—3B 46
Dawson Av. WN6—6A 34
Dawson La. BL1—2E 38
Dawson Rd. SK8—4K 113
Dawson Rd. WA14—6D 100
Dawson St. BL9—6A 26
(in two parts)
Dawson St. M3—5C 4 & 7D 78
(Manchester)
Dawson St. M3—3E 5 & 5F 78
(Salford)
Dawson St. M27—8G 59
Dawson St. M29—5J 55
Dawson St. OL4—3E 64
(Lees)
Dawson St. OL4—2D 64
(Oldham)
Dawson St. OL10—8J 27
Dawson St. OL12—2F 28
Dawson St. SK1—2H 105
Dawson St. SK14—5E 94
Daybrook. WN8—1A 50
Day Dri. M35—1F 80
Dayfield. WN8—1B 50
Day Gro. SK14—3A 96
Daylesford Clo. SK8—9K 103
Daylesford Cres. SK8—9K 103
Daylesford Rd. SK8—9K 103
Deacon Av. M27—7E 58
Deacon Clo. WA14—3A 110
Deacons Clo. SK1—4G 105
Deacons Cres. BL8—5G 25
Deacon's Dri. M6—1K 77
Deacon St. OL16—1H 29
Deakin St. WN3—3E 52
Deal Clo. M10—2D 80
Deal Av. SK5—9H 93
Dealey Rd. BL3—5A 38
Deal St. BL3—6F 38
Deal St. M3—3D 4 & 5E 78
Deal St. SK14—4E 94
Deal St. N. BL9—7B 26
Deal St. S. BL9—8B 26
(in two parts)
Deal Wlk. OL9—2G 63
Dean Av. M10—1B 80
Dean Av. M16—3B 90
Deanbank Av. M19—6M 91
Dean Bank Dri. OL16—9H 29
Dean Clo. BL4—9F 38
Dean Clo. M15—9F 78
Dean Clo. M25—1K 59

Dean Clo. M31—1F 98
Dean Clo. SK9—2J 119
Dean Clo. WN5—4D 68
Dean Clo. WN8—1C 50
Dean Ct. BL1—6G 23
Dean Ct. M15—9D 78
Deancourt. OL11—6F 28
Dean Ct. SK16—6B 82
Dean Cres. WN5—9H 33
Dean Dri. SK9—2J 119
Dean Dri. WA14—3A 110
Deane Av. BL3—4B 38
Deane Av. SK8—8M 103
Deane Av. WA15—8G 101
Deane Chu. Clough. BL3—4A 38
Deane Chu. La. BL3—5B 38
Deane Rd. BL3—4C 38
Deanery Gdns. M7—8D 60
Deanery Way. SK1—3E 104
Deane Wlk. BL3—3E 38
(in two parts)
Dean Ho. BL1—1F 38
Dean La. M10—9B 62
Dean La. SK7—4K 115
Dean Moor Rd. SK7—2G 115
Dean Rd. M3—2D 4 & 4E 78
Dean Rd. M18—2E 92
Dean Rd. M30—8E 86
Dean Rd. SK9—9L 113
Dean Rd. WA3—8G 71
Dean Row Rd. SK9—2J 119
Deanscourt Av. M27—9E 58
Deansgate. BL1—2E 38
Deansgate. M3—5D 4 & 7E 78
(in two parts)
Deansgate. M26—6H 41
Deansgate. WN2—2K 53
Deansgate La. WA14 & WA15
—6E 100
Deanshut Rd. OL8—6A 64
Deans Rd. M27—9D 58
Dean St. BL1—1F 38
Dean St. M1—4G 5 & 6H 79
Dean St. M26—6F 40
Dean St. M35—9E 62
Dean St. OL5—7H 65
Dean St. OL6—4A 82
Dean St. OL16—1H 29
Dean St. SK15—5G 83
Deansway. M27—8E 58
Deanswood Dri. M9—3G 61
Dean Ter. OL6—7B 64
Dean Wlk. M24—7K 43
Deanwater Clo. M13—6G 5 &
8H 79
Deanwater Ct. M32—6K 89
Deanway. M10—8A 62
Deanway. M31—4K 87
Deanway. SK9—2J 119
Deanway Trading Est. SK9
—9K 113
Dean Wood Av. WN5—9E 32
Dearden Av. M28—3G 57
Dearden Fold. BL8—9J 25
Deardens St. BL8—9J 25
Dearden St. BL3—5A 40
Dearden St. OL15—5B 14
Dearden Wlk. M15—9E 78
Deardon Ct. WN8—1A 50
Dearham Av. WA11—8A 68
Dearnley Av. WA11—9E 68
Dearnley Clo OL15—7L 13
Dearnley Pas. OL12—7L 13
Debdale Av. M18—2F 92
Debdale La. M18—2F 92
Debdale La. M29—3M 73
Debenham Av. M10—3C 80
Debenham Ct. BL4—1K 57
Debenham Rd. M32—4G 89
De Brook Ct. M31—5L 87
Dee Av. WA15—8K 101
Dee Dri. BL4—3B 58
Deepcar St. M19—4A 92
Deepdale. OL4—2D 64
Deep Dale. WN7—4J 73
Deepdale Av. M20—6G 91
Deepdale Av. OL2—1J 45
Deepdale Av. OL16—4J 29
Deepdale Av. WA11—6C 68
Deepdale Clo. SK5—5F 92
Deepdale Ct. M9—5B 62
Deepdale Dri. M27—9K 59
Deepdale Rd. BL2—1L 39
Deeping Av. M16—4D 90
Deeplish Cotts. OL11—5F 28
Deeplish Rd. OL11—5F 28
Deeplish St. OL4—1C 64
Deeply Vale La. BL0—9C 10
Deeracre Av. SK2—7J 105
Deerfold Clo. M18—1D 92
Deerhurst Dri. M8—1F 78
Dee Rd. M29—9C 56
Deerpark Clo. M18—9B 80
Deerpark Rd. M16—3E 90
Defence St. BL3—3D 38
Defiance St. M29—5J 55
Deganwy Gro. SK5—9F 92
Deighton Av. M20—6G 91
Delacourt Rd. M14—6G 91
De Lacy Dri. BL2—9H 23
Delafield Av. M12—4A 92
Delaford Clo. SK3—9E 104
Delaford Wlk. M10—3D 80
Delahays Dri. WA15—2H 111
Delahays Range. M18—2F 92
Delahays Rd. WA15—2H 111
Delaine Rd. M20—8J 91
Delamare Av. OL2—1D 46
Delamere Av. M6—1J 77
Delamere Av. M25—9K 41
Delamere Av. M27—6H 59
Delamere Av. M32—4K 89
Delamere Av. M33—2L 101
Delamere Av. WA3—9L 71
Delamere Clo. SK6—9C 94
Delamere Clo. SK7—1A 116
Delamere Clo. SK15—1L 83
Delamere Ct. M9—3G 61
Delamere Gdns. BL1—7D 22
Delamere Rd. M19—6A 92
Delamere Rd. M31—4M 87
Delamere Rd. M34—4H 93
Delamere Rd. OL16—6J 29
Delamere Rd. SK2—9H 105
Delamere Rd. SK7—1A 116
Delamere Rd. SK8—8H 103
Delamere Rd. SK9—8K 113
Delamere St. BL9—5A 26
Delamere St. M11—8F 80
Delamere St. OL6—4B 82
Delamere St. OL8—3B 64
Delamere Way. WN8—1A 50
Delamer Rd. WA14—1C 110
Delaunays Rd. M8 & M9—7G 61
Delaunays Rd. M33—1F 100
Delaware Wlk. M9—9K 61
Delbooth Av. M31—2L 87
Delegarte St. WN3—2E 52
Delft Wlk. M6—2A 78
Delfur Rd. SK7—5F 114
Delhi Rd. M30—6F 86
Dellar St. OL12—1C 28
Dell Av. M27—9K 59
Dell Av. WN6—6L 33
Dellcot Clo. M6—2H 77
Dellcot Clo. M25—6D 60
Dellcot La. M28—2M 75
Dell Gdns. OL12—9B 12
Dell Meadow. OL12—6C 12
Dell Rd. OL12—8B 12
Dell Side. SK6—2L 105
Dellside Clo. WN4—1K 69
Dellside Gro. M28—5L 57
Dell Side Way. OL12—9C 12
Dell, The. BL2—5J 23
Dell, The. WN6—2D 32
Dell, The. WN8—1B 50
Delph Brook Way. BL7—9D 6
Delph Gro. WN7—7D 54
Delph La. BL2—9C 24
Delph La. OL3—4M 47
Delph New Rd. OL3—6L 47
Delph Rd. OL3—2J 47

Delphside Clo. WN5—3D 50
Delphside Rd. WN5—3D 50
Delph St. BL3—4D 38
Delph St. OL16—4M 29
Delph St. WN6—8B 34
Delside Av. M10—8A 62
Delta Clo. OL2—7J 45
Delta Rd. M34—8L 81
Delta Wlk. M10—9A 62
Delvino St. M15—1F 90
Delvino Wlk. M14—2G 91
Delwood Gdns. M22—1D 112
De Massey Clo. SK6—8B 94
Demesne Clo. SK15—6J 83
Demesne Cres. SK15—6J 83
Demesne Dri. SK15—5J 83
Demesne Rd. M16—4E 90
Demmings Ind. Est. SK8
—8M 103
Demmings Rd. SK8—8M 103
Demmings, The. SK8—8M 103
Dempsey Dri. BL9—7B 42
Denbigh Clo. SK7—4J 115
Denbigh Dri. OL2—3M 45
Denbigh Gro. M29—3J 55
Denbigh Pl. M6—5A 78
(in two parts)
Denbigh Rd. BL2—4H 39
Denbigh Rd. M27—6G 59
Denbigh Rd. M34—5M 93
Denbigh St. OL5—8K 65
Denbigh St. OL8—5M 63
Denbigh St. SK4—2D 104
Denbigh Wlk. M15—1E 90
Denbury Dri. WA14—8B 100
Denbury Grn. SK7—3G 115
Denbury Wlk. M9—9J 61
(off Westmere Dri.)
Denbydale Way. OL2—5J 45
(in two parts)
Denby La. SK4—1D 104
Denby Rd. SK16—8C 82
Dencombe St. M13—2M 91
Dene Av. BL8—4J 25
Dene Bank. BL2—5J 23
Dene Brow. M34—6B 94
Dene Ct. SK4—3C 104
Dene Dri. M24—1M 61
Denefield Clo. SK6—4H 107
Denefield Pl. M30—4F 76
Deneford Rd. M20—3G 103
Dene Gro. WN7—3B 72
Dene Hollow. SK5—5G 93
Denehurst Rd. OL11—2B 28
Denehurst St. M12—9M 79
Dene Pk. M20—2G 103
Dene Rd. M20—2G 103
Dene Rd. W. M20—2F 102
Deneside. M10—1K 79
Deneside Cres. SK7—1M 115
Deneside Wlk. M9—7L 61
(off Dalbeattie St.)
Dene St. BL2—5J 23
Dene St. WN7—3B 72
Denesway. M33—2E 100
(in two parts)
Deneway. SK4—3C 104
Deneway. SK6—4F 116
Deneway. SK7—5C 114
Deneway Clo. SK4—3C 104
Deneway M. SK4—3C 104
Denewell Clo. M13—9K 79
Denewood Ct. SK9—5G 119
Denford Clo. WN3—5M 51
Denham Clo. BL1—4G 23
Denham Dri. M30—5G 87
Denham Dri. SK7—5D 114
Denham Dri. WN3—5A 52
Denham St. M13—2K 91
Denham St. M26—3F 40
Den Hill Dri. OL4—2F 64
Denhill Rd. M15—1E 90
Denholme. WN8—1A 50
Denholme Rd. OL11—6F 28
Denholm Rd. M20—5J 103
Denison Rd. OL15—5B 14
Denis Av. M16—4E 90
Denison Rd. M14—3J 91
Denison Rd. SK7—4L 115
Deniston Rd. SK4—9B 92
Den La. OL3—9B 48
Den La. OL4—1F 64
Denman Wlk. M8—1F 78
(off Ermington Dri.)
Denmark Rd. M15—2F 90
Denmark Rd. M33—8H 89
Denmark St. OL4—1C 64
Denmark St. OL9—9J 45
Denmark St. OL16—2G 29
Denmark St. WA14 & WA15
—9D 100
Denmark Way. OL9—9J 45
Denmore Rd. M10—5D 62
Dennington Dri. M31—2C 88
Dennison Av. M20—7H 91
Dennison Rd. SK8—4B 114
Denshaw. WN8—1A 50
Denshaw Av. M34—1K 93
Denshaw Clo. M19—2L 103
Denshaw Rd. OL3—2J 47
Densmead Wlk. M10—2H 5 &
4J 79
Densmore St. M35—9F 62
Denson Rd. WA15—5H 101
Denstone Av. M30—4E 76
Denstone Av. M33—2E 100
Denstone Cres. BL2—8L 23
Denstone Rd. M6—2K 77
Denstone Rd. M31—3C 88
Denstone Rd. SK5—5F 92
Denstone Wlk. M9—5L 61
(off Dam Head Dri.)
Dent Clo. SK5—8J 93
Dentdale Clo. BL1—3K 37
Dentdale Wlk. M22—4C 112
Denton Gro. WN5—9H 33
Denton La. OL9—3G 63
Denton Relief Rd. M34—2K 93
Denton Rd. BL2—3B 40
Denton Rd. M34—1L 93
Denton St. BL9—6M 25
Denton St. OL10—9J 27
Denton St. OL12—1F 28
Denver Av. M10—4K 79
Denver Dri. WA15—7G 101
Denver Rd. OL11—6F 28
Denville Cres. M22—1E 112
Denyer Ter. SK16—6B 82
Depleach Rd. SK8—8K 103
Deptford Av. M23—1A 112
De Quincey Clo. WA14—4D 100
De Quincey Rd. WA14—4D 100
Deramore Clo. OL6—4E 82
Deramore St. M14—3H 91
Derby Av. M6—5L 77
Derby Clo. M30—9C 86
Derby Ct. M33—2J 101
Derby Ct. OL9—3J 63
Derby Gro. M19—5B 92
Derby Ho. M15—1H 91
Derby Ho. WN1—9D 34
Derby Range. SK4—1B 104
Derby Rd. M14—7J 91
Derby Rd. M25—2A 60
Derby Rd. M26—9A 40
Derby Rd. M31—3D 88
Derby Rd. M33—8E 88
Derby Rd. OL6—4D 82
Derby Rd. SK4—1C 104
Derby Rd. SK14—2E 94
Derby Rd. WA3—6J 71
Derbyshire Av. M32—3G 89
Derbyshire Cres. M32—3H 89
Derbyshire Grn. M32—4K 89
Derbyshire Gro. M32—3G 89
Derbyshire La. M32—4J 89
Derbyshire La. W. M32—3G 89
Derbyshire Level. SK13—9K 97
Derbyshire Rd. BL1—7E 22
Derbyshire Rd. M10—3D 80
Derbyshire Rd. M31—3D 98
Derbyshire Rd. M33—1J 101
Derbyshire Rd. S. M33—2J 101

Derbyshire St. M11—8C 80
Derbyshire St. M26—6G 41
Derby St. BL0—5K 9
Derby St. BL3—5D 38
Derby St. BL5—8F 36
Derby St. BL6—9D 20
Derby St. BL9—8M 25
Derby St. M8—2E 78
Derby St. M25—4A 60
Derby St. M29—4J 55
(Atherton)
Derby St. M29—7A 56
(Tyldesley)
Derby St. M34—3K 93
(in two parts)
Derby St. M35—7G 63
Derby St. OL5—8K 65
Derby St. OL7—2A 82
Derby St. OL9—5H 63
(Chadderton)
Derby St. OL9—3J 63
(Oldham)
Derby St. OL10—8H 27
Derby St. OL11—5G 29
Derby St. SK3—5D 104
Derby St. SK6—7F 106
Derby St. SK13—6J 97
Derby St. SK15—4H 83
Derby St. WA14—8E 100
Derby St. WN1—7E 34
Derby St. WN3—4F 52
Derby St. E. WN7—3G 73
Derby St. W. WN7—3G 73
Derby Way. SK6—7F 106
Dereham Clo. BL8—5K 25
Dereham Way. WN3—5K 51
Derg St. M6—5M 77
Derker St. OL1—9A 46
Dermont Murphy Clo. M20
—8F 90
Dernford Av. M19—9M 91
Derngate Dri. WN6—2A 34
Derrett Clo. M11—7A 80
Derrick Walker Ct. OL11—5D 28
Derry Av. M22—9E 102
Derry St. OL1—2M 63
Derville Wlk. M9—8K 61
(off Alderside Rd.)
Derwen Rd. SK3—6E 104
Derwent Av. M21—9D 90
Derwent Av. M25—9B 42
Derwent Av. M35—6E 80
Derwent Av. OL7—3A 82
Derwent Av. OL10—9K 27
Derwent Av. WA3—6J 71
Derwent Av. WA15—8K 101
Derwent Av. WN2—1H 53
Derwent Clo. BL3—6M 39
Derwent Clo. BL6—8C 20
Derwent Clo. M21—9D 90
Derwent Clo. M25—9B 42
Derwent Clo. M28—6H 57
Derwent Clo. M31—1F 98
Derwent Clo. M34—4H 93
Derwent Clo. SK13—6M 97
Derwent Clo. WN7—4E 72
Derwent Dri. BL4—3B 58
Derwent Dri. BL9—2K 41
Derwent Dri. M33—3G 101
Derwent Dri. OL2—1A 46
Derwent Dri. OL9—1G 63
Derwent Dri. OL15—9M 13
Derwent Dri. SK7—7C 114
Derwent Dri. SK9—7J 113
Derwent Ind. Area. M5—6B 4 &
8C 78
Derwent Pl. WN5—1J 51
Derwent Rd. BL4—9F 38
Derwent Rd. M24—6L 43
Derwent Rd. M31—4L 87
Derwent Rd. M32—3K 89
Derwent Rd. OL16—4B 30
Derwent Rd. SK6—4E 116
Derwent Rd. WA11—8B 68
Derwent Rd. WN2—3L 53
Derwent Rd. WN4—2E 70
Derwent Rd. WN5—9F 32
Derwent St. M5—5B 4 & 7C 78
Derwent St. M8—1J 79
Derwent St. M29—9A 56
Derwent St. M35—5D 80
Derwent St. OL12—1F 28
Derwent St. WN7—4E 72
Derwent Ter. SK15—3G 83
Derwent Wlk. M25—9B 42
Derwent Wlk. OL4—1D 64
Desford Av. M21—5C 90
Desford Rd. WA11—8D 68
Design St. BL3—5B 38
Desmond Rd. M22—9E 102
Desmond St. M29—6G 55
(in two parts)
Destructor Rd. M27—7E 58
De Trafford Dri. WN2—9H 35
De Traffords, The. M30—3H 87
Dettingen St. M6—1K 77
Deva Clo. SK7—3K 115
Deva Clo. SK12—8H 115
Devaney Wlk. M34—5L 93
Deva Sq. OL9—3J 63
Devas St. M15—1G 91
Deverill Av. M18—2F 92
Devine Clo. M3—3C 4 & 5D 78
Devine Clo. OL2—3K 45
Devisdale Ct. WA14—1B 110
Devisdale Rd. WA14—9B 100
Devoke Av. M28—6L 57
Devoke Av. WA11—6A 68
Devoke Gro. BL4—9E 38
Devon Av. M19—6M 91
Devon Av. M25—8L 41
Devon Clo. BL3—5B 40
Devon Clo. M6—4G 77
Devon Clo. OL2—2M 45
Devon Clo. SK5—1J 105
Devon Clo. WN2—4K 35
Devon Clo. WN5—2J 51
Devon Dri. BL2—9C 24
Devon Dri. OL3—5B 48
Devon Dri. WN1—9B 18
Devonport Cres. OL2—5M 45
Devon Rd. M29—6M 55
Devon Rd. M30—9D 86
Devon Rd. M31—5L 87
Devon Rd. M35—4G 81
(Droylsden)
Devon Rd. M35—1E 80
(Failsworth)
Devonshire Clo. M31—4E 88
Devonshire Clo. OL10—8G 27
Devonshire Ct. M7—8D 60
Devonshire Ct. SK2—8G 105
Devonshire Dri. M28—1E 74
Devonshire Dri. SK9—7M 119
Devonshire Pk. Rd. SK2
—8G 105
Devonshire Pl. M25—3A 60
Devonshire Pl. M29—4K 55
Devonshire Rd. BL1—9B 22
Devonshire Rd. M6—4G 77
Devonshire Rd. M21—6C 90
Devonshire Rd. M28—2J 57
Devonshire Rd. M29—3J 55
Devonshire Rd. M30—5E 76
Devonshire Rd. OL11—8F 28
Devonshire Rd. SK4—3B 104
Devonshire Rd. SK7—4M 115
Devonshire Rd. WA14—7D 100
Devonshire St. M7—1D 78
Devonshire St. M12—9K 79
Devonshire St. E. M35—1D 80
Devonshire St. N. M12—8K 79
Devonshire St. S. M13—1K 91
Devon St. BL2—2G 39
Devon St. BL4—7K 39
Devon St. BL9—1M 41
Devon St. M27—6F 58
Devon St. OL9—4H 63
Devon St. OL11—4F 28
Devon St. WN2—3L 53
Devon St. WN7—3L 73
Dewar Clo. M11—6A 80
Dewar St. M11—7A 80

Dewberry Clo. M27—6E 58
Dewes Av. M27—6H 59
Dewey St. M11—8D 80
Dewhirst Rd. OL12—7F 12
(in three parts)
Dewhirst Way. OL12—7F 12
Dewhurst Clo. BL7—9D 6
Dewhurst Clough Rd. BL7—9D 6
Dewhurst Rd. BL2—7L 23
Dewhurst St. M8—1E 5 & 3F 78
Dewhurst St. OL10—8L 27
De Wint Av. SK6—5H 107
Dew Meadow Clo. OL12—9E 12
Dewsnap La. SK14—9M 83
Dewsnap La. SK16—9C 82
Dew Way. OL9—1K 63
Dexter Rd. M9—3G 61
Deyne Av. M14—2J 91
Deyne Av. M25—4B 60
Deyne St. M6—5L 77
Dial Ct. BL4—8K 39
Dial Pk. Rd. SK2—9K 105
Dial Rd. SK2—8J 105
Dial Rd. WA15—4J 111
Dialstone La. SK2—6J 105
Diamond Clo. OL6—3D 82
Diamond St. OL6—3D 82
Diamond St. SK2—7G 105
Diamond St. WN6—6A 34
Diamond St. WN7—3E 72
Diamond Ter. SK6—9F 106
Dibberford Wlk. M16—3E 90
Dibden Wlk. M23—8A 102
Dicconson Gro. WN1—8C 34
Dicconson La. WN2 & BL5 —5M 35
Dicconson St. WN1—8C 34
Dicconson Ter. WN1—8C 34
Dicken Grn. OL11—6F 28
Dicken Grn. La. OL11—6F 28
Dickens Clo. SK8—7B 114
Dickens Dri. WN2—8J 53
Dickens La. SK12—9K 115
Dickenson Rd. M14 & M13 —3J 91
Dickenson St. WN2—4L 53
Dickens Pl. WN3—4M 51
Dickens Rd. M30—6D 76
Dickens Rd. PR7—2L 17
Dickens St. OL1—5E 46
Dickinson Clo. BL1—9E 22
Dickinson Clo. WA11—9G 69
Dickinson Ct. BL6—6B 20
Dickinson St. BL1—9E 22
Dickinson St. M1—5E 5 & 7F 78
Dickinson St. M3—1D 4 & 4E 78
Dickinson St. OL4—1B 64
Dickinson St. W. BL6—6A 20
Dickinson Ter. BL1—9E 22
(off Dickinson St.)
Dickins St. OL10—8H 27
Didcot Rd. M22—3C 112
Didley Sq. M12—8A 80
Didsbury Ct. M20—1H 103
Didsbury Gro. WN2—3K 53
Didsbury Pk. M20—3H 103
Didsbury Rd. SK4—3K 103
Digby Rd. OL11—6F 28
Digby Wlk. M11—6M 79
(off Albert St.)
Dig Ga. La. OL16—7L 29
Diggle Mill Cotts. OL3—5F 48
Diggles La. OL11—4L 27
(in two parts)
Diggle St. OL2—3B 46
Diggle St. WN6—8A 34
(in two parts)
Diggle Wlk. SK15—1L 83
Digsby Ct. M20—1H 103
Dijon St. BL3—5C 38
Dilham Ct. BL1—1C 38
Dillicar Wlk. M9—9K 61
Dillmoss Wlk. M15—9D 78
Dillon Dri. M12—1L 91
Dilston Clo. M13—9J 79
Dilworth Clo. OL10—8F 26
Dilworth Ct. SK2—8L 105
Dilworth Ho. M15—1H 91
Dilworth St. M15—1H 91
Dimple Pk. BL7—8D 6
Dinas Wlk. M15—9E 78
(off Ipstone Clo.)
Dingle Av. M34—4B 94
Dingle Av. OL2—9C 30
Dingle Av. SK9—8D 118
Dingle Av. WN6—1E 32
Dingle Av. WN8—9B 32
Dingle Bank Rd. SK7—2D 114
Dinglebrook Gro. SK9—2L 119
Dingle Clo. SK6—3D 106
Dingle Clo. SK13—6G 97
Dingle Dri. M35—4H 81
Dingle Gro. SK8—7F 102
Dingle Hollow. SK6—3E 106
Dingle Rd. M24—2L 61
Dingle Rd. WN8—9B 32
Dingle Ter. OL6—6B 64
Dingle, The. SK7—3C 114
Dingle, The. SK14—8E 94
Dingle Wlk. BL1—1F 38
Dingle Wlk. WN6—5K 33
Dining Room St. M11—8A 80
Dinmore Ct. SK2—8K 105
Dinmor Rd. M22—3D 112
Dinnington Dri. M8—1F 78
Dinorwic Clo. M8—6G 61
Dinsdale Clo. M40—5K 79
Dinsdale Dri. BL3—4D 38
Dinslow Wlk. M8—9F 60
Dinting Av. M20—7G 91
Dinting La. SK13—5G 97
Dinting Lodge Ind. Est. SK13 —4F 96
Dinting Rd. SK13—4F 96
Dinting Vale. SK13—4E 96
Dinton St. M15—6B 4 & 8C 78
Dinwoodie Clo. M15—9G 79
Dipton Wlk. M8—1J 79
(off Smedley Rd.)
Dirty La. OL3—1B 48
Dirty La. OL4—8H 47
Dirty La. WA14—5L 109
Dirty Leech. OL12—5F 12
Disley Av. M20—8F 90
Disley St. OL11—6C 28
Disley Wlk. M34—5A 94
Distaff Rd. SK12—8H 115
Ditchfield La. WA16—9C 108
Ditton Mead Clo. OL12—9H 13
Ditton Wlk. M23—7M 101
Division St. BL3—5F 38
Division St. OL12—9H 13
Dixey St. BL6—7A 20
Dixon Av. M7—1D 78
Dixon Av. WA12—9C 70
Dixon Av. WN6—4G 33
Dixon Clo. M33—3K 101
Dixon Closes. OL11—3M 27
Dixon Ct. SK8—8K 103
Dixon Dri. M27—4E 58
Dixon Dri. WN6—4G 33
Dixon Fold. M25—8L 41
Dixon Fold. OL11—4L 27
Dixon Pl. WN2—7H 53
Dixon Rd. M34—5B 94
Dixon St. BL5—6E 36
Dixon St. BL6—7B 20
Dixon St. M6—1M 77
Dixon St. M10—1B 80
(in two parts)
Dixon St. M24—7A 44
Dixon St. M30—6F 86
Dixon St. OL1—9L 45
Dixon St. OL4—9E 46
Dixon St. OL6—3D 82
Dixon St. OL11—6D 28
Dixon St. WN2—5G 53
Dobb Brow Rd. BL5—1D 54
Dobb Hedge Clo. WA15—6J 111
Dobbinets La. WA15 & M23 —9L 101
Dobb La. WA16—9E 108
Dobcross Clo. M13—4A 92
Dobcross New Rd. OL3—8A 48
Dobhill St. BL4—9K 39
Dobran Wlk. OL1—6D 46
Dobroyd St. M8—8G 61
Dobsen St. BL1—8D 22
Dobson Clo. M13—9K 79
Dobson Clo. WN6—8E 16
Dobson Ct. M10—3B 80
Dobson Rd. BL1—2C 38
Dockray Ho. SK8—5L 113
Doctor Dam Cotts. OL12—8K 11
Doctor Fold La. OL10—3H 43
Doctor La. OL4—8J 47
Doctor La. Head Cotts. OL4 —8J 47
Doctor's Nook. WN7—2F 72
Doddington La. M5—7A 78
Doddington Wlk. M34—5L 93
Dodd La. BL5—6A 36
Dodd St. M5—5K 77
Dodge Fold. SK2—7L 105
Dodge Hill. SK4—3E 104
Dodgson St. OL16—4G 29
Dodhurst Rd. WN2—2M 53
Dodington Clo. M16—2F 90
Dodworth Clo. M15—9F 78
Doe Hey Gro. BL4—7H 39
Doe Hey Rd. BL3—7H 39
Doffcocker Brow. BL1—9M 21
Doffcocker La. BL1—9M 21
Dogford Rd. OL2—4K 45
Dolbey St. M5—6L 77
Dolefield. M3—4D 4 & 6E 78
Dollis Wlk. M11—7M 79
Dollond St. M9—7L 61
Dolman Wlk. M8—1F 78
Dolphin Pl. M12—6H 5 & 8J 79
Dolphin St. M12—6H 5 & 8J 79
Dolwen Wlk. M10—2B 80
Doman St. BL3—4F 38
Dombey Rd. SK12—1K 121
Domett St. M9—6J 61
Dominic Clo. M23—4L 101
Donald Av. SK14—5F 94
Donald St. M1—5F 5 & 7G 79
Dona St. SK1—5G 105
Don Av. M6—5J 77
Doncaster Av. M20—7G 91
Doncaster Clo. BL3—6M 39
Doncaster Wlk. OL1—1M 63
Donhead Wlk. M13—9J 79
Donkey La. SK9—6G 119
Donlan St. M18—9F 80
Donleigh St. M10—1D 80
Donnington. OL11—4E 28
Donnington Av. SK8—7M 103
Donnington Gdns. M28—5K 57
Donnington Rd. M18—1E 92
Donnington Rd. M26—4C 40
Donnison St. M12—9A 80
Donovan Av. M10—1H 5 & 3J 79
Don St. BL3—6D 38
Don St. M24—8C 44
Doodson Av. M30—4G 87
Doodson Sq. BL4—9K 39
Dooley La. SK6—6B 106
Dooleys La. SK9—1B 118
Dootson St. WN2—7H 53
(Bickershaw)
Dootson St. WN2—2A 54
(Hindley)
Dorac Av. SK8—6J 113
Dora St. BL0—7G 9
Dorchester Av. BL2—9L 23
Dorchester Av. M25—6C 60
Dorchester Av. M31—3F 88
Dorchester Av. M34—5M 93
Dorchester Clo. SK9—3K 119
Dorchester Clo. WA15—1J 111
Dorchester Ct. M33—3H 101
Dorchester Ct. SK8—3B 114
Dorchester Dri. M23—4L 101
Dorchester Dri. OL2—7K 45
Dorchester Gro. OL10—1J 43
Dorchester Pde. SK7—3H 115
Dorchester Rd. M27—1F 76
Dorchester Rd. SK7—3H 115
Dorchester Rd. WN8—1A 50
Dorclyn Av. M31—4D 88
Dorfield Clo. SK6—2L 105
Doric Av. SK6—2K 105
Doric Clo. M11—6M 79
Doric Grn. WN5—5D 50
Doris Av. BL2—2K 39
Doris Rd. SK3—5C 104
Doris St. M24—7A 44
Dorking Av. M10—3B 80
Dorking Clo. SK1—6H 105
Dorlan Av. M18—2F 92
Dorland Gro. SK2—6H 105
Dorman St. M11—8D 80
Dormer St. BL1—7F 22
Dorney St. M18—1D 92
Dorning Rd. M27—9G 59
Dorning St. BL4—9M 39
Dorning St. BL6—2M 35
Dorning St. BL8—6H 25
Dorning St. M29—7M 55
Dorning St. M30—6D 76
Dorning St. WN1—9B 34
Dorning St. WN2—7E 72
Dornton Wlk. M8—1F 78
(off Waterloo Rd.)
Dorothy Gro. WN7—3E 72
Dorothy Rd. SK7—1M 115
Dorothy St. BL0—6H 9
Dorothy St. M8—9F 60
Dorothy Way. WN2—8F 52
Dorrington Rd. M33—1D 100
Dorrington Rd. SK3—6A 104
Dorris St. M19—6B 92
Dorrit Clo. SK12—1L 121
Dorset Av. BL4—9J 39
Dorset Av. M14—4G 91
Dorset Av. M29—5M 55
Dorset Av. M34—7J 81
Dorset Av. OL2—2M 45
Dorset Av. OL3—5C 48
Dorset Av. SK5—9J 93
Dorset Av. SK7—2D 114
Dorset Av. SK8—8C 104
Dorset Clo. BL4—9J 39
Dorset Clo. OL10—9G 27
Dorset Clo. WN5—2J 51
Dorset Dri. BL9—1A 42
Dorset Rd. M19—5G 92
Dorset Rd. M29—4J 55
Dorset Rd. M30—9D 86
Dorset Rd. M35—4F 80
(Droylsden)
Dorset Rd. M35—1F 80
(Failsworth)
Dorset Rd. M14—8B 100
Dorset Rd. WN1—9B 18
Dorset St. BL2—2G 39
Dorset St. M27—6F 58
Dorset St. M32—4K 89
Dorset St. OL6—5D 82
Dorset St. OL9—3J 63
Dorset St. OL11—4F 28
Dorset St. WN2—2L 53
(Hindley)
Dorset St. WN2—7F 34
(Wigan)
Dorset St. WN7—3K 73
Dorstone Clo. M10—2C 80
Dorstone Clo. WN2—3B 54
Dorwood Av. M9—3J 61
Dotteral Clo. M23—9A 102
Double Cop. WN7—6D 72
Dougall Wlk. M12—9A 80
Doughty Av. M30—4F 76
Dougill St. BL1—9B 22
Douglas Av. BL6—5C 20
Douglas Av. BL8—8H 25
Douglas Av. M32—3K 89
Douglas Av. WN5—4D 68
Douglas Av. WN6—2F 16
Douglas Bank Dri. WN6—7M 33
Douglas Clo. BL6—6C 20
Douglas Clo. M25—8C 42
Douglas Clo. M35—7H 81
Douglas Dri. WN5—1F 50
Douglas Dri. WN6—4F 32
Douglas Grn. M6—2A 78
Douglas Ho. WN1—1D 52
Douglas Pk. M29—5L 55
Douglas Rd. M28—1C 76
Douglas Rd. M29—6L 55
Douglas Rd. SK3—9E 104
Douglas Rd. SK7—1L 115
Douglas Rd. WN1—8D 34
Douglas Rd. WN6—8H 17
Douglas Rd. WN7—9E 54
Douglas Sq. OL10—9F 26
Douglas St. BL0—5H 9
Douglas St. BL1—5E 22
Douglas St. M7—1D 78
Douglas St. M10—9A 62
Douglas St. M27—9G 59
Douglas St. M29—5L 55
Douglas St. M35—9G 63
Douglas St. OL1—9A 46
Douglas St. OL6—4E 82
(in two parts)
Douglas St. SK14—4E 94
Douglas St. WN2—4J 53
Douglas St. WN5—1A 52
Douglas St. Bk. BL0—5H 9
Douglas Wlk. M33—9C 88
Douglas Way. WN2—6G 53
Douro St. M10—2M 79
Douthwaite Dri. SK6—4E 106
Dove Bank. SK6—7M 107
Dove Bank Rd. BL3—5A 40
Dovecote. M35—4K 81
Dovecote La. M28—5E 56
Dovecote La. OL4—9F 46
Dovecote M. M21—6A 90
Dovedale Av. M20—7G 91
Dovedale Av. M25—5D 60
Dovedale Av. M30—4E 76
Dovedale Av. M31—4D 88
Dovedale Av. M35—5E 80
Dovedale Clo. SK6—5E 116
Dovedale Clo. WN4—8A 52
Dovedale Ct. SK13—5M 97
Dovedale Dri. OL10—5K 13
Dovedale Dri. WN6—8L 17
Dovedale Rd. BL2—9M 23
Dovedale Rd. SK2—6K 105
Dovedale Rd. WN4—8A 52
Dovedale St. M35—9E 62
Dove Dri. BL9—6B 26
Dove Dri. M30—2G 87
Dovehouse Clo. M25—9L 41
Doveleys Rd. M6—3J 77
Dovercourt Av. SK4—1M 103
Dover Gro. BL3—3D 38
Dove Rd. BL3—5B 38
Dover Pk. M31—2D 88
Dover Rd. M27—6G 59
Dover St. BL4—7J 39
Dover St. M13—9H 79
Dover St. M30—5B 76
Dover St. OL9—3J 63
Dover St. OL16—9H 13
Dover St. SK5—6E 92
Dovestone Cres. SK16—8F 82
Dovestone Wlk. M40—7E 62
Doveston Gro. M33—8H 89
Doveston Rd. M33—8H 89
Dove St. BL1—6E 22
Dove St. OL4—3C 64
Dove St. OL11—3D 28
Dove St. WA3—5G 71
Dove Wlk. BL4—8F 38
Dove Wlk. M8—1H 79
Dovey Clo. M29—9C 56
Dower St. WN2—5G 53
Dow Fold. BL8—7F 24
Dow La. BL8—7F 24
Dowling Clo. WN6—6L 33
Dowling St. M19—5C 92
(in two parts)
Dowling St. OL11—4F 28
Downall Grn. WN4—2A 68
Downall Grn. Rd. WN4—1L 69
Downbrook Way. WN4—2D 70
(off North St.)
Downesway. SK9—8K 119
Downfield Clo. BL0—5G 9
Downfields. SK5—5G 93
Downgate Wlk. M8—1G 79
Down Grn. Rd. BL2—7L 23
Downham Av. BL2—1J 39
Downham Chase. WA15 —7H 101
Downham Clo. OL2—7J 45
Downham Cres. M25—5D 60
Downham Gdns. M25—5E 60
Downham Gro. M25—5E 60
Downham Rd. OL10—8G 27
Downham Rd. SK4—9D 92
Downham Wlk. M23—5L 101
Downham Wlk. WN5—7D 50
Downing Clo. OL7—1M 81
Downing Clo. WN2—6G 53
Downing St. M1—6G 5 & 8H 79
Downing St. OL7—2M 81
Downing St. WN7—2F 72
Downley Dri. M4—3H 5 & 5J 79
Downs Dri. WA14—5E 110
Downshaw Rd. OL7—1A 82
Downs, The. M24—2B 62
(in two parts)
Downs, The. M25—6A 60
Downs, The. SK8—1K 113
Downs, The. WA14—1D 110
Downs, The. WN3—4J 51
Downton Av. WN2—4K 53
Dowry Rd. OL3—6M 31
Dowry Rd. OL4—1E 64
Dowry St. OL8—5M 63
Dowson Rd. SK14—7D 94
Dowson St. BL2—2G 39
Dow St. SK14—1D 94
Doyle Av. SK6—2K 105
Doyle Clo. OL1—5E 46
Doyle Rd. BL3—6L 37
Draba Brow. BL0—5J 9
Drake Av. BL4—1K 57
Drake Av. M30—8E 86
Drake Clo. OL1—9M 45
Drake Ct. SK5—1E 104
Drake Hall. BL5—3D 54
Drake Rd. OL15—2C 14
Drake Rd. WA14—5B 100
Drake St. M29—6J 55
Drake St. OL16—3F 28
Draxford Ct. SK9—5H 119
Draycott St. BL1—8E 22
Draycott St. E. BL1—8F 22
Drayfields. M35—5K 81
Drayton Clo. BL1—8D 22
Drayton Clo. M33—3D 100
Drayton Cres. WA11—9D 68
Drayton Dri. SK8—5H 113
Drayton Gro. WA15—9G 101
Drayton Manor. M20—5H 103
Drayton Wlk. M16—1D 90
Drefus Av. M11—5C 80
Dresden St. M10—8C 62
Dresser Cen., The. M11—8B 80
Drewett St. M10—3L 79
Dreyfus St. M10—4L 79
Driffield St. M14—3G 91
Driffield St. M30—7C 76
Drill Wlk. M4—5J 79
(off Kirby Wlk.)
Drinkwater La. BL6—7B 20
Drinkwater Rd. M25—7M 59
Driscoll St. M13—3M 91
Drive, The. BL0—1K 9
Drive, The. BL9—5M 25
Drive, The. M7—7C 60
Drive, The. M20—2J 103
Drive, The. M25—4B 60
Drive, The. M33—4E 100
Drive, The. SK5—1J 105
Drive, The. SK6—2K 105
(Bredbury)
Drive, The. SK6—7E 106
(Marple)
Drive, The. SK8—9C 104
Drive, The. WA13—3D 108
Drive, The. WA15—4K 111
Drive, The. WN7—4F 72
Droitwich Rd. M10—3K 79
Dronfield Rd. M6—3K 77
Dronfield Rd. M22—5D 102
Droughts La. M25—9D 42
Drovers Wlk. SK13—5K 97
Droylesden Rd. M34—6H 81
Droylsden Rd. M10—1C 80
Druids Clo. BL7—8D 6
Druid St. WN4—5C 70
Drummer's La. WN4—9K 51
Drummond Sq. WN5—1L 51
Drummond St. BL1—6E 22
Drury La. OL9—5G 63
Drury St. M19—5A 92
Dryad Clo. M27—6F 58
Drybrook Clo. M13—1L 91
Dryburgh Av. BL1—6D 22
Dry Clough La. OL3—1A 66
Dry Croft La. OL3—2B 48
Dryden Av. M27—9D 58
Dryden Av. SK8—7L 103
Dryden Av. WN4—9M 51
Dryden Clo. SK6—9F 106
Dryden Clo. SK16—8H 83
Dryden Clo. WN3—3A 52
Dryden Ho. WN3—3A 52
Dryden Rd. M16—3C 90
Dryden St. M13—9J 79
Dryden Way. M34—6A 94
Dryfield La. BL6—5A 20
Drygate Wlk. M9—9L 61
(off Orpington Rd.)
Dryhurst Dri. SK12—6K 117
Dryhurst La. SK12—6K 117
Dryhurst Wlk. M15—9G 79
Drymoss. OL8—7A 64
Dryton Wlk. WN2—7G 35
Drywood Av. M28—2A 76
Ducal St. M4—2G 5 & 3H 79
Duchess Pk. Clo. OL2—1B 46
Duchess Rd. M8—8H 61
Duchess St. OL2—1A 46
Duchess Wlk. BL3—5B 38
Duchy Av. BL3—9A 38
Duchy Av. M28—8K 57
Duchy Bank. M6—1K 77
Duchy Rd. M6—1L 77
Duchy St. M6—4M 77
(in two parts)
Duchy St. SK3—6D 104
Ducie Av. BL1—2C 38
Ducie Pl. M5—4B 4 & 6C 78
Ducie St. BL0—4H 9
Ducie St. M1—4G 5 & 6H 79
Ducie St. M25—9M 41
Ducie St. M26—4F 40
Ducie St. OL8—6M 63
Duckshaw La. BL4—9J 39
Duckworth Ho. M8—9G 61
Duckworth Rd. M25—5M 59
Duckworth St. BL3—5C 38
Duckworth St. BL9—6A 26
(in two parts)
Duckworth St. OL2—2C 46
Duddon Av. BL2—9M 23
Duddon Clo. M25—9C 42
Duddon Wlk. M24—7L 43
Dudley Av. BL2—9J 23
Dudley Av. M25—9M 41
Dudley Clo. M15—1E 90
Dudley Rd. M16—4D 90
Dudley Rd. M27—7F 58
Dudley Rd. M30—1D 98
Dudley Rd. M33—8J 89
Dudley Rd. WA15—6H 101
Dudley St. M7 & M8—9E 60
Dudley St. M30—6C 76
Dudley St. M34—2L 93
Dudley St. OL4—2D 64
Dudley St. WN4—2A 70
Dudlow Wlk. M15—9D 78
Duerden St. BL3—7A 38
Duffield Ct. M15—1G 91
Duffield Gdns. M24—3M 61
Duffield Rd. M6—2K 77
Duffield Rd. M24—3M 61
Duffins Clo. OL12—8D 12
Dufton Wlk. M22—3E 112
Dufton Wlk. M24—7L 43
Dugdale Av. M9—4L 61
Duke Av. SK8—6M 113
Duke Av. WA3—8J 73
Duke Clo. M16—1D 90
Duke Ct. M16—1D 90
Dukefield St. M22—5E 102
Duke Pl. M3—5D 4 & 7E 78
Duke Rd. SK14—1F 94
Dukes All. BL1—2F 38
(off Ridgeway Gdns.)
Duke's Av. BL3—5A 40
Dukes Platting. OL6—2F 82
Duke's Row. WN2—5H 35
Duke's Ter. SK16—6B 82
(off Astley St.)
Duke St. BL0—7G 9
Duke St. BL1—1E 38
(in two parts)
Duke St. BL2—9C 24
Duke St. M3—5D 4 & 7E 78
(Manchester)
Duke St. M3—3E 5 & 5F 78
(Salford)
Duke St. M26—7H 41
Duke St. M28—3G 57
Duke St. M29—1C 74
Duke St. M30—3C 76
Duke St. M34—3L 93
Duke St. M35—6H 81
(Droylsden)
Duke St. M35—8G 63
(Failsworth)
Duke St. OL2—3C 46
Duke St. OL5—7L 65
Duke St. OL6—4B 82
Duke St. OL10—8H 27
Duke St. OL12—1F 28
(in two parts)
Duke St. OL15—6A 14
Duke St. SK1—4F 104
Duke St. SK9—7M 119
Duke St. SK13—6J 97
Duke St. SK15—6F 82
Duke St. WA3—6G 71
Duke St. WN1—7G 34
Duke St. WN2—5G 53
Duke St. WN3—4M 51
Duke St. WN4—4C 70
Duke St. WN7—3G 73
Duke St. N. BL1—1E 38
Duke's Wharf. M28—2M 75
Dukinfield Rd. SK14—1C 94
Dukinfield St. WN7—2G 73
Dulford Wlk. M7—1F 78
Dulford Wlk. M13—1J 91
(off Plymouth Gro.)
Dulgar St. M11—7B 80
Dulverton St. M10—1B 80
Dulwich St. M4—2G 5 & 4H 79
Dumbarton Clo. SK5—8F 92
Dumbarton Dri. OL10—9G 27
Dumbarton Grn. WN6—7L 33
Dumbarton Rd. SK5—7F 92
Dumbell St. M27—6F 58
Dumber La. M33—8F 88
Dumers Clo. M26—5K 41
Dumers La. M26 & BL9—5K 41
Dumfries Av. OL3—8J 31
Dumfries Dri. OL3—8J 31
Dumfries Wlk. OL10—9G 27
Dumplington Circ. M31 —8D 76
Dunbar Av. M23—1A 112
Dunbar Gro. OL10—1F 42
Dunbar St. OL1—9L 45
Dunblaine Av. SK4—2D 104
Dunblane Av. BL1—5F 22
Dunblane Av. BL3—4L 37
Dunblane Clo. WN4—3J 69
Dunblane Gro. OL10—1G 43
Duncan Edward Ho. M6—4M 77
(off Sutton Dwellings)
Duncan Edwards Ct. M10—2B 80
(off Eddie Colman Clo.)
Duncan Pl. WN5—1L 51
Duncan Rd. M13—3M 91
(in two parts)
Duncan St. BL1—1F 38
Duncan St. BL6—7C 20
Duncan St. M5—5B 4 & 7C 78
Duncan St. M7—6C 60
Duncan St. OL2—6A 46
Duncan St. WN4—2C 70
Duncan St. SK16—9C 82
Dunchurch Clo. BL6—3K 37
Dunchurch Rd. M33—1E 100
Dun Clo. M3—3C 4 & 5D 78
Duncombe Clo. SK7—1G 115
Duncombe Dri. M40—9B 62
Duncombe Rd. BL3—6E 38
Duncombe St. M7—1E 78
Dundee. M30—5E 76
(off St Andrews Ct.)
Dundee Clo. OL10—9F 26
Dundee La. BL0—5H 9
Dundonald Rd. M20—2J 103
Dundonald Rd. SK8—5A 114
Dundonald St. SK2—7F 104
Dundraw Clo. M24—8H 43
Dundrennan Clo. SK12—7K 115
Dunecroft. M34—2A 94
Dunedin Rd. BL8—9F 8
Dunelm Dri. M33—4K 101
Dungeon Wlk. SK9—4H 119
Dunham Av. WA3—6F 70
Dunham Clo. BL5—3D 54
Dunham Gro. WN7—5L 73
Dunham Lawn. WA14—9B 100
Dunham M. WA14—3M 109
Dunham Rise. WA14—9C 100
Dunham Rd. M31—1K 99
Dunham Rd. SK9—7K 113
Dunham Rd. WA13—6E 98
Dunham Rd. WA14—4L 109
Dunham St. OL4—9E 46
Dunkeld Gdns. M23—7M 101
Dunkeld Rd. M23—7M 101
Dunkerley Av. M35—9F 62
Dunkerleys Clo. M8—3F 60
Dunkerley St. OL2—5K 45
Dunkerley St. OL4—9C 46
Dunkerley St. OL7—2A 82
Dunkery Rd. M22—3D 112
Dunkirk Clo. M34—4G 93
Dunkirk La. SK14—1E 94
Dunkirk Rise. OL12—3E 28
Dunkirk Rd. M25—8M 41
Dunkirk St. M35—6H 81
Dunley Clo. M12—1A 92
Dunlin Clo. BL2—4G 39
Dunlin Clo. OL11—3M 27
Dunlin Clo. SK2—8A 106
Dunlin Clo. SK12—8G 115
Dunlin Dri. M30—3G 87
Dunlin Wlk. WA14—5B 100
Dunlop Av. OL11—6E 28
Dunlop St. M3—4E 5 & 6F 78
Dunmail Av. WA11—6C 68
Dunmail Dri. M24—6L 43
Dunmere Wlk. M9—9J 61
(off Mannington Dri.)
Dunmore Rd. SK8—7H 103
Dunmow Ct. SK2—8L 105
Dunmow Wlk. M23—3A 102
Dunne La. SK13—4L 97
Dunnerdale Wlk. M18—1C 92
Dunnisher Rd. M23—8B 102
Dunnock Clo. SK2—8M 105
Dunollie Rd. M33—2L 101
Dunoon Clo. OL10—9G 27
Dunoon Dri. BL1—5C 22
Dunoon Rd. SK5—7F 92
Dunoon Rd. WN2—4K 35
Dunoon Wlk. M9—9K 61
Dunrobin Clo. OL10—1G 43
Dunscar Clo. M25—1K 59
Dunscore Rd. WN3—5L 51
Dunsdale Dri. WN4—4C 70
Dunsfold Dri. M23—5K 101
Dunsford Ct. OL4—2F 64
Dunsley Av. M10—3D 62
Dunsmore Clo. M16—2D 90
Dunsop Dri. BL1—7M 21
Dunsop Wlk. M15—9F 78
Dunstable. OL12—2E 28
(off Spotland Rd.)
Dunstable St. M19—5B 92
Dunstall Rd. M22—8E 102
Dunstan St. BL2—2J 39
Dunstar Av. M34—8L 81
Dunster Av. M9—4L 61
Dunster Av. M27—5H 59
Dunster Av. OL11—5E 28
Dunster Av. SK5—9J 93
Dunster Clo. SK7—3J 115
Dunster Dri. M31—5J 87
Dunster Pl. M28—9F 56
Dunster Rd. M28—9F 56
Dunsters Av. BL8—5J 25
Dunsterville Ter. OL11—5E 28
(off New Barn La.)
Dunston St. M11—7C 80
Dunton Grn. SK5—8H 93
Dunton Towers. SK5—8H 93
(off Dunton Grn.)
Dunvegan Ct. OL10—9E 26
Dunvegan Rd. SK2—3M 115
Dunwood Av. OL2—1C 46
Dunworth St. M14—3H 91
Durant St. M4—2G 5 & 4H 79
Durban Clo. OL2—3A 46
Durban Rd. BL1—5E 22
Durban St. M29—6G 55
Durban St. OL7—6L 81
Durban St. OL8—5J 63
Durban St. OL11—8C 28
Durban St. WN7—2L 71
Durden M. OL2—3B 46
Durham Av. M31—3E 88
Durham Clo. BL3—5B 40
Durham Clo. M27—6F 58
Durham Clo. M29—5A 56
Durham Clo. SK6—4A 106
Durham Cres. M35—1G 81
Durham Dri. BL0—8H 9
Durham Dri. BL9—1A 42
Durham Dri. OL6—6D 64
Durham Gro. M30—8C 86
Durham Rd. M6—2J 77
Durham Rd. WN2—3L 53
Durhams Pas. OL15—6A 14
Durham St. BL1—8F 22
Durham St. M26—4J 41
Durham St. M35—7G 81
Durham St. OL9—4J 63
(in two parts)
Durham St. OL11—4F 28
Durham St. SK5—4E 92
Durham St. WN1—3E 34
Durham St. Bri. OL11—5G 29
Durham Wlk. M34—5M 93
Durham Wlk. OL13—8G 27
Durley Av. M8—9H 61
Durley Av. WA15—6H 101
Durling St. M12—6H 5 & 8J 79
Durnford Av. M31—4G 89
Durnford Clo. OL12—9K 11
Durnford St. M24—8M 43
Durnford Wlk. M22—1B 112
Durn St. OL15—5C 14
Durrington Wlk. M10—5C 62
(off Sawston Wlk.)
Dursley Dri. WN4—3D 70
Dutton Gro. WN7—5J 73
Dutton St. M3—2E 5 & 4F 78
Duty St. BL2—7E 22
Duxbury Av. BL2—5L 23
Duxbury Av. BL3—4A 40
Duxbury Dri. BL9—8C 26
Duxbury Sq. M15—1G 91
Duxbury St. BL1—8D 22
Duxford Lodge. M8—6F 60
Duxford Wlk. M10—5C 62
Dyche St. M4—2G 5 & 4H 79
Dye Ho. La. OL16—8J 13
Dye La. SK6—3B 106
Dyers Clo. WA13—9A 98
Dyers Ct. OL15—5A 14
Dyers La. WA13—9A 98
Dyer St. M5—6B 4 & 8C 78
Dyer St. M11—7A 80
Dyer St. WA3—6F 70
Dymchurch St. M10—3C 80
Dysarts Clo. OL5—5L 65
Dysart St. OL6—5D 82
Dysart St. SK2—8H 105
Dyserth Gro. SK5—9F 92
Dyson Clo. BL4—9K 39
Dyson Gro. OL4—9F 46
Dyson St. BL4—1K 57
Dyson St. OL1—2M 63
Dyson St. OL5—6H 65
Dystelegh Rd. SK12—6K 117
Eades St. M6—4A 78
Eadingall St. M11—7A 80
Eadington St. M8—7G 61
Eafield Av. OL16—3M 29
Eafield Clo. OL16—3M 29
Eafield Rd. OL15—8L 13
Eafield Rd. OL16—1J 29
Eagar St. M10—1C 80
Eagle Dri. M6—2A 78
Eagle Mill Ct. OL3—4L 47
Eagles Nest. M25—5A 60
Eagle St. BL2—2G 39
Eagle St. M4—3F 5 & 5G 79
Eagle St. OL9—1L 63
Eagle Technology Pk. OL11 —6G 29
Eagley Brow. BL1—4F 22
Eagley Ct. BL7—3G 23
Eagley Dri. BL8—9G 25
Eagley Way. BL1—3F 22
Ealees. OL15—6C 14
Ealees Rd. OL15—6C 14
Ealing Av. M14—4J 91
Ealing Pl. M19—8A 92
Eames Av. M26—9A 40
Eamont Wlk. M9—9K 61
Earby Gro. M9—5M 61
Earle Rd. SK7—2E 114
Earlesden Cres. M28—2G 57
Earle St. OL7—5M 81
Earl Rd. BL0—5H 9
Earl Rd. SK4—1C 104
Earl Rd. SK8—7L 113
Earlscliffe Ct. WA14—9B 100
Earlston Av. M34—3G 93
Earl St. BL0—5K 9
Earl St. BL3—4G 39
Earl St. BL9—8M 25
Earl St. M7—1C 4 & 3D 78
Earl St. M25—4C 60
Earl St. M29—6H 55
Earl St. M34—7L 81
(Audenshaw)
Earl St. M34—2G 93
(Denton)
Earl St. OL5—7H 65
Earl St. OL10—8J 27
Earl St. OL11—1C 44
Earl St. SK3—5D 104
Earl St. WN1—7C 34
Earl St. WN2—1G 53
Earl St. WN7—2G 73
Earlswood Wlk. BL3—5F 38
Earlswood Wlk. M18—9C 80
Earl Ter. SK16—6B 82
(off Astley St.)
Earl Wlk. M12—1M 91
Early Bank. SK15—8J 83
Early Bank Rd. SK16—9H 83
Earney St. WA14—9D 100
Earnshaw Av. OL12—8E 12
Earnshaw Av. SK1—4H 105
Earnshaw St. BL3—6B 38
Earnshaw St. M40—1L 79
Earnshaw St. OL7—2M 81
Earnshaw St. SK14—2D 96
Easby Clo. SK8—6B 114
Easby Clo. SK12—7K 115
Easby Rd. M24—6M 43
Easedale Clo. M31—3M 87
Easedale Rd. BL1—1A 38
Easington Wlk. M10—1A 80
E. Aisle Rd. M17—2J 89
East Av. M19—7M 91
East Av. M25—7L 41
East Av. SK8—3J 113
East Av. SK15—4G 83
(in two parts)
East Av. WA3—6J 71
East Av. WN7—4J 73
E. Bank Rd. BL0—8G 9
(in two parts)
Eastbank St. BL1—8F 22
E. Bond St. WN7—2G 73
Eastbourne Gro. BL1—1A 38
Eastbourne St. OL8—4B 64
Eastbourne St. OL11—5F 28
E. Bridgewater St. WN7—3G 73
Eastbrook Av. M26—5J 41
Eastburn Av. M10—2H 5 & 4J 79
Eastbury Ct. M27—9B 60
E. Central Dri. M27—9H 59
Eastchurch Clo. BL4—1K 57
Eastcote Av. M11—7E 80
Eastcote Rd. SK5—9F 92
Eastcote Wlk. BL4—8L 39
Eastcourt Wlk. M13—9J 79
East Cres. M24—1M 61
Eastdale Pl. WA14—6D 100
E. Downs Rd. SK8—1M 113
E. Downs Rd. WA14—2C 110
East Dri. BL9—5B 42
East Dri. M6—2L 77
East Dri. M21—5M 89
East Dri. M27—9H 59
East Dri. SK6—1F 116
Easterdale. OL4—2C 64
Eastern Av. M27—5K 59
Eastern By-Pass. M11—5C 80
(in two parts)
Eastern Circ. M19—8A 92
Eastfield. M6—3L 77
Eastfield Av. M10—4L 79
Eastfield Av. M24—1A 62
Eastfields. M26—4F 40
Eastford Sq. M10—1H 5 & 3J 79
Eastgarth. WN2—6H 53
Eastgate. OL12—4C 12
Eastgate St. OL7—6A 82
E. Gate St. OL16—2F 28
E. Grange Av. M11—4C 80
East Gro. M13—1J 91
Eastgrove Av. BL1—4E 22
Eastham Av. BL9—4L 25
Eastham Av. M14—5H 91
Eastham Way. M28—3H 57
Eastham Way. SK9—7K 113
Easthaven Av. M11—4C 80
E. Hill St. OL4—2A 64
Eastholme Dri. M19—7B 92
Easthope Clo. M20—7H 91
E. Lancashire Rd. M28 & M27 —8L 57
E. Lancashire Rd. WA3, WN7, M29 & M28—8D 72
E. Lancashire Rd. WA11, WA12 & WA3—7L 69
Eastlands Rd. M9—3K 61
East Lea. M34—3A 94
Eastleigh Av. M7—8E 60
Eastleigh Cres. WN7—4H 73
Eastleigh Dri. M40—4K 79
Eastleigh Gro. BL1—1E 38
Eastleigh Rd. M25—5E 60
(in two parts)
Eastleigh Rd. SK8—3H 113
E. Lynn Dri. M28—5A 58
East Meade. BL3—7E 38
E. Meade. M21—7B 90
E. Meade. M25—6D 60
E. Meade. M27—1E 76
East M. BL2—6K 23
Eastmoor Dri. M10—2E 80
Eastmoor Gro. BL3—7B 38
East Mt. WN5—2F 50
E. Newton St. M4—2H 5 & 4J 79
Eastnor Clo. M15—9D 78
Easton Clo. M24—2C 62
Easton Dri. SK8—8A 104
Easton Rd. M35—5E 80
E. Ordsall La. M5 & M3—4C 4 & 6D 78
E. Over. SK6—5A 106
Eastpark Clo. M13—9J 79
E. Philip St. M3—2D 4 & 4E 78
East Rd. M12—3A 92
East Rd. M18—3B 92
East Rd. M22—6C 112
East Rd. M31—9F 76
East Rd. M32—2H 89
East Rd. SK15—1L 83
Eastry Av. SK5—8H 93
East St. BL9—9M 25
East St. M2—5E 5 & 7F 78
East St. M26—6H 41
East St. M29—7M 55
East St. M34—9M 81
East St. OL6—3D 82
East St. OL12—5J 13
East St. OL15—6C 14
East St. OL16—3K 29
(Firgrove, in two parts)
East St. OL16—2G 29
(Rochdale)
East St. SK3—5D 104
East St. WN2—5B 54
East St. WN4—3D 70
E. Union St. M16—9C 78
East Vale. SK6—8G 107
E. View. BL0—2J 9
E. View. BL8—8J 9
East View. M24—9M 43
East View. M33—2H 101
E. View. OL12—1D 12
(off Market St.)
Eastville Gdns. M19—9L 91
East Wlk. BL7—9D 6
Eastward Av. SK9—5F 118
East Way. BL1—7H 23
Eastway. M24—8M 43
Eastway. M31—3L 87
Eastway. M33—3F 100
Eastway. OL2—3B 46
Eastwell Rd. WN4—4A 70
Eastwell Rd. WN6—6M 33
Eastwood Av. M10—7F 62
Eastwood Av. M28—5G 57
Eastwood Av. M31—4D 88
Eastwood Av. M35—6E 80
Eastwood Clo. BL9—8B 26
Eastwood Ct. BL9—8B 26
Eastwood Dri. SK3—9D 104
Eastwood Gro. WN7—2C 72
Eastwood Rd. M10—7E 62
Eastwood St. M34—8K 81
Eastwood St. OL15—6B 14
Eastwood Ter. BL1—1M 37
Eastwood View. SK15—6H 83
Eatock Way. BL5—2D 54
Eaton Clo. M27—6F 58
Eaton Clo. SK8—1M 113
Eaton Clo. SK12—9A 116
Eaton Ct. WA14—3C 110
Eaton Dri. OL7—3M 81
Eaton Dri. SK9—7K 119
Eaton Dri. WA15—5G 101
Eaton Rd. M8—7F 60
Eaton Rd. M33—1G 101
Eaton Rd. WA14—3C 110
Eaton St. WN2—2L 53
Eaversham St. OL1—9L 45
Eavesford Wlk. M15—9E 78
Eaves Knoll Rd. SK12—3M 117
Eaves La. OL9—3G 63
Ebbdale Clo. SK1—5G 105
Ebberstone St. M14—4G 91
Ebden St. M1—5G 5 & 7H 79
Ebenezer St. M15—6E 5 & 8F 78
Ebenezer St. OL6—4C 82
Ebenezer St. SK13—7K 97
Ebenezer St. WA11—9F 68
Ebnall Wlk. M14—7K 91
Ebor Clo. OL2—1A 46
Ebor Rd. M22—9E 102
Ebor St. OL15—6B 14
Ebsworth St. M10—8A 62
Ebury St. M26—5F 40
Eccles Bri. Rd. SK6—8F 106
Eccles By-Pass. M30—4D 76
Eccles Clo. M11—7C 80
Eccleshall Clo. M15—9G 79
Eccleshall St. M11—6C 80
(in two parts)
Eccles New Rd. M5—5H 77
Eccles Old Rd. M5—5G 77
Eccles Old Rd. M6—4H 77
Eccles Rd. M27—1F 76
Eccles Rd. WN5—8H 33
Eccles St. BL0—5H 9
Eccleston Av. BL2—9H 23
Eccleston Av. M14—5H 91
Eccleston Av. M27—9D 58
Eccleston Clo. BL8—9G 25
Eccleston Pl. M7—8D 60
Eccleston Rd. SK3—9D 104
Eccleston St. M35—8G 63
Eccleston St. WN1—8C 34
Eccleston Way. SK9—8K 113
Eccups La. SK9—3C 118
Echo St. M1—5G 5 & 7H 79
Eckersley Av. WN2—5K 53
Eckersley Fold La. M29—8G 55
Eckersley Rd. BL1—7E 22
Eckersley St. BL3—5C 38
Eckersley St. WN1—8E 34
Eckford St. M8—1H 79
Eclipse Clo. OL16—3J 29
Edale Av. M10—8A 62
Edale Av. M31—5B 88
Edale Av. M34—8K 81
(Audenshaw)
Edale Av. M34—6M 93
(Denton)
Edale Av. SK5—5G 93
Edale Bank. SK13—4E 96
Edale Clo. M29—5J 55
Edale Clo. M30—5G 87
Edale Clo. SK7—3L 115
Edale Clo. SK8—5K 113
Edale Clo. SK13—4E 96
Edale Clo. WA14—3C 110
Edale Cres. SK13—4E 96
Edale Dri. WN6—8L 17
Edale Fold. SK13—4E 96
(off Edale Cres.)
Edale Gro. M33—3E 100
Edale Gro. OL6—1G 83
Edale Rd. BL3—5A 38
Edale Rd. BL4—1J 57
Edale Rd. M32—3H 89
Edale Rd. WN7—3H 73
Edale St. M6—2B 78
Edale St. M35—9E 62
Eddie Colman Clo. M10—2B 60
Eddie Colman Ct. M6—4A 78
(off Meyrick Rd.)
Eddisbury Av. M20—6F 90
Eddisbury Av. M31—2K 87
Edditch Gro. BL2—2J 39
Eddleston St. WN4—1M 69
Eddystone Clo. M15—6A 78
Eden Av. BL0—1K 9
Eden Av. BL1—7E 22
Eden Av. SK6—5E 116
Eden Bank. WN7—1H 73
Edenbridge Rd. M10—3B 80
Edenbridge Rd. SK8—9B 104
Eden Clo. M15—9G 79
Eden Clo. OL10—7H 27
Eden Clo. SK1—5G 105
Eden Clo. SK9—6E 118
Edendale Dri. M22—3D 112
Edenfield Av. M21—1D 102
Edenfield La. M28—2M 75
Edenfield Rd. M25—5E 60
Edenfield Rd. OL11 & OL12 —9J 11
Edenfield Rd. OL12—5C 10
Edenfield St. OL12—1C 28
Eden Gro. BL1—7D 22
Edenhall Av. M19—6M 91
Edenham Wlk. M10—6D 62
Edenhurst Dri. WA15—8H 101
Edenhurst Rd. SK2—7H 105
Eden Lodge. BL1—7E 22
Eden Pl. M33—9H 89
Eden Pl. SK8—7K 103
Eden Rd. WN7—2C 72
Edensor Dri. WA15—1J 111
Eden St. BL0—1K 9
Eden St. BL1—6E 22
Eden St. OL1—1L 63
Eden St. OL12—2D 28
Edenvale. M28—9G 57
Eden Waugh Gdns. OL12—8D 12
Eden Way. OL2—1A 46
Edgar St. BL0—6H 9
Edgar St. BL3—3E 38
Edgar St. OL16—9J 13
Edgar St. W. BL0—6H 9
Edgbaston Dri. M16—3A 90
Edgedale Av. M19—9L 91
Edgefield Av. M9—4L 61
Edge Fold Rd. M28—7K 57
Edge Grn. La. WA3—5F 70
Edge Grn. Rd. WN4—4F 70
Edge Grn. St. WN4—3D 70
Edge Hall Rd. WN5—3E 50
(in two parts)
Edge Hill. SK15—6H 83
Edge Hill Av. OL2—7L 45
Edgehill Chase. SK9—4L 119
Edgehill Clo. M5—5M 77
Edgehill Ct. M32—4L 89
Edgehill Rd. BL3—6B 38
Edgehill Rd. M6—4J 77
Edge Hill Rd. OL2—6L 45
Edgehill St. M4—3F 5 & 5G 79
Edge La. BL1—5J 21
Edge La. BL7—2G 7
Edge La. M11 & M35—5D 80
Edge La. M32 & M21—5K 89
Edge La. SK14—2L 95
Edge La. Rd. OL1—9M 45
Edge La. St. OL2—5L 45
Edgeley Fold. SK3—6C 104
Edgeley Rd. M31—4A 88
Edgeley Rd. SK3—6A 104
Edgeley Rd. Trading Est. SK3 —6A 104
Edgemoor. WA14—2A 110
Edgemoor Clo. M26—4E 40
Edgemoor Clo. OL4—2F 64
Edgemoor Dri. OL11—5M 27
Edgerley Pl. WN4—4A 70
Edgerton Rd. WA3—7M 71
Edge St. M4—3F 5 & 5G 79
Edge View. OL1—8E 44
Edge View La. SK9—9B 118
Edgeview Wlk. M13—6G 5 & 8H 79
Edgeware Av. M25—4F 60
Edgeware Gro. WN3—5K 51
Edgeware Rd. M30—3A 76
Edgeware Rd. OL9—5E 62
Edgeway. SK9—6H 119
Edgeway Rd. WN3—7A 52
Edgewood. WN6—4G 33
Edgeworth Av. BL2—9D 24
Edgeworth Clo. OL10—8G 27
Edgeworth Dri. M14—7L 91
Edgeworth Rd. WA3—6F 70
Edgeworth Rd. WN2—5A 54
Edgmont Av. BL3—5D 38
Edgware Rd. M10—3B 80
Edgworth Dri. BL8—9G 25
Edilom Rd. M8—6E 60
Edinburgh. M30—5E 76
(off St Andrews Ct.)
Edinburgh Clo. SK8—7M 103
Edinburgh Clo. WN2—9G 35
Edinburgh Dri. SK6—9C 94
Edinburgh Dri. WN2—5B 54
Edinburgh Dri. WN5—3K 51
Edinburgh Rd. BL3—7A 40
Edinburgh Sq. M10—3K 79
Edinburgh Wlk. WN2—4K 35
Edinburgh Way. OL11—6D 28
Edington. OL12—2E 28
(off Spotland Rd.)
Edison Rd. M30—6C 76
Edison St. M11—8E 80
Edith Av. M14—3G 91
Edith Cavell Clo. M11—6C 80
Edith Cliff Wlk. M10—7F 62
Edith St. BL1—3C 38
Edith St. BL4—1K 57
Edith St. OL8—5M 63
Edith St. WN3—1B 52
Edleston Gro. SK9—2L 119
Edlin Clo. M12—1L 91
Edlingham. OL11—4E 28
Edlington Wlk. M10—1C 80
Edmonds St. M24—8B 44
Edmonton Ct. SK2—9G 105
Edmonton Rd. M10—3A 80
Edmonton Rd. SK2—9G 105
Edmund Clo. SK4—2E 104
Edmund Dri. WN7—2C 72
Edmunds Pas. OL15—4A 14
Edmund St. BL1—1F 38
Edmund St. M6—4L 77
Edmund St. M26—5J 41
Edmund St. M35—6G 81
(Droylsden)
Edmund St. M35—8F 62
(Failsworth)
Edmund St. OL2—2C 46
Edmund St. OL12—2D 28
Edmund St. OL16—4M 29
Edna Rd. WN7—9C 54
Edna St. SK14—5D 94
Edson Rd. M8—5F 60
Edward Av. M6—4J 77
Edward Av. M21—6M 89
Edward Av. OL15—8M 13
Edward Av. SK6—2L 105
Edward Charlton Rd. M16 —4A 90
Edward Dri. WN4—3B 70
Edward Onyon Ct. M6—4L 77
Edward Rd. M9—3K 61
Edward Rd. OL2—3A 46
Edward Rd. WN1—7C 34
Edwards Clo. SK6—8E 106
Edwards Ct. M22—1D 112
Edward St. BL3—4D 38
Edward St. BL4—7H 39
Edward St. BL5—9E 36
Edward St. BL6—7A 20
Edward St. BL8—7J 25
Edward St. BL9—9M 25
Edward St. M7—1D 4 & 3E 78
Edward St. M9—8L 61
Edward St. M24—7A 44
Edward St. M25—3A 60
Edward St. M26—7H 41
(Radcliffe)
Edward St. M26—9B 40
(Stoneclough)
Edward St. M33—1L 101
Edward St. M34—8K 81
(Audenshaw)
Edward St. M34—2M 93
(Denton)
Edward St. M35—7G 81
(Droylsden)
Edward St. M35—9E 62
(Failsworth)
Edward St. OL6—5E 82
Edward St. OL9—1G 63
(Chadderton)
Edward St. OL9—2J 63
(Oldham)
Edward St. OL12—1D 28
Edward St. OL16—2G 29
Edward St. SK1—5F 104
Edward St. SK6—4G 107
Edward St. SK13—5J 97
Edward St. SK14—3C 94
(in two parts)
Edward St. SK16—9C 82
Edward St. WA11—9G 69
Edward St. WN1—9F 34
Edward St. WN7—3G 73
Edwards Way. SK6—8E 106
Edwin Rd. M11—5L 79
Edwin St. BL9—8L 25
Edwin St. OL9—5K 63
Edwin St. WN1—1E 52
Edzell Wlk. M11—6C 80
Eeasbrook. M31—5D 88
Egbert St. M10—9A 62
Egerton. WA16—7C 108
Egerton Av. WA13—5C 98
Egerton Barn Cottage. BL7 —9E
Egerton Clo. OL10—9K 27
Egerton Ct. M21—7M 89
Egerton Ct. M28—8A 58
Egerton Ct. SK3—9F 104
Egerton Ct. WN2—3L 53
Egerton Cres. M20—7H 91
Egerton Cres. OL10—9J 27
Egerton Dri. M33—9H 89
Egerton Dri. WA15—1G 111
Egerton Gro. M28—5K 57
Egerton M. M3—4C 4 & 6D 7
Egerton M. M35—7G 81
Egerton Pk. M28—9B 58
Egerton Pl. OL2—3A 46
Egerton Rd. BL7—7A 6
Egerton Rd. M14—6K 91
Egerton Rd. M25—1M 59
Egerton Rd. M28—5K 57
Egerton Rd. M30—3D 76
Egerton Rd. SK3—8G 105
Egerton Rd. SK9—2H 119
Egerton Rd. WA15—1G 111
Egerton Rd. N. M16 & M21 —4C
Egerton Rd. N. SK4—9C 92
Egerton Rd. S. M21—6C 90
Egerton Rd. S. SK4—1C 104
Egerton St. BL4—8J 39
Egerton St. M3—4C 4 & 6D
Egerton St. M15—6C 4 & 8D
Egerton St. M24—1J 61
Egerton St. M25—4C 60
Egerton St. M26—7G 41
Egerton St. M30—5B 76
Egerton St. M34—1M 93
Egerton St. M35—6H 81
Egerton St. OL1—1M 63
Egerton St. OL5—6J 65
Egerton St. OL6—4C 82
Egerton St. OL10—9J 27
Egerton St. OL15—6C 14
Egerton St. WN2—9H 53
Egerton Ter. M14—7K 91
Egerton Vale. BL7—9D 6
Eggington St. M10—2J 79
Egham Ct. BL2—9H 23
Egham Ho. BL3—7B 38
Egmont St. M6—1L 77
Egmont St. M8—8G 61
Egmont St. OL5—8J 65
Egremont Av. M20—7G 91
Egremont Clo. M25—8A 42
Egremont Ct. M7—8C 60
Egremont Gro. SK3—5B 104
Egremont Rd. OL16—6L 29
Egret Dri. M30—3G 87
Egyptian St. BL1—5F 22
Egypt La. M25—8D 42
Egypt La. M25—1J 59
Eighth Av. OL8—7K 63
Eighth St. W. M17—9J 77
Eigth St. M17—9K 77
Eileen Gro. M14—4J 91
Eileen Gro. W. M14—4H 91
Elaine Av. M9—6B 62
Elaine Clo. WN4—2D 70
Elbain Wlk. M10—2C 80
Elberton Wlk. M8—9F 60
(off Landfield Dri.)
Elbe St. M12—7J 79
Elbow La. OL11—4G 29
Elbow St. M19—5A 92
Elbow St. Trading Est. M19 —5E
Elbut La. BL9—5F 26
Elcho Ct. WA14—1B 110
Elcho Rd. WA14—1B 110
Elcombe Av. WA3—4L 71
Elcot Clo. M10—2J 79
Elderberry Wlk. M31—2E
Elderburn Dri. M10—1K 79
Elder Clo. SK2—5K 105
Eldercot Gro. BL3—5A 38
Eldercot Rd. BL3—5A 38
Eldercroft Rd. WA15—8J
Elderfield Dri. SK6—1M 10
Elder Gro. M10—6F 62
Elder Mt. Rd. M9—6K 61
Elder Rd. OL4—2E 64
Elder St. OL16—5H 29
Elder Wlk. M33—8C 88
Elderwood. OL9—1E 62
Eldon Clo. M34—8L 81
Eldon Gdns. WN4—1A 70
Eldon Pl. M30—6C 76
Eldon Precinct. OL8—3L 6
Eldon Rd. M30—4G 87
Eldon Rd. SK3—6C 104
Eldon St. BL2—9H 23
Eldon St. BL9—6M 25
Eldon St. OL8—3M 63
Eldon St. WN7—1D 72
Eldridge Dri. M10—2A 80
Eleanor Rd. M21—6M 89
Eleanor Rd. OL2—7L 45
Eleanor St. BL1—5G 23
Eleanor St. OL1—9K 45
Eleanor St. WN3—1A 52
Elevator Rd. M17—9L 77
Eleventh St. M17—9J 77
Elf Mill Clo. SK3—7E 104
Elf Mill Ter. SK3—7E 104
Elford Gro. M18—2G 93
Elgar St. M12—2A 92
Elgin Av. M20—2K 103
Elgin Av. WN4—3K 69
Elgin Clo. WN2—9G 35
Elgin Dri. M33—2L 101
Elgin Rd. OL4—2C 64
Elgin Rd. SK16—9C 82
Elgin St. BL1—8C 22
Elgin St. OL7—3A 82
(in two parts)
Elgin St. OL11—5G 29
Elgin St. SK15—6H 83
Elgol Clo. SK3—8F 104
Elgol Clo. OL10—9G 27
Elgol Dri. BL3—3L 37
Elim St. OL15—4C 14
Eliot Dri. WN3—3A 52
Eliot Rd. M30—6D 76
Eliot Wlk. M24—6C 44
Elisie St. BL0—7G 9
Eli St. OL9—5G 63
Elitex Ho. M7—1D 4 & 3E
Eliza Ann St. M10—1H 5
Elizabethan Ct. M29—7M
(off Market St.)
Elizabethan Dri. WN3—4
Elizabethan Ann St. M30—6
Elizabethan Wlk. WN2—
Elizabethan Way. OL16
Elizabeth Av. M34—1L 9
Elizabeth Av. OL2—6J 45
Elizabeth Av. OL9—5G 63
Elizabeth Av. SK1—5F 10
Elizabeth Av. SK12—7K
Elizabeth Av. SK15—5G
Elizabeth Av. WN2—7L 5
Elizabeth Ct. M14—6K 9
Elizabeth Ct. SK4—5C 10
Elizabeth Gro. OL2—2B 4

Fisherfield. OL12—1M 27
Fishermore Rd. M31—4L 87
Fisher St. OL1—9M 45
Fishwick St. OL16—4G 29
Fistral Av. SK8—4J 113
Fistral Cres. SK15—4K 83
Fitchfield Wlk. M28—5K 57
(off Emlyn St.)
Fitton Av. M21—8B 90
Fitton Cres. M27—5F 58
Fitton Hill Rd. OL8—4A 64
Fitton St. BL3—5E 38
Fitton St. M24—2E 62
Fitton St. OL2—5M 45
(Royton)
Fitton St. OL2—1M 45
(Shaw)
Fitton St. OL16—2G 29
Fitzadam St. WN1—9B 34
Fitzalan St. SK13—5J 97
Fitzgerald Clo. M25—6M 59
Fitzgerald Way. M6—4M 77
Fitzhugh St. BL1—5G 23
Fitzroy St. M35—7H 81
Fitzroy St. OL7—7M 81
Fitzroy St. SK15—3K 83
Fitzwarren Ct. M6—5M 77
Fitzwarren St. M6—4M 77
Fitzwilliam St. M7—1C 4 & 3D 78
Five Fold Pk. OL9—2K 63
Five Quarters. M26—4E 40
Flag Croft Dri. M23—8B 102
Flagg Wood Av. SK6—6D 106
Flag Row. M4—2G 5 & 4H 79
Flake La. OL2—4K 45
Flamborough Wlk. M14—2H 91
Flamingo Clo. M12—9A 80
Flamstead Av. M23—7L 101
Flannel St. OL12—2G 29
Flapper Fold La. M29—4J 55
Flashfields. M25—7M 59
Flash St. M10—1C 80
Flatley Clo. M15—9G 79
Flavian Wlk. M11—7B 80
(off Herne St.)
Flaxcroft Rd. M22—1B 112
Flaxfield Av. SK15—5K 83
Flaxman Rise. OL1—6D 46
Flaxpool Clo. M16—2E 90
Flax St. BL0—7G 9
Flax St. M3—2C 4 & 4D 78
Flaxwood Wlk. M22—1B 112
Fleece St. OL4—1B 64
Fleece St. OL16—3F 28
Fleeson St. M14—3J 91
Fleet Ho. BL1—9E 22
(off Nottingham Dri.)
Fleet St. BL6—7D 20
Fleet St. M18—9F 80
Fleet St. OL4—1C 64
Fleet St. OL6—5A 82
(in two parts)
Fleet St. OL11—1C 44
Fleet St. SK14—2E 94
Fleet St. WN5—2H 51
Fleetwood Rd. M28—5G 57
Fleming Pl. OL9—2K 63
Fleming Rd. M22—2D 112
Flemish Rd. M34—4B 94
Fletcher Av. M27—5G 59
Fletcher Av. M29—3K 55
Fletcher Clo. OL9—2K 63
Fletcher Clo. OL10—8K 27
Fletcher Dri. SK12—6F 116
Fletcher Fold. BL9—3M 41
Fletchers La. WA13—9A 98
Fletchers Pas. OL15—5A 14
Fletchers Pl. OL15—5A 14
(off Hare Hill Rd.)
Fletcher's Rd. OL15—8L 13
Fletchers Sq. OL15—5B 14
(off Sutcliffe St.)
Fletcher St. BL3—4E 38
(Bolton)
Fletcher St. BL3—6B 40
(Little Lever)
Fletcher St. BL4—9K 39
Fletcher St. BL9—8A 26
Fletcher St. M10—2M 79
Fletcher St. M26—5J 41
Fletcher St. M29—5J 55
Fletcher St. OL6—4C 82
Fletcher St. OL11—5G 29
Fletcher St. SK1—4F 104
Fletsand Rd. SK9—5J 119
Flexbury Wlk. M10—2D 80
Flint Clo. M11—5B 80
Flint Clo. SK7—3J 115
Flint Gro. M30—8C 86
Flint St. BL9—7M 25
Flint St. M35—5H 81
Flint St. SK3—5E 104
Flitcroft Ct. BL3—5F 38
Flixton Rd. M31—6L 87
(Carrington)
Flixton Rd. M31—5M 87
(Flixton)
Flixton Wlk. M13—1K 91
Floatshall Rd. M23—7M 101
Floats Rd. M23—9L 101
(in two parts)
Flockton Av. WN6—5K 33
Flora Dri. M7—1C 4 & 3D 78
Floral Av. M19—6B 92
Floral Ct. M7—1D 78
Flora St. BL3—5D 38
Flora St. OL1—1L 63
Flora St. WN4—5B 70
Florence Av. BL1—6F 22
Florence Ct. SK3—7B 104
Florence Pk. Ct. M20—1J 103
Florence St. BL3—5D 38
Florence St. M30—6B 76
Florence St. M33—8H 89
Florence St. M35—7H 81
(Droylsden)
Florence St. M35—8F 62
(Failsworth)
Florence St. OL16—4H 29
Florence St. SK4—3E 104
Florence St. WN1—9E 34
Florence Way. SK14—1D 96
Florida St. OL8—3L 63
Florist St. SK3—6E 104
Flowery Bank. OL8—4B 64
Flowery Field. SK2—9G 105
Floyd Av. M21—8C 90
Foden La. SK7—9D 114
Foden La. SK9—9B 118
Foden Wlk. SK9—1K 119
Fogg La. BL3—5K 39
Fog La. M20 & M19—1H 103
Fold Av. M35—5H 81
Fold Cres. SK15—1M 83
Fold Gdns. OL12—8B 12
Fold Grn. OL9—2G 63
Fold M. SK7—1L 115
Fold Rd. M26—1C 58
Folds La. WA11—8A 68
Folds Rd. BL1—1G 39
(in two parts)
Folds Rd. WA11—9F 68
Folds, The. BL6—7J 19
Fold St. BL4—9L 39
Fold St. BL9—8K 25
Fold St. M10—8A 62
Fold St. OL10—7L 27
Fold St. WA3—6G 71
Fold, The. M9—5K 61
Fold, The. M31—3A 88
Fold View. BL7—1E 22
Fold View. OL8—6A 64
Foleshill Av. M9—9K 61
Foley Gdns. OL10—2L 43
Foley St. WN2—3K 53
Foley Wlk. M22—4E 112
Foliage Cres. SK5—9H 93
Foliage Gdns. SK5—9J 93
Foliage Rd. SK5—1H 105
Folkestone Rd. M11—5D 80
Folkestone Rd. E. M11—5D 80
Folkestone Rd. W. M11—4C 80
Follows St. M18—9D 80
Folly La. M27—2D 76
Folly Wlk. OL12—1F 28
Fonthill Gro. M33—4F 100
Fontwell Clo. M16—3C 90
Fontwell La. OL1—8A 46
Fontwell Rd. BL3—7A 40
Fontwell Wlk. M10—6D 62
Foot Mill Cres. OL12—9D 12
Foot Wood Cres. OL12—9D 12
Forber Cres. M18—3D 92
Forbes Clo. M33—3K 101
Forbes Clo. SK1—5H 105
Forbes Pk. SK7—5D 114
Forbes Rd. SK1—4H 105
Forbes St. SK6—1M 105
Fordbank Rd. M20—3G 103
Fordel Wlk. M7—1D 4 & 3E 78
Ford Gdns. OL11—4B 28
Ford Gro. SK14—2A 96
Fordham Gro. BL1—1C 38
Fordland Clo. WA3—6L 71
Ford La. M6—3A 78
Ford La. M22 & M20—4E 102
(in two parts)
Ford Lodge. M20—3H 103
Fordoe La. OL12—7J 11
Ford's La. SK7—6D 114
Ford St. M3—3C 4 & 5D 78
Ford St. M7—2C 78
Ford St. M12—8K 79
Ford St. M26—9A 40
Ford St. OL16—3G 29
Ford St. SK3—4D 104
Ford St. SK16—9C 82
Fordyce Way. WN2—9G 35
Foreland Clo. M10—2K 79
Forest Av. WN6—6L 33
Forest Dri. BL5—9G 37
Forest Dri. M33—3E 100
Forest Dri. WA15—7F 100
Forest Dri. WN6—8G 17
Forester Dri. SK15—6G 83
Forester Hill Av. BL3—6F 38
(in two parts)
Forester Hill Clo. BL3—6F 38
Foresters Clo. WN2—8L 53
Forest Gdns. M31—2D 98
Forest Range. M19—5A 92
Forest Rd. BL1—7B 22
Forest St. M30—3A 76
Forest St. OL6—3C 82
Forest St. OL8—5M 63
Forest View. OL12—9D 12
Forest Way. BL7—3J 23
Forfar St. BL1—5E 22
Forge Ind. Est. OL4—1B 64
Forge La. M11—4M 79
Forge St. OL4—1B 64
Forge St. WN1—1E 52
Formby Av. M21—7D 90
Formby Av. M29—4K 55
Formby Dri. SK8—4H 113
Formby Rd. M6—1L 77
Forres Gro. WN4—3K 69
Forrester Dri. OL2—1D 46
Forrester Ho. M12—9A 80
(off Blackwin St.)
Forrester St. M28—8A 58
Forrest Rd. M34—5B 94
Forrest St. M11—5M 79
Forshaw Av. M18—9F 80
Forshaw St. M34—2K 93
Forsters St. WA3—6G 71
Forston Wlk. M8—1H 79
Forsythia Wlk. M31—3E 98
Forsyth St. OL12—9L 11
Fortescue Rd. SK2—6K 105
Fortgate Wlk. M13—9K 79
Forth Pl. M26—4F 40
Forth Rd. M26—4F 40
Forth St. WN7—3H 73
Forton Av. BL2—2L 39
Fortran Clo. M5—6A 78
Fort Rd. M25—6D 60
Fortrose Av. M9—5H 61
Fortuna Gro. M19—6M 91
Fortune St. BL3—4H 39
Fortyacre Dri. SK6—2L 105
Forum Gro. M7—2E 78
Fosbrook Av. M20—1J 103
Foscarn Dri. M23—8B 102
Foster Av. WN3—2E 52
Foster Ct. BL9—6D 26
Foster Gro. WA11—9F 68
Foster La. BL2—9M 23
Fosters Bldgs. WN6—9B 34
Fosters Rd. WA11—9F 68
Foster St. M5—6K 77
Foster St. M26—6F 40
Foster St. M34—3M 93
Foster St. OL4—1C 64
Foster St. WN6—8A 34
Foster Ter. BL1—9E 22
(off Barnwood Dri.)
Fotherby Dri. M9—5K 61
Fotherby Pl. WN3—5A 52
Foulds Av. BL8—8G 25
Foundry La. M4—3G 5 & 5H 79
Foundry La. WN3—4K 51
Foundry Rd. M17—2K 89
Foundry St. BL3—4F 38
(Bolton)
Foundry St. BL3—6A 40
(Little Lever)
Foundry St. BL9—8M 25
Foundry St. M26—6G 41
Foundry St. OL8—2L 63
Foundry St. OL10—8J 27
Foundry St. SK16—7C 82
(in two parts)
Foundry St. WN2—3K 53
Foundry St. WN7—3H 73
Fountain Av. WA15—2H 111
Fountain Clo. SK12—9K 115
Fountain Pl. M25—1M 59
Fountain Pl. SK12—8K 115
Fountains Av. BL2—9J 23
Fountains Av. WA11—8M 69
Fountains Clo. M29—9C 56
Fountain Sq. SK12—6J 117
Fountains Rd. M32—3F 88
Fountains Rd. SK8 & SK7 —6B 114
Fountain St. BL8—8J 25
Fountain St. BL9—8A 26
Fountain St. M2—4F 5 & 6G 79
Fountain St. M24—9M 43
Fountain St. M30—7D 76
Fountain St. OL1—1L 63
Fountain St. OL6—3E 82
Fountain St. SK14—3F 94
Fountain St. N. BL9—8A 26
Fountains Wlk. OL9—3G 63
Fountains Wlk. WA3—7B 72
Fount Rd. M15—9E 78
Fouracres. M23—8A 102
Fouracres Rd. M23—8M 101
Four Lanes. SK14—2A 96
Four Lanes Way. OL11—1J 27
Fourteen Meadows Rd. WN3 —1B 52
Fourth Av. BL1—2B 38
Fourth Av. BL3—5M 39
Fourth Av. BL9—6D 26
Fourth Av. M11—4C 80
Fourth Av. M17—9J 77
Fourth Av. M27—2D 76
Fourth Av. OL8—7J 63
Fourth Av. OL9—3G 63
Fourth Av. SK15—1L 83
Fourth St. BL1—6M 21
Fourth St. M17—1K 89
(in two parts)
Fourth St. WN2—9F 52
Fourwaqys Wlk. M10—6B 62
Fourways. M17—9G 77
Four Yards. M2—4E 5 & 6F 78
Fovant Cres. SK5—5E 92
Fowey Wlk. M23—8A 102
Fowey Wlk. SK14—3L 95
Fowler Av. M18—8F 80
Fowler St. OL8—5J 63
Fownhope Av. M33—2F 100
Fownhope Rd. M33—2F 100
Foxall St. M24—1J 61
Fox Bank Ct. SK3—5D 104
Foxbank St. M13—2L 91
Fox Bench Clo. SK8—6C 114
Foxbench Wlk. M21—7D 90
Fox Clo. WA15—7F 100
Foxcroft St. OL15—6M 13
Foxdale Clo. BL7—4L 7
Foxdale St. M11—6C 80
Foxdene Gro. WN3—6L 51
Foxdenton La. M24 & OL9 —2E 62
Foxdenton Wlk. M34—5L 93
Foxfield Clo. BL8—5H 25
Foxfield Rd. M23—1M 111
Foxford Wlk. M22—2E 112
Foxglove Ct. OL12—8D 12
Foxglove Dri. BL9—7D 26
Foxglove Dri. WA14—5B 100
Foxglove Wlk. M31—3F 98
Foxhall Rd. M34—2K 93
Foxhall Rd. WA15—7E 100
Foxham Wlk. M7—1E 78
Foxhill. OL2—1L 45
Foxhill Chase. SK2—8A 106
Foxhill Dri. SK15—7J 83
Foxhill Rd. M30—6M 75
Fox Hill Rd. OL11—1D 44
Foxholes Clo. OL12—1G 29
Foxholes Rd. BL6—6D 20
Foxholes Rd. OL12—1G 29
Foxholes Rd. SK14—6C 94
Foxlair Rd. M22—1B 112
Foxland Rd. SK8—9H 103
Foxley Clo. WA13—2A 108
Foxley Hall M. WA13—3A 108
Foxley Ho. BL5—1A 54
Foxley Wlk. M12—1A 92
Fox Platt Rd. OL5—7H 65
Fox Platt Ter. OL5—8J 65
Fox St. BL6—8C 20
Fox St. BL9—7M 25
Fox St. M30—5F 76
Fox St. OL8—6J 63
Fox St. OL10—8J 27
Fox St. OL16—4L 29
(Milnrow)
Fox St. OL16—2H 29
(Rochdale)
Fox St. SK3—5D 104
Foxton St. M24—1J 61
Foxton Wlk. M23—2A 112
Foxwell Wlk. M8—1H 79
Foxwood Gdns. M19—9L 91
Foynes Clo. M10—2K 79
Foy St. WN4—4B 70
Framingham Rd. M33—2G 101
Frampton Clo. M24—1B 62
Fram St. M6—5L 77
Fram St. M9—8M 61
Frances Av. SK8—7G 103
Francesca Wlk. M18—9C 80
Frances Pl. M29—7G 55
Frances St. M35—9F 62
Frances St. OL1—8A 46
(in two parts)
Frances St. OL16—7K 13
Frances St. SK3—5E 104
Frances St. SK8—7L 103
Frances St. SK14—3C 94
Frances St. W. SK14—3C 94
France St. BL5—2E 54
France St. WN2—2K 53
France St. WN5—1M 51
Francis Av. M28—6M 57
Francis Av. M30—5E 76
Francis Rd. M20—9J 91
Francis Rd. M30—6F 86
Francis St. BL1—8D 22
Francis St. BL4—8J 39
Francis St. M3—2E 5 & 4F 78
Francis St. M29—8D 56
Francis St. M30—9E 86
(Cadishead)
Francis St. M30—4D 76
(Eccles)
Francis St. M34—6B 94
Francis St. WN2—3K 53
Francis Ter. SK16—6C 82
(off Astley St.)
Francis Thompson Dri. OL6 —4B 82
Frandley Wlk. M13—6G 6 & 8H 79
Frankby Clo. M27—9J 59
Frank Cowin Ct. M7—1C 4 & 3D 78
Frankford Av. BL1—8C 22
Frankford Sq. BL1—8C 22
Frank Hulme Ho. M32—5L 89
Frankland Clo. M11—5B 80
Franklin Av. M35—6G 81
Franklin Rd. M18—9E 80
Franklin St. M30—5D 76
Franklin St. OL1—9L 45
Franklin St. OL16—5H 29
Franklin Ter. OL15—6A 14
(off William St.)
Franklyn Av. M31—4L 87
Franklyn Clo. M34—4G 93
Frank Price Ct. M22—1C 112
Frank St. BL1—8D 22
Frank St. BL9—9M 25
Frank St. M1—6E 5 & 8F 78
Frank St. M6—3A 78
Frank St. M35—9E 62
Frank St. OL1—9B 46
Frank St. SK14—4E 94
Frank St. WN1—9C 34
Frank Swift Wlk. M14—3G 91
Frankton Rd. M25—1M 59
Franton Rd. M11—5B 80
Fraser Av. M33—2L 101
Fraser Ho. BL1—9D 22
(off Kirk Hope Dri.)
Fraser Rd. M8—7F 60
Fraser Rd. WN5—1L 51
Fraser St. M27—7G 59
Fraser St. OL2—1A 46
Fraser St. OL6—4C 82
Fraser St. OL16—6H 29
Fraternitas Ter. M35—4E 80
Freckleton Av. M21—1C 102
Freckleton Dri. BL8—1F 40
Freckleton St. WN1—7C 34
Freda Wlk. M11—6M 79
Frederica St. WN2—5G 53
Frederick Av. OL2—4B 46
Frederick Ct. BL4—9L 39
Frederick Rd. M6 & M7—2A 4 & 4B 78
Frederick St. BL0—6H 9
Frederick St. BL4—9K 39
Frederick St. M3—3D 4 & 5E 78
Frederick St. M34—1L 93
Frederick St. OL6—5E 82
Frederick St. OL8—3J 63
Frederick St. OL9—9H 45
Frederick St. OL15—5A 14
Frederick St. WN2—3K 53
Frederick St. WN3—2D 52
Frederick St. WN4—2A 70
Frederic St. WN1—9E 34
Fred Tilson Clo. M14—3G 91
Freehold St. OL11—5E 28
Freelands. M29—7C 56
Freeland Wlk. M11—7C 80
Freeman Av. OL6—4D 82
Freeman Rd. SK16—9C 82
Freemantle St. SK3—5D 104
Freeman Wlk. M15—9G 79
Freestone Clo. BL8—6K 25
Freetown. SK13—6J 97
Freetown Clo. M14—2G 91
Freetrade St. OL11—5E 28
Fremantle Av. M18—3D 92
French Av. OL1—8C 46
French Av. SK15—6J 83
French Barn La. M9—5J 61
French Gro. BL3—4K 39
French St. OL6—3D 82
French St. SK15—6J 83
Frensham Wlk. M23—9M 101
Fresh Ct. SK13—7F 96
Freshfield. SK8—4H 113
Freshfield Av. BL3—7D 38
Freshfield Av. M25—2C 60
Freshfield Av. M29—4J 55
Freshfield Av. SK14—5D 94
Freshfield Clo. SK6—4H 107
Freshfield Gro. BL3—7F 38
Freshfield Rd. SK4—3M 103
Freshfield Rd. WN2—3M 53
Freshfield Rd. WN3—5L 51
Freshfields. M26—4D 40
Freshfield Wlk. M11—5C 80
Freshford Wlk. M22—3B 112
Freshpool Way. M22—7E 102
Freshwater Dri. M34—6B 94
Freshwater St. M18—9E 80
Fresia Av. M28—5F 56
Frew Clo. M10—6B 62
Frewland Av. SK3—9F 104
Freya Gro. M5—5B 4 & 7C 78
Friarmere Rd. OL3—4L 47
Friars Clo. M29—7D 56
Friars Clo. SK9—3E 118
Friar's Ct. M5—5H 77
Friars Cres. OL11—8F 28
Friar's Rd. M33—1H 101
Friar St. WA10—9A 68
Friendship Av. M18—2E 92
Frieston. OL12—2E 28
(off Spotland Rd.)
Frieston Rd. WA14—5E 100
Friezland Clo. SK15—1L 83
Friezland La. OL3—4A 66
Frimley Gdns. M22—1D 112
Frinton Av. M10—5D 62
Frinton Clo. M33—4F 100
Frinton Rd. BL3—6B 38
Frith St. WN5—1A 52
Frobisher Clo. M13—1K 91
Frobisher Pl. SK5—1E 104
Frobisher Rd. OL15—2C 14
Frodesley Wlk. M12—9M 79
Frodsham Av. SK4—2C 104
Frodsham Clo. WN6—6K 33
Frodsham Dri. WA11—9D 68
Frodsham Rd. M33—3L 101
Frodsham St. M14—3H 91
Frodsham Way. SK9—8L 113
Froghall La. WA13 & WA16 —4D 108
Frog La. WN6 & WN1—8A 34
Frogley St. BL2—7H 23
Frogmore Av. SK14—7E 94
Frome Av. M31—5B 88
Frome Av. SK2—8J 105
Frome Clo. M29—1C 74
Frome Dri. M8—9H 61
Frome St. OL4—2C 64
Frostlands Rd. M16—3E 90
Frost St. M4—6K 79
Frost St. OL8—4L 63
Frowde Wlk. M16—2E 90
Froxmer St. M18—9C 80
Fruit Mkt. WN1—9C 34
(off Galleries, The)
Fryent Clo. BL6—8K 19
Fuchsia Gro. M7—1D 78
Fulbeck Av. WN3—6M 51
Fulbeck Wlk. M7—2E 78
Fulbrook Way. M29—7C 56
Fulford St. M16—2C 90
Fulham Av. M10—2B 80
Fulham St. OL4—2C 64
Fullbrook Dri. SK8—6M 113
Fullerton Rd. SK4—3B 104
Full Pot La. OL11—2L 27
Fullwood Rd. WA3—8L 71
Fulmar Clo. BL5—2D 54
Fulmar Clo. SK12—8G 115
Fulmar Dri. M33—3C 100
Fulmar Dri. SK2—8M 105
Fulmards Clo. SK9—4J 119
Fulmar Gdns. OL11—3M 27
Fulmead Wlk. M8—1F 78
(off Kilmington Dri.)
Fulmer Dri. M4—3H 5 & 5J 79
Fulmere Ct. M27—1D 76
Fulneck Sq. M35—7G 81
Fulshaw Av. SK9—5G 119
Fulshaw Ct. SK9—6G 119
Fulshaw Hall Cotts. SK9 —6G 119
Fulshaw Pk. Rd. SK9—7G 119
Fulshaw Pk. Rd. S. SK9—7F 118
Fulshaw Wlk. M13—6G 6 & 8H 79
Fulstone M. SK2—7H 105
Fulthorpe Wlk. M9—3L 61
Fulton Ct. M15—1G 91
(off Brackenbury Wlk.)
Fulton's Ct. OL4—2E 64
Fulwell Av. M29—8L 55
Fulwood Av. M9—4M 61
Fulwood Clo. BL8—9F 24
Furbarn La. OL11—2K 27
Furbarn Rd. OL11—3K 27
Furlong Clo. WN2—9F 52
Furlong Rd. M22—1B 112
Furnace St. SK14—2C 94
Furnace St. SK16—6B 82
Furness Av. BL2—8H 23
Furness Av. M25—9A 42
Furness Av. OL7—2M 81
Furness Av. OL8—4C 64
Furness Av. OL10—7J 27
Furness Av. OL15—5A 14
Furness Clo. OL16—4L 29
Furness Clo. SK12—8J 115
Furness Cres. WN7—7D 54
Furness Gro. SK4—4A 104
Furness Quay. M5—8A 78
Furness Rd. BL1—2B 38
Furness Rd. M14—5J 91
Furness Rd. M24—6M 43
Furness Rd. M31—3D 88
Furness Rd. SK8—6C 114
Furness Sq. BL2—8H 23
Furnival Clo. M34—4G 93
Furnival Rd. M18—1C 92
Furnival St. SK5—4F 92
Furnival St. WN7—9F 54
Furnwood Gro. SK9—3J 119
Further Field. OL11—1K 27
Further Hey Clo. OL4—1E 64
Further La. SK14—3L 95
Further Pitts. OL11—3C 28
Furtherwood Rd. OL1—8J 45
Furze Av. BL5—1F 54
Furze La. OL4—8D 46
(in two parts)
Furze Wlk. M31—2G 99
Fyfield Wlk. M8—1H 79
Fylde Av. BL2—2L 39
Fylde Av. SK8—4J 113
Fylde Ct. M32—6J 89
Fylde Rd. SK4—3A 104
Fylde St. BL3—7K 39
Fylde St. E. BL3—7K 39

Gable Av. SK9—4G 119
Gable Ct. M34—3M 93
Gable Dri. M24—8L 43
Gables, The. M33—2H 101
(Brooklands)
Gables, The. M33—9J 89
(Sale)
Gable St. BL2—5K 23
Gable St. M11—7M 79
Gabriels, The. OL2—2M 45
Gabriel Wlk. M16—3F 90
Gadbury Av. M29—5H 55
Gaddum Rd. M20—2J 103
Gaddum Rd. WA14—3A 110
Gail Av. SK4—3D 104
Gail Clo. M35—2E 80
Gail Clo. SK9—7M 119
Gainford Av. SK8—9H 103
Gainford Gdns. M10—7B 62
Gainford Rd. SK5—5F 92
Gainford Wlk. BL3—5E 38
Gainsboro Rd. M34—6K 81
Gainsborough Av. BL3—6C 38
Gainsborough Av. M20—8J 91
Gainsborough Av. M32—3M 89
Gainsborough Av. OL8—4L 63
Gainsborough Av. SK6—5H 107
Gainsborough Clo. SK9—3K 119
Gainsborough Clo. WN2—5K 51
Gainsborough Dri. OL11—7E 28
Gainsborough Dri. SK3 —7M 103
Gainsborough Rd. BL0—1H 25
Gainsborough Rd. OL9—8E 44
Gainsborough St. M7—9E 60
Gainsborough Wlk. M34—5L 93
Gainsborough Wlk. SK14 —1E 94
Gairlock Av. M32—4H 39
Gair Rd. SK5—1F 104
Gair St. SK14—2D 94
Gaitskell Clo. M12—6L 79
Galbraith Rd. M20—2J 103
Gale Dri. M24—7K 43
Galena St. OL11—6E 28
Gale Rd. M25—5M 59
Gales Ter. OL11—5E 28
Gale St. OL10—8H 27
Gale St. OL12—8E 12
Galey St. BL1—8M 21
Galgate Clo. BL8—9F 24
Galgate Clo. M15—6D 4 & 8E 78
Galgate St. M16—2B 90
Galindo St. BL2—6J 23
Galland St. OL4—9D 46
Galloway Clo. BL3—4L 37
Galloway Clo. OL10—9F 26
Galloway Dri. M27—4F 58
Galloway Rd. M27—1D 76
Gallowsclough Rd. SK15—9L 83
Gallwey Cres. WN1—5C 34
Galston St. M11—7A 80
Galsworthy Av. M8—1G 79
Galvin Rd. M9—5H 61
Galway St. OL1—2M 63
Galway Wlk. M23—2M 111
Gambleside Clo. M28—8H 57
Gamble St. WN7—2G 73
Gambrel Bank Rd. OL6—1B 82
Gambrell Gro. OL6—1B 82
Game St. OL4—3C 64
Games Wlk. M22—3B 112
Gamma Wlk. M11—5B 80
Gandy La. OL12—7C 12
Gan Eden. M7—8E 60
Ganesmoor Clo. M12—9L 79
Gansworth Rd. WA3—6F 70
Gantley Av. WN5—4D 50
Gantley Cres. WN5—5D 50
Gantock Wlk. M14—3J 91
Ganton Av. M25—1K 59
Garbrook Av. M9—3J 61
Garden Av. M32—3K 89
Garden Av. M35—5H 81
Garden City. BL0—9G 9
Garden Clo. M34—9M 81
Garden Clo. OL15—8M 13
Gardenia Sq. M12—9K 79
Garden La. M3—3D 4 & 5E 78
(in two parts)
Garden La. WA14—8D 100
Garden M. OL15—6B 14
(off Industry St.)
Garden Row. OL10—6H 27
Gardens, The. BL1—4F 22
Gardens, The. BL7—7K 7
Gardens, The. M2—3E 5 & 5F 78
Gardens, The. M30—3G 77
Garden St. BL0—5J 9
Garden St. BL4—9L 39
Garden St. BL8—3F 24
Garden St. BL9—8J 9
Garden St. M4—3F 5 & 5G 79
Garden St. M29—8A 56
Garden St. M30—6E 76
Garden St. M34—9M 81
Garden St. OL1—1A 64
Garden St. OL4—3F 64
Garden St. OL10—7J 27
Garden St. OL16—6B 30
Garden St. SK2—8J 105
Garden St. SK14—2E 94
Garden Ter. OL2—2L 45
Garden View. M33—8H 89
Garden Wlk. M31—2E 98
Garden Wlk. M34—3A 94
Garden Wlk. OL6—3C 82
Garden Wall Clo. M5—5B 4 & 7C 78
Garden Way. OL15—9M 13
Gardner. M30—5E 76
Gardner Grange. SK5—1J 105
Gardner Rd. M25—4M 59
Gardner St. M6—3A 78
Gardner St. M12—9B 80
Gareth Av. WA11—9B 68
Garfield Av. M19—5B 92
Garfield Clo. OL11—2L 27
Garfield Gro. BL3—4D 38
Garfield St. M5—9A 78
(in two parts)
Garfield St. SK1—2G 105
Garforth Av. M4—3H 5 & 5J 79
Garforth St. OL9—1J 63
Gargrave Av. BL1—8M 21
Gargrave St. M27—8M 59
Gargrave St. OL4—2B 64
Garland Rd. M22—1E 112
Garlick St. M18—1D 92
Garlick St. OL9—2L 63
(in two parts)
Garlick St. SK14—3F 94
Garner Av. WA15—4G 101
Garner Clo. WA14—2D 110
Garner Dri. M5—4K 77
Garner Dri. M30—4C 76
Garnet St. OL1—9B 46
Garnett Clo. SK14—3M 95
Garnett Rd. SK14—3M 95
Garnett St. BL0—5H 9
Garnett St. BL1—7E 22
Garnett St. M7—1F 78
Garnett St. SK1—4F 104
Garnett Way. SK14—3M 95
(off Garnett Clo.)
Garnet Wolseley Av. M5—6A 4 & 8B 78
Garnham Wlk. M9—3L 61
Garratt Way. M18—1C 92
Garret Gro. OL2—2C 46
Garrett Hall Rd. M28—9E 56
Garrett La. M28—9D 56
Garrett Wlk. SK3—5C 104
Garron Wlk. M22—2A 112
Garrowmore Wlk. M9—5L 61
Garsdale St. M1—6F 5 & 8G 79
Garsden Wlk. M23—9M 101
Garside Av. WA3—8K 71
Garside Gro. BL1—8C 22
Garside Gro. WN3—6L 51
Garside Hey Rd. BL8—4H 25
Garside St. BL1—2E 38
Garside St. M34—4M 93
Garside St. SK14—5E 94
Garstang Av. BL2—3L 39
Garstang Dri. BL8—9F 24
Garstang Ho. M15—1H 91
Garston Av. M29—3H 55
Garston Clo. SK4—2C 104
Garston Clo. WN7—7E 54
Garston St. BL9—5A 26
Garswood Cres. WN5—3E 68
Garswood Dri. BL8—4H 25
Garswood Old Rd. WA11—7C 68
Garswood Rd. BL3—7E 38
Garswood Rd. M14—4F 90
Garswood Rd. WN4 & WA11 —2H 69
Garswood Rd. WN5—2E 68
Garswood St. WN4—4B 70
Garth Av. WA15—7E 100
Garth Heights. SK9—4J 119
Garthland Rd. SK7—1M 115
Garthmere Rd. M29—3M 55
Garthorne Clo. M16—2D 90
Garthorp Rd. M23—4L 101
Garth Rd. M22—9D 102
Garth Rd. SK2—6J 105
Garth Rd. SK6—6G 107
Garth, The. M5—5K 77
Garthwaite Av. OL8—4L 63
Gartland Wlk. M8—8J 61
Garton Dri. WA3—6L 71
Garton Wlk. M9—3L 61
Gartside Gdns. M13—6G 5 & 8H 79
Gartside St. M3—4D 4 & 6E 78
Gartside St. OL3—5L 47
Gartside St. OL4—3B 64
Gartside St. OL7—6L 81
Garwick Rd. BL1—7B 22
Garwood St. M15—6E 5 & 8F 78
Gascoyne St. M14—3H 91
Gaskell Clo. OL15—5A 14
Gaskell Rise. OL1—4E 46
Gaskell Rd. M30—6D 76
Gaskell Rd. WA14—7D 100
Gaskell's Brow. WN4—2L 69
Gaskell St. BL1—1D 38
Gaskell St. M10—2C 80
Gaskell St. M27—6F 58
Gaskell St. SK16—6B 82
Gaskell St. WN1—9E 34
Gaskell St. WN2—1L 53
Gaskill St. OL10—8G 27
Gas St. BL1—2E 38
Gas St. BL4—8K 39
Gas St. OL6—4B 82
Gas St. OL10—8K 27
Gas St. OL11—3E 28
Gas St. SK4—4E 104
Gas St. SK14—1D 96
Gas St. WN2—6H 53
Gas St. WN7—2F 72
Gaston Wlk. M9—3K 61
(off Claygate Dri.)
Gatcombe M. SK9—5G 119
Gatcombe Sq. M14—3J 91
Gateacre Wlk. M23—5L 101
Gate Field Clo. M26—6E 40
Gate Fold Precinct. BL2—5K 23
Gategill Gro. WN5—5D 50
Gatehead Croft. OL3—6M 47
Gatehead M. OL3—6M 47
Gatehead Rd. OL3—7M 47
Gatehouse Rd. M28—4G 57
Gate Keeper Fold. OL7—9A 64
Gatemere Clo. M28—8H 57
Gate Rd. M32—2G 89
Gatesgarth Rd. M24—7J 43
Gateshead Clo. M14—2H 91
Gateside Wlk. M9—3L 61
(off Brockford Dri.)
Gate St. M11—7C 80
Gate St. OL11—5F 28
Gate St. SK16—9A 82
Gateway Ind. Est. M1—4G 5 & 6H 79
Gateway Rd. M18—9C 80
Gathill Clo. SK8—3M 113
Gathurst La. WN6—6G 33
Gathurst Rd. WN5—1E 50
Gathurst St. M18—9E 80
Gatley Av. M14—5G 91
Gatley Brow. OL1—9L 45
Gatley Grn. SK8—8G 103
Gatley Rd. M33—2L 101
Gatley Rd. SK8—8H 103
Gatling Av. M12—4A 92
Gatwick Av. M23—7B 102
Gatwick Clo. BL8—3J 25
Gavel Wlk. M24—8L 43
Gavin Av. M5—6A 78
Gawsworth Av. M20—4J 103
Gawsworth Clo. OL2—2M 45
Gawsworth Clo. SK3—8D 104
Gawsworth Clo. SK7—7E 114
Gawsworth Clo. SK12—1M 121
Gawsworth Clo. WA15—7K 101
Gawsworth Ct. M9—3G 61
(off Deanswood Dri.)
Gawsworth Rd. M33—3L 101
Gawsworth Way. M34—5A 94
Gawsworth Way. SK9—8L 113
Gawthorpe Clo. BL9—4A 42
Gaydon Rd. M33—1D 100
Gayford Wlk. M9—3L 61
(off Brockford Dri.)
Gaynor Av. WA11—8M 69
Gayrigg Wlk. M9—9K 61
Gaythorne St. BL1—7F 22
Gaythorn St. M5—4B 4 & 6C 78
Gayton Clo. WN3—5K 51
Gayton Wlk. M10—6D 62
Gaywood Wlk. M10—1J 79
Gazebo Clo. M28—5F 56
Gee Cross Fold. SK14—7F 94
Gee La. M30—4B 76
Gee St. SK3—6D 104
Gellert Pl. BL5—2E 54
Gellert Rd. BL5—2E 54
Gellifield La. OL3—8D 48
Gendre St. BL7—2E 22
Geneva Rd. SK7—1E 114
Geneva Ter. OL11—2C 28
Geneva Wlk. M8—1H 79
Geneva Wlk. OL9—2J 63
Genista Gro. M7—2D 78
(off Hilton St. N.)
Gennel Stile. WN2—2L 53
Geoff Bent Wlk. M10—1B 80
Geoffrey St. BL0—7G 9
Geoffrey St. BL9—6A 26
George Barton St. BL2—9H 23
George Ct. SK16—6B 82
(off Astley St.)
George La. SK6—1A 106
George Leigh St. M4—3G 5 & 5H 79
George Rd. BL0—6H 9
George's Clo. SK12—9L 115
Georges La. BL6—3D 20
George Sq. OL1—2L 63
George's Rd. M33—2H 101
Georges Rd. SK4—3D 104
George's Rd. E. SK12—9L 115
George's Rd. W. SK12—9K 115
George's Ter. WN5—3D 50
George St. BL3—5F 38
George St. BL4—1L 57
(Farnworth)
George St. BL4—1H 57
(New Bury)
George St. BL5—9F 36
George St. BL6—7C 20
George St. BL9—8M 25
George St. M1—5E 5 & 7F 78
(in two parts)
George St. M3—4C 4 & 6D 78
George St. M8—8E 60
George St. M25—7B 60
(Prestwich)
George St. M25—8L 41
(Whitefield)
George St. M26—6F 40
George St. M29—5K 55
George St. M30—6C 76
(Eccles)
George St. M30—3H 87
(Irlam)
George St. M31—4E 88
George St. M34—3A 94
George St. M35—8F 62
George St. OL1—2L 63
George St. OL2—1C 46
George St. OL5—6J 65
George St. OL6—4C 82
George St. OL9—1G 63
George St. OL10—7H 27
George St. OL12—3C 12
George St. OL15—5B 14
George St. OL16—3L 29
(Firgrove)
George St. OL16—8K 13
(Hurstead)
George St. OL16—2G 29
(Rochdale, in two parts)
George St. SK1—3G 105
George St. SK6—3H 107
George St. SK9—8L 119
George St. SK13—6J 97
George St. SK15—5G 83
George St. WA14—9D 100
George St. WN2—3L 53
(Hindley)
George St. WN2—1F 52
(Ince)
George St. WN4—3C 70
George St. E. SK1—5H 105
George St. W. SK1—5H 105
George St. W. SK14—3C 94
Georgiana St. BL4—7H 39
Georgiana St. BL9—9M 25
Georgian Ct. M29—7M 55
(off Market St.)
Georgian Ct. WN7—3H 73
Georgian Sq. WN2—6G 53
Georgina Ct. BL3—6B 38
Georgina St. BL3—7B 38
Gerald Av. M8—8G 61
Gerald Rd. M6—2A 78
Gerard St. WN4—4B 70
Germain Clo. M9—3J 61
German Bldgs. SK1—7G 105
German La. PR7—1L 17
Gerrard Av. WA15—5G 101
Gerrard Clo. WN2—7K 35
Gerrard Rd. WN5—2E 68
Gerrards Clo. M30—4G 87
Gerrards Gdns. SK14—7E 94
Gerrards Hollow. SK14—7D 94
Gerrard St. BL4—9L 39
Gerrard St. BL5—8E 36
Gerrard St. M6—2A 4 & 4B 78
Gerrard St. OL11—8G 29
Gerrard St. SK15—6H 83
Gerrard St. WN7—2F 72
Gertrude Clo. M5—7A 78
Gervis Clo. M10—2K 79
Ghyll Gro. M28—6L 57
Ghyll Gro. WA11—6B 68
Giants Hall Rd. WN6—6L 33
Gibb Fold. M29—4K 55
Gibb La. SK6—8L 107
Gibbon Av. M22—2D 112
Gibbon's Rd. WN4—5K 69
Gibbon St. BL3—4D 38
Gibbon St. M11—5A 80
Gibb Rd. M28—9B 58
Gibbs St. M3—4C 4 & 6D 78
Gibb St. OL4—2D 64
Gib La. M23—6C 102
Gib La. Cottages. M23—6B 102
Gibraltar La. M34—6B 94
Gibraltar St. BL3—3D 38
Gibraltar St. OL4—3D 64
Gibsmere Clo. WA15—7K 101
Gibson Av. M18—8F 80
Gibson Gro. M28—5G 57
Gibson La. M28—5G 57
Gibson Pl. M3—2F 5 & 4G 79
Gibsons Rd. SK4—1B 104
Gibson St. BL2—9J 23
Gibson St. OL4—2C 64
Gibson St. OL16—2J 29
Gibson St. WN2—7K 53
Gibwood Rd. M22—5C 102
Giddings Rd. M1—5H 5 & 7J 79
Gidlow Av. WN6—7A 34
Gidlow Houses. WN6—4A 34
Gidlow La. WN6—4A 34
Gidlow St. M18—9E 80
Gidlow St. WN2—2K 53
Gifford Av. M9—4M 61
Gifford Wlk. SK7—2G 115
Gigg La. BL9—2L 41
Gilbertbank. SK6—1A 106
Gilbert Rd. WA15—3E 110
Gilbertson Rd. PR7—1E 18
Gilbert St. BL0—2J 9
Gilbert St. M6—6M 77
Gilbert St. M15—6D 4 & 8E 78
Gilbert St. M30—7B 76
Gilbert St. WN2—3J 53
Gilbert White Rd. WA14—9M 99
Gilcrest Rd. M30—8E 86
Gilda Brook Rd. M30—5G 77
(in two parts)
Gilda Cres. Rd. M30—4G 77
Gilda Rd. M28—9E 56
Gildenhall. M35—9G 63
Gilden Wlk. M9—3L 61
Gilderdale Dri. M9—2H 61
Gilderdale St. BL3—5G 39
Gildlow St. WN2—9G 35
Gildridge Rd. M16—5E 90
Gilesgate. M14—3J 91
(off Grelley Wlk.)
Giles St. M12—2A 92
Gillan Rd. WN6—6B 34
Gill Av. WN6—3H 33
Gill Bent Rd. SK8—6A 114
Gillbrook Rd. M20—2H 103
Gillbrow Cres. WN1—8F 34
Gillemere Gro. OL2—2C 46
Gillford Av. M9—7M 61
Gilliburns Wlk. BL5—3F 54
Gillingham Rd. M30—5B 76
Gillingham Sq. M11—6M 79
(off Jobling St.)
Gill St. M9—8M 61
Gill St. SK1—2H 105
Gillwood Dri. SK6—4M 105
Gilman Clo. M9—6J 61
Gilmerton Dri. M10—2C 80
Gilmore Dri. M25—3B 60
Gilmore St. SK3—6E 104
Gilmour St. M24—9A 44
Gilmour Ter. M9—7M 61
Gilnow Gdns. BL1—3C 38
Gilnow Gro. BL1—3D 38
Gilnow La. BL3—3C 38
Gilnow Rd. BL1—3C 38
Gilpin Pl. WN2—6F 52
Gilpin Rd. M31—4F 88
Gilpin Wlk. M24—8K 43
Gilroy St. WN1—9D 34
Giltbrook Av. M10—3K 79
Gilwell Dri. M23—9M 101
Gingham Brow. BL6—6D 20
Gingham Pk. M26—4E 40
Gipsy La. OL11—7C 28
Girton Av. WN4—3M 69
Girton St. BL2—2K 39
Girton St. M7—1D 4 & 3E 78
Girton Wlk. M10—7D 62
Girvan Av. M10—6D 62
Girvan Clo. BL3—6C 38
Girvan Cres. WN4—3J 69
Girvan Wlk. OL10—9F 26
Gisborne Dri. M6—2M 77
Gisburn Av. BL1—8L 21
Gisburn Av. WA3—5F 70
Gisburn Dri. BL8—7E 24
Gisburn Dri. OL11—7G 29
Gisburne Av. M10—6D 62
Gissing Wlk. M9—1K 79
Givendale Dri. M8—6G 61
Glabyn Av. BL6—1F 36
Glade Brow. OL4—2G 65
Gladeside Rd. M22—9C 102
Glade St. BL1—2C 38
Glade, The. BL1—9D 22
Glade, The. SK4—4A 104
Glade, The. WN6—3H 33
Gladstone Clo. BL1—8E 22
Gladstone Clo. M15—2E 90
Gladstone Ct. BL4—8J 39
Gladstone Cres. OL11—7F 28
Gladstone Gro. SK4—2A 104
Gladstone Ho. OL12—5J 13
Gladstone Rd. BL4—8J 39
Gladstone Rd. M30—5E 76
Gladstone Rd. M31—4E 88
Gladstone Rd. WA14—7D 100
Gladstone St. BL1—8E 22
Gladstone St. BL5—8E 36
Gladstone St. BL9—7B 26
Gladstone St. M27—8G 59
Gladstone St. OL4—2B 64
Gladstone St. SK2—9J 105
Gladstone St. SK13—6J 97
Gladstone St. SK14—2G 97
Gladstone Ter. Rd. OL3—4A 66
Gladville Dri. SK8—7A 104
Gladwyn Av. M20—1E 102
Gladys St. BL3—7K 39
Gladys St. M5—8A 78
Gladys St. M16—2C 90
Glaisdale. OL4—2D 64
Glaisdale Clo. BL2—8H 23
Glaisdale Clo. WN4—4C 70
Glaisdale St. BL2—8H 23
Glaister La. BL2—9K 23
Glamis Av. M11—4B 80
Glamis Av. M32—4G 89
Glamis Av. OL10—2L 43
Glamis Clo. WN7—1K 73
Glamorgan Pl. OL9—3J 63
Glandon Dri. SK8—4C 114
Glanford Av. M9—5G 61
Glanton Wlk. M10—7D 62
Glanvor Rd. SK3—5C 104
Glassbrook St. WN6—8A 34
Glasshouse St. M4—2H 5 & 4J 79
Glasson Wlk. OL9—2G 63
Glass St. BL4—1L 57
Glass St. M11—6M 79
Glastonbury. OL12—2E 28
(off Spotland Rd.)
Glastonbury Av. SK8—6B 114
Glastonbury Av. WA3—7C 72
Glastonbury Av. WA15—2H 111
Glastonbury Dri. SK12—8K 115
Glastonbury Gdns. M26—4E 40
Glastonbury Rd. M29—9B 56
Glastonbury Rd. M32—3F 88
Glaswen Gro. SK5—1F 104
Glazebrook Clo. OL10—9J 27
Glazebrook La. WA3—6A 86
Glazebury Dri. M23—8B 102
Glazedale Av. OL2—5J 45
Glaze Wlk. M25—7C 42
Gleave Clo. WA15—9E 100
Gleaves Rd. M30—6E 76
Gleave St. BL1—1F 38
(off Bark St.)
Gleave St. M33—8H 89
Glebe Av. WN4—5C 70
Glebe Clo. WN6—9L 17
Glebe End. WN6—9B 34
Glebe Ho. M24—7A 44
(off Rochdale Rd.)
Glebeland Rd. BL3—4B 38
Glebelands Rd. M23—7M 101
Glebelands Rd. M25—3A 60
Glebelands Rd. M33—8E 88
Glebelands Rd. E. M25—3B 60
Glebe La. OL1—5E 46
Glebe Rd. M31—4D 88
Glebe Rd. WN6—9M 17
Glebe St. BL2—3G 39
Glebe St. BL5—8E 36
Glebe St. M26—6H 41
Glebe St. M34—2M 93
Glebe St. OL2—2B 46
Glebe St. OL6—4C 82
Glebe St. OL9—5G 63
Glebe St. SK1—4G 105
Glebe St. WN7—1F 72
Gleden St. M10—5L 79
(in two parts)
Gledhall St. SK15—5G 83
Gledhill Av. M5—6A 4 & 8A 78
Gledhill Clo. OL2—9A 30
Gledhill St. M20—7H 91
Gledhill Way. BL7—1G 23
Glegg St. WN2—9F 34
Glemsford Clo. M10—1B 80
Glemsford Clo. WN3—5B 52
Glenarm Wlk. M22—2E 112
Glenart. M30—4E 76
Glen Av. BL3—4B 38
Glen Av. BL4—2B 58
Glen Av. M9—7L 61
Glen Av. M27—8D 58
Glen Av. M28—8A 58
Glen Av. M33—8G 89
Glenavon Dri. OL2—1M 45
Glenavon Dri. OL12—8D 12
Glenbarry Clo. M13—9H 79
Glenbarry St. M12—7K 79
Glenbeck Rd. M25—8L 41
Glenboro Av. BL8—8H 25
Glen Bott St. BL1—8D 22
Glenbourne Pk. SK7—7D 114
Glenbrook Gdns. BL4—7K 39
Glenbrook Hill. SK13—4J 97
Glenbrook Rd. M9—3G 61
Glenburn St. BL3—6D 38
Glenby Av. M22—1F 112
Glenby Est. OL9—2J 63
Glencar. BL5—1D 54
Glencar Dri. M10—6D 62
Glencastle Rd. M18—1C 92
Glen Clo. WA3—3B 98
Glencoe. BL2—2H 39
Glencoe Clo. OL10—9F 26
Glencoe Dri. BL2—3M 39
Glencoe Dri. M33—3C 100
Glencoe Pl. OL11—3D 28
Glencoe St. OL8—6J 63
Glen Cotts. BL1—7L 21
Glencoyne Dri. BL1—4D 22
Glencross Av. M21—4A 90
Glendale. M27—6H 59
Glendale Av. BL9—6M 41
Glendale Av. M19—8M 91
Glendale Av. WN4—3C 70
Glendale Clo. M28—9F 56
Glendale Clo. OL10—8K 27
Glendale Dri. BL3—3M 37
Glendale Rd. M28—9F 56
Glendale Rd. M30—4G 77
Glendene Av. M35—4J 81
Glendene Av. SK7—7D 114
Glenden Foot. OL12—9D 12
Glendevon Clo. BL3—4M 37
Glendevon Pl. M25—1B 60
Glendinning St. M6—5L 77
Glendon Cres. OL6—9B 64
Glendore. M5—5J 77
Glendower Dri. M10—2J 79
Glen Dri. WN6—1E 32
Gleneagles. BL3—6M 37
Gleneagles. WA11—9G 69
Gleneagles Av. M11—5C 80
Gleneagles Av. OL10—1K 43
Gleneagles Clo. SK7—5F 114
Gleneagles Clo. SK9—3K 119
Gleneagles Rd. M31—2L 87
Gleneagles Rd. SK8—3J 113
Glenfield. WA14—9B 100
Glenfield Dri. SK12—9K 115
Glenfield Rd. SK4—1D 104
Glenfield Sq. BL4—7H 39
Glenfyne Rd. M6—2K 77
Glen Gdns. OL12—8F 12
Glengarth Dri. BL6 & BL1—3J 37
Glen Gro. M24—1C 62
Glen Gro. OL2—4K 45
Glenham Ct. M15—2E 90
Glenhaven Av. M31—4C 88
Glenholme Rd. SK7—5D 114
Glenhurst Rd. M19—9L 91
Glenlea Dri. M20—5H 103
Glenluce Wlk. BL3—4L 37
Glen Maye. M33—1J 101
Glenmaye Gro. WN2—3A 54
Glenmere Clo. M25—2M 59
Glenmere Rd. M20—5J 103
Glenmoor Rd. SK1—5G 105
Glenmore Av. BL4—7G 39
Glenmore Av. M20—1E 102
Glenmore Clo. BL3—4L 37
Glenmore Clo. OL11—5L 27
Glenmore Dri. M8—9H 61
Glenmore Dri. M35—8H 63
Glenmore Gro. SK16—7C 82
Glenmore Rd. BL0—9F 8
Glenmore St. BL9—9L 25
Glenolden St. M11—5D 80
Glenpark. WN7—1H 73
Glenpark Wlk. M9—9L 61
(off Orpington Rd.)
Glenridding Clo. OL1—8A 46
Glenridge Clo. BL1—8F 22
Glen Rise. WA15—8G 101
Glen Rd. OL4—2C 64
Glen Royd. OL12—1C 28
Glenroy Way. M9—3L 61
Glensdale Dri. M10—7E 62
Glenshee Dri. BL3—4M 37
Glenside. WN6—8B 16
Glenside Av. M18—3D 92
Glenside Dri. BL3—7F 38
Glenside Dri. SK6—9B 94
Glenside Gro. M28—4L 57
Glen St. M5—8A 78
Glen, The. BL1—2L 37
Glen, The. M24—2B 62
Glenthorn Av. M9—2K 61
Glenthorne Dri. OL7—3A 82
Glenthorne St. BL1—9E 22
Glenthorn Gro. M33—2H 101
Glentrees M. BL1—1A 38
Glentrool M. BL1—2A 38
Glent View. SK15—3G 83
Glentwood. WA14—3E 110
Glen View. OL2—4K 45
Glen View. OL12—1C 12
Glenville Wlk. SK15—6G 83
Glenville Way. M34—4A 94
Glenwood Av. SK14—1D 94
Glenwood Dri. M9—9L 61
Glenwood Dri. M24—7C 44
Glenwood Gro. SK2—1H 115
Glenwyn Av. M9—4L 61
Gleyve. WA16—7C 108
Globe La. BL7—8D 6
Globe La. SK16—8A 82
Globe La. Ind. Est. SK16—9B
Globe Sq. SK16—8A 82
Glodwick. OL4—3B 64
Glodwick Rd. OL4—3B 64
Glossop Rd. SK6—5H 107
Glossop Rd. SK13—7D 96
Glossop Ter. M10—5D 62
Gloster St. BL2—2G 39
Gloucester Av. BL6—8D 20
Gloucester Av. M19—6B 92
Gloucester Av. M25—9A 42
Gloucester Av. OL10—1J 43
Gloucester Av. OL12—7K 13
Gloucester Av. SK6—7F 106
Gloucester Av. WA3—6H 7
Gloucester Clo. OL6—8D 64
Gloucester Cres. WN2—2L
Gloucester Dri. M33—1D 10
Gloucester Dri. OL3—5C 48
Gloucester Ho. M7—1D 78
Gloucester Pl. M6—4A 78
Gloucester Pl. M29—4K 55
Gloucester Rise. SK16—8G
Gloucester Rd. M6—3J 77
Gloucester Rd. M24—2A 62
Gloucester Rd. M31—4D 88
Gloucester Rd. M34—4G 93
Gloucester Rd. M35—4G 81
Gloucester Rd. SK8—5J 11
Gloucester Rd. SK12—8K 1
Gloucester Rd. SK14—6E 9
Gloucester Rd. WN5—2J 5
Gloucester St. M1—6E 5 & 8
Gloucester St. M5—5B 4 & 7
Gloucester St. M6—3A 78
Gloucester St. M29—5H 55
Gloucester St. SK3—6D 10
Gloucester St. N. OL9—3J
Gloucester St. S. OL9—3J
Gloucester Way. SK13—6M
Glover Av. M8—1H 79
Glover Ct. M8—8F 60
Glover Field. M7—1D 78
(off Devonshire St.)
Glover Ho. WN7—5E 72
Glover Rd. PR7—3K 17
Glover St. BL6—6B 20
Glover St. WN7—8C 54
Glyn Av. WA15—2G 111
Glyneath Clo. M11—6M 79
Glynis Clo. SK3—7F 104
Glynis Glo. SK3—7F 104
Glynne St. BL4—9J 39
Glynn Gdns. M20—1D 102
Glynrene Dri. M27—7C 58
Glynwood Pk. BL4—8J 39
G.Mex Cen. M2—5E 5 & 7F
Gnat Bank. OL11—5M 27
Goats Ga. Ter. M25—7K 4
Godbert Av. M21—9C 90
Goddard La. SK14—9G 85
Goddard Rd. SK14—2G 97
Goddard St. OL8—4M 63
Godfrey Av. M35—4D 80
Godfrey Range. M18—2F
Godfrey Rd. M6—2J 77
Godlee Dri. M27—9E 58
Godley Clo. M11—7C 80
Godley St. SK14—2F 94
Godson St. OL1—8L 45
Godwin St. M18—9E 80
Goit Pl. OL16—3F 28
Golborne Av. M20—7F 90
Golborne Dri. OL2—1B 46
Golborne Gallery. WN1—
(off Galleries, The)
Golborne Ho. BL1—1F 38
Golborne Ho. OL2—1B 46
(off Cowie St.)
Golborne Ho. WA3—7H 7
Golborne La. WA16—9A
Golborne Pl. WN1—9E 34
Golborne Rd. WA3—7A 68
Goldbourne Rd. WN4—3D
Goldbrook Clo. OL10—9L
Goldcraft Clo. OL10—9L
Goldcrest Clo. M22—8F 1
Goldcrest Clo. M28—9H 5
Goldenhill Av. M11—4C 8
Golden Sq. M30—6D 76
(off Golden St.)
Golden St. M30—6D 76
Golden St. OL2—1E 46
Goldenways. WN1—7C 3
Goldfinch Dri. BL9—5C 2
Goldfinch Way. M35—4J
Goldie Av. M22—2F 112
Goldrill Av. BL2—1M 39
Goldrill Gdns. BL2—1M 3
Goldsmith Av. M5—5K 7
Goldsmith Av. OL1—5E 4
Goldsmith Pl. WN3—3A 5
Goldsmith Rd. SK5—5D 9
Goldsmith St. BL3—5D 3
Goldsmith Way. M34—7
Goldstien Rd. BL6—5H 3
Gold St. M1—4F 5 & 6G 7
Goldsworthy Rd. M31—3
Goldwick Wlk. M23—4L
Golf Rd. M33—1M 101
Golf Rd. WA15—1F 110
Gomer Wlk. M8—1J 79
Gooch Clo. M16—3E 90
Gooch St. BL6—8C 20
Gooden Pl. BL4—7J 39
Gooden St. OL10—9L 27
Goodiers Dri. M5—5A 4 &
Goodier St. M10—2M 79
Goodier St. M33—1G 101
Goodiers View. SK14—1
Good Intent. OL16—5A 3
Goodison Clo. BL9—6B 4
Goodlad St. BL8—6H 25
Goodley Hill Rd. SK14—
Goodman St. M9—8L 61
Goodrich. OL11—4E 28
Goodridge Av. M22—2C
Goodwill Clo. M27—9F 5
Goodwin St. BL1—1G 39
Goodwood Av. M23—5K
Goodwood Av. M33—1C
Goodwood Clo. BL3—6M
Goodwood Ct. M7—1D 7
(off Bury New Rd.)

dwood Cres. WA15—7J 101
dwood Dri. M27—9H 59
dwood Dri. OL1—8B 46
dwood Rd. SK6—8E 106
dworth Wlk. M10—9A 62
(off Hanson Rd.)
e St. M11—7A 80
secote Hill. BL7—9E 6
e Grn. WA14—9D 100
se Grn. Av. PR7—1M 17
ehouse Grn. SK6—2D 106
e La. OL12—2F 28
etrey Clo. SK9—2L 119
trey Av. M20—6G 91
en St. OL11—5G 29
en Ter. M9—8L 61
on Av. BL3—4C 38
on Av. M19—5B 92
on Av. M33—8H 89
on Av. OL4—2B 64
on Av. OL9—5G 63
on Av. SK7—1K 115
on Av. WA11—8M 69
on Av. WN4—3L 69
on Clo. WN5—9L 33
on Pl. M20—9H 91
on Rd. M27—1C 76
on Rd. M30—4D 76
onstoun Cres. WN5—1F 50
on St. BL9—6L 25
on St. M7—1C 4 & 3D 78
on St. M16—1D 90
on St. M18—9E 80
on St. OL2—2C 46
two parts)
on St. OL4—3E 64
es)
n St. OL4—2G 65
ringhead)
n St. OL6—3D 82
n St. OL9—4F 62
n St. OL16—6B 30
n St. SK4—3E 104
n St. SK14—4E 94
n St. SK15—6H 83
n St. WN1—1E 52
n St. WN7—1F 72
n Way. OL10—9F 26
Av. M5—5K 77
Av. M35—8H 63
Cres. M5—4K 77
ale Av. M18—3E 92
Dri. M5—4K 77
La. SK9—8B 118
an Rd. M18—1D 92
La. WA11—1A 68
St. BL9—8C 26
St. M1—4G 5 & 6H 79
St. M3—3D 4 & 6E 78
St. M6—4A 78
St. WN5—2H 51
Av. M18—9D 80
an St. WN6—8A 34
an Wlk. WN3—3M 51
ls Clo. OL11—7D 28
St. OL11—5G 29
s Way. OL11—7D 28
wo parts)
ls Way Ind. Est. OL11 —7D 28
Av. M32—3M 89
Av. M35—5J 81
Av. OL5—7L 65
Av. OL8—5C 64
Av. SK6—7E 106
Bank. BL9—7C 26
Bank Rd. WA15—5J 111
Cres. M32—3M 89
Dri. M28—2F 56
Dri. M32—3M 89
Field Clo. M26—5G 41
ield Dri. M27—9F 58
ield Hey. SK9—3L 119
Hall Clo. SK16—8F 82
Hall Dri. SK15—6F 82
Hall Rd. SK16—8E 82
ands. SK8—7B 114
La. M32—3M 89
Pit. BL9—7C 26
Rd. M27—1E 76
Rd. M28—6L 57
Rd. OL16—4A 30
Dri. WN2—3J 35
Mt. BL2—4J 39
Sq. M31—2D 98
St. M32—3L 89
St. OL9—4F 62
The. WA14—4B 110
Wlk. WN7—2B 72
ay. SK5—1H 105
Way. SK13—6L 97
Av. M22—8C 102
Bank. OL15—4C 14
Bank Rd. SK3—5A 104
Brow. M31—4F 88
Brow. SK6—3A 106
Brow. SK14—5A 96
Brow. WN5—2E 68
Brow. WN6—8H 17
Brow Clo. WN5—2D 68
Brow St. SK1—4G 105
Clough Dri. BL8—5F 24
Clough Wlk. BL8—5F 24
Dri. M22—9C 102
ields. M35—7G 81
Hey. BL5—1E 54
Hill St. OL10—9K 27
La. OL6—1E 82
La. WA13—7G 99
La. WA14—8B 100
Mt. St. SK1—4G 105
Rd. M22—9C 102
Rd. SK9—4F 118
Way. OL6—1E 82
Wlk. M22—4C 112
BL9—8A 42
Cres. M34—4J 93
Cross Cen. M18—1D 92
Gro. M28—3J 57
La. M12 & M18—8A 80
Rd. M11—7M 79
Rd. SK5—7F 92
St. BL2—3G 39
St. BL4—1H 57
St. M3—3E 5 & 5F 78
St. M10—1H 5 & 3J 79
St. M30—6A 76
St. OL7—6M 81
St. OL9—2H 63
St. OL10—8L 27
lla Wlk. M12—9M 79
Clo. BL8—5J 25
Clo. OL1—8A 46
Wlk. M23—4M 101
La. BL9—3M 41
Clo. M16—3F 90
Sq. M7—2D 78
Wlk. M8—1J 79
neaton St.)
St. OL4—2C 64
o. M13—6H 5 & 9J 79
e Clo. SK6—3E 106
e La. SK6—3E 106
lo. SK6—3F 106
OL10—8L 27
SK3—4D 104
Rd. M20—8G 91
St. M4—3G 5 & 5H 79
St. M6—5L 77
Rd. M18—3E 92
M4—2G 5 & 4H 79
M34—3L 93
OL1—9B 46
Dri. SK8—2M 113
M22—4E 102
ri. M24—8K 43
ck's St. BL1—8E 22
d. M16—5E 90
v. SK7—1J 115
le Rd. SK5—9J 93
SK4—1D 104
SK14—5D 94
t. OL16—2H 29

Gower St. BL1—1D 38
Gower St. BL4—8J 39
Gower St. M27—7G 59
Gower St. OL1—1A 64
Gower St. OL6—4C 82
Gower St. WN5—2A 52
Gower St. WN7—3E 72
Gowran Pk. OL4—2D 64
Gowy Clo. SK9—1L 119
Goya Rise. OL1—5D 46
Goyt Av. SK6—9F 106
Goyt Cres. SK1—2H 105
Goyt Cres. SK6—2M 105
Goyt Hey Av. WN5—2E 68
Goyt Rd. SK1—2H 105
Goyt Rd. SK6—9F 106
Goyt Rd. SK12—7K 117
Goyt Valley. SK6—3L 105
Goyt Valley Rd. SK6—2M 105
Goyt Valley Wlk. SK6—2M 105
Grab Brow. M29—5H 55
Grace St. BL6—6B 20
Grace St. OL12—9G 13
Grace St. WN7—2C 72
Grace Wlk. M4—6K 79
Gracie Av. OL1—8B 46
Gradwell St. SK3—5D 104
Gradwell Wlk. M15—1E 90
Grafton Av. M30—3G 77
Grafton Ct. M15—1D 90
Grafton Ct. OL1—5E 46
(off Grafton St.)
Grafton Ct. OL16—4H 29
Grafton Mall. WA14—9D 100
Graftons, The. WA14—9D 100
Grafton St. BL1—1D 38
Grafton St. BL9—1M 41
Grafton St. M13—1H 91
Grafton St. M29—7G 55
Grafton St. M35—8G 63
Grafton St. OL1—5E 46
Grafton St. OL6—5D 82
(in two parts)
Grafton St. OL16—4H 29
Grafton St. PR7—4F 18
Grafton St. SK4—2E 104
Grafton St. SK14—3D 94
Grafton St. SK15—4K 83
Grafton St. WA14—9D 100
Graham Av. WN6—8C 16
Graham Cres. M30—1C 98
Graham Dri. SK12—5J 117
Graham Rd. M6—3J 77
Graham Rd. SK1—5H 105
Graham St. BL1—1F 38
Graham St. M11—7A 80
Graham St. OL7—6M 81
Graham St. WN2—7G 53
Grainger Av. M12—3A 92
Grains Rd. OL2—3C 46
Grains Rd. OL3—3G 47
Gralam Clo. M33—4L 101
Grammar School Rd. OL8 —6H 63
Grammer School La. WA13 —2A 108
Grampian Clo. OL9—3G 63
Grampian Way. OL2—1M 45
Grampian Way. WA3—6K 71
Grampian Way. WN2—6H 53
Granada Rd. M34—3F 92
Granary La. M28—2M 75
Granary Way. M33—3F 100
Granby Houses. M1—5F 5 & 7G 79
Granby Rd. M27—9C 58
Granby Rd. M32—5K 89
Granby Rd. SK2—8H 105
Granby Rd. SK8—4B 114
Granby Rd. WA15—4H 101
Granby Row. M1—5F 5 & 7G 79
Granby St. BL8—6F 24
Granby St. OL9—5G 63
Grandale St. M14—3J 91
Grandidge St. OL11—5E 28
Grand Union Way. M30—7D 76
Grange Av. BL3—6C 40
Grange Av. M19—6M 91
Grange Av. M27—6D 58
Grange Av. M30—3D 76
Grange Av. M31—4L 87
Grange Av. M32—4K 89
Grange Av. M34—4B 94
Grange Av. OL8—4J 63
Grange Av. OL16—6M 29
Grange Av. SK4—9D 92
Grange Av. SK8—1M 113
Grange Av. WA15—6H 101
(Altrincham)
Grange Av. WA15—2G 111
(Hale)
Grange Av. WN3—3B 52
Grange Av. WN5—1H 51
Grange Clo. SK14—5F 94
Grange Clo. WA3—9J 71
Grange Ct. OL8—4K 63
Grange Ct. WA14—3C 110
Grange Cres. M31—5C 88
Grange Dri. M9—5M 61
Grange Dri. M30—3D 76
Grangeforth Rd. M8—8F 60
Grange Gro. M25—9M 41
Grange La. M20—3H 103
Grange La. OL3—3M 47
Grange Mill Wlk. M10—9B 62
Grange Pk. Av. OL6—1F 82
Grange Pk. Av. SK8—8K 103
Grange Pk. Av. SK9—3G 119
Grange Pk. Rd. BL7—4J 23
Grange Pk. Rd. M9—5M 61
Grange Pk. Rd. SK8—8K 103
Grange Pl. M30—9D 86
Grange Rd. BL3—4B 38
Grange Rd. BL4—8G 39
Grange Rd. BL7—3J 23
Grange Rd. BL8—8H 25
Grange Rd. M21—4A 90
Grange Rd. M24—3D 44
Grange Rd. M28—9E 56
Grange Rd. M30—3A 76
Grange Rd. M31—5C 88
Grange Rd. M33—1F 100
Grange Rd. OL12—1D 12
Grange Rd. SK7—1F 114
Grange Rd. WA11—9K 69
Grange Rd. WA14—3C 110
Grange Rd. WA15—6H 101
Grange Rd. WN2—7L 53
Grange Rd. WN4—1M 69
Grange Rd. N. SK14—4F 94
Grange Rd. S. SK14—5F 94
(in two parts)
Grange St. M6—5L 77
Grange St. M35—1D 80
Grange St. OL9—1L 63
Grange St. OL12—9F 12
Grange St. WN2—4K 53
Grange St. WN7—4E 72
Grange, The. M14—3J 91
Grange, The. SK14—5F 94
Grangethorpe Dri. M19—7L 91
Grangethorpe Rd. M14—4J 91
Grangethorpe Rd. M31—5C 88
Grange Valley. WA11—9K 69
Grange Wlk. M24—7L 43
Grangeway. SK9—8K 113
Grange Way. WN2—3A 54
Grangewood. BL7—3J 23
Grangewood Dri. M9—9K 61
Granite St. OL1—9B 46
Gransden Dri. M8—1J 79
Granshaw St. M10—4L 79
Gransmoor Av. M11—8F 80
Gransmoor Rd. M11—8F 80
Grantchester Pl. BL4—8F 38
Grantchester Way. BL2—9L 23
Grant Clo. M9—6K 61
Grant Ct. BL0—4H 9
Grantham Clo. BL1—9E 22
Grantham Dri. BL8—5K 25
Grantham Gro. WN2—7F 34
Grantham Rd. SK4—3C 104
Grantham St. M14—3G 91

Grantham St. OL4—3A 64
Grantley St. WN4—2A 70
Granton. OL11—5F 28
Grant Rd. WN3—5A 52
Grant St. BL3—4G 39
Grant St. BL4—7H 39
Grant St. OL11—8D 28
Grant St. WN2—1F 52
Grantwood. WN4—2A 70
Granville Av. M7—8E 60
Granville Av. M16—4C 90
Granville Clo. OL9—1J 63
Granville Ct. M16—3C 90
Granville Ct. OL16—7B 30
Granville Gdns. M20—3G 103
Granville Gro. WN7—9F 54
Granville Rd. BL3—6C 38
Granville Rd. M14—6J 91
Granville Rd. M31—3E 88
Granville Rd. M34—6H 81
Granville Rd. SK8—8B 104
Granville Rd. SK9—6F 118
Granville Rd. WA15—7J 101
Granville St. BL4—7K 39
Granville St. M27—8F 58
Granville St. M28—5J 57
Granville St. M30—4D 76
Granville St. OL6—5D 82
Granville St. OL9—9J 45
Granville St. PR6—3G 19
Granville St. WN2—3L 53
Granville Ter. OL6—5D 82
Granville Wlk. OL9—9J 45
Grasdene Av. M9—5L 61
Grasmere. WN5—9F 32
Grasmere Av. BL3—5A 40
Grasmere Av. BL4—1F 56
Grasmere Av. M25—1J 59
Grasmere Av. M27—6C 58
Grasmere Av. M31—5L 87
Grasmere Av. OL10—1K 43
Grasmere Av. SK4—8E 92
Grasmere Av. WA11—8B 68
Grasmere Av. WN2—9G 35
Grasmere Av. WN8—1B 50
Grasmere Clo. SK15—3G 83
Grasmere Clo. WA11—8B 68
Grasmere Ct. WA11—8B 68
Grasmere Cres. M30—4B 76
Grasmere Cres. SK6—3E 116
Grasmere Cres. SK7—4E 114
Grasmere Dri. WN4—2B 70
Grasmere Fold. WA11—8B 68
Grasmere Gro. OL7—3M 81
Grasmere Rd. M27—1F 76
Grasmere Rd. M31—2E 98
Grasmere Rd. M32—3K 89
Grasmere Rd. M33—3J 101
Grasmere Rd. OL2—3J 45
Grasmere Rd. OL4—2C 64
Grasmere Rd. SK8—1H 113
Grasmere Rd. SK9—8L 119
Grasmere Rd. WA13—9A 98
Grasmere Rd. WA15—7J 101
Grasmere Rd. WN5—1J 51
Grasmere St. M12—3B 92
Grasmere St. OL12—1F 28
Grasmere St. WN7—2E 72
Grasmere Ter. WN2—8H 53
Grasmere Wlk. M24—7M 43
Grason Av. SK9—2J 119
Grasscroft. SK5—8J 93
Grasscroft Clo. M14—4F 90
Grasscroft Rd. SK15—6G 83
Grasscroft Rd. WN2—4A 54
Grassfield Av. M7—1C 78
Grassholm Dri. SK2—7A 106
Grassingham Gdns. M6—4M 77
Grassington Av. M10—7A 62
Grassington Ct. BL8—6F 24
Grassington Pl. BL2—9G 23
Grass Mead. M34—6B 94
Grassmere St. BL1—7F 22
Grassmoor Cres. SK13—4D 96
Grathome Wlk. BL3—5E 38
Gratrix Av. M5—6A 4 & 8B 78
Gratrix La. M33—2M 101
Gratrix St. M18—2E 92
Gravel Bank Rd. SK6—8B 94
Gravel La. M3—3D 4 & 5E 78
(in two parts)
Gravel La. SK9—7E 118
Gravel Walks. OL4—1B 64
Grave Oak La. WN7—6G 73
(in two parts)
Graver La. M10—2D 80
Graves St. M26—3F 40
Graveyard La. WA16—6A 118
Gray Av. WA11—9K 69
Gray Clo. SK14—3M 95
Gray Ho. BL1—1E 38
(off Gray St.)
Graymar Rd. M28—4G 57
Graymarsh Dri. SK12—1L 121
Graysands Rd. WA15—1F 110
Grayson Av. M25—9A 42
Grayson Rd. M28—4H 57
Grayson's Clo. WN1—8C 34
Grayson Way. OL3—2B 66
Gray St. BL1—1E 38
(in two parts)
Graythorpe Wlk. M5—6A 78
Graythorp Wlk. M14—3H 91
Graythwaite Rd. BL1—8M 21
Greame St. M14—3F 90
Gt. Acre. WN1—8D 34
Gt. Ancoats St. M4—3G 5 & 5H 79
Gt. Arbour Way. M24—8M 43
Gt. Bank Rd. BL5—6D 36
Gt. Bent Clo. OL12—7K 13
Gt. Bridgewater St. M1—5D 4 & 7E 78
Gt. Cheetham E. M7 & M8 —1E 78
Gt. Cheetham St. W. M7—2C 78
Gt. Clowes St. M7 & M3—1C 78
Gt. Ducie St. M3—2E 5 & 4F 78
Gt. Egerton St. SK1—4E 104
Greatfield Rd. M22—1B 112
Gt. Flatt. OL12—1B 28
Gt. Fold. WN7—3L 73
Gt. Gable Clo. OL1—9A 46
Gt. Gates Clo. OL11—6G 29
Gt. Gates Rd. OL11—7G 29
Gt. George St. M3—3C 4 & 5D 78
Gt. George St. OL16—4F 28
Gt. George St. WN3—9B 34
Gt. Hall Clo. M26—5G 41
Gt. Holme. BL3—5F 38
Gt. Howarth. OL12—7H 13
Gt. Howarth Rd. OL12—7J 13
Gt. Jackson St. M15—6D 4 & 8E 78
Gt. John St. M3—5D 4 & 7E 78
Gt. Jones St. M12—9A 80
Great Lee. OL12—8D 12
Gt. Lee Wlk. OL12—8D 12
Gt. Marlborough St. M1—6E 5 & 8G 79
Gt. Marld Clo. BL1—8M 21
Gt. Meadow. OL2—9L 29
Gt. Moor St. BL3 & BL1—3F 38
Gt. Moor St. SK2—8H 105
Gt. Newton St. M10—2C 80
Gt. Norbury St. SK14—3C 94
Gt. Portwood St. SK1—3F 104
Gt. Southern St. M14—3H 91
Greatstone Clo. M26—6D 40
Greatstone Rd. M32 & M16 —2M 89
Gt. Stones Clo. BL7—9E 6
Gt. Underbank. SK1—4F 104
Gt. Western St. M14—2F 90
Greave. SK6—1D 106
Greave Av. OL11—2B 28
Greave Fold. SK6—1C 106
Greave Rd. SK1—5J 105
Greaves Av. BL2—6A 24
Greaves Av. M35—1D 80
Greaves Clo. WN6—1F 32
Greaves Rd. SK9—4C 118
Greaves St. OL1—1M 63

Greaves St. OL2—2C 46
Greaves St. OL4—2F 64
Greaves St. OL5—6J 65
Grebe Clo. SK12—8H 115
Grebe Clo. WN3—4H 51
Grebe Wlk. SK2—9A 106
Grecian Cres. BL3—5F 38
Grecian St. M7—2C 78
Grecian St. N. M7—1C 78
Grecian Ter. M7—2C 78
Greeba Rd. M23—7L 101
Greek St. M1—6G 5 & 8H 79
Greek St. SK3—5E 104
Green Acre. BL5—1F 54
Greenacre La. M28—2M 75
Greenacre Rd. M27—1D 76
Greenacres. BL7—5L 7
Greenacres. WN1—8D 34
Greenacres. WN6—9L 17
Greenacres Clo. WN7—7B 72
Greenacres Ct. OL12—7K 13
Greenacres Dri. M19—1L 103
Greenacres Rd. OL4—1B 64
Greenall St. WN4—2B 70
Green Av. BL3—6H 39
Green Av. M27—9F 58
Green Av. M28—3E 56
Green Av. M29—3M 73
Green Bank. BL2—7L 23
Green Bank. BL4—8J 39
Greenbank. OL12—6C 12
(off Tonacliffe Rd.)
Green Bank. SK4—7D 92
Green Bank. SK13—7F 96
Greenbank. SK14—1F 96
Greenbank. WN2—9H 53
(Abram)
Greenbank. WN2—5A 54
(Hindley)
Greenbank Av. M27—1D 76
Greenbank Av. OL3—8C 48
Greenbank Av. SK4—3L 103
Greenbank Av. SK8—8G 103
Greenbank Av. WN5—5D 50
Greenbank Ct. M29—7M 55
(off Green St.)
Greenbank Cres. SK6—8F 106
Greenbank Dri. OL15—8M 13
Greenbank Rd. BL3—4B 38
(in two parts)
Greenbank Rd. M6—4L 77
Green Bank Rd. M26—4F 40
Greenbank Rd. M33—9E 88
Greenbank Rd. OL12—9F 12
Greenbank Rd. SK6—4H 107
Greenbank Rd. SK8—7G 103
Green Bank St. M29—8B 56
Greenbank Ter. M24—8C 44
Greenbank Ter. SK4—3E 104
Green Barn. BL6—9L 19
Greenbarn Way. BL6—8K 19
Green Beech Clo. SK6—6E 106
Greenbooth Clo. SK16—8F 82
Greenbooth Rd. OL12—8K 11
Green Bri. Clo. OL11—6F 28
Green Bri. La. OL3—3B 66
Greenbrook Clo. BL9—6A 26
Greenbrook St. BL9—6A 26
Greenbrow Pde. M23—9A 102
Greenbrow Rd. M23—8A 102
Greenburn Av. WA11—6C 68
Greenburn Dri. BL2—8L 23
Green Clo. M29—7L 55
Green Clo. SK8—7G 103
Green Comn. La. BL5—2H 55
Greencourt Dri. M28—4F 56
Green Courts. WA14—1B 110
Green Croft. SK6—2D 106
Green Croft La. BL0—1L 9
Greencroft Rd. M30—3B 76
Greendale. M29—4L 55
Greendale Cres. WN7—3J 73
Greendale Dri. M9—5L 61
Greendale Gro. M34—6B 94
Green Dri. BL6—2J 37
Green Dri. M19—5M 91
Green Dri. SK9—1K 119
Green Dri. WA15—6G 101
Green End. M34—6B 94
Green End Rd. M19—9L 91
Greenfield Av. M30—7A 76
Greenfield Av. M31—4D 88
Greenfield Av. WN2—1E 52
Greenfield Clo. BL8—9G 25
Greenfield Clo. SK3—7E 104
Greenfield Clo. SK12—4M 117
Greenfield Clo. WA15—7J 101
Greenfield Ct. OL10—9K 27
Greenfield La. OL2—3B 46
Greenfield La. OL11—6G 29
Greenfield La. OL16—8K 13
Greenfield Rd. M28—4H 57
Greenfield Rd. M29—3L 55
Greenfields. WN6—5A 34
Greenfields Clo. WN2—2M 53
Greenfields Cres. WN4—3B 70
Greenfield St. M34—8K 81
Greenfield St. OL11—6G 29
Greenfield St. SK14—9G 85
(Hadfield)
Greenfield St. SK14—4D 94
(Hyde)
Greenfield Ter. M31—4L 87
Green Fold. M18—9F 80
Greenfold Av. BL4—1H 57
Green Fold La. BL5—1E 54
Greenford Clo. SK8—9B 104
Greenford Clo. WN5—2D 50
Greenford Rd. M8—9G 61
Green Gables Clo. SK8—3H 113
Greengate. M3—2D 4 & 4E 78
(in two parts)
Greengate. M10 & M24—5C 62
Green Ga. SK14—6D 94
Green Ga. WA15—6K 111
Greengate Clo. OL12—7K 13
Greengate La. BL2—1M 39
Greengate La. M25—4A 60
Greengate Lawns. M3—2D 4 & 4E 78
Greengate Rd. M34—2A 94
Greengate St. M24—2D 62
Greengate St. OL4—2A 64
(in three parts)
Greenhalgh La. PR6—2H 19
Greenhalgh Moss La. BL8 —5H 25
Greenhalgh St. M35—1C 80
Greenhalgh St. SK4—3E 104
Greenhalgh Wlk. M4—5J 79
(off Jackroom Dri.)
Green Hall Clo. M29—3M 55
Greenhall M. SK9—5H 119
Greenham Rd. M23—3M 101
Greenhaven. WN8—1B 50
Green Hayes Av. WN1—6C 34
Greenhead Fold. SK6—4A 106
Greenhead Wlk. BL3—5E 38
Greenhey. WN5—1H 51
Greenheys. BL2—7L 23
Greenheys Cres. BL8—1F 24
Greenheys La. M15—9C 78
Greenheys Rd. M28—2E 56
Green Hill. M25—4A 60
Greenhill Av. BL3—4B 38
Greenhill Av. BL4—1J 57
Greenhill Av. M33—8G 89
Greenhill Av. OL2—9L 29
Greenhill Av. OL12—2E 28
Greenhill Cotts. OL5—6K 65
Greenhill Cres. WN5—2F 68
Greenhill La. BL3—5M 37
Greenhill Pas. OL1—2A 64
Green Hill Pl. SK3—6D 104
Greenhill Rd. BL8—9G 25
Greenhill Rd. M8—9G 61
Greenhill Rd. M24—1C 62
Green Hill Rd. SK14—3F 94
Greenhill Rd. WA15—7J 101
Greenhill Rd. WN5—2F 68
Greenhill St. M15—1F 90
Green Hill St. SK3—6D 104
Greenhill Ter. M24—1D 62

Green Hill Ter. SK3—6D 104
Greenhill Terraces. OL4—2A 64
Greenhill Wlk. SK12—6K 117
Greenholme Clo. M10—7D 62
Greenhow St. M35—7F 80
Greenhurst Cres. OL8—6A 64
Greenhurst La. OL6—1E 82
Greenhurst Rd. OL6—9D 64
Green Hythe Rd. SK8—6J 113
Greening Rd. M19—4B 92
Greenland Av. WN6—9L 17
Greenland Clo. M29—9B 56
Greenland La. PR6 & BL6 —5K 19
Greenland Rd. BL3—6F 38
Greenland Rd. M29—1B 74
Greenland St. M6—5L 77
Greenland St. M8—9F 60
Green La. BL3—6F 38
Green La. BL4—1A 58
Green La. BL6—5B 20
Green La. M18—9D 80
Green La. M24—7B 44
(Middleton)
Green La. M24—1D 62
(Middleton Junction)
Green La. M25—8L 41
Green La. M30—9E 86
(Cadishead)
Green La. M30—5C 76
(Eccles)
Green La. M33—8E 88
Green La. M35—3E 80
Green La. OL3—5L 47
Green La. OL4—7F 46
Green La. OL5—4H 65
Green La. OL6—2B 82
Green La. OL8—6K 63
Green La. OL10—8L 27
Green La. OL12—2E 28
Green La. OL16—2G 29
Green La. PR7—3M 17
Green La. SK4—2B 104
Green La. SK6—4B 106
Green La. SK7—1K 115
Green La. SK9—8K 119
(Alderley Edge)
Green La. SK9—4H 119
(Wilmslow)
Green La. SK12—8K 117
(Disley)
Green La. SK12—8C 116
(Poynton)
Green La. SK13—6F 96
Green La. SK14—5G 95
(Godley Green)
Green La. SK14—2F 96
(Hadfield)
Green La. SK14—9D 84
(Hollingworth)
Green La. SK14—4G 95
(Hyde)
Green La. WA3—5A 72
Green La. WA15—1H 111
Green La. WN2—3B 54
Green La. WN5—5D 50
Green La. WN6—1L 33
Green La. WN7—2J 73
(in two parts)
Green La. N. WA15—8H 101
Greenlaw Ct. M16—1C 90
Greenlea Av. M18—3D 92
Green Leach Av. WA11—8B 68
Green Leach Ct. WA11—8B 68
Greenleach La. M28—8L 57
Green Leach La. WA11—8B 68
Greenlea Clo. WN5—3D 50
Greenleaf Clo. M28—1F 74
Greenleas. BL6—3J 37
Greenlees St. OL12—2F 28
Green Meadow. OL12—7K 13
Green Meadows. BL5—9D 36
(in four parts)
Green Meadows. SK6—6F 106
Green Meadows Dri. SK6 —6F 106
Green Meadow Wlk. M22 —3E 112
Greenmount Ct. BL1—1A 38
Green Mt. Dri. BL8—9F 8
Greenmount Dri. OL10—2M 43
Greenmount Ho. BL1—2A 38
Greenmount La. BL1—9M 21
Greenmount Pk. BL4—1A 58
Greenoak. M26—1C 58
Greenoak Dri. M28—3J 57
Greenoak Dri. M33—4J 101
Greenock Clo. BL3—4L 37
Greenock Dri. OL10—9F 26
Greenough's Gdns. WN1—9D 34
Greenough St. M29—7G 55
Greenough St. WN1—9D 34
Green Pk. Clo. BL8—1F 24
Greenpark Rd. M22—4D 102
Green Pastures. SK4—4K 103
Greenpine Ind. Pk. BL6—2D 36
Green Pine Rd. BL6—2D 36
Green Rd. M31—2E 98
Greenroyd Av. BL2—8L 23
Greenroyde. OL11—5E 28
Greens Arms Rd. BL7—3C 6
Greenshall La. SK12—7M 117
Greenshank Clo. OL11—3M 27
Greenside. BL4—8J 39
Greenside. M28—2A 76
Greenside. SK4—4A 104
Greenside Av. BL4—2M 57
Greenside Av. OL4—7D 46
Greenside Clo. BL8—8B 8
Greenside Clo. SK16—7G 83
Greenside Ct. M30—4D 76
Greenside Cres. M35—5F 80
Greenside Dri. BL8—1F 24
Greenside Dri. M30—5F 86
Greenside Dri. WA14—3E 110
Greenside La. M35—4E 80
Greenside Pl. M34—6A 94
Greenside St. BL2—9C 24
Greenside St. M11—7B 80
Greenside Way. M24—3C 62
Green's La. WN5—6E 50
Greenslate Av. WN6—1E 32
Greenslate Ct. WN5—5D 50
(in two parts)
Greenslate Rd. WN5—5E 50
Greensmith Way. BL5—6E 36
Greenson Dri. M24—1L 61
Greenstead Av. M8—8G 61
Greens, The. OL12—2C 12
Greenstone Dri. M6—2M 77
Green St. BL0—1L 9
Green St. BL1—2F 38
Green St. BL4—8J 39
Green St. BL8—6H 25
(Bury)
Green St. BL8—6F 24
(Walshaw)
Green St. M14—7K 91
Green St. M24—8B 44
Green St. M26—6G 41
(in two parts)
Green St. M29—6L 55
(Atherton)
Green St. M29—7A 56
(Tyldesley)
Green St. M30—7B 76
Green St. M32—6J 89
Green St. M35—9E 62
Green St. OL8—2K 63
Green St. OL9—5H 63
Green St. SK3—7F 104
Green St. SK9—8L 119
Green St. SK14—5E 94
Green St. WN2—6H 53
Green St. WN3—1C 52
Green, The. BL8—1F 24
Green, The. M27—6H 59
Green, The. M28—2A 76
Green, The. M31—1F 98
Green, The. OL8—5A 64
Green, The. PR6—1F 18
Green, The. SK4—2C 104
Green, The. SK6—1G 117

Green, The. SK8—4M 113
Green, The. SK9—9L 113
Green, The. SK13—7G 97
Green, The. SK15—3L 83
Green, The. WA15—6J 101
Green, The. WN5—1J 51
(in two parts)
Greenthorne Av. SK4—7D 92
Greenthorne Clo. BL7—4L 7
Greenthorn Wlk. M15—1F 90
(off Botham Clo.)
Green Tree Gdns. SK6—3B 106
Greenvale. OL11—2L 27
Greenvale. WN6—5F 32
Greenvale Cotts. OL15—3D 14
Greenvale Dri. SK8—7J 103
Green View. WA13—8B 98
Greenview Dri. M20—5J 103
Green Villa Pk. SK9—7E 118
Green Wlk. BL6—9K 19
Green Wlk. M16—3C 90
Green Wlk. M32—4H 89
Green Wlk. SK8—7G 103
Green Wlk. WA14—1A 110
Green Wlk. WA15—6F 100
Green Walks. M25—5C 60
Green Way. BL1—7G 23
Greenway. BL6—7F 20
Greenway. M22—5E 102
Greenway. M24—3M 61
Greenway. OL2—9M 29
Green Way. OL11—9B 28
Greenway. SK6—4E 106
Greenway. SK7—6D 114
Greenway. SK9—5H 119
Greenway. SK14—5D 94
Greenway. WA14—8A 100
Greenway. WN4—3B 70
Greenway Av. M19—6B 92
Greenway Clo. BL1—6G 23
Greenway Clo. BL8—7H 25
Greenway Clo. M33—2E 100
Greenway Dri. OL5—6H 65
Greenway Rd. SK8—6J 113
Greenway Rd. WA15—5F 100
Greenways. M10—7D 62
Greenways. OL7—1M 81
Greenways. WN5—5D 50
Greenways. WN6—3A 34
Greenways. WN7—1G 73
Greenwell Rd. WA11—9J 69
Greenwich Clo. M10—3D 80
Greenwich Clo. OL11—4M 27
Greenwood Av. M27—7H 59
Greenwood Av. M28—4J 57
Greenwood Av. OL6—1C 82
(in two parts)
Greenwood Av. SK2—7J 105
Greenwood Av. WN5—1L 51
Greenwood Clo. M28—9E 56
Greenwood Clo. WA15—8K 101
Greenwood Dri. SK9—3K 119
Greenwood Gdns. SK6—2M 105
Greenwood Pl. OL15—6B 14
(off Hare Hill Rd.)
Greenwood Rd. M22—1B 112
Greenwood Rd. WA13—2A 108
Greenwood Rd. WN6—8L 17
Greenwoods La. BL2—6M 23
Greenwood St. BL4—9K 39
Greenwood St. M6—3M 77
Greenwood St. OL4—9C 46
(Oldham, in two parts)
Greenwood St. OL4—3F 64
(Springhead)
Greenwood St. OL8—6M 63
Greenwood St. OL15—6B 14
Greenwood St. WA14—9D 100
Greenwood Vale. BL1—7E 22
Greer St. M11—7C 80
Gregge St. OL10—9L 27
Gregory Av. BL2—1L 39
Gregory Av. M29—3J 55
Gregory Av. SK6—4C 106
Gregorys Row. WA3—7A 72
(off Chapel Wlk.)
Gregory St. BL5—1A 54
Gregory St. M12—9M 79
Gregory St. OL8—5J 63
Gregory St. SK14—1E 94
Gregory St. WN2—2J 53
Gregory St. WN7—3E 72
Gregson Field. BL3—5E 38
(in two parts)
Gregson Rd. SK5—8E 92
Gregson St. OL1—2M 63
Gregson Way. SK5—8F 92
Greg St. SK5—9E 92
Grelley Wlk. M14—3H 91
Grenaby Av. WN2—3A 54
Grendale Av. SK1—4H 105
Grendale Av. SK7—3L 115
Grendale Dri. M16—1C 90
Grendon Av. OL8—4L 63
Grendon St. BL3—6C 38
Grendon Wlk. M12—9A 80
Grenfell Clo. WN3—3A 52
Grenfell Rd. M20—2G 103
Grenfell St. M20—2G 103
Grenham Av. M15—9D 78
Grenvile St. SK3—5D 104
Grenville Rd. SK7—1J 115
Grenville St. SK15—3K 83
Grenville St. SK16—7C 82
Grenville Wlk. OL15—2C 14
Gresford Clo. M21—6A 90
Gresham Clo. M25—1K 59
Gresham Dri. OL9—1J 63
Gresham St. BL1—7F 22
Gresham St. M34—2M 93
Gresham Wlk. SK4—2E 104
Gresty Av. M22—3F 112
Greswell St. M34—2L 93
Greta Av. SK8—6J 113
Greta Wlk. WN2—6G 53
Gretney Wlk. M15—1F 90
Gretton Clo. M13—2L 91
Greville St. M13—2L 91
Grey Clo. SK6—1A 106
Grey Friar Ct. M3—2D 4 & 4E 78
Greyfriars. WN4—3M 69
Greyfriars Rd. M22—2B 112
Greyhound Dri. M6—2C 78
Greylands Clo. M33—1F 100
Greylands Rd. M20—5J 103
Grey Mare La. M11—6M 79
Greymont Rd. BL9—4M 25
Grey Rd. WA14—8B 100
Grey Rd. WN4—3A 70
Greyscroft Dri. M23—9A 102
Greysham Ct. M16—4E 90
Greystoke Av. M19—5C 92
Greystoke Av. M33—2H 101
Greystoke Av. WA15—7K 101
Greystoke Cres. M25—7L 41
Greystoke Dri. BL1—4D 22
Greystoke Dri. M24—7K 43
Greystoke Dri. SK9—7L 119
Greystoke La. M35—1D 80
Greystoke St. SK1—4G 105
Greystone Av. M21—6F 90
Greystone Av. WN2—4J 35
Greystone Wlk. SK4—7D 92
Grey St. M12—9L 79
Grey St. M24—8M 43
Grey St. M25—4C 60
Grey St. M26—6H 41
Grey St. M34—3K 93
Grey St. OL6—5C 82
Grey St. SK15—6J 83
Greyswood Av. M8—9F 60
Greythorne Rd. BL1—9M 21
Greytown Clo. M6—2M 77
Greywood Av. BL9—8B 26
Grierson St. BL1—7E 22
Grierson Wlk. M16—2E 90
Griffe La. BL9—5C 42
Griffin Clo. BL9—6B 26
Griffin Ct. M3—3D 4 & 5E 78
Griffin Gro. M19—6A 92
Griffin St. M7—1C 78
Griffiths Clo. M7—1C 4 & 3D 78
Griffiths St. M10—2C 80

Grimeford La. BL6 & PR6 —5H 19
Grimes Cotts. OL12—1M 27
Grimes St. OL12—1M 27
Grime St. BL0—7G 9
Grimscott Clo. M9—7M 61
Grimshaw Av. M35—8G 63
Grimshaw La. M10—2M 79
Grimshaw La. M24—9A 44
Grimshaw St. M35—8E 62
Grimshaw St. SK1—4G 105
Grimshaw St. WA3—6G 71
Grimstead Clo. M23—7L 101
Grindall Av. M10—6B 62
Grindleford Gdns. SK13—4E 96
(off Buxton M.)
Grindleford Gro. SK13—4E 96
(off Edale Cres.)
Grindleford Lea. SK13—4E 96
(off Edale Cres.)
Grindleford Wlk. M21—9D 90
Grindleford Wlk. SK13—4E 96
(off Edale Cres.)
Grindle Grn. M30—7C 76
Grindley Av. M21—9D 90
Grindlow St. M13—1L 91
Grindlow Wlk. WN3—6J 51
Grindon Av. M7—9A 60
Grindrod La. OL12—6G 13
Grindrod St. M26—5F 40
(in two parts)
Grindrod St. OL12—1E 28
Grindsbrook Rd. M26—2F 40
Grinton Av. M13—4L 91
Grisdale Dri. M24—7L 43
Grisdale Rd. BL3—4C 38
Grisebeck Way. OL1—1L 63
Grisedale Av. OL2—1J 45
Grisedale Ct. M9—4A 62
Grisedale Rd. OL11—6B 28
Gritley Wlk. M22—3C 112
Grizebeck Clo. M18—9C 80
Grizedale Av. WA11—7B 68
Grizedale Clo. BL1—8M 21
Grizedale Clo. SK15—9L 65
Grizedale Rd. SK6—1B 106
Groby Ct. WA14—9C 100
Groby Pl. WA14—8C 100
Groby Rd. M21—6B 90
Groby Rd. M34—8L 81
Groby Rd. WA14—9B 100
Groby Rd. N. M34—7K 81
Groby St. OL8—5A 64
Groby St. SK15—6J 83
Groomsport Dri. M8—2E 78
Groom St. M1—6G 5 & 8H 79
Grosvenor Av. M25—8L 41
Grosvenor Av. WA3—7K 71
Grosvenor Clo. M28—3J 57
Grosvenor Clo. SK9—7G 119
Grosvenor Ct. M7—8D 60
Grosvenor Ct. M33—9F 88
Grosvenor Ct. OL7—6A 82
Grosvenor Cres. SK14—5C 94
Grosvenor Dri. M28—3J 57
Grosvenor Dri. SK12—9J 115
Grosvenor Gdns. M7—1C 4 & 3D 78
Grosvenor Gdns. M22—7E 102
Grosvenor Gdns. SK15—6G 83
Grosvenor Ho. M33—1F 100
Grosvenor Ho. M. M8—6F 60
Grosvenor Pl. OL7—6A 82
Grosvenor Rd. M16—4D 90
Grosvenor Rd. M25—8L 41
Grosvenor Rd. M27—9H 59
Grosvenor Rd. M28—3J 57
Grosvenor Rd. M30—4A 76
Grosvenor Rd. M31—4C 88
Grosvenor Rd. M33—9F 88
Grosvenor Rd. SK4—2A 104
(in two parts)
Grosvenor Rd. SK6—6F 106
Grosvenor Rd. SK8—9C 104
Grosvenor Rd. SK14—5D 94
Grosvenor Rd. WA11—8H 69
Grosvenor Rd. WA14—8E 100
Grosvenor Rd. WN7—1D 72
Grosvenor Sq. M7—1C 4 & 3D 78
Grosvenor Sq. M15—6F 5 & 8G 79
Grosvenor Sq. M33—1F 100
Grosvenor Sq. SK15—6G 83
Grosvenor St. BL2—3G 39
Grosvenor St. BL3—5A 40
Grosvenor St. BL4—9L 39
Grosvenor St. BL9—1M 41
Grosvenor St. M1—6F 5 & 8G 79
Grosvenor St. M25—4C 60
Grosvenor St. M26—5F 40
Grosvenor St. M27—6F 58
Grosvenor St. M32—4K 89
Grosvenor St. M34—2K 93
Grosvenor St. OL7—6M 81
(in two parts)
Grosvenor St. OL10—9J 27
Grosvenor St. OL11—9C 28
Grosvenor St. SK3—5F 104
Grosvenor St. SK7—1K 115
Grosvenor St. SK15—6G 83
(in two parts)
Grosvenor St. WN2—3K 53
Grosvenor St. WN5—2M 51
Grosvenor Way. BL6—7C 20
Grosvenor Way. OL2—7K 45
Grotton Hollow. OL4—2G 65
Grotton Meadows. OL4—3H 65
Grouse St. OL12—1F 28
Grove Arc. SK9—4H 119
Grove Av. M35—2E 80
Grove Av. PR6—3G 19
Grove Av. SK9—4G 119
Grove Clo. M14—3J 91
Grove Cotts. OL3—3D 48
Grove Ct. M33—1K 101
Grove Ct. SK7—1L 115
Grove Cres. PR6—3G 19
Grove Hill. M28—1F 74
Grove Ho. M15—1H 91
Grovehurst. M27—1B 76
Grove La. M20—2G 103
Grove La. SK8—6A 114
Grove La. WA15—6F 100
(Altrincham)
Grove La. WA15—1G 111
(Hale)
Grove La. WN6—1M 33
Grove M. M28—5K 57
Grove Pk. M33—1F 100
Grove Pl. WN6—1M 33
Grove Rd. M24—7B 44
Grove Rd. OL3—1B 66
Grove Rd. SK15—3K 83
Grove Rd. WA15—1E 110
Grove Rd. WN8—9C 32
Grove St. BL1—8D 22
Grove St. BL4—9L 39
Grove St. BL9—6C 26
Grove St. M7—2E 78
Grove St. M35—7F 80
Grove St. OL1—1A 64
(in two parts)
Grove St. OL3—3B 66
Grove St. OL7—2L 81
Grove St. OL10—8L 27
Grove St. OL11—5E 28
Grove St. SK7—1L 115
Grove St. SK9—4H 119
Grove St. SK16—6D 82
Grove St. WN4—3A 70
Grove St. WN7—3H 73
Grove Ter. OL4—9E 46
Grove, The. BL2—4H 39
Grove, The. BL3—6B 40
Grove, The. BL5—9E 36
Grove, The. M20—4H 103
Grove, The. M30—6F 76
Grove, The. M31—5M 87
Grove, The. M33—2H 101
Grove, The. OL2—3A 46
Grove, The. OL3—8M 47
Grove, The. SK2—6E 104

Grove, The. SK8—6A 114
Grove, The. SK14—2F 96
Grove, The. WA3—6K 71
Grove, The. WA14—8D 100
Grove, The. WN2—2F 52
Grove, The. WN6—8C 16
Grovewood Clo. OL7—2L 81
Grovewood Dri. WN6—1E 32
Grundey St. SK7—2L 115
Grundy Av. M25—6L 59
Grundy La. BL9—9A 26
Grundy Rd. BL4—1L 57
Grundy's Clo. M29—2C 74
Grundy's La. PR7—1C 18
Grundy St. BL5—8E 36
Grundy St. M28—5M 57
Grundy St. OL1—1A 64
Grundy St. OL10—1L 43
Grundy St. SK4—3L 103
Grundy St. WA3—8G 71
Grundy St. WN7—3G 73
Guardian Ct. M33—9G 89
Guest Rd. M25—2A 60
Guest St. WN7—2H 73
Guide La. M34—9M 81
Guide Post Sq. M13—9K 79
Guide St. M5—6J 77
Guido St. BL1—8D 22
Guido St. M35—9E 62
Guild Av. M28—6K 57
Guildford Av. SK8—5A 114
Guildford Clo. SK1—6H 105
Guildford Cres. WN6—6M 33
Guildford Dri. OL6—9C 64
Guildford Gro. M24—6C 44
Guildford Rd. BL1—8B 22
Guildford Rd. M6—3H 77
Guildford Rd. M19—4B 92
Guildford Rd. M31—2E 88
Guildford Rd. SK16—8G 83
Guildford St. OL16—3G 29
(in two parts)
Guildhall Clo. M15—1G 91
Guild St. BL7—3G 23
Guilford Rd. M30—6B 76
Guiness Ho. OL16—4H 29
Guinness Rd. M17—7F 76
Guinness Rd. Trading Est. M17 —7G 77
Guiseley Clo. BL9—2L 25
Gullane Clo. M10—9C 62
Gull Clo. SK12—9H 115
Gunson Ct. M10—2H 5 & 4J 79
Gunson St. M10—2H 5 & 4J 79
Gun St. M4—3G 5 & 5H 79
Gunters Av. BL5—2F 54
Gurner Av. M5—6A 4 & 8B 78
Gurney St. M4—6K 79
Gurth St. BL2—2H 39
Gutter La. BL0—4H 9
Guy Fawkes St. M5—6A 4 & 8B 78
Guy St. M8—9F 60
Guywood La. SK6—2C 106
Gwelo St. M11—5A 80
Gwenbury Av. SK1—4H 105
Gwendore Av. M8—5F 60
Gwladys St. SK15—1L 83
Gwynant Pl. M20—7J 91
Gylden Clo. SK14—9H 83
Gypsy La. SK2—7J 105
Gypsy Wlk. SK2—7J 105

Hackberry Clo. WA14—5B 100
Hacken Bri. Rd. BL3—5J 39
Hacken La. BL3—5J 39
Hackford Clo. BL1—1C 38
Hackford Clo. BL8—5K 25
Hacking St. BL9—8A 26
Hacking St. M7—1E 78
Hacking St. M25—4A 60
Hackle St. M11—5C 80
Hackleton Clo. M4—6K 79
Hackness Rd. M21—6M 89
Hackney Av. M10—3C 80
Hackwood Wlk. M8—9F 60
(off Levenhurst Rd.)
Hadbutt La. M29—3M 73
Haddington Dri. M9—5L 61
Haddock St. M26—7G 41
Haddon Av. M10—7F 62
Haddon Clo. BL9—4A 42
Haddon Clo. SK6—6E 116
Haddon Clo. SK9—7K 119
Haddon Grn. SK13—4D 96
(off Haddon M.)
Haddon Gro. M33—1G 101
Haddon Gro. SK5—7E 92
Haddon Gro. WA15—6F 100
Haddon Hall Rd. M35—5E 80
Haddon Ho. M5—4K 77
Haddon Lea. SK13—4D 96
(off Grassmoor Cres.)
Haddon M. SK13—4D 96
Haddon Rd. M21—9D 90
Haddon Rd. M27—1C 76
Haddon Rd. M30—7B 76
Haddon Rd. SK7—3L 115
Haddon Rd. SK8—5J 113
Haddon Rd. WA3—5K 71
Haddon Rd. WN3—5L 51
Haddon St. M6—2B 78
Haddon St. M32—2K 89
Haddon Way. M34—5A 94
Haddon Way. OL2—1C 46
Hadfield Av. OL9—3H 63
Hadfield Cres. OL6—2E 82
Hadfield Pl. SK13—6J 97
Hadfield Rd. SK14—2E 96
Hadfield Sq. SK13—6J 97
Hadfield St. M7—1E 78
Hadfield St. M16—9C 78
Hadfield St. OL8—5L 63
Hadfield St. SK13—6J 97
Hadfield St. SK16—8A 82
Hadfield Ter. OL6—2E 82
Hadleigh Clo. BL1—4G 23
Hadley Av. M13—4L 91
Hadley Clo. SK8—3M 113
Hadley St. M6—2B 78
Hadlow Clo. M10—4L 79
Hadlow Grn. SK5—8H 93
Hadon St. WN4—2M 69
Hadwin St. BL1—9F 22
Hafton Rd. M7—1B 78
Hag Bank La. SK12—6K 117
Hag End Brow. BL2—4J 39
Haggate. OL2—6J 45
Haggate Cres. OL2—6J 45
Hags, The. BL9—4A 42
Hague Bar Rd. SK12—4M 117
Hague Fold. SK12—4M 117
Hague Ho. OL8—3M 63
Hague Pl. SK15—5F 82
Hague Rd. M20—9G 91
Hague Rd. SK14—6B 96
Hague St. M10—2M 79
Hague St. OL4—9E 46
Hague St. OL6—3C 82
Hague St. SK13—7K 97
Haig Av. M30—1C 98
Haigh Av. SK4—9E 92
Haigh Hall Clo. BL0—7H 9
Haigh La. OL9 & OL1—8E 44
Haigh Pk. SK4—9E 92
Haigh Rd. WN2—2H 35
Haigh St. BL1—1F 38
Haigh St. OL11—4G 29
Haigh View. WN1—7D 34
Haigh View. WN3—2E 52
Haig Rd. BL8—8H 25
Haig Rd. M32—3K 89
Haig St. WN3—1B 52
Haile Dri. M28—1F 74
Hailsham Clo. BL8—3J 25
Hailsham St. M11—5M 79
Hail St. BL0—7G 9
Haldene Wlk. M8—1F 78
Haldon Rd. M20—9K 91
Hale Av. SK12—1K 121
Hale Bank Av. M20—7F 90
Hale Clo. WN7—5H 73

Hale Ct. WA14—1D 110
Hale Grn. Ct. WA15—1G 111
Hale Gro. WN4—2M 69
Hale La. M35—8E 62
Hale Low Rd. WA15—1F 110
Hale Rd. WA14 & WA15—1D 110
Hales Clo. M35—5F 80
Halesden Rd. SK4—9D 92
Halesworth Wlk. M10—1H 5 & 3J 79
Haletop. M22—2D 112
Hale Wlk. SK8—9A 104
Halewood Av. WA3—6F 70
Haley Clo. SK5—6F 92
Haley St. M8—9G 61
Half Acre. M26—3E 40
Half Acre Dri. OL11—4C 28
Half Acre Grn. SK9—3H 119
Half Acre La. BL6—8J 19
(in two parts)
Half Acre La. M25—2B 60
(in two parts)
Half Acre La. OL11—4B 28
Half Acre M. OL11—4B 28
Halfacre Rd. M22—9C 102
Half Acre Rd. OL11—4B 28
Half Edge La. M30—4E 76
Half Moon La. SK2—7K 105
Half Moon St. M2—4E 5 & 6F 78
Halford Dri. M10—8B 62
Half St. M3—2D 4 & 4E 78
Half St. M24—8M 43
Halifax Rd. OL4—4F 46
Halifax Rd. OL12 & OL16—1H 29
Halifax Rd. OL15 & HX6—6C 14
Halifax St. BL1—9E 22
Halifax St. OL6—3B 82
Haliwell St. BL1—8D 22
Hallam Rd. M10—2B 80
Hallam St. M26—5K 41
Hallam St. SK2—7G 105
Hall Av. M14—3K 91
Hall Av. M33—8E 88
Hall Av. SK15—2J 83
Hall Av. WA15—6F 100
Hall Bank. M30—5C 76
Hallbottom Pl. SK14—1F 94
Hallbottom St. SK14—1F 94
Hallbridge Gdns. WN8—9B 32
Hall Clo. SK14—1A 96
Hall Coppice, The. BL7—1D 22
Hall Cotts. OL3—2B 66
Hallcroft. M31—1F 98
Hallcroft Gdns. OL16—4L 29
Hall Dri. M24—1M 61
Hall Dri. SK14—1A 96
Halle Mall. M4—5G 79
(off Arndale Cen.)
Halle Sq. M4—5G 79
(off Arndale Cen.)
Hall Farm Av. M31—3B 88
Hall Fold. OL12—3B 12
Hall Fold. SK14—1G 97
Hall Gdns. OL12—9C 12
Hall Ga. BL5—3E 54
Hallgate. WN1—9C 34
Hallgate Dri. SK8—2G 113
Hallgate Rd. SK1—5H 105
Hall Grn. WN8—1B 50
Hall Grn. Clo. SK16—6C 82
Hall Grn. Clo. WN8—1B 50
Hall Grn. Rd. SK16—6C 82
Hall Gro. M14—3K 91
Hall Gro. SK8—7J 103
Hallhouse La. WN7—3J 73
Halliday Ct. OL15—7L 13
Halliday Rd. M10—2B 80
Halliford Rd. M10—1A 80
Hallington Clo. BL3—5E 38
Hall i' th' Wood. BL1—6G 23
Hall i' th' Wood La. BL2—7H 23
Halliwell Av. OL8—5L 63
Halliwell Ind. Est. BL1—7D 22
(off Regan St.)
Halliwell La. M8—9F 60
Halliwell Rd. BL1—7C 22
Halliwell Rd. M25—7M 59
Halliwell's Brow. WA16 —9B 108
Halliwell St. M3—3F 5 & 5G 79
Halliwell St. OL9—7G 63
Halliwell St. OL12—2E 28
(in two parts)
Halliwell St. OL15—6C 14
Halliwell St. OL16—3L 29
Halliwell St. W. M8—9F 60
Halliwell Wlk. M25—7M 59
Hallkirk Wlk. M10—6D 62
Hall La. BL4—7K 39
(in two parts)
Hall La. BL6—2E 36
(Lostock)
Hall La. BL6—1A 20
(Rivington)
Hall La. M23—7B 102
Hall La. M31—1F 98
Hall La. SK6—8B 94
Hall La. WN1—5D 34
Hall La. WN2—1K 53
Hall La. WN3—4F 50
Hall La. WN6—8B 16
Hall La. Gro. WN2—9K 35
Hall Lee Dri. BL5—8G 37
Hallman La. M22—5D 112
Hall Meadow. SK8—3L 113
Hall Meadow Rd. SK13—4K 9
Hall Moss La. SK7—7B 114
Hall Moss Rd. M9—4A 62
Hallows Av. M21—9C 90
Hall Rd. M14—3K 91
Hall Rd. OL6—2C 82
Hall Rd. SK7—3D 114
Hall Rd. SK9—9L 113
(Handforth)
Hall Rd. SK9—4G 119
(Wilmslow)
Hall Rd. WA11—8L 69
Hall Rd. WA14—3C 110
Hallroyd Brow. OL1—9L 45
Hall's Ct. SK13—5J 97
Hall's Pl. OL4—2F 64
Hallstead Av. M28—4E 56
Hallstead Gro. M28—4E 56
Hall St. BL3—7K 39
(in two parts)
Hall St. BL8—6J 25
(Bury)
Hall St. BL8—6F 24
(Walshaw)
Hall St. BL9—9J 9
Hall St. M2—5E 5 & 7F 78
Hall St. M24—9A 44
Hall St. M26—3F 40
Hall St. M27—6F 58
Hall St. M35—1D 80
Hall St. OL2—5K 45
Hall St. OL4—1B 64
Hall St. OL10—9L 27
Hall St. OL12—3C 12
Hall St. SK1—4G 105
Hall St. SK8—7J 103
Hall St. SK14—3B 94
Hall St. WN1—1D 52
Hall St. WN2—9E 52
(Bamfurlong)
Hall St. WN2—9F 34
(Ince)
Hallsville Rd. M19—5C 92
Hallsworth Rd. M30—6A 76
Hallwood Av. M6—2J 77
Hallwood Rd. M23—7A 102
Hall Wood Rd. SK9—1K 119
Hallwood St. OL11—6E 28
Hallworth Av. M34—6H 81
Hallworth Rd. M8—8H 61
Halmore Rd. M10—5K 79
Halsall Clo. BL9—4M 25
Halsall Dri. BL3—7E 38
Halsbury Clo. M12—9L 79
Halsey Clo. OL9—6E 62
Halsey Wlk. M8—9F 60
Halshaw La. BL4—1M 57
Halsmere Dri. M9—5L 61

Halstead Av. M6—3K 77
Halstead Av. M21—7A 90
Halstead Dri. M30—5H 87
Halstead Gro. SK8—9F 102
Halstead St. BL2—2G 39
Halstead Wlk. BL9—5A 26
Halstock Wlk. M10—4K 79
(off Carslake St.)
Halston St. M15—1E 90
Halstone Av. SK9—7E 118
Halton Dri. WA15—4H 101
Halton Flats. OL10—8J 27
(off Pitt St.)
Halton Ho. M5—6M 77
Halton Rd. M11—5C 80
Halton St. BL2—2H 39
Halton St. SK14—3F 94
Halvard Av. BL9—4M 25
Halvard Ct. BL9—4M 25
Halvis Gro. M16—3B 90
Hambledon Clo. BL3—4M 37
Hamble M. M7—9B 60
Hambleton Clo. BL8—9F 24
Hambleton Dri. M23—9A 102
Hambleton Dri. M33—9D 88
Hambleton Rd. SK8—4J 113
Hambleton Wlk. M33—9D 88
Hamblett Lodge. M14—3J 91
Hamblett M. M25—5A 60
Hamblett St. WN7—2B 72
Hambridge Clo. M8—9G 61
Hamel St. BL8—7H 25
Hamel St. SK14—1F 94
Hamer Bldgs. OL1—8H 27
Hamer Clo. OL7—6A 82
Hamer Dri. M16—1D 90
Hamer Hall Cres. OL10—9G 13
Hamer Hill. M9—5J 61
Hamer La. OL16—1H 29
Hamer St. BL0—9H 9
Hamer Ter. M26—5J 41
Hamer Ter. BL9—8J 9
(off Ruby St.)
Hamerton Rd. M10—1H 5 & 3J 79
Hamilcar Av. M30—5E 76
Hamilton Av. M30—1D 98
(Cadishead)
Hamilton Av. M30—6E 76
(Eccles)
Hamilton Av. OL2—6H 45
Hamilton Ct. BL8—7H 25
Hamilton Ct. BL3—6B 40
Hamilton Ct. M23—1H 101
Hamilton Ct. WN5—9L 33
Hamilton Cres. SK4—4B 104
Hamilton Gro. M16—1D 90
Hamilton Ho. WA14—8D 100
Hamilton Lodge. M14—3J 91
Hamilton M. M25—5A 60
Hamilton M. M30—4A 76
Hamilton Pl. OL7—6M 81
Hamilton Rd. M13—3M 91
Hamilton Rd. M25—5A 60
(Prestwich)
Hamilton Rd. M25—9L 41
(Whitefield)
Hamilton Rd. WN2—4M 53
Hamilton Rd. WN4—3J 69
Hamilton Sq. WN5—9L 33
Hamilton St. BL1—5E 22
Hamilton St. BL9—6M 25
Hamilton St. M7—9D 60
Hamilton St. M16—1D 90
Hamilton St. M27—7D 58
Hamilton St. M29—6H 55
Hamilton St. M30—4B 76
Hamilton St. OL4—2A 64
Hamilton St. OL7—6M 81
Hamilton St. OL9—1G 63
Hamilton St. SK15—5F 82
Hamilton St. WN7—1D 72
Hamilton Way. OL10—9E 26
Hamlet. M33—8E 88
Hamlet, The. BL6—1J 37
Hammersmore Rd. M18—9C 80
Hammett Rd. M33—6A 90
Hammond Av. SK4—9E 92
Hammond Flats. OL10—8J 27
(off Ashton St.)
Hamnet Clo. BL1—5G 23
Hamnett Rd. OL10—8D 26
Hamnett St. M11—5C 80
Hamnett St. SK14—3D 94
Hamon Rd. WA14—9E 100
Hampden Ct. M30—5D 76
Hampden Cres. M18—1C 92
Hampden Gro. M30—5D 76
Hampden Pl. WN5—8K 33
Hampden Rd. M24—4B 60
Hampden Rd. M33—2G 101
Hampden Pl. M25—4B 60
Hampden Rd. OL2—3D 46
Hampden Wlk. WN5—8K 33
Hampshire Clo. BL9—1A 42
Hampshire Clo. SK5—9J 93
Hampshire Clo. SK13—6M 97
Hampshire Rd. M31—3D 98
Hampshire Rd. M35—4G 81
Hampshire Rd. SK9—3H 63
Hampshire St. M7—9D 60
Hampshire Wlk. M8—7F 60
Hampson Rd. M30—6B 76
Hampson Clo. WN4—5B 70
Hampson Fold. M26—5F 40
Hampson Mill La. BL9—4M 41
Hampson Pl. OL6—1E 82
Hampson Rd. M32—4J 89
Hampson Rd. OL6—1E 82
Hampson St. M5—4B 4 & 6C 78
Hampson St. M10—3K 79
Hampson St. M26—5G 41
Hampson St. M27—7G 59
Hampson St. M29—5J 55
Hampson St. M30—6B 76
Hampson St. M33—1H 101
Hampson St. M35—5G 81
Hampson St. SK1—5H 105
Hampson St. SK13—7J 97
Hampson St. Trading Est. M5—4C 4 & 6D 78
Hampstead Av. M31—5L 87
Hampstead Dri. SK2—3J 105
Hampstead La. SK2—3J 105
Hampton Gro. BL9—4M 25
Hampton Gro. SK8—2L 113
Hampton Gro. WA14—4F 100
Hampton Gro. WN7—9L 55
Hampton Pl. M15—9D 78
Hampton Rd. BL3—6G 39
Hampton Rd. M21—5M 89
Hampton Rd. M30—1D 98
Hampton Rd. M31—5D 88
Hampton Rd. M35—8G 63
Hampton Rd. OL8—4A 63
Hamsell Rd. M13—6H 5 & 8J 79

Hanborough Ct. M29—8L 55
Hanbury Clo. M19—3M 79
Hanbury Dri. M34—3H 91
Hancock St. M34—3J 91
Handel M. M33—1J 101
Handel Av. M31—4A 88
Handforth Gro. M13—4L 91
Handforth Rd. SK5—9F 92
Handforth Rd. SK9—1L 119
Hand La. WN7—3F 72
Handle Av. M31—4A 88
Handley Av. M14—5H 91
Handley Clo. SK3—6D 104
Handley St. OL12—3B 12
Hands La. OL11—3A 28
Handsworth St. M12—7K 79
Hanging Birch. M24—1H 61
Hanging Bri. M3—5F 78
(off Cateaton St.)
Hanging Chaddar La. OL2—2J 45
Hanging Ditch. M4—3E 5 & 5F 78
Hanging Lees Clo. OL16—6C 30
Hankinson Clo. M31—3F 98
Hankinson Way. M6—4A 78
Hanley Clo. M24—3A 62
Hanley Clo. SK12—7K 117
Hanlith M. M19—9M 91
Hanlon St. M8—7F 60
Hanmer St. WN2—2K 53
Hannah Baldwin Clo. M11—7M 79
Hannah St. M12—4A 92
Hannerton Rd. OL2—1D 46
Hannet Rd. M22—2D 112
Hannington Ct. M7—9B 60
Hanover Ct. BL3—4B 38
(off Greenbank Rd.)
Hanover St. M7—9D 60
Hanover St. M28—1B 76
Hanover Cres. M14—2K 91
Hanover Gdns. M7—8E 60
Hanover Ho. BL3—6B 38
Hanover Ho. WA14—6B 100
Hanover Rd. WN2—2J 53
Hanover St. BL1—2C 38
Hanover St. M4—3F 5 & 5G 79
Hanover St. OL5—6J 65
Hanover St. OL11—8C 28
Hanover St. N. M34—7L 81
Hanover St. S. M34—7L 81
Hanover Ter. SK5—2F 104
Hansdon Clo. M8—6J 78
Hanson Clo. M24—8A 44
Hanson Rd. M10—9A 62
Hanson St. BL9—6M 25
Hanson St. M24—9B 44
(in two parts)
Hanson St. OL4—1C 64
Hanwell Av. M18—4C 92
Hanworth Clo. M13—6G 5 & 8H 79

Hapsford Wlk. M10—2A 80
Hapton Av. M32—5K 89
Hapton Pl. SK4—2C 104
Hapton St. M19—4A 92
Harbern Dri. WN7—6D 54
Harborne Wlk. BL8—1F 24
Harboro Ct. M33—2F 100
Harboro Gro. M33—1F 100
Harboro Rd. M33—2F 100
Harboro Way. M33—1F 100
Harbour Farm Rd. BL7—6K 7
Harbour La. OL16—4M 29
Harbour La. N. OL16—4M 29
Harbourne Av. M28—8J 57
Harbourne Clo. M28—8J 57
Harbury Clo. WN6—7M 33
Harbury Cres. M22—8C 102
Harbury Wlk. WN6—7M 33
Harcombe Rd. M20—8J 91
Harcourt Av. M31—5F 88
Harcourt Clo. M31—5F 88
Harcourt M. BL6—6B 20
Harcourt Rd. M33—8B 89
Harcourt Rd. WA14—7D 100
Harcourt St. BL4—7K 39
Harcourt St. M28—3K 57
(in two parts)
Harcourt St. M32—3L 89
Harcourt St. OL1—9B 46
Hardberry La. SK2—7L 105
Hardcastle Av. M21—8C 90
Hardcastle Gdns. BL2—1A 40
(in two parts)
Hardcastle Rd. SK3—6D 104
Hardcastle St. OL1—1M 63
Harden Dri. BL2—8K 23
Harden Hills. OL2—1D 46
Hardey Rd. M17—7G 77
Hardfield Rd. M24—3A 62
Hardfield St. OL10—8K 27
Hardicker St. M19—7M 91
Harding Av. BL1—1H 57
Harding St. M4—6K 79
Harding St. M6—3A 78
Harding St. SK1—4H 105
Harding St. SK14—1D 94
Harding St. BL3—7B 38
Hard La. WA10—4A 68
Hardman Av. M25—3A 106
Hardman Av. BL6—3F 40
Hardman La. M35—8E 62
Hardmans. BL7—2F 22
Hardman's M. M25—2M 59
Hardman's Rd. M25—2M 59
Hardman St. BL4—1L 57
(in two parts)
Hardman St. BL9—6M 25
Hardman St. M3—4D 4 & 6E 78
Hardman St. M26—5B 40
Hardman St. M35—9D 62
Hardman St. OL9—3H 63
Hardman St. OL10—8K 27
Hardon Gro. M13—4M 91
Hardrush Fold. M35—6C 62
Hardshaw Clo. M13—8H 79
Hardwick Clo. M26—4D 40
Hardwick Clo. SK6—6F 116
Hardwicke Rd. SK12—8B 115
Hardwicke St. OL11—6E 28
Hardwick Rd. M31—2G 99
Hardwick St. OL7—5M 81
Hardy Clo. BL5—6E 36
Hardy Dri. SK7—4G 115
Hardy Farm. M21—8A 90
Hardy Gro. M27—2D 76
Hardy Gro. M28—8F 57
Hardy La. M21—8B 90
Hardy Mill Rd. BL2—6M 23
Hardy St. M30—7B 76
Hardy St. OL6—1E 82
Hardy St. WN6—8A 34
Harebell Av. M28—5F 56
Harebell Clo. OL12—8D 12
Harecastle Av. M30—7E 76
Hare Dri. BL9—5B 42
Harefield Av. OL11—5G 29
Harefield Dri. OL10—8M 27
Harefield Dri. SK9—6H 119
Harefield Rd. SK9—6H 119
Harehill Clo. M13—6G 5 & 8H 79
Hare Hill Ct. OL15—5B 14
Hare Hill Rd. OL15—5A 14
Hare Hill Rd. SK14—3J 95
Harefinch Rd. WA11—9J 69
Harefield Av. OL11—5G 29
Hare St. M4—3G 5 & 5H 79
Hare St. OL11—5F 28
Harewood Av. M33—1D 100
Harewood Av. OL11—9K 11

Harewood Clo. OL11—1K 27
(off Deanswood Dri.)
Harewood Ct. M9—3G 61
(off Deanswood Dri.)
Harewood Dri. OL2—4J 45
Harewood Dri. OL11—1J 27
Harewood Gro. SK5—6E 92
Harewood Rd. M30—4H 87
Harewood Rd. OL2—1C 46
Harewood Rd. OL11—9J 11
Harewood Rd. WN2—2J 53
Harewood Wlk. M34—5A 94
Harewood Way. M27—6F 58
Harewood Way. OL11—1J 27
Harford Clo. SK7—3G 115
Hargate Clo. BL9—9J 9
Hargate Dri. M44—3G 87
Hargate Dri. WA15—3G 111
Hargate Hill La. SK13—7D 96
Hargrave Clo. M9—3J 61
Hargreaves Ho. BL3—3E 38
Hargreaves Rd. WA15—7J 101
Hargreaves St. BL1—8E 22
Hargreaves St. M4—2F 5 & 4G 79
Hargreaves St. OL1—6C 28
Harland Dri. M8—9H 61
Harlea Av. WN2—5A 54
Harlech Av. M25—1B 60
Harlech Av. M45—4A 54
Harlech Clo. M15—1G 91
Harlech Dri. SK7—3J 115
Harlech St. WN4—2M 69
Harlesden Cres. BL3—6E 38
Harleston St. M4—1A 80
Harley Av. BL2—9D 24
(Bolton)
Harley Av. BL2—7L 23
(Harwood)
Harley Av. M14—3L 91
Harley Av. M24—8M 43
Harley Rd. M24—8M 43
Harley St. M11—7D 80
Harley St. OL6—4B 82
Harling Rd. M22—6D 102
Harlington Clo. M23—6K 101
Harlington St. SK6 & SK12—5E 116
Harlyn Av. SK7—5F 114
Harmer Clo. M10—2A 80
Harmol Gro. OL7—2A 64
Harmony St. OL4—4A 64
Harmsworth Dri. SK4—9B 92
Harmsworth St. M6—5L 77
Harmuir Clo. WN6—5L 33
Harold Av. M18—4G 89
Harold Av. SK16—6D 82
Harold Lees Rd. OL10—7M 27
Harold Priestnall Clo. M10—1D 80
Harold St. BL1—8D 22
Harold St. M16—9C 78
Harold St. M24—4M 59
Harold St. M25—4M 59
Harold St. M35—5G 62
Harold St. OL9—1K 63
Harold St. OL16—9J 13
Harold St. SK1—5H 105
Harold St. WN2—4K 35
Haroman Rd. SK5—6F 92
Harper Av. M31—5F 88
Harper Grn. Rd. BL4—7H 39
Harper Pl. OL6—4C 82
Harper Rd. M22—6E 102
Harper's La. BL1—8B 22
Harper Sq. OL2—2C 46
Harper St. BL4—7H 39
Harper St. OL6—4C 82
Harper St. OL8—4L 63
Harper St. OL11—5E 28
Harper Ter. OL11—7E 28
(off William St.)
Hartley Ter. SK15—4K 83
Hartley Ter. WN3—1C 52
Hart Mill Clo. OL5—6H 65
Harton Av. M18—2C 92
Harton Clo. OL2—3A 46
Hart Rd. M14—4G 91
Hartshead Av. OL6—1C 82
Hartshead Av. SK15—4G 83
Hartshead Clo. M11—8G 81
Hartshead Cres. M35—1J 81
Hartshead Rd. OL6—1C 82
Hartshead St. OL4—2F 64
Hartshead View. SK14—5F 94
Hart's La. WN8—9A 32
Hartspot Dri. M24—7J 43
Hartspring Av. M27—9G 59
Hart St. M29—8C 56
Hart St. WA14—8E 100
Hartswood Clo. M34—2A 94
Hartswood Rd. M20—8K 91
Hartwell Clo. BL2—7J 23
Hartwell Clo. M11—7M 79
Harty. M30—5E 76
Harty Rd. WA11—9G 69
Harvard Clo. SK6—9C 94
Harvard St. OL11—6B 28
Harvest Clo. M6—2L 77
Harvey Clo. M11—7M 79
Harvey La. WA3—6A 72
Harvey Rd. SK6—9C 94
Harvey St. BL1—7D 22
Harvey St. BL8—7J 25
Harvey St. M4—6K 79
Harvey St. SK1—4F 104
Harvey St. WN3—2E 52
Harvin Gro. M34—4C 94
Harwich Clo. M19—5B 92
Harwich Clo. SK5—8J 93
Harwin Clo. OL12—8D 12
Harwood Ct. M6—1A 4 & 3B 78
Harwood Ct. SK4—3L 103
Harwood Cres. BL8—3E 24
Harwood Dri. BL8—9E 24
Harwood Gdns. OL10—9K 27
Harwood Gro. BL2—9J 23
Harwood Meadows. BL2—7M 23
Harwood Rd. OL10—9K 27
Harwood Rd. BL8—5C 24
Harwood Rd. M19—8L 91
Harwood Rd. SK4—3L 103
Harwood St. BL1—1F 38
Harwood Vale. BL2—7L 23
Harwood Wlk. BL8—3E 24

Harrow Clo. BL9—4M 41
Harrow Clo. WN5—9F 32
Harrow Cres. WN7—4F 72
Harrowdene Wlk. M9—8K 61
Harrow Dri. M33—3G 101
Harrow Gro. OL11—1J 27
Harrow Gro. SK5—6E 92
Harrow M. OL2—2B 46
Harrow Pl. WN3—4F 52
Harrow Rd. BL1—1B 38
Harrow Rd. M33—3G 101
Harrow St. M8—7H 61
Harrow St. OL11—8H 29
Harry Hall Gdns. M7—1B 4 & 3C 78
Harry Rd. SK5—6F 92
Harry's St. WN7—2D 72
Harry St. OL9—2J 63
Harry St. OL11—7B 28
Harry Thorneycroft Wlk. M11—7L 79
Harrytown. SK6—3A 106
Hart St. M33—1M 101
Hatchmere Clo. SK8—9M 103
Hatchmere Clo. WA15—7K 101
(in two parts)
Hateley Rd. M16—3A 90
Hatfield Av. M19—8M 91
Hatfield Clo. WN3—4F 52
Hatfield Rd. BL1—9C 22
Hathaway Clo. SK8—5M 113
Hathaway Ct. WN7—1H 73
Hathaway Dri. BL1—5G 23
Hathaway Wlk. M13—9J 79
Hatherleigh Wlk. BL2—3M 39
Hatherley Rd. M20—8K 91
Hatherlow. SK6—3A 106
Hatherlow La. SK7—2K 115
Hatherop Clo. M30—3B 76
Hathersage Av. M6—4K 77
Hathersage Cres. SK13—4E 96
Hathersage Rd. M13—2J 91
Hathersage St. OL9—3J 63
Hathersage Way. M34—6A 94
Hathershaw La. OL8—6M 63
Hatro Ct. M31—5G 89
Hattersley Ind. Est. SK14—5K 95
Hattersley Rd. E. SK14—4J 95
Hattersley Rd. W. SK14—4L 95
Hatton Av. M7—2C 4 & 4D 78
Hatton Gro. BL1—5G 23
Hatton's Ct. M3—3E 5 & 5F 78
Hatton St. M12—3J 89
Hattons Rd. M17—5F 77
Hatton St. M12—3A 92
Hatton St. SK9—5G 119
Hatton Ter. SK4—2B 104
Haugh Fold. OL16—6C 30
Haugh Hill Rd. OL4—6E 46
Haugh La. OL16—6C 30
Haugh Sq. OL16—6C 30
Haughton Clo. SK6—8A 94
Haughton Dri. M22—3D 102
Haughton Grn. M34—6A 94
Haughton Hall Rd. M34—3M 93
Haughton St. SK14—5E 94
Hauxwell Gro. WA11—9C 68
Havana Clo. M11—7M 79
Havelock Dri. M7—1C 4 & 3D 78
Haven Clo. M26—4D 40
Haven Clo. OL4—2K 65
Haven Clo. SK7—3J 115
Haven Dri. M35—4E 80
Haven La. OL4—7E 46
Haven St. M6—5L 77
Haven, The. BL3—5A 40
Haven, The. WA15—1F 110
Havercroft Clo. WN3—5L 51
Haverfield Rd. M9—5L 61
Haverford St. M12—4L 79
Havergate Walks. SK2—9M 105
Haverhill Gro. BL2—8H 23
Haversham Rd. M8—6E 60
Haverton Dri. M22—2B 112
Havisham Clo. BL6—5H 37
Hawarden Av. M16—4C 90
Hawarden Rd. WA14—7D 100
Haw Clough La. OL3—2C 66
Hawdraw Grn. SK2—7C 106
Hawes Av. M14—7L 91
Hawes Av. M27—3E 58
Hawes Av. WA11—7C 68
Hawes Clo. SK2—3G 105
Haweswater Av. M29—1C 74
Haweswater Circ. M31—3C 88
Haweswater Cres. WN2—1H 53
Haweswater Clo. M34—4G 93
Hawfinch Gro. M28—9L 57
Hawk Clo. BL8—6E 26
Hawker Av. BL3—6M 37
Hawkeshead Dri. BL3—6A 38
Hawkesheath Clo. BL7—1E 22
Hawke St. SK15—6J 83
Hawk Grn. Clo. SK6—1F 116
Hawkhurst Rd. M13—3M 91
Hawkhurst St. WN7—2J 73
Hawkins St. SK5—1E 104
Hawkley Av. WN3—5M 51
Hawkridge Clo. WN3—2E 52
Hawkshaw Ct. M5—6A 78
Hawkshaw La. BL8—8B 8
Hawkshaw St. BL6—4B 20
Hawkshead Dri. BL3—6A 38
Hawkshead Dri. M24—1K 61
Hawkshead Rd. OL2—3K 45
Hawkshead Rd. SK6—4A 106
Hawksley St. OL8—5J 63
Hawksmoor Clo. WN6—9E 78
Hawkstone Av. M25—1K 59
Hawkstone Av. WA15—4E 80
Hawkstone Clo. BL2—7L 23
Hawkswick Dri. M23—3A 102
Hawksworth Clo. M26—2B 74
Hawk Yd. La. OL3—9D 48
Hawley Dri. WA15—4H 111
Hawley Grn. OL12—9D 12
Hawley La. WA15—4H 111
Haworth Av. BL0—5B 9
Haworth Clo. BL0—5B 9
Haworth Dri. M32—9F 88
Haworth Rd. M18—6C 80
Haworth St. BL4—9H 39
Haworth St. OL12—2D 28
Haworth St. WA14—2D 108
Hawsworth Clo. M15—6H 41
Hawthorn Av. BL0—1L 9
(Edenfield)
Hawthorn Av. BL0—9G 9
(Ramsbottom)
Hawthorn Av. BL9—6J 25
Hawthorn Av. M26—8H 41
Hawthorn Av. M30—4D 76

Haslemere Rd. M31—5E 88
Haslemere Rd. M40—6F 9C
Hassall St. M26—4L 41
Hassall Way. SK9—7L 113
Hassall Way. SK15—6H 83
Hassop Av. M7—9A 60
Hassop Clo. M11—6L 79
Hassop Rd. SK5—5G 93
Hastings Av. M21—6A 90
Hastings Av. M25—1B 60
Hastings Clo. M25—13 60
Hastings Clo. SK1—6H 105
Hastings Clo. SK8—2C 114
Hastings Ct. SK3—5A 104
Hastings Dri. M31—3J 87
Hastings Rd. BL1—1E 38
Hastings Rd. M25—3C 50
Hastings Rd. M30—3A 76
Hastings St. OL11—5F 28
Haston Clo. SK5—1F 104
Hasty La. WA15—5L 111
(in two parts)
Hatchett Rd. M22—3D 112
Haslemere Rd. M31—5E 88
Hawthorn Av. M31—5F 88
Hawthorn Av. SK6—7D 106
Hawthorn Av. SK9—4G 119
Hawthorn Av. WA15—6F 100
Hawthorn Av. WN1—3B 34
Hawthorn Av. WN2—5A 54
Hawthorn Av. WN3—2J 69
Hawthorn Av. WN5—2F 50
Hawthorn Bank. BL2—6L 23
Hawthorn Bank. SK14—2F 96
Hawthorn Clo. M29—7D 56
Hawthorn Clo. WA15—6F 100
Hawthorn Cres. BL8—3F 24
Hawthorn Cres. OL2—3B 46
Hawthorn Cres. OL8—6M 63
Hawthorn Dri. M6—3H 77
Hawthorn Dri. M19—7M 91
Hawthorn Dri. M27—9J 59
Hawthorn Dri. M30—9D 86
Hawthorne Av. OL7—6M 81
Hawthorne Av. BL6—9E 20
Hawthorne Dri. M28—9A 58
Hawthorne Gro. SK6—1L 105
Hawthorne Gro. SK12—8C 116
Hawthorne Gro. SK14—9D 84
Hawthorne Gro. WN7—9E 54
Hawthorne La. OL16—5A 30
Hawthorne La. M21—6M 89
Hawthorne St. BL3—4B 38
Hawthorn Gro. B204—7B 104
Hawthorn Gro. WA3—9K 71
Hawthorn La. M21—6M 89
Hawthorn La. SK9—4G 119
Hawthorn Pk. SK9—4G 119
Hawthorn Rd. BL3—3B 58
Hawthorn Rd. M10—7E 62
Hawthorn Rd. M33—6K 89
Hawthorn Rd. M34—3H 93
Hawthorn Rd. M35—5J 81
Hawthorns, The. M29—5K 55
(off Water St.)
Hawthorns, The. M18—9D 80
Hawthorns, The. M34—9K 81
Hawthorn Ter. SK4—2B 104
Hawthorn Ter. SK9—5G 119
Hawthorn Wlk. M31—2E 98
Hawthorn Wlk. SK9—4G 119
Haxby Rd. M18—3D 92
Hayburn Rd. M23—6B 102
Hayburn Rd. SK2—2J 105
Haycock Clo. SK15—8K 83
Haycroft Clo. SK14—5E 94
Hayden St. M10—2K 79
(off Sedgeford Rd.)
Haydn Av. M14—2J 91
Haydn Fold. SK14—7D 96
Haydn St. BL1—8D 22
Haydock Av. M33—3B 100
Haydock Dri. M28—1H 75
Haydock Dri. SK7—2M 115
Haydock La. WA15—8H 101
Haydock Ho. BL1—1F 38
Haydock La. BL7—1G 23
(in two parts)
Haydock La. WA11—9J 69
Haydock La. WA11—7K 69
(St Helens)
Haydock Pk. Gdns. WA12—6B 70
Haydock St. BL1—1F 38
Haydock St. WN4—5B 70
Haydock Wlk. OL9—1J 63
Haye's Rd. M30—9E 86
Hayes Row. WA3—6A 72
Hayes St. WN7—9E 54
Hayes St. OL12—1D 46
Hayes Wlk. M45—3B 60
(Plank Lane)
Hayeswater Circ. M31—3C 88
Hayeswater Rd. M31—3C 88
Hayfell Av. WN3—7A 52
Hayfield Av. M29—1C 74
Hayfield Clo. BL6—1F 106
Hayfield Clo. OL4—4E 46
Hayfield Rd. M6—3H 77
Hayfield Rd. SK9—3L 119
Hayfield St. M33—7H 81
Hayfield Wlk. M34—6A 94
Hayfield Wlk. WA15—7J 101
Haygrove Wlk. M9—8K 61
Hayley St. M13—2L 91
Hayling Rd. M33—9E 88
Hayman Av. WN7—5D 72
Haymans Wlk. M13—6H 79
Haymarket Clo. M13—1J 91
Haymarket St. BL9—6M 25
Haymarket, The. BL9—8M 25
Haymill Av. M38—1A 57
Haymond Clo. M6—1A 78
Haynes St. BL3—6C 38
Hays St. OL12—2F 28
Haysbrook Av. M38—9H 57
Haythorp Av. M22—1E 112
Hayward Av. BL3—8J 39
Hayward Clo. OL12—1D 46
Hayward St. BL8—4H 25
Haywards Clo. SK13—3J 97
Haywood Av. M34—4C 94
Hayward Way. SK14—3M 95
(off Garnett Clo.)
Haywood Dri. BL3—6A 38
Haywood Way. OL11—1A 28
Hazel Av. BL3—1F 54
Hazel Av. BL5—1F 54
Hazel Av. BL8—6C 24
Hazel Av. M26—3K 41
Hazel Av. OL6—1E 82
Hazel Av. SK6—3D 106
Hazel Av. SK8—8A 114
Hazelbadge Clo. SK12—8J 115
Hazelbadge Rd. SK12—8J 115
Hazelbank Av. M20—8G 91
Hazelbottom Rd. M8—9H 61
Hazel Clo. M45—3D 60
Hazel Clo. SK6—9C 106
Hazeldene Rd. M10—7E 62
Hazel Dri. M22—4G 113
Hazel Dri. SK2—7F 104
Hazel Dri. SK12—9M 113
Hazel Gro. BL4—9H 39
Hazel Gro. M29—4J 55
Hazel Gro. OL4—7M 63
Hazel Gro. WA3—7H 71
Hazel Gro. WN4—5F 70
Hazel Hall La. BL0—7H 9
Hazelhurst Clo. BL0—7H 9
Hazelhurst. BL1—8E 22
Hazelhurst Fold. M28—9C 58
Hazelhurst Rd. M28—4C 70
Hazelhurst Rd. M30—4A 60
Hazelhurst M. OL9—5F 62
(Orrell)
Hazelhurst Rd. WN5—2K 51
(Wigan)
Hazelhurst Rd. OL5—3G 65
Hazelhurst Rd. SK15—3G 83
Hazel La. OL8—6K 63
Hazelmere Av. BL8—9H 25
Hazelmere Gdns. WN2—4L 53
Hazelmere Clo. SK12—6C 116
Hazel Mt. BL7—9E 6
Hazel Rd. M24—7B 44
Hazel Rd. M25—8B 42
Hazel Rd. M29—4J 55
Hazel Rd. SK8—3B 114
Hazel Rd. WA14—8D 100
Hazel Rd. SK7—1D 114
Hazels, The. PR7—1L 17
Hazel View. SK6—1F 116
Hazel Wlk. M31—2E 98
Hazelwood Av. BL2—7L 23
Hazelwood Clo. M31—3D 88
Hazelwood Dri. BL9—3M 25
Hazelwood Dri. M34—9M 81
Hazelwood Rd. BL1—8B 22
Hazelwood Rd. SK7—1M 115
Hazelwood Rd. SK9—3K 119
Hazelwood Rd. M20—7J 91
Hazelwood Rd. SK14—2E 110
Headen Av. WN5—3H 51
Headingley Dri. M16—3A 90
Headingley M. M14—7K 91
Headingley Rd. M14—7K 91
Headingley Way. BL3—6D 38
Headland Clo. WA3—9L 71
Headlands Dri. M25—6A 60
Headlands St. OL12—1E 28
Heady Hill Ct. OL10—8G 27
Heady Hill Rd. OL10—8G 27
Heald Av. M14—3A 90
Heald Clo. OL12—8C 12
Heald Dri. OL15—3A 14
Heald Dri. WA14—2C 110
Heald Gro. M14—3A 90
Heald Gro. SK8—3G 113
Heald La. OL15—7A 14
Heald Pl. M14—2H 91
(in two parts)
Hebden Av. M6—4J 77
Hebden Av. SK13—6M 97
Hebden St. BL1—1E 38
Hebden Wlk. M15—1F 90
(off Arnott Cres.)
Hebdon Clo. WA3—2A 70
Heber St. OL5—6B 14
(off Victoria St.)
Heber St. M26—6G 41
Hebron St. OL4—4A 64
Heddles Av. M19—2H 91
Hector Av. OL16—2H 29
Hector Rd. M13—3M 91
Heddon Clo. SK4—2L 103
Heddon Wlk. M8—7F 60
(off Smedley Rd.)
Hedgehog Ms. M9—7M 77
Hedgelands Wlk. M33—9D 88
Hedgemead. WN6—8A 34
Hedge Rows. OL12—2C 12
Hedges St. M35—8G 63
Hedley St. BL1—8C 22
Hedley Wlk. M8—9F 60
(off Halliwell La.)
Heeley St. WN1—7B 34
Heginbottom Cres. OL6—2C 82
Heights Av. OL12—7F 44
(in three parts)
Heights Clo. OL12—7F 44
Heights La. OL12—3K 47
Heights La. SK9—9L 113
Heights, The. BL6—9D 20
Helena St. M6—2J 77
Helen St. M6—4K 39
Helen St. M30—7B 76
Helen St. WA3—5F 70
Helensville Av. M6—2M 77
Helga St. M10—3K 79
Helias Clo. M28—5F 56
Hellidon Clo. M12—9M 79
Helmclough Way. M28—8J 57
Helmet St. M1—5H 5 & 7J 79
Helmsdale Av. BL3—3M 37
Helmsdale Clo. BL0—7G 9
Helmshore Av. OL4—1A 64
Helmshore Rd. OL2—1B 46
Helmshore Way. WN3—3B 52
Helrose St. M10—2C 80
Helsby Gdns. BL1—4D 22
Helsby Rd. M33—3G 101
Helsby Wlk. M12—7L 79
Helsby Way. SK9—8K 113
Helston Av. WA11—9D 68
Helston Clo. SK7—8D 114
Helston Dri. OL2—4J 45
Helston Gro. SK8—5J 113
Helton Wlk. M24—6H 43
Helvellyn Dri. M24—7K 43
Helvellyn Rd. WN5—2H 51
Helvellyn Wlk. OL1—8M 45
Hembury Av. M19—8M 91
Hembury Clo. M24—2C 112
Hemfield Rd. WN2—1J 53
Hemington Dri. M9—9K 61
Hemlock Av. OL8—3J 63
Hemming Dri. M30—6E 76
Hemmons Rd. M12—4B 92
Hemsby Clo. BL3—9J 37
Hemsley St. M9—8L 61
Hemsley St. S. M9—9L 61
Hemsworth Rd. BL1—1D 38
Hemsworth Rd. M18—9D 80
Henbury Rd. SK9—5K 119
Henbury St. SK6—8B 94
Henbury St. M14—5G 91
Henderson Av. M27—7F 58
Henderson St. M19—6B 80
Henderson St. OL16—6H 13
Henderville St. OL15—5A 14
Hendham Clo. SK7—2H 115
Hendham Dri. WA14—8B 100
Hendham Vale. M9—2J 61
(Lowton)
Hendon Dri. BL9—7L 25
Hendon Dri. SK3—6A 104
Hendon Gro. WN7—8F 54
Hendon Rd. M9—7L 61
Hendriff Pl. OL12—1E 28
Hen Fold Rd. M29—1C 112
Hengist St. M18—3D 92
Hengist St. BL2—3J 71
Henley Av. M16—3B 90
Henley Av. SK8—4D 114
Henley Dri. OL7—3M 81
Henley Dri. WA15—6F 100

Henley Pl. M19—8A 92
Henley St. OL1—9K 45
Henley St. OL9—5G 63
Henley St. OL12—1E 28
Henley Ter. OL11—5C 28
Henlow Wlk. M10—6D 62
Hennelly St. SK14—9A 98
Henniker Rd. BL3—8J 39
Henniker St. M27—7A 56 (?)
Henon St. BL1—9D 22
Henrietta St. BL3—5B 38
Henrietta St. M16—2C 90
Henrietta St. OL6—2B 82
Henrietta St. WN7—2F 72
Henry Herman St. BL3—6A 38
(in two parts)
Henry Lee St. BL3—6C 38
Henry Pk. St. WN1—1E 52
Henry Sq. OL6—5A 82
Henry St. M4—3G 5 & 5H 79
(in two parts)
Henry St. M16—1C 90
Henry St. M24—9M 43
Henry St. M30—3C 60
Henry St. M29—7A 56
Henry St. M30—6C 76
Henry St. M35—6G 81
(Droylsden)
Henry St. M35—9F 62
(Failsworth)
Henry St. OL12—4J 13
Henry St. OL15—8M 13
Henry St. SK1—5H 105
Henry St. SK13—5J 97
Henry St. SK14—4F 52
Henry St. WN7—1C 72
(in three parts)
Henshall La. WA14—7H 99
Henshaw Ct. M16—2B 90
Henshaw St. M32—4K 89
Henshaw St. OL1—1L 63
Henshaw Wlk. BL1—9E 22
(off Ewart St.)
Henshaw Wlk. M13—6G 5 & 8H 79
Henson Gro. WA15—9G 101
Henthorn St. OL2—1A 46
Henthorn St. OL8—4A 64
Henton Wlk. M10—1H 5 & 3J 79
Henwick Hall Av. BL0—7H 9
Henwood Rd. M20—5J 91
Hepley Rd. SK12—9A 116
Hepple Clo. SK4—2L 103
Heppleton Rd. M10—6D 62
Hepple Wlk. OL7—9L 45
Hepton St. OL1—9L 45
Hepworth St. SK14—7E 94
Heraldic Ct. M6—2A 78
Herbert St. BL3—6B 4C
Herbert St. BL7—2F 8
Herbert St. BL6—6A 20
Herbert St. M8—2F 78
Herbert St. M25—4M 59
Herbert St. M26—4F 40
Herbert St. M32—4K 89
Herbert St. M34—2A 94
Herbert St. OL9—1H 63
Herbert St. SK13—6B 4C
Herbert St. BL3—6B 4C
Herbert St. BL6—6A 20
Hereford Av. WA3—7H 71
Hereford Clo. OL2—3M 45
Hereford Clo. OL6—9D 64
Hereford Clo. SK6—4A 106
Hereford Clo. SK9—9L 113
Hereford Cres. BL3—5A 40
Hereford Ct. SK5—3A 40
Hereford Dri. BL9—1M 41
Hereford Dri. M27—1F 76
Hereford Dri. M31—4C 88
Hereford Dri. SK7—5F 114
Hereford Gro. M30—2G 77
Hereford Rd. BL1—1B 38
Hereford Rd. M30—2G 77
Hereford Rd. OL6—9D 64
Hereford Rd. SK3—6A 104
Hereford St. BL3—6B 4C
Hereford St. M33—1F 101
(in two parts)
Hereford St. OL9—3H 63
Hereford Wlk. M34—5M 93
Hereford Wlk. SK6—4A 106
Hereford Way. M24—2C 112
Hereford Way. SK15—8K 83
Herevale Grange. M28—9G 57
Herevale Hall. BL0—7H 9
Heristone Av. M34—3L 93
Herle Dri. M22—3C 112
Hermitage Av. SK6—3E 106
Hermitage Ct. WA15—1F 110
Hermitage Gdns. SK6—3E 106
Hermitage Rd. WA15—1F 110
Hermon Av. OL8—3J 63
Herne St. M11—7A 80
Heron Av. BL4—9F 38
Heron Av. SK16—8E 82
Heron Ct. M6—4H 77
Herondale. M34—9D 92
Heron Dri. M30—3G 87
Heron Dri. M34—6J 81
Heron Dri. WN3—6J 51
Heron Pl. WN5—9J 33
Heron St. M27—2G 59
Heron St. OL8—4J 63
Heron St. SK3—5D 104
Heron's Way. BL3—7E 38
Herries St. OL6—3D 82
Herristone Rd. M8—6G 60
Herrod Av. SK4—7K 93
Herschel St. M10—8A 62
Hersey St. M6—3H 77
Hershan Wlk. M9—7L 61
(off Huncote Dri.)
Herston Av. M7—1F 78
Hertford Gro. M30—8C 86
Hertford Rd. M9—8K 61
Hertfordshire Pk. Clo. OL2—9K 27
Hertford St. OL7—6A 82
Hesford Av. M9—9M 61
Hesketh Av. BL1—5F 22
Hesketh Av. M20—2G 107
Hesketh Av. WA3—9J 71
Hesketh Meadow La. WA3—9J 71
Hesketh Rd. M33—2F 100
Hesketh Rd. OL16—3J 12
Hesketh St. M29—4S 56
Hesketh St. SK4—1C 104
Hesketh St. SK14—1E 94
(in two parts)
Hesnall Clo. WA3—4A 70
Hessall St. M5—6K 77
Hester Wlk. M15—1F 90
Heston Av. M13—4L 91
Heston Dri. M31—3C 98
Heswall Av. M20—2H 91
Heswall Av. WN3—4C 52
Heswall Dri. BL8—9F 24
Heswall Rd. SK5—5F 92
Hetherington Wlk. M12—4L 79
Hethorn St. M10—4L 79
Heversham Av. OL2—1K 45
Heversham Wlk. M18—4D 92
(off Beyer Clo.)

art Clo. M10—2J 79
art Dri. BL9—7C 26
itt Av. M34—3F 92
itt St. M15—6D 4 & 8E 78
lett Av. PR7—1K 17
lett Ct. BL0—9G 9
lett Rd. M21—5A 90
lett St. BL2—2G 39
lett St. BL5—1B 54
lett St. PR7—1L 17
lett St. WN1—9C 34
nam Av. BL1—9M 21
nam Av. WN3—5M 51
nam Clo. M29—4L 55
nam Clo. M33—2D 100
nam Clo. SK2—8L 105
nam Rd. M18—3C 92
worth Wlk. SK7—2G 115
Bottom La. OL12—6F 12
brook. OL12—1H 29
brook Clo. M25—9C 42
brook Rd. M23—8B 102
brook St. OL16—2H 29
brook Wlk. M25—9C 42
Cres. OL4—1F 64
Croft. M25—1J 59
len Bank. SK13—4D 96
f Grassmoor Cres.)
len Fold. SK13—4D 96
f Grassmoor Cres.)
len Ter. SK13—4D 96
s Av. WA11—9K 69
s Av. WA15—6H 101
s Dri. WA15—6H 101
s La. SK9—7L 119
s La. WA15—6H 101
s Leigh. WA15—5H 101
s Rd. WN5—2E 50
s St. WN6—2C 32
s Ter. WA15—5H 101
Flake La. OL3—2L 47
ord Av. M10—6D 62
ord Rd. WN5—9K 33
Head Cotts. BL2—5B 24
Head La. OL15—2B 14
eads New Rd. SK15—9L 65
and Rd. M23—7A 102
a. OL3—8C 48
dge Dri. M22—4D 102
od St. M1—5H 5 & 7J 79
od St. SK15—2K 83
ose Wlk. M15—9D 78
Av. M23—4A 102
Av. M27—6C 58
Av. SK6—2E 106
bank Rd. SK12—6K 117
Clo. N. M27—6C 58
Ct. SK3—5B 104
croft Rd. M20—8J 91
croft Rd. SK4—3A 104
nam Av. M20—7F 90
nam Rd. WN5—1H 51
naw Wlk. M23—4L 101
de. OL2—6A 46
de Av. OL2—6A 46
de Way. BL9—9M 25
La. OL10—8G 27
La. SK6—2E 106
Rd. M25—3A 60
Rd. OL6—4D 82
St. BL8—8K 25
St. WN2—2J 53
The. PR7—1M 17
The. SK5—5G 93
. OL16—2H 29
. WN3—4F 52
. WN6—9B 34
View. M25—4B 60
ood Av. M27—6H 59
ood Av. OL4—9G 47
ood Av. WA3—6H 71
ood Bus. Pk. OL10—1G 43
ood Clo. M24—1G 61
ood Clo. SK9—7M 119
ood Fold Rd. OL4—1F 64
ood Gdns. BL3—5E 38
ood Gdns. M25—4B 60
ood Gdns. WA3—6H 71
ood Gro. M33—8H 89
ood Hall Rd. OL10—7K 27
ood Ho. M6—4J 77
ood Ho. M29—5J 55
ood Ho. OL8—3M 63
ood La. OL4—1G 65
ood Old Rd. M24—8G 43
ood Pk. View. BL3—5E 38
ood Rd. M25—5B 60
od Rd. M33—2H 101
od Rd. OL11—8B 28
od Rd. SK9—7M 119
od's Hollow. BL1—7E 22
od St. BL1—1F 38
od St. BL3—6B 40
od St. BL9—9A 26
od St. M8—9G 61
od St. M27—8E 58
od St. M35—9D 62
od St. OL4—9E 46
od Way. M6—4M 77
rth Av. SK6—2D 106
rth St. M5—6L 77
t Av. M34—1L 93
t Av. SK14—5E 94
t Cres. M35—9G 63
t La. SK6—8F 106
t St. BL1—8F 22
t St. M14—3J 91
t St. OL4—1E 64
t St. SK4 & SK5—9E 92
a St. BL3—4C 38
a Way. M32—1G 89
Av. OL12—9K 11
Clo. OL12—5J 13
i La. PR7—4L 17
ield Rd. SK14—1F 94
Pl. SK14—1F 94
n Dri. WA14—7B 100
Rd. WN1—7E 34
shaw La. OL1 & OL2
—7A 46
shaw Rd. OL1—8M 45
on Rd. SK5—7E 92
on St. WN7—2G 73
Ct. WN1—9E 34
La. SK14—6F 94
St. SK8—3A 114
View. M6—4A 78
Wlk. M10—4K 79
h Gro. M34—8K 81
. BL2—1L 39
nk. BL7—3F 22
nk. M18—1E 92
nk. M27—8J 59
nk. M29—2A 56
nk. M34—4H 93
nk. WA14—8D 100
nk Av. SK15—8K 83
nk Clo. M30—8D 86
nk Cres. M25—5C 60
nk Cres. OL4—3L 65
nk Dri. M20—5H 103
nk Gro. M25—5C 60
nk La. BL6—2H 37
nk Rd. BL9—5M 41
nk Rd. M27—8H 59
nk Rd. M35—7F 80
nk Rd. OL16—6C 30
nk Rd. SK13—7M 97
nk Rd. SK14—3F 94
nkside. SK1—4F 104
nk St. BL2—2J 39
k Trading Est. M11
—8D 80
rn Clo. OL11—5E 28
rn La. OL12—2B 12
old)
rn La. OL12—1C 12
worth)
n Rd. M24—1A 62
rn Rd. OL2—5M 45
rn St. OL2—5L 45
nt Av. SK8—6A 114
ch Ter. OL11—6B 28

Highbridge Clo. BL2—3A 40
High Brindle. M6—3M 77
Highbrook Gro. BL1—9F 22
Highbury. SK4—3M 103
Highbury Av. M30—5G 87
Highbury Av. M31—4L 87
Highbury Rd. M16—5E 90
Highbury Rd. SK4—8C 92
Highbury Way. OL2—4K 45
Highclere Av. M8—1F 78
Highclere Rd. M8—6F 60
Highcliffe Ct. WN6—2M 33
Highcrest Av. SK8—8F 102
Highcroft. SK14—7E 94
Highcroft Av. M20—1E 102
High Croft Clo. SK16—7G 83
Highcroft Rd. SK6—2C 106
Highcroft Way. OL12—7F 12
Highdales Rd. M23—8B 102
High Elm Dri. WA15—4J 111
High Elm Rd. WA15—4J 111
High Elms. SK8—7B 114
Higher Ainsworth Rd. M26
—2E 40
Higher Ardwick. M12—6H 5 &
8J 79
Higher Arthurs La. OL3—2B 66
Higher Bank Rd. OL15—8A 14
Higher Barlow Row. SK1
—5F 104
Higher Barn. BL6—7F 20
Higher Barn Rd. SK14—2E 96
Higher Bents La. SK6—2M 105
Higher Bri. St. BL1—9F 22
Higher Bury St. SK4—3D 104
Higher Calderbrook. OL15
—2C 14
Higher Calderbrook Rd. OL15
—2C 14
Higher Cambridge St. M15
—9G 79
Higher Carr La. OL3—1B 66
Higher Chatham St. M15—9G 79
Higher Cleggswood Av. OL15
—8A 14
Higher Crimble. OL11—6M 27
Higher Croft. M25—2J 59
Higher Croft. M30—7C 76
Higher Crossbank. OL4—9F 46
Higher Cross La. OL3—1C 66
Higher Darcy St. BL2—4J 39
Higher Dean St. M26—6E 40
Higher Downs. WA14—1C 110
Higher Drake Meadow. BL5
—3E 54
Higher Dunscar. BL7—1E 22
Higher Fold. OL2—4A 46
Higher Fulwood. OL1—5D 46
Higher Grn. M6—3M 77
Higher Grn. OL6—3C 82
Higher Grn. La. M29—3C 74
Higher Henry St. SK14—5D 94
Higher Hillgate. SK1—5F 104
Higher Ho. Clo. OL9—4G 63
Higher Kinders. OL3—2B 66
Higher La. M25—9L 41
Higher La. WA13—2A 108
Higher La. WN2—5G 35
Higher La. WN8—1C 50
Higher Lee St. OL8—2K 63
Higher Lime Rd. OL8—8J 63
Higher Lodge. OL12—9K 11
Higher Lomax La. OL10—8G 27
Higher Market St. BL4—9L 39
(in two parts)
Higher Mill Rd. SK15—5H 83
Higher Ormond St. M15—6F 5 &
(in two parts) 9G 79
Higher Pit La. M26—1E 40
Higher Ridings. BL7—2F 22
(in two parts)
Higher Rise. OL2—9A 30
Higher Rd. M31—4D 88
Higher Row. BL9—7B 26
Higher Shady La. BL7—3H 23
Higher Shore Rd. OL15—4L 13
Higher Southfield. BL5—1E 54
Higher Sq. SK14—8G 85
Higher Summerseat. BL0—9H 9
Higher Swan La. BL3—5D 38
Higher Tame St. SK15—5H 83
Higher Turf La. OL4—9H 47
Higher Turf Pk. OL2—6L 45
Higher Wharf St. OL7—5B 82
Higher Wheat La. OL16—2J 29
Higher Wood St. M24—8M 43
Higher York St. M13—9H 79
Highfield. M20—3H 103
Highfield. M33—2J 101
High Field. WA14—2H 109
Highfield. WN5—4K 51
Highfield Av. BL2—7A 24
Highfield Av. M26—8J 41
Highfield Av. M28—9F 56
Highfield Av. M29—3L 55
Highfield Av. M33—2J 101
Highfield Av. OL10—8G 27
Highfield Av. SK6—3M 105
Highfield Av. WA3—7F 70
Highfield Av. WN1—8E 34
Highfield Av. WN6—3G 33
Highfield Av. WN7—4J 73
Highfield Clo. M32—6J 89
Highfield Clo. PR6—3G 19
Highfield Clo. SK3—9F 104
Highfield Clo. SK14—9F 82
Highfield Ct. M25—3B 60
Highfield Cres. SK9—2J 119
Highfield Dri. M24—1M 61
Highfield Dri. M27—9J 59
Highfield Dri. M30—3D 76
Highfield Dri. M31—3C 88
Highfield Dri. OL2—7L 45
Highfield Dri. OL5—8J 65
Highfield Dri. WN6—2M 33
Highfield Est. SK9—2J 119
Highfield Grange Av. WN3
—6K 51
Highfield Gro. WN2—4J 35
Highfield Ho. BL4—9F 38
Highfield Ho. SK3—8F 104
Highfield La. M25—6M 41
Highfield La. WA3—9K 71
Highfield Pk. SK4—3M 103
Highfield Pk. Rd. SK6—1L 105
Highfield Parkway. SK7
—8D 114
Highfield Pl. M18—2F 92
Highfield Pl. M25—3A 60
Highfield Range. M18—2F 92
Highfield Rd. BL0—1K 9
Highfield Rd. BL1—8B 22
Highfield Rd. BL4—9E 38
Highfield Rd. BL6—9L 19
Highfield Rd. M6—4M 77
Highfield Rd. M8—9F 60
Highfield Rd. M19—5C 92
Highfield Rd. M25—2A 60
Highfield Rd. M28—3F 56
Highfield Rd. M30—3D 76
Highfield Rd. M32—6J 89
Highfield Rd. OL11—1L 27
Highfield Rd. OL16—4A 30
Highfield Rd. PR6—2G 19
Highfield Rd. SK6—7F 106
(Marple)
Highfield Rd. SK6—7H 107
(Mellor)
Highfield Rd. SK7—1F 114
(Bramhall)
Highfield Rd. SK7—2A 116
(Hazel Grove)
Highfield Rd. SK8—3L 113
Highfield Rd. SK12—8G 115
Highfield Rd. SK13—6K 97
Highfield Rd. WA15—8H 101
(Altrincham)
Highfield Rd. WA15—2G 111
(Hale)
Highfield Rd. WN2—1K 53
Highfield Rd. Ind. Est. M28
—2F 56
Highfield Rd. N. PR6—2G 19

Highfield St. BL4—2A 58
Highfield St. M24—9B 44
Highfield St. M34—9M 81
(Audenshaw)
Highfield St. M34—1L 93
(Denton)
Highfield St. OL9—1L 63
(in two parts)
Highfield St. SK3—5C 104
Highfield St. SK6—2M 105
Highfield St. SK16—6B 82
Highfield St. W. SK16—6B 82
Highfield Ter. M9—8K 61
Highfield Ter. OL4—7D 46
Highfield Ter. OL7—9M 63
Highgate. BL3—7J 37
Highgate Av. M31—2A 88
Highgate Cres. M18—2D 92
Highgate Cres. WN6—2E 32
Highgate Dri. M28—3E 56
High Gate Dri. OL2—2H 45
Highgate La. M28—3E 56
Highgate La. OL12—5C 12
Highgate Rd. WA14—9B 100
Highgate Rd. WN8—1B 50
Highgrove Clo. BL1—6F 22
Highgrove Ct. M9—3F 60
Highgrove M. SK9—5G 119
High Gro. Rd. OL4 & OL3—3L 65
High Gro. Rd. SK8—8J 103
High Houses. BL1—4D 22
High Hurst Clo. M24—9J 43
Highland Rd. BL6—9E 20
Highland Rd. BL7—2H 23
Highlands. OL2—6J 45
Highlands. OL15—8A 14
Highlands Dri. SK2—7M 105
Highlands Rd. OL2—6J 45
(Royton)
Highlands Rd. OL2—1M 45
(Shaw)
Highlands Rd. OL11—5L 27
Highlands Rd. SK2—7M 105
Highlands, The. OL5—7H 65
Highland View. OL5—6J 65
Highland Wlk. M10—1D 80
High La. M21—6A 90
High La. SK6—9B 94
High La. SK14 & SK13—7E 96
High Lea. SK8—8J 103
High Lea. SK9—8M 119
High Lea Rd. SK12—4M 117
High Lee La. OL4—6H 47
High Legh Rd. M11—7D 80
High Legh Rd. WA13—4C 108
High Level Rd. OL11—4F 28
High Meadow. BL7—2H 23
Highmeadow. M26—8F 40
High Meadow. SK8—4L 113
High Meadows. SK6—2C 106
Highmead St. M18—1D 92
Highmead Wlk. M16—1D 90
High Moor Cres. OL4—8E 46
High Moor La. WN6—6A 16
Highmore Dri. M9—5L 61
High Mt. BL2—7L 23
Highnam Wlk. M22—3A 112
High Pk. WN6—3J 33
High Peak. OL15—6F 14
High Peak Rd. OL6—1G 83
High Peak Rd. OL12—5C 12
High Peak St. M10—1B 80
High Rid La. BL6—1G 37
Highshore Dri. M8—9F 60
High Stile La. OL3—7D 48
High Stile St. BL4—1L 57
Highstone Dri. M8—1J 79
High St. Altrincham, WA14
—9D 100
High St. Aspull, WN2—6H 35
High St. Astley, M29—2B 74
High St. Atherton, M29—5K 55
High St. Bolton, BL3—5D 38
High St. Bury, BL8—7F 24
High St. Cheadle, SK8—7K 103
High St. Dearnley, OL15—6M 13
High St. Delph, OL3—5M 47
High St. Droylesden, M35
—6G 81
High St. E. SK13—5K 97
High St. Goldborne, WA3
—7G 71
High St. Hazel Grove, SK7
—2M 115
High St. Heywood, OL10—8H 27
High St. Hindley, WN2—1L 53
High St. Horwich, BL6—6B 20
High St. Hyde, SK14—3F 94
High St. Ince-in-Makerfield,
WN3—2E 52
High St. Lees, OL4—2E 64
High St. Leigh, WN7—2G 73
High St. Little Lever, BL3
—6B 40
High St. Manchester, M4—4F 5
& 6G 79
High St. Middleton, M24—7A 44
High St. Mossley, OL5—6K 65
High St. Oldham, OL1—1M 63
High St. Rochdale, OL12—2F 28
High St. Royton, OL2—5K 45
High St. Shaw, OL2—3B 46
High St. Stalybridge, SK15
—7E 82
High St. Standish, WN6—9L 17
High St. Stockdale, SK1
—4F 104
High St. Swinley, WN1—7D 34
High St. Turton, BL7—7J 7
High St. Tyldesley, M29—7M 55
High St. Uppermill, OL3—8B 48
High St. W. SK13—5G 97
High St. Worsley, M28—5J 57
High View. M25—5B 60
Highview. SK13—7G 97
Highview St. BL1—4E 22
High View St. BL3—5C 38
Highview Wlk. M9—5L 61
High Wardle La. OL12—2G 13
Highwood. OL11—1L 27
Highwood Clo. SK13—7H 97
Highworth Clo. BL3—4E 38
Highworth Dri. M10—6D 62
Higson Av. M21—7B 90
Higson Av. M30—7C 76
Higson Av. SK6—3M 105
Higson St. BL2—2G 39
Hilary Av. M29—3J 55
Hilary Av. OL8—7M 63
Hilary Av. SK8—4K 113
Hilary Av. WA3—6K 71
Hilary Clo. SK4—3D 104
Hilary Gro. BL4—1J 57
Hilary Rd. M22—3C 112
Hilary St. OL11—9D 28
Hilbre Av. OL1 & OL2—7K 45
Hilbre Av. OL2—7K 45
Hilbre Rd. M19—6M 91
Hilbre Way. SK9—8K 113
Hilbury Av. M9—7K 61
Hilda Av. BL8—4F 24
Hilda Av. SK8—8L 103
Hilda Gro. SK5—1F 104
Hilda Rd. SK14—7D 94
Hilda St. OL9—1K 63
(in two parts)
Hilda St. OL10—7K 27
Hilda St. SK5—1F 104
Hilda St. WN7—1C 72
Hilden Ct. M16—2D 90
Hilden St. BL2—3G 39
Hilden St. WN7—2F 72
Hilditch Clo. M23—7B 102
Hildyard St. WN5—2M 51
Hiley Rd. M30—7M 75
Hilgay Clo. WN3—5K 51
Hillam Clo. M31—5F 88
Hillary Av. OL7—2B 82
Hillary Av. WN5—3K 51
Hillary Rd. SK14—1G 95
Hillbank. WN6—2A 34
Hillbank Clo. BL1—7C 22
Hillbank St. M24—3D 44

Hill Barn La. OL3—6D 48
Hillbeck Cres. WN4—3K 69
Hillbrae Av. WA11—7A 68
Hillbrook Av. M10—6B 62
Hillbrook Rd. SK1—5J 105
Hillbrook Rd. SK7—6D 114
Hillbrow Wlk. M8—9F 60
Hillbury Rd. SK7—3F 114
Hill Carr M. WA14—9B 100
Hill Clo. OL4—3C 64
Hill Clo. WN6—1E 32
Hillcote Wlk. M18—9B 80
Hill Cot Rd. BL1—5F 22
Hillcourt Rd. SK6—5E 116
(High Lane)
Hillcourt Rd. SK6—1C 106
(Romiley)
Hill Cres. M9—5G 61
Hill Cres. WN7—8C 54
Hillcrest. M6—4G 77
Hillcrest. M24—6M 43
Hill Crest. M29—3M 55
Hillcrest. SK14—7F 94
Hillcrest. WN2—6H 53
Hillcrest Av. OL10—7G 27
Hill Crest Av. SK4—3A 104
Hill Crest Av. WN7—8C 54
Hillcrest Cres. OL10—7G 27
Hillcrest Dri. M19—7C 92
Hillcrest Dri. M34—5B 94
Hillcrest Rd. M25—6M 59
Hillcrest Rd. M29—8D 56
Hillcrest Rd. OL11—8D 28
(in two parts)
Hillcrest Rd. SK2—7J 105
Hillcrest Rd. SK7—2F 114
Hillcroft. OL8—7A 64
Hillcroft Clo. M8—8G 61
Hillcroft Ho. M6—4M 77
Hillcroft Rd. WA14—8A 100
Hilldale Av. M9—4K 61
Hilldean. WN8—9C 32
Hill Dri. SK9—9L 113
Hillel Ho. M15—1G 91
Hill End. SK6—1D 106
Hillend La. SK14—5M 95
Hillend Pl. M23—3A 102
Hillend Rd. M23—3A 102
Hill End Rd. OL3—4M 47
Hill Farm Clo. OL8—5A 64
Hillfield. M5—5K 77
Hillfield Clo. M13—1K 91
Hillfield Dri. BL2—9H 23
Hillfield Dri. M28—9G 57
Hillfield Wlk. BL2—9H 23
Hillfoot Wlk. M15—9D 78
Hillgate Av. M5—6A 4 & 8B 78
Hillgate St. OL6—3C 82
Hillhead Wlk. M8—1G 79
(off Barnsdale Dri.)
Hill Ho. Fold La. WN6—5C 16
Hill Ho. La. WN6—3B 16
Hillier St. M9—8L 61
Hillier St. N. M9—8L 61
Hillingdon Clo. OL8—7H 63
Hillingdon Dri. M9—6B 62
Hillingdon Rd. M25—1K 59
Hillingdon Rd. M32—5L 89
Hillington Rd. M33—1E 100
Hillington Rd. SK3—5C 104
Hillkirk St. M11—6L 79
Hill La. BL6—7H 19
Hill La. M9—5K 61
Hill La. SK6—4L 107
Hillman Clo. M10—2K 79
Hill Mt. SK16—7G 83
Hillock Pl. M29—6K 55
(off Wardour St.)
Hillock, The. M29—2B 74
Hillreed. WN6—8M 33
Hill Rise. BL0—7G 9
Hill Rise. SK6—3B 106
Hill Rise. WA14—8A 100
Hillsborough Dri. BL9
—6B 42
Hills Ct. BL8—6H 25
Hillsdale Gro. BL2—7L 23
Hillsdide Clo. M10—7A 62
Hill Side. BL1—2M 37
Hill Side. SK6—9C 94
Hillside Av. BL4—1H 57
Hillside Av. BL6—9L 19
(Blackrod)
Hillside Av. BL6—6C 20
(Horwich)
Hillside Av. BL7—1H 23
Hillside Av. M7—8A 60
Hillside Av. M25—7L 41
Hillside Av. M28—4J 57
Hillside Av. M29—4L 55
Hillside Av. OL2—4L 45
(Royton)
Hillside Av. OL2—2D 46
(Shaw)
Hillside Av. OL3—6B 48
Hillside Av. OL4—3G 65
(Grotton)
Hillside Av. OL4—1C 64
(Oldham)
Hillside Av. SK14—8F 94
Hillside Av. SK15—1M 83
Hillside Av. WN4—8M 51
Hillside Clo. BL2—5L 23
Hillside Clo. BL3—7K 37
Hillside Clo. SK7—5G 115
Hillside Clo. SK14—3E 96
Hillside Clo. WN3—5K 51
Hillside Clo. WN5—2D 68
Hillside Ct. BL1—2M 37
Hill Side Ct. M25—5A 60
Hillside Cres. BL6—6C 20
Hillside Cres. BL9—4M 25
Hillside Cres. OL6—2F 82
Hillside Dri. M24—8B 44
Hillside Dri. M27—1K 77
Hillside Gro. SK6—4H 107
Hillside Rd. BL0—6G 9
Hillside Rd. SK2—6K 105
Hillside Rd. WA15—1G 111
Hillside St. BL3—4D 38
Hillside View. M34—7A 94
Hillside View. OL16—4A 30
Hillside View. SK12—4M 117
Hillside Wlk. OL12—7D 12
Hillside Way. OL12—2C 12
Hills La. BL9—7C 42
Hillsley Wlk. M10—4K 79
Hillstone Av. OL12—7C 12
Hillstone Clo. BL8—9F 8
Hill St. BL8—6F 24
Hill St. BL9—8J 9
Hill St. M6—4M 77
Hill St. M7—1D 78
(in two parts)
Hill St. M20—7H 91
Hill St. M24—6A 44
Hill St. M26—8H 41
(Outwood)
Hill St. M26—5F 40
(Radcliffe)
Hill St. OL2—3C 46
Hill St. OL4—1B 64
Hill St. OL7 & OL6—5A 82
Hill St. OL10—8J 27
Hill St. OL16—3G 29
Hill St. SK6—3B 106
Hill St. SK14—6F 94
Hill St. SK16—6B 82
Hill St. WA14—5C 100
Hill St. WN2—2K 53
(Hindley)
Hill St. WN2—7H 35
(Wigan)
Hill St. WN6—8B 34
Hill St. WN7—2E 72
Hilltop. BL3—5A 40
Hill Top. M29—3M 55
Hilltop. OL12—6C 12
Hill Top. SK6—2B 106
Hill Top. WA15—4G 111
Hilltop Av. M9—5K 61
Hill Top Av. M25—4B 60
(Prestwich)

Hilltop Av. M25—9B 42
(Whitefield)
Hill Top Av. SK8—3A 114
Hill Top Av. SK9—3H 119
Hilltop Ct. M8—6F 60
Hilltop Ct. M14—5K 91
Hill Top Ct. SK8—3B 114
Hilltop Dri. BL8—4E 24
Hill Top Dri. OL11—8F 28
Hill Top Dri. SK6—7C 106
Hill Top Dri. WA15—2G 111
Hill Top Fold. WN2—2L 53
Hilltop Gro. M25—9B 42
Hill Top La. OL3—4G 47
Hill Top Rd. M28—4K 57
Hilltop Rd. SK13—4H 97
Hill View. SK15—9K 83
Hillview Ct. BL1—6E 22
Hill View Dri. PR7—2K 17
Hillview Rd. BL1—6E 22
Hillview Rd. M34—5G 93
Hillwood Av. M8—5F 60
Hillwood Dri. SK13—6M 97
Hillyard St. BL8—7J 25
Hilly Croft. BL7—2F 22
Hilmarton Clo. BL2—5L 23
Hilrose Av. M31—4F 88
Hilson Ct. M35—6G 81
Hilton Arc. OL1—1M 63
Hilton Av. BL6—7A 20
Hilton Av. M31—4D 88
Hilton Bank. M28—5H 57
Hilton Clo. WN7—2G 73
Hilton Cres. M25—6B 60
Hilton Cres. M28—1H 75
Hilton Cres. OL6—2C 82
Hilton Dri. M25—6B 60
Hilton Dri. M30—9C 86
Hilton Fold La. M24—8B 44
Hilton Gro. SK12—8K 115
Hilton La. M25—7M 59
Hilton La. M28—5H 57
Hilton Lodge. M25—6B 60
Hilton Pl. WN2—3J 35
Hilton Rd. BL9—8M 25
Hilton Rd. SK7—2F 114
Hilton Rd. SK12—5H 117
(Disley)
Hilton Rd. SK12—7C 116
(Poynton, in two parts)
Hiltons Farm Clo. M34—9L 81
Hilton Sq. M27—8G 59
Hilton St. BL2—2J 39
Hilton St. BL9—6M 25
Hilton St. M1—4G 5 & 6H 79
Hilton St. M4 & M1—3F 5 & 5G 79
(in two parts)
Hilton St. M7—1D 78
Hilton St. M24—7M 43
Hilton St. M28—4G 57
Hilton St. OL1—9C 46
Hilton St. SK3—5D 104
Hilton St. SK14—1F 94
Hilton St. WN1—8D 34
Hilton St. WN3—2E 52
Hilton St. WN4—4C 70
Hilton St. N. M7—1D 78
Hilton Wlk. M24—9J 43
(in two parts)
Himley Rd. M11—4C 80
Hincaster Wlk. M18—1C 92
Hinchcliffe St. OL12—2D 28
Hinchcliffe Wlk. M16—2E 90
Hinchcombe Clo. M28—2G 57
Hinckley St. M11—7M 79
Hindburn Clo. M25—8B 42
Hindburn Dri. M28—8G 57
Hindburn Wlk. M25—8B 42
Hindell Ter. OL3—5M 47
(off King St.)
Hinde St. M10—8A 62
Hindhead Wlk. M10—3D 80
Hind Hill St. OL10—9K 27
Hindle Dri. OL2—6J 45
Hindles Clo. M29—6G 55
Hindle St. M26—6G 41
Hindley Av. M22—2B 112
Hindley Clo. OL7—6M 81
Hindley Mill La. WN2—1L 53
Hindley Rd. BL5—3C 54
Hindley St. BL4—9J 39
Hindley St. OL7—6M 81
(in two parts)
Hindley St. SK1—5F 104
Hindley Wlk. WN1—9C 34
(off Galleries, The)
Hind Rd. WN5—9K 33
Hindsford Clo. M23—4L 101
Hindsford St. M29—7M 55
Hind's Head Av. WN6—4F 16
Hinds La. M26 & BL8—2J 41
Hind St. BL2—2J 39
Hinkler Av. BL3—6E 38
Hinstock Cres. M18—1D 92
Hinton. OL12—2E 28
(off Spotland Rd.)
Hinton Clo. OL11—4L 27
Hinton St. M4—2G 5 & 4H 79
Hinton St. OL8—3M 63
Hinton St. SK1—4H 105
Hipley Clo. SK6—9A 94
Hirons La. OL4—3G 65
Hirst Av. M28—3J 57
Hitchen Clo. SK16—8F 82
Hitchen Dri. SK16—8F 82
Hitchen Wlk. M13—1K 91
Hive St. OL8—6H 63
Hoade St. WN2—1L 53
Hobart Clo. SK7—8F 114
Hobart St. BL1—8D 22
Hobart St. M18—1D 92
Hobbs Wlk. M8—6E 60
Hob La. BL7—4J 7
Hobroyd. SK13—7H 97
Hobson Ct. M34—9L 81
Hobson Cres. M34—9L 81
Hobson Moor Rd. SK14—9M 83
Hobson St. M11—8G 81
Hobson St. M35—1C 80
Hobson St. OL1—2M 63
Hobson St. SK5—4F 92
Hockley Clo. SK12—9A 116
Hockley Rd. M23—7M 101
Hockley Rd. SK12—9M 115
Hodder Av. OL15—5M 13
Hodder Av. WN2—6F 52
Hodder Bank. SK2—8L 105
Hodder Clo. WA11—8B 68
Hodder Clo. WN5—1K 51
Hodder Sq. M15—9F 78
Hodder Way. M25—9C 42
(in three parts)
Hoddesdon St. M8—9H 61
Hodge La. M6 & M5—6M 77
Hodge La. SK14—7M 95
Hodge Rd. M28—6K 57
Hodge Rd. OL1—6D 46
Hodges St. WN6—6A 34
Hodge St. M9—7M 61
Hodgson Dri. WA15—5G 101
Hodgson St. M8—2F 78
Hodgson St. OL6—5A 82
Hodnet Dri. WN4—4C 70
Hodnett Av. M31—5L 87
Hodnet Wlk. M34—5L 93
Hodson Rd. M27—6E 58
Hodson St. M3—3D 4 & 5E 78
Hodson St. WN3—1B 52
Hogarth Rise. OL1—5C 46
Hogarth Rd. OL11—7F 28
Hogarth Rd. SK6—5H 107
Hogarth Wlk. M8—1J 79
(off Inwood Wlk.)
Holbeach Clo. BL8—5K 25
Holbeach Clo. WN2—4L 53
Holbeck. M29—2B 74
Holbeck Av. OL12—7D 12
Holbeck Gro. M14—2L 91
Holbeton Clo. M8—2E 78
Holbeton Clo. SK7—1G 115
Holborn Av. M26—5D 40
Holborn Av. M35—9H 63
Holborn Av. WN3—3B 52

Holborn Av. WN7—8F 54
Holborn Dri. M8—2H 79
Holborn Gdns. OL11—5D 28
Holborn Sq. OL11—5D 28
Holborn St. OL11—5D 28
Holborn St. SK1—4F 104
Holbrook Av. M28—2G 57
Holcombe Av. BL8—8H 25
Holcombe Av. WA3—7J 71
Holcombe Clo. BL4—2A 58
Holcombe Clo. M6—5A 78
Holcombe Clo. OL4—1G 65
Holcombe Clo. WA14—7B 100
Holcombe Ct. BL0—9F 8
Holcombe Cres. BL4—2A 58
Holcombe Gdns. M19—9L 91
Holcombe Lee. BL0—8G 9
Holcombe Old Rd. BL8—6G 9
Holcombe Rd. BL3—6M 39
Holcombe Rd. BL8—2E 24
Holcombe Rd. M14—7L 91
Holcombe View Clo. OL4—7D 46
Holcombe Village. BL8—5G 9
(off Moor Rd.)
Holcombe Wlk. SK4—7D 92
Holden Av. BL0—6G 9
Holden Av. BL1—4E 22
Holden Av. BL9—6E 26
Holden Brook Clo. WN7—2H 73
Holden Fold La. OL2—7J 45
(in two parts)
Holden Lea. BL5—6E 36
Holden Rd. M7—7D 60
Holden Rd. WN7—1F 72
Holden St. OL6—3C 82
Holden St. OL8—5M 63
Holden St. OL12—9G 13
Holden St. PR7—3F 18
Holder Av. BL3—4B 40
Holderness Dri. OL2—7J 45
Holdgate Clo. M15—1E 90
Holding St. WN2—2K 53
Holdness Clo. M12—1L 91
Holdsworth St. M27—9D 58
Holebottom. OL6—1C 82
Holehouse Fold. SK6—3B 106
Holehouse La. SK10—9H 121
Holford Av. M14—4H 91
Holford Ct. M34—3M 93
Holford St. M6—1B 4 & 3C 78
Holgate Dri. WN5—2E 50
Holgate St. OL4—8E 46
Holgrave Clo. WA16—8C 108
Holhouse La. BL8—9F 8
Holiday La. SK2—7M 105
Holker Clo. M13—1K 91
(in two parts)
Holker Clo. SK12—8M 115
Holker Way. M34—5A 94
Holkham Clo. M4—3H 5 & 5J 79
Holkham Wlk. M4—3H 5 & 5J 79
Hollam Wlk. M16—2E 90
Holland Av. SK15—5G 83
Holland Clo. OL3—5L 47
Holland Ct. M8—6F 60
Holland Ct. SK1—6G 105
(off Ward St.)
Holland Gro. OL6—1B 82
Holland Rise. OL12—2E 28
Holland Rd. M8—6F 60
Holland Rd. SK7—5E 114
Holland Rd. SK14—1F 94
Holland St. BL1—6F 22
Holland St. M5—6A 78
Holland St. M6—2A 78
Holland St. M10—5K 79
Holland St. M26—5J 41
Holland St. M29—6K 55
Holland St. M34—2J 93
Holland St. OL10—8K 27
Holland St. OL12—3E 28
Holland St. OL16—7K 13
Holland Wlk. M6—2A 78
Hollcott Wlk. M8—2E 78
(off Stonefield Dri.)
Hollies Ct. M33—1H 101
Hollies Dri. SK6—8G 107
Hollies La. SK9—4M 119
Hollies, The. M27—1D 76
Hollies, The. M29—5K 55
Hollies, The. SK4—2B 104
Hollies, The. SK8—8H 103
Hollies, The. WN1—6D 34
Hollin Acre. BL5—1F 54
Hollin Bank. SK4—7D 92
Hollinbrook. WN6—7M 33
Hollin Cres. OL3—4L 65
Hollin Cross La. SK13—6J 97
Hollin Dri. M24—5L 43
Holliney Rd. M22—3F 112
Hollinghey Ter. SK14—1C 96
Hollington Way. WN3—6J 51
Hollingwood Clo. WN4—4A 70
Hollingworth Av. M10—6F 62
Hollingworth Clo. SK1—5F 104
(off Mottram Fold)
Hollingworth Dri. SK6—1F 116
Hollingworth Rd. OL15—8B 14
Hollingworth Rd. SK6—1L 105
Hollingworth St. OL9—5H 63
Hollin Hall St. OL4—1C 64
Hollin Hey Clo. WN5—4D 68
Hollin Hey Rd. BL1—7L 21
Hollin Ho. M24—7A 44
Hollinhurst Dri. BL6—2J 37
Hollinhurst Rd. M26—7J 41
Hollin La. M24—4L 43
Hollin La. OL11—4L 27
Hollin La. SK9—6F 112
Hollins. BL4—9D 38
Hollins Av. OL4—9F 46
Hollins Av. SK13—4D 96
(off Hollins M.)
Hollins Av. SK14—7E 94
Hollins Bank. SK13—4D 96
(off Hollins La.)
Hollins Brow. BL9—5M 41
Hollins Clo. M29—8A 56
Hollins Clo. SK13—4D 96
(off Hollins La.)
Hollins Clo. WN4—3K 69
Hollinscroft Av. WA15—8K 101
Hollins Fold. SK13—4D 96
(off Hollins La.)
Hollins Gdns. SK13—4D 96
Hollins Grn. M24—6A 44
Hollins Grn. Rd. SK6—7F 106
Hollins Gro. M12—3A 92
Hollins Gro. M33—1G 101
Hollins Gro. SK13—4D 96
(off Hollins La.)
Hollinshead. M7—1E 78
Hollin's La. BL0—2L 9
Hollins La. BL9—4A 42
Hollins La. OL3—3D 66
Hollins La. OL5—7K 65
Hollins La. SK6—7F 106
(Marple)
Hollins La. SK6—6H 107
(Marple Bridge)
Hollins La. SK13—4D 96
Hollins La. SK16—7F 82
Hollins M. SK13—4D 96
Hollins Mt. SK6—6H 107
Hollins Rd. OL4—9F 46
Hollins Rd. OL8—6H 63
Hollins Rd. WN2—3A 54
Hollins St. BL2—3H 39
Hollins St. OL4—2F 64
Hollins St. SK15—7F 82
Hollins Ter. SK6—7F 106
Hollins, The. SK6—7F 106
Hollins Vale. BL9—3B 42
Hollins Wlk. M22—2D 112
Hollins Way. SK13—4D 96
(off Hollins M.)
Hollinswood Rd. BL2—3H 39
Hollinswood Rd. M28—1H 75
Hollinwood Av. M10 & OL9
—5D 62
Hollinwood Rd. SK12—6K 117
Holloway Dri. M28—7C 58
Hollowell La. BL6—9D 20

Hollow End. SK5—7H 93
Hollow End Towers. SK5
—7H 93
Hollow Field. OL11—1K 27
Hollows Farm Av. OL12—9D 12
Hollowspell. OL12—8J 13
Hollow Vale Dri. SK5—5F 92
Holly Av. M28—6L 57
Holly Av. M31—4B 88
Holly Av. SK8—8K 103
Holly Bank. M33—2J 101
Holly Bank. OL2—3K 45
Holly Bank. SK14—1D 96
Holly Bank. WN7—9G 55
Holly Bank Clo. M15—9C 78
Holly Bank Cotts. M31—1F 98
Holly Bank Ct. SK8—3A 114
Holly Bank Rise. SK16—7F 82
Holly Bank Rd. SK9—2H 119
Holly Bank St. M26—6F 40
Hollybush Sq. WA3—6L 71
Hollybush St. M18—9E 80
Holly Clo. WA15—7G 101
Holly Ct. M20—8H 91
Holly Ct. M30—3H 87
Holly Ct. SK14—4G 95
Hollycroft Av. BL2—4L 39
Hollycroft Av. M22—7D 102
Hollydene. WN2—4H 35
Holly Dene Clo. BL6—2H 37
Holly Dri. M33—1G 101
Hollyedge Dri. M25—6A 60
Holly Fold. M25—8M 41
Holly Grange. SK7—1F 114
Holly Grange. WA14—2D 110
Holly Gro. BL1—9C 22
Holly Gro. BL4—9G 39
Holly Gro. M33—1K 101
Holly Gro. M34—3A 94
Holly Gro. OL4—9E 46
Holly Gro. OL9—9H 45
Holly Gro. SK15—7E 82
Holly Gro. WN7—9E 54
Hollyhedge Av. M22—8D 102
Hollyhedge Ct. Rd. M22—8E 102
Hollyhedge Rd. M23, M22 & SK8
—8M 101
Hollyhey Dri. M23—3C 102
Holly Ho. Dri. M31—4M 87
Hollyhouse Dri. SK6—9A 94
Hollyhurst. M28—1B 76
Holly La. OL8—6J 63
Holly La. SK9—8E 112
Hollymount. M16—2B 90
Hollymount Av. SK2—8J 105
Hollymount Dri. OL4—6E 46
Hollymount Dri. SK2—8J 105
Hollymount Gdns. SK2—8K 105
Hollymount Rd. SK2—8K 105
Holly Rd. M27—1D 76
Holly Rd. SK4—9C 92
Holly Rd. SK6—5F 116
Holly Rd. SK7—7E 114
Holly Rd. SK12—9L 115
Holly Rd. WA3—7J 71
Holly Rd. WA11—9F 68
Holly Rd. WA13—8B 98
Holly Rd. WN2—4H 35
Holly Rd. WN5—1L 51
Holly Rd. N. SK9—5G 119
Holly Rd. S. SK9—6G 119
Holly St. BL1—6F 22
Holly St. BL8—4F 24
Holly St. BL9—8A 26
(Bury)
Holly St. BL9—8J 9
(Summerseat)
Holly St. M11—7L 79
Holly St. M35—5D 80
Holly St. OL12—5J 13
Holly St. OL16—8H 29
Holly St. SK1—4G 105
Holly St. WN2—7F 34
Hollythorn Av. SK8—5C 114
Holly View. M22—8E 102
Holly Wlk. M31—2D 98
Holly Way. M22—5E 102
Hollywood. WA14—2D 110
Hollywood Rd. BL1—8B 22
Hollywood Rd. SK6—5L 107
Hollywood Towers. SK3
(off East St.) —4D 104
Holmbrook. M29—7C 56
Holmbrook Wlk. M8—2G 79
Holm Ct. M6—5A 78
Holmcroft Rd. M18—3D 92
Holmdale Av. M19—9L 91
Holme Av. BL8—5J 25
Holme Av. WN1—7C 34
Holme Cres. OL2—7J 45
Holmefield. M33—1H 101
Holmefield Dri. SK8—4B 114
Holmefield Grn. BL3—6M 37
Holme Ho. St. OL15—2D 14
Holmelyme Ho. SK12—9M 115
Holme Rd. M20—2F 102
Holmes Cotts. BL1—7C 22
Holmes Ho. Av. WN3—5J 51
Holmes Rd. OL12—3D 28
Holmes St. BL3—5G 39
Holmes St. OL12—2D 28
(Rochdale)
Holmes St. OL12—8J 13
(Smallbridge)
Holmes St. SK2—6E 104
Holmes St. SK8—7L 103
Holme St. SK14—4D 94
Holme St. WN1—7C 34
(Swinley)
Holme St. WN1—7C 34
(Water Hayes)
Holmes Way. M34—7M 93
Holmeswood Rd. BL3—7D 38
Holme Ter. OL15—2D 14
Holme Ter. WN1—6B 34
Holmfield. SK9—9L 119
Holmfield Av. M9—9M 61
Holmfield Av. M25—5C 60
Holmfield Av. W. M9—9M 61
Holmfield Clo. SK4—2D 104
Holmfirth Rd. OL3 & HD7—3C 66
Holmfirth St. M13—2M 91
Holmfoot Wlk. M9—9K 61
(off Carisbrook St.)
Holmlea Rd. M35—5E 80
Holmleigh Av. M9—7L 61
Holmpark Rd. M11—8F 80
Holmrook. WA14—8B 100
Holmsfield Clo. WN2—7G 35
Holmside Gdns. M19—1L 103
Holmwood. WA14—1A 110
Holmwood Ct. M20—1H 103
Holmwood Rd. M20—9H 91
Holroyd St. M11—7A 80
Holroyd St. OL16—3G 29
Holset Dri. WA14—8B 100
Holset Wlk. SK7—3G 115
Holst Av. M8—1G 79
Holstein Av. OL12—7D 12
Holt Av. WN5—3D 68
Holtby St. M9—7L 61
Holt Cres. WN5—3D 68
Holthouse Rd. BL8—5E 24
Holt La. M35—1G 81
Holt La. M. M35—9H 63
Holts La. OL4—4D 64
Holts La. SK9—9F 112
Holts Pas. OL15—6A 14
Holts Ter. OL12—9E 12
Holt St. BL0—5K 9
Holt St. BL3—4D 38
Holt St. M10—2M 79
Holt St. M27—6F 58
Holt St. M29—7A 56
Holt St. M30—7C 76
Holt St. M34—7L 81
Holt St. OL4—9C 46
Holt St. OL12—2C 12
Holt St. OL15—1D 14
Holt St. OL16—5A 30
Holt St. SK1—5F 104
Holt St. WA14—5C 100
Holt St. WN1—9F 34

Holt St. WN2—3J 53
Holt St. WN3—4A 52
Holt St. WN5—3D 50
Holt St. WN6—7M 33
Holt St. WN7—9E 54
Holt St. W. BL0—6H 9
Holtswell Clo. WA3—6L 71
Holt Town. M10—5K 79
Holtwood Wlk. SK5—7J 93
Holway Wlk. M9—9J 61
(off Hendham Vale)
Holwick Rd. M23—3M 101
Holwood Dri. M16—6E 90
Holybourne Wlk. M23—5K 101
Holy Harbour St. BL1—8C 22
Holyhurst Wlk. BL1—8E 22
Holyoake Rd. M28—6K 57
Holyoake St. M35—5J 81
Holyoak St. M10—1C 80
Holyrood Clo. WN7—9L 55
Holyrood Ct. M25—2C 60
Holyrood Dri. M25—2C 60
Holyrood Dri. M27—9D 58
Holyrood Gro. M25—2C 60
Holyrood Rd. M25—3B 60
Holyrood St. M10—3E 80
Holyrood St. OL1—8A 46
Holywood St. M14—3H 91
Homebury Dri. M11—5B 80
Home Dri. M24—1M 61
Home Farm Av. SK14—5M 95
Homelands Clo. M33—3F 100
Homelands Rd. M33—3F 100
Homelands Wlk. M9—9K 61
Homer Dri. SK6—5H 107
Homer St. M26—6E 40
Homerton Rd. M10—3B 80
Homestead Av. WA11—8L 69
Homestead Cres. M19—2K 103
Homestead Gdns. OL12—7K 13
Homestead Rd. SK12—6J 117
Homestead, The. M33—9F 88
Homewood Av. M22—4D 102
Homewood Rd. M22—4C 102
Honduras St. OL4—1B 64
Honeybourne. M29—7C 56
Honey Hill. OL4—3F 64
Honey St. M8—1G 5 & 3G 79
Honeysuckle Av. WN6—6M 33
Honeysuckle Wlk. M33—9D 88
Honeysuckle Way. OL12—8D 12
Honeywell La. OL8—5M 63
Honeywood Clo. BL0—8G 9
Honford Rd. M22—9C 102
Honister Av. WA11—7C 68
Honister Dri. M24—7L 43
Honister Rd. M9—9M 61
Honister Way. OL11—6B 28
Honiton Av. SK14—4J 95
Honiton Clo. OL9—8E 44
Honiton Clo. OL10—1J 43
Honiton Clo. WN7—6D 54
Honiton Ct. SK14—4K 95
Honiton Dri. BL2—3A 40
Honiton Gro. M26—4D 40
Honiton Wlk. SK14—4K 95
Honiton Way. WA14—7A 100
Honor St. M13—3M 91
Honsham Wlk. M23—4L 101
Hood Clo. M29—7D 56
Hood Gro. WN7—4H 73
Hood Sq. OL4—3G 65
Hood St. M4—3G 5 & 5H 79
Hood Wlk. M34—7A 94
Hook St. WN2—1F 52
Hoole Clo. SK8—8A 104
Hooley Bri. Ind. Est. OL10
—6J 27
Hooley Clough. OL10—6K 27
Hooley Range. SK4—2B 104
Hooper St. M12—7K 79
Hooper St. OL4—2A 64
Hooper St. SK1—4E 104
Hooten La. WN7—4J 73
Hooton St. BL3—6C 38
Hooton St. M10—4M 79
Hopcroft Clo. M9—2H 61
Hope Av. BL2—3H 39
Hope Av. M28—4J 57
Hope Av. M32—3H 89
Hope Av. SK9—9J 113
Hope Carr La. WN7—5G 73
Hope Carr Rd. WN7—4G 73
(in two parts)
Hopecourt Clo. M6—3J 77
Hope Cres. M6—4J 77
Hope Cres. WN6—3H 33
Hopedale Clo. M11—6M 79
Hopedale Rd. SK5—8F 92
Hopefield Rd. WA13—9B 98
Hopefield St. BL3—5D 38
Hope Fold Av. M29—6H 55
Hopefold Dri. M28—6L 57
Hope Hey La. M28—3F 56
Hope La. SK10—2K 121
Hope La. WN7—5L 73
Hope Pk. Rd. M25—5B 60
Hope Rd. M14—2K 91
Hope Rd. M25—6A 60
Hope Rd. M33—2H 101
Hopes Carr. SK1—4F 104
Hope St. BL0—6H 9
Hope St. BL2—5L 23
Hope St. BL4—9L 39
Hope St. BL6—1L 35
(Blackrod)
Hope St. BL6—6B 20
(Horwich)
Hope St. M1—4G 5 & 6G 79
Hope St. M5—4B 4 & 6C 78
Hope St. M7—9D 60
Hope St. M20—7H 91
Hope St. M27—8G 59
(Pendlebury)
Hope St. M27—9D 58
(Swinton)
Hope St. M28—4G 57
Hope St. M29—2B 74
Hope St. M30—5F 76
Hope St. M34—1M 93
Hope St. OL1—1B 64
Hope St. OL2—2B 46
Hope St. OL6—3D 82
Hope St. OL10—1M 43
Hope St. OL12—2F 28
Hope St. PR6—2H 19
Hope St. SK4—4D 104
Hope St. SK7—1K 115
Hope St. SK13—4L 97
Hope St. SK16—7B 82
(in two parts)
Hope St. WN1—9C 34
(off Galleries, The)
Hope St. WN2—6M 35
(Aspull)
Hope St. WN2—2M 53
(Hindley)
Hope St. WN3—4E 52
Hope St. WN4—2D 70
Hope St. WN7—2F 72
Hope St. N. BL6—5B 20
Hope Ter. SK16—7B 82
Hopgarth Wlk. M10—2D 80
Hopkin Av. OL1—9B 46
Hopkins Field. WA14—3B 110
Hopkinson Av. M34—1K 93
Hopkinson Clo. OL3—9B 48
Hopkinson Rd. M9—3K 61
Hopkins St. M12—3A 92
Hopkins St. SK14—2E 94
Hopkin St. OL1—1M 63
Hoppet La. M35—5J 81
Hopton Av. M22—1E 112
Hopton Ct. M15—9G 79
Hopwood Av. BL6—6C 20
Hopwood Av. M30—4D 76
Hopwood Av. OL10—1K 43
Hopwood Clo. BL9—6M 41
Hopwood Ct. M24—5A 44
Hopwood Ct. OL2—2M 45
Hopwood Rd. M24—5A 44
Hopwood St. M3—3D 4 & 5E 78
Hopwood St. M10—1B 80

Hopwood St. M27—8G 59
Horace Barnes Clo. M14—3G 91
Horace Gro. SK4—1E 104
Horace St. BL1—8D 22
Horatio St. M18—9F 80
Horbury Av. M18—3D 92
Horbury Dri. BL8—8J 25
Horden Wlk. OL2—5L 45
(off Shaw St.)
Hordron Clo. M15—9E 78
Horeb St. BL3—4D 38
Horest La. OL3—1H 47
Horley Clo. BL8—3J 25
Horlock Ct. M6—2A 4 & 4B 78
Hornbeam Clo. M33—9C 88
Hornbeam Clo. WA11—9F 68
Hornbeam Ct. M6—4A 78
Hornbeam Rd. M19—4B 92
Hornby Av. M9—3L 61
Hornby Dri. BL3—7K 37
Hornby Gro. WN7—9K 55
Hornby Rd. M32—2M 89
Hornby St. BL9—5M 25
Hornby St. M8—1E 5 & 3F 78
Hornby St. M24—9A 44
Hornby St. OL8—3K 63
Hornby St. OL10—9K 27
Hornby St. WN1—7C 34
Horncastle Clo. BL8—5K 25
Horncastle Rd. M10—6B 62
Hornchurch Ct. M15—9F 78
(off Bonsall St.)
Horne Dri. M4—3H 5 & 5J 79
Horne Gro. WN3—3M 51
Horne St. BL9—1L 41
Hornet Clo. OL11—7G 29
Hornsea Clo. BL8—8F 24
Hornsea Clo. OL9—8F 44
Hornsea Rd. SK2—8A 106
Hornsea Wlk. M11—6A 80
Hornsey Clo. WN3—5K 51
Horridge Fold. BL7—8E 6
Horridge Fold Av. BL5—7M 37
Horridge St. BL8—6H 25
Horrobin La. BL7—9J 7
Horrobin La. PR6 & BL6—1J 19
Horrocks Fold Av. BL1—4D 22
Horrocks Rd. BL7—4K 7
Horrocks St. BL3—4A 38
Horrocks St. M26—4J 41
Horrocks St. M29—7L 55
(Atherton)
Horrocks St. M29—7M 55
(Tyldesley)
Horrocks St. WN7—2E 72
(Leigh)
Horrocks St. WN7—3A 72
(Plank Lane)
Horsa St. BL2—9H 23
Horsedge St. OL1—9M 45
Horsefield Av. OL12—5C 12
Horsefield Clo. M21—7E 90
Horsefield Way. SK6—8L 93
Horseshoe La. BL7—2G 23
Horseshoe La. SK9—7L 119
Horsfield St. BL3—5A 38
Horsforth La. OL3—4A 66
Horsham Av. SK7—3J 115
Horsham Clo. BL8—3J 25
Horsham Gro. WN2—7F 34
Horsham St. M6—5L 77
Horstead Wlk. M19—4A 92
Horton Av. BL1—4E 22
Horton Rd. M14—4G 91
Horton St. SK1—6G 105
Hortree Rd. M32—4L 89
Horwood Cres. M20—9K 91
Hoscar Dri. M19—7M 91
Hoskers Nook. BL5—1D 54
Hoskers, The. BL5—2D 54
Hoskins Clo. M12—1A 92
Hospital Av. M30—5E 76
Hospital Rd. BL7—2F 22
Hospital Rd. M27—9H 59
Hotel Rd. M22—5C 112
Hotel St. BL1—2F 38
Hothersall Rd. SK5—6F 92
Hothersall St. M7—2D 4 & 4E 78
Hotspur Clo. M14—6G 91
Houghend Av. M21—8C 90
Hough End Cen. M21—7E 90
Houghend Cres. M21—6E 90
Hough Fold Way. BL2—5K 23
Hough Grn. WA15—7E 110
Hough Hall Rd. M10—8M 61
Hough Hill Rd. SK15—6G 83
(in two parts)
Hough La. BL7—3F 22
Hough La. M24—5F 44
Hough La. M29—8C 56
Hough La. SK9—7K 119
Hough La. SK14—9F 82
Hough Rd. M20—7G 91
Hough St. BL3—4A 38
Hough St. M10—2L 79
Hough St. M29—8D 56
Houghton Av. OL8—6K 63
Houghton Av. WN5—7L 33
Houghton La. M27—2D 76
Houghton St. BL3—4E 38
Houghton St. BL9—9L 25
Houghton St. M27—1K 77
Houghton St. OL2—7L 45
Houghton St. WN7—1F 72
Hough Wlk. M7—2B 4 & 4C 78
Houghwood Grange. WN4
—4M 69
Houldsworth Av. WA14
—6E 100
Houldsworth Sq. SK5—7E 92
Houldsworth St. M1—3G 5 &
5H 79
Houldsworth St. M26—4F 40
Houldsworth St. SK5—7E 92
Hounslow Ho. BL1—9E 22
Hourigan Ho. WN7—9E 54
Houseley Av. OL9—5G 63
Housley Clo. WN3—3A 52
Houson St. OL8—3M 63
Houston Pk. M5—6M 77
Hove Clo. BL8—1E 24
Hoveden St. M8—1E 5 & 3F 78
Hove Dri. M14—7L 91
Hove St. BL3—4C 38
Hovey Clo. M8—9F 60
Hoviley. SK14—3E 94
Hoviley Brow. SK14—3E 94
Hovingham St. OL16—2H 29
Hovington Gdns. M19—8L 91
Hovis St. M11—7C 80
Howard Av. BL3—5A 38
Howard Av. BL4—1M 57
Howard Av. M30—4D 76
Howard Av. SK4—8C 92
Howard Av. SK8—3A 114
Howard Av. WA13—9A 98
Howard Clo. SK6—3A 106
Howard Clo. SK13—4H 97
Howard Ct. OL6—4C 82
Howard Dri. WA15—3G 111
Howard Hill. BL9—4A 42
Howard La. M34—2M 93
Howard Pl. OL16—2F 28
Howard Pl. SK13—5H 97
Howard Pl. SK14—4D 94
Howard Rd. M22—4D 102
Howard's La. OL5—6L 65
Howard's La. WN5—1F 50
Howard Spring Wlk. M8—8F 60
Howard St. BL1—9F 22
Howard St. M5—7A 78
Howard St. M8—1E 5 & 3F 78
Howard St. M12—5H 5 & 7J 79
Howard St. M26—6H 41
Howard St. M32—4K 89
Howard St. M34—9M 81
(Audenshaw)
Howard St. M34—1L 93
(Denton)
Howard St. OL2—2A 46
Howard St. OL4—9E 46
Howard St. OL7—3A 82
Howard St. OL12—2F 28

Howard St. SK1—3F 104
Howard St. SK13—5J 97
Howard St. SK15—3K 83
Howard Way. OL15—2C 14
Howarth Av. M28—9C 58
Howarth Clo. M11—6A 80
Howarth Cross St. OL16—9H 13
Howarth Dri. M30—5F 86
Howarth Grn. OL12—8J 13
Howarth Pl. OL11—5D 28
Howarth Sq. OL16—2G 29
Howarth St. BL5—9F 36
Howarth St. M16—2C 90
Howarth St. OL15—5B 14
Howarth St. WN7—3H 73
Howbridge Clo. M28—8J 57
Howbro Dri. OL7—2L 81
Howbrook Wlk. M15—9F 78
Howclough Clo. M28—6M 57
Howclough Dri. M28—6M 57
Howcroft Clo. BL1—1E 38
Howcroft St. BL3—5D 38
Howden Clo. SK5—4E 92
Howden Dri. WN3—4A 52
Howden Rd. M9—3J 61
Howe Dri. BL0—9H 9
Howell Croft N. BL1—2F 38
Howell Croft S. BL1—2F 38
Howells Av. M33—9H 89
Howell's Yd. BL1—2F 38
Howe St. M7—9C 60
Howe St. OL7—7M 81
Howgill St. M11—6D 80
How La. BL9—4L 25
How Lea Dri. BL9—4M 25
Howsin Av. BL2—6H 23
Howton Clo. M12—2A 92
Howty Clo. SK9—2K 119
Hoxton Clo. SK6—1A 106
Hoy Dri. M31—1D 88
Hoylake Clo. M10—8D 62
Hoylake Clo. WN7—5D 72
Hoylake Rd. M33—3M 101
Hoylake Rd. SK3—5A 104
Hoyland Clo. M12—9M 79
Hoyle Av. OL8—3L 63
Hoyle's Ter. OL16—4L 29
Hoyle St. BL1—6E 22
Hoyle St. M12—5H 5 & 7J 79
Hoyle St. M24—2C 62
Hoyle St. M26—8J 41
Hoyle St. OL12—1D 12
Hoyle Wlk. M13—9J 79
Hubert Worthington Ho. SK9 —8L 119
Hucclecote Av. M22—2C 112
Hucklow Av. M23—2A 112
Hucklow Bank. SK13—4D 96
(off Grassmoor Cres.)
Hucklow Clo. SK13—4D 96
(off Grassmoor Cres.)
Hucklow Fold. SK13—4D 96
(off Grassmoor Cres.)
Hucklow Lanes. SK13—4D 96
(off Grassmoor Cres.)
Hudale Clo. M15—9E 78
Huddart Clo. M5—5A 4 & 7B 78
Huddersfield Rd. OL1 & OL4 —1B 64
Huddersfield Rd. OL3—5M 47
(Delph)
Huddersfield Rd. OL3—8K 31
(Denshaw)
Huddersfield Rd. OL3—6B 48
(Diggle)
Huddersfield Rd. OL16—6B 30
Huddersfield Rd. SK15, OL5 &
(Mossley) OL3—2L 83
Huddersfield Rd. SK15—5H 83
(Stalybridge)
Huddleston St. M11—8A 80
Hudgar La. BL9—6A 26
Hudson Rd. BL3—6B 38
Hudson Rd. SK14—7E 94
Hudsons Pas. OL15—4C 14
Hudson St. OL9—6G 63
Hudsons Wlk. OL11—3B 28
Hudswell. M25—9L 41
Huges St. BL9—7A 26
Hughes Av. BL6—6A 20
Hughes St. BL1—8C 22
(in two parts)
Hughes St. M11—7L 79
Hughes Way. M30—7A 76
Hugh Fold. OL4—3E 64
Hugh Lupus St. BL1—5G 23
Hugh Oldham Dri. M7—1C 78
Hugh St. BL3—5C 38
Hugh St. OL16—2G 29
Hugh St. SK13—5H 97
Hughtrede St. OL16—7H 29
Hugo St. BL4—7H 39
Hugo St. M10—9A 62
Hugo St. OL11—8D 28
Hulbert St. BL8—9J 25
Hulbert St. M24—8B 44
Hullet Clo. WN6—1E 32
Hull Mill La. OL3—4M 47
Hull Sq. M3—3C 4 & 5D 78
Hully St. SK15—5F 82
Hulme Gro. WN7—1D 72
Hulme Hall Av. SK8—4A 114
Hulme Hall Cres. SK8—4A 114
Hulme Hall La. M10 & M11 —3L 79
Hulme Hall Rd. M15—6C 4 & 8D 78
Hulme Hall Rd. SK8—2A 114
Hulme Pl. M5—3B 4 & 5C 78
Hulme Rd. BL2—4L 23
Hulme Rd. M26—1C 58
Hulme Rd. M33—2K 101
Hulme Rd. M34—3H 93
Hulme Rd. SK4—8D 92
Hulme Rd. WN7—1C 72
Hulme's La. M34—6L 93
Hulmes Rd. M10 & M35—2E 80
Hulmes Rd. M35—3F 80
Hulme St. BL1—1F 38
Hulme St. BL8—7K 25
Hulme St. M5—4B 4 & 6C 78
Hulme St. M15 & M1
(in three parts)-6D 4 & 8E 78
Hulme St. OL6—3D 82
Hulme St. OL8—4L 63
Hulme St. SK1—6H 105
Hulme Wlk. M15—9E 78
(in three parts)
Hulseheath La. WA16—9F 108
Hulton Av. M28—5G 57
Hulton Clo. BL3—5A 38
Hulton Dri. BL3—6A 38
Hulton Dri. M16—2E 90
Hulton La. BL3—7A 38
Hulton La. Est. BL3—6A 38
Hulton St. M5—6A 4 & 8A 78
Hulton St. M34—2L 93
Hulton St. M35—9E 62
Humber Dri. BL9—2M 25
Humber Pl. WN5—1J 51
Humber Rd. M29—9C 56
Humber Rd. OL16—4A 30
Humberstone Av. M15—6D 4 & 8E 78
Humber St. M5—6K 77
Humber St. M8—9G 61
Hume St. M19—6B 92
Hume St. OL16—4G 29
Humphrey Booth's Gdns. M6 —4L 77
Humphrey Cres. M31—4F 88
Humphrey La. M31—4G 89
Humphrey Pk. M31—4G 89
Humphrey Rd. M16—1B 90
Humphrey Rd. SK7—1E 114
Humphrey St. M8—8F 60
Humps M. OL1—1A 64
Huncoat Av. SK4—8D 92
Huncote Av. WA11—9D 68
Huncote Dri. M9—7L 61
Hungerford Wlk. M23—6K 101
Hunger Hill. OL12—5K 13
Hunger Hill Av. BL3—7L 37
Hunger Hill La. OL12—8M 11
Hunmanby Av. M15—6E 5 & 8F 78
Hunstanton Dri. BL8—5K 25
Hunston Rd. M33—2F 100
Hunt Av. OL7—2B 82
Hunter Rd. WN5—8K 33
Hunters Clo. SK9—2M 119
Hunters Ct. SK15—8K 83
Hunters Grn. BL0—8F 8
Hunters Hill. BL9—5B 42
Hunters Hill La. OL3—3B 48
Hunter's La. M12—1A 92
Hunters La. OL1—1M 63
Hunters La. OL16—2F 28
Hunters La. SK13—6F 96
Hunters M. M33—9G 89
Hunters M. SK9—4J 119
Hunterson Av. M30—5G 77
Hunter St. M24—8A 44
Hunters View. SK9—9J 113
Hunt Fold Dri. BL8—9F 8
Hunt Hill Rd. M26—5F 40
Huntingdon Av. M20—7G 91
Huntingdon Av. OL9—3H 63
Huntingdon Cres. SK5—9J 93
Huntingdon Wlk. BL1—8E 22
Huntingdon Way. M34 —5M 93
Hunt La. OL9—1F 62
Huntley Mt. Rd. BL9—6B 26
Huntley Rd. M8—6E 60
Huntley Rd. SK3—6B 104
Huntley St. BL9—7B 26
Huntley Way. OL10—9E 26
Huntly Chase. SK9—4K 119
Hunton Av. OL6—5E 82
Hunt Rd. SK14—1G 95
Hunt Rd. WA11—9L 69
Huntroyde Av. BL2—9J 23
Hunt's Bank. BL5—2F 54
Hunt's Bank App. M3—3E 5 & 5F 78
Huntsham Clo. WA14—7B 100
Huntsman Dri. M30—7F 86
Hunts Rd. M6—2K 77
Hunt St. M9—7K 61
Hunt St. M29—5K 55
Hunt St. SK3—5C 104
Hunt St. WN1—1E 52
Huntsworth Wlk. M13—1K 91
Hurdlow Av. M7—9A 60
Hurdlow Grn. SK13—5D 96
(off Brassington Cres.)
Hurdlow Lea. SK13—5D 96
(off Brassington Cres.)
Hurdlow M. SK13—5D 96
Hurdlow Wlk. M9—9K 61
Hurdlow Way. SK13—5D 96
(off Brassington Cres.)
Hurdsfield Rd. SK2—9K 105
Hurford Av. M18—9D 80
Hurlbote Clo. SK9—7K 113
Hurley Dri. SK8—2L 113
Hurlston Rd. BL3—7D 38
Hurst Av. M33—2C 100
Hurst Av. SK8—6C 114
Hurst Bank. OL6—3E 82
Hurstbank Av. M19—1K 103
Hurstbourne Av. M11—4B 80
Hurst Brook. PR7—1M 17
Hurstbrook Clo. OL6—3C 82
Hurst Clo. BL5—1M 55
Hurst Ct. M23—9M 101
Hurst Ct. OL6—2D 82
Hurst Cross. OL6—2D 82
Hurstead. OL12—7K 13
Hurstead Grn. OL12—7K 13
Hursted Rd. OL16—4M 29
Hurstfield Ind. Est. SK5 —8E 92
Hurstfield Rd. M28—8H 57
Hurst Fold. M30—3H 87
(off Fiddlers La.)
Hurstfold Av. M19—2K 103
Hurst Grn. Clo. BL8—1F 40
Hurst Gro. OL6—2E 82
Hurst Hall Dri. OL6—2E 82
Hursthead Rd. SK8—5B 114
Hursthead Wlk. M13—6G 5 & 8H 79
Hurst La. WA3—9H 73
Hurst Lea Ct. SK9—7L 119
Hurstmead Ter. M20—3H 103
(off South Rd.)
Hurst Mill La. WA3—7J 73
Hurst Rd. SK13—5M 97
Hurst St. BL3—6C 38
Hurst St. BL4—8J 39
Hurst St. BL9—8A 26
Hurst St. M28—2J 57
Hurst St. OL9—1K 63
Hurst St. OL11—5G 29
Hurst St. SK5—7E 92
Hurst St. WN2—2J 53
Hurst St. WN7—5H 73
Hurstvale Av. SK8—3H 113
Hurstville Rd. M21—8B 90
Hurst Wlk. M23—2A 112
Hurstway Dri. M9—5L 61
Hurstwood Gro. SK2—8M 105
Hurstwood Wlk. M6—5A 78
Hus St. M35—7F 80
Husteads La. OL3—8L 47
Hutchinson Rd. OL11—1K 27
Hutchinson St. M26—5J 41
Hutchinson St. OL11—4B 28
Hutchinson Way. M26—7G 41
Hutton Av. M28—1F 74
Hutton St. WN1—7A 18
Hutton Wlk. M13—9J 79
(off Copeman Clo.)
Huxley Av. M8—1G 79
Huxley Clo. SK7—5E 114
Huxley Dri. SK7—5E 114
Huxley Pl. WN3—3A 52
Huxley St. BL1—8C 22
Huxley St. OL4—3C 64
Huxley St. WA14—6D 100
Huxton Grn. SK7—3G 115
Huyton Rd. PR7—4G 19
Huyton Ter. PR6—3H 19
Hyacinth Clo. SK3—8D 104
Hyacinth Clo. WA11—9M 69
Hyacinth Wlk. M31—3E 98
Hyatt Cres. WN6—7J 17
Hydebank. SK6—4D 106
Hyde By-Pass. SK14—3C 94
Hyde Dri. M28—6J 57
Hyde Fold Clo. M19—8M 91
Hyde Gro. M13—1J 91
Hyde Gro. M28—6J 57
Hyde Gro. M33—1H 101
Hyde Pk. Pl. OL16—3J 29
Hyde Pl. M13—1J 91
Hyde Rd. M12 & M18—6H 5 & 8J 79
Hyde Rd. M24—2E 62
Hyde Rd. M28—6J 57
Hyde Rd. M34—2M 93
Hyde Rd. SK6—9A 94
Hyde Rd. SK14—3M 95
Hyde Sq. M24—9L 43
Hydes Ter. SK15—5H 83
Hyde St. BL3—6C 38
Hyde St. M15—1D 90
(in two parts)
Hyde St. M35—3J 81
Hyde St. OL1—2M 63
Hyde St. SK16—7D 82
Hydon Brook Wlk. OL11 —6C 28
Hydrangea Clo. M33—9C 88
Hyldavale Av. SK8—7H 103
Hylton Dri. OL7—2M 81
Hylton Dri. SK8—4C 114
Hyman Goldstone Wlk. M8 —9F 60
Hyndells Lodge. WN2—2K 53
Hyndman Ct. M5—6K 77
Hypatia St. BL2—1H 39
Hythe Clo. M14—3J 91
Hythe Rd. SK3—5B 104
Hythe St. BL3—5A 38
Hythe Wlk. OL9—2H 63
Ibberton Wlk. M9—7M 61
(off Carnaby St.)
Ibsley. OL12—2E 28
(off Spotland Rd.)
Ice Ho. Clo. M28—5F 56
Iceland St. M6—5L 77
Idiona St. BL1—7D 22
Ilex Gro. M7—1D 78
Ilford St. M11—5B 80
Ilfracombe Rd. SK2—5J 105
Ilfracombe St. M10—1D 80
Ilkeston Dri. WN2—6M 35
Ilkeston Wlk. M10—9A 62
(off Halliford Rd.)
Ilkeston Wlk. M34—6A 94
Ilkley Av. M31—2A 88
Ilkley Clo. BL2—2J 39
Ilkley Clo. OL9—2H 63
Ilkley Cres. SK5—6E 92
Ilkley St. M10—7A 62
Ilk St. M11—5B 80
Illingworth Av. SK15—6J 83
Illona Dri. M7—8A 60
Ilminster. OL11—4E 28
Ilminster Wlk. M9—3L 61
(off Eastlands Rd.)
Ilthorpe Wlk. M10—1A 80
Imogen Ct. M5—5B 4 & 7C 78
Imperial Dri. WN7—1K 73
Imperial Ter. M33—8G 89
Ina Av. BL1—9M 21
Ince Clo. M20—7H 91
Ince Clo. SK4—2E 104
Ince Grn. La. WN3 & WN2 —2E 52
Ince Hall Av. WN2—9F 34
Ince St. SK4—2E 104
Inchcape Dri. M9—4H 61
Inchfield Clo. OL11—2L 27
Inchfield Rd. M10—7A 62
Inchley Rd. M13—6G 5 & 8H 79
Inchwood M. OL4—5E 46
Incline Rd. OL8—6H 63
Independant St. BL1—1G 39
Independent St. BL3—6A 40
India St. BL9—8J 9
Indigo St. M6—2M 77
Indigo Wlk. M6—1M 77
Indoor Mkt. OL16—3F 28
Industrial St. BL0—2J 9
Industrial St. BL5—1F 54
Industry Rd. OL12—1F 28
Industry St. OL9—4G 63
Industry St. OL11—1L 27
Industry St. OL12—1D 12
Industry St. OL15—6B 14
Infant St. M25—4C 60
Infirmary St. BL1—2F 38
Ingham Rd. WA14—5D 100
Inghams La. OL15—6B 14
Ingham St. BL9—9A 26
Ingham St. M10—3E 80
Ingham St. OL1—1A 64
Ingham St. WN7—8E 54
Inghamwood Clo. M8—9F 60
Ingleby Av. M9—4L 61
Ingleby Av. M30—7E 86
Ingleby Clo. OL2—1A 46
Ingleby Ct. M32—5L 89
Ingleby Way. OL2—1A 46
Ingledene Av. M7—7E 60
Ingledene Ct. M7—7E 60
Ingledene Gro. BL1—8A 22
Ingle Dri. SK2—6J 105
Inglefield. OL11—1M 27
Inglehead Clo. M34—4A 94
Ingle Rd. SK8—7A 104
Ingles Fold. M28—9H 57
Ingleton Av. M8—6H 61
Ingleton Clo. BL2—6K 23
Ingleton Clo. BL8—6H 25
Ingleton Clo. OL2—4K 45
Ingleton Clo. SK8—7J 103
Ingleton Dri. WA11—6B 68
Ingleton Gdns. OL2—2D 46
Ingleton Rd. SK3—5C 104
Inglewhite Av. WN1—7C 34
Inglewhite Clo. BL9—1K 41
Inglewhite Cres. WN1—7C 34
Inglewhite Pl. WN1—7C 34
Inglewood Av. WN1—1E 52
Inglewood Clo. OL7—2M 81
Inglewood Rd. OL9—8D 44
Inglewood Wlk. M13—9J 79
(off Brunswick St.)
Inglis St. OL15—5B 14
Ingoe Clo. OL10—7M 27
Ingoldsby Av. M13—2K 91
Ingram Dri. SK4—2L 103
Ingram St. WN2—5G 53
Ingram St. WN6—8M 33
Ingres Wlk. OL1—5C 46
Ings Av. OL12—9B 12
Ings La. OL12—9B 12
Inkerman St. M10—1K 79
(off Topley St.)
Inkerman St. OL12—1F 28
Inkerman St. SK14—2D 94
Ink St. OL16—3F 28
Inman St. BL9—1L 41
Inman St. M34—3M 93
Innes St. M12—3B 92
Innis Av. M10—2C 80
Institute St. BL1—2F 38
Instow Clo. M13—9K 79
Instow Clo. OL9—8F 44
Intake La. OL3—5A 66
Invar Rd. M28—7D 58
Inverbeg Dri. BL2—2A 40
Invergarry Wlk. M11—6C 80
Inverlael Av. BL1—1B 38
Inverness Av. M9—4A 62
Inverness Clo. WN2—4K 35
Inverness Ct. OL8—4M 63
Inverness Rd. SK16—8C 82
Inver Wlk. M10—6D 62
Inward Dri. WN6—4G 33
Inwood Wlk. M8—1J 79
Inworth Wlk. M8—9F 60
(off Highshore Dri.)
Iona Pl. BL2—8J 23
Iona Way. M31—1D 88
Ipstone Clo. M15—9E 78
Ipswich St. OL11—5F 28
Ipswich Wlk. M12—1L 91
(off Martindale Cres.)
Ipswich Wlk. M34—5A 94
Iqbal Clo. M12—1A 92
Irby Wlk. SK8—9A 104
Ireby Clo. M24—7J 43
Iredine St. M11—6C 80
Ireland Rd. WA11—9J 69
Irene Av. SK14—1E 94
Irene Av. WA11—8C 68
Iris Av. BL4—8G 39
(Farnworth)
Iris Av. BL4—3M 57
(Kearsley)
Iris Av. M11—7D 80
Iris St. BL0—5H 9
Iris St. OL8—5M 63
Iris Wlk. M31—3F 98
Irkdale St. M8—1J 79
Irk Pl. M8—9J 61
Irk Vale Dri. OL1—8E 44
Irk Way. M25—7B 42
Irlam Av. M30—6D 76
Irlam-Cadishead By-Pass. M30 —7G 87
Irlam Rd. M31—5H 87
Irlam Rd. M33—9J 89
Irlams Sq. M6—2K 77
Irlam St. BL1—7E 22
Irlam St. M10—2L 79
Irlam Wharf Rd. M30—8G 87
Irma St. BL1—7F 22
Ironmonger La. OL1—2M 63
Ironmonger La. WN3—1C 52
Iron St. BL6—8C 20
Iron St. M10—4L 79
Iron St. M34—3M 93
Irvin Dri. M22—4G 113
Irvine. OL11—6E 28
Irvine Av. M28—1G 75
Irvine St. WN7—1F 72
Irving Clo. SK2—1G 115
Irving St. BL1—8E 22
Irving St. OL8—6H 63
Irvin St. M10—1C 80
Irwell Av. M28—4H 57
Irwell Av. M30—6F 76
Irwell Clo. M26—7H 41
Irwell Gro. M30—6F 76
Irwell Pl. M5—3B 4 & 5C 78
Irwell Pl. M30—6F 76
Irwell Pl. WN2—6F 52
Irwell Pl. WN5—2J 51
Irwell Rd. WN5—1F 50
Irwell St. BL0—5J 9
Irwell St. BL9—8L 25
Irwell St. M3—1D 4 & 5D 78
Irwell St. M6—1A 78
Irwell St. M8—3E 78
Irwell St. M26—9A 40
(Prestolee)
Irwell St. M26—7H 41
(Radcliffe)
Irwell Ter. BL9—2K 41
Irwell Wlk. OL8—5J 63
Irwin Dri. SK9—7J 113
Irwin Rd. WA14—5C 100
Irwin St. M34—3L 93
Isaac Clo. M5—7A 78
Isaac St. BL1—1C 38
Isabella Sq. WN1—9E 34
Isabella St. OL12—9F 12
Isabel Wlk. BL3—4D 38
Isaiah St. OL8—4M 63
Isa St. BL0—7G 9
Isca St. M11—6M 79
Isel Wlk. M24—7K 43
Isherwood Clo. OL10—9K 27
Isherwood Dri. SK6—7D 106
Isherwood Fold. BL7—4K 7
Isherwood Rd. M31—8M 87
Isherwood St. OL10—9L 27
Isherwood St. WN7—8E 54
Island Row. WN2—1H 53
Islands Brow. WA11—9B 68
Islington Rd. SK2—9J 105
Islington St. M3—4C 4 & 6D 78
Isobel Bailey Lodge. M16 —1D 90
Isobel Clo. M30—6B 76
Isobel Wlk. M16—2F 90
Ivanhoe Av. WA3—6K 71
Ivanhoe Ct. BL3—7J 39
Ivanhoe St. BL3—7J 39
Ivanhoe St. OL1—8C 46
Iveagh Ct. OL16—4H 29
Ivor St. OL11—7B 28
Ivory St. M4—1G 5 & 3H 79
Ivory Way. OL1—1M 63
Ivy Bank. OL12—1D 12
Ivy Bank Clo. BL1—5E 22
Ivy Bank Rd. BL1—5E 22
Ivybridge Clo. M13—1K 91
Ivy Clo. M35—4F 80
Ivy Clo. OL2—2B 46
Ivy Cotts. M34—7A 94
Ivy Cotts. OL12—1D 28
Ivy Ct. M21—6B 90
Ivycroft. SK14—2E 96
Ivydale Dri. WN7—2J 73
Ivy Dri. M24—1M 61
Ivygreen Dri. OL4—2F 64
Ivygreen Rd. M21—6M 89
Ivy Gro. BL4—9H 39
(Farnworth)
Ivy Gro. BL4—1M 57
(Kearsley)
Ivy Gro. M28—4F 56
Ivy House Rd. WA3—6K 71
Ivy Leaf Sq. M7—1E 78
Ivylea Rd. M19—1L 103
Ivylodge Clo. SK15—3K 83
Ivy Rd. BL1—9C 22
Ivy Rd. BL5—1F 54
Ivy Rd. BL8—8H 25
Ivy Rd. SK12—9L 115
Ivy Rd. WA3—7H 71
Ivy St. BL3—5C 38
Ivy St. M10—8A 62
Ivy St. M30—6D 76
Ivy St. WN1—9B 34
Ivy St. WN4—4B 70
Ivy Ter. OL15—1D 14
Ivy Ter. WN6—7J 17
Ivy Villa. OL4—3F 64
Ivy Wlk. M31—2D 98
Jackdaw Rd. BL8—9F 8
Jackie Brown Wlk. M10—2K 79
Jackies La. WA13—9A 98
Jack La. M31—6J 87
(Flixton)
Jack La. M31—4E 88
(Urmston)
Jack La. M35—5H 81
(in two parts)
Jack McCann Ct. OL16—2G 29
Jackman Av. OL10—2K 43
Jackroom Dri. M4—3H 5 & 5J 79
Jack's La. BL5—1A 54
Jackson Av. SK16—7D 82
Jackson Clo. BL8—7H 25
Jackson Clo. OL8—3L 63
Jackson Ct. M21—5M 89
Jackson Ct. M31—4A 88
Jackson Cres. M15—6D 4 & 9E 78
Jackson Gdns. M34—4K 93
Jackson Pit. OL1—2L 63
Jackson Pl. OL16—2H 29
Jacksons Bldgs. SK13—6K 97
Jacksons Edge Rd. SK6 & SK12 —5G 117
Jacksons La. SK7—3G 115
Jackson's Row. M2—4E 5 & 6F 78
Jackson St. BL4—9K 39
(Farnworth)
Jackson St. BL4—1M 57
(Kearsley)
Jackson St. M24—8B 44
Jackson St. M25—1M 59
Jackson St. M26—7H 41
Jackson St. M28—4J 57
Jackson St. M32—4J 89
Jackson St. M33—9K 89
Jackson St. M35—1D 80
Jackson St. OL4—1B 64
(Oldham)
Jackson St. OL4—2F 64
(Springhead)
Jackson St. OL12—5J 13
Jackson St. OL16—4H 29
Jackson St. SK8—7L 103
Jackson St. SK13—7J 97
Jackson St. SK14—1J 97
(Hadfield)
Jackson St. SK14—4D 94
(Hyde)
Jackson St. SK14—3A 96
(Mottram)
Jackson St. WA11—8G 69
Jackson St. WN2—1G 53
Jack St. BL2—9J 23
Jacobsen Av. SK14—2F 94
Jacob's Ladder. OL5—7J 65
Jacob St. WN2—2K 53
Jaffrey St. WN7—2E 72
James Andrew St. M24—8B 44
James Bentley Wlk. M10 —2C 80
James Brindley Basin. M1 —6J 79
James Butterworth Ct. OL16 —3H 29
James Butterworth St. OL16 —4H 29
James Clo. SK16—7E 82
James Corbett Rd. M5—6J 77
James Hill St. OL15—6B 14
James Leech St. SK3—5F 104
James Leigh St. M1—5F 5 & 7G 79
Jameson St. OL11—8B 28
James Pl. PR7—1L 17
James Pl. WN6—8K 17
James Rd. OL2—1B 46
James Rd. WA11—8M 69
James Sq. WN6—8K 17
James St. BL3—6B 40
James St. BL4—9M 39
James St. BL5—7E 36
James St. BL6—7M 19
James St. BL7—8D 6
James St. BL9—9A 26
James St. M3—4C 4 & 5D 78
James St. M10—4K 79
James St. M25—3A 60
James St. M26—8G 41
James St. M29—7L 55
(Atherton)
James St. M29—8M 55
(Tyldesley)
James St. M33—1K 101
James St. M34—7L 81
(Audenshaw)
James St. M34—2A 94
(Denton)
James St. M35—5H 81
(Droylsden)
James St. M35—8G 63
(Failsworth)
James St. OL2—4A 46
James St. OL4—8D 46
James St. OL10—7K 27
James St. OL12—7J 13
(Great Howarth)
James St. OL12—2G 29
(Rochdale)
James St. OL12—1D 12
(Whitworth)
James St. OL15—7L 13
James St. OL16—3K 29
James St. SK3—6E 104
James St. SK6—9A 94
James St. SK13—6J 97
James St. SK16—7E 82
James St. WN2—9E 52
James St. WN3—2D 52
James St. S. OL9—1G 63
Jammy La. OL9—2J 63
Jane St. OL9—2H 63
Jane St. OL12—2E 28
Japan St. M8—9F 60
Jarmain St. M12—8A 80
Jarrold St. M11—8A 80
Jarvis St. M11—7M 79
Jarvis St. OL4—2A 64
Jarvis St. OL12—1F 28
Jasmine Av. M35—5J 81
Jasmine Rd. WN5—1K 51
Jasmine Wlk. M31—3F 98
Jasper Wlk. M16—2E 90
Jauncey St. BL3—4C 38
Jay St. M14—3H 91
Jayton Av. M20—6H 103
Jean Av. WN7—5E 72
Jean Clo. M19—4A 92
Jean St. M19—4A 92
Jedburgh Av. BL1—1B 38
Jedburgh Sq. M8—7F 60
Jefferson Way. OL12 —8F 12
Jeffreys Dri. SK16—7D 82
Jeffrey St. WN2—9G 35
Jeffrey Wlk. OL10—8G 27
Jehlum Clo. M8—9H 61
Jellicoe Av. M30—3E 86
Jenkinson St. WN2—2K 53
Jenkyn Wlk. M11—6M 79
Jenner Clo. M15—9E 78
Jennet Hey. WN4—1M 69
Jennet's La. WA3—6J 73
Jennings Av. M5—7A 78
Jennings Clo. M5—7A 78
Jennings Clo. SK14—1H 95
Jennings St. SK3—6D 104
Jennison Clo. M18—9B 80
Jenny Beck Gro. BL3—5E 38
Jenny La. SK7—9E 114
Jenny St. OL8—6J 63
Jepheys Pl. OL12—1F 28
Jepheys St. OL12—1F 28
Jepson St. SK2—7G 105
Jericho Rd. BL9—6E 26
Jermyn St. OL12—2G 29
Jerrold St. OL15—6B 14
Jersey Clo. M19—7M 91
Jersey Pl. SK4—3L 103
Jersey Rd. SK5—1F 104
Jersey St. M4—3G 5 & 5H 79
Jersey St. OL6—3B 82
Jerusalem Pl. M2—5E 5 & 7F 78
Jervas Wlk. OL1—5C 46
Jesmond Av. M25—6B 60
Jesmond Dri. BL8—5J 25
Jesmond Gro. SK8—4B 114
Jesmond Rd. BL1—6B 22
Jesmond St. M35—1C 80
Jesmond Wlk. M9—3K 61
(off Claygate Dri.)
Jespersen St. OL1—1M 63
Jessamine Av. M7—1C 4 & 3D 78
Jessel Clo. M13—9J 79
Jessie St. BL3—4C 38
Jessie St. M10—1A 80
Jessop Dri. SK6—5F 106
Jessop St. M18—1D 92
Jethro St. BL2—1J 39
(Bolton)
Jethro St. BL2—6J 23
(Bradshaw)
Jetson St. M18—9F 80
Jevington. OL11—6F 28
Jevington Wlk. M13—9J 79
(off Dilston Clo.)
Jimmy McMullen Wlk. M14 —3G 91
Jinnah Clo. M11—7C 80
Joan St. M10—9A 62
Jobling St. M11—7M 79
Jocelyn St. M10—1L 79
Joddrell St. M3—4D 4 & 6E 78
Joel La. SK14—7F 94
Johannesburg Dri. M23 —9M 101
Johannesburg Gdns. M23 —9M 101
John Ashworth St. OL12—1H 29
John Atkinson Ct. M5—5K 77
John Av. SK8—8L 103
John Booth St. OL4—3F 64
John Bromley St. BL1—1G 39
John Brown St. BL1—1E 38
John Clynes Av. M10—2H 5 & 4J 79
John Cross St. BL3—5E 38
John Dalton St. M2—4E 5 & 6F 78
John Dalton St. M3—3C 4 & 5D 78
John Dalton St. SK14—1E 96
John Foran Clo. M10—1B 80
John Heywood St. M11—5B 80
John Kemble Ct. OL11—6D 28
John Kennedy Gdns. SK14 —3A 96
John Kennedy Rd. SK14—3M 95
John Knott St. OL4—2F 64
John Lee Fold. M24—8A 44
John Lester Ct. M6—4A 78
(off Meyrick Rd.)
John Nash Cres. M15—9E 78
Johnny King Clo. M10—2K 79
John Robinson Wlk. M10 —9A 62
Johns Av. WA11—8L 69
Johns Clo. M21—6B 90
John Shepley St. SK14—4E 94
John Smeaton Ct. M1—4H 5 & 6J 79
Johnson Av. OL1—4E 46
Johnson Av. WA12—9B 70
Johnson Av. WN2—7L 53
Johnsonbrook Rd. SK14 & SK16 —1C 94
Johnson Clo. WN7—3B 72
Johnson Fold Av. BL1—8L 21
Johnson Gro. M24—9L 43
Johnson's Sq. M10—3K 79
Johnson St. BL1—3F 38
Johnson St. M3—3D 4 & 5E 78
Johnson St. M15—9D 78
Johnson St. M26—7G 41
Johnson St. M27—1K 77
Johnson St. M29—7G 55
(Atherton)
Johnson St. M29—7A 56
(Tyldesley)
Johnson St. WN5—2H 51
John's Pl. SK6—3C 106
Johnston. OL12—2E 28
(off Spotland Rd.)
Johnston Av. OL15—8M 13
John Stone Ct. M32—3G 89
John St. BL3—6B 40
John St. BL4—9L 39
John St. BL7—3G 23
John St. BL9—7M 25
John St. M3—3D 4 & 5E 78
John St. M4—3F 5 & 5G 79
John St. M7—1C 4 & 3D 78
John St. M25—9E 42
John St. M27—8G 59
John St. M28—4K 57
John St. M29—7A 56
John St. M30—9E 86
(Cadishead)
John St. M30—6B 76
(Eccles)
John St. M33—9H 89
John St. M34—2M 93
John St. M35—6F 80
(Droylsden)
John St. M35—7F 62
(Failsworth)
John St. OL2—5K 45
(Royton)
John St. OL2—4A 46
(Shaw)
John St. OL4—2G 65
John St. OL8—2L 63
John St. OL10—8K 27
John St. OL12—1D 12
John St. OL15—6A 14
John St. OL16—2F 28
(Rochdale)
John St. OL16—8J 13
(Smallbridge)
John St. PR7—1L 17
John St. SK1—4F 104
(in two parts)
John St. SK6—9A 94
(Bredbury)
John St. SK6—2H 107
(Compstall)
John St. SK6—8G 107
(Marple)
John St. SK6—3C 106
(Romiley)
John St. SK7—1K 115
John St. SK13—6J 97
John St. SK14—3D 94
(in two parts)
John St. SK15—2J 83
John St. WA3—7G 71
John St. WA14—9D 100
John St. WN1—9D 34
John St. WN2—5B 54
John St. WN4—2D 70
John St. WN5—3K 51
John St. WN7—2F 72
John St. E. OL7—6M 81
(in two parts)
John St. W. OL7—7M 81
John William St. M11—6C 80
John William St. M30—5F 76
Joiner St. M4—4F 5 & 6G 79
Joiner St. M5—4B 4 & 6C 78
Join Rd. M33—1K 101
Jolly Brows. BL2—7K 23
Jolly Tar La. PR7—3M 17
Jonas St. M7—2D 4 & 4E 78
Jones Sq. SK1—6G 105
Jones St. BL6—6B 20
Jones St. M6—4M 77
Jones St. M9—8L 61
Jones St. M26—5H 41
Jones St. OL1—9A 46
Jones St. OL2—7L 45
Jones St. OL16—4G 29
Jones St. SK14—1G 97
Jonquil Dri. M28—6F 56
Jopson St. M24—8B 44
Jordan Av. OL2—9C 30
Jordan St. M15—6D 4 & 8E 78
Jordan St. SK13—5L 97
Joseph Dean Ct. M10—9A 62
Josephine Dri. M27—9G 59
Joseph Mamlock Ho. M8 —7E 60
Joseph St. BL4—8K 39
Joseph St. BL9—7A 26
Joseph St. M24—8M 43
Joseph St. M26—7H 41
Joseph St. M30—6B 76
Joseph St. M34—4H 93
Joseph St. M35—8F 62
Joseph St. OL12—9D 12
Joseph St. OL15—5B 14
Joseph St. SK4—4C 104
Joseph St. SK6—7G 107
Joshua La. M24—1D 62
Josslyn Rd. M5—4K 77
Jo St. M5—4A 4 & 6A 78
Joule Clo. M5—7A 78
Joules Ct. SK1—4F 104
Joule St. M9—7L 61
Jowett St. OL1—8C 46
Jowett St. SK5—1F 104
Jowett's Wlk. OL7—5M 81
Jowkin La. OL11—3K 27
Joyce St. M10—9B 62
Joynson Av. M7—1C 4 & 3D 78
Joynson St. M10—3L 79
Joynson St. M33—9H 89
Joy St. BL0—5H 9
Joy St. OL12—8F 12
Jubilee. OL2—8C 30
Jubilee Av. M26—8J 41
Jubilee Av. SK16—6D 82
Jubilee Av. WN5—4D 50
Jubilee Clo. M30—4D 76
Jubilee Ct. M16—2B 90
Jubilee Ct. OL1—5D 46
Jubilee Ct. SK5—4F 92
Jubilee Cres. WA11—8M 69
Jubilee Ho. BL1—3E 38
Jubilee Houses. M28—5J 57
Jubilee Houses. M29—8L 55
Jubilee Rd. M24—8B 44
Jubilee St. BL3—6C 38
Jubilee St. M3—2E 5 & 4F 78
Jubilee St. M6—5M 77
Jubilee St. OL2—3C 46
Jubilee Ter. M24—7B 44
Jubilee Wlk. OL12—1D 12
Jubilee Way. BL9—8K 25
Juddfield St. WA11—8G 69
Judith St. OL12—8C 12
Judson Av. M21—8C 90
Julia M. BL6—6B 20
Julian Ho. OL1—1M 63
Julia St. BL6—6B 20
Julia St. M3—2E 5 & 4F 78
Julia St. OL12—2E 28
Julius St. M19—6B 92
Junction Rd. BL3—4M 37
Junction Rd. SK1 & SK4—6F 104
Junction Rd. SK3—6F 104
Junction Rd. W. BL6—4J 37
Junction St. M24—2D 62
Junction St. OL6—4C 82
Junction St. OL8—4L 63
Junction St. SK14—1C 94
Junction Ter. WN3—2E 52
June Av. SK4—3B 104
June Av. WN7—1C 72
June St. OL7—5A 82
Juniper Bank. SK5—6G 93
Juniper Clo. OL4—5F 46
Juniper Cres. M35—7E 80
Juniper Dri. WN2—5A 54
Juno St. OL1—8A 46
Jupiter Gro. WN3—6L 51
Jupiter Wlk. M10—2A 80
Jura Clo. SK16—7D 82
Jura Dri. M31—1E 88
Jurby Av. M9—4J 61
Jury St. M8—1E 5 & 3F 78
Jury St. WN7—9E 54
Justin Clo. M13—6G 5 & 8H 79
Jutland Av. OL11—2C 28
Jutland Gro. BL5—8E 36
Jutland St. M1—4G 5 & 6H 79
Kale St. M13—6G 5 & 8H 79
Kalmia Gro. M7—2D 78
(off Hilton St. N.)
Kansas Av. M5—7L 77
Kara St. M6—5L 77
Kate St. BL0—5H 9
Kate St. M9—7K 61
Kathan Clo. OL16—3H 29
Katherine Ho. OL6—4A 82
Katherine Rd. SK2—8J 105
Katherine St. OL7 & OL6—5M 81
Kathkin Av. M8—6H 61
Kathleen Gro. M14—4J 91
Kathleen St. OL12—3D 28
Kay Av. SK6—2K 105
Kay Brow. BL0—5J 9
Kay Brow. OL10—8J 27
Kay Clo. WN1—9D 34
Kayes Av. SK1—4H 105
Kayfields. BL2—6L 23
Kay La. WA13—4B 108
Kayley Ind. Est. OL7—5M 81
Kays Gdns. M3—3C 4 & 5D 78
Kay St. BL0—1K 9
Kay St. BL1—9F 22
Kay St. BL3—6A 40
Kay St. BL7—7J 7
Kay St. BL9—7A 26
(Bury)
Kay St. BL9—8J 9
(Summerseat)
Kay St. M6—1M 77
Kay St. M11—7M 79
Kay St. M29—6K 55
Kay St. OL10—8J 27
Kay St. OL11—5E 28
Kay St. SK15—6G 83
Kay St. SK16—7E 82
Kays Wood Rd. SK6—7D 106
Keal Dri. M30—2G 87
Keane St. OL7—4A 82
Kean Pl. M30—6D 76
Kearsley Dri. BL3—6H 39
Kearsley Hall Rd. M26—1C 58
Kearsley Mt. BL4—2B 58
Kearsley Rd. M8—6G 61
Kearsley Rd. M26—9C 40
Kearsley St. M30—5B 76
Kearsley St. WN6—8B 34
Kearsley St. WN7—2E 72
Kearsley Vale. M26—9B 40
Kearton Dri. M30—5G 77
Keary Clo. M18—9D 80
Keats Av. M34—6A 94
Keats Av. M35—5G 81
Keats Av. WN3—3A 52
Keats Av. WN5—7D 50
Keats Av. WN6—6L 33
Keats Clo. M29—3K 55
Keats Ct. M7—9B 60
Keats Cres. M26—5E 40
Keats Fold. SK16—8H 83
Keats Rd. BL8—9F 8
Keats Rd. M30—6D 76
Keats Rd. OL1—8B 46
Keats St. WN7—9D 54
Keats Wlk. BL1—8E 22
Keats Way. WN2—7H 53
Keb La. OL8—8A 64
Keble Av. OL8—5L 63
Keble Gro. WN7—8C 54
Keble St. WN2—1F 52
Kedington Clo. M10—2J 79
Kedleston Av. M14—2L 91
Kedleston Grn. SK2—6K 105
Kedleston Wlk. M34—5M 93
Keele Clo. M10—2H 5 & 4J 79
Keele Clo. SK2—7H 105
Keeley Clo. M10—3C 80
Keepers Dri. OL12—9L 11
Keighley Av. M35—4G 81
Keighley Clo. BL8—8F 24
Keighley St. BL1—8C 22
Keilder M. BL1—2A 38
Keith Dri. SK3—6B 104
Keith Wlk. M10—4K 79
Kelboro Av. M34—8K 81
Kelbrook Ct. SK2—8L 105
Kelbrook Rd. M11—7B 80
Kelby Av. M23—6B 102
Kelday Wlk. M8—1J 79
(off Smeaton St.)
Keld Clo. BL8—5H 25
Keld Wlk. M18—1C 92
Kelfield Av. M23—3A 102
Kelham Wlk. M10—7C 62
Kellbank Rd. WN3—5L 51
Kellbrook Cres. M7—7B 60
(in two parts)
Kellet's Row. M28—3J 57
Kellet St. OL16—2H 29
Kellett St. BL1—4F 22
Kellett Wlk. M11—5B 80
Kelling Wlk. M15—6C 4 & 8D 78
Kelmarsh Clo. M11—8D 80
Kelmscott Lodge. M31—3B 88
(off Cornhill Rd.)
Kelsall Clo. SK3—7D 104
Kelsall Dri. M35—4F 80
Kelsall Dri. WA15—7J 101
Kelsall St. BL2—2J 39
Kelsall St. M12—9M 79
Kelsall St. M33—1G 101
Kelsall St. OL9—2K 63
Kelsall St. OL16—2F 28
Kelsall Way. SK9—7K 113
Kelsal Rd. SK8—8A 104
Kelsey Flats. OL10—8J 27
(off Fearn St.)
Kelsey Wlk. M9—3H 61
Kelso Clo. OL8—7M 63
Kelson Av. OL7—2A 82
Kelstern Av. M13—3L 91
Kelstern Sq. M13—3L 91
Kelverlow St. OL4—1C 64
Kelvin Av. M24—1H 61
Kelvin Av. M33—1H 101
Kelvin Clo. WN4—2K 69
Kelvindale Dri. WA15—6J 101
Kelvin Gro. M8—1G 79
Kelvin Gro. WN3—6L 51
(in two parts)
Kelvington Dri. M9—1K 79
Kelvin St. M4—3F 5 & 5G 79
Kelvin St. OL7—7M 81
Kelway Ter. WN1—8D 34
Kelwood Av. BL9—5D 26
Kemble Av. M23—4C 102
Kemble Clo. BL6—5B 20
Kemmel Av. M22—8E 102
Kemnay Wlk. M11—6C 80
Kempley Clo. M12—9M 79
Kempnough Hall Rd. M28 —9L 57
Kemp Rd. SK6—5J 107
Kempsey Ct. OL9—1H 63
Kempsey St. OL9—1H 63
Kempsey Wlk. M10—7D 62
Kempster St. M7—1C 4 & 3D 78
Kempston Gdns. BL1—8E 22
Kemp St. M24—9M 43
Kemp St. SK14—2E 94
Kempton Av. BL3—7A 40
Kempton Av. M33—2D 100
Kempton Clo. M35—5J 81
Kempton Clo. SK7—3A 116
Kempton Rd. M19—6A 92
Kempton Way. OL9—1J 63
Kemsing Wlk. M5—6A 78
Kenchester Av. M11—7D 80
Kendal Av. M31—2L 87
Kendal Av. M33—2J 101
Kendal Av. M34—5A 94
Kendal Av. OL7—3M 81
Kendal Av. OL12—9L 11
Kendal Av. SK14—1C 94
Kendal Clo. OL10—1L 43
Kendal Clo. WA15—8K 101
Kendal Dri. BL9—2K 41
Kendal Dri. OL2—2D 46
Kendal Dri. SK7—7C 114
Kendal Dri. SK8—9J 103
Kendal Dri. WA11—7B 68
Kendal Gdns. SK6—1B 106
Kendal Gro. M25—9M 41
Kendal Gro. M28—6M 57
Kendal Gro. WN4—3B 70
Kendal Gro. WN7—2D 72
Kendal Ho. WN2—9G 35
Kendall Rd. M8—5F 60
Kendal Rd. BL0—9F 8
Kendal Rd. BL1—1C 38
Kendal Rd. M6—2J 77
Kendal Rd. M28—9E 56
Kendal Rd. M32—3K 89
Kendal Rd. WN2—3L 53
(Hindley)
Kendal Rd. WN2—9G 35
(Ince)
Kendal Rd. W. BL0—9F 8
Kendal St. WN6—8B 34
Kendal Ter. SK16—6C 82
(off Astley St.)
Kendal Wlk. M24—8L 43
Kendon Gro. M34—3L 93
Kendon Wlk. M8—2E 78
Kendrew Rd. BL3—5A 38
Kendrew Wlk. M9—7L 61
Kendrick Pl. WN1—9E 34
Kenford Wlk. M8—1F 78
Kenhall Rd. WN7—3J 73
Kenilworth. OL11—4E 28
Kenilworth Av. M20—9F 90
Kenilworth Av. M25—2A 60
Kenilworth Av. M27—5H 59
Kenilworth Av. OL9—8E 44
Kenilworth Av. SK8—1A 114
Kenilworth Av. SK9—9K 113
Kenilworth Clo. M26—3F 40
Kenilworth Clo. OL4—3F 64
Kenilworth Clo. SK6—5F 106
Kenilworth Dri. SK7—4K 115
Kenilworth Dri. WN2—4M 53
Kenilworth Dri. WN7—9L 55
Kenilworth Gro. M34—7J 81
Kenilworth Rd. M31—5J 87
Kenilworth Rd. M33—1E 100
Kenilworth Rd. OL16—1J 45
Kenilworth Rd. SK3—6M 103
Kenilworth Rd. WA3—8L 71
Kenilworth Sq. BL1—9B 22
Kenion Rd. OL11—4B 28
Kenion St. OL16—3F 28
Kenley Lodge. SK7—5D 114
Kenley Wlk. M8—1J 79
(off Smedley Rd.)
Kenmay Av. BL3—3M 37
Kenmere Gro. M10—7B 62
Kenmor Av. BL8—1G 41
Kenmore Clo. M25—9B 42
Kenmore Dri. WA15—1G 111
Kenmore Gro. M30—8D 86
Kenmore Gro. WN4—3K 69
Kenmore Rd. M22—6C 102
Kenmore Rd. M25—9B 42
Kenmore Rd. M33—3C 100
Kenmore Way. M25—9B 42
Kennard Clo. M9—7M 61
Kennard Pl. WA14—7E 100
Kennedy Clo. WN6—1M 33
Kennedy Dri. BL3—6C 40
Kennedy Dri. BL9—7B 42
Kennedy Rd. M5—5J 77
Kennedy Rd. WA11—9J 69
Kennedy St. BL2—2J 39
Kennedy St. M2—4E 5 & 6F 78
Kennedy St. OL8—3L 63
Kennedy Way. M34—4K 93
Kennedy Way. SK4—3C 104
Kennerley Ct. SK2—8G 105
Kennerley Lodge. SK3—8F 104
Kennerley Rd. SK2—8F 104
Kennerley's La. SK9—4G 119
Kennet Clo. BL5—8E 36
Kennet Flats. OL10—8J 27
(off Meadow Clo.)
Kenneth Av. WN7—1D 72
Kenneth Gro. WN7—1D 72
Kenneth Sq. M7—1E 78
Kennett Rd. M23—1A 112
Kenninghall Rd. M22—1D 112
Kennington Av. M10—3B 80
Kennington Fold. BL3—6D 38
Kenside Wlk. M16—3F 90
Kensington Av. M14—2K 91
Kensington Av. M26—5D 40
Kensington Av. OL2—3J 45
Kensington Av. OL6—3E 82
Kensington Av. OL9—9E 44
Kensington Av. SK14—5E 94
Kensington Clo. BL8—1F 24
Kensington Clo. OL16—4A 30
Kensington Ct. M7—8C 60
Kensington Ct. M34—2H 93
Kensington Ct. SK9—5G 119
Kensington Ct. SK14—5E 94
Kensington Dri. BL6—7C 20
Kensington Dri. BL8—1G 41
Kensington Dri. M5—4K 77
Kensington Dri. WN7—9L 55
Kensington Gdns. SK14—5F 94
Kensington Gdns. WA15 —3F 110
Kensington Gro. M34—2H 93
Kensington Gro. SK15—6G 83
Kensington Gro. WA14—5E 100
Kensington Pl. BL1—2E 38
(off Kensington St.)
Kensington Rd. M21—4A 90
Kensington Rd. M35—8H 63
Kensington Rd. OL8—4K 63
Kensington Rd. SK3—6B 104
Kensington Rd. WN5—3K 51
Kensington St. BL1—2E 38
Kensington St. M14—3G 91
Kensington St. OL11—6E 28
Kensington St. SK14—5E 94
Kenslow Av. M8—6F 60
Kensworth Clo. BL1—9D 22
Kensworth Clo. M23—7K 101
Kensworth Dri. BL1—9D 22
Kent Av. M35—6E 80
Kent Av. OL9—2G 63
Kent Av. SK8—8C 104
Kent Av. WN2—6G 53
Kent Clo. M28—6H 57
Kent Clo. OL3—5C 48
Kent Ct. BL1—1E 38
Kent Dri. BL4—2B 58
Kent Dri. BL9—1M 41
Kentford Dri. M10—1H 5 & 3J 79
Kentford Gro. BL4—9J 39
Kentford Rd. BL1—9E 22
Kent Gro. M35—1E 80
Kentleigh Wlk. SK14—3L 95
Kentmere Av. OL12—8H 13
Kentmere Av. WA11—7C 68
Kentmere Ct. M9—4A 62
Kentmere Dri. M24—6L 43
Kentmere Dri. M29—9B 56
Kentmere Gro. BL4—1F 56
Kentmere Rd. BL2—9M 23
Kentmere Rd. WA15—7J 101
Kentmore Clo. SK4—3L 103
Kenton Av. M18—2C 92
Kenton Clo. BL1—9D 22
Kenton Clo. M34—8K 81
Kenton Rd. OL2—2A 46
Kenton St. OL8—3B 64
Kent Rd. M29—4J 55
(Atherton)
Kent Rd. M29—6M 55
(Tyldesley)
Kent Rd. M30—9C 86
Kent Rd. M31—3E 98
Kent Rd. M34—4G 93
Kent Rd. SK3—5B 104
Kent Rd. SK13—5K 97
Kent Rd. E. M14—3K 91
Kent Rd. W. M14—3J 91
Kentsford Dri. M26—4B 40
Kentstone Av. SK4—2K 103
Kent St. BL1—1E 38
Kent St. M2—4E 5 & 6F 78
Kent St. M7—1C 4 & 3D 78
Kent St. M27—6F 58
Kent St. OL8—4M 63
Kent St. OL11—4F 28
Kent St. WN1—1D 52
Kent St. WN7—3L 73
Kentucky St. OL4—2C 64
Kent Wlk. OL10—9G 27
Kenwick Dri. M10—6E 62
Kenwood Av. M19—8M 91
Kenwood Av. SK7—7D 114
Kenwood Av. SK8—7G 103
Kenwood Av. WA15—2F 110
Kenwood Av. WN7—2J 73
Kenwood Clo. M32—4L 89
Kenwood Clo. WN7—2J 73
Kenwood Ct. M32—5L 89
Kenwood La. M28—2M 75
Kenwood Rd. BL1—7B 22
Kenwood Rd. M32—5L 89
Kenwood Rd. OL1—8J 45
Kenwood Rd. SK5—4E 92
Kenworthy Av. OL6—2D 82
Kenworthy La. M22—3D 10
Kenworthy St. OL16—3J 29
Kenworthy St. SK15—6G 83
(in two parts)
Kenworthy Ter. OL16—3J 2
Kenwright St. M4—3F 5 & 5
Kenwyn St. M10—4L 79
Kenyon Av. M33—3L 101
Kenyon Av. OL8—5M 63
Kenyon Av. SK16—8E 82
Kenyon Clo. SK14—1F 94
Kenyon Fold. OL11—5L 27
Kenyon Gro. M28—4E 56
Kenyon La. M10—8A 62
Kenyon La. M24—9C 44
Kenyon La. M25—4C 60
Kenyon La. WA3—9E 72
(Kenyon)
Kenyon La. WA3—9L 71
(Lowton)
Kenyon Rd. BL2—4B 40
Kenyon Rd. WN1—7C 34
Kenyon Rd. WN6—8K 17
Kenyon's La. WA11—7M 6
Kenyon St. BL0—4J 9
Kenyon St. BL9—7A 26
Kenyon St. M18—9E 80
Kenyon St. M26—6H 41
Kenyon St. OL6—4A 82
Kenyon St. OL10—8J 27
Kenyon St. SK1—2F 104
Kenyon St. SK16—7B 82
Kenyon St. WN7—8D 54
Kenyon Ter. M28—5E 56
Kenyon Way. BL8—5F 24
Kenyon Way. M28—4E 56
Keppel Rd. M21—5B 90
Kepple St. OL6—4C 82
Kepwick Dri. M22—3E 112
Kerans Dri. BL5—8E 36
Kerenhappuch St. BL0—5
(off Buchanan St.)
Kerfield Wlk. M13—6G 5 & 8
Kerfoot Clo. M22—5E 102
Kerfoot St. WN7—3J 73
Kermishaw Nook. M29—1
Kermoor Av. BL1—4E 22
Kerne Gro. M23—4A 102
Kerrera Dri. M5—6K 77
Kerridge Dri. SK6—1M 105
Kerridge Wlk. M16—3F 90
(off Peachey Clo.)
Kerrier Clo. M30—5G 77
Kerr St. M9—5K 61
Kerry Gro. BL2—1H 39
Kerry Wlk. M23—1M 111
Kersal Av. M27—8J 59
Kersal Av. M28—4H 57
Kersal Bank. M7—8C 60
Kersal Bar. M7—7C 60
Kersal Clo. M25—7A 60
Kersal Crag. M7—7C 60
Kersal Dri. WA15—6J 101
Kersal Gdns. M7—7C 60
Kersal Hall Av. M7—8A 60
Kersal Rd. M25—7M 59
Kersal Vale Ct. M7—8A 6
Kersal Vale Rd. M7—7M 5
Kersal View. M6—3M 77
Kersal Way. M7—9B 60
Kersell Wlk. M10—1A 80
Kersh Av. M19—6B 92
Kershaw Av. BL3—5A 40
Kershaw Av. M25—6M 59
Kershaw Av. M33—3L 10
Kershaw Dri. OL9—5D 62
Kershaw Gro. M34—7H 8
Kershaw La. M34—7H 81
Kershaw Rd. M35—9F 62
Kershaws Pas. OL15—7L
Kershaw St. BL2—5J 23
Kershaw St. BL3—4D 38
Kershaw St. BL9—8A 26
Kershaw St. M29—7A 56
Kershaw St. M35—6F 80
Kershaw St. OL2—4K 45
(Royton)
Kershaw St. OL2—2B 46
(Shaw, in two parts)
Kershaw St. OL4—9C 46
Kershaw St. OL7—7M 81
Kershaw St. OL10—8H 27
Kershaw St. OL12—2F 28
Kershaw St. SK13—6J 97
Kershaw St. WN5—2H 51
Kershaw Wlk. M12—9K 7
Kershope Gro. M5—7A 7
Kersley St. M10—4M 79
Kersley St. OL4—2A 64
Kerwin Wlk. M11—7A 80
Kerwood Dri. OL2—6L 45
Kesteven Rd. M9—9K 61
Keston Av. M9—5A 62
Keston Av. M35—6E 80
Keston Cres. SK5—8H 93
Keston Rd. OL1—8C 46
Kestor St. BL2—1G 39
Kestrel Av. BL4—1F 56
Kestrel Av. M27—6H 59
Kestrel Av. M28—3G 57
Kestrel Av. M34—6J 81
Kestrel Av. OL4—3C 64
Kestrel Clo. M25—2A 60
Kestrel Clo. SK6—1G 117
Kestrel Dri. BL9—6B 26
Kestrel Dri. M30—3G 87
Kestrel Dri. WN4—1C 70
Kestrel M. OL11—3M 27
Kestrel Rd. M17—7F 76
Kestrel St. BL1—1G 39
Kestrel Wlk. M12—9A 8
Keswick Av. M31—5L 8
Keswick Av. M34—2K 9
Keswick Av. OL7—2M 8
Keswick Av. OL8—4A 64
Keswick Av. OL9—1G 63
Keswick Av. SK8—1H 1

140 Greater Manchester

Lemon St. M29—8M 55
Lena St. BL1—8F 22
Lena St. M1—4G 5 & 6H 79
Lenchford Clo. M1—6G 5 & 8H 79
Len Cox Wlk. M4—3G 5 & 5H 79
Lenfield Dri. WA11—9F 68
Leng Rd. M10—2D 80
Lenham Av. M30—5B 76
Lenham Clo. SK5—8H 93
Lenham Gdns. BL2—3L 39
Lenham Towers. SK5—8H 93
Lenham Wlk. M22—4D 112
Lennie Rd. M31—8D 76
Lennox Gdns. BL3—4M 37
Lennox St. M34—9L 81
Lennox St. OL6—4C 82
Lennox Wlk. OL10—9F 26
Lenora St. BL3—5B 38
Lenten Gro. OL10—2L 43
Lenthall Wlk. M8—9F 60
(off Lanbury Dri.)
Lentmead Dri. M10—7A 62
Lenton Gdns. M22—8E 102
Lentworth Wlk. M15—9E 78
Leominster Dri. M22—1E 112
Leominster Rd. M24—2B 62
Leonard Ct. WN7—3B 72
Leonardin Clo. OL2—1M 45
Leonard Pl. WN7—3B 72
(off Plank La.)
Leonard St. BL3—6E 38
Leonard St. OL11—9C 28
Leopold St. WN5—3H 51
Leopold Av. M20—8G 91
Leopold St. OL11—3D 28
Lepp Cres. BL8—4J 25
Lepton Wlk. M9—4L 61
Leroy Dri. M9—6L 61
Lerryn Dri. SK7—3D 114
Lesley Rd. M32—5G 89
Leslie Av. BL9—6M 41
Leslie Av. OL9—5H 63
Leslie Gro. WA15—7G 101
Leslie Hough Way. M6—1A 4 & 3B 78
Leslie St. BL2—9H 23
Leslie St. M14—3H 91
Lessingham Av. WN1—7B 34
Lester Rd. M28—4D 56
Lester St. M32—4K 89
Letchworth Av. OL11—5G 29
Letchworth St. M14—3H 91
Letcombe Ct. M7—9B 60
Letham St. OL8—6M 63
Letitia St. BL6—7A 20
Levedale Rd. M9—4L 61
Leven Clo. BL4—3B 58
Levenhurst Rd. M8—9F 60
Levens Clo. SK8—1H 113
Levens Dri. BL2—9L 23
Levenshulme Rd. M18—2D 92
Levens Pl. WN2—9G 35
Levens Pl. WN5—1J 51
Levens Rd. SK7—2J 115
Levens St. M6—2B 78
Levens St. M10—9A 62
Levens Wlk. OL9—3G 63
Levens Wlk. WN5—1J 51
Leven Wlk. M23—7A 102
Leven Wlk. M25—9C 42
Lever Av. M27—6H 59
Lever Bri. Pl. BL3—4J 39
Lever Dri. BL3—4E 38
Lever Edge La. BL3—7C 38
Leverett Clo. WA14—8A 100
Lever Gdns. BL3—5A 40
Lever Gro. BL2—4G 39
Lever Hall Rd. BL2—2K 39
Leverhulme Av. BL3—6G 39
Lever Pk. Av. BL6—5A 20
Lever Pl. M15—1E 90
Lever St. BL2—4G 39
Lever St. BL3—5E 38
(Bolton)
Lever St. BL3—5A 40
(Little Lever)
Lever St. BL5—6E 36
Lever St. BL9—7M 25
Lever St. M1—4F 5 & 6G 79
Lever St. M24—8A 44
Lever St. M26—4F 40
Lever St. M29—7M 55
Lever St. SK7—2K 115
Lever St. WN1—9C 34
Lever Wlk. M24—1M 61
Levington Dri. OL8—8A 64
Levi St. BL1—9M 21
Lewes Av. M34—5M 93
Lewes Wlk. OL9—2H 63
Lewis Av. M9—7L 61
Lewis Av. M31—1D 88
Lewis Clo. PR7—4E 18
Lewis Clo. WN3—3A 52
Lewis Dri. OL10—9F 26
Lewisham Av. M10—3B 80
Lewisham Clo. OL2—3J 45
Lewis Rd. M35—5E 80
Lewis Rd. SK5—5F 92
Lewis St. M10—4K 79
Lewis St. M30—6D 76
Lewis St. OL2—3B 46
Lewis St. OL10—7L 27
Lewis St. SK14—3E 94
Lewtas St. M30—6E 76
Lexton Av. M8—6H 61
Leybourne Av. M19—4B 92
Leybourne M. M7—1E 78
Leybourne St. BL1—8E 22
Leybrook Rd. M22—1C 112
Leyburn Av. M31—5A 88
Leyburn Av. M32—3J 89
Leyburn Av. OL2—5K 45
Leyburn Clo. M25—9L 41
Leyburne Rd. SK2—7K 105
Leyburn Gro. BL4—8K 39
Leyburn Gro. SK6—3C 106
Leyburn Rd. M10—6C 62
Leycett Dri. M23—4A 102
Ley Cres. M29—1B 74
Leyden Wlk. M23—9A 102
Ley Dri. OL10—2L 43
Leyfield Av. SK6—3C 106
Leyfield Ct. SK6—3C 106
Leyfield Rd. OL16—4K 29
Ley Hey Av. SK6—6F 106
Ley Hey Rd. SK6—6F 106
Leyland Av. M20—2K 103
Leyland Av. M30—2H 87
Leyland Av. SK8—7H 103
Leyland Av. WN2—5K 53
Leyland Grn. Rd. WN4—2H 69
Leyland Gro. WA11—9H 69
Leyland Mill La. WN1—6C 34
Leylands La. SK14—8M 95
Leyland St. BL9—5M 41
Leyland St. WN2—4J 53
(Hindley)
Leyland St. WN2—7G 53
(Platt Bridge)
Leyland St. WN6—9B 34
Ley La. SK6—4J 107
Ley Rd. M29—9M 55
(in two parts)
Leys Rd. WA14—5E 100
Leyton Av. M10—9B 62
Leyton Clo. BL4—8G 39
Leyton Dri. BL9—4M 41
Leyton St. OL12—9F 12
Library La. OL9—9K 45
Library St. BL5—9F 36
Library St. WN1—9C 34
Library Wlk. M2—4E 5 & 6F 78
Libra St. BL1—8D 22
Lichens Cres. OL8—5A 64
Lichfield Av. BL2—8H 23
Lichfield Av. M29—9C 56
Lichfield Av. OL6—8D 64
Lichfield Av. SK5—7E 92
Lichfield Av. WA3—7K 71
Lichfield Av. WA15—1J 111
Lichfield Clo. BL4—8G 39
Lichfield Clo. M26—4D 40
Lichfield Dri. BL8—6K 25
Lichfield Dri. M8—9H 61
Lichfield Dri. M25—6C 60
Lichfield Dri. M27—1F 76
Lichfield Dri. OL9—8G 45
Lichfield Gro. WN4—5C 70
Lichfield Rd. M26—4D 40
Lichfield Rd. M30—3F 76
Lichfield Rd. M31—2D 88
Lichfield St. M6—2A 78
Lichfield St. WN5—3J 51
Lichfield Ter. OL16—6J 29
Lichfield Wlk. SK6—4A 106
Lidbrook Wlk. M12—9L 79
Liddington Hall Dri. BL0—7H 9
Lidgate Clo. WN3—5K 51
Lidgate Gro. BL4—9J 39
Lidgate Gro. M20—2G 103
Lidgett Clo. M28—3J 57
Lidiard St. M8—7G 61
Liffey Av. M22—1E 112
Lifton Av. M10—3L 79
Light Alders La. SK12—5G 117
Lightbirches La. OL5—6H 65
Lightborne Rd. M33—1D 100
Lightbounds Rd. BL1—7M 21
Lightbourne Av. M27—9F 58
Lightbowne Rd. M10—8H 101
Lightburn Av. OL15—7L 13
Lightburne Av. BL1—4B 38
Lightburne Av. WN7—4E 72
Lightfoot Wlk. M11—6M 79
Lighthorne Av. SK3—6M 103
Lighthorne Gro. SK3—6M 103
Lighthorne Rd. SK3—6M 103
Lighthouse. OL15—2C 14
Light Oaks Rd. M6—3H 77
Light Oaks Rd. WA3—9J 73
Lightowlers La. OL15—4D 14
Lightshaw La. WN7—3M 77
Lightwood. M28—8H 57
Lightwood Clo. BL4—8L 39
Lignum Av. OL9—9H 45
Lilac Av. BL9—2K 41
Lilac Av. M27—8G 59
Lilac Av. OL16—7A 30
Lilac Av. WN4—2K 69
Lilac Av. WN6—6A 34
Lilac Av. WN7—9E 54
Lilac Ct. M6—5A 78
Lilac Gro. M10—7A 62
Lilac Gro. M25—2A 60
Lilac Gro. OL9—9H 45
Lilac Gro. WN5—3D 68
Lilac La. OL8—6K 63
Lilac Rd. OL11—8F 28
Lilac Rd. WA3—6G 71
Lilac Rd. WA15—1G 111
Lilac St. SK2—7F 104
Lilac View Clo. OL2—3C 46
Lilac Wlk. M31—2E 98
Lila St. M9—9M 61
Lilburn Clo. BL0—7J 9
Liley St. OL16—3G 29
Lilford Clo. M12—9A 80
Lilford St. M29—6H 55
Lilford St. WN7—3E 72
Lilian Dri. WN2—6A 34
Lilian St. M16—2C 90
Lillian Gro. SK5—6F 92
Lilly St. BL1—1D 38
Lilly St. SK14—6F 94
Lilmore Av. M10—1C 80
Lilstock Wlk. M9—5L 61
Lily Av. BL4—8H 39
Lily Clo. SK3—8D 104
Lily Hill St. M25—7L 41
Lily La. M9—9M 61
Lily La. OL6—1B 82
Lily La. WN2—9E 52
(Bamfurlong)
Lily La. WN2—8G 53
(Platt Bridge)
Lily Lanes. OL6—8E 64
Lily Pl. WN4—5C 70
Lily St. M24—9C 44
Lily St. M30—6B 76
Lily St. OL1—8L 45
Lily St. OL16—4M 29
Lily St. WN4—2E 70
Lily Thomas Ct. M11—8D 80
Lima St. BL9—8C 26
Lime Av. M25—1M 59
Lime Av. M27—1C 76
Lime Av. M31—4B 88
Lime Av. WN7—8E 54
Lime Bank St. M12—7K 79
Limebrook Clo. M11—8E 80
Lime Clo. SK16—9D 82
Lime Clo. WA3—3B 98
Lime Clo. WN2—9J 53
Lime Ct. M6—4A 78
Lime Cres. M16—2B 90
Lime Ditch Rd. M35—7G 63
Limefield. M24—9L 43
Limefield. OL16—3L 29
Limefield. WN1—9D 34
Limefield Av. BL4—8K 39
Limefield Brow. BL9—3M 25
Limefield Clo. BL1—6B 22
Limefield Ct. M7—7D 60
Limefield Rd. BL1—6B 22
Limefield Rd. BL9—3M 25
Limefield Rd. M7—7D 60
Limefield Rd. M26—6D 40
Limefield Ter. M19—5A 92
Lime Gdns. M24—9L 43
Lime Gdns. SK16—7B 82
Lime Ga. OL8—6J 63
Lime Grn. OL8—7K 63
Lime Grn. Rd. OL8—8J 63
Lime Gro. BL0—4K 9
Lime Gro. BL9—3M 25
Lime Gro. M15—1H 91
Lime Gro. M16—2B 90
Lime Gro. M25—2A 60
Lime Gro. M28—7K 57
Lime Gro. M34—2M 93
Lime Gro. OL2—3K 45
Lime Gro. OL6—2C 82
Lime Gro. OL10—7J 27
Lime Gro. OL15—5M 13
Lime Gro. SK8—7K 103
Lime Gro. SK15—7E 82
Lime Gro. WA3—9K 71
Lime Gro. WA15—6H 101
Lime Gro. WN2—5M 53
Limehurst Av. OL7—1A 82
Limehurst Rd. OL7—1A 82
Limekiln La. M12—7K 79
Lime Kiln La. SK6—8G 107
Lime La. OL8 & M35—7J 63
(in two parts)
Lime Pl. SK16—7B 82
Lime Rd. M32—5K 89
Limerston Dri. M10—2M 79
Limes Av. WN6—3B 34
Limeside Rd. OL8—6J 63
Limesdale Av. M8—8G 61
Limes, The. OL5—7H 65
(Fox Platt)
Limes, The. OL5—7L 65
(Mossley)
Limes, The. WN6—3A 34
Limes, The. WN7—9G 55
Lime St. BL4—9L 39
Lime St. BL9—4M 25
Lime St. M10—4K 79
Lime St. M29—7M 55
Lime St. M30—6D 76
Lime St. OL1—8J 45
Lime St. OL11—6C 28
Lime St. SK16—1L 105
Lime St. SK16—7B 82
(in two parts)
Lime St. WN1—9D 34
Lime Tree Clo. M31—5E 88
Lime Tree Gro. M35—9H 63
Limetree La. WA16—6D 108
Limetrees Rd. M24—9M 43
Limetree Wlk. M11—6M 79
Lime Vale Rd. WN5—4C 68
Lime Wlk. M31—2D 98
Lime Wlk. SK9—2K 119
Limley Gro. M21—7C 90
Linacre Av. BL3—7E 38
Linacre Way. SK13—7M 97
Linbeck Gro. WA3—6L 71
Linburne St. WN2—7K 53
Linby St. M15—6D 4 & 8E 78
Lincoln Av. BL3—7A 40
Lincoln Av. M19—5B 92
Lincoln Av. M30—1C 98
Lincoln Av. M32—3F 88
Lincoln Av. M34—5M 93
Lincoln Av. M35—4G 81
Lincoln Av. SK8—4H 113
Lincoln Av. WA3—6K 71
Lincoln Clo. M29—6A 56
Lincoln Clo. OL6—8D 64
Lincoln Clo. OL11—4G 29
Lincoln Clo. WN7—7C 72
Lincoln Ct. M7—7E 60
Lincoln Ct. M10—3B 80
Lincoln Cres. WA11—9B 68
Lincoln Dri. BL9—1M 41
Lincoln Dri. M25—6C 60
Lincoln Dri. WA15—8H 101
Lincoln Dri. WN2—4J 35
Lincoln Dri. WN4—5C 70
Lincoln Grn. SK5—8H 93
Lincoln Gro. BL2—6M 23
Lincoln Gro. M13—1J 91
Lincoln Gro. M29—5H 55
Lincoln Gro. M33—1L 101
Lincoln Minshull Clo. M23—3M 101
Lincoln Pl. WN5—8J 33
Lincoln Rise. SK6—4A 106
Lincoln Rd. BL1—1B 38
Lincoln Rd. M24—3C 62
Lincoln Rd. M27—9E 58
Lincoln Rd. M35—1G 81
Lincoln Rd. SK9—2L 119
Lincoln Rd. WN2—3L 53
Lincoln St. BL1—9F 22
Lincoln St. M13—2M 91
Lincoln St. M30—6C 76
Lincoln St. OL9—3H 63
Lincoln St. OL11—4G 29
Lincoln Towers. SK1—5F 104
Lincoln Wlk. OL10—8G 27
Lincoln Way. SK13—6M 97
Lincombe Rd. M22—4C 112
Lincroft Rd. WN2—5A 54
Lincroft St. M14—2G 91
Linda Dri. SK7—2K 115
Lindale. SK14—1C 94
Lindale Av. BL1—1M 37
Lindale Av. BL9—6A 42
Lindale Av. M10—6D 62
Lindale Av. M31—3M 87
Lindale Av. OL2—1J 45
Lindale Av. OL9—2G 63
Lindale Clo. M28—9E 56
Lindale Dri. M24—6L 43
Lindale Rise. OL2—2D 46
Lindale Rd. M28—9E 56
Lindbury Av. SK2—6J 105
Linden Av. BL0—5K 9
Linden Av. BL3—4A 40
Linden Av. M6—1L 77
Linden Av. M29—6H 55
Linden Av. M33—1F 100
Linden Av. M34—8K 81
Linden Av. OL4—9D 46
Linden Av. WA15—8E 100
Linden Av. WN4—1M 69
Linden Av. WN5—2E 50
Linden Clo. BL0—1K 9
Linden Clo. WN3—9A 98
Linden Croft. OL8—4J 63
Linden Dri. M5—7A 78
Linden Dri. E. M5—5A 4 & 7B 78
Linden Gro. M5—7A 78
Linden Gro. M14—6K 91
Linden Gro. M30—9D 86
Linden Gro. SK2—9H 105
Linden Gro. SK7—8D 114
Linden Gro. WN5—4C 68
(Billinge)
Linden Gro. WN5—2E 50
(Orrell, in two parts)
Linden Gro. WN7—9E 54
Linden Lea. M33—3H 101
Linden M. M28—1F 74
Linden Pk. M19—6M 91
Linden Rd. M20—1G 103
Linden Rd. M28—1F 74
Linden Rd. M34—3A 94
Linden Rd. SK8—1A 114
Linden Rd. SK15—8K 83
Linden Rd. WN2—1L 53
Linden St. M27—9D 58
Linden St. WN5—3J 51
Linden Wlk. BL2—5H 23
Linden Wlk. WN5—2E 50
Linden Way. SK6—5G 117
Lindenwood. OL9—9E 44
Lindeth Av. M18—2D 92
Lindfield Dri. BL1—8E 22
Lindfield Est. N. SK9—5G 119
Lindfield Est. S. SK9—5G 119
Lindfield Rd. SK5—5F 92
Lindinis Av. M5—3A 4 & 5A 78
Lindisfarne. OL12—2E 28
(off Spotland Rd.)
Lindisfarne Av. WA3—7C 72
Lindisfarne Clo. M33—4H 101
Lindisfarne Dri. SK12—8K 115
Lindisfarne Pl. BL3—8J 23
Lindisfarne Rd. OL7—2L 81
Lindley Av. WN5—3C 50
Lindley St. BL3—6B 40
Lindley St. BL4—2B 58
Lindley Wood Rd. M14—6L 91
Lindon Av. M34—4K 93
Lindon Clo. M34—3A 94
Lindon Way. M35—7E 80
Lindop Rd. WA15—3F 110
Lindow Clo. BL8—8G 25
Lindow Ct. SK9—3E 118
Lindow Fold Dri. SK9—7D 118
Lindow La. SK9—4E 118
Lindow Pde. SK9—5F 118
Lindow Rd. M16—3C 90
Lindow St. M33—2M 101
Lindow St. WN7—1D 72
Lindrick Av. M25—2K 59
Lindrick Clo. M10—9C 62
Lindrick Ter. BL3—4D 38
Lindsay Av. M19—5M 91
Lindsay Av. M27—9E 58
Lindsay Av. SK8—3B 114
Lindsay Clo. OL4—7D 46
Lindsay Rd. M19—6M 91
Lindsay St. BL6—9D 20
Lindsay St. SK15—5H 83
Lindsell Rd. WA14—5C 100
Lindsey Ter. WN2—4H 35
Lindsgate Dri. WA15—6H 101
Lindside Wlk. M9—5L 61
Lind St. M10—5L 79
Lindum Av. M16—2C 90
Lindum Ct. OL10—8L 27
Lindum St. M14—3H 91
Lindwall Clo. M23—3B 102
Lindy Av. M27—5F 58
Linear Walkway. M30—3E 76
Linehan Clo. SK4—3K 103
Lineholme. OL2—7J 45
Lines Rd. M30—6F 86
Lines Rd. M35—6H 81
Linfield Clo. BL2—6K 23
Linfield St. M11—6B 80
Linford Av. M10—6C 62
Linford Gro. WA11—9C 68
Lingard Clo. M34—7J 81
Lingard La. SK6—9K 93
Lingard Rd. M22—4D 102
Lingards Dri. M29—3A 74
Lingards La. M29—3A 74
Lingard St. SK5—6F 92
Lingard St. WN7—3H 73
Lingard Ter. M34—7J 81
Lingbeck Cres. M15—1E 90
Lingcrest Clo. M19—7C 92
Lingdale Rd. SK8—2M 113
Lingdale Wlk. M10—9A 62
Lingfield Av. M33—3B 100
Lingfield Av. SK7—2M 115
Lingfield Clo. BL4—1J 57
Lingfield Clo. BL8—3J 25
Lingfield Cres. WN6—5C 33
Lingfield Rd. M11—5C 80
Lingfield Wlk. OL9—1J 63
Lingholme Dri. M24—7J 43
Lingmell Av. WA11—6B 68
Lingmell Clo. BL1—1M 37
Lingmell Clo. M24—7K 43
(in two parts)
Lingmell Clo. M31—2A 88
Lingmoor Clo. M24—7J 43
Lingmoor Clo. WN3—7A 52
Lingmoor Dri. M29—9B 56
Lingmoor Rd. BL1—9M 21
Lingmoor Wlk. M15—9F 78
Lings Wlk. M22—3E 112
Linhope Clo. SK4—2L 103
Link Av. M31—5G 89
Link Av. WA11—9E 68
Linkfield Dri. M28—1F 74
Link La. OL8—6L 63
Link Rd. M33—4D 100
Link Rd. OL4—1F 64
Links Av. M35—2F 80
Links Cres. M25—6E 60
Links Dri. BL6—2H 37
Linksfield. M34—1M 93
Linkside Av. OL2—4K 45
Links Pl. OL6—1E 82
Links Rise. M31—2A 88
Links Rd. BL2—6A 24
Links Rd. BL3—6M 37
Links Rd. BL6—2H 37
Links Rd. OL10—1K 43
Links Rd. SK6—9F 106
(Marple)
Links Rd. SK6—2D 106
(Romiley)
Links Rd. SK9—8E 118
Links, The. M10—9C 62
Links View. M25—7A 60
Links View. OL11—4B 28
Links View Ct. M25—1K 59
Linksway. M25—6D 60
Linksway. M27—1G 77
Linkway. OL9—9J 45
Linksway. SK8—9G 103
Linksway Clo. SK4—9A 92
Linksway Dri. BL9—6A 42
Link, The. OL2—1M 45
Link, The. SK5—8J 93
Link, The. SK9—9K 113
Link Wlk. M31—3D 98
Linkway. WN4—2E 70
Linley Clo. WN6—5J 33
Linley Dri. OL4—4D 64
Linley Rd. M33—9H 89
Linley Rd. SK8—4B 114
Linley St. M26—4L 41
Linnell Dri. OL11—2L 27
Linnet Clo. M34—6J 81
Linnet Clo. SK2—8M 105
Linnet Dri. BL9—6B 26
Linnet Dri. M30—3G 87
Linnet Hall. BL8—9E 24
Linnet Hill. OL11—4C 28
Linnett Clo. M12—2M 91
Linney Gro. BL0—9G 9
Linney La. OL2—2C 46
Linney Rd. SK7—2D 114
Linney Sq. WN1—9E 34
Linn St. M8—7G 61
Linnyshaw Ind. Est. M28—5M 57
Linnyshaw La. M28—4L 57
Linslade Gdns. BL3—4E 38
Linslade Wlk. M9—9K 61
(off Foleshill Av.)
Linsley St. M3—3D 4 & 5E 78
Linstead Dri. M8—1F 78
Linstock Way. M29—5H 55
Linthorpe Wlk. BL3—5B 38
Linton Av. BL9—5M 25
Linton Av. M34—3G 93
Linton Av. WA3—5F 70
Linton Clo. M4—7K 79
Linton Rd. M33—9G 89
Linton Wlk. M7—8M 59
Linwood Clo. M10—4K 53
Linwood Gro. M12—4A 92
Lion Brow. M9—6K 61
Lion Fold La. M9—5K 61
Lion La. BL6—8J 19
Lions Dri. M27—8F 58
Lion St. M9—6K 61
Liptrot St. WN5—1M 51
Lisbon St. OL12—2C 28
Lisburn Av. M21—5C 90
Lisburn Av. M33—2G 101
Lisburne Av. SK2—7K 105
Lisburne Clo. SK2—7K 105
Lisburne Ct. SK2—7K 105
Lisburne La. SK2—8J 105
Lisburn Rd. M10—8A 62
Liscard Av. M14—5H 91
Liscard St. M29—5H 55
Lisetta Av. OL4—3B 64
Liskeard Av. OL2—6M 45
Liskeard Clo. OL16—1J 29
Liskeard Dri. SK7—5F 114
Liskeard Rd. WA15—9J 101
Lisle St. OL12—2G 28
Lismore Av. BL3—4M 37
Lismore Av. SK3—6B 104
Lismore Rd. SK16—8D 82
Lismore Wlk. M22—4E 112
Lismore Way. M31—1E 88
Lissadel St. M6—1A 4 & 3A 78
Lisson Gro. WA15—2E 110
Lister Rd. M24—2H 61
Lister St. BL3—6B 38
Liston St. SK16—7F 82
Litcham Clo. M1—6G 5 & 8H 79
Litchfield Clo. OL3—8J 31
Litchfield Gro. M28—9A 58
Litherland Cres. WA11—8C 68
Litherland Rd. BL3—7E 38
Litherland Rd. M33—2L 101
Lit. Ancoats St. M1—3G 5 & 5H 79
Lit. Bank St. OL4—2B 64
Littlebourne Wlk. BL1—4G 23
Lit. Bridge St. M3—2E 5 & 4F 78
Lit. Brook Clo. SK8—9C 104
Littlebrook Clo. SK14—2G 97
Lit. Brook Rd. M33—4C 100
Lit. Brow. BL7—3G 23
Lit. Church St. WN5—2H 51
Lit. Clegg Rd. OL15—9L 13
Littledale St. OL12—2E 28
(in two parts)
Lit. David St. M1—5F 5 & 7G 79
Lit. Ees La. M33—8F 88
Lit. Egerton St. SK1—3E 104
Lit. Factory St. M29—7M 55
Littlefields. SK14—2A 96
Lit. Flatt. OL12—1C 28
Little Ga. BL5—3E 54
Littlegreen Ho. M6—4M 77
Littleham Wlk. M18—1C 92
Lit. Harwood Lee. BL2—7K 23
Littlehaven Clo. M12—1L 91
Lit. Hey St. OL2—5A 46
Littlehills Clo. M24—8L 43
Lit. Holme St. M4—6K 79
Lit. Holme Wlk. BL3—5F 38
Lit. John St. M3—4D 4 & 6E 78
Little La. M9—4H 61
Little La. WN5 & WN3—3L 51
Lit. Lever St. M1—4G 5 & 6H 79
Lit. London. WN1—8C 34
Lit. Meadow. BL7—3F 22
Lit. Meadow Rd. WA14—3B 110
Lit. Moor Clough. BL7—9E 6
Littlemoor Cotts. SK1—5H 105
Littlemoor La. OL4—9C 46
Littlemoor Rd. SK14—4A 96
Little Moss La. M27—5F 58
Littlemoss Rd. M35—4J 81
Lit. Oak Clo. OL4—2E 64
Lit. Pasture. WN7—9D 54
Lit. Peter St. M15—6D 4 & 8E 78
Lit. Pitt St. M1—4G 5 & 6H 79
Lit. Quay St. M3—6E 78
Littler Av. M21—9C 90
Littler Rd. WA11—9F 68
Lit. Scotland. BL6—8H 19
Lit. Stones Rd. BL7—9E 6
Little St. OL16—9J 13
Little St. SK2—5H 105
Littleton Gro. WN6—8L 17
Littleton Rd. M7 & M6—8M 59
Littletown. OL8—4J 63
Lit. Underbank. SK1—4F 104
Lit. Western St. M14—2H 91
Littlewood Av. BL9—5M 25
Littlewood Rd. M22—9C 102
Littlewood St. M6—5L 77
Litton Bank. SK13—5E 96
(off Litton M.)
Littondale Clo. OL2—4L 45
Litton Fold. SK13—5E 96
(off Riber Bank)
Litton Gdns. SK13—5E 96
Litton M. SK13—5E 96
Liverpool Clo. SK5—7E 92
Liverpool Rd. M3—5C 4 & 7D 78
Liverpool Rd. M30—7E 76
Liverpool Rd. WA3 & M30—2C 98
Liverpool Rd. WA11—8G 69
Liverpool Rd. WN2—6J 53
Liverpool Rd. WN4—5L 69
Liverpool St. M5 & M6—4A 4 & 5K 77
Liverpool St. SK5—7E 92
(in two parts)
Liverpool St. WN2—7H 35
Liverstudd Av. SK5—6F 92
Liverton Ct. M9—3H 61
Liverton Dri. M9—3H 61
Livesey St. M4—2H 5 & 4J 79
Livesey St. M19—6B 92
Livesey St. OL1—9C 46
Livingstone Av. OL5—7H 65
Livingstone St. OL4—3E 64
(Lees)
Livingstone St. OL4—2G 65
(Springhead)
Livingstone St. WN4—2A 70
Livsey Ct. BL1—9F 22
Livsey La. OL10—8G 27
Livsey St. OL16—3G 29
Lizard St. M1—4G 5 & 6H 79
Liza St. WN7—8E 54
Lizmar Ter. M9—8M 61
Llanberis Rd. SK8—3L 113
Llanfair Rd. SK3—5C 104
Lloyd Av. SK8—7G 103
Lloyd Rd. M19—7B 92
Lloyd's Ct. WA14—9C 100
Lloyd's Gdns. WA14—1D 110
Lloyd Sq. WA14—9D 100
Lloyd St. M2—4E 5 & 6F 78
Lloyd St. OL10—9K 27
Lloyd St. OL11—6D 28
Lloyd St. OL12—2C 12
Lloyd St. SK4—2D 104
Lloyd St. WA11—9F 68
Lloyd St. WA14 & WA15—9D 100
Lloyd St. N. M15—2G 91
Lloyd St. S. M14—5G 91
Lobden Cres. OL12—4C 12
Lobelia Av. BL4—8G 39
Lobelia Wlk. M31—3E 98
Lobley Clo. OL12—9H 13
Lochawe Clo. OL10—9G 27
Lochinver Gro. OL10—9G 27
Lochmaddy Clo. SK7—3M 115
Loch St. WN5—2H 51
Lock Clo. OL10—1L 43
Lockerbie Pl. WN3—5L 51
Locker La. WN4—2F 70
Lockett Gdns. M3—3C 4 & 5D 78
Lockett Rd. WN4—1B 70
Lockett St. M6—2A 78
Lockett St. M8—1D 4 & 3E 78
Lockhart Clo. M12—1A 92
Lockhart St. OL16—5H 29
Lockingate St. OL6—1B 82
Locking Ga. Rise. OL4—8E 46
Lock La. BL6 & BL5—5J 37
Lock La. M31—2D 98
Lock Rd. WA14—7C 100
Lockside. SK6—7G 107
Locksley Clo. SK4—3M 103
Lockstock Ct. SK9—8K 113
Lockton Clo. M1—6G 5 & 8H 79
Lockton Clo. SK5—8F 92
Lockton Ct. M1—6G 5 & 8H 79
Lockwood St. M12—3B 92
Loddon Wlk. M9—8L 61
Lodge Av. M31—3B 88
Lodge Bank. SK14—9G 85
Lodge Bank Rd. OL15—8M 13
Lodge Brow. M26—7H 41
Lodge Brow. SK10—9M 121
Lodge Clo. SK16—8E 82
Lodge Ct. M22—8E 102
Lodge Ct. SK14—2A 96
Lodge Dri. M29—3G 57
Lodge Farm Clo. SK7—2E 114
Lodge Grn. SK16—8E 82
Lodge Gro. M29—7L 55
Lodge La. M29—7K 55
Lodge La. OL3—4L 47
(in two parts)
Lodge La. SK14—2D 94
Lodge La. SK16—7D 82
Lodge La. WA12—6B 70
Lodge La. WN7—2L 73
Lodge Mill La. BL0—2A 10
Lodgepole Clo. M30—7M 75
Lodge Rd. M26—7H 41
Lodge Rd. M29—7L 55
Lodge Rd. WN5—4E 50
Lodges, The. M28—8A 58
Lodge St. BL0—5J 9
Lodge St. BL9—7A 26
Lodge St. M10—2L 79
Lodge St. M24—8A 44
Lodge St. OL7—6M 81
Lodge St. OL12—5J 13
Lodge St. OL15—6E 14
Lodge St. SK14—1E 94
Lodge, The. SK14—9G 85
Loeminster Pl. WN2—1F 52
Loen Cres. BL1—7C 22
Logan St. BL1—5E 22
Logendale Rd. WN6—1K 33
Logwood Av. BL8—7K 25
Logwood Av. WN5—1K 51
Logwood Ho. WN5—9L 33
Logwood Pl. WN5—9L 33
Loisine Clo. OL11—7B 28
Lois St. OL9—7G 63
Lomas Clo. M19—2L 103
Lomas St. M24—8B 44
Lomas St. M30—7G 63
Lomas St. SK3—6E 104
Lomax St. BL1—8E 22
Lomax St. BL4—7J 39
Lomax St. BL8—1F 24
Lomax St. BL9—7A 26
Lomax St. M1—4H 5 & 6J 79
Lomax St. M26—7G 41
Lomax St. OL12—1F 28
Lomax St. OL15—4A 14
Lomax St. WN2—6G 53
Lombard Gro. SK6—1M 105
Lombard Gro. M14—6J 91
Lombard St. M29—5H 55
Lombard St. OL1—1L 63
Lombard St. OL12—2D 28
Lombardy Ct. M6—4A 78
Lomond Av. M32—3K 89
Lomond Av. WA15—1G 111
Lomond Clo. SK2—1G 115
Lomond Rd. M22—5H 103
Lomond Pl. BL3—3L 37
Lomond Rd. M22 & SK8—2F 112
Lomond Ter. OL16—6J 29
London Clo. WN5—9K 33
London Fields. WN5—2E 68
London Pl. SK1—4F 104
London Rd. M1—4G 5 & 6H 79
London Rd. OL1—8B 46
London Rd. SK7—1K 115
London Rd. SK9—8L 119
London Rd. SK10 & SK12—9H 121
London Rd. N. SK12—8L 115
London Rd. S. SK12—1K 121
London Sq. SK1—4F 104
London St. BL3—5E 38
London St. M6—1A 4 & 3B 78
London St. M25—1M 59
Longacres Dri. OL12—2D 12
Longacres La. OL12—1D 12
Longacres Rd. WA15—5J 111
Longacre St. M1—4H 5 & 6J 79
Longbow Ct. M7—2D 78
Longbridge Rd. M17—9G 77
Longbrook. WN6—2H 33
Longbutt La. WA13—1A 108
Long Causeway. BL4—1K 57
Long Causeway. M29—9G 55
Longcliff Wlk. BL1—9F 22
Longclough Dri. SK13—6G 97
Longcrag Wlk. M15—1G 91
Longcroft. M29—3L 73
Longcroft Dri. WA14—9B 100
Longcroft Gro. M23—6M 101
Longcroft Gro. M34—7H 81
Long Croft La. SK8—4L 113
Longdale Clo. OL2—5J 45
Longdale Dri. SK14—3A 96
Longdell Wlk. M9—8L 61
(off Moston La.)
Longden Av. OL4—6E 46
Longden Rd. M12—4A 92
Longden St. BL1—1C 38
Long Dri. M29—9B 56
Longfellow Av. BL3—6B 38
Longfellow Cres. OL1—5D 46
Longfellow St. M6—1B 4 & 3C 78
Longfellow Wlk. M34—7A 94
Longfield. BL9—5A 26
Longfield. M25—3A 60
Longfield Av. M31—5C 88
Longfield Av. PR7—1L 17
Longfield Av. SK8—5J 113
Longfield Av. WA15—7J 101
Longfield Clo. SK14—9E 82
Longfield Cotts. M31—4B 88
(off Stamford Rd.)
Longfield Cres. OL4—8C 46
Longfield Dri. M31—8B 88
Longfield Gdns. M30—1D 98
Longfield Pk. OL2—3A 46
Longfield Rd. BL3—7A 38
Longfield Rd. M23—5M 101
Longfield Rd. OL2—3A 46
Longfield Rd. OL11—2C 28
Longfield St. WN2—7G 35
Longford Av. BL1—8C 22
Longford Av. M32—4L 89
Longford Clo. M32—3L 89
Longford Cotts. M32—4M 89
Longford Ho. M21—5M 89
Longford Pl. M14—2L 91
Longford Rd. M21—5A 90
Longford Rd. M32—3K 89
Longford Rd. SK5—5F 92
Longford Rd. W. M19 & SK5—5D 92
Longford St. M18—9D 80
Longford St. OL10—8K 27
Longford Trading Est. M32—3K 89
Long Grain Pl. SK2—8K 105
Longham Clo. M11—6L 79
Longham Clo. SK7—3C 114
Long Hey. WA15—1G 111
Longhey Rd. M22—8D 102
Long Heys La. WN8—4A 32
Long Hill. OL11—6D 28
Longhill Wlk. M10—1A 80
Longhirst Clo. BL1—7B 22
Longhope Rd. M22—1B 112
Longhurst La. SK6—7H 107
Longhurst Rd. M9—4H 61
Longhurst Rd. WN2—4M 53
Long La. BL2—4K 39
Long La. BL5—7C 36
Long La. OL3—7A 48
(Dobcross)
Long La. OL3—2D 66
(Tunstead)
Long La. OL9—5F 62
Long La. PR6—1J 19
Long La. SK12—8K 117
Long La. SK14—6B 96
Long La. WN8—5A 50
Long Levens Rd. M22—2C 112
Longley Dri. M28—1B 76
Longley La. M22 & SK8—5D 102
Longley St. OL1—2M 63
Longley St. OL2—4B 46
Longmead Av. SK7—2K 115
Longmead Av. WN4—3C 70
Longmeade Gdns. SK9—5J 119
Long Meadow. BL7—3J 23
Longmeadow. SK8—5C 114
Long Meadow. SK14—9F 82
Longmeadow Gro. M34—4L 93
Long Meadow Pas. SK14—3D 94
Longmead Rd. M6—2K 77
Longmere Av. M22—1D 112
Long Millgate. M3—3E 5 & 5F 78
Longmoor Rd. SK13—7G 97
Longnor Grn. SK13—4D 96
(off Longnor M.)
Longnor M. SK13—4D 96
Longnor Rd. SK7—4L 115
Longnor Rd. SK8—4K 113
Longport Av. M20—7F 90
Longridge. BL7—2J 23
Longridge Av. SK15—3G 83
Longridge Av. WA11—9D 68
Longridge Av. WN6—1M 33
Longridge Cres. BL1—8M 21
Longridge Dri. BL8—1G 41
Longridge Dri. OL10—8F 26
Longridge Dri. WN6—1M 33
Longridge Pl. WN4—2A 70
Longridge Way. WN6—1M 33
Long Row. SK12—9M 115
Long Rushes. OL2—1M 45
Longshaw. WN5—7E 50
Longshaw Av. M27—7F 58
Longshaw Av. WN5—7E 50
Longshaw Clo. WN5—7E 50
Longshaw Comn. WN5—7E 50
Longshaw Dri. M28—4G 57
Longshaw Ford Rd. BL1—5L 21
Longshut La. SK1—6F 104
Longshut La. W. SK1—6F 104
Long Sides Rd. WA15—5J 111
Longsight. BL0—8G 9
Longsight. BL2—7K 23
Longsight Ind. Est. M12—2M 91
Longsight La. BL2—7K 23
Longsight La. SK8—7M 113
Longsight Rd. M18—3B 92
Longsight St. SK4—3D 104
Longsons, The. SK5—2F 104
Longson St. BL1—9G 23
Long St. M18—9E 80
Long St. M24—8A 44
(in two parts)
Long St. M27—9F 58
Longton Av. M20—9G 91
Longton Av. WA3—7J 71
Longton Rd. M6—2J 77
Longton Rd. M9—3J 61
Longton St. BL9—5M 41
Longton St. WN2—4J 53
Longtown Gdns. BL1—8E 22
(off Gladstone St.)
Longview Dri. M27—7C 58
Long Wlk. M31—2D 98
Longwall Av. M28—8H 57
(in two parts)
Longwood Av. SK2—7H 105
Longwood Clo. SK6—2E 106
Long Wood Rd. M17—9H 77
Longwood Rd. M22—1E 112
Long Wood Rd. Est. M17—9G 77
Longworth Av. BL6—7J 19
Longworth Av. PR7—1A 18
Longworth Clo. M33—5L 87
Longworth Rd. BL6—6C 20
Longworth Rd. BL7—7A 6
Longworth St. BL2—2J 39
Longworth St. M3—5D 4 & 7E 78
Lons Av. WN7—5D 72
Lonsdale Av. M27—2D 76
Lonsdale Av. OL16—5H 29
Lonsdale Av. SK5—3F 92
Lonsdale Av. M31—2B 88
Lonsdale Gro. BL4—9J 39
Lonsdale Rd. BL1—1B 38
Lonsdale Rd. M19—4B 92
Lonsdale Rd. OL8—6J 63
Lonsdale St. BL8—8J 25
Lonsdale St. M10—1C 80
Lonsdale Wlk. WN5—9H 33
Loom St. M4—3G 5 & 5H 79
Loonies Ct. SK1—4F 104
Lord Av. M29—7M 55
Lord Byron Sq. M5—6M 77
Lord Derby Rd. SK14—8E 94
Lord Gro. M29—7M 55
Lord Kitchener Ct. M33—8H 89
Lord La. M35—3E 80
(Droylsden)
Lord La. M35—9F 62
(Failsworth)
Lord Napier Dri. M5—6A 4 & 8B 78
Lord North St. M10—3L 79
Lord's Av. M5—5K 77
Lordsfield Av. OL7—3B 82
Lordship Clo. M9—7M 61
Lordsmead St. M15—9D 78
Lord's Stile La. BL7—3H 23
Lords St. M30—8C 86
Lord St. BL3—6B 40
Lord St. BL4—9L 39
Lord St. BL5—8E 36
Lord St. BL6—8D 20
Lord St. BL9—8M 25
(Bury)
Lord St. BL9—8C 26
(Heap Bridge)
Lord St. M3 & M4—1E 5 & 3F 78
Lord St. M7—1B 4 & 3C 78
Lord St. M25—8L 41
Lord St. M26—6G 41
Lord St. M29—7M 55
(Atherton, off Short St.)
Lord St. M29—1M 73
(Tyldesley)
Lord St. M34—2G 93
Lord St. OL1—9M 45
(in three parts)
Lord St. OL6—3B 82
Lord St. OL15—6C 14
Lord St. SK1—4F 104
Lord St. SK13—5J 97
Lord St. SK14—2D 96
Lord St. SK16 & SK15—7F 82
Lord St. WN1—8C 34
Lord St. WN2—3K 53
(Hindley)
Lord St. WN2—1G 53
(Ince)
Lord St. WN4—3D 70
Lord St. WN7—2F 72
Lord St. SK7—2G 115
Loreto Wlk. M15—1F 90
(off Moss Side Shopping Cen.)
Loretto Rd. M31—5F 88
Lorgill Clo. SK3—9F 104
Loring St. M10—2C 80
Lorland Rd. SK3—6B 104
Lorna Gro. SK8—7F 102
Lorna Rd. SK8—2B 114
Lorne Av. OL2—6H 45
Lorne Gro. M31—4E 88
Lorne Gro. SK3—7E 104
Lorne Rd. M14—6J 91
Lorne St. BL1—2F 38
Lorne St. BL4—7J 39
Lorne St. M13—1J 91
Lorne St. M30—7B 76
Lorne St. OL5—7J 65
Lorne St. OL8—4L 63
Lorne St. OL10—9K 27
Lorne St. OL12—8H 13
Lorne St. WN1—9E 34
Lorne Way. OL10—9F 26
Lorraine Clo. OL10—1L 43
Lorraine Rd. WA15—8J 101
Lorton Av. WA11—7A 68
Lorton Clo. M24—7J 43
Lorton Clo. M28—1F 74
Lorton Gro. BL2—1M 39
Lostock Av. M19—5B 92
Lostock Av. M31—3B 88
Lostock Av. M33—1L 101
Lostock Av. SK7—3H 115
Lostock Av. SK12—8H 115
Lostock Clo. OL10—7H 27
Lostock Clo. WN5—2E 68
Lostock Ct. M32—2F 88
Lostock Dene. BL6—1H 37
Lostock Dri. BL9—4M 25
Lostock Gro. M32—3H 89
Lostock Hall Rd. SK12—9H 115
Lostock Ind. Est. BL6—2D 36
Lostock Junct. La. BL6—3J 37
Lostock La. BL5—4D 36
Lostock Pk. Dri. BL6—2G 37
Lostock Rd. BL5—5C 36
Lostock Rd. M5—4L 77
Lostock Rd. M26—1L 59
Lostock Rd. M31—2C 88
Lostock Rd. SK9—8K 113
Lostock Rd. SK12—1K 121
Lostock St. M10—4K 79
Lostock Wlk. M25—7C 42
Lottery St. SK3—4D 104
Lottie St. M27—8G 59
Loughfield. M31—4A 88
Loughman Wlk. M15—9E 78
Loughrigg Av. OL2—1J 45
Loughrigg Av. WA11—6B 68
Louisa St. BL1—8E 22
Louisa St. M11—7D 80
Louisa St. M28—4K 57
Louis Av. BL9—6M 25
Louise Clo. OL12—8H 13
Louise Gdns. BL5—2F 54
Louise Gdns. OL12—8H 13
(in three parts)
Louvaine Av. BL1—6M 21
Louvaine Clo. M18—9E 80
Louvain St. M35—9E 62
Lovalle St. BL1—9C 22
Lovat Rd. BL2—2A 40
Love La. BL0—2L 9
Love La. SK4—3E 104
Loveless Ho. M29—4K 55
(off Brooklands Av.)
Lovell Ct. M8—6F 60
Lovell Dri. SK14—2F 94
Lovers La. M29—6F 54
Lovers La. OL4—2J 65
Lovett Wlk. WA15—9E 100
Lovett Wlk. M22—5E 102
Low Bank. OL12—8J 13
Low Bank Rd. WN4—3M 69
Lowbrook La. OL4—8F 46
(in two parts)
Lowcock St. M7—1D 4 & 3E 78
Low Crompton Rd. OL2—3K 45
Lowcross Rd. M10—1A 80
Lowe Grn. OL2—4L 45
Lowe Mill La. WN2—3K 53
Lwr. Alma St. SK16—6B 82
Lwr. Bamford Clo. M24—7A 44
Lwr. Bank. M34—1M 93
Lwr. Bank. SK13—6K 97
Lwr. Bank Clo. SK14—3F 96
Lwr. Bank St. BL9—8L 25
Lwr. Barn Rd. SK14—2E 96
Lwr. Bennett St. SK14—2C 94
Lwr. Bents La. SK6—1M 105
Lwr. Bridgeman St. BL2—3G 39
Lwr. Broadacre. SK15—9L 83
Lwr. Brooklands Pde. M8—6E 60
Lwr. Broughton Rd. M7—2C 78
Lwr. Bury St. SK4—3D 104
Lwr. Byrom St. M3—5D 4 & 7E 78
Lwr. Calderbrook. OL15—2C 14
Lwr. Carr La. OL3—2B 66
Lwr. Carrs. SK1—4F 104
Lwr. Chatham St. M1 & M15 (in two parts)—6F 4 & 8G 79
Lwr. Crimble. OL11—6L 27
Lwr. Croft. M25—2J 59
Lowercroft Rd. BL8—8E 24
Lwr. Crossbank. OL4—9F 46
Lwr. Darcy St. BL2—4J 39
Lwr. Dingle. OL1—5C 46
Lwr. Drake Field. BL5—3E 54
Lwr. Edge Av. OL1—9L 45
Lwr. Falinge. OL12—2E 28
Lowerfield. M34—4A 94
Lowerfield Dri. SK2—8M 105
Lowerfields. OL3—8A 48
Lowerfields. OL8—4B 64
Lwr. Fold. SK6—5H 107
Lowerfold Av. OL2—5A 46
Lowerfold Clo. OL12—7C 12
Lowerfold Cres. OL12—7C 12
Lowerfold Way. OL12—7C 12
Lwr. Fullwood. OL1—4D 46
Lwr. Goodwin Clo. BL2—7L 23
Lwr. Grn. M6—3M 77
Lwr. Green. M24—3M 61
Lwr. Green. OL6—3C 82
Lower Grn. OL12—1C 28
Lwr. Green La. M29—5C 74
Lwr. Greenshall La. SK12—6M 117
Lwr. Hague. SK12—4L 117
Lwr. Hardman St. M3—4D 4 & 6E 78
Lwr. Healey La. OL12—9E 12
Lwr. Hey La. OL5—5L 65
Lwr. Hill Dri. PR6—1H 19
Lwr. Hillgate. SK1—4F 104
Lwr. House Dri. BL6—2J 37
Lwr. House St. OL1—9B 46
Lwr. House Wlk. BL7—2G 23
Lwr. Jowkin La. OL11—3K 27
Lwr. Knoll Rd. OL3—4D 48
Lwr. Knowl La. OL12—6J 11
Lwr. Landedmans. BL5—1F 54
Lower La. OL16—7J 29
Lwr. Leigh Rd. BL5—3F 54
Lwr. Lime Rd. OL8—8J 63
Lwr. Longshoot. WN1—9D 34
Lwr. Lyndon Av. WN6—3G 33
Lwr. Makinson Fold. BL6—8D 20
Lwr. Market St. SK14—6A 96
Lwr. Marlands. BL7—2F 22
Lwr. Mead. BL7—1F 22
Lwr. Meadow. BL7—5K 7
Lwr. Mill Cotts. OL15—7M 13
Lwr. Moat Clo. SK4—2E 104
Lwr. Monton Rd. M30—5E 76
Lwr. Mosley St. M2—5E 5 & 7F 78
Lwr. Moss La. M15—6C 4 & 8D 78
Lwr. Moss La. M25—9M 41
Lwr. New Rd. M28—7G 57
Lwr. Ormond St. M1 & M15 (in two parts)—6F 5 & 8G 79
Lwr. Park Cres. SK12—6J 115
Lwr. Park Rd. M14—2J 91
Lwr. Park Rd. SK12—7H 115
(in three parts)
Lwr. Rawson St. BL4—8L 39
Lwr. St Stephen St. WN6—9A 34
Lwr. Seedley Rd. M6—4L 77
Lwr. Sheriff St. OL12—2E 28
Lwr. Southfield. BL5—1E 54
Lwr. Square. SK14—8G 85
Lwr. Standrings. OL11—2A 28
Lower St. BL4—1J 57
Lower St. OL16—6G 29
Lwr. Strines Rd. SK6—8G 107
Lwr. Sutherland St. M27—8E 58
Lwr. Tenterfield. OL11—9K 11
Lwr. Tong. BL7—3F 22
Lwr. Turf La. OL4—1G 65
Lwr. Tweedale St. OL11—4F 28
Lwr. Vickers St. M10—4K 79
Lwr. Victoria St. OL9—1H 63
Lwr. Wharf St. OL6—5B 82
Lwr. Wheat End. OL16—2H 29
Lwr. Woodhill Rd. BL8—7K 25
(in two parts)
Lwr. Wood La. BL2—9H 23
Lowe's Ho. WN1—9D 34
Lowesside Av. BL1—3J 37
Lowes Rd. BL9—4M 25
Lowestead Rd. M11—5C 80
Lowes, The. WA14—3B 110
Lowestoft St. M14—4H 91
Lowe St. M26—5F 40
Lowe St. M34—3B 94
Lowe St. SK1—4F 104
Lowe St. WA3—7G 71
Loweswater Av. M29—9A 56
Loweswater Cres. WA11—9G 69
Loweswater Rd. SK8—1H 113
Loweswater Ter. SK15—3G 83
Lowfell Wlk. M18—3D 92
Lowfield Av. M35—4F 80
Lowfield Av. OL6—2F 82
Lowfield Gdns. WA3—8J 73
Lowfield Gro. SK2—6F 104
Lowfield Rd. SK3—7E 104
Lowfield Wlk. M9—5L 61
(off White Moss Rd.)
Low Ga. La. OL3—9M 31
Lowgill Wlk. M18—1D 92
Low Grn. M29—3M 55
Low Hall Gdns. WN2—5H 53
Low Hill. OL12—8J 13
Lowhouse Clo. OL16—3A 30
Lowick Av. BL3—6G 39
Lowick Clo. SK7—2K 115
Lowick Grn. SK6—8M 93
Lowland Gro. OL7—1A 82
Lowland Rd. SK2—9H 105
Lowlands Clo. M24—3B 62
Low Lea Rd. SK6—6H 107
Lowndes Clo. SK2—7H 105
Lowndes La. SK2—6H 105
Lowndes St. BL1—1B 38
Lowndes Wlk. M13—9J 79
Lownorth Rd. M22—4E 112
Lowood Av. M31—2M 87
Lowood Clo. OL16—4M 29
Lowood St. WN7—2D 72
Lowrey Wlk. M9—9L 61
(off Broadwell Dri.)
Lowry. M30—5E 76
Lowry Dri. M27—7F 58
Lowry Dri. SK6—4F 106
Lowry Gro. SK14—3M 95
Lowry Ho. M16—1D 90
Lowry Wlk. BL1—9D 22
Lowside Av. SK6—8C 94
Lowside Dri. OL4—3B 64
Low's Pl. OL12—9G 13
Lowstern Clo. BL7—1E 22
Lows, The. OL4—3B 64
(in two parts)
Low St. BL0—5J 9
Lowther Av. M18—3B 92
Lowther Av. OL2—1J 45
Lowther Av. WA15—7G 101
Lowther Ct. M25—5M 59
Lowther Cres. M24—8K 43
Lowther Dri. WN7—9L 55
Lowther Gdns. M31—3K 87
Lowther Rd. M8—7G 61
Lowther Rd. M25—5M 59
Lowther Rd. OL11—6E 28
Lowther St. BL3—7G 39
(in two parts)
Lowther Ter. WN6—1C 32
Lowthorpe St. M14—3G 91
Lowton Av. M9—9M 61
Lowton Ho. BL1—1F 38
(off Gray St.)
Lowton Rd. M33—3D 100
Lowton Rd. WA3—5H 71
Lowton St Mary's By-Pass. WN7—7D
Lowton St. M26—5G 41
Low Wood Clo. SK7—3C 114
Low Wood Rd. M34—2G 93
Loxford Ct. M15—6E 5 & 9F
Loxford Gdns. M15—9F 78
Loxford St. M15—6E 5 & 9F
Loxham St. BL3 & BL4—7K
Loxton Cres. WN3—5B 52
Loxton Wlk. M7—1E 78
Loyalty Pl. WA14—4F 104
Loynd St. BL0—5K 9
Lubeck St. M9—8L 61
Lucas Rd. BL4 & M28—9G 3
Lucas St. BL9—7A 26
Lucas St. OL4—1B 64
Lucas Wlk. M11—7M 79
Lucerne Clo. OL9—2J 63
Lucerne Rd. SK7—1E 114
Lucien Clo. M12—1L 91
Luciol Clo. M29—7C 56
Lucknow St. OL11—5F 28
Lucy St. BL1—9A 22
Lucy St. BL9—6K 39
Lucy St. M7—2D 78
Lucy St. M15—9D 78
Lucy St. SK3—5E 104
Ludford Gro. M33—3F 100
Ludgate Hill. M4—2G 5 & 4H
Ludgate Rd. M10—3C 80
Ludgate Rd. OL11—8G 29
Ludgate St. M4—2F 5 & 4G
Ludlow Av. M25—2B 60
Ludlow Av. M27—6G 59
Ludlow Av. WN2—4A 54
Ludlow Dri. WN7—9L 55
Ludlow Pk. OL4—2D 64
Ludlow Rd. SK2—5J 105
Ludlow St. WN6—7J 17
Ludlow Towers. SK5—7J 93
Ludovic Ter. WN1—9C 34
Ludwell Wlk. M8—1G 79
Lugano Rd. SK7—1E 114
Luke Kirby Ct. M27—7F 58
Luke Rd. M35—6H 81
Luke St. BL3—4E 38
Luke St. WN4—2D 70
Luke Wlk. M8—1H 79
Lullington Rd. M6—3K 77
Lulworth Av. M31—4M 87
Lulworth Clo. BL8—4J 25
Lulworth Cres. M35—8H 63
Lulworth Dri. WN2—4A 54
Lulworth Gdns. M23—5M 1
Lulworth Rd. BL3—8A 38
Lulworth Rd. M24—7A 44
Lulworth Rd. M30—4C 76
Lumb Carr Av. BL0—7G 9
Lumb Carr Rd. BL8—8G 9
Lumb Clo. SK7—6E 114
Lumber La. M28—8L 57
Lumb Ho. SK7—6E 114
Lumb La. M34—4J 81
Lumb La. M35—4J 81
(in three parts)
Lumb La. SK7—6E 114
Lumley Clo. M14—2H 91
Lumn Gro. BL9—2M 25
Lumn Hollow. SK14—4E 94
Lumn Rd. SK14—4E 94
Lumn's La. M27—6J 59
Lumsden St. BL3—4E 38
Luna St. M4—3G 5 & 5H 79
Lundale Wlk. M10—1A 80
Lund Av. M26—9H 41
Lund St. M16—9C 78
Lundy Av. M21—9C 90
Lune Clo. M25—8A 42
Lunedale. WN2—6H 53
Lunedale Grn. SK2—7K 105
Lune Dri. M25—9A 42
Lune Gro. OL10—7H 27
Lune Gro. WN7—2C 72
Lunehurst. WA3—7L 71
Lune Rd. WN2—6F 52
Lune St. M29—8M 55
Lune St. OL8—4L 63
Lune Wlk. M25—9A 42
Lune Wlk. M35—7H 81
Lune Way. SK5—9F 92
Lunn Av. M18—9F 80
Lupin Av. BL4—8G 39
Lupin Dri. WA11—9M 69
Lupton St. M3—3C 4 & 5D
Lupton St. M34—2M 93
Lupton Wlk. M15—9F 78
Lurden Wlk. OL9—4H 63
Lurdin La. WA6 & WN1—
Lurgan Av. M33—2J 101
Lutener Av. WA14—5J 100
Luton Dri. M23—9A 102
Luton Gro. M29—5H 55
Luton Rd. SK5—6F 92
Luton St. BL3—5G 39
Luton St. BL8—9H 25
Luxhall Wlk. M10—2B 80
Luxor Gro. M34—3F 92
Luzley Rd. OL5 & OL6—8H
Luzley Rd. SK15—4H 83
Lyceum Pas. OL16—3F 28
Lychgate. WN5—3L 51
Lychgate M. SK4—3L 103
Lydbrook Clo. BL1—3E 38
Lydden Av. M11—4D 80
Lydford. OL11—4E 28
Lydford Gdns. BL2—4M 3
Lydford Grn. WN6—1M 33
Lydford St. M6—1A 4 & 2
Lydford Wlk. M13—9J 79
(off Torquay Clo.)
Lydgate Av. BL2—1L 39
Lydgate Clo. M25—8A 42
Lydgate Clo. M34—5J 94
Lydgate Clo. SK15—1L 83
Lydgate Dri. OL4—3C 64
Lydgate Rd. M33—3J 101
Lydgate Rd. M35—4E 80
Lydgate Wlk. M25—8A 42
Lydiat La. SK9—9L 119
Lydney Av. SK8—5J 113
Lydney Rd. M31—3K 87
Lyefield Av. WN1—8F 34
Lyefield Wlk. OL16—4H 2
Lymbridge Dri. BL6—8K
Lyme Av. SK9—2H 119
Lymefield Dri. M28—9G 5
Lymefield Gro. SK2—7H
Lyme Gro. M33—6F 80
Lyme Gro. SK1—6F 104
(Marple)
Lyme Gro. SK6—8F 106
(Marple)
Lyme Gro. SK6—3D 106
(Romiley)
Lyme Gro. WA14—9C 100

ne Rd. SK7—3L 115
ne Rd. SK12—5G 117
isley)
e Rd. SK12—9D 116
oynton)
e St. SK4—3L 103
e St. SK7—1K 115
e St. WA11—9L 69
e Ter. SK16—6B 82
ewood Ct. WA11—8K 69
ewood Dri. SK9—3L 119
ewood Dri. SK12—6J 117
ington Clo. M24—3B 62
ington Dri. M23—4K 101
m Clo. M28—5G 57
m Clo. SK3—7D 104
m Rd. WA13 & WA14
—3E 108
m Wlk. SK8—8A 104
combe Clo. SK8—6B 114
dale Av. M27—1D 76
dale Av. SK5—3F 92
dale Dri. OL15—5A 14
dene Av. M28—8A 58
dene Gdns. SK8—7H 103
dene Rd. M22—8D 102
dhurst Av. M25—5E 60
dhurst Av. M30—3H 87
dhurst Av. M31—2C 88
dhurst Av. M33—2F 100
dhurst Av. M34—3L 93
hurst Av. OL6—2B 82
hurst Av. OL9—3F 62
hurst Av. OL11—1D 44
hurst Av. SK6—1M 105
hurst Av. SK7—3J 115
hurst Clo. SK9—6D 118
hurst Dri. WA15—2G 111
hurst Gdns. M24—9L 43
hurst Rd. M20—1G 103
two parts)
hurst Rd. M32—4H 89
hurst Rd. OL8—5K 63
hurst Rd. SK5—4E 92
hurst St. M5—5L 77
hurst View. SK16—6C 82
on Av. WN6—3G 33
on Clo. BL8—4F 24
on Clo. OL4—9H 47
on Rd. M30—4F 86
Av. SK13—6G 97
Edge Cres. SK16—8F 82
Edge Rd. SK15—7F 82
Edge Rd. SK16—8G 83
Gro. M33—2J 101
ham Wlk. M8—1F 78
ham Wlk. M9—3L 61
View. SK14—9F 82
ard Clo. SK9—2L 119
arth Ho. WA14—7E 100
ate Clo. SK1—5G 105
Gro. OL10—7H 27
am Dri. OL10—1K 43
outh Av. M20—8G 91
outh Av. M31—6B 88
outh Av. OL2—6J 45
outh Av. OL8—5M 63
outh Av. SK5—7E 92
outh Clo. M26—5J 41
outh Clo. OL9—8E 44
outh Clo. WN6—7A 34
outh Ct. M25—5M 59
outh Gro. M25—5M 59
Av. M33—8K 89
Dri. M35—5E 80
Clo. SK13—6M 97
field Ho. WA14—8D 100
St. OL9—4J 63
St. WN2—5H 53
wood Dri. OL11—2B 28
wood Rd. M19—3K 103
yle Way. OL11—7D 28
de Wlk. M22—5E 112
ade Av. M31—3M 87
ed Av. BL3—6G 39
ock Way. BL6—3E 36
orpe Av. M30—8D 86
orpe Rd. M10—5D 62
n Av. M27—7F 58
n Av. M30—8E 86
n Av. M31—4J 87
n Av. OL2—6J 45
n Av. OL8—6J 63
n Av. OL11—7B 28
n Av. SK14—4J 95
n Av. WN6—6A 34
n Clo. OL9—8F 44
n Cres. M28—7K 57
n Dri. M19—7M 91
n Dri. M25—2C 60
n Dri. SK6—4E 116
n Gro. WA15—8F 100
n La. SK9—7L 119
n Lee. M26—5J 41
n M. SK9—7L 119
n Pk. Rd. SK8—4M 113
n Rd. BL3—7C 38
n Rd. M21—5A 90
n Rd. M27—7F 58
n Rd. M29—8D 56
n Rd. SK4—9C 92
n Rd. SK8—8H 103
n Rd. WN2—2M 53
n St. M14—4H 91
n St. WN7—2D 72
nvale Av. SK8—7G 103
n Wlk. SK14—4J 95
own Trading Est. M30
—5D 76
wn Trading Est. OL11
—7D 28
y Dri. M20—9H 91
ll Rd. M30—5D 76
ood. WA15—4G 111
ood Av. BL3—7H 39
ood Av. M16—4C 90
ood Av. M30—5D 76
ood Av. WA3—9L 71
ood Ct. M8—6F 60
ood Dri. OL4—9D 46
ood Gro. BL2—6K 23
ood Gro. M29—5H 55
od Gro. M33—9J 89
od Gro. M34—6J 81
od Gro. SK4—8C 92
Gro. M28—8A 58
Rd. BL4—3L 57
Rd. WA14—6C 100
Dri. BL8—9G 25
Fold. M33—8H 89
Rd. M17—8G 77
t. M27—9E 58
t. OL2—2B 46
t. WN3—1B 52
t. WN4—8G 35
Way. SK5—8E 92
der Clo. M14—6H 91
n Av. M21—7C 90
n Clo. OL6—1E 82
n Dri. OL10—9J 27
n Dri. SK7—5G 115
n Rd. M19—5M 91
n Rd. M31—4J 87
n Rd. SK8—3H 113
n Rd. WN4—2M 69
n St. OL12—8E 12
n St. SK3—7F 104
ton Av. M30—1D 98
t. M5—5C 4 & 7D 78
t. M14—7K 91
Av. M8—1G 79
Rd. M35—5G 81
St. BL1—8D 22
Av. BL3—6G 39
Av. M28—9A 58
Rd. M35—7G 63
s Brow. BL4—1L 57
wo parts)
St. BL1—1C 38
St. BL5—1F 54
St. OL12—9D 12

Mabel St. WN5—2L 51
Maberry Clo. WN6—2D 32
Mabfield Rd. M14—5J 91
Mabledon Clo. SK8—4K 113
Mable St. M10—2D 80
Mabs Ct. OL6—5D 82
Macaulay Way. M34—6A 94
Macauley Clo. SK16—8G 83
Macauley Pl. WN3—4M 51
Macauley Rd. M16—4B 90
Macauley Rd. SK5—5D 92
Macauley St. OL2—5L 45
Macauley St. OL11—8D 28
McCall Wlk. M11—5B 80
Maccles Ct. OL15—5A 14
Macclesfield Clo. WN2—3J 53
Macclesfield Rd. SK7—5L 115
Macclesfield Rd. SK9—8L 119
(Alderley Edge)
Macclesfield Rd. SK9—4J 119
(Wilmslow)
McConnell Rd. M10—9A 62
McCormack Dri. WN1—9D 34
Macdonald Av. BL4—1G 57
Macdonald Av. WN3—5A 52
Macdonald Rd. M30—7E 86
Macdonald St. OL8—4M 63
Macdonald St. WN5—2H 51
McDonna St. BL1—7C 22
McDowall Wlk. M8—6H 61
Macefin Av. M21—1D 102
Macfarren St. M12—3A 92
McKean St. BL3—5G 39
Mackenzie Av. WN3—5A 52
Mackenzie Gro. BL1—6D 22
Mackenzie Rd. M7—1B 78
Mackenzie St. BL1—5D 22
Mackenzie St. M12—3A 92
Mackenzie Wlk. OL1—4E 46
Mackeson Dri. OL6—3E 82
Mackeson Rd. OL6—3E 82
Mackintosh Way. OL1—1M 63
Maclaren Dri. M8—6E 60
Maclaren Ho. M6—4M 77
(off Sutton Dwellings)
McLean Dri. M30—2G 87
Maclure Clo. M16—3E 90
Macnair M. SK6—8G 107
McNaught St. OL16—4H 29
McOwen Pl. OL16—3G 29
McOwen St. OL16—3G 29
Madam Wood Rd. M28—5F 56
Maddison Rd. M35—6F 80
Madeley Clo. WA14—4E 110
Madeley Clo. WN3—5L 51
Madeley Dri. OL9—2J 63
Madeley Gdns. BL1—8E 22
Madeley Gdns. OL12—1D 28
Madeline St. BL3—7K 39
Maden St. M29—1M 73
Maden Wlk. OL9—9H 45
Madison Av. M34—7J 81
Madison Av. SK8—2A 114
Madison Gdns. M35—9E 62
Madison St. M18—9E 80
Madras Rd. SK3—6C 104
Mafeking Av. BL9—5A 26
Mafeking Pl. WN4—4C 70
Mafeking Rd. BL2—2L 39
Mafeking St. OL8—5J 63
Magdala St. OL1—9L 45
Magdala St. OL10—1L 43
Magdalen Dri. WN4—3M 69
Magdalen Wlk. M15—6D 4 &
8E 78
Magda Rd. SK2—8J 105
Mag La. WA16 & WA13—7A 108
Magna Carta Ct. M6—1H 77
Magnolia Clo. M31—3E 98
Magnolia Clo. M33—8C 88
Magnolia Clo. WA11—9F 68
Magnolia Ct. M6—5A 78
Magnolia Ct. M33—9C 88
(off Magnolia Clo.)
Magnolia Dri. M8—1G 79
Magpie Clo. M35—4J 81
Magpie Wlk. M11—6M 79
Mahogony Wlk. M33—9C 88
Mahood St. SK3—6D 104
Maida St. M12—4B 92
Maiden Clo. OL7—1A 82
Maiden M. M27—9F 58
Maidford Clo. M4—6K 79
Maidstone Av. M21—5A 90
Maidstone M. M21—5A 90
Maidstone Rd. SK4—2K 103
Maidstone Wlk. M34—5A 94
Main Av. M17—2J 89
Main Av. M19—7M 91
Main Clo. WA11—9G 69
Maine Rd. M14—4G 91
Mainhill Wlk. M10—2C 80
Main La. WA3—9E 72
Mainprice Clo. M6—3M 77
Main Rd. M27—5K 59
Main Rd. OL9—1J 63
Mains Av. WN2—9F 52
Main St. M35—8F 62
Main St. SK14—2D 94
Main St. WN5—3D 68
Mainwaring Dri. SK9—3K 119
Mainway. M24—2M 61
Mainway E. M24—2C 62
Mainwood Rd. WA15—8J 101
Mainwood Sq. M13—6G 5 &
8H 79
Maismore Ct. M22—3A 112
Maismore Rd. M22—3B 112
Maitland Av. M21—9C 90
Maitland Clo. OL12—8J 13
Maitland St. SK1—6H 105
Maitland Wlk. OL9—9H 45
Major St. BL0—5H 9
Major St. M1—5F 4 & 7G 79
Major St. OL16—4M 29
Major St. WN5—2J 51
Makants Clo. M29—2M 55
Makant St. BL1—7C 22
Makepiece Wlk. M8—6E 60
Makerfield Way. WN2—1H 53
Makin Ct. OL10—9K 27
Makinson Arc. WN1—9C 34
(off Galleries, The)
Makinson Av. BL6—8E 20
Makinson Av. WN2—1K 53
Makin St. M1—5F 5 & 7G 79
Malakoff St. SK15—6E 82
Malbrook Wlk. BL3—5F 38
Malbrook Wlk. M13—9J 79
(off Ardeen Wlk.)
Malby St. OL1—9M 45
Malcom Av. M27—5G 59
Malcom Dri. M27—6G 59
Malcom St. OL11—7D 28
Malden Gro. M23—6A 102
Maldon Clo. SK2—7A 106
Maldon Clo. WN2—7F 34
Maldon Cres. M27—1F 76
Maldon Dri. M30—3E 76
Maldon Rd. WN6—1M 33
Maldon St. OL11—5F 28
Maldwyn Av. BL3—7B 38
Maldwyn Av. M8—6G 61
Malford Dri. M8—1F 78
Malgam Dri. M20—5H 103
Malham Av. WN3—6A 52
Malham Clo. OL2—5K 45
Malham Clo. WN7—2C 72
Malham Ct. SK2—7K 105
Malham Gdns. BL3—6C 38
Mallaig Wlk. M11—7C 80
Mallard Clo. OL8—6K 63
Mallard Clo. SK2—8A 106
Mallard Clo. SK16—8E 82
Mallard Ct. SK8—4H 113
Mallard Cres. SK12—8G 115
Mallard Dri. BL6—7A 20
Mallard Grn. WA14—5B 100
Mallard St. M1—6F 5 & 7G 79
Mallet Cres. BL1—8M 21
Malley Wlk. M9—5L 61
(off Greendale Dri.)
Malling Rd. M23—9A 102

Mallison St. BL1—7F 22
Mallory Av. OL7—2B 82
Mallory Ct. WA14—1C 110
Mallory Dri. WN7—2J 73
Mallory Gro. WA11—9D 68
Mallory Rd. SK14—1G 95
Mallory Wlk. M23—5K 101
Mallowdale. M28—8H 57
Mallowdale Clo. BL1—2K 37
Mallowdale Clo. M15—9F 78
Mallowdale Rd. SK2—8L 105
Mallow Wlk. M31—2F 98
Mall, The. BL9—8M 25
Mall, The. M30—5F 76
Mall, The. M33—9H 89
Mall, The. SK14—4D 94
Mall, The. SK15—9L 83
Malmesbury Clo. SK12—8K 115
Malmesbury Rd. SK8—6B 114
Malpas Av. WN1—8E 34
Malpas Clo. SK8—9A 104
Malpas Clo. SK9—2L 119
Malpas Dri. WA14—4E 100
Malpas St. M12—9A 80
Malpas St. OL1—1M 63
Malpas Wlk. M16—1D 90
Malsham Rd. M23—3M 101
Malta Clo. M24—9D 44
Malta St. M4—6K 79
Malta St. OL4—2D 64
Maltby Dri. BL3—6C 38
Maltby Rd. M23—7M 101
Malton Av. BL3—5A 38
Malton Av. M21—6B 90
Malton Av. M25—7M 41
Malton Av. OL9—8F 44
Malton Av. WA3—8L 71
Malton Clo. M25—7M 41
Malton Clo. WN7—1C 72
Malton Dri. SK7—5K 115
Malton Dri. WA14—7A 100
Malton Rd. M28—9E 56
Malton Rd. SK4—1A 104
Malton St. OL8—3K 63
Malt St. M15—6C 4
Malus Ct. M6—4A 78
Malvern Av. BL1—9A 22
Malvern Av. BL9—5M 25
Malvern Av. M29—3M 55
Malvern Av. M31—3B 88
Malvern Av. M35—5J 81
Malvern Av. OL6—9C 64
Malvern Av. SK8—8F 102
Malvern Av. WN2—4A 54
Malvern Clo. BL4—9F 38
Malvern Clo. BL6—5C 20
Malvern Clo. M25—3C 60
Malvern Clo. M27—1K 77
Malvern Clo. OL2—6J 45
(Royton)
Malvern Clo. OL2—2M 45
(Shaw)
Malvern Clo. OL16—3A 30
Malvern Clo. SK4—2D 104
Malvern Clo. WN3—5J 51
Malvern Clo. WN4—3B 70
Malvern Cres. WN3—4F 52
Malvern Dri. WA14—8B 100
Malvern Gro. M6—4J 77
Malvern Gro. M20—8G 91
Malvern Gro. M28—5K 57
Malvern Rd. M24—3M 61
Malvern Row. M15—9D 78
Malvern St. M15—9D 78
Malvern St. OL8—3K 63
Malvern St. WN6—7K 17
Malvern St. E. OL11—3C 28
Malvern St. W. OL11—3C 28
Malvern Ter. WN7—4F 72
Manby Rd. M18—2B 92
Manby Sq. M18—2B 92
Manchester Ind. Cen. M3—5C 4
& 7D 78
Manchester International
Airport. M22, SK9 & WA15
(Ringway) —7B 112
Manchester International Bus.
Cen. M22—5G 113
Manchester New Rd. M24
—3L 61
Manchester New Rd. M31
—1F 98
Manchester Old Rd. BL9—9L 25
Manchester Old Rd. M24—1H 61
Manchester Rd. BL0 & BL9
—5L 9
Manchester Rd. BL2 & BL3
—3G 39
Manchester Rd. BL4—9L 39
(Farnworth)
Manchester Rd. BL4 & M27
(Kearsley) —2A 58
Manchester Rd. BL5—2M 35
(Hilton House)
Manchester Rd. BL5—6E 36
(Westhoughton)
Manchester Rd. BL6—8K 19
Manchester Rd. BL9 & M25
—9L 25
Manchester Rd. M21 & M16
(in two parts) —6A 90
Manchester Rd. M28 & M27
(Walkden) —5K 57
Manchester Rd. M29—7A 56
Manchester Rd. M31—1F 98
Manchester Rd. M34—2G 93
Manchester Rd. M34 & OL7
—8G 81
Manchester Rd. M35—6E 80
Manchester Rd. OL2—4A 46
Manchester Rd. OL3—4M 65
Manchester Rd. OL5—1J 83
Manchester Rd. OL8 & OL9
—6H 63
Manchester Rd. OL10—5J 43
Manchester Rd. OL11—7C 28
Manchester Rd. OL11 & OL12
(in three parts) —5D 28
Manchester Rd. SK4—8C 92
Manchester Rd. SK8—5K 103
Manchester Rd. SK9—4H 119
Manchester Rd. SK14—9E 84
(Hollingworth)
Manchester Rd. SK14—3B 94
(Hyde)
Manchester Rd. WA3—4A 98
Manchester Rd. WA14—7D 100
Manchester Rd. WN1 & WN2
—9E 34
Manchester Rd. WN7 & M29
—3J 73
Manchester Rd. E. M28—4G 57
Manchester Rd. N. M34—2J 93
Manchester Rd. S. M34—2J 93
Manchester Rd. W. M28—2D 56
Manchester Science Pk. M15
(off Lloyd St. N.) —1G 91
Manchester St. M16—1C 90
Manchester St. OL8 & OL9
—3K 63
Manchester St. OL10—8K 27
Manchet St. OL11—9B 28
Mancroft Av. BL3—5D 38
Mancroft Wlk. M1—6G 5 &
8H 79
Mancunian Rd. M34—6A 94
Mancunian Way. M15, M1 &
M12—6D 4 & 8E 78
Mandalay Gdns. SK6—6D 106
Mandarin Grn. WA14—5B 100
Mandarin Wlk. M6—2A 4 &
4A 78
Manderville Clo. WN3—6K 51
Mandeville St. M19—6B 92
Mandley Av. M10—6D 62
Mandley Clo. BL3—4A 40
Mandley Pk. Av. M8—9E 60
Mandon Clo. M26—4E 40
Manesty Clo. M24—7J 43
Manet Wlk. OL1—5D 46
Mangle St. M1—4G 5 & 6H 79
Manifold Dri. SK6—6F 116
Manifold St. M6—2B 78

Manilla Wlk. M11—6M 79
Manipur St. M11—7M 79
Manley Av. M27—4E 58
Manley Av. WA3—5F 70
Manley Clo. BL9—9J 9
Manley Clo. SK3—7C 104
Manley Clo. WN7—8D 54
Manley Cres. BL5—8H 37
Manley Gro. SK7—6E 114
Manley Rd. M21 & M16—5C 90
Manley Rd. M33—4E 100
Manley Rd. OL8—4L 63
Manley Rd. OL11—7C 28
(in two parts)
Manley Row. BL5—8H 37
Manley St. M7—1D 78
Manley St. WN3—2E 52
Manley Ter. BL1—6E 22
Manning Av. WN6—7A 34
Manningham Rd. BL3—4B 38
Mannington Dri. M9—9J 61
Mannion Ho. WN1—9D 34
Mannock St. OL8—2K 63
Manor Av. BL3—6C 40
Manor Av. M16—4D 90
Manor Av. M31—5D 88
Manor Av. M33—9D 88
Manor Av. WA3—7J 71
Manor Clo. M34—4B 94
Manor Clo. OL4—2L 65
Manor Clo. OL9—9J 45
Manor Clo. SK8—4C 114
Manor Clo. SK9—3E 118
Manor Clo. WN4—4J 69
Manor Ct. M32—5H 89
Manor Ct. M33—9D 88
Manor Ct. WA3—7J 71
Manordale Wlk. M10—1K 79
Manor Dri. M21—1D 102
Manor Dri. M28—2E 56
Manor Dri. OL2—6L 45
Manor Farm Clo. OL7—1M 81
Manor Farm Rise. OL4—1D 64
Manorfield Clo. BL1—9A 22
Manor Fold. M29—5J 55
Manor Gdns. SK9—4K 119
Manor Ga. Rd. BL2—1M 39
Manor Gro. WN2—4H 35
Manor Gro. WN5—9H 33
Manor Gro. WN7—4J 73
Manor Heath. M7—8C 60
Manor Hill Rd. SK6—6F 106
Manor Ho. Clo. WA11—6A 68
Manor Ind. Est. M32—6J 89
Manor Lodge. M27—8K 59
Manor Pk. M31—5D 88
Manor Pk. Rd. SK13—5L 97
Manor Pl. WN3—2F 52
Manor Rd. BL6—6D 20
Manor Rd. M6—3K 77
Manor Rd. M19—4B 92
Manor Rd. M24—2M 61
Manor Rd. M27—1F 76
Manor Rd. M29—1C 74
Manor Rd. M32—5H 89
Manor Rd. M33—9H 89
Manor Rd. M34—8H 81
(Audenshaw)
Manor Rd. M34—4B 94
(Denton)
Manor Rd. M35—6E 80
Manor Rd. OL2—2A 46
Manor Rd. OL4—4C 64
Manor Rd. SK5—1J 105
Manor Rd. SK6—6F 106
(Marple)
Manor Rd. SK6—9B 94
(Woodley)
Manor Rd. SK8 & SK7—3C 114
Manor Rd. SK9—3E 118
Manor Rd. SK14—1F 94
Manor Rd. WA11—8M 69
Manor Rd. WA15—9E 100
Manor Rd. WN2—3M 53
Manor Rd. WN6—3F 32
Manor St. BL0—4H 9
Manor St. BL1—2F 38
Manor St. BL4—1J 57
(Farnworth)
Manor St. BL4—3B 58
(Kearsley)
Manor St. BL9—8A 26
Manor St. M12—6H 5 & 8J 79
(in two parts)
Manor St. M24—7A 44
Manor St. M34—8M 81
Manor St. OL1—9A 46
Manor St. OL5—6J 65
Manor St. SK13—5K 97
Manor St. WA3—6H 71
Manor St. WN1—9C 34
Manor St. WN5—2M 51
Manor View. SK6—9B 94
Manor Wlk. M34—8M 81
Manor Yd. OL3—9B 48
(off High St. Uppermill)
Manse Av. WN6—5F 16
Mansell Way. BL6—1E 36
Mansfield Av. BL0—9H 9
Mansfield Av. M34—1K 93
Mansfield Clo. M34—1K 93
Mansfield Clo. OL7—6M 81
Mansfield Cres. M34—2K 93
Mansfield Dri. M9—4L 61
Mansfield Gro. BL1—9B 22
Mansfield Rd. M9—4K 61
Mansfield Rd. M31—5B 88
Mansfield Rd. OL5—7L 65
Mansfield Rd. OL8—3B 64
Mansfield Rd. OL11—3L 27
Mansfield Rd. SK14—5E 94
Mansfield St. OL7—7L 81
Mansfield St. WA3—6F 70
Mansfield View. OL5—7L 65
Mansford Dri. M10—2M 79
Manshaw Cres. M34—8G 81
Manshaw Rd. M11—8G 81
Mansion Av. M25—6L 41
Mansley's Pas. WN7—2F 72
(off King St.)
Manson Av. M15—6C 4 & 8D 78
Manstead Wlk. M10—5L 79
Manston Dri. SK8—2A 114
Manswood Dri. M8—9G 61
Mantell Wlk. M10—2A 80
Manton Av. M9—5B 62
Manton Av. M34—3G 93
Manton Clo. M8—1F 78
Manvers St. SK5—2E 104
Manwaring St. M35—8E 62
Maple Av. BL1—9B 22
Maple Av. BL6—9E 20
Maple Av. BL9—7B 26
Maple Av. M21—6B 90
Maple Av. M25—1M 59
Maple Av. M29—4H 55
Maple Av. M30—3A 76
Maple Av. M32—5K 89
Maple Av. M34—6H 81
(Audenshaw)
Maple Av. M34—3L 93
(Denton)
Maple Av. SK6—9F 106
Maple Av. SK8—2M 113
Maple Av. SK12—6M 117
(New Mills)
Maple Av. SK12—9M 115
(Poynton)
Maple Av. SK15—7F 82
Maple Av. WA3—8M 71
Maple Av. WA11—8H 69
Maple Av. WN2—5M 53
(Hindley)
Maple Av. WN2—2F 52
(Ince)
Maple Bank. WA14—1B 110
Maple Clo. BL4—3M 57
Maple Clo. M6—4M 77
Maple Clo. M24—9D 44
Maple Clo. M33—1C 100
Maple Clo. OL2—1M 45
Maple Clo. OL9—8H 45
Maple Clo. SK2—7H 105

Maple Clo. WN5—2D 68
Maple Cres. WN7—9E 54
Maple Croft. SK1—5H 105
Maple Dri. WN2—9H 53
Maplefield Dri. M28—9H 57
Maple Gro. BL0—6K 9
Maple Gro. BL8—5G 25
Maple Gro. M10—6F 62
Maple Gro. M25—2A 60
Maple Gro. M35—2E 80
Maple Gro. WA15—8L 101
Maple Gro. WN6—6A 34
Maple Rd. BL4—9G 39
Maple Rd. M23—5J 101
Maple Rd. M27—1E 76
Maple Rd. M31—2E 98
Maple Rd. OL9—8H 45
Maple Rd. SK7—7E 114
Maple Rd. SK9—8H 119
Maple Rd. W. M23—5J 101
Maple St. BL2—5J 23
Maple St. BL3—4D 38
Maple St. OL8—5J 63
Maple St. OL11—4D 28
Maple St. WN4—1A 70
Maple Wlk. M23—5J 101
Maplewood Gdns. BL1—9E 22
Maplewood Ho. BL1—8E 22
Maplewood Rd. SK9—3L 119
Mapley Av. M22—5D 102
Maplin Clo. M13—8J 79
Maplin Dri. SK2—8A 106
Mapperton Wlk. M16—3F 90
Marble St. M2—4F 5 & 6G 79
(in two parts)
Marble St. OL1—9B 46
Marbury Av. M14—5H 91
Marbury Clo. M31—3K 87
Marbury Dri. WA14—4E 100
Marbury Gro. WN6—1L 33
Marbury Rd. SK4—8D 92
Marbury Rd. SK9—2H 119
Marcer Rd. M10—5K 79
March Av. SK4—3B 104
Marchbank. WN2—7G 35
Marchbank Dri. SK8—7J 103
March Dri. BL8—5K 25
Marchioness St. M18—9F 80
Marchmont Clo. M13—9K 79
March St. OL16—3G 29
Marchwood Av. M21—5D 90
Marcliffe Dri. M19—5C 92
Marcliffe Dri. OL11—4B 28
Marcliffe Ind. Est. SK7—3L 115
Marcliff Gro. SK4—3B 104
Marcroft Pl. OL11—6G 29
Marcus Gro. M14—4J 91
Marcus St. BL1—9B 22
Mardale Av. M20—9J 91
Mardale Av. M27—6C 58
Mardale Av. M31—3M 87
Mardale Av. OL2—1J 45
Mardale Av. WA11—7B 68
Mardale Clo. BL2—9M 23
Mardale Clo. M25—1C 60
Mardale Clo. M29—3J 55
Mardale Clo. OL4—9D 46
Mardale Clo. SK15—4G 83
Mardale Cres. WA13—1A 108
Mardale Dri. BL2—9M 23
Mardale Dri. M24—8L 43
Mardale Dri. SK8—7H 103
Mardale Rd. M27—1D 76
Marden Rd. M23—8A 102
Mardyke. OL12—2E 28
Mardyke Dri. M8—2E 78
Marefield. M33—2M 101
Marfield Av. OL9—3G 63
Marfield Ct. M31—5L 87
Marfield St. M9—7L 61
Marford Clo. M22—7D 102
Marford Cres. M33—3F 100
Margaret Av. OL16—3J 29
Margaret Av. WN6—5J 33
Margaret Ho. OL6—5A 82
Margaret Rd. M34—2A 94
Margaret Rd. M35—5E 80
Margaret St. BL9—9M 25
Margaret St. OL2—3B 46
Margaret St. OL6—4A 82
Margaret St. OL7—5A 82
Margaret St. OL8—6H 63
Margaret St. OL10—8H 27
Margaret St. SK5—7E 92
Margaret St. WN2—2K 53
Margaret St. WN6—8A 34
Margaret Ter. OL6—5A 82
Margaret Ward Ct. OL11—5G 29
Margate Av. M10—2B 80
Margate Rd. SK5—7F 92
Margrove Rd. M6—3J 77
Marguerita Rd. M10—3D 80
(in two parts)
Marham Clo. M21—7E 90
Marian Rd. WA11—8L 69
Maria St. BL1—8E 22
Marie Clo. M34—4M 93
(in two parts)
Marie St. M8—9E 60
Marigold St. OL11—5F 28
(in two parts)
Marigold St. WN5—1K 51
Mariman Dri. M8—6G 61
Marina Av. M34—5A 94
Marina Clo. SK9—7K 113
Marina Cres. M11—4B 80
Marina Dri. SK6—6C 106
Marina Dri. WN5—3K 51
Marina Rd. M35—5H 81
Marina Rd. SK6—1L 105
Marine Av. M31—2D 98
Marion Pl. WN2—8F 52
Marion St. BL3—7J 39
Marion St. OL8—5M 63
Maritime Ct. M33—1F 100
Marjorie Clo. M18—9B 80
Mark Av. M6—1A 4 & 3B 78
Markendale St. M5—9A 78
Markenfield Dri. OL2—2M 45
Markerside Clo. M21—6C 90
Market Arc. WN7—2F 72
Market Av. OL1—1M 63
Market Av. OL6—4B 82
Market Brow. M9—6K 61
Market Cen., The. M2—4F 5 &
6G 79
Market Hall. WN1—9C 34
(off Galleries, The)
Market Pde. BL9—8M 25
Market Pl. BL0—1K 9
(Edenfield)
Market Pl. BL0—4J 9
(Ramsbottom)
Market Pl. BL4—9K 39
Market Pl. BL9—8L 25
Market Pl. M4—3E 5 & 5F 78
Market Pl. M24—8A 44
Market Pl. M27—7G 59
Market Pl. M29—5K 55
Market Pl. M34—3L 93
Market Pl. M35—6G 81
Market Pl. OL1—1L 63
Market Pl. OL2—5K 45
(Royton)
Market Pl. OL2—3B 46
(Shaw)
Market Pl. OL10—8K 27
Market Pl. OL16—3E 28
Market Pl. SK1—3F 104
(in two parts)
Market Pl. SK6—4G 107
Market Pl. SK14—4D 94
(in two parts)
Market Pl. WN1—9C 34
Market St. BL0—1K 9
Market St. BL1—2F 38
Market St. BL3—6A 40
Market St. BL4—8K 39
Market St. BL5—9E 36
Market St. BL8—3F 24
Market St. BL9—8L 25
(in four parts)
Market St. M1—4F 5 & 6G 79

Market St. M24—8M 43
(in two parts)
Market St. M26—9B 40
Market St. M27—7G 59
Market St. M29—5J 55
(Atherton)
Market St. M29—7M 55
(Tyldesley)
Market St. M34—3M 93
Market St. M35—7G 81
Market St. OL2—5K 45
(Royton)
Market St. OL2—3B 46
(Shaw)
Market St. OL5—7J 65
Market St. OL6—4B 82
Market St. OL10—8J 27
Market St. OL12—5C 12
(Rochdale)
Market St. PR7—4G 19
Market St. SK6—7F 106
Market St. SK12—6K 117
Market St. SK13—6J 97
Market St. SK14—6A 96
(Broadbottom)
Market St. SK14—1C 96
(Hollingworth)
Market St. SK14—3D 94
(Hyde)
Market St. SK14—2A 96
(Mottram)
Market St. SK15—5G 83
Market St. WA14—9D 100
Market St. WN1—9C 34
Market St. WN2—3K 53
Market St. WN6—9L 17
Market St. WN7—2F 72
Market Wlk. M33—9H 89
Market Way. M4—5G 79
(off Arndale Cen.)
Market Way. M6—4M 77
Market Way. OL16—3F 28
Markfield Av. M13—1K 91
Markfield Cres. WA11—9C 68
Markham Clo. M12—7L 79
Markham Clo. SK14—9D 82
Markham St. SK14—9D 82
Markington St. M14—3G 91
Mark Jones Wlk. M10—2B 80
Markland Hill. BL1—1L 37
Markland Hill Clo. BL1—9M 21
Markland Hill La. BL1—9M 21
Marklands Rd. M29—3A 74
Markland St. BL3—3F 38
(off Soho St.)
Markland St. BL3—4G 39
(off Thynne St.)
Markland St. SK14—5E 94
Markland St. WN1—9E 34
Mark La. OL2—3C 46
Marks St. M26—6G 41
Mark St. M28—9F 56
Mark St. OL9—1K 63
Mark St. OL12—1H 29
Markwood. OL3—5M 47
Marland Av. OL8—7A 64
Marland Av. OL11—6B 28
Marland Av. SK8—2M 113
Marland Clo. OL11—5B 28
Marland Cres. SK5—6F 92
Marland Fold. OL11—6B 28
Marland Fold La. OL8—7M 63
Marland Grn. OL11—6B 28
Marland Hill Rd. OL11—5C 28
Marland Old Rd. OL11—6B 28
Marlands Sq. M29—7M 55
(off Lime St.)
Marland St. OL9—5G 63
Marland Tops. OL11—6B 28
Marlborough Av. M16—4C 90
Marlborough Av. SK8—2B 114
Marlborough Av. SK9—7M 119
Marlborough Av. WN3—4F 52
Marlborough Clo. BL0—8J 9
Marlborough Clo. M34—3M 93
Marlborough Clo. OL7—7L 81
Marlborough Clo. OL12—4C 12
Marlborough Clo. SK6—6D 106
Marlborough Ct. M9—3G 61
Marlborough Dri. M35—1E 80
Marlborough Dri. SK4—1D 104
Marlborough Gdns. BL4—9G 39
Marlborough Gro. M35—5J 81
Marlborough Rd. M7 & M8
—1F 78
Marlborough Rd. M29—4L 55
Marlborough Rd. M30—3G 77
(Eccles)
Marlborough Rd. M30—3H 87
(Irlam)
Marlborough Rd. M31—3M 87
Marlborough Rd. M32—3J 89
Marlborough Rd. M33—1H 101
Marlborough Rd. OL2—7L 45
Marlborough Rd. SK14—6E 94
Marlborough Rd. WA14
—2D 110
Marlborough St. BL1—1C 38
Marlborough St. OL4—2A 64
Marlborough St. OL7—7L 81
Marlborough St. OL10—1L 43
Marlborough St. OL12—1C 28
Marlbrook Dri. BL5—3E 54
Marlcroft Av. SK4—3B 104
Marld Cres. BL1—8M 21
Marle Av. OL5—7L 65
Marle Croft. M25—2J 59
Marle Rise. OL5—7L 65
Marler Rd. SK14—2E 94
Marley Clo. WA15—6F 100
Marley Dri. M33—8G 89
Marleyer Rise. SK6—5A 106
Marley Hey. BL7—6K 7
Marley Rd. M19—6B 92
Marley Rd. SK12—1L 121
Marlfield Rd. OL2—1L 45
Marlfield Rd. WA15—5K 111
Marl Gro. WN5—4D 50
Marlheath Wlk. M15—8E 78
(off Jackson Cres.)
Marlhill Clo. SK2—8L 105
Marlhill Ct. SK2—8L 105
Marlinford Dri. M10—2C 80
Marlor Ct. OL10—8H 27
Marlor St. M34—2L 93
Marlow Brow. SK14—2G 97
Marlow Clo. BL2—9M 23
Marlow Clo. M31—2B 88
(in four parts)
Marlow Clo. SK8—2M 113
Marlow Dri. M27—1E 76
Marlow Dri. M30—3G 87
Marlow Dri. SK9—7J 113
Marlow Dri. WA14—2M 109
Marlowe Dri. M20—1H 103
Marlowe Wlk. M34—7A 94
Marlowe Walks. SK6—3L 105
Marlow Rd. M9—7M 61
Marlow St. SK14—1G 97
Marlton Wlk. M9—5L 61
(off Leconfield Dri.)
Marlwood Rd. BL1—8M 21
Marmaduke St. OL9—9K 45
Marmion Clo. WA3—6L 71
Marmion Dri. M21—6A 90
Marne Av. M22—8E 102
Marne Av. OL6—2F 82
Marne Cres. OL11—3C 28
Marnland Gro. BL3—5L 37
Maroon Rd. M22—5F 112
Marple Av. BL1—6G 23
Marple Clo. WN6—8H 17
Marple Ct. SK1—6G 105
Marple Gro. M32—3J 89
Marple Hall Dri. SK6—6D 106
Marple Old Rd. SK2—7A 106
Marple Rd. SK2—6K 105
Marple Rd. SK14—9M 95
Marquis Av. BL9—6L 25
Marquis Dri. SK8—5K 113
Marquis St. M19—5D 92
Marrick Av. SK8—8J 103
Marrick Clo. WN3—6A 52

Marriott's Ct. M2—4F 5 & 6G 79
Marriott St. M20—8H 91
Marriott St. SK1—5F 104
Mars Av. BL3—6C 38
Marsden Clo. OL5—6H 65
Marsden Clo. OL7—2L 81
Marsden Clo. OL16—1J 45
Marsden Ct. M4—5G 79
(off Arndale Cen.)
Marsden Dri. WA15—7J 101
Marsden Rd. BL1—2E 38
Marsden Rd. SK6—2C 106
Marsden's Sq. OL15—5B 14
(off Sutcliffe St.)
Marsden St. BL5—9E 36
Marsden St. BL9—7M 25
Marsden St. M2—4E 5 & 6F 78
Marsden St. M24—1C 62
Marsden St. M28—9F 56
(Mosley Common)
Marsden St. M28—6B 58
(Worsley)
Marsden St. M30—4C 76
Marsden St. SK14—2G 97
Marsden St. WN1—9C 34
Marsden St. WN3—4F 52
Marsden St. WN5—1M 51
Marsden Wlk. M26—5F 40
Marsden Way. M4—5G 79
(off Arndale Cen.)
Marsett Clo. OL12—1M 27
Marsett Wlk. M23—3M 101
Marshall Ct. OL1—9L 45
Marshall Rd. M19—5A 92
Marshall Stevens Way. M17
—9H 77
Marshall St. M4—3G 5 & 5H 79
Marshall St. M34—2L 93
Marshall St. OL16—3J 29
Marshall St. WN7—3E 72
Marsham Clo. M13—1L 91
Marsham Clo. OL4—3H 65
Marsham Dri. SK6—8G 107
Marsham Rd. SK7—3H 115
Marshbank. BL5—8E 36
Marsh Brook Fold. BL5—1A 54
Marshbrook Rd. M31—3C 88
Marshdale Rd. BL1—1M 37
Marshfield Rd. WA15—8J 101
Marshfield Wlk. M13—9J 79
(off Lauderdale Cres.)
Marsh Fold La. BL1—1C 38
Marsh Grn. WN5—8K 33
Marsh Head. OL3—4E 48
Marsh La. BL3—5B 40
Marsh La. BL4—9G 39
Marsh La. WA16—9M 109
Marsh La. WN1—9C 34
Marsh Lea. OL3—4E 48
Marsh Rd. BL3—5A 40
Marsh Rd. M28—4H 57
Marsh Row. WN2—4A 54
Marsh St. BL1—8E 22
Marsh St. BL5—8E 36
Marsh St. BL6—6A 20
Marsh St. M28—6M 57
Marsh St. WN3—4A 52
Marsland Av. WA15—5H 101
Marsland Clo. M34—3H 93
Marsland Grn. La. M29—3L 73
Marsland Rd. M33—2G 101
Marsland Rd. SK6—6E 106
Marsland Rd. WA15—7H 101
Marsland St. SK1—2F 104
(in two parts)
Marsland St. SK7—2K 115
Marsland St. N. M8—9F 60
Marsland St. S. M8—9F 60
Marsland Ter. SK1—5H 105
Mars St. BL7—5L 7
Mars St. OL9—1J 63
Marston Clo. BL6—1F 36
Marston Clo. M25—9C 42
Marston Dri. M30—4H 87
Marston Rd. M7—8E 60
Marston Rd. M32—4L 89
Marston St. M10—2K 79
Marsworth Dri. M4—3H 5 &
5J 79
Martens Rd. M30—9E 86
Marthall Dri. M33—3L 101
Marthall Way. SK9—7L 113
Martham Dri. SK2—8A 106
Martha's Ter. OL16—8J 13
Martha St. BL3—5D 38
Martha St. OL1—9K 45
Martin Av. BL3—6C 40
Martin Av. BL4—1F 56
Martin Av. OL4—2C 64
Martin Av. WA10—9A 68
Martin Av. WA12—9B 70
Martin Clo. M34—1M 93
Martin Clo. SK2—8A 106
Martindale Clo. OL2—4L 45
Martindale Cres. M12—9L 79
Martindale Cres. M24—6K 43
Martindale Cres. WN5—2M 51
Martindale Gdns. BL1—8E 22
Martindale Rd. WA11—5B 68
Martindale Way. M35—4K 81
Martin Dri. M30—2G 87
Martin Gro. BL4—1M 57
Martin La. OL12—1B 28
Martin Rd. M27—6H 59
Martinsclough. BL6—3J 37
Martinscroft Rd. M23—8B 102
Martin St. BL7—7K 7
Martin St. BL9—7D 26
Martin St. M5—5K 77
Martin St. M29—5K 55
Martin St. M34—8M 81
Martin St. SK14—4E 94
Martland Av. WN6—4F 32
Martland Cres. WN6—6L 33
Martland Mill La. WN5—7K 33
Martland Mill La. WN6—6L 33
Martlesham Wlk. M4—3F 5 &
5G 79
Martlet Av. OL11—3L 27
Martlet Clo. M14—5H 91
Martlets Av. SK12—6J 117
Martlew Dri. M29—4M 55
Martock Av. M22—1E 112
Marton Av. BL2—1J 39
Marton Av. M20—3J 103
Marton Dri. M29—4L 55
Marton Ga. M25—6D 60
Marton Grn. SK3—7D 104
Marton Gro. SK4—8E 92
Marton Pl. M33—1G 101
Marton St. WN1—8C 34
Marton Way. SK9—7L 113
Martsland Av. WA3—8K 71
Marus Av. WN3—5M 51
Marvic Ct. M13—3L 91
Marwood Clo. M26—9A 40
Marwood Clo. WA14—7B 100
Marwood Dri. M23—1M 111
Mary Anne Clo. OL7—1A 82
Maryfield Ct. M16—6E 90
Maryland Av. BL2—2K 39
Marylebone Pl. WN1—6C 34
Marylon Dri. M22—5E 102
Mary St. BL0—6H 9
Mary St. BL4—1K 57
Mary St. BL9—4M 25
Mary St. M3—2E 5 & 4F 78
Mary St. M29—7A 56
Mary St. M34—2A 94
Mary St. M35—5H 81
Mary St. OL10—8J 27
Mary St. OL16—7K 13
Mary St. SK8—7K 103
Mary St. SK14—3D 94
Mary St. SK16—6B 82
Mary St. E. BL6—6B 20
Mary St. W. BL6—5A 20
Masbury Clo. BL1—3E 22
Masefield Av. M25—5M 59
Masefield Av. M26—5E 40
Masefield Av. WN5—2G 51
Masefield Av. WN7—9D 54
Masefield Clo. SK16—8H 83

Masefield Cres. M35—6G 81
Masefield Dri. BL4—1H 57
(in two parts)
Masefield Dri. WN3—3M 51
Masefield Gro. SK5—5E 92
Masefield Ho. WN3—3M 51
Masefield Rd. BL3—5B 40
Masefield Rd. M35—6G 81
Masefield Rd. OL1—7B 46
Masmyth St. BL6—7C 20
Mason Clo. WN4—3D 70
Mason Gdns. BL3—3E 38
Mason La. M29—6L 55
Mason Row. BL7—9D 6
Mason St. BL6—7A 20
Mason St. BL9—8A 26
Mason St. M3—3C 4 & 5D 78
Mason St. M4—3G 5 & 5H 79
Mason St. OL10—8H 27
Mason St. OL16—3F 28
Mason St. WN2—8H 53
Mason St. WN3—1B 52
Mason St. Ind. Est. WN3—1B 52
(off Mason St.)
Massey Av. M35—8H 63
Massey Av. OL6—1C 82
Massey Croft. OL12—3C 12
Massey Rd. M33—1L 101
Massey Rd. WA15—9E 100
Massey St. BL9—7A 26
Massey St. M5—5C 78
Massey St. SK9—8L 119
Massey Wlk. M22—3F 112
Massie St. SK8—7K 103
Matchmoor La. BL6—6F 20
Matham Wlk. M15—9G 79
(off Chevril Clo.)
Mather Av. M25—6C 60
(Prestwich)
Mather Av. M25—7M 41
(Whitefield)
Mather Av. M30—5E 76
Mather Av. WA3—9L 71
Mather Clo. M25—8M 41
Mather Fold Rd. M28—7H 57
Mather La. WN7—3G 73
Mather Rd. BL9—3M 25
Mather Rd. M30—5E 76
Mather St. BL3—3E 38
Mather St. BL4—9L 39
Mather St. M26—6G 41
Mather St. M29—5K 55
Mather St. M35—9E 62
Mather Way. M6—4A 78
Matheson Dri. WN5—9K 33
Matley Clo. SK14—1H 95
Matley Gro. SK5—8J 93
Matley La. SK14 & SK15—1H 95
Matley Pk. La. SK15—9K 83
Matlock Av. M7—9A 60
Matlock Av. M20—8F 90
Matlock Av. M31—6B 88
Matlock Av. M34—6A 94
Matlock Av. OL6—1F 82
Matlock Bank. SK13—5E 96
(off Riber Bank)
Matlock Clo. BL4—8L 39
Matlock Clo. M29—6K 55
Matlock Clo. M33—1J 101
Matlock Dri. SK7—4L 115
Matlock Gdns. SK13—5E 96
(off Riber Bank)
Matlock La. SK13—5E 96
(off Riber Bank)
Matlock M. WA14—8E 100
Matlock Pl. SK13—5E 96
(off Riber Bank)
Matlock Rd. M32—3G 89
Matlock Rd. SK5—5G 93
Matlock Rd. SK8—5J 113
Matlock St. M30—7C 76
Matson Wlk. M22—2A 112
Matt Busby Clo. M27—9H 59
Matterdale Ter. SK15—3G 83
Matthew Moss La. OL11—6B 28
Matthews Av. BL4—1M 57
Matthews La. M12 & M19
—4A 92
Matthew's St. M12—8M 79
Matthew St. BL4—7J 39
Matthew St. SK6—7G 107
Matthias Ct. M3—2C 4 & 4D 78
Maudsley St. BL9—9L 25
Maud St. BL2—5J 23
Maud St. OL12—9G 13
Mauldeth Clo. SK4—2A 104
Mauldeth Ct. SK4—2A 104
Mauldeth Rd. M20 & M19—7J 91
(Withington & Burnage)
Mauldeth Rd. SK4 & M19—9M 91
(Heaton Mersey & Green End)
Mauldeth Rd. W. M21 & M20
—8C 90
Maunby Gdns. M28—5J 57
Maureen Av. M8—8G 61
Maurice Clo. SK16—7E 82
Maurice Dri. M6—3M 77
Maurice Pariser Wlk. M8
—9F 60
Maurice Rd. OL11—4F 28
Maurice St. M6—3M 77
Maveen Ct. SK2—9G 105
Maveen Gro. SK2—9G 105
Mavis Dri. PR7—1L 17
Mavis Gro. OL16—4A 30
Mavis St. OL11—9C 28
Mawdsley Dri. M8—8J 61
Mawdsley St. BL1—2F 38
Maxton Ho. BL4—9L 39
Maxwell Av. SK2—8J 105
Maxwell St. BL1—6E 22
Maxwell St. BL9—7B 26
Max Woosnam Wlk. M14
—3G 91
Mayall St. OL5—7J 65
Mayall St. E. OL4—1C 64
Mayan Av. M3—3C 4 & 5D 78
May Av. SK4—3B 104
May Av. SK8—6B 114
May Av. WN7—1D 72
Maybank Clo. M15—1F 90
Maybank St. BL3—4D 38
Mayberth Av. M8—6G 61
Maybrook Wlk. M9—8K 61
Mayburn Clo. M24—3C 62
Maybury St. M18—9E 80
Maycroft. SK5—8H 93
Maycroft Av. M20—9J 91
May Dri. M19—8M 91
Mayering Ct. SK4—1C 104
Mayer St. SK2—6J 105
Mayes Gdns. M4—6K 79
Mayes St. M4—3F 5 & 5G 79
(in two parts)
Mayfair. BL6—7D 20
Mayfair Av. M6—4H 77
Mayfair Av. M25—1M 59
Mayfair Av. M26—5D 40
Mayfair Av. M31—4B 88
Mayfair Clo. SK16—7G 83
Mayfair Cres. M35—8H 63
Mayfair Dri. M29—4M 55
Mayfair Dri. M30—4G 87
Mayfair Dri. M33—3E 100
Mayfair Dri. OL2—7K 45
Mayfair Dri. WN2—7K 35
Mayfair Dri. WN3—6M 51
Mayfair Gdns. OL11—5D 28
Mayfair Gro. M25—1A 60
Mayfair Pk. M20—2F 102
Mayfair Rd. M22—1E 112
Mayfield. BL2—5K 23
Mayfield. M26—7E 40
Mayfield Av. BL3—6H 39
Mayfield Av. BL4—1J 57
Mayfield Av. M27—1C 76
Mayfield Av. M28—5K 57
Mayfield Av. M32—5H 89
Mayfield Av. M33—1L 101
Mayfield Av. M34—7A 94
Mayfield Av. OL4—1G 65
Mayfield Av. PR6—3G 19
Mayfield Av. SK5—9F 92

Mayfield Clo. BL0—9G 9
Mayfield Clo. WA15—7H 101
Mayfield Ct. WA15—7H 101
Mayfield Ct. WN5—8H 33
Mayfield Dri. WN7—7C 72
Mayfield Gro. M18—2F 92
Mayfield Gro. SK5—8F 92
Mayfield Gro. SK9—6E 118
Mayfield Rd. BL0—9G 9
Mayfield Rd. M7—7B 60
Mayfield Rd. M16—3E 90
Mayfield Rd. OL1—8B 46
Mayfield Rd. SK6—4H 107
Mayfield Rd. SK7—8E 114
Mayfield Rd. WA15—7H 101
Mayfield Rd. WN5—9H 33
Mayfield Rd. WN8—1A 50
Mayfield St. M29—5J 55
Mayfield St. M34—1L 93
Mayfield St. OL16—1H 29
(in two parts)
Mayfield Ter. M33—1G 101
Mayfield Ter. OL16—1H 29
Mayfield View. WA13—2A 108
Mayflower Cotts. WN1—1C 34
Mayford Rd. M19—4A 92
Maygate. OL1—9K 45
May Gro. M19—6B 92
Mayhill Dri. M6—3G 77
Mayhill Dri. M28—8A 58
Mayhurst Av. M21—1D 102
Mayorlowe Av. SK5—1J 105
Mayor's Rd. WA15—9E 100
Mayor St. BL1 & BL3—3D 38
Mayor St. BL8—7J 25
Mayor St. OL9—1J 63
Mayo St. M12—7K 79
May Pl. OL11—6G 29
(off Oldham Rd.)
May Pl. OL15—7L 13
Maypole Ind. Est. WN2—9J 53
Maypool Dri. SK5—8F 92
May Rd. M16—3D 90
May Rd. M27—1H 77
May Rd. SK8—6B 114
Maysmith M. M7—1D 78
May St. BL2—2G 39
May St. BL7—5L 7
May St. M10—2C 80
(in two parts)
May St. M26—6G 41
May St. M30—3C 76
May St. OL8—4J 63
May St. OL10—1L 43
(in two parts)
May St. WA3—5H 71
May St. WN7—2C 72
Mayton St. M11—7A 80
Mayville Dri. M20—9H 91
May Wlk. M31—2E 98
Maywood. SK9—7E 118
Maywood Av. M20—5H 103
Maze Ct. OL1—9L 45
Maze St. BL3—4J 39
Meachin Av. M21—8C 90
Meade Clo. M31—4C 88
Meade Gro. M13—3M 91
Meade Hill Rd. M25—5E 60
Meade, The. BL3—7E 38
Meade, The. M21—7B 90
Meade, The. SK9—3J 119
Meadfoot Av. M25—5C 60
Meadfoot Rd. M18—9D 80
Meadland Gro. BL1—6F 22
Meadon Av. M27—7H 59
Meadow Av. SK14—5E 94
Meadow Av. WA15—1H 111
Meadow Bank. BL9—1L 41
Meadow Bank. M21—7A 90
Meadow Bank. SK4—3B 104
Meadow Bank. SK6—2M 105
Meadow Bank. SK13—7F 96
Meadow Bank. SK14—9D 84
Meadow Bank. WA15—6G 101
Meadowbank Av. M29—4L 55
Meadow Bank Ct. M32—5G 89
Meadowbank Gdns. WA3
—8J 73
Meadowbank Rd. BL3—7B 38
Meadowbrook Clo. BL6—6H 37
Meadow Brow. SK9—7L 119
Meadow Clo. BL3—7B 40
Meadow Clo. M32—5L 89
Meadow Clo. M34—7A 94
Meadow Clo. OL5—5L 65
Meadow Clo. OL10—8J 27
Meadow Clo. SK6—4F 116
(High Lane)
Meadow Clo. SK6—9A 94
(Woodley)
Meadow Clo. SK9—7E 118
Meadow Clo. WA15—1H 111
Meadow Clo. WN7—5E 72
Meadow Cotts. OL12—1D 12
Meadow Ct. M6—4H 77
Meadow Ct. WA15—1J 111
Meadowcroft. BL5—1F 54
Meadow Croft. M25—2J 59
Meadowcroft. M26—4F 40
Meadowcroft. M33—8H 89
Meadow Croft. SK7—1L 115
Meadowcroft. SK14—2A 96
Meadowcroft. WN4—1M 69
Meadowcroft La. OL11—4M 27
Meadowfield. BL6—2H 37
Meadowfield Clo. SK13—3F 96
Meadowfield Dri. M28—1H 75
Meadow Fold. OL3—9C 48
Meadowgate. M28—8M 57
Meadowgate. M31—5D 88
Meadowgate Rd. M6—4H 77
Meadow Head Av. OL12—5D 12
Meadow La. BL2—2A 40
Meadow La. M28—2M 75
Meadow La. M34—6A 94
Meadow La. OL8—6L 63
Meadow La. SK12—6K 117
Meadow La. SK16—7D 82
Meadow La. WA14—9G 99
Meadow Pit La. WN2—1E 34
Meadow Rise. OL2—9A 30
Meadow Rise. SK13—7F 96
Meadow Rd. M7—2B 4 & 4C 78
Meadow Rd. M24—2L 61
Meadow Rd. M31—5D 88
Meadowside. M21—8B 90
Meadowside. OL16—6C 30
Meadowside. SK7—2C 114
Meadowside. SK12—6M 117
Meadowside Av. BL2—1J 39
(in two parts)
Meadowside Av. M22—9D 102
Meadowside Av. M28—4L 57
Meadowside Av. M30—4G 87
Meadowside Av. WN4—8A 52
Meadowside Gro. M28—5L 57
Meadows La. BL2—7M 23
Meadows Rd. M33—8J 89
Meadows Rd. SK4—7C 92
Meadows Rd. SK8—4M 113
(Cheadle Hulme)
Meadows Rd. SK8—3H 113
(Heald Green)
Meadows, The. M24—2B 62
Meadows, The. M25—4B 60
Meadows, The. M26—4E 40
Meadows, The. M30—8E 86
Meadows, The. OL3—1B 66
Meadows, The. OL4—2G 65
Meadows, The. SK14—2F 96
Meadow St. M16—2E 90
Meadow St. OL8—7H 63
Meadow St. SK2—8J 105
Meadow St. SK14—5E 94
Meadow St. WN6—8A 34
Meadow, The. BL1—2J 37
Meadow, The. OL12—2C 12
Meadow View. OL12—1A 28
Meadow Wlk. M29—2B 74
Meadow Wlk. M31—2E 98
Meadow Wlk. OL15—6M 13
Meadow Wlk. SK6—2M 105
Meadow Way. BL6—9L 19

Meadow Way. BL7—5K 7
Meadow Way. BL8—4E 24
Meadow Way. BL9—9J 9
Meadow Way. M10—7A 62
Meadow Way. PR7—2K 17
Meadow Way. SK9—7E 118
Meadow Way. WA15—1H 111
Meads Gro. BL4—9E 38
Meads Gro. M29—1C 74
Meads, The. OL9—2G 63
Mead, The. M5—5K 77
Meadway. BL0—2J 9
Meadway. BL4—8M 39
Meadway. BL9—3M 41
Meadway. M29—7D 56
Meadway. M33—2E 100
Mead Way. M34—6M 93
Meadway. OL9—6E 62
Meadway. OL11—6C 28
Meadway. SK6—4F 116
Meadway. SK7—7E 114
Meadway. SK12—7H 115
Meadway. SK15—9L 83
Meadway. SK16—8E 82
Meadway. WA3—7K 71
Meadway. WN2—1F 52
Meadway Clo. M33—3E 100
Meadway Rd. SK8—1B 114
Mealhouse Brow. SK1—4F 104
Mealhouse Ct. M29—5J 55
Mealhouse La. BL1—2F 38
Mealhouse La. M29—5J 55
Meal St. SK4—2E 104
Meanley Rd. M29—9L 55
Meanley St. M29—7A 56
Meanwood Brow. OL12—2C 28
(in two parts)
Meanwood Fold. OL12—2D 28
Measham Clo. WA11—9C 68
Meddings Clo. SK9—9K 119
Medina Clo. SK8—9B 104
Medley St. OL12—1F 28
Medley Wlk. M13—8H 79
(off Hanworth Clo.)
Medlock Ct. M15—1F 90
(off Lingbeck Cres.)
Medlock Ct. OL4—1E 64
Medlock Dri. OL8—7A 64
Medlock Rd. M35—3F 80
Medlock St. M15—6E 5 & 8F 78
Medlock St. M35—5G 81
Medlock St. OL1—1A 64
Medlock Way. M25—9C 42
Medlock Way. OL4—2E 64
Medlock Way WN2—6G 53
Medway Clo. BL6—7D 20
Medway Clo. M5—4K 77
Medway Clo. OL8—5J 63
Medway Clo. WN4—1M 69
Medway Clo. WN7—7C 72
Medway Cres. WA14—7C 100
Medway Dri. BL4—3B 58
Medway Dri. BL6—7D 20
Medway Pl. WN5—1K 51
Medway Rd. M28—8H 57
Medway Rd. OL2—1A 46
Medway Rd. OL8—5J 63
Medway, The. OL10—7H 27
Medway Wlk. M10—4K 79
Medway Wlk. WN5—1K 51
Meech St. M11—7C 80
Meek St. OL1—7A 46
Meersbrook Rd. SK3—5A 104
Mee's Sq. M30—7D 76
Megfield. BL5—2E 54
Melandra Castle Rd. SK13 —5D 96
Melandra Cres. SK14—4L 95
Melanie Clo. SK13—6G 97
Melanie Dri. SK5—6F 92
Melba St. M11—7E 80
Melbecks Wlk. M23—3L 101
Melbourne Av. M32—4K 89
Melbourne Av. OL9—1G 63
Melbourne Clo. BL6—7C 20
Melbourne Clo. OL11—8G 29
Melbourne Gro. BL6—7C 20
Melbourne M. M7—2D 78
Melbourne Rd. BL3—4B 38
Melbourne Rd. OL11—8G 29
Melbourne Rd. SK7—6E 114
Melbourne St. M7—2D 78
Melbourne St. M9—8L 61
Melbourne St. M15—6D 4 & 8E 78
Melbourne St. M27—8H 59
Melbourne St. M34—4L 93
Melbourne St. OL9—1H 63
Melbourne St. SK5—6F 92
Melbourne St. SK15—5G 83
Melbourne St. N. OL6—3C 82
Melbourne St. S. OL6—3C 82
Melbourne Wlk. M5—5A 4 & 7B 78
Melbury. OL11—6F 28
Melbury Av. M20—1K 103
Melbury Dri. BL6—1F 36
Melbury Rd. SK8—6B 114
Meldon Rd. M13—4L 91
Meldreth Dri. M12—2M 91
Meldrum St. OL8—4M 63
Meldrum Wlk. OL8—4M 63
Melford Av. M10—7E 62
Melford Dri. WN4—3A 70
Melford Dri. WN5—5D 50
Melford Ho. BL1—9E 22
(off Nottingham Dri.)
Melford Rd. SK7—3M 115
Melfort Av. M32—5L 89
Meliden Cres. BL1—9B 22
Meliden Cres. M22—1E 112
Mellalieu St. M24—8L 43
Mellalieu St. OL2—7L 45
Mellalieu St. OL10—7J 27
Melland Av. M21—9C 90
Melland Rd. M18—3C 92
Meller Rd. M13—4M 91
Melling Av. OL9—8E 44
Melling Av. SK4—8E 92
Melling Clo. WN7—6F 72
Melling Rd. OL4—2C 64
Mellings Av. WN5—7E 50
Melling St. M12—2A 92
Melling St. WN5—3L 51
Mellington Av. M20—5H 103
Mellish Wlk. M8—2F 78
Mellor Brow. OL10—8J 27
Mellor Clo. M16—1D 90
Mellor Clo. OL6—4E 82
Mellor Ct. SK2—6L 105
Mellor Dri. BL9—2K 41
Mellor Dri. M28—7J 57
Mellor Gro. BL1—9B 22
(in two parts)
Mellor Ho. OL2—5L 45
(off Royton Hall Wlk.)
Mellor Rd. OL6—5E 82
(in two parts)
Mellor Rd. SK8—3B 114
Mellors Rd. M17—8H 77
Mellor St. M10—4K 79
Mellor St. M25—4M 59
Mellor St. M26—7H 41
(in two parts)
Mellor St. M30—6D 76
Mellor St. M32—2L 89
Mellor St. M35—6F 80
(Droylsden)
Mellor St. M35—1D 80
(Failsworth)
Mellor St. OL2—4K 45
Mellor St. OL4—2E 64
Mellor St. OL8—6J 63
Mellor St. OL11 & OL12—2D 28
Mellor Way. OL9—4H 63
Mellowdew St. OL1—5E 46
Mellowstone Dri. M21—6F 90
Melloy Pl. M8—1F 5 & 3G 79
Melmerby Clo. WN4—4M 69
Melmerby Ct. M5—6M 77
Melrose. OL12—2E 28
(off Spotland Rd.)
Melrose Av. BL1—9A 22
Melrose Av. BL8—7J 25
Melrose Av. M20—2J 103
Melrose Av. M30—3A 76
Melrose Av. M33—1H 101
Melrose Av. OL10—7J 27
Melrose Av. OL15—4A 14
Melrose Av. SK3—6M 103
Melrose Av. WN7—7D 54
Melrose Clo. M25—7M 41
Melrose Ct. OL9—4G 63
Melrose Cres. SK3—9D 104
Melrose Cres. WA15—3H 111
Melrose Cres. WN4—4J 69
Melrose Dri. WN3—5J 51
Melrose Gdns. M26—4E 40
Melrose Rd. BL3—6M 39
Melrose Rd. M26—4E 40
Melrose St. BL9—9H 9
Melrose St. OL1—8B 46
Melrose St. OL11—3D 28
Melsomby Rd. M23—3A 102
Meltham Av. M20—8G 91
Meltham Clo. SK4—4L 103
Meltham Pl. BL3—5C 38
Meltham Rd. SK4—4L 103
Melton Av. M31—3K 87
Melton Av. M34—3G 93
Melton Clo. M28—6J 57
Melton Clo. M29—8B 56
Melton Clo. OL10—9H 27
Melton Dri. BL9—4A 42
Melton Rd. M8—7E 60
Melton St. M9—7M 61
Melton St. M26—5F 40
Melton St. OL10—9H 27
Melton St. SK5—1F 104
Melverley Dri. WN7—2J 73
Melverley Rd. M9—3G 61
Melverley St. WN3—1A 52
Melville Clo. M11—8E 80
Melville Rd. BL4—2M 57
Melville Rd. M30—9C 86
Melville Rd. M32—3H 89
Melville St. BL3—5G 39
Melville St. M3—3C 4 & 5D 78
Melville St. OL4—3E 64
Melville St. OL6—4B 82
Melville St. OL11—9D 28
Melvin Av. M22—9E 102
Memorial Rd. M28—6K 57
Menai Gro. SK8—7A 104
Menai Rd. SK3—7E 104
Menai St. BL3—5B 38
Mendip Av. M22—9F 102
Mendip Av. WN3—5J 51
Mendip Clo. BL2—2A 40
Mendip Clo. BL6—5C 20
Mendip Clo. OL2—6J 45
Mendip Clo. OL9—3H 63
Mendip Clo. SK4—2E 104
Mendip Clo. SK8—5H 113
Mendip Ct. SK4—2E 104
Mendip Ct. WN2—5H 53
Mendip Cres. BL8—7G 25
Mendip Dri. BL2—3A 40
Mendip Dri. OL16—4A 30
Mendips Clo. OL2—1M 45
Menston Av. M10—7E 62
Mentmore Rd. OL16—3K 29
Mentone Cres. M22—9E 102
Mentone Rd. SK4—2B 104
Mentor St. M13—3M 91
Mercer La. OL11—2L 27
Mercer Rd. M35—5H 81
Mercer Rd. OL10—2K 43
Mercer Rd. WA11—9J 69
Mercer St. M18—1D 92
Mercer St. M19—5B 92
Merchants Cres. WA3—6L 71
Merchants Quay. M5—9M 77
Mercian Way. OL6—4B 82
Mercian Way. SK3—6D 104
Mercia St. BL3—4C 38
Mercury Way. M31—1F 88
Mere Av. M6—5L 77
Mere Av. M24—2A 62
Mere Av. M35—7E 80
Mere Av. WN7—2D 72
Mere Clo. M33—2M 101
Mere Clo. M34—3H 93
Mereclough Av. M28—7M 57
Meredew Av. M27—1E 76
Meredith St. BL3—6F 38
Meredith St. M14—7K 91
Mere Dri. M20—1H 103
Mere Dri. M27—6G 59
Merefield Rd. WA15—8J 101
Merefield Ter. OL11—5E 28
Mere Fold. M28—5H 57
Mere Gdns. BL1—1E 38
Mere Gro. WA11—6B 68
Merehall Clo. BL1—1E 38
Merehall Dri. BL1—9E 22
Merehall St. BL1—9D 22
Mereland Av. M20—1J 103
Mere La. OL11—5F 28
Merepool Clo. SK6—6D 106
Mere Rd. WN4—3C 70
Mere Side. SK15—3F 82
(in four parts)
Mereside Clo. SK8—9M 103
Mereside Gro. M28—5L 57
Mereside Rd. WA16—9J 109
Mereside Wlk. M15—9D 78
Mere St. OL11—4F 28
(in three parts)
Mere St. WN5—2M 51
Mere St. WN7—2D 72
Mere, The. OL6—1E 82
Mere, The. SK8—9M 103
Mere Wlk. BL1—1E 38
Merewood Av. M22—7D 102
Merfield Av. OL11—5E 28
Meridan Clo. WA11—9D 68
Meriden Clo. M26—3F 40
Meriden Gro. BL6—3K 37
Merinall Clo. OL16—3J 29
Meriton Rd. SK9—8J 113
Meriton Wlk. M18—2B 92
Merlewood. BL0—1L 9
Merlewood Av. M19—7C 92
Merlewood Av. M34—6H 81
Merlewood Av. OL3—9B 48
Merlewood Dri. M27—1C 76
Merlewood Dri. M29—8B 56
Merlin Clo. OL8—8A 64
(in two parts)
Merlin Clo. OL15—9A 14
Merlin Clo. SK2—7A 106
Merlin Dri. M27—6H 59
Merlin Gro. BL1—9B 22
(in two parts)
Merlin Rd. M30—2G 87
Merlin Rd. OL16—4M 29
Merlyn Av. M20—1J 103
Merlyn Av. M33—8J 89
Merlyn Av. M34—4L 93
Merlyn Ct. M20—1G 103
Merrick Av. M22—9E 102
Merrick St. OL10—9L 27
Merridale, The. WA15—4G 111
Merridge Wlk. M8—1F 78
Merrill St. M4—6K 79
Merriman Clo. M16—2E 90
Merriman Hall. OL16—9H 13
Merrion St. BL4—7J 39
Merrow Wlk. M1—8H 79
(off Grosvenor St.)
Merrybent Clo. SK2—8K 105
Merry Bower Rd. M7—8E 60
Merrydale Av. M30—3E 76
Mersey Bank. SK14—1F 96
Merseybank Av. M21—9C 90
Mersey Bank Rd. SK14—2F 96
Mersey Clo. M25—8B 42
Mersey Clo. WN2—5C 54
Mersey Cres. M20—2D 102
Mersey Dri. M25—8B 42
Mersey Dri. M31—1G 99
Mersey Ho. SK3—6A 104
Mersey Meadows. M20—2F 102
Mersey Rd. M20—2F 102
Mersey Rd. M33—8H 89
Mersey Rd. SK4—3M 103
(in two parts)
Mersey Rd. WN2—6F 52
Mersey Rd. WN5—1F 50
Mersey Rd. N. M35—7G 63
Mersey Sq. M25—8B 42
Mersey Sq. SK1—4E 104
Mersey St. M11—8E 80
Mersey St. SK1—3G 105
Mersey St. WN7—3C 72
Mersey View. M31—6L 87
Merseyway. SK1—4E 104
Merston Dri. M20—5J 103
Mersy Ct. M33—9L 89
Mersy St. SK1—4F 104
Merton Av. OL8—5K 63
Merton Av. SK6—1A 106
Merton Av. SK7—4M 115
Merton Clo. BL3—4C 38
Merton Dri. M35—6E 80
Merton Gro. M29—1C 74
Merton Gro. OL9—5D 62
Merton Gro. WA15—7H 101
Merton Rd. M25—3C 60
Merton Rd. M33—8G 89
Merton Rd. SK3—6B 104
Merton Rd. SK12—8H 115
Merton Rd. WN3—4H 51
Merton St. BL8—7K 25
Merton Wlk. M9—9L 61
(off Trongate Wlk.)
Merville Av. M10—7M 61
Mervyn Pl. WN3—4A 52
Mervyn Rd. M7—1A 78
Merwell Rd. M31—5L 87
Merwood Av. SK8—4K 113
Merwood Gro. M14—2L 91
Mesnefield Rd. M7—8A 60
(in two parts)
Mesne Lea Gro. M28—8L 57
Mesne Lea Rd. M28—7L 57
Mesnes Av. WN3—3A 52
Mesnes Pk. Ter. WN1—8C 34
Mesnes Rd. WN1—7C 34
Mesnes St. WN1—8C 34
Mesnes Ter. WN1—9C 34
Metal Box Way. BL5—7F 36
Metcalfe St. OL16—3K 29
Metcalfe Ter. BL2—9D 24
Metfield Pl. BL1—1C 38
Metfield Wlk. M10—6D 62
Methuen St. M12—3B 92
Methwold St. BL3—5C 38
Metroplex Bus. Pk. M5—7L 77
Metropolitan Ho. OL1—2M 63
Mevagissey Wlk. OL4—9C 46
Mews, The. M10—4M 79
Mews, The. M25—5B 60
Mews, The. M33—2J 101
Mews, The. SK8—8H 103
Mews, The. WN2—3K 53
Meyer St. SK3—7F 104
Meynell Dri. WN7—5F 72
Meyrick Rd. M6—4A 78
Meyrick St. WN5—2M 51
Miall St. OL11—4F 28
Micawber Rd. SK12—1L 121
Michaels Hey Pde. M23—5J 101
Michael St. M24—9M 43
Michael Wife La. BL0—1M 9
Michigan Av. M5—7M 77
Mickleby Wlk. M10—4K 79
Micklehurst Av. M20—1E 102
Micklehurst Grn. SK2—8L 105
Micklehurst Rd. OL5—8K 65
Mickleton. M29—4L 55
Midbrook Wlk. M22—3B 112
Middlebourne St. M6—5L 77
Middlebrook Dri. BL6—3J 37
Middle Calderbrook. OL15 —2C 14
Middlefell St. BL4—7K 39
Middlefield. OL8—8A 64
Middle Field. OL11—1L 27
Middlefields. SK8—9B 104
Middle Fold. BL7—4K 7
Middlegate. M10—5D 62
Middle Ga. OL8—6L 63
Middle Grn. OL6—3C 82
Middleham St. M14—4G 91
Middle Hill. OL12—7F 12
Middle Hillgate. SK1—5F 104
Middle Holly Gro. OL3—6C 48
Middle La. M31—3D 98
Middle Rd. M31—9E 76
Middlesex Dri. BL9—1M 41
Middlesex Rd. M9—6K 61
Middlesex Rd. SK5—8H 93
Middlesex Wlk. OL9—2K 63
Middlestone Dri. M9—9K 61
Middle St. OL12—2C 12
Middleton Av. M35—9F 62
Middleton Clo. M26—2F 40
Middleton Dri. BL9—6M 41
Middleton Gdns. M24—9M 43
Middleton Old Rd. M9—5K 61
Middleton Rd. M8 & M24—7F 60
Middleton Rd. OL2—6H 45
Middleton Rd. OL9—8E 44
Middleton Rd. OL10—1L 43
Middleton Rd. SK5—4F 92
Middleton View. M24—9B 44
Middleton Way. M24—9M 43
Middleway. OL4—3H 65
Middlewich Wlk. M18—1C 92
Middlewood. WA3—7M 71
Middlewood Dri. SK4—4A 104
Middle Wood La. OL12—5L 13
Middlewood Rd. SK6—5D 116
Middlewood Rd. SK12—9A 116
Middlewood St. M5—4B 4 & 6C 78
Middlewood View. SK6—4D 116
Middlewood Wlk. M9—9K 61
Midfield Ct. M7—9E 60
Midford Av. M30—5B 76
Midford Dri. BL1—3E 22
Midford Wlk. M8—1G 79
Midge Hall Dri. OL11—4A 28
Midgley Av. M18—9E 80
Midgley Gro. OL6—3E 82
Midgley St. M27—1D 76
Midgrove. OL3—5M 47
Midgrove La. OL3—6M 47
Midhurst Av. M10—3B 80
Midhurst Clo. BL1—9E 22
Midhurst Clo. SK8—4M 113
Midhurst St. OL11—5F 28
Midhurst Way. OL9—2H 63
Midland Clo. WN7—1C 72
Midland Cotts. SK7—3C 116
Midland Rd. SK5—4F 92
Midland Rd. SK7—9E 104
Midland St. M12—8K 79
Midland Ter. WA14—2D 110
Midland Wlk. SK7—1E 114
(in two parts)
Midlothian St. M11—5B 80
Midmoor Wlk. M9—5L 61
(off Levedale Rd.)
Midville Rd. M11—4C 80
Midway. SK8—7B 114
Midway. SK12—1K 121
Midwood Hall. M6—4M 77
(off Sutton Dwellings)
Milan St. M7—1E 78
Milbourne Rd. BL9—4M 25
Milburn Av. M23—3B 102
Milburn Dri. BL2—1M 39
Milbury Dri. OL15—9A 14
Milden Clo. M20—1J 103
Mildred Av. M25—6C 60
Mildred Av. OL2—7L 45
Mildred Av. OL4—3H 65
Mildred St. M7—2C 78
Mile End La. SK2—8H 105
Mile La. BL8—9F 24
Miles La. WN6—1D 32
(Appley Bridge)
Miles La. WN6—3F 32
(Shevington)
Miles St. BL4—9J 39
Miles St. M12—8A 80
Miles St. OL1—9B 46
Miles St. SK14—4F 94
Milfoil Clo. M28—3K 57
Milford Av. OL8—6J 63
Milford Brow. OL4—1E 64
Milford Cres. OL15—5B 14
Milford Dri. M19—7B 92
Milford Gro. SK2—6J 105
Milford Rd. BL2—6M 23
Milford Rd. BL3—6E 38
Milford Rd. WN2—7F 34
Milford St. M6—5L 77
Milford St. M9—4H 61
Milford St. WN3—2E 52
Milking La. BL3—7C 38
Milkstone Pl. OL11—4F 28
Milkstone Rd. OL11—4F 28
(in two parts)
Milk St. BL0—6H 9
Milk St. M2—4F 5 & 6G 79
Milk St. M29—7A 56
Milk St. OL4—1C 64
Milk St. OL11—4F 28
Milk St. SK14—4D 94
Milk St. WN3—1C 52
Milkwood Gro. M18—2D 92
Millais St. M10—8A 62
Millard St. OL9—1G 63
Millard Wlk. M18—2D 92
Millbank. WN6—2D 32
Millbank Ct. OL10—8H 27
Millbank St. M1—4H 4 & 6J 79
Millbank St. OL10—8H 27
Millbeck Ct. M24—7K 43
Millbeck Gro. BL3—5E 38
Millbeck Gro. WA11—5B 68
Millbeck Rd. M24—7K 43
Millbrook Av. M29—3L 55
Millbrook Av. M34—4K 93
Millbrook Bank. OL11—1K 27
Millbrook Gro. SK9—2K 119
Millbrook Ho. BL4—9L 39
Mill Brook Ind. Est. M23 —7L 101
Millbrook Rd. M23—1A 112
Millbrook St. SK1—5F 104
Millbrook Towers. SK1—5F 104
Mill Brow. M9—6J 61
Mill Brow. M28—1M 75
Mill Brow. OL1—7G 45
Mill Brow. OL6—7C 64
Mill Brow. SK6—5K 107
Mill Brow. SK14—6A 96
Mill Brow Rd. SK6—5K 107
Millbrow Ter. OL1—7G 45
Mill Ct. M31—4E 88
Mill Croft. BL1—1D 38
Millcroft. OL2—3C 46
Millcroft Av. WN5—3D 50
Mill Croft Clo. OL11—9J 11
Millcroft La. OL3—2M 47
Milldale Clo. M29—5J 55
Milldale Rd. WN7—7B 72
Millerhouse. OL2—4B 46
Miller Rd. OL8—5L 63
Millers Brook Clo. OL10—7K 27
Millers Clo. M33—2A 102
Miller's Ct. M5—5G 77
Millersdale Ct. SK13—5M 97
Miller's La. M29—6K 55
(Atherton)
Miller's La. M29—8K 55
(Tyldesley)
Millers La. WA13—8B 98
Miller's La. WN2—6F 52
Millers St. M30—5C 76
Miller St. BL6—2L 35
Miller St. BL9—9J 9
Miller St. M4—3F 5 & 4G 79
Miller St. M26—3F 40
Miller St. OL6—3B 82
Miller St. OL10—8K 27
Millet St. BL0—4K 9
Millett St. BL9—8K 25
Millfield Dri. M28—1H 75
Millfield Gro. OL16—4H 29
Millfield La. WN4—5L 69
Millfield Rd. BL2—2A 40
Millfield Wlk. M10—6C 62
Millfold. OL12—1D 12
Mill Fold Rd. M24—9M 43
Millford Av. M31—4L 87
(in two parts)
Millford Gdns. M31—4L 87
Millford St. OL12—1F 28
Millgate. BL7—9D 6
Millgate. OL3—5M 47
Mill Ga. OL8—5K 63
Mill Ga. OL16—9H 13
Millgate. SK1—3F 104
Millgate. WN1—9C 34
Millgate Cen. OL3—5M 47
Millgate La. M20—4H 103
(in two parts)
Mill Grn. St. M12—7K 79
Millhalf Clo. M15—1E 90
Millhead Av. M10—5L 79
Mill Hill. M28—2E 56
Mill Hill Av. SK12—5K 115
Mill Hill Caravan Pk. BL1
(off Mill Hill St.) —1G 39
Mill Hill Gro. SK14—4M 95
Mill Hill Hollow. SK12—5K 115
Mill Hill St. BL2—1G 39
Mill Hill Ter. BL2—1G 39
Mill Hill Way. SK14—4M 95
Millhouse Av. M23—9A 102
Mill Ho. Clo. OL12—7K 13
Mill Ho. View. WN8—1C 50
Millingford Av. WA3—5F 70
Millingford Gro. WN4—4B 70
Millington Hall La. WA14 —7H 109
Millington La. WA14—5H 109
Millington Rd. M17—8J 77
Millington Wlk. M15—9D 78
(off Shawheath Clo.)
Mill La. BL2—1G 39
Mill La. BL5—3E 54
Mill La. BL6—6D 20
(Horwich)
Mill La. BL6—2F 36
(Lostock, in two parts)
Mill La. BL8—6H 25
Mill La. M22—4E 102
Mill La. M34 & SK14—5B 94
Mill La. M35—9C 62
Mill La. OL2—5J 45
Mill La. OL3—8K 47
Mill La. OL5—6J 65
Mill La. OL6—5B 82
Mill La. OL9—4J 63
Mill La. PR7—1L 17
(Coppull)
Mill La. PR7—1G 17
(Wrightington Bar)
Mill La. SK5—5F 92
(North Reddish)
Mill La. SK5—7G 93
(Reddish Vale)
Mill La. SK6—6A 106
(Chadkirk)
Mill La. SK6—9A 94
(off Hyde Rd)
Mill La. SK6—8A 94
(off Lambeth Gro., in two parts)
Mill La. SK7—4M 115
Mill La. SK8—7K 103
(Cheadle)
Mill La. SK8—1B 114
(Cheadle Hulme)
Mill La. SK10—5E 120
(Adlington)
Mill La. SK10—8B 120
(Mottram)
Mill La. WA13—8C 98
Mill La. WA15—8K 111
Mill La. WN2—6M 35
Mill La. WN6—2C 32
Mill La. WN7—3H 73
Mill La. WN8—8A 32
Mill Meadow. WN1—1D 52
Millom Av. M23—4B 102
Millom Clo. OL16—1J 29
Millom Ct. WA15—7K 101
Millom Dri. BL9—7A 42
Millom Pl. SK8—1H 113
Millow St. M4—2F 5 & 4G 79
Millpool Wlk. M9—8K 61
(off Alderside Rd.)
Millrise. OL1—9L 45
Mill Rd. BL9—2M 25
Mill Rd. SK9—4H 119
Mill Rd. WN5—3D 50
Mills Hill Rd. M24—8D 44
Mills St. M25—9M 41
Mills St. OL10—8H 27
Mills St. OL12—2D 12
Millstone Clo. SK12 —7M 115
Millstone Rd. BL1—9M 21
Millstream La. M10—3E 80
Mill St. BL0—7G 9
Mill St. BL1—2G 39
Mill St. BL4—9J 39
Mill St. BL7—2F 22
Mill St. M6—3A 78
Mill St. M11—4M 79
Mill St. M26—7H 41
(in two parts)
Mill St. M28—9G 57
(Boothstown)
Mill St. M28—2D 56
(Greenheys)
Mill St. M29—7L 55
Mill St. M35—9D 62
Mill St. OL2—5K 45
Mill St. OL3—9B 48
Mill St. OL5—7J 65
Mill St. OL15—8M 13
Mill St. PR6—2G 19
Mill St. PR7—1L 17
Mill St. SK6—9A 94
(in two parts)
Mill St. SK7—1K 115
Mill St. SK9—4H 119
Mill St. SK13—5K 97
Mill St. SK14—1E 94
Mill St. SK15—6J 83
Mill St. WA3—7G 71
Mill St. WA14—8E 100
Mill St. WN2—2K 53
Mill St. WN3—1B 52
Mill St. WN4—5C 70
Mill St. WN7—3G 73
Milltown. SK13—5K 97
Milltown Clo. M26—7H 41
Milltown St. M26—7H 41
Millview. OL3—5C 48
Millwall Clo. M18—1D 92
Millway. WA15—5J 111
Millway Wlk. M10—2C 80
Millwood Ct. BL9—3M 41
Millwood View. SK15—5H 83
Millwright St. M10—2B 80
Mill Yd. BL9—7A 26
Milly St. M31—4C 88
Milne Clo. M12—9A 80
Milner Av. BL9—5M 25
Milner Av. WA14—6B 100
Milner St. M16—2D 90
Milner St. M26—6E 40
Milner St. M27—8F 58
Milner St. OL12—3C 12
Milnes Av. WN7—5F 72
Milne St. OL1—7A 46
Milne St. OL2—3B 46
Milne St. OL9—8J 45
(Busk)
Milne St. OL9—1H 63
(Chadderton)
Milne St. OL9—3J 63
(Oldham)
Milne St. OL11—8C 28
Milnrow Clo. M13—6G 5 & 8H 79
Milnrow Rd. OL2—2B 46
Milnrow Rd. OL15—9M 13
Milnrow Rd. OL16—3F 28
Milnthorpe Rd. BL2—1L 39
Milnthorpe St. M6—2B 78
Milnthorpe Way. M12—9L 79
Milo St. M9—5K 61
Milsom Av. BL3—6C 38
Milstead Wlk. M10—2A 80
Milton Av. BL3—6B 38
(Bolton)
Milton Av. BL3—5B 40
(Little Lever)
Milton Av. M5—5K 77
Milton Av. M30—8E 86
Milton Av. M35—6G 81
Milton Av. SK15—3L 83
Milton Clo. M29—3K 55
Milton Clo. M32—3L 89
Milton Clo. SK6—9F 106
Milton Clo. SK16—8H 83
(in two parts)
Milton Ct. M7—7E 60
Milton Ct. PR7—1L 17
Milton Cres. BL4—2H 57
Milton Cres. SK8—8J 103
Milton Dri. M33—8G 89
Milton Dri. OL9—2G 63
Milton Dri. SK12—8K 115
Milton Dri. WA15—4G 101
Milton Gro. M16—4C 90
Milton Gro. M33—8G 89
Milton Gro. WN1—6C 34
Milton Gro. WN5—7D 50
(Billinge)
Milton Gro. WN5—2F 50
(Orrell)
Milton Mt. M18—2D 92
Milton Pl. M6—2A 4 & 4B 78
Milton Rd. M25—3C 60
Milton Rd. M26—5D 40
Milton Rd. M27—7D 58
Milton Rd. M32—3L 89
Milton Rd. M34—6K 81
Milton Rd. PR7—2L 17
Milton Rd. SK7—5E 114
Milton Rd. WA3—8K 71
Milton St. BL0—5H 9
Milton St. BL8—7K 25
Milton St. M7—1D 4 & 3E 78
Milton St. M24—8M 43
Milton St. M30—5D 76
Milton St. M34—2L 93
Milton St. OL2—4L 45
Milton St. OL5—6J 65
Milton St. OL16—2F 28
Milton St. SK14—2D 94
Milton St. WN7—2E 72
Milton View. OL5—6J 65
Milverton Av. SK14—4J 95
Milverton Clo. BL6—4K 37
Milverton Dri. SK7—7B 114
Milverton Rd. M14—2K 91
Milverton Wlk. SK14—4J 95
Milwain Dri. SK4—8C 92
Milwain Rd. M19—6M 91
Milwain Rd. M32—5J 89
Mimosa Dri. M27—6F 58
Mincing St. M4—2F 5 & 4G 79
Minden Clo. BL8—8H 25
Minden Clo. M20—1J 103
Minden Pde. BL9—8M 25
Minden St. M6—1L 77
Minehead Av. M20—7F 90
Minehead Av. M31—6B 88
Minehead Av. WN7—6D 54
Minerva Rd. BL4—8F 38
Minerva Rd. OL6—5C 82
Minerva St. BL2—2H 39
Minerva Ter. OL15—6A 14
(off William St.)
Mine St. OL10—6J 27
Mine Way. WA11—3M 69
Minford Clo. M10—1B 80
Minnie St. BL3—6C 38
Minnie St. OL12—1D 12
Minoan Gdns. M7—2C 78
Minorca Av. M11—5D 80
Minorca Clo. OL11—2L 27
Minorca St. BL3—5E 38
Minor St. M35—8G 63
(in two parts)
Minor St. OL8—3L 63
Minor St. OL11—9C 28
Minshull St. M1—4F 5 & 6G 79
Minshull St. S. M1—5G 5 & 7H 79
Minsmere. SK2—8M 105
Minsmere Wlk. M8—1F 78
(off Alderford Pde.)
Minstead Wlk. M22—2B 112
Minster Clo. BL2—8J 23
Minster Dri. SK8—8A 104
Minster Gro. M29—9B 56
Minsterley Pde. M22—3C 112
Minster Rd. BL2—8J 23
Minster Way. OL9—8G 45
Minton St. OL4—3A 64
Minto St. OL7—3A 82
(in two parts)
Mintridge Clo. M11—8E 80
Mint St. BL0—1K 9
Mirabel St. M3—2E 5 & 4F 78
Miranda Ct. M5—5B 4 & 7C 78
Mirefield Clo. WA3—8K 71
Mirfield Av. M9—4K 61
Mirfield Av. OL8—4L 63
Mirfield Av. SK4—3B 104
Mirfield Dri. M24—8M 43
Mirfield Dri. M30—3D 76
Mirfield Dri. M31—2C 88
Mirfield Rd. M9—4K 61
Miriam St. BL3—5B 38
Miriam St. M35—1D 80
Miry La. BL5—3D 54
(in two parts)
Miry La. WN6 & WN3—9A 34
Mission St. OL10—8J 27
Missouri Av. M5—6L 77
Misterton Wlk. M23—6L 101
(off Sandy La.)
Mistletoe Gro. M3—3C 4 & 4D 78
Mistral Ct. M30—4E 76
Mitcham Av. M9—5A 62
Mitchell Gdns. M22—9E 102
Mitchell Hey. OL12—3E 28
Mitchell Rd. WN5—2E 68
Mitchell St. BL8—6J 25
Mitchell St. M10—2B 80
Mitchell St. M24—8M 43
Mitchell St. M30—4C 76
Mitchell St. OL1—9K 45
Mitchell St. OL12—2D 28
Mitchell St. OL16—8J 13
Mitchell St. WA3—7G 71
Mitchell St. WN2—1G 53
Mitchell St. WN4—5C 70
Mitchell St. WN5—2L 51
Mitchell St. WN7—2B 72
Mitcheson Gdns. M6—4M 77
Mitford Ct. M14—7J 91
Mitford Rd. M14—7J 91
Mitford St. M32—5J 89
Mitre Rd. M13—2M 91
Mitre St. BL1—6E 22
Mitre St. BL8—7K 25
Mitton Clo. BL8—8E 24
Mitton Clo. OL10—8F 26
Mizpah Gro. BL8—8H 25
Mizzy Rd. OL12—1E 28
Moadlock. SK6—1C 106
Moat Av. M22—8C 102
Moat Gdns. M22—9C 102
Moat Hall Av. M30—7A 76
Moat Ho. St. WN2—1G 53
Moat Rd. M22—9C 102
Moat Wlk. SK5—7J 93
Mobberley Clo. M19—1L 103
Mobberley Rd. BL2—1K 39
Mobberley Rd. SK9—3B 118
Mobberley Rd. WA14 & WA15 —9E 110
Mocha Pde. M7—2C 4 & 4D 78
Modbury Clo. SK7—3G 115
Modbury Wlk. M8—1G 79
Mode Hill La. M25—9C 42
Mode Hill Wlk. M25—9C 42
Model Ter. WN2—5G 53
Mode Wheel Rd. M5—6K 77
Mode Wheel Rd. S. M5—7K 77
Moelfre Dri. SK8—5C 114
Moffat Clo. BL2—3M 39
Moffat Ct. SK16—6B 82
Moisant St. BL3—6D 38
Mold St. BL1—7E 22
Mold St. OL1—9L 45
Molesworth St. OL1—9A 46
Molesworth St. OL16—3G 29
Mollets Wood. M34—1A 94
Mollington Rd. M22—4E 112
Molyneux Rd. BL5—8G 37
Molyneux Rd. M19—5C 92
Molyneux St. OL12—2D 28
Molyneux St. WN1—9D 34
Mona Av. M32—3J 89
Mona Av. SK8—3K 113
Monaco Dri. M22—3D 102
Monarch Trading Est. M17 —9M 77
Monart Rd. M9—7L 61
Mona St. BL1—8E 22
Mona St. M6—3A 78
Mona St. SK14—4E 94
Mona St. WN1—9B 34
Moncrieffe St. BL3—4G 39
Monde Trading Est. M17—9G 77
Mond Rd. M30—2H 87
Money Ash Rd. WA15—1D 110
Monfa Av. SK2—9G 105
Monica Av. M8—5F 60
Monica Ct. M30—4F 76
Monica Gro. M19—6M 91
Monica Ter. WN4—5B 70
Monk Clo. M29—9B 56
Monks Clo. M8—6H 61
Monk's Ct. M5—5H 77
Monksdale Av. M31—4B 88
Monks Hall Gro. M30—4F 76
Monks La. BL2—8K 23
Monks Rd. SK13—8E 96
Monkswood. OL1—1L 63
Monkton Av. M18—2C 92
Monkwood Dri. M9—8L 61
Monmouth Av. BL9—5M 25
Monmouth Av. M33—9F 88
Monmouth Cres. WN4—5C 70
Monmouth Rd. SK8—3B 114
Monmouth St. M24—9C 44
Monmouth St. OL9—3J 63
Monmouth St. OL11—4F 28
Monroe Clo. WN3—5A 52
Monsal Av. M7—9A 60
Monsal Av. SK2—6K 105
Monsall Clo. BL9—7A 42
Monsall Rd. M10—1L 79
Monsall St. M10—2K 79
Monsall St. OL8—5L 63
Mons Av. OL11—2C 28
Monster Rd. WN5—2H 51
Montague Ct. M33—1J 101
Montague Ho. SK3—5D 104
(off East St.)
Montague Rd. M16—1A 90
Montague Rd. M33—1H 101
Montague Rd. OL6—5D 82
Montague St. BL3—6B 38
Montague Way. SK15—5G 83
Montagu Rd. SK2—6K 105
Montagu St. SK6—3H 107
Montana Sq. M11—8E 80
Montcliffe Cres. M16—5F 90
Monteagle St. M9—4H 61
Montford Rise. WN2—7G 35
Montford St. M5—6M 77
Montgomery. OL11—4E 28
Montgomery Dri. BL9—7B 42
Montgomery Rd. M13—4M 91
Montgomery St. OL8—6H 63
Montgomery Way. M26—4C 40
Monton Av. M30—4E 76
Monton Fields Rd. M30—4C 76
Monton Grn. M30—3C 76
Monton La. M30—5E 76
Montonmill Gdns. M30—4C 76
Monton Rd. M30—4D 76
(in two parts)
Monton Rd. SK5—1J 105
Monton St. BL3—6E 38
Monton St. M14—2G 91
(in two parts)
Monton St. M26—6F 40
Montpellior Rd. M22—2D 112
Montreal St. M19—5B 92
Montreal St. OL8—4M 63
Montreal St. WN7—3L 71
Montrey Cres. WN4—4J 69
Montrose. M30—5E 76
(off St Andrews Ct.)
Montrose Av. BL0—9G 9
Montrose Av. BL2—9J 23
Montrose Av. M20—9G 91
Montrose Av. M32—4H 89
Montrose Av. SK2—1G 115
Montrose Av. SK16—8C 82
Montrose Av. WN5—9H 33
Montrose Dri. BL7—3H 23
Montrose Gdns. OL2—5M 45
Montrose Ho. OL8—4M 63
Montrose St. OL11—9C 28
Montserrat Brow. BL1—8K 21
Montserrat Rd. BL1—8L 21
Monument Rd. WN1—7D 34
Monyash Ct. SK13—5D 96
(off Monyash M.)
Monyash Gro. SK13—5D 96
(off Monyash M.)
Monyash Lea. SK13—5D 96
(off Monyash M.)
Monyash M. SK13—5D 96
Monyash Pl. SK13—5D 96
(off Monyash M.)
Monyash Way. SK13—5E 96
(off Ashford M.)
Moody St. WN6—9L 17
Moon Gro. M14—3K 91
Moon St. OL9—1J 63
Moor Av. WN6—1E 32
Moor Bank La. OL16—6K 29
Moorbottom Rd. BL8—5E 8
Moorby Av. M19—1L 103
Moorby St. OL1—9A 46
Moorby Wlk. BL3—4F 38
Moor Clo. M26—4E 40
Moorclose St. M24—9C 44
Moorclose Wlk. M9—9K 61
(off Heathersett Dri.)
Moorcock Av. M27—8H 59
Moor Cres. OL3—5C 48
Moorcroft. BL0—1K 9
Moorcroft. OL11—7F 28
Moorcroft Dri. M19—1M 103
Moorcroft Rd. M23—4M 101
Moorcroft Sq. SK14—9E 82
Moorcroft St. M35—6G 81
Moorcroft St. OL8—6J 63
Moorcroft Wlk. M19—1L 103
Moordale Av. OL4—8E 46
Moordale St. M20—9G 91
Moordown Clo. M8—1H 79
Moore Cres. WA13—8B 98
Moor Edge Rd. OL5 & OL3 —6M 65
Mooredge Ter. OL2—7L 45
Moore Dri. WA11—9M 69
Moore Ho. M30—7D 76
Moor End. M22—5D 102
Moor End Av. M7—8C 60
Moor End Ct. M7—8C 60
Moor End Rd. SK6—7M 107
Moores La. WN6—8K 17
Moore St. OL16—3F 28
Moore St. WN1—7D 34
Moore St. E. WN1—8E 34
Moore Wlk. M34—7A 94
Moorfield. BL7—5K 7
Moorfield. M7—7C 60
Moorfield. M28—9F 56
(Mosley Common)
Moorfield. M28—8M 57
(Worsley)
Moorfield. WN2—5H 53
Moorfield Av. M14—7J 91
Moorfield Av. M34—5A 94
Moorfield Av. OL15—4A 14
Moorfield Av. SK15—8K 83
Moorfield Clo. M27—1D 76
Moorfield Clo. M30—6D 76
(Eccles)
Moorfield Clo. M30—3H 87
(Irlam)
Moorfield Cres. WA3—8A 72
Moorfield Dri. SK9—6E 118
Moorfield Dri. SK14—1E 94
Moorfield Gro. BL2—9H 23
Moorfield Gro. M33—2J 101
Moorfield Gro. SK4—1B 104
Moorfield Pde. M30—3H 87
Moorfield Pl. OL12—1E 28
Moorfield Rd. M6—3K 77
Moorfield Rd. M20—1F 102
Moorfield Rd. M27—1C 76
Moorfield Rd. M30—3H 87
Moorfield Rd. OL8—6H 63
Moorfield St. M20—7H 91
(in two parts)
Moorfield St. OL2—2B 46
Moorfield St. SK14—1D 96
Moorfield Ter. SK14—1D 96
Moorfield Ter. SK15—9L 65
Moorfield View. OL15—5A 14
Moorfield Wlk. M31—4D 88
Moorgate. BL2—5K 23
Moorgate. BL9—7M 25
Moorgate Av. M20—7F 90
Moorgate Av. OL11—3A 28
Moorgate Ct. BL2—9H 23
Moorgate Dri. M29—1C 74
Moorgate Dri. SK15—1L 83
Moor Ga. La. OL15—4L 13
Moorgate Rd. M26—1E 40
Moorgate Rd. SK15—1L 83
Moorgate St. OL3—9B 48
Moorhead St. M4—2G 5 & 4H 79
Moorhey Rd. M28—2F 56
(in two parts)
Moorhey St. OL4—2B 64
Moor Hill. OL11—1M 27
Moorhill Ct. M7—7C 60
Moorhouse Fold. OL16—4L 29
Moorings, The. M28—2A 76
Moorland Av. M8—6F 60
Moorland Av. M33—2J 101
Moorland Av. M35—6E 80
Moorland Av. OL11—2M 27
Moorland Av. OL12—4C 12
Moorland Av. OL16—4A 30
Moorland Cres. OL12—4C 12
Moorland Dri. BL6—7F 20
Moorland Dri. M28—2F 56
Moorland Dri. SK8—4M 113
Moorland Gro. BL1—8A 22
Moorland Rd. M20—2H 103
Moorland Rd. SK2—9H 105
(in two parts)
Moorland Rd. SK15—2L 83
Moorland Rd. WN2—3J 53
Moorland Rd. WN4—3E 70
Moorlands Av. M31—3B 88
Moorlands Av. WN7—4F 72
Moorlands Cres. OL5—7K 65
Moorlands Rd. OL5—5L 65
Moorland St. OL2—2B 46
Moorland St. OL12—1E 28
Moorland St. OL15—4C 14
Moorlands View. BL3—7A 38
Moorland Ter. OL12—1A 28
Moor La. BL3 & BL1—3E 38
Moor La. M7—8M 59
Moor La. M23—3A 102
Moor La. M31—3A 88
Moor La. OL3—9M 31
(Denshaw)
Moor La. OL3—7C 48
(Dobcross)
Moor La. OL12—8M 11
Moor La. SK7—8D 114
Moor La. SK9—6C 118
Moor La. WN7—8E 54
Moor Nook. M33—2K 101
Moor Pk. Av. OL11—8B 28
Moor Pk. Rd. M20—4J 103
Moor Platt Clo. BL6—7F 20
Moor Rd. BL8—5G 9
Moor Rd. M23—4L 101
Moor Rd. OL15—2C 14
Moor Rd. WN5—3D 50
Moorsbrook Gro. SK9—2L 119
Moorsholme Av. M10—9A 62
Moorside. OL5—7L 65
Moorside. OL11—7F 28
Moorside. OL15—5D 14
Moorside Av. BL1—8A 22
(in two parts)
Moorside Av. BL2—9D 24
Moorside Av. BL4—1H 57
Moorside Av. BL6—6C 20
Moorside Av. M35—4J 81
Moorside Av. OL4—5F 46
Moorside Ct. M33—1H 101
Moorside Cres. M35—5J 81
Moorside Ho. WA15—6J 101
Moor Side La. BL0—4A 10
Moorside La. M34—2A 94
(in two parts)
Moorside Lodge. M27—8D 58
Moorside Rd. BL7—2J 7
Moorside Rd. BL8—4E 24
Moorside Rd. M7—7C 60
Moorside Rd. M27—9C 58
Moorside Rd. M31—3L 87
Moorside Rd. SK4—3A 104
Moorside St. M35—5H 81
Moorside Wlk. WN5—9H 33
Moor St. BL9—7M 25
Moor St. M27—9F 58
Moor St. M30—6B 76
Moor St. OL1—1B 64
Moor St. OL2—3A 46
Moor St. OL10—8H 27
Moor St. WN2—4K 35
Moors View. BL0—5H 9
Moorton Av. M19—7M 91
Moorton Pk. M19—7M 91
Moortop Clo. M9—3J 61
Moor Top Pl. SK4—2B 104
Moor Way. BL8—8B 8
Moorway. SK9—6E 118
Moorway Dri. M9—4A 62
Moorwood Dri. M33—2E 100
Mora Av. OL9—8H 45
Moran Wlk. M15—9F 78
Morar Dri. BL2—2A 40
Morar Rd. SK16—8D 82
Mora St. M9—8M 61
Moravian Clo. SK16—6C 82
Moravian Field. M35—7G 81
Moray Clo. BL0—7G 9
Moray Rd. OL9—4G 63
Moray Wlk. OL8—4M 63
Morden Av. M11—5C 80
Morden Av. WN4—3A 70
Morecombe Clo. M10—1B 80
Moresby Clo. WN7—2D 72
Moresby Dri. M20—5H 103
Morestead Wlk. M10—2H 5 & 4J 79
Moreton Av. M25—8M 41
Moreton Av. M32—4K 89
Moreton Av. M33—2E 100
Moreton Av. SK7—7E 114
Moreton Clo. WA3—6F 70
Moreton Dri. BL8—7H 25
Moreton Dri. SK9—9L 113
Moreton La. SK2—6J 105
Moreton St. OL9—9F 44
Moreton Wlk. SK2—6J 105
Morgan Pl. SK5—1F 104
Morgan St. OL15—6B 14
Morillon Rd. M30—2G 87
Morland Rd. M16—2C 90
Morley Av. M14—5G 91
Morley Av. M27—1E 76
Morley Grn. Rd. SK9—1C 118
Morley Ho. M6—4M 77
(off Sutton Dwellings)
Morley Rd. M26—5D 40
Morley's La. M29—4M 73
Morley St. BL3—3D 38
Morley St. BL9—1M 41
Morley St. M25—9M 41
Morley St. M29—5J 55
Morley St. OL4—8E 46
Morley St. OL16—1H 29
Morley St. SK13—6K 97
Morley Way. OL3—3B 66
Morna Wlk. M12—7K 79
Morningside Clo. M35—7G 81
Morningside Dri. M20—5J 103
Mornington Av. SK8—9K 103
Mornington Ct. OL1—9L 45
Mornington Cres. M14—6G 91
Mornington Rd. BL1—1B 38
Mornington Rd. M29—2M 55
Mornington Rd. M33—9K 89
Mornington Rd. OL11—8F 28
Mornington Rd. PR6—2H 19
Mornington Rd. SK8—9K 103
Mornington Rd. WN2—3M 53
Morpeth Clo. OL7—3L 81
Morpeth St. M27—1E 76
Morpeth Wlk. M12—1L 91
Morrell Rd. M22—5D 102
Morris Clo. WA11—9F 68
Morris Fold Dri. BL6—3H 37
Morris Grn. BL3—7C 38
Morris Grn. La. BL3—6C 38
Morris Grn. St. BL3—7C 38
Morris Gro. M31—6L 87
Morris Ho. WN1—9D 34
Morrison St. BL3—6E 38
Morrison Wlk. M10—2A 80
(off Eldridge Dri.)
Morris Rd. WN8—1A 50
Morris St. BL1—2G 39
Morris St. M20—7H 91
Morris St. M26—4L 41
Morris St. M29—7M 55
Morris St. OL4—3A 64
Morris St. WN1—9D 34
Morris St. WN2—3K 53
Morris St. WN3—4E 52
Morrowfield Av. M8—9F 60
Morrwell Rd. M22—5E 102
Morse Rd. M10—2B 80
Mortar St. OL4—9C 46
(in two parts)
Mort Ct. BL1—7C 22
Mortfield Gdns. BL1—1D 38
Mortfield La. BL1—1D 38
(in two parts)
Mort Fold. M28—3G 57
Mortimer Av. M9—4L 61
Mortimer St. OL1—8A 46
Mortlake Clo. M28—5F 56
Mortlake Dri. M10—2B 80
Mort La. M29—7E 56
Morton Av. WN3—3B 52
Morton Clo. WN3—6J 51
Morton Dri. SK12—8M 115
Mortons, The. BL5—7E 36
Morton St. BL2—2G 39
Morton St. M24—7A 44
Morton St. M26—7H 41
Morton St. M35—9C 62
Morton St. OL16—3G 29
Morton St. SK4—1E 104
Morton Ter. SK6—9B 94
Mort St. BL4—9H 39
Mort St. BL6—6B 20
Mort St. M29—7M 55
Mort St. WN2—3A 54
Mort St. WN6—7A 34
Mort St. WN7—2B 72
Morven Av. SK7—1M 115
Morven Dri. M23—8A 102
Morven Gro. BL2—2M 39
Morville Dri. WN3—4B 52
Morville Rd. M6—2J 77
Morville Rd. M21—5D 90
Moschatel Wlk. M31—2G 99
Moscow Rd. SK3—6D 104
Moscow Rd. E. SK3—6D 104
Mosedale Av. WA11—6B 68
Mosedale Clo. M23—7L 101
Mosedale Rd. M24—7K 43
Moseldene Rd. SK2—8K 105
Moseley Grange. SK8—1M 11
Moseley Rd. M14 & M19—6K 9
Moseley Rd. SK8—1M 113
Moseley St. SK3—5E 104
Mosley Arc. M1—6G 79
(off Piccadilly Plaza)
Mosley Av. BL0—9H 9
Mosley Av. BL9—5M 25
Mosley Clo. WA15—6F 100
Mosley Comn. Rd. M29 & M2 —8E
Mosley Rd. M17—9J 77
Mosley Rd. WA15—7H 101
Mosley Rd. N. M17—8J 77
Mosley St. M2—4F 5 & 6G 79
Mosley St. M26—4F 40
Mossack Av. M22—3D 112
Moss Av. OL16—4J 29
Moss Av. WN5—5D 50
Moss Av. WN7—2H 73
Moss Bank. M8—8G 61
Moss Bank. OL2—3B 46
Moss Bank. SK6—6J 107
Moss Bank. SK7—7C 114
Moss Bank Av. M35—5J 81
Moss Bank Clo. BL1—6D 22
Mossbank Clo. SK14—2E 96
Moss Bank Ct. WN7—2C 72
Moss Bank Gro. M27—6D 58
Mossbank Gro. OL10—7J 27
Moss Bank Rd. M27—6D 58
Moss Bank Rd. WA11—7A 68
Moss Bank Trading Est. M28 —4L
Moss Bank Way. BL1—9L 21
Mossbray Av. M19—1K 103
Moss Bri. Rd. OL16—5H 29
Mossbrook Dri. M28—2E 56
Moss Brook Rd. M9—9L 61
Moss Clo. M26—4D 40
Moss Clo. OL7—6L 81
Mossclough Ct. M9—9L 61
Moss Colliery Rd. M27—5E 5
Mosscot Clo. M13—6G 5 & 8H
Moss Croft Clo. M31—3L 87
Mossdale Rd. M23—4M 101
Mossdale Rd. M33—4E 100
Mossdale Rd. WN4—8A 52
Mossdown Rd. OL2—6A 46
Moss Dri. BL6—7F 20
Mossfield Clo. BL9—6C 26
Mossfield Clo. SK4—3B 104
Mossfield Dri. M9—4A 62
Mossfield Grn. M30—2J 87
Mossfield Rd. BL4—9H 39
(Farnworth)
Mossfield Rd. BL4—3M 57
(Kearsley)
Mossfield Rd. M27—6E 58
Mossfield Rd. WA15—7K 10
Moss Fold. M29—9C 56
Moss Ga. Rd. OL2—1M 45
(in two parts)
Moss Grange Av. M16—2D 9
Moss Grn. M31—8M 87
Moss Gro. BL9—7B 26
Moss Gro. OL2—9L 29
Moss Gro. WA13—9B 98
Moss Gro. WN6—1L 33
Moss Gro. Ct. M15—2E 90
(off Moss La. W.)
Mossgrove Rd. WA15—6F 1
Mossgrove St. OL8—6K 63
Mosshall Clo. M15—9D 78
Moss Hall Rd. BL9 & OL10 —9D
Moss Hey Dri. M23—4C 102
Moss Hey St. OL2—3B 46
Moss Ho. La. M28—2F 74
Moss Ind. Est. OL16—5H 29
Moss Ind. Est. WN7—6B 72
Mossland Clo. OL10—1K 43
Mossland Gro. BL3—7K 37
Moss La. BL1—7A 22
Moss La. BL4—3B 58
Moss La. BL6—8M 19
Moss La. M24—3M 61
(in two parts)
Moss La. M25—9M 41
Moss La. M27—6D 58
Moss La. M28—4L 57
(in two parts)
Moss La. M29—6M 73
Moss La. M30—9D 86
Moss La. M31—1D 88
Moss La. M31 & WA13—2F
Moss La. M33—2D 100
(Sale)
Moss La. M33—3C 100
(Woodhouses)
Moss La. OL2—6A 46
Moss La. OL7—3K 81
(in two parts)
Moss La. OL12—3B 12
Moss La. OL16—4G 29
Moss La. PR7—1L 17
Moss La. SK7—7B 114
Moss La. SK9—8M 119
(Alderley Edge)
Moss La. SK9—7D 112
(Wilmslow)
Moss La. SK14—6M 95
Moss La. WA13—4E 98
Moss La. WA14 & WA15
(Altrincham) —9D
Moss La. WA15—6F 100
(Timperley)
Moss La. WA16—6E 108
(High Legh)
Moss La. WA16—7A 118
(Mobberley)
Moss La. WN2—5G 53
Moss La. WN6—6C 16
Moss La. E. M15 & M14—2
Moss Lane Ind. Est. M25 —8
Moss Lane Trading Est. M2 —8
Moss La. W. M15—2D 90
Moss Lea. BL1—6D 22
Moss Lea Fold. WN6—7G
Mosslee Av. M8—5F 60
Mossley Rd. OL5 & OL4—4
Mossley Rd. OL6—4C 82
Moss Lodge La. OL7—5K 8
Moss Lynn. OL4—1G 65
Moss Manor. M33—2E 100
Moss Meadow. BL5—7E 3
Moss Meadow Rd. M6—3J
Mossmere Rd. SK8—9A 1
Moss Mill St. OL16—5H 29
Moss Nook Ind. Area. M22 —4
Moss Pk. Rd. M32—4G 89
Moss Pit Row. WN2—5H 3
Moss Pl. BL9—1L 41
Moss Rd. BL4—1L 57
(in two parts)
Moss Rd. M30—5B 86
Moss Rd. M32—2J 89
Moss Rd. M33—1B 100
Moss Rd. SK9—7M 119
Moss Rd. WN5—5D 50
Moss Rose. SK9—7M 119
Moss Row. BL9—9M 25
Moss Row. OL11—1K 27
Moss Shaw Way. M26 —4
Moss Side. BL8—5G 25
Moss Side Cres. M15—1G
Moss Side La. OL16—5J 2
Moss Side La. WA3—2A 9
Moss Side Rd. M30—8D 8
Moss Side Shopping Cen. —
Moss St. BL4—8L 39

Oakington Av. M14—3H 91
Oakland Av. M6—3G 77
Oakland Av. M16—2A 90
Oakland Av. M19—1L 103
Oakland Av. SK2—7J 105
Oakland Cotts. M7—8B 60
Oakland Ct. SK12—8K 115
Oakland Ct. WN2—5M 53
Oakland Gro. BL1—8A 22
Oakland Ho. M16—1A 90
Oaklands. BL1—2M 37
Oaklands. BL6—1H 37
Oaklands. SK9—4K 119
Oaklands Av. SK6—5J 107
Oaklands Av. SK8—2A 114
Oaklands Clo. SK9—2L 119
Oaklands Dri. M25—4B 60
Oaklands Dri. M33—9G 89
Oaklands Dri. SK7—3L 115
Oaklands Dri. SK14—4G 95
Oaklands Pk. OL4—3M 65
Oaklands Rd. BL0—1K 9
Oaklands Rd. M7—9A 60
Oaklands Rd. M27—1D 76
Oaklands Rd. OL2—7L 45
Oaklands Rd. OL3 & OL4 —3M 65
Oaklands Rd. WA3—8M 71
Oaklands, The. WN2—5A 54
Oakland Ter. OL11—9C 28
Oak La. M25—9B 42
Oak La. SK9—5F 118
Oaklea. WN6—8G 17
Oak Lea Av. SK9—6G 119
Oaklea Rd. M33—8E 88
Oakleigh. SK3—9F 104
Oakleigh Av. BL3—7G 39
Oakleigh Av. M19—7M 91
Oakleigh Av. WA15—6G 101
Oakleigh Clo. OL10—2L 43
Oakley Av. WN5—1E 68
Oakley Clo. M26—9G 41
Oakley Pk. BL1—2M 37
Oakley St. M5—5K 77
Oakley St. OL15—7L 13
Oakley Vs. SK4—2B 104
Oak Lodge. SK7—5F 114
Oakmere Av. M30—3C 76
Oakmere Clo. M22—9D 102
Oakmere Rd. SK8—9M 103
Oakmere Rd. SK9—7K 113
Oak M. SK9—2J 119
Oakmoor Dri. M7—8A 60
Oakmoor Rd. M23—7A 102
Oakridge Wlk. M9—9K 61
Oak Rd. M7—1C 78
Oak Rd. M20—9H 91
Oak Rd. M31—3D 98
Oak Rd. M33—1K 101
Oak Rd. M35—1F 80
Oak Rd. OL8—6J 63
Oak Rd. SK8—7L 103
Oak Rd. SK10—9A 120
Oak Rd. WA15—1E 110
Oaks Av. BL2—6J 23
Oaksey Wlk. M7—9B 60
Oakside Clo. SK8—7K 103
Oaks La. BL2—5H 23
Oaks, The. SK8—2G 113
Oak St. BL0—6H 9
Oak St. M4—3F 5 & 5G 79
(in two parts)
Oak St. M24—1D 62
Oak St. M26—8J 41
Oak St. M27—7G 59
Oak St. M29—7G 55
(Atherton)
Oak St. M29—7A 56
(Tyldesley)
Oak St. M30—6D 76
Oak St. M34—9M 81
Oak St. OL2—2C 46
Oak St. OL10—7H 27
Oak St. OL15—6C 14
(Littleborough)
Oak St. OL15—8M 13
(Smithy Bridge)
Oak St. OL16—6B 30
(Newhey)
Oak St. OL16—3F 28
(Rochdale)
Oak St. SK3—5B 104
Oak St. SK7—1K 115
Oak St. SK13—5J 97
Oak St. SK14—2E 94
Oak St. WN1—9E 34
Oak St. WN7—4F 72
Oak Tree Clo. M29—7G 55
Oak Tree Clo. SK2—5K 105
Oak Tree Ct. SK8—8K 103
Oak Tree Cres. SK15—7G 83
Oak Tree Dri. SK16—8F 82
Oak View Rd. OL3—3B 66
Oakville Dri. M6—3G 77
Oakville Ter. M40—7M 61
Oakway. M20—5J 103
Oakwell Dri. BL9—6B 42
Oakwell Dri. M8—7E 60
Oakwood. M33—1C 100
Oakwood. OL9—1E 62
Oakwood. SK13—6F 96
Oakwood Av. M10—7D 62
Oakwood Av. M27—4E 58
Oakwood Av. M28—6M 57
Oakwood Av. M34—8L 81
Oakwood Av. SK8—8G 103
Oakwood Av. SK9—5E 118
Oakwood Av. WN4—5A 70
Oakwood Av. WN6—4F 32
Oakwood Clo. BL8—7H 25
Oakwood Ct. WA14—4B 110
Oakwood Dri. BL1—1M 37
Oakwood Dri. M6—2H 77
Oakwood Dri. M28—6M 57
Oakwood Dri. WN7—6F 72
Oakwood Ho. M21—6C 90
Oakwood La. WA14—4B 110
Oakwood Rd. SK6—3C 106
Oakwood Rd. SK12—6K 117
Oakworth Croft. OL4—5F 46
Oakworth St. M9—6J 61
Oatlands. SK9—9M 119
Oatlands Rd. M22—2C 112
Oat St. SK1—6G 105
Oats Wlk. M13—2J 91
Oban Av. M10—3B 80
Oban Av. OL1—8B 46
Oban Cres. SK3—9D 104
Oban Dri. M33—2L 101
Oban Dri. WN4—3J 69
Oban Gro. BL1—5E 22
Oban St. BL1—7D 22
Oban Way. WN2—4K 35
Oberlin St. OL4—1D 64
Oberlin St. OL11—5D 28
Oberon Clo. M30—5D 76
Occleston Clo. M33—4L 101
Occupation Rd. M17—8F 76
Ocean St. WA14—7B 100
Ocean Wlk. M15—1F 90
Ockenden Dri. M9—8K 61
O'Connell Clo. WA11—9J 69
Ocshell Ho. M16—4M 77
Octagon Ct. BL1—3F 38
Octavia Dri. M10—3C 80
Octavia Ho. M6—4M 77
(off Sutton Dwellings)
Oddies Yd. OL12—9G 13
Odell St. M11—8B 80
Odessa Av. M6—2H 77
Odette St. M18—1C 92
Off Duke St. OL5—7L 65
Offerton Dri. SK2—7K 105
Offerton Fold. SK2—6J 105
Offerton Grn. SK2—7M 105
Offerton La. SK2—5H 105
Offerton Rd. SK7 & SK2—1A 116
Offerton St. BL6—7A 20
Offerton St. SK1—3H 105
Off Green St. M24—8A 44
Off Grove Rd. SK15—3K 83
Off Kershaw St. OL2—2B 46
(off Kershaw St., in two parts)
Off Lees St. OL2—2B 46
(off Lees St.)
Off Ridge Hill La. SK15—5F 82
Off Stamford St. SK15—3K 83
Ogbourne Wlk. M13—9J 79
(off Lauderdale Cres.)
Ogden Clo. M25—8A 42
Ogden Clo. OL10—8G 27
Ogden Ct. SK14—4E 94
Ogden Gdns. SK16—7E 82
Ogden Gro. SK8—9F 102
Ogden La. M11—8D 80
Ogden La. OL16—5D 30
Ogden Rd. M35—1F 80
Ogden Rd. SK7—7C 114
Ogden's Bldgs. SK15—5J 83
Ogden Sq. SK16—7B 82
Ogden St. M15—9C 78
Ogden St. M20—2H 103
Ogden St. M24—9A 44
Ogden St. M25—4C 60
Ogden St. M27—9F 58
Ogden St. OL4—2D 64
Ogden St. OL6—2D 82
Ogden St. OL9—9J 45
Ogden St. OL11—8C 28
Ogden Wlk. M25—9A 42
Ogmore Wlk. M10—6C 62
Ogwen Dri. M25—3B 60
Ohio Av. M5—7M 77
Oil Works Rd. WA14—6D 100
O'Kane Ho. M30—6D 76
Okehampton Clo. M26—4C 40
Okehampton Cres. M33—9D 88
Okell Gro. WN7—1D 72
Okeover Rd. M7—8D 60
Olaf St. BL2—9H 23
Old Bank. SK12—6M 117
Old Bank St. M2—4E 5 & 6F 78
Old Barn Pl. BL7—2G 23
Old Barton Rd. M31—9C 76
Oldbridge Dri. WN2—2K 53
Old Broadway. M20—9H 91
Old Brook Clo. OL2—1D 46
Old Brow. OL5—7J 65
(in two parts)
Old Brow. OL16—8J 13
Oldbury Clo. M10—4K 79
Oldbury Clo. OL10—2K 43
Oldcastle Av. M20—6G 91
Old Chapel St. SK3—6C 104
Old Church St. M10—1B 80
Old Chu. St. OL1—1M 63
Old Clough La. M28—8M 57
(in two parts)
Old Colliery Yd. WN4—4J 69
Old Cottage Clo. M28—2F 74
Old Crofts Bank. M31—2C 88
Old Cross. SK13—4L 97
Old Cross St. OL6—4C 82
Old Delph Rd. OL11—1L 27
Old Doctors St. BL8—3F 24
Old Eagley M. BL1—4F 22
Old Edge La. OL2 & OL1—7L 45
Old Elm St. M13—9J 79
Old Engine La. BL0—5K 9
Oldershaw Dri. M9—1K 79
Old Farm Cres. M35—7F 80
Old Farm Rd. SK2—7M 105
Oldfield Clo. BL5—9F 36
Oldfield Dri. WA15—7F 100
Oldfield Gro. M33—9J 89
Oldfield La. WA14—9J 99
Oldfield M. WA14—8C 100
Oldfield Rd. M5—5B 4 & 7C 78
Oldfield Rd. M25—1C 60
Oldfield Rd. M33—9J 89
Oldfield Rd. WA14—8A 100
Oldfield St. M11—6B 80
Old Fold. M30—3C 76
Old Fold. SK7—1K 115
Old Fold. WN5—2H 51
Old Fold Rd. BL5—1B 54
Old Fold Rd. WN2—4K 35
(in two parts)
Old Gdns. St. SK1—5F 104
Oldgate Wlk. M15—9D 78
Oldgreave Wlk. M15—9E 78
Old Green. BL8—1F 24
Old Greenwood La. BL6 —9D 20
Old Ground St. BL0—5J 9
Old Hall Clo. SK13—4K 97
Old Hall Clough. BL6—2J 37
Old Hall Ct. M33—1L 101
Old Hall Dri. M18—2D 92
Old Hall Dri. SK2—7L 105
Old Hall Dri. WN4—5A 70
Old Hall La. BL5—2E 54
Old Hall La. BL6—9J 21
Old Hall La. M14, M13 or M19 —5K 91
Old Hall La. M25 & M24—1E 60
(Prestwich)
Old Hall La. M25—2J 59
(Whitefield)
Old Hall La. SK6—8H 107
Old Hall La. SK7—2D 120
Old Hall La. SK14—1A 96
Old Hall La. WA15—6M 109
Old Hall Mill La. M29—8G 55
Old Hall Rd. M7—7D 60
Old Hall Rd. M10—9B 62
Old Hall Rd. M25—1J 59
Old Hall Rd. M32—2F 88
Old Hall Rd. M33—1L 101
Old Hall Rd. SK8—7G 103
Old Hall Sq. SK14—1G 97
Old Hall St. BL4—1L 57
Old Hall St. M11—8E 80
Oldhall St. M24—9M 43
(in two parts)
Old Hall St. SK16—8A 82
Old Hall St. WN3—2E 52
Old Hall St. N. BL1—2F 38
Oldham Av. SK1—4H 105
Oldham Central Trading Pk. OL1—9A 46
Oldham Ct. M10—2H 5 & 4J 79
Oldham Dri. SK6—1A 106
Oldham Ho. OL2—4B 46
Oldham Rd. M4 & M10—3G 5 & 5H 79
Oldham Rd. M24—9A 44
Oldham Rd. OL2—5L 45
(Royton)
Oldham Rd. OL2—5B 46
(Shaw)
Oldham Rd. OL3—3G 47
Oldham Rd. OL4 & OL3—9J 47
(Scouthead & Dobcross)
Oldham Rd. OL4 & OL3—2F 64
(Springhead & Uppermill)
Oldham Rd. OL7—9A 64
Oldham Rd. OL7 & OL6—2A 82
Oldham Rd. OL11—9H 29
Oldhams Ter. BL1—5D 22
(in three parts)
Oldham St. BL3—3D 38
Oldham St. M1 & M4—4F 5 & 6G 79
Oldham St. M5—4C 4 & 6D 78
Oldham St. M29—8A 56
Oldham St. M34—4J 93
Oldham St. M35—5H 81
Oldham St. OL8—6J 63
Oldham St. SK5—7E 92
Oldham St. SK14—4D 94
Oldham Way. OL9, OL8, OL1 & OL4—9K 45
Oldheyes Rd. WA15—5H 101
Old Ho. Ter. OL6—2E 82
Old Kiln La. BL1—8J 21
Oldknow Rd. SK6—7G 107
Old La. BL5—1D 54
Old La. BL6—8F 20
(in three parts)
Old La. BL9—2M 25
Old La. M11—7D 80
Old La. M28—2F 56
Old La. OL3—7B 48
(Dobcross)
Old La. OL3—8D 48
(Pobgreen)
Old La. OL4—9F 46
(Austerlands)
Old La. OL4—2L 65
(Grasscroft)
Old La. OL9—4H 63
Old La. SK13—7G 97
Old La. WN1—5B 34
Old La. WN6—3G 33
Old Lansdowne Rd. M20 —1F 102
Old Lees St. OL6—2D 82
Old Lord's Cres. BL6—5B 20
Old Market Pl. WA14—8D 100
Old Market St. M9—6J 61
Old Meadow Dri. M34—1M 93
Old Meadow La. WA15—1H 111
Old Medlock St. M3—5C 4 & 7D 78
Old Mill Clo. M27—8H 59
Old Mill Ho. OL4—3G 65
Old Mill La. OL4—3G 65
Old Mill La. SK7—4A 116
Old Mill La. WN6—4A 16
Old Mills Hill. M24—8D 44
Old Mill St. M4—4H 5 & 6J 79
Oldmill St. OL12—2F 28
Old Moat La. M20—7G 91
Oldmoor Rd. SK6—9L 93
Old Moss La. WA3—9K 85
Old Mount St. M4—2G 5 & 4G 79
Old Nans La. BL2—8M 23
Old Nook La. WA11—9E 68
Old Oake Clo. M28—6L 57
Old Oak St. M20—2H 103
Old Packhorse Rd. HX6—4K 15
Old Parrin La. M30—4B 76
Old Penny La. WA11—7B 70
Old Pepper La. WN6—8H 17
Old Quarry La. BL7—1F 22
Old Rake. BL6—5D 20
Old Rectory Gdns. SK8—8K 103
Old Rd. BL1—6E 22
Old Rd. M35—9E 62
Old Rd. OL6—2F 82
Old Rd. OL16—7L 13
Old Rd. SK4—2E 104
Old Rd. SK8—7M 103
Old Rd. SK9—9K 113
(Handforth)
Old Rd. SK9—3H 119
(Wilmslow)
Old Rd. SK14—1D 94
(Hyde)
Old Rd. SK14—9M 83
(Mottram)
Old Rd. SK14—8G 85
(Tintwistle)
Old Rd. SK15—7J 83
Old Rd. SK16—6C 82
(in two parts)
Old Rd. WN4—3A 70
Old Rd. WN5—7E 50
Old School La. PR7—5E 18
Old Sq. OL6—4C 82
Oldstead Gro. BL3—5M 37
Oldstead Wlk. M9—1K 79
(off Parkstead Dri.)
Old St. OL4—3D 64
Old St. OL6—5A 82
Old St. SK14—6A 96
Old St. SK15—5G 83
Old Swan Clo. BL7—9E 6
Old Swan Cotts. BL7—9E 6
Old Thorn La. OL3—2D 66
Old Vicarage. BL5—3E 54
Old Vicarage Gdns. M28—5K 57
Old Vicarage M. BL5—3E 54
Old Vicarage Rd. BL6—7F 20
Oldway Wlk. M10—2B 80
Old Wellington Rd. M30—5D 76
Old Wells Clo. M28—2G 57
Old Well Wlk. M33—3C 100
Old Whint Rd. WA11—9G 69
Old Wood La. BL2—1K 23
Old Wool La. SK8—9M 103
Olerton Dri. M35—1F 80
Olga St. BL1—8D 22
Olivant St. BL9—1L 41
Olive Bank. BL8—6H 25
Olive Gro. WN6—6M 33
Oliver Clo. OL15—6M 13
Olive Rd. WA15—5G 101
Oliver St. M29—5K 55
Oliver St. OL1—2M 63
Oliver St. SK3—5E 104
Olive St. BL3—5D 38
Olive St. BL8—8K 25
Olive St. M35—8E 62
Olive St. OL8—2K 63
Olive St. OL10—8L 27
Olive St. OL11—9D 28
Olive Wlk. M33—8C 88
Olivia Gro. M14—3K 91
Ollerbarrow Rd. WA15—2E 110
Ollerbrook Ct. BL1—8F 22
Ollerton. OL12—2E 28
(off Spotland Rd.)
Ollerton Av. M16—3C 90
Ollerton Av. M33—8D 88
Ollerton Clo. M22—4E 102
Ollerton Clo. WN2—7G 35
Ollerton Rd. SK9—7K 113
Ollerton St. BL1—4F 22
Ollerton St. PR6—1G 19
Ollerton Ter. BL1—4F 22
(off Ollerton St.)
Ollier Av. M12—4A 92
Olney. OL11—4E 28
Olney Av. M22—7D 102
Olney St. M13—2K 91
Olverston Rd. WN3—5M 51
Olwen Av. M12—1A 92
Olwen Cres. SK5—6F 92
Olympia Trading Est. M15 —6D 4 & 8E 78
Olympic Ct. M5—7M 77
Omer Av. M13—4M 91
Omer Dri. M19—7L 91
Onchan Av. OL4—2B 64
One Ash Clo. OL12—9F 12
Oneoak Ct. SK7—2D 114
One Oak La. SK9—4M 119
Ongar Way. M9—5H 61
Onslow Av. M10—7E 62
Onslow Clo. OL1—9L 45
Onslow Rd. SK3—5C 104
Onslow St. OL11—6C 28
Onward St. SK14—4D 94
Oozewood Rd. OL2—4G 45
Opal Gro. WN7—3E 72
Opal St. M19—6B 92
Openshaw Fold Rd. BL9—2K 41
Openshaw La. M30—8E 86
Openshaw Pl. BL4—9H 39
Openshaw St. BL9—9A 26
Openshaw Wlk. M11—7C 80
Oracle Ct. M28—6J 57
Orama Av. M6—3G 77
Oram St. BL9—6A 26
Orange Hill Rd. M25—3C 60
Orange St. M6—4A 78
Orange St. OL6—4B 82
Orchard Av. BL1—7F 22
Orchard Av. M28—9H 57
Orchard Av. M31—1F 98
Orchard Av. WA13—1A 108
Orchard Brow. WA3—3A 98
Orchard Clo. SK8—5C 114
Orchard Clo. SK9—6F 118
Orchard Clo. SK12—9L 115
Orchard Clo. WA11—8D 68
Orchard Clo. WN6—2G 33
Orchard Clo. WN7—9F 54
Orchard Ct. WA15—6H 101
Orchard Dri. SK9—1L 119
Orchard Dri. WA15—1G 111
Orchard Gdns. BL2—7M 23
Orchard Grn. SK9—8M 119
Orchard Gro. M20—9F 90
Orchard Gro. OL2—2A 46
Orchard Ind. Est. M6—2A 78
Orchard La. WN7—9F 54
Orchard Pl. M33—9H 89
Orchard Pl. WA15—6H 101
Orchard Rd. M35—9F 62
Orchard Rd. SK6—3H 107
Orchard Rd. WA13—8B 98
Orchard Rd. WA15—8E 100
Orchard Rd. E. M22—3D 102
Orchard Rd. W. M22—3D 102
Orchards, The. OL2—2M 45
Orchard St. BL4—1L 57
Orchard St. M6—2A 78
(in two parts)
Orchard St. M20—9F 90
Orchard St. OL10—7L 27
Orchard St. SK1—4F 104
Orchard St. SK14—4E 94
Orchard St. WN1—9D 34
Orchard St. WN4—4C 70
Orchard, The. BL5—8E 36
(off Gerrard St.)
Orchard, The. SK9—9M 119
Orchard Trading Est. M6 —2M 77
Orchid Av. BL4—8H 39
Orchid Clo. M30—6E 86
Orchid St. M9—9K 61
Orchid Way. OL12—8D 12
Ordell Wlk. M9—5L 61
Ordsall Av. M28—4H 57
Ordsall Dri. M5—6A 4 & 8B 78
Ordsall La. M5—6A 4 & 9A 78
Oregon Av. OL1—8L 45
Oregon Clo. M13—9J 79
Orford Av. SK12—6K 117
Orford Clo. SK6—5E 116
Orford Rd. M10—2C 80
Orford Rd. M25—3B 60
Organ St. WN2—5B 54
Organ St. WN7—2E 72
Organ Way. SK14—1D 96
Oriel Av. OL8—5L 63
Oriel Clo. OL9—3G 63
Oriel Clo. SK2—7H 105
Oriel Ct. M33—9G 89
Oriel Rd. M20—1G 103
Oriel Rd. WN4—3M 69
Oriel St. BL3—4C 38
Oriel St. OL11—5G 29
Orient Rd. M6—3G 77
Orient Sq. M1—7G 79
(off Samuel Ogden St.)
Orient St. M8—9F 60
Oriole Dri. M28—8H 57
Orion Pl. M7—1B 4 & 3C 78
Orion Trading Est. M17—7G 77
Orkney Clo. WA11—8D 68
Orkney Dri. M31—1D 88
Orlanda Av. M6—3G 77
Orlando St. BL3 & BL2—4F 38
(in two parts)
Orleans Way. OL1—1L 63
Orley Wlk. OL1—5D 46
Orme Av. M6—2H 77
Orme Av. M24—1A 62
Orme Clo. M11—6L 79
Ormerod Av. OL2—6L 45
Ormerod Clo. SK6—4M 105
Ormerod St. M10—4E 80
Ormerod St. OL10—9L 27
Orme St. M11—6L 79
Orme St. OL4—3A 64
Orme St. SK1—3G 105
Orme St. SK9—8L 119
Ormonde Av. M6—3H 77
Ormonde St. OL6—3C 82
Ormond St. BL3—4K 39
Ormond St. BL9—7A 26
Ormrod St. BL2—6J 23
Ormrod St. BL3—3E 38
Ormrod St. BL4—8J 39
Ormrod St. BL9—8A 26
Ormrod St. OL1—1L 63
Ormsby Av. M18—2B 92
Ormsby Clo. SK3—9E 104
Ormsby Clo. WN6—8L 17
Ormsgill Clo. M15—9F 78
Orms Gill Pl. SK2—7L 105
Ormside Clo. WN2—4B 54
Ormskirk. WN8—1A 50
Ormskirk Av. M20—8F 90
Ormskirk Clo. BL8—1G 41
Ormskirk Rd. SK5—8F 92
Ormskirk Rd. WN5—2H 51
Ormston Av. BL6—5B 20
Ormston Gro. WN7—9F 54
Ormstons La. BL6—4D 20
Ornatus St. BL1—5F 22
Ornsay Wlk. M11—6C 80
Oronsay Gro. M5—6K 77
Orpington Dri. BL8—9H 25
Orpington Rd. M9—9L 61
Orpington St. WN5—2J 51
Orrell Arc. WN1—9C 34
(off Galleries, The)
Orrell Gdns. WN5—2F 50
Orrell Hall Clo. WN5—9H 33
Orrell Rd. WN5—1D 50
Orrell St. BL8—7J 25
Orrell St. M11—7D 80
Orrell St. WN1—1D 52
Orrel St. M5—5L 77
Orrishmere Rd. SK8—1M 113
Orron St. OL15—6A 14
Orr St. M11—7D 80
Orsett Clo. M10—2H 5 & 4J 79
Orthes Gro. SK4—9D 92
Orton Av. M23—4A 102
Orton Rd. M23—4A 102
Orton Way. WN4—4M 69
Orvietto Av. M6—3G 77
Orville Dri. M19—7M 91
Orwell Av. M22—7D 102
Orwell Av. M34—3G 93
Orwell Clo. BL8—6K 25
Orwell Rd. BL1—8B 22
Osborne Clo. BL4—8K 39
Osborne Clo. BL8—1H 41
Osborne Dri. M27—9J 59
Osborne Gro. BL1—9C 22
Osborne Gro. SK8—1G 113
Osborne Gro. WN7—1K 73
Osborne Ho. M30—5C 76
(off Police St.)
Osborne Pl. SK14—1G 97
Osborne Rd. M6—5G 77
Osborne Rd. M19—5M 91
Osborne Rd. M34—2M 93
Osborne Rd. OL8—3K 63
Osborne Rd. SK2—6F 104
Osborne Rd. SK14—5E 94
Osborne Rd. WA3—8L 71
Osborne Rd. WA15—8E 100
Osborne Rd. WN4—3A 70
Osborne St. M6—4M 77
Osborne St. M10—1H 5 & 3J 79
Osborne St. M20—2G 103
Osborne St. OL2—3B 46
Osborne St. OL9—9J 45
Osborne St. OL10—9K 27
Osborne St. OL11—5E 28
Osborne St. SK6—2K 105
Osborne Ter. M33—1H 101
Osborne Wlk. M26—6E 40
Osbourne Pl. WA14—9D 100
Oscar St. BL1—8C 22
Oscar St. M10—9A 62
(in two parts)
Oscott Av. M28—2G 57
Oscroft Clo. M8—1F 78
Oscroft Wlk. M14—7K 91
(off Ladybarn La.)
Osmond St. OL4—1C 64
Osmund Av. BL2—2K 39
Osprey Av. BL5—2C 54
Osprey Clo. M15—1E 90
Osprey Clo. SK16—8E 82
Osprey Dri. M30—3G 87
Osprey Dri. M35—4J 81
Osprey Dri. SK9—3J 119
Osprey's, The. WN3—4J 51
Osprey Wlk. M13—9J 79
Ossington Wlk. M23—3A 102
Ossory St. M14—3H 91
Osterley Rd. M9—5M 61
Ostlers Ga. M35—5K 81
Ostrich La. M25—5C 60
O'Sullivan Cres. WA11—9E 68
Oswald Clo. M6—2A 78
Oswald La. M21—5B 90
Oswald Rd. M21—5A 90
Oswald St. BL3—5C 38
(in two parts)
Oswald St. M4—6K 79
(Ancoats)
Oswald St. M4—2F 5 & 4G 79
(Manchester)
Oswald St. OL2—1C 46
Oswald St. OL9—9K 45
Oswald St. OL16—2G 29
Oswald St. SK5—3F 92
Oswestry Clo. BL8—2F 24
Otago St. OL4—8C 46
Otford Dri. M5—5A 78
Othello Dri. M30—5D 76
Otley Av. M6—4J 77
Otley Clo. OL9—2H 63
Otley Gro. SK3—9D 104
Otmoor Way. OL2—5A 46
Otranto Av. M6—3H 77
Ottawa Clo. M23—9M 101
Otterburn Clo. M15—9F 78
Otterburn Ho. M30—4E 76
Otterburn Pl. SK2—7K 105
Otterbury Clo. BL8—8F 24
Otter Dri. BL9—5B 42
Otterham Wlk. M10—2D 80
Otterspool Rd. SK6—4B 106
Oughtrington Cres. WA13 —9B 98
Oughtrington La. WA13 —2A 108
Oughtrington View. WA13 —9B 98
Oulder Hill. OL11—3B 28
Oulder Hill Dri. OL11—3A 28
Ouldfield Clo. OL16—4H 29
Oulton Av. M33—9L 89
Oulton St. BL1—5G 23
Oulton Wlk. M10—4K 79
Oury St. SK3—5E 104
Ouse St. M5—6J 77
Outdoor Mkt. OL16—3E 28
Outfield Rd. WA15—8E 100
Outram Clo. SK6—9F 106
Outram Ho. M1—6J 79
Outram Rd. SK16—9B 82
Outram Sq. M35—7G 81
Outrington Dri. M11—7A 80
Outterside St. PR7—4G 19
Outwood Av. M27—4D 58
Outwood Dri. SK8—4G 113
Outwood Gro. BL1—5E 22
Outwood La. M22—4B 112
Outwood Rd. M26—8G 41
Outwood Rd. SK8—4H 113
Oval Dri. SK16—8B 82
Oval, The. SK8—4H 113
Oval, The. WN6—4F 32
Overbridge Rd. M7—1D 4 & 3E 78
Overbrook Av. M10—2K 79
Overbrook Dri. M25—5B 60
Overcombe Wlk. M10—1J 79
(off Westmount Clo.)
Overdale. M27—1G 77
Overdale. SK6—4M 105
Overdale Cres. M31—4M 87
Overdale Dri. BL1—2A 38
Overdale Rd. M22—8D 102
Overdale Rd. SK6—4A 106
Overdale Rd. SK12—6M 117
Overdell Dri. OL12—8C 12
Overdene Clo. BL6—3H 37
Overens St. OL4—1B 64
Overfield Way. OL12—9F 12
Overgreen. BL2—7L 23
Overhill Dri. SK9—4L 119
Overhill La. SK9—4L 119
Overhill Rd. OL9—9F 44
Overhill Rd. SK9—4K 119
Overhill Way. WN3—5K 51
Overhouses. BL7—5H 7
Overlea Dri. M19—9L 91
Overlinks Dri. M6—2H 77
Overshores Rd. BL7—4G 7
Overstone Dri. M8—9F 60
Overton Av. M22—8D 102
Overton Cres. M33—3D 100
Overton Cres. SK7—9L 105
Overton Rd. M22—8D 102
Overton St. WN7—3E 72
Overton Way. SK9—7K 113
Over Town La. OL12—8G 11
Overt St. OL11—5F 28
Overwood Rd. M22—5D 102
Ovington Wlk. M10—2J 79
Owenington Gro. M28—2G 57
Owens Clo. OL9—9E 44
Owen St. M6—2A 78
Owen St. M30—6B 76
Owen St. OL1—6E 46
Owen St. SK3—4D 104
Owen St. WN7—2D 72
Owen Wlk. M16—2F 90
Owlerbarrow Rd. BL8—7G 25
Owler La. OL9—5D 62
Owlwood Clo. M28—5E 56
Owlwood Dri. M28—5E 56
Oxburgh Rd. WN3—3F 52
Oxendale Dri. M24—8K 43
Oxendon Av. M11—4B 80
Oxenhurst Grn. SK2—8L 105
Oxford Av. M25—9A 42
Oxford Av. M33—1D 100
Oxford Av. M35—4F 80
Oxford Av. OL11—4A 28
Oxford Clo. BL4—9F 38
Oxford Ct. M2—5E 5 & 7F 78
Oxford Ct. M16—1D 90
Oxford Ct. WN1—8D 34
Oxford Dri. SK6—1C 106
Oxford Gro. BL1—9C 22
Oxford Gro. M30—8C 86
Oxford Gro. SK2—7G 105
Oxford Ho. OL9—2J 63
Oxford Pl. M14—2J 91
Oxford Pl. OL16—5G 29
Oxford Rd. BL3—6M 39
Oxford Rd. BL6—1F 36
Oxford Rd. M1, M15 & M13 —6F 5 & 8G 79
Oxford Rd. M6—3G 77
Oxford Rd. M29—3H 55
Oxford Rd. SK14—6E 94
Oxford Rd. SK16—7D 82
Oxford Rd. WA14—1D 110
Oxford Rd. WN5—9F 32
Oxford Rd. Sta. App. M1 —6F 5 & 7G 79
Oxford St. BL1—2F 38
Oxford St. BL9—9A 26
Oxford St. M1—5E 5 & 7F 78
Oxford St. M16—1D 90
Oxford St. M30—5E 76
Oxford St. OL2—2B 46
Oxford St. OL9—3H 63
Oxford St. PR7—4G 19
Oxford St. SK15—3K 83
(Millbrook)
Oxford St. SK15—6J 83
(Stalybridge)
Oxford St. WN2—1M 53
Oxford St. WN7—1F 72
Oxford St. E. OL7—7M 81
Oxford St. W. OL7—7M 81
Oxford Wlk. M34—5A 94
Oxford Way. SK4—2D 104
Ox Ga. BL2—5K 23
Oxhey Clo. BL0—4J 9
Ox Hey Clo. BL6—1E 36
Ox Hey La. BL6—1E 36
Ox Hey La. OL3—9K 31
Oxhill Wlk. M10—6D 62
Oxhouse Rd. WN5—4D 50
Oxlea Gro. BL5—1E 54
Oxley St. M11—5A 80
Oxney Rd. M14—2J 91
Ox St. BL0—6H 9
Oxted Wlk. M8—1G 79
Oxton Av. M22—9D 102
Oxton St. M11—8F 80

Pacific Rd. WA14—7A 100
Pacific Way. M5—7J 77
Packer St. BL1—8C 22
Packer St. OL16—3F 28
Padbury Clo. M31—3K 87
Padbury Wlk. M10—2M 79
Padbury Way. BL2—8K 23
Padden Brook. SK6—3B 106
Paddington Av. M10—2B 80
Paddington Clo. M6—5A 78
Paddison St. M27—8E 58
Paddock Av. M5—5A 4 & 7B 78
Paddock Av. S. M5—5A 4 & 7B 78
Paddock Chase. SK12—6M 115
Paddock Clo. M29—3L 55
Paddock Dri. M5—5A 4 & 7B 78
Paddock Field. M5—7B 78
Paddock Head. OL15—7L 13
Paddock Hill. WA16—8A 118
Paddockhill La. WA16—7A 118
Paddock La. M35—2F 80
Paddock La. WA13—5B 98
Paddock La. WA14—8G 99
Paddock Rd. SK14—6D 94
Paddock Rise. WN6—6L 33
Paddocks End. WA15—4G 111
Paddock Shopping Precinct, The. SK9—8K 113
Paddock St. M12—6H 5 & 8J 79
Paddock, The. BL0—4H 9
Paddock, The. M25—1J 59
Paddock, The. OL3—4M 65
Paddock, The. SK3—8G 105
Paddock, The. SK8—8L 103
Paddock, The. SK14—1F 96
Paddock, The. WA13—9C 98
Paddock, The. WN4—1M 69
(in two parts)
Paderborn Ct. BL1—3E 38
Padfield Ga. SK13—7K 97
Padfield Main Rd. SK14—9G 85
Padiham Clo. BL9—2K 41
Padstow Clo. SK14—3K 95
Padstow Dri. SK7—5F 114
Padstow St. M10—4L 79
Padstow Wlk. SK14—3K 95
Padworth Wlk. M23—5K 101
Pagefield Clo. WN6—8A 34
Pagefield Ind. Est. WN6—8M 33
Pagefield St. WN6—8A 34
Pagen St. OL16—2F 28
Paget St. M10—2K 79
Pagnall Ct. OL9—3H 63
Paignton Av. M19—6M 91
Paignton Av. SK14—4J 95
Paignton Clo. WN5—8E 50
Paignton Dri. M33—9D 88
Paignton Gro. SK5—7E 92
Paignton Wlk. SK14—4J 95
Pailin Dri. M35—5J 81
Pailton Clo. BL6—3K 37
Painswick Rd. M22—3B 112
Paisley Av. WA11—8D 68
Paisley Ter. M8—8F 60
Paiton St. BL1—2C 38
Palace Arc. WN4—4B 70
(off Bryn St.)
Palace Gdns. OL2—7K 45
Palace Gro. WN7—1K 73
Palace Rd. M33—9G 89
Palace Rd. OL6—2D 82
Palace St. BL1—1F 38
Palace St. BL9—8A 26
Palace St. OL9—1J 63
Palatine Av. M20—8H 91
Palatine Av. OL11—2A 28
Palatine Clo. M30—5F 86
Palatine Cres. M20—9H 91
Palatine Dri. BL9—2M 25
Palatine M. M20—8H 91
Palatine Rd. M22 & M20 —4C 102
Palatine Rd. OL11—2A 28
Palatine Sq. WN7—2D 72
Palatine St. BL1—2F 38
Palatine St. M34—1L 93
Palatine St. OL16—3J 29
Palatine Ter. OL11—2A 28
Paley St. BL1—2F 38
Palfrey Pl. M12—6H 5 & 8J 79
Palgrave Av. M10—2K 79
Palin St. WN2—5B 54
Palin Wood Rd. OL3—4M 47
Pall Mall. M2—4E 5 & 6F 78
(in two parts)
Palm Av. WN4—2K 69
Palm Clo. M33—9C 88
Palmer Av. SK8—7M 103
Palmer Clo. M8—6H 61
Palmer Gro. WN7—7E 54
Palmerston Av. M16—4D 90
Palmerston Clo. BL0—7H 9
Palmerston Clo. M34—3H 93
Palmerston Rd. SK2—1G 115
Palmerston St. M12—7K 79
Palmer St. M7—2C 78
Palmer St. M33—9H 89
Palmer St. SK16—6B 82
Palm Gro. OL9—9H 45
Palm Gro. WN5—2K 51
Palm St. BL1—7E 22
Palm St. M13—3M 91
Palm St. M35—5D 80
Palm St. OL4—9C 46
Pandora St. M20—9G 91
Panfield Rd. M22—9C 102
Pangbourne Av. M31—3E 88
Pankhurst Wlk. M14—3H 91
Panmure St. OL8—4M 63
Pansy Rd. BL4—9G 39
Panton St. BL6—9D 20
Paper Mill Rd. BL7—3G 23
Parade Rd. M22—5C 112
Parade, The. M27—8F 58
Parade, The. SK6—4A 106
Paradise St. BL0—5J 9
Paradise St. M34—8M 81
Paradise St. SK14—1F 96
Paradise Wharf. M1—4G 5 & 6H 79
Paragon Ho. WN7—2G 73
(off Lord St.)
Paragon Ho. WN7—2G 73
(off Princess St.)
Parbold Av. M20—7G 91
Parbold Av. WA11—9D 68
Parbrook Clo. M10—2K 79
Parcel St. M11—5M 79
Pardoner's Ct. M5—5H 77
Pares Land Wlk. OL16—4H 29
Paris Av. M5—6A 4 & 8B 78
Parisian Way. M15—1F 90
(off Moss Side Shopping Cen.)
Paris St. BL3—5B 38
Park Av. BL0—5K 9
Park Av. BL1—6E 22
Park Av. M8—8F 60
Park Av. M16—1C 90
Park Av. M19—5A 92
Park Av. M25—4B 60
(Prestwich)
Park Av. M25—2K 59
(Whitefield)
Park Av. M26—5K 41
Park Av. M27—9G 59
Park Av. M31—4C 88
Park Av. M33—8G 89
Park Av. M35—8D 62
Park Av. OL9—8H 45
Park Av. SK3—6M 103
Park Av. SK6—2C 106
Park Av. SK7—7C 114
Park Av. SK8—3M 113
Park Av. SK9—3J 119
Park Av. SK12—8L 115
Park Av. SK14—2D 94
Park Av. WA3—5F 70
Park Av. WA11—9G 69
Park Av. WA14—5E 100
Park Av. WA15—3F 110
Park Av. WN5—7E 50
Park Av. WN6—2H 33
Park Bank. M5—5K 77
Park Bank. M29—2M 55
Parkbridge Wlk. M13—9H 79
Parkbrook La. WN6—2H 33
Parkbrook Rd. M23—6B 102
Park Brow Clo. M21—6C 90
Park Bungalows. SK6—8F 106
Park Clo. M25—2M 59
Park Clo. SK13—4K 97
Park Clo. SK15—4F 82
Park Clo. WA14—5F 100
Park Cotts. BL1—7C 22
Park Cotts. OL2—1M 45
Park Cotts. OL3—3L 65
Park Ct. M22—1D 112
Park Ct. M33—9G 89
Park Ct. OL11—4E 28
Park Ct. M. SK8—9L 103
Park Cres. M14—3J 91
Park Cres. OL6—5E 82
Park Cres. OL9—8F 44
Park Cres. SK9—2H 119
Park Cres. SK13—3H 97
Park Cres. WN1—8B 34
Park Cres. W. WN1—8B 34
Parkdale. OL9—8H 45
Parkdale Av. M18—1C 92
Parkdale Av. M34—8K 81
Parkdale Rd. BL2—9J 23
Parkdene Clo. BL2—6K 23
Park Dene Dri. SK13—4J 97
Park Dri. M16—4C 90
Park Dri. M30—3D 76
Park Dri. SK4—3B 104
Park Dri. SK14—2D 94
Park Dri. WA15—6G 101
(Altrincham)
Park Dri. WA15—2F 110
(Hale)
Park Edge. BL5—1G 55
Parkend Dri. WN7—5D 72
Parkend Rd. M23—8A 102
Parker Arc. M1—6G 79
(off Piccadilly Plaza)
Parker St. BL9—8A 26
Parker St. M1—4F 5 & 6G 79
Parkfield. M5—5K 77
Parkfield. M24—9M 43
Parkfield. M30—2J 87
Parkfield. OL9—8G 45
Parkfield. WN6—2H 33
Parkfield Av. BL4—1H 57
Parkfield Av. M14—3H 91
Parkfield Av. M25—5D 60
Parkfield Av. M29—1B 74
Parkfield Av. M31—5B 88
Parkfield Av. OL8—6H 63
Parkfield Av. SK6—7F 106
Parkfield Clo. M29—1B 74
Parkfield Clo. WN7—9G 55
Parkfield Ct. WA14—9C 100
Parkfield Dri. M24—9L 43
Parkfield Dri. M29—7D 56
Parkfield Est. M27—1G 77
Parkfield Ind. Est. M24—9L 43
Parkfield Rd. BL3—6F 38
Park Field Rd. OL4—2L 65
Parkfield Rd. SK8—3M 113
Parkfield Rd. WA14—9C 100
Parkfield Rd. N. M40—5A 62
Parkfield Rd. S. M20—1G 103
Parkfields. SK15—4K 83
Parkfields. WN2—9H 53
Parkfield St. M14—3H 91
Parkfield St. OL16—8H 29
Parkgate. BL8—5E 24
Parkgate. OL9—8H 45
Park Ga. Av. M20—8H 91
Parkgate Dri. BL1—5F 22
Parkgate Dri. M27—9G 59
Parkgate Dri. SK2—9H 105
Park Gates Av. SK8—3C 114
Park Gates Rd. SK8—3C 114
Parkgate Way. OL2—2D 46
Parkgate Way. SK9—8K 113
Park Gro. M19—4A 92
Park Gro. M26—5F 40
Park Gro. M28—8K 57
Park Gro. SK4—1B 104
Park Hey Dri. WN6—2E 32
Parkhill. OL12—1F 28
Parkhill Av. M8—6H 61
Parkhill Dri. M25—9L 41
Park Hill Rd. WA15—3G 111
Parkhills Rd. BL9—1L 41
Park Hill St. BL1—1D 38
Parkhill Ter. SK15—4K 83
Park Ho. M29—7M 55
Park Ho. Bri. Rd. M6—1L 77
Parkhouse St. M11—7B 80
Parkhouse St. Ind. Est. M11 —7B 80
Parkhurst Av. M10—7E 62
Parkin Clo. SK16—7C 82
Parkinson St. BL3—4C 38
Parkinson St. BL9—5M 25
Parkin St. M12—3A 92
Park Lake Av. M7—8E 60
Parklands. M25—9L 41
Parklands. OL2—2J 45
(Royton)
Parklands. OL2—1D 46
(Shaw)
Parklands. SK9—4J 119
Parklands. SK12—8L 115
Parklands Cres. OL10—1G 43
Parklands Dri. M33—3D 100
Parklands Ho. OL2—3J 45
Parklands Rd. M23—5M 101
Parklands, The. SK4—1E 104
Parklands Way. OL10—1G 43
Parklands Way. SK12—8L 115
Park La. BL6—7D 20
Park La. M6—2J 77
Park La. M7—8E 60
Park La. M27—9K 59
Park La. M28—9D 56
Park La. OL2—4K 45
(in four parts)
Park La. OL3—3C 66
Park La. OL8—6M 63
Park La. OL16—2F 28
Park La. SK1—5H 105
Park La. SK12—6G 117
(Disley)
Park La. SK12—8L 115
(Poynton)
Park La. SK16—6C 82
Park La. WA14—2H 109
Park La. WA15—3G 111
Park La. WN2—9H 53
Park La. WN7—3J 73
Park La. Ct. M7—8D 60
Park La. Ct. M25—1K 59
Park La. W. M27—9K 59
Park Lea Ct. M7—7E 60
Parkleigh Dri. M10—6E 62
Park Lodge. M7—8D 60
Park Lodge. M19—5A 92
Park Lodge Clo. SK8—9L 103
Park Meadow. BL5—9G 37
Park M. M16—4C 90
Park Mt. SK8—8G 103
Parkmount Rd. M9—7L 61
Park Pde. OL2—9C 30
Park Pde. OL7 & OL6—5A 82
Park Pl. M4—2F 5 & 4G 79
Park Pl. M6—4G 77
Park Pl. M25—3C 60
Park Pl. SK4—3M 103
Park Range. M14—3K 91
Park Rise. SK6—2C 106
Park Rise. SK15—4F 82
Park Rd. BL1—2C 38
Park Rd. BL3—5M 39
Park Rd. BL5—9F 36
Park Rd. BL7—6L 7
Park Rd. BL9—6L 25
Park Rd. M24—9M 43
Park Rd. M25 & M8—5D 60
Park Rd. M28—7J 57
Park Rd. M30—3D 76
Park Rd. M30 & M6—3G 77
Park Rd. M31—2G 99
Park Rd. M32—3J 89
Park Rd. M33—8G 89
Park Rd. M34—7K 81
(Audenshaw)
Park Rd. M34—3L 93
(Denton)
Park Rd. OL8 & OL4—2M 63
Park Rd. OL12—9G 13
Park Rd. OL15—5B 14
Park Rd. PR7—4F 18
(Adlington)
Park Rd. PR7—1L 17
(Coppull)
Park Rd. SK4—9B 92
Park Rd. SK6—2C 106
Park Rd. SK8—7L 103
(Cheadle)
Park Rd. SK8—3C 114
(Cheadle Hulme)
Park Rd. SK8—7F 102
(Gatley)
Park Rd. SK9—4G 119
Park Rd. SK12—6F 116
Park Rd. SK14—2G 97
(Hadfield)
Park Rd. SK14—2D 94
(Hyde)
Park Rd. SK16—6C 82
Park Rd. WA3—8F 70
Park Rd. WA13—4D 108
(Lymm)
Park Rd. WA13—5B 98
(Warburton)
Park Rd. WA14 & WA15 —5E 100
(Altrincham)
Park Rd. WA14—1A 110
(Bowdon)
Park Rd. WA15—3E 110
Park Rd. WN2—4K 53
Park Rd. WN5—7E 50
(Billinge)
Park Rd. WN5—2G 51
(Orrell)
Park Rd. WN6—1L 33
Park Rd. WN6 & WN1—8A 34
Park Rd. N. M31—3C 88
Park Rd. S. M31—4C 88
Park Row. BL1—4F 22
Park Row. SK4—3L 103
Park Seventeen. M25—8M 41
Parkside. M24—2L 61
Parkside. OL12—1D 12
Parkside. WN2—2L 53
Parkside Av. M7—8E 60
Parkside Av. M28—7K 57
Parkside Av. M30—6C 76
Parkside Av. M35—2E 80
Park Side Av. OL2—1C 46
Parkside Av. WN4—8M 51
Parkside Clo. M26—5K 41
Parkside Clo. SK6—4D 116
Parkside Cres. WN5—2F 50
Parkside Ho. OL2—5L 45
Parkside Ind. Est. OL2—5L 45
Parkside La. SK6—7J 107
Parkside Rd. M14—4F 90
Parkside Rd. M33—2K 101
Parkside St. BL2—9J 23
Parkside St. M12—6H 5 & 8J 79
Parkside Wlk. BL9—9M 25
Parkside Wlk. SK7—1E 114
(in two parts)
Parks Nook. BL4—1J 57
Park Sq. M16—4A 90
Park Sq. OL6—3E 82
Parkstead Dri. M9—1K 79
Parkstone Av. M18—9F 80
Parkstone Av. M25—2K 59
Parkstone Dri. M27—1H 77
Parkstone La. M28—2M 75
Parkstone Rd. M30—3G 87
Park St. BL1—1D 38
Park St. BL4—8K 39
Park St. BL9—7M 25
Park St. M3—2E 5 & 4F 78
(Manchester)
Park St. M3—3C 4 & 5D 78
(Salford)
Park St. M7—8C 60
Park St. M25—4C 60
Park St. M26—5J 41
Park St. M27—9G 59
Park St. M29—4L 55
(Atherton)
Park St. M29—7A 56
(Tyldesley)
Park St. M34—3K 93
Park St. M35—5J 81
(Droylsden)
Park St. OL2—5L 45
(Royton)
Park St. OL2—2B 46
(Shaw)
Park St. OL5—8J 65
Park St. OL7—6A 82
(in two parts)
Park St. OL8—3L 63
Park St. OL10—1L 43
Park St. OL16—4F 28
Park St. SK1—3F 104
Park St. SK6—2M 105
Park St. SK15—6H 83
Park St. WA11—9F 68
Park St. WN3—2B 52
Park St. WN4—9M 51
Parkway. M9—3H 61
Parkway. M25—6C 60
Parkway. M27—1J 77
Parks Yd. BL9—8L 25
Park Ter. BL1—4F 22
Park Ter. BL5—8F 36
Park Ter. M25—1K 59
Park Ter. OL5—8J 65
Park Ter. OL10—7K 27
Park Ter. SK13—6J 97
Park Ter. WN6—7K 17
Park, The. OL3—3C 66
Park, The. OL4—2K 65
Park View. BL1—4F 22
(in two parts)
Park View. BL4—8K 39
(Farnworth)
Park View. BL4—1M 57
(Kearsley)
Park View. M5—6A 4 & 8B 78
Park View. M9—1J 79
Park View. M14—7L 91
Park View. OL2—1M 45
Park View. OL9—8G 45
Park View. SK3—6M 103
Park View. SK6—2J 105
Park View. SK7—4B 116
Park View. SK8—7L 103
Park View. WA14—1H 109
Park View. WN2—1H 53
(Ince)
Park View. WN2—7H 53
(Platt Bridge)
Park View. WN4—5B 70
Park View Clo. M25—5A 60
Park View Ct. M21—5M 89
Parkview Ct. M32—5M 89
Park View Ho. M29—5J 55
Park View Rd. BL3—5C 38
Park View Rd. M25—5B 60
Park View Ter. M18—2C 92
Parkville Rd. M20—9J 91
Parkville Rd. M25—1C 60
Parkway. BL5—2D 54
Park Way. M28—4E 56
(in two parts)
Park Way. M31, M32 & M17 —2F 8
Parkway. OL9—8G 45
Parkway. OL11—2B 28
Parkway. SK3—6M 103
Parkway. SK7—2E 114
Parkway. SK9—5H 119
Parkway. WN6—8G 17
Parkway Bus. Cen. M14—4F 9
Parkway Four Ind. Est. M17 —9G 7
Parkway Gro. M28—4E 56
Parkway Ind. Est. M17—9G 77
Parkwood. BL7—9D 6
Parkwood Dri. BL5—1M 55
Parkwood Rd. M23—6C 102
Parliament Pl. BL9—9L 25
Parliament St. BL9—9L 25
Parliament St. WN3—2E 52
Parnam Wlk. M9—5L 61
Parndon Dri. SK2—6J 105
Parnell Av. M22—5C 102
Parnham Clo. M26—4B 40
Parrbrook Clo. M25—8A 42
Parrbrook Wlk. M25—8B 42
Parr Clo. BL4—9H 39
Parrenthorn Rd. M25—9C 42
Parrfield Rd. M28—9A 58
Parr Fold. BL9—7B 42
Parr Fold Av. M28—7J 57
Parr Gro. WA11—9G 69
Parr Ho. OL8—3M 63
Parrin La. M30—4B 76
Parr La. BL9—7A 42
Parrot St. BL3—4E 38
Parrott St. M11—6C 80
Parrs Ct. M30—4F 86
Parrs Mt. M. SK4—3M 103
Parr St. M11—8E 80
Parr St. M30—6D 76
Parrs Wood Av. M20—4J 103
Parrs Wood La. M20—4J 103
Parrs Wood Rd. M20—5H 103
Parry Mead. SK6—1A 106
Parry Rd. M12—2A 92
Parry Wlk. OL6—3D 82
Parslow Av. M8—8G 61
Parsonage. M3—3E 5 & 5F 78
Parsonage Clo. BL9—7A 26
Parsonage Clo. M5—5B 4 & 7C 7
Parsonage Ct. M20—8H 91
Parsonage Ct. SK4—1B 104
Parsonage Dri. M28—6J 57
Parsonage Gdns. M3—4E 5 & 6F
Parsonage Gdns. SK6—9G 10
Parsonage Grn. SK9—4H 119
Parsonage La. M3—3E 5 & 5F 7
Parsonage Rd. M20—8H 91
Parsonage Rd. M26—1C 58
Parsonage Rd. M28—6J 57
Parsonage Rd. M31—5L 87
(in two parts)
Parsonage Rd. SK4—1B 104
Parsonage Rd. WN8—1A 50
Parsonage St. BL9—7A 26
Parsonage St. M8—7F 60
Parsonage St. M15—1E 90
Parsonage St. M26—5G 41
Parsonage St. SK4—3D 104
Parsonage St. SK14—4D 94
Parsonage Ter. OL16—3M 29
(off Parsonage Wlk.)
Parsonage Wlk. OL16—3M 2
Parsonage Way. SK8—8A 10
Parson's Dri. M24—7M 43
Parsons Field. M6—1A 78
Parsons La. BL9—8M 25
Parsons St. BL8—7K 25
Parsons St. OL9—2J 63
Parson's Wlk. WN1—8B 34
Parth St. BL9—9D 26
Partington Ct. BL4—8J 39
Partington Ct. SK13—5M 97
Partington La. M27—9E 58
Partington Pl. M33—9H 89
Partington Shopping Cen. M —2F
Partington St. BL3—7C 38
Partington St. M10—2M 79
Partington St. M28—9C 58
Partington St. M35—9F 62
Partington St. OL1—1A 64
Partington St. OL10—8G 27
Partington St. OL11—8B 28
Partington St. WN5—9L 33
Partridge Av. M23—7C 102
Partridge Clo. M30—2G 87
Partridge Clo. OL11—3M 27
Partridge Rise. M35—4K 81
Partridge Rd. M35—1J 81
Partridge St. M32—1M 89
Partridge Way. OL9—9D 44
Part St. BL5—7E 36
Parvet Av. M35—4F 80
Pascal St. M19—6A 92
Passmonds Cres. OL12—2B
Pass St. OL9—2K 63
Pass, The. OL16—2G 29
Passway. WA11—7C 68
Paston Rd. M22—6D 102
Pasture Clo. OL10—9H 27
Pasture Clo. WN4—1L 69
Pasturefield Clo. M33—2M
Pasture Field Rd. M22—2F
Pastures La. OL4—9H 47
Patch Croft Rd. M22—3F 11
Patchett St. M29—7A 56
Patch La. SK7—7D 114
(in two parts)
Pateley Sq. WN6—7B 34
Patey St. M12—3A 92
Pathfield Wlk. M9—8K 61
(off Coningsby Dri.)
Patience St. OL12—1C 28
Paton Av. BL3—6G 39
Paton M. BL3—6G 39
Paton St. M1—4G 5 & 6H 79
Paton St. OL12—8D 12
Patricia Dri. M28—6L 57
Patrick Roddy Ct. M18—1C
Patricroft Rd. WN2—1F 52
Patten St. M20—8H 91
Patterdale Av. M31—2B 88
Patterdale Av. OL7—2M 81
Patterdale Clo. OL1—8A 46
Patterdale Clo. OL11—7B 2
Patterdale Clo. SK15—4G 8
Patterdale Dri. BL9—2L 41
Patterdale Dri. M24—7L 43
Patterdale Pl. WN2—1G 53
Patterdale Rd. BL2—6M 23
Patterdale Rd. M22—5E 102
Patterdale Rd. M31—2E 98
Patterdale Rd. OL7—2M 81
Patterdale Rd. SK1—6H 105
Patterdale Rd. SK6—1B 106
Patterdale Rd. WN4—8A 52
Patterdale Rd. WN7—3J 73
Patterdale Wlk. WA15—8K
Patterson Av. M21—5A 90
Patterson St. BL3—5A 38
Patterson St. BL5—1B 54
Patterson St. M34—2M 93
Pattishall Clo. M4—6K 79
Pattison Clo. OL12—8D 12
Patton Clo. BL9—7B 42
Patton Ct. M7—1B 4 & 3C 7
Paul Ct. SK1—4G 105
Paulden Av. M23—7B 102
Paulden Av. OL4—8E 46
Paulden Dri. M35—9G 63
Paulette St. BL1—8E 22
Paulhan Rd. M20—1K 103
Paulhan St. BL3—6D 38
Pauline St. WN2—7B 54
Paul Row. OL15—2C 14
Pavilion Clo. OL12—9F 12
Pavilion Dri. OL6—2D 82
Pavilion Lodge. M16—3A 9
Pavilion Wlk. M26—5F 40
Pawn St. OL8—2K 63

ford Pl. SK9—6G 119
thorne Grn. SK2—8L 105
body St. SK2—5E 28
cefield. SK6—8E 106
cehaven Av. M11—5C 80
ce St. BL3—4D 44
ce St. M29—5L 55
(Atherton)
ce St. M29—9M 55
(Tyldesley)
ce St. M35—7G 63
ceville Rd. M19—9M 91
ch Bank. M24—9A 44
ch Rd. OL4—8D 46
ch Tree St. M6—5A 78
chy Clo. M16—2F 90
cock Av. M11—2K 79
cock Clo. M18—9C 80
cock Clo. SK8—6H 113
cock Fold. WN7—1D 72
cock La. WA16—6C 108
cock M. M18—1D 92
xdale Av. SK8—3H 113
xdale Rd. M35—4E 80
xdale Rd. SK6—9G 107
xnaze Clo. SK13—3E 96
xnaze Clo. SK13—6G 97
x St. BL1—8D 22
x St. M1—4G 5 & 6H 79
x St. OL9—2J 63
x St. SK3—3G 105
nock La. OL15—9M 13
Av. BL9—7C 26
Av. TE 60
Mill Clo. BL0—4B 64
St. M34—3L 93
St. OL11—2C 28
St. SK7—9L 105
St. WN6—6A 34
ly Bank. M19—9M 91
Mill Ind. Est. SK6—3J 105
n Av. M19—9M 91
n Rd. M19—9M 91

son Clo. M31—2G 99
son Clo. OL16—3M 29
son Gro. OL4—3D 64
son Ho. M30—7D 76
son St. BL9—7B 26
son St. OL16—2J 29
son St. SK5—2E 104
son St. SK16—9C 82
St. M25—3C 60
t Av. SK6—8C 94
Tree Clo. M6—5A 78
Tree Clo. SK6—5H 107
Tree Clo. SK14—2E 96
Tree Ct. M6—5A 78
Tree Grn. M29—7D 56
Tree Wlk. M22—9B 102
Tree Wlk. M33—9C 88
St. M34—3L 93
Pendleton Ho. M6—3A 78
(off Broughton Rd.)
Pendleton Way. M6—4M 77
field Wlk. M9—5L 61
(off Sanderstead Dri.)
field Wlk. M15—1F 90
e Clo. SK15—3G 83
worth Gro. M24—3M 61
ford Dri. M10—2A 80
forton Clo. SK8—8G 103
forth Clo. SK9—2L 119
milti Clo. SK9—1L 119
er St. BL1—9C 22
er Brow La. OL12—5L 13
ey Hill. SK10—4M 121
ey Wlk. M13—6G 6 & 8H 79
Penhale M. SK7—5F 114
les Clo. WN4—3J 69
les Dri. M10—8D 80
Av. BL0—6G 9
Av. WA14—2D 110
Brow. BL0—5K 9
Cen., The. SK1—3G 105
Clo. M29—5L 55
Dri. SK2—7G 105
Cross Rd. M5—6A 78
Dri. M28—4F 56
Dri. M33—1L 101
ate Dri. SK8—2G 113
Grn. Rd. M30—7B 76
Gro. M12—2A 92
Hall Rd. M9—9H 9
Hall Rd. M22—1E 112
Ho. M30—5F 76
Av. M8—1F 5 & 3G 79
Av. M29—3B 74
two parts)
e. OL10—7H 27
Moat Dri. SK4—1B 104
Moat Rd. SK4—9B 92
Mt. M6—2A 4 & 4B 78
Pk. Cres. M28—4F 56
Rd. M28—4F 56
Av. OL4—1G 65
Sq. M18—1D 92
St. BL4—9J 39
St. M26—7H 41
St. M29—3B 74
St. SK14—9L 81
denshaw)
St. M34—2J 93
nton, in two parts)
St. M7—7D 80
oylsden)
St. OL10—1D 80
ilsworth)
St. OL2—2A 46
St. OL6—4B 82
St. OL10—8H 27
St. OL12—2E 28
St. OL15—6B 14
St. PR6—2H 19
St. SK14—1J 97
dfield)
St. SK14—5E 94
de)
St. SK15—6F 82
St. SK16—6C 82
St. WN2—6G 53
St. WN7—1E 72
er. BL5—7E 36
er. SK16—6B 82
(off Astley St.)
ew. BL8—4G 25
ood Av. M28—3G 57
ood Gro. BL6—6L 55
ow Pk. Est. SK14—5E 100
Clo. M31—2K 87
Dri. BL4—5F 24
St. BL8—8J 25
St. OL2—3H 23
aus St. M7—2B 4 & 4C 78
e's La. SK10—8K 121
(veldi Dri. M7—2E 78)
St. OL6—3C 82
m Pl. M8—6H 61
n Clo. BL3—6C 38
St. OL7—7L 81
e Rd. OL8—4L 63
Av. M27—6C 58
Wlk. M10—2K 79
ton Ho. OL2—1B 46
Napier St.)
ton Rd. WN5 & WN6—
—8G 51
ton St. BL1—6E 22
rton St. M16—2C 90
ton St. M28—4H 57

Pemberton St. OL11—8C 28
Pemberton Way. OL1—4M 61
Pembridge Av. M9—4M 61
Pembro Av. M30—5D 76
Pembroke Av. M33—9F 88
Pembroke Clo. M13—9F 79
Pembroke Clo. M27—8H 59
Pembroke Clo. OL12—1F 28
Pembroke Cres. WN4—3B 70
Pembroke Dri. BL9—2L 41
Pembroke Dri. OL4—5E 46
Pembroke Gro. M30—8C 86
Pembroke Rd. WN2—5C 54
Pembroke Rd. WN5—8K 33
Pembroke St. BL1—1D 38
Pembroke St. M6—1E 77
Pembroke St. M28—5J 57
Pembroke St. OL15—5B 14
Pembroke Way. SK1—5A 94
Pembry Clo. SK5—9H 93
Pembury Clo. M22—1J 112
Penarth Rd. BL3—5B 38
Pencombe Clo. M12—1A 92
Pencroft Way. M15—1G 91
Pendeen Clo. M29—9A 56
Pendennis. OL11—4E 28
Pendennis Av. OL4—4B 46
Pendennis Clo. M26—4C 40
Pendennis Cres. WN2—5A 54
Pendennis Rd. SK4—2C 104
Pendine Wlk. M7—1E 78
Pendle Av. BL1—4E 22
Pendle Av. M9—9D 68
Pendlebury Clo. M26—6M 59
Pendlebury Ct. SK3—9G 105
Pendlebury Fold. BL3—7K 37
Pendlebury Ind. Est. M27—
—8G 59
Pendlebury La. WN2—3C 34
Pendlebury Rd. M27—8F 58
Pendlebury Rd. SK3—7G 103
Pendlebury St. BL1—7F 22
Pendlebury St. M26—6G 41
Pendlebury Towers. SK5—
—2F 104
Pendle Clo. BL8—7H 25
Pendle Clo. OL4—3D 64
Pendlecroft Av. M27—8J 59
Pendle Dri. BL6—5C 20
Pendlegreen Clo. M11—7M 79
Pendle Gro. OL2—4J 45
Pendle Ho. M34—4M 93
Pendle Rd. M34—4M 93
Pendleton Way. M6—4M 77
Pendle Wlk. M22—9B 102
Pendle Wlk. M40—9C 88
Pendragon Pl. M35—9G 63
Pendrell Wlk. M9—5L 61
(off Sanderstead Dri.)
Penelope Rd. M6—2E 77
Penerley Dri. M9—1K 79
Penfair Clo. M11—6A 80
Penfield Clo. M1—6G 5 & 8H 79
Penfold Wlk. M12—9M 79
Pengarth Rd. BL6—6C 20
Pengham Wlk. M23—4A 102
Penhale M. SK7—5F 114
Penhall Wlk. M9—5L 61
(off Limerston Dri.)
Pen Ho. Clo. SK7—4E 114
Penistone Av. M6—4J 77
Penistone Av. M9—9A 62
Penketh Av. M18—2A 92
Penketh Av. M29—1B 74
Penketh St. WN6—7A 34
Penleach Av. WN7—2H 73
Penmere Gro. M33—4E 100
Penmore Chase. SK7—3H 115
Penmore Clo. OL2—2C 46
Pennant Dri. M25—3A 60
Pennant St. OL1—9D 46
Pennant St. OL1—8J 46
Pennell Dri. M19—4B 92
Penn Grn. SK8—3B 114
Pennie Rd. SK6—9C 94
Pennine Av. WN3—5J 51
Pennine Clo. BL9—6C 26
Pennine Clo. M9—4M 61
Pennine Clo. OL2—2C 46
Pennine Clo. M27—7G 59
Pennine Ct. OL4—2A 64
Pennine Dri. OL12—5J 13
Pennine Dri. WA14—8B 100
Pennine Gro. OL6—1E 82
Pennine La. WA3—6J 71
Pennine Rd. SK6—5C 20
Pennine Rd. SK6—9C 94
Pennine Rd. SK7—3H 115
Pennine Rd. SK6—9G 97
Pennine Ter. SK16—6C 82
(off Astley St.)
Pennine Vale. OL2—1C 46
Pennine View. M34—1L 93
Pennine View. OL2—5L 45
Pennine View. OL7—7K 65
Pennine View. SK15—3J 83
Pennine Wlk. WN2—6H 53
(off Rivington Rd.)
Pennington Av. WN7—4E 72
Pennington Clo. M28—4E 56
Pennington Clo. M30—8L 35
Pennington Gdns. WN7—4E 72
Pennington Grn. La. WN2—
—7L 35
Pennington Ho. WN7—3E 72
Pennington La. WN2—1E 34
(Haigh)
Pennington La. WN2—9G 35
(Ince)
Pennington M. WN7—5E 72
Pennington Rd. BL3—8B 38
Pennington Rd. WN7—5E 72
Pennington St. BL8—6E 24
Pennington St. M12—4A 92
Pennington St. M28—6L 57
Pennington St. WN2—2K 53
Pennington St. OL9—9J 63
Penn St. BL0—9J 39
Penn St. BL6—7C 20
Penn St. M10—8B 61
Penn St. OL8—3N 63
Penn St. OL10—9K 27
Penn St. OL16—9H 29
Penny La. SK5—3F 104
(in two parts)
Penny La. WA11—8M 69
Penny Meadow. OL6—4C 82
(in two parts)
Pennymoor Dri. WA14—7B 100
Penrhos Av. OL4—8F 102
Penrhyn Av. M24—5A 62
Penrhyn Av. M35—4A 113
Penrhyn Cres. SK7—4J 115
Penrhyn Dri. M25—3J 55
Penrhyn Gro. M29—3J 55
Penrhyn Rd. SK3—5B 104
Penrice Clo. M26—4D 40
Penrice Fold. M28—4G 57
Penrith Av. BL1—9A 22
Penrith Av. M11—4B 80

Penrith Av. M25—1B 60
Penrith Av. M28—6M 57
Penrith Av. M33—3J 101
Penrith Av. OL7—2M 81
Penrith Av. OL8—4J 63
Penrith Av. SK5—5F 92
Penrith Cres. WN4—3B 70
Penrith Clo. M31—1E 98
Penrith St. OL11—5F 28
Penrod Pl. M6—1A 4 & 3B 78
Penrose Av. BL2—2J 39
Penrose Av. M20—2D 102
Penroy Av. M20—2D 102
Penroyson Clo. M12—9M 79
Penruddock Wlk. M13—2M 91
(off St John's Rd.)
Penry Av. M30—8E 86
Penryn Av. M33—4J 101
Penryn Av. OL2—6M 45
Penryn Ct. M7—7D 60
Pensarn Av. M14—6L 91
Pensarn Gro. SK5—1F 104
Pensby Clo. M27—9J 59
Pensby Wlk. M7—9E 54
Pensford Rd. M23—1M 111
Penshaw Av. WN3—5B 52
Penshurst Wlk. M34—5A 94
Penson St. WN1—7H 34
Penthorpe Dri. OL2—6M 45
Pentland. BL1—9E 22
Pentland Av. M10—6C 62
Pentland Clo. SK7—3G 115
Pentlands Av. M7—3B 78
Penton Wlk. M16—3F 90
Pentwyn Gro. M23—6B 102
Penworthan St. M10—4L 79
Penzance St. M10—4L 79
Peover Av. M33—1L 101
Peover Rd. SK9—7L 113
Peover Wlk. SK8—8A 104
Peploe Wlk. M23—4K 101
Peover Av. M23—3B 102
Pepper La. WN6—6H 33
Pepperhill Wlk. M16—2F 90
Pepper Mill La. WN1—1D 52
Pepper Rd. SK7—9C 106
Pepper St. WA13—1A 108
Percival Av. OL2—6L 45
Percy Dri. M5—4A 4 & 8B 78
Percy Rd. M34—4L 93
Percy St. BL0—9J 39
Percy St. BL1—8F 22
Percy St. BL9—7A 26
Percy St. OL1—1G 64
Percy St. OL5—1J 65
Percy St. OL16—5H 29
Percy St. SK1—3F 104
Percy St. SK15—5H 83
Peregrine Cres. M35—4J 81
Peregrine Dri. M30—2G 87
Peregrine Rd. M29—9M 105
Periton Wlk. M9—5L 61
(off Levedale Rd.)
Perkins Av. M7—2D 78
Permain St. OL4—1C 64
Perrin St. SK14—4D 94
Perry Av. SK14—2G 95
Perrybrook Wlk. WN4—3D 70
(off North St.)
Perrygate Av. M20—8G 91
Perrymeed. OL15—1F 90
Perrymead. SK8—1F 90
Perrys Pl. WN6—9M 17
Perry Rd. WA14—7H 101
Pershore. OL12—2E 28
(off Spotland Rd.)
Persian Clo. M15—1G 91
Perth. M30—5E 76
(off St Andrews Ct.)
Perth Av. OL9—4G 63
Perth Clo. SK7—7E 114
Perth Rd. OL11—8H 29
Perth St. BL3—6B 38
(in two parts)
Perth St. M27—9D 58
Peru St. M3—4A 4 & 5D 78
Peterborough Clo. OL6—1B 82
Peterborough Dri. BL1—9F 22
Peterborough St. M18—9F 80
Peterborough Wlk. BL1—9F 22
(off Charnock Dri.)
Peterchurch Wlk. M11—7C 80
Peterhead Clo. BL1—9D 22
Peterhead Wlk. M5—1C 90
Peterhouse Gdns. SK6—1C 106
Peterhouse Wlk. WN4—3M 69
Peterloo Ter. M24—7A 44
Petersburg Rd. SK3—7D 104
Peters Ct. WA15—8K 101
(off Norwood Dri.)
Petersfield Dri. M23—6K 101
Petersfield Wlk. WN1—9F 22
Petersen St. BL9—7A 26
Peters St. BL5—1A 54
Peter St. BL9—7G 71
Peter St. M2—5E 5 & 7F 78
Peter St. M29—7M 55
Peter St. M34—6D 76
Peter St. OL11—4M 79
Peter St. WA3—7G 71
Petersfield. SK15—5A 14
Petheridge Dri. M22—3B 112
Petrel Av. SK12—8H 115
Petrel Clo. SK12—8H 115
Petrie Ct. M6—1A 4 & 3B 78
Petrie St. OL12—2F 28
Petrock Wlk. M10—2C 80
Petticoat La. WN1—1H 53
Petts Cres. OL15—5A 14
Petunia Wlk. M28—5F 56
(off Madam Wood Rd.)
Petworth Av. WN3—6J 51
Petworth Rd. OL9—2H 63
Pevensey Ct. M9—6A 62
Pevensey Rd. M6—1L 77
Pevensey Wlk. OL9—2H 63
Peveril Av. BL3—6C 38
Peveril Clo. WN4—4M 69
Peveril Cres. M21—4M 89
Peveril Ct. SK13—6M 97
Peveril Cres. M21—4M 89
Peveril Dri. SK7—4M 115
Peveril Rd. M5—5K 77
Peveril Rd. OL7—1J 65
Peveril St. BL3—5F 38
Peveril Ter. SK14—6E 94
Peveril M. SK12—6M 117
Peveril M. SK12—6M 117
Pewfist Spinney, The. BL5
Pewfist, The. BL5—2E 54

Pexwood. OL1—1E 44
Pheasant Dri. M21—6B 90
Pheasant Dri. M21—7D 90
Pheasant Rise. WA14—3D 110
Pheasant Wlk. WA16—8B 108
Phelan Clo. M10—2J 79
Phethean St. BL2—2G 39
Phethean St. BL4—8J 39
Philip Av. M34—1K 93
Philip St. BL3—4D 38
Philip St. M33—3H 101
Philip Howard Rd. SK13—6J 97
Philips Av. BL4—1K 57
Philips Dri. M25—2K 59
Philip's Rd. M11—5L 79
Philip's Dri. M18—2D 92
Philip St. OL6—3H 29
Philip St. OL9—9G 45
Philip St. OL10—8K 27
Philip St. OL15—5B 14
Philip St. OL16—7B 30
Phillimore St. M3E 64
Phillips Pk. Rd. E. M25—2M 59
Phillips Pk. Rd. W. M25—3J 59
Phillips St. WN7—8E 54
Phillip Way. SK14—1L 95
Phipps St. M28—4J 57
Phoebe Clo. M15—2M 91
Phoebe St. M5—4A 4 & 7A 78
Phoenix Clo. OL10—9M 27
Phoenix Clo. OL10—9M 27
Phoenix Pl. OL4—1F 64
Phoenix St. BL1—3K 39
Phoenix St. BL4—1K 57
Phoenix St. BL9—8L 25
Phoenix St. M2—4F 5 & 6G 79
Phoenix St. OL1—2M 63
Phoenix St. OL4—1F 64
Phoenix St. OL12—1C 28
Phoenix St. OL15—5B 14
Phoenix Way. M26—7G 41
Phyllis St. M24—1C 62
Phyllis St. OL12—1B 28
Phythian St. WA11—9F 68
Picadilly. WN5—2E 68
Piccadilly. M1—4F 5 & 6G 79
(in two parts)
Piccadilly. SK1—4F 104
Piccadilly Pl. M1—5F 5 & 5G 79
Piccadilly Plaza. M1—
—6G 79
Piccadilly Trading Est. M1
—5H 5 & 7J 79
Piccadilly Village. M1—5F 5 &
6J 79
Pickering Clo. BL8—5H 25
Pickering Clo. M26—9A 40
Pickering Clo. M31—4B 88
Pickering Clo. WA15—6G 101
Pickering St. M6—2L 77
Pickford Av. BL8—6C 40
Pickford Ct. M15—1E 90
Pickford La. SK16—7C 82
Pickford M. SK16—7C 82
Pickford's Brow. SK1—4F 104
(off High Bankside)
Pickford St. M4—3G 5 & 5H 79
Pickford St. OL16—3G 29
Pickford Wlk. OL16—3G 29
Picklehill La. OL3—9B 48
Picklehill N. OL3—9B 48
Pickley Grn. WN7—7E 54
Pickmere Av. M20—6H 91
Pickmere Clo. M33—3M 101
Pickmere Clo. SK5—7C 104
Pickmere Ct. SK9—7K 113
Pickmere Gdns. SK8—8B 103
Pickmere Rd. SK9—7K 113
Pickmere Way. SK9—7K 113
Picksley St. WN7—3H 73
Pickthorn Clo. WN2—5H 53
Pickup St. WN2—1F 52
Pickwick Pl. BL2—4J 9
Pickwick Rd. SK12—9K 115
Picton Clo. M3—4D 4 & 5E 78
Picton Dri. SK9—2L 119
Picton Sq. OL4—2M 63
Picton St. M7—4D 78
Picton St. OL7—1A 82
Piele Rd. WA11—8K 69
Pierce St. OL1—8C 46
Piercy Av. M7—1C 4 & 3D 78
Piercy St. M4—6K 79
Piercy St. WA3—8G 71
Pierhorne Clo. OL16—4D 30
Pigeon St. M1—4G 5 & 6H 79
Piggott St. BL4—1J 57
Pigot St. WN5—2H 51
Pike Av. M35—1J 81
Pike Fold La. M9—6J 61
Pike Mill Est. BL3—5E 38
Pike's La. SK13—6H 97
Pike St. OL11—5F 28
Pike St. SK14—3D 94
Pike View Clo. OL4—3B 64
Pilgrim Dri. M11—6M 79
Pilkington Rd. M25—7B 42
Pilkington Rd. BL4—2M 57
Pilkington Rd. M9—6A 62
Pilkington St. BL0—6H 9
Pilkington St. BL3—6E 38
Pilkington St. M24—8B 44
Pilkington St. WN2—2K 53
Pilkington Way. M26—6G 41
Pilling Field. BL7—1L 23
Pilling St. BL8—7J 25
Pilling St. M10—2M 79
Pilling St. M34—3M 93
Pilling St. OL12—2D 28
Pilling St. WN7—2G 73
Pilning St. BL3—6B 38
Pilot St. BL9—9A 26
Pilsworth Av. BL9—6A 26
Pilsworth Rd. BL9—3A 42
Pilsworth Rd. OL10—2F 42
Pimblett Rd. WA11—8L 69
Pimblett St. M3—2E 5 & 4F 78
Pimblett St. WA3—8G 71
Pimbo La. WN8—6A 50
Pimhole Fold. BL9—8A 26
Pimhole Rd. BL9—8A 26
Pimlico Clo. M7—1D 78
Pimlott Gro. M25—3A 60
Pimlott Gro. SK7—2D 114
Pimlott Rd. SK14—1D 94
Pimlott Rd. BL1—7H 23
Pimmcroft Way. M33—2M 101
Pincher Wlk. M11—6F 80
Pinder Wlk. M15—9F 78
Pineapple St. SK7—2L 115
Pine Av. M25—1M 59
Pine Av. WA10—9A 68
Pine Clo. M34—9L 81
Pine Clo. SK6—9E 106
Pine Clo. OL1—1G 99
Pine Ct. SK7—2D 114
Pine Gro. BL4—9H 39
Pine Gro. BL5—1E 54
Pine Gro. M14—2L 91
Pine Gro. M25—2A 60
Pine Gro. M27—8L 57
Pine Gro. M28—8L 57
Pine Gro. M30—3D 76
Pine Gro. OL4—4K 65
Pine Gro. OL16—4C 100
Pine Gro. SK14—5F 94
Pine Lodge. SK7—5F 114
Pine Rd. M20—1G 103
Pine Rd. SK7—1L 115
Pine Rd. WN3—9L 33
Pine St. OL4—4F 114
Pine St. SK16—7E 82
Pine St. WN5—2L 51
Pinehurst Rd. M10—2L 79
Pine St. BL1—8F 22

Pine St. BL1—8F 22
Pine St. BL4—5F 6 & 5G 79
Pine St. BL8—8B 26
Pine St. M3—2C 4 & 4D 78
Pine St. M24—1C 62
Pine St. M29—7A 56
Pine St. OL6—3B 82
Pine St. OL9—9G 45
Pine St. OL10—8K 27
Pine St. OL15—5B 14
Pine St. OL16—7B 30
(Milnrow)
Pine St. OL16—3H 29
(Rochdale)
Pine St. SK6—9B 94
Pine St. SK14—1D 94
Pine St. N. BL9—8B 26
Pine St. S. BL9—8B 26
Pine Tree Rd. OL8—7K 63
Pinetree St. M18—1C 92
Pine View. WN3—7H 51
Pine Wlk. M31—2E 98
Pineway. OL4—2F 64
Pinewood. M33—1D 100
Pinewood Av. M10—2G 80
Pinewood Av. M34—5A 70
Pinewood Clo. BL1—8E 22
Pinewood Clo. SK4—2A 104
Pinewood Clo. SK6—8C 82
Pinewood Cres. WN2—9J 53
Pinewood Cres. WN5—2F 52
Pinewood Rd. M21—7A 90
Pinewood Rd. SK9—2L 119
Pinewood Way. M26—7G 41
Pinfold. OL11—4E 28
Pinfold Av. M9—5A 62
Pinfold Clo. WA15—3A 114
Pinfold Dri. M25—2A 60
Pinfold Dri. SK8—3A 114
Pinfold La. M25—9L 41
Pinfold La. OL10—1D 106
Pinfold La. WA15—6M 111
Pinfold La. WN7—3F 57
Pingate Dri. SK8—6A 114
Pingate La. SK8—6A 114
Pingate La. S. SK8—6A 114
Pingle La. OL3—4L 47
Pingot. OL2—9D 30
Pingot Av. M23—3B 102
Pingot La. SK14—5B 96
Pingot La. WN5—2E 68
Pingot, The. WN7—2D 72
Pingott La. SK14—1L 97
Pink Bank La. M12—2A 92
Pin Mill Brow. M12—7K 79
Pinnacle Dri. BL7—9D 6
Pinner Pl. M19—8A 92
Pinnington La. M32—5K 89
Pinnington Rd. M18—9D 80
Pioneer Rd. M27—6K 59
Pioneers St. OL4—3A 64
Pioneers St. OL11—4C 29
Pioneer St. M11—4B 80
Pioneer St. M24—4A 44
Pioneer St. OL15—6B 14
Pioneers Villa. OL16—6E 30
Pioneers Yd. OL16—4M 29
Piperhill Av. M22—4D 102
Pipers, The. WA3—7M 71
Pipit Clo. M34—5J 81
Pirie Wlk. M10—1C 80
Pitcairn Ho. M30—6D 76
Pitcombe Rd. M22—2B 112
Pitfield Gdns. M23—6M 101
Pitfield La. BL2—6M 23
Pitfield St. BL2—2H 39
Pithouse La. OL12—9J 11
Pit La. OL2—1J 45
(in two parts)
Pitman Clo. M11—7A 80
Pitmore Wlk. M10—6D 62
Pitney Wlk. M16—3E 90
Pitsford Rd. M10—2L 79
Pit St. M34—9M 81
Pitt St. E. OL4—3E 64
Pitt St. M26—6E 40
Pitt St. M34—3M 93
(Denton)
Pitt St. OL10—8J 27
Pitt St. OL12—2F 28
Pitt St. SK5—5D 104
Pitt St. SK14—3D 94
Pitt St. SK14—9M 81
(Lower Ince)
Pitt St. SK14—1C 94
(Wallgate)
Pixmore Av. BL1—6H 23
Place Rd. WA14—7C 100
Plaine Av. WN5—1L 51
Plain Pit St. SK14—1C 94
(in two parts)
Plainsfield Clo. M16—2F 90
Plane Av. OL2—4A 64
Plane St. M35—5A 78
Plane St. OL4—1D 64
Plane Tree Clo. SK6—8D 106
Plane Tree Gro. WA11—8A 70
Plane Tree Rd. M31—2D 98
Planetree Rd. WA15—2G 111
Planet Way. M34—1L 93
Plank La. WN7—3A 72
Plantagenet St. M40—1D 80
Plantation Av. M28—4J 57
Plantation Gates. WN1—7E 34
Plantation St. M18—1D 82
Plantation St. M18—5D 82
Plantation View. BL9—8J 9
Plant Hill Rd. M9—3J 61
Plantree Wlk. M23—5J 101
Plant St. M1—4G 5 & 6H 79
Plato St. OL9—1K 63
Platt Av. OL6—2K 45
Platt La. M14—2K 91
Platt La. OL3—3M 101
Platt La. WN1—7B 18
(Standish)
Platt La. WN1—8E 34
(Wigan)
Platt La. WN2—3K 53
Platts Dri. M31—5G 99
Platt St. SK8—7L 103
Platt St. SK15—4H 83
Platt St. WN7—1F 72
Plattwood Wlk. M15—9D 78
Playfair Clo. OL10—2L 43
Playfair St. M14—2H 91
Play Fair St. BL1—4F 22
Pleachway. SK4—3M 103
Pleasant Gdns. BL1—1E 38

Pleasant St. BL8—6F 24
Pleasant St. M9—4N 61
Pleasant St. OL10—6J 27
Pleasant St. M26—9H 41
Pleasant Ter. SK16—6C 82
(off Astley St.)
Pleasant View. BL3—4K 39
Pleasant View. M9—4L 61
Pleasant View. M26—9H 41
Pleasant View. OL2—3D 46
Pleasant View. OL4—1F 64
Pleasant View. OL10—7H 27
Pleasant View. M33—2H 101
Pleasant Way. SK8—6C 114
Pleasington Dri. BL8—8C 24
Pleasington Dri. M10—6C 62
Plevna St. BL2—2G 39
Plodder La. BL4—9F 38
Plodder La. BL5 & BL4—8A 38
Ploughbank Dri. M21—7D 90
Ploughfields. BL5—6E 36
Plough St. SK16—7D 82
Plover Clo. BL9—8D 26
Plover Dri. BL9—8D 26
Plover Dri. WA14—5B 100
Plover Ter. M21—7D 90
Plowden Clo. BL3—6C 38
Plowden Rd. M22—2B 112
Plowley Clo. M20—3H 103
Plucksbridge Rd. SK6—9A 80
Plumbley Dri. M16—3C 90
Plumbley St. M11—8E 80
Plumley Clo. M33—2M 101
Plumley Clo. SK3—8F 104
Plumley Rd. SK9—7K 113
Plummer Av. M21—8B 90
Plumpton Clo. OL2—7L 45
Plumpton Dri. BL9—4L 25
Plumpton Rd. OL11—1H 45
Plumpton Wlk. M13—2M 91
(off St John's Rd.)
Plum St. OL8—3K 63
Plum Tree Clo. M6—5A 78
Plunge Rd. BL0—1L 9
Plymouth Av. M13—1L 91
Plymouth Clo. OL6—9B 64
Plymouth Dri. BL4—9F 38
Plymouth Dri. SK7—5E 114
Plymouth Gro. M13—9J 79
Plymouth Gro. SK3—6B 104
Plymouth Gro. W. M13—1K 91
Plymouth Rd. M33—9D 88
Plymouth St. OL8—4M 63
Plymouth View. M13—9J 79
Plymtree Clo. M8—6E 60
Pobgreen La. OL3—8D 48
Pochard Dri. SK12—8H 115
Pochard Dri. SK14—6B 100
Pocket Nook La. WA3—7A 72
Pocket Nook Rd. BL6—6A 56
Pocket Workshops, The. BL3
—3C 38
Pocklington Dri. M23—6M 101
Podnor La. SK6—7M 107
Podsmead Pl. M22—2B 112
Poets Nook. WN7—3E 72
Poise Brook Dri. SK2—8M 105
Poise Brook Rd. SK2—8M 105
Poise Clo. SK7—1A 116
Poke St. WN5—1L 51
Poland St. M34—7L 81
Poland St. M4—7L 81
Poland St. Ind. Est. M4—3H 5 &
5J 79
Polden Wlk. M9—7M 61
Polding St. WN3—3E 52
Poleacre La. SK6—3C 94
Pole Ct. BL9—6C 42
Polefield App. M25—2B 60
Polefield Gdns. M25—2B 60
Polefield Gro. M25—2B 60
Polefield Hall Rd. M25—2B 60
Polefield Rd. M9—6K 61
Polefield Rd. M25—1B 60
Polefield St. M35—9E 62
Pole La. OL6—1C 82
Pole La. OL10—2F 28
Pole La. WN7—2F 72
Pole St. BL2—3J 57
Pole St. N. OL6—4A 82
Pole St. S. OL6 & OL7—
—5A 82
Polesworth Clo. M12—9A 80
Portloe Rd. SK8—5H 113
Portman Clo. M16—3E 90
Portman Rd. M16—3E 90
Porton Wlk. M22—3B 112
Portrea Clo. SK3—8E 104
Portree Clo. M30—5B 76
Portree Ct. OL10—9C 27
Portrush Rd. M22—1C 112
Portside Clo. M28—1H 75
Portslade Wlk. M23—8M 101
Portsmouth Clo. M7—2D 78
Portsmouth St. M13—9H 79
(in two parts)
Port Soderick Av. M5—4A 78
Portsone Clo. M16—2E 90
Port St. M1—4G 5 & 6H 79
Port St. OL8—4M 63
Port St. SK1—3E 104
Portugal Rd. M25—6B 60
Portugal St. M29—3H 29
Portugal St. M4—3H 5 & 5J 79
(in two parts)
Portugal St. OL7—6M 81
Portugal St. E. M1—5H 5 & 7J 79
Portville Rd. M19—4A 92
Portway. M22—2B 112
Portwood Ind. Est. SK1—3G 105
Portwood Pl. SK1—3F 104
Portwood Wlk. M9—5F 61
Posnett St. SK3—5C 104
Postal Clo. M11—4G 5 & 6J 79
Postbridge Clo. M13—9J 79
Post Office St. WA14—8D 100
Post St. SK14—1H 97
Potato Wharf. M3—5A 4 & 7D 78
Pot Green. OL6—3C 82
Pot Hill. OL6—3C 82
Pot Hill Sq. OL6—3C 82
Pot Ho. La. OL12—8F 12
Pot St. WA14—9D 100
Potter Ho. OL8—3M 63
Potter's La. M9—9L 61
Potter St. BL9—7A 26
Potter St. M26—4K 17
Pottery La. M11 & M12—8B 80
Pottery Row. M11—5L 79
Pottery Ter. WN3—1G 52
Pottinger St. OL7—6M 81
Pott St. M10—2B 80
Poulton Av. BL2—2J 39
Poulton Dri. M24—6M 69
Poulton St. M11—8E 80
Pool St. BL1—1E 38
Powell Av. SK14—3C 110
Powell Dri. WN5—4D 68
Powell St. BL1—1B 38
Powell St. BL9—5M 25
Powell St. OL8—3L 63
Powell St. SK9—3E 118
Powell St. M30—6E 76
Pownall Av. M20—6G 91
Pownall Av. SK7—7B 26
Pownall Ct. SK9—3D 118
Pownall Grn. SK7—7C 114
Pownall Rd. SK9—3E 118
Pownall Rd. WA14—1K 115
Pownall St. SK7—7C 114
Pownall St. WN7—2G 73

Powys St. M29—7L 55
Poynings Dri. M22—3C 112
Poynt Chase. M28—1H 75
Poynter St. M10—7C 62
Poynton Clo. BL9—9A 26
Poynton Clo. M15—9F 78
Praed Rd. M17—9J 77
Prark Ct. OL16—4F 28
Pratt Wlk. M11—6M 79
(off Turnpike Wlk.)
Precinct Cen. M13—9G 79
Precinct, The. SK2—7K 105
Precinct, The. SK6—8D 104
Precinct, The. SK8—2B 114
Preece Clo. SK14—2G 95
Preesall Av. SK8—1A 114
Preesall Clo. BL8—1F 40
Premier Rd. M8—1E 5 & 3F 78
Premier St. M16—2D 90
Prentice Clo. OL5—8L 65
Prenton St. M11—6A 80
Prenton Way. BL8—5F 24
Presall St. BL2—1J 39
Presbyterian Fold. WN2—2K 53
Prescot Av. M29—3L 55
(Atherton)
Prescot Av. M29—7D 56
(Tyldesley)
Prescot Clo. BL9—9A 26
Prescot Rd. M9—9K 61
Prescot Rd. WA15—2F 110
Prescott Av. WA3—5F 70
Prescott La. WN5—9H 33
Prescott Rd. SK9—2H 119
Prescott Rd. WN8—3A 50
Prescott St. BL3—5C 38
Prescott St. M28—5H 57
Prescott St. WN7—1F 72
Prescott Wlk. M34—5B 94
Press St. M11—8D 80
Prestage St. M12—4B 92
Prestage St. M16—1C 90
(in four parts)
Prestbury. OL11—6F 28
Prestbury Av. M14—5F 90
Prestbury Av. WA15—2F 110
Prestbury Clo. SK2—9K 105
Prestbury Dri. OL1—8K 45
Prestbury Clo. SK2—9K 105
Prestbury Rd. BL1—5G 23
Prestbury Rd. SK2—9K 105
Prestbury Rd. BL6—6L 119
Prestfield Rd. M26—1A 60
Presto Gdns. BL3—5B 38
Prestolee Rd. BL3—4B 40
Prestolee Rd. M26—4E 94
Preston Av. M30—4G 77
Preston Clo. M30—4G 77
Preston Rd. M19—6A 92
Preston Rd. PR7 & WN6—1J 17
Preston St. M18—9D 80
(Eccles)
Preston St. WN3—1C 52
Preston St. WN2—2G 73
Preston Clo. M30—4G 77
Prestwich Av. WN7—2H 73
Prestwich Clo. SK2—6H 105
Prestwich Hills. M25—5A 60
Prestwich Pk. Rd. S. M25—
—5A 60
Prestwich St. M29—4H 55
Prestwich St. M34—2L 93
Prestwood Clo. BL1—9D 22
Prestwood Rd. BL4—8G 39
Prestwood Rd. M6—3J 77
Preswick Wlk. M10—6C 62
Pretoria Rd. BL2—2L 39
Pretoria Rd. OL6—5J 63
Pretoria Rd. WN4—3B 70
Pretoria St. OL12—1C 28
Price St. BL4—8K 39
Price St. M4—6K 79
Price St. M26—2A 106
Prichard St. M32—4K 89
Prickshaw La. OL12—5A 12
Pridmouth Rd. M20—8J 91
Priest Av. SK8—9G 103
Priest Hill St. OL1—1L 63
Priest La. SK10—9A 120
Priestley Rd. M28—8B 58
Priestley Way. OL2—2D 46
Priestnall Ct. SK4—2A 104
(off Priestnall Rd.)
Priestnall Rd. SK4—2M 103
Priestwood Av. OL4—5F 46
Primley Wlk. M9—8L 61
(off Edward St.)
Primrose Av. BL4—8G 39
Primrose Av. M28—6H 57
Primrose Av. M31—4D 88
Primrose Av. SK14—7E 106
Primrose Bank. BL8—3E 24
Primrose Bank. M28—6H 57
Primrose Bank. OL8—3L 63
Primrose Bank. WA14—3C 110
Primrose Bungalow. SK13
—6H 97
Primrose Clo. BL6—6A 24
Primrose Clo. M11—5M 77
Primrose Clo. OL11—9C 28
Primrose Cotts. WA14—3C 110
Primrose Cres. SK13—6H 97
Primrose Cres. SK14—6D 94
Primrose Dri. BL9—6D 26
Primrose Dri. M35—4J 81
Primrose Gro. WA11—8L 69
Primrose Gro. WN5—1L 51
Primrose Hill Cotts. OL10
—6A 28
Primrose La. SK6—9M 107
Primrose La. SK13—5G 97
Primrose La. OL6—2D 82
Primrose Pl. WN4—5B 70
(off Violet St.)
Primrose St. BL1—1F 22
Primrose St. BL9—4A 42
Primrose St. OL9—4C 53
Primrose St. M31—9C 76
Primrose Ter. M31—9C 76
Primrose Ter. SK13—6H 83
Primrose Ter. SK15—5H 83
Primrose View. WN4—5B 70
Primrose Wlk. OL8—3L 63
Primrose Wlk. SK6—7E 106
Primula St. BL1—1F 22
Prince Albert Av. M19—4A 92
Prince Charlie St. OL1—9B 46
Princedom St. M9—8L 61
Prince Edward Av. OL4—1C 64
Prince Edward Av. M34—4M 93
Prince George St. OL1—8C 46
Prince Rd. SK12—7C 116
Prince's Av. BL9—6C 26
Princes Av. M20—1J 103
Princes Av. M30—3J 87
Princes Av. SK6—2A 106

Prince's Bri. M3—5C 4 & 7D 78
Princes Ct. M30—4D 76
Princes Clo. M34—2K 101
Princes Ct. M30—4D 76
Princes Dri. SK6—6E 106
Prince's Incline. SK12—8L 115
Prince's Pk. M6—5F 32
Princes Rd. M23—2J 101
Princes Rd. SK4—1A 104
Princes Rd. WA14—7D 100
Princess Av. BL4—2M 57
Princess Av. M25—6C 60
Princess Av. M29—3J 55
Princess Av. M34—3L 93
Princess Clo. OL12—7J 13
Princess Clo. SK8—1A 114
Princess Clo. WN4—4C 70
Princess Clo. OL5—8L 65
Princess Clo. OL9—9K 27
Princess Clo. SK16—7D 82
Princess Ct. M15—9D 78
Princess Dri. M24—9L 43
Princess Dri. M23—1J 39
Princess Gro. BL4—9K 39
Princess Pde. BL9—8M 25
Princess Pde. M14—5F 90
Princess Parkway. M23
—6C 102
Princess Rd. BL6—2H 37
Princess Rd. M15 & M14—6E 5 &
Princess Rd. WN4—4C 70
Princess Rd. M25—4C 60
Princess Rd. M31—3B 88
Princess Rd. OL4—3A 46
Princess Rd. OL9—5E 62
Princess Rd. SK9—6F 118
Princess St. M25—9M 59
Princess St. WN7—1F 72
Princess St. M34—5B 94
Princess St. M2 & M1—4E 5 &
6F 78
Princess St. M6—3A 78
Princess St. M10—3L 79
Princess St. M15—9C 78
Princess St. M26—6E 40
Princess St. M27—9C 76
Princess St. M35—5C 76
Princess St. OL4—9E 82
Princess St. OL5—1J 65
Princess St. M28—5H 57
Princess St. OL12—3C 12
(off Albert St.)
Princess St. OL12—2F 28
(Rochdale, in two parts)
Princess St. SK13—6H 97
Princess St. SK14—4E 94
Princess St. WA14—5C 100
Princess St. WN2—3J 53
Princess St. WN3—1C 52
Princess St. WN2—2G 73
Prince's Wlk. SK7—5F 114
Prince St. BL0—9M 9
Prince St. BL1—1E 38
Prince St. OL1—1A 64
Prince St. OL10—8K 27
Prince St. OL16—2D 30
Prince St. WN4—2A 70
Princes Wlk. SK7—5F 114
Princethorpe Clo. BL6—3K 37
Prince Way. OL2—3J 45
Pringle St. OL16—3G 29
Prinknash Rd. M22—2D 112
Printers Ct. BL7—7K 7
Printers Fold. SK14—1D 96
Printer St. M11—7D 80
Printer St. OL1—2M 63
Printon Av. M9—4H 61
Printshop La. M29—7L 55
Printworks La. M19—5C 92
Printworks Rd. SK15—4H 83
Prior St. M11—8D 80
Priorswood Pl. WN8—4A 50
Priory Av. M7—1C 78
Priory Av. M21—6B 90
Priory Av. M25—6B 60
Priory Av. SK9—3E 118
Priory Av. OL4—3A 46
Priory Clo. M33—8K 89
Priory Clo. OL9—9D 62
Priory Clo. SK16—9D 82
Priory Ct. BL4—8K 39
Priory Ct. M30—5E 76
Priory Ct. SK5—6E 92
Priory Ct. WA14—3C 110
Priory Gdns. M20—1H 103
Priory Gdns. WA14—3A 68
Priory Gro. M7—1C 78
Priory Gro. OL9—4G 63
Priory Nook. WN8—1C 50
Priory Pl. BL2—3J 23
Priory Pl. M7—1C 78
Priory Rd. M27—7E 58
Priory Rd. M33—8K 89
Priory Rd. SK9—3E 118
Priory Rd. WN4—2M 69
Priory, The. M7—1C 78
Pritchard St. M1—5F 5 & 7G 79
Privet St. OL4—8D 46
Proctor Clo. WN5—3L 33
Proctor Way. M30—8M 75
Proctor St. BL8—9J 25
Prodesse Ct. SK4—2A 104
Proffitt St. BL3—3D 38
Pros Ct. WN1—9D 34
Progress Av. M34—9M 81
Progress St. BL1—9F 22
Progress St. OL6—4A 82
Progress St. OL11—9C 28
Progress St. WN3—4K 53
Promenade St. OL10—8J 27
Propps Hall Dri. M35—1D 80
Prospect Av. BL2—7H 23
Prospect Av. M26—2F 40
Prospect Dri. M33—2G 99
Prospect Hill. OL10—6A 28
Prospect Pl. BL4—1J 57
Prospect Pl. BL9—4A 42
Prospect Pl. M29—9G 59
Prospect Pl. OL6—2D 82
Prospect Pl. SK16—6D 82
Prospect Rd. M30—8E 86
Prospect Rd. OL6—2E 82
Prospect Rd. SK16—6D 82
Prospect St. BL1—9F 22
Prospect St. M29—7M 55
Prospect St. OL10—9L 27
Prospect St. OL11—6E 28
Prospect St. OL15—5B 14
Prospect Ter. OL12—9J 11
Prospect Vale. SK8—3H 113
Prospect View. M27—9D 58
Prospect Villas. M9—6G 61
Prosperity St. M29—6G 55
Prout St. M12—3A 92
Providence St. BL3—4F 38
Providence St. M4—8K 79
Providence St. M34—8M 81
Providence St. OL6—3D 82
Provident Av. M19—5C 92
Provident St. OL2—3A 46
Provident Way. WA15—7G 101
Provis Rd. M21—7B 90

Prubella Av. M34—1L 93
Pryce Av. WN2—1F 52
Pryce St. BL1—9D 22
Pryme St. M15—6D 4 & 8E 78
Pudding La. SK14—3J 95
(in two parts)
Puffin Av. SK12—8H 115
Pugin Wlk. M9—1K 79
(off Parkstead Dri.)
Pulborough Clo. BL8—3H 25
Pulford Av. M21—1D 102
Pulford Rd. M33—3J 101
Pullman Clo. M19—6B 92
Pullman St. OL11—5F 28
Pump St. M10—5L 79
Pump St. OL9—6H 63
Pump St. WN2—3K 53
Punch La. BL3—7K 37
(in three parts)
Punch St. BL3—3D 38
Purbeck Dri. BL6—9F 20
Purbeck Dri. BL8—4J 25
Purbeck Way. M29—9B 56
Purcell Clo. BL1—9D 22
Purcell St. M12—3A 92
Purdon St. BL9—4M 25
Purdy Ho. OL8—3M 63
Puritan Wlk. M10—2J 79
(off Elcot Clo.)
Purley Av. M23—4B 102
Purley Dri. M30—9C 86
Purslow Clo. M12—6L 79
Purton Wlk. M9—9L 61
(off Norbet Wlk.)
Putt St. M27—6F 58
Pye Clo. WA11—7B 70
Pyegreave Clo. M15—6D 4 & 8E 78
Pyegrove. SK13—5M 97
Pyegrove Rd. SK13—5L 97
Pyes Gdns. WA11—8B 68
Pyke St. WN1—8D 34
Pymgate Dri. SK8—2G 113
Pymgate La. SK8—2G 113
Pym St. M10—8M 61
Pym St. M30—5D 76
Pym St. OL10—9K 27
Pyramid Ct. M7—1D 78
Pyrus Clo. M30—7M 75
Pytha Fold Rd. M20—9J 91

Quadrant, The. M9—5A 62
Quadrant, The. M32—3A 90
Quadrant, The. M35—6F 80
Quadrant, The. SK1—4H 105
Quadrant, The. SK6—3A 106
Quail Dri. M30—3G 87
Quail St. OL4—2C 64
Quakerfields. BL5—1D 54
Quakers Field. BL8—2F 24
Quakers Pl. WN6—9L 17
Quakers Ter. WN6—7K 17
Quantock Clo. M16—2E 90
Quantock Clo. SK4—3E 104
Quantock Clo. WN3—6J 51
Quarlton Dri. BL8—8B 8
Quarmby Rd. M18—2F 92
Quarry Bank Rd. SK9—9F 112
Quarry Clo. SK13—5K 97
Quarry Clough. SK15—7J 83
Quarry Hill. OL12—8E 12
Quarry Pl. WN1—9E 34
Quarry Pond Rd. M28—5F 56
Quarry Rise. SK15—7F 82
Quarry Rd. BL4—1A 58
Quarry Rd. SK6—3B 106
Quarry St. BL0—5K 9
(in three parts)
Quarry St. M26—6H 41
Quarry St. OL12—1E 28
Quarry St. SK6—9B 94
Quarry St. SK15—6F 82
Quarry View. OL12—8E 12
Quarry Wlk. M11—6M 79
(off Pilgrim Dri.)
Quayside Clo. M28—2H 75
Quays, The. M5—8L 77
Quay St. M3—4D 4 & 6E 78
(Manchester)
Quay St. M3—3D 4 & 5E 78
(Salford)
Quay St. SK15—6F 82
Quebec Pl. BL3—4C 38
Quebec St. BL3—4D 38
Quebec St. M34—2L 93
Quebec St. OL9—9J 45
Queen Alexandra Clo. M5—5B 4 & 7C 78
Queen Ann Dri. M28—9H 57
Queenhill Dri. SK14—1G 95
Queenhill Rd. M22—4E 102
Queen's Av. BL3—5A 40
Queen's Av. BL7—3G 23
Queen's Av. M29—3J 55
Queens Av. OL12—7J 13
Queens Av. SK6—2A 106
Queen's Av. WA3—8J 73
Queen's Av. WN4—4B 70
Queensbrook. BL1—2E 38
Queensbury. OL11—6E 28
Queensbury Ct. M10—4K 79
Queensbury Pde. M10—4L 79
Queens Clo. M28—9F 56
(Mosley Common)
Queen's Clo. M28—4K 57
(Walkden)
Queens Clo. SK4—3A 104
Queen's Ct. M20—1G 103
Queen's Ct. SK4—3A 104
Queens Ct. SK6—7G 107
Queens Ct. SK9—5G 119
Queen's Dri. M25—6C 60
Queens Dri. OL11—7E 28
Queen's Dri. SK4—3A 104
Queen's Dri. SK8—2A 114
Queen's Dri. SK13—5M 97
Queens Dri. SK14—7F 94
Queens Dri. WA3—7J 71
Queens Dri. WA12—9B 70
Queensferry St. M10—1C 80
Queens Gdns. SK8—7L 103
Queens Gdns. WN7—2J 73
Queensgate. BL1—1C 38
Queensgate. SK7—7E 114
Queensgate Dri. OL2—3J 45
Queen's Gro. M12—2A 92
Queensland Rd. M18—1B 92
Queen's Pk. Rd. OL10—6K 27
Queens Pk. St. BL1—1D 38
Queens Pl. BL9—9J 9
Queen Sq. SK1—3G 105
Queens Rd. BL3—5B 38
Queen's Rd. M8, M9 & M10—2G 79
Queen's Rd. M31—5D 88
Queens Rd. M33—9F 88
Queens Rd. OL6—2D 82
Queens Rd. OL8—3A 64
Queens Rd. OL9—1G 63
Queen's Rd. OL15—6B 14
Queens Rd. SK6—2A 106
Queen's Rd. SK7—1L 115
Queen's Rd. SK8—9M 103
Queens Rd. SK9—5G 119
Queens Rd. WA11—8A 70
Queen's Rd. WA15—1E 110
Queen's Rd. WN2—5G 53
Queen's Rd. WN4—3B 70
Queens Rd. WN5—3C 50
Queen's Rd. Ter. OL15—6B 14
(off Queen's Rd.)
Queens Ter. SK9—8K 113
Queens Ter. SK16—6B 82
Queenston Rd. M20—1G 103
Queen St. BL0—5H 9
Queen St. BL1—2E 38
Queen St. BL4—9K 39
Queen St. BL5—9E 36
Queen St. BL6—7A 20
Queen St. BL8—5G 25
Queen St. BL9—8A 26
Queen St. M2—4E 5 & 6F 78
Queen St. M3—3D 4 & 5E 78
Queen St. M6—2K 77
Queen St. M24—9C 44
Queen St. M26—7J 41
Queen St. M28—5H 57
Queen St. M30—6F 76
Queen St. M34—9M 81
(Audenshaw)
Queen St. M34—2L 93
(Denton, in two parts)
Queen St. M35—9E 62
Queen St. OL1—1M 63
Queen St. OL2—5K 45
(Royton)
Queen St. OL2—3B 46
(Shaw)
Queen St. OL4—2F 64
Queen St. OL5—7J 65
Queen St. OL6—4C 82
Queen St. OL10—7K 27
Queen St. OL12—2F 28
Queen St. OL15—6B 14
Queen St. SK1—3G 105
(in two parts)
Queen St. SK6—7G 107
Queen St. SK8—7M 103
Queen St. SK13—6H 97
Queen St. SK14—2G 97
(Hadfield)
Queen St. SK14—4E 94
(Hyde)
Queen St. SK15—5G 83
Queen St. SK16—6B 82
Queen St. WA3—7H 71
Queen St. WN1—1C 52
Queen St. WN2—2K 53
(Hindley)
Queen St. WN2—6G 53
(Platt Bridge)
Queen St. WN5—2G 51
(Orrell)
Queen St. WN5—3K 51
(Pemberton)
Queen St. WN7—2G 73
Queen St. W. M20—7H 91
Queen's Wlk. M35—6G 81
Queensway. BL4—3M 57
Queensway. M19—3K 103
Queensway. M27—6G 59
Queensway. M28—8H 57
Queensway. M30—4F 86
Queensway. M31—2E 88
Queensway. OL3—2B 66
Queensway. OL5—8K 65
Queensway. OL11—8C 28
Queensway. SK8—4H 113
Queensway. SK12—9K 115
Queensway. SK16—8F 82
Queensway. WA11—7A 68
Queensway. WN1—7B 34
Queens Way. WN2—9G 35
Queensway. WN6—5F 32
Queensway. WN7—2K 73
Queen Victoria St. M30—5C 76
Queen Victoria St. OL11—6G 29
Quenby St. M15—6C 4 & 8D 78
Quendon Av. M7—1C 4 & 3E 78
Quick Edge La. OL4—4H 65
Quickedge Rd. OL5—6J 65
Quick Rd. OL5—4K 65
Quick View. OL5—5L 65
Quilter Gro. M9—6J 61
Quinney Cres. M16—2E 90
Quinn St. M11—6A 80
Quinton. OL12—2E 28
(off Spotland Rd.)
Quinton Wlk. M13—9H 79
Quixall St. M11—5A 80

Rabbit La. SK14—9A 84
Raby St. M14—2F 90
Raby St. M16—2E 90
Racecourse Pk. SK9—5F 118
Racecourse Rd. SK9—4E 118
Racecourse Wlk. M26—5F 40
Race Ct. WA13—1A 108
Racefield Clo. WA13—1A 108
Racefield Hamlet. OL1—5H 45
Racefield Rd. WA14—9C 100
Race, The. SK9—1K 119
Rachel Rosing Wlk. M8—8F 60
Rachel St. M12—5H 5 & 7J 79
Rackhouse Rd. M23—4B 102
Radbourne Clo. M12—9A 80
Radcliffe Gro. WN7—9F 54
Radcliffe Moor Rd. BL2 & M26—3B 40
Radcliffe New Rd. M25—7J 41
Radcliffe Pk. Cres. M6—2J 77
Radcliffe Pk. Rd. M6—2H 77
Radcliffe Rd. BL2 & BL3—2G 39
Radcliffe Rd. BL9—2K 41
Radcliffe Rd. OL4—7D 46
Radcliffe St. OL1—9M 45
Radcliffe St. OL2—5K 45
Radcliffe St. OL4—2G 65
Radcliffe View. M5—8B 78
(off Ordsall Dri.)
Radclyffe St. M24—7A 44
Radclyffe St. OL9—9H 45
Radclyffe Ter. M24—7A 44
Radelan Gro. M26—5D 40
Radford Clo. SK2—6K 105
Radford Dri. M9—8L 61
Radford Dri. M30—3G 87
Radford St. M7—8C 60
Radium St. M4—5J 79
Radlet Dri. WA15—5G 101
Radlett Wlk. M13—1J 91
(off Plymouth Gro.)
Radley Clo. BL1—9A 22
Radley Wlk. M16—3F 90
(off Quinney Cres.)
Radnor Av. M34—3H 93
Radnor Clo. WN2—5A 54
Radnor Dri. WN7—2C 72
Radnormere Dri. SK8—9M 103
Radnor St. M15—1F 90
Radnor St. M18—2C 92
Radnor St. M32—4K 89
Radnor St. OL9—3J 63
Radstock Clo. BL1—3E 22
Radstock Clo. M14—5H 91
Radstock Rd. M32—4J 89
Radway. M29—7C 56
Raeburn Dri. SK6—5H 107
Rae St. SK3—5C 104
Raglan Av. M25—1B 60
Raglan Av. M27—6H 59
Raglan Clo. M11—6M 79
Raglan Dri. WA14—5E 100
Raglan Rd. M32—3H 89
Raglan Rd. M33—2F 100
Raglan St. BL1—8D 22
Raglan St. OL11—9C 28
Raglan St. SK14—4C 94
Raglan Wlk. M15—9F 78
Ragley Clo. SK12—8M 115
Raikes La. BL3—5H 39
(in two parts)
Raikes Rd. BL3—4K 39
Railton Av. M16—3D 90
Railton Ter. M9—9M 61
Railway App. M26—6H 41
Railway App. OL11—8C 28
Railway Brow. OL11—9C 28
Railway Rd. M31—4D 88
Railway Rd. M32—1L 89
Railway Rd. OL9—6G 63
(Chadderton)
Railway Rd. OL9—2K 63
(Oldham)
Railway Rd. PR7 & PR6—3G 19
Railway Rd. SK1—5E 104
Railway Rd. SK6—7D 106
Railway Rd. WA3—7H 71
Railway Rd. WN7—2E 72
Railway St. BL0—5J 9
Railway St. BL4—8L 39
Railway St. BL9—9J 9
Railway St. M18—9C 80
Railway St. M26—6G 41
Railway St. M29—4H 55
Railway St. OL10—9L 27
Railway St. OL15—6B 14
Railway St. OL16—6B 30
(Newhey)
Railway St. OL16—4G 29
(Rochdale)
Railway St. SK4—3E 104
Railway St. SK13—5J 97
Railway St. SK14—1G 97
(Hadfield)
Railway St. SK14—4D 94
(Hyde)
Railway St. SK16—6B 82
Railway St. WA14—9D 100
Railway St. WN2—1K 53
Railway St. WN6—8A 34
Railway St. W. BL9—9H 9
Railway Ter. BL9—9J 9
(off Miller St.)
Railway Ter. M21—4B 90
Railway Ter. OL10—9K 27
Railway Ter. PR7—1M 17
Railway Ter. SK12—6K 117
Railway View. OL4—2F 64
Railway View. SK5—4E 92
Railway View. SK14—5C 94
Railway View. SK16—9C 82
Raimond St. BL1—7C 22
Rainbow Clo. M21—7B 90
Rainbow Way. SK9—2K 119
Raincliff Av. M13—4M 91
Raines Crest. OL16—4M 29
Rainford. OL11—6E 28
Rainford Av. M20—6G 91
Rainford Av. WA15—7G 101
Rainford Ho. BL1—1F 38
(off Beta St.)
Rainford La. BL0—5L 9
Rainford Rd. WA11 & WN5—2B 68
Rainford St. BL2—4J 23
Rainforth St. M13—3M 91
Rainham Dri. BL1—9E 22
Rainham Dri. M8—9G 61
Rainham Gro. BL1—9E 22
(off Rainham Dri.)
Rainham Way. OL9—2H 63
Rainham Way SK5—8H 93
Rainhill Wlk. M10—2D 80
Rainow Av. M35—6E 80
Rainow Rd. SK3—8C 104
Rainsdale Flats. OL10—8J 27
(off Meadow Clo.)
Rainshaw St. BL1—6F 22
Rainshaw St. OL2—5K 45
Rainshaw St. OL4—9D 46
Rainsough Av. M25—7A 60
Rainsough Brow. M25—7M 59
Rainsough Clo. M25—7A 60
Rainton Wlk. M10—6D 62
Rainwood. OL9—9E 44
Raithby Dri. WN3—5A 52
Raja Clo. M8—9H 61
Rake. OL11—3K 27
Rakehead Wlk. M15—1G 91
(off Botham Clo.)
Rake La. M27—5G 59
Rake St. BL9—6M 25
Rake Ter. OL15—5C 14
Rake Top. OL12—1C 28
Rakewood Dri. OL4—5E 46
Rakewood Rd. OL15—8B 14
Raleigh Clo. OL1—9M 45
Raleigh Gdns. OL15—2C 14
Raleigh St. M32—4K 89
Raleigh St. SK5—1E 104
Ralli Ct. M3—4D 4 & 6E 78
Ralli Quays. M3—4D 4 & 6E 78
Ralph Av. SK14—7E 94
Ralph Sherwin Ct. OL12—7K 13
Ralphs La. SK16—8C 82
Ralph St. BL1—8D 22
Ralph St. M11—6D 80
Ralph St. OL12—1G 29
Ralston Clo. M8—8E 60
Ralstone Av. OL8—4M 63
Ramage Wlk. M12—6L 79
Ramillies Av. SK8—3B 114
Rampit Clo. WA11—8M 69
Ramp Rd. E. M22—5C 112
Ramp Rd. S. M22—5C 112
Ramp Rd. W. M22—5B 112
Ramsay Av. BL4—1G 57
Ramsay St. BL1—6E 22
Ramsbottom La. BL0—4J 9
Ramsbottom Rd. BL6—7C 20
Ramsbottom Rd. BL7 & BL8—9M 7
Ramsbury Dri. M10—6D 62
Ramsdale Rd. SK7—4E 114
Ramsdale St. OL9—1G 63
Ramsden Clo. OL1—1L 63
Ramsden Clo. SK13—4J 97
Ramsden Clo. WN3—3A 52
Ramsden Cres. OL1—9L 45
Ramsden Fold. M27—6F 58
Ramsden Rd. OL12—4J 13
(in two parts)
Ramsden St. OL1—1L 63
Ramsden St. OL6—3B 82
Ramsey Av. M19—5D 92
Ramsey Clo. M29—6L 55
Ramsey Clo. WN4—5B 70
Ramsey Gro. BL8—8H 25
Ramsey Pl. OL16—2G 29
Ramsey Rd. WN7—3G 73
Ramsey St. M10—9B 62
Ramsey St. OL1—9B 46
Ramsey St. OL9—3H 63
Ramsey St. OL16—2G 29
Ramsey Ter. OL16—2G 29
Ramsgate Rd. M10—3C 80
Ramsgate Rd. SK5—7F 92
Ramsgate St. M7—2E 78
Ramsgill Clo. M23—4L 101
Ramsgreave Clo. BL9—2K 41
Ram St. M28—4F 56
Ramwell Gdns. BL3—4D 38
Ramwells Brow. BL7—2F 22
Ranby Av. M9—4M 61
Randale Dri. BL9—6A 42
Randall Av. WN6—4G 33
Randall Wlk. M11—6M 79
(off Turnpike Wlk.)
Randal St. BL3—5C 38
Randal St. SK14—3E 94
Randerson St. M12—6H 5 & 8J 79
Randlesham St. M25—4C 60
Randle St. WN2—1K 53
Randolph Pl. SK3—6E 104
Randolph Rd. BL4—1M 57
Randolph St. BL3—3C 38
Randolph St. M19—4B 92
Randolph St. OL8—6J 63
Rands Clough Dri. M28—1H 75
Rand St. OL1—8D 46
Ranelagh Rd. M27—9H 59
Ranelagh St. M11—5B 80
Ranford Rd. M19—6A 92
Range Dri. SK6—8C 94
Rangefield Wlk. M15—1F 90
Range Hall Ct. SK1—4G 105
Range La. OL3—9K 31
Rangemoor Av. M22—5E 102
Range Rd. M16—3E 90
Range Rd. SK3—6E 104
Range Rd. SK16 & SK15—8H 83
(in two parts)
Range St. BL3—5D 38
Range St. M11—7C 80
Ranicar St. WN2—5C 54
Rankin Clo. M15—1E 90
Rankine Ter. BL3—3D 38
Ranley Gro. OL11—8G 29
Ranmore Av. M11—7D 80
Ranmore Av. WN4—3K 69
Rannoch Rd. BL2—2M 39
Ransfield Rd. M21—4B 90
Ranulph Ct. M6—2K 77
Ranworth Av. SK4—3M 103
Ranworth Clo. BL1—4G 23
Ranworth Clo. M11—7M 79
Raper St. OL4—9C 46
Rapes Highway. OL3—5K 31
Raphael St. BL1—8D 22
Rappax Rd. WA15—4G 111
Rasbottom St. BL3—4E 38
Raspberry La. M30—1G 87
Rassbottom Brow. SK15—5F 82
Rassbottom St. SK15—5F 82
Rassey Gro. WN6—2A 34
Rastell Wlk. M9—5L 61
(off Ravenswood Dri.)
Ratcliffe Av. M30—4G 87
Ratcliffe Rd. WN2—3J 35
Ratcliffe St. M19—5B 92
Ratcliffe St. M29—7B 56
Ratcliffe St. SK1—5F 104
(in two parts)
Ratcliffe St. WN6—8A 34
Ratcliffe St. WN7—9F 54
Ratcliffe Ter. OL5—8J 65
Ratcliffe Towers. SK1—5F 104
Rathan Rd. M31—2C 88
Rathbone St. OL16—3J 29
Rathbourne Av. M9—4K 61
Rathen Av. WN2—8G 35
Rathen Rd. M20—9H 91
Rathmell Rd. M23—3M 101
Rathmore Av. M10—2L 79
Rathvale Dri. M22—4C 112
Rath Wlk. M10—2C 80
Rattenbury Ct. M6—2J 77
Ravald St. M3—2D 4 & 4E 78
Raveden Clo. BL1—7C 22
Raveley Av. M14—6K 91
Ravelston Dri. M9—1K 79
Raven Av. OL9—3G 63
Raven Clo. M35—4J 81
Raven Ct. WA13—1A 108
Ravendale Clo. OL12—1A 28
Raven Dri. M30—3G 87
Ravenfield Gro. BL1—1D 38
Ravenhead Clo. M14—6K 91
Ravenhead Dri. WN8—1A 50
Ravenhead Sq. SK15—2L 83
Ravenhurst. M7—7E 60
Ravenhurst Dri. BL1—3K 37
Ravenna Av. M23—6K 101
Ravenoak Av. M19—5C 92
Ravenoak Pk. Rd,. SK8—4B 114
Ravenoak Rd. SK2—9G 105
Ravenoak Rd. SK8—4B 114
Raven Rd. BL3—5A 38
Raven Rd. WA15—4H 101
Ravensbury St. M11—5B 80
Ravenscar Cres. M22—4D 112
Ravenscar Wlk. BL4—1K 57
Ravens Clo. M25—6E 60
Ravenscraig Rd. M28—2H 57
Ravensdale Gdns. M30—4E 76
Ravensdale Rd. BL1—2K 37
Ravensdale St. M14—3J 91
Ravenstone Dri. M33—9L 89
Ravenstone Dri. OL3—6C 48
Raven St. BL9—6M 25
Raven St. M12—5H 5 & 7J 79
Raven St. OL11—1L 27
Ravensway. M25—6D 60
Ravenswood Av. SK4—4A 104
Ravenswood Av. WN3—5K 51
Ravenswood Ct. SK3—9F 104
Ravenswood Dri. BL1—1L 37
Ravenswood Dri. M9—5L 61
Ravenswood Dri. SK8—4B 114
Ravenswood Dri. WN2—1L 53
Ravenswood Rd. M32—1M 89
Ravenswood Rd. SK9—7E 118
Raven Ter. SK16—6C 82
(off Astley St.)
Raven Way. M6—4A 78
Ravenwood. OL9—1D 62
Ravenwood Dri. M34—9L 81
Ravenwood Dri. WA15—5K 111
Ravine Av. M9—9L 61
Rawcliffe Av. BL2—2M 39
Rawcliffe St. M14—3H 91
Rawdon Av. M19—5B 92
Rawlinson La. PR7—1E 18
Rawlinson La. PR7 & PR6—1F 18
Rawlyn Rd. BL1—8A 22
Rawpool Gdns. M23—6A 102
Rawson Av. BL4—8L 39
Rawson Rd. BL1—9C 22
Rawsons Rake. BL0—5G 9
Rawson St. BL4—8K 39
Rawsthorne Av. BL0—1K 9
Rawsthorne St. BL1—8E 22
Rawsthorne St. M29—8D 56
Rawstron St. OL12—2C 12
Rawthey Pl. WN2—6F 52
Rayburn Way. M8—2G 79
Raycroft Av. M9—6A 62
Raydale Clo. WA3—6L 71
Rayden Cres. BL5—2E 54
Raydon Av. M10—2K 79
Raylees. BL0—7J 9
Rayleigh Av. M11—8F 80
Raymond Av. BL9—5M 25
Raymond Av. OL9—4H 63
Raymond Rd. M23—3B 102
Raymond St. M27—7F 58
Rayner Av. WN2—6K 53
Rayner La. OL7—5K 81
Rayner St. SK1—5H 105
Raynham St. OL6—4C 82
Rayson St. M9—6J 61
Reabrook Clo. M12—9M 79
Reach, The. M28—6L 57
Read Clo. BL9—2K 41
Reade Av. M31—5M 87
Reade Ho. M31—5M 87
Reading Dri. M33—1D 100
Reading St. M6—2B 78
Reading Wlk. M34—5M 93
Read St. SK14—3C 94
Read St. W. SK14—3C 94
Reaney Wlk. M12—9A 80
Rear Grn. M27—6H 59
Reather Clo. M10—2H 5 & 4J 79
Rebecca St. M8—8G 61
Recreation Av. WN4—3D 70
Recreation Dri. WN5—2E 68
Recreation Rd. M35—7G 63
Recreation St. BL2—5L 23
Recreation St. BL3—5E 38
Recreation St. M25—4C 60
Rectory Av. M8—7G 61
Rectory Av. M25—4B 60
Rectory Av. WA3—7J 71
Rectory Clo. M26—5K 41
Rectory Clo. M34—4A 94
Rectory Fields. SK1—4G 105
Rectory Gdns. BL5—3E 54
Rectory Gdns. M25—4B 60
Rectory Grn. M25—4A 60
Rectory Grn. SK1—4G 105
Rectory Gro. M25—5B 60
Rectory La. BL9—6D 26
Rectory La. M25—3A 60
Rectory La. M26—6H 41
Rectory La. WN6 & WN1—9L 17
Rectory M. M22—4F 102
Rectory Rd. M8—7F 60
Rectory Rd. WN4—2K 69
Rectory St. M24—8M 43
Redacre. SK12—6L 115
Redacre Rd. M18—9E 80
Red Bank. M4 & M8—2F 5 & 4G 79
Red Bank Rd. M26—4F 40
Redbarn Clo. SK6—1M 105
Red Barn Rd. WN5—1B 68
Redbourne Dri. M31—2M 87
Redbrick Ct. OL7—6A 82
Red Bri. BL2—9A 24
Redbridge Gro. M21—6A 90
Redbrook Av. M10—2L 79
Redbrook Clo. BL4—8L 39
Redbrook Gro. SK9—2K 119
Redbrook Rd. M31—3E 98
Redbrook Rd. WA15—7K 101
Red Brook St. OL11—3D 28
Redbrook Way. SK10—6J 121
Redburn Clo. WN3—2B 52
Redburn Rd. M23—6B 102
Redcar Av. M20—8H 91
Redcar Av. M31—2A 88
Redcar Clo. OL1—8B 46
Redcar Clo. SK7—2M 115
Redcar Rd. BL1—6B 22
Redcar Rd. BL3—6A 40
Redcar Rd. M27—9J 59
Redcar St. OL12—2E 28
Red Cat La. WA11—2A 68
Redcliffe Ct. M25—6B 60
Redclyffe Av. M14—3J 91
Redclyffe Rd. M20—9G 91
Redclyffe Rd. M31—7D 76
Redcot Ct. M25—1J 59
Redcote St. M10—8A 62
Redcourt. SK13—6J 97
Redcourt Av. M20—1H 103
Redcroft Gdns. M19—1L 103
Redcroft Rd. M33—8E 88
Redcross St. OL12—2F 28
Redcross St. N. OL12—1E 28
Reddish Clo. BL2—4L 23
Reddish Cres. WA13—9A 98
Reddish La. M18—2E 92
Reddish La. WA13—9A 98
Reddish Rd. SK5—7F 92
Reddish Vale Rd. SK5—7F 92
Reddy La. WA14—5G 109
Redesmere Clo. M35—6H 81
Redesmere Clo. WA15—7K 101
Redesmere Dri. SK8—9M 103
Redesmere Dri. SK9—8K 119
Redesmere Pk. M31—6B 88
Redesmere Rd. SK9—7K 113
Redfern Av. M33—2L 101
Redfern Cotts. OL11—1K 27
Redfern St. M4—3F 5 & 5G 79
Redfern Way. OL11—1K 27
Redfield Clo. M11—6M 79
Redford Clo. WN7—2G 73
Redford Dri. SK7—2G 115
Redford Rd. M8—4F 60
Redford St. BL8—7J 25
(in two parts)
Redgate. SK14—6D 94
(Hyde)
Redgate. SK14—2J 97
(Padfield)
Redgate La. M12—9M 79
(in two parts)
Redgate Rd. WN4—1B 70
Redgates Wlk. M21—5B 90
Redgrave Pl. OL4—9D 46
Redgrave Rise. WN3—5K 51
Redgrave St. OL4—9C 46
Redgrave Wlk. M19—5C 92
Red Hall St. OL4—2C 64
Redhill Dri. SK6—2K 105
Redhill Gro. BL1—9E 22
Redhill St. M4—3G 5 & 5H 79
Red Hill Way. WN2—2K 53
Redhouse La. SK6—1M 105
Redhouse La. SK12—5L 117
Red Ho. La. WA14—5J 99
Redisher La. BL8—8E 8
Redland Av. SK5—9F 92
Redland Clo. OL15—5B 14
Redland Ct. WN2—9F 52
Redland Cres. M21—8E 90
Red La. BL2—9K 23
Red La. OL3—3C 48
Red La. OL12—9H 13
Red La. SK12—7H 117
Red Lion St. M4—3F 5 & 5G 79
Red Lodge. SK12—6G 117
Red Lumb St. OL12—7G 11
Redlynch Wlk. M8—9G 61
Redmain Gro. WA3—7L 71
Redmere Gro. M14—6J 91
Redmire M. SK16—8F 82
Redmires Ct. M5—6A 78
Redmond Clo. M34—8L 81
Redmoor La. SK12—8M 117
Redmoor Sq. M13—6G 6 & 8H 79
Rednal Wlk. WN3—2B 52
Red Pike Wlk. OL1—9A 46
Redpoll Clo. M28—9H 57
Red Rock Brow. WN1—1C 34
Red Rock La. M26—2D 58
Red Rock La. WN1 & WN2—1B 34
Red Rose Cen. M5—4A 4 & 6B 78
Redrose Cres. M19—7C 92
Red Rose Gdns. M28—4G 57
Red Row. SK7—4B 116
Redruth Av. WA11—8D 68
Redruth St. M14—4H 91
Redscar Wlk. M24—8K 43
Redshaw Bank. SK2—8K 105
Redshaw Clo. M14—5K 91
Redstock Clo. BL5—8G 37
Redstone Rd. M19—2K 103
Red St. M29—5L 55
Redthorn Av. M19—7M 91
Redvales Rd. BL9—2L 41
Redvale Wlk. M7—1E 78
Redvers St. M11—7L 79
Redvers St. OL1—9K 45
Red Waters. WN7—1G 73
Redwing Rd. BL8—9F 8
Redwood. BL5—2D 54
Redwood. M33—1C 100
Redwood. OL9—1D 62
Redwood. WN6—3H 33
Redwood Av. WN5—2G 51
Redwood Av. WN6—6M 33
Redwood Clo. OL12—8B 12
Redwood Dri. M8—2H 79
Redwood Dri. SK6—1M 105
Redwood Dri. WA11—9F 68
Redwood La. OL4—1E 64
Redwood Rd. OL3—1C 66
Redwood St. M6—3A 78
Reece Ct. SK16—7D 82
Reedbank. M26—9G 41
Reed Ct. OL1—9L 45
Reed Cres. WN3—4A 52
Reedham Clo. BL1—1C 38
Reedham Wlk. M10—3L 79
(off Lifton Av.)
Reedham Wlk. OL9—4J 63
Reed Hill. OL16—2F 28
Reedmace Clo. M28—7L 57
Reedsmere Clo. WN5—2M 51
Reed St. M18—9D 80
Reed St. OL1—1M 63
Reeman Clo. SK6—1A 106
Reepham Clo. WN3—5K 51
Reeve Clo. SK2—8M 105
Reeve's Ct. M5—5G 77
Reeves Rd. M21—7B 90
Reeves St. WN7—1F 72
Reeve St. WA3—7B 72
Reevey Av. SK7—2J 115
Reform St. OL12—2F 28
Reform Wlk. M11—7B 80
Refuge St. OL2—3B 46
Regaby Gro. WN2—3A 54
Regal Clo. M25—9B 42
Regal Ind. Est. M12—8A 80
Regal Wlk. M10—1C 80
Regan Av. M21—7D 90
Regan St. BL1—7D 22
Regan St. M26—7H 41
Regatta St. M6—1M 77
Regency Clo. M10—2K 79
Regency Clo. OL8—4K 63
Regency Ct. WN1—9D 34
Regent Av. M14—4G 91
Regent Av. M28—4J 57
Regent Av. WN4—2M 69
Regent Bank. SK9—6F 118
Regent Clo. SK7—8D 114
Regent Clo. SK8—9C 104
Regent Clo. SK9—6F 118
Regent Ct. M7—7D 60
Regent Ct. SK4—9C 92
Regent Cres. M35—1E 80
Regent Cres. OL2—7K 45
Regent Dri. BL6—2H 37
Regent Dri. M34—5K 93
Regent Dri. OL5—8K 65
Regent Dri. WN7—9K 55
Regent Ho. M14—3K 91
Regent Pl. M14—2J 91
Regent Rd. BL6—3H 37
Regent Rd. M5 & M3—5A 4 & 6B 78
Regent Rd. SK2—7G 105
Regent Rd. WA14—9C 100
Regent Rd. WN2—5G 53
Regent Rd. Ind. Area. M5—7D 78
Regents Av. WA11—8H 69
Regents Pl. M5—4A 4 & 6B 78
Regent Sq. M5—5A 4 & 7B 78
Regent St. BL0—7G 9
Regent St. BL9—6M 25
Regent St. M10—2D 80
Regent St. M24—7M 43
Regent St. M29—6L 55
Regent St. M30—5F 76
Regent St. OL1—1A 64
Regent St. OL2—2B 46
Regent St. OL10—9H 27
Regent St. OL12—1F 28
Regent St. OL15—6B 14
Regent St. PR7—1L 17
Regent St. SK14—1H 97
Regent St. WN2—3J 53
(in two parts)
Regent Wlk. BL4—9K 39
Regina Av. SK15—5G 83
Regina Ct. M6—4G 77
Regina Cres. WN7—1L 73
Reginald Latham Ct. M10—4K 79
Reginald St. BL3—7A 38
Reginald St. M11—8F 80
Reginald St. M27—7D 58
Reginald St. M30—7A 76
Reid Clo. M34—6A 94
Reigate Clo. BL8—9H 25
Reigate Rd. M31—6L 87
Reins Lea Av. OL8—6A 64
Reins Lee Rd. OL7—1A 82
Reliance St. M10—1C 80
Rembrandt Wlk. OL1—5C 46
Rena Clo. SK4—2D 104
Renfrew Av. WA11—8D 68
Renfrew Clo. WN3—5A 52
Renfrew Rd. WN2—4K 35
Rennell St. OL16—3G 29
Rennie Clo. M32—4K 89
Renshaw Av. M30—6D 76
Renshaw Dri. BL9—7C 26
Renshaw Sq. M30—6C 76
Renshaw St. M12—9A 80
Renshaw St. M30—6D 76
Renshaw St. WA14—8E 100
Rensherds Pl. WA16—7C 108
Renton Rd. M22—9D 102
Renton Rd. M32—4L 89
Renwick Gro. BL3—6C 38
Renwick Sq. WN4—4M 69
Repton Av. M10—7E 62
Repton Av. M31—4K 87
Repton Av. M34—3G 93
Repton Av. M35—4D 80
Repton Av. OL8—5K 63
Repton Av. SK14—3E 94
Repton Av. WN3—4F 52
Repton Clo. WA16—8C 108
Reservoir Rd. SK3—6D 104
Reservoir St. M3—2D 4 & 4E 78
Reservoir St. M6—5M 77
Reservoir St. OL16—2J 29
Reservoir St. WN2—6M 35
(Aspull)
Reservoir St. WN2—9G 35
(Wigan)
Resevoir St. WN4—4C 70
Restormel Av. WN2—4K 35
Retford Av. OL16—6H 29
Retford Clo. BL8—5K 25
Retford St. OL4—3B 64
Retiro St. OL1—1M 63
Retreat, The. SK6—4C 106
Reuben St. SK4—1E 104
Revers St. BL8—7K 25
Reveton Grn. SK7—2G 115
Rex Bldgs. SK9—5H 119
Rex Ct. OL4—2H 65
Reynard Rd. M21—7B 90
Reynard St. SK14—3D 94
Reynell Rd. M13—4M 91
Reyner Sq. OL6—5E 82
Reyner Stephens Way. OL6—4B 82
Reyner St. M1—5F 5 & 7G 79
Reynolds Clo. BL5—2M 55
Reynolds Dri. BL5—1M 55
Reynolds Dri. M18—9D 80
Reynolds Dri. SK6—5H 107
Reynolds M. SK9—3L 119
Reynolds Rd. M16—2C 90
Reynold St. SK14—4D 94
Rhine Clo. BL8—3F 24
Rhiwlas Dri. BL9—1M 41
Rhodehouses. SK6—1F 116
Rhodes Av. OL3—8C 48
Rhodes Av. OL4—3F 64
Rhodes Bank. OL1—2M 63
Rhodes Cres. OL11—7F 28
Rhodes Dri. BL9—7A 42
Rhodes Hill. OL4—3F 64
Rhodes St. M10—3L 79
Rhodes St. OL1—1A 64
Rhodes St. OL2—6A 46
Rhodes St. OL4—1F 64
Rhodes St. OL12—8H 13
Rhodes St. SK14—1H 97
(Hadfield)
Rhodes St. SK14—3C 94
(Hyde)
Rhodes St. N. SK14—3C 94
Rhode St. BL8—4F 24
Rhos Av. M14—6L 91
Rhos Av. M24—1A 62
Rhos Av. SK8—3L 113
Rhos Dri. SK7—3K 115
Rhosleigh Av. BL1—6D 22
Rhyl St. M11—7A 80
Rialto Gdns. M7—1E 78
Rial Wlk. M15—9G 79
Ribbesford Rd. WN3—4J 51
Ribble Av. BL2—2L 39
Ribble Av. OL9—8F 44
Ribble Av. OL15—5M 13
Ribble Dri. BL4—3A 58
Ribble Dri. BL9—2M 25
Ribble Dri. M25—8A 42
Ribble Dri. M28—1F 74
Ribble Dri. WN5—1J 51
Ribble Gro. OL10—7G 27
Ribble Gro. WN7—2C 72
Ribble Rd. OL8—5J 63
Ribble Rd. WN2—6G 53
Ribble Rd. WN6—8H 17
Ribblesdale Dri. M10—2J 79
Ribblesdale Rd. BL3—5D 38
Ribble St. OL11—6D 28
Ribbleton Clo. BL8—9F 24
Ribble Wlk. M35—7G 81
Ribchester Dri. BL9—2K 41
Ribchester Gro. BL2—9L 23
Ribchester Wlk. M15—9F 78
Riber Bank. SK13—5E 96
Riber Clo. SK13—5E 96
(off Riber Bank)
Riber Fold. SK13—5E 96
(off Riber Bank)
Riber Grn. SK13—5E 96
(off Riber Bank)
Rice St. M3—5D 4 & 7E 78
Richard Burch St. BL9—7M 25
Richardson Clo. M25—7M 41
Richardson Rd. M30—5E 76
Richardson St. SK1—6G 105
Richards Rd. WN6—7H 17
Richard St. M26—6F 40
Richard St. OL2—4A 46
Richard St. OL11—4F 28
Richard St. SK1—3F 104
(in two parts)
Richard St. WN3—2D 52
Richbell Clo. M30—7E 86
Richborough Clo. M7—2E 78
Richelieu St. BL3—5G 39
Richmond Av. M25—7C 60
Richmond Av. M31—4E 88
Richmond Av. OL2—5K 45
Richmond Av. OL9—4G 63
Richmond Av. SK9—7K 113
Richmond Av. WA11—8H 69
Richmond Clo. BL8—4F 24
Richmond Clo. M25—1K 59
Richmond Clo. M33—2M 101
Richmond Clo. OL2—4B 46
Richmond Clo. SK15—8L 65
(Mossley)
Richmond Clo. SK15—6G 83
(Stalybridge)
Richmond Clo. SK16—9D 82
Richmond Clo. WA13—9B 98
Richmond Clo. WN1—2B 34
Richmond Ct. M9—3G 61
(off Deanswood Dri.)
Richmond Ct. SK8—8J 103
Richmond Ct. WA14—2B 110
Richmond Cres. SK15—8L 65
Richmond Dri. M28—8C 58
Richmond Dri. WA13—9B 98
Richmond Dri. WN7—9K 55
Richmond Gdns. BL3—6H 39
Richmond Gro. BL4—8G 39
Richmond Gro. M12—1L 91
Richmond Gro. M13—2K 91
Richmond Gro. M30—4E 76
Richmond Gro. SK8—2M 113
Richmond Gro. WN7—9L 55
Richmond Hill. SK14—5F 94
(in two parts)
Richmond Hill. WA14—2B 110
Richmond Hill. WN5—2J 51
Richmond Hill Rd. SK8—8J 103
Richmond Ho. M29—7M 55
Richmond Ho. SK15—6G 83
Richmond Rd. M14—6K 91
Richmond Rd. M17—8G 77
Richmond Rd. M28—9E 56
Richmond Rd. M34—3G 93
Richmond Rd. M35—8G 63
Richmond Rd. SK4—3M 103
Richmond Rd. SK6—2C 106
Richmond Rd. SK16—9C 82
Richmond Rd. WA14—8D 100
(Altrincham)
Richmond Rd. WA14—2B 110
(Bowdon)
Richmond Rd. WN2—5A 54
Richmond Rd. WN4—2M 69
Richmond St. BL6—7B 20
Richmond St. BL9—1L 41
Richmond St. M1—5F 5 & 7G 79
Richmond St. M3—2D 4 & 4E 78
Richmond St. M29—5J 55
Richmond St. M34—9L 81
Richmond St. M35—5J 81
Richmond St. OL7 & OL6—3M 81
Richmond St. SK14—4E 94
Richmond St. SK15—5H 83
Richmond St. WN1—9B 34
Richmond St. WN3—3A 52
Richmond Ter. SK6—4H 117
Richmond Ter. SK9—8L 119
Richmond Wlk. M26—3F 40
Richmond Wlk. OL9—2K 63
Rickford Av. WN7—9D 54
Ricroft Rd. SK6—2H 107
Ridd Cotts. OL11—2H 27
Riddell Ct. M5—5J 77
Ridding Av. M22—2E 112
Ridding Clo. SK2—7K 105
Riddings Ct. WA15—5F 100
Riddings Rd. WA15—5F 100
(Altrincham)
Riddings Rd. WA15—3F 110
(Hale)
Riders Ga. BL9—6F 26
Ridge Av. SK6—9G 107
Ridge Av. WA15—6K 111
Ridge Av. WN1—2B 34
Ridge Clo. SK6—3E 106
Ridge Clo. SK14—2E 96
Ridge Cres. M25—9B 42
Ridge Cres. SK6—1F 116
Ridgedale Cen. SK6—7F 106
Ridgefield. M2—4E 5 & 6F 78
Ridgefield St. M35—9D 62
(in two parts)
Ridge Gro. M25—9B 42
Ridge Hill La. SK15—5F 82
(in two parts)
Ridge La. OL3—4D 48
Ridgemont Av. SK4—2B 104
Ridgemont Dri. M28—1F 74
Ridgemont Wlk. M23—3M 101
Ridge Pk. SK7—6D 114
Ridge Rd. SK6—9G 107
Ridge Wlk. M9—5K 61
Ridgeway. M27—6H 59
Ridgeway. SK9—4M 119
Ridgeway. WA3—8M 71
Ridgeway Gates. BL1—2F 38
Ridgeway Rd. WA15—8J 101
Ridgeway, The. SK6—4A 106
Ridgeway, The. SK12—6J 117
Ridgewell Av. WA3—7J 71
Ridgewood. OL9—9E 44
Ridgewood Av. M10—2K 79
Ridgmont Clo. BL6—7F 20
Ridgmont Dri. BL6—7F 20
Ridgmont Rd. SK7—7E 114
Ridgway. BL6—8J 19
Ridgway St. M10—5K 79
Ridgway St. E. M4—5K 79
Riding Clo. M29—9D 56
Ridingfold La. M28—2A 76
Riding Ga. BL2—4L 23
Riding Ga. M. BL2—4L 23
Riding Head La. BL0—3M 9
Riding La. WN4—1E 70
Ridings Rd. SK14—1F 96
Ridings St. M10—2M 79
Riding St. M3—3D 4 & 5E 78
Ridley Dri. WA14—4E 100
Ridley Gro. M33—2M 101
Ridley La. L40—1A 16
Ridley St. OL4—2A 64
Ridley Wlk. M15—1G 91
Ridling La. SK14—4E 94
Ridsdale Av. M20—8G 91
Ridsdale Wlk. M6—2A 78
Ridyard St. M28—4H 57
Ridyard St. WN2—5H 53
Ridyard St. WN5—1K 51
Rifle Rd. M33—9M 89
Rifle St. OL1—9M 45
Riga Rd. M14—5J 91
Riga St. M4—3F 5 & 5G 79
Rigby Av. BL6—8J 19
Rigby Av. M26—4J 41
Rigby Ct. BL3—5F 38
(in two parts)
Rigby Ct. OL12—1L 27
Rigby Gro. M28—4E 56
Rigby La. BL2—4J 23
Rigbys La. WN4—4D 70
Rigby St. BL3—5F 38
Rigby St. M7—9D 60
(in two parts)
Rigby St. WA3—7G 71
Rigby St. WA14—1D 110
Rigby St. WN2—2L 53
Rigby St. WN4—4A 70
Rigby's Yd. WN5—2H 51
Rigby Wlk. M7—1E 78
Rigel Pl. M7—2B 4 & 4C 78
Rigel St. M4—2H 5 & 4J 79
Rigi Mt. OL2—3K 45
Rigton Clo. M12—1A 92
Riley Clo. M33—4B 100
Riley Ct. BL1—9F 22
Riley La. WN2—1H 35
Riley Sq. WN1—8D 34
Riley St. M29—7G 55
Riley Wood Clo. SK6—4M 105
Rimington Av. WA3—6J 71
Rimmington Clo. M9—6A 62
Rimsdale Clo. SK8—1G 113
Rimsdale Wlk. BL3—4L 37
Rimworth Dri. M10—1H 5 & 3J 79
Rinbble Cres. WN5—4C 68
Rindle Rd. M29—5C 74
Ringcroft Gdns. M10—7B 62
Ringfield Clo. M16—2E 90
(in two parts)
Ringford Wlk. M10—2L 79
Ringley Av. WA3—6F 70
Ringley Chase. M25—9L 41
Ringley Clo. M25—9K 41
Ringley Dri. M25—1K 59
Ringley Gro. BL1—5E 22
Ringley Hey. M25—9K 41
Ringley Meadows. M26—1C 58
Ringley Old Brow. M26—1C 58
Ringley Pk. M25—9K 41
Ringley Rd. M26—9B 40
(in three parts)
Ringley Rd. W. M26—9E 40
Ringley St. M9—8K 61
Ringlow Av. M27—9C 58
Ringlow Pk. Rd. M27—1C 76
Ring Lows La. OL12—7F 12
Ringmer Dri. M22—3C 112
Ringmere Ct. OL1—9L 45
Ringmore Rd. SK7—2G 115
Ring-O-Bells La. SK6—6K 117
Rings Clo. M35—1F 80
Ringstead Dri. M10—1H 5 & 3J 79
Ringstone Clo. M25—5A 60
Ringway Av. WN7—8F 54
Ringway Gro. M33—3L 101
Ringway Rd. M22—5C 112
Ringway Rd. W. M22—4C 112
Ringway Trading Est. M22—4E 112
Ringwood Av. BL0—7G 9
Ringwood Av. M12—4B 92
Ringwood Av. M26—8H 41
Ringwood Av. M34—6J 81
Ringwood Av. SK7—3H 115
Ringwood Way. OL9—9J 45
Rink St. M14—7K 91
Ripley Av. SK2—9H 105
Ripley Av. SK8—7B 114
Ripley Clo. M4—7K 79
Ripley Clo. M5—3A 4 & 5B 78
Ripley Clo. SK7—4L 115
Ripley Cres. M31—1M 87
Ripley Dri. WN3—4J 51
Ripley Dri. WN7—1F 72
Ripley St. BL2—6H 23
Ripley Way. M34—6M 93
Ripon Av. BL1—9M 21
Ripon Av. M25—7M 41
Ripon Av. WA3—7K 71
Ripon Av. WN6—6B 34
Ripon Clo. BL3—6M 39
Ripon Clo. M25—7M 41
Ripon Clo. M26—4K 41
Ripon Clo. OL9—2H 63
Ripon Clo. SK1—5F 104
Ripon Clo. WA15—3J 111
Ripon Cres. M32—3F 88
Ripon Dri. BL1—9M 21
Ripon Dri. WN4—5D 70
Ripon Gro. M33—8F 88
Ripon Hall Av. BL0—7H 9
Ripon Rd. M32—3F 88
Ripon St. M15—1G 91
Ripon St. OL1—9K 45
Ripon St. OL6—4C 82
Ripon Wlk. SK6—4A 106
Rippenden Av. M21—4A 90
Rippingham Rd. M20—7H 91
Rippleton Rd. M22—9E 102
Ripponden Rd. OL1 & OL4—9C 46
Ripponden Rd. OL3—8J 31
Ripponden St. OL1—8C 46
Ripton Wlk. M9—4H 61
(off Selston Rd.)
Risbury Wlk. M10—1C 80
Rises, The. SK14—1F 96
Rise, The. OL4—1F 64
Rise, The. WN6—6J 33
Rishton Av. BL3—7F 38
Rishton Av. M10—2L 79
Rishton La. BL3—5F 38
Rishworth Clo. SK2—8K 105
Rishworth Dri. M10—8E 62
Rishworth Rise. OL2—9M 29
Rising La. OL8—6L 63
Rising La. Clo. OL8—6L 63
Risley Av. M9—8K 61
Risley St. OL1—9M 45
Risque St. SK4—2D 104
Rita Av. M14—3H 91
Ritson Clo. M18—9B 80
Riva Rd. M19—3K 103
Riverbank Dri. BL8—6K 25
Riverbank Lawns. M3—2D 4 & 4E 78
Riverbank Tower. M3—2D 4 & 4E 78
Riverbank Wlk. M20—1D 102
Riverbank Way. SK13—7M 97
Riverdale. WN6—5K 33
Riverdale Ct. M9—5H 61
Riverdale Rd. M9—5G 61
River La. M31—1F 98
River La. M34—3B 94
Rivermead Av. WA15—6J 111
Rivermead Clo. M34—7A 94
Rivermead Rd. M34—6A 94
Riverpark Rd. M10—4A 80
River Pl. M15—6D 4 & 8E 78
River Pl. OL16—4M 29
Riversdale Ct. M25—4A 60
Riversdale Dri. OL8—7A 64
Riversdale Rd. SK8—7J 103
Riversdale View. SK6—8A 94
Rivershill. M33—8G 89
Rivershill Dri. OL10—9H 27
Rivers Hill Gdns. WA15—6K 111
Riverside. M7—2B 4 & 4C 78
Riverside. OL1—8E 44
River Side. SK16—5C 82
Riverside Av. M21—1D 102
Riverside Av. M30—5H 87
Riverside Av. WN1—8D 34
Riverside Ct. M20—2F 102
Riverside Dri M31—6B 88
Riverside Dri. BL9—9H 9
Riverside Dri. M26—9B 40
Riverside Rd. M26—5K 41
Riverside Works. SK9—3H 119
Rivers La. M31—1B 88
Riversleigh Clo. BL1—7M 21
Riversmeade. BL7—3J 23
Riversmeade. WN7—1G 73
Rivers St. WN5—2E 50
Riverstone Dri. M23—6K 101
River St. BL2—2G 39
River St. M12—5H 5 & 7J 79
River St. M15—6E 5 & 8F 78
River St. M26—6H 41
River St. OL10—6K 27
River St. OL16—3F 28
River St. SK1—2H 105
River St. SK9—3H 119
River St. WN7—3G 73
Riverton Rd. M20—5H 103
River View. SK5—7G 93
River View Clo. M25—6M 59
Riverview Cotts. SK13—7J 97
(off Turnlee Dri.)
River View Ct. M7—8C 60
River Way. WN1—9C 34
Riviera Ct. OL11—9J 11
Rivington. M6—3J 77
Rivington Av. M27—8J 59
Rivington Av. PR6—3H 19
Rivington Av. WA3—6J 71
Rivington Av. WA10—9A 68
Rivington Av. WN1—7B 34
Rivington Av. WN2—5H 53
Rivington Cres. M27—8J 59
Rivington Dri. BL8—9G 25
Rivington Dri. OL2—2D 46
Rivington Dri. WN2—7M 53
Rivington Dri. WN8—1C 50
Rivington Gro. M30—8D 86
Rivington Gro. M34—7J 81
Rivington Ho. BL6—6B 20
Rivington La. BL6—1M 19
Rivington La. PR6—4K 19
Rivington Pl. PR7—4K 17
Rivington Rd. M6—3J 77
Rivington Rd. OL4—1G 65
Rivington Rd. WA15—2F 110
Rivington St. BL6—8K 19
Rivington St. M29—6G 55
Rivington St. OL1—8M 45
Rivington St. OL12—1F 28
Rivington Wlk. M12—1M 91
Rivington Way. WN6—1M 33
Rixson St. OL4—7D 46
Rix St. BL1—8E 22
Rixton Ct. M16—3B 90
Rixton Dri. M29—8B 56
Rixton St. M5—9B 78
Roach Bank Rd. BL9—2B 42
Roaches Way. OL5—5L 65
Roach Grn. WN1—8E 34
Roachill Clo. WA14—8B 100
Roach Pl. OL16—2G 29
Roach St. BL9—5M 41
(Bury)
Roach St. BL9—8C 26
(Heap Bridge)
Roachwood Clo. OL9—1E 62
Roading Brook Rd. BL2—7B
Road La. OL12—7D 12
Roads Ford Av. OL16—3M 29
Roadside Clo. WA3—6J 71
Roaring Ga. La. WA15—1L 1
Robert Adam Cres. M15—9E
Robert Hall St. M5—5A 4 & 7B
Robert Malcolm Clo. M10—2K
Robert Moffat. WA16—7C 10
Robert Owens Gdns. M22—5D 1
Robert Owen St. M35—5J 81
Roberts Av. M14—2H 91
Roberts Av. WA11—9F 68
Robert Saville Ct. OL11—4B
(off Half Acre M.)
Robertscroft Clo. M22—9C 1
Robertshaw Av. M21—8B 90
Robertshaw St. WN7—9E 54
Robertson Clo. M18—1C 92
Robertson St. M26—5G 41
Roberts Pas. OL15—1D 14
Roberts Pl. OL15—8M 13
Roberts St. M30—5D 76
Robert St. BL0—2J 9
Robert St. BL1—1G 39
Robert St. BL2—5L 23
Robert St. BL4—9L 39
Robert St. BL8—7J 25
Robert St. M3—2E 5 & 4F 78
Robert St. M10—2M 79
Robert St. M25—3C 60
Robert St. M26—5G 41
Robert St. M29—7L 55
Robert St. M33—1L 101
Robert St. M35—7G 63
Robert St. OL8—5H 63
Robert St. OL10—1L 43
Robert St. OL16—2G 29
Robert St. SK14—3C 94
Robert St. SK16—7B 82
Robert St. WN2—5G 53
Robe Wlk. M18—9D 80
Robina Clo. M30—7M 75
Robin Clo. BL4—1F 56
Robin Croft. SK6—2K 105
Robin Dri. M30—3G 87
Robin Hill Dri. WN6—8H 17
Robin Hill La. WN6—7J 17
Robin Hood La. WN6—7B 1
Robin Hood St. M8—8F 60
Robin La. M25—1M 59
(in two parts)
Robin Pk. Rd. WN5—9L 33
Robin Rd. BL9—8H 9
Robinsbay Rd. M22—4E 11
Robins Clo. M35—4J 81
Robins Clo. SK7—5E 114
Robins Hill. SK7—5D 114
Robins La. SK7—5D 114
Robin's La. WN8—8A 50
Robinson La. OL7—4M 81
Robinsons Fold. OL4—1H 6
Robinson St. BL6—6B 20
Robinson St. M29—7A 56
Robinson St. OL1—2M 63
Robinson St. OL6—3B 82
Robinson St. OL8—5M 63
Robinson St. OL9—2H 63
Robinson St. OL16—3G 29
Robinson St. SK3—6D 104
Robinson St. SK14—3F 94
Robinson St. SK15—7E 82
Robinson St. WN7—3G 73
Robin St. OL1—9L 45
Robinsway. WA14—3C 110
Robinswood Rd. M22—2D
Rob La. WA12—9E 70
Robson Av. M31—8E 76
Robsons Pl. WN2—8H 53
Roby Mill. WN8—6B 32
Roby Rd. M30—7C 76
Roby St. M1—4G 5 & 6H 79
Roby Well Way. WN5—2D
Roch Av. OL10—8G 27
Rochbury Clo. OL11—4M 2
Roch Clo. M25—8B 42
Roch Cres. M25—7B 42
Rochdale Ind. Cen. OL11—
Rochdale La. OL2—4K 45
Rochdale La. OL10—8K 27
Rochdale Old Rd. BL9—7C
Rochdale Rd. BL0—1L 9
Rochdale Rd. BL9—8M 25
Rochdale Rd. HX6—2K 15
Rochdale Rd. M4, M10 & M—2G 5 & 4
Rochdale Rd. M24—7A 44
Rochdale Rd. OL1 & OL9—
Rochdale Rd. OL2—2J 45
(Royton)
Rochdale Rd. OL2—9L 29
(Shaw)
Rochdale Rd. OL3—7H 31
Rochdale Rd. OL10—8K 27
Rochdale Rd. OL16—3K 29
Rochdale Rd. E. OL10—8L
Roche Gdns. SK8—6B 114
Roche Rd. OL3—4L 47
Rochester Av. BL2—9L 23
Rochester Av. M25—6C 60
Rochester Av. M28—7J 57
Rochester Clo. OL6—9C 64
Rochester Clo. SK16—8G
Rochester Dri. WA14—4E
Rochester Gro. SK7—1L 1
Rochester Rd. M31—2D 88
Rochester Way. OL9—2H
Rochford Av. M22—4D 112
Rochford Av. M25—1K 59
Rochford Clo. M25—1K 59
Rochford Rd. M30—7M 75
Roch Mills Cres. OL11—5C
Roch Mills Gdns. OL11—5
Roch Pl. WN2—6F 52
Roch St. OL16—1H 29
Roch Valley Way. OL11—
Roch Wlk. M25—8B 42
Roch Way. M25—8B 42
Rockall Wlk. M11—6M 79
Rock Av. BL1—8C 22
Rock Bank. OL5—7J 65
Rockbourne Clo. WN2—4

🔵 **ramp** for 0.41 mile(s) / 0.66 km(s)At the roundabout, take the third exit onto ramp

⬇️ **M6** for 37.14 mile(s) / 59.77 km(s)Continue onto M6

↰ **M61** for 21.44 mile(s) / 34.5 km(s)Bear left onto M61

↰ **M60** for 2.3 mile(s) / 3.7 km(s)Bear left onto M60

⬇️ **Eccles Interchange** for 0.4 mile(s) / 0.64 km(s)Continue onto Eccles Interchange

⬇️ **M602** for 3.65 mile(s) / 5.87 km(s)Continue onto M602

➡️ **ramp (J3)** for 0.21 mile(s) / 0.34 km(s)Exit onto ramp (J3)

⬇️ **Trafford Road A5063** for 0.18 mile(s) / 0.29 km(s)Continue onto Trafford Road A5063

⬅️ **Broadway** for 0.04 mile(s) / 0.06 km(s)Turn right onto Broadway

⬇️ **Broad Way** for 0.08 mile(s) / 0.13 km(s)Continue onto Broad Way

↱ **Broadway** for 0.04 mile(s) / 0.06 km(s)Bear left onto Broadway

🔵 **The Quays** for 0.54 mile(s) / 0.87 km(s)At the roundabout, take the first exit onto The Quays

🔵 **The Quays** for 0.03 mile(s) / 0.05 km(s)At the roundabout, take the second exit onto The Quays

Quays

🏁 for 0.0 mile(s) / 0.0 km(s)Arrive at your destination

Lock your car and don't leave valuables on display

RAC's Accident Care helpline

Save 0800 0966 999 to your mobile and call us for help if you're involved in an accident

Broken down?

RAC members who have broken down should call 0800 828282†

If you are not an RAC member, you can still join and get Roadside Assistance immediately. Please call 0800 197 7815† to speak to an advisor, quoting WJ0003.

† Calls may be recorded and/or monitored

RAC

Route Planner

UK, European & Overseas Route Planner

Total Distance: 73.12 mile(s), 117.68 km(s) - about: 1 hour(s) 18 minute(s)

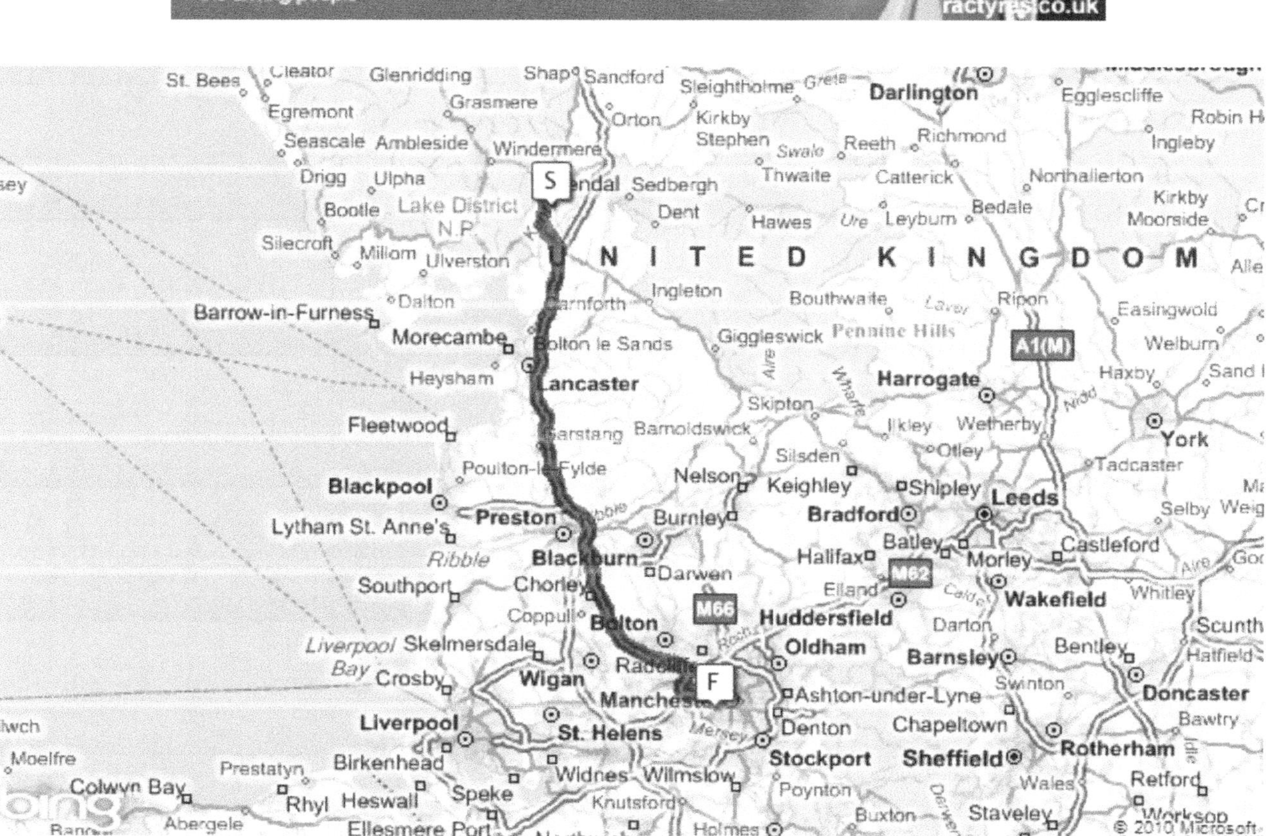

Stage 1

La9 5jj to M50 3az - 73.12 mile(s), 117.68 km(s) - about: 1 hour(s) 18 minute(s)

S	**Wattsfield Avenue** for 0.04 mile(s) / 0.06 km(s)	Depart on Wattsfield Avenue
	Wattsfield Road for 0.11 mile(s) / 0.18 km(s)	Bear right onto Wattsfield Road
→	**Milnthorpe Road A6** for 0.84 mile(s) / 1.35 km(s)	Turn left onto Milnthorpe Road A6
⟳	**ramp** for 0.17 mile(s) / 0.27 km(s)	At the roundabout, take the first exit onto ramp
⬇	**A591** for 2.23 mile(s) / 3.59 km(s)	Continue onto A591
⬇	**A590** for 3.24 mile(s) / 5.21 km(s)	Continue onto A590

kdove Av. M15—6E 5 & 8F 78
kfield Dri. M9—8L 61
k Fold. BL7—1F 22
khampton St. M18—1D 92
khaven Av. BL6—6C 20
khouse Clo. M30—7C 76
kingham Clo. OL2—1L 45
kland Wlk. M10—6C 62
kley Gdns. M6—1A 4 & 3B 78
klyn Av. M10—6C 62
klynes. SK6—3B 106
kmead Dri. M9—5L 61
k Nook. OL15—2D 14
k Rd. M28—4G 75
k Rd. M31—4F 88
k St. BL6—7B 20
k St. M7—1D 78
k St. M11—7E 80
k St. OL1—1M 63
n two parts)
k St. OL7—2A 82
k St. OL10—9L 27
k St. SK14—7E 94
k St. WA3—5G 71
k Ter. BL7—1F 22
k Ter. OL5—1J 83
k Ter. WN6—3F 16
k, The. BL9—8M 25
n three parts)
ky Bank Ter. WN3—3E 52
ff Warrington Rd.)
ky La. M30—2D 76
a St. M9—9M 61
borough Gdns. M23—1M 111
borough Rd. M23—1M 111
eheath Clo. SK9—4K 119
en Ct. M25—4C 60
enhurst Dri. M10—9A 62
epool Clo. SK9—1K 119
ford Wlk. M7—1F 78
gers Clo. BL5—2E 54
gers Way. BL5—2E 54
nell Av. M10—2K 79
nell Clo. BL7—3F 22
mill Dri. SK8—1G 113
ney Ct. M4—2H 5 & 4J 79
ney Dri. SK6—9A 94
ney St. M3—4C 4 & 6D 78
ney St. M4—3H 5 & 5J 79
ney St. M29—6J 55
ney St. OL5—6J 65
ney St. OL6—3D 82
ney St. OL11—8B 28
ney St. WN1—1C 52
way Wlk. M7—1F 78
acre St. OL10—8L 27
buck Gdns. M33—1G 101
buck La. M33—1G 101
buck La. OL4—6G 47
buck Low. OL4—6G 47
buck M. M33—1H 101
buck St. WN2—5C 54
burn Wlk. M25—9C 42
burn Wlk. WN2—6F 52
cliffe Clo. WN3—2B 52
Cross Grn. SK14—1M 95
Cross Rd. SK14—9M 83
dean Gdns. M31—4J 87
ield. OL12—2C 28
ield Ter. OL12—2C 28
Grn. M28—8M 57
Grn Av. M28—8A 58
Hey Dri. PR7—1M 17
La. OL4—3D 64
St. OL12—1C 28
ate Dri. M23—8A 102
er Byrne Clo. M10—2B 80
er Clo. SK6—4M 105
erstead. BL3—3C 38
er St. M4—2F 5 & 4G 79
erton Clo. WN7—3H 73
eby Av. M32—5K 89
eby Av. WA3—6K 71
er Av. M13—4M 91
er Pk. Av. M34—8K 81
nd Av. WA11—8C 68
nd Rd. BL3—5C 38
nd Rd. SK5—7F 92
Row. M25—7B 60
a St. M3—3D 4 & 5E 78
esby Clo. BL8—5K 25
eston Av. M10—5K 79
ns La. SK6—4G 107
s Cres. M15—9E 78
swood Dri. M10—1A 80
an Clo. WN3—4M 51
an Ct. M7—2D 78
an Rd. M25—7A 60
an Rd. M35 & OL8—8G 63
an Rd. OL2—6K 45
an Rd. SK4—3E 104
an Rd. WN4—2A 70
ans, The. OL5—7K 65
an St. M4—3F 5 & 5G 79
an St. M26—6E 40
an St. OL5—5K 65
er Av. M10—7E 62
er St. BL2—2J 39
ord Av. M34—2A 94
ord Av. WN7—1F 72
ord Clo. OL8—3L 63
ord Pl. WN2—3L 53
ford Rd. M33—8E 88
ford St. WN2—3K 53
ford Wlk. M9—5G 61
ley Cres. BL2—1K 39
ley Dri. BL2—1K 39
eightmet)
ley Dri. BL2—2G 39
ill Hill)
ley Sq. WN6—1L 33
ley St. M6—2K 77
ley St. SK1—2H 105
ey Precinct. SK6—3C 106
ey Rd. M31—2D 88
ney Av. OL11—8F 28
ney Rd. BL1—8L 21
ney St. M6—2B 78
ney St. M10—8A 62
ney St. OL6—4C 82
ney Wlk. OL9—2H 63
ney Way. SK5—8H 93
ney Way. WN1—6B 34
sey. OL12—2E 28
f Spotland Rd.)
sey Av. M24—6M 43
sey Dri. SK8—6C 114
sey Gdns. M23—7M 101
sey Gro. WN3—6K 51
sley Clo. M12—9A 80
sley Dri. BL3—6C 38
ldsay Gdns. M5—6L 77
ld St. M11—6D 80
ld St. OL4—1C 64
ld St. OL11—9C 28
Wlk. M12—1L 91
in Clo. M12—7L 79
is Mt. OL7—9A 64
on Wlk. M8—8J 61
roft Sq. BL6—8J 19
roft St. BL1—9D 22
s La. OL11—1J 27
ery Av. M18—9F 80
ery Av. WN4—5B 70
ery Av. WN6—1E 32
ery Clo. SK15—8L 83
erypool Clo. SK9—1K 119
e St. M30—7A 76
field. M33—9J 89
field Av. M33—9J 89
ley Wlk. M14—3J 91
St. BL0—4J 9
St. BL9—6M 25
St. OL4—3C 64
swood Dri. OL11—7B 28
way. M24—1M 61
wood. OL1—8E 44
wood Av. M23—6M 101
wood Hill. SK7—3E 114
y Moor Rd. OL12—1K 11
Rooley St. OL12—1C 28
Rooley Ter. OL12—2C 28
Roosevelt Rd. BL4—1M 57
Rooth St. SK4—3D 104
Rope St. OL12—2F 28
Ropley Wlk. M9—7M 61
(off Oak Bank Av.)
Rosa Gro. M7—1D 78
Rosalind Ct. M5—5B 4 & 7C 78
Rosamond Dri. M3—3C 4 & 5D 78
Rosamond St. BL3—5C 38
Rosamond St. W. M15—9G 79
Rosary Clo. OL8—7M 63
Rosary Rd. OL8—7A 64
Roscoe Ct. BL5—1F 54
Roscoe Lowe Brow. PR6—3K 19
Roscoe Pk. Est. WA14—5E 100
Roscoe Rd. M30—5E 86
Roscoe St. OL1—2M 63
(in two parts)
Roscoe St. SK3—5D 104
Roscoe St. WN1—1E 52
Roscow Av. BL2—1L 39
Roscow Rd. BL4—1A 58
Rose Acre. M28—9H 57
Roseacre Clo. BL2—1J 39
Roseacre Dri. SK8—3J 113
Rose Av. BL4—8J 39
Rose Av. M30—5F 86
Rose Av. OL11—9K 11
Rose Av. OL15—8M 13
Rose Av. WA11—9L 69
Rose Av. WN2—9H 53
Rose Av. WN6—6M 33
Rose Bank. BL6—2J 37
Rose Bank. M31—9C 76
Rosebank. WA13—1A 108
Rosebank Clo. BL2—9C 24
Rose Bank Clo. SK14—1D 96
Rose Bank Rd. M10—3B 80
Rosebank Rd. M30—1C 98
Roseberry Av. OL1—8B 46
Roseberry Clo. BL0—8J 9
Roseberry Rd. WN4—2A 70
Roseberry St. BL3—5C 38
Roseberry St. OL8—2K 63
Rosebery St. BL5—9F 36
Rosebery St. M14—3F 90
Rosebery St. SK2—9K 105
Rosebury Av. WN7—2G 73
Rose Cottage Rd. M14—6H 91
Rose Cotts. M14—6K 91
(off Ladybarn La.)
Rose Cres. M30—5F 86
Rosecroft Clo. SK3—9E 104
Rosedale Av. BL1—5E 22
Rosedale Av. M29—5J 55
Rosedale Av. WA3—8J 71
Rosedale Clo. OL1—8B 46
Rosedale Ct. M34—3L 93
Rosedale Dri. WN7—2J 73
Rosedale Rd. M14—4G 91
Rosedale Rd. SK4—9D 92
Rosefield Cres. OL16—3J 29
Rosegarth Av. M20—1D 102
Rosegate Clo. M16—3F 90
Rose Grn. SK13—5L 97
Rose Gro. BL4—1M 57
Rosehay Av. M34—4M 93
Rose Hey La. M35—3E 80
Rose Hill. BL2—4G 39
Rose Hill. M34—3K 93
Rose Hill. M35—7G 63
Rose Hill. OL3—6M 47
Rose Hill. SK15—7G 83
Rose Hill. WN4—9M 51
Rose Hill Av. M10—3B 80
Rose Hill Av. WN5—2J 51
Rose Hill Clo. BL7—3G 23
Rosehill Clo. M5—5M 77
Rose Hill Clo. OL6—2E 82
Rosehill Ct. M6—5M 77
Rose Hill Ct. OL4—8E 46
Rose Hill Cres. OL6—2F 82
Rose Hill Dri. BL7—3G 23
Rosehill M. M27—6F 58
Rosehill Rd. M27—6F 58
Rose Hill Rd. OL6—2F 82
Rose Hill St. OL10—8H 27
Rose Hill Ter. M29—5K 55
Roseland Av. M20—1H 103
Roseland Dri. M25—2C 60
Roselands Av. M33—3F 100
Rose La. SK6—7E 106
Rose Lea. BL2—6L 23
Roseleigh Av. M19—7M 91
Rosemary Cres. WN1—7D 34
Rosemary Dri. SK14—7D 94
Rosemary Gro. M7—2C 78
Rosemary La. BL5—3A 56
Rosemary La. SK1—4G 105
Rosemary Wlk. M31—2F 98
Rosemead Ct. SK5—8F 92
Rosemount. M24—7M 43
Rosemount. SK14—1D 94
Rosemount Cres. SK14—1C 94
Roseneath Av. M19—5C 92
Roseneath Gro. BL3—7D 38
Roseneath Rd. BL3—6D 38
Rosen Sq. OL9—1H 63
Rose Rd. M31—3C 88
Rose St. M24—9C 44
Rose St. OL9—5G 63
Rose St. SK5—2F 104
Rose St. WN1—1F 52
Rose St. WN2—3K 53
Rose Ter. SK15—6G 83
Rosette Wlk. M27—9F 58
Rose Vale. SK8—3H 113
Rosevale Av. M19—8L 91
Rose Wlk. M31—2E 98
Rose Wlk. SK6—7E 106
Roseway. SK7—2F 114
Rosewell Clo. M10—3K 79
Rosewood. BL5—2C 54
Rosewood. M34—3K 93
Rosewood. OL11—1L 27
Rosewood Av. M35—4J 81
Rosewood Av. SK4—4A 104
Rosewood Clo. SK16—9D 82
Rosewood Clo. WN2—9H 53
Rosewood Cres. OL9—8H 45
Rosewood Gdns. M33—2M 101
(off Marefield)
Rosewood Wlk. M23—5J 101
Rosford Av. M14—4H 91
Rosgill Clo. SK4—3L 103
Rosgill Wlk. M18—1C 92
Rosina St. M11—8F 80
Rosley Rd. WN3—5B 52
Roslin Gdns. BL1—7C 22
Roslin St. M11—5D 80
Roslyn Av. M31—6L 87
Roslyn Rd. SK3—8E 104
Rossall Av. M26—8J 41
Rossall Av. M32—3J 89
Rossall Clo. BL2—1J 39
Rossall Ct. SK7—6E 114
Rossall Cres. WN7—4G 73
Rossall Dri. SK7—6E 114
Rossall Rd. BL2—1J 39
(in two parts)
Rossall Rd. OL12—9G 13
Rossall St. BL2—1J 39
Rossall Way. M6—4A 78
Ross Av. M19—5M 91
Ross Av. M25—2M 59
Ross Av. OL9—5F 62
Ross Av. SK3—8E 104
Ross Clo. WN2—7F 34
Ross Clo. WN5—1E 68
Ross Dri. M27—4E 58
Rossenclough Clo. SK9—2K 119
Rossendale Av. M9—7M 61
Rossendale Clo. OL2—2D 46
Rossendale Rd. SK8—4J 113
Rossendale Way. OL2—1B 46
Rossett Av. M22—4D 112
Rossett Av. WA15—5G 101
Rossett Clo. WN3—6K 51
Rossett Dri. M31—2M 87
Rossetti Wlk. M34—7A 94
Ross Gro. M31—4C 88
Rosshill Wlk. M15—9D 78
Rossington St. M10—2D 80
Rossini St. BL1—7D 22
Rosslane Wlk. SK5—7J 93
Rosslare Rd. M22—2E 112
Ross Lave La. M34—6H 93
Rosslyn Gro. WA15—7G 101
Rosslyn Rd. M10—7A 62
Rosslyn Rd. M16—4A 90
Rosslyn Rd. SK8—3K 113
Rossmere Av. OL11—4C 28
Rossmill La. WA15—6H 111
Ross St. BL1—9E 22
Ross St. OL8—3K 63
Rostherne. SK9—7G 119
Rostherne Av. M14—5G 91
Rostherne Av. M16—3C 90
Rostherne Av. SK6—4E 116
Rostherne Av. WA3—7K 71
Rostherne Gdns. BL3—5B 38
Rostherne Rd. M33—2M 101
Rostherne Rd. SK3—8E 104
Rostherne Rd. SK9—6F 118
Rostherne St. M6—5L 77
Rostherne St. WA14—1D 110
(in two parts)
Rosthernmere Rd. SK8—9M 103
Rosthwaite Clo. WN3—6A 52
Rosthwaite Gro. WA11—6B 68
Rosthwwaite Clo. M24—8J 43
Roston Ct. M7—8E 60
Roston Rd. M7—8E 60
Rostrevor Rd. SK3—8E 104
Rostron Brow. SK1—4F 104
(off Churchgate)
Rostron Clo. M12—9L 79
Rostron Rd. BL0—5H 9
Rostron St. M19—5B 92
Rostron St. M26—5G 41
Rothay Clo. BL2—9M 23
Rothay Dri. M24—6L 43
Rothay Dri. SK5—6F 92
Rothay St. WN7—3H 73
Rothbury Av. OL7—3L 81
Rothbury Clo. BL8—8F 24
Rothbury Ct. BL3—6B 38
Rotherby Rd. M22—9E 102
Rotherdale Av. WA15—8K 101
Rothermere Wlk. M23—6L 101
Rotherwood Av. M32—3L 89
Rotherwood Rd. SK9—5C 118
Rothesay Av. SK16—8C 82
Rothesay Clo. WA11—8E 68
Rothesay Cres. M33—3C 100
Rothesay Rd. BL3—6B 38
Rothesay Rd. M8—6E 60
Rothesay Rd. M27—9J 59
Rothesay Rd. OL1—8C 46
Rothesay Ter. OL16—6J 29
Rothiemay Rd. M31—5L 87
Rothley Av. M22—8D 102
Rothman Clo. M10—1C 80
Rothwell Cres. M28—2E 56
Rothwell La. M28—3E 56
Rothwell Rd. PR6—3H 19
Rothwell Rd. WA3—6J 71
Rothwell St. BL0—5H 9
Rothwell St. BL3—4E 38
Rothwell St. M10—1C 80
Rothwell St. M28—5M 57
Rothwell St. M35—9F 62
Rothwell St. OL2—6J 45
Rothwell St. OL12—1G 29
Rottingdene Dri. M22—3C 112
Rough. OL15—6F 14
Rough Bank. OL12—6C 12
Roughey Gdns. M22—9C 102
Rough Hey La. OL3—7K 31
Rough Hey Wlk. OL16—4H 29
Rough Hill La. BL9—6D 26
Roughlee Av. M27—9D 58
Roughtown Rd. OL5—6K 65
Roundcroft. SK6—2E 106
Roundham Wlk. M9—8L 61
Round Hey. OL5—8J 65
Roundhey. SK8—4H 113
Round Hill Clo. SK14—3F 96
Roundhill Way. OL4—8E 46
Roundhouse Av. WN1—8E 34
Roundmoor Rd. WN6—2A 34
Roundthorn Ct. M23—6H 105
Roundthorn Ind. Est. M23—6L 101
Roundthorn Rd. M23—7M 101
Roundthorn Rd. M24—1B 62
Roundthorn Rd. OL4—2B 64
Roundway. SK7—6D 114
Roundwood Rd. M22—6D 102
Roundy La. SK10—6M 121
Rousden Clo. M10—2K 79
Rouse St. OL11—6C 28
Routledge Wlk. M9—8L 61
Rowan Av. BL6—9E 20
Rowan Av. M16—3D 90
Rowan Av. M31—3D 88
Rowan Av. M33—3J 101
Rowan Av. WA3—8M 71
Rowan Av. WN6—6M 33
Rowan Clo. M6—5A 78
Rowan Clo. M35—1F 80
Rowan Clo. OL12—8A 12
Rowan Clo. WA11—8D 68
(Haydock)
Rowan Clo. WA11—9F 68
(St Helens)
Rowan Cres. SK16—8F 82
Rowan Dri. SK8—4C 114
Rowanhill. WN1—8D 34
Rowan Pl. M25—5B 60
Rowanside Dri. SK9—3L 119
Rowans St. BL8—6J 25
Rowans, The. BL1—2L 37
Rowans, The. M28—9E 56
Rowan St. SK14—5F 94
Rowan Tree Dri. M33—4H 101
Rowan Tree Rd. OL8—7K 63
Rowan Wlk. M31—2E 98
Rowan Wlk. SK14—2F 96
Rowanwood. OL9—1E 62
Rowany Clo. M25—6A 60
Rowarth Av. M34—6A 94
Rowarth Av. SK13—4D 96
(off Eyam La.)
Rowarth Bank. SK13—4D 96
(off Grassmoor Cres.)
Rowarth Clo. SK13—4D 96
(off Grassmoor Cres.)
Rowarth Fold. SK13—4D 96
(off Eyam La.)
Rowarth Rd. M23—2M 111
Rowarth Way. SK13—4D 96
(off Eyam La.)
Rowbotham St. SK14—6E 94
Rowbottoms Sq. WN1—9C 34
Rowbottom Wlk. OL8—3L 63
Rowcon Clo. M34—1L 93
Rowdell Wlk. M23—3B 102
Rowden Rd. OL4—4E 64
Rowe Grn. M34—3M 93
Rowell Sq. M3—3C 4 & 5D 78
Rowell St. M3—3C 4 & 5D 78
Rowena St. BL3—7J 39
Rowendale St. M1—7E 78
Rowe St. M29—8B 56
Rowfield Dri. M23—1M 111
Rowland Av. M31—3E 88
Rowland Ct. OL16—4H 29
Rowland Ho. OL2—5M 45
Rowlands Rd. BL9—9J 9
Rowland St. M5—7A 78
Rowland St. M29—5K 55
(in two parts)
Rowland St. OL16—4H 29
Rowlands Way. M22—2D 112
Rowland Way. OL4—1E 64
Rowley Bank La. WA16—9B 108
Rowley Dri. SK7—4L 115
Rowley St. OL6—1D 82
Rowlsey Clo. SK13—4E 96
(off Melandra Castle Rd.)
Rowood Av. M8—1H 79
Rowood Av. SK5—4F 92
Rowrah Cres. M24—8H 43
Rowsley Av. BL1—9A 22
Rowsley Av. M20—1E 102
Rowsley Grn. SK13—4E 96
(off Melandra Castle Rd.)
Rowsley Gro. SK5—7E 92
Rowsley Gro. SK13—4E 96
Rowsley M. SK13—4E 96
Rowsley Rd. M30—7C 76
Rowsley Rd. M32—3G 89
Rowsley St. M6—2B 78
Rowsley St. M11—5L 79
Rowsley Wlk. SK13—4E 96
(off Melandra Castle Rd.)
Rowson Ct. M33—1K 101
Rowson Dri. M30—8D 86
Rowton Rise. WN1—1B 34
Rowton St. BL2—7H 23
Roxalina St. BL3—5E 38
Roxburgh St. M18—1D 92
Roxbury Av. OL4—3D 64
Roxby Clo. M28—5H 57
Roxby Wlk. M10—6D 62
Roxholme Wlk. M22—4C 112
Roxton Clo. BL6—4B 20
Roxton Rd. SK4—8C 92
Roxwell Wlk. M9—8K 61
(off Alderside Rd.)
Royal Arc. WN1—9C 34
(off Galleries, The)
Royal Av. BL9—5M 25
Royal Av. M21—6A 90
Royal Av. M31—4D 88
Royal Av. M35—5H 81
Royal Av. OL10—9K 27
Royal Carr Flats. SK6—2A 106
(off Wild St.)
Royal Dri. WN7—1K 73
Royal Exchange. M2—3E 5 & 5F 78
Royal Exchange Arc. M2—6F 78
Royal George Cotts. OL3—3L 65
(off Church Rd.)
Royal George St. SK3—5E 104
Royal Oak Rd. M23—6M 101
(in two parts)
Royal Oak Yd. SK1—4F 104
Royal Rd. SK12—7K 117
Royal St. OL16—8J 13
Royalthorn Av. M22—7D 102
Royalthorn Dri. M22—7C 102
Royalthorn Rd. M22—7C 102
Royce Av. WA15—8E 100
Royce Ind. Est. M17—8F 76
Royce Rd. M15—9D 78
Roydale St. M10—4L 79
Royden Av. M9—3K 61
Royden Av. WN3—6A 52
Roydes St. M24—7B 44
Roydon Av. M30—6F 86
Roydon Cres. WN5—2E 68
Roydon Rd. WN5—2E 68
Royds Clo. M13—1K 91
Royds Pl. OL16—5G 29
Royds St. BL8—3F 24
Royds St. OL15—6C 14
Royds St. OL16—5A 30
(Milnrow)
Royds St. OL16—5H 29
(Rochdale)
Royds St. S. BL8—3F 24
Royds St. W. OL16—5G 29
Royd St. OL8—4J 63
Roy Grainger Ct. M16—3E 90
Royland Av. BL3—6G 39
Royle Av. SK13—5K 97
Royle Barn Rd. OL11—8C 28
Royle Clo. SK2—8H 105
Royle Grn. Rd. M22—4E 102
Royle-Higginson Ct. M31—5C 88
Roylelands Bungalows. OL11—7C 28
Royle Pennine Trading Est. OL11—7D 28
Royle Rd. OL11—7C 28
Royles Cottages. M33—2H 101
Royle St. M6—6M 77
Royle St. M14—7K 91
Royle St. M28—6K 57
Royle St. M34—1M 93
Royle St. SK1—6F 104
Royley. OL2—6J 45
Royley Cres. OL2—6J 45
Royley Rd. OL8—4L 63
Royley Way. OL2—6J 45
Roynton Rd. BL6—4B 20
Royon Dri. SK3—6B 104
Royston Av. BL2—1H 39
Royston Av. M16—3D 90
Royston Av. M34—3G 93
Royston Clo. BL8—1F 24
Royston Clo. WA3—7L 71
Royston Rd. M16—3B 90
Royston Rd. M31—3E 88
Roy St. BL3—5B 38
Roy St. M35—8G 63
Roy St. OL2—5K 45
Royton Av. M33—3L 101
Royton Hall Wlk. OL2—5L 45
Royton Ho. OL2—4B 46
Rozel Sq. M3—5D 4 & 7E 78
Ruabon Cres. WN2—4M 53
Ruabon Rd. M20—3J 103
Ruby St. BL1—7F 22
Ruby St. BL9—8J 9
Ruby St. M34—4L 93
Ruby St. WN7—3E 72
Ruby St. Pas. OL11—4E 28
Rudcroft Clo. M13—6G 5 & 9H 79
Rudding St. OL2—7A 46
Ruddpark Rd. M22—3D 112
Rudd St. M10—9A 62
Rudford Av. M11—7E 80
Rudford Gdns. BL3—5F 38
Rudgwick Dri. BL8—3J 25
Rudheath Av. M20—7G 91
Rudkin St. M11—7A 80
Rudman Dri. M5—5B 4 & 7C 78
Rudman St. OL12—9E 12
Rudolph St. BL3—6F 38
Rudston Av. M10—6B 62
Rudyard Av. M24—6C 44
Rudyard Av. WN6—8L 17
Rudyard Gro. M33—3E 100
Rudyard Gro. OL11—8F 28
Rudyard Gro. SK4—8D 92
Rudyard Rd. M6—2J 77
Rudyard St. M7—1D 78
Ruebens Clo. SK6—5H 107
Rufford Av. OL11—6D 28
Rufford Av. SK14—4F 94
Rufford Clo. M25—7A 42
Rufford Clo. OL2—2M 45
Rufford Clo. OL6—9C 64
Rufford Dri. BL3—7D 38
Rufford Dri. M25—7L 41
Rufford Gro. BL3—7D 38
Rufford Pl. M18—2F 92
Rufford Pl. M29—3M 73
Rufford Rd. M16—3D 90
Rufford St. WN4—2M 69
Rufford Way. WA11—9E 68
Rufus St. M14—7L 91
Rugby Dri. M33—3G 101
Rugby Dri. WN5—9F 32
Rugby Rd. M6—4G 77
Rugby Rd. OL12—1G 29
Rugby Rd. WN7—4F 72
Rugby Rd. Ind. Est. OL12—1G 29
Rugby St. M7—1D 4 & 3E 78
Rugeley St. M6—2B 78
Ruins La. BL2—6L 23
Ruislip Clo. OL8—4B 64
Rumbles La. OL3—5M 47
Rumbold St. M18—9E 80
Rumbold St. OL11—5F 28
Rumford St. M13—9H 79
(in two parts)
Rumworth Rd. BL6—3J 37
Rumworth St. BL3—5D 38
Runcorn St. M15—6B 4 & 8C 78
Runger La. WA15—5M 111
Runhall Clo. M12—9A 80
Runimead Ct. OL2—5L 45
Running Hill Ga. OL3—8D 48
(in two parts)
Running Hill La. OL3—7D 48
Runnymeade. M27 & M6—1G 77
Runnymede Clo. SK3—6C 104
Runnymede Ct. BL3—4D 38
Runnymede Ct. SK3—7C 104
Runnymede Dri. WA11—9G 69
Runshaw Av. WN6—1E 32
Rupert St. BL3—5E 38
Rupert St. M10—3E 80
Rupert St. M26—8G 41
Rupert St. OL12—1C 28
Rupert St. SK5—7E 92
(in two parts)
Rupert St. WN1—1E 52
Rupert Ter. SK5—7E 92
Rush Acre Clo. M26—6E 40
Rushall Wlk. M23—2M 111
Rush Bank. OL2—1M 45
Rushbrooke Av. M11—4C 80
Rushcroft Ct. M9—6A 62
Rushcroft Rd. OL2—1M 45
Rushdene. WN3—4A 52
Rushden Rd. M19—4B 92
Rushen St. M11—6C 80
Rushes, The. SK14—2F 96
Rushey Av. M22—7C 102
Rushey Clo. WA15—5K 111
Rushey Field. BL7—2F 22
Rushey Fold La. BL1—8D 22
Rushey Rd. M22—8C 102
Rushfield Rd. SK8—5M 113
Rushford Av. M19—4A 92
Rushford Gro. BL1—6F 22
Rushford St. M12—2A 92
Rushgreen Rd. WA13—9A 98
Rush Hill. OL3—1B 66
Rush Hill Rd. OL3—1B 66
Rush Hill Ter. OL3—1B 66
Rushlake Dri. BL1—9E 22
Rushley Av. M7—1B 78
Rushmere. OL6—1E 82
Rushmere Av. M19—5B 92
Rushmere Dri. BL8—5J 25
Rushmere Wlk. M16—1D 90
Rushmoor Av. WN4—3E 70
Rushmoor Clo. M30—4G 87
Rush Mt. OL2—1M 45
Rusholme Gro. M14—3J 91
Rusholme Gro. W. M14—3J 91
Rusholme Pl. M14—2J 91
Rushside Rd. SK8—6M 113
Rush St. SK16—7F 82
Rushton Av. WN7—8D 54
Rushton Clo. SK6—8G 107
Rushton Dri. SK6—8F 106
(Marple)
Rushton Dri. SK6—2C 106
(Romiley)
Rushton Dri. SK7—1D 114
Rushton Gdns. SK7—1D 114
Rushton Gro. M11—8E 80
Rushton Gro. OL4—6E 46
Rushton Rd. BL1—9B 22
Rushton Rd. SK3—6B 104
Rushton Rd. SK8—6A 114
Rushton St. M20—3H 103
Rushton St. M28—6K 57
Rushwick Av. M10—1L 79
Rushworth Ct. SK4—9C 92
Rushworth St. M10—4K 79
Rushyfield Cres. SK6—2D 106
Rushy Hill View. OL12—1C 28
Ruskin Av. BL4—1M 57
Ruskin Av. M14—2H 91
Ruskin Av. M34—8J 81
(Audenshaw)
Ruskin Av. M34—5K 93
(Denton)
Ruskin Av. OL9—5F 62
Ruskin Av. WN3—5M 51
Ruskin Cres. M25—5M 59
Ruskin Cres. WN2—7H 53
Ruskin Gdns. SK6—2A 106
Ruskin Gro. SK6—2A 106
Ruskington Dri. M9—9K 61
Ruskin Rd. BL3—5B 40
Ruskin Rd. M16—3C 90
Ruskin Rd. M25—5L 59
Ruskin Rd. M35—5G 81
Ruskin Rd. OL11—8F 28
Ruskin Rd. SK5—5E 92
Ruskin St. M26—5J 41
Ruskin St. OL1—9K 45
Rusland Ct. M9—5A 62
Rusland Ct. M33—9G 89
Rusland Dri. BL2—8L 23
Rusland Wlk. M22—2C 112
Ruslip Av. M10—2L 79
Russeldene Rd. WN3—5L 51
Russell Av. M16—4D 90
Russell Av. M33—9K 89
Russell Av. SK6—5E 116
Russell Clo. BL1—1C 38
Russell Ct. BL4—9L 39
Russell Ct. M28—5J 57
Russell Dri. M30—4G 87
Russell Gdns. SK4—4B 104
Russell Ho. WN1—9D 34
(off School St.)
Russell Rd. M6—2H 77
Russell Rd. M16—3D 90
Russell Rd. M31—2G 99
Russell St. BL1—1D 38
Russell St. BL4—9L 39
Russell St. BL9—6M 25
Russell St. M8—1D 4 & 3E 78
Russell St. M16—3F 90
Russell St. M25—4B 60
Russell St. M28—5J 57
Russell St. M29—4H 55
Russell St. M30—5F 76
Russell St. M34—3M 93
Russell St. OL5—7J 65
Russell St. OL6—3D 82
Russell St. OL9—1H 63
Russell St. OL10—8L 27
Russell St. OL11—5E 28
(off Grove St.)
Russell St. SK2—7G 105
Russell St. SK6—2H 107
Russell St. SK14—3D 94
Russell St. SK16—7C 82
Russell St. WN1—9D 34
Russell St. WN2—6C 54
(Hindley)
Russell St. WN2—9G 35
(Ince)
Russet Rd. M9—7K 61
Rustons Wlk. M10—7E 62
Ruth Av. M10—7E 62
Ruthen La. M16—2B 90
Rutherford Av. M14—3H 91
Rutherford Dri. BL5—1M 55
Rutherglade Clo. M10—1J 79
Rutherglen Dri. BL3—3M 37
Rutherglen Wlk. M10—2L 79
Ruthin Av. M9—3J 61
Ruthin Av. M24—1A 62
Ruthin Av. SK8—2L 113
Ruthin Clo. M6—5A 78
Ruthin Clo. OL8—6H 63
Ruthin Ct. M6—5A 78
Ruth St. BL0—1K 9
Ruth St. BL1—1E 38
Ruth St. M18—3D 92
Ruth St. OL1—9M 45
Ruth St. OL12—2C 12
Rutland. OL11—4E 28
Rutland Av. M16—3A 90
Rutland Av. M20—8G 91
Rutland Av. M27—6F 58
Rutland Av. M29—3M 55
Rutland Av. M31—4E 88
Rutland Av. M34—4A 94
Rutland Av. WA3—8K 71
Rutland Clo. BL3—5B 40
Rutland Clo. OL6—5D 82
Rutland Clo. SK8—7H 103
Rutland Ct. M20—2H 103
Rutland Ct. SK2—8G 105
Rutland Cres. SK5—9K 93
Rutland Dri. BL9—1A 42
Rutland Dri. M7—7C 60
Rutland Dri. WN4—3C 70
Rutland Gro. BL1—9C 22
Rutland Gro. BL4—1J 57
Rutland La. M33—1M 101
(in two parts)
Rutland Rd. M28—7J 57
Rutland Rd. M29—6M 55
Rutland Rd. M30—9D 86
(Cadishead)
Rutland Rd. M30—3F 76
(Eccles)
Rutland Rd. M31—3E 98
Rutland Rd. M35—4E 80
Rutland Rd. SK7—4L 115
Rutland Rd. WA14—7D 100
Rutland Rd. WN2—2M 53
Rutland St. BL3—5D 38
Rutland St. M18—9E 80
Rutland St. M27—7E 58
Rutland St. M35—7H 81
(Droylsden)
Rutland St. M35—8F 62
(Failsworth)
Rutland St. OL6—5D 82
Rutland St. OL9—3J 63
Rutland St. OL10—7K 27
Rutland St. SK14—1D 94
Rutland St. WA10—9A 68
Rutland St. WN7—3L 73
Rutter's La. SK7—2J 115
Rutter St. BL4—2A 58
Ryall Av. M5—5A 6 & 7B 78
Ryall Av. S. M5—5A 4 & 7B 78
Ryan St. M11—8E 80
Ryburn Flats. OL10—8J 27
(off Meadow Clo.)
Ryburn Sq. OL11—4L 27
Rydal Av. M24—2M 61
Rydal Av. M30—3B 76
Rydal Av. M31—6A 88
Rydal Av. M33—9F 88
Rydal Av. M35—6E 80
Rydal Av. OL2—1J 45
Rydal Av. OL9—8E 44
Rydal Av. SK6—4E 116
Rydal Av. SK7—1J 115
Rydal Av. SK14—1C 94
Rydal Av. WN2—3L 53
Rydal Av. WN5—1F 50
Rydal Clo. BL6—7J 19
Rydal Clo. BL9—2L 41
Rydal Clo. M29—9A 56
Rydal Clo. M34—4H 93
Rydal Clo. SK8—1H 113
Rydal Clo. WN4—3C 70
Rydal Cres. M27—1F 76
Rydal Cres. M28—7L 57
Rydal Dri. WA15—4K 111
Rydal Gro. BL4—1F 56
Rydal Gro. M25—9A 42
Rydal Gro. OL7—3M 81
Rydal Gro. OL10—1K 43
Rydal Gro. WA11—8A 68
Rydal Mt. SK5—4F 92
Rydal Mt. SK9—8E 118
Rydal Pl. WN2—9H 35
Rydal Rd. BL1—9A 22
Rydal Rd. BL3—6A 40
Rydal Rd. M32—3K 89
Rydal Rd. OL4—1C 64
Rydal St. WN7—2E 72
Rydal Wlk. OL4—1D 64
Rydal Wlk. SK15—4G 83
Ryde Av. M34—6B 94
Ryde Av. SK4—3B 104
Ryder Av. WA14—6E 100
Ryder Brow. M18—2D 92
Ryderbrow Rd. M18—2D 92
Ryder Gro. WN7—5J 73
Ryder St. BL1—8C 22
Ryder St. M10—1H 5 & 3J 79
Ryder St. M26—6K 41
Ryder St. OL10—8K 27
Ryde St. BL3—5A 38
Ryde St. WN5—2L 51
Rydings La. OL12—5G 13
Rydings Rd. OL12—7H 13
Rydley St. BL2—3H 39
Ryebank Gro. OL6—2D 82
Ryebank M. M21—5M 89
Rye Bank Rd. M16—4A 90
Ryebank Rd. M21—5M 89
Ryeburn Av. M22—1D 112
Ryeburne St. OL4—1C 64
Ryeburn Wlk. M31—2M 87
Rye Croft. M25—1J 59
Ryecroft. WA3—6L 71
Ryecroft Av. BL8—4F 24
Ryecroft Av. M6—4J 77
Ryecroft Av. OL10—8L 27
Ryecroft Clo. OL9—5F 62
Ryecroft Dri. BL5—5D 36
Ryecroft Gro. M23—6A 102
Ryecroft La. M28—3M 75
Ryecroft La. M34—8L 81
Ryecroft Rd. M32—5J 89
Ryecroft St. OL7—6M 81
Ryecroft View. M34—7J 81
Ryedale Av. M10—2K 79
Ryedale Clo. SK4—2B 104
Ryefield. M6—1K 77
Ryefield. OL7—6M 81
Ryefield Clo. WA15—8J 101
Ryefield Rd. M33—3C 100
Ryefields. OL12—7K 13
Ryefields Dri. OL3—8B 48
Ryefield St. BL1—9G 23
Rye Hill. BL5—9F 36
Ryelands. BL5—9F 36
Ryelands Clo. OL16—6H 29
Ryelands Ct. BL5—9F 36
(off Ryelands)
Rye St. OL10—7L 27
Rye Wlk. M13—1J 91
Rye Wlk. OL9—2G 63
Rygate Wlk. M8—1F 78
Ryhope Wlk. M7—2E 78
Rylance St. M11—6L 79
Ryland Clo. SK5—5F 92
Rylands Ct. M15—9D 78
Rylands St. WN6—7A 34
Rylane Wlk. M10—2K 79
(off Ridgewood Av.)
Rylatt Ct. M33—9G 89
Ryley Av. BL3—4B 38
Ryleys La. SK9—8K 119
Ryley St. BL3—3C 38
Rylstone Av. M21—2D 102
Ryther Gro. M9—3H 61
Ryton Av. M18—3C 92
Ryton Clo. WN3—2B 52
Sabden Clo. BL9—3M 25
Sabden Clo. M10—4L 79
Sabden Clo. OL10—8G 27
Sabden Rd. BL1—8L 21
Sabrina St. M8—2E 78
Sack St. SK14—1D 94
Sackville Clo. OL2—9A 30
Sackville St. BL2—2J 39
Sackville St. BL9—7A 26
Sackville St. M1—5F 5 & 7G 79
(in three parts)
Sackville St. M3—3D 4 & 5E 78
Sackville St. OL6—4B 82
Sackville St. OL11—9C 28
Saddleback Clo. M28—1H 75
Saddleback Cres. WN5—2H 51
Saddleback Rd. WN5—1H 51
Saddlecote. M28—3A 76
Saddle Ct. WN5—2M 51
Saddle Gro. M35—4K 81
Saddle St. BL2—8H 23
Saddlewood Av. M19—3K 103
Sadie Av. M32—2G 89
Sadler Clo. M14—3G 91
Sadler St. BL3—5G 39
Sadler St. M24—8M 43
Saffron Dri. OL4—7D 46
Saffron Wlk. M22—3D 112
Saffron Wlk. M31—3F 98
Sagars Rd. SK9—8H 113
Sagar St. M8—1E 5 & 3F 78
Sahal Ct. M7—1C 4 & 3D 78
St Agnes Rd. M13—4M 91
St Agnes St. SK5—3F 92
St Aidans Clo. M26—8G 41
St Aidan's Clo. OL11—5C 28
St Aidan's Clo. WN5—1F 68
St Aidan's Gro. M7—1B 78
St Albans Av. M10—2B 80
St Albans Av. OL6—9B 64
St Alban's Av. SK4—9C 92
St Albans Clo. WA11—8M 69
St Alban's Cres. WA14—5C 100
St Albans Ho. OL16—4E 28
(off St Albans St.)
St Albans St. OL16—4E 28
St Alban's Ter. M8—2E 78
St Alban's Ter. OL11—4E 28
St Aldates. SK6—3M 105
St Aldwyn's Rd. M20—9H 91
St Ambrose Gdns. M6—5M 77
St Ambrose Rd. M29—2A 74
St Ambrose Rd. OL1—8C 46
St Andrews Av. M30—6E 76
St Andrew's Av. M35—6E 80
St Andrew's Av. WA15—6E 100
St Andrews Clo. BL0—6J 9
St Andrews Clo. M33—4C 100
St Andrews Clo. SK4—1B 104
St Andrew's Clo. SK6—4B 106
St Andrew's Ct. BL1—2F 38
(off Chancery La.)
St Andrews Ct. WA15—1F 110
St Andrew's Cres. WN2—3K 53
St Andrew's Dri. OL10—1K 43
St Andrew's Dri. WN6—7M 33
St Andrews Dri. WN7—2J 73
St Andrews Gro. WA11—9B 68
St Andrews Rd. BL6—2G 37
St Andrew's Rd. M26—3F 40
St Andrews Rd. M32—4H 89
St Andrews Rd. SK4—1B 104
St Andrew's Rd. SK8—3J 113
St Andrew's Sq. M1—7J 79
St Andrew's St. M1—5H 5 & 7J 79
St Andrew's St. M26—3F 40
St Andrews View. M26—3F 40
St Anne's Av. M6—4L 77
St Anne's Av. M29—7L 55
St Anne's Av. OL2—6L 45
St Annes Ct. M6—3M 77
St Annes Ct. M33—1J 101
St Annes Ct. WN6—4F 32
St Anne's Cres. OL4—3J 65
St Anne's Dri. M34—2A 94
St Anne's Dri. WN6—4G 33
St Annes Gdns. OL10—8M 27
St Annes Rd. BL6—6C 20
St Annes Rd. M21—7B 90
St Anne's Rd. M34—1M 93
(Denton)
St Annes Sq. OL3—5M 47
St Annes's Rd. M34—9M 81
(Audenshaw)
St Anne's St. BL9—6M 25
St Anne's St. M10—2M 79
St Anne St. M12—9A 80
(off Hyde Rd.)
St Ann's All. M2—6F 78
(off St Ann's Pl.)
St Ann's Arc. M2—6F 78
(off St Ann's Sq.)
St Ann's Chyd. M2—6F 78
(off St Ann St.)
St Anns Clo. M25—5A 60
St Ann's Pl. M2—4E 5 & 6F 78
St Ann's Rd. OL16—2J 29
St Anns Rd. SK7—3J 115
St Ann's Rd. N. SK8—3J 113
St Ann's Rd. S. SK8—4J 113
St Ann's Sq. M2—4E 2 & 6F 78
St Ann's Sq. SK8—4J 113
St Ann's St. M27—8E 58
St Ann's St. M33—2M 101
St Ann St. BL1—9E 22
St Ann St. M2—4E 5 & 6F 78
St Asaph's Dri. M8—8F 60
St Asaph's Dri. OL6—1B 82
St Aubin's Rd. BL2—3H 39
St Aubyn's Rd. WN1—5C 34
St Augustine's Rd. SK3—5B 104
St Augustine St. BL1—8D 22
St Augustine St. M10—2L 79
St Austell Av. M29—8C 56
St Austell Dri. BL8—9F 8
St Austell Dri. SK8—4H 113
St Austell Rd. M16—5E 90
St Austells Dri. M25—3B 60
St Austell's Dri. M27—9J 59
St Barnabas Pl. OL15—5A 14
St Barnabas Sq. M11—7B 80
St Bartholomew's Dri. M5—5B 4 & 7C 78
St Bartholomew St. BL3—5G 39
St Bedes Av. BL3—7B 38
St Bees Clo. M14—2G 91
St Bees Clo. SK8—1H 113
St Bees Rd. BL2—8J 23
St Bees Wlk. M24—7L 43
St Bernards Clo. M6—2C 78
St Bernards St. M6—2C 78
St Boniface Rd. M7—1B 4 & 2C 78
St Brannock's Rd. M21—5C 90
St Brannocks Rd. SK8—5B 114
St Brelades Dri. M8—8F 60
St Brendan's Rd. M20—7H 91
St Brendian's Rd. N. M20—7H 91
St Bride St. M16—1D 90
St Brides Way. M16—1D 90
St Catherine's Rd. M20—7H 91
St Chads Av. SK6—3C 106
St Chad's Clo. OL16—3F 28
St Chads Cres. OL3—9C 48
St Chads Cres. OL8—7K 63
St Chads Gro. SK6—3C 106
St Chads Rd. M20—7K 91
St Chads St. M8—1F 5 & 3G 79
St Charles Clo. SK14—1F 96
St Christopher's Av. OL6—1E 82
St Christopher's Dri. SK6—3A 106
St Christopher's Rd. OL6—1D 82
St Clair Rd. BL8—8F 8
St Clement's Ct. M25—4C 60
St Clements Ct. M30—3H 87
St Clements Ct. OL8—3M 63
St Clements Ct. WN3—3A 52
(off Worsley Mesnes Dri.)
St Clement's Dri. M5—6A 4 & 8B 78
St Clement's Rd. M21—6A 90
St Clement's Rd. WN1—5C 34
St Clement's St. WN3—4F 52
St Davids Av. SK6—3B 106
St David's Clo. OL6—9D 64
St David's Cres. WN2—4H 35
St Davids Rd. SK7—3J 115
St David's Rd. SK8—8M 103
St David's Wlk. M32—4G 89
St Domingo St. OL9—1L 63
St Dominic's M. BL3—6C 38
St Dominics Way. M24—1A 62
St Dunstan Wlk. M10—1A 80
(off Rollswood Dri.)
St Edmund's Rd. M10—1L 79
St Edmund St. BL1—2E 38
St Edmund's Wlk. M28—4H 57
St Elizabeth's Rd. WN2—3H 35
St Elizabeth's Way. SK5—6E 92
St Elmo Av. SK2—6K 105
St Elmo Pk. SK12—8C 116
St Ethelbert's Av. BL3—4B 38
St Gabriel Clo. WN8—6C 32
St Gabriels Clo. OL11—9D 28
St Gabriel's Ct. OL11—8C 28
(off Atkinson St.)
St Georges Av. BL5—2E 54
St George's Av. M15—6C 4 & 8D 78
St George's Av. WA15—6G 101
St Georges Cen. M6—1A 4 & 3B 78
St George's Ct. BL1—1E 38
St Georges Ct. BL9—5C 42
St Georges Ct. M30—6F 76
St George's Ct. M32—5J 89
St George's Ct. WA14—6B 100
St George's Cres. M6—4G 77
St George's Cres. M28—6K 57
St George's Cres. WA15—5G 101
St George's Dri. M10—9B 62
St Georges Dri. SK14—5D 94
St George's Gdns. M34—5A 94
St Georges Pl. M6—2A 78
St George's Pl. M29—4H 55
St George's Rd. BL1—1E 38
St George's Rd. BL9—5C 42
St George's Rd. M14—7L 91
St George's Rd. M31—8K 87
St Georges Rd. M32—4J 89
St George's Rd. M35—4F 80
St George's Rd. OL11—2M 27
St Georges Sq. BL1—1E 38
(off All Saints St.)
St George's Sq. OL9—5E 62
St George's St. BL1—1F 38
St George's St. M29—8M 55
St George's St. SK15—4F 82
St George St. M4—2H 5 & 4J 79
St Georges Way. M6—2A 78
(in two parts)
St Germain St. BL4—9J 39
St Giles Dri. SK14—4F 94
St Helena Rd. BL1—2E 38
(in two parts)
St Helens Clo. WA3—2B 98
St Helens Rd. BL3—8A 38
St Helens Rd. WN7—7C 72
St Helier's Dri. M8—8F 60
St Helier St. BL3—5D 38
St Herberts Ct. OL9—1H 63
St Hilda's Clo. M22—4E 102
St Hilda's Dri. OL1—9K 45
St Hilda's Rd. M16—1C 90
St Hilda's Rd. M22—4D 102
St Hilda's Rd. M34—9M 81
St Hilda's View. M34—1L 93
St Hughe's Clo. WA14—5E 100
St Ignatius Wlk. M5—5A 4 & 7B 78
St Ives Av. SK8—7M 103
St Ives Cres. M33—4G 101
St Ives Rd. M14—4H 91
St James Av. BL8—6H 25
St James Clo. M6—4H 77
St James Clo. OL16—1J 45
St James Clo. SK13—6J 97
St James Ct. M20—5H 103
St James Ct. OL4—9C 46
St James Cres. WN2—8M 53
St James Dri. SK9—5G 119
St James Gro. OL10—8J 27
St James Gro. WN3—2B 52
St James Ho. SK4—2D 104
St James Rd. SK4—9B 92
St James Rd. WN5—4D 50
St James's Av. BL2—1L 39
St James's Gro. WA14—4F 100
St James's Rd. M7—1E 78
St James's Sq. M2—4E 5 & 6F 78
St James St. BL4—1H 57
St James St. BL5—3F 54
St James St. M1—5F 5 & 7G 79
St James St. M5—9A 78
St James St. M30—5E 76
St James St. OL1—1B 64
St James St. OL2—2B 46
St James St. OL6—5D 82
St James St. OL10—8J 27
St James St. OL16—4M 29
St James Ter. OL10—8J 27
St James Way. SK8—6M 113
St John's Av. BL5—6D 36
St Johns Av. M35—5H 81
St Johns Clo. SK6—3B 106
St Johns Clo. SK16—7E 82
St John's Ct. M7—1C 78
St John's Ct. M26—7H 41
St Johns Ct. OL4—1F 64
St John's Ct. OL16—4H 29
St John's Ct. WA14—1D 110
St John's Dri. OL16—4H 29
St Johns Dri. SK14—3F 94
St John's Gdns. OL5—6K 65
St John's Ind. Est. OL4—2E 64
St John's Pas. M3—4D 4 & 6E 78
St John's Pl. SK4—3L 103
St John's Rd. BL6—6H 37
St John's Rd. M13—2M 91
St John's Rd. M16—2C 90
St John's Rd. M28—9E 56
St John's Rd. M34—1M 93
St John's Rd. SK4—3L 103
St Johns Rd. SK7—3H 115
St John's Rd. SK9—8E 118
St John's Rd. WA14—1C 110
St John's Rd. WN2—4H 35
St John's St. BL4—9L 39
St John's St. M7—9D 60
St John's St. M26—7H 41
St John's St. OL9—3J 63
St John's St. WN2—8H 53
St John St. BL6—7B 20
St John St. M3—5D 4 & 7E 78
St John St. M27—1K 77
St John St. M28—4J 57
St John St. M29—5K 55
St John St. M30—6D 76
(Eccles)
St John St. M30—4G 87
(Irlam)
St John St. M35—7F 80
St John St. OL4—2E 64
St John St. SK16—7E 82
(in two parts)
St John's Wlk. OL9—2J 63
St Johns Wlk. SK3—5B 104
(off Oak St.)
St Johns Wood. SK15—7E 82
St Joseph's Av. M25—1C 60
St Joseph's Dri. M5—5A 4 & 7B 78
St Joseph St. BL1—8D 22
St Katherine's Dri. BL6—7J 19
St Kilda Av. BL4—2M 57
St Kilda's Av. M35—4F 80
St Kilda's Dri. M8—8F 60
St Lawrence Ct. M34—4M 93
St Lawrence Rd. M34—3M 93
St Leonard's Av. BL6—9F 20
St Leonard's Ct. M33—1F 100
St Leonards Dri. WA15—7F 100
St Leonards Rd. SK4—9D 92
St Leonards St. M24—8A 44
St Leonard St. M13—9J 79
St Lesmo Ct. SK3—6C 104
St Lesmo Rd. SK3—5B 104
St Luke's Av. WA3—7K 71
St Lukes Ct. BL1—1C 38
St Lukes Ct. OL11—5F 28
St Lukes Cres. SK16—7C 82
St Luke's Dri. WN5—4D 50
St Luke's Rd. M6—5K 77
St Lukes St. OL11—5F 28
St Lukes Wlk. M10—1A 80
St Magaret's Rd. M25—2C 60
St Malo Rd. WN1—5C 34
St Margaret's Av. M19—8M 91
St Margarets Clo. BL1—1B 38
St Margarets Clo. WA14—9C 100
St Margaret's Rd. BL1—1B 38
St Margaret's Rd. M10—5D 62
St Margaret's Rd. SK8—7A 104
St Margaret's Rd. WA14—1C 110
St Marks Av. OL2—5A 46
St Mark's Av. WA14—8A 100
St Mark's Av. WN5—1M 51
St Marks Clo. OL2—5A 46
St Mark's Ct. OL9—9H 45
St Mark's La. M8—9F 60
St Marks Sq. BL9—6M 25
St Mark's St. BL3—4F 38
St Mark's St. M19—4C 92
St Mark's St. SK6—1A 106
St Mark's St. WA11—9G 69
St Mark St. SK16—6B 82
St Mark's View. BL3—4F 38
St Mark's Wlk. BL3—5E 38
St Martin's Av. SK4—3C 104
St Martin's Clo. M35—4F 80
St Martin's Clo. SK14—4F 94
St Martin's Dri. M8—8F 60
St Martins Rd. M33—8D 88
St Martin's Rd. OL8—6A 64
St Martin's Rd. SK6—7G 107
St Martins St. OL11—9D 28
St Marys'. SK1—4G 105
St Mary's Av. BL3—4B 38
St Mary's Av. M34—6A 94
St Mary's Av. WN5—3C 68
St Mary's Clo. M29—6L 55
St Mary's Clo. SK1—4G 105
St Mary's Clo. WN2—4H 35
St Mary's Ct. M8—7F 60
St Mary's Ct. M10—8B 62
St Marys Ct. WN7—6C 72
St Mary's Crest. OL3—3C 66
St Mary's Dri. OL3—3C 66
St Mary's Dri. SK5—8F 92
St Mary's Dri. SK8—7M 103
St Mary's Ga. M1—3E 5 & 5F 78
St Marys Ga. OL2—2B 46
St Mary's Ga. OL3—9B 48
St Mary's Ga. OL16—3E 28
St Marys Ga. SK1—4F 104
St Mary's Hall Rd. M8—7F 60
St Mary's Parsonage. M3—4D 4 & 6E 78
St Mary's Pl. BL9—8L 25
St Mary's Rd. M10—9B 62
St Mary's Rd. M25—4A 60
St Mary's Rd. M28—3J 57
St Marys Rd. M30—5F 76
St Mary's Rd. M33—9F 88
St Mary's Rd. SK12—7K 117
St Mary's Rd. SK13—6J 97
St Mary's Rd. SK14—1E 94
St Mary's Rd. WA14—2B 110
(in two parts)
St Mary's Rd. WN2—3H 35
St Mary's St. M3—4E 5 & 6F 78
(Manchester)
St Mary's St. M15—1E 90
St Mary's St. M27—8G 59
St Mary's St. OL1—9M 45
St Mary St. M3—3C 4 & 5D 78
(Salford)
St Mary's Way. OL1—1L 63
St Marys Way. SK1—3G 105
St Mary's Way. WN7—2F 72
St Matthew's Clo. WN3—4J 51
St Matthews Ct. M32—5J 89
St Matthews Dri. OL1—7G 45
St Matthew's Rd. SK3—5D 104
St Matthews Ter. BL1—9E 22
(off St Matthews Wlk.)
St Matthew's Ter. SK3—5D 104
St Matthews Wlk. BL1—9E 22
(in two parts)
St Michael's Av. BL3—7H 39
St Michael's Av. M29—7G 55
St Michael's Av. SK7—5E 114
St Michael's Clo. BL8—1G 41
St Michael's Ct. M30—7A 76
St Michaels Ct. M33—8E 88
St Michaels Rd. SK14—4F 94
St Michael's Sq. M4—2F 5 & 4G 79
St Michael's Sq. OL6—4C 82
St Modwin Rd. M32—1F 88
St Nicholas Rd. WA3—6A 72
St Osmund's Dri. BL2—2L 39
St Osmund's Gro. BL2—2L 39
St Oswalds Rd. M19—4B 92
St Oswald's Rd. WN4—5A 70
St Patrick St. WN1—9D 34
St Patricks Way. WN1—9D 34
St Paul's Av. WN3—4M 51
St Pauls Clo. M26—8G 41
St Paul's Clo. PR6—2G 19
St Paul's Clo. SK15—4J 83
St Paul's Ct. M7—7C 60
St Paul's Ct. M28—6K 57
St Pauls Ct. OL8—4M 63
St Paul's Hill Rd. SK14—4F 94
St Paul's Pl. BL1—7C 22
St Paul's Rd. M7—7C 60
St Paul's Rd. M20—8J 91
St Paul's Rd. M28—6L 57
St Paul's Rd. SK4—1B 104
St Paul's St. BL9—7A 26
St Paul's St. SK1—2G 105
St Pauls St. SK14—3E 94
St Paul's St. SK15—5J 83
St Paul's Vs. BL9—7A 26
St Peter Quay. M5—8A 78
St Peter's Av. BL1—8A 22
St Peter's Clo. WA13—9A 98
St Peter's Dri. SK14—4F 94
St Petersgate. SK1—4E 104
St Peter's Rd. BL9—2L 41
St Peter's Rd. M27—9E 58
St Peter's Sq. M2—5E 5 & 7F 78
St Peter's Sq. SK1—4E 104
St Peters St. OL6—5A 82
St Peter's St. OL16—4H 29
St Peter's Ter. BL4—1K 57
St Peter's Way. BL1, BL2 & BL3—9F 22
St Philip's Av. BL3—5D 38
St Philip's Pl. M3—3C 4 & 5D 78
St Phillip's Dri. OL2—8L 45
St Quen Precinct. M28—5K 57
St Saviour's Rd. SK2—8J 105
Saintsbridge Rd. M22—2C 112
St Simons Clo. SK2—5J 105
St Simon St. M3—2C 4 & 4D 78
St Stephen's Av. M34—7L 81
St Stephen's Av. WN1—7E 34
St Stephens Clo. BL2—4J 39
St Stephens Clo. M29—2A 74
St Stephens Gdns. BL4—2A 58
St Stephen's Gdns. M24—7A 44
St Stephens Rd. WN6—9J 17
St Stephen's St. BL4—2A 58
St Stephen St. M3—3C 4 & 5D 78
St Stephen St. OL1—9A 46
St Stephen's Way. WN3—3L 51
St Teresa's Rd. M16—3A 90
St Thomas Circ. OL8—3K 63
St Thomas Ct. BL9—8A 26
St Thomas's Pl. M8—1F 5 & 3G 79
St Thomas's Pl. SK1—5F 104
St Thomas St. BL1—8D 22
St Thomas St. WN1—1C 52
St Thomas St. N. OL8—3K 63
St Thomas St. S. OL8—3K 63
St Vincent St. M4—3H 5 & 5J 79
St Vincent St. WA15—9E 100
St Westburgh's Rd. M21—5C 90
St Wilfrid's Pl. WN6—9L 17
St Wilfrid's Rd. WN6—9M 17
St William's Av. BL3—6E 38
St Winifred's Pl. SK15—5F 82
Salcombe Av. BL2—9D 24
Salcombe Clo. M33—9E 88
Salcombe Clo. WN1—7E 34
Salcombe Gro. BL2—3A 40
Salcombe Rd. M11—7D 80
Salcombe Rd. SK2—5J 105
Salcot Wlk. M10—2H 5 & 4J 79
Sale Eastern & Northenden By-Pass. M33, M23 & M22—7J 89

Sale Heys Rd. M33—2F 100
Sale La. M29—8D 56
Salem Gro. OL4—2D 64
Sale Rd. M23—3A 102
Salesbury Way. WN3—5A 52
Sales's La. BL9—9B 10
Sale St. OL15—5B 14
Salford App. M3—3E 5 & 5F 78
Salford Rd. BL5—9A 38
Salford Rd. M28—1C 56
Salford St. BL9—6A 26
Salford St. OL4—3C 64
Salisbury Av. OL10—1J 43
Salisbury Av. WN2—2M 53
Salisbury Cotts. SK14—1G 97
Salisbury Cres. OL6—9D 64
Salisbury Dri. M25—6C 60
Salisbury Dri. SK16—8G 83
Salisbury Rd. BL6—9F 20
Salisbury Rd. M21—5B 90
Salisbury Rd. M25—9M 41
Salisbury Rd. M26—4E 40
Salisbury Rd. M27—9E 58
Salisbury Rd. M30—3F 76
Salisbury Rd. M31—2D 88
Salisbury Rd. OL4—2B 64
Salisbury Rd. WA11—7L 69
Salisbury Rd. WA14—6D 100
Salisbury Rd. WN4—2A 70
Salisbury St. BL3—3D 38
Salisbury St. M14—2G 91
Salisbury St. M24—8B 44
Salisbury St. OL2—1M 45
Salisbury St. SK5—6F 92
Salisbury St. SK14—1G 97
Salisbury St. WA3—7G 71
Salisbury Ter. BL3—6B 40
Salisbury Way. M29—8B 56
Salix Ct. M6—4A 78
Salkeld Av. WN4—4M 69
Salkeld St. OL11—5F 28
Salley St. OL15—1C 14
Sallowfields. WN5—3D 50
Salmesbury Clo. BL0—7H 9
Salmon Fields. OL2—6M 45
Salmon St. M4—3F 5 & 5G 79
Salmon St. WN1—8E 34
Salop St. BL2—3G 39
Salop St. M6—3A 78
Saltash Clo. M22—3D 112
Saltburn Wlk. M9—8L 61
(off Naunton Wlk.)
Saltdene Rd. M22—3C 112
Saltergate M. M5—5A 78
Saltersbrook Gro. SK9—2L 119
Saltersgate Clo. BL3—5L 37
Salter Sq. M15—9F 78
Salterton Wlk. M10—9A 62
Salteye Rd. M30—6A 76
Saltford Av. M4—3H 5 & 5J 79
Saltford Ct. M4—5K 79
Salthill Av. OL10—2L 43
Salthill Dri. M22—2E 112
Salthouse Clo. BL8—4J 25
Saltire Gdns. M7—8E 60
Saltney Av. M20—7F 90
Salt Pit La. L40—1A 16
Saltram Clo. M26—4C 40
Saltram Rd. WN3—4J 51
Saltrush Rd. M22—2D 112
Salts Dri. OL15—5A 14
Salts St. OL2—2A 46
Saltwood Gro. BL1—9F 22
Salvin Wlk. M9—5L 61
Sam Cowan Clo. M14—3G 91
Sam Fritton Way. OL1—1M 63
Samian Gdns. M7—2C 78
Samlesbury Clo. OL2—2M 45
Sammy Cookson Clo. M14
(in two parts) —3G 91
Samouth Clo. M10—4K 79
Sampson Sq. M14—2G 91
Sam Reid Wlk. M16—2E 90
Sam Rd. OL3—4C 48
Samson St. OL16—2J 29
Samuel La. OL2—1L 45
Samuel Ogden St. M1—5F 5 & 7G 79
Samuel St. BL3—5A 40
Samuel St. BL9—7A 26
Samuel St. M19—6B 92
Samuel St. M24—7A 44
Samuel St. M29—7M 55
(in two parts)
Samuel St. M35—8F 62
Samuel St. OL10—8J 27
Samuel St. OL11—8C 28
Samuel St. SK4—2D 104
Samuel St. SK14—2C 96
Samwoods Ho. WN4—2A 70
Sanby Av. M18—2C 92
Sanby Dri. SK6—5H 107
Sanby Rd. M18—2C 92
Sandacre Rd. M23—6B 102
Sandal Ct. M10—4L 79
Sandal St. M10—4L 79
Sandalwood Dri. WN6—6M 33
Sandbach Av. M14—6F 90
Sandbach Rd. M33—2M 101
Sandbach Rd. SK5—4E 92
Sandbach Wlk. SK8—9A 104
Sandbank Gdns. OL12—1C 12
Sand Banks. BL1—4F 22
Sandbed La. OL3—4A 48
Sandbed La. OL5—6J 65
Sandbrook Gdns. WN5—3D 50
Sandbrook Rd. WN5—3C 50
Sandbrook Way. M34—1M 93
Sanderling Clo. BL5—2D 54
Sanderling Rd. SK2—8A 106
Sanderson Av. M10—2L 79
Sanderson Clo. M28—9A 58
Sanderson Ct. M10—2L 79
Sanderson La. PR7—1A 16
Sanderson's Croft. WN7—3J 73
Sanderson St. BL9—7A 26
Sanderson St. M10—2L 79
Sanderson St. WN7—2E 72
Sanderstead Dri. M9—5L 61
Sandfield Clo. WA3—7M 71
Sandfield Cres. WA3—8J 73
Sandfield Dri. BL6—3J 37
Sandfield Rd. OL16—5H 29
Sandfold. SK5—4E 92
Sandfold La. M19—4C 92
Sandfold La. SK5—4D 92
(in two parts)
Sandford Av. M18—9D 80
Sandford Clo. BL2—6L 23
Sandford Rd. M33—2M 101
Sandford Rd. WN5—3C 50
Sandford St. M3—2D 4 & 4E 78
Sandford St. M26—5K 41
Sandgate Av. M11—5D 80
Sandgate Clo. WN7—1F 72
Sandgate Dri. M31—2C 88
Sandgate Rd. M25—1B 60
Sandgate Rd. OL9—2H 63
Sandham St. BL3—5F 38
Sandham Wlk. BL3—5F 38
Sandheys. M34—1M 93
Sandheys Gro. M18—2E 92
Sandhill Clo. BL3—5F 38
Sandhill La. SK6—3L 107
Sandhill St. SK14—2F 94
Sandhill Wlk. M22—2B 112
Sand Hole La. OL11—5L 27
(Kenyon Fold)
Sand Hole La. OL11—9F 28
(Kirkholt)
Sand Hole Rd. BL4—2A 58
Sandhurst Av. M20—8G 91
Sandhurst Ct. BL2—3L 39
Sandhurst Dri. BL2—3L 39
Sandhurst Rd. BL8—7H 25
Sandhurst Rd. M20—3H 103
(in two parts)
Sandhurst Rd. SK2—8H 105
Sandhurst St. OL8—4C 64
Sandhutton St. M9—7K 61
Sandiacre. WN6—1L 33
Sandilands Rd. M23—5K 101
Sandileigh Av. M20—9H 91
Sandileigh Av. SK5—1H 105
Sandileigh Av. SK8—7A 104
Sandileigh Av. WA15—1F 110
Sandileigh Dri. WA15—1F 110
Sandiway. M5—8C 78
(off Ordsall Dri.)
Sandiway. M30—4G 87
Sandiway. OL10—8L 27
Sandiway. SK6—2M 105
Sandiway. SK7—2E 114
Sandiway. SK13—7M 97
Sandiway Clo. SK6—5F 106
Sandiway Dri. M20—2G 103
Sandiway Pl. WA14—8D 100
Sandiway Rd. M33—1F 100
Sandiway Rd. SK9—7K 113
Sandiway Rd. WA14—7D 100
Sandmere Wlk. M9—5L 61
Sandon St. BL3—5D 38
Sandown Av. M6—5L 77
Sandown Clo. OL1—8A 46
Sandown Clo. SK9—3K 119
Sandown Cres. BL3—7A 40
Sandown Cres. M18—3D 92
Sandown Dri. M33—2E 100
Sandown Dri. M34—6B 94
Sandown Dri. WA15—6K 111
Sandown Gdns. M31—4A 88
Sandown Rd. BL2—7L 23
Sandown Rd. BL9—6A 42
Sandown Rd. SK3—5B 104
Sandown Rd. SK7—2M 115
Sandown Rd. WN6—6L 33
Sandown St. M18—9E 80
Sandpiper Clo. OL11—3M 27
Sandpiper Clo. SK16—8E 82
Sandpiper Rd. WN3—4H 51
Sandpits. OL10—1M 43
Sandray Clo. BL3—4M 37
Sandray Gro. M5—6L 77
Sandridge. OL11—6E 28
Sandridge Wlk. M12—9L 79
Sandringham Av. M34—9K 81
(Audenshaw)
Sandringham Av. M34—3G 93
(Denton)
Sandringham Av. SK15—4G 83
Sandringham Clo. WN5—3L 51
Sandringham Ct. M9—3G 61
(off Deanswood Dri.)
Sandringham Ct. M33—5J 101
Sandringham Ct. SK9—5G 119
Sandringham Dri. BL8—1G 25
Sandringham Dri. OL16—4A 30
Sandringham Dri. SK4—4A 104
Sandringham Dri. SK12 —9K 115
Sandringham Dri. SK16—8F 82
Sandringham Dri. WN7—9L 55
Sandringham Grange. M25 —5E 60
Sandringham Rd. BL6—8D 20
Sandringham Rd. M28—1G 75
Sandringham Rd. SK6—2J 105
Sandringham Rd. SK7—2M 115
Sandringham Rd. SK8—1A 114
Sandringham Rd. SK14—7E 94
Sandringham Rd. WN2—4L 53
Sandringham St. M18—2C 92
Sandringham Way. OL2—3J 45
Sandringham Way. SK9 —5G 119
Sands Av. OL9—8D 44
Sands Clo. SK14—5K 95
Sandsend Clo. M8—2E 78
Sandsend Rd. M31—3C 88
Sandstone Rd. OL16—3M 29
Sandstone Rd. WN3—6K 51
Sandstone Way. M21—7D 90
Sand St. M10—1H 5 & 3J 79
Sand St. SK15—7F 82
Sands Wlk. SK14—5K 95
Sandway. WN6—7M 33
Sandwich Cres. BL3—4D 38
Sandwich Rd. M30—4F 76
Sandwich St. M28—6K 57
Sandwith Clo. WN3—6B 52
Sandwood Av. BL3—3L 37
Sandyacre Clo. BL5—2A 56
Sandy Bank. OL2—1M 45
Sandy Bank Av. SK14—5K 95
Sandybank Clo. SK14—2E 96
Sandy Bank Ct. SK14—5K 95
Sandy Bank Rd. BL7—6K 7
Sandy Bank Rd. M8—8F 60
Sandy Bank Wlk. SK14—5K 95
Sandybrook Clo. BL8—4F 24
Sandy Brow. M9—6K 61
Sandy Clo. BL9—5M 41
Sandycroft Av. WN1—7C 34
Sandy Ga. Clo. M27—9E 58
Sandy Gro. M6—3L 77
Sandy Gro. M27—8F 58
Sandy Gro. SK16—6D 82
Sandy Haven Clo. SK14—5K 95
Sandy Haven Wlk. SK14—5K 95
Sandyhill Ct. M9—5G 61
Sandyhill Rd. M9—5G 61
Sandylands Dri. M25—7A 60
Sandy La. M6—4L 77
Sandy La. M21—6B 90
Sandy La. M23—6K 101
Sandy La. M24—9C 44
Sandy La. M25—5M 59
Sandy La. M29—6B 74
(Astley Green)
Sandy La. M29—3A 74
(Astley)
Sandy La. M30—3G 87
Sandy La. M32—5H 89
Sandy La. M35—4J 81
Sandy La. OL2—5K 45
Sandy La. OL3—7A 48
Sandy La. OL11—3C 28
Sandy La. PR7—3D 18
Sandy La. SK5—2E 104
Sandy La. SK6—3C 106
Sandy La. SK9—3D 118
Sandy La. SK14—9M 95
Sandy La. SK16—7D 82
Sandy La. WA3—7E 70
(Golborne)
Sandy La. WA3—5A 72
(Lowton)
Sandy La. WA11—6A 68
Sandy La. WA13—8B 98
Sandy La. WN2—2M 53
Sandy La. WN5—4D 50
Sandy Meade. M25—5M 59
Sandy Pk. WN2—2A 54
Sandys Av. OL8—5K 63
Sandyshot Wlk. M22—1F 112
Sandy Vale. SK16—6E 82
Sandy Wlk. OL2—5K 45
Sandy Way. M25—5A 60
Sandy Way. WN2—2M 53
Sandywell Clo. M11—8D 80
Sandywell St. M3—2D 4 & 4E 78
Sandywell St. M11—7D 80
Sangster Ct. M5—7A 78
Sankey Gro. M9—5H 61
Sankey Rd. WA11—9E 68
Sankey St. BL9—8K 25
Sankey St. WA3—7G 71
Santiago St. M14—3H 91
Santley St. M12—3A 92
Santon Av. M14—6L 91
Santon Dri. WA3—7L 71
Sapling Gro. M33—3D 100
Sapling Rd. BL3—7B 38
Sapling Rd. M27—2D 76
Sarah Ann St. M11—6M 79
Sarah Butterworth Ct. OL16 —3H 29
Sarah Butterworth St. OL16 —4H 29
Sarah Jane St. OL16—4M 29
Sarah St. BL0—1L 9
Sarah St. M11—7M 79
Sarah St. M24—9M 43
Sarah St. M30—6B 76
Sarah St. OL2—4A 46
Sarah St. OL11—4G 29
Sarah St. WN2—6B 54
Sargent Dri. M16—2E 90
Sargent Rd. SK6—3K 105
Sark Rd. M21—4A 90
Sarn Av. M22—9D 102
Sarnesfield Clo. M12—2A 92
Sarnia Ct. M7—9D 60
Sarsfield Av. WA3—7K 71
Satinwood Rd. WN4—4M 69
Saunton Av. BL2—7M 23
Saunton Rd. M11—7D 80
Sautridge Clo. OL11—2D 44
Savernake Rd. SK6—9C 94
Savick Av. BL2—2L 39
Saville Rd. M26—2F 40
Saville Rd. SK8—7H 103
Saville St. BL2—2G 39
Saville St. M24—1D 62
Saviours Ter. BL3—4C 38
Savio Way. M24—1A 62
Savoy Ct. M25—7L 41
Savoy Dri. OL2—7K 45
Savoy St. M12—9A 80
Savoy St. OL4—3B 64
Savoy St. OL11—2C 28
Sawley Av. M25—7M 41
Sawley Av. OL4—4D 64
Sawley Av. OL15—4A 14
Sawley Av. WA3—6K 71
Sawley Av. WN6—7M 33
Sawley Dri. SK8—6C 114
Sawley Rd. M10—3K 79
Sawpit St. WA13 & WA14 —6G 99
Sawston Wlk. M10—5C 62
Sawyer Brow. SK14—2F 94
Sawyer St. BL8—6H 25
Sawyer St. OL12—1F 28
Saxbrook Wlk. M22—1F 112
Saxby St. M6—2J 77
Saxelby Dri. M8—9H 61
Saxfield Dri. M23—7C 102
Saxholme Wlk. M22—2C 112
Saxon Av. M8—6G 61
Saxon Av. SK16—7C 82
Saxon Clo. BL8—8H 25
Saxon Dri. M34—8L 81
Saxon Dri. OL9—9E 44
Saxonholme Rd. OL11—2C 44
Saxon Ho. OL15—6C 14
Saxonside. M24—6L 43
Saxon St. M10—4L 79
Saxon St. M24—9B 44
Saxon St. M26—6F 40
Saxon St. M34—3M 93
Saxon St. M35—5H 81
Saxon St. OL4—1C 64
Saxon St. OL5—5K 65
Saxon St. OL11—3D 28
Saxthorpe Clo. M33—9D 88
Saxthorpe Clo. WN3—5K 51
Saxthorpe Wlk. M12—1L 91
Saxwood Av. M9—7K 61
Saxwood Clo. OL12—1M 27
Scafell Av. OL7—3M 81
Scafell Clo. OL1—8M 45
(in two parts)
Scafell Clo. SK6—4E 116
Scafell Dri. WN5—2H 51
Scafell Gro. WN2—6H 53
Scafell Rd. WA11—7A 68
Scalby Wlk. M22—3D 112
Scale St. M5—4A 4 & 6A 78
Scarborough St. M10—8A 62
Scarcroft Rd. M12—1A 92
Scaresdale Av. BL1—9A 22
Scarfield Dri. OL11—1L 27
Scargill Clo. M14—6J 91
Scargill Rd. BL3—5A 38
Scarisbrick Rd. M19—6M 91
Scarisbrick St. WN1—8C 34
Scarisbrook Av. M20 —2K 103
Scarr Av. M26—7J 41
Scarr Dri. OL12—8F 12
Scarr La. OL2—2C 46
Scarr Ter. OL12—1D 12
Scarr Wheel. M7—9C 60
Scarsdale Rd. M14—2L 91
Scarsdale St. M6—2A 4 & 4B 78
Scarth Wlk. M15—9F 78
Scarthwood Clo. BL2—5L 23
Scawfell Av. BL2—8H 23
Scawton Wlk. M9—3H 61
Sceptre St. M10—2C 80
Schofield Av. M31—5F 88
Schofield Gdns. WN7—4E 72
Schofield Hall Rd. OL15—1D 30
Schofield La. M29—5F 54
Schofield Pl. OL15—1D 14
Schofield Rd. M30—6A 76
Schofield Rd. M35—6H 81
Schofield St. M3—3C 4 & 5D 78
Schofield St. M11—6C 80
Schofield St. M29—8A 56
Schofield St. M35—8F 62
Schofield St. OL2—4K 45
Schofield St. OL8—5L 63
Schofield St. OL10—8K 27
Schofield St. OL11—6G 29
Schofield St. OL15—5C 14
(Littleborough)
Schofield St. OL15—1D 14
(Summit)
Schofield St. OL16—5A 30
Schofield St. SK14—1G 95
Schofield St. WN7—3E 72
Scholar's Way. M24—8M 43
Scholefield La. WN1—9D 34
Scholes. WN1—9D 34
Scholes Bank. BL6—5A 20
Scholes Clo. M8—8F 60
Scholes Dri. M10—6E 62
Scholes La. M25—5B 60
Scholes St. BL8—7J 25
Scholes St. M27—8F 58
Scholes St. M35—7G 63
Scholes St. OL9—4G 63
Scholes St. OL11—9C 28
Scholes Wlk. M25—5B 60
Scholes Walker St. BL9—6M 25
Scholey St. BL2—4G 39
School Av. M32—3M 89
School Av. OL6—1D 82
School Av. WN1—8E 34
School Brow. BL9—8M 25
School Brow. M28—1M 75
School Brow. SK6—3A 106
School Brow. WN5—2E 68
School Clo. SK12—8M 115
School Cres. SK15—4F 82
School Dri. WN5—2E 68
School Gro. M20—8J 91
School Gro. M25—6A 60
School Gro. W. M20—8J 91
School Hill. BL1—1E 38
School Ho. Flats. OL8—6J 63
School La. BL7—3K 7
School La. BL9—2L 25
School La. M20—2H 103
School La. M30—9D 86
(Cadishead)
School La. M30—4F 86
(Irlam)
School La. M31—8L 87
School La. OL11—2J 27
School La. OL16—3F 28
School La. SK4—9C 92
School La. SK6—2H 107
School La. SK8—4M 113
School La. SK10—9A 120
School La. SK12—8M 115
(in two parts)
School La. SK14—7E 94
School La. SK15—9L 65
School La. WA3—3A 98
School La. WA14—6K 99
School La. WN1—9D 34
School La. WN2—1E 34
School La. WN4—4J 69
School La. WN6—9K 17
School La. WN8—1C 50
(Roby Mill)
School La. WN8—6B 32
(Up Holland)
School Rd. M30—7C 76
School Rd. M32—4J 89
School Rd. M33—9H 89
(in two parts)
School Rd. M35—9F 62
School Rd. OL8—6H 63
School Rd. SK9—8K 113
School Rd. WA15—1F 110
Schools Hill. SK8—1K 113
Schoolside La. M24—1H 61
Schools Rd. M18—1E 92
School St. BL0—6H 9
School St. BL3—6B 40
School St. BL5—9E 36
School St. BL6—7C 20
School St. BL7—3F 22
School St. BL9—9B 26
School St. M4—2F 5 & 4G 79
School St. M7—1D 4 & 3E 78
School St. M26—6F 40
School St. M29—6H 55
(Atherton)
School St. M29—9M 55
(Gin Pit)
School St. M29—8M 55
(Tyldesley)
School St. M30—4B 76
School St. OL1—1A 64
School St. OL3—9B 48
School St. OL4—2G 65
School St. OL8—3K 63
School St. OL10—8J 27
School St. OL12—2F 28
School St. OL15—6L 13
School St. SK7—2L 115
School St. WA3—7G 71
School St. WA11—9F 68
School St. WN1—9D 34
School St. WN2—1F 52
School St. WN4—2D 70
School St. WN7—8E 54
School Ter. OL12—2C 12
(off Lloyd St.)
School Ter. WA3—7G 71
School Wlk. M15—1D 90
School Way. WN5—2J 51
School Yd. SK4—4L 103
Schwabe St. M24—9J 43
Scobell St. BL8—5F 24
Scope o' th' La. BL2—6J 23
Scopton St. BL1—1C 38
Score St. M11—6A 80
Scorton Av. BL2—2M 39
Scorton Wlk. M10—6D 62
Scotforth Clo. M15—6D 4 & 8E 78
Scotland. M4—2F 5 & 4G 79
Scotland Hall Rd. M10—2B 80
Scotland St. M10—2C 80
Scotland St. OL6—4C 82
Scot La. WN2 & BL6—4J 35
Scot La. WN5—9L 33
Scot La. WN5 & WN6—8L 33
Scotta Rd. M30—7B 76
Scott Av. BL9—3M 41
Scott Av. M21—4B 90
Scott Av. M30—4C 76
Scott Av. WN2—2L 53
Scott Clo. SK5—1F 104
Scott Dri. SK6—5H 107
Scottfield. OL8—3L 63
Scottfield Rd. OL8—3M 63
Scott Ga. M34—8L 81
Scott Rd. M25—5M 59
Scott Rd. M34—5L 93
Scott Rd. M35—5G 81
Scott Rd. WA3—6K 71
Scott St. BL5—7E 36
Scott St. M6—1B 4 & 3C 78
Scott St. M26—1D 58
Scott St. M29—3C 74
Scott St. M34—8M 81
Scott St. OL8—3M 63
Scott St. OL16—6M 29
Scott St. WN6—8B 34
Scott St. WN7—2D 72
Scout Dri. M23—9M 101
Scout Rd. BL0—1M 9
Scout Rd. BL1—1A 22
Scout View. BL8—4G 25
Scovell St. M7—1D 78
Scowcroft La. OL2—4A 46
Scowcroft St. BL2—9H 23
Scowcroft St. BL4—1K 57
Scroggins La. M31—1E 98
Scropton St. M10—1K 79
Seabright Wlk. M11—6M 79
Seabrook Cres. M31—2C 88
Seabrook Rd. M10—3C 80
Seacombe Av. M14—5G 91
Seacombe Gro. SK3—5B 104
Seaford Rd. BL2—4K 23
Seaford Rd. M6—1A 4 & 2B 78
Seaford Wlk. OL9—2H 63
Seaford Way. M9—5J 61
Seaforth Av. M29—4J 55
Seaforth Rd. BL1—5E 22
Seaham Dri. BL8—5J 25
Seaham Wlk. M14—3H 91
Sealand Clo. M33—3L 101
Sealand Dri. M30—7A 76
Sealand Rd. M23—3M 101
Sealand Way. SK9—8K 113
Seale Av. M34—8K 81
Sealey Wlk. M10—3L 79
(off Filby Wlk.)
Seal Rd. SK7—4F 114
Seamons Dri. WA14—8B 100
Seamons Rd. WA14—7A 100
Seamons Wlk. WA14—8B 100
Searby Rd. M18—2B 92
Searness Rd. M24—7J 43
Seascale Av. M11—4B 80
Seascale Cres. WN1—6C 34
Seascale Wlk. M24—7L 43
Seathwaite Clo. M29—9A 56
Seathwaite Wlk. M18—1C 92
Seatoller Ct. OL2—5L 45
(off Shaw St.)
Seatoller Dri. M24—8J 43
Seatoller Pl. WN5—1H 51
Seaton Clo. SK7—3K 115
Seaton M. OL7—3L 81
Seaton Rd. BL1—8C 22
Seaton Way. M14—2G 91
Sebastopol Wlk. M4—3H 5 & 5J 79
Second Av. BL1—2B 38
Second Av. BL3—5M 39
Second Av. BL9—6D 26
Second Av. M11—4C 80
Second Av. M17—1K 89
Second Av. M27—2D 76
Second Av. M29—4K 55
(Atherton)
Second Av. M29—3B 74
(Tyldesley)
Second Av. OL8—6J 63
Second Av. SK10—2K 121
Second Av. SK15—2L 83
Second Av. WN6—7A 34
Second St. BL1—6M 21
Second St. M17—1K 89
Sedan Clo. M5—6A 78
Sedbury Clo. M23—4L 101
(in two parts)
Seddon Av. M18—9D 80
Seddon Av. M26—4K 41
Seddon Clo. M29—5J 55
Seddon Gdns. M26—9A 40
Seddon Ho. Dri. WN6—6L 33
Seddon La. M26—9A 40
Seddon Rd. WA14—2D 110
Seddons Av. BL8—1G 41
Seddon St. BL3—6B 40
Seddon St. BL5—6E 36
Seddon St. M12—4B 92
Seddon St. M26—6G 41
Seddon St. M28—3F 56
Seddon St. WA10—8A 68
Sedgeborough Rd. M16—2E 90
Sedge Clo. SK5—6G 93
Sedgefield Clo. M5—5A 78
Sedgefield Dri. BL1—7B 22
Sedgefield Dri. WN6—6L 33
Sedgefield Pk. OL4—2D 64
Sedgefield Rd. M26—9F 40
Sedgefield Wlk. M23—3M 101
Sedgeford Rd. M10—2K 79
Sedgeley. WN6—2A 34
Sedgemoor Clo. SK8—2E 114
Sedgemoor Vale. BL2—8M 23
Sedgemoor Way. OL1—1L 63
Sedgley Av. M25—6C 60
Sedgley Av. OL16—6H 29
Sedgley Clo. M24—1C 62
Sedgley Ct. M24—1C 62
Sedgley Dri. BL5—3E 54
Sedgley Pk. Rd. M25—6C 60
Sedgley Rd. M8—8G 61
Sedgley St. M24—1C 62
Sedgwick Clo. M29—5L 55
Sedon St. M11—5M 79
Sedwyn St. WN1—8D 34
Seedfield Rd. BL9—5M 25
Seedley Av. M28—4H 57
Seedley Pk. Rd. M6—5L 77
Seedley Rd. M6—4L 77
Seedley St. M14—3H 91
Seedley Ter. M6—4L 77
Seedley View Rd. M6—4L 77
Seed St. BL1—2C 38
Seel St. OL5—7H 65
Sefton Av. M29—3J 55
Sefton Av. WN5—3D 50
Sefton Clo. M13—9H 79
Sefton Clo. M24—9L 43
Sefton Clo. WN5—3D 50
Sefton Cres. M33—8H 89
Sefton Dri. BL9—4A 26
Sefton Dri. M27—1D 76
Sefton Dri. M28—2A 76
Sefton Dri. SK9—1J 119
Sefton Fold Dri. WN5—2D 68
Sefton Fold Gdns. WN5—2D 68
Sefton Ho. BL1—1E 38
(off School Hill)
Sefton La. BL6—1D 36
(in two parts)
Sefton Rd. BL1—8B 22
Sefton Rd. M21—6B 90
Sefton Rd. M24—9L 43
Sefton Rd. M26—2E 40
Sefton Rd. M27—7E 58
Sefton Rd. M33—9H 89
Sefton Rd. WN3—4M 51
Sefton Rd. WN4—1M 69
Sefton Rd. WN5—3D 50
Sefton St. BL9—4M 25
Sefton St. M8—8G 61
Sefton St. M25—1M 59
Sefton St. M26—8J 41
Sefton St. OL9—6H 63
Sefton St. OL10—9L 27
Sefton St. OL11—5F 28
Sefton St. SK13—6J 97
Sefton St. WN7—2F 72
Sefton View. WN5—3D 50
Selborne Rd. M21—5E 90
Selbourne Clo. BL5—8G 37
Selbourne Clo. SK5—4E 92
Selbourne St. OL8—7M 63
Selbourne St. WN7—9F 54
Selby Av. M25—7M 41
Selby Av. OL9—8F 44
Selby Clo. M26—4K 41
Selby Clo. M32—3G 89
Selby Clo. OL16—4L 29
Selby Clo. SK12—7K 115
Selby Dri. M6—4H 77
Selby Dri. M31—1M 87
Selby Dri. WN3—4J 51
Selby Gdns. SK8—6C 114
Selby Rd. M24—6M 43
Selby Rd. M32—3G 89
Selby St. M11—7A 80
Selby St. OL16—2H 29
Selby St. SK4—1D 104
Selby Wlk. BL8—8F 24
Selden St. OL8—3K 63
Selham Wlk. M13—6H 5 & 8J 79
Selhurst Av. M11—5C 80
Selkirk Av. OL8—4K 63
Selkirk Av. WN4—3K 69
Selkirk Dri. M9—5M 61
Selkirk Gro. WN5—9H 33
Selkirk Pl. OL10—9G 27
Selkirk Rd. BL1—5D 22
Selkirk Rd. OL9—4F 62
Sellars Sq. M35—7G 81
Sellers Way. OL9—5G 63
Selsby Av. M30—5B 76
Selsey Av. M33—2F 100
Selsey Av. SK3—6M 103
Selsey Dri. M20—5J 103
Selside. WN3—6B 52
Selside Wlk. M14—6J 91
Selstead Rd. M22—3C 112
Selston Rd. M9—4H 61
Selvesen Ho. WN7—2G 73
Selwood Wlk. M9—9K 61
(off Carisbrook St.)
Selworth Av. M33—1L 101
Selworth Clo. WA15—7E 100
Selworthy Rd. M16—2E 90
Selwyn Av. M9—8K 61
Selwyn Clo. OL8—3L 63
Selwyn Dri. SK8—5C 114
Selwyn St. BL2—3G 39
Selwyn St. OL8—3L 63
Selwyn St. WN7—1F 72
Senior Av. M14—7L 91
Senior Rd. M30—7A 76
Sennicar La. WN1 & WN2 —4C 34
Senoir St. M3—2D 4 & 4E 78
Sepal Clo. SK5—5G 93
Sephton St. WN3—2F 52
Sequoia St. M9—8M 61
Sergeants La. M25—1J 59
Serin Clo. SK2—8M 105
Serpentine Wlk. WA12—7D 70
Service St. SK3—5B 104
Set St. SK15—6F 82
Settle Clo. BL8—8F 24
Settle St. BL3—6D 38
(Bolton)
Settle St. BL3—6C 40
(Little Lever)
Settle Wlk. M15—9F 78
Settstones La. OL3—8D 48
Sevenacres. OL3—4M 47
Seven Acres La. OL12—9L 11
Sevenoaks. WN7—1G 73
Sevenoaks Av. M31—2D 88
Sevenoaks Av. SK4—1A 104
Sevenoaks Dri. M27—1G 77
Sevenoaks Rd. SK8—7H 103
Sevenoaks Wlk. M13—1J 91
(off Lauderdale Cres.)
Seven Stars Rd. WN3—1A 52
Seven Stiles Dri. SK6—6E 106
Seventh Av. OL8—7J 63
Severn Clo. BL9—3M 25
Severn Clo. WA14—7C 100
Severn Clo. WN5—4D 68
Severn Dri. OL16—4A 30
Severn Dri. SK7—6C 114
Severn Dri. WN2—5C 54
Severn Dri. WN5—1J 51
Severn Rd. OL8—7H 63
Severn Rd. OL9—9F 44
Severn Rd. OL10—7G 27
Severn Rd. WN4—2E 70
Severnside Trading Est. M17 —1H 89
Severn St. WN7—3H 73
Severn Way. BL4—2B 58
Severn Way. SK5—9F 92
Sevilles Bldgs. OL5—6J 65
Seville St. OL2—7L 45
(Royton)
Seville St. OL2—4A 46
(Shaw)
Sewerby Clo. M16—2F 90
Sexa St. M11—7D 80
Sexton St. OL10—8J 27
Seymour Av. M11—5D 80
Seymour Clo. M16—1C 90
Seymour Ct. M7—8F 60
Seymour Ct. M26—6H 41
Seymour Ct. SK4—3L 103
Seymour Dri. BL2—4J 23
Seymour Gro. BL4—8G 39
Seymour Gro. M16—1B 90
Seymour Gro. M33—1H 101
Seymour Gro. OL16—7H 29
Seymour Gro. SK6—7E 106
Seymour Gro. WA15—8G 101
Seymour Pl. M16—1B 90
Seymour Rd. BL1—7E 22
Seymour Rd. M8—7F 60
Seymour Rd. SK2—8H 105
Seymour Rd. SK8—4A 114
Seymour Rd. S. M11—5D 80
Seymour St. BL2—4J 23
Seymour St. M18—9D 80
Seymour St. M26—6H 41
(in two parts)
Seymour St. M34—3K 93
(in two parts)
Seymour St. OL10—9J 27
(in two parts)
Shackcliffe Rd. M10—6B 62
Shackleton Ct. M10—3C 80
Shackleton Gro. BL1—8L 21
Shackleton St. M30—4C 76
(in two parts)
Shaddock Av. OL12—1M 27
Shade La. PR7—1D 18
Shade St. SK7—2L 115
Shade Ter. SK6—5F 116
Shadow Moss Rd. M22—5E 112
Shadows La. OL5—4L 65
Shadwell Gro. WN7—8C 54
Shadwell St. E. OL10—7K 27
Shadwell St. W. OL10—7K 27
Shadworth La. OL3—5M 65
Shady La. BL7—4H 23
Shady La. M23—6K 101
(in two parts)
Shady Oak Rd. SK2—7M 105
Shaftesbury Av. BL6—1F 36
Shaftesbury Av. M30—7C 76
Shaftesbury Av. OL15—8M 13
Shaftesbury Av. SK8—3C 114
Shaftesbury Av. WA15—8H 101
Shaftesbury Clo. BL1—9E 22
Shaftesbury Clo. BL6—1F 36
Shaftesbury Dri. OL10—1J 43
Shaftesbury Dri. OL12—5K 13
Shaftesbury Gdns. M31—4K 87
Shaftesbury Ho. M6—4M 77
Shaftesbury Rd. M8—9G 61
Shaftesbury Rd. M27—9F 58
Shaftesbury Rd. SK3—7A 104
Shaftesbury St. WN6—6M 33
Shafton Wlk. M10—6D 62
Shaftsbury Rd. WN5—9G 33
Shaftway Clo. WA11—8M 69
Shakerley La. M29—4M 55
Shakerley Rd. M29—7M 55
Shakespeare Av. BL9—3M 41
Shakespeare Av. M26—5E 40
Shakespeare Av. M34—6M 93
Shakespeare Av. SK15—3L 83
Shakespeare Clo. OL15—2C 14
Shakespeare Cres. M30—5D 76
Shakespeare Cres. M35—5G 81
Shakespeare Dri. SK8—7M 103
(in two parts)
Shakespeare Gro. WN3—3A 52
Shakespeare Rd. M25—5M 59
Shakespeare Rd. M27—8D 58
Shakespeare Rd. M35—5G 81
Shakespeare Rd. OL1—7B 46
Shakespeare Rd. SK6—2L 105
Shakespeare Wlk. M13—9J 79
Shakleton Av. M9—5A 62
Shalbourne Rd. M28—5J 57
Shaldon Dri. M10—3E 80
Shalfleet Clo. BL2—5L 23
Shalford Dri. M22—4D 112
Shambles Sq. M3—3E 5 & 5F 78
Shamrock Ct. M28—5H 57
Shandon Av. M22—4C 102
Shanklin Clo. M21—5A 90
Shanklin Clo. M34—6B 94
Shanklin Wlk. BL3—4J 39
Shanklyn Av. M31—4C 88
Shannon Clo. OL10—7G 27
Shannon Rd. M22—9E 102
Shap Av. WA15—8K 101
Shap Cres. M28—7M 57
Shap Dri. M28—6M 57
Shap Ga. WN5—1H 51
Shapwick Clo. M9—8K 61
Sharcott Wlk. M16—2F 90
Shardlow Clo. M10—3K 79
Shared St. WN1—1D 52
Sharman St. BL3—4H 39
Sharnbrook Wlk. BL2—9H 23
Sharnbrook Wlk. M8—6E 60
Sharnford Clo. BL2—3H 39
Sharnford Sq. M12—9A 80
Sharon Av. OL4—3L 65
Sharon Clo. OL7—6L 81
Sharon Sq. WN2—8F 52
Sharples Av. BL1—4E 22
Sharples Dri. BL8—6F 24
Sharples Grn. BL7—5K 7
Sharples Hall. BL1—4F 22
Sharples Hall Dri. BL1—4F 22
Sharples Hall Fold. BL1—5F 22
Sharples Hall M. BL1—4F 22
Sharples Hill. OL4—8D 46
Sharples Meadow. BL7—5K 7
Sharples Pk. BL1—6D 22
Sharples St. SK4—2E 104
Sharples Vale. BL1—7E 22
Sharples Vale Cotts. BL1 —7E 22
Sharp St. M4—2G 5 & 4H 79
Sharp St. M24—9A 44
Sharp St. M25—4A 60
Sharp St. M28—5L 57
Sharp St. WN3—2E 52
Sharrington Dri. M23—7L 101
Sharrow Wlk. M9—9K 61
(off Ockendon Dri.)
Sharston By-Pass. M22 & SK8 —6C 102
Sharston Grn. M22—7E 102
Sharston Ind. Area. M22 —6E 102
Sharston Rd. M22—7D 102
Shaving La. M28—7K 57
Shaw Av. SK14—6F 94
Shawbrook Av. M28—8H 57
Shawbrook Rd. M19—8M 91
Shawbury Clo. BL6—9K 19
Shawbury Clo. M24—1C 62
Shawbury Gro. M33—3F 100
Shawbury Rd. M23—9B 102
Shawclough Clo. OL12—8D 12
Shawclough Dri. OL12—8C 12
Shawclough Rd. OL12—7C 12
Shawclough Way. OL12—8C 12
Shawcroft Clo. OL2—4A 46
Shawcross La. M22—5E 102
Shawcross St. M6—6M 77
Shawcross St. SK1—5F 104
Shawcross St. SK14—6F 94
Shawdene Rd. M22—5C 102
Shawe Hall Av. M31—6A 88
Shawe Hall Cres. M31—6A 88
Shawe Rd. M31—4A 88
Shawes Dri. PR6—3J 19
Shawe View. M31—4A 88
Shawfield Clo. M14—6G 91
Shawfield Ct. SK2—8K 105
Shawfield La. OL12—9M 11
Shawfield Rd. SK14—3F 96
Shawfields. SK15—4K 83
Shawfold. OL2—2B 46
Shawford Cres. M10—6C 62
Shawford Rd. M10—6C 62
Shaw Ga. OL3—1D 66
Shawgreen Clo. M15—9D 78
Shaw Hall Av. SK14—1H 95
Shaw Hall Bank Rd. OL3 —3M 65
Shaw Hall Clo. OL3—3M 65
Shawhead Dri. M35—1F 80
Shaw Heath. SK3 & SK2 —5E 104
Shawheath Clo. M15—9D 78
Shawhill Wlk. M10—5L 79
Shaw Ho. M29—4K 55
(off Brooklands Av.)
Shaw Ho. OL2—4B 46
Shaw La. OL16—1A 30
Shaw La. SK13—4E 96
Shawlea Av. M19—8L 91
Shaw Lee. OL3—5D 48
Shaw Moor Av. SK15—6J 83
Shaw Rd. BL6—5B 20
Shaw Rd. OL1—8A 46
Shaw Rd. OL2—6L 45
Shaw Rd. OL16—7B 30
(Newhey)
Shaw Rd. OL16—9H 29
(Rochdale)
Shaw Rd. SK4—9B 92
Shaw Rd. Est. OL1—8M 45
Shaw Rd. S. SK3—7E 104
(in two parts)
Shaws Fold. OL4—1H 65
Shaws Fold. SK9—9F 112
Shaws La. OL3—9B 48
Shaw's Rd. WA14—9D 100
Shaw St. BL3—4E 38
Shaw St. BL4—7J 39
Shaw St. BL9—7B 26
Shaw St. M3—2E 5 & 4F 78
Shaw St. OL1—9M 45
Shaw St. OL2—5L 45
Shaw St. OL3—2B 66
Shaw St. OL4—2G 65
Shaw St. OL6—4D 82
Shaw St. OL12—9H 13
Shaw St. SK13—6J 97
Shaw St. SK14—2A 96
Shaw St. WA11—9L 69
Shaw St. WN1—8C 34
Shaw St. WN4—2B 70
Shaw Ter. SK16—6C 82
Shay Av. WA15—3L 111
Shayfield Av. M22—8D 102
Shayfield Av. OL9—9E 44
Shayfield Dri. M22—7D 102
Shayfield Rd. M22—8D 102
Shay La. WA15—3J 111
Sheader Dri. M5—5J 77
Sheaf Field Wlk. M26—5G 41
Sheard Av. OL6—1D 82
Sheardhall Av. SK12—7L 117
Shearing Av. OL12—1M 27
Shearsby Clo. M15—1E 90
Shearwater Dri. BL5—2D 54
Shearwater Dri. M28—5J 57
Shearwater Gdns. M30—7A 76
Shearwater Rd. SK2—7M 105
Sheddings, The. BL3—5G 39
Shed St. BL3—4F 38
Shed St. OL12—2D 12
Shed St. WN3—4E 52
Sheepfoot La. M25—5D 60
Sheepfoot La. OL1—8K 45
Sheep Gap. OL12—1B 28
Sheepgate Dri. BL8—5E 24
Sheep Ho. La. BL6—1M 19
Sheep La. M28—8F 56
Sheerness St. M18—1D 92
Sheffield Rd. SK13—5L 97
Sheffield Rd. SK14—2F 94
(in two parts)
Sheffield St. M1—5G 5 & 7H 79
Sheffield St. SK4—2E 104
Shefford Clo. M11—7M 79
Shefford Cres. WN3—6J 51
Sheiling Ct. WA14—9C 100
Sheilings, The. WA3—7M 71
Shelbourne Av. BL1—9B 22
Shelden Clo. SK13—5D 96
Shelden Fold. SK13—5D 96
(off Brassington Cres.)
Shelden M. SK13—5D 96
Shelden Pl. SK13—5D 96
(off Brassington Cres.)
Shelderton Clo. M10—9A 62
Sheldon Av. M31—4B 88
Sheldon Av. WN6—8L 17
Sheldon Clo. BL4—7H 39
Sheldon Clo. M31—2F 98
Sheldon Ct. OL7—2B 82
Sheldon Rd. SK7—5L 115
Sheldon St. M11—5B 80
Sheldrake Clo. SK16—8E 82
Sheldrake Rd. WA14—5B 100
Shelfield. OL11—1M 27
Shelfield Clo. OL11—2M 27
Shelfield La. OL11—1L 27
Shelford Av. M18—2B 92
Shellbrook Gro. SK9—2K 119
Shelley Av. M24—7B 44
Shelley Clo. PR7—2M 17
Shelley Ct. SK8—3A 114
Shelley Dri. WN2—7H 53
Shelley Dri. WN5—2G 51
Shelley Gro. M35—5G 81
Shelley Gro. SK14—1D 94
Shelley Gro. SK15—3L 83
Shelley Rise. SK16—8H 83
Shelley Rd. M25—5M 59
Shelley Rd. M27—8D 58
Shelley Rd. M28—3G 57
Shelley Rd. OL1—8C 46
Shelley Rd. OL9—5F 62
Shelley Rd. SK5—5D 92
Shelley St. M10—8C 62
Shelley St. WN7—9C 54
Shelley Wlk. BL1—9D 22
Shelley Wlk. M29—3K 55
Shelley Way. M34—6M 93
Shelmerdine Gdns. M6—3J 77
Shelmerdine St. WN1—1D 52
Shelton Av. M33—1D 100
Shenfield Wlk. M10—4K 79
Shenton Av. WA11—9D 68
Shentonfield Rd. M22—7E 102
Shenton Pk. Av. M33—3C 100
Shenton St. SK14—2C 94
Shepherd Ct. OL16—3H 29
Shepherd Cross St. BL1—9C 22
Shepherds Brow. WA14 —1A 110
Shepherds Clo. BL6—7J 19
Shepherds Clo. BL8—1F 24
Shepherds Cross St. Ind. Est. BL1—8D 22
(off Shepherds Cross St.)
Shepherd's Dri. BL6—7G 21
Shepherd St. BL8—2F 24
Shepherd St. BL9—8M 25
Shepherd St. M9—7L 61
Shepherd St. OL2—5L 45
Shepherd St. OL10—8J 27
Shepherd St. OL11—1K 27
Shepherd St. OL12—2F 28
Shepherd Wlk. M34—6M 93
Shepley Av. BL3—4C 38
Shepley Clo. SK7—4K 115
Shepley Clo. SK16—7D 82
Shepley Dri. SK7—3K 115
Shepley Ind. Est. N. M34 —8M 81
Shepley Ind. Est. S. M34—9A 82
Shepley La. SK6—9F 106
Shepley Rd. M34—9M 81
Shepley St. M1—5G 5 & 7H 79
Shepley St. M34—8M 81
Shepley St. M35—7G 63
Shepley St. OL4—2E 64
Shepley St. SK13—4L 97
(Glossop)
Shepley St. SK13—3E 96
(Hollingworth)
Shepley St. SK14—4E 94
Shepley St. SK15—5G 83
Shepton Av. WN2—7G 53
Shepton Dri. M23—2A 112
Shepway Ct. M30—5B 76
Sheraton Rd. OL8—4L 63
Sherborne Av. WN2—3A 54
Sherborne Ho. M24—6A 44
Sherborne Rd. M24—6M 43
Sherborne Rd. SK3—6A 104
Sherborne Rd. WN5—9G 33
Sherborne St. M3 & M8—1D 4 & 3E 78
Sherborne St. Trading Est. M8 —2G 79
Sherborne St. W. M3—2D 4 & 4E 78
Sherbourne Clo. M26—4D 40
Sherbourne Clo. SK8—6B 114
Sherbourne Ct. M25—4A 60
Sherbourne Dri. OL10—7G 27
Sherbourne Pl. WN3—3E 52
Sherbourne Rd. BL1—9A 22
Sherbourne Rd. M31—3E 88
Sherbrooke Av. OL3—8C 48
Sherbrook Rise. SK9—5J 119
Sherbrook Rd. SK12—6K 117
Sherdley Ct. M8—7G 61
Sherdley Rd. M8—7G 61
Sherford Clo. SK7—2G 115
Sheridan Av. WA3—8K 71
Sheridan Ct. M10—2L 79
Sheridan Way. M34—6M 93
Sheridan Way. OL9—9E 44
Sheriffs Dri. M29—7D 56
Sheriff St. BL2—9H 23
Sheriff St. OL12—2E 28
Sheriff St. OL16—5A 30
Sheringham Dri. BL8—5K 25
Sheringham Dri. M27—1F 76
Sheringham Pl. BL3—4D 38
Sheringham Rd. M14—7K 91
Sherlock Av. WA11—8L 69
Sherlock St. M14—7K 91
Sherratt St. M4—3G 5 & 5H 79
Sherrington St. M12—3A 92
Sherway Dri. WA15—7J 101
Sherwell Rd. M9—5H 61
Sherwin St. M12—9M 79
Sherwin Way. OL11—9D 28
Sherwood Av. M7—9B 60
Sherwood Av. M14—6J 91
Sherwood Av. M26—1F 40
Sherwood Av. M29—1A 74
Sherwood Av. M33—9J 89
Sherwood Av. M35—5J 81
Sherwood Av. SK4—4A 104
Sherwood Av. SK8—2M 113
Sherwood Av. WN4—3C 70
Sherwood Clo. BL8—3F 24
Sherwood Clo. M5—4K 77
Sherwood Clo. OL6—9C 64
Sherwood Clo. SK6—9F 106
Sherwood Cres. WN2—6G 53
Sherwood Cres. WN5—1K 51
Sherwood Dri. M27—9H 59
Sherwood Dri. WN5—2K 51
Sherwood Fold. SK14—7D 96
Sherwood Gro. WN5—1K 51
Sherwood Gro. WN7—5H 73
Sherwood Ho. WN2—6G 53
Sherwood Rd. M9—6K 61
Sherwood Rd. M34—3H 93
Sherwood Rd. SK6—9B 94
Sherwood St. BL1—7F 22
Sherwood St. M14—6J 91
Sherwood St. OL1—9K 45
Sherwood St. OL11—5G 29
(off Durham St)
Sherwood St. OL11—8D 28
(off Queensway)
Sherwood Way. OL2—1L 45
Shetland Rd. M10—3K 79
Shetland Way. M31—1C 88
Shevington Gdns. M23—4B 102
Shevington La. WN6—3H 33
Shevington Moor. WN6—8G 17
Shieldburn Dri. M9—9L 61
Shield Clo. OL8—9L 45
Shield Dri. M28—8C 58
Shield St. SK3—5E 104
Shields View. M5—8B 78
(off Ordsall Dri.)
Shiel St. M28—5K 57
Shiers Dri. SK8—9L 103
Shiffnal St. BL2—3F 38
Shildon Clo. WN2—7F 34
Shilford Dri. M4—2H 5 & 4J 79
Shillingstone Clo. BL2—7M 23
Shillington Clo. M28—5F 56
Shiloh La. OL4—7H 47
Shilton Gdns. BL3—4E 38
Shilton St. BL0—6H 9
Shilton Wlk. M10—6D 62
Shipgates Cen. BL1—2F 38
Shipham Clo. WN7—8D 54
Shipley Av. M6—4J 77
Shipley View. M31—1M 87
Shipper Bottom La. BL0—6K 9
(in two parts)
Shippey St. M14—7K 91
Shipston Clo. BL8—7G 25
Shipton St. BL1—9B 22
Shirburn. OL11—4E 28
Shirebrook Dri. M26—5H 41
Shirebrook Dri. SK13—6M 97
Shireburn Av. BL2—1J 39
Shireburn Av. WA11—8B 68
Shiredale Clo. SK8—9B 104
Shiredale Dri. M9—9K 61
Shiregreen Av. M10—2J 79
Shirehills. M25—5A 60
Shireoak Rd. M20—7K 91
Shires, The. M35—4K 81
Shire Way. SK13—3L 97
Shirley Av. M7—9A 60
Shirley Av. M27—9J 59
Shirley Av. M30—7C 76
Shirley Av. M32—3M 89
Shirley Av. M34—7J 81
(Audenshaw)
Shirley Av. M34—3F 92
(Denton)
Shirley Av. OL9—6E 62
Shirley Av. SK6—7E 106
Shirley Av. SK8—6J 113
Shirley Av. SK14—1D 94
Shirley Clo. SK7—2J 115
Shirley Ct. M33—1J 101
Shirley Gro. SK3—8E 104
Shirley Rd. M8—9G 61
Shirley St. OL11—8C 28
Shoecroft Av. M34—4L 93
Shofield St. M26—5H 41
Sholver Hey La. OL1—5D 46
Sholver Hill Clo. OL1—5E 46
Sholver La. OL1—5D 46
Shone Av. M22—2F 112
Shore Av. OL2—9C 30
Shoreditch Clo. SK4—9B 92
Shorefield Clo. OL16—3M 29
Shorefield Mt. BL7—2E 22
Shore Fold. OL15—5M 13
Shoreham Clo. BL8—3J 25
Shoreham Wlk. M16—2E 90
Shoreham Wlk. OL9—2G 63
Shore Hill. OL15—5C 14
Shore La. OL15—6C 14
Shore Lea. OL15—5M 13
Shore Mt. OL15—5M 13
Shore Rd. OL15—5M 13
Shore St. OL1—1A 64
Shore St. OL16—4M 29
Shoreswood. BL1—5D 22
Shore View. OL16—4L 29
Shorland St. M27—9C 58
Shorrocks St. BL8—7F 24
Short Av. M35—7F 80
Shortcroft St. M15—6E 5 & 8F 78
Shortland Cres. M19—2K 103
Shortlands Av. BL9—9M 25
Short St. M4—4F 5 & 6G 79
Short St. M7—2D 4 & 4E 78
(in two parts)
Short St. M29—6L 55
Short St. OL6—4B 82
Short St. OL10—9H 27
Short St. SK4—2D 104
(in two parts)
Short St. SK7—1K 115
Short St. WA3—6H 71
Short St. WA11—9L 69
Short St. WN5—2H 51
Short St. E. SK4—2E 104
Shortwood Clo. M10—1A 80
Shottery Wlk. SK6—2M 105
Shotton Wlk. M14—3J 91
Shrewsbury Clo. WN2—2M 53
Shrewsbury Ct. M16—1D 90
Shrewsbury Gdns. SK8—6C 11
Shrewsbury Rd. BL1—1B 38
Shrewsbury Rd. M25—5A 60
Shrewsbury Rd. M33—3G 101
Shrewsbury Rd. M35—4G 81
Shrewsbury St. M16—1C 90
Shrewsbury St. OL4—9C 46
Shrewsbury St. SK13—5J 97
Shrewsbury Way. M34—5A 9
Shrigley Clo. SK9—2K 119
Shrigley Rd. SK12—9C 116
Shrigley Rd. N. SK12—9C 116
Shrivenham Wlk. M23—6M 10
Shropshire Av. SK5—8J 93
Shropshire Dri. SK13—6M 97
Shropshire Rd. M35—1G 81
Shrowbridge Wlk. M12—5A 8
Shrub St. BL3—7C 38
Shude Hill. M4—3F 5 & 5G 79
Shudehill Rd. M28—7G 57
Shurdington Rd. M29 & BL5 —2M 5
Shurmer St. BL3—5C 38
Shutt La. OL3—7M 47
Shuttle Cen. M25—9B 42
Shuttle St. M29—7M 55
Shuttle St. M30—5F 76
Shuttle St. WN2—2L 53
(in two parts)
Shuttleworth Clo. M16—6E 9
Shutts La. SK15—7K 83
Siam St. M11—7M 79
Sibley Av. WN4—3D 70
Sibley Rd. SK4—2B 104
Sibley St. M18—1D 92
Siblies Wlk. M22—3B 112
Sibson Ct. M21—5A 90
Sibson Rd. M21—5A 90
Sibson Rd. M33—1G 101
Sicklefield. WN1—4C 34
Sickle St. M2—4F 5 & 6G 79
Sickle St. OL4—2A 64
Sidbrook St. WN2—2J 53
Sidbury Rd. M21—6C 90
Sidcup Rd. M23—8M 101
Siddall St. M12—4A 92
Siddall St. M34—3M 93
Siddall St. OL1—9M 45
Siddall St. OL2—2B 46
Siddall St. OL10—1L 43
Siddal St. M26—5G 41
Siddeley St. WN7—2D 72
Siddington Av. M20—6G 91
Siddington Av. SK3—7C 104
Siddington Rd. SK9—7K 113
Siddington Rd. SK12—1M 12
Siddow Comn. WN7—4G 73
(in two parts)
Side Av. WA14—3C 110
Sidebottom St. M35—6F 80
Sidebottom St. OL4—9E 46
Sidebottom St. SK6—1M 105
Sidebottom St. SK15—5G 83
Side St. M11—6B 80
Side St. OL8—6J 63
Sidford Clo. BL3—4K 39
Sidings, The. M28—2A 76
Sidley Av. M9—4M 61
Sidley Pl. SK14—3F 94
Sidley St. SK14—3F 94
Sidmouth Av. M31—3L 87
Sidmouth Dri. M9—6K 61
Sidmouth Gro. SK8—5M 113
Sidmouth Gro. WN3—5L 51
Sidmouth Rd. M33—9D 88
Sidmouth St. M34—8K 81
(in two parts)
Sidmouth St. OL9—3J 63
Sidney James Ct. M10 —7C 6
Sidney Rd. M9—7K 61
Sidney St. BL3—4F 38
Sidney St. M1—6F 5 & 8G 79
Sidney St. M3—3C 4 & 5D 78
Sidney St. OL1—8A 46
Sidney St. WN7—2G 73
Sidwell Wlk. M4—5K 79
Siemens Rd. M30—9E 86
Siemens St. BL6—8C 20
Sighthill Wlk. M9—8K 61
Signet Wlk. M8—2H 79
Silas St. OL6—2D 82
Silbury Wlk. M8—2F 78
Silchester Dri. M10—1K 79
Silchester Wlk. OL1—1M 63
Silchester Way. BL2—9L 23
Silcock St. WA3—6G 71
Silfield Clo. M11—6L 79
Silkin Clo. M13—6G 5 & 8H 7
Silkin Ct. M13—8H 79
(off Silkin Clo.)
Silk St. BL5—8E 36
Silk St. M3—2C 4 & 4D 78
Silk St. M4—3H 5 & 5J 79
Silk St. M24—9M 43
Silk St. M30—6F 76
Silk St. OL11—6C 28
Silk St. SK13—5L 97
Silk St. WN7—2F 72
Sillavan Way. M3—3D 44 & 5E
Silsbury Gro. WN6—1A 34
Silsden Av. M9—3H 61
Silsden Av. WA3—7B 72
Silsden Wlk. M27—8M 59
Silton St. M9—9M 61
Silver Av. WA11—9G 69
Silverbirch Clo. M33—3D 10
Silver Birch Gro. M27—1H 7
Silver Clo. SK16—8B 82
Silvercroft St. M15—6D 4 & 8E
Silverdale. M27—6G 59
Silverdale. WN1—7C 34
Silverdale Av. M25—6E 60
Silverdale Av. M28—3G 57
Silverdale Av. M30—2H 87
Silverdale Av. M34—4A 94
Silverdale Av. OL9—2G 63
Silverdale Av. WN2—9G 35
Silverdale Clo. SK6—4E 116
Silverdale Ct. WN1—9D 34
Silverdale Dri. OL4—2F 64
Silverdale Dri. SK9—7G 119
Silverdale Gro. WA11—7A 6
Silverdale Rd. BL1—2C 38
Silverdale Rd. BL4—8G 39
Silverdale Rd. M21—5C 90
Silverdale Rd. SK4—1C 104
Silverdale Rd. SK8—9H 103
Silverdale Rd. WN2—3M 53
Silverdale Rd. WN5—1H 51
Silverdale St. M11—8F 80
Silver Hill. OL16—3M 29
Silver Hill Rd. SK14—5E 94
Silver Jubilee Wlk. M4—3G 5H
Silvermere. OL6—1E 82
Silver Spring. SK14—6F 94
Silverstone Dri. M10—3D 80
Silver St. BL9—8L 25
Silver St. M1—5F 5 & 6G 79
Silver St. M25—8L 41
Silver St. M30—2H 87
Silver St. OL1—2M 63
Silver St. OL12—2D 28
Silver St. WN2—6G 53
Silverthorne Clo. SK15—6G

erton Clo. SK14—4L 95
(in two parts)
erton Gro. BL1—6F 22
erwell La. BL1—2F 28
erwell Rd. BL6—6B 20
erwell St. BL1—6F 28
erwood. OL9—1E 62
ine Wlk. M10—3L 79
(off Bednal Av.)
ington Way. WN2—7G 35
eon St. M4—2G 5 & 4H 79
eon St. OL16—4M 29
ster Dri. SK6—6J 97
ster Dri. BL9—7L 42
ster St. M25—8E 42
ster St. M35—9F 62
mondley Gro. SK13—6G 97
mondley La. SK13—6G 97
mondley New Rd. SK13
—7G 97
ms Clo. M3—3C 4 & 5D 78
ms Yd. WN2—5L 35
(spull)
olly Nook. M4—4J 35
bury Clo. BL8—8F 24
on Freeman Clo. M19
—7C 92

Sledmoor Rd. M23—4M 101
Sligo St. BL1—1G 39
Slimbridge Clo. BL2—9A 24
Sloane Av. OL4—4B 46
Sloane St. BL3—6B 38
Sloane St. M11—5A 80
Sloane St. OL6—4C 82
Slough Ind. Est. M5—5B 4 &
7C 78
Smallbrook. OL2—1C 46
Smallbrook La. WN7—5D 54
Small Brook Rd. OL2—8C 30
Smalldale Av. M16—3F 90
Smalley St. OL11—8C 28
Smalley St. WN6—9L 17
Smallfield Dri. M9—8K 61
Smallridge Clo. M10—4K 79
Smallshaw Fold. OL6—2B 82
Smallshaw La. OL6—2B 82
Smallshaw La. OL12—7A 12
Smallshaw. OL6—2B 82
Smallwood. M10—1C 80
Smart St. M12—3A 92
Smeaton Clo. M32—4L 89
Smeaton St. BL6—2C 20
Smeaton St. M8—1H 79
Smedley Av. M8—1H 79
Smedley La. BL3—6G 39
Smedley Av. M8—1H 79
Smedley Pl. SK13—4L 97
Smedley St. M8—1H 79
Smethurst St. BL3—7B 38
(off Smethurst La.)
Smethurst Hall Pk. WN5—6C 50
Smethurst La. BL3 & BL5
—7B 38
Smethurst La. WN5—3J 51
Smethurst Rd. WN5—6B 50
Smethurst La. BL2—1H 39
Smethurst Rd. BL2—1G 75
Smith Av. WN5—9H 33
Smith Brow. BL6—7J 19
Smithfold La. M28—4G 57
Smith Hill. OL16—4M 29
Smithies Av. M24—7A 44
Smithies St. OL10—8L 27
Smithills Croft Rd. BL1—7A 22
Smithills Dean Rd. BL1—1A 22
Smithills Dri. BL1—8M 21
Smithills Hall Clo. BL0—6J 9
Smith La. BL7—2F 22
Smith's La. WN2—7A 54
Smith's Pl. M29—5K 55
Smith's Rd. BL0—6H 9
Smith St. BL9 & BL8—8A 26
Smith St. M5—4A 78
Smith St. M16—9C 78
Smith St. M28—5K 57
Smith St. M29—5J 55
Smith St. M34—4M 93
Smith St. OL4—6E 46
Smith St. OL9—6H 65
Smith St. OL7—6M 81
Smith St. OL10—8K 27
Smith St. OL15—6B 14
Smith St. OL16—3E 28
Smith St. PR7—4F 18
Smith St. SK8—7M 103
Smith St. SK14—1D 94
Smith St. SK16—1A 82
Smithwood Av. WN2—2M 53
Smithy Bri. Rd. OL16 & OL15
—7L 13
Smithy Brow. WN6—2C 16
Smithy Clo. SK13—5K 97
Smithy Croft. BL7—2F 22
Smithy Field. OL15—5A 14
Smithy Fold. OL12—1C 28
Smithy Fold Rd. SK14—5E 94
Smithy Grn. OL6—3E 30
Smithy Grn. SK6—9B 94
Smithy Grn. WN2—1F 52
Smithy Grn. OL6—3C 82
Smithy Hill. BL3—5A 38
Smithy La. M3—4E 5 & 6F 78
Smithy La. M31—2F 98
Smithy La. SK6—4M 107
Smithy Nook. OL15—2C 14
Smithy St. OL15—8M 13
Smithy Wlk. WN7—3F 72
Smock La. WN4—3J 69
Smyrna St. M6—6J 77
Smyrna St. OL4—2C 64
Smyrna St. WN5—3K 51
Snapebrook Gro. SK9—2L 119
Snape St. M26—3F 40
(in two parts)
Snell St. M4—6K 79
Snipe Av. M22—3M 101
Snipe Clo. SK12—8G 115
Snipe Rd. OL8—6B 64
Snipe St. BL3—2C 38
(in two parts)
Snowberry Wlk. M31—2E 98
Snowden Av. M31—6B 88
Snowden Av. WN3—4M 51
Snowden Av. M10—3A 80
Snowden Wlk. M10—6C 62
Snowdon Av. BL2—3B 40
Snowdon Rd. M30—4G 75
Snow Hill Rd. BL3—4K 39
Snow Hill Ter. M25—4C 60
Snowshill Dri. WN2—4J 51
Snydale Clo. BL6—7G 37
Snydale Way. BL3—6J 37
S. Hall St. M5—5B 4 & 7C 78
S. Hill St. OL4—2A 64
S. King St. M2—4E 5 & 6F 78
S. King St. SK12—1A 121
S. Lancashire Ind. Est. WN4
—1H 70
Southlands. BL2—1L 39
Southlands Av. M30—7M 75
Southlands Av. WN6—1L 33
South La. M29—2A 74
S. Langworthy Rd. M5—7L 77
Southlink Bus. Pk. OL4—2A 64
S. Lonsdale St. M32—3C 112
S. Marlow St. SK14—2G 97
S. Mead. SK12—7H 115
S. Meade. M25—7B 42
S. Meade. M33—6D 60
S. Meade. M27—1E 76
S. Meade. WA15—6G 101
S. Meadway. SK6—5F 116
Southmere Clo. M10—5C 62
Southmill St. M2—5E 5 & 7F 78
Southmoor Wlk. BL3—4E 38
(off Parrot St.)
Southover. BL5—7M 37
S. Oak La. SK9—5F 118
Southolme Gdns. M19—1L 103
Southover. BL5—7M 37
S. Parade. SK14—2F 97
South Pde. SK7—2F 114
South Pk. Rd. SK8—7H 103
S. Park Dri. SK12—8L 115

S. Park Rd. SK8—7H 103
South Pl. OL16—2G 29
Southpool Clo. SK7—2G 115
S. Pump St. M1—5G 5 & 7H 79
S. Radford St. M7—9A 60
Southreay Av. WN3—5K 51
South Ridge. M34—3M 93
South Rd. M17—2J 89
South Rd. M20—3H 103
South Rd. M27—6K 59
South Rd. PR7—7L 17
South Rd. WA14—4D 110
(Bowdon, in two parts)
South Rd. WA14—4D 110
(Hale)
South Row. M25—7M 59
Southsea St. M11—8D 80
Southside. SK6—8L 93
South St. BL0—5K 9
South St. BL3—6E 38
South St. M11—7B 80
(in two parts)
South St. M12—1L 91
South St. M29—7L 55
South St. OL7—7L 81
South St. OL8—6H 63
South St. OL10—8H 27
South St. OL16—2G 29
South St. SK9—8L 119
South Ter. BL0—1J 9
South Ter. M25—2K 41
South Ter. OL16—5G 29
South Vale. SK14—8F 100
South View. M29—5J 55
S. View. OL1—6F 94
S. View. SK5—3F 92
S. View. SK6—8C 94
S. View. SK15—1M 83
S. View Rd. SK13—7H 97
S. View Ter. OL16—7L 13
S. View Ter. OL16—2J 39
Southview Wlk. OL4—8D 46
Southview Wlk. SK15—6G 83
Southward Rd. WA11—8A 70
Southway. M10—6F 62
Southway. M30—5F 76
Southway. M35—7G 81
Southway. OL7—1B 82
Southway. WA14—7E 100
Southwell Clo. BL1—1D 38
Southwell St. M9—6L 61
Southwell Gdns. OL6—9B 64
Southwell St. M9—9L 61
Southwick Rd. M23—3A 102
Southwold Clo. M19—5C 92
Southwood Clo. BL3—5E 38
Southwood Dri. M9—3G 61
Southwood Rd. SK2—9H 105
Sovereign Enterprise Pk. M50
—7A 78
Sovereign Fold Rd. WN7—7E 54
Sovereign Ho. BL3—7M 103
Sovereign Rd. WN1—1D 52
Sovereign St. M6—1A 78
Sowerby Wlk. M9—4H 61
(off Chapel La.)
Spa Clo. SK5—5C 92
Spa Cres. M28—2F 56
Spa La. M28—2G 57
Spa La. OL16—8B 13
Spa La. OL4—3D 64
Spa Rd. BL1—3D 38
Spadeling Dri. M23—2A 112
Sparkford Av. M23—4K 101
Sparkle St. M1—5G 5 & 6H 79
Spark Rd. M23—6B 102
Sparrow Clo. SK5—4E 92
Sparrow Hill. OL16—3E 28
Sparrow Hill. WN6—8A 16
Sparrow St. OL2—4L 45
Sparta Av. M28—6J 57
Sparta Wlk. M11—7A 80
Sparth Bottoms Rd. OL11
—4D 28
Sparth St. SK4—2D 104
Sparthfield Av. OL11—5E 28
Sparthfield Rd. SK4—2D 104
Spath Clo. SK7—3F 114
Spath Cres. SK7—2F 114
Spath Holme. M20—6G 103
Spath La. SK8—7M 113
Spath La. E. SK8—7B 114
Spath Rd. M20—1F 102
Spath Wlk. SK8—7B 114
Spawell Clo. WA3—6L 71
Spaw St. M3—3D 4 & 5E 78
(in two parts)
Speakman Av. WN7—2H 73
Speakmans Dri. WN6—3C 32
Spean Wlk. M11—6C 80
Spear St. M1—4F 5 & 6G 79
Spectator St. M4—5K 79
Specton Wlk. M12—3B 92
Speedwell Clo. SK14—8F 84
Speke Wlk. M34—5L 93
Spelding Dri. WN6—5K 33
Spencer Av. BL3—6C 40
Spencer Av. M25—7L 41
Spencer Clo. WN2—7H 35
Spencer Rd. OL5—7H 65
Spencer Rd. W. WN1—6B 34
Spencer's La. WN5—1D 50
Spencer St. BL0—6H 9
Spencer St. BL9—7J 25
Spencer St. M26—5J 41
Spencer St. M30—6C 76
Spencer St. OL1—4M 64
Spender Av. M8—1G 79
Spendmore La. PR7—2K 17
Spen Fold. BL8—1G 41
Spenleach La. BL8—7C 8
Spenlow. WN7—4J 73
Spenlow Clo. SK12—1A 121
Spennithorne Rd. M31—4B 88
Spenser Av. M26—5E 40
Spenwood Rd. OL15—6M 13
Spibby Sq. WN3—6A 52
Spindle Av. SK15—4J 83
Spindle Croft. BL4—1D 56
Spindle Hillock. WN4—2K 69
Spindles Shopping Cen., The.
OL1—1E 63
Spindles Brow. PR7—5K 17
Spingside. SK4—7D 92
Springside Gro. M28—5L 57
Springside Clo. M28—5L 57
Springside Rd. B...
Springside Wlk. M15—9D 78

Spinning Jenny Wlk. M4—5J 79
(off Slate Av.)
Spinning Meadows. BL1—1D 38
Spion Kop. WN4—4B 70
Spire Hollin. SK13—4J 97
Spire Wlk. M12—7L 79
Spirewood Gdns. SK6—4A 106
Spodden Cotts. OL12—1D 12
Spodden St. OL12—2D 28
Spodegreen La. WA3—2J 109
Spod Rd. OL12—1C 28
Spooner Rd. M30—6C 76
Spooner St. M28—5C 57
Sporton Clo. M28—5M 57
Sportside Av. M28—4K 57
Sportside Clo. M28—4K 57
Sportside Gro. M28—4K 57
Sportsman Dri. OL8—5A 64
Sportsman St. WN7—2D 72
Spotland Rd. OL12—2D 28
Spotland Tops. OL12—1B 28
Spout Brook. S...
Spreadbury St. M10—9A 62
Spring Av. M25—7L 41
Spring Bank. M29—1B 74
Spring Bank. OL12—2M 81
Springbank. BL4—9A 40
Springbank. OL9—1G 63
Springbank. BL8—4E 24
Springbank. OL12—7D 12
(Healey)
Spring Bank. OL12—2D 12
(Whitworth)
Spring Bank. SK13—7H 97
Spring Bank. SK14—1F 96
Spring Bank. WN6—1C 32
Spring Bank Av. M34—8J 81
Spring Bank Av. SK16—2B 82
Springbank Clo. SK6—8C 94
Spring Bank Ct. M8—7F 60
Springbank Pl. SK1—5E 104
Spring Bank Rd. SK6—8C 94
Spring Bank St. M35—6H 83
Spring Bank Ter. M34—8J 81
Spring Bri. Rd. M16—4F 90
Spring Clough. M27—2B 76
Spring Clough Av. M28—6M 57
Spring Clough Dri. M28—6M 57
Spring Clough. OL16—3H 29
Spring Gdns. OL3—4L 47
Spring Gdns. M27—1H 77
Spring Gdns. OL9—8E 44
Springwell Gdns. SK14—5L 95
Springwell Way. SK14—5L 95
Springwood. OL3—4L 47
Springwood. SK13—6F 96
Springwood Av. M27—1H 77
Springwood Cres. SK6—3E 106
Springwood Hall Rd. OL8
—6A 64
Springwood La. SK6—3E 106
Springwood Way. OL7—1A 82
Sprodley Dri. WN6—8B 16
Spruce Av. BL9—8B 26
Spruce Clo. SK6—4A 54
Spruce Clo. OL4—3D 64
Spruce Lodge. SK8—7K 103
Spruce Rd. BL0—6G 9
Spruce St. OL16—3H 29
Spruce Wlk. M33—8B 88
Spurn La. OL3—4B 48
Spurstow M. SK8—4C 114
Spur Wlk. M8—5F 60
Square Fold. M35—5H 81
Square, The. BL0—5J 9
Square, The. BL3—8M 37
Square, The. M34—1L 93
Square, The. M25—9L 41
Square, The. OL6—3D 82
Square, The. SK7—1K 115
Square, The. SK2—9E 96
Square, The. WN7—1D 72
Square, The. SK5—7E 92
Square, The. WA13—8B 98
Square, The. SK5—7E 92
(Dobcross)
Square, The. OL3—9B 48
(Uppermill)
Squire's Ct. M5—... 77
Squires La. M29—8L 55
Squirrel La. BL6—9D 19
Squirrels Jump. SK9—8M 119
Stablefold. OL5—8J 65
Stablefold. M28—3C 76
Stable M. M25—5C 60
Stables, The. M35—4K 81
Stable St. M10—3D 4 & 5E 78
Stable St. OL9—7E 44
Stablings, The. SK9—6G 119
Stafford Clo. SK13—6M 97
Stafford Rd. N. PR7—1L 17
Stafford Rd. M27—8F 58
Stafford Rd. M28—7J 57
Stafford Rd. M30—9M 81
Stafford Rd. M35—2G 81
Stafford St. M29—2H 55
Stafford View. M5—4A 4 &
8B 78
Stage La. WA13—9B 98
Stage St. WA14—7B 100
Stainburn Clo. WN6—3D 32
Stainburn Rd. SK2—7J 105
Staindale Clo. OL4—2D 64
Stainer St. M12—3A 92
Stainforth St. M11—7D 80
Stainmoor Ct. SK2—7K 105
Stainmore Av. M18—2E 92
Stainsbury St. BL3—5C 38
Stainton Av. M18—4D 92
Stainton Clo. M26—4E 40
Stainton Rd. M26—4F 40
Stalbridge Clo. OL16—5B 14
Staley Clo. SK15—5J 83
Staley Dri. SK15—5J 83
Staley Hall Rd. SK15—4J 83
Staley Rd. OL4—2F 64
(Oldham)
Staley Ter. SK15—4H 83
(Springhead)
Staley Rd. SK15—4H 83
Stalham Clo. M10—4K 79
Stalmine Av. SK8—4H 113
Stalybridge Rd. SK14—...
Stalyhill Dri. SK15—8L 83
Stamford Arc. OL6—4C 82
Stamford Ct. OL6—50 82
(Springhead)
Spring Rd. SK12—1M 121
Spring Rd. WA14—2D 110
Spigby Sq. WN3—6A 52
Springs. OL11—9L 27
Springs Brow. PR7—5K 17
Springside Gro. SK15—4F 82
Springside Rd. BL9—6E 10
Spring Side Rd. BL8—3H 25
Springside Wlk. M15—9D 78
Springs La. SK15—3F 82
(in four parts)
Springs Rd. M24—8K 43
(in two parts)
Spring St. BL0—5H 9
Spring St. BL8—3F 24

Stamford St. M16—1C 90
(in two parts)
Stamford St. M27—7G 59
Stamford St. M29—4L 55
Stamford St. M33—8G 89
Stamford St. OL4—2E 64
Stamford St. OL5—8H 65
Stamford St. OL6—4C 82
(in two parts)
Stamford St. OL10—9L 27
Stamford St. OL16—4H 29
Stamford St. M32—2K 89
Stamford St. M35—5F 104
Stamford St. Flats. M32—2K 89
Stamford St. Central. OL6
—5B 82
Stamford St. OL6—5A 82
(Millbrook)
Stamford St. SK15—5E 82
(Stalybridge, in two parts)
Stamford Way. WA14—8D 100
(off Berkshire Rd.)
Stancliffe Gro. WN2—3J 35
Stancliffe Rd. M22—8E 102
Stancross Rd. M23—4J 101
Stanwell St. M9—7L 61
Stand Av. M25—8L 41
Stand Clo. M25—9J 41
Standedge Clo. BL0—7J 9
Standedge Rd. OL3—6B 48
Standedge St. M11—7D 80
Standedge Wlk. SK15—1L 83
(off Crowswood Dri.)
Standfield Dri. M28—9G 57
Standford Hall Clo. BL0—7H 9
Standish Av. WN5—2D 50
Standish Gallery. WN1—9C 34
(off Galleries, The)
Standishgate. WN1—9C 34
Standish La. M14—6K 91
Standish St. M29—8A 56
Standish Wlk. M34—8K 93
Standish Wood La. WN6—2L 33
Standmoor Ct. M25—1K 59
Standmoor Rd. M25—1K 59
Standon Wlk. M10—6D 62
Standring Av. BL3—1G 41
Standmoor M8—1G 79
Stand Rise. M25—9L 41
Stanedge Gro. WN3—6B 52
Stangate Wlk. M11—7M 79
Stanhope Av. M34—9L 81
Stanhope Clo. SK9—3K 119
Stanhope Ct. M25—3A 60
Stanhope Rd. M6—2L 77
Stanhope Rd. WA14—2A 110
Stanhope St. M19—5B 92
Stanhope St. M34—8E 92
Stanhope St. OL6—3D 82
Stanhope St. OL11—5F 28
(Broadley)
Stanhope St. OL12—1D 12
(Whitworth)
Stanhope Way. M35—8F 62
Stanhorne Av. M8—6G 61
Stanhurst. M30—4E 76
Stanier Av. M30—4D 75
Stanier St. M9—8B 61
Stanion Gro. SK16—7G 41
Stanley Av. M14—3J 91
Stanley Av. N. M25—2A 60
Stanley Av. S. M25—2A 60
Stanley Bank Rd. WA11—7M 69
Stanley Clo. M16—1B 90
Stanley Clo. BL4—1F 24
Stanley Clo. M45—... 61
Stanley Clo. WN2—5C 112
Stanley Dri. SK8—3A 66
Stanley Dri. M45—2A 60
Stanley Dri. WA15—8G 101
Stanley Gro. BL6—9D 20
Stanley Gro. M29—2M 91
Stanley Gro. OL1—7A 46
Stanley Gro. M12—8A 92
Stanley Gro. SK4—1B 104
Stanley Hall La. SK12—6J 117
Stanley La. WN2—2H 35
Stanley Mt. M33—2G 101
Stanley Pl. OL11—4F 28
Stanley Pl. WN1—9E 34
Stanley Rd. BL1—9B 22
Stanley Rd. BL4—9E 38
Stanley Rd. M7—6E 60
Stanley Rd. M16—8F 90
Stanley Rd. M26—8G 41
Stanley Rd. M27—... 58
Stanley Rd. M32—2K 89
Stanley Rd. OL4—2G 65
(Oldham)
Stanley Rd. OL15—6B 14
(Lees)
Stanley Rd. OL9—1H 63
Stanley Rd. WA14—7B 100
Stanley Rd. SK1—3G 105
Stanley Rd. SK4—1B 104
Stanley Rd. SK6—3B 106
(Marple)
Stanley Rd. SK8—2A 114
Stanley Rd. SK9—1H 119
(Handforth)
Stanley Rd. WN2—5G 53
(Aspull)
Stanley Rd. WN3—2J 35
(Platt Bridge)
Stanley Sq. SK15—2J 117
Stanley St. M4—2D 112
Stanley St. M8—... 79
Stanley St. M25—8M 41
Stanley St. M29—6J 55
(Atherton)
Stanley St. M29—7E 80
(Tyldesley)
Stanley St. M35—7E 80
Staton Av. BL2—9J 23
Staton St. M11—7C 80
Staveleigh Way. OL6—4B 82
Staveley Av. SK15—4G 83
Staveley Av. BL1—4B 22
Staveley Clo. M24—7L 43
Staveley Clo. OL2—7H 45
Staveley Wlk. OL2—5L 45
(off Shaw St.)
Staveton Clo. SK7—1G 115
Stavordale. OL2—2E 28
(off Spotland Rd.)
Staycott St. M16—8C 78
Staythorpe Wlk. M7—8E 60
Stead St. M11—8D 80
Steadway. OL3—3C 30
Steam St. M11—6L 79
Stedman Clo. M11—5L 79
Steele Gdns. BL2—4L 39
Steeple Dri. M5—4A 78
Stefan Clo. M11—5K 79
Stelfox Av. M14—8J 91
Stelfox Av. WA15—5F 100
Stelfox La. M34—5K 93
Stelfox St. M30—9A 76
Stelling St. M18—1D 92
Stenbury Clo. M14—2H 91
Stenner La. M20—9G 103
Stenson Sq. M11—4D 80
Stephen Clo. BL8—8J 25

Stephenson Av. M35—6G 81
Stephenson Rd. M32—4L 89
Stephenson Sq. BL6—8B 20
Stephenson St. M35—7G 63
Stephenson St. M30—8H 53
Stephens Av. M5—... 77
Stephens Rd. M20—9J 91
Stephens Rd. SK15—3F 82
Stephens St. BL2—2K 39
Stephen Ter. M20—2H 103
Stephen St. BL8—8J 25
Stephen St. M3—1E 5 & 3F 78
Stephen St. M31—4E 88
Steps Meadow. OL12—7J 13
Sterndale Av. WN6—3L 17
Sterndale Rd. M28—1F 74
Sterndale Rd. SK3—8K 104
Sterndale Rd. SK6—4B 106
Sterratt St. BL1—2D 38
Stetchworth Dri. M28—9H 57
Stevenson Clo. M3—3A 52
Stevenson Dri. OL1—5E 46
Stevenson Pl. M1—4F 5 & 6G 79
Stevenson Rd. M27—8E 58
Stevenson Sq. M1—4G 5 &
6H 79
Stevenson St. M3—4C 4 & 6D 78
Stevens St. SK9—8L 119
Stewart Av. BL4—1H 57
Stewart Av. M19—5A 92
Stewart Rd. WN3—5A 52
Stewart St. BL1—8E 22
Stewart St. BL8—7H 25
(in two parts)
Stewart St. OL7—5M 81
Stewart St. WA14—6F 62
Stewart St. OL9—7H 72
Stile Clo. M31—4J 87
Stiles Av. SK6—6E 106
Stiles Clo. SK14—1E 96
Stilton Dri. M11—7A 80
Stirling. M30—5F 76
(off St Andrews Ct.)
Stirling Av. M20—6F 90
Stirling Av. SK6—8F 106
Stirling Av. SK7—3K 115
Stirling Av. WN2—9G 35
Stirling Clo. WN7—1K 73
Stirling Ct. SK4—3F 92
Stirling Dri. SK15—4G 83
Stirling Gro. M25—9K 69
Stirling Pl. OL10—9F 26
Stirling Rd. BL3—5E 22
Stirling Rd. OL9—4F 62
Stirling St. OL9—1J 63
Stirrup Brook Gro. M28—2F 74
Stirrup Ga. M28—2K 76
Stitch La. SK4—2D 104
Stiups La. OL16—6H 29
Stobart Av. M25—6B 60
Stockbury Gro. BL1—9F 22
(off Lindfield Dri.)
Stockdale Av. SK3—8F 104
Stockdale Gro. BL2—9M 23
Stockdale Rd. M9—4L 61
Stockfield Mt. OL9—2H 63
Stockfield Rd. OL9—2H 63
Stockholm Rd. SK3—6B 104
Stockholm St. M11—5B 80
Stockland Clo. M13—6B 5 &
8H 79
Stock La. OL9—1H 63
Stockley Av. BL2—8L 23
Stockley Dri. WN6—1E 32
Stockley Wlk. M15—9D 78
Stockport Rd. E. SK6—1M 105
Stockport Rd. M12, M13 & M19
—9J 79
Stockport Rd. M34—3M 93
Stockport Rd. OL5 & OL4—6J 65
Stockport Rd. OL7—7M 81
(Marple)
Stockport Rd. SK6—3B 106
(Diggle)
Stockport Rd. SK8 & SK3
—7K 103
Stockport Rd. SK14—7D 94
(Gee Cross)
Stockport Rd. SK14—5H 95
(Hattersley)
Stockport Rd. SK14—5E 94
(Hyde)
Stockport Rd. WA15—8E 100
Stockport Trading Est. SK6
—4B 104
Stockport Trading Est. SK4
—4C 104
Stockport Village. SK14—1E 104
Stocks Av. SK14—8G 85
Stocksfield Dri. M9—5L 61
Stocks La. SK15—6H 83
Stocks Pk. Dri. BL6—7C 20
Stocks Pk. Ho. BL6—7C 20
Stocks St. M8—1F 5 & 4G 79
Stocks St. E. M8—1F 5 & 3G 79
Stock St. M26—3D 42
Stockton Dri. BL8—5B 104
Stockton Pk. OL4—2D 64
Stockton Rd. M21—6A 90
Stockton Rd. OL9—7F 118
(Hadfield)
Stockton Rd. SK14—1G 97
(Hyde)
Stockton Rd. WA11—8D 68
Stockton St. M16—2E 90
Stockton St. OL15—6A 14
Stockwood Wlk. M9—5K 61
Stoke Abbot Clo. SK7—5E 114
Stoke Abbot Lodge. SK7
—... 114
Stokesay Clo. BL9—4M 41
Stokesay Dri. SK7—1L 115
Stokesay Rd. M33—9E 88
Stokesley Wlk. BL3—5E 38
(in two parts)
Stokes St. M11—6D 80
Stokoe Av. WA14—8A 100
Stolford Wlk. M8—1F 78
(off Ermington Dri.)
Stonall Av. M15—9D 78
Stoneacre. BL6—1F 36
Stoneacre Rd. M22—2C 112
Stonebeck Ct. M9—3H 61
Stonebeck Rd. M23—8M 101
Stone Breaks Av. OL4—1G 65
Stone Breaks Rd. OL4—2G 65
Stonebridge Clo. BL6—3J 37
Stonechat Clo. M28—9J 57
Stonechat Clo. M35—4J 81
Stonechat Clo. WA3—7M 71
Stonecliffe Av. SK15—5G 83
Stonecliffe Ter. SK15—4G 83
Stone Clo. BL0—7G 9
Stoneclough Rd. BL4 & M26
—1M 57
Stonecroft. OL1—1L 63
Stone Cross La. WA3—... 71
Stonedale Clo. OL2—4L 45
Stonedelph Clo. BL8—1G 24
Stonefield. OL15—... 13
Stonefield Dri. M8—2E 78
Stonefield St. OL16—5M 29
Stonehaven. WN3—6K 51

Stonehead St. M9—9M 61
Stonehewer St. M26—7H 41
Stonehill Cres. OL12—8A 12
Stonehill Dri. OL12—8A 12
Stone Hill La. OL12—9A 12
Stone Hill Rd. BL4—2K 57
Stonehill Rd. OL12—8A 12
Stonehouse Wlk. M23—6L 101
(off Sandy La.)
Stonehurst Clo. M12—9A 80
Stoneleigh Av. M33—9D 88
Stoneleigh Dri. M26—1B 58
Stoneleigh Rd. OL4—1G 65
Stoneleigh St. OL1—8B 46
Stonelow Clo. M15—9F 78
Stonemead. SK6—2E 106
Stone Mead Av. WA15 —5J 111
Stonemead Clo. BL3—5F 38
Stonemill Ter. SK5—2F 104
Stonepail Clo. SK8—8F 102
Stonepail Rd. SK8—8G 103
Stone Pit Clo. WA3—6M 71
Stone Pit La. WA3—9E 72
Stone Pits. BL0—1M 9
Stoneridge. SK14—1F 96
Stone Row SK6—7G 107
(in two parts)
Stone Row. WN2—6G 35
Stones Bank Rd. BL7—6A 6
Stonesby Clo. M16—2D 90
Stonesteads Dri. BL7—2G 23
Stonesteads Way. BL7—2G 23
Stone St. BL2—9H 23
Stone St. M3—5D 4 & 7E 78
Stone St. OL16—5M 29
Stoneswood Rd. OL3—6L 47
Stonewaite Clo. WN3—6A 52
Stoneway. M5—8B 78
(off W. Park St.)
Stoneyboyd. OL12—2D 12
Stoney Brow. WN8—6B 32
(in two parts)
Stoneycroft Av. BL6—6D 20
Stoneycroft Clo. BL6—5D 20
Stoneyfield. SK15—3G 83
Stoneyfield Clo. M16—4F 90
Stoneygate La. WN6—8B 16
Stoneygate Wlk. M11—8D 80
Stoney Knoll. M7—1D 78
Stoney La. OL3—2L 47
Stoney La. PR7—6E 18
Stoney La. SK9—6F 118
Stoneyside Av. M28—4L 57
Stoneyside Gro. M28—4L 57
Stonie Heyes Av. OL12 —9H 13
Stonor Rd. PR7—3F 18
Stonyford Rd. M33—1K 101
Stony Head. OL15—1C 14
(off Calderbrook Rd.)
Stonyhurst Av. BL1—5E 22
Stonyhurst Av. WN3—2D 52
Stonyhurst Clo. M15—9F 78
Stonyhurst Clo. WA11—8B 68
Stony La. WN6—6A 16
Stopes Rd. BL3 & M26—6C 40
Stopford Av. OL15—7L 13
Stopford St. M11—7E 80
Stopford St. SK3—5D 104
Stopford St. WN2—1F 52
Stopford Wlk. M34—3M 93
Stopforth St. WN6—8A 34
Stopley Wlk. M11—7A 80
Stores Cotts. OL4—2L 65
Stores St. M25—4C 60
Store St. BL6—6C 20
Store St. M1—5G 5 & 7H 79
Store St. M11—8B 80
Store St. OL2—1C 46
Store St. OL7—1A 82
Store St. OL11—1L 27
Store St. SK2—9J 105
Storey Pas. Rd. OL15—6M 13
Stortford Dri. M23—3B 102
Storth Bank. SK13—7F 96
Storth Meadow Rd. SK13 —7F 96
Stothard Rd. M32—5H 89
Stott Dri. M31—5K 87
Stottfield. OL2—6H 45
Stott Ho. OL8—3L 63
Stott La. BL2—9H 23
Stott La. M6—4H 77
Stott La. M24—4M 43
Stott Milne St. OL9—3H 63
Stott Rd. M27—1D 76
Stott Rd. OL9—5E 62
Stott's La. M10—1D 80
Stott St. M11—5M 79
Stott St. M35—1D 80
Stott St. OL12—1F 28
Stott St. OL16—8K 13
Stourbridge Av. M28—2G 57
Stour Clo. WA14—7C 100
Stourport St. OL1—8A 46
Stour Rd. M29—8B 56
Stout St. WN7—2C 72
Stovell Av. M12—4A 92
Stovell Rd. M10—8A 62
Stow Clo. BL8—5K 25
Stowell St. BL1—9E 22
Stowell St. M5—6L 77
Stowfield Clo. M9—4H 61
Stow Gdns. M20—8G 91
Stracey St. M10—4L 79
Stradbroke Clo. M18—1B 92
Strain Av. M9—4K 61
Straits, The. M29—1C 74
Strand Av. WN4—3B 70
Strand Ct. M32—6J 89
Strand La. M26—8J 41
Strand, The. BL6—7D 20
Strand, The. OL11—8F 28
Strand, The. WN4—3B 70
Strand Way. OL2—7K 45
Strange Rd. WN4—4K 69
Strange St. WN7—3B 72
Strangford St. M26—5D 40
Stranraer Rd. WN5—8J 33
Stranton Dri. M28—8C 58
Stratfield Av. M23—4K 101
Stratford Av. BL1—9A 22
Stratford Av. BL9—2L 25
Stratford Av. M20—9F 90
Stratford Av. M30—7C 76
Stratford Av. OL8—5L 63
Stratford Av. OL11—5E 28
Stratford Clo. BL4—8F 38
Stratford Gdns. SK6—2M 105
Stratford Rd. M24—3B 62
Stratford Sq. SK8—5J 113
Stratford St. WN6—8A 34
Strathaven Pl. OL10—9F 26
Strathblane Clo. M20—7H 91
Strathfield Dri. M11—5C 80
Strathmere Av. M16—4B 90
Strathmore Av. M32—3K 89
Strathmore Av. M34—4B 94
Strathmore Av. WN4—2A 70
Strathmore Clo. BL0—7J 9
Strathmore Rd. BL2—9L 23
Stratton Dri. WN2—7F 52
Stratton Gro. BL6—5B 20
Stratton Rd. M16—4B 90
Stratton Rd. M27—7F 58
Stratton Rd. SK2—5J 105
Strawberry Bank. M6—2A 4 & 4B 78
Strawberry Clo. WA14—6B 100
Strawberry Hill. M6—2A 4 & 4B 78
Strawberry Hill Rd. BL2—4H 39
Strawberry La. OL5—4J 65
Strawberry La. SK9—5E 118
Strawberry Rd. M6—2A 4 & 4A 78
Stray, The. BL1—6H 23
Stream Ter. SK1—4H 105
Street Bri. Rd. OL1—7G 45
Streetgate. M28—3F 56
Streethouse La. OL3—8M 47
Street La. M26—1E 40
Street La. SK10—3J 121
Stretford By-Pass. M28 & M30 —2M 75
Stretford-Eccles By-Pass. M31 —3F 88
Stretford Motorway Est. M32 —1G 89
Stretford Pl. OL12—8E 12
Stretford Rd. M16 & M15—1C 90
Stretford Rd. M31—5D 88
Stretton Av. M20—2J 103
Stretton Av. M32—3G 89
Stretton Av. M33—1E 100
Stretton Av. WA3—8K 71
Stretton Av. WN5—2E 68
Stretton Clo. M10—2K 79
Stretton Clo. WN6—1L 33
Stretton Rd. BL0 & BL8—9G 9
Stretton Rd. BL3—5B 38
Stretton Way. SK9—7K 113
Striding Edge Wlk. OL1—8A 46
Strines Ct. SK14—2E 94
Strines Rd. SK6—7G 107
Strines Rd. SK6 & SK12 —2H 117
Stringer Av. SK14—4M 95
Stringer Clo. SK14—4M 95
Stringer St. SK1—3G 105
Stringer St. WN7—2F 72
Stringston Wlk. M16—3E 90
(off Westerling Wlk.)
Stroma Gdns. M31—1C 88
Stromness Gro. OL10—9F 26
Strong St. M7—1D 4 & 3E 78
Strongstry Rd. BL0—1J 9
Strontian Wlk. M11—6C 80
Stroud Av. M30—4B 76
Stroud Clo. M24—3A 62
Stroud Clo. WN2—7F 34
Struan Ct. WA14—8C 100
Stuart Av. M30—4F 86
Stuart Av. SK6—6D 106
Stuart Av. WN2—5B 54
Stuart Cres. WN5—2D 68
Stuart Rd. M32—3K 89
Stuart Rd. SK6—8K 93
Stuart St. M11—5M 79
(in two parts)
Stuart St. M24—9C 44
Stuart St. OL8—3L 63
Stuart St. OL16—4G 29
(in two parts)
Stuart St. WN1—9D 34
Stuart Wlk. M24—1M 61
Stubbins Clo. M23—4L 101
Stubbins La. BL0—4J 9
Stubbins St. BL0—2J 9
Stubbins Vale Rd. BL0—3J 41
Stubbins Vale Ter. BL0—2H 9
Stubley La. OL15—6M 13
Stubley Mill Fold. OL15—7M 13
Stubley Mill Rd. OL15—7L 13
Studforth Wlk. M15—1G 91
(off Botham Clo.)
Studland Rd. M22—9F 102
Studley Clo. OL2—5A 46
Studley Ct. M29—7M 55
Sturton Av. WN3—5L 51
Styal Av. M32—3G 89
Styal Av. SK5—8F 92
Styal Gro. SK8—1G 113
Styal Rd. M22 & SK8—6F 112
Styal Rd. SK9—9G 113
Styhead Dri. M24—6K 43
Style St. M4—2F 5 & 4G 79
Style View. SK9—1H 119
Sudbury Clo. M16—1C 90
Sudbury Clo. WN3—6B 52
Sudbury Dri. BL6—3J 37
Sudbury Dri. SK8—4K 113
Sudbury Rd. SK7—4L 115
Sudden St. OL11—6C 28
Sudell St. M4 & M10—2G 5 & 4H 79
Sudley Rd. OL11—5C 28
Sudlow St. OL16—9H 13
Sudren St. BL8—7F 24
Sue Patterson Wlk. M10 —2K 79
Suffield St. M24—9M 43
Suffield Wlk. M22—3D 112
Suffolk Av. M35—4G 81
Suffolk Clo. BL3—4B 40
Suffolk Clo. WN1—1B 34
Suffolk Dri. SK5—8J 93
Suffolk Dri. SK9—2J 119
Suffolk Gro. WN7—2C 72
Suffolk Rd. WA14—9B 100
Suffolk St. M6—2A 78
Suffolk St. OL9—4H 63
Suffolk St. OL11—4F 28
Sugar La. OL3—7A 48
Sugar La. SK10—6M 121
Sugden St. OL6—4D 82
Sulby Av. M32—4L 89
Sulby St. M10—8A 62
Sulby St. M26—9B 40
Sulgrave Av. SK12—8M 115
Sullivan St. M12—3A 92
Sullivan Way. WN1—8D 34
Sultan St. BL9—1L 41
Sulway Clo. M27—9G 59
Sumac St. M11—5D 80
Sumbland Ho. M27—6H 59
Summer Av. M31—4E 88
Summer Castle. OL16—3F 28
Summer Ct. M29—9B 56
Summercroft. OL9—5H 63
Summerdale Dri. BL0—9H 9
Summerfield Av. M35—4E 80
Summerfield Dri. M24—7C 44
Summerfield Dri. M25—7A 60
Summerfield Dri. M29—8B 56
Summerfield La. M29—8B 56
Summerfield Pl. SK9—5G 119
Summerfield Rd. BL3—5H 39
Summerfield Rd. M22—2C 112
Summerfield Rd. M28—9A 58
Summerlea. SK8—4B 114
Summer Pl. M14—4J 91
Summers Av. SK15—5J 83
Summerseat Clo. M5—7A 78
Summerseat La. BL0—8G 9
Summersgill Clo. OL10—9L 27
Summershades La. OL4—2K 65
Summers St. OL9—1J 63
Summers St. SK15—7E 82
Summer St. BL6—6B 20
Summer St. OL16—3G 29
Summer St. SK13—6J 97
Summerville Av. M9—9M 61
Summerville Rd. M6—2L 77
Summit Clo. BL9—6F 26
Summit St. OL10—8F 26
Sumner Av. BL2—9D 24
Sumner Rd. M6—2K 77
Sumners Pl. SK13—5H 97
Sumner St. BL3—7B 38
Sumner St. M29—5J 55
Sumner St. OL2—4B 46
Sumner St. WA11—9G 69
Sumner St. WN2—4K 35
Sunbank Clo. OL12—9D 12
Sunbank La. WA15—7K 111
Sunbeam Wlk. M11—6M 79
(off Hopedale Clo.)
Sunbury Clo. SK16—7F 82
Sunbury Dri. M10—3D 80
Sundance Ct. M5—7L 77
Sunderland Av. OL6—3C 82
Sunderland Pl. WN5—8K 33
Sundew Pl. M24—1D 62
Sundial Clo. SK14—3K 95
Sundial Rd. SK2—6K 105
Sundial Wlk. SK14—3K 95
Sundown Clo. SK12—4M 117
Sunfield. SK6—2B 106
Sunfield Av. OL4—6E 46
Sunfield Cres. OL2—6L 45
Sunfield Dri. OL2—6M 45
Sunfield Est. OL3—5C 48
Sunfield La. OL3—5C 48
Sunfield Rd. OL1—9M 45
Sunfield Way. OL4—1E 64
Sun Ga. OL15—1M 29
Sunk La. M24—1A 62
(in two parts)
Sunlaws St. SK13—6H 97
Sunleigh Rd. WN2—2L 53
Sunlight Rd. BL1—2C 38
Sunningdale Av. M11—5B 80
Sunningdale Av. M25—1J 59
Sunningdale Av. M26—4D 40
Sunningdale Av. M33—2L 101
Sunningdale Clo. BL8—1G 41
Sunningdale Clo. SK14—1F 94
Sunningdale Ct. M34—2H 93
Sunningdale Dri. M6—2G 77
Sunningdale Dri. M25—3A 60
Sunningdale Dri. M30—3F 86
Sunningdale Dri. OL10—1K 43
Sunningdale Dri. SK7—5F 114
Sunningdale Gro. WN7—9K 55
Sunningdale Ho. M33—2L 101
Sunningdale Rd. M31—5B 88
Sunningdale Rd. M34—5A 94
Sunningdale Rd. SK8—5A 114
Sunningdale Wlk. BL3—4D 38
Sunninghill St. BL3—5D 38
Sunny Av. BL9—5M 25
Sunny Bank. M26—9A 40
Sunny Bank. OL4—3E 64
Sunnybank. SK9—5G 119
Sunnybank Av. M30—4F 76
Sunny Bank Av. M35—6F 80
Sunny Bank Av. SK4—1M 103
Sunnybank Dri. SK9—7D 118
Sunnybank Rd. BL1—8C 22
Sunny Bank Rd. BL9—6M 41
Sunny Bank Rd. M13—3L 91
Sunnybank Rd. M29—9B 56
Sunny Bank Rd. M35—6F 80
Sunny Bank Rd. WA14—3C 110
Sunny Banks. SK13—6H 97
Sunny Bower St. BL8—4E 24
Sunny Brow. PR7—1A 18
Sunny Brow Rd. M18—1C 92
Sunny Brow Rd. M24—9L 43
Sunny Dri. M25—4M 59
Sunny Dri. WN5—2F 50
Sunnyfield Rd. M25—1C 60
Sunnyfield Rd. SK4—2M 103
Sunnyfields. WN3—6J 51
Sunny Garth. BL5—9E 36
Sunnylea Av. M19—9L 91
Sunny Lea M. SK9—5G 119
Sunnymead Av. BL1—6F 22
Sunnymede Vale. BL0—8G 9
Sunny Side. M18—2E 92
Sunnyside. M35—4F 80
Sunnyside. OL7—2M 81
Sunny Side Cotts. M32—4M 89
Sunny Side Cotts. OL12—9H 11
Sunnyside Ct. M5—6A 4 & 8B 78
Sunnyside Ct. M35—4F 80
Sunnyside Cres. OL6—5D 82
Sunnyside Gro. OL6—5D 82
Sunnyside La. M35—3F 80
Sunnyside Rd. BL1—8C 22
Sunnyside Rd. M35—4F 80
Sunnyside Rd. WN4—1M 69
Sunnywood Dri. BL8—4G 25
Sunnywood La. BL8—4G 25
Sunrise View. OL15—2D 14
Sunset Av. M22—3D 102
Sun St. BL0—4H 9
Sun St. OL5—7J 65
Sunwell Ter. SK6—1F 116
Surbiton Rd. M10—3B 80
Surrey Av. M35—4F 80
Surrey Av. OL2—2M 45
Surrey Av. WN7—3L 73
Surrey Clo. BL3—5B 40
Surrey Dri. BL9—1M 41
Surrey Pk. Clo. OL2—1B 46
Surrey Rd. M9—6K 61
Surrey St. M9—6J 61
Surrey St. OL6—2D 82
Surrey St. OL9—3J 63
Surrey St. SK13—5H 97
Surrey Way. SK5—9J 93
Surridge. WA16—7C 108
Surtees Rd. M23—3A 102
Sussex Av. BL9—9E 26
Sussex Av. M20—1H 103
Sussex Clo. M27—6F 58
Sussex Clo. M31—3E 98
Sussex Clo. OL9—2H 63
Sussex Clo. WN1—9B 18
Sussex Clo. WN2—3A 54
Sussex Dri. BL9—1M 41
Sussex Dri. M35—4G 81
Sussex Pl. M29—5A 56
Sussex Pl. SK14—1F 94
Sussex Rd. M30—8C 86
Sussex Rd. SK3—5B 104
Sussex St. M2—4E 5 & 6F 78
Sussex St. M7—2C 4 & 4D 78
(in two parts)
Sussex St. OL16—4F 28
Sussex St. WN7—3L 73
Sutch La. WA13—1A 108
Sutcliffe Av. M12—4B 92
Sutcliffe St. BL1—8E 22
Sutcliffe St. M24—9C 44
Sutcliffe St. OL2—6A 46
(Heyside)
Sutcliffe St. OL2—4A 46
(Shaw Side)
Sutcliffe St. OL7—6M 81
Sutcliffe St. OL8—3L 63
Sutcliffe St. OL15—5B 14
Sutherland Clo. OL8—7M 63
Sutherland Flats. OL10—8J 27
(off Meadow Clo.)
Sutherland Gro. BL4—9J 39
Sutherland Rd. BL1—9A 22
Sutherland Rd. M16—3A 90
Sutherland Rd. OL10—9E 26
Sutherland Rd. WN3—5A 52
Sutherland St. BL4—9J 39
Sutherland St. M27—7E 58
Sutherland St. M30—4B 76
Sutherland St. OL6—4E 82
Sutherland St. WN2—3J 53
Sutherland St. WN5—2M 51
Suthers St. M26—8J 41
Suthers St. OL9—2J 63
Sutton Dri. M35—4E 80
Sutton Dwellings. M6—4M 77
Sutton Ho. M6—4M 77
(off Sutton Dwellings)
Sutton La. PR6—1H 19
Sutton Rd. BL3—5M 37
Sutton Rd. M18—3C 92
Sutton Rd. SK4—2C 104
Sutton Rd. SK9—7K 119
Sutton Rd. SK12—1M 121
Suttons La. SK6—8G 107
Sutton St. M12—9A 80
Sutton Way. M6—4A 78
Sutton Way. SK9—7L 113
Swailes St. OL4—2B 64
Swaindrod La. OL15—4E 14
Swaine St. SK3—4E 104
Swainsthorpe Dri. M9—8L 61
Swain St. OL12—1E 28
Swalecliff Av. M23—4K 101
Swaledale Clo. OL2—4L 45
Swale Dri. WA14—7C 100
Swallow Bank Dri. OL11 —7B 28
Swallow Clo. SK15—9M 65
Swallow Dri. BL9—6B 26
Swallow Dri. M30—3G 87
Swallow Dri. OL11—3M 27
Swallowfield. WN7—2G 73
Swallowfields. WN5—3D 50
Swallow La. SK15—9M 65
Swallow St. M12—4A 92
Swallow St. OL8—6K 63
Swallow St. SK1—6F 104
Swanage Av. M23—5K 101
Swanage Av. SK2—7K 105
Swanage Clo. BL8—4J 25
Swanage Rd. M30—4B 76
Swanbourne Gdns. SK3 —7C 104
Swan Clo. SK12—8H 115
Swan Ct. OL2—3B 46
Swanhill Clo. M18—9F 80
Swan La. BL3—5D 38
Swan La. WN2—4B 54
Swanley Av. M10—2L 79
Swan Meadow Rd. WN3—1B 52
Swann Ct. SK8—3B 114
Swann Gro. SK8—3B 114
Swann La. SK8—3A 114
Swann St. OL6—4C 82
Swann St. WN3—1B 52
Swan Rd. BL8—9F 8
Swan Rd. WA15—4G 101
Swansea St. OL8—4B 64
Swan St. M4—3F 5 & 5G 79
Swan St. M26—7H 41
Swan St. SK9—4H 119
Swan Ter. M30—7C 76
Swanton Wlk. M8—1F 78
(off Kenford Wlk.)
Swarbrick Rd. M25—6M 59
Swarthdale Ho. M6—4M 77
(off Sutton Dwellings)
Swayfield Av. M13—3M 91
Swaylands Dri. M33—4H 101
Sweet Briar Clo. OL12—9E 12
Sweet Briar La. OL12—9E 12
Sweetlove's Gro. BL1—5E 22
Sweetlove's La. BL1—5E 22
Sweetnam Dri. M11—5B 80
Swettenham Rd. SK9—7K 113
Swift Clo. SK6—9C 94
Swift Rd. OL1—5E 46
Swift Rd. OL11—3M 27
Swift St. OL6—2D 82
Swift Wlk. M10—1C 80
Swinbourne Gro. M20—7J 91
Swinburne Av. M35—4G 81
Swinburne Grn. SK5—5D 92
Swinburne Way. M34—7A 94
Swinburn Gro. WN5—7D 50
Swinburn St. M9—7M 61
Swindell's St. M11—8E 80
Swindells St. SK14—1E 94
Swindon Clo. M18—1D 92
Swineyard La. WA16—7A 108
Swinfield Av. M21—6M 89
Swinford Gro. OL2—4A 46
Swinford Wlk. M9—5L 61
Swinley Chase. SK9—2M 119
Swinley La. WN1—7C 34
Swinley Rd. WN1—7C 34
(in two parts)
Swinside. WN1—8F 34
Swinside Clo. M24—7J 43
Swinside Rd. BL2—1M 39
Swinstead Av. M10—2L 79
Swinton Cres. BL9—8A 42
Swinton Gro. M13—1J 91
Swinton Hall Rd. M27—8F 58
Swinton Pk. M6—2H 77
Swinton St. BL2—2L 39
Swinton St. OL4—3C 64
Swiss Hill. SK9—8M 119
Swithemby St. BL6—6A 20
Swithin Rd. M22—4E 112
Swythamley Clo. SK3 —5A 104
Sybil St. OL15—5A 14
Sycamore Av. M25—2M 59
(off Beech Av.)
Sycamore Av. M26—9F 40
Sycamore Av. M34—4M 93
Sycamore Av. OL4—9D 46
Sycamore Av. OL9—5F 62
Sycamore Av. OL10—1L 43
Sycamore Av. OL16—7A 30
Sycamore Av. WA3—6G 71
Sycamore Av. WA11—9F 68
Sycamore Av. WA14—8A 100
Sycamore Av. WN2—5M 53
Sycamore Av. WN6—5M 33
Sycamore Clo. OL15—6M 13
Sycamore Clo. SK9—2H 119
Sycamore Clo. SK16—7F 82
Sycamore Ct. M6—4A 78
Sycamore Ct. M10—4L 79
Sycamore Cres. OL6—2C 82
Sycamore Cres. WA3—3B 98
Sycamore Dri. M35—5J 81
Sycamore Dri. WN3—6H 51
Sycamore Gro. M35—9H 63
Sycamore Lodge. SK7—5F 114
Sycamore Pl. M25—2M 59
Sycamore Rd. BL8—5F 24
Sycamore Rd. M29—5L 55
Sycamore Rd. M30—3A 76
Sycamore Rd. M31—2E 98
Sycamore Rd. SK6—1A 106
Sycamores, The. M33—2J 101
Sycamores, The. OL4—9E 46
Sycamores, The. OL5—7L 65
Sycamores, The. SK14—3F 96
Sycamores, The. SK15—7H 83
Sycamore St. M33—1L 101
Sycamore St. SK3—5B 104
Sycamore St. SK15—6F 82
Sycamore Wlk. BL6—8E 20
Sycamore Wlk. SK8—7K 103
Syddal Clo. SK7—7D 114
Syddal Cres. SK7—8D 114
Syddal Grn. SK7—7D 114
Syddall Av. SK8—4K 113
Syddall St. SK14—5D 94
Syddall St. WA10—8A 68
Syddal Rd. SK7—7D 114
Sydenham St. OL1—8A 46
(in two parts)
Sydenham Ter. OL12—8D 12
Sydney Av. M30—5D 76
Sydney Av. WN7—5D 72
Sydney Gdns. OL15—2C 14
Sydney Rd. SK7—7F 114
Sydney St. M6—5L 77
Sydney St. M27—9D 58
Sydney St. M32—4K 89
Sydney St. M35—9E 62
Sydney St. OL5—8K 65
Sydney St. SK2—6J 105
Sydney St. WN2—5G 53
Syke Croft. SK6—2D 106
Syke La. OL12—7F 12
Syke Rd. OL12—7F 12
Syke Rd. OL15—9C 14
Sykes Av. BL9—5B 42
Sykes Clo. OL3—3B 66
Sykes Ct. OL16—4H 29
Sykes Meadow. SK3 —7D 104
Sykes St. BL9—7A 26
Sykes St. OL16—6A 30
(Milnrow)
Sykes St. OL16—4H 29
(Rochdale)
Sykes St. SK5—6F 92
Sykes St. SK14—5F 94
Sykes Wlk. SK5—6F 92
(off Sykes St.)
Sylvan Av. M16—3D 90
Sylvan Av. M31—3D 88
Sylvan Av. M33—2J 101
Sylvan Av. M35—2E 80
Sylvan Av. SK9—6F 118
Sylvan Av. WA15—5F 100
Sylvandale Av. M19—5A 92
Sylvan Gro. WA14—8D 100
Sylvan St. OL9—1J 63
Sylvester Av. SK2—7H 105
Sylvester Clo. SK14—4L 95
Sylvester St. BL1—1E 38
Sylvester St. BL6—8K 19
Sylvester Way. M34—7A 94
Sylvester Way. SK14—4L 95
Sylvia Gro. SK5—7E 92
Symms St. M6—3B 78
Symond Rd. M9—3L 61
Symons Rd. M33—9H 89
Symons St. M7—9E 60
Syndall Av. M12—9K 79
Syndall St. M12—9K 79
Syresham St. WN2—5H 53
Syston Av. WA11—9C 68
Taberner Clo. WN6—9M 17
Taberner St. WN2—6H 53
Tabley Av. M14—4H 91
Tabley Gdns. M35—6H 81
Tabley Gdns. SK6—9G 107
Tabley Gro. M13—4M 91
Tabley Gro. SK5—7E 92
Tabley Gro. WA15—4F 100
Tableymere Gdns. SK8—1M 113
Tabley Rd. BL3—5B 38
Tabley Rd. M33—3L 101
Tabley Rd. SK9—7K 113
Tabley St. M6—2B 78
Tabley St. OL5—8K 65
Tabley St. SK16—7E 82
Tabor St. M24—7M 43
Tackler Clo. M27—9F 58
Tadcaster Wlk. OL1—1M 63
Taddington Bank. SK13—5E 96
(off Castleton Cres.)
Taddington Clo. SK13—5E 96
(off Castleton Cres.)
Taddington Pde. SK13—5E 96
(off Castleton Cres.)
Taddington Pl. SK13—5E 96
(off Castleton Cres.)
Tadlow Wlk. M10—2H 5 & 4J 79
Tadman Gro. WA14—7A 100
Tadmor Clo. M28—4F 56
Tagge La. M27—1L 77
Tagore Clo. M13—2L 91
Tahir Clo. M8—9H 61
Tait M. SK4—3M 103
Talavera St. M7—2D 78
Talbot Av. BL3—5A 40
Talbot Clo. OL4—9C 46
Talbot Ct. BL1—6F 22
Talbot Ct. M32—3L 89
Talbot Gro. BL9—4A 26
Talbot Pl. M16—1B 90
Talbot Rd. M14—7L 91
Talbot Rd. M32 & M16—3L 89
Talbot Rd. M33—1L 101
Talbot Rd. SK9—8M 119
Talbot Rd. SK13—4J 97
Talbot Rd. SK14—1E 94
Talbot Rd. WA14—2B 110
(in two parts)
Talbot Rd. WN7—3A 72
Talbot St. M24—7M 43
Talbot St. M30—6E 76
Talbot St. OL6—4A 82
Talbot St. OL11—4F 28
Talbot St. SK7—9K 105
Talbot St. SK13—5J 97
Talbot St. WA3—7G 71
Talbot St. WN4—3D 70
Talbot Vs. SK13—5J 97
Talford Gro. M20—9G 91
Talgarth Rd. M10—1H 5 & 3J 79
Talkin Dri. M24—6L 43
Talland Wlk. M13—1K 91
Tallarn Clo. M20—7J 91
Tallis St. M12—3A 92
Tall Trees. M7—7D 60
Tall Trees Pl. SK2—7J 105
Talmine Av. M10—2L 79
Talock Clo. WN5—2E 68
Tamar Clo. BL4—3B 58
Tamar Ct. M15—9D 78
Tamar Dri. M23—9A 102
Tamarin Clo. M27—7C 58
Tamar Rd. WA11—9J 69
Tamar Way. OL10—7G 27
Tame Barn Clo. OL16—4A 30
Tame Clo. SK15—4J 83
Tame Ct. SK15—5H 83
Tame La. OL3—2J 47
Tamer Gro. WN7—8C 54
Tamerton Dri. M8—1G 79
Tame St. M4—6K 79
Tame St. M34—8M 81
(Audenshaw)
Tame St. M34—1L 93
(Denton)
Tame St. OL3—9B 48
Tame St. OL5—5L 65
Tame St. SK15—6E 82
Tame View. OL5—6J 65
Tame Wlk. SK9—1L 119
Tamewater Vs. OL3—7M 47
(off Brook La.)
Tamworth Av. M5—5A 4 & 7B 78
Tamworth Av. M25—1A 60
Tamworth Av. W. M5—7A 78
Tamworth Clo. M15—1E 90
Tamworth Clo. SK7—4J 115
Tamworth Ct. M15—1E 90
Tamworth Ct. OL9—3L 63
Tamworth Dri. BL8—5J 25
Tamworth Dri. WN2—7F 34
Tamworth Grn. SK1—3H 105
Tamworth St. OL9—3J 63
Tamworth St. SK1—3H 105
Tamworth Wlk. M5—5A 4 & 7B 78
Tandis Ct. M6—3G 77
Tandle Hill Rd. OL2—3H 45
Tandlewood M. M10—2C 80
Tandlewood Pk. OL2—3H 45
Tanfield Rd. M20—6H 103
Tangmere Clo. M10—5C 62
Tangshutts La. SK6—3D 106
Tang, The. SK6—3B 106
Tanhill La. OL8—6A 64
Tanhouse Av. M29—9D 56
Tan Ho. Dri. WN3—6J 51
Tan Ho. La. WN3—6J 51
Tanhouse Rd. M31—3K 87
Tanner Brook Clo. BL3—5E 38
Tanners Brow. BL6—9L 19
Tannersfield Lodge. M35 —1E 80
Tanners Fold. OL8—6A 64
Tanners Grn. M6—4M 77
Tanner's La. WA3—7G 71
Tanners St. BL0—5H 9
Tanners St. M18—1E 92
Tanner St. SK14—3D 94
Tannock Ct. SK7—3M 115
Tannock Rd. SK7—3M 115
Tan Pit Cotts. OL10—5K 27
Tanpits Rd. BL9—7L 25
Tanpit Wlk. M22—2C 112
Tansey Gro. M8—9F 60
Tansley Av. PR7—1K 17
Tansley Rd. M8—6H 61
Tansley Sq. WN5—3K 51
Tanthill Clo. SK2—7L 105
Tanworth Wlk. BL1—8E 22
Tan Yd. Brow. M18—2E 92
Tanyard Clo. PR7—1K 17
Tanyard Dri. WA15—5J 111
Tanyard La. WA15—7F 110
Taper St. BL0—5H 9
Tape St. BL0—5H 9
Tapley Av. SK12—1L 121
Taplow Gro. SK8—2M 113
Taplow Wlk. M14—3L 91
Tarbet Dri. BL2—2M 39
Tarbet Rd. SK16—8C 82
Tarbet Wlk. M8—1F 78
Tarbolton Cres. WA15—1J 111
Tariff St. M1—4G 5 & 6H 79
Tarland Wlk. M11—6C 80
Tarleton Av. M29—3H 55
Tarleton Clo. BL8—9F 24
Tarleton Ho. M6—3J 77
Tarleton Pl. BL3—6A 38
Tarleton Wlk. M13—9K 79
Tarnbrook Clo. M25—9C 42
Tarnbrook Wlk. M15—1G 91
(off Wellhead Clo.)
Tarn Clo. WN4—2B 70
Tarn Dri. BL9—3L 41
Tarn Gro. M28—7M 57
Tarn Gro. WA11—7B 68
Tarnrigg Clo. WN3—5L 51
Tarnside Clo. SK2—7M 105
Tarnside Fold. SK13—7G 97
Tarnside Rd. WN5—2E 50
Tarns, The. SK8—1H 113
Tarnway. WA3—8M 71
Tarporley Av. M14—6G 91
Tarporley Clo. SK3—8D 104
Tarporley Wlk. SK9—1L 119
Tarran Grn. M34—5B 94
Tarran Gro. M34—5B 94
Tarran Pl. WA14—7E 100
Tarrant Clo. WN3—6K 51
Tarrington Clo. M12—1A 92
Tartan St. M11—5B 80
Tarves Wlk. M11—6B 80
Tarvin Av. M20—7G 91
Tarvin Av. SK4—7D 92
Tarvin Clo. WA3—8L 71
Tarvin Dri. SK6—1L 105
Tarvington Clo. M10—1J 79
Tarvin Rd. SK8—8A 104
Tarvin Wlk. BL1—8E 22
Tarvin Way. SK9—7K 113
Tasle Av. M2—4E 5 & 6F 78
Tatchbury Rd. M35—9G 63
Tate St. OL8—4B 64
Tatham St. OL16—3G 29
Tatland Dri. M22—1F 112
Tattenhall Wlk. M14—6K 91
Tattersall Av. BL1—8L 21
Tattersall St. OL9—2K 63
Tatton Clo. SK7—9M 105
Tatton Clo. SK8—9A 104
Tatton Ct. M14—6K 91
Tatton Ct. SK4—1C 104
Tatton Ct. SK9—7L 113
Tatton Dri. WN4—2M 69
Tatton Gdns. SK6—9C 94
Tatton Gro. M20—8H 91
Tatton Mere Dri. M35—6H 81
Tattonmere Gdns. SK8—9A 104
Tatton Pl. M33—9H 89
Tatton Rd. M33—9H 89
Tatton Rd. M34—5A 94
Tatton Rd. SK9—7L 113
Tatton Rd. N. SK4—9C 92
Tatton Rd. S. SK4—1C 104
Tatton St. M5—5A 4 & 7B 78
Tatton St. M15—6C 4 & 9D 78
Tatton St. SK1—4F 104
Tatton St. SK14—7E 94
Tatton St. SK15—5H 83
(in two parts)
Tatton Ter. SK16—6B 82
Tatton View. M20—8H 91
Taunton Av. M30—4B 76
Taunton Av. M31—6B 88
Taunton Av. OL7—3A 82
Taunton Av. OL11—3B 28
Taunton Av. SK5—9J 93
Taunton Av. WN7—6D 54
Taunton Clo. BL1—9C 22
Taunton Clo. SK7—2A 116
Taunton Dri. BL4—8F 38
Taunton Grn. OL7—2M 81
Taunton Gro. M25—2A 60
Taunton Hall Clo. OL7—2M 81
Taunton Pl. OL7—2M 81
Taunton Rd. M33—1D 100
Taunton Rd. OL7—3A 82
Taunton Rd. OL9—7G 45
Taunton St. M4—6K 79
Taunton Wlk. M34—5A 94
Taurus St. OL4—9C 46
Tavern Ct. M35—9H 63
Tavern Ct. Av. M35—9H 63
Tavery Clo. M4—5K 79
Tavistock Clo. SK14—4L 95
Tavistock Dri. OL9—8F 44
Tavistock Rd. BL1—3D 38
Tavistock Rd. M33—9D 88
Tavistock Rd. OL11—7F 28
Tavistock Rd. WN2—4A 54
Tavistock Sq. M9—9K 61
(off Grangewood Dri.)
Tavistock St. M29—4H 55
Tawton Av. SK14—3L 95
Tay Clo. OL8—3L 63
Tayfield Rd. M22—2C 112
Taylor Av. OL11—2M 27
Taylor Bldgs. BL4—2B 58
Taylor Grn. Way. OL4—1F 64
Taylor Gro. WN2—5C 54
Taylor La. M34—2K 93
Taylor Rd. M31—8E 76
Taylor Rd. WA11—9L 69
Taylor Rd. WA14—8A 100
Taylor Rd. WN2—5C 54
Taylor's La. BL2—2A 40
Taylor's La. M10—2C 80
Taylor's La. WN3—5E 52
Taylorson St. M5—6A 4 & 9B 78
(in two parts)
Taylorson St. S. M5—9A 78
Taylor's Pl. OL4—2A 64
Taylors Pl. OL12—1F 28
Taylor's Rd. M32—2K 89
Taylor St. BL6—7B 20
Taylor St. BL9—6A 26
Taylor St. M18—9C 80
Taylor St. M24—9A 44
Taylor St. M25—4B 60
Taylor St. M26—6G 41
Taylor St. M34—2M 93
Taylor St. M35—6F 80
Taylor St. OL1—9C 46
Taylor St. OL2—4K 45
Taylor St. OL4—2E 64
Taylor St. OL9—1G 63
Taylor St. OL10—8J 27
Taylor St. OL12—1F 28
(Rochdale)
Taylor St. OL12—3D 12
(Whitworth)
Taylor St. SK14—1D 96
(Hollingworth)
Taylor St. SK14—3F 94
(Hyde)
Taylor St. SK15—6H 83
Taylor St. WA3—6J 71
Taylor St. WN3—9B 34
Taylor St. WN7—8D 54
Taylor Ter. OL15—6C 14
(off Ealees Rd.)
Taylor Ter. SK16—6B 82
(off Astley St.)
Tayton Clo. M29—7C 56
Taywood Rd. BL3—7K 37
Teak Dri. BL4—4D 58
Teak St. BL9—8B 26
Teal Av. SK12—8G 115
Tealby Av. M16—2C 90
Tealby Ct. M21—6C 90
Tealby Rd. M18—2B 92
Teal Clo. SK2—8M 105
Teal Clo. WA14—5B 100
Teal Clo. WN3—4H 51
Teal Ct. OL11—3M 27
Teal St. BL3—5F 38
Teasdale Clo. OL9—5E 62
Tebbutt St. M4—2G 5 & 4H 79
Tedburn Wlk. M10—6D 62
Tedder Clo. BL9—7B 42
Tedder Dri. M22—5F 112
Teddington Rd. M10—7C 62
Ted Jackson Wlk. M11—7M 79
Teesdale Av. M31—2A 88
Teesdale Clo. SK2—7L 105
Teesdale Dri. WN7—2J 73
Teesdale Rd. WA11—8J 69
Teesdale Wlk. M9—5L 61
Tees St. OL16—4H 29
Tees Wlk. OL8—3L 63
Teignmouth Av. M10—1H 5 & 3J 79
Telegraphic Ho. M5—8A 78
Telegraph Rd. M17—9G 77
Telfer Av. M13—4L 91
Telfer Rd. M13—4L 91
Telford Clo. M34—8L 81
Telford Cres. WN7—8D 54
Telford Rd. SK6—9G 107
Telford St. BL6—8C 20
Telford St. M8—2J 79
Telford St. M29—6G 55
Telford Wlk. M16—2D 90
Telford Way. OL11—8G 29
Telham Wlk. M23—8A 102
Tellson Clo. M6—1K 77
Tellson Cres. M6—1K 77
Tell St. OL12—3D 28
Telryn Wlk. M8—8J 61
(off Stakeford Dri.)
Temperance Sq. SK14—2A 96
Temperance St. M12—5H 5 & 7J 79
Temperance Ter. SK6—7F 106
Tempest Rd. BL6—6H 37
Tempest Rd. SK9—8M 119
Tempest St. BL3—5B 38
Temple Av. SK14—1J 97
Temple Clo. OL4—9E 46
Templecombe Dri. BL1—4D 22
Temple Dri. BL1—7C 22
Temple Dri. M27—9H 59
Temple La. OL15—2C 14
Temple Rd. BL1—7C 22
Temple Rd. M33—1K 101
Temple Sq. M8—1H 79
Temple St. M24—8B 44
Temple St. OL1—1B 64
Temple St. OL10—8K 27
Temple St. SK14—1J 97
Templeton Dri. WA14—7B 100
Templeton Rd. WN2—6H 53
Temsbury Wlk. M10—2L 79
Ten Acre La. M25—1K 59
Ten Acres La. M10—2A 80
Tenax Rd. M17—8H 77
Tenbury Dri. WN4—3M 69
Tenby Av. BL1—9A 22
Tenby Av. M20—8H 91
Tenby Av. M32—2M 89
Tenby Ct. M15—9C 78
Tenby Dri. M6—2K 77
Tenby Dri. SK8—3B 114
Tenby Gro. OL12—1C 28
Tenby Rd. OL8—6H 63
Tenby Rd. SK3—6B 104
Tenby St. OL12—1C 28
Tenement La. SK7—1C 114
Tenement St. WN2—7H 53
Teneriffe St. M7—2D 78
Ten Foot Clo. SK13—4H 97
Tenham Wlk. M9—5L 61
(off Ravenswood Dri.)
Tennis St. BL1—7D 22
Tennis St. M16—2B 90
Tennyson Av. BL9—3M 41
Tennyson Av. M26—5E 40
Tennyson Av. M34—7A 94
Tennyson Av. SK16—8G 83
Tennyson Av. WN7—8C 54
Tennyson Dri. WN1—6C 34
Tennyson Dri. WN5—7D 50
Tennyson Gdns. M25—5M 59
Tennyson Rd. BL4—2H 57
Tennyson Rd. M24—7B 44
Tennyson Rd. M27—8D 58
Tennyson Rd. M35—5G 81
Tennyson Rd. SK5—5D 92
Tennyson Rd. SK8—7M 103
Tennyson St. BL1—9D 22
Tennyson St. M6—1B 4 & 3C 78
Tennyson St. OL1—8C 46
Tennyson St. OL11—5G 29
Tennyson Wlk. BL1—8E 22
Tensing Av. M29—3J 55
Tensing Av. OL7—2B 82
Tensing St. OL8—8A 64
Tenter Brow. SK15—5F 82
Tentercroft. OL1—1L 63
Tentercroft. OL12—3E 28
Tenterden St. BL9—8K 25
(in two parts)
Tenterden Wlk. M22—1C 112
Tenter Dri. WN6—2B 34
Tenterhill La. OL12—9K 11
Tenters St. BL9—8K 25
Tenth St. M17—9J 77
Terence St. M10—2D 80
Terling Wlk. M10—2L 79
(off Lodge St.)
Terminal Rd. E. M22—5C 112
Terminal Rd. N. M22—5B 112
Terminal Rd. S. M22—5B 112
Tern Av. BL4—9F 38
Tern Clo. OL11—3M 27
Tern Clo. SK16—8E 82
Tern Clo. WA14—5B 100
Tern Dri. SK12—8H 115
Ternhill Ct. BL4—9K 39
Terrace St. OL4—1B 64
Terrace, The. M25—5B 60
Terrington Clo. M21—7E 90
Tetbury Dri. BL2—9M 23
Tetbury Rd. M22—3B 112
Tetlow Gro. M30—6C 76
Tetlow La. M7 & M8—8E 60
Tetlow St. M10—2C 80
Tetlow St. M24—9A 44
Tetlow St. OL8—2K 63
Tetlow St. SK14—1E 94
Tetlows Yd. OL15—1D 14
Tetsworth Wlk. M10—6D 62
Teviot St. M13—1L 91
Tewkesbury Av. M24—6M 43
Tewkesbury Av. M31—2D 88
Tewkesbury Av. M35—4G 81
Tewkesbury Av. OL6—9C 64
Tewkesbury Av. OL9—7G 45
Tewkesbury Av. WA15—1J 111
Tewkesbury Clo. SK8—6B 114
Tewkesbury Clo. SK12—7K 115
Tewkesbury Dri. M25—6C 60
Tewkesbury Rd. M10—4K 79
Tewkesbury Rd. SK3—7B 104
Tewkesbury Rd. WA3—7H 71
Texas St. OL6—5C 82
Textile St. M12—8A 80
Textilose Rd. M17—1H 89
Teynham Wlk. M22—3C 112
Thackeray Clo. M8—1G 79
Thackeray Gro. M35—5G 81
Thackeray Ho. WN3—3A 52
Thackeray Pl. WN3—3A 52
Thackeray Rd. OL1—8C 46
Thames Av. WN7—6F 72
Thames Clo. BL9—2M 25
Thames Clo. M11—7B 80
Thames Ct. M15—9D 78
Thames Dri. WN5—1F 50
Thames Rd. OL16—4B 30
Thames St. OL1—9A 46
Thames St. OL16—4H 29
Thames St. WN2—3H 35
Thanet Clo. M7—2E 78
Thanet Gro. WN7—2G 73
Thankerton Av. M34—6K 81
Thatcher St. OL8—4A 64
Thatch Leach. OL9—3F 62
Thatch Leach La. M25—1A 60
Thaxmead Dri. M10—3D 80
Thaxted Dri. SK2—8A 106
Thaxted Pl. BL1—1C 38
Thaxted Wlk. M22—4C 112
Theatre St. OL1—1M 63
Thekla St. OL9—9K 45
Thelma St. BL0—5H 9
Thelwall Av. BL2—1K 39
Thelwall Av. M14—6F 90
Thelwall Clo. WN7—3B 72
Thelwall Rd. M33—2L 101
Thelwell Clo. WA15—7E 100
Theobald Rd. WA15—3D 110
Theodore Wlk. M12—9K 79
Theta Clo. M11—5B 80
Thetford. OL12—2E 28
(off Spotland Rd.)
Thetford Clo. BL8—5K 25
Thetford Clo. WN2—4L 53
Thetford Dri. M8—9G 61
Thicketford Brow. BL2—9K 23
Thicketford Clo. BL2—8J 23
Thicketford Rd. BL2—9H 23
Thicknesse Av. WN6—6M 33
Thimble Clo. OL12—7K 13
Thimbles, The. OL12—7K 13
Third Av. BL1—2B 38
Third Av. BL3—5M 39
Third Av. BL9—6D 26
Third Av. M11—4C 80
Third Av. M17—1K 89
Third Av. M27—2E 76
Third Av. M29—3B 74
Third Av. OL8—6J 63
Third Av. SK10—2K 121
Third Av. SK15—1L 83
Third Av. WN6—7A 34
Third St. BL1—6M 21
Third St. M17—1K 89
(in two parts)
Third St. WN2—9F 52
Thirkhill Pl. M30—5F 76
Thirlby Dri. M22—3D 112
Thirlestone Av. OL4—5F 46
Thirlmere Av. BL6—8C 20
Thirlmere Av. M27—9G 59
Thirlmere Av. M29—9A 56
Thirlmere Av. M32—3J 89
Thirlmere Av. OL7—3M 81
Thirlmere Av. WA11—7B 68
Thirlmere Av. WN2—8H 53
(Abram)
Thirlmere Av. WN2—1H 53
(Ince)
Thirlmere Av. WN4—3C 70
Thirlmere Av. WN5—9F 32
Thirlmere Av. WN6—2A 34
Thirlmere Av. WN8—1B 50
Thirlmere Clo. PR6—2H 19
Thirlmere Clo. SK9—8K 119
Thirlmere Clo. SK15—3G 83
Thirlmere Dri. BL9—2L 41
Thirlmere Dri. M24—7L 43
Thirlmere Dri. M28—3G 57
Thirlmere Dri. WA13—1A 108
Thirlmere Gro. BL4—9E 38
Thirlmere Gro. OL2—3K 45
Thirlmere Rd. BL5—1M 55
Thirlmere Rd. BL6—7J 19
Thirlmere Rd. M31—1E 98
(Partington)
Thirlmere Rd. M31—3L 87
(Urmston)
Thirlmere Rd. OL11—6B 28
Thirlmere Rd. SK1—6H 105
Thirlmere Rd. WA3—6J 71
Thirlmere Rd. WN2—3L 53
Thirlmere Rd. WN5—1H 51
Thirlmere St. WN7—2E 72
Thirlspot Clo. BL1—4E 22
Thirsfield Dri. M11—5C 80
Thirsk Av. M33—2C 100
Thirsk Av. OL9—8F 44
Thirsk Clo. BL8—5H 25
Thirsk M. M7—1D 78
Thirsk Rd. BL3—6A 40
Thirsk St. M12—6H 5 & 8J 79
Thistle Clo. SK15—8L 83
Thistle Sq. M31—3E 98
Thistleton Rd. BL3—6M 37
Thistle Wlk. M31—3E 98
Thistlewood Dri. SK9—4K 119
Thistleyfield. OL16—3L 29
Thistley Fields. SK14—6C 94
Thomas Clo. M34—2A 94
Thomas Dri. BL3—4D 38
Thomas Gibbon Clo. M32 —5J 89
Thomas Greenwood Clo. M11 —7L 79
Thomas Henshaw Ct. OL11 —6C 28
Thomas Holden St. BL1—1D 38
Thomas Ho. OL2—5L 45
(off Royton Hall Wlk.)
Thomason Fold. BL7—5K 7
Thomason Sq. OL15—6A 14
Thomas Regan Ct. M18—9D 80
Thomasson Clo. BL1—9E 22
Thomas St. BL3—4D 38
Thomas St. BL4—9L 39
(Farnworth)
Thomas St. BL4—1L 57
(Kearsley)
Thomas St. BL5—6E 36
Thomas St. M4—3F 5 & 5G 79
Thomas St. M8—8F 60
Thomas St. M26—6H 41
Thomas St. M29—5K 55
Thomas St. M32—2K 89
Thomas St. M35—8G 63
Thomas St. OL2—6M 45
(Royton)
Thomas St. OL2—3C 46
(Shaw)
Thomas St. OL4—3E 64
Thomas St. OL12—1D 12
Thomas St. OL15—7L 13
Thomas St. OL16—2G 29
Thomas St. SK1—6F 104
Thomas St. SK6—2M 105
(Bredbury)
Thomas St. SK6—3H 107
(Compstall)
Thomas St. SK13—5L 97
Thomas St. SK14—4E 94
Thomas St. WA3—7G 71
Thomas St. WA15—9E 100
Thomas St. WN2—5B 54
Thomas St. W. SK1—6F 104
Thomas Telford Basin. M1 —4H 5 & 6J 79
Thompson Av. BL2—9D 24
Thompson Av. M25—1A 60
Thompson Clo. M34—3H 93
Thompson Dri. BL9—7C 26
Thompson Ho. M29—5J 55
Thompson La. OL9—4G 63
Thompson Rd. BL1—9B 22
Thompson Rd. M17—7E 76
Thompson Rd. M34—3H 93
Thompson St. BL3—4F 38
Thompson St. BL6—7A 20
Thompson St. M3—2E 5 & 4F 78
Thompson St. M4—3G 5 & 4H 79
Thompson St. M10—2M 79
Thompson St. OL9—1K 63
Thompson St. WN1—8E 34
Thompson St. WN3—4A 52
Thompson St. WN4—3D 70
Thompson St. WN7—2B 72
Thomson Rd. M18—2C 92
Thomson St. M13—9J 79
Thomson St. SK3—5E 104
Thoralby Clo. M12—1A 92
Thorburn Dri. OL12—4B 12
Thorburn Ho. WN5—1J 51
(off Green, The)
Thorburn La. WN5—1K 51
Thorburn Rd. WN5—2J 51
Thoresby Clo. M26—4C 40
Thoresby Clo. WN3—5L 51
Thoresway Rd. M13—3L 91
Thoresway Rd. SK9—6F 118
Thorgill Wlk. M10—9A 62
Thor Gro. M5—5B 4 & 7C 78
Thorley Clo. OL9—6F 62
Thorley Dri. M31—4D 88
Thorley Dri. WA15—8H 101
Thorley La. WA15—1H 111
Thorley La. WA15 & M22
(Ringway) —3M 111
Thorley La. WA15—1H 111
(Timperley)
Thorley M. SK7—5F 114
Thorley St. M35—8F 62
Thornaby Wlk. M9—1K 79
(off Kirklington Dri.)
Thornage Dri. M10—1H 5 & 3J 79
Thornam New Rd. OL11—1D 44
Thorn Av. M35—1E 80
Thornbank. M30—4E 76
Thornbank Clo. OL10—2L 43
Thornbank E. BL3—4C 38
(off Deane Rd.)
Thornbank Est. BL3—3C 38
Thornbeck Dri. BL1—9M 21
Thornbeck Rd. BL1—9M 21
Thornbridge Av. M21—6B 90
Thornbury. OL11—4E 28
Thornbury Av. SK14—4L 95
Thornbury Av. WA3—8L 71
Thornbury Rd. M32—2L 89
Thornbury Way. M18—1C 92
Thornbush Clo. WA3—6L 71
Thornbush Way. OL16—2J 29
Thornby Wlk. M23—8A 102
Thorncliff Av. OL8—5L 63
Thorncliffe Av. OL2—3J 45
Thorncliffe Av. SK16—8C 82
Thorncliffe Gro. M19—5C 92
Thorncliffe Ho. M15—1H 91
Thorncliffe Pk. OL2—2J 45
Thorncliffe Rd. BL1—5E 22
Thorncliffe Rd. SK14—2F 96
Thorn Clo. OL10—7H 27
Thorncombe Clo. M16—3E 90
Thorn Ct. M6—3A 4 & 5B 78
Thorncross Clo. M15—6B 4 & 8C
Thorndale Ct. WA15—8G 101
Thorndale Gro. WA15—8G 10
Thornden Rd. M10—3K 79
Thorn Dri. M22—4G 113
Thorndyke Av. BL1—5E 22
Thorndyke Wlk. M25—5B 60
Thorne Av. M31—3A 88
Thorne Ho. M14—4K 91
Thorneside. M34—1M 93
(in two parts)
Thorne St. BL4—8J 39
Thorneycroft. WN7—2J 73
Thorneycroft Av. M21—9B 90
Thorneycroft Clo. WA15 —8H 1
Thorneycroft Rd. WA15 —8H 1
Thorney Dri. SK7—6C 114
Thorney Hill Clo. OL4—2A 64
Thorneyholme Clo. BL6—3J
Thorneylea. OL12—2D 12
Thornfield. BL2—1L 39
Thornfield Clo. WA3—7J 71
Thornfield Cres. M28—3F 56
Thornfield Dri. M27—9E 58
Thornfield Gro. M28—3F 56
Thornfield Gro. OL6—4E 82
Thornfield Gro. SK8—2A 114
Thornfield Hey. SK9—3L 119
Thornfield Rd. BL8—3D 24
Thornfield Rd. M19—9L 91
Thornfield Rd. SK4—2A 104
Thornfield St. M5—6K 77
Thornfield Ter. OL6—5C 82
Thornford Wlk. M10—6D 62
Thorn Gro. M14—6K 91
Thorn Gro. M33—1H 101
Thorn Gro. SK8—6A 114
Thorn Gro. WA15—1E 110
Thorngrove Av. M23—6K 10
Thorngrove Dri. SK9—5J 119
Thorngrove Hill. SK9—5J 11
Thorngrove Ho. M23—6K 10
Thorngrove Rd. SK9—5J 119
Thornham Clo. BL8—4J 25
Thornham Dri. BL1—4G 23
Thornham La. M24—3D 44
Thornham La. OL2—1J 45
Thornham Old Rd. OL2—2G 4
Thornham Rd. M33—3E 100
Thornham Rd. OL2—2K 45
Thornhill. OL11—6E 28
Thornhill Clo. BL1—7C 22
Thornhill Clo. M34—4G 93
Thornhill Dri. M28—8L 57
Thornhill Rd. BL0—1G 25
Thornhill Rd. M35—5H 81
Thornhill Rd. SK4—3M 103
Thornhill Rd. WN4—3J 69
Thornholme Clo. M18—3B 9
Thornholme Rd. SK6—9F 10
Thorniley Brow. M4—3F 5 & 5G
Thorn Lea. BL2—6K 23
Thornlea Av. M27—1D 75
Thornlea Av. OL8—7J 63
Thorn Lea Clo. BL1—2M 37
Thornlee Ct. OL4—3H 65
Thornleigh Rd. M14—5G 91
Thornley Av. BL1—8C 22
Thornley Clo. OL4—3G 65
Thornley Cres. OL4—3G 65
Thornley Cres. SK6—1A 106
Thornley La. OL4—3G 65
Thornley La. N. SK5—3F 92
Thornley La. S. SK5 & M34 —4F
Thornley Pk. Rd. OL4—3G 65
Thornley Rd. M25—1C 60
Thornley Rd. M34—2A 94
Thornley St. M24—8B 44
Thornley St. M26—7H 41
Thornley St. SK14—5E 94
Thornmere Clo. M27—6C 58
Thorn Pl. M6—3A 4 & 5B 78
Thorn Rd. M27—1E 76
Thorn Rd. OL8—5C 64
Thorn Rd. SK7—7D 114
Thorns Av. BL1—6E 22
Thorns Clo. BL1—7D 22
Thorns Clough. OL3—4C 48
Thornsett Clo. M9—8L 61
Thornsgreen Rd. M22—4D 1
Thorns Rd. BL1—7D 22
Thorns, The. M21—7B 90
Thorn St. BL1—8F 22
Thorn St. BL9—8J 9
Thorn St. WN2—4K 53
Thornton Av. BL1—9M 21
Thornton Av. M31—4A 88
Thornton Av. M34—7J 81
Thornton Clo. BL3—6C 40
Thornton Clo. BL4—1H 57
Thornton Clo. M28—9E 56
Thornton Clo. WN4—3M 69
Thornton Clo. WN7—6F 72
Thornton Dri. SK9—9K 113
Thornton Ga. SK8—7G 103
Thornton Pl. SK4—1B 104
Thornton Rd. M14—4G 91
Thornton Rd. M28—9E 56
Thornton Rd. SK8—3J 113
Thornton St. BL2—2G 39
Thornton St. M10—1H 5 & 3
Thornton St. M11—7A 80
Thornton St. OL4—3M 63
Thornton St. OL11—5F 28
Thornton St. N. M10—1H 5 & 2
Thorntree Clo. M9—9L 61
Thorntree Pl. OL12—2D 28
Thornvale. WN2—9J 53
Thorn View. BL9—7C 26
Thorn Wlk. M31—3E 98
Thornway. M28—8G 57
Thornway. SK6—5F 116
Thornway. SK7—4C 114
Thorn Well. BL5—1E 54
Thornwood Av. M18—2E 92
Thorold Gro. M33—1L 101
Thorp Av. M26—4K 41
Thorpe Av. M27—7E 58
Thorpebrook Rd. M10—1A
Thorpe Clo. M34—2M 93
Thorpe Clo. OL4—9G 47
Thorpe Gro. SK4—8D 92
Thorpe Hall Rd. SK14—9F 8
Thorpe Hill. OL1—1L 63
Thorpe La. M34—1M 93
Thorpe La. OL4—9F 46
Thorpeness Sq. M18—9D 8
Thorpe St. BL0—6H 9
Thorpe St. BL1—8D 22
Thorpe St. M16—2C 90
Thorpe St. M24—1J 61
Thorpe St. M28—4K 57
Thorpe St. SK13—4L 97
Thorpe View. M5—8C 78
(off Ordsall Dri.)

Virginia Clo. M23—6K 101
Virginia Ho. BL4—1K 57
Virginia St. BL3—5B 38
Virginia Way. WN5—9J 33
Viscount Dri. SK8—5A 113
Viscount St. WA15—5M 111
Viscount St. M14—3J 91
Vista Rd. WA11 & WA12—8A 70
Vista, The. M30—1C 98
Vivian Pl. M14—2L 91
Vivian St. OL11—5E 28
Vixen Clo. M21—7D 90
Voewood Ho. SK14—5H 105
Voltaire Av. M6—4H 77
Vulcan Dri. WN1—1D 52
Vulcan Rd. WN5—9K 33
Vulcan St. OL1—8B 46
Vulcan St. SK14—4D 94
Vulcan Ter. OL15—6M 13
Vyner Gro. M33—8F 88

Wadcroft Wlk. M9—8L 61
Waddicor Av. OL6—1E 82
Waddington Rd. BL8—2E 24
Waddington St. OL9—9J 45
Wade Bank. BL5—9F 36
Wadebridge Av. M23—6K 101
Wadebridge Rd. BL2—9G 23
Wadebrook Gro. SK8—2L 119
Wade Clo. M30—6D 76
Wadeford Clo. M4—2H 5 & 4J 79
Wade Hill La. OL3—9J 47
Wade Ho. OL3—9B 48
(off Wade Clo.)
Wade Row Top. OL3—9B 48
(off Wade Row)
Wadesmill Wlk. M13—6G 5 & 8H 79
Wadeson Rd. M13—6G 5 & 8H 79
Wade St. BL3—6F 38
Wade St. M24—2D 62
Wade Wlk. M11—7A 80
Wadham Gdns. SK6—9C 94
Wadham Way. WA15—3F 110
Wadhurst Wlk. M13—1E 38
Wadsley St. BL1—1E 38
Wagg Fold. OL15—5M 13
Waggon Rd. OL15—2K 23
Waggon Rd. BL5—6J 65
Wagner St. BL1—7D 22
Wagon La. WA11—9H 69
Wagstaff St. M35—9F 69
Wagstaffe St. M24—8A 44
Wagstaff St. SK15—6E 82
Waincliffe Av. M21—1D 102
Wain Clo. M30—5B 76
Waine St. WA11—9F 68
Wainfleet Clo. WN3—5L 51
Waingap Cres. OL12—3D 12
Waingap Rise. OL12—7E 12
Wainman St. M6—4H 77
Wain Stones Grn. SK2—8L 105
Wainwright Av. M34—1G 65
Wainwright Clo. OL4—1G 65
Wainwright Rd. WA14—8B 100
Wainwright St. OL8—3J 63
Wainwright St. SK16—6D 82
Waithlands Rd. OL16—4H 29
Wakefield Cres. SK6—4A 106
Wakefield Dri. M27—3D 58
Wakefield Dri. OL1—8J 45
Wakefield Dri. SK15—5G 83
Wakefield St. M1—5F 5 & 7G 79
Wakefield St. OL1—6L 45
Wakefield St. WA3—8G 71
Wakefield Wlk. M34—5A 94
Wakeling Rd. M34—6L 93
Walcote Av. WN3—6M 51
Walcott Clo. M13—1L 91
Wald Av. M14—7J 91
Waldeck Wlk. M9—8J 73
(off Ravenswood Dri.)
Walden Av. OL4—7D 46
Walden Clo. M14—6G 91
Walden Cres. SK7—1J 115
Walden Flats. OL10—8J 27
(off Fox St.)
Waldon Av. M10—9A 62
Waldon Av. SK8—8K 103
Waldon Clo. BL3—5C 38
Waldorf Clo. WN3—6K 51
Waldorf St. M12—9L 79
Wales St. OL1—4E 46
Walford Clo. M16—2E 90
Walford Rd. WN4—4C 70
Walkden Av. M11—7B 34
Walkden Av. E. WN1—7C 34
Walkden Dri. M4—6K 79
(off Harrison St.)
Walkdene Dri. M28—5H 57
Walkden Ho. WN4—2M 69
Walkden Rd. M28—6K 57
Walkdens Av. M46—6G 55
Walkden St. OL12—1F 28
Walker Av. BL3—6F 38
Walker Av. M25—2A 60
Walker Av. M35—1H 81
Walker Av. SK15—5J 83
Walker Clo. BL4—2A 58
Walker Clo. M14—4E 90
Walker Fold Rd. BL1—7J 21
Walker Grn. M30—6D 76
Walker La. M30—6D 76
Walker La. SK14—4E 94
Walker Rd. M9—4L 61
Walker Rd. M30—3A 76
(Eccles)
Walker Rd. M30—7F 86
(Irlam)
Walker Rd. OL9—6F 62
Walkers Bldgs. M1—4G 5 & 6H 79
Walkers Ct. BL4—9B 39
Walkers Ct. OL8—5L 63
Walkers Croft. M3—3E 5 & 5F 78
Walker's La. OL4—2G 65
Walker's La. OL6—6J 63
Walker St. BL1—1D 38
Walker St. BL5—9E 36
Walker St. BL9—1L 41
Walker St. M3—2C 4 & 4C 78
Walker St. M9—8L 61
Walker St. M24—1H 61
(in two parts)
Walker St. M26—8J 41
Walker St. M34—2L 93
Walker St. OL8—2K 63
Walker St. OL10—1G 27
Walker St. OL16—3G 29
Walker St. SK14—1G 97
Walkers View. OL4—1G 65
Walk Mill Clo. OL12—7K 13
Walk St. M9—5K 55
Walk, The. M15—7E 28
Walkway, The. M34—8M 37
(in two parts)
Wallace Av. M14—3K 91
Wallace La. WN1—8E 34
Wallace St. OL8—4M 63
Wallace St. M15—9E 78
Wallasey Av. M14—5G 91
Wallbank Dri. OL12—8H 12
Wallbank Rd. SK7—3G 115
Wallbrook St. BL8—3F 24
Wallbrook Cres. M28—4E 40
Wallbrook Gro. BL4—7H 39
Walsall Rd. M22—7E 102
Wallgarth Clo. WN3—6L 51
Wallgate. WN5, WN3 & WN1—1A 52

Wallgate La. WN3—1B 52
Wall Hill Rd. OL3—8L 47
Wallingford Rd. M31—3E 88
Wallingford Rd. SK9—7J 113
Wallis St. OL9—4G 63
Wallshaw Pl. OL1—1A 64
Wallshaw St. OL1—1A 64
(in two parts)
Walls St. WN2—6C 54
Wall St. M6—5M 77
Wall St. OL8—3M 63
Wallsuches La. BL6—6E 20
Wallwork Clo. OL11—1J 27
Wallwork Rd. M29—1D 74
Wallwork St. M11—7E 80
Wallwork St. M26—5G 41
Wallwork St. SK5—4F 92
Wallworth Ter. SK9—3E 118
Wally Sq. M7—1E 78
Walmer Dri. SK7—3F 114
Walmersley Ct. SK6—7F 106
Walmersley Old Rd. BL9—2M 25
Walmersley Rd. BL9—9L 9
Walmersley Rd. M10—6E 62
Walmer St. WN2—3H 91
Walmer St. E. M14—3J 91
Walmer St. M18—9D 80
Walmesley Dri. BL9—8J 9
Walmesley Rd. WN2—1H 53
Walmesley Rd. WN1—1D 52
Walmsley Av. OL16—1D 92
Walmsley Clo. BL5—8M 13
Walmsley Dri. M31—4D 88
Walmsley St. BL8—6H 25
Walmsley St. SK5—2F 104
Walmsley St. SK15—7G 83
Walney Rd. M22—9D 102
Walney Rd. WN3—6K 51
Walnut Av. BL9—7B 26
Walnut Av. OL4—9D 46
Walnut Av. WN1—7D 34
Walnut Clo. M27—4D 58
Walnut Gro. WN7—8F 54
Walnut Rd. M30—3A 76
Walnut St. BL1—2D 98
Walnut St. M18—9D 80
Walnut Tree Rd. SK3—4A 104
Walnut Wlk. M32—6J 89
Walpole Av. WN3—5M 51
Walpole St. OL16—3G 29
Walsall St. M6—2A 78
Walsden St. M11—5C 80
Walsh Av. M9—6J 61
Walshaw Brook Clo. BL8—6F 24
Walshaw Rd. BL8—6F 24
Walshaw Rd. BL8—5F 24
Walshaw Wlk. BL8—5F 24
Walshe St. BL9—8K 25
Walsh St. M29—4K 55
(off Brooklands Av.)
Walsh St. BL6—6B 20
Walsh St. OL9—2H 63
Walsingham Av. M20—1F 102
Walter Greenwood Ct. M6—4A 78
(off Meyrick Rd.)
Walter La. BL9—8A 42
Walter Scott Av. WN1—5B 34
Walter Scott St. OL1—9B 46
Walter St. BL4—7H 39
Walter St. M18—9E 80
Walter St. M25—4M 59
Walter St. OL1—2M 63
Walter St. OL10—1K 43
Walter St. SK1—6F 104
Walter St. WN4—2F 40
Walter St. M28—6K 57
Walter St. WN7—2B 72
Waltham Av. WA3—8J 73
Waltham Av. WN6—6M 33
Waltham Dri. SK8—6B 114
Waltham Gdns. M26—5E 40
Waltham Rd. M16—5E 90
Waltham St. OL4—4C 64
Walton Clo. M24—3J 43
Walton Clo. OL10—1K 43
Walton Ct. BL3—5F 38
Walton Dri. BL9—2L 25
Walton Ho. SK6—6D 106
Walton Pl. BL4—1L 57
Walton Rd. M9—3K 61
Walton Rd. WA14—9B 78
Walton St. M24—4F 100
Walton St. OL10—1K 43
Walton Way. M34—5B 94
Walworth St. BL3—5C 38
Walwyn Clo. M32—5L 89
Wandsworth Av. M11—5D 80
Wanley Wlk. M9—5L 61
Wansbeck Clo. M32—5L 89
Wansfield Wlk. M4—5K 79
Wansford St. M14—3G 91
Wanstead Av. M9—5M 61
Wapping St. BL1—8D 22
Warbeck Clo. SK5—4G 93
Warbeck Clo. WN2—5L 53
Warbeck Rd. M10—6D 62
Warbreck Gro. M33—2K 101
Warburton Clo. SK6—4M 105
Warburton Clo. WA15—6K 111
Warburton Dri. WA15—6K 111
Warburton La. WA13 & M31—5D 98
Warburton Pl. M29—5K 55
Warburton Rd. SK9—3A 118
Warburton St. BL1—2F 38
Warburton St. M5—9B 78
Warburton St. M20—2H 103
Warburton St. M31—2B 88
Warburton St. SK1—3K 101
Warburton View. WA3—3A 98
Warcock Rd. OL4—1C 64
Wardale Ct. M33—1J 101
Ward Ct. OL3—5C 48
(off Ward La.)
Warden La. WA15—3E 110
Warden St. M26—7J 81
Warden's Bank. BL5—3E 54
Ward La. M10—1B 80
Ward La. SK12—1E 63
Ward La. SK1—1B 121

Wardley Hall Rd. M28 & M27—7B 58
Wardley Ind. Est. M28—7B 58
Wardley Rd. M29—8D 56
Wardley Sq. M29—8D 56
Wardley St. M27—7F 58
Wardley St. WN5—3H 51
Wardlow Av. SK13—5D 96
(in two parts)
Wardlow Fold. SK13—5D 96
(off Wardlow M.)
Wardlow Gdns. SK13—5D 96
(off Wardlow M.)
Wardlow Gro. SK13—5D 96
(off Wardlow M.)
Wardlow M. SK13—5D 96
Wardlow St. BL3—5B 38
Wardlow Wlk. SK13—5D 96
(off Wardlow M.)
Wardour Sq. M29—6J 55
(in two parts)
Ward Rd. M10—3B 80
Ward St. M3—2E 5 & 4F 78
Ward St. M9—1J 61
Ward St. M10—8M 61
Ward St. M20—2H 103
Ward St. M35—8E 62
Ward St. OL1—9A 45
Ward St. OL9—1J 63
Ward St. SK1—6G 105
Ward St. SK6—2M 105
Ward St. E. M14—3J 91
Ward St. WN2—1K 53
Wareham Gro. M30—4C 76
Wareham St. M8—7H 61
Wareing St. M29—8M 55
Wareing Way. BL3—3E 38
Warfield Wlk. M9—5L 61
Warford Av. SK12—9A 116
Warford La. WA15—1G 97
Warhurst Fold. SK14—1G 97
Warke, The. M28—1M 75
Warley Clo. SK8—7L 103
Warley Rd. SK16—7C 82
Warley Rd. M16—3A 90
Warley St. OL15—5B 14
Warlingham Clo. BL8—9H 25
Warlow Crest. OL3—4A 66
Warlow Dri. OL3—4A 66
(in two parts)
Warmington Dri. M12—1L 91
Warmley Rd. M23—5K 101
Warne Av. M35—5J 81
Warner Wlk. M11—6M 79
(off Hopedale Clo.)
Warnford Clo. M10—3D 80
Warnford St. WN1—7C 34
War Office Rd. OL11—4L 27—9D 46
Warp Wlk. M4—6J 79
(off Cardroom Rd.)
Warren Av. SK8—8K 103
Warren Bank. M9—5K 61
Warren Clo. M29—3L 55
Warren Clo. M34—4K 93
Warren Clo. SK12—8H 115
Warren Ct. SK7—2D 114
(off Warren Lea)
Warren La. OL8—4B 64
Warren Lea. SK6—3H 107
Warren Lea. SK12—7L 115
Warren Rd. M27—2D 76
Warren Rd. WA15—5K 111
Warrener St. M33—1K 101
Warren Hey. SK9—3L 119
Warren Rd. SK7—2D 114
Warren St. M9—5K 61
Warren St. OL12—2M 27
Warren St. SK1—3E 104
Warren St. SK3—7F 104
Warrington La. WA13—1D 108
Warrington La. WN1—9D 34
Warrington Rd. M9—4J 61
Warrington Rd. WA12 & WA3—9H 71
Warrington Rd. WN1, WN3 & WN2—1D 52
(Ince-in-Makerfield)
Warrington Rd. WN2—6G 53
(Platt Bridge)
Warrington Rd. WN5—5M 51
(Goose Green)
Warrington St. M5—8B 70
Warrington St. WN7 & WA3—6H 73
Warrington Rd. Ind. Est. WN3—3L 51
Warsall Rd. M22—7E 102
Warslow Dri. M33—1L 101
Warsop Av. M22—8E 102
Warstead Wlk. M13—1J 91
(off Plymouth Gro.)
Warth Cotts. OL3—5C 48
(off Huddersfield Rd.)
Warth Fold Rd. M26—3J 41
Warth Rd. BL9—2K 41
Warton Clo. BL8—8F 24
Warton Clo. SK7—5G 115
Warton Dri. M23—8A 102
Warwick Av. M20—1F 102
Warwick Av. M25—1A 60
Warwick Av. OL2—5A 46
Warwick Av. SK4—4M 103
Warwick Clo. BL8—1G 25
(Greenmount)
Warwick Clo. OL12—2A 62
Warwick Clo. OL2—2M 45
Warwick Clo. SK4—1D 104
Warwick Clo. SK8—5M 113
Warwick Ct. M16—4M 89
Warwick Dri. WA15—3E 110
Warwick Dri. WN2—2M 53
Warwick Gdns. BL3—7B 38
Warwick Ho. M19—4A 92
Warwick Mall. SK8—7K 103
Warwick Pl. M11—1M 89
Warwick Rd. M16—1M 89
Warwick Rd. M21—5B 90
Warwick Rd. M26—3F 40
Warwick Rd. M28—7J 57
Warwick Rd. OL12—3C 12
Warwick Rd. OL16—4M 29
Warwick Rd. SK14—3D 94
Warwick Rd. WA3—5C 88
Warwick Rd. S. M16—3A 90

Warwick St. M15—1F 90
Warwick St. M25—4A 60
Warwick St. M27—7F 58
Warwick St. OL9—4J 63
(in two parts)
Warwick St. PR7—4F 18
Warwick St. M31—3L 73
Warwick Ter. SK16—6B 82
(off Astley St.)
Watkin St. M3—2C 4 & 4D 78
Watkin St. OL6—6G 29
Watkin St. WN1—9C 34
Watkin St. SK14—1G 95
Watkin Av. M14—4H 91
Watling St. BL8—9M 7
(Affetside)
Watling St. BL5—1F 54
(Bury)
Watsacre. BL5—1F 54
Washacre Clo. BL5—1F 54
Wash Brook. OL9—4H 63
Washbrook Ct. BL9—2H 25
Washbrook Dri. M32—4H 89
Washbrook Ho. M6—4M 77
(off Sutton Dwellings)
Wash Brow. BL8—5H 25
Washburn Clo. BL7—7F 36
Washford Dri. M23—5K 101
Washington Ct. BL9—7M 25
Washington St. BL3—3C 38
Washington St. OL1—9C 28
Wash La. BL9—7A 26
Wash La. WN7—1H 73
(in two parts)
Wash Ter. BL8—5H 25
Washway La. WA10 & WA11—8A 68
Washway Rd. M33—1D 100
Washwood Clo. M28—7H 57
Wasp Av. OL11—7G 28
Wastdale Av. BL9—6A 42
Wastdale Rd. M23—9M 101
Wast Water St. OL1—8A 46
Watch Hall St. OL16—9J 13
Waterbeck Clo. WN1—8F 34
Waterbridge. M28—7H 57
Watercroft. OL11—1K 27
Waterdale Clo. M28—1H 75
Waterfield Clo. BL9—3M 25
Waterfoot Cotts. SK14—2A 96
Waterford Av. M20—2D 102
Waterford St. OL8—4K 63
Waterfront Quay. M5—8M 77
Watergate. M34—7J 81
(in two parts)
Watergrove Rd. SK16—8F 82
Waterhead. OL4—9E 46
Waterhouse Clo. OL12—6J 13
Waterhouse Rd. M18—2E 92
Waterhouse St. OL12—2F 28
Water La. BL0—1K 9
Water La. BL4—1L 57
Water La. M26—5F 40
Water La. M35—6E 80
Water La. OL16—5A 30
Water La. SK9—4G 119
Water La. SK14—1D 96
Water La. SK26—6F 40
Waterloo Ct. BL1—1L 41
Waterloo Est. M8—1G 79
Waterloo Rd. SK9—9C 26
Waterloo Pde. M8—1E 5 & 3F 78
Waterloo Pk. SK1—4G 105
Waterloo Pl. M34—1F 104
(off Watson Sq.)
Waterloo Rd. M8—1E 5 & 3F 78
Waterloo Rd. OL6—2B 82
Waterloo Rd. SK1—2E 104
Waterloo St. BL1—1L 41
Waterloo St. M1—3F 5 & 5G 79
Waterloo St. M9—2L 61
Waterloo St. M7—8A 60
Waterloo St. OL6—3M 63
Waterloo St. OL1—1M 63
Waterloo St. SK1—3F 104
Waterloo St. SK12—4A 116
Waterloo St. SK15—5G 83
Watermans Clo. M9—5G 61
Watermead. WN5—5E 50
Watermeetings La. SK6
Watermill Clo. OL16—4K 29
Watermillock Gdns. BL1—6F 22
Watersedge. BL4—7G 39
Watersedge Clo. SK8—5M 113
Watersfield Clo. SK8—4M 113
Watersheddings St. OL4—8D 46
Waterside. BL3—4J 39
Waterside. SK6—9F 106
Waterside. SK14—4K 95
(Hyde)
Waterside Av. SK6—8F 106
Waterside Clo. M21—1D 102
Waterside Clo. M26—5K 41
Waterside Clo. SK14—4K 95
Watersmeade Clo. BL1—8F 22
Water's Nook Rd. BL5—9G 37
Waterson Av. M10—9A 62
Waters Reach. SK6—5E 116
Waters Reach. SK12—7M 115
Water St. BL0—6H 9
Water St. BL1—2F 38
Water St. BL7—9D 6
Water St. M3—5C 4 & 5 & 7D 78
(Manchester)
Water St. M3—3E 5 & 5 & 5F 78
(Salford)
Water St. M9—8K 61
Water St. M24—8M 43
Water St. M31—8M 81
(Audenshaw)
Water St. M34—2J 93
(Denton)
Water St. OL1—1L 63
Water St. OL2—5A 46
Water St. OL9—1J 63
Water St. SK1—5F 104
Water St. SK13—6M 97
Water St. SK14—3D 94
Water St. SK9—6J 61
Waterton La. OL6—6H 65
Waterton La. OL5—6H 65
Waterway Enterprise Pk. M17
Waterworks Rd. OL4—8E 46

Watfield Wlk. M9—9K 61
(off Foleshill Av.)
Watford Av. M14—4H 91
Watford Clo. BL1—8E 22
(off Sham Av.)
Watford Rd. M19—8A 92
Watkin Clo. M13—9J 79
Watkins Dri. M25—2C 60
Watkinson's Yd. BL5—3E 36
Watson Av. M31—4K 87
Watson Av. WN4—8A 52
Watson Gdns. OL12—9D 12
Watson Rd. M30—5L 75
Watson Sq. SK1—4F 104
(in two parts)
Watson St. M3 & M2—5E 5 & 7F 78
Watson St. M26—5G 41
Watson St. M27—7F 53
Watson St. M30—5C 76
Watson St. OL3—9C 46
Watson St. OL6—6G 29
Watson St. SK14—1G 95
Watts St. M19—6B 92
Watts St. OL6—4C 64
Watts St. M6—4C 76
Watts St. OL12—2G 29
Wavell Av. SK5—5G 83
Wavell Dri. BL9—8A 42
Wavell Rd. M22—1D 112
Waveney Flats. OL10—4J 27
(off Fox St.)
Waveney Rd. M22—9E 102
Waveney Rd. OL2—1A 46
Waverley Av. BL4—2M 57
Waverley Av. M32—3L 89
Waverley Av. WN4—4A 54
Waverley Ct. M9—3G 61
Waverley Cres. M35—4G 81
Waverley Cres. M43—6B 81
Waverley Dri. SK8—6E 114
Waverley Pl. OL11—5G 29
Waverley Rd. BL1—7E 22
Waverley Rd. M9—9M 61
Waverley Rd. M24—4H 75
Waverley Rd. M33—9F 88
Waverley Rd. SK14—6D 94
Waverley Rd. SK5—4D 92
Waverley Rd. W. M9—9M 61
Waverley Sq. BL4—2M 57
Waverton Av. SK4—7D 92
Waverton Rd. M14—5G 91
Wavertree Av. M43—6A 82
Wavertree Ho. BL1—1E 38
(off Prince St.)
Wayfarers Dri. M29—4J 61
Wayford Wlk. M9—5U 61
Wayland Rd. M18—2D 92
Wayland Rd. S. M18—3D 92
Wayne Clo. M35—3J 81
Wayne St. M11—7E 80
Wayoh Croft. BL7—7J 7
Wayside Av. M12—9M 61
Wayside Dri. SK12—6J 115
Wayside Gro. M28—6F 57
Wayville Clo. OL12—2E 28
(off Spotland Rd.)
Weald Clo. M13—9J 79
Wealdstone Gro. BL2—8H 23
Wearhead Clo. WA3—4J 77
Wearhead Row. M5—6M 77
Weardale Rd. M9—6A 62
Weary Wlk. M11—6D 80
Weaste Av. M28—4H 57
Weaste Dri. M5—5K 77
Weaste La. M5 & M6—4J 77
(in three parts)
Weaste Rd. M5—5K 77
Weaste Trading Est. M5—5K 77
Weatherall St. N. M8—9F 60
(in two parts)
Weatherley Dri. SK6—7D 106
Weaver Av. M28—7J 57
Weaver Ct. M15—9D 78
Weaver Dri. BL9—8A 42
Weaver Gro. WN7—3C 72
Weaver Rd. WA14—8M 61
Weaverham Clo. M13—3M 91
Weaverham Wlk. M9—5L 61
Weavers Ct. M24—3M 43
Weavers Grn. BL4—9K 39
Weavers Grn. M24—8M 43
Weaver Wlk. M11—6D 80
Webb La. SK1 & SK6—4G 105
Webb La. SK6—7C 20
Webb St. BL8—7K 25
Webdale Dri. M10—6A 62
Webster Arc. OL1—1M 63
Webster Gro. M25—9M 59
Webster St. BL3—4H 39
Webster St. M15—1G 91
Webster St. OL5—6, 65
Webster St. OL8—3M 63
Webster St. WN2—5G 53
Wedge St. WA11—6G 69
Wedgewood Dri. WN6—6K 33
Wedgwood Rd. M27—6J 59
Wedhurst St. OL4—1C 64
Wedneshough. SK14—1C 96
Weedall Av. M5—9M 77
Weedon St. OL16—2H 29
Weeton Av. BL2—7L 23
Weeton Av. M23—2M 39
Weint, The. WA3—2B 98
Weir Rd. OL16—3L 29
Weir St. M35—9E 62
Welbeck Av. M31—3E 88
Welbeck Av. OL9—5D 62
Welbeck Av. WN5—8G 45
Welbeck Clo. OL15—7M 41
Welbeck Gdns. BL2—8H 23
Welbeck Gro. M7—1E 78
Welbeck Rd. BL6—7H 21
Welbeck Rd. M30—2E 76
Welbeck Rd. OL6—1A 38
Welbeck St. BL1—1A 38
Welbeck St. M18—3D 80
Welbeck St. S. OL6—3B 64
Welburn St. SK3—7F 104
Welbury Rd. M23—4M 101
Welby St. M13—1K 91
Welch Hill St. WN7—3K 72
Welch Rd. SK14—2F 94
Welcomb Clo. SK6—1M 105
Welcomb St. M11—8B 80
Welcome Pde. OL8—5C 64
Welcroft St. SK1—5F 104
Weldon Av. BL3—7A 38
Weldon Cres. SK3—9E 104
Weldon Dri. M9—3K 61
Weldon Gro. WN3—6L 51
Weldon Rd. WA14—7C 100
Weld Rd. M20—7K 91
Welfold Ho. OL4—3B 64

Welford Av. WA3—8J 71
Welford Clo. SK9—3L 119
Welford Gro. M44—6J 91
Welford Rd. M8—4F 60
Welford St. M6—1A 4 & 3B 78
Welham Rd. WN3—5B 52
Welkin Rd. SK6—2J 105
Wellacre Av. M31—4K 87
Welland Av. OL10—7G 27
Welland Clo. M15—9D 78
Welland Ct. M15—9D 78
(off Eastnor Clo.)
Welland Rd. WN4—2E 70
Welland St. M11—7D 80
Welland St. SK5—5F 92
Welland, The. BL9—8K 26
Wellbank. SK15—7J 83
Wellbank Av. OL6—1E 82
Wellbank St. BL8—4F 24
Wellbank View. OL12—1M 27
Wellbridge Rd. SK16—9B 82
Wellbrow Ter. OL12—9D 12
Wellbrow Wlk. M9—5L 61
Wellcroft. BL8—6B 103
Wellcross Rd. WN8—2B 50
Wellens Way. M24—1J 59
Weller Av. M21—7D 90
Weller Av. SK12—1K 121
Weller Gdns. M21—7D 90
Wellesbourne Dri. M23—6M 101
Wellesley Av. M18—9D 80
Wellesley Gro. WN5—9J 33
Wellfield. SK6—1C 106
Wellfield Clo. BL9—3L 41
Wellfield Gdns. WA15—1J 111
Wellfield La. WA15—3J 111
Wellfield Rd. Pl. OL11—5G 29
Wellfield Rd. BL9—2G 39
Wellfield Rd. M8—8G 61
Wellfield Rd. M23—6A 102
Wellfield Rd. SK2—7J 105
Wellfield St. OL11—4G 29
Wellgate Av. M19—6B 92
Wellgreen Clo. WA15—1J 111
Wellgreen Lodge. WA15—1J 111
Welling Rd. M10—6A 62
Welling St. BL2—9H 23
Wellington Av. M16—5B 90
Wellington Bldgs. OL1—2M 63
Wellington Clo. BL8—4H 25
Wellington Clough. OL7—1A 82
Wellington Cres. M16—3C 90
Wellington Gdns. BL8—4H 25
Wellington Gro. M15—9D 78
Wellington Gro. SK2—6F 104
Wellington Lodge. OL15—5B 14
(off Lodge St.)
Wellington Pde. SK16—6B 82
(off Astley St.)
Wellington Pl. M3—5D 4 & 7E 78
Wellington Pl. OL16—2G 29
Wellington Pl. WA14—9D 100
Wellington Rd. BL7—7J 7
Wellington Rd. BL9—1L 41
Wellington Rd. M14—1F 90
Wellington Rd. M16—3C 90
Wellington Rd. M27—1F 76
Wellington Rd. M30—5D 76
Wellington Rd. M31—1D 92
Wellington Rd. OL9—2H 63
Wellington Rd. SK4—9D 92
Wellington Rd. WA14—7C 100
Wellington Rd. N. SK4—7B 92 & 2E 104
Wellington Rd. S. SK1, SK3 & SK2—4E 104
Wellington Sq. BL3—3D 38
Wellington St. BL3—3D 38
Wellington St. BL7—7J 7
Wellington St. BL9—1L 41
Wellington St. M18—3D 80
Wellington St. M26—1D 92
Wellington St. M29—2S 89
Wellington St. M35—7G 63
Wellington St. OL6—2H 77
Wellington St. OL7—6A 82
Wellington St. E. M7—9D 60
Wellington St. W. M7—9C 60
Wellington Ter. M5—5K 77
Wellington Ter. SK16—6B 82
(off Astley St.)

Welwyn Dri. M6—2G 77
Welwyn Wlk. M10—5K 79
Wembley Gro. M14—6J 91
Wembley Rd. M18—3C 92
Wembury St. M9—6L 61
Wem St. OL9—4G 63
Wemyss Av. SK5—5F 92
Wenderholme Lodge. BL1—1L 37
Wendlebury Grn. OL2—4A 46
Wendon Rd. M23—8B 102
Wendover Dri. BL3—4J 37
Wendover Ho. M5—6A 78
Wendover Rd. M23—4K 101
Wendover Rd. M31—4C 88
Wenfield Dri. M9—6B 62
Wenlock Av. OL7—6J 77
Wenlock Clo. SK2—7M 105
Wenlock Gro. WN2—6G 53
Wenlock Rd. M33—3G 101
Wenlock St. M27—8D 58
Wenlock Way. M12—9M 79
Wensley Ct. M7—7A 60
Wensleydale Av. BL9—6A 42
Wensleydale Clo. OL2—4A 46
Wensleydale Rd. WN7—2J 73
Wensley Dri. SK7—4K 115
Wensley Rd. SK5—7J 103
Wensley Rd. WA3—8L 71
Wensley Way. OL16—4H 29
Wentbridge Rd. BL1—1D 38
Wentworth Av. M18—9E 80
Wentworth Av. M35—1J 81
Wentworth Av. M44—4H 91
Wentworth Av. M6—4J 77
Wentworth Clo. M24—4J 43
Wentworth Clo. BL8—2H 63
Wentworth Ct. SK14—5E 94
Wentworth Rd. M30—5L 87
Wentworth Rd. M6—4L 77
Wentworth Rd. SK5—5B 92
Wentworth Wlk. SK14—4D 38
Werneth Av. M14—4H 91
Werneth Clo. M34—4M 93
Werneth Clo. SK7—5G 115
Werneth Cres. OL8—4J 63
Werneth Gro. WN3—3D 52
Werneth Hall Rd. OL8—3K 63
Werneth Hollow. SK6—8D 94
Werneth Low Rd. SK6 & SK14—1D 106
Werneth Rise. SK6—9C 94
Werneth Rd. SK14—6G 97
Werneth St. M34—1M 93
Werneth St. SK1—3H 105
Werneth View. SK7—4C 116
Werneth Wlk. M34—4M 93
Wescoe Clo. WN6—3L 69
Wesley Av. WA11—8L 69
Wesley Clo. BL5—7E 36
Wesley Clo. OL16—4M 29
Wesley Clo. OL12—8H 13
Wesley Ct. BL8—3E 24
Wesley Ct. M28—4J 57
Wesley Ct. SK8—4M 113
Wesley Dri. OL6—1D 82
Wesley Dri. M28—4J 57
Wesley Grn. M5—4F 5 & 6G 78
Wesley M. BL2—2G 39
Wesley Mt. SK4—3E 104
(off Dodge Hill)
Wesley Sq. M31—4A 88
Wesley St. BL3—4L 57
Wesley St. BL5—7E 36
Wesley St. BL7—2G 23
Wesley St. BL9—9L 25
Wesley St. M11—7A 80
Wesley St. M29—6J 61
Wesley St. M30—1C 54
Wesley St. M31—3J 73
Wesley St. M35—7G 63
Wesley St. OL12—4B 12
Wesley St. OL16—4J 27
Wesley St. SK5—7E 92
Wesley St. SK14—1G 97
Wesley St. WA14—1J 105
Wessenden Bank E. SK2—8K 105
Wessenden Bank W. SK2—8K 105
Wessex Clo. WN1—9B 18
Wessex Pk. Clo. OL2—1A 46
Wessex Rd. WN5—8K 33
Wessington Bank. SK13—4E 96
(off Wessington M.)
Wessington Fold. SK13—4E 96
(off Langsett La.)
Wessington M. SK13—4E 96
(off Wessington M.)
West Av. M19—7M 91
West Av. M25—7L 41
West Av. M34—3F 5 & 5G 78
West Av. M29—4B 56
West Av. WA14—8A 100
West Av. M10—8D 62
West Av. M18—1E 92
West Av. WN4—8A 52
West Bank. M11—8G 81
West Bank. SK9—9M 119
W. Bank. SK16—3K 103
W. Bank St. M5—5B 4 & 7C 78
Westbank Rd. BL6—3K 37
Westbourne Av. BL3—6G 39
Westbourne Av. M27—3D 58
Westbourne Av. WN7—9E 54
(in two parts)
Westbourne Gro. M9—8K 61
Westbourne Gro. M20—3G 103
Westbourne Gro. WN7—9C 54
Westbourne Pk. M31—3D 88
Westbourne Range. M18

Westbrook Wlk. M20—1G 103
Westbury Av. M33—4C 100
Westbury Av. WN3—6K 51
Westbury Clo. BL5—6G 37
Westbury Clo. BL8—4H 25
Westbury Dri. SK6—7E 106
Westbury Rd. M8—7G 61
Westbury St. OL6—4C 82
Westbury St. SK14—1C 94
Westbury Way. OL2—7K 45
Westby Clo. SK7—4G 115
Westby Gro. BL2—1J 39
West Central Dri. M27—9H 59
W. Charles St. M5—4A 4 & 6B 78
W. Church St. OL10—8J 27
Westcliffe Ho. OL1—4F 22
Westcliffe Rd. BL1—7C 22
West Clo. M29—7L 55
West Cotts. OL3—3B 65
Westcott Av. M20—2H 103
Westcott Clo. BL2—5L 23
Westcott Ct. WN3—4J 51
Westcott Gro. OL2—4A 46
Westcourt Rd. BL3—6D 38
Westcourt Rd. M33—8F 88
Westcroft Rd. M20—8G 91
W. Craven St. M5—6A 4 & 7B 78
West Cres. M24—1H 61
West Dean St. M5—4B 4 & 6C 78
Westdene. M8—1F 78
(off Kilmington Dri.)
W. Downs Rd. SK8—1M 113
W. Dri. M6—5L 77
W. Dri. M21—7H 89
W. Dri. M27—9H 59
W. Dri. M31—3B 88
W. Dri. M35—6F 80
W. Dri. SK8—9G 103
W. Duke St. M5—4C 4 & 6D 78
W. Egerton St. M5—4A 4 & 6B 78
West End Av. SK8—7G 103
West End Av. WA11—9F 68
West End Rd. M35—4H 39
West End St. OL9—9K 45
Westerdale. OL2—6C 64
(in two parts)
Westerdale Dri. BL3—4A 38
Westerdale Dri. OL2—6C 64
(in two parts)
Westerham Av. M5—6A 78
Westerling Wlk. M16—3E 90
Western Access Trading Est. M17—7G 77
Western Av. M27—6K 59
Western Circ. M19—8M 91
Western Rd. M31—5L 87
Western St. M6—3L 77
Western St. M18—9E 80
Westerton Ct. BL3—4D 38
Westfield. WA14—1C 110
Westfield Av. M24—9A 44
Westfield Clo. OL11—1M 27
Westfield Dri. OL4—3L 65
Westfield Dri. SK6—9C 94
Westfield Gro. M34—1L 93
Westfield Lodge. WA14—5E 100
(off Park Rd.)
Westfield Rd. BL3—7B 38
Westfield Rd. M21—5B 90
Westfield Rd. M29—7L 55
Westfield Rd. SK8—6D 114
Westfields. WA15—4F 110
Westfield St. M7—7D 60
West Gate. M5—5B 4 & 7B 78
Westgate. M33—1G 101
Westgate. OL12—6G 119
Westgate. SK9—6G 119
Westgate. WA15—2E 110
Westgate Av. BL0—9G 9
Westgate Av. BL9—9L 25
Westgate Dri. M27—1F 76
Westgate Rd. M6—2H 77
Westgate St. OL7—6A 82
West Grn. M24—1H 61
West Gro. M13—9K 79
West Gro. M28—2H 57
West Gro. M33—2H 101
West Gro. SK15—7J 65
Westgrove Av. BL1—4E 22
Westhide Wlk. M9—7M 61
West Hill. OL11—4B 28
Westhill Clo. SK15—5F 82
Westhold Clo. OL1—4F 22
Westholm Av. SK4—7B 92
West Holme Ct. SK9—7L 119
Westholme Rd. M20—4H 91
West King St. M3—3D 4 & 5E 78
Westlake St. M10—2D 80
Westland Av. BL1—9A 22
Westland Av. BL4—2J 57
Westland Av. SK1—4H 105
Westland Dri. M9—4K 61

Westlands. M25—2M 59
Westlands, The. M27—1H 77
West La. M9—2H 61
West La. WA16 & WA13—8B 108
West Lea. M34—3A 94
Westlea Dri. M18—3D 92
Westleigh La. WN7—6D 54
Westleigh St. WN7—6D 54
Westleigh View. WN7—7L 61
Westman Clo. BL1—9E 22
W. Marwood St. M7—1E 78
Westmead. WN6—1L 33
Westmead Dri. M8—2C 78
Westmeade Rd. WA15—6K 101
W. Meade. BL3—7B 38
W. Meade. M21—6D 90
W. Meade. M25—6D 60
W. Meade. M27—1E 76
W. Meadow. SK5—5J 39
W. Mt. SK4—3E 104
W. Mt. WN5—7D 50
Weston Av. M10—7E 62
Weston Av. M27—4E 58
Weston Av. M31—5M 89
Weston Av. OL16—6H 29
Weston Av. M34—3A 94
Weston Dri. SK8—9D 104
Weston Gro. M22—5E 102
Weston Gro. SK4—8C 92
Weston Rd. SK9—5K 119
Weston St. BL3—5B 38
Weston St. M11—9E 80
Weston St. OL1—9B 46
Weston St. SK5—1E 104
W. Over. SK6—5A 106
Westover Rd. M31—3C 68
Westover St. M27—7E 58
West Pde. M33—2C 100
W. Park. SK14—7D 94
W. Park Av. SK12—4G 115
W. Park Est. OL7—6A 82
W. Park Rd. SK1—3H 105
W. Park Rd. SK7—2D 114
W. Park St. M5—6A 4 & 8B 78
W. Point Enterprise Pk. M17—8J 77
West Point Ind. Est. OL9—2J 63
Westray Cres. M5—6L 77
Westray Rd. M13—4L 91
Westress. WN7—9G 55
West Rd. M25—3M 59
West Rd. M31—8E 76
West Row. M25—7M 59
W. Starkey St. OL10—7J 27
W. Stockport Rd. SK6—1L 19
West St. BL0—6H 9
West St. BL1—2C 38
West St. BL4—3C 58
West St. M9—5G 61
West St. M11—5B 60
West St. M24—2F 62
West St. M26—6G 41
West St. M29—7L 55
West St. M35—6D 80
West St. OL6—2H 77
West St. OL16—3K 29
West St. OL7—6A 82
West St. SK3—4D 104
West St. SK9—3L 119
West St. SK14—8F 84
(Hadfield)
West St. SK14—1G 97
(Hyde)
West St. SK15—5F 82
West St. SK16—6B 82
West St. WN2—5B 54
(Hindley)
West St. WN2—9G 35
(Ince)
West St. WN6—8B 34
W. Towers St. M6—6M 77
W. Vale. M26—4M 41
W. Vale Rd. WA15—7F 100
W. View. BL0—1J 9
West View. M34—8L 61
West View. OL16—4M 29
Westview Gro. M25—8K 41
W. View Rd. M22—5E 102
Westville Gdns. M19—9L 91
Westward Ho. OL16—4M 29
Westward Rd. SK9—5F 119
West Way. BL1—7H 23
Westway. M9—2H 61
West Way. M28—3G 57
Westway. M38—7G 81
Westway. OL4—3B 64
Westway. OL2—3B 46
Westwell St. WN7—8E 54
(off Halliwell Rd.)
W. Whitehill St. M9 & M8—4K 61

Westminster Rd. M28—6K 57
Westminster Rd. M30—4E 76
Westminster Rd. M31—2D 88
Westminster Rd. M35—8H 63
Westminster Rd. WA15—1G 111
Westminster St. BL4—9J 25
Westminster St. M15—9E 78
Westminster St. M19—5B 92
Westminster St. M27—7D 58
Westminster St. OL1—9B 46
Westminster St. OL11—5D 28
Westminster Wlk. M34—9J 3
Westminster Way. SK16—9C 82
Westmoor Gables. SK4—4M 103
Westmoor St. WN1—8B 18
Westmorland Av. OL7—3B 82
Westmorland Clo. SK16—2C 82
Westmorland Clo. BL9—4J 25
Westmorland Dri. OL12—5D 12
Westmorland Rd. M33—3J 101
Westmorland Rd. M20—1K 103
Westmorland Rd. M30—5C 86
(Urmston)
Westmorland Rd. M30—8M 91
(Partington)
Westmorland Wlk. OL2—5J 45
W. Mosley St. M2—5E 5 & 8F
(in two parts)
W. Mt. WN5—7D 34
W. Oak Pl. SK8—3M 113
Weston Av. PR7—1K 17
West End Av. SK8—7G 103
W. End End Av. WA11—9F 68
Westend St. BL4—8H 39
Weston St. OL9—9K 45
Westerdale. OL2—6C 64
(in two parts)
Weston Clo. BL3—4C 64
Weston St. OL16—4L 29
(in two parts)
W. Over. SK6—5A 106
Westover St. M27—7E 58
W. Pde. M33—2C 100
W. Pk. SK14—7D 94
W. Park Av. SK12—4G 115
W. Park Est. OL7—6A 82
W. Park Rd. SK1—3H 105
W. Park St. M5—6A 4 & 8B 78
W. Point Enterprise Pk. M17—8J
Westville Gdns. M19—9L 91
West Way. BL1—7H 23
Westway. M9—2H 61
Westward Rd. SK9—5F 119
Westwell St. WN7—8E 54
Westwick Ter. BL1—2E 22
Westwood Av. M7—5B 60
Westwood Av. M10—7E 62
Westwood Av. M30—3M 75
Westwood Av. M40—9A 52
Westwood Av. WN3—2C 52
Westwood Bus. Cen. OL9
Westwood Clo. BL4—9K 3
Westwood Cres. M30—3M 75
Westwood Dri. M27—1J 59
Westwood Dri. M33—3J 57
Westwood Dri. OL9—1N 63
Westwood La. WN3—2D 52
Westwood Rd. BL1—1C 38
Westwood Rd. M32—4H 89
Westwood Rd. SK2—9H 105
Westwood Rd. SK8—5C 114
Westwood St. M14—3G 91
Westwood Ter. WN3—3E
W. Works Rd. M17—2J 77
Wetheral Dri. BL3—6C 38
Wet Earth Grn. M27—1J 75
Wetherall St. M19—5B 92

herby Dri. OL2—4J 45
herby Dri. SK7—2A 116
herby St. M11—8E 80
xford Wlk. M22—2E 112
bourne Av. M9—6A 62
bourne Dri. SK6—1M 105
bourne Dri. WN3—5L 51
bourne Gro. BL2—6H 23
bridge Clo. BL1—1E 38
bridge Rd. M4—3H 5 & 5J 79
brook Dri. SK4—7B 92
croft Clo. BL2—3A 40
Gates Dri. WA15—5J 111
hill Rd. M23—8A 102
lands Gro. M6—2H 77
mouth Dri. WN2—4A 54
mouth Rd. M30—4B 76
mouth Rd. OL6—1E 82
mouth St. BL1—8E 22
thorne Dri. BL1—6F 22
thorne Dri. BL9—5F 26
lley Av. BL1—7M 21
lley Av. M16—3D 90
lley Av. M19—4B 92
lley Av. M21—6C 90
lley Av. M31—3E 88
lley Av. M33—9J 89
lley Av. OL15—5A 14
lley Av. WA3—8J 73
lley Clo. M25—8M 41
lley Clo. WA15—5F 100
lley Clo. WN3—5A 52
lley Cotts. BL6—1L 35
lley Dri. BL8—8F 24
lley Gdns. OL12—1B 28
lley Gro. M16—4D 90
lley Gro. OL6—8C 64
lley Gro. WN7—7D 54
ley Rd. BL0—1K 9
ley Rd. M16—3C 90
ley Rd. M24—6M 43
ley Rd. M25—8M 41
ley Rd. OL10—8G 27
ley Rd. OL12—1B 28
ley Rd. SK2—6J 105
ley Rd. WA15—2G 111
ley St. OL1—1M 63
ly Clo. OL16—4L 29
m Bar Dri. OL10—8H 27
m Bottom La. OL12—7D 12
n La. OL3—9K 31
n St. OL10—8H 27
f Clo. WA14—6D 100
fedale. BL5—7F 36
fedale Av. M10—7A 62
fedale Rd. SK5—6E 92
f Rd. M33—9J 89
f Rd. WA14—6D 100
f St. OL9—5H 63
f St. SK4—2E 104
f St. SK14—3C 94
f St. SK16—6B 82
f St. WN7—3G 73
mby Rd. WA11—9L 69
mton Rise. OL4—2K 65
mton View. OL3—2A 66
ncliffe St. WN2—3K 53
ton Av. M21—7D 90
ton La. M28—4D 56
ton Lodge. M30—4E 76
t Clo. M13—1J 91
t Croft. SK3—8F 104
tcroft. SK14—2E 96
ter's Cres. M7—1B 4 & 3C 78
ter's St. M7—1C 4 & 3D 78
ter's Ter. M7—1C 4 & 3D 78
tfield. SK15—8L 83
tfield Clo. BL9—3M 25
tfield Clo. SK6—1A 106
tfield Cres. OL2—6J 45
tfield St. BL2—4H 39
thill St. OL16—6G 29
tley Rd. M27—6D 58
tley Wlk. M12—9M 79
tsheaf Cen. ,The. OL16—2F 28
tsheaf Ind. Est. M27—7H 59
dale. OL4—2D 64
dale Clo. BL1—8E 22
don St. M14—3G 91
lock Clo. SK9—2K 119
ton Clo. BL8—9G 25
wright Clo. OL11—6B 28
wright Clo. SK6—5F 106
n Av. BL9—2L 41
n Clo. BL9—2L 41
r St. M11—7D 80
ey. WN1 & WN2—8E 34
nar Est. SK8—1B 114
nar Ho. WN7—2G 73
neside Av. OL6—9C 64
nside Av. M10—7A 62
nside Clo. SK4—2E 104
norhurst Rd. SK6—8L 107
tone Hill Clo. OL1—7B 46
tone Hill La. OL1—8C 46
tone Hill Rd. OL1—7B 46
ell Av. M26—4K 41
ell St. M29—7A 56
y St. M13—2M 91
berry Lee La. OL3—2D 48
orel Rd. M29—9B 56
orel Rd. SK2—9A 106
erry Rd. WA14—6B 100
erry Way. OL4—5E 46
hat Clo. SK2—9A 106
ell Dri. M24—8H 43
eld Clo. WN6—9A 34
roves Wlk. M10—9A 62
moor Wlk. M10—9B 62
Av. BL4—9E 38
Crest. BL6—2J 37
ee Dri. BL6—2J 37
tone Way. OL1—8E 44
ey La. BL8—9D 8
y Clo. SK4—9D 92
ey St. WN2—5H 53
n Dri. BL2—3J 39
n Rd. M8—7H 61
ker St. M24—9M 43
ook Way. M24—4D 44
rn Av. M13—4L 91
rn Clo. BL3—5L 37
rn Clo. WN4—3K 69
rn Dri. BL8—5J 25
rn Rd. M23—9A 102
Av. M6—4J 77
Av. M14—6L 91
Av. M16—3D 90
Av. M31—4E 88
Av. OL10—7J 27
Clo. BL8—8F 24
Clo. SK8—7J 103
Clo. SK12—8J 115
Rd. M14—6K 91
Rd. OL8—5C 64
St. M24—8C 44
St. OL11—5G 29
urch Dri. M16—1D 90
urch Gdns. BL1—8E 22
Gladstone St.)
urch Rd. M20—7F 90
urch St. M3—2D 4 & 4E 78
cre. WN6—8G 17
cres. M27—9C 58
cres Rd. OL6—4C 82
cre Wlk. M15—1E 90
Shearsby Clo.)
ank Av. SK5—1J 105
Bank Rd. OL8—6K 63
arn Rd. SK9—9M 119
eam Clo. M6—4A 78
eam Clo. OL16—7A 30
eam Ct. M6—4A 78
eam Wlk. BL5—7F 36
eam Wlk. M33—9D 88
eck Ct. M9—4A 62
irk Clo. BL8—9F 8

White Bri. SK16—9C 82
White Brook La. OL3—2D 66
(Greenfield)
White Brook La. OL3—9C 48
(Uppermill)
Whitebrook Rd. M14—5H 91
White Broom. WA13—9B 98
White Brow. BL9—4M 41
Whitecar Av. M10—7E 62
Whitecarr La. WA15 & M23—1K 111
Whitechapel Clo. BL2—2L 39
Whitechapel St. M20—2H 103
White City Retail Pk. M16—1A 90
White City Way. M16—1A 90
Whitecliff Clo. M14—3J 91
Whitecroft Av. OL2—2D 46
Whitecroft Av. WA3—6L 71
Whitecroft Dri. BL8—7F 24
Whitecroft Gdns. M19—1L 103
Whitecroft Rd. BL1—9M 21
Whitecroft Rd. SK12—3J 117
Whitecroft Rd. WN3—6A 52
Whitecroft St. OL1—8C 46
Whitecroft Vs. M31—3E 98
Whitefield. M6—1K 77
Whitefield. SK4—2C 104
Whitefield. WA13—9A 98
Whitefield Bottoms. OL16—7B 30
Whitefield Cen. M25—9B 42
Whitefield Clo. WA3—7G 71
Whitefield Clo. WA13—8A 98
Whitefield Cres. OL16—7B 30
Whitefield Gro. WA11—9G 69
Whitefield Gro. WA13—9A 98
Whitefield Rd. BL9—2K 41
(in two parts)
Whitefield Rd. M33—9F 88
Whitefield Rd. SK6—1L 105
White Friar Ct. M3—2D 4 & 4E 78
Whitefriars Wlk. M22—4D 112
Whitegate. BL3—7J 37
Whitegate. OL15—7L 13
Whitegate Av. OL9—4F 62
Whitegate Dri. BL1—5F 22
Whitegate Dri. M5—4K 77
Whitegate Dri. M27—6H 59
Whitegate La. OL9—4F 62
(in two parts)
Whitegate Pk. M31—4L 87
Whitegate Rd. OL9—5D 62
Whitegates Clo. WA15—8H 101
Whitegates Rd. M24—5C 44
Whitegates Rd. SK8—8K 103
Whitehall. OL4—5F 46
Whitehall Av. WN6—1E 32
Whitehall Clo. SK9—6G 119
(in two parts)
Whitehall La. BL6—8K 19
Whitehall La. OL4—5F 46
Whitehall Rd. M20—2J 103
Whitehall Rd. M33—3H 101
Whitehall St. OL1—9M 45
Whitehall St. OL12 & OL16
(in two parts) —1F 28
Whitehall St. WN3—2E 52
White Hart Meadow. M24—7A 44
White Hart St. SK14—2D 94
Whitehaven Gdns. M20—3G 103
Whitehaven Pl. SK14—1C 94
Whitehaven Rd. SK7—7C 114
Whitehead Cres. BL8—4J 25
Whitehead Cres. M26—1C 58
Whitehead Pl. OL4—1F 64
Whitehead Rd. M21—6M 89
Whitehead Rd. M27—6H 59
Whitehead St. M24—8C 44
Whitehead St. M28—4K 57
Whitehead St. M34—8L 81
Whitehead St. OL2—1M 45
Whitehead St. OL16—3L 29
(Milnrow, in two parts)
Whitehead St. OL16—6D 30
(Newhey)
Whitehill Clo. OL12—7D 12
Whitehill Cotts. BL1—4D 22
Whitehill Dri. M10—9A 62
Whitehill Ind. Est. SK4—9E 92
Whitehill La. BL1—4D 22
Whitehill St. SK4—1D 104
Whiteholme Av. M21—1D 102
White Horse Clo. BL6—5C 20
White Horse Gdns. M27—1C 76
White Horse Gro. BL5—7G 37
White Ho. Av. M8—5E 60
Whitehouse Av. OL4—2C 64
Whitehouse Clo. OL10—2K 43
White Ho. Clo. WA11—9H 69
Whitehouse Dri. M23—8A 102
Whitehouse Dri. WA15—4H 111
Whitehouse La. M31—6K 99
Whitehouse Rd. WA16—9H 109
White Houses. BL1—9M 21
Whitehouse Ter. M9—7M 61
Whitehurst Rd. SK4—1M 103
Whitekirk Clo. M13—9H 79
White Lady Clo. M28—5F 56
Whitelake Av. M31—4M 87
Whitelake View. M31—3M 87
Whiteland Av. BL3—4C 38
Whitelands. OL6—5C 82
Whitelands Rd. OL6—5C 82
Whitelands Ter. OL6—5C 82
Whitelea Dri. SK3—8D 104
Whitelees Rd. OL15—6A 14
Whitelegge St. BL8—6H 25
Whiteleggs La. WA13—3B 108
Whiteley Dri. M24—1C 62
Whiteley Pl. WA14—7D 100
Whiteleys Pl. OL12—2E 28
Whiteley St. M11—5B 80
Whiteley St. OL9—4H 63
White Lion Brow. BL1—2E 38
White Lodge Dri. WN4—3E 70
Whitelow Rd. BL9—5L 9
Whitelow Rd. M21—6A 90
Whitelow Rd. SK4—2A 104
White Meadows. M27—9F 58
White Moss Av. M21—6C 90
White Moss Gdns. M9—6A 62
White Moss Rd. M9—5L 61
Whiteoak Clo. SK6—6E 106
Whiteoak Rd. M14—6J 91
Whites Croft. M27—8F 58
Whiteshead Clo. SK12—7K 117
Whiteside Av. WA11—9E 68
Whiteside Av. WN2—1K 53
Whiteside Av. WN6—8A 34
Whiteside Rd. WA11—9H 69
Whitestone Clo. BL6—3K 37
Whitestone Wlk. M13—1K 91
White St. BL8—9J 25
White St. M6—6L 77
White St. WN5—2H 51
White St. WN7—3J 73
White Swallows Rd. M27—1G 77
Whitethorn Av. M16—3D 90
Whitethorn Av. M19—7M 91
Whitethorn Clo. SK6—6E 106
Whiteway St. M9—9L 61
Whitewell Clo. OL16—2J 29
Whitfield Av. OL11—2M 27
Whitfield Av. SK13—7J 97
Whitfield Brow. OL15—4C 14
Whitfield Cross. SK13—7K 97
Whitfield Rise. OL2—9A 30
Whitfield St. M3—2F 5 & 4G 79
Whitfield St. WN7—3J 73
Whitford Wlk. M10—4K 79
Whiting Gro. BL3—3L 37
Whitland Dri. OL8—6H 63
Whit La. M6—1M 77
(in two parts)
Whitledge Grn. WN4—2A 70
Whitledge Rd. WN4—2A 70
Whitley Cres. WN1—5B 34
Whitley Cres. WN2—9H 53
Whitley Gdns. WA15—5H 101

Whitley La. WN8—8D 32
Whitley Pl. WA15—6H 101
Whitley Rd. M10—1H 5 & 3J 79
Whitley Rd. SK4—2B 104
Whitley Rd. WN8—6C 32
Whitley St. BL3—7K 39
Whitlow Av. WA3—6F 70
Whitlow Av. WA14—5B 100
Whitman St. M9—8M 61
Whitmore Rd. M14—5H 91
Whitnall Clo. M16—2E 90
Whitnall St. SK14—1D 94
Whitsbury Av. M18—3D 92
Whitsbury Av. WN2—4K 53
Whitstable Clo. OL9—2H 63
Whitstable Rd. M10—7C 62
Whitsundale. BL5—7F 36
Whitswood Clo. M16—3E 90
Whittaker Clo. M25—4C 60
Whittaker Dri. OL15—9M 13
Whittaker La. M25—4C 60
Whittaker La. OL11—1K 27
Whittaker La. OL15—7E 14
Whittaker St. M10—8M 61
Whittaker St. M12—7K 79
Whittaker St. M26—5H 41
Whittaker St. OL2—5K 45
Whittaker St. OL6—2D 82
Whittaker St. OL11—1L 27
Whittingham Dri. BL0—7J 9
Whittingham Gro. OL1—9K 45
Whittington St. OL7—6A 82
Whittle Av. WA11—9G 69
Whittlebrook Gro. OL10—2L 43
Whittle Brow. PR7—1J 17
Whittle Dri. M28—3J 57
Whittle Dri. OL2—1D 46
Whittle Gro. BL1—9B 22
(in two parts)
Whittle Gro. M28—5L 57
Whittle Hill. BL7—8E 6
Whittle La. OL10—4G 43
Whittle La. WN6—6A 16
Whittles Av. M34—3A 94
Whittle's Croft. M1—4G 5 & 6H 79
Whittle's Ter. BL5—8E 36
Whittles Ter. OL16—6B 30
Whittle St. BL8—7J 25
Whittle St. M4—5H 79
Whittle St. M27—9E 58
Whittle St. M28—5K 57
Whittle St. OL15—6M 13
Whittles Wlk. M34—4A 94
Whitton M. BL6—6B 20
Whitwell Bank. SK13—4D 96
(off Eyam La.)
Whitwell Clo. BL9—2K 41
Whitwell Clo. SK13—4D 96
Whitwell Fold. SK13—4E 96
(off Melandra Castle Rd.)
Whitwell Gdns. BL6—5B 20
Whitwell Grn. SK13—4E 96
(off Hathersage Cres.)
Whitwell Lea. SK13—4D 96
(off Melandra Castle Rd.)
Whitwell Wlk. M13—2L 91
Whitwell Way. M18—1C 92
Whitworth Clo. OL6—3C 82
Whitworth La. M14—5K 91
Whitworth Pk. Mans. M14—2G 91
Whitworth Rake. OL12—3D 12
Whitworth Rd. OL12—7D 12
Whitworth Rd. OL16—4M 29
Whitworth Sq. OL12—3D 12
Whitworth St. BL6—8C 20
Whitworth St. M1—5F 5 & 7G 79
Whitworth St. M11—8A 80
(in two parts)
Whitworth St. OL16—9J 13
Whitworth St. W. M1—5D 4 & 7E 78
Whoolden St. BL4—8J 39
Whowell Fold. BL1—7C 22
Whowell St. BL3—3E 38
Wibbersley Pk. M31—4M 87
Wichbrook Rd. M28—5F 56
Wicheaves Cres. M28—5F 56
Wicheries, The. M28—5F 56
Wicken Bank. OL10—2L 43
Wickenby Dri. M33—1G 101
Wicken St. SK2—6J 105
Wickentree La. M35—7F 62
Wicker La. WA15—4H 111
Wickham Clo. M14—3H 91
Wickliffe Pl. OL11—4F 28
Wickliffe St. BL1—1E 38
Wicklow Av. SK3—6B 104
Wicklow Dri. M22—2E 112
Widcombe Dri. BL2—4M 39
Widdop St. OL9—1K 63
Widdow's St. WN7—3H 73
Widdrington Rd. WN1—7D 34
Widecombe Clo. M31—2B 88
Widford Wlk. BL6—9K 19
Widgeon Clo. M14—6H 91
Widgeon Clo. SK12—8H 115
Widgeon Rd. WA14—5B 100
Wiend. WN1—9C 34
Wiend Hall. BL5—7E 36
Wigan Cen. Arc., The. WN1
(off Galleries, The) —9C 34
Wigan La. PR7—4C 18
Wigan La. WN1—4B 34
Wigan Lwr. Rd. WN6—5J 33
Wigan Pier. WN3—1A 52
Wigan Rd. BL3—7K 37
Wigan Rd. BL5—1A 54
Wigan Rd. M29—5F 54
Wigan Rd. WA3—5H 71
Wigan Rd. WN2—6G 35
(Aspull)
Wigan Rd. WN2—2J 53
(Hindley)
Wigan Rd. WN4—8M 51
Wigan Rd. WN5—9F 50
Wigan Rd. WN6—3H 33
(Shevington)
Wigan Rd. WN6—1L 33
(Standish)
Wigan Rd. WN7—8C 54
Wigan Sq. WN1—9C 34
(off Galleries, The)
Wigan St. WN2—7G 53
Wiggins Teape Rd. BL9—3B 42
Wiggins Wlk. M14—3J 91
Wighurst Wlk. M22—3D 112
Wigley St. M12—8L 79
Wigmore Rd. M8—9H 61
Wigmore St. OL6—3D 82
Wigsby Av. M10—6C 62
Wigsey La. WA13—6A 98
Wigston Wlk. M8—2E 78
(off Fairy La.)
Wigwam Clo. SK12—8J 115
Wike St. BL8—7K 25
Wilberforce Clo. M15—1F 90
Wilbraham Rd. M21, M16 & M14—5A 90
Wilbraham Rd. M28—5K 57
Wilbraham St. WN7—2C 72
Wilburn St. M5—5C 4 & 7D 78
(in two parts)
Wilby Av. BL3—4A 40
Wilby Clo. BL8—5K 25
Wilby St. M8—1H 79
Wilcock Clo. M16—2E 90
Wilcock Rd. WA11—7B 70
Wilcock St. WN3—1A 52
Wilcott Dri. M33—9E 88
Wilcott Dri. SK9—7F 118
Wilcott Rd. SK8—8G 103
Wildbank Chase. SK15—8L 83
Wildbrook Clo. M28—5E 56
Wildbrook Cres. OL8—5A 64
Wildbrook Gro. M28—5E 56
Wildbrook Rd. M28—4E 56
Wildcroft Av. M10—7A 62
Wilderswood Av. BL6—6C 20
Wilderswood Ct. BL6—6C 20
Wilderswood Rd. M20—9J 91
Wilde St. OL6—3B 82

Wild Ho. OL8—3M 63
Wildhouse Ct. OL16—2M 29
Wild Ho. La. OL16—2M 29
Wilding St. WN3—2E 52
Wildman La. BL4—9F 38
Wildmoor Av. OL4—4E 64
Wilds Bldgs. OL16—3K 29
Wild's Pas. OL15—7L 13
(Littleborough)
Wilds Pas. OL15—1D 14
(Summit)
Wild's Pas. WN7—3F 72
Wild St. M26—5K 41
Wild St. M34—3M 93
Wild St. OL1—1A 64
Wild St. OL2—3C 46
Wild St. OL4—2E 64
Wild St. OL10—8L 27
Wild St. SK2—7G 105
Wild St. SK6—3M 105
Wild St. SK7—2K 115
Wild St. SK16—7D 82
Wildwood Clo. BL0—7G 9
Wileman Ct. M5—5K 77
Wilford Av. M33—3G 101
Wilfred Dri. BL9—6A 26
Wilfred Rd. M28—6K 57
Wilfred Rd. M30—7A 76
Wilfred St. BL7—3G 23
Wilfred St. M3—1D 4 & 3E 78
Wilfred St. M10—8A 62
Wilfred St. M35—7H 81
Wilfred St. WN5—1M 51
Wilfrid St. M27—8F 58
Wilham Av. M30—6D 76
Wilkesley Av. WN6—1K 33
Wilkes St. OL1—5D 46
Wilkin Croft. SK8—3L 113
Wilkins La. SK9—7E 112
Wilkinson Av. BL3—4A 40
Wilkinson Gdns. BL1—5D 22
Wilkinson Rd. BL1—5D 22
Wilkinson Rd. SK4—3E 104
Wilkinson St. M24—8M 43
Wilkinson St. M33—1K 101
Wilkinson St. OL4—1B 64
Wilkinson St. OL6—5A 82
Wilkinson St. WN7—2E 72
Wilks Av. M22—2F 112
Willand Clo. BL2—3A 40
Willand Dri. BL2—4A 40
Willan Ind. Est. M5—6M 77
Willan Rd. M9—3J 61
Willan Rd. M30—5E 76
Willard Av. WN5—5D 50
Willard St. SK7—1K 115
Willaston Clo. M21—7A 90
Willaston Way. SK9—7K 113
Willbutts La. OL11—2C 28
Willdale Clo. M11—5A 80
Willdor Gro. SK3—7B 104
Willenhall Rd. M23—3C 102
Willerby Rd. M7—2E 78
Willert St. M10—2K 79
Willesden Av. M13—3L 91
Will Griffiths Wlk. M11—7L 79
William Chadwick Clo. M10—2H 5 & 4J 79
William Coates Ct. M16—3D 90
William Henry St. OL11—6G 29
William Jessop Ct. M1—4H 5 & 6J 79
William Kay Clo. M16—2E 90
William Kent Cres. M15—9E 78
William Lister Clo. M10—3D 80
William Murray Ct. M4—5J 79
(off Jackroom Dri.)
William Rd. WA11—9F 68
Williams Cres. OL9—5F 62
Williamson Av. M26—3F 40
Williamson Av. SK6—1A 106
Williamson La. M35—7H 81
Williamson St. M4—2G 5 & 4H 79
Williamson St. OL6—4B 82
Williamson St. SK5—7F 92
Williamson's Yd. OL1—1B 64
Williams Pas. OL15—2D 14
Williams Rd. M10—9B 62
Williams Rd. M18—1C 92
Williams St. BL3—6B 40
Williams St. M18—1C 92
William St. BL0—2J 9
William St. BL6—7A 20
William St. M1—6E 5 & 8F 78
William St. M3—3D 4 & 5E 78
William St. M12—7K 79
William St. M20—2H 103
William St. M24—9B 44
William St. M26—5H 41
William St. M31—4C 88
William St. M34—2A 94
William St. M35—7G 63
William St. OL7—5M 81
William St. OL11—4F 28
(in two parts)
William St. OL12—2C 12
William St. OL15—6A 14
William St. OL16—7K 13
William St. SK1—6H 105
William St. WN2—3L 53
William St. WN3—2D 52
William St. WN7—2G 73
William Wlk. WA14—1D 110
Willingdon Clo. BL8—3J 25
Willingdon Dri. M25—3B 60
Willink Rd. WA11—8C 68
Willis Rd. OL8—8A 64
Willis Rd. SK3—7E 104
Willis St. BL3—5C 38
Williton Wlk. M22—1F 112
Willock St. M7—1E 78
Willoughby Av. M20—1J 103
Willoughby Clo. M33—9G 89
Willow Av. M24—1C 62
Willow Av. M29—1A 74
Willow Av. M31—4E 88
Willow Av. SK5—1F 104
Willow Av. SK8—2M 113
Willow Bank. M9—8L 61
(off Church La.)
Willow Bank. M14—6J 91
Willowbank. M26—9F 40
Willowbank. M27—6G 59
Willow Bank. OL4—9E 46
(in two parts)
Willow Bank. SK8—6A 114
Willow Bank. WA15—7G 101
Willowbank Av. BL2—3H 39
Willow Bank Ct. M20—5H 103
Willowbrook Av. M10—9A 62
Willowbrook Dri. WN6—2H 33
Willow Clo. BL3—5B 38
Willow Clo. PR6—2H 19
Willow Clo. SK12—9L 115
Willow Ct. M14—6J 91
Willow Ct. M33—9L 89
Willow Cres. WN7—8E 54
Willowcroft Av. WN2—6M 35
Willowdale Av. SK8—2H 113
Willowdene Clo. BL7—2F 22
Willowdene Clo. M10—2J 79
Willow Dri. M33—3E 100
Willow Dri. SK9—9K 113
Willow Dri. WN2—5M 53
Willowfield Gro. WN4—5A 70
Willowfield Rd. OL4—7D 46
Willow Fold. M35—7H 81
Willow Gro. M18—2E 92
Willow Gro. M34—3L 93
Willow Gro. OL9—9H 45
Willow Gro. SK6—8F 106
Willow Gro. WA3—6G 71
Willow Gro. WN4—2E 70
Willow Hey. BL7—3J 23
Willow Hill Rd. M8—6G 61
Willow La. WN2—7H 53
Willow Lawn. SK8—1A 114
Willowmead Ct. SK4—1B 104
Willowmoss Clo. M28—7L 57
Willow Pk. M14—6J 91
Willow Rise. OL15—8M 13
Willow Rd. M25—2A 60

Willow Rd. M30—3A 76
Willow Rd. M31—3E 98
Willow Rd. OL3—1C 66
Willow Rd. SK6—5F 116
Willow Rd. WA11—8L 69
Willow Rd. WN6—5M 33
Willows Dri. M35—2F 80
Willows La. BL3—5B 38
Willows La. OL16—4K 29
Willows Rd. M5—5K 77
Willows, The. M21—7A 90
Willows, The. M29—5K 55
(off Water St.)
Willows, The. M31—2F 98
Willows, The. OL4—3F 64
Willows, The. OL5—7L 65
Willows, The. OL12—6C 12
(off Tonacliffe Rd.)
Willows, The. PR7—2L 17
Willow St. BL9—8B 26
(in two parts)
Willow St. M7—1D 4 & 3E 78
Willow St. M11—6A 80
Willow St. M27—2D 76
Willow St. M28—9C 58
Willow St. M29—4J 55
Willow St. M35—9D 62
Willow St. OL1—1A 64
Willow St. OL10—8K 27
Willow St. WN2—7H 53
Willow Tree Ct. M33—2H 101
Willowtree Rd. WA14—1D 110
Willow Wlk. M35—5J 81
Willow Way. M20—2J 103
Willow Way. SK7—5C 114
Wilma Av. M9—4J 61
Wilmcote Clo. BL6—3K 37
Wilmcote Gdns. SK6—2M 105
Wilmcote Rd. M10—3K 79
Wilmers. OL15—1D 14
Wilmington Rd. M32—4H 89
Wilmot St. BL1—7C 22
Wilmott St. M15—6E 5 & 8F 78
(in two parts)
Wilmslow Av. BL1—5E 22
Wilmslow Old Rd. SK10—9A 120
Wilmslow Old Rd. WA15—6M 111
Wilmslow Pk. Rd. SK9—4J 119
Wilmslow Rd. M14—2J 91
Wilmslow Rd. SK7—3B 120
Wilmslow Rd. SK8—7K 103
Wilmslow Rd. SK8 & SK9—2K 113
Wilmslow Rd. SK9—7L 119
Wilmslow Rd. SK10—5C 120
(Butley)
Wilmslow Rd. SK10—8A 120
(Mottram)
Wilmslow Rd. WA15 & SK9—6M 111
Wilmur Av. M7—1E 78
Wilmur Av. M25—1A 60
Wilna Ter. M5—4A 4 & 6B 78
Wilpshire Av. M12—3B 92
Wilsford Clo. WA3—6H 71
Wilshaw Gro. OL7—1A 82
Wilshaw La. OL7—2A 82
Wilshaw Pl. OL7—2A 82
Wilson Av. M27—6H 59
Wilson Av. OL10—8G 27
Wilson Av. WN6—7B 34
Wilson Clo. SK16—8F 82
Wilson Fold Av. BL6—9F 20
Wilson Gro. OL6—3E 82
Wilson Rd. M9—7K 61
Wilson Rd. SK4—1B 104
Wilsons Brow. BL4—8M 39
Wilson's Ter. SK13—6H 97
Wilson St. BL4—9L 39
Wilson St. BL6—6A 20
Wilson St. BL9—9A 26
Wilson St. M10—2L 79
Wilson St. M11—7A 80
Wilson St. M13—9J 79
Wilson St. M18—1D 92
Wilson St. M26—5F 40
Wilson St. M32—2L 89
Wilson St. M33—9H 89
Wilson St. OL3—3A 66
Wilson St. OL8—4L 63
Wilson St. OL12—2F 28
Wilson St. SK14—4E 94
Wilson Way. OL1—9M 45
Wilsthorpe Clo. M19—8C 92
Wilton Av. M16—3A 90
Wilton Av. M25—6D 60
Wilton Av. M27—9J 59
Wilton Av. SK8—5J 113
Wilton Av. WN2—7F 34
Wilton Ct. M9—5G 61
Wilton Ct. M34—2G 93
Wilton Cres. SK9—7K 119
Wilton Dri. BL9—4A 42
Wilton Dri. WA15—4J 111
Wilton Gdns. M26—4J 41
Wilton Gro. M34—2G 93
Wilton Gro. OL10—9K 27
Wilton La. WA3—9B 72
Wilton Paddock. M34—2G 93
Wilton Pl. M7—3C 4 & 5D 78
Wilton Polygon. M8—7F 60
Wilton Rd. BL1—5E 22
Wilton Rd. M6—3H 77
Wilton Rd. M8—6F 60
Wilton Rd. M21—6B 90
Wilton Rd. WN6—3G 33
Wilton St. BL1—7F 22
Wilton St. BL9—4A 42
Wilton St. M5—6A 78
Wilton St. M24—1H 61
Wilton St. M25—4C 60
(Prestwich)
Wilton St. M25—1M 59
(Whitefield)
Wilton St. M34—2L 93
Wilton St. OL9—5H 63
Wilton St. OL10—8H 27
Wilton St. SK5—4F 92
Wilton St. WN1—1D 52
Wilton St. WN4—1A 70
Wilton Ter. OL12—2E 28
Wiltshire Av. SK5—1J 105
Wiltshire Clo. BL9—1A 42
Wiltshire Dri. SK13—6M 97
Wiltshire Pl. WN5—2J 51
Wiltshire Rd. M31—3E 98
Wiltshire Rd. M35—1G 81
Wiltshire Rd. OL9—3H 63
Wiltshire St. M7—1E 78
Wimberry Hill Rd. BL5—6D 36
Wimbledon Dri. SK3—6C 104
Wimbledon Rd. M35—8G 63
Wimbledon Ter. M10—3B 80
Wimborne Av. M31—2D 88
Wimborne Av. OL9—8G 45
Wimborne Clo. BL6—9F 20
Wimborne Clo. SK8—9C 104
Wimborne Rd. WN5—9G 33
Wimborne Wlk. M5—5A 78
Wimbourne St. M10—3M 79
Wimpenny Ho. OL8—3L 63
Wimpole St. OL1—8A 46
Wimpole St. OL6—4C 82
(in three parts)
Wimpory St. M11—8D 80
Winbolt St. SK2—9J 105
Wincanton Av. M23—5K 101
Wincanton Dri. BL1—3D 22
Wincanton Pk. OL4—2D 64
Wincebrook. M24—9A 44
Wince Clo. M24—2C 62
Wincham Clo. M15—9D 78
Wincham Rd. M33—3E 100
Winchester Av. M25—6C 60
Winchester Av. M29—9C 56
Winchester Av. M34—5M 93
Winchester Av. OL6—8D 64
Winchester Av. OL9—8F 44
Winchester Av. OL10—1J 43
Winchester Av. WN4—4A 70
Winchester Clo. BL8—3J 25

Winchester Clo. OL11—3A 28
Winchester Clo. SK9—6E 118
Winchester Clo. WN5—1F 50
Winchester Cres. SK16—8G 83
Winchester Dri. M33—1D 100
Winchester Dri. SK4—3B 104
Winchester Gro. WN3—2D 52
Winchester Pk. M20—1F 102
Winchester Rd. M6—3J 77
Winchester Rd. M26—4D 40
Winchester Rd. M30—2G 77
Winchester Rd. M31 & M32—3D 88
Winchester Rd. SK16—8G 83
Winchester Rd. WA11—6L 69
Winchester Rd. WA15—3J 111
Winchester Rd. WN5—6D 50
Winchester Way. BL2—9K 23
Wincle Av. SK12—1M 121
Wincombe St. M14—4H 91
Windale. M28—5H 57
Windcroft Clo. M11—7M 79
Winder Dri. M4—3H 5 & 5J 79
Windermere. BL4—9E 38
Windermere Av. BL3—5A 40
Windermere Av. M27—9G 59
Windermere Av. M29—3K 55
Windermere Av. M33—3K 101
Windermere Av. M34—4G 93
Windermere Av. WA11—7A 68
Windermere Clo. M11—7A 80
Windermere Cres. OL7—3M 81
Windermere Dri. BL0—4J 9
Windermere Dri. BL9—2L 41
Windermere Dri. PR6—1H 19
Windermere Dri. SK9—8K 119
Windermere Gro. WN7—1E 72
Windermere Pl. WA11—7A 68
Windermere Rd. M24—7H 43
Windermere Rd. M31—5C 88
Windermere Rd. OL2—2K 45
Windermere Rd. SK1—6H 105
Windermere Rd. SK6—4E 116
Windermere Rd. SK9—8J 113
Windermere Rd. SK14—1C 94
Windermere Rd. SK15—4G 83
Windermere Rd. WA11—9H 69
Windermere Rd. WN2—8H 53
(Abram)
Windermere Rd. WN2—3L 53
(Hindley)
Windermere Rd. WN2—1G 53
(Ince)
Windermere Rd. WN5—9F 32
Windermere Rd. WN7—2E 72
Windermere St. BL1—7F 22
Windermere St. OL12—9F 12
Windermere St. WN1—8E 34
Windermere Wlk. OL4—9C 46
Winders Way. M6—1A 4 & 3B 78
Windfields Clo. SK8—1B 114
Windham St. OL16—8J 13
Windle Av. M8—5F 60
Windle City. WA10—9A 68
Windle Ct. SK2—8L 105
Windle Hall Dri. WA10—8A 68
Windlehurst Ct. SK6—5D 116
Windlehurst Dri. M28—9H 57
Windlehurst Old Rd. SK6—2F 116
Windlehurst Rd. SK6—4D 116
Windleshaw St. WN3—2E 52
Windley St. BL2—1G 39
Windley St. Caravan Site. BL1
(off Windley St.) —1G 39
Windmill Av. M5—6A 4 & 8B 78
Windmill Clo. M28—3J 57
Windmill Clo. M34—4H 93
Windmill Clo. WN1—9D 34
Windmill Ct. OL16—4H 29
Windmill Field. M5—8B 78
(off W. Park St.)
Windmill La. M29—3M 73
Windmill La. SK5 & M34—5F 92
Windmill La. Ind. Est. M34—3J 93
Windmill Rd. M28—3J 57
Windmill Rd. M33—2M 101
Windmill Rd. WN8—1A 50
Windmill St. M2—5E 5 & 7F 78
Windmill St. OL16—4H 29
Windover Clo. BL5—1A 56
Windover St. BL3—5A 38
Windrush Av. BL0—9G 9
Windrush Dri. BL5—8F 36
Windrush Dri. M9—9K 61
Windrush, The. OL12—7C 12
Windsor Av. BL3—6A 40
Windsor Av. M25—1A 60
Windsor Av. M27—6H 59
Windsor Av. M28—3H 57
Windsor Av. M29—1A 74
Windsor Av. M30—3H 87
Windsor Av. M31—4M 87
Windsor Av. M33—8H 89
Windsor Av. M35—8H 63
Windsor Av. OL9—4G 63
Windsor Av. OL10—8H 27
Windsor Av. PR7—4F 18
Windsor Av. SK4—2A 104
Windsor Av. SK8—8F 102
Windsor Av. SK9—4F 118
Windsor Clo. BL8—1G 25
Windsor Clo. SK12—8K 115
Windsor Ct. M9—3F 60
Windsor Ct. M33—9F 88
Windsor Cres. M25—5E 60
Windsor Cres. WN2—4K 35
Windsor Dri. BL6—8E 20
Windsor Dri. BL8—1H 41
Windsor Dri. M34—6K 81
Windsor Dri. OL7—3M 81
Windsor Dri. SK6—2J 105
(Bredbury)
Windsor Dri. SK6—8E 106
(Marple)
Windsor Dri. SK15—4G 83
Windsor Dri. SK16—8F 82
Windsor Dri. WA11—8A 70
Windsor Dri. WA14—5F 100
Windsor Gdns. WA15—8L 101
Windsor Gro. BL1—9C 22
Windsor Gro. M26—1B 58
Windsor Gro. OL6—9C 64
Windsor Gro. SK6—3E 106
Windsor Gro. SK8—4M 113
Windsor Gro. WN2—5B 54
Windsor Rd. BL7—3G 23
Windsor Rd. M9—9L 61
Windsor Rd. M10—3E 80
Windsor Rd. M19—5M 91
Windsor Rd. M25—6E 60
(in two parts)
Windsor Rd. M34—2G 93
Windsor Rd. M35—5D 80
Windsor Rd. OL8—3K 63
Windsor Rd. SK7—2M 115
Windsor Rd. SK14—7D 94
Windsor Rd. WA3—7J 71
Windsor Rd. WA15—9E 100
Windsor Rd. WN4—5B 70
Windsor Rd. WN5—2E 68
Windsor Rd. WN7—1L 73
Windsor Rd. WN8—9A 32
Windsor St. M5—4A 4 & 6B 78
Windsor St. M10—3E 80
Windsor St. M18—2C 92
Windsor St. M29—6L 55
Windsor St. M35—8G 63
Windsor St. OL1—8A 46
Windsor St. OL11—5G 29
Windsor St. SK2—7F 104
Windsor St. WN1—8D 34
Windsor Ter. OL16—4L 29
(Milnrow)
Windsor Ter. OL16—3J 29
(Rochdale)
Windsor Ter. SK2—7G 105
(off Russell St.)
Windsor Wlk. SK2—7F 104
(off Windsor St.)
Windward St. BL5—8E 36
Windybank. M9—3J 61

Windybank. WA3—7L 71
Windycroft. BL7—2H 23
Windy Harbour La. BL7—2H 23
Winfell Dri. M10—4K 79
Winfield Av. M20—8K 91
Winfield Dri. M18—9D 80
Winfield Gro. SK6—4H 107
Winfield St. SK14—4F 94
Winford Rd. M24—2C 62
Winford St. M9—8L 61
Wingate Av. BL8—8H 25
Wingate Dri. M20—3J 103
Wingate Dri. M25—8L 41
Wingate Dri. WA15—8G 101
Wingate Rd. M28—4H 57
Wingate Rd. SK4—1C 104
Wingates Gro. BL5—6D 36
Wingates La. BL5—4E 36
Wingates Rd. WN1—4C 34
Wingates Sq. BL5—6E 36
Wingate St. OL11—1L 27
Wingfield Av. SK9—5E 118
Wingfield Dri. M27—1G 77
Wingfield Dri. SK9—5E 118
Wingfield Gro. SK13—7M 97
Wingfield St. M32—2K 89
Wingfield Vs. OL15—4C 14
Wingham St. M7—1D 4 & 3E 78
Wingrave Ho. M5—5M 77
Wings Gro. OL10—2K 43
Winifred Av. BL9—6E 26
Winifred Kettle Ho. BL5—1F 54
Winifred Rd. BL4—8G 39
Winifred Rd. M10—9B 62
Winifred Rd. M20—2H 103
Winifred Rd. M31—4D 88
Winifred Rd. SK2—8G 105
Winifred St. BL0—6H 9
Winifred St. M30—6B 76
Winifred St. OL12—1B 28
Winifred St. SK14—7E 94
Winifred St. WN3—2E 52
Winmarith Dri. WA15—5K 111
Winmarleigh Clo. BL8—9F 24
Winmarleigh Gdns. WN7—4E 72
Winnall Wlk. M10—1C 80
Winnats Clo. SK13—6M 97
Winnie St. M10—8A 62
Winnington Grn. SK2—7K 105
Winnington Rd. SK6—5F 106
Winnipeg Quay. M5—8M 77
Winnows, The. M34—3K 93
Winscombe Dri. M10—1H 5 & 3J 79
Winser St. M1—5F 5 & 7G 79
Winsfield Rd. SK7—4K 115
Winsford Clo. WA11—8M 69
Winsford Dri. OL11—5M 27
Winsford Gro. BL3—4M 37
Winsford Rd. M14—5G 91
Winsford Wlk. M33—2L 101
Winskill Rd. M30—6G 87
Winslade Clo. SK7—2G 115
Winsley Rd. M23—3M 101
Winslow Av. SK14—4M 95
Winslow Pl. M19—8M 91
Winslow Rd. BL3—6J 37
Winslow St. M11—7A 80
Winson Clo. BL3—5E 38
Winstanley Clo. M6—2K 77
Winstanley Pl. WN3—2E 52
Winstanley Rd. M10—4K 79
Winstanley Rd. M33—9J 89
Winstanley Rd. WN2—8F 52
Winstanley Rd. WN4 & WN5—1H 69
Winstanley Rd. WN5—4E 50
Winstanley St. WN5—2M 51
Winster Av. M7—1B 78
Winster Av. M20—1E 102
Winster Av. M32—3G 89
Winster Clo. BL2—9M 23
Winster Clo. M25—9B 42
Winster Dri. BL2—9L 23
Winster Dri. M24—7L 43
Winster Grn. M30—7B 76
Winster Gro. SK2—6G 105
Winster Ho. WN5—1J 51
Winster M. SK13—4E 96
(off Melandra Castle Rd.)
Winster Rd. M30—7B 76
Winston Av. BL3—6C 40
Winston Av. OL11—4L 27
Winston Clo. M26—4E 40
Winston Clo. M33—9F 88
Winston Clo. SK6—6D 106
Winston Rd. M9—7M 61
Winswell Clo. M11—5B 80
Winterbottom Gro. SK14—4M 95
Winterbottom St. BL3—4E 38
Winterbottom St. OL9—1K 63
Winterbottom Wlk. SK14—4M 95
Winterburn Av. M21—1C 102
Winterburn Grn. SK2—8L 105
Winterdyne St. M9—9L 61
Winterford Av. M13—1K 91
Winterford La. OL5—6K 65
Winterford Rd. M8—9F 60
Winterford Rd. OL5—6K 65
Wintergreen Wlk. M31—2F 98
Winter Hey La. BL6—7B 20
Wintermans Rd. M21—7D 90
Winterslow Av. M23—4K 101
Winter St. BL1—7D 22
Winterton Clo. BL5—8G 37
Winterton Rd. SK5—5G 93
Winthorp Av. M10—2K 79
Winton Av. M10—7D 62
Winton Av. M34—8K 81
Winton Av. WN5—3K 51
Winton Clo. SK7—3C 114
Winton Ct. WA14—2C 110
Winton Grn. BL6—1F 36
Winton Gro. BL3—5L 37
Winton Rd. M6—1K 77
Winton Rd. WA14—2C 110
Winton St. OL6—4B 82
Winton St. OL15—6B 14
Winton St. SK15—6H 83
Winward St. BL3—5A 38
Winward St. WA3—5H 71
Winward St. WN7—2B 72
Winwick La. WA3—9L 71
Winwood Rd. M20—5J 103
Wireworks St. M10—8C 62
Wirral Clo. M27—6G 59
Wirral Cres. SK3—5A 104
Wirral Dri. WN3—6J 51
Wisbech Dri. M23—4M 101
Wisbeck Rd. BL2—1J 39
Wiseley St. M11—7L 79
Wiseman Ter. M25—4C 60
Wishaw Sq. M21—7E 90
Wisley Clo. SK5—6F 92
Wistaria Rd. M18—1D 92
Withall Ho. WN1—9D 34
Witham Av. M22—8E 102
Witham Clo. OL10—7G 27
Witham St. OL6—3E 82
Withenfield Rd. M23—5M 101
Withens Grn. SK2—7L 105
Withern Flats. OL10—8J 27
(off Fox St.)
Withies, The. M30—5B 76
Withington Dri. M29—9C 56
Withington Grn. M24—5A 44
Withington La. WN2—6G 35
Withington Rd. M16—2D 90
Withington Rd. M21 & M16—6D 90
Withington St. M6—2A 4 & 4B 78
Withington St. OL10—1L 43
Withins Av. M26—4J 41
Withins Clo. BL2—1L 39
Withins Dri. BL2—1L 39
Withins Gro. BL2—1L 39
Withins La. BL2—1L 39
Withins La. M26—4J 41
Withins Rd. OL8—6H 63

Withins Rd. WA11—7L 69
Withins St. M26—5J 41
Withnell Dri. BL8—9G 25
Withnell Rd. M19—2K 103
Withycombe Pl. M6—2A 78
Withy Gro. M4—3F 5 & 5G 79
Withypool Dri. SK2—8H 105
Withytree Gro. M34—4A 94
Witley Dri. M33—8D 88
Witley Rd. OL16—3H 29
Witney Clo. BL1—8E 22
Wittenbury Rd. SK4—3B 104
Witterage Clo. M12—9M 79
Witton Wlk. M8—1F 78
Woburn Av. BL2—7J 23
Woburn Av. WN7—7D 54
Woburn Clo. M16—3F 90
Woburn Clo. OL16—4L 29
Woburn Clo. WA11—8M 69
Woburn Dri. BL9—4M 41
Woburn Dri. WA15—2H 111
Woburn Rd. M16—3A 90
Woden's Av. M5—5B 4 & 7C 78
Woden St. M5—6B 4 & 8C 78
Woking Gdns. BL1—9E 22
Woking Rd. SK8—6M 113
Woking Ter. BL1—9E 22
(off Bk. Woking Gdns.)
Wolfenden St. BL1—8E 22
Wolfenden Ter. BL1—8E 22
Wolford Dri. M29—7C 56
Wolfreton Cres. M27—5G 59
Wolfson St. WN4—3M 69
Wollaton Wlk. M34—5L 93
Wolmer St. WN4—3A 70
Wolseley Ho. M33—8J 89
Wolseley Pl. M20—9H 91
Wolseley Rd. M33—8H 89
Wolseley St. OL16—6B 30
Wolsely St. BL8—9H 25
Wolsey Clo. M26—6G 41
Wolsey St. M26—6G 41
Wolsey St. OL10—9J 27
Wolstenholme Av. BL9—4M 25
Wolstenholme Coalpit La. OL11—9H 11
Wolstenholme La. OL12 & OL11—9J 11
Wolstenvale Clo. M24—8B 44
Wolver Clo. M28—2H 57
Wolverton Av. OL8—5K 63
Wolverton St. M11—8M 79
Wolvesey. OL11—4E 28
Woodacres Ct. SK9—5F 118
Woodall Clo. M33—1K 101
Woodbank. BL2—8K 23
Woodbank Av. SK1—5J 105
Woodbank Av. SK6—2L 105
Woodbank Ct. M31—3B 88
Woodbank Dri. BL8—6J 25
Woodbank Pk. SK1—4H 105
Woodbank Rd. OL15—8B 14
Woodbank Ter. OL5—6K 65
Woodbine Av. M30—1D 98
Woodbine Cres. SK2—6F 104
Woodbine Pas. OL15—6A 14
(off William St.)
Woodbine Rd. BL3—6C 38
(in two parts)
Woodbine Rd. WA13—9B 98
Woodbine St. M14—2G 91
Woodbine St. OL16—5G 29
(in two parts)
Woodbine St. E. OL16—5H 29
Woodbine Ter. M30—4H 87
Woodbourne Rd. M33—3G 101
Woodbourne Rd. SK4—8C 92
Woodbourne Rd. SK12—6M 117
Woodbray Av. M19—9L 91
Woodbridge Av. M34—8K 81
Woodbridge Dri. BL2—9H 23
Woodbridge Gdns. OL12—9C 12
Woodbridge Gro. M23—4A 102
Woodbridge Rd. M31—3K 87
Woodbrook Av. OL4—1G 65
Woodbrook Dri. WN3—4K 51
Woodbrooke Av. SK14—4F 94
Wood Brook La. OL4—1H 65
Wood Brook Rd. OL4—1G 65
Woodbrook Rd. SK9—8M 119
Woodburn Dri. BL1—7B 22
Woodburn Rd. M22—5D 102
Woodburns. M29—4C 74
Woodbury Rd. SK3—6B 104
Woodchurch. WN1—8F 34
Woodchurch Clo. BL1—9E 22
Woodchurch Wlk. M33—2M 101
Woodchurch Wlk. OL9—2H 63
Woodcock Clo. M35—4J 81
Woodcock Clo. OL11—3M 27
Woodcock Dri. WN2—6H 53
Woodcock Gro. SK13—5M 97
Woodcock Ho. WN1—9D 34
Woodcock Sq. M15—9F 78
Woodcock Sq. WN1—9C 34
(off Galleries, The)
Woodcote Av. SK7—2C 114
Woodcote Rd. WA14—4D 100
(off Manchester Rd.)
Woodcote Rd. WA14 & M31
(off Sinderland Rd.)—4A 100
Woodcote Wlk. M8—8J 61
(off Crescent Rd.)
Wood Cottage Clo. M28—5F 56
Woodcott Gro. SK9—2L 119
Wood Ct. WN3—2B 52
Wood Cres. OL4—5E 64
Woodcroft. SK2—7K 105
Woodcroft. WN6—3E 32
Woodcroft Av. M19—1L 103
Wooddagger Clo. WN2—3M 53
Woodeaton Clo. OL2—5A 46
Wooded Clo. BL9—5M 25
Woodedge. WN4—4M 69
Wood End. SK7—2D 114
Woodend Ct. SK14—5D 94
Woodend La. OL12—5K 13
Woodend La. SK14—5C 94
Wood End La. SK15—8K 83
Woodend Rd. M22—9D 102
Woodend Rd. SK3—9F 104
Woodend St. OL1—8L 45
Woodend St. OL4—3F 64
Woodend View. OL5—6K 65
Woodfield. M22—1D 112
Woodfield Av. OL12—9E 12
Woodfield Av. SK6—1A 106
Woodfield Av. SK14—6D 94
Woodfield Clo. OL8—4J 63
Woodfield Clo. SK14—2F 96
Woodfield Ct. SK2—9G 105
Woodfield Cres. SK6—3M 105
Woodfield Cres. WN4—5A 70
Woodfield Dri. M28—1H 75
Woodfield Gro. BL4—2J 57
Woodfield Gro. M30—6C 76
Woodfield Gro. M33—8G 89
Woodfield M. SK14—6D 94
Woodfield Rd. M6—3K 77
Woodfield Rd. M8—7G 61
Woodfield Rd. M24—2L 61
Woodfield Rd. SK8—5B 114
Woodfield Rd. WA14—7C 100
Woodfields. WN7—9G 55
Woodfields Ter. BL9—7M 25
Woodfield St. BL3—6G 39
Woodfield St. WN2—6G 35
Woodfield Ter. OL10—7L 27
Wood Fold. BL7—4J 23
Woodfold Av. M19—4A 92
Woodford Av. M30—4B 76
Woodford Av. M34—2A 94
Woodford Av. OL2—2D 46
Woodford Av. WA3—8K 71
Woodford Dri. M27—6E 58
Woodford Gdns. M20—3G 103
Woodford Gro. BL3—5C 38
Woodford La. SK10—5C 120
Woodford Rd. M35—8G 63
Woodford Rd. SK7—7E 114
Woodford Rd. SK9—3A 120
Woodford Rd. SK12—8G 115

Woodford St. WN2—2L 53
Woodford St. WN5—2H 51
Woodgarth. WN7—2C 72
Woodgarth Av. M10—2D 80
Woodgarth Dri. M27—1E 76
Woodgarth La. M28—2M 75
Woodgate Av. BL9—6D 26
Woodgate Av. OL11—4A 28
Woodgate Clo. SK6—2M 105
Woodgate Dri. M25—2C 60
Woodgate Hill Rd. BL9—7C 26
(Bury)
Woodgate Hill Rd. BL9—6D 26
(Woodgate Hill)
Woodgate Rd. M16—5E 90
Woodgate St. BL3—6G 39
Woodgrange Clo. M6—5L 77
Woodgreen Clo. WN2—4K 53
Woodgreen Dri. M26—9G 41
Wood Gro. M25—6L 41
Wood Gro. M34—2M 93
Wood Gro. SK6—9A 94
Woodhall Av. M20—7G 91
Woodhall Av. M25—2K 59
Woodhall Clo. BL2—7J 23
Woodhall Clo. BL8—5K 25
Woodhall Clo. SK7—9E 114
Woodhall Cres. SK5—1G 105
Woodhall Rd. SK5—1F 104
Woodhall St. M35—8F 62
Woodhalt Rd. M8—8G 61
Woodham Rd. M23—4M 101
Woodham Wlk. BL3—4D 38
Woodhead Clo. BL0—7J 9
Woodhead Clo. M16—2E 90
Woodhead Dri. WA15—3F 110
Woodhead Gro. WN3—6B 52
Woodhead Rd. SK13 & SK14—4K 97
Woodhead Rd. SK14—8H 85
Woodhead Rd. WA15—3F 110
Wood Hey Clo. M26—6D 40
Wood Hey Gro. M34—4A 94
Wood Hey Gro. OL12—7E 12
Woodhey Rd. BL0—8G 9
Woodheys. SK4—2M 103
Woodheys Dri. M33—4D 100
Woodheys Rd. OL15—9A 14
Woodheys St. M6—6M 77
Wood Hill. M24—7M 43
Wood Hill Clo. M12—2B 92
Woodhill Clo. M24—7M 43
Woodhill Dri. M25—6B 60
Woodhill Fold. BL8—7K 25
Woodhill Gro. M25—5B 60
Woodhill Ho. M6—4M 77
Woodhill Rd. BL8—7K 25
Woodhill St. BL8—6K 25
Woodhouse Ct. M31—2A 88
Woodhouse Dri. WN6—6L 33
Woodhouse Farm Cotts. OL12—9K 11
Woodhouse Knowle. OL3—5L 47
Woodhouse La. M22—9D 102
Woodhouse La. M33—3B 100
(in three parts)
Woodhouse La. OL12—9K 11
Woodhouse La. WA14—9H 99
(Dunham Massey)
Woodhouse La. WA14—9L 99
(Dunham Town)
Woodhouse La. WA15—4G 101
Woodhouse La. WN6—7L 33
Woodhouse La. N. M22—4D 112
Woodhouse La. S. M22—5D 112
Woodhouse Rd. M22—4D 112
Woodhouse Rd. M31—2M 87
Woodhouse St. M10—2M 79
Woodhouse St. M18—1E 92
Woodhouse St. M29—6K 55
Woodhouse St. OL8—3M 63
Wooding Clo. M31—1G 99
Woodlake Av. M21—1C 102
Woodland Av. BL3—7H 39
Woodland Av. M18—2E 92
Woodland Av. WA13—2A 108
Woodland Av. WN2—5A 54
Woodland Cres. M25—6B 60
Woodland Cres. WA16—8C 108
Woodland Dri. WA13—2A 108
Woodland Dri. WN4—2B 70
Woodland Dri. WN6—8L 17
Woodland Grn. BL7—9D 6
Woodland Gro. WN1—7D 34
Woodland Pk. OL2—3H 45
Woodland Rd. M18—2E 92
Woodland Rd. M19—6A 92
Woodland Rd. OL6—9D 64
Woodland Rd. OL10—7L 27
Woodland Rd. OL12—9C 12
Woodlands. M31—3C 88
Woodlands. M35—3E 80
Woodlands. OL16—8J 13
Woodlands Av. M25—8L 41
Woodlands Av. M27—1C 76
Woodlands Av. M30—7A 76
(Eccles)
Woodlands Av. M30—3G 87
(Irlam)
Woodlands Av. M31—4J 87
Woodlands Av. M32—4K 89
Woodlands Av. OL11—4A 28
Woodlands Av. SK6—9A 94
Woodlands Av. SK7—3K 115
Woodlands Av. SK8—2A 114
Woodlands Av. WN3—2F 52
Woodlands Av. WN7—4F 72
Woodlands Clo. M28—9L 57
Woodlands Clo. SK14—5M 95
(Broadbottom)
Woodlands Clo. SK14—9F 84
(Tintwistle)
Woodlands Clo. SK15—8K 83
Woodlands Ct. WA15—8F 100
Woodlands Dri. M29—3M 55
Woodlands Dri. M33—4J 101
Woodlands Dri. SK2—5J 105
Woodlands Dri. SK6—9A 94
Woodlands Dri. WN6—5F 32
Woodlands Gro. BL8—7H 25
Woodlands Gro. SK14—5M 95
Woodlands La. WA15—8E 100
Woodlands Pk. Rd. SK2—5K 105
Woodlands Parkway. WA15—8E 100
Woodlands Rd. BL0—1K 9
Woodlands Rd. M8—8G 61
Woodlands Rd. M16—5E 90
Woodlands Rd. M28—9L 57
Woodlands Rd. M29—9B 56
Woodlands Rd. M33—9J 89
Woodlands Rd. OL16—5L 29
Woodlands Rd. SK4—3K 103
Woodlands Rd. SK9—9L 113
(Handforth)
Woodlands Rd. SK9—2F 118
(Wilmslow)
Woodlands Rd. SK12—6G 117
(Disley)
Woodlands Rd. SK12—4M 117
(New Mills)
Woodlands Rd. SK15—8J 83
Woodlands Rd. WA11—9B 68
Woodlands Rd. WA14 & WA15—8D 100
Woodlands St. M8—8G 61
Woodlands, The. BL6—1J 37
Woodlands, The. BL8—5K 25
Woodlands, The. M35—4E 80
Woodlands, The. WN1—6D 34
Woodland St. M7—2E 78
Woodland St. M12—1B 92
Woodland St. OL10—8K 27
Woodland St. OL12—9G 13
Woodland Ter. M31—2E 98
Woodland View. BL7—2H 23
Woodland Way. M24—2M 61
Wood La. M24—1B 62
Wood La. M31—2D 98
Wood La. OL6—2B 82
Wood La. PR7 & WN6—1E 16

Wood La. SK6—8D 106
Wood La. WA15—8G 101
Wood La. S. SK10—4M 121
Wood La. W. SK10—3L 121
Woodlawn Ct. M16—3C 90
Woodlea. M28—8L 57
Woodlea. M30—3C 76
Woodlea. OL9—1D 62
Woodlea Av. M19—8L 91
Woodleigh. WA14—8A 100
Woodleigh Ct. SK9—7L 119
Woodleigh Dri. M35—3J 81
Woodleigh Rd. OL4—1G 65
Woodleigh St. M9—7M 61
Woodley Av. M26—8H 41
Woodley Clo. SK2—6K 105
Woodley Gro. WN7—2D 72
Woodley Precinct. SK6—9A 94
Woodley St. BL9—1M 41
Woodliffe St. M16—1C 90
Woodlinn Wlk. M9—9K 61
Woodman Dri. BL9—4L 25
Woodman St. SK1—3E 104
Woodmeadow Ct. OL5—6J 65
Woodmere Dri. M9—5L 61
Wood Mt. WA15—8H 101
Woodmount Clo. SK6—3E 106
Wood Newton Clo. M18—2C 92
Woodnook Rd. WN6—1E 32
Woodpark Clo. OL8—5A 64
Woodridings. WA14—1B 110
Wood Rd. M16—3C 90
Wood Rd. WA15 & M33—4H 101
(in two parts)
Wood Rd. La. BL8 & BL9—2H 25
Wood Rd. N. M16—3C 90
Woodrow Wlk. M12—9M 79
Woodrow Way. M30—7F 86
Woodroyd Clo. SK7—3D 114
Woodroyd Dri. BL9—7C 26
Woodruffe Gdns. SK6—5A 106
Woodruff Wlk. M31—2F 98
Woodrush Rd. WN6—5K 33
Woodseats La. SK14—7A 96
Woodsend Circ. M31—3K 87
(in two parts)
Woodsend Cres. M31—4K 87
Woodsend Grn. M31—3K 87
Woodsend Rd. M31—2K 87
Woodsend Rd. S. M31—4L 87
(in two parts)
Woods Gro. SK8—5B 114
Woodshaw Gro. M28—8J 57
Woodside. OL2—1D 46
Woodside. OL16—5C 30
Woodside. SK4—4M 103
Woodside Av. M19—9M 91
Woodside Av. M28—6M 57
Woodside Av. WA11—7A 68
Woodside Av. WN4—8A 52
Woodside Clo. WN8—9C 32
Woodside Dri. BL0—6G 9
Woodside Dri. M6—4J 77
Woodside Dri. SK6—5E 116
Woodside Dri. SK14—5E 94
Woodside Gdns. M31—1F 98
Woodside M. SK7—2C 114
Woodside Pl. BL2—4J 39
Woodside Rd. M16—4B 90
Woodside Rd. WA11—8L 69
Woodside St. SK15—1L 83
Woods La. OL3—8A 48
Woods La. SK8—5B 114
Woods La. WN4—3D 70
Woods Lea. BL1—2M 37
Woodsley Rd. BL1—8M 21
Woods Moor La. SK3 & SK2 —1F 114
Woodsmoor Rd. M27—9D 58
Woods Pas. OL15—6M 13
Wood Sq. M35—7G 81
Wood Sq. OL3—2B 66
Woods Rd. M30—6F 86
Woods Rd. WN2—5J 35
Wood's St. WN3—1C 52
Woods, The. OL4—2H 65
Woods, The. OL11—7C 28
Woods, The. WA14—7E 100
Woodstock Av. SK5—9F 92
Woodstock Av. SK8—5A 114
Woodstock Clo. OL10—8L 27
Woodstock Cres. SK6—9A 94
Woodstock Dri. BL1—9A 22
Woodstock Dri. BL8—3D 24
Woodstock Dri. M27—1G 77
Woodstock Dri. M28—2A 76
Woodstock Grn. SK5—8G 93
Woodstock Rd. M10—7C 62
Woodstock Rd. M16—3B 90
Woodstock Rd. SK6—9A 94
Woodstock Rd. WA14—5C 100
Woodstock St. OL4—3M 63
Woodstock St. OL12—1C 28
Wood St. BL0—6H 9
Wood St. BL1—2F 38
Wood St. BL4—7K 39
Wood St. BL5—9E 36
Wood St. BL6—7C 20
Wood St. BL8—7J 25
Wood St. M3—4D 4 & 6E 78
(Manchester)
Wood St. M3—3D 4 & 5E 78
(Salford)
Wood St. M11—7B 80
Wood St. M24—7K 43
Wood St. M26—9E 40
Wood St. M29—4H 55
(Atherton)
Wood St. M29—8B 56
(Tyldesley)
Wood St. M30—6F 76
Wood St. M34—2M 93
Wood St. OL1—9B 46
Wood St. OL2—1L 45
Wood St. OL6—5B 82
Wood St. OL10—8K 27
Wood St. OL15—6B 14
Wood St. OL16—6C 30
(Newhey)
Wood St. OL16—3G 29
(Rochdale)
Wood St. SK3—5D 104
Wood St. SK8—7K 103
Wood St. SK13—6J 97
Wood St. SK14—1D 96
(Hollingworth)
Wood St. SK14—4E 94
(Hyde)
Wood St. SK15—5G 83
Wood St. SK16—9C 82
Wood St. WA3—7H 71
Wood St. WA14—9D 100
Wood St. WN2—5B 54
Wood St. WN3—1C 52
Wood St. WN5—1M 51
Wood Ter. BL2—9D 24
Woodthorpe Dri. SK8—1A 114
Wood Top Av. OL11—5M 27
Woodvale. M24—5A 44
Woodvale Av. BL3—7D 38
Woodvale Av. M29—3H 55
Woodvale Av. WN2—6M 35
Woodvale Dri. BL3—7D 38
Woodvale Gdns. BL3—7D 38
Woodvale Gro. BL3—7D 38
Woodvale Wlk. M11—6M 79
(off Limetree Wlk.)
Wood View. M22—4D 102
Wood View. OL10—6J 27
Wood View. WN6—3H 33
Woodview Av. M19—9M 91
Woodville Dri. M33—9G 89
Woodville Dri. SK6—8D 106
Woodville Dri. SK15—4K 83
Woodville Gro. SK5—8F 92
Woodville Rd. M33—9G 89
Woodville Rd. PR6—1F 18
Woodville Rd. WA14—9C 100
Woodville Ter. M10—7M 61
Woodward Clo. BL9—5M 25
Woodward Ct. M4—5K 79
Woodward Pl. M4—3H 5 & 5J 79
Woodward Rd. M25—6M 59
Woodwards Rd. BL5—2F 54
Woodward St. M4—3H 5 & 5J 79
Woodwise La. M23—4L 101
Wood Yd. OL16—9K 29
Woodyates Ter. WN5—2M 51
Woolden Rd. M30—6B 86
Woolden St. M27—6E 58
Woolden St. M30—4B 76
Woolden St. WN5—2M 51
Wooley Clo. SK14—2D 96
Wooley Ter. SK16—6B 82
Woolfall Clo. M12—9M 79
Woollacot St. OL1—1M 63
Woollam Pl. M3—6C 4 & 7D 78
Woolley Av. SK12—1K 121
Woolley Bri. Rd. SK14—2E 96
Woolley La. SK14—9D 84
(Hollingworth)
Woolley La. SK14—2C 96
(Woolley Bridge)
Woolley Mill La. SK14—8E 84
Woolley St. M8—1E 5 & 3F 78
Woolley St. OL6—1E 82
Woolpack Clo. WN7—2F 72
Woolpack Grn. M6—4M 77
Wool Rd. OL3—8B 48
Woolston Dri. M29—8C 56
Woolston Ho. M6—3J 77
Woolton Clo. M10—6C 62
Woolton Clo. WN4—2M 69
Wootton St. SK14—2D 94
(in two parts)
Worcester Av. M34—5A 94
Worcester Av. SK5—9J 93
Worcester Av. WA3—7H 71
Worcester Av. WN2—2M 53
Worcester Clo. M6—3J 77
Worcester Clo. OL6—8D 64
Worcester Clo. SK6—4A 106
Worcester Gro. SK13—6M 97
Worcester Rd. BL3—6M 39
Worcester Rd. M6—3J 77
Worcester Rd. M24—2M 61
Worcester Rd. M27—6D 58
Worcester Rd. M33—2D 100
Worcester Rd. SK8—9A 104
Worcester St. BL1—9E 22
Worcester St. BL8—6K 25
Worcester St. OL9—3H 63
Worcester St. OL11—5E 28
Wordsworth Av. BL4—1H 57
Wordsworth Av. BL9—3M 41
Wordsworth Av. M8—1G 79
Wordsworth Av. M26—5E 40
Wordsworth Av. M29—4K 55
Wordsworth Av. M35—5G 81
Wordsworth Av. WN1—6C 34
Wordsworth Av. WN5—7D 50
(Billinge)
Wordsworth Av. WN5—2F 50
(Orrell)
Wordsworth Av. WN7—9D 54
Wordsworth Clo. SK16—8G 83
Wordsworth Cres. OL7—2L 81
Wordsworth Cres. OL15 —9M 13
Wordsworth Gdns. M25—5M 59
Wordsworth Rd. M16—3B 90
Wordsworth Rd. M24—7B 44
Wordsworth Rd. M27—7D 58
Wordsworth Rd. M28—3H 57
Wordsworth Rd. M34—7A 94
Wordsworth Rd. OL1—8B 46
Wordsworth Rd. SK5—5D 92
Wordsworth St. BL1—9D 22
Wordsworth St. M6—1B 4 & 3C 78
Wordsworth Way. OL11—4L 27
Workesleigh St. M10—2C 80
Worrall St. M5—6B 4 & 8C 78
Worrall St. M10—1A 80
Worrall St. SK3—6E 104
Worral St. OL12—9D 12
Worrell Clo. M26—5F 40
Worsefold St. M10—8A 62
Worsel St. BL3—5C 38
Worsley Av. M10—7M 61
Worsley Av. M28—5G 57
Worsley Brow. M28—1M 75
Worsley Clo. WN5—3H 51
Worsley Cres. SK2—6H 105
Worsley Grn. WN5—3H 51
Worsley Gro. M19—5A 92
Worsley Gro. M28—6G 57
Worsley Mesnes Dri. WN3 —3M 51
Worsley Pl. OL2—3A 46
Worsley Pl. OL16—3H 29
Worsley Rd. BL3—5A 38
Worsley Rd. BL4—2K 57
Worsley Rd. M28 & M27—2M 75
Worsley Rd. M30—3A 76
Worsley Rd. N. M28—3K 57
Worsley St. BL8—3E 24
Worsley St. M3—5D 4 & 7E 78
(Manchester)
Worsley St. M3—3D 4 & 5E 78
(Salford)
Worsley St. M15—6C 4 & 8D 78
Worsley St. M27—9G 59
(Pendlebury)
Worsley St. M27—6F 58
(Swinton)
Worsley St. OL8—3B 64
Worsley St. OL16—3H 29
Worsley St. WA3—7G 71
Worsley St. WA11—9F 68
Worsley St. WN5—3H 51
Worsley Ter. WN1—8C 34
Worston Av. BL1—7M 21
Worthenbury Wlk. M13—3L 91
Worthing Clo. SK2—7K 105
Worthing Gro. M29—5H 55
Worthing St. M14—4H 91
Worthington Av. M31—2F 98
Worthington Av. OL10—2L 43
Worthington Clo. OL7—2A 82
Worthington Clo. SK14—4L 95
Worthington Ct. M33—1L 101
Worthington Dri. M7—7D 60
Worthington Fold. M29—5H 55
Worthington Rd. M33—1L 101
Worthington Rd. M34—4B 94
Worthington St. BL3—6C 38
Worthington St. M16—2C 90
Worthington St. OL7—2A 82
Worthington St. OL8—2K 63
Worthington St. SK15—6F 82
Worthington St. WN2—2K 53
Worthington Way. WN3—6L 51
Worth's La. M34—7A 94
Worth St. WN3—1A 52
Wortley Av. M6—4J 77
Wortley Gro. M10—6B 62
Wragby Clo. BL8—5K 25
Wraxhill Cres. WN7—9D 54
Wray Pl. OL16—4J 29
Wraysbury Wlk. M10—9A 62
(off Hugo St.)
Wray St. WN1—9E 34
Wrayton Lodge. M33—3H 101
Wrekin Av. M23—1A 112
Wren Av. M27—5H 59
Wrenbury Av. M20—7F 90
Wrenbury Clo. WN5—2H 51
Wrenbury Cres. SK3—7C 104
Wrenbury Dri. BL1—4F 22
Wrenbury Dri. SK8—7L 103
Wrenbury Wlk. M33—2L 101
Wren Clo. BL4—9F 38
Wren Clo. M34—6J 81
Wren Clo. SK2—8M 105
Wren Dri. BL9—6B 26
Wren Dri. M30—2G 87
Wren Grn. OL16—4H 29
Wren Nest Ter. SK13—5J 97
Wrenshot La. WA16—7C 108
Wrens Nest Av. OL2—1C 46
Wren St. OL4—2C 64
Wren St. OL9—9H 45
Wrexham Clo. OL8—6H 63
Wrigglesworth Clo. BL8—7F 24
Wright Robinson Clo. M11 —7L 79
Wrights Bank N. SK2—3K 105
Wrights Bank S. SK2—3L 105
Wright St. BL6—6B 20
Wright St. M16—9C 78
Wright St. M26—6F 40
Wright St. M34—7L 81
Wright St. M35—8F 62
Wright St. OL6—3D 82
Wright St. OL9—3H 63
Wright St. WA14—6C 100
Wright St. WN1—8E 34
Wright St. WN2—9H 63
(Abram)
Wright St. WN2—5G 53
(Platt Bridge)
Wright St. WN4—1M 69
Wright Tree Vs. M30—9D 86
Wrigley Cres. M35—9F 62
Wrigley Head. M35—8F 62
Wrigley Head Cres. M35—8F 62
Wrigley Pl. OL15—8M 13
Wrigley Rd. WA11—9L 69
Wrigley's Pl. OL8—5L 63
Wrigley Sq. OL4—2F 64
Wrigley's Sq. OL12—2F 28
Wrigley St. OL4—2E 64
(Lees)
Wrigley St. OL4—1B 64
(Oldham)
Wrigley St. OL4—9H 47
(Scouthead)
Wrigley St. OL6—3B 82
Wrigley St. SK16—7D 82
Wrington Clo. WN7—8D 54
Writhington St. WN1—8C 34
Wroe St. M3—4C 4 & 6D 78
Wroe St. M27—5F 58
Wroe St. OL4—2F 64
Wrotham Clo. M5—6A 78
Wroxeter Wlk. M12—9M 79
(off Wenlock Way)
Wroxham Av. M31—3B 88
Wroxham Av. M34—3G 93
Wroxham Clo. BL8—5K 25
Wroxham Rd. M9—5H 61
Wuerdle Clo. OL16—7L 13
Wuerdle Pl. OL16—7L 13
Wuerdle St. OL16—7L 13
Wyatt Av. M5—6B 4 & 8B 78
Wyatt St. SK4—3D 104
Wyatt St. SK16—7C 82
Wybersley Rd. SK6—4G 117
Wychbury St. M5—5L 77
Wychelm Rd. M31—2F 98
Wycherley Rd. OL12—9B 12
Wych Fold. SK14—7E 94
(in two parts)
Wych La. SK10—6K 121
Wych St. OL6—5B 82
Wychwood. WA14—3B 110
Wychwood Clo. M24—1B 62
Wycliffe Av. SK9—4G 119
Wycliffe Ct. M31—4C 88
Wycliffe Rd. M31—4C 88
Wycliffe Rd. WA11—8L 69
Wycliffe St. M30—5C 76
Wycliffe St. SK4—3D 104
Wycliffe Wlk. M12—9L 79
Wycombe Av. M18—9E 80
Wycombe Clo. M31—1C 88
Wycombe Dri. M29—9B 56
Wye Av. M35—9F 62
Wyecroft Clo. SK6—9B 94
Wyedale Rd. WA11—8J 69
Wye St. OL8—3K 63
Wykeham Gro. OL12—1B 28
Wykeham M. BL1—2A 38
Wykeham St. M14—3G 91
Wyken Gro. WA11—9C 68
Wyke Pk. OL4—2D 64
Wylam Wlk. M12—3B 92
Wylde, The. BL9—8L 25
Wynard Av. WN1—8D 34
Wynchgate Rd. SK7—1A 116
Wyndale Dri. M35—2F 80
Wyndale Rd. OL8—5M 63
Wyndcliff Dri. M31—5L 87
Wyndham Av. BL3—7A 38
Wyndham Av. M27—5F 58
Wyndham Clo. SK7—5F 114
Wyndham St. BL9—9M 25
Wyne Clo. SK7—1A 116
Wynfield Av. M22—5F 112
Wynford Sq. M5—6M 77
Wyngate Rd. SK8—3M 113
Wyngate Rd. WA15—4F 110
Wynne Av. M27—5F 58
Wynne Clo. M11—7M 79
Wynne Clo. M34—5M 93
Wynne Gro. M34—5L 93
Wynne St. BL1—8E 22
Wynne St. M6—1A 4 & 3B 78
Wynne St. M28—4G 57
Wynne St. M29—7M 55
Wynnstay Gro. M14—6J 91
Wynnstay Rd. M33—9H 89
Wynn St. M10—7E 62
Wynton Clo. WN7—5E 72
Wynt, The. M31—1F 98
Wynyard Clo. M33—3K 101
Wynyard Rd. M22—1C 112
Wyre Av. WN2—6G 53
Wyre Clo. M25—8B 42
Wyre Dri. M28—9H 57
Wyresdale Rd. BL1—1C 38
Wyresdale Wlk. M15—9E 78
(off Ipstone Clo.)
Wyre St. M1—5G 5 & 7H 79
Wyre St. OL5—7H 65
Wyrevale Clo. WN4—4C 70
Wythall Av. M28—2H 57
Wythburn Av. BL1—9A 22
Wythburn Av. M8—1J 79
Wythburn Av. M31—3B 88
Wythburn Cres. WA11—7B 68
Wythburn Rd. M24—6L 43
Wythburn Rd. SK1—6H 105
Wythburn St. M5—5L 77
Wythenshawe Rd. M23—5L 101
Wythenshawe Rd. M33—1L 101
Wythens Rd. SK8—4H 113
Wythop Gdns. M5—6A 78
Wyvern Av. SK5—9E 92
Wyverne Rd. M21—5D 90
Wyville Av. M27—1E 76
Wyville Clo. SK7—1A 116
Wyville Dri. M6—4M 77
Wyville Dri. M9—2H 61

Yarburgh St. M16—3E 90
Yardley. OL11—6E 28
Yardley Av. M32—4G 89
Yardley Clo. M32—4G 89
Yarmouth Dri. M23—4B 102
Yarn Croft. M29—8B 56
Yarnton Clo. OL2—4A 46
Yarn Wlk. M4—6J 79
(off Kirby Wlk.)
Yarrow Clo. OL11—5F 28
Yarrow Gro. BL6—6B 20
Yarrow Pl. BL1—9D 22
Yarrow St. WN2—4J 53
Yarrow Wlk. M25—8C 42
Yarrow Wlk. WN2—6F 52
Yarwell. OL12—2E 28
(off Spotland Rd.)
Yarwood Av. M23—6M 101
Yarwood Clo. OL10—7L 27
Yarwoodheath La. WA14 —4L 109
Yarwood St. BL9—8A 26
Yarwood St. WA14—1D 110
Yates Gro. WN6—5M 33
Yates St. BL2—9G 23
Yates St. M24—1J 61
Yates St. OL1—9A 46
Yates St. SK1—2H 105
Yates St. WN3—1A 52
Yates St. WN7—9E 54
Yates Ter. BL8—5L 25
Yattendon Av. M23—5K 101
Yeadon Rd. M18—3D 92
Yealand Av. SK4—2D 104
Yealand Clo. OL11—4B 28
Yealand Rd. WN2—3A 54
Yeardsley Clo. SK7—1E 114
Yellow Lodge Dri. BL5—8H 37
Yelverton Wlk. M13—9J 79
(off Lowndes Wlk.)
Yeoford Dri. WA14—7B 100
Yeoman Clo. SK7—1K 115
Yeoman's Clo. OL16—3M 29
Yeoman Wlk. M11—6M 79
Yeovil Wlk. M16—3F 90
Yewbarrow Rd. OL1—9A 46
Yew Clo. BL3—5B 38
Yew Ct. OL12—9H 13
Yew Cres. OL4—9D 46
Yewdale. M27—6H 59
Yewdale. WN6—3H 33
Yewdale Av. BL2—8M 23
Yewdale Av. WA11—6B 68
Yewdale Cres. WN1—6B 34
Yewdale Dri. M24—8L 43
Yewdale Gdns. BL2—8M 23
Yewdale Gdns. OL11—6B 28
Yewdale Rd. SK1—6H 105
Yewdale Rd. WN4—9A 52
Yew Gro. WN6—5M 33
Yewlands Av. M9—3K 61
Yew St. BL9—7C 26
Yew St. M7—1C 78
Yew St. M34—9M 81
Yew St. OL10—8H 27
Yew St. SK4—4C 104
Yew Tree Av. M14—4G 91
Yew Tree Av. M19—5A 92
Yew Tree Av. M22—4D 102
Yew Tree Av. M29—4J 55
Yew Tree Av. SK7—3M 115
Yew Tree Clo. OL7—1A 82
Yew Tree Clo. SK6—8E 106
Yew Tree Cotts. OL3—3C 48
Yew Tree Cres. M14—5H 91
Yew Tree Dri. BL6—3H 37
Yew Tree Dri. M22—4D 102
Yew Tree Dri. M25—4B 60
Yew Tree Dri. M31—2M 87
Yew Tree Dri. M33—1L 101
Yew Tree Dri. OL9—1D 62
Yew Tree Dri. SK6—2K 105
Yewtree Gro. SK8—1G 113
Yew Tree La. BL1—5G 23
Yew Tree La. M23 & M22 —3B 102
Yewtree La. SK12—1L 121
Yewtree La. SK16—8E 82
Yewtree La. WA15—5M 111
Yew Tree Pk. Rd. SK8—6B 114
Yew Tree Rd. M14—3H 91
Yew Tree Rd. M34—5L 93
Yew Tree Rd. SK3—1F 114
Yew Tree Trading Est. WA11 —7A 70
Yew Wlk. M31—3E 98
York Arc. M1—6G 79
(off Piccadilly Plaza)
York Av. BL3—6A 40
York Av. M16—4C 90
York Av. M25—6D 60
York Av. M27—6D 58
York Av. M29—6M 55
York Av. M31—3E 88
York Av. M33—9H 89
York Av. OL8—4K 63
York Av. OL11—4A 28
York Clo. M34—2M 93
York Clo. SK8—8A 104
York Cres. SK9—3J 119
Yorkdale Rd. OL4—1D 64
York Dri. BL0—7G 9
York Dri. SK7—2M 115
York Dri. WA14—3D 110
York Dri. WA15—5M 111
York Ho. M33—9H 89
York Pl. OL6—5A 82
York Pl. PR6—2G 19
York Rd. M21—6B 90
York Rd. M30—9D 86
York Rd. M33—9G 89
York Rd. M34—2L 93
York Rd. M35—4F 80
York Rd. OL9—9F 44
York Rd. SK4—9B 92
York Rd. SK14—6E 94
York Rd. WA14—3C 110
York Rd. WN2—2M 53
York Rd. WN4—4C 70
York Rd. E. M24—3C 62
York Rd. W. M24—3C 62
Yorkshire Rd. M31—3E 98
Yorkshire St. M3—3D 4 & 5E
Yorkshire St. OL1—1M 63
Yorkshire St. OL6—3B 82
(in two parts)
Yorkshire St. OL16 & OL12
(in three parts) —3F
Yorkshire Way. SK13—6M 97
York Sq. OL2—5K 45
York St. BL4—9L 39
York St. BL9—8A 26
York St. M1—5F 5 & 7G 79
(in two parts)
York St. M2 & M1—4F 5 & 6G
York St. M9—8L 61
(in two parts)
York St. M15—6D 4 & 8E 78
York St. M19—6A 92
York St. M20—2H 103
York St. M25—9M 41
York St. M26—4K 41
York St. M29—5K 55
York St. M34—7L 81
York St. M35—8G 63
York St. OL9—2L 63
York St. OL10—8K 27
York St. OL16—4H 29
York St. SK3—5E 104
York St. SK13—5L 97
York St. WA3—6G 71
York St. WA15—1D 110
York St. WN1—9B 34
York St. WN7—3K 73
York St. S. WN4—5C 70
York Ter. BL1—8E 22
York Ter. M33—8G 89
York Ter. SK13—6J 97
Youd St. WN7—2E 72
Youlgreave Cres. SK13—5D
Young St. BL0—5H 9
Young St. BL4—1L 57
Young St. M3—4D 4 & 6E 78
Young St. M26—4F 40
Young St. WN7—3L 73
Yulan Dri. M33—1C 100
Yule St. SK3—5D 104
Yvonne Clo. WN4—2D 70

Zama St. BL0—7G 9
Zealand St. OL4—8C 46
Zebra St. M8—9F 60
Zedburgh. OL12—2E 28
(off Spotland Rd.)
Zennor. OL11—6E 28
Zero Av. M17—1K 89
Zeta St. M9—9M 61
Zetland Av. BL3—7B 38
Zetland Av. N. BL3—7B 38
Zetland Pl. OL16—2H 29
Zetland Rd. M21—6B 90
Zetland St. SK16—6C 82
Zinnia Dri. M30—6E 86
Zion Cres. M15—9E 78
Zion Ter. OL12—1L 27
Zurich Gdns. SK7—1E 114
Zyburn Ct. M6—4G 77

156 Greater Manchester

Printed and bound in Great Britain by
BPC Consumer Books Ltd
A member of
The British Printing Company Ltd